The Lost History of Washington and Lee:

New Discoveries

A Historical Performance Audit

Kent Wilcox

Rev. date: 05/31/2018

To order additional copies of this book, contact:
Xlibris
1-888-795-4274
www.Xlibris.com
Orders@Xlibris.com
776761

The Lost History of Washington and Lee:

New Discoveries

(A Historical Performance Audit)
2018

(Including, a Brief Sketch of the Origins of Washington
and Lee University, Based on Primary Sources)

Petition of the Liberty Hall Academy Trustees to
the Virginia Synod,[1] September 1792:
(An extract)

*<u>For it was under Wm. Graham that our Academy
first received its existence</u> and it is chiefly owing to
his extraordinary exertions that it has persevered
through all the convulsions of a calamitous War
and the many vicissitudes which have taken place
through the operations of various causes for the
space of about 16 years .. . .[2]*

Samuel Lyle
Alex. Campbell
Wm. McKee
Wm Alexander
James Ramsay
Jno. Wilson
Joseph Walker
John Lyle
Samuel Houston
Claverhouse Associates
East Lansing, Michigan

---

1   The Synod of the Presbyterian Church.

2   A copy is on file at the Leyburn Library of Washington and Lee University. Technically, the date
of establishment is Oct. 13, 1774, See, Hanover Presbytery meeting minutes record book, pg. 55.

Contents

---

3   The initial report will only contain assessments of only about half of the seventy-six authors that were assessed due to time and space constraints. The first twenty are highlighted, and a then an additional ten were selected from the original list for inclusion based on their significance. The remainder (shown separately below) are intended to be released at a later date in a supplement.

4   John B. Hoge wrote a biography of his father Rev. Moses Hoge. While it contains many extracts from Moses Hoge's diaries as well as various manuscripts Moses drafted, the essence of the biography is the product of his son, John B. Hoge. Written in the early 1820s, it was not published until 1963.

6. *Rev. Dr. Henry Ruffner*   [1840-]
7. Rev. Robert Davidson   [1847]
8. * *William Henry Foote*[5]   [1850 and 1855]
9. Rev. Samuel Houston[6]   [unknown]
10. Charles Campbell   [1860]
11. * Anon, Charter and Laws . . . of Washington College   [1865]
12. * *Bolivar Christian*[7]   [1869]
13. Hugh Blair Grigsby   [1870]
14. Rev. E. D. Junkin   [1871]
15. Samuel Davies Alexander   [1872]
16. Rev. J. G. Craighead, DD   [1878]
17. S. P. Miller   [1883]
18. Alfred Nevin, DD, LLD, (Editor)   [1884]
19. Dean, Charles A. Graves (W&L Law School)   [1885]
20. William McLaughlin   [1888]

****

---

5   *The accentuation of Mr. Foote is occasioned by the auditor's conclusion that he is the culprit most responsible for the bastardization of the early history of Washington and Lee University that repudiated seventy-five years of documented and reliable history without notice to his readers, and without providing any compelling evidence to support his actions in this regard. The evidence to support our conclusion is scattered throughout this audit report, especially in the Author's Errors Section and some of the attached appendices. Evidence is also located in the exceedingly important Prolegomenon, and the Executive Summary.*

6   The auditor here provides an important caveat, which is that several conclusions about Mr. Foote are premised on the assumption that Mr. Houston indeed wrote the letter alluded to and extracted, in part, in Foote's two volumes on Virginia history. An assumption that may very well be incorrect. This so-called letter is at best dubious and may actually be a hoax, or even possibly a forgery. Readers are referred to the author's Errors Section and the subsection pertaining to William H. Foote, and also to the related Appendix.

7   *Trustee Bolivar Christian is highlighted because the auditor believes he was either the single driving force, or one of them, who was a part of the University that expanded upon Mr. Wm. H. Foote's 1850 & 1855 bastardization of the university's history and he initiated the university's repudiation of the long-established history of its founding, and early history. Again, like Mr. Foote, Trustee Bolivar Christian failed to acknowledge what he was doing in altering the history, or upon what evidence he based his assertions.*

(From here forward, the authors are taken out of the original order)[8]

To this list might well be added the Washington and Lee University's website (2017) because here the university, once again, restates the history of its founding incorrectly by predating its origins by twenty-five years.

****

---

8   This break in order was deemed expedient by the auditor in order to facilitate the report's timely release while ensuring the inclusion of several of the most import authors and their works.

9   Carter J. Harris A.M., Prof. Of Latin and Roman History. James J. White, Prof. Of Greek and Greek History. It seems odd that Adams did not identify these co-authors by their full names, but Dr. Ollinger Crenshaw, author of General Lee's College, identifies them in his unpublished Appendix 'A', that was part of his original two volume manuscript typescript that included footnotes not published by Random House in their 1969, edition. In addition, Dr. Adams referenced in his bibliography of W&L an Article, "A Virginian University Town," published in the _Overland Monthly_ magazine (May, 1883) which includes numerous errors about the origins of W&L.

Below is a list of authors/sources who were assessed and found to have also made serious errors concerning the founding of Washington and Lee University or about its founding first president William Graham but are not included in the report due to time and space requirements. In all, seventy-four assessments were conducted.

1a.	William H. Whitsett	[1888]
2a.	Judge James Patton	[1890]
3a.	Rev. James A. Waddell (not the "blind preacher")	[1890]
4a.	Kaleidoscope (A Hampden Sydney Annual)	[1893]
5a.	Wm. Henry Ruffner	[1893]
6a.	J. B. Henneman	[1896]
7a.	Robert E. Withers	[1907]
8a.	Arista Hoge	[1908]
9a.	Henry Jones Ford	[1915]
10a.	A. J. Morrison,	[1917]
11a.	Oren F. Morton	[1920]
12a.	S. Gordon Smyth (New Prov.)	[1922]
13a.	Charles E. Kemper	[1922]
14a.	Edgar Knight	[1922]
15a.	Robert G. Albion and Leonidas Dodson[10]	[1934]
16a.	Edgar Erskine Hume	[1934]
17a.	Henry Boley	[1936]
18a.	Freeman Hart	[1942]
19a.	Bayless Hardin	[1942]
20a.	Donald Robert Come	[1945]
21a.	Thomas Jefferson Wertenberger	[1946]
22a.	Samuel Holt Monk	[1946]
23a.	Edmund P. Thompkins, MD	[1952]
24a.	Ernest Trice Thompson	[1963]
25a.	Rebecca K. Pruett	[1966]
26a.	Dr. George West Diehl	[1970]
27a.	Robert Goggin Gillespie Jr.	[1970]
28a.	Howard McKnight Wilson	[1971]
29a.	Philip Lightfoot Scruggs	[1971]
30a.	J. R. Hildebrand, [Historical map of Rockbridge Co.][11]	[1973]

---

10 These gentlemen are the Princeton University Press editors of Rev. Philip Vicker Fithian's Published Journal for 1775–1776. In regards to the early history of Washington and Lee University and that school's first president, they contribute to unjustifiable denigrating of one of Princeton's premier graduates of the eighteenth century, Rev. William Graham. Their editorializing in at least two instances are embarrassingly in error and provide succor to those who have repeated the monumental errors of William H. Foote, mistakenly linking Liberty Hall Academy to earlier peripatetic primary schools.

11 This map contains many annotations about Liberty Hall Academy that are importantly incorrect.

31a. Herbert C. Bradshaw	[1976]
32a. Durward T. Stokes	[1976]
33a. Patricia Givens Johnson	[1976]
34a. Royster Lyle Jr., and Pamela H. Simpson	[1977]
35a. John White Stuart III, PhD	[1980]
36a. David W. Robson, PhD	[1980]
37a. Earle W. Crawford	[1980 and 1983]
38a. Betty Ruth Kondayan	[1980]
39a. James William Hagy	[1981]
40a. James H. Smylie	[1985]
41a Vincent Stanley McCluskey	[1991]
42a. John Luster Brinkley PhD	[1994]
43a. Helen Chavis Othow	[2001]
44a. Preservation Master Plan [W&L]	[2005]

Note: Any of the above-named authors who wrote after 1850 and referred to the university's founding, incorrectly deemed its origins to be twenty-years (or thereabouts)[12] prior to when the university was actually founded.

---

12 *Virtually all of these listed authors/sources incorrectly dated the founding to have occurred sometime between1748 and 1752, with most adopting the year 1748. Most of these errors are traceable to the mistakes of William Henry Foote in one or both of his* Sketches of Virginia: Historical and Biographical, *Series One (1850) or Series Two (1855). No one is known to have made this mistake in print before 1850.*

Preface

A performance audit typically provides for an independent review of someone or something. This performance audit is particularly unique and, in a broad sense, may be unprecedented because it addresses the broad spectrum of the major historical treatments of an institution instead of its operations in light of regulatory requirements or financial matters. Its utilitarian value will no doubt be determined by the way in which this report's legitimacy and objectivity is received by the institution and the history community. Irrespective of how it is received, however, the accuracy of the audit's findings should not be ignored because they are incontrovertible and consistent with all of the best evidence known to exist.

It is entirely reasonable to subject a public institution's represented history to the same standards that are commonly applied in commercial settings because representations of what purports to be true may or may not, in fact, be accurate. The value of an audit will depend entirely upon several criteria. These criteria include the following: the expertise of the firm or auditor conducting the audit; the reputation of the auditors for applying close and careful scrutiny and analysis of selected aspects of that which is being assessed; the reputation of the auditors for possessing a willingness to publish controversial or embarrassing results that might otherwise be suppressed or couched in vagaries designed to obscure uncomfortable facts, as well as the recognized independence of the auditor.[13]

This historical performance audit was designed to specifically examine and analyze written historical accounts of the origins and early history of Washington and Lee University. The audit covers historical accounts included in published histories as well as those accounts that were authorized histories created at the behest of the university's governing body, which was initially the Hanover Presbytery of Virginia,[14] but which was transferred, in the main, to a Board of Trustees.[15] In addition, this assessment includes commentary about the institution's founder and first president, Rev. William Graham, and because Mr. Graham and the school are so intertwined during the college's important first twenty years,

---

13   In this auditor's view, no auditor can be considered as being independent, if the auditor has any financial connection to the entity being audited other than underwriting the expenses for conducting the audit. In regulated environments the regulator should ensure that the auditor is selected by an independent entity. Claverhouse Associates is an independent performance auditing firm recognized by the Federal Trade Commission and various state government regulatory agencies including California, Ohio, and Florida.

14   The Hanover Presbytery, at the time, was an organization comprised of all the Presbyterian ministers in Virginia, as well as selected Elders.

15   That Board of Trustees, like the college, was created by the Hanover Presbytery. That creation took place on May 6, 1776.

it follows that anything written about either Mr. Graham or the school may very well impact upon the perceived character and reputation of the other.

The principal auditor is Kent S. Wilcox, who is currently president and co-owner of Claverhouse Associates, a national performance auditing firm since 1991.* Claverhouse Associates has conducted numerous performance audits pursuant to the Magnuson-Moss Federal Warranty Act and various regulations promulgated by the Federal Trade Commission and also at the behest of several state regulatory entities pursuant to various state regulatory authorities. In this regard, Claverhouse Associates has conducted more than fifty federal and state audits of national and state arbitration programs representing several Fortune 500 companies. The firm's twenty-five years of existence has resulted in a multitude of institutional changes implemented for the purpose of either enhancing the quality of the programs under review or, in many cases, bringing a company or institution into compliance with federal or state law. In some cases, regulators have even initiated changes in their methods of applying the regulations under which they operate as a result of Claverhouse recommendations.

This historical performance audit was initiated and designed by the firm's president, Mr. Wilcox. It is a unique design created for this specific purpose. The nature of the numerous suspected inconsistencies, errors, and inappropriate omissions necessitated the unique design of the audit review process and the report.

The genesis of the audit project was occasioned by the principal auditor being made aware of the rather unique fact that Washington and Lee University appears to have the unique characteristic of being possessed of not one but two entirely different and inconsistent early histories, a fact that immediately struck the auditor as necessarily improper. This unique characteristic was brought to the auditor's attention by Dr. Ollinger Crenshaw, who had written a two-volume history of Washington and Lee, entitled _General Lee's College_,[16] which originally included an appendix entitled "The Problem of the Origins." This provocative appendix title led, in part, to the auditor initiating a preliminary investigation into this seeming paradox which, in turn, led eventually to this performance audit project.

This audit was independently initiated and has been written on an entirely pro bono basis. The report is copyrighted, and any errors contained herein are the sole responsibility of the principal auditor, Kent S. Wilcox. The report was not initiated by or on behalf of Washington and Lee University and, therefore, Washington and Lee University bears no responsibility for the text of the audit.

There are several historical authors who deserve special recognition for their important contributions to the history of Washington and Lee University and/or, its founding first president,[17] Rev. William Graham, and the terribly important and unique role played by the Presbyterian Church in promoting public education in

---

16   This version was not published, but the published version (Random House) does not include the critically important Appendix A, nor the informative and extensive footnotes.

17   Technically his title was then "rector," which, however, today would be "president." They are functional equivalents.

the British colonies of North America and then later in the United States. Some of the authors included in the report deserve special recognition despite any historical mistakes they may have made about the college's founding or concerning the character of the institution's founding first president, William Graham. They include Justice (Rev.) Caleb Wallace, whose understandably brief first authorized institutional history of the founding of what was initially and unofficially referred to by the Hanover Presbytery as Augusta Academy,[18] and later, officially, as "Liberty Hall Academy" is free of error; Professor and Trustee Edward Graham, Esq., who wrote the first published history of the college's founding included in his *Memoir of the Late President William Graham*, which included much important information pertaining to the early history of the college; Dr. Henry Ruffner, often referred to as the first true historian of Washington College. His important manuscript history was written in the 1840s at the suggestion of the Trustees but was allowed by the Board of Trustees to lie unpublished, not because of the quality of the work, but to spite the work's author, with whom the Trustees were unhappy. Eventually, the Trustees ordered the publication of Ruffner's manuscript, and it was included in the first volume of the institution's Historical Papers in 1890.[19] Despite Ruffner's several errors, his history is a valuable record of events. His understanding of the character of the college's first president, however, is embarrassingly flawed in many instances and based upon incorrect information and highly biased and unreliable sources.

Dr. Ruffner's valuable contribution is terribly tainted by his numerous mistakes concerning the college's founding first president and his inexplicable final (1857) editing that caused much confusion about the origins of the college. The Trustees' failure to publish Ruffner's "Early History of Washington College," as it was written, denied the public access to this important work of history for many years.[20] It is entirely possible, however, that the published history was substantively edited (altered) by his well-meaning but, in this case, misguided son and Trustee, William Henry Ruffner; Rev. George Junkin, whose published

---

18   The important unofficial name "Augusta Academy," used by Presbytery in slightly variant forms, first appeared in the Presbytery's meeting minutes after the creation of a second seminary., (Academy) in Prince Edward County, thereafter necessitating a means by which to distinguish the Academies, one from the other, in the meeting minutes. Later, nineteenth century authors became confused and began to inappropriately use the name Augusta Academy to refer to other private preparatory schools, which contributed to a widespread misunderstanding and confusion about the various different private schools in Augusta County during the eighteenth century. Attaching the name of a vast county to a local common school, however, never happened in Virginia in the eighteenth century. This is an obvious oversight missed by many historians of both the nineteenth and twentieth centuries.

19   Ruffner's history was published posthumously and therefore its authenticity is open to question insofar as his son, who edited the final version had the opportunity to make modifications as he deemed appropriate. As explained in the main body of the report there are reasons to believe he may have taken inappropriate liberties in this regard.

20   The article was eventually published by the Trustees, but not until fifty-years after it was written.: Henry Ruffner, "Early History of Washington College," *Washington & Lee University Historical Papers*, Vol. 1, Baltimore, John Murphy & Co. 1890.

inaugural address was the occasion for the college's first authorized published history of the college's founding;[21] Dr. Ollinger Crenshaw, whose important history entitled _General Lee's College_ is comprised of two different versions: (1) The unpublished typescript version in two volumes, with footnotes and an appendix; and, (2) the published Random House version, which bears an imprint date of 1969 and which was released without footnotes and without the vastly important appendix A, "The Problem of the Origins"; and finally, Dr. I. Taylor Sanders who provided the world with the most definitive treatment of the institution's first president, Rev. William Graham in the first two chapters of his _Now Let the Gospel Trumpet Blow_.[22] Notwithstanding these last two listed authors' important contributions to the university's history, it is disappointing that they also failed to realize that the post–Civil War version of the origins of the college was wrong in dating the founding before the October 13, 1774. Importantly they both also failed by assuming a link between Liberty Hall Academy and one or both of the local preparatory schools of Robert Alexander and/or Rev. John Brown, when in fact no such link whatsoever exists. This fact was never in doubt during the college's first ninety years of existence, and none of the several authors who published a history of the college before 1850 made that mistake.

Surprisingly, neither Dr. Crenshaw nor Dr. Sanders cited Liberty Hall Academy's first authorized history written by Rev. (Later Justice) Caleb Wallace, whose brief written history was created at the behest of the Hanover Presbytery, then the governing authority of the Academy. This historical account constitutes the institution's first authorized written history. Amazingly, this inchoate history, as best the auditor could ascertain, has never been published or even cited as an authority by any historian, and yet its existence is palpable and its legitimacy is beyond question. The account is understandably cursory because the school was only founded in October of 1774 and Wallace's history was written in May of 1776, less than two years after its nativity. Given Wallace's status as a paragon of virtue and integrity as well as his professional standing in both the legal and clerical professions, it came as a great shock that his vastly important history had gone unheralded even to this day. It is entirely inexplicable that this critically important document seems to have been overlooked by virtually everyone given its appearance in the first few pages of the college's record book containing the Board of Trustees' very first meeting minutes.

The Presbytery's directive to Clerk Caleb Wallace is found in the Presbytery's meeting minutes.[23] This rather significant oversight is surprising in that the

---

21   Rev. George Junkin, DD, _Christianity The Patron of Literature and Science: An Address Delivered February 22, 1849. On the Occasion of the Author's Inauguration as President of Washington College, Virginia_, Philadelphia, The Board of Trustees, 1849. [pamphlet pp. 39.] The Junkin Inaugural Address includes an important Appendix: "_A Brief Sketch of the Early History of Washington College_." (ordered printed by the Board of Trustees). This constitutes the college's first authorized, _published_ History.

22   I. Taylor Sanders, II, _Now Let the Gospel Trumpet Blow_, Lexington, Virginia, New Monmouth Presbyterian Church, 1986.

23   Hanover Presbytery Meeting Minutes, pg. 72, para one. Ordered that the clerk furnish the Clerk of the Trustees of the Prince Edward Academy with a copy of all of our Minutes relative

historical sketch, based on documentary records of the founding and patronizing Presbytery, is located in the Board of Trustees record book containing the Trustees' meeting minutes covering its earliest years and is easily located in the first several pages of the Trustees' first record book. The Presbytery's recorded directive, in this regard, was admittedly only in reference to the Prince Edward Academy, but the two Academies were created at nearly the same time and the clerk obviously realized that what he was directed to provide to Prince Edward Trustees should also be provided to the Augusta Academy's Trustees. It is not uninteresting that the clerk who created the first authorized documentary history for both of these venerable institutions of higher learning was also the only man in Virginia who served as a Trustee on the Boards of Trustees of both of these colleges. Caleb Wallace would go on to become a Justice of the then highest court in Kentucky.

The opening lines of Judge Wallace's history of Liberty Hall Academy deserve to be repeated frequently, which this report has done. They are:

> **The Present Academy of Liberty Hall began under the Direction and Patronage of the Presbytery of Hanover as the following minutes fully evince.**

> **At a session of the Pby of Hanover at Cub Creek Oct. 13, 1774, the Pby resumed consideration of a school for the liberal education of youth which we unanimously judge to be of great importance. We do therefore agree to establish and patronize a public school which shall be confined to the county of Augusta in this colony. At present it shall be managed by Mr. William Graham, a Gentleman properly recommended . . .[24]** (Emphasis added)

Note: Not one author who has asserted that Washington and Lee University's origins are to be found in the local common or preparatory schools of Robert Alexander and/or Rev. John Brown bothered to provide any credible evidence in support of that claim. Most who have made such a claim have also erred by asserting Robert Alexander was a graduate of one of two possible European Colleges located in the British Isles, but Dr. Ollinger Crenshaw investigated those claims and concluded that Mr. Alexander attended neither of these institutions. (See Dr. Crenshaw's General Lee's College, "Typescript version, Appendix A," "The Problem of the Origins.")[25] Their failure in this additional regard reflects poorly on their credulity generally.

---

to that Academy, to be entered in their book. Apparently, Wallace realized that the Presbytery intended that he provide the same information for its other seminary in Augusta County, which he obviously did.

24 ***Rev. Caleb Wallace, Liberty Hall Academy Record Book, containing the meeting minutes of the Board of Trustees of Liberty Hall Academy, pg. 3. The history was organized and written down by Rev. Caleb Wallace, Clerk of the Hanover Presbytery. It is signed by Mr. Wallace and dated May of 1776. The second paragraph is an extract taken from the Hanover Presbytery's meeting minutes.***

25 *Dr. Ollinger Crenshaw, General Lee's College,* typescript, unpublished version in two volumes with Appendix 'A', "The Problem of the Origins" (pg. 524 of entire typescript, but Appendix 'A' is also paginated separately as pages 1-13). This typescript is housed at the Leyburn Library of Washington and Lee University.

Claverhouse Associates wishes to acknowledge the cooperation and assistance of the library staffs of Washington and Lee University (Leyburn Library), Union Theological Seminary in Richmond, Virginia, and Princeton Theological Seminary—all of which have provided important assistance in locating scarce and early records of the Hanover Presbytery, as well as records of the Trustees of Liberty Hall Academy (now Washington and Lee University.) Of paramount importance is the assistance of the Library at Princeton Theological Seminary which provided a photocopy of the original manuscript of Rev. Archibald Alexander's manuscript "Memoir of Rev. William Graham" written in the 1840s.[26]

The research foundation upon which this audit was constructed was built over the course of more than forty years. The auditor has had the distinct advantage of time, computer technology, and the cooperation of many individuals associated officially and unofficially with Washington and Lee University. From the beginning of this process in 1972 until the present, the auditor has enjoyed the willing cooperation of the university, its administrators, and its faculty. In the earliest days of this project, the auditor communicated with the librarian, Betty Ruth Kondayan, who provided much valuable material, and the auditor had an unscheduled on-site interview at the university with the venerable Dean, James G. Leyburn for whom the current library is named. Many years ago, the auditor communicated with the late Dr. Diehl, the well-known local Rockbridge County historian. More recently, the auditor has communicated with both Dr. Taylor Sanders, Dr. McDaniel, and Dr. Theodore DeLaney whose works and helpful comments are herein acknowledged and have been most appreciated.[27] The auditor also acknowledges the assistance and cooperation of the staff of the Library at Princeton Theological Seminary who made copies of rare and valuable manuscript resources available for the auditor's use in conducting this audit.

The auditor has been a rare book hobbyist/dealer for over forty years and has relied heavily on numerous scarce and even rare written materials that he has in his own personal library. Many of these books, pamphlets, and journals are now available online through various vendors like Google Books, and the auditor has downloaded several of these in order to print selected pages containing possible material to be extracted and then quoted in our report. Since the auditor possessed most of the original materials, we have only cited in the report's bibliography and footnotes the printed source originally relied upon. There are some materials referred to in the report that we obtained via Google Books and are not in the

---

26 This critically important and extensive document does not appear to have ever been published, although many extracts were published in Archibald Alexander's biography listed in this report's bibliography. The biography is no substitute for the original memoir of William Graham because the biographer/editor occasionally took inappropriate liberties that are of important consequence, as is discussed elsewhere in this report. The original manuscript memoir of Rev. William Graham written by Archibald Alexander is housed at the Princeton Theological Seminary Library. A spiral-bound photocopy of the original handwritten memoir is housed at the Leyburn Library of Washington and Lee University.

27 None of the individuals named, endorsed, or in any way articulated agreement with any of the Author's findings. Their endorsements were neither asked for nor were voluntarily expressed.

auditor's library, but none that comes to mind was of critical importance to the reports' fundamental conclusions. Where the auditor relied solely on material from one of Google's Books, he has acknowledged Google Books as his source for the material. If the auditor has overlooked any of these, he extends his apologies to Google Books and to Google's founder Mr. Page. Mr. Page grew up in the auditor's East Lansing, Michigan, neighborhood. Thanks to Mr. Page and his Google Books, those who may want to fact-check this report will be able to do so with much greater ease than in the past.

*Claverhouse Associates is a national performance-auditing firm that has been in business since 1991. The firm is an independent, well-known enterprise, widely recognized by numerous federal and state regulators that regulate national and state arbitration programs operating pursuant to the Federal Magnuson-Moss Warranty Act and its associated administrative regulation CFR Part 703. Most audits conducted by Claverhouse Associates are mandated by Federal or state law, and the principal recipients of the audit reports are the governing regulatory agencies. The purpose of the audits is to ensure annually that the arbitration program administrators and their trained arbitrators have carried out their regulated programs in compliance with the governing regulatory requirements. The primary recipients of the audit reports generated by Claverhouse Associates are the United States Federal Trade Commission and selected state regulatory agencies.

Some of the corporate entities that have been a part of audits conducted by Claverhouse Associates include Acura, Ford Motor Co., Chrysler Corp., General Motors, Honda, Toyota, Lexus, Mercedes Benz, Porsche, Suzuki, Mitsubishi, and Volkswagen.

The founding president and senior auditor is Kent S. Wilcox. Mr. Wilcox was for many years director of an agency in the State of Michigan named the Michigan Consumers Council, which had the responsibility for advising the governor, the Secretary of State, the Attorney General, and both houses of the Michigan Legislature, on all pending legislation that impacted Michigan consumers, including banking, public utilities, insurance, and retail sales, as well as all licensed occupations. In this capacity, Mr. Wilcox sat on the public policy committee of the National Association of Consumer Agency Administrators. In addition, Mr. Wilcox was appointed to numerous Boards and Commissions, task forces, and special committees by governors and various regulatory agency administrative heads. A recognized expert on Consumer Law, he has lectured on and taught classes on Consumer Law at Eastern Michigan University. He was also appointed by the Michigan Supreme Court's administrative division to a special advisory committee concerning administrative rules and procedures where he served for several years.

During his tenure in state government, Mr. Wilcox appeared on hundreds of television and radio programs, including multiple appearances on national broadcasting programs like, NBC's The Today Show and CBS Morning News. His national performance-auditing firm is the longest operating firm of its type in the nation, and his company's mandated performance audits have gone unquestioned and unchallenged by any federal or state regulator for twenty-five years.

Disclosure: The auditor, Kent S. Wilcox, is related to several families who long ago lived in Rockbridge County, Virginia. His fifth great-grandfather, for example, is that Samuel Lyle who was one of the original Trustees of Liberty Hall Academy and was for many years the Trustees' treasurer. The enclosed assessments, however, are in most every case not subject to any form of significant familial bias because they are in most every case based on incontrovertible documentary records, as well as the published eyewitness testimony of unimpeachable witnesses most of whom testified in print or in eighteenth-century letters.

Statement of Purpose

Claverhouse Associates' original purpose in conducting this historical performance audit was to reveal the true nature of the irreconcilable assertions[28] referenced by the preeminent historian of Washington and Lee University, Dr. Ollinger Crenshaw, in the following true statement below:

> *It is evident even from cursory investigation that the institution* [W&L] *had adhered to_ one version of its history prior to 1865, and to another in the post-bellum era.*[29] (O. Crenshaw, General Lee's College, Typescript version, Appendix, "The Problem with the Origins") (Emphasis added here does not represent an error.)

In addition, to identify the more egregious of the inexplicable and seemingly innumerable written historical mistakes as they relate to the early history of Washington and Lee and its founding first president, Rev. William Graham, that have been repeated in variant forms by historians, genealogists, and pamphleteers of every imaginable sort since 1850. This includes significant errors of omission concerning the first black college graduate in America as well as the first female college student in America and concerning the university's founding first president, Rev. William Graham.

Note: The two currently competing versions of the founding are as follows:

CORRECT VERSION

a) The college was created by the Hanover Presbytery, an association of ministers and church elders to establish and

---

28 It is axiomatic that an institution cannot have two conflicting histories of their founding that are both accurate reflections of that event. To legitimately supplant one with another suggests the appropriateness of an explanation clarifying which version is true. Washington and Lee University, however, in 1865 repudiated the college's seventy-five year consistent history without having announced its repudiation, and further, without bothering to explain why the earlier history was inaccurate, or why the revised history was true. This is a situation that cries out for clarification, which this auditor attempts to provide.

29

patronize a public Academy in Augusta County, Virginia, on October 13, 1774, under the direction of Rev. William Graham;

INCORRECT VERSION

b) The college began with a private preparatory school conducted by a Mr. Robert Alexander in Augusta County in 1748, 1749, or 1752, which was subsequently conducted by Rev. John Brown and which later evolved into Washington and Lee University. *Note: This version appears in various forms, some of which may only refer to one or the other of these two named educators.*

Quite obviously, both renditions cannot be true. As the audit will demonstrate, version (a) is undeniably correct while version (b) is demonstrably incorrect.

Note: The principal errors of omission refer to students John Chavis and Sarah Priestley. Both of these students were accepted at Liberty Hall by its first president William Graham. The only two such college students who attended chartered institutions of higher learning in the United States during the eighteenth century. They also include other various failures of the university to adequately recognize and honor the many important contributions made by the university's founding first president William Graham. His contributions to higher education as well as to Virginia and to the nation as a political philosopher and an advocate for religious freedom and civil liberties associated with the nation's Bill of Rights. Moreover, as a leading proponent of the American Revolution who took to the field as a captain of militia on more than one occasion during the war. Finally, the university has failed to make their founding first president's known writings available to the public by reprinting his known works.

Introduction

In 1972, the author received a letter from his barely known father announcing that he had been diagnosed with terminal cancer. Thus began a forty-year investigation that was precipitated by a desire to learn more about the man I then only vaguely knew and about the family I had never known.

During a quickly arranged visit to Oklahoma for a final visit, I was introduced to my eldest living relative, a great-aunt from Muskogee, who put me in touch with her younger sister in Sacramento that possessed a rare family history. This book turned out to be an astounding tome filled with amazing revelations, one of which led me the Great Valley of Virginia. Here, I discovered several links to Washington and Lee University, including the fact that my fifth great-grandfather, Samuel Lyle, was one of the original Trustees, appointed two months before the Continental Congress approved the Declaration of Independence. This was how the author discovered why the then college was initially named Liberty Hall Academy. But that was just the first of a series of discoveries that would stretch to over forty years of periodic amazing revelations.

In time, my research unearthed certain disturbing anomalies and inconsistencies that could not be reasonably rectified. As a professional performance auditor, these inconsistencies were becoming increasingly annoying, and I became plagued by a need to rectify representations that did not seem to be possible. These fragmentary miscues began to appear as pieces to a puzzle. As each small error was corrected, a place into the partial picture the actual image began to form a recognizable form. In time, everything became clear. What began as a series of small mistakes became a monstrous hoax as inconsistencies began to call into question professional reputations and historians with an agenda that went into a predictable cover-up mode. Most of the historians that have been assessed and discovered to have added to the long list of errors went astray due to carelessness. Only a few knew or should have known that what they were publishing was not true. Unfortunately, one of them was an author of great reputation who was relied upon when he should not have been.

Fortunately, there are extant records and documents that allow for correcting the mistakes of the past; but for some unknown reason, historians, genealogists, and researchers since 1850 neglected to consult these obscure archival treasures. Hopefully, once the existence of the records that are now being highlighted are consulted and analyzed by professional historians, a cogent history of the founding of Washington and Lee will be published and with it a restoration of the true history of that period.

Perhaps the most egregious mistakes that have been identified herein relate to the unmerciful maligning of the character of the man who was most responsible for the erecting the first institution of higher learning south of the Potomac and west of the Blue Ridge Mountains, Rev. William Graham.

Rev. Graham was summoned by the leading Presbyterians of Virginia, to come south for the stated purpose of managing the launching of an educational institution. The envisioned seminary or "college[30]"—if you were able to obtain a charter from the governing authorities—was to be for the purpose of preparing educators and clergymen. There was, at the time, an increasing demand for ministers and teachers as the nation was realizing its manifest destiny to expand its environs both southward and westward.

This noble objective Mr. Graham met and indeed far exceeded its original intent. In the end, he had become the most sought-after educator and divine south of the Potomac. A fact, that today is mostly obscured from view in the vicinage of the Valley of Virginia. At the same time, this fact was well recognized by the leading men of that early period. Men like Patrick Henry, James Madison, George Mason, Edmund Randolph, and Rev. Archibald Alexander, founding president of the Princeton Theological seminary, all of Virginia. Even founding fathers like Graham's preceptor, Rev. John Witherspoon, president of Princeton and signer of our famous Declaration of Independence, and Witherspoon's son-in-law, who succeeded Witherspoon as president of Princeton, Samuel Stanhope Smith understood the unusual gifts of Rev. Graham. It was this Smith who had the honor of summoning Graham to Virginia at the behest of the Presbyterian Clergymen of Virginia. Smith and Graham and their mutual schoolmate at Princeton, James Madison, were all critically involved in Virginia's great struggle for religious liberty that flowered into the establishment clause of the nation's Bill of Rights. These men knew Rev. Graham in ways that today's leading men of the Great Valley do not.

It is one of the author's objectives to shine a bright light on obscurities that have hidden Graham from view and allowed fictionalized characterizations to camouflage from view the true nature of the man who deserves to be feted as the father of that institution known to many in that day as the "Princeton of the South." As these facts emerge, they will assist in appropriately assigning to the dung-heap of history the great fabrication that Rev. William Graham was a "defender of African slavery." An invidious distinction that could only come

---

30   British authorities, in that day, typically only awarded official charters with degree granting authority to educational institutions that were patronized by the "established" Church of England, which was then denominated the Anglican Church. Other such institutions of the higher order were therefore denominated "Academy." Common schools were labeled variously as "English schools," "grammar schools," "Latin Schools," etc., the most common denomination among Presbyterians was the "grammar school" which was a preparatory school. These schools and their curriculum was determined by the skills of the instructors that conducted them. Many basic common schools that offered fundamental classes in elementary mathematics, English composition, geography, history, and literature were often simply referred to as a school. At Princeton and later at Liberty Hall, the grammar school operated in conjunction with the college was a precollege preparatory school that, in addition to basic mathematics and English composition, offered elementary Latin and Greek. A grasp of these languages, in that day, was a prerequisite for entry into college.

from someone who did not know the measure of this man. A discovery that will allow for a well-deserved restoration of the unstained character of the university's founding father.

A later unearthing that will do much for the prestige of Washington and Lee is the unchallengeable fact that Graham's Liberty Hall Academy holds the distinct honor of being the first and only degree-granting college in North America to have accepted into its undergraduate ranks, a man that would be distinguished as the first black college graduate in the United States of America. The documentary evidence that makes this a certainty emerged from the rich storehouse of ancient archival records located in various libraries in Virginia. Records that will allow posterity an opportunity to reevaluate many questionable notions that have served to distort and misinterpret various important historical occurrences in Virginia during the last half of the eighteenth century.

In the course of the author's research, it was also revealed that it was at Washington and Lee that women in America first found an open door to higher education. Indeed, a married woman, Mrs. Sarah (McBride) Priestley, found in Rev. William Graham a welcoming educator who made her a member of the college's regular academic program. This disclosure will open the door to more in-depth research into Washington and Lee's unprecedented foray into progressive education and into the colorful lives of Mrs. Priestley and her husband. Dr. James Priestley.[31] Together these two early students at Liberty Hall later oversaw educational endeavors for men and women in various parts of the country. Mrs. Priestley burdened, at the time of her matriculation with two young children, was unable to complete her program at Liberty Hall, but she advanced sufficiently that she later oversaw a successful school for women in Baltimore. This school was operated in conjunction with her husband's Academy there.

The importance of the matriculation of Mr. Chavis and Mrs. Priestley has heretofore not been fully appreciated in the history of higher education in America. That this occurred under Rev. William Graham without any known associated social disturbances in the then-largest slaveholding state in the nation is an astounding revelation pregnant with research possibilities. The author determined that these shocking realities deserved to be placed before the reading public.

Analysis of the extant historical literature covering the second half of eighteenth-century Virginia made clear that some of the existing assumptions about affairs in the Valley relied upon by historians were not sustainable when scrutinized. Highly significant hoaxes and dishonesty also emerged that are shocking due to the participation by some important historians will call into question numerous sacred cows, like the reliability of the long accepted legitimacy of the works of William Henry Foote. A careful study of his two heretofore valued *Sketches of Virginia, Historical and Biographical* will henceforth become a much more cautiously cited source. Foote's monumental historical misdeeds played a central role in the 1865 inappropriate and surreptitious repudiation of Washington

---

31   Mrs. Priestley's husband was one of Graham's earliest students at Liberty Hall who Graham educated and boarded at his own expense because Priestley's father was poor.

and Lee's original and now proven legitimate history of its founding. This and the institution's misguided adoption of a fictionalized and easily proven bogus account of its founding by a credulous Board of Trustees in 1865 embarrassingly resulted in an apparent magical expansion of the university's life by twenty-five years. The culmination of the embarrassment was the celebration and fanfare that took place in Lexington throughout the 1998–99 academic year.[32]

The necessary redundancies associated with the unfortunate repetitions by so many different writers, each presenting their variations on the same theme, are regrettable. This rather comprehensive collection of assessments, however, will serve as a handy reference guide for avoiding further repeats of the same common mistakes.

The author laments not being possessed of the writing skills this endeavor deserves. His hope is that his findings and discoveries will assist someone more worthy with the important task of rewriting the early history of the university and its founding first president, William Graham—a man who Dr. Samuel L. Campbell once described thus:

> Mr. Graham came to this country with the character of a gentleman of genius, scholarship, and piety, which character he supported through life.[33]

(Dr. Samuel L. Campbell, "History of Washington College . . ."
Southern Literary Messenger, 1838.)

---

32 See W&L website for "A Brief History" April 1, 2018. In 2024, W&L can rightfully celebrate their 250th Anniversary of its nativity. On October 13 of that year, they can celebrate its 250th birthday.

33 Dr. Samuel L. Campbell, of Rockbridge, . . . enjoyed opportunities of acquaintance with Mr. Graham equal to those enjoyed by any other man . . . Campbell was brought up under the tuition of Mr. Graham from his youth and was perfectly acquainted with all his excellencies and his foibles. He not only pursued his academical studies under the direction of Mr. G but also studied theology under his guidance for several years . . ." (Alexander, Mss. "Memoir of Rev. William Graham," pp 48,49.)

Prolegomenon

(A Critical Introduction)

> *__For it was under Wm. Graham that our Academy first received__
> __its existence__ and it is chiefly owing to his extraordinary
> exertions that it has persevered through all the convulsions of
> a calamitous War and the many vicissitudes which have taken
> place through the operations of various causes for the space of
> about 16 years . . .*
>
> (Liberty Hall Academy Board of Trustees' Petition
> to the Virginia Synod of the Presbyterian Church,
> Sept. 1792)

The multifarious nature of this historical performance audit report suggests
the appropriateness of providing a rather critical introduction in order to better
understand the several laudatory revelations that emerged from the investigation
upon which the reports' findings are based. Clearly, Washington and Lee
University's reputation will be greatly enhanced by the findings in two material
ways. First, because it has been revealed that without question Washington and
Lee University was the only eighteenth-century chartered American college that
accepted a black college student. The student, John Chavis, is not just the only
known black student to have been accepted into the regular academic course
of a recognized college in the United States, he also "went through the regular
academic course."[34] As such, he is the first black college graduate in the nation.
This fact, Chavis himself asserted as part of a court filing, and fortunately it was
officially recorded and memorialized in a Rockbridge County Court order, signed
by every one of the then sitting magistrates, one of whom, William Lyle, was also
a Trustee of Washington College. Many years later, Chavis' status as a college
graduate of Washington and Lee University was alluded to in a written essay by

---

34   A euphemism for *college graduate*, common in the American colonies around the time of the
     American Revolution. In rural America in the eighteenth century, formal graduations were
     often impractical and the printing of documents like diplomas was uncommon. Moreover,
     at that time, certifying a student for graduation was not a prevalent procedure. The fact that
     Chavis "went through the regular academic program" at Liberty Hall Academy was widely
     recognized in that time, as the local court records from that period evince. The Lexington
     Presby recognized this fact as well when they accepted Chavis for "Trials" to certify his
     scholarly attainments and his Christian rectitude and faith. Presbyterian ministers were all
     expected to have acquired higher lever scholarship as a prerequisite to being licensed to peach
     the gospel. It is recorded in church records that Rev. Chavis preached to numerous Virginia
     congregations in the early part of the nineteenth century where he was well received without
     exception.

yet another Trustee of the college, William Henry Ruffner[35] whose father had been an early president of the college.

Secondly, Washington and Lee was the only American college in the eighteenth century to accept a female student, Sarah (McBride Priestley) into its regular academic program. In both cases, our audit uncovered records that prove both of these assertions. That Mrs. Priestley was enrolled as a regular student in the regular academic program is unassailable.[36] The auditor's exhaustive search failed to locate any other college that claims to have had a regular undergraduate black student in the eighteenth century or a female student.

There is also a significant finding that calls for a major correction by the administration to restore the university's correct narrative that describes the institution's origins and its official founding by those responsible for its existence. The early account (1776) was consistently provided to the administrators, governors (Trustees), students, faculty, alumni, and the public during the college's first seventy-five years. This well-documented history was, however, radically repudiated and inappropriately revised in 1865 without explanation and without the support of any credible evidence or justification. This revisionism took place in the aftermath of a great conflagration that engulfed our nation between 1861 and 1865 and which decimated the lives and infrastructure of Virginia, including the college destined to become Washington and Lee University. Today, much of the true history has been restored as a result of this audit. A more thorough history remains to be properly written by others more suited to the task, but now, that can be accomplished based on documentary-based facts. The current public representation is based entirely on fragments of mere assumptions, gossip, gratuitous assertions, and easily disproved hearsay. The history of the college's founding and its origins as currently represented in most-published histories and by the university is an absurd and easily proven fiction.

Dr. Ollinger Crenshaw

To date (Summer 2017), the undisputed premier published history of Washington and Lee University is _General Lee's College,_ by Dr. Ollinger Crenshaw, late professor of history at Washington and Lee published by Random

---

35   , unpublished manuscript article _"An Educated Negro Preacher of a Century Ago,"_ n.d., cite: William Henry Ruffner Papers, 1848–1907, Accession 24814, personal papers, collection, The Library of Virginia, Richmond, Virginia. 5pg. [no.88]. The University's Catalog of the Alumni fails to reference Chavis as a graduate. Apparently, the university is unaware of that which was quite plain to the various magistrates of Rockbridge County as well as to two early Trustees with impeccable reputations and which was obviously apparent to the Lexington Presbytery, which licensed Chavis as a Presbyterian minister. As a general rule, the Presbyterian Church only licensed individuals with a college degree. Moreover, Claverhouse could not find any claim that Chavis did not complete his education at Liberty Hall Academy(W&L)., excepting, of course, those Chavis family biographers who mistakenly believed that Chavis was educated at Princeton. An idea exposed for the error that it is within this report.

36   Its truth was testified to by the venerable Rev. Dr. Archibald Alexander who was a schoolmate of Mrs. Priestley. See Alexander's "Memoir of Rev. William Graham."

House in 1969. More important, however, in many ways, is a slightly earlier version written by Crenshaw, which, in its typescript form, contains a multitude of enlightening footnotes and an invaluable appendix entitled "The Problem of the Origins." This version has yet to be published.[37]

Crenshaw's book in either format comprises the broadest and most thoroughly researched historical treatment of Washington and Lee University that currently exists. At the same time, the book's initial chapters on the early days of the college are inexplicably sprinkled with several of the worst common errors committed by Dr. Crenshaw's antecedent sources, most of whom arose in the aftermath of the Civil War. The lone exception being the earlier and fallacious account of the college's founding published by William Henry Foote in 1850. Foote based his repudiation of the long-established documentary-based institutional history, on a brief phrase in a very dubious letter, ostensibly written by Rev. Samuel Houston. Relying on this scant piece of evidence, if indeed it actually exists, Foote repudiates all of the numerous historical published articles and institutional records that were created between 1774 and 1849. All of the early records and publications were generally consistent as regards to who created the college and when it was created, and importantly, they all contained a completely contrary account to that perpetrated by the grossly mistaken Mr. Foote. The records and publications which all agreed that the college was founded by the Hanover Presbytery in October of 1774 had been the universally accepted account during the college's first seventy-five years.

It was Dr. Ollinger Crenshaw who discovered the amazing fact that the university holds the distinction of being the only known long-established American University that possesses two entirely unique histories of its founding and its origins. One that was consistently maintained during the institution's first seventy-five years, and the other one astoundingly fashioned in the fertile imaginations of a credulous Board of Trustees in 1865. It was this 1865 Board which, in that same year, presumably authorized the rewrite of the history of the college's nativity.[38] A revision based, in the main, on the utterly false undocumented narratives published by William Henry Foote.[39] Crenshaw, however, made no attempt to unravel the mystery of these Trustees' motivations or to explain who were the driving forces behind the revisionism.

Disappointingly, Crenshaw declined to declare that the account of the founding currently represented by most modern-day historians is clearly false. Instead, he mysteriously adopted the incorrect account currently represented by

---

37 In the 1980s, Dr. Crenshaw's widow donated the typescript to the University's Leyburn Library. The appendix deserves to be published and historians deserve to have easy access to it.

38 We use "presumably" because while the revised history was published in a university-sponsored pamphlet, there was no recorded directive or decision to alter the previously represented history; It simply appeared without explanation.

39 William Henry Foote, DD, *Sketches of Virginia, Historical and Biographical*, First Series, Philadelphia, William S. Martien., 1850. See also John Knox Press reprint edition 1966, with index; Sketches of Virginia, Historical and Biographical, Second Series, second edition Revised, Philadelphia, JB Lippincott & Co., 1856.

Washington and Lee and left the responsibility of calling that current account exactly what it is to others. Of course, what the currently represented history is, is an inexcusably incorrect fiction lacking any credible eighteenth-century evidence to support its accuracy.

Any serious assessment of the founding by an experienced auditor would quickly discover the undeniable truth of all of this report's major findings including the fact that the university' currently asserted history of the founding is undeniably false and foundationless. A consideration of the full complement of the important known facts leads inescapably to our conclusions. Moreover, no credible evidence exists to support the university's current claim that the college was founded earlier than 1774.[40] Neither is there any credible evidence to support the idea that the college was linked in any way to the eighteenth-century educational endeavors of either Robert Alexander or Rev. John Brown.

Robert Alexander's educational endeavors are indistinguishable from most all of the other early private efforts in rural America to provide elementary instruction to the local rural residents, including those of his brother, Archibald ("Old Ersbel")Alexander. "Ersbel" as he was referred to, provided elemental instruction to one of Liberty Hall's original Trustees, Samuel Lyle, in the same period and same neighborhood where Robert was carrying out his educational instruction. These facts were related by Mr. Lyle to Ersbel's grandson, Archibald Alexander, who provides a cursory description of these efforts by his grandfather in his "Memoir of Rev. William Graham." Certainly, Archibald Alexander, a noted historian of early Presbyterian educational activities in Colonial America, would hardly have failed to credit his grandfather's brother Robert if he had any reason to believe that Robert's educational endeavors were worthy of being noted as anything exceptional, but, of course, he did no such thing. The well-published Rev. Archibald Alexander had myriad opportunities to credit his close relations in print had he thought it appropriate. Indeed, he did just the opposite, as is noted in his vastly important Address to the Alumni of Washington College, wherein he gives all the credit to William Graham for being the school's father and first chief executive officer.[41] A sentiment shared by the entire eighteenth-century Board of Trustees as reflected in its petition to the Virginia Synod of the Presbyterian Church in the early 1790s.

Crenshaw, concerning the vastly important notion of the college's founding, declined to bring the embarrassing truth to the attention of the university that

---

40   The university which adopted the revised version in 1865, thereafter, made slight modifications by changing the year they claimed the school began (e.g., 1748, 1749, 1752, etc.); but all their assertions, in this regard were, of course, all wrong for the same reason.

41   Some might question this based on the biography of Rev. Archibald Alexander, but they would be mistaken. Indeed, the biography written by Alexander's son, James, does quote his father as saying that the school, Augusta Academy, had existed before Mr. Graham's coming, but James's quotation is a mistake and possibly a forged manipulation of his father's words executed in a ridiculous attempt to correct what James believed to have been a mistake made by his father. This subject is thoroughly discussed and analyzed in this report's section addressing the various author's mistakes in the subsection devoted to Archibald Alexander.

was both his employer and his financially supporting partial underwriter for conducting the research necessary for writing *General Lee's College*. It comes as no great shock then that Crenshaw demurred when confronted with the embarrassing reality that no one at the university, after 1865, had ever bothered to thoroughly research their own early records in order to discover their proper history. Instead, they all essentially relied upon William Henry Foote or Foote's many credulous adherents including Trustee Bolivar Christian.

Unfortunately, when Random House decided to publish *General Lee's College*, it purged Crenshaw's original manuscript version of *General Lee's College* of its numerous and important footnotes and its vastly important appendix A entitled "The Problem of the Origins." The rationale for the publishing house's decision in this regard is unknown to the auditor. Its decision, whatever its reasons, served to conceal from public view the true history of the university's founding.

If the institution's history department had exercised proper due diligence, however, someone on the faculty would have long ago revealed that which this report makes abundantly clear, which is that the university's earliest records contain all that is necessary to establish what entity created the college and precisely when it took place. Alas, no one in the History Department or any other university official, after 1865, ever cited, or even referenced the institution's first written and authorized history of the founding of the college.

While the college was created on October 13, 1774, the creators, the members of the Hanover Presbytery, withheld giving the school an official name, reserving that honor for the prospective Board of Trustees. The Board of Trustees was created by the Hanover Presbytery on May 6, 1776,[42] and then at the Trustees' first meeting a week later (May 13), the Board's first official and recorded Act was to give its school the name Liberty Hall Academy. These facts are easily located in the university's first record book which was used to record the meeting minutes of the Board of Trustees. Embarrassingly, the facts are located on this precious artifact's first page of text,[43] which is undeniably the college's first

---

42   Interestingly, the Presbytery acted to create the Board of Trustees just as the buildings that were to comprise the campus were being completed at Timber Ridge. This suggests that Presbytery and the college administration (William Graham) were operating in concert with a well-conceived plan that was intricately timed to establish Graham as the pastor of Timber Ridge congregation prior to the buildings being constructed on lands adjacent to Timber Ridge that were donated by members of the same congregation. As pastor, Graham's initial and immediate expenses were also being covered separately, allowing the raised funds to cover institutional costs related to construction and academic materials including a library and science and mathematics laboratory apparatus.

43   As this report reveals, one page of text in this venerable record book, now precedes the institution's first authorized history of the school's creation, but it only appeared in this location by the infamous and grossly inappropriate act to paste in a ridiculous sheet of notes about which almost nothing is known for certain. The culprit responsible for this travesty, according to Dr. Crenshaw, was Trustee Bolivar Christian, a noted lawyer who should have known better. This egregious misdeed is thoroughly discussed in the main body of the report. Christian's claims about this document defy reason and are contradicted by the man he names as its author, Edward Graham. Professor Edward Graham's views on the topic of the school's founding were widely known during the last decades of his life, and they bore no resemblance to the contents of this unsigned and undated document

authorized history, is a clear and concise detailing of the events leading up to and including the official decision to "establish and patronize" a public seminary for the education of young men, and especially those who were predisposed to preaching the Holy Gospel. A history that as far as the auditor could determine has never been published, nor even cited as an authority during the last two hundred years. This fact is admittedly as astonishing as it is incomprehensible.

In appendix A, Dr. Crenshaw explained that Washington and Lee University, unlike any other institution in the nation, has represented to the public two altogether conflicting histories detailing how and when the institution was founded. The university's earliest representation of the founding and it activities during its early years is based on official documentary records of the last quarter of the eighteenth century. Records of both the Hanover Presbytery, which created the school, and served as its first governing authority and those of the college's Board of Trustees which accepted most of the governance responsibilities once the incipient operation was transferred from its temporary headquarters at Mount Pleasant to the new campus buildings on lands adjacent to the Timber Ridge Presbyterian Meeting House.

The second and conflicting history was adopted by the college in the iconic year of 1865. At this time, the college's misguided Trustees arbitrarily altered the university's birthdate by extending its existence by twenty-five years. Somehow, the world of American history seems to have failed to take cognizance of the seemingly paradoxical inconsistency of claiming to have two entirely different dates of birth. A difference of two-and-a-half decades. Crenshaw left to posterity the means by which to begin solving the mystery of two competing histories, but he declined to rock the Lexington community's boat, so to speak. He was a messenger who apparently sought to avoid the likely wrath of some in the greater Lexington community for delivering an unpopular message that would likely ruffle the feathers of some influential local Lexington area families. Some of these families, it seems, have long been representing an ancient connection to the university that actually does not exist. His reluctance, in this regard, is, therefore, more understandable than justified.

The revised adopted history of Washington and Lee that the university has adhered to since 1865 is an unadulterated fiction bearing little resemblance to the truth. It is an incontestably embarrassing representation, and like fairytale air castles, it was built without the benefit of any historical foundation whatsoever. Indeed, the revision was an action of paramount significance that went entirely unnoticed to and unexplained to the public. Instead, the Trustees buried their newly revised history of the founding in a mostly in-house article in a larger piece called in its short title, Charter and Laws.[44]

---

44   The official title of this publication is *Charter and Laws and Trustees and Alumni of Washington College at Lexington, Virginia, A. D. 1865,* Richmond, 1865. The number of copies printed is unknown to the auditor, but its title does not suggest that it enjoyed a wide public circulation. The few who may have seen the publication would not likely realize that the opening article constituted a complete repudiation of a long-established contrary history. The article's unprovocative title is "Historical Statistics."

Crenshaw in his *appendix A*, "The Problem of the Origins" then, did not include the inescapable conclusion and chose to merely point out the inconsistency between what the university represents today and what the college's institutional guardians represented during its first seventy-five years of existence. In other words, he didn't say the 1865 Trustees were wrong. He said its action in this regard was inconsistent.

This report, however, explains what transpired in this regard and demonstrates just how all the collected documentary evidence known to exist on the subject is consistent with the institution's early history as originally represented. It also demonstrates that the currently represented institutional history is ***inconsistent*** with all the known eighteenth-century documentary evidence known to exist. The currently asserted history is offered without benefit of authority, and this is for good cause, which is that there is no credible authority or evidence to support the revised account. None that is, which existed prior to Foote's publishing of his two books on Virginia. Thereafter, there were many such accounts, but all were, at its root, based on Foote's false account, and none of them ever bothers to even identify the inconsistency between the 1865 revised history and the one adhered to by the institution for nearly a century (1774–1865.)

The first public appearance of a published revised version of the college's founding took place in the 1850 publication of William Henry Foote and was contained in the first volume of *Sketches of Virginia, Historical and Biographical*. The second appearance of any note also came from Foote. This account appeared when he released his second Series of *Sketches of Virginia* . . ., in 1855. While Foote's two accounts vary, they are, nevertheless, both wrong. Neither of Foote's published accounts of the college's founding was based upon any credible evidence, and both seriously conflict with all known previous publications and all of the known documentary evidence created in the eighteenth century.

Foote, who eschewed the use of citations of authority, fully admits this amazing fact in the introduction to the first volume of his two Virginia historical treatments. Understandably, he fails to provide any credible substantiation for his inconsistent account. He implies, however, that his account is based upon an alleged letter, supposedly written by Rev. Samuel Houston. We say "supposedly" because as best as the auditor was able to learn, no one but Mr. Foote has ever had the pleasure of seeing the referenced letter. This "letter" is a topic thoroughly treated with in this report. In sum, if indeed the letter ever existed, its content, as represented by Foote, is both replete with easily demonstrated historical errors of consequence, and its content in the first book, as represented by Foote, was altered and corrected by Foote without notice or acknowledgment in his second book. It is, therefore, neither credible nor competent evidence in support of Foote's preposterously mistaken representations about the origins of Washington and Lee University.

Foote quotes from Houston's alleged letter full of significant errors and then later publishes another altered version as though no changes had been made. In short, Foote altered what he said the letter contained in an apparent attempt to make the letter seem more credible. Had he acted in this way before a Court of law, Foote would have found himself in jail for, at least, perjury, and possibly for forgery. As it stands, he is simply an unmitigated obvious fraud. His guilt is proven by his own conflicting quotations of the same original text. Foote simply wanted the letter to say something other than what it apparently did say. The original quoted text is so patently false that the letter's author would have no credibility as a knowledgeable source pertaining to the creation of the college. This was apparently a fact that Foote discovered some time after he released his first volume of Virginia history. The "Houston letter" is the only possible evidence ever presented in print that Foote could possibly have relied upon for revising the university's early history that was consistently represented for seventy-five years[45](1774–1849).[46]

Institutional representations of the origins of the institution did not change from the original accounts until the landmark year of 1865. It was at this time that the Board of Trustees apparently experienced their extraordinary historical epiphany. Then, without fanfare or even a recognition of what was about to happen, the Board of Trustees of Washington College published in an official institutional document[47] an entirely different history of the school's founding, one that silently repudiated all of the early documentary evidence and the credible evidence written by Presbyterian Church leaders and early students of the institution who had matured into eminent scholars (e.g., Professor Edward Graham, Rev. Dr. Archibald Alexander, Dr. Samuel. Campbell, and John Holt Rice).

The Trustees chose instead to embrace a series of undocumented foundation less theories postulated by a misguided attorney and amateur historian named Bolivar Christian. Mr. Christian—having been appointed a Trustee of the college several years prior to the conflict between the States, and who had the distinction of being a law partner of John Randolph Tucker—made the unfortunate decision to expand his amateur status as would-be historian and apparently persuaded his colleagues on the Board of Trustees that all their predecessors had been wrong about when and how the college was founded.

Mr. Christian's venture into history as fiction does not reflect his only misadventure that seriously and negatively impacted the college's history; however, because, as pointed out by Dr. Crenshaw, he also perpetrated the so-called

---

45   Technically, for about ninety years since the University did not alter its represented history published in 1849 until they published the "Charter and Laws . . ." article in 1865.

46   Foote obviously was influenced by someone whose identity he wished to conceal. It would serve no useful purpose for the auditor to speculate on the subject of Foote's secret source.

47   *Charter and Laws and Trustees and Alumni of Washington College at Lexington, Virginia,* Richmond, 1865
       While the pamphlet lists no author or editor, the copy reviewed by the auditor is housed in the Leyburn Library of Washington and Lee University, and it is bound in a volume which bears the following legend upon its spine, "Washington and Lee University, Catalogs, 1865–1879." The volume includes an 1855 catalogue and also catalogues for 1865–1879 in chronological order, and a few additional miscellaneous items. The auditor has understandably accepted the authenticity of these various catalogues as having been produced at the behest of the university's administration.

"Edward Graham manuscript" hoax[48] which culminated in Mr. Christian pawning off an old sheet of undated and unsigned rough draft notes as a long-lost history written by a professor of the college.[49] Not content with writing a preposterous advocacy piece[50] falsely representing the document and its contents, Trustee Mr. Christian also desecrated one of the university's most sacred archives by inserting into the college's very first record book (the Trustees' only record of their first meeting minutes) this spurious document, which now, thanks to the misdeeds of Mr. Christian, is placed in the position of *page one* of the book's text despite the fact that it has no provenance, and its author and the date it was written are both mysteries. It is very much akin to the millions of sheets of paper stuffed into faculty file cabinets bearing discarded notes without a signature or any indication as to what the sheet represents, if anything.

By this act, Christian rendered this archive a partial forgery, passing it off as the college's first authorized history, when in fact, the document has no historical value whatsoever. No one knows what it is, what it represents, what its purpose was, or when and by whom it was written. Forensically, we only know that it is foolscap with writing on it.[51] Trustee Christian's actions make the university's

---

48   Crenshaw, however, does not label Christian's actions a "hoax." That is a conclusion reached by the auditor.

49   This episode should serve as a warning to all university professors to destroy all their old rejected rough drafts in order to avoid having someone decades after their death, presenting them to the public as being something they intended to publish. In this case, the sheet Mr. Christian claims to represent the historical views of Edward Graham contradict the known views of Edward Graham during the last twenty years of his life; these views are expressed repeatedly and consistently in letters to authors who later published histories that reflected Graham's thoughts on the origins of W&L, all of which contradict Mr. Christian's mystery document. Hence, the auditor's conclusion that the document, as represented by Mr. Christian, is a hoax. There is no simple basis upon which to conclude that this document is worthy of serious consideration.

50   A series of articles on the history of Washington College published in the Southern Collegian.

51   Dr. Crenshaw suggests in an unsigned article that it was likely written by Bolivar Christian. Titled, "The origins," it appeared in the Southern Collegian, February 7, 1874 [a W&L Newspaper]. It contains for the first time a printed version of the "Edward Graham manuscript," which is called *"a very recent discovery" of an early - virtually contemporaneous MS., whose antiquity 'proves itself'*; it is now prefixed to vol. 1 of the minutes of the Board of Trustees, and we here put it in print." Indeed! And how very convenient that Mr. Christian bases his nonsensical complete revision of the college's history on an unsigned, undated, series of notes, which Mr. Christian alone ascribes to Professor Edward Graham and which dubious document he himself appears to have pasted into the college's oldest record book, and which is now, thanks to Mr. Christian, located on the book's very first page. Had Mr. Christian bothered to read what had originally been the record book's very first page, prior to his meddling, he would have read the beginning of the college's first authorized history of the establishment and origins of the college, which clearly contradicts the claims of Mr. Christian's mystery document, misnamed, the "Edward Graham manuscript." Mr. Christian also conveniently neglects to mention that Edward Graham wrote the first *published* history of the college's origins in his "A Memoir of the Late Rev. William Graham, A.M." *The Evangelical and Literary Magazine and Missionary Chronicle*, IV (1821), p.75 et Seq, and that the published memoir completely contradicts the one-page mystery document relied upon by Mr. Christian, and which he inappropriately attributed to Edward Graham.

guardians (Trustees) appear foolish for credulously accepting the representations of one of their own who had completely altered the long-established history of the college without bothering to authenticate any of the numerous gratuitous assertions upon which his revised history is based.

This report will explain in some detail that Mr. Christian's supposed source, Edward Graham, wrote a memoir of his elder brother William Graham in 1821, which was published by another early student of Liberty Hall, John Holt Rice. Edward Graham's 1821 article delineates precisely when the college was established and by whom. This account is in direct contravention of the revisionist narrative published by Foote in 1850 and by the college in 1865.[52]

Noteworthy is the fact that Edward Graham was later credited by several historians with having supplied them with valuable information concerning the college's earliest years, and in every case, these authors subsequently published accounts consistent in all important respects with Edward's 1821 account and inconsistent with Mr. Christian's baseless assertions. The subsequent accounts published by the historians who had relied upon Edward Graham's written communications stretched over time until shortly before Edward's death in 1840; therefore, the inconsistent narrative jotted down on a scrap of foolscap upon which Mr. Bolivar Christian relied for his evidence overturning seventy-five years of documentary history, do not, and could not represent Edward's permanent view about the founding of the college.[53] Since the document is unsigned and undated, history will likely never be able to know what the document truly represents. The truth about what this document is, or means, is likely not discoverable. Regardless, it does not repudiate the many official records still extant that were created by the authorities that created the college.

A century and a half later, Dr. Crenshaw wrote out his shocking twentieth-century exposé in a dedicated appendix entitled "The Problem of the Origins." That appendix lay dormant for yet another forty-five years. It was this appendix A that served as the seminal precipitating impetus behind the conducting of this historical performance audit. The auditor came upon this revealing document somewhat accidentally, but upon reading it, he realized immediately that the reality which Dr. Crenshaw describes is not simply a historical paradox but constitutes a historical inconsistency that is seemingly without parallel in the history of American higher education, an inconsistency that is factually, irreconcilable. *Note: Numerous historians have attempted to reconcile these seeming inconsistencies including the renowned late Dr. Herbert B. Adams of the University of Virginia who tried valiantly to untangle the frustrating web of faulty assumptions and gross misinterpretations of official records of the Hanover*

---

52   *Charter and Laws and Trustees and Alumni of Washington College at Lexington, Virginia, A. D. 1865,* Richmond, 1865, includes a sketch of the early history of the college under the strange title, *"Historical Statistics.*

53   This is true even if the document is in Edward Graham's handwriting because we still have no idea when it was drafted and for what purpose. The possibilities are infinite. Certainly, Edward Graham never publicly acknowledge it to be his.

Presbytery between 1771 and the end of 1776, but as Dr. Crenshaw explains, even Dr. Adams threw up his hands in despair and gave up.[54]

What is abundantly clear is that either the initial seventy-five-year history was wrong, or the revised history is in error, they simply cannot both be true. The audit was designed, in part, to discover which history, if either, was true. The task of discovery, while in this case proving to be inordinately time-consuming, in retrospect, need not have been as difficult as it proved to be. Had the auditor only done that which he and all Valley historians should all have done and started by researching the earliest extant records, he and all of the others would have quickly discovered that the official documentary evidence unquestionably debunks the revised history of 1865. As it stands, it has taken more forty years to bring this assessment to fruition.

The process can reasonably be said to have begun in 1973 when the auditor received a letter from Betty Ruth Kondayan in response to an earlier inquiry. Ms. Kondayan, the university's then-librarian, listed several sources of obscure information concerning Washington and Lee University and President Graham that could be copied for a nominal charge. Thus began the forty-year investigation and assessment.

Background

This historical performance audit's results are, in some respects, very welcome news for Washington and Lee University, but they also reveal some deeply disturbing realities. By way of example, consider that the university's current representation of its early history in the eighteenth century is a grossly inaccurate one not based upon any credible eighteenth-century evidence. In over 160 years, not one author treating this subject seems to have provided one solid piece of reliable evidence to support the notion that the college has existed since the 1740s or thereabouts.[55] The fact is, this representation is not accurate and is mistaken by approximately twenty-five years.

---

54   *Crenshaw probably discovered the troubling anomaly of the university having had two entirely different histories late in process of researching General Lee's College,* and like Professor Adams, he too threw up his hands but not in bewilderment or despair but rather in surrender because for reasons which he refused to disclose. In his early chapters, he adopted the status quo ante, and he decided to not challenge the then status quo ante. Hence, the need for this historical performance audit, for the truth deserves to be restored to public view because Crenshaw's account of the founding is not distinguishable from all the other erroneous accounts that have been published since 1850. Nevertheless, he deserves credit for leaving to posterity a monumentally important clue to solving the mystery of two histories, in the form of his Appendix A.

55   The erroneous representations predating the college's actual birthday of October 13, 1774, include several different erroneous dates including 1748, 1749, and 1752. Trustee Bolivar Christian mistakenly thought, initially, to date the origins to 1752, and then later to 1749. Understandably, in neither case did Mr. Christian bother to inform his readers upon what evidentiary foundation he constructed these fictions. Although, he inappropriately pasted a dubious document in the college's first record book that seemed to some to support his theory, Christian was careful not to actually claim that this was his source. This subject is explored in detail within this report.

The essence of the university's currently represented and, quite obviously, inaccurate history of the institution's founding appeared for the first time in 1850 in a book (_Sketches of Virginia_ . . .) authored by William Henry Foote.[56] Fifteen years later, the college published its own seriously inaccurate account of its founding.[57] In so doing, the then-college's unnamed institutional author (probably Bolivar Christian) adopted the essence of William Henry Foote's error made in his first and second series of _Sketches of Virginia: Historical and Biographical_, 1850 and 1855. Over time, the university introduced some additional embellishments to Mr. Foote's great fiction. The university's embellishments were not offered with any explanation, justification, or citation of authority. They are addressed in detail, however, in various sections of this report.

The source of the above-referenced mistaken representation of the university's founding remains technically unknown to the auditor.[58] The responsibility for publishing this revolutionary fictionalized account, however, lies at the feet of the 1865 Board of Trustees in general, with particular emphasis upon the role of the Board's Chairman, Judge John W. Brockenbrough,[59] aided mostly by Trustee Bolivar Christian, but also by Professor James Jones White (a.k.a., "Old Zeus")— all of whom should have realized that the college's new statement of its early history was pure fairy-dust, notwithstanding Mr. Foote's two varying accounts in his two published historical treatments concerning Virginia.[60] They should

---

56   William Henry Foote, **Sketches of Virginia, Historical and Biographical**, First Series, Philadelphia, J.B. Lippincott & Co., 1850.

57   _Charter and Laws and Trustees and Alumni of Washington College at Lexington, Virginia,_ Richmond, 1865
       While the pamphlet lists no author or editor, the copy reviewed by the auditor is housed in the Leyburn Library of Washington and Lee University, and it is bound in a volume that bears the following legend upon its spine, "Washington and Lee University, Catalogs, 1865–1879." The volume includes an 1855 catalogue and also catalogues for 1865–1879 in order, as well as a few miscellaneous items. The auditor has understandably accepted the authenticity of these various catalogues as having been produced at the behest of the university's administration.

58   All the evidence the auditor has unearthed suggests that the originator of the false history narrative within the university is Trustee Bolivar Christian, who was undoubtedly led astray by the chronicler William Henry Foote when he published the first false history of the college in 1850 (Sketches of Virginia . . . see bibliography) and then added to it in his second volume published in 1855. Still, Mr. Christian, himself an amateur historian, was aware of the numerous earlier accurate histories he chose to ignore.

59   Judge Brockenbrough was appointed a Trustee of Washington College in 1852 and undoubtedly became aware that the only existing authorized published history of the college's founding was that which was included as an appendix to the Inaugural Address of Pres. George Junkin, Christianity, The Patron of Literature and Science: An Address Delivered February 22, 1849. On the Occasion of the Author's Inauguration as President of Washington College, Virginia, Philadelphia, the Board of Trustees'1849. The Junkin Inaugural Address includes an important Appendix: **"A Brief Sketch of the Early History of Washington College"** (ordered printed by the Board of Trustees). It begins on page 39. This constitutes the college's first authorized, published history.

60   Many decades later, Professor White ("Old Zeus") coauthored a history with Prof. Carter Harris that is inconsistent with the representation authorized by the Trustees in 1865. This gross inconsistency, however, has gone undetected until now.

have known because of the existence of the critically important and venerable documentary records that demonstrate that this new revised history was wrong. They are as follows: (1) The meeting minutes of the Hanover Presbytery from 1771 to 1776 that contain all the minutes pertaining to the establishment of the college; (2) Rev. Caleb Wallace's first authorized history written into the Board of Trustees' oldest record book containing their first meeting minutes comprised of the book's first several pages (3–7) signed and dated "May 1776"; (3) The Board of Trustees' 1792 petition to the Virginia Synod of the Presbyterian Church seeking their assistance in preserving William Graham as their president; and (4) President Graham's 1796 letter drafted on behalf of the Trustees addressed to Pres. George Washington containing a brief sketch of the early history of the college; and the aforementioned first authorized published historical sketch of the college. It is noteworthy that not one of these most venerable early documents contains the name of Robert Alexander or Rev. John Brown or mentions of their schools; and nowhere in these early documents is there a claim of a link between the college and any private preparatory school in Virginia.

When the Trustees authorized the printing of *Charter and Laws and Trustees and Alumni of Washington College at Lexington, Virginia*, Richmond, 1865, which contains the institution's first false publication of its early history, it, in effect, repudiated entirely the most recent prior "authorized publication" of 1849, located in the pamphlet containing President Junkin's inaugural address,[61] and all of the previous accounts known to exist. Certainly, Trustee Bolivar Christian deserves to be highlighted as an intimately involved participant because he was well schooled in the early history of the institution and its community, having not only researched the subject for many years, but he having also published works on related subjects as early as 1860.[62] He, of all the other Trustees, should

---

61   Rev. George Junkin, DD, <u>Christianity, the Patron of Literature and Science: An Address Delivered February 22, 1849. On the Occasion of the Author's Inauguration As President of Washington College, Virginia</u>, Philadelphia, the Board of Trustees, 1849 [pamphlet pp. 39.] The Junkin Inaugural Address includes an important appendix: "A Brief Sketch of the Early History of Washington College" (ordered printed by the Board of Trustees).

62   Col. Bolivar Christian, "The Scotch-Irish Settlers in the Valley of Virginia," Alumni Address at Washington College, Alumni Association, 1860. (Also published in the book below); *Washington and Lee University, Historical Papers*, No. 3 - 1892, "The Scotch-Irish Settlers in the Valley of Virginia" originally published by the Alumni Association, 1860. [33pps.]; "Historical Sketch," *Catalogue of Alumni of Washington College of Virginia for the year 1869*, Baltimore, John Murphy & Co, 1869. Esp. At pp. 3–13; *Christian Bolivar Esq., is also the presumptive author of an unsigned article on the origins of Washington and Lee in "Southern Collegian," [Washington And Lee Univ. College newspaper, vol. VI, No. 9, Feb. 7, 1874]. The article contains a quote (within the article) from an unsigned manuscript said to be in the handwriting of Edward Graham, brother of William Graham, setting forth a very brief sketch of a series of schools evolving into Liberty Hall Academy and referring to a list of early students, to wit: Samuel Doak....etc. And Archibald Alexander, son of Robert's..." So, it was not referring to Rev. Archibald Alexander, DD. More importantly, the unsigned author's hypothesis and reasoning are absurd in the extreme. The contentions in the last analysis are merely concern a one-page unsigned and undated memo about which almost nothing is known or knowable. Its legitimacy is beyond dubious and is of no historical value whatsoever.*

have known better, and he unquestionably must have known better. Had he not read Edward Graham's published "Memoir of the Late Rev. William Graham" or "Rev. Archibald Alexander's Address to the Alumni of Washington College?" Was he not aware that the college maintained the meeting minutes of the Board of Trustees? Did he fail to consult the meeting minutes of the institution that created the college? All and each one of these sources is virtually consistent in asserting an entirely different account than what Christian provides. Not one of the then-known writings claimed the college was founded earlier than October of 1774. How could a student of the history of the Valley of Virginia in the 1850s not be aware of the first authorized and published history of the founding of Washington and Lee University contained in the inaugural address of Pres. George Junkin, published in 1849? Junkin, after all, was still president of the college in 1858 when Col. Christian was appointed a Trustee.

It could be the scribbling of some unknown drunkard crumbled and tossed in the trash of a wayside inn, or it could be almost anything the mind can conjure up, but what it is not is a sound basis upon which to revise seventy-five years of published and documented history left by historians and custodians of institutional records of reputable bodies. Nevertheless, this silly little unsigned, undated memorandum, mortared together with W. H. Foote's un-evidenced and unauthenticated revised version of Liberty Hall's founding, formed the very foundation of the post-modern version represented by the University since 1869. The source upon which the auditor relied re: this presumption is Dr. Ollinger Crenshaw, author of General Lee's College (see the 2 vol. Typescript version w/ footnotes.) Lending further credence to the presumption that Bolivar Christian played a singular role in the revised history, as if more were needed, is this important note from Dr. Crenshaw: **"Bolivar Christian, Trustee from 1858 to 1891, wrote adjacent to this manuscript,** *"This paper (pasted in this page) I found among the files of MSS of the College: It is endorsed 'found among the papers of Edward Graham in his handwriting.; It corroborates the other accounts (traditional & otherwise) of the origins of the College." (Dr. Ollinger Crenshaw, General Lee's College, the unpublished Typescript version, Vol. I, pg. 30, footnote no. 12, see bibliography.) [Emphasis added]. Note: Of course, the final sentence is a preposterous error because all the known published histories at the time of Edward Graham's death in 1840, **do not corroborate Mr. Christian's mystery document,** they contradict it, especially the one written by Edward Graham and published by Rev. John Holt Rice, both of whom were students of William Graham at Liberty Hall Academy. Moreover, Edward Graham's numerous letters to inquiring historians, written in his mature years, also contradict the so-called, Edward Graham manuscript, that was foisted on an unknowing and unsuspecting public by Col. and Trustee Bolivar Christian. This is not asserted lightly, but it is inconceivable that one as familiar with the Lexington, Virginia, local history, as was Mr. Christian, would not have been aware of the numerous documentary-based histories of the college's founding, all of which contradict Mr. Christian's mystery document, as well as his own written false history of the college's origins. Christian based his accounts entirely on William Henry Foote's travesty, in conjunction with his mystery document, to the exclusion of all published and unpublished known written histories of the college's origins written prior to 1850, as well as the official documentary records of the college, and the Hanover Presbytery that created the college (i.e., Academy). Mr. Christian's claimed date for the college's establishment varies from 1748 o 1752, but his accounts are all outside the realm of possibility, and none are based on authenticated records.*

The Why of It All

Unfortunately, several Trustees and faculty members are implicated in this wholesale unjustified and false historical revisionism. This is especially so, insofar as these otherwise venerated faculty members who apparently were unable to locate the institution's early records were nevertheless willing to publish articles in various forms that were directly related to the early history of the college. These include Trustee Bolivar Christian, Professor J. J. White, and Trustee William McLaughlin. McLaughlin, as editor, is credited with having been the principle person in charge of the very erroneous "Historical Sketch" that begins on page 7 of the Catalogue of the Officers and Alumni of Washington and Lee University, Lexington Virginia, 1749–1888 published in 1888. All of the heretofore named gentlemen failed to exercise due diligence as institutional guardians by researching their institution's own early records.

If, in fact, the college's guardians in 1865 were unaware of the truth in regard to the founding, then they were also completely unqualified to author, or coauthor, histories on a subject about which they apparently knew very little, if anything, worthwhile. They nevertheless did author such historical pieces. It is also true, however, that these gentlemen were probably all too credulous concerning the representations of Trustee Bolivar Christian that began in 1865 and—instead of conducting their own research— simply accepted Mr. Christian's disingenuous analysis of obviously dubious sources (the so-called *Edward Graham manuscript* or memorandum[63]) and so-called "traditions" instead of relying on easily authenticated documentary sources that emanated from the institution that was responsible for establishing the college, and, of course, the institution's own early records, including the Trustees' early meeting minutes.

Another thing the 1865 Trustees did not do was explain to the public what they were doing and why they had repudiated seventy-five years of history that had appeared first in 1776, and finally in 1849, a history consistently related and based entirely upon documentary evidence. In addition, the Trustees did not mention the name of the person who wrote the first (1865) revised history[64] or did they bother to announce that the revised version amounted to a wholesale repudiation of a long-venerated history dating back to 1774. Finally, in this regard, these Trustees failed to mention any evidence upon which they relied to reach their surreptitiously revised history. This is a fact curiously not mentioned in the literature of American History since this repudiation first appeared in 1850.

---

63   This irrelevant unsigned and undated document, whatever it is, does not in any case trump Edward Graham's published memoir of the university's first president, Rev. William Graham (see bibliography). That Mr. Christian would adopt an unauthenticated document with no provenance in place of a published article, as well as other published articles that relied upon later letters from Edward Graham, and to rely instead on a dubious source speaks loudly and reveals that Mr. Christian was up to mischief. It is also rather telling that Christian failed to note his deviation from well-documented sources or bother to explain himself in this regard since all other known earlier sources contradict Mr. Christian's preferred mystery source.

64   Rev. Caleb Wallace—then (1776) operating as clerk of the institution that created the college, the Hanover Presbytery—was ordained at the same meeting, at which, the Presbytery created the college. An event he would hardly not remember since it transpired at the church he had just, the day before, become the pastor of.

It is patently obvious that the primary reason that the participants in this embarrassing revisionism allowed themselves to engage in unacceptable selective perception—and, therefore, saw only what they wanted to see—was that they were blinded by their passionate desire to procure the acceptance of the presidency of the college in the person of their venerated recent commander, General Robert E. Lee.

It had become known to the Trustees that General Lee had earlier rebuffed the advances of another college and gave as his reason for refusing the position that the school (Sewanee) was denominational. Washington College's origins were then recognized to have been the direct result of the actions of a Presbyterian institution comprised mostly of Presbyterian clergymen. This—together with the fact that the region in which the college was located was, at the time, almost entirely Presbyterian—suggested that the school was, in effect, denominational. It is true that the faculty and Trustees from Washington College's inception had been almost entirely Presbyterian, and apparently, this made for a potentially serious barrier that, in these gentlemen's view, needed to be overcome.[65]

Mr. Foote's _Sketches of Virginia_, had by this time (1865), gained wide acceptance as one of the most valuable collections of reprinted rare and important documents[66] of its type, related to Virginia history, notwithstanding its seemingly unknown erroneous historical accounts of the college's founding. At any rate, the college's post–Civil War Board of Trustees readily embraced Foote's fiction, although silently in the beginning. Bolivar Christian was later to draft yet another similar new historical account that simply ignored the college's long-established Presbyterian connections. Indeed, Mr. Christian's 1869 brief sketch never mentions the word _Presbyterian_, [67] but he undoubtedly relied in great measure upon Foote's unsubstantiated nonsense.

Judge Brockenbrough, having also embraced the newly crafted history, was thereafter able to present the college's offer of the presidency of the college to his close friend Gen. Robert E. Lee with an assurance that the school was entirely undenominational in nature and with his fellow Trustees' assurances that it would remain such. Assurances that Mr. Christian no doubt realized, as an able lawyer and judge, that he and the Trustees had no authority whatsoever to make. Nevertheless, the offer with these assurances gained General Lee's acceptance. These chain of events, however, could not alter the fact that the history of the college's founding was written down at the time the college was created

---

65   Had anyone researched the issue, they should have discovered that the college's official connections to the Presbyterian Church had long ago been severed. The link between the college and the Presbyterian Church was a gradual separation and effectively ended when William Graham died in 1799. The final break can be legitimately argued to have occurred once the Virginia legislature acted to involve itself in the college's affairs, as is described by Dr. Crenshaw in _General Lee's College_. Thereafter, the church's records are devoid of references to the college being within its sphere of influence.

66   A collection of documents will hereafter exist under a dark cloud of suspicion as a result of this audit which discovered that Foote's materials can no longer be accepted as presumptively accurate.

67   Dr. Crenshaw asserts that Trustee Christian authored the historical sketch contained in the Alumni directory for 1869, but he was apparently not so certain about the 1865 sketch, "Historical Statistics." The auditor believes but cannot evidence Mr. Christian's authorship of the 1865 sketch. There is no other obvious and likely candidate for that dubious honor.

on page 55, of the Presbytery's record book containing their official meeting minutes and recorded by the Hanover Presbytery's clerk, Rev. Caleb Wallace, later Justice of Kentucky's Supreme Court. "Facts," as has been so often said, "are stubborn things," and the facts clearly demonstrate that the college owes its existence to an official institution of the Presbyterian Church comprised, in the main, by Presbyterian clergymen acting as agents of the Presbyterian Church. Its Presbyterian roots, therefore, cannot be denied.

Admittedly, the underlying cause discussed in this subsection of the prolegomenon is speculative and is but one of the several possibilities, but something caused these gentlemen to suspend their normal sense of reason and cautious application of skepticism; and having done so, they thereafter embraced an otherwise preposterous notion that, in effect, concludes that prior to 1865, the college's administrators, faculty, and friends, as well as the Presbyterian church leaders in Virginia, had deliberately represented a false account of the founding of the college to the public, the president of the United States, and to the Virginia Legislature. The facts and evidence found in the original eighteenth-century records of the Hanover Presbytery and those of the college, however, indisputably demonstrate that the originally represented history was completely accurate while the narrative first published in 1865 by the Board of Trustees has no basis in fact or in competent evidence. Untruths, after all, do not actually become less so simply by virtue of systematic repetition.

William Henry Foote, a _qualified_ excellent chronicler, but not so eminent a historian[68] (DO NOT FAIL TO READ THIS FOOTNOTE)

William Henry Foote, the author of the first seriously flawed history of the college's founding was palpably mistaken about the founding of Washington and

---

68   It was discovered late in the editing process of this report that Mr. Foote was not quite the excellent chronicler he has been made out to be because the auditor discovered that he quoted the same paragraph of an important (so-called letter from Rev. Samuel Houston) and quoted the single most important paragraph differently at different times and did this without bothering to bring any attention to this serious content-altering change. In both instances the paragraph in question appears inside quotation marks. They appear in his two separate volumes of _Sketches of Virginia_, Series 1 & 2 (1850 & 1855 respectively) _[for details, see appendix re Rev. Samuel Houston]_. The question then is: Are either one of the vastly different versions of the exact same quoted paragraph correct, and if so, which one? A very substantive mistake for one who, we are told, saved many rare and fragile documents from extinction. It must now be asked, how many of these rare documents did Foote copy incorrectly? As for the "Houston Letter," Mr. Foote's two seriously different characterizations renders the letter inadmissible, and it may not be afforded any serious consideration absent the original being found so as to allow for authentication. Foote's error in this one respect was rendered even more problematic by the fact that one of the names included in his 1850 supposed reprinting of Houston's letter was conveniently left out of the reprinting of the letter in the 1855 volume. This expurgation was carried out without notice. Presumably it was left out by Mr. Foote because he had, apparently, discovered that the person named originally as a student, Ebenezer Smith was in fact an instructor, not a student. The mistake was so great that it would have undermined the author's credibility and, in effect, it would have called into question his entire testimony as it was represented in 1850. Of course, historians are not permitted to substantively alter their sources' quoted claims, but then Mr. Foote clearly did not believe that these widely accepted standards applied to him.

Lee University, and yet the institution inexplicably decided in 1865 to follow Foote's lead. Apparently, no one bothered to review the evidence Mr. Foote relied upon in formulating his historical representation of the college's founding. It is entirely possible, it must be supposed, that most of the Trustees in 1865 were fully ignorant of their institution's founding. This audit report, however, will demonstrate the truth of our inescapable conclusion that the university's origin is precisely October 13, 1774. Moreover, if many of the Trustees were ignorant of the existence of a long-standing earlier documentary-based history, it could only be that they failed to consult the school's earliest records.

The assessment methodology used in this report applies incontrovertible documentary evidence, supplemented by the incontestable testimony of eighteenth-century eyewitnesses which are of the highest credibility and unquestioned veracity. The institution's current representation is based upon erroneous speculation and creative fantasy evidenced by virtually nothing. All this will be presented in this report in tireless and sometimes in admittedly tiresome but necessary detail. One all-important fact needs to be constantly kept in mind, which is that the institution (i.e., W&L) correctly and consistently represented its founding from its beginning in 1774 and for seventy-five years thereafter.

Some Results and a Restoration

One particularly welcome result of this historical performance audit is that the university's true history, as represented by the college, and also by all the numerous authors who wrote historical accounts during the school's first seventy-five years (1774–1849) can now be restored to its rightful place. The true history was never actually lost; it was first misplaced, subsequently replaced, and then subjected to benign neglect by many generations of credulous and sometimes misguided institutional guardians of the university's early history.

The audit also reveals some amazingly interesting and important cultural and historical dimensions that, to date, for all intents and purposes, have gone virtually unrecognized by published historians. These discoveries reveal institutional characteristics that are far more interesting and noteworthy than any of the institution's friends would expect to find among their storehouse of treasured antiquities. These new discoveries will no doubt elevate the university's prestige and enhance its national reputation. This aspect of the audit, to be fully realized, will necessitate the university's embracing the several incontrovertible findings that are set forth in detail below concerning Rev. John Chavis and Mrs. Sarah (McBride) Priestley.

The audit report is divided into two parts to be issued separately: (part 1) the main body of the report together with the major written errors concerning the Institution or its founding president Rev. William Graham, found in thirty works (mostly published) and several appendices that explore more deeply issues already touched upon in the main body of the report; and (part 2) a supplement, to be released at a later date containing approximately forty additional assessments of the author's errors contained in articles and books published in the nineteenth and twentieth centuries. The authors assessed in the supplement essentially commit the same mistakes as those found in part 1. Major errors concerning the institution or its founding first president, Rev. William Graham, are found in part 1, and it may be legitimately considered as complete.

The supplement demonstrates the extent of the auditors' research into the subjects under consideration and will hopefully assist subsequent researchers.

Ten Key Findings of the Audit

1. Washington and Lee University was created by an organization of Presbyterian Ministers (Hanover Presbytery) in Virginia on October 13, 1774, not, as more recently represented by Washington and Lee University, sometime in either 1748, 1749, or 1752.

(Note: The university, after 1865, adopted from time to time, all three of these erroneous dates as the date of its founding. There is no competent evidence to support any of the ideas that the institution was founded before the 1770s or that the school was in any way linked to a preexisting precollege educational endeavor.)

2. All known published histories that addressed the founding of Washington and Lee University from the date of its founding on October 13, 1774, up to 1850 did so correctly, in the main,[69] and those histories were based upon all of the documentary evidence and official records of the Hanover Presbytery and the Board of Trustees of the university as the school was constituted in the eighteenth century.

3. All of Washington and Lee University's eighteenth-century records accurately reflect the institution's origins and founding for nearly a century. The college accurately represented its origins and founding until 1865, when the college published the *Charter and Laws and Trustees and Alumni of Washington College at Lexington, Virginia*, Richmond, 1865, which contained a radically

---

69   One notable exception is that Edward Graham in his memoir of President William Graham incorrectly maintained that Prince Edward Academy (Hampden Sydney) was founded prior to Liberty Hall Academy (W&L).

incorrect and revised history of the founding of the college.

4. From the founding of the college until the autumn of 1796, the only president of Washington and Lee University (Liberty Hall Academy) was Rev. William Graham. Mr. Graham was originally appointed in absentia as the chief operations officer with the title "manager." (Oct. 1774); subsequently, as "rector"[70] (1776). In both cases, these titles reflected his position as the chief operations officer of the college, which in later years was referred to as "president."

5. Washington and Lee University currently misrepresents that Mr. Robert Alexander of Augusta County, Virginia, is the institution's first president, or rector. In fact, there is no eighteenth-century evidence that Robert Alexander had any connection, direct or indirect, to Washington and Lee University or any of its antecedents (Augusta Academy, Liberty Hall Academy, and Washington College, Virginia.)[71]

6. The so-called "Edward Graham Memorandum" or "Edward Graham Manuscript" is not what it is represented to be. Whatever it is, its contents do not, and

---

70   The term "rector" connoted, at the time in question, a chief operations officer of an educational institution who was also a cleric that conducted religious services for the students under their charge. In this capacity, William Graham reported directly to the Hanover Presbytery from 1774 to May of 1776, when the Presbytery created the first Board of Trustees to which Mr. Graham reported thereafter, as rector. Mr. William Graham was the only president of the university during his entire connection with the institution.

71   No author published before 1850 ever made this dubious claim, and no author subsequent to 1850, has ever presented any credible evidence to support the notion that Alexander's school had any direct link to W&L. All the known documentary evidence demonstrates that no such link exists. A few have invoked the canard of "tradition" to justify the claim of a link but invoked the term improperly because the so-called 'tradition' cannot be found in the eighteenth-century literature including correspondence. All such claims are nineteenth-century retrospective fabrications. To be taken at all seriously, a "tradition" needs to be traceable to sources that are rooted in the period to which the tradition refers. In this case, there is but one demonstrably erroneous assertion traceable to the eighteenth century (i.e., the infamous "Houston letter.") See the appendix devoted to this palpable mistake. In sum, the so-called Houston letter as represented by Foote is not credible in the least and may well be a certifiable hoax as presented.

could not, possibly represent the views of Professor Edward Graham pertaining to the founding of Washington College. His contrary views are well-known to history, and these contrary views were long held by Edward Graham even until his death.

Note: By inserting this dubious document into an official record of the college, Trustee Bolivar Christian defiled a precious historical artifact, virtually as old as the college itself. Its placement is now the first page on which text appears which suggests to any researcher who is unaware of how it was inserted surreptitiously many decades after the records were created, that it represents the institution's official statement of its history. In truth, the document has no historical value whatsoever. It is uncertain what it is, who wrote the words, when it was written, and for what purpose. Was the document meant to be history, or is it simply notes taken down based upon an interview with some unknown person? The possibilities are quite simply infinite. What it is not and cannot possibly be is a statement of Edward Graham's beliefs in his mature years because the assertions contained in the mystery document contradict his published views reiterated in his correspondence to several historians seeking advice and information throughout his adult life. As a scholar and a lawyer, Edward Graham would not repudiate his long-held views without bothering to explain such an astounding reversal to his friends, family, or colleagues at the college, and especially his collaborator and brother-in-law, Rev. Archibald Alexander.[72] For these reasons, the document should be considered as specious.

7. Washington and Lee University currently misrepresents that Rev. John Brown was a president, or rector, of the institution as well as a Trustee. In fact, by his own choice, Rev. John Brown held no position at Washington and Lee University or any of its antecedents (Augusta Academy, Liberty Hall Academy, or Washington College, Virginia).[73] No credible evidence is known to exist that supports a contrary conclusion.

---

72 *Edward Graham and Archibald Alexander lived in the college president's home while students at Liberty Hall Academy. Edward later married Archie Alexander's sister. They collaborated on the biography of Rev. William Graham, although both wrote their own "Memoirs" of the college's first president (see our bibliography). Alexander having relied on Edward's treatment of the Graham family and President William Graham's affairs prior to his coming to Virginia. Also, Alexander would later correct Edward's mistake about the sequence of establishment of the Hanover Presbytery's two eighteenth-century Academies in Virginia.*

73 Rev. John Brown was appointed by the Presbytery to several positions of responsibility, including that of Trustee, but Mr. Brown refused to accept any of these appointments, as is clear from the meeting minutes of the Hanover Presbytery and those of the Board of Trustees, an important fact apparently overlooked by all previously published historians. Rev. Brown and his family's animus in regard to Rev. William Graham, which was personal, palpably affected his views toward the Academy. Mr. Brown's sons were all sent elsewhere for their education, and Rev. Brown advised others, in writing, to do the same. This is reflected in his extant correspondence. See John W. Stuart's biography of Rev. Brown in bibliography.

8. Virtually all significant histories that address the origins of Washington and Lee University, since 1850, contain grossly incorrect accounts of the university's origins. *(This report assesses thirty of these histories, but there are many more contained in additional books, articles, and newspaper columns numbering into the hundreds.*

9. The first black (African American) College Graduate in North America was Mr. (Rev.) John Chavis, whose entire undergraduate instruction took place at Washington and Lee University (then Liberty Hall Academy). This fact was asserted by Mr. Chavis in his court filing, and his assertion was affirmed by all of the sitting magistrates of the Rockbridge County (Va.) Court, all of whom knew Mr. Chavis, including magistrate, Col. William Lyle, who was then also a Trustee of Liberty Hall Academy. Mr. Lyle had firsthand knowledge of the school's affairs while Mr. Chavis was a student at the Academy, which was then under the direction of Rev. William Graham.[74]

Note (a): Readers are forewarned that most-published accounts of John Chavis mistakenly claim that he attended college at Princeton. Mr. Chavis himself initiated the court proceeding in Rockbridge County, Virginia, and Chavis's court record speaks for itself. In brief, the plan to educate Chavis privately at Princeton went awry for reasons explained in this report. Princeton representatives concur that there is no evidence in their files that Chavis ever attended classes or received private

---

74   Rockbridge County Court Order Book 6, pg. 10, April Term 1802, The Library of Virginia., Reel 36. A photocopy of this official court record can be seen on pg. 45 of Helen Chavis Othow's book, *John Chavis, African American, Patriot, Preacher, Teacher and Mentor (1763–1838)*, but this copy has unfortunately cropped off part of the name, "William Lyle," rendering it nearly indecipherable. The Library of Virginia's copy does not have this defect. In addition, Mr. John Chavis was also a student at the Lexington Theological Seminary, served as an adjunct to Liberty Hall and was licensed by the Lexington Presbytery based on his educational and theological preparations under the direction of rector, William Graham. Rev. Chavis was the first black Presbyterian minister in America. Like so many early W&L Alumni, Mr. Chavis has not as yet received, posthumously, an acknowledgment of his formal degree. There were few commencements held in those days and many of the alumni never received any formal certificate of degree. On request, however, many know alumni were acknowledged as such by the Board of Trustees. Those who might question this claim should consult the aforementioned Rockbridge County Court record of 1802 signed by several magistrates including Trustee, Wm. Lyle, and also review William Henry Ruffner's *article,"An Educated Negro of a Hundred Years Ago,"* n.d., William Henry Ruffner Papers, 1848–190, Accession 24814, personal papers, collection, The Library of Virginia, Richmond, Virginia. 5pg. [no.88].

instruction there. See Professor John M. Murrin's introduction to Princetonians *1784–1790, 1991, pg. liii of the introduction.*

Note (b) *Note: Commencements were not regularly held in this period, but a sure indicator of whether a student had "gone through the regular academic program" was when a student applied for licensure as a candidate for the Presbyterian ministry because such advanced education was a prerequisite for licensure. The Presbyterians in particular were firm in their resolve that their ministers be scholars because they were expected, as part of their pastorate, to conduct schools for the congregation's youth. Mr. Chavis, having gone through the regular program, also became a theological student under Rev. Graham in preparation for the ministry. At the first opportunity following Rev. Graham's sudden unexpected death in 1799, Mr. Chavis applied for and was taken into the Lexington Presbytery for his trials. Such acceptance is a recognition by the Lexington Presbytery that Mr. Chavis had indeed* gone through the regular academic program at Liberty Hall Academy. *This formal acceptance, together with the local court's recognition, constitutes a far better case of a student's having graduated with a BA than would be the case for most of the college's listed alumni from that period. The common suggestion that Mr. Chavis attended Princeton is refuted in other sections of this report. The evidence on this matter is incontrovertible and clearly exceeds the evidence upon which many other Alumni were granted their B A certificates by the college long after their matriculation.*

Note:(c) The Chavis "family tradition," often referred to, asserts incorrectly that John Chavis attended Princeton,[75] as revealed in a County Court record initiated by Rev. John Chavis. That is, Mr. Chavis or his legal representative filed this action and the content of the order reflects what Chavis's motion avers. It is Chavis himself who represented that he had gone through the regular academic program at Liberty Hall Academy and this assertion was then confirmed by several sitting magistrates, one of whom was, at the time, in addition to being a Court Magistrate, a Trustee of Washington College (Academy). Chavis would hardly initiate a court action by falsely claiming that he obtained his college education at Liberty Hall Academy if he actually obtained it at Princeton. Just as surely, Magistrate, Capt. Wm. Lyle would not have perjured himself so as to embellish the résumé of a prior student, if that man had not, in fact, "gone through the regular academic program at the same college where Lyle was a Trustee. Lyle was a Trustee whose position was obtained in

---

75   *Professor John M. Murrin,* Princetonians 1784–1790, *Princeton, N.J., Princeton University Press, writing in the Introduction, pg. liii; said this:*

> On September 27, 1792, the trustees voted to use the Lesley Fund ("for the education of poor and pious youth with a view to the ministry of the Gospel in the Presbyterian Church") on behalf of John Chavis, a light-skinned free black and Revolutionary War Veteran from Virginia. One of the most remarkable African-Americans of the antebellum era, Chavis became a noted Latinist and a tutor to prominent white boys, particularly in the Magnum family of North Carolina. ***His name appears on no*** [Princeton] ***class list***, but strong family tradition insists that he attended. ***If so***, he was the College's only black student before the mid-twentieth century, but ***he did not stay long. The one semester he would most likely have been at Princeton was the summer term of 1793***, for which no class list survives. In other words, the family tradition may well be accurate and has been accepted by several generations of archivists at Princeton University. But unless Chavis entered with junior class standing, which seems highly improbable, he would necessarily have been assigned to the class of 1795 or 1796. For this reason, his biography does not appear in these volumes. (Emphasis added)

> ***Note: John Chavis's name does appear on one of the few Liberty Hall Academy surviving class lists for the year 1795. In Virginia, Rev. Chavis preached at numerous regular Presbyterian Churches to whites and to blacks, both free and*** *slave, as the records of the Virginia Synod clearly indicate. After his move to North Carolina, laws were enacted that served to interfere with his profession, and unfortunately, his teaching and preaching were both severely affected. He, nevertheless, remained officially connected to the Presbyterian Church throughout his life.*

order to replace his father, Samuel Lyle, one of the college's original Trustees, who was appointed two months prior to the signing of the Declaration of Independence in 1776. To think that Captain Lyle would dishonor his father, his college and his court, by signing his name to a falsehood is beyond preposterous. Moreover, to believe that Rev. John Chavis—the first black college graduate in America and the first black Presbyterian minister in the world—would not be aware of where he attended college is an absurdity that is simply beyond comprehension.

Mr. Chavis's twentieth-century relatives were probably aware that there indeed had been a plan to send Mr. Chavis on scholarship to Princeton where he was to be privately tutored by the retired president, John Witherspoon, but Dr. Witherspoon's health was rapidly failing at the time. Witherspoon had also become blind. Chavis's sponsor and preparatory preceptor Rev. Henry Pattillo and Rev. William Graham had a long-term professional relationship dating back to 1775, and Graham obviously was willing to accept John Chavis as a regular student at nearby Liberty Hall Academy. Given Witherspoon's unavailability, Liberty Hall was clearly a preferable alternative plan. This change in plans was apparently not fully understood by Mr. Chavis's twentieth-century descendants. Obviously, the best evidence on the question is that offered by the college, via Trustee Lyle, and by Mr. Chavis himself in conjunction with the Rockbridge County Court of 1802. All of these gentlemen were eyewitnesses to Mr. Chavis's completed matriculation.

On the other hand, there is no documentary evidence known that demonstrates that John Chavis ever stepped foot on the campus of Princeton, let alone attended a class there. A conclusion entirely consistent with the research done by Princeton's eminent professor of history, John Murrin, who looked into the question for the Princeton University Press, and who is quoted in one of the adjacent footnotes.

10. The first female student to be enrolled into a chartered college in the United States was Sarah (McBride) Priestley, who was enrolled by Rev. William Graham into the regular academic program at Liberty Hall Academy (circa 1787), long after the college's charter as a degree-granting institution had been granted by the Virginia legislature. Mrs. Priestley's husband, James Priestley, was a graduate of Liberty Hall and subsequently a tutor under his preceptor, Rev. Graham. James, was later president of Cumberland College. Mrs. Priestley did not complete her studies at Liberty Hall but was far enough advanced in her studies that she later founded a school for young women in Baltimore.

(Note: See Archibald Alexander Mss "The Reverend William Graham," a handwritten manuscript memoir on file at Leyburn Library Washington and Lee University. Mr. Alexander testifies to these facts as a postgraduate theological student and an eyewitness to her matriculation at Liberty Hall Academy in the regular academic program. This evidence is highly persuasive, and to date, no one has proffered any case that another female student preceded Mrs. Priestley as a regular academic student enrolled into a properly chartered college.)

The three known eighteenth-century historical accounts of Washington and Lee's origins:

1. The handwritten meeting minutes of the Hanover Presbytery between 1771 and 1776.
2. The account written by Rev. Caleb Wallace in May of 1776.[76]
3. Rev. William Graham's Letter (written on behalf of the Trustees) to Pres. George Washington in 1796.

Note: These accounts, were all authorized by the institution's first two consecutive guardians: First, the Virginia Hanover Presbytery, and second, the Board of Trustees of the college (Liberty Hall Academy) that was created by the Hanover Presbytery prior to its having turned over its primary responsibility as guardians to the new Trustees in May of 1776. None of these three sources even hints at the possibility of there being a link between the Hanover Presbytery's eighteenth-century established and patronized seminary and any preexisting private school: not when it was unofficially referred to as Augusta Academy and not when it was named Liberty Hall Academy.

Note: Wallace and Graham were both graduates of Princeton and were also, as Trustees of Liberty Hall and members of the Hanover Presbytery, eyewitnesses to the events which they describe, as well as active participants in the early activities of the Presbytery's first patronized seminary designed from its inception to be patterned after Princeton. In neither account do these authors mention Liberty Hall Academy having ever been linked to the schools of Robert Alexander or Rev. John Brown.

Any claims that are contrary to the accounts of Rev. Caleb Wallace and Pres. (Rector) William Graham concerning any of the ten key findings listed above have no basis in any credible fact or known documentary evidence that dates from the eighteenth century. All such contrary claims emanate from the nineteenth century, well, after all of the events in question had transpired, and after most, if not all, of the original participants were deceased. In addition, all such claims are purely gratuitous and typically amount to mere speculation or, in many cases, nothing more than one misguided nineteenth-century or later author, quoting yet another equally misguided scribe, none of whom were eyewitnesses to the matters addressed in these findings. The pertinent facts concerning the establishment

---

76   Rev. Caleb Wallace's memorandum history of Liberty Hall Academy is a handwritten document copied into the record book of the newly established Board of Trustees of Liberty Hall Academy by the Board's clerk, in which is found the original handwritten meeting minutes of the Board of Trustees. It is located at the Leyburn Library of Washington and Lee University, pps. 3–7. The copyist says this was signed "Caleb Wallace, Clerk, May 1776." Here, Rev. Wallace was acting as clerk of the Hanover Presbytery. Rev. Caleb Wallace is a witness of the highest caliber, for he is the only member of the Hanover Presbytery who was appointed a Trustee of both Liberty Hall Academy and Hampden Sidney Academy. Rev. Wallace afterwards became a Justice of Kentucky's highest Court. (Note: The Caleb Wallace memorandum documentary history of the origins of the college appear to all be in the same handwriting as the early minutes which suggests that the text was written into the record book by the board's clerk.

of Liberty Hall Academy are all rooted in the eighteenth century and are both consistent with one another and incontrovertible. These facts have been subjected to thorough scrutiny, and their implications are simply unassailable.

The rationales for various findings set forth in this report, along with the associated supporting evidence, are laid out in admittedly tiresome but nonetheless essential detail. The rather burdensome details result from the multitude of existing variant false representations that have emerged over time as one ill-informed author after another built upon the fictions of those who went before them. It calls to mind Sir Walter Scott's admonition: "Oh what a tangled web we weave when first we practice to deceive." It cannot be said in this case, however, that the principal culprit in creating the variant false narratives, Mr. William Henry Foote, concocted his erroneous depictions with the intent to deceive, but whether intentional or not, they certainly had the same effect on the subsequently published early histories of Washington and Lee.[77]

Someone apparently led Mr. Foote astray concerning the founding of Liberty Hall Academy, but who that may have been is currently unknown to history.[78] It appears that, initially, Mr. Foote was principally influenced by a rather dubious, error-ridden letter ostensibly written[79] by Rev. Samuel Houston, referred to above,

---

77 An arguably additional contributor to the revised history, albeit in directly, is Rev. William Hill, who is credited as the author of a brief history of Washington College, Virginia, published in 1838 by the American Historical Quarterly, Vol. 10, pp. 145–150. The article lists several extracts from the 1775 meeting minutes of the Hanover Presbytery, which—by their placement in the same paragraph— suggests that the extracts are all connected, when, in fact, they were not, but Hill undoubtedly believed that were connected. Hill's mistake in this regard could have created the false impression that the Presbytery's minutes were referring to only one school when Hill's listed extracts actually addressed two entirely different schools, in different locations, and of different types and calibers. Furthermore, the two different schools were directed by different individuals. Mr. Hill, if he is indeed the author as Dr. Crenshaw says he is, mislead his readers by inappropriately including the reference to Brown's school among the several extracts that dealt with Liberty Hall Academy. Mr. Foote did not feel compelled, as a rule, to identify his sources, so it is not known whether he was, or was not, misled by Rev. Hill. Of the extracts, Hill listed all refer to the Presbytery's seminary under Graham, save the one 1775 reference to Brown's private Latin school. Perhaps Hill thought that the meeting in question, which began at Timber Ridge meeting House continued there, but after the first day, the members moved several miles away lodging with Rev. John Brown at his commodious estate at New Providence. Of course, Liberty Hall was near Liberty Hall while Brown's school was next door to his home. By failing to take note of the meeting having been moved, Mr. Hill may have confused the schools with each other. This seems to be the only scenario that would explain why Hill included the extract pertaining to Brown's school.

78 By the time Mr. Foote issued his second volume of *Sketches of Virginia . . .* in 1855, he had obviously been influenced by an additional, albeit unnamed source. Here he expands upon his nonsensical theme associating local private preparatory and common schools of the Valley with the founding of Washington and Lee., a mistake not emulated by W&L's sister college, in Prince Edward County, Hampden Sydney, where there were also local private preparatory schools conducted by members of the Hanover Presbytery prior to the Presbytery's establishment of Prince Edward Academy. Hampden Sydney has been content to present an accurate accounting of their founding even until today without attempting to predate their history by inappropriately linking the college to earlier common schools.

79 The dubious nature of the letter Mr. Foote attributes to Rev. Houston requires study and authentication given that Mr. Foote inexplicably quotes a section of the so-called Houston

but that doesn't excuse Mr. Foote's incompetent reading of the meeting minutes of the Hanover Presbytery, which he clearly misconstrues, nor does it excuse his failure to consult the several publications then in print that were in direct conflict with his own novel narrative, including Edward Graham's memoir of Rev. William Graham, and the published histories written by Rev. William Hill and Dr. Samuel L. Campbell, as well as the published address of Archibald Alexander, delivered to the college's Alumni Association seven years before the publication of Mr. Foote's unfortunate account. Nor does it excuse Mr. Foote's ignoring Caleb Wallace's brief documentary history of the origins. It is also imperative to point out here that Mr. Foote was either ignorant or unpersuaded by the letter written by Pres. (Rector) William Graham, which was sent to Pres. George Washington advocating for Liberty Hall Academy to become the recipient of Washington's intended gift of an endowment. This prospective endowment was the largest ever to be granted in America, at that time. Graham's letter to the president, on behalf of the Trustees, contained a brief historical sketch of the college's origins and makes no mention of his colleague of long-standing, Rev. John Brown. This historical sketch contained no reference whatsoever to a school operated by Robert Alexander.[80]

Finally in this regard, some attention should be given to the message sent by the Board of Trustees to the Virginia Synod in 1792, in the form of a petition, which is included below in its entirety due to its overwhelmingly compelling and illuminating message:

*Note: The readers' special attention is drawn to that portion of the petition that appears in **bold italics with underline** below.* A few words are seemingly indecipherable and are referred to in brackets:

Rockbridge County 1792

A petition from the Board of Trustees of the Academy of Liberty Hall to the Rev'd Synod of Virginia.
Moderator

We would call your attention to the consideration of an affair which deeply concerns us and which from the importance merits the most serious attention of Synod.

---

letter differently from one book and then later, from the other. So different in fact that this peculiarity hints at foul play. Under normal circumstances, forensics would suggest the very real possibility that forgery is involved. Mr. Foote places the concluding sentences of the same paragraph within quotation marks, but in each case, he provides two entirely different conclusions. He then compounds his misdeed by not providing notice of his different versions of the same quote, nor does he offer any explanation. The differences in textual content could not possibly amount to a clerical error. The subject is dealt with more particularly elsewhere in this report. See especially the appropriate appendix.

80   Crenshaw seems to have at one time or another believed that the initial school organized by William Graham was an outgrowth of Rev. Brown's school, but he offered no serious argumentation or evidence to support the speculation. Sometimes long-accepted myths are difficult to dispense with, and perhaps Crenshaw found it hard to believe that so many could have been wrong for so long.

Through the Presbytery of Lexington we are informed of the attempts of the Board of Trustees of the college of Hampden Sydney to deprive us of our Rector the Rev. Wm. Graham in order to convince him to take the presidency of their college. We also are informed that the [issue?] of this event depends upon a decision of your Rev'd Body. In our objecting to the removal of Mr. Graham we would not in the least reflect on Trustees of Hampden Sydney for attempting to obtain our Rector from us for we think him qualified for such a place and that they need such a gentleman. But this so far from leading us to freely give him up as they wish does considerably increase our desire to retain him over our Academy. It is true Hampden Sydney can plea many things in their favour; But we are not without our arguments too. They can at certain times boast of their numerous students; But out of our smaller numbers we can say that God has been pleased to bring more useful men upon the stage of public actors, and especially into the ministry of the Gospel, yea in this respect we have supplied every seat of learning in the state which we conceive must and ought to have much weight with Synod to countenance our institution.

Hampden Sydney can plead her wealth; of this we Have what has been considerable advantage and still have it in a safe condition with the hope especially if Synod were to take us under their patronage of an increase (to?) our friends. Hampden Sydney can urge their flattering prospects; our imagination can [paint?] [minds?] and if [former experience can furnish any arguments to pinpoint [??] we can [venture??] more safely on what only [??] in expectations, than they can. Hampden Sydney can plead the necessity. On this [??] surely we are not behind them. *__For it was under Wm. Graham that our Academy first received its existence and it is chiefly owing to his extraordinary exertions that it has persevered through all the convulsions of a calamitous War and the many vicissitudes which have taken place through the operations of various causes for the space of about 16 years, and here we cannot forebear asking the question would it be wisdom or duty in Synod to destroy our Academy which has been the most useful to the church of any in the state and which is at this time more promising to the church in point of numbers than ever it has been, and this too on the bare probability that another may or nearly so must be the consequence unless providence preserveth it if our Rector be removed at this juncture__*.[81]

---

81 The emphasis was added by the auditor

We would now inform this Rev'd Body that we have maturely considered the place for a seminary proposed by the Synod last year and that we are so highly pleased with its principles and design that we have adopted its part relative to education and as far or nearly so of the rest as considered with our Act of Incorporation. But as it appears that the Synod had not a [distinct/direct??] view to our legal [constitution??] and therefore that some things in their plans are not consistent with it we therefore wish the Synod to review their plan and to make such alterations in it as will make it agree with the law which will be laid before you for that purpose. And upon such alterations being made we shall be happy in applying our library which consists of about 300 well chosen volumes many of these are large ones and our mathematical and philosophical apparatus are nearly complete together with other property in land [??] buildings of considerable value belonging to our Academy to promote the pious and well conceived design proposed by Synod for training young men to preach the everlasting gospel. Further in order to convince Synod that our designs are reasonable we would mention the [healthiness of the situation ??]of the Academy of Liberty Hall that the low price of provisions, the convenience of the place to acquire information from distant parts and necessaries of almost every kind. Altho the compact state of the neighborhood and the ease with which young men can attend upon public worship every Sabbath day. All which shew that our Academy is the place where Wm Graham can most successfully execute the design of Synod. Besides which seems to have been an object fully contemplated in the Synod Plan, it often happens that young men [designing or desiring??] the Gospel ministry are under a necessity to be very frugal during the acquisition of an education.

Now if this ought to be considered we can say in our favour that expenses would be less with us than at Hampden Sydney. Moderately speaking they would be 3 to 4 or at least 4 to 5 which in the cause of an education will be will be of considerable moment. We also believe should Mr. Graham be removed that it will operate to deprive some hopefully pious young men of the benefit of his instruction.

We have again to urge that in the providence of God, Mr. Graham is settled upon a tract of good land of his own within a few poles[82] of the seat of the Academy for the benefit [business??] of which therefore he can attend with little inconvenience to his domestic concerns. The President both of Hampden Sydney & of Liberty

82   The rod, perch, *or pole* is a surveyors tool and unit of length equal to 5 ½ yards, 16 ½ feet, 1/320 of a statute mile.

Hall must make a sacrifice of his time and labour [sic] because
there are no funds for their support in either of the seminaries. A
young man who has much to hope and little to lose may venture,
but to send a man away a good living who has a large family to
support, not to sacrifice his time and labour only hath private
estate too and then to accomplish no greater [???] good than may
be obtained where he enjoys his estate will we hope to [??] of
feeling and experiences appear altogether inescapable.

For these and such reasons your petitioners earnestly pray that
this Rev'd Synod would not remove Wm Graham from his present
charge of the Academy and we hope and trust that you will see
reasons to grant the prayer of your petitioners. And that the great
head of the church may direct you in all things to seek and promote
his glory as the object and prayer of the Trustees of Liberty Hall.
We appoint Mr. John Wilson a member of our Board
Commissioner on our behalf to present our petition and to give
such information as may be required.

Samuel Lyle
Alex. Campbell
Wm. McKee
Wm Alexander
James Ramsay
Jno. Wilson
Joseph Walker
John Lyle
Samuel Houston
*Andrew Moore**

Petition presented to
the Synod from the
Board of Trustees
Sept. 1792

[* Signature added later. Hence, the italics.[83]]
****

In the parlance of today, this petition "speaks volumes" on many issues, but
none of them of greater significance than the clear esteem that these eighteenth-
century community leaders and Trustees of the Academy had for their rector,
William Graham, all of whom clearly recognized that ***it was under Wm. Graham
that our Academy first received its existence and it is chiefly owing to his
extraordinary exertions that it has persevered through all the convulsions of a
calamitous War and the many vicissitudes which have taken place through the
operations of various causes for the space of about 16 years***.

---

83   This notation is the auditor's.

Of course, the unstated but clear inference is that these early Trustees, even after the college, had received its incorporation and degree-granting charter from the Virginia legislature, nonetheless recognized the overarching authority of the Virginia Synod to reassign their rector to Hampden Sydney College, if they so choose. This denominational feature of the college changed dramatically, however, after Graham's resignation and then even more so when Graham died in 1799. Thereafter, the college's connection to the church slowly dissipated into eventual oblivion. A clear case of nineteenth-century benign neglect on the part of the Synod. The separation does not appear to have ever been a formal one but rather a willing withering on the vine.

As Dr. Crenshaw has explained in *General Lee's College*, the connection that had been reestablished between the college and the Presbyterian Synod was viewed by some as inappropriate. It came about as the result of a scheme to obtain patronage from the Synod and as a means by which to secure funds for the construction of the stone campus buildings that were erected on Mulberry Hill in the early 1790s, the remains of which are still standing. The reconnection was also accomplished for the purpose of establishing the Lexington Theological Seminary as an adjunct of Liberty Hall Academy.[84] That objective was realized, but the reconnection to the church was objected to by numerous non-Presbyterians and was eventually resolved by the death of the seminary's first rector, Rev. William Graham. Thereafter, the seminary died out along with the demise of its rector, and no attempt was made to restore it.[85]

Importantly, from this time circa 1799, the college's intermittent formal connection to the Presbyterian Church languished into oblivion. The Lee Chapel constructed later, therefore, has no connections to any denomination and serves Christians generally.

Foote's Inexplicable Refusal to Acknowledge the Existing Historical Accounts

For Mr. William Henry Foote to ignore the historical depiction of the founding of the college provided by the venerable Rev. Dr. Archibald Alexander, founder of the Princeton Theological Seminary and early student of Liberty Hall Academy, as well as the first published memoir of the college's founding first president, William Graham, written by his younger brother, Edward, is simply inexplicable. This is specially so in light of the fact that William Foote frequently quotes passages from both the *Memoir of the Late Rev. William Graham,* written by Professor Edward Graham. He also ignored the important assertions of Dr. Archibald Alexander, who was also an early student at Liberty Hall Academy, and who along with Edward Graham, lived with the rector's family while a student. Foote, however, also quotes

---

84 Records of the college and of the Synod demonstrate that the Virginia Synod and the Lexington Presbytery held some of their meetings at the college during the early and mid-1790s.

85 Notice of President Washington's endowment gift arrived just prior to President Graham's retirement and resignation. The Trustees, to honor Washington's generous gift, changed the college's name from Liberty Hall Academy to Washington Academy. This was followed by some political wrangling that inevitably concluded with the name being changed to Washington College.

freely from Alexander's writings whenever he believed the text advanced his bias, but he did not feel obliged to credit the author.[86] Foote also ignored all the historical accountings of the founding authorized by the Board of Trustees of the college during the institution's first seventy-five years. That he did so, persuaded the auditor that Mr. Foote was relying on someone, or something, in addition to the so-called Houston letter. If so, he failed to identify the source(s). The college's first authorized and published history of its origins was published in 1849, and like all other depictions written up to this time, the college's origins are clearly stated to be the result of the actions of the Hanover Presbytery in October of 1774.[87]

The fact that none of the following: Rev. Caleb Wallace, Rev. William Graham, Rev. Archibald Alexander, Professor Edward Graham, Dr. Samuel L. Campbell, Rev. William Hill,[88] or Rev. Robert Davidson, in their well-known histories ever claimed a link between Washington College and the schools of either Robert Alexander or Rev. John Brown should have served as a cautionary red flag concerning Mr. Foote's decision to claim such a link. When he found no credible evidence to support his early notion, he failed or refused to abandon his dubious contention, but instead proceeded to publish, what is herein established to be pure rubbish about when Washington and Lee University was founded and by whom.[89]

The earliest authors (pre-1850) personally knew several of the participants or were themselves eyewitnesses to many of the pertinent events associated with the founding of the college that were assessed in this audit. While some of these early authors err in minor ways, most of their errors are of little consequence, and none relates to the general date of origin or to just how the institution came to exist.[90] Consequential errors, where pertinent, have been identified and explained in the

---

86   The auditor became so familiar with the memoirs of William Graham that were written by Edward Graham and Archibald Alexander that he immediately recognized the quoted text when it appeared in Foote's two books. Foote presents this material within quotation marks, but typically does not identify the authors.

87   Rev. George Junkin, DD, *Christianity the Patron of Literature and Science: An Address Delivered February 22, 1849. On the Occasion of the Author's Inauguration as President of Washington College, Virginia*, Philadelphia, The Board of Trustees, 1849 [pamphlet pps. 39.] The Junkin Inaugural Address includes an important Appendix: "A Brief Sketch of the Early History of Washington College." (ordered printed by the Board of Trustees) This constitutes the college's first authorized, published History.

88   Rev. Hill's 1838 article on the history of Washington College (see bibliography) does include a brief and unfortunate reference to Rev. John Brown's school, but the reference was as unfortunate as it was inappropriate and confusing. Still, it does not claim a direct link to the College. His mere mention of it, however, implies a connection, but whatever Hill's intent, he does not actually claim one. If Mr. Hill thought that Rev. Brown's school at New Providence and Graham's Academy at Mount Pleasant were one and the same, he would have been sorely mistaken. Some, however, admittedly may have read his reference to mean just that, albeit mistakenly.

89   It is worthy of notice that in contrast to the numerous pre-1850 published histories listed above, no published history during the college's first seventy-five years had ever claimed that Liberty Hall was linked to Robert Alexander or Rev. John Brown.

90   The lone exception of consequence being Edward Graham's mistake concerning the sequence of establishment between Liberty hall and Hampden Sydney. He reversed the true order and mistakenly claimed that Hampden Sydney was established first.

Author's Errors Section of this report. We repeat, however, that all these early accounts accurately report that the founding of Washington and Lee University took place in October of 1774, and there are no pre-1850 accounts that suggest that the college's origin is earlier than 1774 or that the Presbytery's new seminary in Augusta County, Virginia, is possessed of a "germ"[91] that predates October of 1774. Any person who suggests otherwise today should provide evidence to support their claim, but the auditor is confident that no such evidence exists. That is because none has appeared in two hundred years that tend to support the fiction penned by those who claim an earlier date than that found in the appendix embodied within the pamphlet: _Christianity the Patron of Literature And Science: An Address Delivered February 22, 1849. On the Occasion of the Author's Inauguration as President of Washington College, Virginia_, Philadelphia, The Board of Trustees, 1849 pamphlet pps. 39, by, Rev. George Junkin, DD.[92] This pamphlet includes the important Appendix: "A Brief Sketch of the Early History of Washington College." It was ordered to be printed by the Board of Trustees, and its central assertion concerning the time and circumstances of the college's founding remained unchallenged and unchanged by the college from that time until the embarrassing revision took place in 1865. It would seem, in retrospect, that it was incumbent upon the rector and Board of Trustees in 1865 to have deigned to explain their rash and bold decision to rewrite seventy-five years' worth of consistent documentary-based history, but truth be told, they did no such thing. They refused to even acknowledge what they had done, let alone attempt to justify their actions in this regard. In retrospect is plain to see that those particular Trustees failed the alumni and all of the friends of the college by not protecting the long-established documentary history of the college's founding.

Finally in regards to the late arrived suggestion of a link between Rev. Brown and his school to the establishment of Augusta Academy/Liberty Hall, readers need to keep in mind that there are extant letters written by Rev. John Brown that prove beyond a shadow of doubt that Brown opposed the Presbytery's decision to

---

91   The only way that _the germ theory_ might be seen as applicable to Liberty Hall academy is if one contends that the seminary created by the Hanover Presbytery in October of 1774, originally referred to as "Augusta Academy" is the germ from which Liberty Hall Academy sprang, but even that argument technically fails because "Augusta Academy" is the same institution as Liberty Hall Academy. In the very beginning it was operating in its initial organizing phase in the form of a temporary and officially unnamed grammar school. The Presbytery, at the time, unofficially referred to the school as _Augusta Academy_ in their meeting minutes to distinguish it from their Academy in Prince Edward County.

        Colleges typically do not suddenly appear in their final form; they must be built, brick by brick, and evolve until at long last there appears a freshman class; then a year later is added a sophomore class, and so on and so forth. So too, was Washington and Lee University carefully nurtured during its nativity as Augusta Academy. This formulation, of course, was molded by its rector William Graham soon after his arrival in Virginia.

92   Who actually authored the appendix is unknown, but it was published along with the Inaugural Address by order of the Trustees.

        It was very likely penned by past president Dr. Henry Ruffner who had already researched and written a comprehensive history of the college that was then still an unpublished manuscript. It was later published in Volume One of the University's Historical Papers.

create a seminary of learning in Virginia during the period in which it was created. Over time he went so far as to urge his relations to send their sons to places other than the Academy under the Direction of Rev. Graham. This too is made all too clear in existing letter written during the early years of the Academy's operations. It is difficult to comprehend how someone confronted with this evidence could fail to comprehend that there could not have been any direct connection between Rev. Brown and Liberty Hall Academy given Brown's unquestionable animus toward the college and its director, William Graham. Certainly Rev. Brown never made such a preposterous suggestion.

The implication of the irreconcilable alternate accounts presented to the public

There needs to be a full public accounting for what has transpired, and this historical performance audit's release is an attempt to do just that. Hopefully, upon mature and careful consideration, Washington and Lee University will, forthwith, right this embarrassing wrong, and in so doing, restore that which so many worked diligently to record in the spirit of Dr. Archibald Alexander, who explained in these aptly formed words written nearly two hundred years ago:

> *Mount Pleasant should be considered as a kind of consecrated spot; and altho' it is now, like Shilo of old,*[93]*a desolation; yet it would be well, especially for the surviving pupils of Mr. Graham, to erect a monument on that spot,* as a memorial of the first classical school instituted in the Valley, But stone, marble, & brass are perishable substances: we want a memorial more enduring than those; and this can only be erected by a faithful history of this institution & its founder* [William Graham] *which we are now attempting to furnish.*

> (Rev. Archibald Alexander D. D., Mss Memoir of Rev. William Graham pg. 45.)[94]

---

93   *"Shilo of old" is an ancient biblical reference found in the Old Testament books of Joshua and Judges and refers to ancient ruins of the capital of Israel before Jerusalem.*

94   Mss, "Memoir of William Graham," handwritten by A. A. and paginated by the auditorr. Pg. 45.

The location of the university's birthplace at
"Mount Pleasant" (Rockbridge County)

Note: A local resident, Mrs. J. P. Alexander, was interviewed by the McDaniel group (see bibliography), and on that subject they inform as follows: ". . . *interviews . . . now allow us to pinpoint the location more precisely.*"

Mrs. Alexander also indicated that:

> the school was located at the source of a stream that crosses a railroad grading, approximately five hundred yards to the southwest of the point where county highway 724 now crosses the grading. (FN no. 20)[95] There are no roads, and no industrial development has taken place in this area; *it is probable that archaeological investigation would provide valuable data.*" (McDaniel et al., Liberty Hall Academy . . . Lexington, Va., Liberty Hall Press 1979, pg. 5)

One can only wonder at the curious fact that the university has yet to purchase this small parcel of land in order to preserve it as suggested by Mr. Alexander, "*as a memorial of the first classical school instituted in the Valley . . .*"

****

The Two Conflicting Versions of Washington and Lee's History

As pointed out by the eminent historian and author of *General Lee's College*, Dr. Ollinger Crenshaw, there are two conflicting versions of the early history of Washington and Lee University.[96] One version, however, is patently incorrect and lacks any credible foundation. The correct version is based upon the official institutional records of the period of the founding, together with all known written and or published accounts written before 1850, with one unimportant exception. The one possible exception is a portion of an undated letter ostensibly written by a misguided and misinformed elderly minister, Rev. Samuel Houston, but its contents have never been verified and it does not appear to be extant.

If Rev. Houston actually wrote such a letter, he obviously had not consulted the official records of the institution or any of the other existing published or unpublished histories, two of which were written by his friends, colleagues, and

---

95   FN no. 20 reads as follows: "Interview with Mrs. Alexander—Dr. John McDaniel, Washington and Lee University, Lexington, Virginia, Winter 1974."

96   Ollinger Crenshaw, Appendix A, "The Problem of the Origins" in Typescript unpublished version of *General Lee's College*, vol. II, pg. 524 et seq. (Separately paginated 1–13.) Located at Leyburn Library, Washington and Lee University, Lexington, Virginia.

fellow alumni. This report contains an appendix dedicated to the debunking of, the alleged, error-riddled letter, said to have been written by Rev. Houston. Rev. Houston was somewhat fond of expounding upon historical occurrences in an impromptu fashion. His off-the-cuff recollections, however interesting, are understandably unreliable as historical evidence. This alleged letter to Rev. Morrison of New Providence Church, would be just such an occurrence, and as represented by Mr. Foote, is riddled with obvious and easily demonstrated mistakes. This mystery letter, however, is the only basis upon which the absurd notion that Washington and Lee University evolved from the private "Latin School" of Rev. John Brown, was ever offered. Foote reprinted the same part of this letter in both of his two books on Virginia the content of which mysteriously and substantively changed from one volume to the next.[97] In one case, Foote apparently corrects Houston by deleting a name from a list of students printed in his first volume and in his second book completely alters an important aspect bearing on the founding of the college. He did this, however, without notice or explanation. It was only recently discovered by the auditor. As such, the ideas proffered by Mr. Foote on the subject of the founding are beyond absurd. In truth, the representations as presented by Mr. Foote are deceptive and totally unreliable. It is simply astounding for Foote to think that he could substantively change the quoted text of someone else's letter. This comparison of the two quotes is detailed in the main body of this report. That Foote committed this unforgivable error is unmistakable when the two quoted extracts are viewed side by side.

Rev. John Brown's "Latin School" actually operated contemporaneously with the school later named "Liberty Hall Academy," as evidenced by Rev. Philip Vicker Fithian in his written testimony found in his journal for 1775 and 1776.[98] This testimony was written by Mr. Fithian while lodging, intermittently, in the home of Rev. John Brown in late 1775 and early 1776. His eyewitness observations were written at the time in question. Fithian was a schoolmate of both William Graham and Samuel Doak, and he was possessed of an impeccable reputation as both a scholar and a reputable eyewitness who recorded the events in question at the time they transpired. His recorded testimony is incontrovertible and refutes the version offered by Mr. Foote. Fithian's account is also consistent with virtually all the records and published histories dating from 1774 through 1849. Moreover, as a frequent houseguest Rev. Brown during his visit to the Valley in 1775 and early 1776, he was obviously well aware of Brown's Latin school conducted on the grounds of the Brown estate. In fact, he reported that another schoolmate from Princeton, Samuel Doak, was conducting the classes in Brown's school in early December of 1775.

---

97   As discussed previously and elsewhere in this report, the text, as reproduced varies importantly, in volume one and volume two. And because the variance is located in the same sentence, neither extract can be considered reliable.

98   Philip Vickers Fithian, *The Journal & Letters of Philip Vickers Fithian, "Written on the Virginia-Pennsylvania Frontier and in the Army Around New York, [1775–1776]*, Princeton, Princeton University Press, 1934.

Then came William Henry Foote who laid the groundwork for the complete repudiation of the long-standing consistent history that was then well established. Astoundingly, Foote's version became canon despite his failure to authenticate his gratuitous assertions. That not one scholar in the nineteenth century bothered to fact-check the foundation of Foote's ridiculous claims is an embarrassment to the field of history. That embarrassment was expanded upon by all, but one of the scholars of the twentieth century who wrote on the early history of education in Virginia. Dr. Crenshaw was the first to recognize the disparity of historical treatments of the university's founding, but he demurred in the face of potential controversy and retreated into academic safety, leaving the responsibility to announce the unjustifiable disparity in the early history as represented by the institution, to others.

WASHINGTON AND LEE FOUNDING VARIANTS

VERSION 1: (Below is the correct version)

The correct version of Washington and Lee's origins is based on documentary evidence and all the known published accounts before 1850. It can be found in the college's first authorized and official institutional history. Below are the opening lines:

> *The Present Academy of Liberty Hall **began***
> ***under the Direction and Patronage of the***
> ***Presbytery of Hanover** as the following*
> *minutes fully evince.*

***At a session of the Pby. of Hanover at Cub Creek Oct. 13, 1774**, the Pby resumed consideration of a school for the liberal education of youth which we unanimously judge to be of great importance. **We do therefore agree to establish and patronize a publick school which shall be confined to the county of Augusta in this colony**.* Source: Rev. Caleb Wallace, Clerk, Hanover Presbytery written May 1776.[99]

Note: This opening by Rev. Wallace is followed by four pages of text, mostly comprised of extracts from the meeting minutes of the Hanover Presbytery that were deemed by Clerk Wallace to address all those aspects that bore directly upon the establishment of the Presbyterian Church's new, and first, Virginia Seminary [Academy of higher education]. As such, it is the institution's first authorized, written history. Later, the Hanover Presbytery would create a governing Board of Trustees, but initially governance was retained within the province of the Hanover Presbytery.

VERSION 2: This fallacious and unsupported version may, or may not, contain two parts, depending upon the particular author asserting the claim. Some asserted part 1, some part 2, and some assert a combination of both parts linking the two men and their schools. All of the known similar versions lack any credible

---

99   This written history is located in the Liberty Hall Academy Board of Trustees' meeting minutes record book on file at the Leyburn Library of Washington and Lee University. The man who wrote this cursory history was the then Clerk of the Hanover Presbytery. He explains that he constructed it using extracts from all the sections of the Presbytery's meeting minutes that he determined pertinent to the college's founding. It was written by Wallace at the behest of the Presbytery and provided to the newly created Board of Trustees in May of 1766.

foundation, and none of these authors had even been born when the college was created. Their understanding therefore was based upon idle hearsay, speculation, unreliable secondary sources, or upon misreading of extracts from documents that were unclear without the benefit of the associated contexts.

Part 1-   **(Below is one variation of the false version)**

The ***germ of Washington College was a classical school established about 1752 (?) by Robert Alexander***, at first near Greenville, Augusta County; and "***was the first classical school in the valley of Virginia.***" *It was removed "shortly before the revolution" to Mt. Pleasant*, near Fairfield, Rockbridge County, where October *12*, 1774, *it was formally adopted by Hanover Presbytery*, with its original name of the Augusta Academy, and arrangements were made to support it, while it remained under the patronage of the Presbytery, by "liberal contributions."[100] [Washington College, Virginia, Charter and Laws . . .. 1865.] [emphasis added]

Part 2 -   **(Below is another variation of the false version)**

As Principal of Augusta Academy, Mr. Alexander was succeeded by Rev. John Brown, D. D., his (i.e., Alexander's) pastor[101], who was called to Providence and Timber Ridge Churches in 1753. During the administration of Mr. Brown, the Academy was successively removed a few miles westward, first to Old Providence, *then to New Providence,*[102] *Church and "shortly before the Revolution" to Mt. Pleasant, near Fairfield*, in (now) Rockbridge County, *where in 1774, Mr. Wm. Graham became his assistant*, and *in 1776*,

---

100   *100 . The Charter and Laws and Trustees and Faculty of Washington College at Lexington, Va. A. D. 1865*, Richmond: Chas. H. Wynne, Printer, 1865.

101   [101.] Robert Alexander was a recorded vestryman and therefore most likely an Anglican, unlike his brother Archibald who was a Presbyterian. Christian then would be incorrect in claiming that Brown was Robert Alexander's pastor. Archibald signed Rev. Brown's call to be the church's pastor, Robert did not.

102   *The term "New Providence" is technically not an official geographically designated location. Rather, it refers connotatively to the close vicinity of the New Providence Presbyterian Church in Rockbridge County, Virginia.*

succeeded him as Principal."[103] (Washington College,
Va., 1869, Bolivar Christian, Trustee.) (Emphasis added.)

Note: The numerous mistakes embodied within the two parts of the erroneous version shown above are highlighted in bold and italicized typeface. The first part, "Historical Statistics" was written anonymously,[104] *but like the other was published under the imprimatur of the college. In 1869, the second part appeared, four years after the university's Charter and Laws . . . and, according to Dr. Crenshaw, it was authored by Trustee, Col. Bolivar Christian. In neither variant does the author acknowledge that he is repudiating all the university's prior historical accounts, nor does the author provide any evidence to justify his repudiation of the university's consistent seventy-five-year history identifying the institution's date of origin to be October of 1774. The probability is that both erroneous versions were written by Bolivar Christian. One of them in 1865 and the other in 1869.*

The two incorrect variations shown above are both asserted without the benefit of any serious authority other than an easily detected fictitious "tradition."[105] The correct version is reflected in the applicable historical literature dating from 1796 to 1850, and in the earliest records of those institutions associated with the university's founding. All the early literature and the records are, in every important respect,[106] consistent concerning the institution's founding. The founding occurred as a result of the actions of the Hanover Presbytery in October of 1774. There is no sound basis for believing that the university's history extends further backward than October of 1774. The University's current claim is, without doubt, incorrect. The basis of the current rendition lacks even one particle of fact rooted in the eighteenth century. In the parlance of today, the current representation emanating from the university is a Madison Avenue- like, public relations "wag-the-dog" example of *postmodern spin*. Simply put, it isn't true. The facts supporting the report's conclusion that the currently presented early history isn't true are quite clearly incontrovertible.

Amazingly, the accurate rendition was widely known and well publicized during the institution's first seventy-five years. There were several published histories during this time period and they all consistently represented the origin of the institution as being the product of the actions of the Hanover Presbytery in October of 1774. These publications include those authored by Edward Graham, Esq. (Prof & Trustee of Washington College, Va.- 1821; Rev. Archibald Alexander, president

---

103 Christian, Col. Bolivar, "Historical Sketch," *Catalogue of Alumni of Washington College of Virginia for the year 1869*, Baltimore, John Murphy & Co, 1869. Esp. At pp. 3–13.

104 *The auditor suspects but cannot confirm that Bolivar Christian was the author of both variants.*

105 In any typical historical context, the word *tradition* is generally speaking a euphemism for an assertion that has no basis in fact or evidence and which is usually unreliable but has been passed down from earlier times. In the case of the erroneous history of W&L, which is the current official version, tradition means gratuitous assertions with no basis in fact whatsoever, and which only emerged after 1850 in the mind of some unknown person(s) but were then relied upon by William Henry Foote. At the time, no such tradition was known to exist, so in fact, it was not an actual tradition, it was merely a retrospective erroneous and baseless assertion.

106 The lone exception to the rule is that several of the earliest histories erroneously represent that Washington and Lee University was established after Hampden Sydney College, but the reverse is unquestionably true.

of both Hampden Sydney College, and later Princeton Theological Seminary- 1843; noted author and Presbyterian historian Rev. William Hill (1835); Dr. Samuel L. Campbell acting president of Washington College -1838; and noted historian Rev. Robert Davidson, author of a history of the Churches of the Valley[107] - 1847.

Finally, in this regard, there is the first authorized published account in 1849.[108] All of these published accounts assert that the founding of Washington College occurred in October of 1774 by the actions of the Hanover Presbytery. Moreover, no contrary credible claims or assertions are known to have existed during these first seventy-five years of the university's existence.

As previously mentioned (version 1), the presbytery presented in its first official history in May of 1776. This history is located in the official record book of the Liberty Hall Academy's Board of Trustees. The Board of Trustees, like the school, was also created by the actions of the Hanover Presbytery, but that did not occur immediately upon the school's creation. The school was created on October 13, 1774, and was organized informally thereafter at Mount Pleasant while buildings were being constructed at Timber Ridge. The Board of Trustees was not created until May of 1776. At that time, the Hanover Presbytery presented its first official history to their newly created Board of Trustees, and the Trustee's sought to ensure its preservation by having it written down as an introduction to the record book that was to contain their official meeting minutes. That first official historical sketch remains where it was placed in May of 1776,[109] at the record book's opening pages, 3–7. Written by Rev. Caleb Wallace, it was likely copied from a memorandum into the record book by the rector, Mr. Graham, or whoever was acting as the Trustees' Clerk. Mr. Wallace was also an early Trustee of Liberty Hall Academy and later became a Justice of Kentucky's highest Appellate Court. It is not without interest that Rev. Caleb Wallace was the only member of the Hanover Presbytery who became a Trustee of both of the Hanover Presbytery's seminaries, Liberty Hall and Hampden Sydney. Another interesting fact is that the author of this first authorized history, Caleb Wallace was ordained at the same meeting when the Academy was created, and in addition, it took place in his own church. Presumably, the author of the sketch was unlikely to have been mistaken about the events of that meeting because it may very well have been the most memorable meeting of his life.

---

107 Rev. Robert Davidson, *History of the Presbyterian Church in the State of Kentucky; (with a preliminary Sketch of the Churches in the Valley of Virginia,)* New York, Robert Carter, 1847.

108 Rev. George Junkin, DD, *Christianity the Patron of Literature And Science: An Address Delivered February 22, 1849, On the Occasion of the Author's Inauguration as President of Washington College, Virginia,* Philadelphia, The Board of Trustees, 1849 [pamphlet pp. 39.] The Junkin Inaugural Address includes an important Appendix: entitled, *"A Brief Sketch of the Early History of Washington College."* (ordered printed by the Board of Trustees) This appendix constitutes the College's first, authorized and published History.)

109 The historical sketch is five pages in length and occupies pages three through seven. The book contains no title page, as is typical with record books, and no flyleaf. There are no pages numbered, one or two.

Mr. Wallace's historical sketch[110] is understandably a brief one since the institution was then only nineteen months old. He begins his sketch with the actions of the Hanover Presbytery in 1771 to initiate a process that today we might well describe as a feasibility and desirability study. The sketch is comprised of extracts of the Presbytery's meeting minutes that the Presbytery's Clerk Caleb Wallace, deemed pertinent to the establishment of the Academy. As such, it is the first authorized documentary-based history of the institution and a valid one. Amazingly, we did not locate any published work that cited this most important primary source for delineating an accurate early history of Washington and Lee University. We found this fact the most striking and disturbing of all our findings given its prominent location in the college's oldest and first record book.

The first few lines of this authorized institutional history of Washington and Lee University by Clerk, are repeated:

> *The Present Academy of Liberty Hall*[111] *began under the Direction and Patronage of the Presbytery of Hanover as the following minutes fully evince.* (Rev. Caleb Wallace, Clerk, Hanover Presbytery, May 1776) (Emphasis added.)

Rev. Wallace, following the actual meeting minutes, dates the establishment of Augusta Academy as having taken place on October 13, 1774. Moreover, there is no mention in this account of the local schools directed by either Robert Alexander, or Rev. John Brown. The reason that Caleb Wallace fails to mention these two men or their schools is because there is no connection between them and the new public seminary, which was unofficially referred to by the Presbytery as Augusta Academy.[112] Representations to the contrary are not based upon either facts or credible evidence.

****

---

110 Introduction, Liberty Hall Academy, Trustee minutes book, pg. 3, dated May 1776, and the author is identified as "Caleb Wallace, Clerk."

111 *That Mr. Wallace refers to the school as "Liberty Hall Academy" suggests that this history was created contemporaneously with the first meeting of the new Board of Trustees, because it was only then that the Trustees gave the Academy its first official name, Liberty Hall Academy. That the sketch was copied into the Trustee's own record book on pages immediately before their first meeting's minutes means that this history was presented with the full knowledge and the approval of both the Hanover Presbytery and the Board of Trustees of Liberty Hall Academy. As such, its status as the preeminent primary source of authority is, in the auditor's view, incontrovertible. Wallace provided the same kind of history to the new Trustees of Hampden Sydney, and of course, at the Presbytery's direction.*

112 The name "Augusta Academy is not found in any eighteenth-century Virginia sources except in relation to the Presbytery's new seminary in Augusta County. No eighteenth-century source is known to have used that name to refer to either the school of Robert Alexander or to the "Latin School" of Rev. John Brown. The denomination was a convention adopted by the Hanover Presbytery to distinguish in its minutes between the Presbytery's two new Virginia seminaries in Augusta and Prince Edward Counties, respectively., hence the names, "Augusta Academy" and "Prince Edward Academy." Those who used the name "Augusta Academy" to refer to either Mr. Alexander's or Mr. Brown's schools only did so retroactively, and after 1850. Such usage of the name is laughably inappropriate.

The Current (Jan. 2015) Washington and Lee University Official History
(Based on the false version, number Two shown above.)

Below is the opening part of the university' current (early 2015) official
statement of the institution's early history and its founding. This 2015 account
contradicts the representations made by the institution from 1776 until 1865,
and it **lacks any evidentiary support that is based on eighteenth-century
sources.**[113] **What appears below in *bold italics* is demonstrably incorrect, and
the incontrovertible evidence that proves it is scattered throughout the report.

> *Washington and Lee is a small, private, liberal arts University
> nestled between the Blue Ridge and Allegheny Mountains in
> Lexington, Va. **It is the ninth oldest institution of higher
> learning in the nation.***[114]
>
>   ***In 1749, Scotch-Irish pioneers who had migrated deep
> into the Valley of Virginia founded a small classical school
> called Augusta Academy,** some 20 miles north of what is now
> Lexington. **In 1776, the Trustees, fired by patriotism, <u>changed</u>
> the name of the school to Liberty Hall.***[115]
>
>   *Four years later the school was moved to the vicinity of
> Lexington, where in 1782 it was chartered as Liberty Hall
> Academy by the Virginia Legislature and empowered to grant
> degrees. A Limestone building, erected in 1793 on the crest
> of a ridge overlooking Lexington, burned in 1803, though
> its ruins are preserved today as a symbol of the institution's
> honored past.*" (From the Washington and Lee website, posted
> on January 31, 2015) (emphasis added)

Contrary to the university's representation, Washington and Lee is not the
ninth oldest institution of higher learning in the nation, if that distinction was

---

113   **John M. McDaniel, Charles N. Watson, David T.** Moore, <u>Liberty Hall Academy, The Early
      History of the Institutions Which Evolved Into Washington and Lee University</u>, Lexington,
      Virginia, Liberty Hall Press, 1979, pg. 4 "evidence of direct ties between the sites [Alexander's
      school & Brown's School(s)] has not been found in eighteenth-century sources."

114   *It is assumed that this self-ranking is incorrect because the correct date of origin is off by
      twenty-five years.*

115   *The trustees, in 1776, did give the school the name Liberty Hall Academy, but they did not
      change its name because, in truth, it had no earlier name. It was unofficially referred to
      as Augusta Academy, but the use of that denomination was merely a convention used by
      the Presbytery to distinguish the Academy in Augusta County from the other Academy in
      Prince Edward County. This subtle distinction is important because the Presbytery was
      reserving the honor of naming its two new schools (Academies) for the yet-to-be appointed
      Boards of Trustees, which they intended to create once it was clear that the schools were
      viable educational endeavors. For all important purposes, the only "official name" of the
      college in the eighteenth century was Liberty Hall Academy, although it was inappropriately
      denominated as Washington Academy by the Virginia legislature in 1798; thereafter, it was
      given the name Washington College. Still, the college Liberty Hall Academy had been vested
      with degree-granting authority since 1782.*

predicated on a founding date earlier than the 1770s. Additionally, no small classical school founded by pioneers in the Valley was called Augusta Academy[116] during that era. Moreover, The first Board of Trustees did not "change" the name of the school because prior to the name "Liberty Hall Academy," the school had no official name to change. That is, the official records demonstrate that the Presbytery never made a formal decision to give the school a name.

The school was referred to by the Hanover Presbytery under several denominations similar to Augusta Academy, but this was merely a convention used by the Presbytery's clerk and its other members to distinguish between its two academies during meetings and in its minutes. The members of the Presbytery consciously did not name their two academies in order to allow their prospective Boards of Trustees to have the honor of giving the schools their first official names. In the case of both academies, the unofficial denominations were often similar variants, but most often, the variants included the names of the counties wherein the academies were located. Hence the early labels Augusta Academy and Prince Edward Academy. These unofficial names were only in used by the Presbytery for a very brief period. By June of 1776 both schools had operating Boards of Trustees and official names, Liberty Hall Academy and Hampden Sydney College.

Note: The College's Website's statement of history is also incorrect in the seventh paragraph, but on an entirely different subject. The current Website states that the first female students who matriculated at W&L did so in 1985. This too is essentially incorrect. The institution's first female student, Sarah (McBride) Priestley, matriculated in the late 1780s, two hundred years earlier. Mrs. Priestley's husband was an alumnus of Liberty Hall, and an early tutor under Rev. William Graham. Mr. James Priestley's wife, the former Sarah McBride of Kentucky, was enrolled in the regular academic program by Rev. William Graham. Here she matriculated for some time, where she occasionally encountered Archibald Alexander, who was an alumnus, then studying theology under Rev. Graham. Dr. Alexander wrote about this in his Mss "Memoir of the Rev. Wm Graham, it is available to the public in spiral-bound form at the Leyburn Library, Washington and Lee University. At the time of her matriculation, Sarah Priestley had two children, "one at the breast," according to Dr. Alexander. Alexander claims that Sarah did not complete her studies but was so far advanced in her studies as to allow her to organize a successful school for young women in Baltimore. Mrs. Priestley is the first female College student ever enrolled into a regular academic program in a chartered college in America. That Mrs. Priestley's matriculation was long a singular unmatched event does not detract from the reality of her matriculation nor does it alter the fact, that the college's president, by this example of enrolling Mrs. Priestley, proved his willingness to accept a properly prepared female student. Whether subsequent presidents were as progressive and open-minded as President Graham in this regard is unknown to the auditor.

****

---

116   Common local school were not typically given names. There are no known letters or documents from the Valley prior to the creation of the Presbytery's seminary that contain a name and none that was referred to in letters or publications as, Augusta Academy.

THE ESTABLISHMENT: VERSION 1 vs. VERSION 2

The evidence in support of version 1 (date of founding is October 13, 1774)

Below are ten selected and credible authorities in support of version 1 (i.e., the 1774 establishment). Cumulatively, they represent overwhelming and incontrovertible evidence in support of version 1. (Five of these authorities are eighteenth-century authorities; the remainder are pre-1850.)[117]

- The official records (Meeting Minutes) of the Hanover Presbytery between 1771 and 1776

- The official records (Meeting Minutes) of the Liberty Hall Academy Board of Trustees from its inception in May of 1776

- The written memorandum (Historical Sketch) of Liberty Hall Academy's founding by Rev. Caleb Wallace, Clerk of the Hanover Presbytery (May 1776)

- The eyewitness, written testimony of Rev. Philip Vickers Fithian[118] in his journal for 1775–1776 (not published until 1934)

- William Graham's letter written on behalf of the Board of Trustees and communicated to President George Washington, containing a brief historical sketch[119] (1796)

- The first published historical account of Liberty Hall, written in 1821 by Edward Graham

  ("A Memoir of the Late Rev. William Graham, AM." *The Evangelical and Literary Magazine and Missionary Chronicle*, IV (1821), p.75 et Seq)

- Rev. William Hill's published article, "History of Washington College, Virginia"[1838][120]

---

117   There are other eighteenth-century supporting authorities for Version A, including extant letters too numerous to mention.

118   Philip Vickers Fithian, *The Journal & Letters of Philip Vickers Fithian, "Written on the Virginia-Pennsylvania Frontier and in the Army Around New York, [1775–1776]*, Princeton, Princeton University Press, 1934 (Written in 1775–76]

119   The sketch is intentionally vague about the Presbyterian church's establishment because President Washington was an Anglican, but there is no mention of Robert Alexander, Rev. John Brown, or their schools.

120   Dr. Crenshaw provides in his unpublished footnotes (typescript) Washington & Lee University Archives/Library] "Vol. II, "Appendix "A"] [hand-paginated in pencil as Pg. no. 526] that this article is based in large measure upon an article by Rev. Dr. William Hill, published in 1835. The editors also relied upon a letter from Mr. Edward Graham. See bibliography under Rev. Wm. Hill. The auditor was not able to locate a copy of the 1835 article by Rev. Hill.

- The unpublished manuscript "Memoir of William Graham" written by Rev. Archibald Alexander (Pres. Princeton Theological Seminary, and Presbyterian Church historian) (1840s)

- Rev. Archibald Alexander DD, "An Address before the Alumni of Washington College," Virginia. Delivered June 29, 1843, limited-edition pamphlet in wraps ("wraps" is a term of art used by antiquarian book dealers to describe flexible, usually heavy-stock paper binding (i.e., covers)

- Rev. Robert, Davidson's *History of the Presbyterian Church in the State of Kentucky*; *__with a preliminary Sketch of the Churches in the Valley of Virginia__*, New York, Robert Carter, 1847. (Emphasis added.)

- The college's first authorized ***published*** history of the founding and early days of Liberty Hall Academy, *A Brief Sketch of the Early History of the College*, in 1849. (See bibliography, Rev. George Junkin, Inaugural Address, *Appendix,* "A Brief Sketch of the Early History of the College." For full citation, see bibliography.)

Note: All of these various materials listed above support the viability of version 1 (i.e., Oct. 1774) and not one of these cited writings implies, or asserts, any link between Augusta Academy/ Liberty Hall and the schools of either Robert Alexander or Rev. John Brown. All of these identified sources appeared between 1774 and 1849. During this seventy-five-year period, not one inkling is heard anywhere, or at any time, that suggests any date of origin other than October of 1774.

Conclusion regarding the evidentiary foundation for Version 1

The evidence provided above in support of version "One" is contained mostly in published, histories and all are authored by eminent professionals spanning seventy-five years of history. All essentially date the origins of Washington and Lee University to October of 1774 and not one, mentions Robert Alexander, or Rev. John Brown as having any meaningful connection to the Presbytery's seminary, Liberty Hall Academy. In addition, version 1, appears consistently in records and publications of the late eighteenth and early nineteenth century and is supported by eyewitness testimony written down at the time of the events in question by Rev. Philip Vickers Fithian, a man of unquestioned character and reputation. The identified evidence is also consistent with contemporary letters of Rev. John Brown. It is also consistent with the meeting minutes of both the Hanover Presbytery covering the years 1771–1776, and the meeting minutes of the Board of Trustees, from the Board's creation. Version "One" reflects precisely the representation of the Clerk of the Hanover Presbytery, Rev. Caleb Wallace,[121]

---

121   Rev. Caleb Wallace is a most credible eyewitness who later became a Justice of Kentucky's highest [Supreme] Court.

written in 1776, and, finally, it is consistent with the first authorized published historical sketch, issued by order of the Board of Trustees in 1849.[122]

The list above constitutes an impressive array of persuasive historical authorities. This highly persuasive evidence should not have, but did go unnoticed by virtually all historians, including numerous representatives of the university since 1865. This impressive collection of persuasive evidence seems all the more striking when it is compared to the paltry little upon which the incorrect version 2 is based.

****

The Scant Evidence in Support of Version 2
Note: There is no known eighteenth-century documentary evidence to support the current false history.

There is no credible evidence to support the widely publicized fiction that the institution dates to 1749 or any other year prior to 1774. There are no known witnesses that were party to the establishment of Washington and Lee University or who were among the adults involved in the establishment of the university who might have, but did not, leave any letter, manuscript, or publication describing events in a manner consistent with the claims embodied in any component of version 2. Moreover, there was no official document created by any institution existing at or even near that era that is even remotely reflective of the representations made in version 2.

In truth, not one author we have reviewed over the course of forty years of research ever offered or referenced any credible authority that existed in the eighteenth century and claimed directly, or indirectly, that the origin of Washington and Lee University began before October 13, 1774. Those few contrarians who cite the Hanover Presbytery's 1770 minutes either rely upon an extract taken out of context, or they palpably misinterpret the minutes. In such cases, we have gone to great lengths to demonstrate in the Author Errors Section of this report the precise nature of various authors' mistakes in this regard.

One common error that led people astray in this regard stems from a misread of the minutes of the Hanover Presbytery for April of 1775. One can easily see that several historians failed to note that the multiday meeting, which began at Timber Ridge, was subsequently moved from Timber Ridge to Rev. John Brown's capacious home on Moffett's Creek near the New Providence Church. Here, on the last day of the Presbytery's spring meeting, the Presbytery accepted Rev. Brown's offer to visit his private Latin School next door at New Providence, and unfortunately the acting Clerk, William Irving, noted this unofficial activity in the meeting minutes. This notation has been misread by several authors who failed to

---

122 Junkin, Rev. George, DD, *Christianity the Patron of...*, Philadelphia, The Board of Trustees, 1849 [pamphlet pps. 39.] The Junkin Inaugural Address includes an important Appendix: "A Brief Sketch of the Early History of Washington College," (ordered printed by the Board of Trustees.)

note that the meeting had been moved and therefore assumed, albeit incorrectly, that the Presbytery on that day visited the school at Mount Pleasant. Instead, the Presbytery visited Rev. Brown's private "Latin School" at New Providence. These authors, most prominent being Rev. William Hill are responsible for later authors confusing the Presbytery's new "public" seminary, initially and temporarily, at "Mount Pleasant," near Timber Ridge, with Rev. Brown's preparatory Latin School at New Providence,[123] which was a private school that had no connection whatsoever to the Presbytery's seminary (Academy) at Mount Pleasant or to the Presbytery. The public seminary at Mount Pleasant was, at the time (April 1775) under the "Care and tuition of William Graham." See the Hanover Presbytery Meeting Minutes for 1775, all of which, make this abundantly clear.

Mr. Foote's only identified source *(The Dubious Houston Letter)*

The only known so-called evidence that the sponsor of version 2, William Henry Foote, appears to have relied upon, is printed, in part, in both of Mr. Foote's two volumes of, *Sketches of Virginia, Historical and Biographical*, Series One and Series Two, 1850 and 1855, respectively.[124] This source is the previously mentioned ostensible letter written by Rev. Samuel Houston to Rev. James Morrison, pastor of New Providence Presbyterian Church. Mr. Foote, does not specifically represent that he relied upon this letter, or any other particular authority, but it can be reasonably argued that his authority, at least in part, is Rev. Samuel Houston's alleged letter, which has already been demonstrated to be, at best, a dubious source.

The reason Mr. Foote supplies no credible authority, is the fact that no such evidence, or authority exists. The simple truth is, there is no direct link between Liberty Hall Academy and any other school because Liberty Hall Academy was created in its entirety by the Hanover Presbytery in October of 1774, just as they created their second Academy in Prince Edward County, the following year (i.e., 1775). In neither case did the Presbytery patronize an existing preparatory school, and, why would they? If there had been some benefit to patronizing an existing small local preparatory school then the Presbytery would have considered doing that when establishing both of its two academies. There were local preparatory schools in Prince Edward County just as there was in what is now Rockbridge County, but in the case of Hampden Sydney, the subject was never mentioned in the Presbytery's minutes. If truth be told, the subject never came up in regards to Liberty Hall's establishment either, as the meeting minutes make all too clear. The real problem is, that most authors who have made the spurious claim that the

---

123 The Presbytery's meeting minutes for the following year's Spring meeting at Timber Ridge are noticeably different in their description of the Presbytery's sitting in review of its seminary's operations and in its assessment of both the Presbytery's students and the faculty under the "Care and Tuition" of Rev. William Graham.

124 These are two distinctly different books by Foote that were both named *Sketches of Virginia, Historical and Biographical* were dated 1850 and 1855 respectively. The 1850 volume is subtitled "Series One," while the second is sub-titled Series Two.

Presbytery patronized Rev. Brown's Latin school never bothered to review the Presbytery's actual meeting minutes. Instead, they relied on extracts devoid of highly meaningful context, which had been reprinted by others, especially those extracts provided by Foote. What Foote actually relied upon is unknown because he mostly refused to use citations of authority.

In the case of Liberty Hall Academy, there is ample evidence that this school was operating under William Graham at Mount Pleasant at the same time (Dec. 1775) that Rev. Brown's private Latin School was being taught by Samuel Doak at New Providence. Therefore, Liberty Hall Academy could not possibly have evolved from Rev. Brown's Latin School. If it had, perhaps Brown would not have shunned the Presbytery's new Academy and sent at least one of sons to Liberty Hall instead of sending them off to Princeton, William and Mary and elsewhere.

Rev. Houston's letter, if it exists or existed, is, as shown by Foote, a memory-based historical narrative of the early days of the New Providence Presbyterian Church. Most of the content is classic hearsay (i.e., "tradition") and obviously written when Rev. Houston no longer had an opportunity to compare his memory or the traditions he had heard from others, with living adult eyewitnesses to the event. Rev. Houston also obviously did not compare his memories to the contradictory documentary evidence possessed by either the Hanover Presbytery, or the Board of Trustees of the Academy. In addition, the small portion of Rev. Houston's letter that refers to Liberty Hall Academy is so vague that its meaning cannot be discerned with any degree of specificity. For example, it is unclear whether Rev. Houston means to refer to the school directed by Rev. John Brown, or the school conducted by Rev. William Graham. It is true that both of these schools had been located at the place called Mount Pleasant, but Rev. Brown's school had been moved from Mount Pleasant to his home and church at New Providence several miles away from Fairfield long before the Presbytery established their new seminary, Augusta Academy. A fact, seemingly unknown to mid-nineteenth century historians and virtually all those who followed them, up to our own times.

The aspect of Houston's letter that pertains to Liberty Hall Academy, is exceedingly brief and yet contains several unquestionably erroneous statements, which are included in the following excerpt reprinted by Foote,[125] from the dubious "Rev. Houston's letter:"

> ***This grammar school was moved to the place, near Fairfield, called Mount Pleasant; about which time the Presbytery of Hanover patronized it.*** (printed in Foote, series 1, pg. 442,443; It is also found, in part, in series 2, pg. 60, although as explained elsewhere, Foote deleted the last three words and replaced them with words of his own. Shockingly,

---

125 Keeping in mind that Foote provably changed the content of the letter to fit his own agenda, printing it one way in 1850 and in another way in 1855, and by failing to inform his readers of his literary crime, he perjures himself and undermines his own credibility.

Foote placed his own words within the quotation marks meant
to convey that they were Houston's assertion.)

(Note: This statement above is patently false. If it were true, there would be some indication made in the Presbytery's minutes but, of course, no such indication exists. Perhaps, that is why Foote removed that claim from the text of what he represented was a letter from Houston when he released his second volume of Sketches of Virginia... in 1855. At this point, Foote reprinted the same basic extract as he had in 1850, but this time he removed two inescapable errors[126] that had obviously been brought to his attention since the release of his earlier edition. To do this without informing his readers of what he did and why he did it constitutes a serious breach of ethics, and is without question, unprofessional. It is also unethical not to explain that he had removed the only basis upon which he had earlier formulated the link between Liberty Hall and a preexisting school. Astoundingly, Foote wrote an entirely new concluding phrase to replace the one he had removed, and passed his creation off as the work of Rev. Houston by placing his words within in content of Houston's letter. All of it in the same quotation marks. This elevates Foote's ethical breach from a literary high misdemeanor to what equates to a felonious hoax, because what he did had to have been premeditated forgery. The victims in this case are his readers, and, of course, all those authors who followed in his footsteps. It is amazing that his mischief and/or incompetence went undetected for so long.)

Foote obviously believed it was within his province to correct other's errors, ex post facto, as though the errors had never been made in the first instance. This is an inexcusable thing for any author to do in the way Mr. Foote appears to have done it. It constitutes a serious breach of professional ethics, and at the same time, it renders the extract he attributes to Rev. Houston of no value whatsoever. The letter is apparently not extant and therefore its content cannot be authenticated. We only have Foote's word about Houston's letter, and his word is unreliable given his serious breach of ethics. This is not the only example of Foote's prestidigitations and manipulations of the truth. Others are addressed in the Author's Errors Section of this report. In addition to deliberate falsifying the writings of others, Foote also mixes his interpretations of events into introductory comments preceding extracts from others and, whether intentional or not, changes the meaning of the text which follows his introductory material. Examples of this are set forth in the subsection devoted to Foote in Authors Errors Section.

The statement by Rev. Houston, if indeed he made any part of it,[127] is not correct in four critically important ways:

> 1. In the decade during which Liberty Hall Academy was established and patronized by the Hanover Presbytery, no grammar school, or for that matter any other school, had been moved to the local spot called "Mount Pleasant," as is

---

126 *He removed the name of Ebenezer Smith whose name had been incorrectly included in a list of students and he removed the false claim that the Presbytery had patronized an existing school at Mount Pleasant" Of course, the second item he removed is the sole basis upon which he had incorrectly formulated his notion that Rev. Brown's Latin School was the germ from whence Liberty Hall sprang.*

127 Earlier, in this report, it was explained that Mr. Foote's referenced "Houston Letter" has no historical value due to the fact that Mr. Foote failed to quote from it, in a consistent manner, and because no original is apparently extant.

asserted in the letter. At least, no record exists from that time to authenticate such a school.

2. Rev. Brown's private school had indeed been moved, but not_ _to_ Mount Pleasant as the letter suggests. Rather, the school had been moved in the other direction, _from_ Mount Pleasant to New Providence. Here Mr. Brown's school remained for as long as it operated. So, Brown's own letters of that period demonstrate.

3. Rev. Brown's school was not, as the letter says "a grammar school"[128] but was rather a "Latin School." This was a label used consistently by Rev. John Brown who had created this private school, but labels aside, the Hanover Presbytery's meeting minutes covering the time period 1771 to 1776 clearly demonstrate that the Presbytery never "patronized" any existing school. The seminary established on October 13, 1774, was an entirely new and entirely unprecedented educational endeavor undertaken by the Hanover Presbytery. _Note: Brown's school was preparatory for prospective college students. The Presbytery's Augusta Academy/Liberty Hall was designed and established, from its inception to provide a college education like that of the college of New Jersey. See, Hanover Presbytery meeting minutes between 1771 and 1775._

4. The "Houston letter," as presented by Foote, asserts that one of the early students was Ebenezer Smith, which is a preposterous and inexplicable mistake, because Ebenezer Smith was educated at his father's Academy in Pennsylvania and he was one of Rev. Brown's hired Tutors, not a student as is claimed in the letter. It is a clear indicator that whoever was responsible for this account was a completely unreliable scribe. It also suggests that Houston did not write the letter because this is a fact he should have been aware of. If Houston actually wrote this assertion, it calls into question the status of his faculties at the time he wrote it, or that he had been misled by someone else. Whatever Houston wrote or did not write in this regard, the letter as presented by Foote, is clearly wrong about Ebenezer Smith being a student in the Valley. We know from unimpeachable evidence that all three of these Smith brothers received their preparatory education from their father, Rev. Robert Smith in Pennsylvania and college education at Princeton. He was an instructor for a time at Rev. John Brown's Latin school.

---

128 The term "grammar school" connotes a general curriculum of classical studies while the term "Latin school" connotes a narrowly focused course in the basic Latin and Greek grammar, which was then typically required for any student applying to a college.

> Note: Ebenezer Smith was the brother of both Rev. Samuel Stanhope Smith, first President of Hampden Sydney and his brother John Blair Smith, his successor. As a later Trustee of Liberty Hall, it is difficult to believe that Rev. Houston would not have been aware of the connection between these three Smith brothers. Whoever wrote the content of the so-called Houston letter, however, was clearly not well informed on the subject of the early history of Liberty Hall Academy, given this colossal blunder concerning Ebenezer Smith. In sum, the so-called "Houston letter" is no sound basis upon which to re-write seventy-five years of consistent documentary-based history, irrespective of its authorship or its provenance.

Rev. John Brown's congregation, it should be remembered, was composed of numerous members Rev. Houston's close family members, and was this Samuel Houston was undoubtedly baptized and married by his pastor, Rev. Brown, and yet he does not mention Rev. Brown's name in connection with the establishment of Liberty Hall Academy in this alleged letter to Rev. Morrison.

If Mr. Houston actually believed that his family's pastor deserved to be considered as the college's first president, he had several opportunities during his lifetime to recognize his old pastor in this regard. For example, Houston composed the letter of dismissal (Brown' retirement) from his pastorate of the New Providence congregation, but in that letter, Mr. Houston made no mention of Rev. Brown's having played any role in the establishment of Liberty Hill Academy. This oversight would certainly not have been made if Mr. Brown had indeed played such a pivotal role as has been represented by so many later historians and the university.

An entirely different letter which actually was written by Houston, and on behalf of the Lexington Presbytery, acknowledging Rev. Brown's retirement was signed by Houston and is extant. He also cosigned a letter with Rev. William Graham that was sent to Pres. George Washington which contained a brief history of the college. In neither of these two letters signed by Rev. Houston is there any reference whatsoever to Rev. John Brown nor to Robert Alexander as having had any connection to Liberty Hall Academy. This, too, is easily explained by the simple fact that there was no connection.

(Note: Rev. John Brown was one of many members of the Hanover Presbytery that created "Augusta Academy," but he is the only known member of the Presbytery to have opposed the creation of this seminary (i.e., Academy). Brown's opposition is revealed in his known correspondence from that period, which is abstracted in Mr. John White Stuart's important biography of Rev. Brown (see bibliography). Many of Brown's letters from this period are housed in the famous Draper Collection of manuscripts. See bibliography entry for John White Stuart, Brown's only biographer.)

Rev. Samuel Houston is an aptly venerated early graduate of Liberty Hall and a long-serving friend of the college from which he graduated under his preceptor and friend, Rev. William Graham. He is remembered for his several attainments as a man, a father, and as a pious patriarch of the Presbyterian Church. He is not, however, an historian, notwithstanding his fondness for yarn spinning. If he did in fact write a letter to Rev. Morrison referring to the founding of Liberty Hall, he was relying on secondhand information (hearsay) because, he was a teenager living on his family's farm near Timber Ridge when the founding took place approximately eighty miles from Timber Ridge, at the Cub Creek Presbyterian Meeting House in Charlotte County. This was where the Hanover Presbytery, comprised of Presbyterian ministers and selected Elders acted to establish their first Seminary (Academy) in Virginia.

Young mister Houston would hardly have been in attendance at a meeting of Presbyterian leaders, and it also unlikely that such a young lad asked to review the Presbytery's meeting minutes record book during his youth. Such records are comprised of important institutional information that eighteenth-century teenage boys in the mountains of Virginia would not typically find of interest. His hearsay understanding then is hardly any basis upon which to repudiate all the official records created by the institutions involved in the creation of Liberty Hall. Quite possibly, Rev. Houston never wrote that the seminary (academy) which was created by the Hanover Presbytery in Augusta had any connection to Rev. John Brown's or Robert Alexander's private schools, but if he did, he would have been wrong.

Rev. Houston did write one interesting and valuable article, however, which was later published as an appendix to a larger history of Virginia. This piece was based upon his own experiences during the Revolutionary War and he wrote it using his journal/diary kept during the experience. It is interesting and useful because it is a firsthand account based upon his recorded thoughts written when or shortly after the events occurred. With that having been admitted, it nevertheless does not alter the fact that the "Houston letter" referred to by Mr. Foote is either a complete hoax or an internally inconsistent rambling and error-ridden document that cannot possibly be relied upon as concerns the founding of Washington and Lee University. As evidence that is in direct conflict with all official records and every published account written by those who made a serious study of the events surrounding the founding before 1850, it is utterly unpersuasive.

Rev. Philip V. Fithian visits the Valley in 1775–1776.
(His 1775–1776 Journal is a valuable primary source.)

In December of 1775, a guest in Rev. Brown's home, Rev. Philip Vickers Fithian wrote in his Journal that there were two distinctly different schools in the area. One, directed by Rev. Graham, the other organized but not taught by Fithian's host, Rev. John Brown. These were two different schools that Fithian makes abundantly clear were of different types, and also were conducted at different locations, albeit in the same neighborhood.[129] The "Latin School" that

---

129   Philip Vickers Fithian, *The Journal & Letters of Philip Vickers Fithian, "Written on the Virginia-Pennsylvania Frontier and in the Army Around New York, [1775–1776]*, Princeton, Princeton University Press, 1934 [considered by publisher to be vol. II] While this volume stands alone and has its own index, it is volume two, the first volume being published in 1900.

Rev. Houston, presumably refers to as a "grammar school," was where the students that he references by name in that same letter, had attended. Some of these students would have attended classes at Mount Pleasant while others were later, instructed at New Providence because Brown had moved the school sometime in the late 1760s. Brown's school was under his administrative direction, but he did not conduct the classes. Instructors, or tutors at Brown's school were hired by Brown whose scholarly attainments were insufficient and somewhat superficial. Marginally acceptable for a Presbyterian country Parson, perhaps, but far below the standards expected of graduates from Princeton under Dr. Witherspoon. See, John White Stuart's biographical Dissertation on John Brown.

Rev. Brown's school, at the time that the Hanover Presbytery established their new seminary in Augusta, had long since been moved from Mount Pleasant to New Providence, a location from which it was never again moved. This fact is made obvious by the extant correspondence of Rev. John Brown during these years. [130] For this reason alone, it is fair to say that there was no school operating at or even near Mount Pleasant when Mr. Graham arrived in the Valley in late 1774 or early 1775. In addition, Rev. Fithian explains that in December of 1775, Brown's "Latin School" was being taught by Mr. Samuel Doak, a 1775 Princeton graduate. A few weeks earlier (Oct. 31), Mr. Doak, had been married to a Miss Montgomery, who was a sister of John Montgomery who was a teaching assistant of Rev. Graham. Mr. Montgomery was also a classmate of Mr. Doak at Princeton. Fithian knew all of these named individuals and interacted with them while in Virginia. His familiarity these ministers and educators was not casual but they were on intimate terms as friends, colleagues and classmates.

It is probably worth mentioning here that both Mr. Doak and Mr. Montgomery studied theology under Rev. Graham's direction, even though both of these men were lifelong members of Rev. Brown's Church. It is hardly possible that Rev. Fithian, who knew all of these Princeton men, would have been wrong in describing Samuel Doak's role as the tutor at Rev. Brown's Latin School in December of 1775, since Fithian was then lodging at Rev. Brown's home which was virtually next door to his school at the same time Fithian made his journal entries for December of 1775.

These facts were not generally known to historians until after the Princeton University Press published Fithian's Journal in 1934, which explains why his eyewitness testimony contradicting Foote's false representations were not taken

---

(The editors, in a footnote, erroneously challenged Mr. Fithian concerning Samuel Doak being in Augusta in December of 1775. The editor's challenge is not supported by the demonstrable facts surrounding the starting date of classes at Hampden Sydney Academy. Simply put, the Princeton editors were wrong to challenge Mr. Fithian in this regard. Philip Vickers Fithian was a scholar, and eye-witness to the events he describes in his Journal written at the time in question. The Princeton editors, writing more than a century after the fact, rather foolishly challenged a highly credible source with first-hand knowledge.)

130   Stuart, John White *The Rev. John Brown of Virginia (1728–803): His Life and selected sermons,* Doctoral Dissertation, University of Massachusetts, 1988, passim. This biography contains numerous important extracts from Brown's letters.

into consideration by the numerous nineteenth-century historians who were misled by Foote. It does not, however, excuse them from failing the authenticate Foote's preposterous repudiation of a long-standing contrary account of the founding of Washington and Lee.

The Hanover Presbytery's meeting minutes between 1771 and 1776 make clear that the Presbytery did not patronize any existing school in the Valley of Virginia in the 1770s. Indeed, they did not patronize any schools in that century other than the two they created in Augusta and Prince Edward counties.

What the Hanover Presbytery did do was to establish not one, but two, public seminaries of higher learning. These two colleges can fairly be described as sister Colleges for they were created within a few months of one another, on the same general plan, and in much the same manner by the same body of Presbyterian ministers.

The first Presbyterian seminary to be established was the one in Augusta County in October of 1774, which the Presbytery informally called "Augusta Academy." The second was established on the east side of the Blue Ridge Mountains in Prince Edward County, in February of the following year, 1775. Both of these ventures were entirely new schools, and in neither case were these schools related to any other schools. Importantly, for seventy-five years after these two schools' establishments, no other writing is known to exist that asserts any scenario consistent with Rev. Samuel Houston's demonstrably erroneous letter to Rev. Morrison, and alluded to by Foote, if indeed, Houston actually wrote such words.

This letter, said by Mr. Foote to have been written by Rev. Houston, is the sum total of all the evidence ever offered by the multitude of authors who have written on this subject since 1850. Most, do not even cite this dubious piece of evidence. Most merely cite Mr. William. Henry Foote—if they cite any authority at all—and Mr. Foote's representations concerning the origins of Washington and Lee University are an embarrassment in the annals of history. Foote's assertions in this regard are simply not credible when scrutinized in light of credible, documentary history. In sum, Rev. Houston's claim, if he ever made it, was not correct, and could not possibly be correct given how much real historical evidence there is to contradict it.

Dr. Crenshaw Too Stumbles

Houston's erroneous letter includes a mistake also made by Dr. Ollinger Crenshaw in the published version of his *General Lee's College* (Random House version). Crenshaw engages in some analytical gymnastics in attempting to explain Mr. Graham's and the Board of Trustees' meaning when they invoked the term "grammar school,"[131] in the letter to President Washington, written by Graham on behalf of the Trustees. Graham too was a Trustee, ex officio.

---

131 Ollinger Crenshaw, *General Lee's College*, New York, Random House, 1969, pg. 10, paragraph three.

In the published version of _General Lee's College_, Dr. Crenshaw butchers the subject of the founding. The first two chapters of the Random House version (1969) are inconsistent with the facts set forth in his unpublished "Appendix A: The Problem of the Origins," which is part of volume 2 of the unpublished typescript version (see bibliography). The known facts concerning the founding are also inconsistent with Crenshaw's unpublished version. Crenshaw's original version (typescript) includes extensive and important footnotes and appendix A, but he clearly equivocated on the subject of the founding.

It seems that Crenshaw was mistaken about the founding of the college during most of the years in which he was researching his subject, but clearly, he began to see at some point that something about the second version linking the college with earlier schools was out-of-joint, but even so, he declined to attempt to resolve the ever more apparent inconsistencies. In the end, he unfortunately turned his back on the conflicting versions and left it to others to figure out. Hopefully, this audit assessment will provide all the necessary ingredients for a proper historian to construct or restore the initial accurate history and explain the process by which both the university and post-1850 historians that addressed the college's origins both went so far astray. Because, Crenshaw wrote his vastly important "The Problem of the Origins" appendix which was attached to the typescript version of _General Lee's College_, he may perhaps be forgiven for his reluctance to confront a predictably hostile community in which he lived and worked. He left posterity with enough information exposing the incompatible two variant histories of the college's origins, that it was inevitable that, at some point, the true picture would re-emerge and take its proper place in the literature of the Valley. If Crenshaw had not absolutely concluded that the then-current history as depicted by the university was incorrect, he must surely have suspected it.

The known and undisputed facts of the matter paint a fairly clear picture of a man (Dr. Crenshaw) who had decided he did not want to become engaged in controversy with the extended families of the purveyors of the pervasive but false history of the college's origins. That is precisely why his first two chapters, especially in the published version, make little sense in regards to the founding of the college. Crenshaw's few but important errors in this regard are treated in detail in the Author's Errors Section of this report.

Provincialism's clear negative connotations seem to have been at work here. In the parlance of the millennium, his footnotes and appendix A, "_speak volumes._" In his appendix, Dr. Crenshaw identifies the two variant histories and provides an important overview of many of the sources responsible for version 1 (i.e., Oct 1774). He also gives a fair accounting of the dubious version 2 (1748 or thereabouts).

What Crenshaw obviously knew about the origins, he was not willing to address in the published version. His appendix A can be found at Washington and Lee University's Leyburn Library. It is a pity that the published Random House version has the effect of perpetuating a fraudulent accounting of the university's founding. Perhaps out of a sense of guilt, Dr. Crenshaw left to posterity most all of the essential clues for setting things right. Whatever his reasons, the auditor has attempted to do just that. Two clues Crenshaw apparently and surprisingly never unearthed, however, are Rev. Philip Vickers Fithian's Journal from 1775 to 1776, and the Caleb Wallace memorandum that is the first authorized institutional history of Liberty Hall Academy located in the Trustees' meeting minutes record book, pps. 3–7. The auditor is at a loss as to how Dr. Crenshaw could have missed these two important sources. Fithian's name does not appear in the index to the Random House edition of General Lee's College, or in the indexes of either of the two volumes of the typescript version, and Wallace's first authorized history is not included in his list of sources that is part of the unpublished version.

Note: In his appendix A, Crenshaw discusses the document that some mistakenly refer to as the Edward Graham memorandum which Crenshaw says Trustee Bolivar Christian pasted into the Trustees' first record book containing its meeting minutes. So he obviously reviewed this page. The very next page, which is the books actual first page, is where one finds Wallace's first authorized history of the founding of the college. It rather astounding therefore, that Crenshaw could have missed it.)

Conclusion Regarding Versions 1 and 2 of the History of the Origins

All of the credible evidence leads to the inescapable and incontrovertible conclusion that Washington and Lee University's founding took place on Oct. 13, 1774. It was the first school created to provide a college education for students west of the Blue Ridge Mountains, and it has no common link to any other school in the Valley of Virginia. Its first administrative leader was William Graham of Pennsylvania, who was summoned to Virginia by the Hanover Presbytery for the very specific purpose of implementing the Presbytery's plan to provide educational opportunities for Virginia students designed from the beginning to be on a par with the education offered by the College of New Jersey [now Princeton]. All representations to the contrary are false and have no basis in fact or credible evidence.

Those who claim that Rev. Brown's school was moved back to Mount Pleasant from New Providence are all post-1850 authors who were apparently ignorant of the existence of Rev. Philip Vickers journal covering 1775 and 1776.[132] After that

---

132 It is apparent that a few twentieth-century authors were aware of Rev. Fithian's 1775–1776 Journal, published for the first time in 1934, but those who reference it, clearly were blinded by what communication theorists call "selective perception." That is, these authors read his journal based upon preconceived notions about the schools in the valley and read into the text only that which comported with their preconceptions. Any fair reading by someone not aware of the erroneous representations of mid-nineteenth century revisionists of W&L's founding would see that there were two different schools operating in the neighborhood of Timber Ridge and New Providence churches, one that was "public" under the direction of William Graham at Mount Pleasant, and under the patronage of the Hanover Presbytery; and, the other, a private Latin School under the direction of Rev. John Brown at New Providence. In December 1775, the latter school was taught by Samuel Doak, who was then studying theology under William Graham. This is an important distinction lost to most nineteenth-century historians after 1850, who were all misled by William H. Foote (Sketches of Virginia.) Importantly, Rev. Fithian was personally acquainted with all the central figures involved in these educational endeavors, and when he wrote his Journal entries in this regard, it was mostly while lodging with Rev. John Brown and his family. Fithian's contemporaneous testimony in this regard is simply unimpeachable,

important book was published by the Princeton University Press in 1934, authors who were aware of the book made rather humorous attempts to manipulate the text's meaning to conform to their preconceived beliefs. These later authors apparently could not reconcile the conflicts of this eyewitness testimony with a hundred and fifty years of false representations made by terribly misguided historians who couldn't be bothered with checking the available documentary sources housed at Washington and Lee University and Union Theological Seminary in Richmond. Fithian's commentary on the schools in the Valley was entirely consistent with the various letters of Rev. John Brown that were abstracted by John White Stuart in his valuable biography of Rev. John Brown.[133]

These post-1850 authors apparently failed to locate Dr. Archibald Alexander's original manuscript "Memoir of William Graham," that is housed at Princeton Theological Seminary.[134] Instead, they relied on the biography of Dr. Archibald Alexander written by his son, James W. Alexander and published by Charles Scribner in 1854, which contains many extensive extracts from the manuscript. Many of the later authors believed they were quoting Archibald Alexander on the founding of Washington and Lee, but in truth, they were relying on his son's inappropriate and unauthorized revised commentary. At least, in the narrow context of the history of the founding of Liberty Hall Academy.

The best way to determine Archibald Alexander's views on the origins of Liberty Hall Academy is to compare the manuscript "Memoir of William Graham" to Rev. Alexander's "Address to the Alumni" published originally in 1843. Where these two items agree, that is clearly what Rev. Archibald Alexander wanted to leave to posterity. One thing in that regard is certain, and that is that Archibald Alexander believed that the founder and first president of what was in 1843 Washington College was Rev. William Graham, not his own great-uncle, Robert Alexander, and certainly not Rev. John Brown who eschewed all things "Liberty Hall Academy."

Archibald Alexander knew Rev. Brown refused to send any of his children to Liberty Hall Academy and for twenty years never attended a meeting of the Board of Trustees, which, initially, was held in his own neighborhood (i.e., the immediate vicinity of New Providence and Timber Ridge Presbyterian congregations.) The hordes of mid to late-nineteenth- and twentieth-century historians who slavishly followed Foote's unsupported claims concerning the mythical link between Rev. Brown and his school to Liberty Hall, all overlooked the embarrassing fact that Brown had no connection whatsoever to Liberty Hall Academy. Not one of these misguided historians who touted Brown's appointment as a Trustee noticed that Brown's name is consistently absent from the Trustees who were in attendance

---

notwithstanding the misguided footnote no.19, of the Princeton University Press editor who challenges Fithian's use of the word "neighborhood." The editor is wrong, and Fithian was correct, as the auditor has explained elsewhere in this report.

133   While valuable, Dr. Stuart was nevertheless, also mistaken about there being a connection between Brown's school and Liberty Hall.

134   A photocopy was obtained by the auditor in the late 1980s and was thereafter recopied and bound for the Leyburn Library at Washington and Lee University.

at the meetings of that body held from the Board's creation on May 6, 1776, until Brown left Virginia to retire among his family in Kentucky. There is a very good reason for Brown's seeming absence from the Trustees' meetings which is that he never accepted the appointment. It is truly inexplicable that so many scholars could have failed to notice that Rev. John Brown was never present at any meeting of the Liberty Hall Academy Board of Trustees. Their failure in that regard is frankly unfathomable.

Rev. Archibald Alexander, an early graduate of Liberty Hall and an eminent church historian, explains Rev. Brown's animus for Liberty Hall Academy and its rector, William Graham in his mss. "Memoir of Rev. William Graham." This illuminating memoir was unfortunately never published, but it is housed at the Library of the Princeton Theological Seminary, in Princeton, New Jersey, and a spiral-bound photocopy was presented to Washington and Lee University by the auditor.

The published biography[135] of Archibald Alexander put together by his son, James W. Alexander contains several unfortunate editorial alterations that, in effect, repudiate both his father's manuscript memoir of his preceptor, Rev. William Graham and also his father's 1843 published "Address to the Alumni." James obviously had in his possession his father's published Address to the Alumni..., in which his father discusses the founding of Liberty Hall Academy. James obviously assumed that the notorious William Henry Foote, upon whom he obviously relied, knew more about the history of Liberty Hall Academy than did his father. It would have been more helpful if the son had bothered to explain to his readers that he had modified his fathers repeated representations concerning Liberty Hall's establishment. Alas, he did not. Instead, James W. Alexander changed his father's text from which he was quoting. In this way, he misled his readers. In effect, he put his own words into his father's mouth. In so doing, James' quotations of his father came, in time, to comport with the false depictions published by William Henry Foote, and may have played some part in Foote's mistaken beliefs about the college's founding. James Alexander was supposed to destroy his father's memoir upon his death and James undoubtedly intended to do just that, but as so often happens, the memoir was kept by James as a reference tool which he used while putting together his father's biography. James died without having destroyed it. Fortunately for history, the memoir was preserved, and then in the late 1980s, it was gifted to the Princeton Theological Seminary Library by one of Alexander's relations. The memoir's authenticity is beyond question. Its consistency when compared to Alexander's Address to the Alumni Association is compelling evidence that his son's depictions on this subject are not believable. Keeping mind that correctness of Alexander's Address to the Alumni on the subject of the college's founding and first president, William Graham was, in effect, reiterated by Archibald Alexander himself shortly before his death in a message reprinted along with Alexander's submission to the editor of Sprague's

---

135   Archibald Alexander, D. D., Mss "Memoir of Rev. Wm Graham," [written in longhand]. The Rev. Graham portions of this manuscript constitute the largest part of a writing entitled, *Great Valley of Virginia.*

Annals of the American Pulpit,[136] Alexander died two years later. Foote's infamous claims about Washington and Lee's founding was published in 1850, so Archibald Alexander was therefore unable to explain to the world how wrong Foote was in this regard. It is a sad commentary that Alexander's credulous son adopted Foote's version as opposed to that of his father especially since Foote provided no compelling evidence to support his novel notions on the subject.

In sum, altering another's written words without acknowledgment, is simply not an accepted practice. James compounded his error in judgment by then publishing the altered texts within quotation marks that were meant to identify the written sentiments of his father. James Alexander altered his father's words to conform to what he himself believed to be true. By these acts, James was both presumptuous and dishonest. That he probably thought he was simply fixing his father's errors does not diminish his culpability for having misrepresented what his father had actually written. The result of James' actions was to underscore and emphasize the errors of William Henry Foote, and by doing that, he aided in both creating and in perpetuating a false history of Washington and Lee University.

The fact is that Archibald Alexander who was an eyewitness to much of Liberty Hall Academy's early years knew precisely how and when the school was created and by whom. He learned of this history from the lips of the school's first rector William Graham and from the rector's younger brother Edward Graham, who was to later become his brother-in-law when Edward married Alexander's sister, Margaret.

Archibald Alexander and Edward Graham both lived in the rector's home during the American Revolution. Both of these schoolmates later wrote memoirs of their preceptor at Liberty Hall.[137] Their mostly consistent memoirs were primarily based on their personal experiences as early students at Liberty Hall Academy and their accounts are in direct conflict with the secondhand speculations of William Henry Foote and virtually all post-1850 historians who addressed the issues of the founding of Liberty Hall Academy. At the same time, their accounts comport with most all of the official records of both the Hanover Presbytery and the early records of the Liberty Hall Academy's Board of Trustees, the important exception being Edward Graham's error concerning the sequence of establishment between Liberty Hall Academy and Hampden Sydney. His mistake in this regard is revealed in detail in the Author's Errors Section of this report.[138]

---

136 William B. Sprague, *Annals of the American Pulpit; or Commemorative Notices of Distinguished American Clergymen*.Volume III, New York, Robert Carter & Brothers, 1858, pg. 366, [note appears on pg. 365, sketch by Rev. Archibald Alexander D. D., dated Nov. 23, 1849.

137 Edward Graham's memoir of William Graham was published in 1821 (see bibliography) and Alexander in later life realized his earlier written memoir of Rev. Graham was imprudently too frank and potentially embarrassing, so he decided to rewrite some aspects of his memoir in the form of a eulogy of his late preceptor and included it in an "Address to the Alumni . . ." which he delivered at a meeting of the Alumni Association in 1843 and which was published in a limited edition pamphlet. It was also reprinted in the W&L Historical Papers, No. 2, 1890.

138 The reasons Edward made this mistake is that he had not yet arrived in Virginia when the formal decisions of the Presbytery to establish these two Academies took place, and the fact of his youth when he arrived. His error was a mistaken assumption.

The auditor knows what Archibald Alexander did because he has in his possession a photocopy of Archibald's handwritten manuscript memoir. James informs the readers that his father directed him to destroy this manuscript upon his death. Obviously, James ignored his father's directive. How it managed to survive remains a mystery, but in any event, a descendant who obtained ownership donated it to the institution that Archibald Alexander founded, the Princeton Theological Seminary. The auditor having learned about its existence had a copy bound for himself and for the Leyburn Library at Washington and Lee. With this photostatic copy of the original it was now possible to discover that James' published biography includes quotes which were clearly modified by James W. Alexander. Therefore, James' biography of his father is rendered a somewhat dubious book in its entirety, and it definitely includes forged quotations concerning the founding of Washington and Lee.[139] James obviously assumed, albeit incorrectly, that his father had erred and sought to correct him. His judgment in this regard was a blunder. Fortunately, James neglected to destroy the evidence (i.e., his father's actual manuscript that James says he was quoting from) that would later demonstrate his unethical conduct, although the auditor is unaware of any published recognition of James's inappropriate conduct in this regard.

Here below are Rev. Dr. Archibald Alexander's two particularly important and accurate quotes on the subject of the founding. The bold italics are included to emphasize the importance, not to identify errors:

1.   "Mount Pleasant should be considered as a kind of consecrated spot; and altho' it is now, like Shilo of old,[140] a desolation; yet it would be well, **especially for the surviving pupils of Mr. Graham, to erect a monument on that spot, as a memorial of the first classical school instituted in the Valley,** But stone, marble, & brass are perishable substances: we want a memorial more enduring than those; **and this can only be erected by a faithful history of this institution & its founder,** [William Graham] **which we are now attempting to furnish**." (Alexander, Mss "Memoir of Rev. William Graham pg. 45.) (emphasis added)

Note to the current administration and all of the university's Trustees: The above underlined quote was written by the preeminent early graduate of Liberty Hall Academy, the Reverend Dr. Archibald Alexander, the founding first president of

---

139   This revelation casts doubt on the reliability of anything attributed to Archibald Alexander or J. A. Alexander in the manuscript "Notices of Distinguished Graduates," referring here to Princeton graduates. This mss. is held by the Princeton Firestone Library. This item includes a palpably false depiction of the character of Rev. William Graham. While the author may have relied, in part, on notes of Archibald Alexander, he nevertheless gives a completely unjustified and a-historical of Graham, that misuses and misinterprets Archibald Alexander's Mss "Memoir of Rev. William Graham." Its author(s) are likely one or both, sons of Archibald Alexander.

140   "Shilo of old" is an ancient biblical reference found in the Old Testament books of Joshua and Judges and refers to ancient ruins of the capital of Israel before Jerusalem.

Princeton Theological Seminary, who obviously knew something about "founding first presidents."

2.   "When the Presbytery of Hanover determined to establish a school in this Valley, for the rearing of young men for the ministry, they applied to the Reverend Samuel Stanhope Smith, then itinerating in the State, to recommend a suitable person to take charge of their school, upon which he at once recommended Mr. Graham; and at their request wrote to him to come on to the Valley of Virginia. **Before this time,** a classical school had been taught at the place called Mount Pleasant, near the little town of Fairfield. **Here Mr. Graham commenced his labours as a teacher; and here we find the germ**[141] **whence sprung this college.**"[142] (A. Alexander, Address...pg. 21 of the scarce 1843 pamphlet, and pg. 129 of the reprint in the W&L Historical Papers]) (emphasis added)

What appears above is entirely different from what James Alexander claims in his biography that his father said. Our report discusses and explains the vastly important difference in the related appendix and in the author's errors section of the report. In sum, James says his father said that the school at Mount Pleasant under Mr. Graham had existed prior to Graham's arrival but his father did not say that. His father said "a school" had existed at Mount Pleasant, in earlier days, which is true, but it was not "the school" established by the Hanover Presbytery and conducted by Mr. Graham, as was suggested by James. The difference is of vast significance.

Note: The only school known to have been located at Mount Pleasant other than the Presbytery's seminary was Rev. John Brown's Latin school, but when the Presbytery made its decision to "establish" and "patronize" a school in Augusta County, in 1774, Rev. Brown's school had long since been moved from Mount Pleasant to New Providence. This is the school "that had been taught at a place called Mount Pleasant" that Archibald Alexander was referring to in his Address to the Alumni Association. Brown's school did not exist at "Mount Pleasant" in the 1770s. It had been permanently moved to New Providence about 1767, and it was thereafter never again moved. When Mr. Graham arrived in Virginia in early 1775, there was no school operating at Mount Pleasant. At least, not until Mr. Graham began to organize classes at Mount Pleasant, which were in the form of a grammar school. This school was designed to continue as an adjunct to the college once the campus buildings were completed at Timber Ridge. The grammar school component did continue as an adjunct to the college all during Graham's tenure as the college's president (rector). This feature Graham adopted from a similar one conducted at The College of New Jersey under his preceptor, Dr.

---

141   **The "germ" to which Alexander refers is the initial educational endeavor initiated by William Graham in the "form of a grammar school," as Mr. Graham styled it in the letter he wrote to President Washington on behalf of the Trustees of Liberty Hall in early 1796, requesting to be considered as a possible recipient of a prospective endowment. This grammar school served as the foundation upon which was built the superstructure that became known as Liberty Hall Academy.**

142   Alexander, Archibald DD, an Address before Alumni of Washington College, Delivered June 29, 1843, Washington and Lee Historical Papers No. 2, Lexington, Va., 1890 [Note that the auditor's copy is in wraps & includes two articles: Alexander's Address, published in a Limited edition, 1843. & "The Founders of Washington College" by Hon. Hugh Blair Grigsby, delivered June 22, 1870.]

John Witherspoon. Most post-1850 authors confused this school under Graham at Mount Pleasant with Rev. Brown's school at New Providence. These schools, however, were altogether different. That they were both located in the same neighborhood added to the confusion.

Note: In November of 1849, Rev. Alexander submitted this introductory testimonial to be included in an abbreviated sketch of Rev. Wm. Graham for inclusion in Sprague's Annals of the American Pulpit (Presbyterian) Clergymen Vol. 3, 1858 [See bibliography for full citation]

> In complying with your request for some notices of ...Rev. William Graham... I shall avail myself chiefly to an Address which I delivered ...some years ago before the Alumni of Washington College (1843), and which, upon examination, I find to be entirely in accordance with my present impressions.
>
> (Sprague's Annals..., Vol. 3, pg. 365. (1849) [but not published until 1858].

Clearly then, Dr. Alexander's views and representations about the founding of Washington College, and his view that Rev. William Graham was the founder and first president[143] of the school remained constant until the year prior to the publication of Mr. Foote's bastardization of the college's origins. The item immediately above is what Alexander believed only two years before his death and it appears to be his last public comment on the subject. It is somewhat ironic that Dr. Archibald Alexander's last statement on the subject and the college's first authorized and published historical treatments were both published the year before Mr. Foote's first volume on Virginia was published. Astoundingly, historians would later adopt Mr. Foote's unauthenticated bastardized history of the college's founding, none of them seems to have felt that it was incumbent on them to explain why they accepted Foote's version when it stood in stark contrast to the 1849 accounts of both Archibald Alexander and the college. This phenomenon is dismaying in and of itself, but even more stupefying when one considers that the two aforementioned 1849 accounts were both consistent with all previous published accounts, and also consistent with the documentary records of both the college and the Hanover Presbytery which no one seems to have doubted, at the time, was the institution that created the college.

****

---

143 The title "president" is synonymous with rector, at the time in question. Arguments about the title are irrelevant here, for Mr. Graham was unquestionably the chief operations officer of Liberty Hall Academy. This fact explains why Graham is the only Trustee who was denominated as "ex officio," a status usually only applied to the person who is the functional equivalent to the position of President. Juliet, after all is indubitably correct in saying "a rose by any other name would smell as sweet."

The Generally Unknown Brown/Graham Scandal[144]

Rev. John Brown's immediate family was estranged from both Liberty Hall Academy and the Academy's director, William Graham, an outgrowth of a romantic affair in which Rev. Graham broke off his engagement to Rev. Brown's much sought-after daughter, Ms. Betsy. This affair is detailed in the mss. "Memoir of Rev. William Graham," written but not published by Rev. Archibald Alexander.[145]

Without going into the intimate details, suffice to say that the breakup was not occasioned by the actions or desires of either the prospective bride, the groom, or the prospective father-in-law. It was the direct result of a malevolent, unwarranted attack on the character of Rev. William Graham.

Rev. Graham, a recent arrival into the Valley, was about to take charge of an aspiring new college, and two local Presbyterian congregations while, at the same time, providing theological instruction to prospective Presbyterian ministers. It would not have been prudent for Mr. Graham under those circumstances to enter into a marriage rife with discord due to a meddling, vexatious, and resentful member of his affianced's prominent and influential family.

According to Dr. Alexander, Mrs. Brown resented Mr. Graham's scholarly attainments that far and away eclipsed those of her husband. She apparently felt that Graham's presence in the community had severely affected her social standing in the Valley. While coming from a prominent family it was her husband's social standing that had maintained her influential position in the community, and it was quickly apparent that her prospective son-in-law was a man of genius who was a magnetic personality with possess extraordinary gifts as a scholar, theologian, and even as an agriculturist adept in the mechanical skills so important to successful farming. These characteristics of the recently arrived rector of the Presbytery's

---

144 **While a broken proposal of marriage was indeed scandalous in eighteenth-century America, it hardly arises to that degree of significance today, but to understand the event and its consequences demands that we view the matter in its eighteenth-century context. To the Brown family in that day, Graham's request that he be allowed to withdraw his previous offer of marriage to Ms. Betsy Brown, their eldest and highly sought-after daughter was tantamount to a slap in the face, although Mr. Graham probably did not mean it to have that effect. He was a new arrival in the community about to launch a new college and assume the pastorate of the Timber Ridge church, and he sagaciously understood that Mrs. Brown's whispered attacks on his character would undermine his ability to succeed in either venture and would undermine the marriage as well. The real suffering, however, accrued mostly to the two young sweethearts both of whom were brokenhearted by the socially well-connected Mrs. Brown's petulant and baseless character attacks whispered to her social coterie. This unfortunate circumstance explains the subsequent alienation of Rev. Brown from the affairs of Liberty Hall Academy.**

145 Alexander, Archibald DD, Mss "Memoir of the Rev. William Graham," [written in longhand]. The Reverend Graham portions of this manuscript constitute the largest part of a writing entitled *Great Valley of Virginia*. This copy came from the Princeton Seminary Library in 1989. It is also available in spiral-bound form at the Leyburn Library, Washington and Lee University. The author is the founding president of Princeton Theological Seminary and an eminent historian of early American Presbyterian schools.

new seminary (i.e., college) stood in clear contrast to Mrs. Brown's husband who for some time had been the only resident Presbyterian cleric west of the Blue Ridge mountains, and even though he was a classic country parson, his somewhat limited scholarship placed him well above the members of his flock, which at the time included the congregations of Timber Ridge and New Providence.[146]

With Graham's arrival in the neighborhood of Timber Ridge and New Providence congregations, the community shifted its customary reliance on Rev. Brown to the newly arrived man of genius whose reputation for unusual knowledge and understanding of theology caused many every young candidate for the Presbyterian ministry in Virginia to seek his assistance with their theological studies in preparation for the ministry. Mrs. Brown, whose own standing was so intertwined with her husband's, quickly began to see Mr. Graham as a threat and a nuisance and forgetting the romantic interests of her highly sought-after daughter, Betsey, she began a campaign to cut her prospective son-in-law down to size. Relying on her gift for satire and character assassination she took every opportunity to try and make Graham seem ridiculous. Predictably, word got back to Graham about these attacks upon himself.

Mr. Graham realized that his recent appointments as pastor and seminary rector of a new institution of higher learning would require broad community support. He could ill-afford to begin upon such momentous challenges and at the same be caught up in a tumultuous domestic environment that included the family of the other Presbyterian minister located in the same community. His new bride would be placed in an impossible position of conflict of affections pitting her new husband's interest against those of her parents. Graham obviously recognized that Mrs. Brown's attacks upon his character would be nearly irreconcilable, so he decided to ask the woman he loved to release him from his proposal of marriage. The bride-to-be, of course, reluctantly agreed. This scuttled venture into the waters of romance and domesticity would become one of the few defeats experienced by William Graham during his many years in the Valley of Virginia.

As events unfolded, however, it can be seen that Rev. Graham's successes over the long course of twenty-two years as clergyman and as educator, were achieved without any assistance from the family of Rev. John Brown. Rev. Brown and Rev. Graham, however, do not appear to have let this coolness in their personal relationship affect their ability to work together as fellow clergymen when circumstances called for their mutual cooperation. The records of the Lexington Presbytery and the Virginia Synod during the entire fourth quarter of the eighteenth century provide no evidence of any professional rancor existing between the Reverends John Brown and William Graham, although Dr. John White Stuart quite obviously views their relationship in a more disputatious mode than this auditor. Stuart's views are ably put forth in his dissertation biography of Rev. John Brown which is listed in this report's bibliography.

Rev. Alexander's description of the relationship that existed between Rev. William Graham and the family of Rev. John Brown reflects a reality that was

---

146 While his pastorate of the Timber Ridge congregation had recently been severed, Brown still serviced many of the members of that congregations in the absence of anyone to replace him.

widely known to that community made up of the congregations of Timber Ridge and New Providence during the last quarter of the eighteenth century. That explains why no one from that area in that period made the colossal error of claiming that Rev. Brown was involved with affairs of Liberty Hall Academy. This error could only have been made by individuals who had no direct involvement in the affairs of these two congregations during the period under consideration. The auditor's view is that there was little open animosity between Rev. Brown and Graham and points to Graham being invited to preside over a communion service held before Brown's congregation, which actually came about.[147] Despite having been given an opportunity to complain to the church authorities, Rev. Brown chose not to file a formal complaint with the Lexington Presbytery. Neither did any other member of Brown's congregation, and for good reason, which is that Rev. Graham's conducting of this holy service was blameless and entirely in keeping with the policies of the national Presbyterian Church.

A serious breach in archival protocols at Washington and Lee University
(The bogus and so-called "Edward Graham Memorandum" or "Edward Graham Manuscript")

At some point after 1857 and before 1874, a mysterious and clearly bogus document surfaced which was introduced by, and inaccurately identified by, Trustee Bolivar Christian as a cursory sketch of the college's origins, written, he believed by Professor Edward Graham, Esq. This claim has no basis whatsoever in fact, or credible evidence, and is contradicted by all known documented evidence. The document is not, and cannot be, what it has been represented to be for well over a hundred years. It is a great hoax that can be easily proven to be so. The perpetrators, not content with simply misrepresenting the nature of the unsigned and undated document, went so far as to retrospectively insert the document into the college's oldest official record of its founding, which is the Liberty Hall Academy's Board of Trustees meeting minutes record book.[148]

The claim that the document is a history written by Edward Graham representing his views on the subject matter contained therein is contradicted by easily ascertainable and well-established facts. The most important of which involve written communications from Edward Graham to various historians who subsequently published histories based in large measure on Mr. Graham's letters. These authors' published histories, reflecting in most ways the views of Mr. Graham, contradict the contents of the so-called "Edward Graham memorandum."

---

147 The service became a bit of a controversy, but a close study of this event demonstrates that it was but a tempest in a teapot that actually had little to do with Rev. Graham except in the minds of a few malcontents that were looking for an excuse to bolt from Brown's congregation. This affair is treated within several parts of this report, see esp. the subsection devoted to Archibald Alexander in the Author's Errors Section.

148 Technically, it could be argued that the Hanover Presbytery's meeting minutes predate the Trustees' minutes, but those records are the property of the Presbytery, not the college. The Presbytery, however, created the college, and its actions in that regard are recorded in earlier minutes of the Presbytery (1774). The Board of Trustees was not created by the Presbytery until May 6 of 1774.

Instead, their histories reflect Mr. Graham's 1821 published views and Graham's consistently held point of view concerning the origins of Washington College, Virginia, from the date of his own Article in 1821, up to shortly before he died in 1840. The authors to whom we refer include Rev. Archibald Alexander (Edward Graham's brother-in-law), Rev. William Hill, Rev. Robert Davidson, and the editor John Holt Rice, who published *The Evangelical and Literary Magazine and Missionary Chronicle* in the early part of the nineteenth century.

For further details, readers are referred to the aforementioned Appendix devoted to debunking this rather transparent hoax.[149]

Reasons why this mystery document should not be taken seriously:

- It is not known what it is.
- It is not known who wrote it.
- It is not known when it was written.
- It is not known for what purpose it was written.[150]
- The document has no established provenance.
- There is no known credible evidence that supports the claim that the document's content was created by Edward Graham or even that its contents were written down by him.[151]

---

149   The document itself is not the hoax, rather it is the false depictions of what the document represents, and the way in which Col. Christian describes the document and then surreptitiously and without authorization retroactively inserts the document into the ancient record book of the Liberty Hall Academy's Trustees that constitutes the hoax. Had Mr. Christian or any historian bothered to consult the first pages of text in the record book, they would have discovered that the document he retroactively imposed into the book containing the college's most precious and venerable records completely contradicts the claims embodied in this document. An undated, unsigned document lacking any provenance whatsoever thereafter precedes the college's first authorized history written at the behest of the organization that created the college, the Hanover Presbytery. That is what constitutes the hoax.

150   Consider, for example, the possibility that the words were written down by Edward Graham during or immediately following an interview with a mistaken local resident whom Edward interviewed when preparing his "Memoir of the Late Rev. William Graham," reflecting not his own views but those of another. This entirely possible assertion is rather obvious because the founding of Liberty Hall Academy took place when Edward was a young boy living in Pennsylvania, so he had no firsthand knowledge of the Presbytery's activities in regard to creating a new Academy and, at the time, probably no serious interest in the institutional machinations of a group of Presbyterian clergymen. In 1821, Edward was asked by his friends and colleagues to prepare a memoir of his dead older brother for publication. Presumably, he consulted with others more intimately familiar with the early history, and in doing so, he likely took notes. Of course, there are a myriad other possibilities, but the truth of the matter is that, at this late date, it will most likely remain unknowable. Since the document is unsigned and undated, we know little, if anything, that can be ascertained with any degree of confidence. This is especially so, insofar as the document is at odds with all known institutional documentary evidence from the eighteenth century.

151   It is entirely possible that the document is in Edward Graham's, but even if so, it could be notes scribbled down from an interview with others or possibly early research notes that were later discarded. The possibilities are infinite but irrelevant given what is actually known about what Edward Graham believed about the founding of his Alma Mater. He shared those thoughts with

- The document, suggested by its champion to reflect the views of Edward Graham, is entirely inconsistent with all of the known, and in one case published, views of Professor Graham about the early history of Washington College held during the last twenty years of his life.

* *

Two Critically Important Official Eighteenth-century Records
(Documentary evidence that aids in ascertaining the correct history of the college's founding)

1. Official Minutes of the Meetings of the Hanover Presbytery (1771–1776):[152]

The original, handwritten manuscript Minutes of the Hanover Presbytery from 1771 through 1776. These particular minutes detail the entire establishment process, from the Presbytery's first thoughts in 1771 through its decision and actions to establish a Seminary, including the appointment of a Board of Trustees to oversee the operations of its Seminary [Reviewed in a scanned PDF format provided by: Reference / Archives; William Smith Morton Library; Union Presbyterian Seminary; Richmond, Virginia].

It appears that very few historians who follow W. H. Foote's erroneous contentions about the origins of W&L predating October 13, 1774, have viewed the actual text of the Hanover Presbytery's minutes. Even those later authors who quote from the minutes appear to have simply repeated someone else's quoted extract. Very few publications include the minutes in their citation of authorities. [These minutes are available at Reference / Archives; William Smith Morton Library; Union Presbyterian Seminary, Richmond, Va.]. The meeting minutes serve as a direct contradiction of any claim that Washington and Lee began before October of 1774.

2. Official Minutes of the Meetings of the Board of Trustees (Liberty Hall Academy)

The original handwritten manuscript record book containing the first minutes of the Board of Trustees of Liberty

---

several, and they are reflected in those others published histories. They are not what Bolivar Christian obviously hoped they were.

152 Having read the earlier transcribed minutes of the Hanover Presbytery published in *The Virginia Magazine of History and Biography*, Vol. 63, nos. 1, and 2, edited by Mr. William Munford Ellis Rachal, we found that the only pertinent minutes concerning Liberty Hall Academy's origins were those from the years 1771 through 1776. We realize that this leaves the Hanover minutes for the years 1762 to 1770 unread by the auditors, but to date nothing has been found in any eighteenth-century history suggesting that any matters pertaining to the creation of Liberty Hall Academy were dealt with by the Presbytery during that period.

Hall [beginning in May 1776], which includes, in the form of a preface, a brief memorandum of the College's founding, written into the Board's record book by the Hanover Presbytery's Clerk Rev. Caleb Wallace and dated May 1776. Caleb Wallace later migrated to Kentucky, where he became a long-serving justice of that state's Court of Appeals. As an eyewitness to the affairs of Liberty Hall Academy and the Hanover Presbytery during the years 1771–1776, he was a Presbyterian minister, a scholar, and later, an Appellate-level Justice of Kentucky's highest Court, and his testimony is thereby exceedingly persuasive. The records contained in this book,[153] including the meeting minutes, serve as a direct contradiction of the claim that Washington and Lee began before October of 1774.

These two vastly important primary sources do not support the notion that Washington and Lee University's founding and origins are earlier than the 1770s, nor that the school was linked in any way to any private preparatory school of Robert Alexander or Rev. John Brown.

Note: Any serious researcher investigating the early history of Washington and Lee University is herein advised to avoid, at all costs, relying on secondary sources for determining what was actually said and or done, by either the Hanover Presbytery or the Liberty Hall Academy Board of Trustees in the eighteenth century. Those who erred with respect to the early history of Liberty Hall Academy were often led astray by inaccurate depictions written by others of what these two organizations did, decided, or ordained. These record books speak for themselves and they say nothing whatsoever about the institution being connected to either Robert Alexander, Rev. John Brown, or either of their private schools.

****

W&L'S HISTORY INTERRUPTED

Washington and Lee University's true early history was first inappropriately repudiated by Rev. William Henry Foote in 1850. It seems unlikely that Mr. Foote had any idea how egregious his erroneous depiction of Washington College's

---

153   The one exception is the nineteenth-century defacing of the college's first record book that is manifested by the paste-in document about which virtually nothing is known except that it is located on the front inside cover of the record book, to the everlasting shame of Bolivar Christian, who had the audacity to place it there. Dr. Ollinger Crenshaw in *General Lee's College*, in the typescript version identifies Trustee Bolivar Christian as the man responsible. Christian's culpability is not mitigated by his having left a short note admitting that he pasted it in the book, because he exacerbates his misdeed by stating that document "corroborates" the other accounts (traditional and otherwise) of the origins of the college, "when in fact it does neither. For one thing, there were no traditional accounts because legitimate traditions date from the period of the events in question, not nearly a century afterward. In addition, all of the accounts that would make up "or otherwise" are contradictory accounts. No post-1850 accounts are even worthy of consideration because none are based on eighteenth-century evidence. His note is irrational in the extreme.

founding was when he published *Sketches of Virginia, Historical and Biographical,* Philadelphia, J. B. Lippincott & Co., 1850, Series One. On him alone, however, lies the blame for perpetuating a palpable and fraudulent revisionist early history of the Commonwealth of Virginia's first chartered institution of higher learning, which is Washington College in Lexington, Virginia. It is regrettable that the auditor has been unable to discover how, or by whom, Mr. Foote was led astray concerning the early days of Liberty Hall Academy. While his error in this regard may have been an honest mistake in the beginning, surely his obviously intentional rewrite and publishing of a letter ostensibly written by Rev. Samuel Houston in his second Volume of *Sketches of Virginia,* and passing his changes in the text off as the product of Rev. Houston constitutes intentional deception. The letter's content, as originally reprinted by Foote in 1850, contained such obvious errors that it undermined the credibility of Foote's only apparent source for having offered a revised history of Washington and Lee's founding. So, Foote rewrote the erroneous sections of the letter and then reprinted the letter as though it was the original. Houston was dead and Foote apparently had possession of the letter, so he apparently thought he could get away with his fraud, and amazingly, he did, until now.

Below, is a copy of the monumental error made by Mr. Foote, who says in his *Sketches of Virginia, Historical and Biographical,* Series One, that:

> the Presbytery having, in 1771, taken up the subject of education, and in 1772, having deferred action, and in 1773, having located it in Staunton, and in 1774 having determined to locate the school in another place, ***appointed Rev. William Graham the tutor under supervision***[154] ***of Mr. John Brown*** of New Providence, ***and directed the Seminary to be carried on near Fairfield, where Brown had been conducting a classical school.***
>
> (W. H. Foote, Sketches of Virginia, Historical and Biographical, Series One, pg. 393.) (Here the bold and italics emphasis was added to indicate error.)

---

154 *In deference to the descendants of the long-serving Rev. Brown, the auditor will simply point out that the academics at Princeton had changed considerably from its earliest days when Mr. Brown attended and the vastly expanded program offered under the illustrious John Witherspoon when Mr. Graham matriculated at Nassau Hall. At Liberty Hall, Mr. Graham taught many classes not offered when Mr. Brown attended the school. It is difficult to envision on what matters Mr. Brown might have been in a position to supervise Mr. Graham, who had conducted the preparatory Academy at Princeton even while he was himself a student in the college. Mr. Brown organized his school, but it was always taught by others.*

This statement by Mr. Foote is riddled with errors. The Presbytery did not, as he suggests, locate the school in one place ("Staunton") and then move it to another. The 1773 action to which he alludes was merely a preliminary decision, but since the school did not yet exist, it did not then actually exist in Staunton or anywhere else. In 1774, the Presbytery did not "locate the school in another place," but it did decide to "establish and patronize a public school" somewhere in the vast county of Augusta that reached from the Blue Ridge Mountains all the way to the Ohio River. Foote's commentary suggests a school was moved from one place to another, when in fact, no physical school yet existed. Foote also incorrectly states that William Graham was appointed a "tutor" when, in reality, he was appointed as the chief administrative officer with the nominal title of "manager." The Presbytery appointed Rev. John Brown to the nebulous responsibility of "inspector," but the uncertainty of the meaning of this nomination is of no importance because, whatever the Presbytery's intent, the appointment was not accepted by Rev. Brown. The question then as to what the Presbytery meant by "inspector" is moot because the school never had an "inspector" in the eighteenth century. Indeed, Brown actually refused all such appointments in connection with the Presbytery's new academy under William Graham. Also, in regard to this extract, the Presbytery, contrary to Mr. Foote's assertion, did not direct the seminary (Academy) to be "carried on" at any specific location, but Mr. Graham, in cooperation with various local residents, launched the school's initial organizational operations on the farm of Mr. James Wilson on a spot called "Mount Pleasant."

The presbytery's meeting minutes are silent about the subject of the initial temporary headquarters of its work in progress, which they had begun to refer to as "Augusta Academy." Classes began at Mount Pleasant in the Spring shortly after the Presbytery decided to establish a second seminary east of the mountains of Virginia. The location of temporary operations in Augusta was left to its manager in cooperation with local residents, who were located near the Timber Ridge Congregation. We know this because there was no meeting of the Presbytery between April and October of 1775 and yet the October meeting minutes contain a decision of Presbytery that "Mr. Graham continue to have the Care and Tuition of said school" referring of course to their school in Augusta. See page 67 of the Hanover Presbytery minutes for their October 1775 meeting. Timber Ridge, of course, was the targeted congregation with which Mr. Graham was seeking to establish a connection between himself and the then pastorless church.[155]

Contrary to Mr. Foote's claim, Mr. John Brown had not been conducting" a "classical" school near Fairfield at this time. Instead, Brown's Tutor was conducting Brown's Latin school at New Providence quite a few miles away.[156]

---

155 The Hanover Presbytery did not have the financial resources to pay Graham a salary, so it was imperative that Graham be attached to a nearby congregation, as its pastor, in order to supplement whatever meager monies that might be had from tuition.

156 This was the meeting after which the members of the Presbytery made an unofficial courtesy "visit" to Brown's school next door to his home at New Providence. The Presbytery's school under Mr. Graham, at this time, was operating at the place near Timber Ridge called Mount

Foote was probably confused on this point by the fact that Brown had sometime earlier organized his Latin school in the same vicinity of Timber Ridge. Brown's pastorate of Timber Ridge, however, was not a happy one and in 1763 he sought to be dismissed from his charge there. His dismissal was finally approved in 1767. During the period between 1763 and 1767 Brown had moved his school and his family to new quarters on Moffett's Creek. By 1774, when the Presbytery established the Academy in Augusta, Brown's "Latin school" had for some time been located at New Providence adjacent to Brown's newly acquired but existing home several miles distant from where the Presbytery's newly established seminary was temporarily located near Fairfield. Foote's egregious error in this regard was replicated repeatedly and without exception by historians throughout the second half of the nineteenth and all of the twentieth century. The fault for this travesty rests with reliance on secondary sources when primary sources would have made things, in this regard quite clear, provided the researcher read the Presbytery's meeting minutes carefully. No one after 1849 seems to have done so, until now.

> Here again in the same volume but different section, Mr. Foote erroneously said this:
>
> In the fall of 1774, on the recommendation of Rev. Samuel Stanhope Smith, employed in founding Hampden-Sidney [sic] College, in Prince Edward, **Mr. Graham was invited to engage in a classical school, in Augusta County, <u>under the direction</u> <u>of the Rev. John Brown</u>**, pastor of New Providence and formerly of Timber Ridge. (W. H. Foote, Sketches of Virginia...Series One, pg. 441.)
> (Here the bold and italics emphasis was added to indicate error.)

Foote implies in the above quoted text that Samuel Smith was already employed in founding Hampden Sydney when he recommended William Graham to take charge of the Presbytery's Seminary deigned to be established in Augusta County. The truth of the matter is that Smith recommended Mr. Graham prior to 1774 when the Presbytery's design was to merely create one school in Virginia. One that was to serve as Virginia's version of Princeton. A fact made clear in the Presbytery's meeting minutes between 1771 and 1774. The creation or establishment of a second seminary east of the mountains was an afterthought never mentioned in the Presbytery's minutes until the day after the Presbytery established its seminary in Augusta County, and appointed William Graham, in absentia, to manage the project.

In addition, Mr. Graham was not, as suggested by Foote, "invited to engage in a classical school under the direction of Rev. John Brown." Search for any provision in the Presbytery's meeting minutes from the period in question, and the careful researcher will not discover any provision of those minutes that even

---

Pleasant. Understandably, this brief reference to Brown's private school is the only reference to it in any of the Presbytery's meeting minutes because the school was a private affair that had no connection to the Presbytery.

remotely suggests such a thing.[157] The best and consistent evidence from the time in question is that the Hanover Presbytery requested that Samuel Smith write to his old schoolmate and fellow instructor from Princeton and offer him the opportunity to take charge of erecting a college in Virginia designed to emulate the program at Princeton where both Smith and Graham had been instructors under Princeton's eminent educator, Rev. John Witherspoon. Mr. Graham, having conducted Princeton's preparatory school, had demonstrated the administrative and academic attainments desirable for an academic administrator. As Graham soon proved, he was an able instructor capable of providing college-level instruction in the classical languages, sciences, mathematics, government, history, and philosophy necessary to carry on a full curriculum for that age. He would hardly have accepted a position in which he was to be a subordinate to a country parson of exceedingly limited scholarly attainments.

A few of Graham's early students went on to serve as college presidents. Students at Rev. Brown's Latin school were merely preparing for their collegiate studies. Moreover, Brown didn't even teach the students in the local school he had organized. Instructors were hired by Brown to instruct students in elementary Latin and Greek grammar which was then a prerequisite for being accepted into a college's regular academic program. It seems safe to assume that Brown was not sufficiently qualified to do the instructing himself because when Brown's instructors resigned, the school typically closed until he could find a replacement. For example, it closed for the duration of the Revolutionary War when there were simply not enough qualified and available young men to hire and si Brown simply closed his school, rather than conduct it himself.

He took steps several years later to reopen his school, as his correspondence proves, but no further useful information on that subject could not be located by the auditor. It may have been that the universe of potential preparatory students had come to rely on Liberty Hall Academy's preparatory grammar school, and after the war, there was simply no further need of a Latin school in that vicinage.

Mr. Foote continues his erroneous account thus:

> By the act of Presbytery in 1774, *the grammar school, conducted by the Rev. John Brown, or under his supervision and his charge, became the center of operations for literary and theological improvement in the Valley.*
> The Rev. Samuel Houston in his letter to Rev. James Morrison tells us:

---

157 The one qualifying parenthetical in the minutes that seems to be at the root of many having mistakenly concluded that Rev. Graham was to be under Brown's direction or supervision is not what it seems. The phrase is "and under the *inspection* of Rev. John Brown. As explained in detail elsewhere in this report, the meaning of the phrase is unimportant in the last analysis because Brown did not accept the appointment. Its meaning therefore is moot. If it had meant "direction or supervision" Graham would most assuredly have never accepted the Presbytery's offer.

that shortly before the war, some men whose sons were growing up, felt a desire for having them or part of them educated liberally, chiefly with a view to the ministry of the gospel. Accordingly a small grammar school was formed in the neighborhood of Old Providence, composed of Samuel Doak, John Montgomery, Archibald Alexander James Houston, William Tate, Samuel Greenlee, William Wilson, *Ebenezer Smith*, and some others, which greatly increased and drew youths from distant neighborhoods. This grammar school was moved to the place, near Fairfield, called Mount Pleasant; *about which time the Presbytery of Hanover patronized it.*[158]

(Foote, Sketches of Virginia... Series One, pg. 442–443.)

The quoted text above, supplied by Foote, is wrong in many important ways and is terribly misleading. Of course, Rev. Brown's school, given its limited curriculum, was not, as Mr. Foote would have us believe, a "grammar school," and

---

158 *Mr. Houston, if Mr. Foote quotes him accurately, which is open to question, has mixed apples and oranges. All of the men he named as students attended schools other than the one created by the Hanover Presbytery in 1774. There was no school at Mount Pleasant at the time that the Presbytery created their new seminary (Academy), and the Presbytery did not "fix" any location for its initial operations (See the Presbytery's meeting minutes). That decision was obviously made by the seminary's first "manager," William Graham, in cooperation with residents living within the bounds of the Timber Ridge congregation. The new seminary's temporary headquarters was located on the farm of Mr. James Wilson, at a spot that local residents called "Mount Pleasant." Here, some years earlier, Rev. John Brown organized a "Latin School" while pastor of Timber Ridge Congregation. When Rev. Brown moved and relinquished his pastorate of the Timber Ridge congregation, he moved his Latin School to his new residence on Moffett's Creek several miles distant. The school ostensibly referenced by Rev. Houston was conducted from that time forward at New Providence, not at "Mount Pleasant."*

Rev. Brown had no role at the Presbytery's seminary at Mount Pleasant. Moreover, the *"centre of operations for literary and theological improvement"* that Foote refers to was not Rev. Brown's peripatetic Latin School. Foote's description aptly applies only to the Presbytery's seminary under the "Care and Tuition" of its "manager," Rev. William Graham. This seminary, Augusta Academy, was conducted initially at Mount Pleasant, several miles away from Rev. Brown's Latin school at New Providence. Brown's school in December of 1775 was being conducted by Mr. Samuel Doak. A fact supplied to later historians by the Rev. Philip Vicker Fithian. Unfortunately, Foote did not have access to the contents of Fithian's Journal for 1775 and 1776 because it was not published until 1934.

Note the emphasis the auditor has placed on the name *Ebenezer Smith above* in the list of early students, for it is of critical importance that the writer of the letter could have been so ignorant of the affairs of the schools under discussion, that he could mistake a Tutor for a student. This monumental error, Foote would fix when reprinting the erroneous letter in his second volume in 1855. Unfortunately, Foote fixed it surreptitiously and passed the reprinted letter as the original. Suddenly, Mr. Houston's supposed letter is purged of the egregious mistakes, rendering his source a far more credible one than what he was. This example of Foote's behavior is an operational definition of forgery.

It seems that Mr. Foote could not make up his own mind on the subject of the early history of Liberty Hall Academy. Five years later (1855), Mr. Foote, continuing along in the same fallacious manner in his second volume, said this:

> and Mr. Robert Alexander taught in the bounds of Timber Ridge the first classical school in the valley. Mr. Brown kept up a flourishing *"grammar school"* near his residence. His dwelling was about three-fourths of a mile from the south end of the present village of Fairfield, in a westward direction; and the *Academy* stood about a mile from his house, and about the same distance from the north end of the village. *In 1774 the Presbytery of Hanover adopted the school, and appointed William Graham teacher, under the care of Mr. Brown.* In 1777 the school was removed to Timber Ridge. From thence it was removed to the neighborhood of Lexington. (Foote, W. H., _Sketches of Virginia . . . . Series Two_, 1855 pp. 96 and 97.) (Here the bold and italics emphasis was added to indicate error.)

In one fell swoop, Mr. William Henry Foote, without any credible authority to justify his claim, repudiated the history passed down by the university's founding institutional body, the Hanover Presbytery of Virginia. His revision was a fraud propped up with a forgery.

The late Rev. Houston was in no position to correct the now dubious letter, supposedly penned by him so, Foote took the liberty of correcting it for him, but in so doing, he concealed his forgery and passed off his own new text as being Houston's original text. The new text constitutes the evidence that convicts Foote of duplicity and further demonstrates that his actions were premeditated. Foote had to first discover that his source's letter contained embarrassing mistakes. He then had to have removed the mistakes. He, thereafter, added some new text to replace the erroneous text. He completed his crime by placing the new text in quotation marks so as to make his new text appear to have been written by Mr. Houston. This scenario could not possibly be a typographical error.

In fact, neither Rev. Brown nor Robert Alexander, who had, it is said by some, pioneered common school education in the Valley of Virginia, played any role in the affairs of the Hanover Presbytery's new seminary, Augusta Academy. The fiction that they were, understandably, did not arise during either man's lifetime. If it had, there is little doubt that either man would have squelched this ridiculous myth making.

Robert Alexander was not active in the affairs of the Hanover Presbytery because he wasn't a Presbyterian minister or Elder. In fact, he was probably not even a Presbyterian. He was, however, an elected vestryman in Augusta County which suggests that he adhered to the Anglican (later, called Episcopal) church. Moreover, Robert Alexander's name does not appear on the list of Presbyterians from his neighborhood who "called" Rev. John Brown to be pastor of Timber Ridge and New Providence congregations. Robert's brother Archibald Alexander's name, however, is among those early Presbyterians who called for Rev. Brown to be their pastor. If he Robert Alexander who resided within the bounds of Timber Ridge and New Providence congregations adhered to the Presbyterian Church, then his name should have been included on the list of those who were requesting his services. That it was not, suggests that he was not one of the Valley's numerous Presbyterians. Keeping in mind that Brown did not live in the area at the time he received the "call" so his decision would likely be affected by the number of persons whose signature appeared on the list because this was an indicator of the areas ability to provide sufficient financial support for the prospective pastor. It is, therefore, not insignificant that Robert Alexander's name was not included in this important list.

More importantly, there is no eighteenth century evidence known that supports the idea that Robert Alexander's educational endeavors, were linked to, or had evolved into Rev. Brown's Latin school. A fact revealed by Professor McDaniel's University supported archaeological study that produced two published monographs of great value and interest. See this report's bibliography.[159]

Note: Despite the value of the McDaniel group's extensive study, they too were taken in by Foote's fraud and continued to adhere to the university's revised history that dates the university's origins

---

159   John M. McDaniel., Charles N. Watson, David T. Moore, *Liberty Hall Academy, The Early History of the Institutions which Evolved into Washington and Lee University,* Lexington, Virginia, Liberty Hall Press, 1979. A most unfortunate title because, in truth, no institution "evolved" into Washington and Lee University.

to a time prior to October 13, 1774, and linking the university to Rev. John Brown's private school. This group's failure in this regard is inexplicable because there was no such connection and they referenced no credible evidence that supported the university's post-1865 adherence to the false history.

It is indeed difficult to comprehend how Foote came to stoop so low as to commit such an egregiously deceptive literary concoction. His motives are not apparent, but his actions speak for themselves. It is disappointing, however, that his deceptions, for so long escaped detection. Selective perception does not account for forgery. His actions in this regard, however, redounds to his newfound infamy, and his infamy undercuts the value of his heretofore venerated two volumes of *Sketches of Virginia, Historical and Biographical.*

Foote Unaware of Rev. John Brown's Views about the Presbytery's New Seminary in Augusta

Rev. Brown, as a member of the Hanover Presbytery, quietly but tenaciously opposed the creation of the seminary (Augusta Academy) and refused to be involved in the school's affairs virtually from the onset of its establishment.[160] In a still extant letter, Brown informed his influential brother-in-law, Col. William Preston of his opposition to establishing the school the Presbytery was considering creating. Later, he urged the same person to avoid sending his sons to Liberty Hall. Brown's animus by this time was quite palpable, insofar as he refused to participate in the school's affairs. It is a fact that most later historians completely missed and led to their several faulty assumptions about the founding of Liberty Hall. This letter is abstracted in John White Stuart's biography of Brown. See bibliography for a complete citation.

Mr. Foote never bothered to explain why the Liberty Hall Board of Trustees' meeting minutes fail to indicate Mr. Brown's presence at any of the Trustees' meetings during the school's entire eighteenth century existence. It seems fair to ask, if this supposed superintendent and Trustee, was ever present at a Trustee meeting. If Mr. Foote had sought an answer to this seeming inconsistency, he would have discovered that there is no record of Mr. Brown having ever attended a Board meeting of the Trustees of the college. This fact is punctuated by another, which is that every one of the Liberty Hall Academy Board meetings conveniently took place in Rev. Brown's own greater neighborhood. This astounding reality seems to have gone unnoticed by every administration and every Board of Trustees that has represented that this man was one of the school's first two presidents. This is applicable to every administration, and every Board of Trustees since the

---

160 Rev. Brown was inexplicably in attendance at a reported informal prayer meeting held at Mount Pleasant in January of 1776, at which prayers for the new seminary were offered. Perhaps the breech in the personal relationship between Rev. Graham and Rev. Brown had not yet fully ripened. However this happened, it was a unique occurrence never again repeated. It may have been that Rev. Brown had little professional choice, since all the other attendees were his friends and many had been members of his congregation when he had been pastor of the Timber Ridge church, where Rev. Graham was the new pastor. This was reported by Rev. Fithian in his Journal for 1775–1776, pg. 170. (See bibliography.)

college's claim of Brown's Presidency first surfaced in 1865. Of course, in fairness to the reputation of Rev. John Brown, he himself never claimed having had any connection to Liberty Hall Academy. Several of his descendants, however, did but they were obviously misled by someone. They provided no evidence from their ancestor's files or extant letters that would tend to support their baseless suppositions.

For auditing purposes, Claverhouse Associates reviewed the institution's records and also the various authorized published histories that emanated from the university during the 1770s. These inquiries proved both interesting and revealing. We noted, for example, that notwithstanding the order of the Board of Trustees to publish an historical account of their own origins in the year 1849,[161] Mr. Foote nevertheless published his fantastical contrary account, the year afterwards. His bold and rather shocking action in this regard, however, should have come as no great surprise, for Mr. Foote forewarns his readers in his introduction thus:

> Comparatively little has been taken from any political history in general circulation . . . . ***Traditions have been compared with written documents***, and ***nothing has been received from conjecture,*** or preconceived hypothesis . . . To a great extent, and generally as far as is practicable, or useful, **the important facts *are given in the words of the original writer, or author of the tradition***, that the reader may make his own construction. ***By this means numerous footnotes are avoided***, the *searching out **authorities for verification less necessary,** and the liability to misconstruction greatly lessened*. (Foote, Sketches of Va....Series. One, 1850 pp. 2–4] (Emphasis added) (The underlining above is added to indicate nonsense.)

While it can be accepted that Mr. Foote generally means what he says, nevertheless, when he says that "***nothing has been received from conjecture,***" this representation is pure rubbish, as we have demonstrated in regards to the Rev. Houston letter to Rev. Morrison. That letter is pure conjecture on Houston's part, at least insofar as he treats the college's origins, and as such, it is demonstrably incorrect as it relates to the misconception about the Hanover Presbytery's patronizing of an already existing school in Augusta County, which never happened. What is revealed in this audit report's assessment of Mr. Foote's two books on Virginia is that nothing contained therein that is not a quote from the text of institutional documentary records can be safely relied upon without independent verification of its authenticity. The prudent researcher, however, should be sure to compare such documents with originals whenever possible.

---

161 Junkin, Rev. George, DD, _Christianity The Patron of Literature and Science: An Address Delivered February 22, 1849. On the Occasion of the Author's Inauguration as President of Washington College, Virginia_, Philadelphia, The Board of Trustees, 1849 [pamphlet pps. 39.] The Junkin Inaugural Address includes an important Appendix: (ordered printed by the Board of Trustees) "A Brief Sketch of the Early History of Washington College." This constitutes the College's first ***published*** History.

Now it can be seen how most of the errors concerning the early history of Washington and Lee came to be. Mr. Foote simply threw out all the rules of accurate history making and declared himself the arbiter for determining when it was appropriate to provide evidence in support of any of his unauthenticated claims and assertions. True to his word, Mr. Foote eschews the modern methodology of Mr. Edward Gibbon and instead pontificates unencumbered by the time-consuming "**searching out authorities for verification**" which he denigrates in his introduction to his first book on Virginia.

Mr. Foote's arrogance was exceeded only by his faulty reasoning in rejecting well-established verification methodologies (i.e., using footnotes and citing relied upon sources.)[162] With this insight, the reader can easily see how Washington and Lee's early history was purloined under its Trustees' collective noses. This does not, however, explain why Washington and Lee's own historians failed to challenge Foote's unsupported and unauthenticated repudiation of the institution's previously well-established history.

The plain fact is that the college's many historians after 1865, each and every one of them, did fail in this regard, and in so doing, became a good example for the institution's history instructors to show students how not to create an honest and accurate history.

It is difficult to construct a more embarrassing scenario for any institution of higher learning's history department than Washington and Lee's abandonment of well-established fact-checking methods when researching the various extant historical treatments of the institution's origins. Presumably, the university will very soon take appropriate steps to correct this shameful failure to act with due diligence to ensure that what they represent about its founding is actually true.

The reader may recall the incontestable fact that no historian in the last one hundred and fifty years has cited as authority the first authorized history of Washington and Lee University written by Rev. Caleb Wallace, the Hanover Presbytery's Clerk in May of 1776. The history is not hidden in some dark corner of the library, rather, it is located on the first pages of text in the college's first official record book containing the first Board of Trustees' meeting minutes. This, of course, is the place one would expect that a historian studying the college's founding would initiate his or her research. Nevertheless, even Dr. Crenshaw, then the Chair of the History Department, failed to include in his references the single most important primary source that exists concerning the founding of Washington and Lee University. It is absent from his unpublished bibliography and is not included in any of his voluminous footnotes or in his Appendix, "The Problems of the Origins."[163]

---

162 As mentioned elsewhere, Mr. Foote admits in his introduction to Volume One, that he abstained from citing authorities, and he boldly asserts that for him they were not necessary. He says this in different words, but ones that have the same meaning. How his admission failed to serve as a red-flag to the University's own history department is indeed baffling.

163 These materials are located in Crenshaw's Typescript version of *General Lee's College* but was not included in the Random House published edition.

The auditor cannot fathom how any historian, let alone the premier historian of the institution, Dr. Ollinger Crenshaw, who was concerned with the early history of Washington and Lee could fail to even acknowledge the existence of the university's first authorized statement of its history. This documentary-based history contains all the pertinent extracts from the meeting minutes of the institution that created the college, and it was written by a man with an unimpeachable reputation, Rev. Caleb Wallace. A graduate of Princeton under Dr. Witherspoon, who served as a Trustee of both Liberty Hall and Hampden Sydney. He was also a Presbyterian minister and was later a Justice of Kentucky's highest appellate Court. Anyone who seeks to challenge Justice Wallace's history written at the behest of the Hanover Presbytery only two years after the college was created must necessarily accept the great burden associated with an attempt to impeach him on a subject with which he was intimately familiar. To date, no one has had the temerity to directly challenge Judge Wallace's account. Rather, they have all pretended his account did not exist. Its existence, however, is proven by the unchallengeable fact that it is the college's earliest documentary record. Located in its very first record book created in May of 1776.

Note: There are a few rare records that pertain to the college that predate this book, but they are the records of the Hanover Presbytery, some of which, are housed in the university's archives, including original subscription lists that contain signatures of individuals who pledged their financial support for such things as purchasing a library and laboratory equipment for teaching natural science (i.e., "natural philosophy") mathematics, geometry, and astronomy. No early record of the Hanover Presbytery pertaining to the college, that is known to exist, suggests a date of establishment prior to October of 1774. Claims to the contrary all surface only after the original participants were all deceased and therefore were unable to challenge the attempts to revise the history of the school's origins.

First Suspicion that Something Is "Rotten in the state of Denmark."

Dr. Ollinger Crenshaw, a history professor at Washington and Lee, seems to have suspected that something was seriously amiss concerning the founding, but he elected to gloss over this aspect of the college's history in his published version of *General Lee's College* (Random House, 1969). To his credit, he left to the university's library,[164] his two-volume typescript version of *General Lee's College*, which includes the very valuable appendix A, "The Problem of the Origins," which at least alerts subsequent researchers to the fact that something is not quite right with respect to the post–Civil War history of the college.

Crenshaw also left his valuable related footnotes for the book. Random House unfortunately declined to include either the appendix or the footnotes in their published version. History, it should be said, is indebted to Dr. Crenshaw for having identified many of the fundamental errors identified in this audit report. He should not, however, have missed that there is no evidence of a connection between Liberty Hall Academy and the Latin School of Rev. John Brown. If, on

---

164 Technically, it was gifted to the Library by Dr. Crenhaw's widow after his death, but it is assumed that she gifted it consistent with his expressed desire.

the other hand, Dr. Crenshaw did not actually miss this obvious error, then he apparently elected to let local sleeping dogs lie, as it were.[165] Auditors, however, who conduct investigations are obligated to search for and report hard truths. Their reputations depend upon a record of having revealed that which is found irrespective of how the findings might be received.

William Henry Foote's Historical Debacle

Rev. William Henry Foote, among all the authors who have written about Washington and Lee University, did more than any other author to annihilate a long and honorable true history of the university. To be sure, he also ranks very high among those important chroniclers and archivists who preserved many valuable eighteenth-century documentary treasures that came from various obscure yet important, colonial Virginia records. He should forever be remembered on both accounts. As an historian, however, he was an utter failure. His own words, in both of his Virginia books, are often both unreliable, and, perhaps, as often as not, erroneous. Mr. Foote demonstrates repeatedly that he should have left analysis of the materials he chronicled to others. Mr. Foote tended to see what he wanted to see rather than what was actually there. It is highly likely that he consulted politically important individuals who led him astray. Whether such actions, in this regard, were intentional or not is beyond the auditor's central concerns. Mr. Foote's own words are, in many instances, grossly misleading on important matters of institutional history. The more significant errors are explained in the Author's Errors Section of the report as well as in selected Appendices.

For purposes of this historical performance audit, it is Mr. Foote's gross errors with which we are most concerned. His historical misdeeds are so great and so complex as they relate to the early history of Washington and Lee that they must be discussed in detail elsewhere than in this introduction. Here, it is sufficient to point out that Mr. Foote discarded seventy-five years of authorized, authenticated documentary history and foisted on an unsuspecting public an utterly preposterous narrative explaining just how Washington and Lee University was created. Of course, in so doing, he shunned evidence in favor of gossip and ignored institutional records in favor of fabulous fictions formed by unnamed sources that Mr. Foote credulously deemed reliable.

Before the published appearance of Mr. Foote, in his two separate volumes of _Sketches of Virginia: Historical and Biographical_ in 1850 and 1855 respectively, the world had been blessed with numerous fairly accurate historical accountings of the origins of Washington and Lee University. Afterward, there are virtually

---

165 It has been whispered by a few that Col. Bolivar Christian et al. were intent on persuading General Lee to accept the presidency of the College in 1865, and that this cabal had concluded that it was imperative in this regard to gloss over the college's strong historical ties to the Presbyterian Church in light of Lee's family being Episcopalians. For that reason, Col. Christian may have penned his historical sketch so as to link the college's origins to Robert Alexander and his private preparatory school rather than to ascribe it to the actions of the Hanover Presbytery. A lawyer, Col. Christian was not unfamiliar with creative argumentation in defense of clients in untenable situations.

no accurate published accounts of the early history of the college or, as it was first informally known, "Augusta Academy." What is abundantly clear in the last analysis is that William Henry Foote, more than any other source, is responsible for the bastardization of the early history of Washington and Lee University while Colonel and Trustee Bolivar Christian is nearly as responsible because he is obviously the culprit that championed Foote's insistence that the college was much older than it was and stewarded that puerile narrative into the institution's embrace in 1865. The university has misrepresented its history ever since. Trustee Christian's credulous acceptance of Foote's false narrative was most likely caused by selective perception when he heard what he wanted to hear.

Prior to Mr. Foote's venture into Virginia history, earlier historians explained that Washington and Lee was created by the Hanover Presbytery in October of 1774, which was unquestionably accurate. The reference to "historians," in this context, means all those authors who wrote on the subject of the origins of Washington and Lee from the day of its establishment until the day that William Henry Foote appeared with his altogether new notion. Mr. Foote, the reader will no doubt recall, did not bother to mention that his version of the college's origins was at serious odds with all known previous writings on the subject, including the college's first authorized history (1776) and the college's last authorized and accurate early history published the year before the arrival of Mr. Foote (1849).[166]

Here again, is the opening of the first authorized account written in 1776:

> The Present Academy of Liberty Hall began under the Direction and Patronage of the Presbytery of Hanover as the following minutes fully evince.

> At a session of the Pby. of Hanover at Cub Creek Oct. 13, 1774, the Pby resumed consideration of a school for the liberal education youth which we unanimously judge to be of great importance. We do therefore agree to establish and patronize a publick school which shall be confined to the county of Augusta in this colony.[167]

Here below is the last authorized account (1849) before Mr. Foote's appearance in 1850:

---

166 Rev. George Junkin, DD, *Christianity the Patron of Literature and Science: An Address Delivered February 22, 1849. On the Occasion of the Author's Inauguration As President of Washington College, Virginia*, Philadelphia, The Board of Trustees, 1849 [pamphlet pp. 39]. The Junkin Inaugural Address includes an important Appendix: "A Brief Sketch of the Early History of Washington College" (ordered printed by the Board of Trustees). This constitutes the College's First authorized published History.

167 Rev. Caleb Wallace, Record Book, containing the minutes of the Board of Trustees of Liberty Hall Academy, pg. 3, This opening is written down and organized by Rev. Caleb Wallace, Clerk of the Hanover Presbytery.

Oct. 12, 1774. At a meeting of the Hanover Presbytery, at Cub Creek, in Charlotte, Presbytery resumed consideration of a school for the liberal education of youth, and unanimously judge it to be of great and immediate importance. We do therefore agree to establish and patronize a public school, which shall be confined to the county of Augusta in this colony. And we order, that at present, it be managed by Mr. William Graham, a gentleman, who has been well recommended to this body, . . .[168]

Now comes Mr. Foote, and he informs his readers thus:

By the act of Presbytery in 1774, the grammar school, conducted by the Rev. John Brown, *or under his supervision and his charge, became the centre (sic) of operations for literary and theological improvement in the Valley.* The Rev. Samuel Houston in his letter to Rev. James Morrison explains "that shortly before the war, some men whose sons were growing up, felt a desire for having them or part of them educated liberally, chiefly with a view to the ministry of the gospel. *Accordingly a small grammar school was formed in the neighborhood of Old Providence, composed of Samuel Doak, John Montgomery, Archibald Alexander James Houston, William Tate, Samuel Greenlee, William Wilson, Ebenezer Smith, and some others*, which greatly increased and drew youths from distant neighborhoods. *This grammar school was moved to the place, near Fairfield, called Mount Pleasant; about which time the Presbytery of Hanover* patronized it."[169] (Foote, *Sketches of Virginia . . .* Series One, pg. 442, 443] (Emphasis added here in bold italics represent error.)

---

168 Junkin, Rev. George, DD, *Christianity The Patron Of Literature And Science: An Address Delivered February 22, 1849. On the Occasion of the Author's Inauguration As President of Washington College, Virginia*, Philadelphia, The Board of Trustees, 1849 [pamphlet pps. 39.] The Junkin Inaugural Address includes an important Appendix: "A Brief Sketch of the Early History of Washington College" (ordered printed by the Board of Trustees).

169 Houston has mixed apples and oranges. All of the men he named as students in this letter attended schools other than the one created by the Hanover Presbytery in 1774. There was no school at Mount Pleasant at the time that the Presbytery created their new seminary (Academy), and the Presbytery did not "fix" the location for its initial operations. That decision was made by the new seminary's "manager" William Graham in cooperation with residents living within the bounds of the Timber Ridge congregation. The new seminary's temporary headquarters was located on the farm of Mr. James Wilson, which local residents called "Mount Pleasant." Here, some years earlier, Rev. John Brown organized a "Latin School" while pastor of Timber Ridge Congregation. When Rev. Brown moved and relinquished his pastorate of Timber Ridge he moved his school to his new residence on Moffett's Creek several miles distant. The school referenced by Rev. Houston was conducted from that time forward at New Providence, not at Mount Pleasant.

Note: The above indented paragraph contains a quote within a quote. The second quote follows the underlined passage and continues on for the remainder of the paragraph. Technically, however, the second quote is probably not an accurate quotation because Mr. Foote changed the wording in his second volume published five years later. Foote failed to alert the readers of the second volume that he had failed to quote that passage consistent with his earlier volume, or how and why he failed in this regard.

Mr. Foote's paragraph above is more wrong than it is right. In the author's errors section of the report, his many mistakes are explained in detail. The reader will note, however, that Mr. Foote provides the introduction to the above paragraph, and the report is essentially false in every important aspect. For example, Rev. John Brown did not "conduct" any school, at any time or anywhere. Rather, he **organized** two schools at two different times and in two separate locations, but both of these schools **were conducted by qualified tutors, not by Rev. Brown**. Rev. John Brown was neither a teacher nor a scholar. As a writer, Rev. Brown candidly admitted to the fact that "I am no scribe."[170] Rev. Brown was a country parson who knew that congregations expected that their minister would see to it that the children of the congregation had at least some measure of basic instruction. His schools were peripatetic because he depended on others to serve as instructors, and the men he hired rarely stayed long at his school. Rev. Brown explains in some of his correspondence that on occasion he sent his own sons to schools other than his own private Latin School, for instruction in basic English writing and mathematics. He refused, however, to send his sons to Liberty Hall Academy or even to that Academy's grammar school, both of which were under the care and tuition of Rev. William Graham. Both of the schools under Mr. Graham[171] were initially located in Rev. Brown's own neighborhood.

Mr. Foote was also incorrect to say that Rev. Brown's school became the "centre (sic) for literary and theological improvement in the Valley" after 1774. From the time that William Graham arrived in the Valley of Virginia, wherever he happened to be was the center, and where he organized those operations was initially, and temporarily at a place locally called, *Mount Pleasant*. Here, Mr. Graham's students attended instruction while awaiting the much-anticipated construction of the seminary's first permanent buildings on Timber Ridge.[172]

Ironically, Mr. Graham's temporary operations were conducted near the spot where Rev. Brown had at an earlier time organized a Latin School, but Mr.

---

170   Stuart, John White, *The Rev. John Brown of Virginia (1728–1803): His Life and Selected Sermons*, Doctoral Dissertation, University of Massachusetts, 1988. (See, J. Brown letters extracts, passim)

171   Referring here to the grammar school and its associated college. The grammar school was part of the college from its inception and was initially erected in rude quarters at Mount Pleasant while the college's campus buildings were being constructed at Timber Ridge. The Mount Pleasant location served as Mr. Graham's operations headquarters during his earliest days in Virginia.

172   It was at this location that Dr. Samuel L. Campbell observed the school's operations which formed the basis of his retrospective memoir, published in the Southern Literary Messenger in1838. See the attached bibliography.

Brown had moved that school to his new home on Moffett's Creek several years earlier. Foote seems completely ignorant of Rev. John Brown's location in 1774 and thereafter. After Mr. Foote published his books on Virginia, many later historians were clearly as ignorant as Mr. Foote about the location of Rev. Brown's Latin School during the 1770s. Fortunately, one person, Rev. Philip V. Fithian, was not ignorant in this regard, and he left a written journal created in 1775 and 1776 while visiting the Valley of Virginia, and often while lodging in the home of Rev. Brown.[173]

Fithian's Journal contains a useful and accurate depiction of the two different schools then being conducted in the neighborhood of Timber Ridge and New Providence congregations. Mr. Fithian knew both Brown and Graham, and he knew and understood their two different schools as well. Fithian accurately refers to Brown's school as a "Latin School." Graham's school is referred to either as an Academy, or as a seminary. Rev. Fithian understood that these terms were, in that time, functional equivalents.

As for theological instruction, William Graham's theological attainments were widely known and virtually all of Virginia's young men interested in the Presbyterian ministry flocked to Graham almost as soon as he arrived in Virginia.[174] From 1774 onward, most all new Presbyterian ministers in Virginia were, for the next twenty years, products of William Graham's theological instruction. That's why when the Presbyterian Church created its first college-affiliated theological Seminary in North America at Lexington, Virginia, they chose the rector of Liberty Hall Academy (Graham) as its president.[175] It is also why the Virginia Synod appointed Graham Chairman of the Committee on Missions that oversaw most young Virginia missionaries' church-sponsored activities. Rev. William Hill mentions Graham in this regard in the journal he kept while conducting his missionary requirements.[176]

Finally, in regards to Mr. Foote's incomprehensible ignorance of the affairs in the Valley of Virginia during the last quarter of the eighteenth century, and contrary to Mr. Foote's views on educational matters in the Valley, he was wrong

---

173 Philip Vickers Fithian, *The Journal & Letters of Philip Vickers Fithian, "Written on the Virginia-Pennsylvania Frontier and in the Army Around New York, [1775–1776]*, Princeton, Princeton University Press, 1934 [I was considered by the publisher to be vol. II] .While this volume stands alone and has its own index, it is volume two, the first volume being published in 1900. Unfortunately, the journal was not published until 1934, and therefore many important historians had already published their treatments.

174 Alexander, Archibald DD, Mss "Memoir of The Rev. Wm Graham," [written in longhand]. The Rev. Graham portions of this manuscript constitute the largest part of a writing entitled, *Great Valley of Virginia*. Auditor's photocopy came from the Princeton Seminary Library in 1989. It is now available in spiral-bound form at the Leyburn Library, W&L.

175

176 Hill, William, Autobiographical sketches of Dr. William Hill: together with his account of the revival of religion in Prince Edward County, and biographical sketches of the life and character of the Reverend Dr. Moses Hoge of Virginia, Richmond, 1968. Rev. Hoge, too, received his "regular academic courses" at Liberty Hall, and also his theological instruction under Rev. William Graham.

to say that Brown's school during this period *"was moved to the place, near Fairfield, called Mount Pleasant* (emphasis added). Brown first established his school at Mount Pleasant, and then shortly after 1767, the school was moved from Mount Pleasant to New Providence. From this location it was never again moved. In other words, Rev. Brown's school was not moved *to* Mount Pleasant but *from* there, to New Providence. This fact is well demonstrated in Rev. Brown's extant correspondence from that period.[177]

There are, indeed, numerous examples of such colossal blunders made by Mr. Foote concerning the origins of Washington and Lee University and her first president, Rev. William Graham, most of which are detailed in the author's errors section of the audit report together with persuasive corresponding evidence to support our determinations.

It will likely remain a mystery why Mr. Foote's unsupported new contentions went unchecked and unchallenged for over a hundred and fifty years. It certainly did not result from a broad conspiracy to rewrite the institution's early history because so much of the institutional documentary evidence debunking Mr. Foote's gross mistakes was left hiding in plain sight for anyone who was interested enough to search for it. Instead, it appears that the revision was caused by a host of institutional guardians' failure to exercise due diligence in carrying out their assigned responsibilities. The first manifestation of the institution having been hoodwinked about its own creation occurred in the iconic year 1865, suggesting the very real possibility that the institution's guardians were suffering mental fatigue from the devastation all around them and had perhaps lost most of their normal instinct for healthy skepticism.

Today, however, is a new dawn, and it is altogether timely enough to set things right. That was not, however, the course that was taken in 1865, when an unnamed source[178] wrote the college's first incorrect history, which was published in, Charter and Laws and Trustees and Alumni of Washington College at Lexington, Virginia, Richmond, 1865 (see below). It is to be regretted that the auditor's review did not unearth clear evidence concerning the identity of the author of that first institutional false rendition of its own history. Col. Bolivar Christian, who wrote the second false institutional rendition, might well have also been the author of the first false history because he was a Trustee when it was published in 1865, and he was an amateur historian who had written on the history of the Valley, but we located no evidence to support that possibility. Had Col. Christian exercised due diligence in researching his own historical treatment published four years later (1869), he would have quickly discovered that the 1865 rendition published in the

---

177 John White Stuart, The Rev. John Brown of Virginia (1728–1803): His Life and selected sermons, Doctoral Dissertation, University of Massachusetts, 1988 passim.

178 Quite likely the author was Col. Bolivar Christian who was an amateur historian and had been a Trustee since 1858. Four years later Col. Christian wrote a similar account for the college's Alumni directory, and while it, too was written anonymously, Dr. Crenshaw definitely attributed that article to Trustee Col. Christian. Mr. Christian had several historical articles published while a Trustee that at least touched upon the history of the community surrounding the college. (See the attached bibliography.)

Charter and Laws publication, was bogus because it is inconsistent with all prior accounts known to exist and all of the known pertinent documentary records of the college and the Presbytery that created the college.

****

Washington College Adopts Wm. H. Foote's Folly [1865]
(Repudiates its own eighty-five years of history without explanation)

In 1865, Washington College turned its back on its long-standing history, including its own earlier authorized histories written first in 1776 and then its last accurate account in 1849. The college did this without any explanation. Presumably, the decision to adopt an entirely new history, was based on William Henry Foote's, *Sketches of Virginia: Historical and Biographical*, Series One and Series Two, 1850 & 1855, because this is the published account of the origins that is fairly consistent with the new accounts adopted by the college in 1865 and repeated in similar but variant forms thereafter.

The 1865 New Inappropriately Authorized version:
(The errors below appear in bold italics.)

> *(The Charter and Laws and Trustees and Faculty of Washington College at Lexington, Va. A. D. 1865*, Richmond: Chas. H. Wynne, Printer, 1865)

HISTORICAL STATISTICS

The *germ of Washington College was a classical school established about 1752 (?) by Robert Alexander*, at first near Greenville, Augusta County; and *was the first classical school in the valley of Virginia. It was removed "shortly before the revolution" to Mt. Pleasant*, near Fairfield, Rockbridge County, where October *12*,[179] 1774, *it was formally adopted by Hanover Presbytery, with its original name of the Augusta Academy, and arrangements were made to support it, while it remained under the patronage of the Presbytery, by "liberal contributions."* In its records of May 13, 1776, it is styled

---

[179] *The autumn meeting of the Hanover Presbytery was a three-day meeting. The action to establish Augusta Academy took place on October 13, 1774. Some simply refer to the event as "the meeting of October 12, 1774." This statement, however, is incorrect when it includes an assertion that the Hanover Presbytery formally adopted the school of Robert Alexander on the day of October 12, 1774. In fact, the Presbytery never "adopted" any school in Virginia, a fact confirmed by the meeting minutes.*

"Liberty Hall Academy as it is hereafter to be called, instead
of The Augusta Academy," and lands were accepted for its new
site, near the Timber Ridge Church. (Charter and Laws . . . pg. 3.)
(emphasis added above indicate error)

The words above that are in **bold and italics** are demonstrable mistakes.
Washington College had no "germ"[180] that predates the creation of the college
on October 13, 1774. It was intended from inception to be a college, which
was clearly explained in the Presbytery's meeting minutes leading up to its
creation. Admittedly, the school went through an evolutionary process, but then
most colleges do that, although in varying ways. For example, many agricultural
college's that were established in response to the Morrill Agricultural Act, like
Michigan State University, which during the first of its first emendations involved
freshmen spending much of their first year clearing land and constructing barns
of various types. Nevertheless, Michigan State dates their school's establishment
to that first year (1855). Obviously, there was no commencement that year since
the school only had a freshman class. The 1855 class, however, is not a "germ"
in the germ-theory sense of that concept. Moreover, local common schools that
may have been located at an earlier date on a portion of the same lands where the
college was initially located are not in any sense a germ from whence Michigan
State University sprung. The Presbytery's seminary, Augusta Academy, was an
entirely new venture designed from inception to be a college.[181] In 1775, William
Graham initiated classroom instruction in the form of a grammar school, but that
was part and parcel of the college, and remained so as long as Rev. Graham was
its president (rector.) Still, some might contend that this was the college's germ.

In addition, and also contrary to Foote's assertion, Robert Alexander had
no connection to the Augusta Academy, and no school was moved to Mount
Pleasant shortly before the Revolution from some other locale. Moreover, the

---

180 Unless one assigns that unfortunate denomination ("germ") to the seminary created on October
13, 1774, in its incipient temporary form at "Mount Pleasant" in anticipation of its new buildings
still under construction, but in that case, the seminary is still the same entity. It was merely
referred to by some by the informal name Augusta Academy. The grammar school was the
foundation upon which the superstructure was to be erected. At the end of 1776, the grammar
school students were transferred from Mount Pleasant to the new campus buildings built
on property adjacent to the Timber Ridge Meeting House. The grammar school format was
continued, however, as an adjunct to the college and it was conducted on the same grounds
as the college. There is no known record of its specific location on the new Campus, but at
Princeton where Graham had conducted the grammar school while a student in the college,
was located in the lower level of the main building.

181 At the time the Presbytery decided to "establish and patronize" the new seminary (Oct. 1774),
it also initiated a fund-raising campaign in its name, that was, among other things, was also
specifically for the purpose of procuring laboratory equipment of various types associated with
college level instruction in various mathematical and science classes, as well as for purchasing
books to supply a new library. The books purchased were all college level books. These items
were purchased by the new director of the college, William Graham, in Philadelphia a few
months after he was appointed to head up the actual physical creation of the new Academy
(i.e,. college).

Hanover Presbytery records clearly demonstrate that it never "adopted" any existing educational entity during the period under consideration. The only schools patronized by the Hanover Presbytery in eighteenth-century Virginia were the exclusive creations of the Hanover Presbytery, as its meeting minutes clearly indicate to anyone who reads them with an objective eye. Representations to the contrary, like Foote's quoted above, are in every case asserted without any credible evidence or reliable authority to support them. In short, his assertions are gross errors based on inappropriate assumptions and or false representations of unidentified sources.

Note: Above, the standard quotation marks are the auditor's designation, in this section of material we are quoting. However, in this section, We use the single quotation mark to indicate a quotation within a quotation, or in other words, a quotation used by the unnamed author(s) being quoted.

****

The Two Schools in the Neighborhood of Timber Ridge and New Providence

Much of the mid-nineteenth century confusion about Liberty Hall Academy stems from the fact that early researchers failed to comprehend that there were two schools, and two ministers in the general neighborhood of the Presbyterian congregations of Timber Ridge and New Providence Presbyterian churches in the 1770s. Adding to the possible confusion is the fact that both of these schools had at one time been located on the same farm near Fairfield, Virginia, which location was called locally Mount Pleasant.[182] These schools, however, were of two entirely different types, and they were under the direction of the different minsters namely, Rev. John Brown and Rev. William Graham.

Rev. Brown's private school was a preparatory school that he labeled a Latin School. Rev. Graham's school, on the other hand, was intended from its inception to be a "public" college-level school patterned after the College of New Jersey. Fund-raising campaigns conducted in the name of the Hanover Presbytery were initiated at the time of the Academy's creation for the purpose of purchasing a library and the kinds of scientific laboratory equipment only used in institutions of higher learning. Contributions were received from many Virginian residents that lived far from the Valley because it was widely known that the Presbyterian Church was intent on establishing a college in Virginia that would provide the same kind of educational opportunities in Virginia that students received at the College of New Jersey at Princeton. At this time, the early 1770s, the only college in Virginia was William and Mary, and that institution was primarily focused on the study of law.

---

182 This farm was then owned by a Mr. James Wilson. Se: Pilcher, Margaret Campbell, _Historical Sketches of the Campbell, Pilcher, and kindred families_, Press of Marshall & Bruce Co., Nashville, Tennessee, 1911. 444 pp. [Important because she locates the property on whichAugusta Academy was first located at Mount Pleasant, near Fairfield, Va. The Wilson and Campbell families had close ties to Washington College for many of its early years.]

Colleges, as is well known, do not appear suddenly with the stroke of a pen, but rather students must be cultivated from freshman-level instruction gradually on up to the senior class level. The difference between freshman-level instruction and grammar school (preparatory) instruction can in certain venues be virtually indecipherable. During the new academy's first year or so, much of the instruction at the school's temporary quarters at Mount Pleasant might have appeared, to the untrained eye, much like the "Latin School" that had been conducted there by Rev. Brown several years earlier. These schools were, however, working from an entirely different mission. Brown's school was intended to prepare students for entrance into schools like the College of New Jersey (Princeton) while Mr. Graham's school was intended to provide from the onset an opportunity for students to "finish their classical studies."[183] In 1775, the academy was in its initial evolutionary stage of development or incipient state. Colleges and universities rarely, if ever, begin with a full complement of freshmen, sophomores, juniors, and seniors. A fact rarely emphasized in institutional accountings of a school's origins.

These confusing elements were exacerbated by two additional facts: (1) The schools were both directed by Presbyterian ministers, and (2) both of the ministers involved were members of the Hanover Presbytery that had created the school under the "Care and Tuition of Mr. Graham." Mr. Graham, however, who came to Virginia from Pennsylvania, was not initially a member of the Hanover Presbytery because he had not yet been hired [i.e., "Called"] by a local Presbyterian congregation, and he had not yet gone through what the Presbyterian Church refers to as "Trials," that precede Licensing as a probationer.

One person from outside the Valley of Virginia who was not confused about these two different schools located at two different places in the same neighborhood was Rev. Philip Vickers Fithian, who spent several weeks in the Valley in 1775 and 1776. Fortunately, he kept a journal and knew personally most all of the central players in this confusing drama centering around educational endeavors in the Valley between 1774 and 1776. His entries for December of 1775 and 1776 clearly delineate the differences between these schools and their directors. Unfortunately, Fithian's Journal, written in 1775 and 1776, was not published until 1934.[184] This was nearly a century after various authors had published vastly incorrect histories based on their having been so confused that many incorrectly assumed that these two schools were one and the same. However, they could hardly have been more different, even in the academy's first year, which difference can be amusingly seen in the literary memoir of the early days at Washington College written by one of its early graduates, Dr. Samuel L. Campbell.[185] According to Dr. Archibald

183   The phrase "finish their classical studies" was a euphemistic way of referring to obtaining a college education.

184   Philip Vickers Fithian, The Journal & Letters of Philip Vickers Fithian, "Written on the Virginia-Pennsylvania Frontier and in the Army Around New York, [1775–1776], Princeton, Princeton University Press, 1934.

185   Dr. Samuel L Campbell.,(M.D.)[i.e., "Senex"], "Washington College, Lexington, Virginia," Southern Literary Messenger, June 1838, beginning at pg. 364. Campbell later became a

Alexander, "Dr. Campbell was for many years a trustee of Washington College, and knew as much of its early history as any other person in the world. Shortly before his death he drew up a brief history of his Alma Mater, and published it in the Southern Literary Messenger." Campbell said:

> About threescore years ago[186] (i.e., circa 1770s) The Hanover Presbytery taking into consideration the low state of literature in this commonwealth, **conceived a project of establishing a seminary of learning in the upper country.** They wisely concluded that **such an establishment** in the limestone valley **would afford to all classes an opportunity of acquiring a liberal education, thereby rendering unnecessary the inconvenience and extra expense of resorting to northern colleges** . . . it was readily foreseen that the times were unfavorable for making collections of money for any public purpose . . . . The Presbytery, however, considering the necessity of the case, thought that something might be done; and on making experiment something was done.[187]

Dr. Campbell in the same section of the article says:

> Mr. Graham came to this country with the character of a gentleman of genius, scholarship, and piety, which character he supported through life.
>
> A number of students from this and the neighboring counties now resorted to Mount Pleasant. In a short time a very respectable grammar school was formed. **This was the first germ of Washington College.** (Dr. Samuel L. Campbell, "History of Washington College," Southern Literary Messenger, Vol. IV, 1838, pp. 107–108.] (emphasis added)

Note: Lest the reader be confuse by the use of the term "germ," it is important to point out that the school to which Campbell refers here is not a different school. The "grammar school" is what Rev. Graham refers to as the college's foundation upon which is to be constructed the college's superstructure. To Mr. Graham, who designed and formed this foundation, it was part and parcel of one unit.

---

long-serving Trustee of W&L and served as "acting President" during the interregnum between President Graham's resignation in the Fall of 1796 and the appointment of the college's second President, George A. Baxter, at the very close of the eighteenth-century. Campbell's father, was one of President Graham's most intimate friends. Dr. Campbell was an eyewitness and the only such person who published an account of the actual class activities that took place at the Augusta Academy in 1775 & 1776. His memoir's few errors are limited to allusions to activities he did not actually observe.

186   Sixty years ago would make the time period the 1770s.

187   Alexander, Memoir of Rev. William Graham . . . pps 49, 50, wherein he quotes from Campbell's article.

Campbell in the same article further elucidates:

> Here (Mount Pleasant) Washington College drew its first breath. On this spot, Mount Pleasant, commenced the establishment of a seminary of learning.

Campbell's apt conclusion in this regard is as follows:

> **_Mr. Graham now resumed the business of the academy_**, over which he had heretofore watched with parental care and solicitude. He had led it cautiously and tenderly through many difficulties to a certain stage of its existence. Besides the labor of teaching, and governing, there devolved upon him the task of planning, buildings,; making contracts with the workmen; attending to the faithful execution of the contracts; the devising ways and means for fulfilling those engagements; **_and, in a word, all that was to be done for the academy fell chiefly on him . . ._**
>
> During this long period he had, for the most part, performed all the duties in person, which in other public seminaries are confided to a faculty consisting of several professors. **_He not only gave instruction in the scientific and classical departments, but paid special attention to the grammar school. "Here," said he, "should be laid a substratum on which to build a superstructure of learning."_** (Campbell, Dr. Samuel L., "Washington College, Va." Southern Literary Messenger, June 1838, beginning at pg. 364. [reprinted in W&L Hist. Papers No. 1, 1890, pg. 115.) [Emphasis added here due to its importance.)

With this picture in mind consider the view of another eyewitness, Rev. Philip Vickers Fithian who was a friendly acquaintance and schoolmate of Mr. Graham's at Princeton who happened to be visiting the Valley in 1775 and early 1776 while on a missionary tour, and who kept a journal while residing at Rev. Brown's home. Fithian had this to say:

> Dec. 24, 1775   **Mr. Graham, lately initiated a brother** [minister]**, is appointed Director of a school in the neighborhood of Mr. Brown's** –(He thinks to enlarge his Method of Education so much as to finish Youth in their classical, Philosophical Studies.
>
> (Fithian's Journal 1775–1776. pg. 150)
> (Emphasis here does not indicate error.)
>
> Jan. 18, 1776   Mr. Graham is here—Sage, deep-studied, Mr. Graham. **He is Director of the small Academy in this neighborhood.** He retains, with Dignity, the inherent Gravity

which he always supported in every Part of his Conduct while he was a Student at Nassau [Princeton]. The Lines of Method & Discipline have been inscribed & are yet visible & legible upon his countenance.

(Fithian's Journal, pg.171)
(Emphasis here does not indicate error.)

Unfortunately for maintaining the true history of Washington and Lee, Mr. Fithian's journal entries, written in 1775 and 1776, was not published for public consumption until 1934.[188] Perhaps, if Foote and those who misguidedly followed him in the latter half of the nineteenth century had been privy to Fithian's Journals, history would have been spared their embarrassing historical faux pas and there would never have been a need to purge from historical accounts the utter nonsense of Rev. John Brown having had a connection or link with Liberty Hall Academy. Not that there are not others persuasive and documentary sources from which to ascertain the history of the founding because many of these records exist, but a published book issued by the Princeton University Press would be far easier for historians to access.

The longtime unavailability of Fithian's Journal to the general public, however, does not excuse the failure on the part of those historians who neglected to review the primary and documentary sources, which were well-known to exist. These primary sources are rarely confusing except to those who relied only upon often misleading excerpts that were not considered in the full context of their creator's written records. Had the early researchers for example, referred to the first meeting minutes of the Board of Trustees, they could not have failed to note Rev. Caleb Wallace's historical sketch that occupies the Trustees meeting minutes record book's first five pages.[189] These illuminating pages inform us of all that we need to know in order to accurately ascertain the college true history of its founding.

Similarly, if the many historians who touched on the subject had bothered to review the meeting minutes of the organization that created Liberty Hall Academy, they would have noticed how the Hanover Presbytery's minutes demonstrate that the "Care and Tuition of Augusta Academy" (Liberty Hall Academy) had been with Rev. William Graham from the school's inception.

The same meeting minutes also reveal that Rev. John Brown had virtually no interaction with the Presbytery concerning Liberty Hall, even though the Presbytery's made several attempts to bring him into the school's activities by

---

188 Fithian, Philip Vickers, The Journal & Letters of Philip Vickers Fithian, "Written on the Virginia-Pennsylvania Frontier and in the Army Around New York [1775–1776], Princeton, Princeton University Press, 1934.

189 At least that was true until Trustee Bolivar Christian inappropriately inserted his mystery document, with a false and error-ridden handwritten document, ex post facto, and by doing this, he attempted to rewrite history in a way more suitable to his pet theories that have utterly no basis in fact. The inserted (pasted-in) document is unsigned and undated with no ability to authenticate its provenance. For Christian, it was an excuse that created s a blank canvass upon which to paint his own narrative. The document is as bogus as is Christian's fanciful fiction.

appointing him to various position, none of which he accepted.[190] All the business affairs of the new seminary in those first years were seemingly conducted between Rev. Graham and the Presbytery, at least, as far as the meeting minutes reveal. This reality should have given rise to a heightened sense of skepticism about the undocumented claims of Foote and his many subsequent adherents.

Note: The Hanover Presbytery attempted to involve Rev. Brown in the affairs of the new seminary by appointing him to various responsibilities, but he responded to none of their overtures. They even appointed him as one of the school's Trustees, but as the Trustee minutes demonstrate, Rev. Brown was never present at a Board of Trustees meeting, not once, not ever. Yet, the university to this very day continues to propagate that this man who refused to have anything to do with Liberty Hall Academy was either "a president" or "the first president" of that institution. This same fictitious president, by the way, also refused to send any of his several sons to attend Liberty Hall. An absurd notion, that would seem comical if it wasn't so terribly pathetic. Rev. Brown not only refused all attempts by the Hanover Presbytery to involve him in the Academy's affairs, he even refused to attend any meetings of the Board of Trustees during his lifetime, as is proven by the Board's meeting minutes, where his name never appears. Among those listed as being present. This is a fact that seems to have escaped the attention of hundreds of historians, and other authors from 1850 to the present, including most every member of the university's History Department since the department was first organized. This embarrassing fact even seems to have even eluded Dr. Crenshaw and his colleague, Dr. I. Taylor Sanders. Sanders is the author of Now Let the Gospel Trumpet Blow, which is a history of New Monmouth Presbyterian Church, and it contains two chapters on this church's first pastor, Rev. Wm. Graham, the president of Liberty Hall. Sanders' book constitutes the most extensive published treatment of Rev. William Graham other than the 1821 biographical memoir published by Graham's younger brother Edward. See bibliography. There are at least four academic dissertations that provide biographical treatments of Rev. Graham but all of these are inadequate and include some serious errors passed on from the infamous Rev. W. H. Foote.

In fairness to Rev. John Brown, it is not suggested that he himself ever asserted any direct connection to the college, for he did not, at least as far as his recorded activities are concerned. That includes his numerous extant letters that refer to his educational endeavors in the Valley during his tenure in that locale. Mr. Brown did acknowledge the seminary (Academy) in some of his letters, but his comments in this regard reflect his opposition to the school's founding, and he went so far as to encourage his friends and family to send their sons elsewhere than to Liberty Hall Academy. (For extensive extracts from the letters of Rev. John Brown, see Stuart, John White, *The Rev. John Brown of Virginia (1728–1803): His Life and selected sermons*, Doctoral Dissertation, University of Massachusetts, 1988, for a thorough treatment of these letters of Rev. Brown in which these sentiments are expressed.)[191] This, of course,

---

190   Such Presbyterial appointments all required the appointee to accept the appointment in order to make the appointment official. Because acceptance was not a formal process, its reality is not easily discernable. If the appointment was to some form of committee then it would normally be determined by the appointee's presence and participation. With careful study it can be readily seen that Rev. John Brown eschewed all appointments associated with the Seminary/college, called Augusta Academy, or Liberty Hall Academy. His own private Latin school, like most such ventures, had no name.

191   We do not mean to suggest that Mr. Stuart seemed aware of Rev. Brown's alienation from Liberty Hall for he does not, but he provides a valuable service by publishing many important facts about Rev. Brown's life and service as a Presbyterian minister. In our view, however, Mr. Stuart misconstrued Rev. Philip V. Fithian's journal entries concerning both Brown's role vis-a-vis Liberty Hall and about Fithian's depictions of Rev. William Graham.

is the same Rev. Brown that so many later historians have embarrassingly insisted was an early president of Washington and Lee, when, in truth, it may fairly be said that was the only known person in Virginia who actively opposed the creation of the college.[192]

****

Misuse of The Name Augusta Academy
[Note: The name Augusta Academy did not exist in the literature of the Valley of Virginia before 1775.]

Robert Alexander's school in the Valley, like most common schools in eighteenth-century America, was never given a formal name. Contrary to assertions made by several later nineteenth, and many twentieth-century authors, his school was not referred to as Augusta Academy during the time that Robert Alexander conducted it or, for that matter, at any time in the eighteenth century. No known author has provided any evidence to the contrary. Every author known to the auditor who suggested otherwise only appeared in print at least seventy-five years after the real Augusta Academy was established in October of 1774, and all of these authors either offer no authority for associating that name with the school of Robert Alexander or with Rev. John Brown's Latin School, or they cite other similar latecomers, who in turn either cited no authority, or they cited yet another nineteenth-century author. No one can point to any letter, advertisement, or other publication referring to any school in Augusta County by the name Augusta Academy other than the new academy established by the Hanover Presbytery in October of 1774. Used by the Presbytery of that unofficial name only occurred during the two years that the Academy was housed at Mount Pleasant (i.e., 1775–1776). In May of 1776, the Hanover Presbytery created a Board of Trustees for Augusta Academy and the Trustees first administrative act at their first meeting on May 13, 1776, was to give the academy its first official name, and they chose the name Liberty Hall Academy. Much confusion about these eighteenth-century Valley schools has resulted from the careless use of the name Augusta Academy.

The only reason the name "Augusta Academy" exists resulted from the Hanover Presbytery's decision to establish a second Academy in Prince Edward County on Feb. 1, 1775. After doing this, the Presbytery found it expedient to adopt, as a convention, the practice of referring to these two schools as Augusta Academy and Prince Edward Academy respectively, in order to be able to distinguish between them in their meeting minutes. The names were never adopted officially. The Presbytery had wisely reserved the honor of naming the Academies for the anticipated Boards of Trustees. In the interregnum, the Presbytery used the county names, but before that time these names did not exist, at least not in the literature of eighteenth-century Virginia.

In the eighteenth century in North America, there was a vast array of confusing and confounding terms used to describe schools, and unfortunately

---

192 Presumably, most of Brown's immediate family shared his sentiments regarding Liberty Hall Academy. The likely exception would be Brown's daughter, Betsy, who had been engaged to Rev. Graham and whose broken marital plans were caused by her own mother, according to Archibald Alexander. See his Mss. "Memoir of Rev. William Graham."

there were no widely accepted standards by which to accurately distinguish schools of varying types. To be sure, the terms "college" and "university" were only used in reference to higher education. All other types were referred to without regard to precise nomenclature. The term "academy" in eighteenth-century America, however, was, more often than not, limited in its applicability to institutions offering higher education but lacking a charter from the Crown's authorities. In British North America colonies it was deemed inappropriate to use the term "college" in reference to a school unless it had received a charter from the governing authorities. That tradition changed, of course, following the Revolution, but the practice in the new United States in some cases was held over for a time after the Revolution, as was the case with Liberty Hall Academy, which after obtaining its incorporation and charter with degree-granting authority, elected to retain the then well-established name, Liberty Hall Academy.

It would have been viewed as exceedingly presumptuous in eighteenth-century Virginia for a school to invoke the term "academy" if that school was merely preparatory in nature. Presumably, that is one reason why Rev. John Brown always referred to the school that he organized as his "Latin School," not an academy. In fact, most of the schools operated by Presbyterian pastors in connection with their pastorate were common schools and were rarely given a name. For this reason, authors in the latter half of the nineteenth century should have suspected that the name "Augusta Academy" did not refer to Robert Alexander's common school or to Rev. John Brown's "Latin School."

Many authors have inappropriately used the name Augusta Academy when referring to the schools of Robert Alexander or Rev. John Brown, and in so doing, they added to the confusion surrounding the various schools conducted in the Valley of Virginia in the late eighteenth and early nineteenth century. That name should only be used to refer to the academy founded by the Hanover Presbytery in Augusta County in 1774.

Robert Alexander and his brother Archibald Alexander (Old Ersbel), as he was known, both gave instruction to young people who lived in the vicinity of Timber Ridge or Old Providence congregations, but very little useful information has been passed down about either of these their educational endeavors. Neither Augusta Academy nor its successor, Liberty Hall Academy, was ever located near or adjacent to the New Providence Congregation's Meeting House where Brown's Latin school was conducted after it was relocated there in the 1760s, by Rev. John Brown, and there is no eighteenth-century evidence to the contrary. Contrary representations did not begin to appear until after Foote published his *Sketches of Virginia, Historical and Biographical*, in 1850.[193]

****

---

193 Foote's second series published in 1855 was published under the same basic title as Foote's First Series published in 1850. In the second book, he embellished his earlier mistaken representations about the origins of Washington College, now Washington and Lee. University. The second book is entitled *Sketches of Virginia, Historical and Biographical, Series Two*.

Liberty Hall & Hampden Sydney Academies: the Sequence of Establishment & Sequence of Chartering Errors as between These two Academies

Sequence of Establishment

Numerous authors, beginning with Edward Graham in his 1821 "Memoir of the Late Rev. William Graham, A.M."[194] mistakenly assert that the first Academy established by the Hanover Presbytery in Virginia was the seminary established in Prince Edward County under the leadership of Rev. Samuel Stanhope Smith. Those who claimed this were quite clearly mistaken. The Hanover Presbytery that was responsible for establishing both of these seminaries also created and maintained official meeting minutes that are recorded in a record book from that period, and in no way are they uncertain or unclear about the dates of their respective creations. The meeting minutes inform that Liberty Hall Academy (temporarily called Augusta Academy) was established, or created, on October 13, 1774. Hampden Sydney Academy (earlier Prince Edward Academy), on the other hand, was not established until Feb. 1, 1775.[195]

On the day following the establishment of Augusta Academy (October 14, 1774), the Hanover Presbytery discussed the possibility of establishing a second seminary on the other side of the Blue Ridge Mountains and, toward that end, authorized a campaign to obtain subscriptions for establishing such a seminary somewhere east of the Mountains, but this was merely a feasibility study and was clearly only a provisional campaign. In other words, the Presbytery indicated that it was predisposed to establishing a second seminary, provided that the requisite funds could be secured and further provided that a suitable candidate could be secured to take charge of such a venture. On this, the meeting minutes are crystal clear. It then set a date in April for their subsequent spring meeting to be held at Timber Ridge Meeting House. Thus, the 1774 autumn meeting of the Presbytery ended.

Early the next year, a select group of members of the Presbytery sought to convene a special previously unscheduled meeting pro re nata, which met on February 1, 1775. The purpose was to establish the hoped-for academy east of the mountains. At this meeting, the members who were present got slightly ahead of themselves and selected Samuel Stanhope Smith in absentia to take charge of the prospective seminary, but they lost sight of the fact that, technically, they should have first decided to "establish" the school. Supposedly, the school was later assumed to have been "established" at that meeting by virtue of their having selected someone to manage the intended school. It would have been better if they had first formally decided to establish and patronize a second seminary of learning in Virginia. This group also failed to properly secure the meeting minutes for this

---

194   Edward Graham, "A Memoir of The Late Rev. William Graham, A.M." *The Evangelical and Literary Magazine and Missionary Chronicle*, IV (1821), pg.75 et Seq.

195   The Presbytery's February 1, 1775, meeting was a special and previously unscheduled one and was called for the very specific purpose of formally deciding to establish and patronize a second seminary in Virginia, which was to be located east of the Blue Ridge Mountains.

special meeting, and they were, for a time, assumed to be lost. The minutes were eventually either found or they were retrospectively reconstructed, and minutes were inserted into their record book, but they are not located in the record book in the proper chronological order. Such are the various vicissitudes that are common to the early stages of Revolutions.

Liberty Hall Academy, as has been explained, was established before Hampden Sydney Academy, not as some have represented it, the other way around. In both cases, once the schools were formally "established and patronized" by the Presbytery, and it became clear that plans were well under way to erect the Academies, the Presbytery created for each of the schools, a Board of Trustees. At this time, both academies were, for a brief time, institutions that existed merely "on paper." This condition, of course, is the way most colleges begin. A full complement of classes (freshmen through seniors) cannot possibly exist by simply waving a magic wand. They must be cultivated over the course of three or four years. Still, it seems entirely reasonable to date one's origins to the time when its founders declare that it is hereby established.

Classes at Augusta Academy were conducted by William Graham in 1775 and 1776 "in the form of a preparatory grammar school" at a place called locally Mount Pleasant. Here, in rude temporary quarters learning began while campus buildings were being constructed on lands adjacent to the Timber Ridge Meeting House. Classes at Hampden Sydney were anticipated to have begun the last part of 1775, but in fact, they did not actually begin until January of 1776. Liberty Hall's classes were also continuing on at Mount Pleasant in 1776, but the school's classes were transferred from Mount Pleasant to the newly constructed buildings at Timber Ridge in January of 1777. From this time forward, Liberty Hall Academy began distinguishing between the Academy and its associated grammar school, which had been created by Mr. Graham as a "substratum upon which to construct its superstructure."[196] In this, Mr. Graham was following a principle he had learned from his Princeton preceptor, Dr. John Witherspoon. Witherspoon appointed Graham to conduct Princeton's associated grammar school even while Graham was himself a student in the regular academic program.

Sequence of Chartering:

There has also been some confusion as to the correct sequence of the legislature's granting of charters to these two academies after the Revolutionary War. Following the same sequence, Liberty Hall Academy, under the leadership of Rev. William Graham in Augusta County, was granted a charter with college-degree-granting authority in the fall of 1782. Prince Edward Academy, then under the leadership of Rev. John Blair Smith, was granted a Charter the following year in 1783. In both cases, the institutional records of these two institutions and

---

196 "He [Graham] not only gave instruction in the scientific and classical departments, but paid special attention to the grammar school. "Here," said he, "should be laid a substratum on which to build a superstructure of learning." [Campbell, Dr. Samuel L., "Washington College, Va." reprinted in W&L Hist. Papers No. 1, 1890, pg 115.

those of the Hanover Presbytery are absolutely clear. It is therefore a mystery as to why so many historians seem to have been unable to accurately report when each academy was established.

Liberty Hall was unquestionably established, incorporated and chartered before Hampden Sydney as is evinced by the Hanover Presbytery's meeting minutes between 1771 and 1776. In each case, Liberty Hall's status predates that of her sister Academy in Prince Edward County. Those few who have suggested otherwise were demonstrably incorrect.

****

Further Published Historical Errors that Concern Liberty Academy's Rector (i.e., first president) Rev. William Graham.

Included below are a few basic findings that will be detailed in the main body of the report concerning written historical errors in regards to the university's founding first president, William Graham.

- Contrary to the mistaken representations of many, Liberty Hall's president, Rev. William Graham's tenure as a Presbyterian minister is free of any notice that he was ever censured by the church. This did not occur, not once, not ever.

  > *Note: Some authors misread a notice in the official records of the Presbyterian Church that failed to emphasize that a complaint lodged against Graham by the infamous Rev. Hezekiah Balch, had improperly proceeded and a committee had made improper comments that were printed in the record. This matter was begun in an improper Ecclesiastical Court but that court, having subsequently realized its jurisdictional error, withdrew the incomplete case and transferred it to the proper court. The proper court held a complete review and acquitted Rev. Graham. He was not censured.*[197]

- Contrary to the representations of many, Rev. William Graham did not precipitate a schism within the New Providence

---

[197] This matter is discussed in detail in the main body of the report. It is noteworthy that Rev. Balch, who knew better, intentionally filed his complaint against Graham in the wrong court. The improper Synod committee inappropriately commented on the case after only hearing from the complainant Rev. Balch. Embarrassingly, the committee's premature comments were printed in the published proceedings even though the Synod having recognized their error in accepting the case had withdrawn the matter and transferred it to the proper court. This was the proximate cause of the historical mistake. The final determination was to acquit Graham which was, by inference, a rebuke against Balch, who later became notorious as a serial disputatious rabble-rouser.

Congregation of Rev. John Brown. This calumny is disproved in the main body of this report.

> *Note: A significant clue in this regard is that Rev. Brown who had the most to lose as a result of this schism, did not complain to church officials charging Graham with having brought about the division in his congregation which he obviously would have done, if there was any such case to be made. The same is true for Brown's congregation's Elders, any one of whom could have lodged a complaint, but no such claim was ever made by a member of Brown's congregation. The only claims that Graham was the proximate cause of the schism were made by persons who were not involved or even alive at the time of the events surrounding the affair.*

- Contrary to the representations of many, Rev. William Graham was not out of step with his brethren in regard to his playing a pivotal role in the politics related to the formation of the United States Government. Mr. Graham's political involvement was limited in scope and entirely consistent with the activities of his mentor and preceptor at Princeton, Dr. John Witherspoon, who was the only clergyman signer of the Declaration of Independence, and who was a member of the first Continental Congress as well as a Presbyterian minister. Graham, along with his friend Patrick Henry, George Mason, and Richard Henry Lee, was an ardent anti-federalist who opposed ratification of the proposed new Constitution that did not then contain the Bill of Rights.

- Contrary to the representations of some, Rev. William Graham's ministerial colleagues agreed with him in the matter of the Whiskey Rebellion resolution of Rev. Moses Hoge and consequently, the Virginia Synod decided that the matter was, as Rev. Graham contended, a purely civil matter outside the jurisdiction of their ecclesiastical court. His opposition to Hoge's proposed resolution, was based, in the main, upon jurisdictional grounds. Graham contended the issue was of a purely civil nature. Some have suggested that Graham's opposition was based on his support for the "Whiskey Rebels." Moses Hoge was Graham's earlier student, Hoge's son assures his readers that the dispute between his father and Rev. Graham centered around the jurisdictional issue.

- Contrary to the representations of some, William Graham's lectures were never written down or transcribed. Copies of lectures at Washington and Lee University that are said to be those of Rev. Graham are not William Graham's lectures; they are the lectures of Dr. John Witherspoon, President of Princeton, transcribed by William Graham when he was a student at Princeton. These lectures were distributed by William Graham and others at Liberty Hall Academy and used as textbooks. They were later misinterpreted as being those written by and "delivered by Rev. William Graham." Based on one essay in a packet of essays, One twentieth-century author, Dr. David Robson libeled Rev. Graham as a defender of slavery. This matter is addressed and repudiated in detail in an Appendix to this report.

•   Contrary to the 1890 representations of Mr. Joseph A. Waddell, there exists no known evidence to support his contention that Rev. William Graham was an "imprudent man." Rather, Rev. Graham succeeded, against great odds, in accomplishing his every known major professional objective during his joint careers as a Presbyterian minister, Founding College President, Founding Theological Seminary President, leader of the Presbyterian coup d' etat that reversed the Hanover Presbytery's 1784 last-minute acquiescence on separation of church and state and educational and social innovator. This latter role is made evident by his enrolling and educating the first black college graduate in America, and then enrolling the first black Presbyterian ministerial candidate in America into the theological seminary in Lexington affiliated with Liberty Hall Academy. As a result, that student, John Chavis, became the first black Presbyterian minister in America.

Earlier, President Graham enrolled into his chartered degree-granting college the first female member of a regular academic college program and consequently was the first female college student in North America. In the early 1790s, the Virginia Synod created the first church patronized theological seminary in America with President Graham as its President. Graham's final major endeavor on behalf of the college he had given birth to was to persuade his Board of Trustees to allow him to draft a letter to President, George Washington, in their name, advocating that Liberty Hall be awarded a large financial endowment that the President was preparing to bestow upon a worthy educational endeavor. Washington subsequently did award the endowment to Liberty Hall Academy. Perhaps, Mr. Waddell, held the view that some, or all of these actions by Rev. Graham were "imprudent." If so, the auditor respectfully disagrees.

Note: The above does not comprise an exhaustive list of Pres. William Graham's professional achievements but is merely a generous sample of his many accomplishments. At the same time, Graham was indeed once unsuccessful when he offered himself up as a candidate for delegate to the

Virginia convention held to consider ratification of the proposed new US Constitution. Graham was an anti-federalist aligned Patrick Henry, George Mason, and others; they opposed ratifying original draft on several counts, the most compelling of which was the absence of a Bill of Rights. Their opposition revealed the degree of dissatisfaction with not having a Bill of Rights included in the Constitution and caused James Madison to publicly promise, if ratified, that such a Bill of Rights would be one of the first orders of business of the new Congress. A promise he quickly made good. If their anti-Federalist campaign against ratification in this regard is considered by Waddell to be "imprudent," the auditor respectfully disagrees. Other than this example, the auditor was unable to identify any significant personal or professional act by Rev. Graham that could even remotely be interpreted as having been imprudent.[198] If not winning one particular election constitutes "imprudence" then, the United States is riddled with imprudent men, including several presidents of the United States, one of whom wrote and delivered the Gettysburg Address.

- Contrary to many nineteenth- and twentieth-century historians, Rev. William Graham did not follow his misguided colleagues who had acquiesced on the churches long-standing opposition to any form of taxation to support churches or church-sponsored schools. Instead, he mounted a successful grassroots campaign to repudiate actions of his colleagues in this regard and led the fight to obtain the Presbyterian Church's support for passing Jefferson's Bill for Religious Freedom. This concerted effort in opposition to the Bill is now credited as being the key factor in breaking the Bill loose from the log-jam that had kept it languishing for several years in committee, despite Mr. Madison's repeated efforts to obtain its passage. Mr. Graham's leadership of the successful campaign, which later defeated his friend Patrick Henry's Bill, was the reason why the general convention of Virginia Presbyterians had earlier selected Rev. William Graham to draft its final official message to the Virginia Legislature announcing their final position in opposition to any assessments (i.e., taxes) that would be used to support religion and its absolute unqualified opposition to taxing the citizens to support the any church. This message written at the behest of all Presbyterians in Virginia together with the ten thousand signatures on petitions opposing any assessment to support the church is viewed by several twentieth-century scholars as being the key to the defeat of Henry's Bill on assessment. It was President Graham's leadership that is credited with the Presbyterian Church in Virginia reversing the ill-advised course of Graham's fellow ministers. This reversal and Graham's

---

198 *The Graham v Balch affair has been discussed in detail elsewhere. Graham's public letter accusing Rev. Balch of improper behavior as an instigator of mob violence and burnings or hanging of two rival Presbyterian ministers was determined by an ecclesiastical Court to have been, essentially correct in every respect. This court rejected Rev. Balch's complaint. The judgment in this case was not appealed by Rev. Balch.*

associated petition campaign, joined by the Baptists, that is seen as the key to Jefferson's Bill for religious Freedom being rescued from virtual oblivion, and then passed into law. This law, in turn, became the model used by Graham's old Princeton schoolmate James Madison, to formulate the establishment clause of the First Amendment in our nation's Bill of Rights.

Princeton's professor Charles Grier Sellers astutely said this concerning Liberty Hall Academy's President William Graham:

> In the spring of 1784, just as the assessment movement was gaining headway, John Smith drew up for the Presbyterian clergy an ambiguous memorial to the legislature. . . . coupled with one for "an equal protection and favor of government to all denominations of Christians . . . .When the Presbytery convened at Timber Ridge in October, just before the meeting of the legislature, the general assessment idea was attacked by William Graham, John Smith's Princeton classmate whom Samuel Smith had brought to Virginia to superintend the Valley Presbyterian's Liberty Hall Academy. Graham was a radical democrat and a born agitator, . . ." (Sellers, John Blair Smith, pps. 211–212)

Sellers continues:

> **Smith's defeat** was a triumph for William Graham, who drafted the convention's vehement denunciation of any legislation on religion . . . The final blow to assessment was the loss of its strongest legislative champion through Patrick Henry's election as governor. "It was . . . In July, 1788, that Smith, . . . withdrew from active supervision of the College [Hampden-Sydney] . . . With Smith out of the way, Patrick Henry undertook to get the state's grants to William and Mary divided with Hampden-Sydney, and Henry's crony and fellow opponent of the Constitution,[199] William Graham, was offered the Presidency." [200] (Emphasis Added)

(Sellers, ibid.)

[Auditor's note: Graham declined his friend Henry's offer and stayed with Liberty Hall.]

---

199 President Graham joined with other antifederalists, Patrick Henry, George Mason, et al., in opposition to the original draft of the proposed Constitution, due in large measure to the fact that it did not yet contain a Bill of Rights. It is generally accepted that the opposition to ratification of the Constitution by antifederalists was responsible for the Congress's passage of the Bill of Rights as proposed amendments to the newly ratified United States Constitution.

200 [Charles G. Sellers, jr., "John Blair Smith," Journal of The Presbyterian Historical Association, Vol. XXXIV, No. 4., Dec. 1956, pp. 201–225)] esp. pg. 214, 217–18.

Auditor's Note: Prior to Liberty Hall Academy's rector, Rev. Wm. Graham initiating his campaign to reverse the 1784 action of his brethren, which was, in effect, a surrender on the assessment question, Patrick Henry's Bill that would have taxed the citizenry to support religion and religious schools was viewed as most likely to pass and become the law in Virginia. His brethren, in fact, had expressed their view that the Bill's passage was a foregone conclusion and that consequently it was prudent and expedient to "get on board" lest they be left out in the cold, so to speak, and therefore, they agreed to alter their earlier unqualified opposition to any assessment. They then asked the leader of the movement, Rev. John B. Smith, to alter their position and draft the communication or "memorial" to the Virginia legislature announcing their change-of-heart. The Presbytery also appointed Rev. Graham to the drafting committee, presumably because of his active opposition, in hopes of smoothing any ruffled feathers of Mr. Graham. If so, their plan failed in this regard because Rev. Graham demurred and elected instead to circumvent the Presbytery by appealing to the much wider organization of Virginia Presbyterians which required the Presbyterians to come together in an unprecedented general convention. In this, Rev. Graham was exceedingly successful. Indeed, it soon became readily apparent that the larger body of Presbyterians were fairly well in universal agreement with Mr. Graham, and consequently the Hanover Presbytery abandoned the idea of acquiescing on assessment. The outcome strained the relations between Rev. Graham and Rev. Smith for some time. (See Charles Grier Sellers, *"John Blair Smith,"* Journal of the Presbyterian Historical Society, Vol. XXXIV, No. 4., December 1956, pp. 201–225.)

Conclusion of Prolegomenon:

Hopefully, this introduction will be useful in providing a more accurate foundation for studying the massive number of mistakes concerning the founding of Washington and Lee University and also concerning the university's eminently successful first president, Rev. William Graham. The various mistakes discussed in this report were replicated by numerous authors which were published and then republished over the course of a hundred and fifty years. As historians know, lies repeated endlessly over time have a way of eventually seeming to be true, but of course, facts are indeed stubborn things. These particular false narratives needed to be corrected and brought into conformity with all the early official records in order to for the true history to once again be revealed.

As has been demonstrated herein, the official records, in the main, are consistent with all the known eyewitness' eighteenth-century testimony (written by men of the highest character) who substantiate the written histories pertaining to the college's origins that were written during the university's first seventy-five years.[201] Moreover, these same witnesses' testimony repudiate with certainty virtually all of the histories pertaining to the institution's founding that were printed after 1849.[202]

---

201 The one serious exception pertains to the sequence of establishment between Augusta Academy (Liberty Hall Academy) and Prince Edward Academy (Later, Hampden Sydney College). Several authors mistakenly followed Edward Graham on this issue, but Edward, who was not in Virginia at the time of the establishment of either school, misunderstood the sequence and incorrectly assumed that Prince Edward Academy was established before Augusta Academy. The accurate order is just the reverse.

202 There have been a few exceptions, but typically these are cursory representations made in minor and nonserious pieces appearing in newspapers or popular magazines which are almost never cited as authorities by historians.

The auditor's analysis of several published attacks pertaining to the character of the university's founder and first president, Rev. William Graham, reveal in every case that they are baseless and contrary to the pertinent facts and evidence. Astoundingly, the auditor could not locate even one case wherein a published indictment of Mr. Graham was, or possibly could be, sustained by any known credible evidence. In each case, the authors of these indictments provide no persuasive evidence to support the truth of their claim, and in some cases, the indictment is completely illogical. One suspects that Mr. Graham's few but influential enemies and their descendants waged a relentless campaign to traduce the character of the man, Rev. William Graham. Perhaps, this apparent animus was because of his reluctant withdrawal of an accepted proposal of marriage to a daughter of Rev. John Brown or possibly because of his decision to enroll and educate the nation's first black college graduate. Ultimately, the rationale behind this campaign of character assassination against a deceased man who could not defend himself, is, and will likely remain unknown with any degree of certainty. Fortunately, the facts of Rev. William Graham's life, once revealed, speak for themselves.

The best example of an indictment of Rev. Graham that is illogical is the charge that Rev. Graham was responsible for the schism that occurred in the New Providence Church's congregation (circa late 1780s) when he, as a visiting minister, introduced a hymn into the service, the author of which, a few members found offensive. Supposedly then, a failed attempt to interrupt the service caused a permanent schism within the congregation, and Rev. Graham, it is suggested, was the proximate cause. This conclusion is so absurd that it is stupefying.[203] Why would any group of sane congregants punish themselves, their fellow congregants, and their own minister by leaving the congregation due to a minor act of a visiting minister to use a hymn written by someone whose hymns were authorized by the national organization of Presbyterians?[204] That this puerile notion has persisted is truly astounding.

It was also found during this investigation that in virtually every known case, the published attacks upon President Graham's character came at the hands of men who did not know Mr. Graham and who had misinterpreted either official eighteenth-century records or the written works of others who had come before them. By far, the most ridiculous and the most egregious attack against President Graham was the series of attacks made by Professor David W. Robson, in an article published by the William and Mary Quarterly in 1980. Robson's primary charge being that Washington and Lee's first president was the first academic defender of slavery in America and that he lectured to his college's students in defense of slavery. A charge which is patently absurd and demonstrably false. Mr.

---

203 Archibald Alexander criticized his preceptor on this subject in his manuscript memoir of Graham, but his criricism was based on a misconception which is dealt with and explained in the author's errors section of the report. The treatment is located in the subsection devoted to Archibald Alexander.

204 The author of the Hymn that appears to have been offensive is none other than Rev. Isaac Watts, the author of the hymn, *Joy to the World.*

Robson made the colossal blunder of attacking someone he obviously knew next to nothing about, based upon a handwritten packet of lectures that he didn't bother to appropriately research and authenticate.[205] If he had, he would have discovered that the lectures he relied upon were not those of his subject, but instead were the lectures of his subject's own preceptor, the venerable Rev. John Witherspoon, president of Princeton.[206]

As stated clearly by both Professor Edward Graham and Rev. Dr. Archibald Alexander, founding and first president of the Princeton Theological Seminary, William's Graham's lectures were never written down. He delivered his lectures, like his sermons, after extensive study, extemporaneously. The packet of lectures that Dr. Robson relied upon, was not an original set of the lectures or even a copy of the originals. They were, at best, a copy of a copy made by other students and then in 1896 recopied by a professor, a century after they were last copied by a student.[207] They are principally a set of lectures originally written by Dr. Witherspoon, not William Graham.[208] The packet of lectures was used as a sort

---

205 It is true that the lecture relied upon by Dr. Robson is part of a packet of numerous lectures that has a cover page that asserts that the packet contains the lectures delivered by William Graham in 1796. It is also true that the staff at the library have relied upon the accuracy of that cover page, but that cover page was created a century after the student named on that page first transcribed the lectures, and as an 1896 creation of the last copyist the cover page itself has no provenance, and the language of the assertions are nothing more than that. That is extremely problematic because the claims are persuasively untrue. The evidence and argumentation are detailed in the report. The assertions moreover, contradict well established facts. No Lectures by Graham were ever written. The packet contains lectures originally written by Dr. Witherspoon, President of Princeton, and they were transcribed there by Mr. Graham when he was a student. Graham in turn used them as a template which students at Liberty Hall copied and used as textbooks.

206 As discussed in greater depth elsewhere in this report, the specific lecture that was Dr. Robson's primary concern while in many ways similar to Dr. Witherspoon's own writings on the subject may have been authored by someone else, and if so, it was most likely a revised version of an essay, written by professor Edward Graham, the president's younger brother. Edward's essay was written as a submission to the Governor of Virginia, Mr. Randolph, who had sponsored an essay contest, and of course, young Edward Graham, wrote with the objective of winning a prize. His true sentiments, therefore, cannot be ascertained based on the essay alone. As a professor at Washington College, Edward, would certainly have had his students copy the lectures of Dr. Witherspoon, and the template he used was likely the same one he himself had made while a student, with a couple of lectures he may have added for his own purposes. The packet of lectures used at Washington and Lee in those days was used a textbook, and every student made their own copy. This allowed each possessor of such a packet to modify their own packet as they saw fit.

207 The instructor who recopied this particular packet in 1896, Mr. Pratt, apparently, assumed they were Rev. Graham's lectures, but they were not, as one can readily discern from the two early memoirs of Rev. Graham written by Graham's younger brother, Professor Edward Graham and that of Rev. Archibald Alexander, the Presbyterian historian and president of Princeton Theological Seminary, who was an early student at Liberty Hall Academy. Both of these authors insisted that Graham's lectures were all delivered without notes and none were ever transcribed, much to their regret.

208 All students at Liberty Hall copied a set of these lectures. They were then used as a textbook. Needless to say, anyone who had such a packet was free to add material of their own or to edit them as they saw fit. The lecture relied upon by Dr. Robson was quite likely an addition inserted

of textbook at Liberty Hall much like at Princeton. Graham, like numerous of his classmates at Princeton who went on to become educators of various types, made use of those lectures in the same manner as Dr. Witherspoon. In some cases, like Samuel Doak, in Tennessee, his set of lectures obtained at Princeton would also later be mistakenly attributed to the student (Doak) who originally copied them at Princeton.

The cover sheet upon which Dr. Robson foolishly relied and which is his only supporting evidence has no provenance whatsoever, and the text of the cover page is so grossly inaccurate that it is hardly possible that it is a copy of the original cover, if such a cover ever existed, made by the Liberty Hall student who copied them from a template.

Because each set of lectures is handwritten and gathered together by whomever possessed them, it is virtually impossible to know whether any given set of lectures had been edited, added to, or had been partially deleted from its original form. In this particular case, it is entirely possible that the one lecture that Robson based his article upon was not Witherspoon's lecture. It may well be a slightly modified or edited version of an essay written by the then student, Edward Graham, for the purpose of winning a prize. It may not have even reflected Edward's views since the objective was to earn a prize. Edward Graham, it is believed, was the named student's instructor while at Liberty Hall, and Edward Graham may have been the instructor who made his own copy of Witherspoon's lectures, available to Joseph Glass. What is quite certain is that Rev. William Graham did not write any lecture of give any lecture defending African slavery in America. If he had, history can be certain that such an item would not have escaped the attention of his early biographers, but for obvious reasons, no one ever made a claim that William Graham was a defender of slavery in either the eighteenth or nineteenth century. This glaring fact should have put the overcredulous Mr. Robson on his guard, but instead he assumed that he alone had discovered what everyone else had missed for nearly two centuries. In truth, Robson was simply wrong, and being so, he severely traduced a man of eminent worth and smeared him unmercifully. Indeed, he magnified his character assassination of Graham in several other ways dragging his character through the mud of history. His vile attacks on Graham's character seem to have been personal but the n. of course, he never knew the subject of his venom. His motivations aside, Robson's every attack was subjected to intense scrutiny with the result that his every charge against

---

by Edward Graham into his own packet after he became a professor at Washington College. The subject matter and argumentation found in this essay is nearly identical to that used by Edward Graham in a prize-winning essay he crafted as an entry into a contest initiated by Gov. Randolph. Edward was undoubtedly an instructor of the student, Joseph Glass, who had made the copy in 1796. A later instructor, Mr. Pratt, recopied Glass's packet a century later. Pratt foolishly attributed the entire packet to William Graham. The auditor cannot prove this scenario, but it the most likely scenario given that the student Glass would hardly have claimed the lectures were delivered by Graham when Graham was mostly absent from the campus during the time the cover page claims that he "delivered" the lectures. Mr. Pratt obviously just assumed that they were delivered by Graham, but that claim cannot possibly be true.

Graham was false and his every derogatory assertion can and was, herein, easily disproved, his current reputation as an historian notwithstanding.

(Note: See the appendix dedicated to the false allegation that Graham was a defender of African slavery in America for details about the many reasons why Robson's only source for support of his main thesis, was not what Robson believed it to be.)

The authors selected for assessment in this report include historians, genealogists, chroniclers and church record keepers, as well as institutional archivists and even one of the university's librarians. None of these authors correctly reported the date of the college's founding after 1849, and most of them mistakenly believed that Rev. John Brown's Latin School was directly linked to Liberty Hall Academy and confused the public school operating at Mount Pleasant under the patronage of the Hanover Presbytery, in 1775 and 1776, with Rev. Brown's private Latin School operating on the grounds of the New Providence Presbyterian Church, which was then located at Moffett's Creek.

As a group, the historians of W&L's founding, writing after 1850, constitute in large measure the proverbial blind leading the blind concerning the founding of Washington and Lee. This does not mean, however, that many of their works were in vain because the errors we have focused on relate, in the main, to the institution's first seventy-five years. Historians like Dr. Ollinger Crenshaw, Dr. Taylor Sanders, Dr. John M. McDaniel, Rev. George West Diehl, and many others left many historical treasures for which posterity must be eternally grateful. It does mean, however, that all the histories associated with Washington and Lee need to be reread, analyzed, and tested for validity, including, of course, those authors just mentioned. The earliest histories, however, will stand up well under the closest scrutiny. Those after 1850 are universally in error about the college's founding and also on many points about the college's first president, Rev. William Graham. The numerous errors concerning Rev. William Graham are mostly errors made by authors who relied on tradition and gossip to fashion their own disparaging remarks about the first president. In this they repeatedly missed the mark, as it were. They seem to have ignored the inconsistency of their attacks on Graham's character and the fact that Rev. Graham was consistently selected by his colleagues and peers during his entire tenure as college president and Presbyterian theologian and divine for the highest positions related to his profession. For example, President Washington bestowed the largest educational endowment in the nation's history to Graham's College in the mountains, Patrick Henry sent several delegations on a mission to purloin Graham's services to be the president of Hampden Sydney, the Virginia Synod selected Graham to be president of the first church patronized theological seminary in America. These are testaments of the highest order, and the entire body of Virginia Presbyterian selected Graham to draft their final memorial on separation of church and state and in support of Jefferson's Bill for religious liberty.

It seemed appropriate at this juncture to provide the reader with but a small sample of the views of the man that is this university's founding father and first president, William Graham, who published these words while other American founding fathers were attempting to fashion a constitution for the new nation in 1786:

Quotes from President William Graham

(Written at or about the time of the founding of the United States of America)

A Republic is a government, by equal and just laws, made by common consent, for the common benefit, ***and not the dominion of one community over another community***, ...which is founded in the perfect, political equality of all the citizens.

*Note: Could Graham's phrase, ".***and not the dominion of one community over another community*** refer to anything other than the institution of slavery?*

Every violation of the perfect equality of the citizens, is a step towards tyranny.

That government is excellent, ***which inviolably preserves the equality of the citizens***, both in civil and a religious respect.

Let us try to know our rights and assert our privileges, free from the heat of passion, or the prejudice of party. Let us remember that we are acting for ages; and let us endeavour to secure the applause and gratitude of posterity, ***by securing to them a precious birth right of perfect freedom and political equality***.

(William Graham, *An Essay on Government*, Phil. 1786.) (Emphasis added)

These are but a few of the views of the man who the Virginia Presbyterian Clergymen asked to come to the Valley of Virginia from his family's home in Pennsylvania in 1774, to accept the honor of implementing their proposal to establish a new institution of higher education west of the Blue Ridge Mountains. This was an endeavor that they hoped would provide Virginia with the opportunity to provide a college education for their young men on a par with that instruction then being offered at the College of New Jersey (Princeton.) Mr. Graham accepted the offer of these educated clergymen, and to this task he devoted his entire professional career. When he retired twenty-two years later (1796), Rev. William Graham had guided the Hanover Presbytery's project from proposal to complete fruition. He left in the hands of the institution's guardian Trustees a noble campus with a then modern stone main building representing the first chartered institution in the new State of Virginia with degree-granting authority authorized by the Commonwealth of Virginia's first state legislature. He also left and a long list of admirable alumni, many of whom went on to found some of the most eminent colleges and Academies of the south and the West.

Just as his preceptor Rev. John Witherspoon had done as president of his college, Graham delved into the politics of the new nation in his adopted state of Virginia. Witherspoon met with the Continental Congress and signed the Declaration of Independence while Graham drafted a proposed state Constitution (Frankland/Franklin) and led the successful grassroots campaign to defeat the proposal to tax the people in support of religion and subsequently to enact

Jefferson's Bill for Religious Liberty. In the process, Graham was invited by the General Convention of Virginia Presbyterians to write their final communication on religious freedom and liberty.

With these two major political successes, the president of Liberty Hall withdrew from the political scene and devoted his remaining years to the college and to establishing a patronized Theological Seminary in association with the college which he administered for several years prior to his death.

At the pinnacle of his career, Graham was the most sought-after college president in Virginia. Gov. Patrick Henry along with Board of Trustees of Hampden Sydney repeatedly sent delegations to Lexington appealing to President Graham to leave Liberty Hall for the greener financial pastures east of the Blue Ridge Mountains by accepting their offers of the Presidency of Hampden Sydney College.

As the leading Presbyterian minister in Virginia, the Virginia Synod established, and patronized the first active Theological Seminary in the nation connected to a college and appointed Graham as its president. Numerous Congregations appealed to Rev. Graham to accept a call from their churches on both sides of the Blue Ridge Mountains. He chose to remain in Lexington with his college and his congregations while presiding over the new Theological Seminary. When, the Synod initiated a comprehensive missionary program they appealed to Rev. Graham to chair the Committee created to oversee these probationary ministers' missionary experiences.

In this regard, we have these interesting insights from one of the well-known Virginia ministers, Rev. William Hill, written during his missionary experiences, the following is from Hill's Autobiographical Journal:

> Mon July 25 1791, I rode to Lexington, spent the day with Mr. Graham.

> Tues July 26, 1791, I spent the greatest part of my day at Mr. Saml Lyles[209],[sic] In the afternoon I rode to Lexington and spent the night at Mr. Alexanders. (.pg. 79)

> Fr. July 29, 1791, I rode to Lexington, **spent the day, enjoying the edifying conversation of the great and good man Mr. Graham.** (Autobiog....pg. 79.)

> Mr. Graham, of Lexington, was present and preached on Saturday; *and on Sabbath,*

> ***Mr. Graham preached in the forenoon, one of the greatest sermons I ever heard. I sat under it with great delight, and***

---

209   Samuel Lyle, Trustee and long-time treasurer of Liberty Hall Academy. Mr. Lyle was the father-in-law of Mr. Graham's brother, Michael Graham. Michael Graham was married to Elizabeth Lyle as was much esteemed for her learning and wit [see Philip V. Fithian, Journal 1775–1776]

its fruit was sweet to my taste. (Rev, William Hill, _Autobiographical Sketches of Dr. William Hill: together with his account of the revival of religion in Prince Edward County, and biographical sketches of the life and character of the Reverend Dr. Moses Hoge of Virginia_, Richmond, 1968. Also, published, in part, in Foote's _Sketches of Virginia_, Second Series, pg. 185.) (Emphasis added here above does not indicate error.)

The remains of the university's founder and first president, Rev. William Graham' lie beneath a large marble slab surrounded by a wrought-iron fence just outside the Lee Chapel on the current campus of Washington and Lee University. These remains had been reinterred in 1911 when they were removed from the St. John's Episcopal cemetery in Richmond, where Mr. Graham had been buried following his sudden demise from pneumonia. He died in June of 1799 while on a business visit to that city. His remains had been reinterred in 1911 when they were removed from the St John's Episcopal cemetery in Richmond where he had been buried following his sudden demise from pneumonia in 1799. Trustee, William A. Anderson chaired the committee responsible for the reinterment and his article detailing the momentous occasion is housed in the holdings of the Leyburn Library at Washington and Lee University.[210] Below is the text included upon the Tombstone of the university's founding first president William Graham:

Epitaph of William Graham

Sacred
to the Memory
of the
Rev. William Graham
*Founder and twenty years Rector of
Washington Academy*[211] in
Rockbridge County
Virginia.

---

210   William A. Anderson, An article, "Rev. William Graham, Founder, and Rector of Washington and Lee" published in the, Lexington Gazette, Vol 107, No. 19, May, 10, 1911; also, An article "William Graham, Founder of Washington and Lee, Teacher, Preacher, and Patriot," The Rockbridge County News, May 5, 1911. William. A. Anderson's remarks made on March 5, 1911, in the University Chapel during the ceremony associated with the reinterment of the remains of Rev. William Graham. Trustee, Anderson was in charge of the reinterment of President Graham's remains from St. Johns Churchyard cemetery in Richmond, Virginia. Anderson was the Attorney General of Virginia and he realized that the college's first President was Rev. William Graham.

211   *The college's only official name during Rev. Graham's tenure was Liberty Hall Academy. Prior to the creation of the Board of Trustees, the institution was unofficially referred to as Augusta Academy or designations similar in nature. The newly created Board of Trustees' first official action took place on May 13, 1776, and that action was to name the school, "Liberty Hall Academy." The name Washington Academy did not exist in Virginia until after Mr. Graham had resigned the Presidency of the college in 1796.*

He was born in the State of Pennsylvania
December 19th 1746
And died in the City of Richmond
June 17th 1799
He was distinguished for the strength and
originality of his genius
And the successful tenor of his exertions
in behalf of solid literature and
evangelical piety.

President Graham's remains are buried just outside the
Lee Chapel on the campus of the university.

**********************************finis**********************************

Chapter One

Key Historical Facts
(Concerning Washington and Lee University)

Introduction:

Section 1 includes twenty important facts simply stated, and without the comprehensive listing of evidence and arguments that support them. The evidence and supporting arguments are found scattered throughout this report, and in some cases in the attached appendices.

FACT no. 1 Every known writing on the subject of the founding of Washington and Lee University published before 1850[212] contains an assertion[213] that the founding, or the establishment, of Washington and Lee University was the result of the actions of the Hanover Presbytery (Va.), which took place at its autumn meeting in October of 1774.[214]

FACT no. 2 An important fact that gives lie to the common assertion, from 1850 onward, that Washington and Lee University is the outgrowth of a private Latin school operated by Rev. John Brown *is that every such published or written assertion that is known to exist was presented without reference to any credible historical evidence to support that assertion.*[215] (Emphasis added)

FACT no. 3 An important fact that gives lie to the common assertion, from 1850 onward, that Washington and Lee University is the outgrowth of a private school operated by Robert Alexander *is that every such published or written assertion that is known to exist was presented without reference to any credible historical evidence to support that assertion.*[216] (Emphasis added)

---

212 The dubious Rev. Samuel Houston letter should not be considered as an exception to this rule. It is completely unreliable, and the alleged content is open to serious doubt, as has been demonstrated within this report.

213 In a couple of cases the assertion may be more properly labeled *an inference*, but in such cases the inference, in its proper context, is both clear and comprehensible.

214 .To be precise, the Presbytery acted to establish the new academy on the second day of its multiday meeting, which was October 13, 1774. Occasionally, early authors cited the wrong day of that meeting, but they all agreed that it was in October of 1774.

215 *After Foote's 1850 Sketches of Virginia was published, authors who made this claim either cite the erroneous Mr. Foote, someone else who had relied on Foote, or cited no authority at all, but none provided any credible or compelling evidence to support that notion.*

216 .*This fiction was not known in the Valley of Virginia in the eighteenth century. It has no basis in fact, or credible evidence, and the first published author to assert this preposterous unsupported notion is Col. Bolivar Christian, a trustee of Washington College beginning*

FACT no. 4   At the time that the Hanover Presbytery acted to formally "establish" the first and only Presbyterian-patronized Seminary in Virginia, on October 13, 1774, there was no known school operating at the place called Mount Pleasant near the Village of Fairfield. Therefore, there cannot be any Mount Pleasant-based germ from whence the college evolved.[217]

Note: Rev. Brown's Latin school, at that time, was being conducted at New Providence on Moffett's Creek. Rev. Brown had moved his family, school, and farm from Mount Pleasant to the Moffett's Creek location several miles away after his separation from the Timber Ridge congregation in 1767. (See Rev. Brown's letters in the Draper Collection, extracts from which are included in Dr. Stuart's doctoral dissertation biography of Rev. John Brown.[218])

FACT no. 5   From October of 1774 until the 1850 publication of W. H. Foote's *Sketches of Virginia*, no eighteenth-century record of the proceedings of the Hanover Presbytery had ever been presented to the public, which claimed that there was any connection between Rev. John Brown's Latin school and the presbytery's newly established Seminary in Augusta County (Liberty Hall Academy)."[219] All claims to the contrary only arise after the 1850 Foote publication, and by then all those actually responsible for creating the college were all deceased and therefore unable to raise objections to Foote's fanciful claims.[220]

FACT no. 6   No letter or public statement is known to exist that claims that Rev. John Brown, himself, ever asserted or suggested that the presbytery's newly established "Augusta Academy" emanated or evolved from his unnamed "Latin school" in the Valley of Virginia, at either Mount Pleasant (prior to 1767) or

---

in 1758. He is responsible for the hoax referred to as the "Edward Graham Memorandum," which is exposed and debunked in other sections of this report.

217 .Some have confusingly asserted that Augusta Academy was such a germ. Augusta Academy, however, is part and parcel of the presbytery's seminary and operated as an adjunct to the presbytery's establishment and appointment of William Graham to assume the "care and tuition" of that academy from its inception. During its incipiency at Mount Pleasant, it took the form of a grammar school, and according to Graham, "Here" (referring to the grammar school), 'said he,' "should be laid a substratum on which to build a superstructure of learning." (Dr. Samuel L. Campbell, "Washington College, Va.," *Southern Literary Messenger*, re-printed in W&L Historical Papers No. 1, 1890, p. 115.) Augusta Academy is Washington and Lee in its infancy, which is a reality made apparent in the meeting minutes of both the organization that created the university, and those of the institution's first board of trustees.

218 .*John White Stuart III, The Rev. John Brown of Virginia (1728 –1803): His Life and Selected Sermons*, doctoral dissertation, University of Massachusetts, 1988.

219 Rev. William Hill's article on the history of Washington College (Va.), includes an inappropriate reference to an unofficial visit that the Hanover Presbytery made to Rev. Brown's private Latin school after their April 1775 meeting, but he merely confused that school with the public seminary several miles away from Brown's school. The presbytery that created the college, however, never confused the one school with the other.

220 .Excepting, of course, the possibility of the infamous and so-called letter of Rev. Samuel Houston, which is, however, irrelevant for reasons explained thoroughly elsewhere in this report.

at New Providence (after 1767). In the same vein, no letter or public statement is known to exist in which Rev. John Brown ever asserted that he "directed," "supervised," or even, "inspected" the "Augusta Academy" under the "care and tuition" [i.e., "management"] of William Graham.

FACT no. 7   Rev. John Brown opposed the presbytery's plan to establish a seminary in Augusta County, as his extant letters clearly demonstrate. In this, he never relented or acquiesced, and he sent none of his sons to that academy. He even suggested in letters to close friends and relatives that they do the same. Rev. John Brown was no friend of Liberty Hall Academy, and from the day it was first created by the Hanover Presbytery in 1774, he and his family stood aloof from activities associated with the college during the eighteenth century.[221]

FACT no. 8   Rev. John Brown did not accept any appointment offered by the Hanover Presbytery in connection with the presbytery's new seminary in Augusta County, and for that reason, Rev. Brown's name never appears in the board of trustees' meeting minutes as having been "present."

FACT no. 9   On May 6, when the Hanover Presbytery announced the names of their "appointees" to the board of trustees of Augusta Academy, its members also appointed an all-important executive committee to carry out the essential business necessary for moving the academy from its temporary embryonic phase at Mount Pleasant into full-scale academy operations at Timber Ridge. Rev. Brown, the presbytery's then-only voting member living in Augusta County, *was noticeably left off the executive committee.*[222]

---

221   After Gen. Robert E. Lee became the president of Washington College, the Brown family of the nineteenth century ironically began to claim that their immigrant ancestor, Rev. John Brown, was actually the founder of the college. Of course, the Brown family's claim, in this regard, is specious and contrary to all the known evidence. In fact, it is doubtful that Rev. Brown ever stepped foot inside the halls of Liberty Hall Academy despite its close proximity to his own home.

222   *Generally, the presbytery minutes will include a direction for some particular person(s) to notice appointees and solicit the appointee's acceptance because technically most appointments are conditioned upon the appointee's acceptance. Another convention of the Hanover Presbytery in that day was to frequently appoint opposing parties in a matter under dispute to a working committee after a decision on the matter was rendered. Presumably, the members thought that by involving both parties, or leading opposition advocates to committees designed to carry out the policy under consideration, their working together might help defuse any lingering resentments. It didn't work, but it has caused many historians to misread certain situations that involved such appointments. For example, during the religious liberty struggle in the 1780s in Virginia, at a critical time just before the matter was resolved, the presbytery altered a long-standing position on assessment [taxation] for support of churches. Rev. John Blair Smith advocated for the change, but Rev. Wm. Graham opposed it. Smith won round one, and the presbytery appointed both Smith and Graham to draft a memorial to the legislature, whose appointment was included in the minutes, and many historians mistakenly read this as Mr. Graham having demurred in his opposition, but that is untrue. Mr. Graham ignored the appointment and launched instead a campaign to call a general convention, which he did, and in that larger arena the Presbyterians of Virginia repudiated Rev. Smith's proposal to alter the presbytery's*

Note: It seems, from this, that the presbytery had finally accepted that Rev. Brown was intractable in his opposition to the new seminary. Rev. Brown obviously recognized the inevitable effect the seminary would have on his existing Latin school operating in the same neighborhood.[223]*In this, at least, Rev. Brown, or his more socially conscious wife, was prescient, and his refusal to participate in its affairs is understandable. A year after the presbytery established Liberty Hall, Brown lost his instructor, Samuel Doak, and because of the impending Revolutionary War he was not able to find a replacement instructor. Unable to conduct the classes himself, Brown suspended his Latin school for the duration of the war. After the treaty of Paris, effectively ending the war, Brown announced his intention to reopen the school at the same New Providence location, but it is unclear whether that plan came to fruition. See, Brown's correspondence in the Draper collection or John White Stuart's biographical dissertation on John Brown.*

FACT no. 10   Rev. William Graham, the administrative leader (rector/president) of Liberty Hall Academy from its inception in 1774 until his resignation in 1796, left no letter, memorandum, lecture, or publication, including his drafted letter to President Washington,[224] which included a brief sketch of the academy's history, wherein he intimated, hinted at, or asserted that there was any connection or link between Liberty Hall and any other school in the Valley of Virginia.[225]

FACT no. 11   No lectures given by Rev. William Graham were ever written down or transcribed verbatim or even approximating a verbatim transcription; therefore, there is no such thing as a written lecture, or lectures, of Rev. William

---

long-standing opposition to the legislature having any role in church policy or finance. See: Seller, Dr. Charles G., "John Blair Smith," Journal of the Presbyterian Historical Society, Vol. XXXIV, No. 4., December 1956, pp. 201–225.

223   *Rev. Brown's Latin school at New Providence, like most schools, discontinued its operations during the Revolutionary War. Rev. Brown announced to his brother-in-law, the influential Col. William Preston, that he was re-opening his "Latin school" at New Providence in 1783, and requested Col. Preston's assistance in obtaining supplies for the school. At that time, the Presbytery's Academy at Mount Pleasant, initially referred to unofficially as "Augusta Academy," had been in operation for nearly a decade. Once the presbytery's academy at Mount Pleasant was moved from its temporary quarters to the school's new buildings at Timber Ridge in late 1776, Rev. Graham continued the grammar school aspect of the academy, which thereafter functioned as a preparatory school, just as his preceptor, Dr. Witherspoon had wisely done at Princeton.*

224   The letter was drafted by Mr. Graham in 1796, for, and on behalf of, the board of trustees of Liberty Hall Academy.

225   Some, including Dr. Crenshaw, mistakenly assumed that the Rev. Graham's letter to George Washington, which included a reference to an earlier "grammar school," was a veiled reference to Rev. Brown's private Latin school. Mr. Graham's allusion was merely referring to the classes he initially organized and taught at "Mount Pleasant," which were simply preparing young men for their eventual matriculation at the academy while it was still a work-in-progress, and these rudimentary classes were referred to by the presbytery in the interregnum (1775–1776) as the "grammar school" in its minutes and denominated it as Augusta Academy. Mr. Graham, in his letter seeking President Washington's prospective endowment for Liberty Hall, was appropriately being as precise as possible, and by invoking the term "grammar school," he correctly described the school's earliest activities and dated them to a point in time antedating the Revolutionary War. This fact was thought to be important to President Washington, who subsequently did grant the endowment to Liberty Hall Academy.

Graham. This fact is noted and regretted by both of Rev. Graham's earliest biographers, Edward Graham and Rev. Archibald Alexander,[226] two eminent eighteenth-century students of Graham, both of whom resided in the rector's home while students during the Revolutionary War. They were eyewitnesses to the early years who became eminent scholars. These men's written and consistent testimony clearly trump the mere speculations of mid-nineteenth-century authors with no direct connection to the college's early days. (See the bibliography.)

Note: The same thing is true with respect to his sermons, which were never written down before or after they were delivered.

Note: A checklist of Rev. William Graham's writings may be found in an attached appendix devoted to that subject.

FACT no. 12   The first president of Washington and Lee University, Rev. William Graham, was never censured by his church, contrary to the repeated false claims made by numerous historians that only emerged seventy-five years after the college was founded and fifty years after Mr. Graham's death. No supporting evidence has ever been provided for the simple reason that there isn't any eighteenth-century evidence to support the spurious claim that Rev. Graham was censured. Rev. William Graham was never censured by the Presbyterian Church.[227]

FACT no. 13   Washington and Lee University never ceased to operate from the time it was first organized at the place locally called "Mount Pleasant" to the effective date of the resignation of its first president in the autumn of 1796, which is contrary to the oft-repeated false claim that the school was closed during the Revolutionary War.[228] Its operation at Timber Ridge was suspended during the war, but the instruction continued nonetheless, temporarily at the rector's home and then in an abandoned house. Later, a frame structure was constructed for holding classes, near the rector's home. Subsequently, the stone buildings were

---

226   This means that the "copy" of a packet of lectures housed at Washington and Lee University, which include an ex post facto cover page attributing the lectures to Rev. William Graham, is not what it is claimed to be. They are undoubtedly the oft-copied lectures originally written by Pres. John Witherspoon of Princeton, that were copied by all students at Liberty Hall Academy and used as a sort of textbook. These copies were based on William Graham's own packet made by him while a student at Princeton (circa 1768–1773).

227   Some writers have re-printed some preliminary findings of a committee, but the committee had only heard from the complainant and it was soon discovered that the committee had no proper jurisdiction to review the matter and the case was then referred to the proper authorities who declined to censure Graham. The matter is detailed in this report in several locations.

228   The instruction at Timber Ridge ceased during the war, but the school was merely transferred to the farm of its president, William Graham. The enrollment, of course, suffered greatly, but some students were still receiving instruction throughout the war, as is made clear by President Graham's famous letter to President George Washington, written on behalf of the trustees in early 1796, which included a brief sketch of the college's continuous operation from its inception prior to the revolution and throughout the war to 1796. *This phase of the college's operations is also discussed in some detail by Rev. Archibald Alexander in his memoir of his old preceptor, Mr. Graham.*

erected on Mulberry Hill, which was the campus where Graham submitted his resignation in 1796.

FACT no. 14   When Washington and Lee University was still named "Liberty Hall Academy," but well after it was chartered and granted college-degree-granting authority, the college's president, Rev. William Graham, enrolled the new nation's first black undergraduate college student, Mr. John Chavis of North Carolina, into its regular academic program, and Chavis thereafter became the nation's first black college graduate, as evidenced by the Rockbridge County Court in 1802. (See John Chavis appendix.)

Note: By this and other actions, Washington and Lee University may claim the mantle of the single most socially progressive American college in the eighteenth century. Nearly a hundred years later, colleges like Harvard, Yale, Princeton, and Columbia began to consider enrolling black students into their prestigious institutions.

FACT no. 15   When Washington and Lee University was still named "Liberty Hall Academy," but well after it was chartered, and granted college-degree-granting authority, the college's president enrolled the new nation's first female undergraduate student, Mrs. Sarah (McBride) Priestley, into the college's regular academic program, and she attended the institution for some time before the challenges of motherhood interrupted her schooling, but not before she had obtained sufficient attainments to allow her to create, and conduct a successful school for young women in Baltimore. *(See the appendix devoted to Mrs. Priestley.)*

Note: By these, and other actions, Washington and Lee University claims the mantle of the single most socially progressive American college in the eighteenth century.

FACT no. 16   The legacy of Washington and Lee University's founding first president, William Graham, has been largely overlooked, in good measure as a result of an ongoing, misguided, but nonetheless effective campaign carried out by descendants of the rector's few but powerful eighteenth-century enemies. Among the several erroneous attacks on Rev. William Graham's character are these unsupportable calumnies: (1) That he was "censured" by his church; (2) that he precipitated a schism within New Providence Presbyterian Church; (3) that he was motivated by avarice; (4) that he was possessed of an irascible temperament; (5) that he had little regard for the educational utility of books and reading; and of a more current variety, (6) that he was an advocate for and defender of the American form of African slavery. All of these claims are indisputably disproved by proofs embedded throughout this report.

FACT no. 17   In 1890 the Virginia Synod published an embarrassingly incompetent ahistorical depiction of the origins of Washington College (Virginia) included in "Contributions to the History of the Synod of Virginia"[229] by the

---

229 *Contributions to the History of the Synod of Virginia*, Waddell, Rev. James A., ed. Waddell, James A., Washington: John F. Sheiry, Printer, 1890. Waddell was one of three committee

Rev. James A. Waddell, editor (not to be confused with the eighteenth-century Virginia minister of the same name, whom William Wirt characterized as the "blind preacher"). Instead of relying on the Presbyterian Church's own records, Rev. Waddell relied on Mr. William H. Foote's mistaken accounts provided in his *Sketches of Virginia: Historical and Biographical*, Series One and Series Two, 1850 and 1855 respectively. This gross error by the Synod is inexplicable since the primary evidence is located in the records of the Hanover Presbytery.[230]

FACT no. 18   Rev. William Graham, president of Liberty Hall Academy, oversaw the fund-raising, planning, and construction of the college's first four campuses: (1) The "Mount Pleasant" planning headquarters and grammar school (1775–1776); (2) the Timber Ridge series of buildings (circa 1776–1778); (3) the frame buildings near Rev. Graham's home on Whistle Creek (1782–1788); (4) the Stone buildings built on Mulberry Hill (circa 1792–1802) referred to in the present day as "the remains."[231]

Note: This fact goes a long way toward explaining why Dr. Samuel L. Campbell M.D.[232] wrote for publication this statement:

> _**Mr. Graham now resumed the business of the academy**_, over which he had heretofore watched with parental care and solicitude. He had led it cautiously and tenderly through many difficulties to a certain stage of its existence. Besides the labor of teaching, and governing, there devolved upon him the task of planning, buildings; making contracts with the workmen; attending to the faithful execution of the contracts; the devising ways and means for fulfilling those engagements;_ **and, in a word, all that was to be done for the academy fell chiefly on him** . . ._

---

members who, it appears, functioned as writers, editors, and collators of this article. Other committee members were Rev. Wm. Wirt Henry and Rev. P. B. Price, both trustees of Hampden-Sydney College. Henry, grandson of Patrick, was president of the American Historical Association. This unfortunate piece is riddled with errors and omissions concerning the origins of Washington and Lee University. An attached article is a reprinted address by John Randolph Tucker given originally at the Centennial Meeting of the Virginia Synod in October of 1888 at New Providence Presbyterian Church in Rockbridge County, Virginia.

230   The Hanover Presbytery may have been remiss by not providing the synod with requested information.

231   It seems that the classes may also have been conducted for a time in an abandoned home near Graham's farm on Whistle Creek.

232   *Dr. Campbell was the man selected by the college's trustees as "acting president" after Pres. Graham's resignation in 1796. He was an eyewitness to Liberty Hall Academy's operations at Mount Pleasant; an early student of Liberty Hall; an eighteenth-century trustee of Liberty Hall; an eminent physician; and a leading citizen of the eighteenth-century Lexington, Virginia, community.*

During this long period he had, for the most part, performed all the duties in person, which in other public seminaries are confided to a faculty consisting of several professors. ***He not only gave instruction in the scientific and classical departments, but paid special attention to the grammar school. "Here," said he, "should be laid a substratum on which to build a superstructure of learning.***" (Dr. Samuel L. Campbell, "Washington College, Va." *Southern Literary Messenger*, June 1838, beginning at p. 364. [reprinted in W&L Hist. Papers No. 1, 1890, p. 115.) [Emphasis added here due to its importance.)

FACT no. 19   The three most important figures in Virginia's rejection of an established church, the related proposed assessment (taxation) of the citizenry for support of the church and its patronized schools, and the related passage of Mr. Jefferson's bill for religious freedom were Thomas Jefferson, James Madison, and Washington and Lee's Rev. William Graham.

Note: Rev. William Graham, president of Liberty Hall Academy, was the man most responsible for ensuring the inclusion of the religious liberty provision in the nation's Bill of Rights. His actions in this regard began with the defeat of the eighteenth-century legislative attempts to tax Virginia's citizens for the support of religion, that resulted from a statewide campaign engineered by President Graham and included his unsuccessful candidacy, as an anti-Federalist candidate, to be a delegate to the Virginia ratification convention, along with his friend Patrick Henry and George Mason, the author of Virginia's Declaration of Rights. As part of his anti-tax campaign, he engineered the calling of a General Convention of the Presbyterian Church in Virginia, which overturned a dangerous decision of their ministers that would have virtually assured passage of the proposed tax scheme in support of religion. They then elected Mr. Graham to draft a final message on behalf of the Virginia Presbyterians in general convention. The message conveyed the Presbyterians' strong, unqualified opposition to any form of taxation in support of religion, and at Mr. Graham's urging, they added a plea for the passage of Thomas Jefferson's Bill for Religious Freedom that James Madison, acting on behalf of Mr. Jefferson, had long been unable to even bring up for a vote. Upon the legislature's receipt of Mr. Graham's drafted message from the Presbyterians, in conjunction with the associated petition signatures from more than 10,000 voters, the legislature forthwith, quietly abandoned the taxation bill, and shortly thereafter passed Mr. Jefferson's Bill for Religious Freedom. These actions were the impetus for Mr. Madison ensuring that a religious liberty provision would be incorporated into the Bill of Rights. Had the Virginia Bill to tax the citizens in support of the church passed, it is difficult to envision the inclusion of a religious liberty provision in the Bill of Rights. Thankfully, Rev. Graham's amazing and unprecedented campaign successfully ensured its defeat.

FACT no. 20   Rev. William Graham, president of Liberty Hall Academy, wrote for publication a proposed state constitution in 1785, which has been described by modern-day scholars as one of the most democratic constitutions published in North America in the eighteenth century. The constitution was the provisional constitution for the proposed state of Frankland/Franklin. He also published thereafter an *"Essay on Government"* (1786), which was occasioned by his earlier proposed constitution. See the bibliography for a detailed citation.

Note: Below are a few selections from the Essay on Government included at the conclusion of the Prolegomenon, one of which is repeated below:

> *A Republic is a government, by equal and just laws, made by common consent, for the common benefit, <u>and not the dominion of one community over another community</u>, . . . which is founded in the perfect, political equality of all the citizens.*[233]

(William Graham, first president of Washington
and Lee University, 1786)

Note: This essay by Graham was published before the ratification of the U.S. Constitution.

This published comment hardly reflects the sentiments of a defender of African slavery in America.

****

In addition to the twenty facts identified above, it is perhaps appropriate to conclude this section with two selected quotes from two impressive sources:

> "Mount Pleasant should be considered as a kind of consecrated spot; and altho' it is now, like Shilo of old, a desolation; yet it would be well, especially for the surviving pupils of Mr. Graham, to erect a monument on that spot, as a memorial of the first classical school instituted in the Valley. <u>*But stone, marble, & brass are perishable substances: we want a memorial more enduring than those; and this can only be erected by a faithful history of this institution & its founder,*</u> [Wm. Graham] which we are now attempting to <u>furnish</u>."[234] (Emphasis added)

> [Dr. Archibald Alexander, president of Princeton Theological Seminary and the most published scholar on the educational endeavors of the Presbyterian Church in early America during his lifetime.]

The Present Academy of Liberty Hall began under the Direction and Patronage of the Presbytery of Hanover as the following minutes fully evince.

At a session of the Pby. of Hanover at Cub Creek Oct. 13, 1774, the Pby resumed consideration of a school for the liberal education of youth which we unanimously judge to be of great importance. **We do therefore agree to establish and patronize**

---

233 Copy provided to the auditor by W&L Librarian Betty R. Kondayan in the 1970s.

234 Alexander, Archibald DD, Mss, "Memoir of William Graham" [written in longhand]. The Rev. Graham portions of this manuscript are part of a larger writing entitled *Great Valley of Virginia*. The auditor's photocopy came from the Princeton Seminary Library in 1989. It is now also available in spiral-bound form at the Leyburn Library, Washington and Lee University.

a publick school which shall be confined to the county of Augusta in this colony.

> (Rev. Caleb Wallace, clerk of the Hanover Presbytery, from the record book, containing the earliest meeting minutes of the board of trustees of Liberty Hall Academy. This extract is from a several-page history of the establishment of Liberty Hall Academy, which constitutes the first authorized history of the founding of Washington and Lee University. The history, as written by Rev. Caleb Wallace, is located on the very first pages of the Liberty Hall Academy's first record book, begun in May of 1776. Its author, as clerk, was writing on behalf of the Hanover Presbytery, who had directed that the record book be presented to the new board of trustees then created by the Hanover Presbytery for keeping a record of the board's activities carried out at its official meetings. It is, therefore, the primary authoritative source concerning the early history of Liberty Hall Academy.) (*Emphasis in most every case above, was added by the auditor.*)

Chapter Two

Key Errors

(Concerning the History of the Origins of Washington and Lee University and the university's founding first president, William Graham)

NOTE: The attached report will demonstrate why each of the listed mistakes listed below is clearly an error. In most cases, the report's contentions are supported by official records and documents created by either the Hanover Presbytery or the board of trustees of Liberty Hall Academy in the eighteenth century. This evidence is then supplemented by all known eighteenth- and early-nineteenth-century published accounts of Liberty Hall academy's origins. Taken together, the performance audit presents an incontrovertible case that the mistakes herein enumerated all constitute significant errors. These errors have contributed to a false characterization of the founding of Washington and Lee University since 1850.

This section is divided into two parts: (A) A brief list of the key errors made by both the institution and various and sundry writers, some of which are historians, and (B) a list of the errors, with a brief explanation of the reason(s) why the auditor deems these claims to be erroneous.

Part A *(Part B includes argumentation and evidence)*
The following are all mistakes: [Twenty principal errors]

1. It is an error to assert that Liberty Hall Academy's history extends any further back than the 1770s. This error has been made by many authors and the university.

2. It is an error to assert that the Hanover Presbytery's establishment of its first sponsored seminary in Virginia was somehow connected to earlier existing private primary schools. This error has been made by many authors and the university.

3. It is an error to assert that Liberty Hall Academy had more than one administrative leader during its first twenty-two years of existence. This error has been made by many authors and the university.

4. It is an error to assert that Rev. William Graham was not the first chief administrator, rector, and or president[235] of the

---

235 In North America during the eighteenth century, these two labels or titles, were, generally speaking, functional equivalents used to identify an organization's chief administrative officer.

academy that evolved into Washington and Lee University. This error has been made by many authors and the university.

5. It is an error to assert that Robert Alexander operated a school in Augusta County, Virginia, that had any connection whatsoever to Liberty Hall Academy. This error has been made by many authors and the university.

6. It is an error to assert that the Prince Edward Academy [Hampden Sidney Academy] was established prior to the founding of Augusta Academy [Liberty Hall]. This error has been made by many authors.

7. It is an error to assert that Rev. John Brown's Latin school was conducted at "Mount Pleasant" at any time in the 1770s. This error has been made by many authors.

(Note: In part of the 1760s, however, Brown's Latin school, was located, at "Mount Pleasant," but it was moved permanently to New Providence on Moffett's Creek before 1770. See, Brown's correspondence abstracted in John White Stuart's biography of Rev. John Brown. (See the bibliography.)

8. It is an error to assert that Rev. John Brown ever accepted any appointment made by the Hanover Presbytery in connection with its new seminary, "Augusta Academy" (i.e., Liberty Hall Academy). This error has been made by many authors and the university.

9. It is an error to assert that there was any private school operating at "Mount Pleasant" (near Fairfield, Virginia) after Rev. Brown's Latin school was moved from there to New Providence. This error has been made by many authors and the university.

(Note: On October 13, 1774, the Hanover Presbytery formally "decided" to establish its new and first-ever "public"[236] patronized seminary in Augusta County. Shortly thereafter, the presbytery's appointed "manager," William Graham, established his first and temporary headquarters at "Mount Pleasant" and upon this spot he oversaw the development of an idea into a reality. Here, Graham began planning the campus and during its construction at Timber Ridge, he created a grammar school as the foundation upon which the college

---

236 The distinction in this context is a bit murky, but the Hanover Presbytery created its seminary and patronized it, in part, by fund-raising in its name, and the school was open to students of any Christian denomination. Brown's "private school was exclusively his own school and it had no official connection to any organization.

was to be built. The college's first academic activities took place at Mount Pleasant beginning in early 1775. The college's origin, however, dates to the presbytery's formal decision to establish the college on October 13, 1774, as asserted by the presbytery's clerk, Caleb Wallace, in the college's first authorized history, a copy of which was written into the college's first record book of the Liberty Hall Academy's first board of trustees. The board of trustees was created by the presbytery on May 6, 1776.)

10. It is an error to assert that William Henry Foote, the authority most referred to by W&L historians after 1850, relied upon any credible authority[237] for his preposterous claim, by inference, that all the published histories of the early days of Liberty Hall Academy, the official documents of Liberty Hall Academy, and the official documents of the Hanover Presbytery during that same time period were incorrect in regard to the institution's founding. He did not. Foote's claims about the founding of the college are merely gratuitous assertions that have no basis in facts or credible evidence. This error has been made by many authors and the university.

11. It is an error to claim that any eighteenth-century student who did not matriculate under William Graham at "Augusta Academy" or Liberty Hall Academy is an alumnus of Washington and Lee University, with the possible exception of anyone who may have matriculated there during the four-year period between 1796 and 1800.[238] This error has been made by many authors and the university.

Note: The university's catalogue of alumni lists several persons as alumni whose only assumed connection to the university is based on a false notion that the private instruction they received in that community while attending schools operated by Robert Alexander or Rev. John Brown was in some way linked to the university in its earliest forms. This notion is patently false.

---

237 Mr. Foote embarrassingly presented two conflicting histories of the college's founding, one in his first volume, the other in his second volume published five years later. In both cases he cites the exact same source, from which he quotes, but shockingly, he quotes the same paragraph differently resulting in two entirely different accounts. Simply put, either one, or both of these small extracts, is a forgery. As a result, neither of the variant accounts can be trusted to be true because Foote offered no explanation for the gross discrepancy. Unfortunately, Foote's first account is the one that is most wrong, and damaging to the college's history, and ironically it is the one most referred to by later historians. Had Mr. Foote done this under oath in court, he would be subject to perjury.

     Those innumerable historians citing Foote as their authority concerning the founding of W&L, cite his first volume, and based upon it, collectively emaciate the college's true early history. This variation in accounts is a historical blunder of colossal proportions.

238 Many records for this period are either missing or were never created.

12. It is an error to claim that Rev. William Graham, rector of Liberty Hall Academy, was ever censured by the Presbyterian Church. This error has been made by many authors.

13. It is an error to claim that any school in Virginia was known in the eighteenth century as the "Augusta Academy" other than the seminary established by the Hanover Presbytery on October 13, 1774. This error has been made by many authors.

Note: The notion that the name Augusta Academy was the traditional name associated with private preparatory schools operated by Robert Alexander or Rev. John Brown was the retrospective product of the fertile imaginations of writers in the mid- to late-nineteenth century. Their assumption in this regard is not supported by facts, evidence, or traditions that arose in the eighteenth century.

14. It is an error to claim that William Graham was ever a subordinate appointee of the Hanover Presbytery, to a "director," "supervisor," or any other person. This error has been made by many authors and the university. There is a reason why this mistake has frequently been made, which is explained in other sections of this report.

Note: Mr. Graham, in his capacity as the chief administrative officer of the academy in Augusta County, Virginia, reported initially to the entity that first appointed him, the Hanover Presbytery. Subsequently, Rev. Graham, in the same capacity, reported directly to the board of trustees created by the Hanover Presbytery on May 6, 1776. This fact is evinced by the eighteenth-century meeting minutes of the Hanover Presbytery.

15. It is an error to claim that the Hanover Presbytery in the eighteenth century ever "established," "patronized," or otherwise officially connected itself to any school organized or operated by Rev. John Brown, pastor of New Providence Presbyterian Church. This error has been made by many authors and the university.

16. It is an error to claim that Rev. John Brown's private Latin school, located in 1775 at or adjacent to New Providence Church, was thereafter returned to Mount Pleasant near Fairfield, Virginia, from where it originated. This error has been made by many authors.

Note: Brown's Latin school was located first at Mount Pleasant, and then subsequently and permanently at New Providence.

17. It is an error to claim that the Hanover Presbytery "visited" the "Augusta Academy" on April 15, 1775.[239] It did not. This error has been made by many authors.

Note: Rev. William Irvin was the clerk at that April meeting, and it was he who mistakenly inserted a reference to the "visit" to Brown's school into the meeting minutes. Irvin was educated by Brown's old friend, Rev. John Todd, in Louisa, Virginia. Irvin would clearly have known that Rev. Brown privately opposed the presbytery's creation of an academy in Augusta, and this was likely Brown's last and not too subtle of an effort to persuade his colleagues that his preparatory Latin school, in connection with Princeton, was a better way to prepare young men for the Presbyterian ministry than a new institution in Virginia. Irvin's inappropriate reference to this unofficial "visit" confused later historians who mistakenly concluded that the reference meant that Brown's school was the Augusta Academy, but that entity was located at "Mount Pleasant," not at New Providence where Brown's school was located.

18. It is an error to claim that the transcribed handwritten packet of lectures that are attributed to Rev. William Graham, and housed at the Leyburn Library on the campus of Washington and Lee University, are what the packet's cover page suggests they are (i.e., lectures written by, or "delivered by," Rev. William

---

239 The presbytery did "visit" Rev. Brown's private Latin school after the conclusion of the presbytery's spring meeting (April 15, 1775). Mr. Brown had hosted his colleagues at his capacious home and after the meeting, the members accepted their host's invitation to "visit" his private school, which was being conducted next door at the New Providence Meeting House. Some authors who failed to note that the first day's meeting held at Timber Ridge had been moved from there to New Providence several miles distant and in so doing confused the presbytery's seminary at Mount Pleasant with Brown's school at New Providence. The presbytery's clerk caused the confusion by inappropriately including a reference to the "visit" in the presbytery's meeting minutes. The presbytery had no connection to the private school, and the "visit" was, therefore, not the official business of the presbytery. Consequently, the "visit" should not have been reference by the clerk.

Graham.)[240] This error has been made by many authors and the university.[241]

19. It is an error to claim that the Liberty Hall Academy's rector, Rev. William Graham, was a proponent of, or defender of, the institution of slavery, or that he lectured on or wrote about that subject.[242] This error has been made several later

---

240 These are, principally, a packet of transcribed lectures of Dr. John Witherspoon, copied by the students at Princeton and then later, recopied by students at Liberty Hall Academy and used at as a textbook. The packet's provenance is not thorough or complete. Rev. William Graham copied Witherspoon's lectures while at Princeton and he used his personal copy as a template. This particular packet, according to the current cover page, was copied by Mr. Joseph Glass in 1796. Unfortunately, the packet was again re-copied by professor or instructor Waddell in 1896. An interesting artifact, it is, however, not all that the cover page asserts, and it likely contains at least two lectures that were added to the packet, which were not written by Dr. Witherspoon. Quite possibly they were written by and added to the packet by Professor Edward Graham, but this notion is purely conjectural. What they were not are lectures written by William Graham who, according to his earliest biographers who knew him well, regretfully, never wrote his lectures down for posterity. Both lived in the president's home and one was Graham's brother, Edward Graham. Two unimpeachable eyewitnesses.

241 The error made by faculty and staff of the library was occasioned by Professor Harry Waddell Pratt's 1896 copying of the original packet copied one hundred years earlier by the student Joseph Glass in 1796. Glass would not have asserted that the packet contained lectures "delivered by William Graham in 1796" because he would have known better. William Graham was rarely, if ever, lecturing the students during his last year as the college's president. Indeed, he was frequently absent from Lexington in 1796. Glass's instructor that year was probably, more often than not, the president's younger brother, Professor Edward Graham. Edward had earlier been Glass's instructor at the New London Academy in Bedford County and he had been instrumental in bringing Glass to Liberty Hall. (See, Read, Daisy I., *New London, Today and Yesterday*, J.P. Bell Company, Lynchburg, Virginia, 1950.) [This book concerns New London Academy where Edward Graham of Lexington, Virginia, was the first president and an instructor.]

242 While historians may engage in speculation on the subject of William Graham's views on African slavery in America, they will soon discover that there is but a paucity of extant historical evidence upon which to draw any definitive conclusions. Archibald Alexander engaged in some admitted speculation on the question in his unpublished "Memoir of Rev. William Graham," but at a later date he crossed through his speculation without comment. The fact is that Alexander did not know for sure what Graham's views on the subject were. The content of some of his extant papers referring to one black couple and any of their offspring for whom he listed as "tithables" does not mean that he must therefore have supported the institution of slavery because Presbyterian ministers in the South who had slaves in their congregations were occasionally asked by slaves to take possession of their immediate family when they suspected they were about to be separated and sold. Such cases constituted distinctions of enormous consequential differences.
     Emancipation was often out of the question because an emancipated slave(s) would, by law, have had to then leave the state of Virginia. This reality created a "Sophie's Choice" for some slaves with extended families still in bondage nearby. Such individuals may truly have been slaves "in name only." This important distinction was often completely lost on citizens then living in non-slave states. It is also significant that the only written comment Rev. Graham is known to have made on that subject was in a letter to Col. Arthur Campbell in which he alludes to "the horrors of slavery." Perhaps even more important is the fact that Graham's

twentieth-century authors beginning with Dr. David Robson in 1980.[243]

20. It is an error to believe that Rev. William Graham was complicit with his brethren in the Hanover Presbytery when, in October of 1784, at the urging of Rev. John B. Smith, the body approved a new position amending its long-standing opposition to taxing the people to support the church. He was not.[244] Quite the contrary. This error has been made by many nineteenth- and twentieth-century authors.

****

BELOW IS A REFERENCE TO AN ACTION THAT IS ASSERTED TO HAVE TRANSPIRED IN 1780, BUT IT WAS WRITTEN (ASSERTED) MUCH EARLIER OR PERHAPS LATER, EITHER IN THE 1840S, OR CIRCA 1890.

The error was committed by either President Henry Ruffner, or his son, William Henry Ruffner who edited his father's manuscript while preparing it for publication many decades after it was originally written. This matter is further confused by the fact that in 1857, long after it was originally written, Henry Ruffner made a number of edits to the original, which he never bothered to identify. This fact was revealed by Henry Ruffner in a notice printed along with the publication of his "History of Washington College" that is located in Volume 1 of the Washington and Lee University Historical Papers.

Note: The auditor decided to insert this here rather than in the Author's Errors section because it is unclear to whom the error should be assigned.

An erroneous representation by one of the Ruffners (father & son); it isn't clear which was is responsible for this error "*__in the course of the year 1780, the operations of the academy were wholly suspended, and were never resumed at Timber Ridge.__* Thus in the fourth year of its new existence, the this

---

proposed state Constitution for the proposed state of Frankland (generally, Tennessee and part of Kentucky) pointedly did *not contain a provision for preserving the property interest slaves, like most state constitutions, at that time, contained.* That may very well explain why Graham was hung in effigy by an angry mob after the convention rejected Graham's Constitution. (See the bibliographic entries for William Graham, especially since Graham was not in attendance or even in the vicinage.)

243 David W. Robson, "An Important Question Answered: William Graham's Defense of Slavery in Post-Revolutionary Virginia," William and Mary Quarterly, 3rd Series, 37, No. 4, pp. 644–652. (October 1980). [Note: An erroneous piece throughout.]

244 Rev. Graham led an insurgency against the action in which he successfully obtained a complete repudiation of the amended policy, and even went much further by demanding passage of Jefferson's long-stalled Bill for Religious Liberty, which is explained in detail in the appendix on church and state.

young seminary of learning fainted under the hard pressure
of the times; . . . But some of the students being anxious to
complete their studies, the library and apparatus were removed
to Mr. Graham's residence, where he continued to give private
instruction . . . Among the pupils who followed their teacher,
were Moses Hoge and Archibald Alexander . . . This private
school prevented extinction of the academy . . . While the
academy lay in this state of suspended animation, the people of
Virginia were more than ever agitated by the alarms of war."[245]

*This odd entry is included here for reference purposes only. Its text seems to be entirely misleading
because the school was never actually closed. It was merely relocated. A distinction of the greatest
significance to the school's true history.*

Part B (Nearly identical errors as shown above, but with explanations.)

Introduction:

The general subject about which so many of the errors are concerned is the
origin of Washington and Lee University and the date of its founding. Central
to the formulating of many, if not most, of the errors is the generally unknown
fact that Rev. John Brown, pastor of New Providence Presbyterian Church, as
well as most of the pastor's immediate family, were personally estranged from
both Rev. William Graham and the seminary ("Augusta Academy") under Rev.
Graham's management and direction. The important background for appreciating
this phenomena is provided by Rev. Archibald Alexander, the founder and first
president of the Princeton Theological Seminary, as follows:

"Here I think it proper to relate what I have heard, that may cast
some light on this subject. The Rev. Mr. Brown had a daughter
just grown, when Mr. G. came into the neighborhood. Great pains
had been taken with her education at home, so that she had learned
everything which her brothers learned, not excepting Latin &
Greek. And she was not destitute of personal attractions. As Mr.
Graham was once in the family, and was of an engaging person
and able to make himself agreeable in the company of ladies,

---

245 Ibid [Note: It is unclear to this auditor why Pres. Ruffner invokes the term "private" here
because it appears the only real change is that of place. This appellation, "private," in this
context is what the U.S. Supreme Court has called "a distinction without a difference." Aren't
the Mssrs. Hoge and Alexander who both matriculated for a time at Graham's home, considered
by all to be graduates of Liberty Hall Academy? The point is that, due to the American
Revolution, Liberty Hall Academy avoided going into suspended animation by continuing
classes under William Graham at his home a few miles south of the original campus. When
Graham petitioned the new Virginia Legislature (General Assembly) for a charter afer the
Treaty of Paris concluded hostilities, he did so in the name of Liberty Hall Academy and its
trustees. Moreover, classes by then were being held in separate quarters from Graham's home.]

it is not strange that a mutual attachment should arise between two young persons, apparently so well suited to each other. The report was that a matrimonial engagement had actually taken place between them. But of this no certain knowledge is possessed by the author. The mother, Mrs. Brown however had taken up some prejudice against young Mr. G. And preferred another person for her son-in-law. She was also an extraordinary woman. Possessed of a keen wit & power of satyr & sarcasm, which have seldom been exceeded. When she pleased could turn any person into ridicule. Something wh[ich] she had said respecting Mr. G. having come to his ears, wh[ich] he considered disrespectful, or calculated to expose him to ridicule, he was so much offended, that he took the first occasion wh[ich] offered, to propose that all further proceedings between himself & Miss B [Betsy] should cease; wh[ich] of course was consented to by the lady." [A. Alexander, Mss Memoir of William Graham, pp. 65–66].

Note: Alexander makes it clear that this rupture in the relationship between most of the Brown family and Rev. Graham was never healed. If this information had been readily available to nineteenth-century historians, the revision of the accurate history of Washington and Lee's origins may never have occurred.

Upon reflection of this important but generally unknown backdrop, one cannot fail to appreciate the significance of the fact that Rev. Brown never attended a Liberty Hall Academy board of trustees meeting during the entire twenty-two years of Rev. Graham's tenure at the college. It is regrettable that so few had access to Rev. Alexander's unpublished manuscript memoir of his old preceptor, but fortunately, the auditor learned that the Princeton Theological Seminary library had obtained the manuscript from a descendant of Dr. Alexander. The auditor received a photocopy of the manuscript in 1989. According to Alexander's son and biographer, James W. Alexander, the manuscript was not intended to be published, but history will be well-served by its retention for the benefit of posterity.

Note: Alexander's handwriting is at times challenging, but over the course of several years, the auditor generally was able to discern the author's words. It is clear that Archibald Alexander often referred to it and made subsequent edits as well. In some cases, marginalia notations are also included, but it is not clear who made these notations. On occasion, Alexander lined through material that he had learned was incorrect, or in which he no longer had confidence.

If most of the mid-nineteenth-century and later authors who blindly followed Mr. Foote, or took from his sometimes conflicting accounts of the same events, had been given access to Alexander's manuscript memoir of William Graham, they apparently ignored those accounts that conflict with those histories written after 1850, and especially accounts that pertain to the founding of Washington and Lee. With this in mind, we repeat the errors listed above and provide cursory explanations as to why they are mistakes.

It is a mistake: [Twenty principal errors with explanation]

1. It is an error to assert that Liberty Hall Academy's history extends any further back than the 1770s.

Explanation: On October 13, 1774, the Hanover Presbytery, an association comprised of all active Presbyterian ministers and elders in Virginia, following a three-year study, formally announced its decision in the form of an ordination to establish and patronize a public academy (i.e., "college") in Augusta County, Virginia, under the direction of Mr. William Graham. This was the first such endeavor ever conceived or realized by the Presbyterian Church in Virginia. The new academy had no link or connection of any type to any other school, a fact made clear by a reading of the presbytery's official meeting minutes covering the years 1771–1776. For a citation of authority, see this report's bibliography. For a more detailed explanation and argument, see appendices dedicated to this subject.

2. It is an error to assert that the Hanover Presbytery's establishment of its first sponsored seminary in Virginia was somehow connected to earlier existing private primary schools.

Explanation: See the explanation above (no. 1) and, moreover, there is no known evidence of an eighteenth-century link between Robert Alexander's private school and Rev. John Brown's private Latin school. In addition, there is no known eighteenth-century evidence of a link between Rev. Brown's private school and the Hanover Presbytery's public Augusta Academy that was under the "care and tuition" of William Graham from its very inception and for twenty-two uninterrupted years. In addition, Rev. John Brown refused to associate with Augusta Academy from the day of its inception.[246]

3. It is an error to assert that Liberty Hall Academy had more than one administrative leader during its first twenty-two years of existence.

Explanation: The initial organization of that educational endeavor that became Liberty Hall Academy began in 1775 with the arrival of William Graham, a recent Princeton graduate who had conducted the Princeton preparatory academy

---

[246] *Brown, however, did attend a prayer meeting at the Augusta Academy on one inexplicable occasion in early 1776, but from that day, there is nothing to suggest that he ever after attended a class or a meeting of the board of trustees of Liberty Hall Academy. He opposed its creation and he refused to send any one of his sons to the school sitting in his own neighborhood encompassing the Timber Ridge and New Providence Presbyterian congregations.*

(grammar school) under his preceptor, president of Princeton, and noted American founding father, Dr. John Witherspoon. Mr. Graham made his initial temporary headquarters at a place informally called "Mount Pleasant" in the "neighborhood" comprised of two Presbyterian congregations, Timber Ridge, and New Providence. These temporary headquarters were made available by the generosity of Mr. James Wilson on his farm near Fairfield, Virginia. Here Mr. Graham began the rudimentary instruction of students who anxiously awaited the completion of the academy's new buildings, which were being built at Timber Ridge.

As the Hanover Presbytery's meeting minutes make abundantly clear, Mr. Graham had the "care and tuition" of the academy from its very inception throughout the Revolutionary War and thereafter until after twenty-two years he tendered his resignation in the autumn of 1796. This assertion comports with the meeting minutes of the Hanover Presbytery between October of 1774 through 1796, and with the recorded eyewitness testimony of Rev. Philip Vicker Fithian, who wrote out his account in his journal maintained during his extended trip to Virginia in 1775 and 1776. While in the neighborhood of Timber Ridge and New Providence, Rev. Fithian lodged in the home of Rev. John Brown. He describes his interactions with the principals of the two different schools then conducted in that neighborhood: the private preparatory Latin school organized by Rev. John Brown at New Providence, and the public academy organized at Mount Pleasant under Rev. William Graham. Unfortunately, the journal of Rev. Fithian was not published until 1934. Careless historians writing after 1850 became confused and mistakenly failed to distinguish between these two schools, which led to a widely held false view that the two different schools were one and the same.

4. It is an error to assert that Rev. William Graham was not the first chief administrator, rector, and or president[247] of the academy that evolved into Washington and Lee University.

Explanation: *There are two principal reasons why historians after 1850 mistakenly believed that Rev. John Brown (New Providence Pby. Church) was involved in the affairs of Liberty Hall Academy. First, they misinterpreted the Hanover Presbytery meeting minutes that included an unfortunate and misleading statement, which is as follows:*

---

247 In North America during the eighteenth century, these two labels or titles were functional equivalents used to identify an organization's chief administrative officer.

> *"We therefore agree to establish and patronize a publick (sic) school . . . At present it shall be managed by Mr. William Graham, a Gentleman properly recommended to this pby. . . <u>and under the Inspection of the Rev. Mr. John Brown</u>."*
> *(Pby. Minutes, p. 55) (Emphasis added)*

Historians failed to grasp that such appointments are provisional in nature and, as in this case, the appointee may not accept the appointment. Rev. John Brown did not accept this, or any other appointment, related to the presbytery's academy in Augusta County, Virginia. Notations in the minutes make this clear by stating that the recipients of the appointments be notified and their acceptance solicited.

Secondly, historians after 1850 failed to realize that while Rev. Brown had indeed organized a private Latin school at the same location, (i.e., Mount Pleasant) that he had later (circa 1767) moved that school from Mount Pleasant to New Providence after he had separated himself from the Timber Ridge Congregation.[248] When the presbytery added the phrase "under the Inspection of Rev. John Brown" in its meeting minutes, that wording did not represent a fait accompli, but rather it was operationally more of a nomination, which, as it turns out, was never accepted by Rev. John Brown. In fact, Mr. Brown refused to accept any nomination to serve in any capacity, in connection with Liberty Hall Academy. That is why his name never appears in the meeting minutes of the Liberty Hall Academy Board of Trustees indicating that he was present. Not once in the twenty-two years of the first president's tenure did Rev. John Brown attend a meeting of the college's trustees, even though the meetings were held in Rev. Brown's own neighborhood. In fact, Rev. Brown and his family were estranged from all things associated with Liberty Hall Academy. He sent none of his sons to the academy, and he encouraged others to do the same, as his extant letters make abundantly clear. See John White Stuart's biography of Rev. John Brown which extracts pertinent letters of Brown.

In 1775, there were two separate and distinctly different schools operating in the neighborhood of the two congregations,

---

248 *See, John White Stuart, <u>The Rev. John Brown of Virginia (1728–1803): His Life and Selected Sermons,</u>* doctoral dissertation, University of Massachusetts, 1988. Dr. Stuart abstracts many extant letters of Rev. John Brown, which make it abundantly clear that Rev. Brown's school had been moved from Mount Pleasant to New Providence on Moffett's Creek, and that it was never again moved.

Timber Ridge and New Providence, which is an embarrassingly overlooked fact by all W&L historians since 1850. These historians of the college frequently made the mistake of assuming Brown's school and Graham's school were one and the same school.

5. It is an error to assert that Robert Alexander operated a school in Augusta County, Virginia, that had any connection whatsoever to Liberty Hall Academy.

Explanation: What is of the greatest importance here is the fact that not one historian has ever presented any evidence from the eighteenth century that supports the gratuitous assertion that Alexander's school was linked to Rev. Brown's. Some who realize this embarrassing fact nonetheless insist on adhering to the nonsensical notion, and they attribute their belief to "tradition," which, in this case, is absurd. No such eighteenth-century tradition is known to exist. Tradition, of course, is generally little more than a lazy man's euphemism for gossip. In this case, the so-called tradition is not rooted in the time of the events to which they are said to relate, but rather it was a narrative concocted by later nineteenth-century historians more interested in writing a history that suited their desires than one that comported with documented facts. Traditions, as it were, to be given any credence should be traceable to the times of the events to which they refer. There are, however, no known traditions linking either Robert Alexander's or Rev. John Brown's schools to Liberty Hall Academy that existed during Liberty Hall Academy's first quarter century (i.e., 1775–1800).

6. It is an error to assert that the Prince Edward Academy [Hampden Sidney Academy] was established prior to the founding of Augusta Academy [Liberty Hall].

Explanation: *Augusta Academy was established October 13, 1774; Prince Edward Academy was established February 1, 1775, as the official records (meeting minutes) of the body that created both academies (the Hanover Presbytery) clearly demonstrate.*

7. It is an error to assert that Rev. John Brown's Latin school was conducted at "Mount Pleasant" at any time in the 1770s.

Explanation: *Rev. Brown's Latin school at Mount Pleasant was of a peripatetic nature, and it only operated at that location* *in the 1760s. Rev. Brown's pastorate at the Timber Ridge Church was dismissed in 1767, he had moved the school to New Providence several miles away at some time during the process of his dismissal. From that time, Brown's school remained at New Providence as long as it existed.*

8. It is an error to assert that Rev. John Brown ever accepted any appointment made by the Hanover Presbytery in connection with its new seminary, "Augusta Academy" (i.e., Liberty Hall Academy).

Explanation: A review of all the Hanover Presbytery's Meeting Minutes from 1771 to 1776 and all of the meeting minutes of the Liberty Hall Academy Board of Trustees from 1776 until Rev. Brown retired to Kentucky in 1796[249] will demonstrate that Rev. John Brown refused [250] all appointments of the Hanover Presbytery in connection with the presbytery's Academy (Liberty Hall Academy) in Augusta County.

9. It is an error to assert that there was any school operating at "Mount Pleasant" (near Fairfield, Virginia) after Rev. Brown's Latin school was moved from there to New Providence until the Hanover Presbytery established its new and first-ever patronized seminary on October 13, 1774.

Explanation: Rev. John Brown organized what he designated a "Latin school" at a place locally called "Mount Pleasant" when he lived nearby and ministered to both the Timber Ridge and New Providence congregations. Rev. Brown's pastorate at Timber Ridge came to an end in 1767, due in part to his having moved to a different farm near the New Providence congregation. When Mr. Brown moved, he moved his "Latin school" to his new residence adjacent to New Providence. Here his school remained as long as it existed. This fact is demonstrated in Rev. Brown's various letters written during this period. (See, John White Stuart, *The Rev. John Brown of Virginia (1728-1803): His Life and Selected Sermons*, Doctoral Dissertation, University of Massachusetts, 1988, passim)

---

249 *The Hanover Presbytery only held two meetings a year, as a general rule.*

250 *There is no formal refusal noted in the minutes, but there is also no evidence in the minutes to suggest that he accepted, which should not be the case. For example, Brown's appointment as trustee is not followed by any reference to his being present at one of the meetings of the trustees despite those being present having been noted.*

As can be readily seen, there was no school at Mount Pleasant at the time the Hanover Presbytery "established" and "patronized" its first seminary in Virginia on October 13, 1774. The new seminary (academy) took up temporary quarters at "Mount Pleasant" while certain preliminaries to the organizing of the academy were transpiring, including the construction of the academy's new buildings at Timber Ridge.

Note: The first mistake to appear in print concerning the Hanover Presbytery "visiting" Rev. Brown's "Latin school" at New Providence that the auditor has located is found in the "History of Washington College, Virginia," written by Rev. William Hill, <u>American Historical Quarterly</u>, Vol. X [1838], pp. 145–150. What Rev. Hill did was include a spring 1775 meeting minutes extract that only related to a courteous last-minute "visit" to the presbytery's host's private school close by its meeting, along with a list of extracts from various meeting's minutes pertaining to the presbytery's new seminary that was located several miles away, under the direction of Rev. William Graham. This confusion was occasioned by the misguided decision of the presbytery's clerk to include a reference to the "visit" to its host's private school because Rev. Brown's private Latin school had no connection whatsoever to the Hanover Presbytery. The references to these two schools in the minutes are not from the same paragraph, but Mr. Hill publishes them as though they were, thereby creating the appearance that two entirely different schools were the same. They were not the same: one was private and exclusively preparatory; the other was a public academy intended from inception to be a college. The public school was created by, and patronized by, the Hanover Presbytery. The private school of John Brown was not created by nor ever patronized by the Hanover Presbytery, as the eighteenth-century meeting minutes of the presbytery, properly read, clearly demonstrate.

10. It is an error to assume or assert that William Henry Foote, the authority most referred to by W&L historians after 1850, relied upon a credible authority[251] for his preposterous claim,

---

251 Mr. Foote embarrassingly presented two conflicting histories of the college's founding, one in his first volume, the other in his second volume published five years later. In both cases he cites the exact same source from which he quotes, but shockingly, he quotes the same paragraph differently, resulting in two entirely different accounts. Simply put, either one or both of these small extracts is a forgery. As a result, neither of the variant accounts can be trusted to be true because Foote offered no explanation for the gross discrepancy. Unfortunately, Mr. Foote's first account is the one that is most wrong and damaging to the college's history, and tragically, it is the one most referred to by later historians. Had Mr. Foote done this under oath in court, he would be subject to perjury.

Those innumerable historians, citing Mr. Foote as their authority concerning the founding of W&L, cite his first volume, and based upon it, they collectively eviscerate the college's true early history. This variation in accounts is a historical blunder of colossal proportions. Arguably, Mr. Foote, by seriously contradicting himself, in presenting what is ostensibly the same quote with two very different words and phrases, calls into question the reliability of everything he wrote, and everything he reprinted.

by inference, that all the published histories of the early days
of Liberty Hall Academy, all the official documents of Liberty
Hall Academy, and all the official documents of the Hanover
Presbytery during that same time period were incorrect.

*Explanation: Mr. Foote fully admits in his introduction to the
first series of* Sketches of Virginia, Historical and Biographical
*(1850) that he does not bother to provide the normally expected
citations of authority to validate the various contents of his
book. Most of the documents Mr. Foote reprints appear to be
quite accurate reproductions, but the auditor discovered that
virtually everything in Mr. Foote's two volumes on Virginia
history that appears within quotation marks must be checked
for accuracy prior to using the text as a source of authority.
He also extracts a great deal of material that he received as
contributions from various sources, that he carelessly quotes
from and intermixes with his own commentary and editorial
revisions of those contributions. In this way, he sometimes
distorts what others have said, and consequently confuses
and misguides later historians. The great value of his having
preserved some rare documents that might otherwise have
been lost does not justify his numerous distortions and gross
misrepresentations, including placing some of his own words
within quotation marks and thereby designating them as the
words of someone else.*

*Mr. Foote, more than anyone else, is responsible for distorting
the early history of Washington College and for libeling the
college's founding first president, Rev. William Graham. Many,
if not most, of the errors made by more than sixty authors
identified in the main body of this report are directly attributable
to either the irresponsible gossip-mongering of Mr. Foote, or
to his inexplicable quoting of the identical small portion of a
critically significant important statement ostensibly made by the
same person, but with two entirely different conclusions. Said
another way, Mr. Foote quotes precisely the same lines from the
exact same document, but the quote reads entirely differently in
the first volume than it does in the second volume.*

*Astoundingly, the first time Foote quotes from the particular
paragraph in the alleged Rev. Houston letter, he has Mr.
Houston saying that the school to which Houston is ostensibly
alluding was" patronized" by the Hanover Presbytery, and
that it later became Liberty Hall Academy. In his 1855 second
volume, however, quoting from the exact same portion of the*

same paragraph, Foote presents the quote with an entirely different conclusion, which of course, is an unquestionable impossibility. It is analogous to quoting from the same final section of a brief paragraph of the same speech delivered by President Kennedy:

> **In Vol. 1**: "Ask not what your country can do for you, but what you can do for your country."

and then five years later, writing that the president on that same occasion in the same portion of the same paragraph said,

> **In Vol. 2**: "Ask not what your country can do for you, but how can we continue to raise taxes in a recession?"

Foote's changes to Houston's letter is equally disturbing as is the example above.

While most adult Americans in the second half of the twentieth century would immediately realize that something is terribly wrong here, no one seems to have caught this colossal blunder by Mr. Foote. Nonetheless it is a blunder of monumental historical significance to the history of Washington and Lee University, because the repudiation of the long-standing early history known during the college's first seventy-five years (1774–1850) was accomplished only because later historians relied unquestioningly on the reputation of Mr. Foote and blindly accepted his several accountings in his two volumes. In both cases that was a narrative based solely on the portion of the Houston letter that he irresponsibly edited out of the letter, an edit he made without acknowledgment, or explanation. However, more importantly, Mr. Foote edited out the only statement upon which he relied to justify his earlier repudiation of all the earlier histories. This should have been followed by an apology for misquoting Rev. Houston earlier, and a revision of the incorrect history he had presented in Vol. 1. Shockingly, Foote did none of these things. Instead, he simply quotes Houston differently in Vol. 2 and repeats his earlier false and indefensible narrative, and even embellishes the earlier false history, while ignoring the fact that he told his readers in Vol. 1 that Rev. Houston's letter said one thing and subsequently told them that it said something else entirely. One of the versions he presented may be accurate, but both cannot be, because they vary, and the variances are consequential. Accuracy, in cases such as this, demands that the same quote, repeated at different times be precisely the same or noticed and explained.

11. It is an error to claim that any eighteenth-century student who did not matriculate under William Graham at "Augusta Academy" or Liberty Hall Academy is an alumnus of Washington and Lee University. The limited possible exceptions being a student who may have matriculated there during the four-year period between 1796 and 1800, but then, the school was operating without a permanent president, and the classes were mostly underclassmen taught by tutors. Few records are extant from this period.

Explanation: *The catalogues of alumni clearly include the names of some students who attended preparatory schools in Augusta County prior to the establishment of Liberty Hall Academy in 1774. These schools are not linked to Liberty Hall Academy. Insofar as these preparatory schools have no link to Liberty Hall Academy, the students who attended these common schools of various types under various instructors do not warrant the status of alumni of Washington and Lee University. Moreover, no instructor in the eighteenth century who was not hired by the Hanover Presbytery, the trustees of Liberty Hall Academy, or the rector (president) Rev. William Graham or his successors deserves to be listed as an instructor or faculty member of Washington and Lee University.*

12. It is an error to claim that Rev. William Graham, rector of Liberty Hall Academy, was ever censured by the Presbyterian Church.

Explanation: *Many later historians have referred to Washington and Lee's founder, Rev. William Graham, as having been censured by his church. These misguided historians failed to sufficiently research the official records of the Presbyterian Church.*

The misguided and mistaken attacks upon Rev. Graham's character, in this regard, stem from the perjured testimony of one of Rev. Graham's brethren, the Rev. Hezekiah Balch, whose shenanigans in this matter eventually emerged during the only official hearing before the appropriate ecclesiastical court. After taking the evidence from both parties and selected witnesses, the church declined to censure Rev. Graham.

Earlier, an improperly appointed committee of an inappropriate church body had deigned to take testimony in a one-sided, improper presentation, and had erred so far as to make prejudicial remarks about the dispute without having proper jurisdiction, and without having received the other half of the case. In sum, the complaint was dismissed and Rev. Graham was acquitted, and, the complainant, Rev. Balch, marked the beginning of a career in which he was perpetually in dispute with his colleagues. Mr. Balch's lone witness, Col. William Cocke, was a man who was forced from the United States Army for cowardice in the face of the enemy under the threat of a court martial disposition, and was subsequently impeached as a judge in Kentucky's Supreme Court. Such was the character of Balch's only witness.

This is the only complaint ever lodged against the president of Liberty Hall Academy, Rev. William Graham, within the province of the Presbyterian Church. He was never censured by the Presbyterian Church.

13. It is an error to claim that any school in Virginia in the eighteenth century was known as the "Augusta Academy" other than the seminary established by the Hanover Presbytery on October 13, 1774.

Explanation: In America in the eighteenth century, it was inappropriate to denominate a preparatory or precollege school as "academy," because in that era it was the terminology used to describe a school of higher learning but one that the British Crown had not "chartered." Those institutions that received official "charters" were afforded the privilege of bestowing upon their graduates a degree of bachelor of arts. Charters were nearly impossible to obtain in the British colonies of North America unless the school was established and patronized by the Anglican Church of England.[252]

14. It is an error to claim that William Graham was ever a subordinate appointee of the Hanover Presbytery, to any "director," "supervisor," or any other person.

Explanation: Mr. William Graham answered initially to but one single authority in matters pertaining to the affairs of the new academy in Augusta County, Virginia, and that was the

---

252 *For a complicated set of political reasons, the College of New Jersey was the most notable, if not the only, exception to this general rule.*

*Hanover Presbytery. Once ordained as a Presbyterian minister,
of course, he answered in part to the Virginia Synod, and to
some degree to the national Presbyterian General Assembly.
After May of 1776, Rev. Graham was also subject to the oversight
of the newly created board of trustees. At no time during his
tenure at Liberty Hall Academy was Mr. Graham under the
supervision of any single person because he was from the date
of the college's inception the chief administrative officer. This
is a fact made abundantly clear in the meeting minutes of both
the Hanover Presbytery from October of 1774[253] and the Liberty
Hall Academy Board of Trustees, until his resignation in the
fall of 1796.*

15. It is an error to claim that the Hanover Presbytery in
the eighteenth century ever "established," "patronized," or
otherwise officially connected itself to any school organized
or operated by Rev. John Brown, pastor of New Providence
Presbyterian Church.

Explanation: *Many authors after 1850 have made the mistake
of claiming a link between the Hanover Presbytery's new
public academy in Augusta County, Virginia, and Rev. John
Brown's "Latin school" in that same county. There is no such
link, however, as the official records of both the Hanover
Presbytery and the Liberty Hall Academy's board of trustees
demonstrate. In addition, Rev. John Brown and his family were
very early estranged from the academy due to a heartbreaking
engagement breakup between the academy's new director,
Rev. William Graham, and Rev. John Brown's highly esteemed
eldest daughter, "Betsy," which is detailed in the unpublished
"Memoir of Rev. William Graham," written by one of Mr.
Graham's earliest students, Rev. Dr. Archibald Alexander.
Suffice to say that the breakup left two broken hearts, neither
of which was responsible for the unfortunate outcome. The
Brown family was thereafter never reconciled in their negative
feelings toward the academy or its rector, Mr. Graham. Rev.
Brown did not send any of his sons to the academy despite the
fact that it was located in his own neighborhood, and further,
for the academy's first twenty-two years, he never attended a
meeting of the board of trustees of Liberty Hall Academy.[254]*

---

253 *The meeting minutes reference to Rev. John Brown serving as an "inspector" in connection
with Mr. Graham's initial appointment was rendered a moot question, by virtue of Rev. Brown's
failure to accept the appointment, whatever it may have meant.*

254 *In the 1790s, the Lexington Presbytery held some of its meetings at the then-new stone main
building of Liberty Hall Academy, and it is possible that Rev. Brown may have attended one of*

16. It is an error to claim that Rev. John Brown's private Latin school, located in 1775 at, or adjacent to, New Providence Church, was thereafter returned to Mount Pleasant near Fairfield, Virginia, from where it originated.

Explanation: *Many authors writing after 1850 have mistakenly claimed that Rev. John Brown's Latin school, prior to October of 1774, was moved from New Providence to Mount Pleasant, where it was merged with, adopted by, or joined with the Liberty Hall Academy.*

The evidence on this is abundantly clear. Rev. Brown's Latin school was operating at New Providence in April of 1775, as evidenced by the Hanover meeting minutes of that spring meeting. Rev. Brown's Latin school was being conducted at New Providence in December of 1775, as evidenced by the journal entries of Rev. Philip Vickers Fithian, who met with the school's instructor at the time, Mr. Samuel Doak, in the home of Rev. John Brown. (See bibliography re Philip Vicker Fithian's Journal, written in 1775 & 1776.) In addition, Mr. William Graham was at the same time conducting classes at Mount Pleasant several miles from New Providence. Here Mr. Fithian met with his old schoolmate, William Graham, at, as he styles it, "his school." There were therefore two schools and two different locations operating at the same time, rendering it impossible for the one to have evolved from the other.

While Rev. Brown was forced by the effects of the Revolutionary War to close his school during the war's duration, Rev. Brown writes to his brother-in-law Col. William Preston in 1783 of his intention to reopen his Latin school, and requests assistance in securing some necessary books and materials. This was at the time that Rev. William Graham, on behalf of the trustees, was seeking to secure a charter for Liberty Hall Academy from the new Virginia legislature. He was successful in this regard and in October of 1782, the new Virginia Legislature granted the charter and bestowed upon the college the authority to grant the degree of bachelor of arts. Mr. Graham's Liberty Hall was then operating at his property near Whistle Creek just outside of Lexington, and Mr. Brown's reopening of his Latin school was still to be at New Providence, but whether that plan ever came to fruition or not, the auditor was unable to ascertain.

---

these meetings at the school's new building. If so, it would be his last and probably only visit, for he very soon resigned his pastorate and membership in the Presbytery. Shortly thereafter (mid-1790s), he and his wife moved to Kentucky to live among their children.

The school facility on Mr. Wilson's farm denominated locally as "Mount Pleasant" had long since been abandoned. Mr. Brown, after all, had no good reason to move his school once again to its earlier location miles away from his home, and the Meeting House at New Providence.

Brown's school was always peripatetic because Brown relied exclusively on others as tutors, so when a tutor resigned, the school's operation was held in abeyance until another tutor could be obtained by Rev. Brown. After Samuel Doak resigned as tutor in late December of 1775, Brown apparently was unable to obtain a tutor due to the rapidly emerging Revolutionary War. Brown's school was suspended for the duration of the war but in 1782, with the war coming to a close, Brown announced to his relatives his intention to reopen the school. Its activities thereafter, if any, are unknown and unrecorded.

17. It is an error to claim that the Hanover Presbytery "visited" the "Augusta Academy" on April 15, 1775.

Explanation: The spring meeting of the Hanover Presbytery began on its first day at the Timber Ridge Meeting House. After adjourning, the members traveled to the home of Rev. John Brown on Moffett's Creek, where many of them lodged in his capacious home. The remaining parts of the meeting were held at Rev. Brown's home. After concluding all their business and adjourning until their next scheduled meeting in the fall, they accepted their host's invitation to visit his Latin school next door, where the preparatory students studying basic Latin and Greek grammar were in session. Many authors have mistakenly assumed this visit took place at the presbytery's seminary at Mount Pleasant, but it did not. To visit the presbytery's new school would have meant returning toward Timber Ridge several miles distant. Nevertheless, many authors failed to recognize that the second and subsequent day's meetings were not at the same location as the first day's meeting. The school "visited" on that last day was Rev. Brown's Latin school, not Rev. Graham's Academy at Mount Pleasant. Insofar as there was no official connection between Rev. Brown's private school and the Hanover Presbytery, the visit was entirely unofficial.

It was a mistake for the presbytery's clerk, Mr. Irvine, to have even referenced the "visit" to Brown's school in the presbytery's minutes because it was a private affair and it had no connection to the presbytery. It was likely noted, only because of Brown's

*belief that his colleagues were making a mistake by establishing
the seminary at Mount Pleasant and the clerk simply thought it
appropriate to show that the members gave him an opportunity
to showcase his school. Brown clearly viewed the new seminary
as a threat to his private Latin school's continued success. In
that, he was prescient because within a short time, his school
was discontinued, but its closing surely had more to do with the
commencement of the Revolutionary War.*

*Sometimes, as in this case, extending a simple courtesy ends up
causing unintended consequences.*

18. It is an error to claim that the transcribed handwritten
lectures that are attributed to Rev. William Graham and housed
at the Leyburn Library on the campus of Washington and Lee
are what the packet's cover page suggests that they are (i.e.,
lectures written by or "delivered by" Rev. William Graham).[255]

*Explanation: For details, readers are referred to the appendix,
"William Graham's non-existent defense of slavery." This
appendix explains why Dr. David Robson mistakenly believed
that Rev. William Graham was a defender of slavery. Dr. Robson
believed that a written lecture embedded within a packet of extant
lectures in the archives of the library at Washington and Lee
University were in fact what the packet's cover page claims them
to be, to wit: lectures delivered by Rev. William Graham at Liberty
Hall Academy in 1796, which is an entirely misguided belief.*

*Rev. William Graham did not write out any of his lectures.
The packet of lectures from which Dr. Robson has extracted
one particular lecture is comprised, in the main,[256] of lectures*

---

255 These are primarily a packet of transcribed lectures of Dr. John Witherspoon, copied by the
students at Princeton, including President Graham, and then later, re-copied by students at
Liberty Hall Academy and used as a textbook. Rev. Graham's lectures were never written
down. This fact was first explained by Rev. Graham's younger brother Edward in his memoir
of his late brother, published in 1821, and also by Dr. Archibald Alexander in his unpublished
memoir (see bibliography). The Joseph Glass packet's provenance is not thorough or complete.
Rev. William Graham used his personal copy as a template for his own students to copy. This
particular packet, according to the current cover page, was copied by Mr. Joseph Glass in 1796.
Unfortunately, the packet was again recopied by professor or instructor, Waddell in 1896. An
interesting artifact, it is not all that the cover page asserts. For example, contrary to the cover
page, Rev. Graham did not deliver a series of lectures at the college in 1796, because he was
rarely in Lexington that year. The J. Glass packet likely contains at least two lectures that were
added to the packet after Witherspoon's death, which were not written by Dr. Witherspoon.

256 *Whether the particular instructor who made this packet available to students at Liberty Hall
Academy in 1796 had edited or added to the packet he used as a template cannot now be*

written by Dr. John Witherspoon, president of Princeton College, and they were transcribed from a template by William Graham while a student at Princeton under Dr. Witherspoon. These lectures were later used as a sort of textbook by Rev. Graham at Liberty Hall Academy, just as Witherspoon had used them at Princeton.

*There is only one currently known written document written by Rev. Graham that directly addresses slavery, and the only expression on that subject in the letter is **Rev. Graham's belief in the "horrors of slavery**," a sentiment clearly at odds with Dr. Robson's libelous attack on the founding first president of Washington and Lee University. Robson fails to appreciate the importance of the fact that Rev. Graham was the only eighteenth-century president of an American-chartered college (then named Liberty Hall Academy) that enrolled a black student, Mr. John Chavis, in the college's regular academic course. The fact of his college education is attested to by Mr. Chavis and several sitting court magistrates in Rockbridge County, Virginia (Lexington), in 1802.* See appendix devoted to John Chavis for details and citations pertaining to the official court record. Robson's dismissive treatment of this monumental and unprecedented enrollment decision taken by Rev. Graham and his college is frankly shocking and inexplicable.

In addition, Rev. Graham wrote and had published a proposed state constitution for the state of Franklin, which was the most democratic constitution published in North America in the eighteenth century, and it is the only proposed state constitution in the South that did not contain a specific provision for protecting slaveholders property rights in their slaves, an odd omission for an author, if they were indeed, as Dr. Robson contends, a defender of slavery. Dr. Robson's attack on the president of Liberty Hall Academy will not withstand professional scrutiny in regards to his main thesis, or respecting any of his other subsidiary claims against a man he obviously did not know or understand. Dr. Robson's unfortunate article stands as the preeminent example of an unprofessional historical article that is essentially wrong about every charge he made against the subject of his diatribe.

---

determined with any degree of certainty. What is certain is that no evidence has surfaced in the last two hundred and some odd years, which suggests that Rev. William Graham ever publicly advocated for any point of view on the subject of slavery.

19. It is an error to claim that the Liberty Hall Academy's rector, Rev. William Graham, was a proponent or defender of the institution of slavery, or that he lectured on or wrote about that subject. [257]

Explanation: See no. 18 above.

20. It is an error to believe that Rev. William Graham was complicit with his brethren in the Hanover Presbytery when in October of 1784, at the urging of Rev. John B. Smith, the body approved a new position amending its long-standing opposition to taxing the people to support the church.[258]

Explanation: Dr. F. J. Hood, who relied heavily on the works of Charles G. Sellers of Princeton and the University of California at Berkeley, explains what actually happened in Virginia during the struggle for religious liberty. In his biography of Rev. John Blair Smith, he explains the correct sequence of events:

> Smith at one time favored the assessment. Graham on the other hand was at least one Presbyterian minister who had consistently opposed the assessment.[259] Graham was

---

257 While historians may engage in speculation on the subject of William Graham's views on African slavery in America, they will soon discover that there is but a paucity of extant historical evidence upon which to draw any definitive conclusions. Essentially one can mostly only infer from his written words. Indeed, Archibald Alexander initiated some admitted speculation on the question in his unpublished "Memoir of Rev. William Graham," but at a later dated crossed through his speculation without comment. The fact is that even he did not know for sure what his views were, his possession of papers on one black couple and any of their offspring does not mean that he must therefore have supported the institution because Presbyterian ministers in the South who had slaves in their congregations were frequently asked by the slaves to take possession of their immediate family when they suspected they were about to be separated and sold. Such cases constituted distinctions of enormous consequential differences.

  Emancipation was often out of the question because the emancipated slave(s) would, by law, have had to then leave the state of Virginia. This reality created a "Sophie's Choice" for those slaves with extended families still in bondage nearby. *These individuals were truly slaves "in name only," an important distinction often completely lost on citizens then living in non-slave states. It is also significant that the only written comment Rev. Graham is known to have made was in a letter to Col. Arthur Campbell in which he alludes to "the horrors of slavery." (See the bibliography entry for William Graham.)*

258 Rev. Graham led an insurgency against the action in which he successfully obtained a complete repudiation of the amended policy, and even went much further by demanding passage of Jefferson's long-stalled Bill for Religious Liberty, which is explained in detail in the appendix on church and state.

259 It should be pointed out here that one of Dr. Hood's principal sources, Dr. Charles G. Sellers, cited herein, had mistakenly assumed that Mr. Graham was momentarily persuaded that Dr.

of western Pennsylvania and a radical
democrat who wrote the constitution for the
proposed state of Franklin.[260] (Fred J. Hood,
"Revolution and Religious Liberty: The
Conservation of the Theocratic Concept in
Virginia," Church History, p. 180.)

Dr. F. J. Hood continues:

In October, [1785] [Rev.] John Blair Smith
and [Rev.] William Graham presented the
new Presbyterian position in the Assembly
at a meeting of a committee of the whole.[261]

Dr. Charles G. Sellers said this:

"In the spring of 1784, just as the assessment
movement was gaining headway, John
Smith drew up for the Presbyterian
clergy an ambiguous memorial to the
legislature . . . . coupled with one for "an equal
of the protection and favor of government to
all denominations of Christians . . . .When
the Presbytery convened at Timber Ridge
in October, just before the meeting of the
legislature, the general assessment idea was
attacked by William Graham, John Smith's
Princeton classmate whom Samuel Smith
had brought to Virginia to superintend the
Valley Presbyterian's Liberty Hall Academy.
Graham was a radical democrat and a born
agitator, . . ." (Sellers, "John Blair Smith,"
pp. 211–212.)

John Smith was correct in regards to what policy the church should adopt in light of the apparent
inevitability of the passage of the bill for a general assessment. In truth, Dr. Hood was correct
to say that Graham's opposition to any assessment was consistent, and that is why Mr. Graham
attacked John B. Smith's proposal to modify their long-standing position of opposition to any
and all assessment to support the church.

260 Fred J. Hood, *"Revolution and Religious Liberty: The Conservation of the Theocratic Concept
in Virginia,"* Church History, Vol. 40, NO. 2 (Jun. 1971) p. 180.

261 Fred J. Hood, *"Revolution and Religious Liberty: The Conservation of the Theocratic Concept
in Virginia,"* Church History, Vol. 40, NO. 2 (Jun. 1971) p. 180.

Dr. Sellers continues:

> "As soon as the presbytery adopted his [John Smith's] memorial [Oct. 1784] John Smith and one of the other ministers departed to present it to the legislature. He had no sooner reached Richmond, however than he was overtaken by anti-assessment petitions from large numbers of Presbyterian laymen in the Valley counties of Rockingham and Rockbridge, where William Graham's influence was strong . . . . Though the assessment movement seemed assured of success at first, dissenter resistance to any legislation on religion was greatly stiffened . . . . This development and the anti-assessment backfire that William Graham had lit in the Valley were too much for Smith's hot temper. . ." (Sellers, "John Blair Smith," p. 213)

Dr. Sellers again:

> "The spring of 1785 produced a violent public reaction against assessment, especially in the Valley, where the Presbyterian laity rose in rebellion against the position into which John Smith had maneuvered Hanover Presbytery . . . . Hanover Presbytery voted unanimously against assessment at its May meeting and called a great convention of Presbyterian ministers and laymen . . . to memorialize against it." (Sellers, "John Blair Smith," p. 214)

Dr. F. J. Hood adds this:

> "This convention, composed largely of laymen, sent to the Virginia Assembly the first decisive Presbyterian statement [composed by Rev. Wm. Graham] calling for disestablishment. The memorial began, The Ministers and Lay Representatives of the Presbyterian Church in Virginia, assembled in Convention. . . The memorial was as extraordinary for Presbyterianism of the day

as was the "convention" that drafted it."[262]
(Fred J. Hood, "Revolution and Religious
Liberty: The Conservation of the Theocratic
Concept in Virginia," p. 180.)

Dr. Sellers concludes with this:

"Smith's defeat was a triumph for William
Graham who drafted the convention's
vehement denunciation of any legislation on
religion . . . . A deluge of anti-assessment
petitions from all over the state, . . . buried
the assessment bill in committee and sent
Jefferson's long-deferred bill for establishing
religious freedom racing through both houses.
Thus John Smiths defeat helped pave the way
for the classic statement of the emerging
American doctrine of separation of church
and state." (Sellers, "John Blair Smith," p. 214)

Conclusion on this important point

Liberty Hall Academy's president Rev. William Graham's triumph paved
the way for the new nation's embracing of the doctrine of religious liberty, and
provided his Princeton schoolmate, James Madison, with the requisite armaments
for ensuring that the religious liberty doctrine would be the first provision set forth
in the American *Bill of Rights*, commonly referred to as "the establishment clause."
Absent the intervention by Rev. William Graham of Liberty Hall Academy, the
law of the land in the United States would undoubtedly have been that all citizens
would be taxed to support the church, a virtual fact that has been missed by
most historians interested in religious liberty in the United States. History and
Washington and Lee have Dr. Charles Sellers to thank for having discovered this
heretofore well-kept secret about the important role played by the university's
founding first president, William Graham.

*Note: As the table of contents indicate, there are appendices attached that address some of the
main subject areas referenced in the above enumerated findings.*

All of the findings listed above are easily proven by clear and convincing
evidence, as the main body of this audit report demonstrates. Nevertheless, these
listed mistakes continued to abound throughout the literature of the second half
of the nineteenth century and up to the present day.

****

---

262   The actual drafting of the convention's memorial was carried out by Rev. William Graham,
president of Liberty Hall Academy.

Five Errors of Omission

1. A failure of the university to publicly recognize the critically important and vitally significant role played by their founder, William Graham, in the struggle for religious liberty in Virginia, and consequently in securing the United States Bill of Rights and especially the establishment clause of the first amendment. In this regard, he was second only to Thomas Jefferson and his schoolmate at Princeton, James Madison.

2. A failure of the university to publicly recognize the critically important publication of one of, if not the then most democratic state Constitution west of the Blue Ridge Mountains, written by its founding first president, William Graham. (See Thomas Perkins Abernethy, *From Frontier to Plantation in Tennessee: A Study in Frontier Democracy*, Chapel Hill, The University of North Carolina Press, 1932.)

3. A failure of the university to publically recognize the critically important publication of *An Essay on Government*, written by their first president, William Graham. (See Rev. William Graham, *Essay on Government,* Philadelphia, 1786. [A copy is on file at Leyburn Library at Washington and Lee University.]

4. A failure of the university to publically recognize the critically important decision of Rev. William Graham to enroll into Liberty Hall Academy's regular academic program the first black college student in America. (See appendix concerning Rev. John Chavis.)

5. A failure of the university to publically recognize the critically important decision of Rev. William Graham to enroll into Liberty Hall Academy's regular academic program the first female college student in America. (See appendix concerning Mrs. Sarah [McBride] Priestley.)

****

Chapter Three

A Baker's Dozen (13) of Key Historical Sources
(Prior to 1850)

Thirteen Important Sources Prior to W. H. Foote (1850)

1. **Official Minutes of the Meetings of the Hanover Presbytery [1771–1776]**

2. **Rev. Philip Vickers Fithian's Published Journal [1775–1776]**
   Philip Vickers Fithian, *Journal, 1775-1776: Written on the Virginia-Pennsylvania Frontier and in the Army Around New York,* Princeton, Princeton University Press, 1934

3. **Official Minutes of the Board of Trustees (Liberty Hall Academy) (Includes the college's first authorized history dated May 1776)**
   Note: The college's first authorized history composed by Rev. Caleb Wallace appears on the first several pages of text (pages 37). Wallace composed this history at the behest of the Hanover Presbytery of which he was then its clerk. Never published, this manuscript history was copied into Liberty Hall Academy's first record book, which was where the board of trustees kept its earliest official meeting minutes. This venerable record book is extant and housed in the archives at the university's Leyburn Library.

4. **Board of Trustees of Liberty Hall Academy (petition re Wm. Graham (1792))**

5. **William Graham Letter, Written for the Trustees to President George Washington [1796]** (Includes a brief history of the college)

6. **Edward Graham's "Memoir of Rev. William Graham A.M."**
   The Evangelical and Literary Magazine and Missionary Chronicle, IV (1821), p.75 et seq.

7. **Samuel L. Campbell's "Washington College, Lexington, Virginia"**
   Southern Literary Messenger, June 1838, beginning at p. 364.

8. **Rev. William Hill's** "History of Washington College, Virginia"
   American Historical Quarterly, Vol. X, [1838], pp. 145–150 [author's name not listed][263]

---

263 Cited in Crenshaw, Ollinger, General Lee's College [unpublished footnotes (typescript) Washington & Lee University Archives/Library] "Vol. II, "Appendix "A"] [hand-paginated in pencil as p. no. 526. [based in large measure upon an article by Rev. Dr. William Hill [Hampden Sydney] in ***Southern Religious Telegraph*** [Richmond] Dec. 19, 1834, Jan. 2, 23, Feb. 6, 1835 [serialized form] and also relying on a letter to the unnamed author from Edward Graham, Esq. of Lexington, Virginia. These articles, according to Ollinger Crenshaw, both date the history of the college from the 1770s and the actions of the Hanover Presbytery.

9.   **Rev. Archibald Alexander's: An Address before Alumni of Washington College,**

Archibald Alexander DD, _Address delivered before the Alumni Association of Washington College, Virginia_, delivered June 29, 1843, Lexington, Va., R. H. Glass, 1843, 31 pp.; also later in Washington and Lee Historical Papers No. 2, Lexington, Va., 1890.

10. **Henry Howe's, _Historical Collections of Virginia_.**

Charleston, S. C., Babcock & Co., 1845

11. **Davidson's History, Presbyterian Church in Ky. & the Valley of Va.**

Rev. Robert Davidson, _History of the Presbyterian Church in The State of Kentucky: With a Preliminary Sketch of the Churches in the Valley of Virginia_, New York, Robert Carter, 1847.

12. **"A Brief Sketch of Washington College"**

On the Occasion of the Author's Inauguration As President of Washington College, Virginia, Philadelphia, The Board of Trustees, 1849 [pamphlet pp. 39. The Junkin Inaugural Address includes an important appendix: "_A Brief Sketch of the Early History of the College_" (ordered printed by the board of trustees). This constitutes the college's first published history.

13. **President Henry Ruffner's _manuscript_ and _published_** "Early History of Washington College."[264] Henry

Ruffner, ed. _Washington & Lee University Historical Papers_, Vol. 1, "Early History of Washington College," Baltimore, John Murphy & Co. 1890. Note: While published in 1890, Ruffner's history was written in the 1840s with 1857 revisions.

**Thirteen Sources with Pertinent Extracts Therefrom**

1. Official Minutes of the Meetings of the Hanover Presbytery [1771–1776]:

> "_We do therefore agree to establish and patronize a publick [sic] school which shall be confined to the County of Augusta. At present it shall be managed by Mr. William Graham._"[265] (_Minutes, Hanover Presbytery of Virginia_, 1771–1776)

Note: This is the original, handwritten manuscript minutes of the Hanover Presbytery from 1771 through 1776. These particular minutes detail the entire process from the presbytery's first thoughts in 1771 through their actions to establish a seminary including the appointment of a board of trustees to oversee the operations of their seminary. [Reviewed in a scanned Pdf file made available to the auditor by Union Theological Seminary, Richmond.]

---

264   We treat them together [i.e., the published and mass. versions] because there are few differences, and none that are material. The originals were written in the 1840s and are so designated by President Ruffner's son, Wm. Henry Ruffner, in marginalia accompanying the manuscript.

265   .Minutes, Hanover Presbytery of Virginia, 1771–1776, scanned images of handwritten minutes from William Smith Morton Library, Union Presbyterian Seminary, Richmond, Va.00

2. Rev. Philip Vickers Fithian's Published Journal [1775–1776]

> December 24, 1775 *Mr. Graham, lately initiated a brother,*
> *is appointed Director of a school in the neighborhood of*
> *Mr. Brown's—He thinks to enlarge his Method of Education*
> *so much as to finish Youth in their classical, Philosophical*
> *Studies*— [Written at the time, December 1775.]

3. Record Book Official Minutes of the Board of Trustees - Introduction [1776] (Liberty Hall Academy)

> *The Present Academy of Liberty Hall began under the*
> *Direction and Patronage of the Presbytery of Hanover as the*
> *following minutes fully evince."* This is followed by a series of
> extracts from the minutes of Hanover Presbytery, dating the
> establishment to Oct. 13, 1774, and signed and dated, [Rev.]
> "Caleb Wallace, Clerk, May 1776)."[266]

4. Petition of the Liberty Hall Academy Board of Trustees (in re Wm Graham 1792)[267]

Note: Written and signed by every trustee of Liberty Hall Academy during the
college's first twenty years.

Through the Presbytery of Lexington we are informed of the
attempts of the board of trustees of the college of Hampden
Sydney to deprive us of our Rector the Rev. Wm. Graham
in order to convince him to accept the presidency of their
college . . . . In our objecting to the removal of Mr. Graham, we
would not in the least reflect on Trustees of Hampden Sydney
for attempting to obtain our Rector from us for we think him
qualified for such a place and that they need such a gentleman.
But this so far from leading us to freely give him up as they
wish does considerably increase our desire to retain him over
our Academy. . . . Hampden Sydney can plead the necessity. On
this [??] surely we are not behind them. ***For it was under Wm.***
Graham that our Academy first received its existence and
it is chiefly owing to his extraordinary exertions that it has
persevered through all the convulsions of a calamitous War
and the many vicissitudes which have taken place through the
operations of various causes for the space of about 16 years, and

---

266 Rev. Caleb Wallace, record book, containing the minutes of the board of trustees of Liberty Hall
   Academy, p. 3, This opening is written down and organized by Rev. Caleb Wallace, clerk of
   the Hanover Presbytery. This introduction is the first written account of the origins of Liberty
   Hall Academy other than the actual meeting minutes. The introduction is signed and dated by
   the presbytery's clerk, Rev. Caleb Wallace, May 1776.

267 On file at Washington and Lee's Leyburn Library (archives) [file 41].

here we cannot forebear asking the question would it be wisdom or duty in Synod to destroy our Academy which has been the most useful to the church of any in the state and which is at this time more promising to the church in point of numbers than ever it has been, and this too on the bare probability that another may or nearly so must be the consequence unless providence preserveth it if our Rector be removed at this juncture . . . .

For these and such reasons *your petitioners earnestly pray that this Rev'd Synod would not remove Wm Graham from his present charge of the Academy and we hope and trust that you will see reasons to grant the prayer of your petitioners*. And that the great head of the church may direct you in all things to seek and promote his glory as the object and prayer of the Trustees of Liberty Hall.

We appoint Mr. John Wilson a member of our Board [??] on our behalf to present our petition and to give such information as may be required. (Emphasis added)

5. William Graham Letter Written on Behalf of the Board of Trustees of Liberty Hall Academy, to President George Washington in 1796 [1796]

*From a conviction of the necessity and utility of a public Seminary to complete the education of youth in this upper part of the State; as early as the year 1776, a seminary **before conducted in these parts as a grammar school**, received the nominal title of an Academy*[268]. . .[269] (Emphasis added)

This constitutes the institution's [Washington and Lee University, then Liberty Hall Academy] first representation of its earliest history.

Note no. 1: This brief history of the origins was written by the school's first rector at the direction of the board of trustees. The letter is signed by both Rev. Graham and Rev. Samuel Houston. Mr. Houston had every opportunity to insist that the section of letter devoted to a brief sketch of the origins include a reference to the school of Rev. John Brown, but he did not, and therefore the letter does not mention Mr. Brown in connection with Liberty Hall Academy. Similarly, Houston signed the presbytery's letter of recognition of Rev. John Brown's service while within the bounds of the presbytery, written at the time of Brown's retirement and dismissal from the presbytery occasioned by his move to Kentucky in 1796. This letter is also noticeably devoid of any mention of Rev. John Brown in connection with the affairs or origins of Liberty Hall Academy. These two facts tend to question Houston's later letter to Rev. Morrison in which he shares recollections of his childhood and in so doing mistakenly claims that the Augusta Academy and Rev. Brown's school were one and

---

268

269 Taken from the official record of board of trustees as reprinted in Foote's Sketches of Virginia, 1850.

the same, when they were not. Moreover, the Lexington Presbytery's letter of dismission, concerning Rev. Brown's resignation and removal to Kentucky in 1795, includes the presbytery's recognition of Rev. Brown's long service as pastor of his congregation at New Providence, but tellingly omits any mention of Rev. Brown's connection's to the Presbyterian Church's seminary, Liberty Hall. Even more interesting is that the letter is signed by Mssrs. Rev. William Wilson and Rev. Samuel Houston, both of whom were baptized by Rev. Brown and whose families were members of Mr. Brown's church. Of course, Rev. Houston is the author of the notorious letter to Rev. Morrison many years later that mistakenly asserts that Liberty Hall Academy was an extension of the school conducted earlier at Mount Pleasant. Rev. Houston apparently forgot that the school he was referencing had been moved from Mount Pleasant several years before the Hanover Presbytery established their new seminary that began its operations in the same general area where Brown's earlier school had been located. Hence, the confusion in Rev. Houston's mind when writing his letter many years after the events had transpired. A mistake, his colleagues, friends, and relations who published histories on the subject did not make, including Professor Edward Graham, Rev. Archibald Alexander, and Dr. Samuel L. Campbell.

*Note no. 2: In bold and italics above appears the term "**grammar school**," which may have caused, for some historians, confusion as to why this term was invoked by the rector, Rev. Graham. It may be properly explained as Mr. Graham's scrupulous attention to accuracy, given that the proposed endowment was being competed for, and Graham was referencing the term, because it had been used by the Hanover Presbytery in their minutes of 1775. They used the term "grammar school" to refer to the temporary and initial school at Mount Pleasant, under the care and tuition of Mr. Graham, who, of course, had no upper-class students available in the very beginning, and those earliest students likely all required some measure of preparatory instruction, while the new academy's buildings were being constructed. To fail to properly disclose this true depiction, would have invited competitors to claim misrepresentation by Liberty Hall Academy.*

6. Edward Graham's "Memoir of Rev. William Graham A.M." *The Evangelical and Literary Magazine and Missionary Chronicle*, IV, (1821), p.75 et seq. [1821]

The presbytery of Hanover, the only presbytery, then and for many years afterwards, in the colony, took the subject [a new Seminary] into consideration. There seemed to be a difficulty in obtaining a suitable person to manage its interests. Mr. Smith [Rev. Samuel Stanhope], informed them that he knew a young man whom he thought eminently qualified for the station, and who he supposed could be induced to accept it. **He wrote immediately to Mr. Graham, informed him of the state of things in Virginia, and urged him to come without delay. Accordingly he came and a school was soon formed for him.** He commenced teaching at a place called Mount Pleasant, an eminence in the vicinity of the pleasant village of Fairfield . . .

The presbytery of Hanover turned its attention particularly to this school, and at a meeting of that body held at Cub Creek, in October 1774, they came to the resolution "To

establish and patronize a public school, which shall be confined to the county of Augusta in this colony–At present it shall be managed by Mr. William Graham, a gentleman properly recommended to this presbytery." (Edward Graham, "Memoir of William Graham A. M."[270]) (Emphasis added)

This constitutes the first published account of the founding of Liberty Hall Academy.

7. Samuel L. Campbell's "Washington College, Lexington, Virginia," *Southern Literary Messenger*, June 1838, beginning at p. 364.

Note no. 1: "Dr. Campbell was for many years a trustee of Washington College, and knew as much of its early history as any other person in the world. Shortly *before his death he drew up a brief history of his Alma Mater, and published it in the Southern Literary Messenger"*
(Alexander, Memoir, pp. 49, 50. Written in the 1840s.)

Note no. 2: "Dr. Samuel L. Campbell, of Rockbridge, who enjoyed opportunities of acquaintance with Mr. Graham equal to those enjoyed by any other man. The father of Doctor Campbell, Charles Campbell, Esq., was one of Mr. Graham's most intimate friends, who agreed with him in all his sentiments, and at whose house he made his home when in the neighborhood. And Dr. Campbell was brought up under the tuition of Mr. Graham from his youth, and was perfectly acquainted with all his excellences and his foibles. He not only pursued his academical studies under the direction of Mr. G, but also studied theology under his guidance for several years. . ." [Alexander, Mss. Memoir of William Graham, pp. 48, 49.]

Here below is the 1838 testimony of Dr. Campbell:

About threescore years ago[271] (i.e., circa 1770s) the Hanover Presbytery taking into consideration the low state of literature in this commonwealth, *conceived a project of establishing a seminary of learning in the upper country. They wisely concluded that such an establishment in the limestone valley would afford to all classes an opportunity of acquiring a liberal education, thereby rendering unnecessary the inconvenience and extra expense of resorting to northern colleges* . . . it was readily foreseen that the times were unfavorable for making collections of money for any public purpose. . . . The Presbytery, however, considering the necessity of the case, thought that something might be done; and on making experiment something was done. The trustees soon determined to erect a building; and

---

270 .Edward Graham, "Memoir of Rev. William Graham, A.M." *The Evangelical and Literary Magazine and Missionary Chronicle*, IV, (1821), p.75 et seq. No authorship attribution appears in the magazine. [Note: Attributed to Edward Graham (Rev. Wm.'s brother) by Archibald Alexander upon whom one can rely. Moreover, the authorship has been generally accepted by the historians of this locale and this period.]

271 Sixty years ago would make the time period the 1770s.

a site was chosen in a grove, on a summit of Timber Ridge, about one mile northwest of the present Village of Fairfield . . . and appropriately denominated Mount Pleasant . . . A teacher was now employed. The first whose name I remember was William Graham. He was a graduate of Nassau Hall, during the administration of the celebrated Doctor Witherspoon.

Mr. Graham came to this country with the character of a gentleman of genius, scholarship, and piety, which character he supported through life.

A number of students from this and the neighboring counties now resorted to Mount Pleasant. In a short time a very respectable grammar school was formed. **This was the first germ of Washington College**. (Emphasis added)

Here (Mount Pleasant) Washington College drew its first breath. On this spot, Mount Pleasant, commenced the establishment of a seminary of learning. (Dr. Samuel L. Campbell, History of Washington College," *Southern Literary Messenger*, Vol. IV, 1838, pp. 107—108.) (Emphasis added)

8. Rev. William Hill's "History of Washington College, Virginia" [1838]

The following extracts from the records of the Presbytery of Hanover, Va.

> Oct. 4th, 1773, the presbytery agree to fix the public seminary for the liberal education of youth in Staunton, Augusta county." 'Augusta included then what is now the county of Rockbridge.' "Oct. 12th (13th) 1774, the presbytery resume the consideration of a public school for the liberal education of youth, judging it to be of great and immediate importance. We do, therefore agree to establish, and patronize a public school, which shall be confined to the county of Augusta. At present it shall be managed by Mr. William Graham, a gentleman properly recommended to this presbytery . . . etc., etc." [pp. 145–146] (The entire paragraph is taken from the article, the single quotation marks represent text from the Hanover Presbytery minutes)

Note: It is of paramount importance to take notice of a footnote in this article on page 147, which reads as follows:

> *"The Augusta Academy was first taught in a log-building, situated in a forest, on a lofty eminence, about a mile and a*

*half or two miles north of the village of Fairfield in Rockbridge
County." –Ms. Letter to the writer from Edward Graham, Esq.
of Lexington."*

*Note: This article was published in 1838 and Edward Graham died in 1840, so very near the end of
his life Edward communicates to Rev. William Hill to aid in his research for the article. Similarly
Rev. Davidson corresponded with Edward Graham numerous times concerning his history of the
Churches in the Valley, in conjunction with his history of the Presbyterian Church in Kentucky. If
Edward had altered his views about the origin of Liberty Hall Academy, certainly he would have
informed Rev. Hill, or Rev. Davidson, of his views. It is noteworthy then, that two Presbyterian
clergymen authors had received intelligence from Edward Graham on the early history of Liberty
Hall Academy, and yet neither of them refer to the schools of Rev. John Brown, or Robert Alexander,
in connection with Liberty Hall Academy.*

*Note: Davidson mistakenly refers to the presbytery, having twice visited their seminary so, he
obviously thought the "visit" referred to in the presbytery's minutes covering the April 1775 meeting
was referring to the seminary, Augusta Academy, but that is incorrect. The April 1775 visit was an
unofficial one regretfully referenced in the meeting minutes. Brown was their host for several days
and the visit was to Brown's Latin school next door to his residence. In fact, the presbytery only
visited their seminary in Augusta County once prior to its having created a board of trustees for this
school. The one visit to its own school was in the spring of 1776.[272]*

Rev. Hill's article appeared in the, American Historical
Quarterly, Vol. X, [1838], pp. 145-150. Authorship is therein
unspecified, but cited in Ollinger Crenshaw's, *General Lee's
College* [unpublished footnotes (typescript) Washington &
Lee University Archives/Library], "Vol. II, "Appendix "A"]
[hand-paginated in pencil as p. no. 526 [based in large measure
upon an article by Rev. Dr. William Hill [Hampden Sydney] in_
Southern Religious Telegraph [Richmond], Dec. 19, 1834, Jan.
2, 23, Feb. 6, 1835 [serialized form] and also relying on a letter
to the unnamed author from Edward Graham, but the letter's
whereabouts is unknown. Both articles, according to Ollinger
Crenshaw, date the history of the college from the 1770s and the
actions of the Hanover Presbytery. Crenshaw accepted that Rev.
Hill was likely responsible, in the main, for the contents of this

---

272   *Davidson lived in Kentucky and was possibly misled by descendants of Rev. John Brown who
     had somehow become confused about their ancestor Rev. John Brown's role in the educational
     activities that existed in the neighborhood of Timber Ridge and New Providence Presbyterian
     congregations. However this family came to misunderstand Rev. Brown's relationship with
     the founders of Liberty Hall Academy is unknown, but there can be no mistake about the fact
     that Rev. John Brown of New Providence congregation, by his own free choice, had absolutely
     no connection whatsoever with the affairs of the Hanover Presbytery's seminary in Augusta
     County. Brown shunned all appointments related to the seminary and from the date of its
     establishment in October of 1774 until his departure from Virginia to Kentucky in 1796, he
     never attended a meeting of that school's board of trustees. He refused to send any of his sons
     to Liberty Hall and wrote to others imploring them to send their sons elsewhere. In sum, Rev.
     John Brown was never a friend of Augusta Academy or Liberty Hall Academy, as the school
     had been named by the new trustees in 1776.*

unsigned article. This review relied on the article in *Southern Religious Telegraph* and we accepted Dr. Crenshaw's word that the *Southern Religious Telegraph* article was the basis upon which the other article was written, and especially in regards to the date of origin of the college. We were unable to locate a copy of the older of these two articles. We are, however, content to rely upon Dr. Crenshaw's belief on this matter.

9. Rev. Archibald Alexander's "An Address before Alumni of Washington College," Delivered June 29, 1843, limited edition; also later in Washington and Lee Historical Papers No. 2, Lexington, Va., 1890 [1843]

I cannot conclude this address without pronouncing a brief eulogy **on the man who deserves to be called the father of this College, and whose memory should be venerated by all its alumni. I mean the Rev. William Graham.** [p. 128]

When the Presbytery of Hanover determined to establish a school in this Valley, for the rearing of young men for the ministry, they applied to the Reverend Samuel Stanhope Smith, then itinerating in the State, to recommend a suitable person to take charge of their school, upon which **he at once recommended Mr. Graham; and at their request wrote to him to come on to the Valley of Virginia. Before this time,** a ***classical*** school had been taught at the place called Mount Pleasant, near the little town of Fairfield. Here Mr. Graham commenced his labours as a teacher; and here we find the germ whence sprung this college." (p. 129) (Emphasis added)

Note no. 1: That "classical" school had been moved to New Providence by Rev. John Brown long before Mr. Graham came to Virginia and continued there well after "Augusta Academy" was established on October 13, 1744.

Note no. 2: The address delivered in 1843 was published then [1843], in a limited edition by R. H. Glass.

10. Henry Howe's "Historical Collections of Virginia," 1845

"Washington College, one of the oldest literary institutions south of the Potomac,[273] was established as an academy in the year 1776, under the name of Liberty Hall, by the Hanover Presbytery (then embracing the whole of the Presbyterian Church in Virginia). Its first rector was the Rev. William Graham, a native of Pennsylvania and a graduate of Nassau Hall, N.J. [Princeton]. Mr. Graham was a man of extensive

---

273 It is probably the second oldest institution of higher learning south of the Potomac, second only to William and Mary, which was chartered by authorities of the British Crown.

acquirements, great originality of thought, warm patriotism, and indomitable energy; and to his exertions, more than to those of any other man, the institution owes its establishment, and its continuance during troublous times of our revolutionary struggle. Liberty Hall received its charter from the state in the year 1782, still retaining the name of an academy, although its charter authorized it 'to confer literary degrees, to appoint professors, as well as masters and tutors, and, in short, to perform all the acts which properly belong to a college.'" (p. 57)

11. Davidson's History, Presbyterian Church in Ky. and The Valley of Va.

Rev. Robert Davidson, *History of The Presbyterian Church in The State of Kentucky: With a Preliminary Sketch of the Churches in the Valley of Virginia*, New York, Robert Carter, 1847.

> A single seminary being deemed inadequate to the growing wants of so extensive a country, ***another was opened under the patronage of Hanover Presbytery, in what is now Rockbridge county*** . . . "A single seminary being deemed inadequate to the growing wants of so extensive a country, ***another was opened under the patronage of Hanover Presbytery, in what is now Rockbridge county*** but was then part of Augusta, in ***November 1774.*** Its location was then on Mount Pleasant . . . and it was at First called Augusta Academy" [p. 40] (Emphasis added here represents error.)

The above quote is wrong on one point, which is that Davidson is asserting that another patronized school had already been established in 1774, but the one he alludes to is the first school established by the presbytery of Hanover. Davidson's error stems from one of his principal sources, Edward Graham, who mistakenly believed that the seminary in Prince Edward County, under Rev. Samuel Stanhope Smith, predates the establishment of the seminary in Augusta County. In fact, the reverse is true, and this fact is clearly demonstrated in the Hanover Presbytery's own meeting minutes covering 1774–1775. Our report details this in the main body of the report. What Davidson does report accurately is that the seminary (Augusta Academy) was established by the presbytery in 1774 and it was during that time denominated, unofficially, in the minutes as "Augusta Academy."[274] Unfortunately Davidson reports its origin in November of 1774, when the presbytery's records clearly demonstrate that it was established on October 13, 1774.

---

274 The name "Augusta Academy" was used to distinguish between the Hanover Presbytery's two recently established seminaries, the one from the other.

> In 1776, the Presbytery, who had shown much
> interest in the school, and had *twice attended
> the examinations*, made the appointment
> [Wm. Graham's appointment] permanent,
> and as Mr. Graham had now taken charge of
> Timber Ridge congregation, in connection
> with Hall's Meeting House, the Academy
> was transferred thither, and suitable buildings
> provided. [Davidson, History of the Presb. Church,
> Ky] (Emphasis added here represents errors)

In the section of Rev. Davidson's book devoted to the history of Presbyterian Churches in the Valley of Virginia, he relies heavily for his authority on eight separate letters he had received from Edward Graham. Davidson's treatment of the establishment assigns to that event the founding date of November of 1774. In that, he was one month beyond the actual date. Importantly, however, Davidson relies, in large part, upon eight letters from Edward Graham[275] and he does not date the origin of Liberty Hall Academy earlier than 1774. If, as the advocates of the so-called Edward Graham memorandum contend, Edward had abandoned his published view on the date of origin, it is difficult to reconcile why Rev. Davidson, relying so heavily on Edward Graham's letters, publishes his 1847 account, which follows Edward's earlier 1821 published account. Instead, Davidson became yet another in a growing list of early historians that date the school's founding to the actions of the Hanover Presbytery in 1774.

Note: The above reference to Edward Graham letters is of singular importance when analyzing the so-called Edward Graham memorandum that some mid-nineteenth-century writers contend represents a view of Edward Graham held since the eighteenth century. The assessment in this regard, however, is completely wrong. The referenced memorandum is of no historical value whatever, a fact we describe in detail within the main body of the report. It is important to keep a few dates in mind when considering Edward Graham's views. (1) Edward wrote his "Memoir of Rev. William Graham A.M." in 1821, and it contains his only, and the first published account, of the founding of Washington and Lee (then "Augusta Academy," or later, Liberty Hall Academy) and, in essence, is an entirely different account from that set forth on the alluded to document of unknown provenance and authorship; (2) Edward Graham died in November of 1840 and Davidson's book was published in 1847; Davidson says in his preface that the book was based on nine years of research. Davidson relied heavily on eight letters from Edward Graham in the section of the book devoted to the Presbyterian Churches of the Valley of Virginia. The most important fact, in this regard, is that Davidson's account bears no resemblance whatever to that contained in the mysterious, unsigned, and undated memorandum attributed to Edward Graham by Col. Bolivar Christian. If Mr. Christian's unauthenticated speculation is what he says it is, it is highly unlikely that Rev. Davidson would have relied so heavily on Edward Graham, and then elected not to follow Edward's early published version. There is no compelling reason to believe Edward Graham materially altered his 1821 published belief that Liberty Hall Academy [Washington College/Washington and Lee] was founded by the Hanover Presbytery in 1774 under Edward's brother, William Graham. This notion

---

275 (See Davidson's footnotes) in Davidson, Rev. Robert, *History of The Presbyterian Church in The State of Kentucky: With a Preliminary Sketch of the Churches in the Valley of Virginia*, New York, Robert Carter, 1847. See the special section devoted to the Churches of the Valley of Virginia.

is dealt with at length in the main body of the report. In truth, the evidence is incontrovertible that Edward's view on the date of the college's origins remained steadfast from the date of his published memorial in 1821 until his death in 1840. Anything he may have said or written on the subject in earlier times is absolutely irrelevant.

It is worthwhile to point out that Rev. Davidson does err in at least one regard concerning Washington and Lee's early history in that he follows Edward's long-standing mistaken idea that Hampden Sydney College [Prince Edward Academy] was established shortly before Washington and Lee University [Liberty Hall Academy]. Both Edward Graham and Robert Davidson would have been wise to consult the presbytery's meeting minutes where they would have discovered that they had the establishments in reverse order. Washington and Lee was established on October 13, 1774. Hampden Sydney was established on February 1, 1775. About this fact, the Hanover Presbytery could not have been more clear. Rev. Davidson did get the Washington and Lee founding date correct, but then, mistakenly, represents that Hampden Sydney had already been established.

12. First authorized and published history of Washington College,[276] "A Brief Sketch of Washington College"[277] (Washington College's first authorized and first history published at the direction of the college)

> "As the dark clouds of the Revolution seemed to be gathering on the mountains' brow, many sober and reflecting minds, on both sides of the Blue Ridge, began to feel deeply interested in the question of education. The state of alienated affection between them and the mother country, must diminish the influx of educated intellect: and men inquired, "who shall be our teachers in the higher departments of learning, science and religion?" Various attempts at classical instruction were made by private persons, and with considerable success, in the Valley. But no movement resulting in permanancy [sic] occurred until 1771: when the presbytery of Hanover (then embracing all the Presbyterians in Virginia) took the subject into serious consideration, and after three years' consultation and experimenting, came to decided action, as appears by the following minute:

---

276   The first authorized history of the college, written by Caleb Wallace in 1776, was, technically, not published, but it was recorded in the Liberty Hall Academy's record book containing the board of trustees' earliest meeting minutes, beginning on the book's first page of text.

277   .Rev. George Junkin, DD, *Christianity: The Patron of Literature and Science: An Address Delivered February 22, 1849. On the Occasion of the Author's Inauguration as president of Washington College, Virginia,* Philadelphia, The Board of Trustees, 1849 [pamphlet p. 39.] The Junkin inaugural address includes an important appendix: "*A Brief Sketch of the Early History of the College*" (ordered printed by the board of trustees). This constitutes the college's first published history of their school.

"**Oct. 12, 1774.** At a meeting of the Presbytery of Hanover, at Cub Creek, in Charlotte, Presbytery resumed the consideration of a school for the liberal education of youth, and unanimously judge it to be of great and immediate importance. _We do therefore agree to establish and patronize a public school, which shall be confined to the county of Augusta in this colony. And we order, that at present, it shall be managed by Mr. William Graham, a gentleman who has been well recommended to this body_, and under the general inspection of the Rev. Mr. Brown." [Appendix, "A Brief Sketch of the Early History of Washington College" p. 35] (Emphasis added)

Note: It should be pointed out here that both Edward Graham and Archibald Alexander's published histories of the college during these early years dropped the final qualifier in the minutes about the school being "under the inspection of Rev. John Brown" because they knew that Brown never accepted this appointment, whatever it may have meant, and it would therefore simply create confusion on that point. The meeting minutes demonstrate that Brown never communicated with the presbytery concerning the academy.

The institution's [Washington College, Va.] first _published_ history of its origins and founding is published in: Junkin, Rev. George, DD, "Christianity: The Patron of Literature and Science: An Address Delivered February 22, 1849. On the Occasion of the Author's Inauguration As President of Washington College, Virginia," Philadelphia, The Board of Trustees, 1849. This pamphlet contains an appendix entitled "A Brief Sketch of the Early History of Washington College" (ordered printed by the board of trustees). This constitutes the college's first published history [pp. 35–39].[278] This first authorized institutional history identifies the origin as being October 12, 1774. [Note: In truth, it was done the next day, October 13, 1774. The meeting, however, began on the twelfth.]

---

278 This sketch is, by and large, accurate and consistent with the meeting minutes of the Hanover Presbytery and the Liberty Hall Academy board of trustee minutes in every respect, save one, which is that in citing the single most significant minute noting the establishment and appointment of William Graham as manager, they include in their afterthought of naming Rev. John Brown as the presbytery's inspector the inaccurate qualified term, "general inspection," when the actual minutes do not include the word "general" in conjunction with the word "inspection." An error of little significance because like the presbytery's other appointments of Rev. Brown to various and sundry responsibilities, Mr. Brown rejected these assignments, including his appointment as a trustee. His name does not appear as being in attendance at even one of the board of trustees' meetings. Moreover, there is no record of Mr. Brown ever reporting on the early activities of the new seminary. All business of this school is discussed in the minutes as matters between the presbytery and Mr. Graham excepting the heretofore referenced appointments of Rev. Brown that went unacknowledged by Mr. Brown.

Note: Twenty years after this authorized sketch, above, was published at the direction of the board of trustees, Bolivar Christian, then a trustee, in effect, repudiates this first sketch. He does so without explanation or even acknowledgment of the earlier sketch, and substitutes his own version, following the unauthenticated W. H. Foote's Sketches of Virginia . . . Series One and Series Two, published in 1850 and 1855, respectively. Christian's sketch was published in the university's Catalogue of the Alumni . . . from 1869 onward in a series of mostly erroneous variants.

13. President Henry Ruffner's Manuscript and published "Early History of Washington College."

[Note: We treat them together because there are few differences, and none that are material. The originals were written in the 1840s, and are so designated by President Ruffner's son, Wm. Henry Ruffner, in marginalia accompanying the manuscript.]

The Presbytery therefore resolved to 'fix a seminary for the education of youth in Staunton.' But they adopted no measure for carrying this resolution into effect until their meeting in October, 1774. (Ruffner, Hist. Papers. V. 1, p. 13.)

The Presbytery resumed the consideration of a public school for the education of youth, judging it to be of great immediate importance. **We do therefore agree to establish and patronize a public school, which shall be managed by William Graham**, *(a gentleman properly recommended to this Presbytery and to be* under the inspection of the Rev. John Brown;[279] *and the Presbytery reserve to themselves, the liberty at a future session more particularly to appoint the person by whom it shall be conducted and where it shall be fixed.* [Ruffner, Hist. Papers V. 1, p. 13] (Emphasis added)

As William Graham, *above named,* **was the first rector [President]** *of the academy, and the principal agent in giving it permanent success, we shall introduce him to the reader by presenting a sketch of his early life.* [Ruffner, Hist. Papers, V. 1, p. 15] (Footnote explains that a rector was then ex officio president of the board of trustees.]

Rev. Henry Ruffner's published version of the early history of Washington College appeared in Washington and Lee University Historical Papers, Vol. 1, "Early History of

---

279 *Readers should avoid placing any significant meaning to this parenthetical because Rev. Brown did not accept this responsibility, whatever it might have meant. This can easily be gleaned by a review of the presbytery's meeting minutes covering the period in question. Rev. Brown eschewed any involvement in the new seminary, which he had opposed from its inception. Mr. Brown sent none of his sons to Liberty Hall Academy and advised others to follow his lead, in that regard. A more detailed discussion on this subject appears in the main body of the report.*

Washington College," Baltimore, John Murphy & Co. 1890 et
seq, edited by his son William Henry Ruffner. The manuscript
version was written in the 1840s, and before the publication of
W. H. Foote's mistaken accounts of the college's origins in 1850
and 1855. To be sure, Dr. Ruffner, the college's oft-referred-to
"first historian" made a host of inexplicable errors in writing his
historical account, but to his credit, he purposefully avoided the
mistake of dating the school's origin to a time before 1774. Not
so, however, his son who modified his father's account of the
origins and, unfortunately, did so without noting what he had
done, or explaining his decision to rewrite his father's text. In so
doing, William Henry Ruffner left his father open to criticism
for presenting a false history. In all likelihood, the son, William
Henry Ruffner, was following the grave error of William Henry
Foote in this regard.

Above are thirteen important authorities that were written seventy-five years
prior to Foote's first book on Virginia and more than ninety years before the college
decided to change its date of birth by adding twenty-five years. They all have one
important thing in common, to wit: None of these early authorities suggested an
origin for Washington and Lee University that predates the actions of the Hanover
Presbytery in establishing its new seminary in Augusta County Virginia, on
October 13, 1774. Moreover, every one of these authorities remained unchallenged
in any known publication until Foote's disastrous unsubstantiated assertions
published in his *Sketches of Virginia, Historical. . .,* 1850 and then elaborated on
in his series no. 2, in 1855. Whether Washington College based its decision to
expand its history by twenty-five years based on Foote's unsubstantiated history
is unknown because the college failed or refused to explain what they had done
or why they had done it. They simply replaced its original history that had been
adhered to for ninety years with an entirely different one, for no apparent reason.[280]

Conclusion

These listed sources are not only significant sources, they constitute all
of the known credible sources that exist. These sources consistently show that
Washington and Lee University was founded by the actions of the Hanover
Presbytery that culminated in a formal decision by that organization of
Presbyterian church leaders in Virginia to create a college in Virginia that was
envisioned to be able to provide the same educational opportunities then offered
by the College of New Jersey at Princeton. These representations reflected the

---

280   The auditor speculates on the reason for this precipitous decision by the college in the report,
      but truth be told, no living person appears to know precisely why the college thought that the
      thirteen reputable sources the auditor has cited, and which should have all been known to the
      trustees, had suddenly become unreliable, a reality that is as unacceptable as it is inexplicable,
      and as unjustified as it is presumptuous.

general understanding held by virtually everyone living between 1774 and 1849. If there were any exceptions, they were generally unknown.

In 1850, William Henry Foote published his now-infamous contrary accounts that appeared in his published *Sketches of Virginia, Historical and Biographical*. Fifteen years later, in 1865, Washington College published ***Charter and Laws and Trustees and Alumni of Washington College at Lexington, Virginia, A. D. 1865***, Richmond, 1865, which included a sketch of the early history of the college under the strange title, *"Historical Statistics."* In essence, the college adopted the most egregiously mistaken aspects of Mr. Foote's unsubstantiated novel notions about the origins of Washington College. Like Foote, the college offered no explanation in this new publication concerning their decision to abandon the institution's long-standing consistent history that it had adhered to since the college's inception. In this new publication, the college did not cite any earlier authority to justify its decision to adopt an entirely new history extending its life by twenty-five years. Of course, there was no such authority upon which it could have relied because as has been shown above, all the known earlier sources would not support the newly adopted nonsensical statement of its history. To the contrary, all of the known sources had made it abundantly clear that the college was created by the Hanover Presbytery in its autumn meeting of 1774. This stands as an incontrovertible fact of history.

Postscript:

Take note of **Robert Stuart Sanders' biography of Rev. Robert Stuart** that contains quotes from before 1850 that refer to Liberty Hall's establishment in ways that are consistent with all the above. As a student at Liberty Hall, he discusses Robert Stuart's matriculation under Graham and with no reference to his own minister, Rev. John Brown, nor any reference to Robert Alexander. See bibliography for citation of this important biography. As more and more of similar documents find their way into the public sphere, it is interesting and instructive how none of them that come from these eighteenth-century Valley residents ever refer to Robert Alexander or Rev. John Brown's schools having had a connection to Liberty Hall Academy. That innovation only appears after Mr. Foote put that notion into play without having provided any evidence to support that ridiculous notion. How this glaring failure escaped the attention of so many late-nineteenth- and twentieth-century historians boggles the mind.

Chapter Four

Brief Sketch of Washington and Lee University's Early History

In mid-October of 1774, leading men of the American colonies and several leading clergymen met in Philadelphia and near Richmond in Virginia, respectively, determined to lay enduring foundations for the erection of a new nation and a new American college. In Virginia near Richmond, the Hanover Presbytery resolved to establish and patronize a college in Virginia on October 13, 1774,[281] while at Carpenter's Hall in Philadelphia on the next day was approved our nation's first American Bill of Rights.[282]

The university was created by the Hanover Presbytery in Charlotte County, Virginia, on October 13, 1774, when, after three years study, it decided to establish and patronize a public school capable of finishing a student's liberal education.[283] Also decided that day, was the appointment of William Graham as the seminary's chief administrative officer, and that the seminary[284] be located in Augusta County.

The new seminary (academy) was initially located in temporary quarters located on James Wilson's farm, near Fairfield, referred to as "Mount Pleasant." Here in 1775 Graham designed and implemented the first operational phase of the college in the form of a grammar school to serve as the college's foundation. At the time, the presbytery referred to the school informally as Augusta Academy. The initial phase was the formation of a grammar school component of the college following the plan initiated at Princeton by Graham's preceptor, President John Witherspoon.

At the time of the school's establishment, a fund-raising campaign was authorized by the presbytery, in their name, to underwrite the costs associated with college-level instruction, including buildings, a library, and laboratory equipment required for teaching science, mathematics, and surveying. The planning and implementation of all these aspects was overseen by Mr. Graham. The embryonic

---

281 This new educational endeavor was to headed by a man from Pennsylvania, Rev. William Graham.

282 Denominated A Declaration of Rights, the document included ten resolves, including the right to life, liberty, and property.

283 This decision was memorialized in the organization's official meeting minutes.

284 In the eighteenth century, the term "seminary" was an imprecise term, but it was used in connection with higher-level schools and was synonymous with academy and college, although in some venues the term "academy" was also applied to preparatory schools.

school at Mount Pleasant was conducted simultaneously with the fund-raising and construction of the prospective campus buildings, and the securing of a library and laboratory apparatus. The initial applicants were assessed by the lone academic principal and thereafter instructed based upon the new student's various readiness for instruction. By October 27, 1775, the presbytery appointed, having acquainted itself with its selected leader, Mr. Graham, ordained him, and made his appointment permanent, and appointed John Montgomery, another recent graduate from Princeton, to be Graham's assistant.

On May 6, 1776, the presbytery created a board of trustees for the school and nominated numerous prospective trustees, of whom many declined to accept. Of those new trustees who accepted their nomination, several gathered quickly for their first meeting on May 13, 1776. Noticeably absent from this historic meeting was the only member of the Hanover Presbytery, who lived in the Great Valley of Virginia, west of the Blue Ridge Mountains, other than the academy's rector and newly ordained minister, Rev. Graham, the nominated Rev. John Brown. Brown declined his nomination by virtue of his absence, a status he maintained for the remaining twenty years of his tenure in Virginia.

The trustees' first order of business was to give the academy its first official name, Liberty Hall Academy.

Also in May of 1776, the first authorized history of the academy was written by Rev. Caleb Wallace, acting as clerk of Hanover Presbytery. His brief sketch is a narrative heavily interspersed with extracts taken from the official meeting minutes of the Hanover Presbytery between October of 1774 and May of 1776.[285] Wallace's sketch was copied into the official new record book obtained for keeping the first board of trustees' meeting minutes. It comprises the first few pages of text in this historic record book. Wallace was an eyewitness to the event who was ordained at that meeting. Wallace's instructive opening states:

> **The Present Academy of Liberty Hall began under the Direction and Patronage of the Presbytery of Hanover as the following minutes fully evince.**
> **"At a session of the Pby. Of Hanover at Cub Creek Oct. 13, 1774, the Pby resumed consideration of a school for the liberal education of youth which we unanimously judge to be of great importance. We do therefore agree to establish and patronize a publick school which shall be confined to the county of Augusta in this colony. _At present it shall be managed by Mr. William Graham, a Gentleman properly recommended_."** (Rev. Caleb Wallace, clerk of the Hanover Presbytery, May 1776)

---

285 The actual "establishment" on October 13, 1774, was the culmination of a three-year investigation by the Hanover Presbytery that took the form of what might well be labeled today as a desirability and feasibility study. From the very beginning, the focus was on creating an institution on a par with the College of New Jersey but in Virginia.

The moving of the school from Mount Pleasant to its newly constructed campus at Timber Ridge campus began in late 1776, culminating in the winter of 1777. By that time, the country was fully engaged in the American Revolution, which interrupted the anticipated flow of enrollment. In addition, the devaluing of currency created economic chaos that forced the rector to secure a farm upon which he could engage in agricultural pursuits necessary for providing for his family. The trustees authorized Mr. Graham to move the academy several miles away so as to be near his new farm, and here the academy continued during the remainder of the war. Initially, instruction took place in the rector's home.

In the meantime, Rector Graham continued raising money for the school, and with these proceeds had a new frame building constructed in which to hold classes. In 1782, with the revolution having all but ended, Mr. Graham moved with dispatch to request incorporation and a charter from the new "free Virginia legislature, in the name of the Liberty Hall Academy Board of Trustees." The requested charter, with degree- granting authority, was granted shortly thereafter in the autumn of 1782. Liberty Hall Academy had the distinction of being the first institution of higher learning in Virginia, to be granted this honor following the revolution. Liberty Hall thereby joined with the College of William and Mary[286] as the only two college-degree-granting institutions in Virginia. Hampden Sydney, however, followed closely behind her sister college, obtaining its charter the following year, in 1783. At this time, the school was conducted in a framed schoolhouse near Graham's farm.

The schoolhouse near "Whistle Creek" farm burned in 1783 and was replaced by a similar structure, but once again, the school was destroyed by fire in 1790. In December of 1790, the rector and trustees Samuel Lyle and John Wilson formed a committee that planned for the construction of a campus on Mulberry Hill,[287] which was completed by Christmas of 1793. This campus included several other buildings, but the main building housed the dormitory and the classrooms, while the smaller refectory and steward's quarters, also of stone, was located nearby.[288]

This new campus served multiple functions, housing the grammar school, the regular academic program, and the Virginia Presbyterian Synod's newly established Lexington Theological Seminary. This arrangement was necessitated by the financial considerations associated with the construction of the new campus. President Graham was appointed president of the new Theological Seminary by Virginia Synod. He therefore occupied two presidential positions

---

286 William and Mary, of course, was chartered before the war by the British Crown.

287 The remains of the main building are still standing at the Mulberry Hill site. An architectural rendering is included in Lyle. Royster Jr. and Simpson, Pamela H., *The Architecture of Historic Lexington*, Charlottesville.

288 Here, the first steward was the rector's younger brother, Edward Graham, but Edward had married Archibald Alexander's sister, Margaret, on New Year's Eve, the year before (1792) and as newlyweds, they likely didn't occupy the steward's quarters. The steward's quarters was quite likely where rector's new student, John Chavis, a nontraditional much older student, resided. A student that just happened to be the first black college student enrolled in a degree-granting chartered college in the United States.

at Liberty Hall Academy, appointed rector (president) of the regular academic college by the Hanover Presbytery, and president of the Theological Seminary by the Virginia Synod. At the same time, Liberty Hall Academy was established with the understanding that the college was to be Christian but nondenominational in character and in its operations. That is, students would not be pressured or recruited to become members of the Presbyterian Church.

After serving as the college's only administrative head for twenty-two years, Rev. Graham, rather unexpectedly, resigned his position as president of the college in the autumn of 1796. He continued, however, overseeing the instruction of the theological students after his resignation as president of the college, and he maintained his connection to the Lexington Presbytery until his untimely death from pneumonia during a trip to Richmond in June of 1799.

As his final major initiative on behalf of the college, Rev. Graham prepared an application, in the form of a letter, addressed to the United States' first president, George Washington, urging the president to select Liberty Hall Academy as the recipient of a large endowment that the president was intending to bestow upon a worthy educational endeavor. This letter, signed by Rev. Graham and countersigned by trustee Rev. Samuel Houston on behalf of the trustees of Liberty Hall Academy, together with the advocacy efforts of several local political leaders, and private efforts by General Henry ("light-Horse-Harry Lee[289]) resulted in President Washington's decision to award this endowment to Liberty Hall Academy. It is said to have been the largest such endowment then ever given to a college in America.

After Graham's resignation and his unexpected death three years later, the Virginia Synod's connection to the academy thereafter slowly dissipated and finally disappeared prior to the academy's appointment of Rev. Graham's successor in late 1799.

At the Mulberry Hill location, the impressive new campus stood for nearly a decade. It was the institution's final campus during the tenure of the college's founding first president, Rev. William Graham. Originally buried in Richmond, Graham's remains were ceremoniously reinterred to Liberty Hall's campus in 1911, and his remains were placed just outside the Lee Chapel, over which was placed a large stone monument with the following epitaph:

Sacred
To the Memory
of the
Rev. William Graham
Founder and Twenty Year Rector of
Washington Academy.
He was born in the State of Pennsylvania
December 19th 1746

---

289 General Henry Lee of revolutionary fame was the father of Gen. Robert E. Lee. Henry Lee was a classmate of President Graham when they were at Princeton, and Graham as an advanced scholar is known to have tutored Lee at Lee's request in preparation for their final exams.

And died June 17th 1799.
He was Distinguished for the Strength and
Originality of his Genius[290]
And the successful tenor of his exertions
in behalf of solid literature and
evangelical piety.

Thus was ended Washington and Lee University's eighteenth-century history from its inception in October of 1774 to the appointment of its second president, Rev. George Addison Baxter, who was an early student at Liberty Hall Academy under President Graham, and who also obtained his theological instruction from Rev. Graham.

---

290 President Graham was selected by Princeton's president, Witherspoon, to address his 1773 classmates on the question of "the infinite divisability of matter," a question that lies at the heart of atomic theory. It is not known whether that address is extant.

Chapter Five

Analysis of Authors' Errors, Part 1
"The First Twenty"
(Arranged chronologically by date of publication)

Below is an assessment of twenty of the earliest authors who provided inaccurate information about the origins of Washington and Lee and/or concerning the institution's founding first president, William Graham:

> Professor/Trustee Edward Graham, Esq., Rev. Dr. Archibald Alexander, Rev. William Hill, Trustee, Dr. Samuel L. Campbell, President, Dr. Henry Ruffner, Rev. Robert Davidson, William Henry Foote, Trustee, Rev. Samuel Houston, Charles Campbell, Anon. Charter and Laws . . . (probably Bolivar Christian), Trustee, Bolivar Christian, Hugh Blair Grigsby, E. D. Junkin, and Samuel D. Alexander.

In all, the audit selected seventy authors or works that contain significant errors, but in most cases the errors made were based upon the mistakes much earlier by the fifteen authors assessed in this section of the report. Only David W. Robson greatly expanded upon the nineteenth-century errors of those list above.

Several of these authors also provided much accurate and invaluable historical information and eyewitness accounts of events that are immensely important to history's understanding of both people and events that occurred in eighteenth-century Virginia. In most cases, this report does not intend to diminish the value of the contributions of the listed authors, their errors notwithstanding.

Note: In all, the auditor studied and assessed the works of well over seventy authors. In addition to the first grouping listed chronologically above, this main part of the report will include an additional assessment off numerous others that were selected from the complete chronological list of seventy-five authors based on their seeming historical significance either to the public or to the university. A supplement including evaluations of all of the authors reviewed is envisioned to come at a later date.

Introduction:

In this section of the report, the auditor identifies important mistakes made by fifteen of the seventy-five authors deemed significant enough in some respect to warrant an assessment. The mistakes made by these thirteen authors all pertain in some way to the early history of Washington and Lee University and or about the college's founding first president (rector), William Graham. Many of the authors included in this assessment have provided valuable additions to history, notwithstanding our criticisms, and in no way does the auditor's criticisms mean to impute a conclusion about the relative merit of the authors' overall specifically selected work product, with two notable exceptions.[291]

The authors, generally speaking, are listed chronologically, in order of the date of publication of the work(s) assessed. The auditor lays no claim to bibliographic expertise, but for reference purposes has adopted in basic form the style used by historians generally. The auditor apologizes for any failure to have structured a footnote improperly, but trusts the information included will provide the researcher ample and accurate enough information for the reader to be able to locate the referenced material.

Early in the auditor's research, it became clear that the life of Rev. William Graham was so inextricably linked with the early history of the university that reflections on his character necessarily impacted on perceptions of the university in its earliest emendations. For that reason, mistakes made by these authors concerning Graham during his long association with the institution were deemed to be mistakes pertaining to Liberty Hall Academy, as the institution was named in those early days.[292]

---

291   The exceptions are: (1) **Dr. David W. Robson**. The article,"An Important Question Answered: William Graham's Defense of Slavery in Post-Revolutionary Virginia," by David W. Robson, *William and Mary Quarterly*, 3rd Series, 37, No. 4, pp. 644–652 (October 1980). [An erroneous piece throughout, and mostly based on the author's incorrect assumption that his referenced Joseph Glass's "lecture notes" are transcriptions of William Graham's lectures, when they are not. This article is mostly incorrect in every important respect concerning the several assertions made about Rev. William Graham, the author's recognized contemporary reputation as a scholar notwithstanding. The article is among the author's early work, and does not appear to represent his later scholarship. The article is an incredible embarrassment, or it should be, for reasons that are provided in the appendix devoted to critiquing Mr. Robson's unfortunate article. There is no evidence known to exist that supports a claim that Rev. William Graham ever publicly defended slavery. His known private beliefs on that subject are limited to one cursory comment in a letter to a friend, Col. Arthur Campbell, wherein he refers to "the horrors of slavery," a reference rather inconsistent with the views of a defender of slavery but nevertheless, they constitute the only words known to have been written by Rev. Graham on the subject of slavery. Robson's other claims about Graham are in most every case absurdly incorrect. Robson went on from this work to complete what appears to be an important body of work, none of which has been studied by the auditor; and (2) **William Henry Foote**. Our criticisms of Foote are indeed of a serious nature, but this subject must be analyzed more deeply and broadly because of Foote's long-standing importance to the history of the eighteenth-century Virginia and North Carolina. For the time being, however, his works must be treated with great scepticism because of the revelations about him contained in this report. Foote's re-printing of documents in these two volumes appears to have generally been done quite accurately, with two notable exceptions. See the subsection devoted to Foote and especially concerning what may now be called the infamous Rev. Samuel Houston letter.

292   The institution was initially referred to, unofficially, as "Augusta Academy" or denominations similar in nature by the clerks of the Hanover Presbytery when they drafted the presbytery's meeting minutes. This convention was adopted in 1775 after the presbytery established its second seminary of learning, which was located in Prince Edward County, and the decision to adopt this convention was, no doubt, adopted in order for the clerks to be able distinguish between the presbytery's two seminaries in its meeting minutes. Prior to 1775, the name "Augusta Academy" was not in general use in Virginia. Indeed, prior to 1776, other than the College of William and Mary, it is doubtful if any other school in Virginia was given an official

Here below then are the auditor's historical assessments of the first thirteen selected authors,[293] arranged chronologically based in the main, on the date of publication. The mistakes identified in these assessments include most of the major errors made by the selected authors, varying only in the writing style of each author. In other words, the same basic errors are repeated ad infinitum by authors over the last one hundred and fifty-plus years, with only a few notable exceptions. The auditor has completed preliminary assessments of the works of over seventy authors, which may be added as an addendum or as a second volume somewhat later. Decisions have not been finalized in that regard, but any additional materials would not substantively affect the overall findings as they relate to the early history and founding of Washington and Lee University, or the findings as they relate to the life of the university's founding first president, Rev. William Graham.

Subsection One:

1. EDWARD GRAHAM ESQ. (b. Oct. 29, 1765, d. Nov. 5, or Nov. 26, 1840)[294]
(Edward Graham, "Memoir of the Late Rev. William Graham, A.M.," *Virginia Literary and Evangelical Magazine*, vol. 4, 1821 et seq. [serialized])

Author of first *published* account of the founding of Washington and Lee University.[295]

Edward Graham's memoir of his much older brother is of immense importance because it is the first published account of the founding of Washington and Lee University and also the first published account of the life of Rev. William Graham. It has an added importance for those interested in the early life of Rev. William Graham and the Graham family history, and that particular genealogical line in America.

Edward Graham's memoir is, overall, the only history of William Graham's early family life and an accurate account based on a young man's eyewitness

---

name. Many nineteenth-century authors mistakenly associated the name "Augusta Academy" with other private preparatory schools simply because the private school was located in that county.

293   The authors selected are all of the generally known authors who wrote about the early history of the university or its first president, William Graham, and who made serious mistakes about the institution's origins or about Graham.

294   .Edward died in 1840. This is proven by a letter of condolence sent by Rev. Archibald Alexander to his sister, Margaret, who was Edward Graham's wife, dated in 1840. A copy in the auditor's files was made from an original in the Graham Family Papers, Perkins Library, Duke University.

295   **The first written history of Liberty Hall Academy, other than the meeting minutes of the Hanover Presbytery, was created by Rev. Caleb Wallace in May of 1776, and can be found in the original meeting-minutes book of the Liberty Hall Academy Board of Trustees, pp. 3–7. Readers are cautioned to beware of the pasted-in sheet that now precedes the Wallace memo. The paste-in is falsely described by some to be an Edward Graham memorandum reflecting his views. The attribution is false and lacks any supporting evidence. See the appendix dedicated to this subject for a more detailed treatment of this unsigned, undated document.**

perspective, but it does contain one significant and two rather minor errors. In general, Edward Graham's memoir of his older brother is correct on matters concerning the founding of Liberty Hall Academy. His two minor errors were not factual mistakes, but are rather the kind of fault-finding one hears from the children of famous fathers. Because Edward's article is the first published account of Liberty Hall Academy's founding, as well as the first biographical sketch of the school's founding first president, William Graham, it was deemed worthy to examine even Edward's minor errors of judgment concerning his older brother.

His only major mistake concerns his inaccurate report that Hampden Sydney Academy [at the time Prince Edward Academy] was established (i.e., created) before Liberty Hall Academy (then Augusta Academy), which is demonstrably wrong. The creation of these two Presbyterian-sponsored seminaries was carried out in exactly the reverse order from that which Edward Graham reported. The establishments took place prior to Edward's arrival in Virginia, and he was simply confused about this subject. The records of the Hanover Presbytery (i.e., meeting minutes) are very clear on this point. Unfortunately, Edward's memoir was so important, and he was deemed to be such a rich source of historical information on the subject of the early history of Washington College that several later authors repeated his one significant error concerning the sequence of the presbytery's actions to establish its two eighteenth-century seminaries in Virginia. Today, that mistake is rarely repeated, but it is still worth noting for the sake of historical accuracy, and to aid researchers' ability to understand how the mistake happened to creep into several early-nineteenth-century histories.

Of far less importance are two mistakes, or at best questionable judgments, concerning personal characteristics of Rev. Graham. One of Edward's published judgments in this regard concerns Rev. Graham's views and habits concerning books and reading; the other concerns Rev. Graham's disposition concerning the accumulation of wealth. We assume that Edward bent over backward, as it were, to avoid being suspected of hero worship of his older brother, but if so, he unintentionally provided fodder for his brother's few but influential enemies by rendering them a valuable assist in their rather persistent attempts to reduce Rev. Graham's influence and legacy in the Valley of Virginia.

We opted to include these two minor mistakes only because later historians have been misled in important ways as a direct result of these mistakes having been expanded upon and embellished so as to alter the true nature of the historical character, Rev. William Graham.

It is worth noting that Edward Graham's interest in the early history of Washington College, as it was known in his day, was keen, and it was probably precipitated by his necessary research conducted prior to submitting his manuscript to Mr. John Holt Rice, his publisher of *A Memoir of the Late Rev. William Graham*. His interest never thereafter waned, and history informs us that several important authors consulted him by mail while working on histories of their own. His last letters of this type appear to have been directed to Rev. Robert Davidson, who was working on his manuscript history of the Presbyterian Church in Kentucky, with an important section devoted to the Valley of Virginia in the eighteenth century. This fact is alluded to by Mr. Davidson in the publication that came out after Edward Graham's death in 1840. Nothing in the works of the men who consulted and relied on Edward Graham as a major source of information comports with the dubious so-called Edward Graham Manuscript. It is a sheet of paper disproved by all the known documentary evidence of the college, as well as the documentary evidence located in the early archives of the institution that created the college, the Hanover Presbytery of Virginia.

Note: The auditor has not, in this section, dealt with a curious hoax perpetrated, either knowingly or not, by one of the college's mid-nineteenth-century trustees, so-called Col. Bolivar Christian, whose rank is of the dubious type that today is associated with Kentucky Fried Chicken Madison Avenue icons. The hoax is often referred to as "The Edward Graham Memorandum" or "The Edward Graham Manuscript." In fact, this one-page, undated, and unsigned document's true nature is unknown and probably will always be unknowable. What it is not is an asserted repudiation of everything Edward Graham was known to believe about the founding of Washington and Lee University. This silly sheet of notes is analyzed and explained in an appendix that exposes it for what it is. Whether Mr. Christian's motives were pure or not is mostly left to the reader to decide, but suffice to say that Trustee Christian, an attorney, should have known that, as evidence of anything historical, no competent court in the land would accept such a document as evidence of anything important without its presenter having some means by which to authenticate it, which has never been offered by any person referring to it. The reason for this is that there is no known means by which to authenticate the one-page, unsigned, and undated document. The same thing can be said about any number of sheets of notes found in the miscellaneous papers of authors long after their death. The possibilities are only limited by the boundaries of one's imagination without some other associated evidence that points to the document's purpose and/or authorship. Historians often sketch an early working hypothesis on a matter under consideration, which they then later dismiss as having been erroneous. In this case, no one has ever published any evidence that even directly links this document to Edward Graham, let alone evidence that goes to its date or its intended purpose. What is known however, is that the document in question is contradicted by Edward Graham's only published writing issued in 1821, and it is also contradicted by the information that Edward Graham supplied to authors writing up to and even after Edward's death in 1840.[296]

ERROR (no. 1): Edward Graham wrongly asserts that Liberty Hall Academy [W&L] was established after the founding of Hampden Sydney Academy, *when precisely the opposite is true.*

Note: *Edward Graham was the younger brother of Rev. William Graham. He did not leave his father's home in Pennsylvania to live with his older brother's new family until after the Hanover Presbytery announced its establishment of a new seminary in Augusta County, Virginia, in October of 1774. This explains why he could have easily been mistaken about the sequence of establishment between Liberty Hall Academy and Hampden Sydney Academy. Edward would, no doubt, have heard from his older brother how Samuel S. Smith had recommended him to the presbytery, and Edward must have assumed that since Samuel Smith was already in Virginia, that Hampden Sydney had been created first. The schools were, after all, created within months of one another, but the presbytery's minutes clearly indicate that the idea to create a second seminary east of the*

---

296 *This assertion is inferred from the referenced authors' own writings, which contradict the information contained in the mystery document wrongfully believed by some to reflect the views of Edward Graham pertaining to the establishment of Liberty Hall Academy.*

*mountains was an afterthought that arose in the final stages of the three-year
process that culminated in the establishment of Liberty Hall Academy.*

Below is what Edward Graham mistakenly asserted:

> The presbyterian clergy of the colony had for some time, felt the
> importance of having a seminary within its limits conducted
> upon what they considered proper principles; but there was some
> difficulty in selecting the place, and in obtaining a suitable person
> to superintend it. **These difficulties were removed soon after
> Mr. Smith (Samuel Stanhope Smith) came to Virginia**. . . .
> **His popular talents and literary attainments rendered him
> a fit person to take charge of the seminary which had been
> for some time in contemplation.** Subscriptions were circulated
> with considerable success, for the purpose of raising funds; and
> a college was established in the county of Prince Edward. Mr.
> Smith was invited to take upon himself its superintendence. This
> invitation he accepted and the seminary was put into operation.
> (Edward Graham, "Memoir of the Late Rev. William Graham A.M.," p. 253)
> (Emphasis added here to indicate error.)

The above constitutes a serious error by Edward Graham. Liberty Hall
Academy (nee Augusta Academy) was established (i.e., created) on October 13,
1774, by the Hanover Presbytery, then in the following year, the same presbytery
met on February 1, 1775, and at that meeting, Prince Edward Academy, later,
Hampden Sidney (i.e., Hampden Sydney) was established. Therefore, Edward's
understanding is incorrect, and the reverse sequence is what is in fact correct.
His error can be demonstrated in the presbytery's minutes at page 55, in regards
to Liberty Hall, and page 135 et seq. concerning the minutes of October 13, 1774,
and those of February 1, 1775. This subject is not open to debate because the best
documentary evidence pertaining to the issue is abundantly clear.

Here, according to its meeting minutes, is what the Hanover Presbytery
actually did:

> *The Pby resume the Consideration of a School for the liberal
> Education of Youth, judged to be of great and immediate
> importance.* ***We do therefore agree to establish and patronize
> a publick School which shall be confined to the County of
> Augusta, at present it shall be managed by William Graham****, a
> Gentleman properly recommended to this Pby. . . (Hanover Pby
> minutes,* p. 55) (Emphasis added but does not indicate an error.)

*Note: The above extract from Edward Graham's memoir is quoting from the Hanover Presbytery's
meeting minutes, but it stops in midsentence and does so for a very good reason. The portion that is
deliberately excluded from Edward's quotation, is the following, now irrelevant, qualifier:*

"*. . . under the inspection of Rev. John Brown.*"

The reason that phrase was irrelevant then, as it is now, is that Rev. John Brown did not accept this appointment. Brown, at the time, was the presbytery's only member residing in the vast country that was then Augusta County, so it was only prudent that the presbytery appoint Brown to serve as its eyes and ears during the initial period of Graham's services to launch the seminary's new educational venture in the Valley of Virginia. After all, Graham was a stranger to these Virginians and was hired sight unseen. Brown and his family, however, became estranged from Graham over a failed matrimonial engagement between William Graham and Brown's eldest daughter, Betsy, which is discussed in greater detail elsewhere in this report.

What is of great significance, however, is that Brown very soon avoided having any involvement in the affairs of the presbytery's new seminary. That is why Brown's name is absent from all the meeting minutes of the board of trustees of Liberty Hall Academy from the board's inception. This fact was well known to both Edward Graham and also to Archibald Alexander, the two early authors of published accounts of Liberty Hall Academy as well as Graham, who excluded mentioning that the presbytery's meeting minutes had included what had become an irrelevant and possibly misleading qualifier about Brown's being referred to as an inspector. Unfortunately, numerous later authors failed to take note of these two important biographers' exclusion, and obviously failed to comprehend the exclusion's significance. In so doing, they joined an ever-increasing herd of credulous historical lemmings as they plunged into a deep gorge of literary and historical fallacy that this audit, in important part, seeks to correct. These later historians mistakenly assumed that the appointment came to fruition, and also mistakenly assumed that the presbytery intended that Graham was to serve as a subordinate to Brown.

Note: Those who made this mistake in the first instance failed to comprehend that Rev. John Brown, pastor of New Providence congregation, was not much of a scholar, but was merely a country parson. He was an alumnus of the College of New Jersey, but he attended in its earliest emendation when its curriculum was devoted, in the main, to theology, Latin, and Greek. His educational attainments were such that his "Latin school" in the Valley was taught by instructors Mr. Brown hired, not being qualified to serve in that capacity himself. He was therefore in no position to supervise the much more highly educated and trained Mr. Graham, who taught the college-level philosophy, theology, science, astronomy, government, English composition, and mathematics offered at Liberty Hall. Most of these subjects were not a part of Rev. Brown's matriculation at the College of New Jersey. Rev. Brown was in no position to supervise the experienced educator and theologian William Graham. At Princeton, William Graham oversaw the college's preparatory academy under the supervision of one of the foremost educators in the country, Dr. John Witherspoon. Mr. Graham would hardly have accepted a position that required him to move from Pennsylvania to mountainous Virginia only to serve as an assistant to a country parson, a poignant fact seemingly overlooked by a host of later historians.

On the following day, the presbytery confirmed the sequence of establishment in its minutes in the following manner when referring to the possible establishment of a second seminary east of the Blue Ridge Mountains:

> The Pby taking into consideration the great extent of this Colony, *judge that a publick School for the Liberal Education of Youth would be* of great importance on the south side of the

blue ridge, *__notwithstanding of the Appointment of one already__*
__made in the county of Augusta__ . . . . (*Hanover Presbytery minutes*, p.
57) (Emphasis added here is not an error.)

What is contained in the first extract above from the presbytery's minutes constitutes an actual "establishment," along with the "appointment" of a specified "manager" of that school. In the second extract from those minutes, dated the day following, the presbytery acknowledges its previous establishment in Augusta County (i.e., Augusta Academy, later Liberty Hall) and then proceeds to announce its desire to initiate a study to determine if conditions can be met to establish a second school of the exact same type east of the Blue Ridge. Could these statements by the presbytery be any clearer about the sequence of establishment between the academy west of the mountains in Augusta County and the second academy established the following year (1775) in Prince Edward County, Virginia (i.e., Hampden Sydney)?

It should be emphasized that the Hanover Presbytery did not establish a second school on October 14, 1774, but only agreed, at that time, that such an establishment would be of great importance, *provided* that [297] sufficient funds could be raised and a suitable manager could be induced to oversee such a theoretical endeavor. Subsequently, the presbytery held a special meeting (pro re nata) in February of 1775 and acknowledged that the conditions had been met that were earlier deemed essential to creating a second school, therefore they appointed a manager, Samuel Stanhope Smith, and gave him the title of rector. The minutes, however, are devoid of any reference to the presbytery technically announcing its establishment and patronization of a school for Mr. Smith to take charge of. We assume that this technicality is just that, an administrative oversight, most likely occasioned by the special meeting participants not having the actual minutes in their possession at the time of this special meeting and operating on the misconception that the establishment had already been accomplished. Nevertheless, it is clear from the above extracts that there is no question as to which of these two academies was established first. That honor accrues to the school informally called "Augusta Academy"[298] and which later became officially named *Liberty Hall Academy* in May of 1776.

The error we have numbered 1, is amplified in another part of Edward Graham's m*emoir* of his brother wherein he describes the establishment of Augusta Academy. This mistake is in essence just part of the same mistake but described in a different context. We include the language for reference and apologize for what may appear to be redundancy.

---

297   *Indicating a theoretical possibility, not a reality.*

298   The presbytery adopted, as a convention, the names "Augusta Academy" and "Prince Edward Academy" after the establishment of its second school in order to better distinguish the schools from one another in their minutes. The presbytery understandably reserved the honor of officially naming the schools to the prospective boards of trustees of each school once the presbytery created a board of trustees and announced the appointments of the prospective trustees, which, in the beginning, it apparently believed to be premature.

Here are Edward Graham's words in that regard:

> "*It was soon perceived, however, that this institution would*
> *be insufficient to supply the literary and religious wants of*
> *the colony. Another seminary, to be located westward of the*
> *Blue Ridge, was thought to be necessary. The presbytery*
> *of Hanover,... . . . They selected the county of Augusta...as*
> *the place where it should be established.*" (Edward Graham.
> "Memoir of... . . . p. 253) (Note: The underlined emphasis, here,
> indicates what is an error.)

The entire statement in italics above constitutes an error. The presbytery
made no pronouncement suggesting that one seminary was insufficient to meet
the needs of the colony. Indeed, the establishment of two seminaries at that time
was a foolish and imprudent decision. It is somewhat of a miracle that under these
circumstances, they both survived and continue to exist. It is doubtful if Graham
would have ever agreed to accept the presbytery's offer to head up their new
educational venture to create a college in the Mountains of Virginia if there was
a prospect that a second such venture would soon be launched in that part of the
state likely to supply the most student applicants. The decision to investigate the
feasibility and desirability of a second school was a last-minute one, obviously
made by wealthy and influential members east of the mountains.

Note: It is inexplicable that Smith agreed to accept the presbytery's 1775 offer of the presidency of
the second school, after having encouraged his friend and schoolmate at Princeton, Graham, to
accept the presbytery's offer to head up its rather risky venture to create a Presbyterian-patronized
college in Virginia on the eve of the American Revolution. In effect, Smith set his friend Graham up
for likely failure. Of course, Graham could not have known that the presbytery would make such a
foolish and imprudent decision at the time of his acceptance, for he was undoubtedly in route from
Pennsylvania to Virginia when the possibility was first raised, and by the time he arrived, it was a fait
accompli. He simply had to make the best of a bad bargain. To his credit and against all odds, Liberty
Hall Academy survived the vicissitudes of the war, and went on to fame and a monumental success.

Edward then describes how Smith recommended Graham to superintend
the operation, but once again he has the order of establishment in the wrong
sequence. Below are the actual words contained in the presbytery's minutes that
relate specifically to Hampden Sydney:

> The Pby taking into consideration the great extent of this
> Colony, judge that a publick School for the Liberal Education
> of Youth **would be** of great importance on the south side of
> the blue ridge, **notwithstanding of the Appointment of one**
> **already made in the county of Augusta** . . . . (Hanover Pby
> minutes, p. 57) (Emphasis here does not indicate error.)

It is obvious from the extracts included above that Edward Graham in 1821
had not researched the Hanover Presbytery's meeting minutes, and that he was
uninformed as to the establishment of the academy in Prince Edward County. The
issue, however, is not open to dispute because of the unmistakable and undebatable

fact that Liberty Hall was established before Prince Edward Academy (Hampden Sydney). Liberty Hall was founded in 1774 while Prince Edward Academy was established the following year, 1775. This fact is easily demonstrated in the Hanover Presbytery's meeting minutes covering its meetings held in 1774 and 1775.

The presbytery held a special (pro re nata) meeting February 1, 1775, and at that meeting confirmed that the provisional requirements had been met and therefore went ahead to establish the seminary in Prince Edward County and appointed Samuel Stanhope Smith to superintend the presbytery's second seminary. Those who may doubt the sequence as we have outlined it and as the presbytery's minutes describe it are directed to the language in the minute above where they will note the phrase, "***notwithstanding of the appointment of one already made in the county of Augusta.***"

This phrase leaves no room for doubt on the question of establishment. It is Augusta Academy first, Prince Edward Academy second. This assertion is confirmed by the records of the entity that created both of these seminaries, the Hanover Presbytery.

CONCLUSION REGARDING EDWARD GRAHAM

Edward Graham's "A Memoir of The Late Rev. William Graham, A.M." *The Evangelical and Literary Magazine and Missionary Chronicle*, IV(1821), p.75 et seq. is of the utmost importance. It is not only the first published account of the life of Rev. William Graham, but it also contains the first ***published*** account of the creation of that institution that has evolved into Washington and Lee University.

Edward not only lived with the family of the college's first president, who was his much older brother, but he was also among the school's earliest students,[299] and he was associated with the institution from his arrival in Virginia in late 1776 until his retirement from the faculty, and later from his position as trustee shortly before his death in 1840. He appears to have served under all of the first six presidents of the college, but he was absent for a couple of short periods and may have not been there during the tenure of either Pres. Vethake or possibly Marshall, both of whom had short tenures. Clearly, no other man was better suited to write this first memoir, and none knew the events and the central characters involved with the early history of either the college or its first president better than Edward Graham. He was not, however, an eyewitness to the events surrounding the organizational efforts of the college when it was located at "Mount Pleasant" in temporary quarters while the first campus buildings were being constructed

---

299 Edward Graham did not arrive in Virginia until late 1776, which is when his father, Michael (Sr.), brought the Pennsylvania family south, traveling through Virginia before settling farther south in the Haw River settlement near his eldest daughter, Mary (Graham) Sharp. Edward, then only eleven years old, was left in the care of his older brother, William, in order to receive from him a college education. Another brother, Michael (Jr.), fresh returned from the Revolutionary War, also stayed in Lexington with William's family. Young Edward undoubtedly began instruction at Liberty Hall in the attached grammar school, and would have had no first-hand knowledge of the initial operations at "Mount Pleasant," when the school was informally referred to as Augusta Academy (1775 and 1776).

because he did not arrive in Virginia to join his older brother William's family until late 1776 or early 1777.[300]

Edward Graham's only published error of significant consequence is that pertaining to the sequence of establishment by the Hanover Presbytery, which our audit demonstrates was precisely the opposite of what Edward thought when he published his memoir of his late brother. Fortunately, his brother-in-law, Rev. Archibald Alexander, with whom he collaborated and corresponded, eventually discovered their earlier misconceptions about the sequence of establishment, and published a more accurate account in his 1843 "Address to the Alumni of Washington College" (see bibliography). Unfortunately, Edward Graham did not live to witness Alexander's address. The auditor was unable to learn whether Edward Graham ever discovered his mistake concerning the sequence of establishment between the presbytery's two seminaries.

Edward included in his published memoir of his elder brother William a few ill-advised comments of a more personal nature that were later blown out of his intended proportions by some of William Graham's enemies. Later, historians mysteriously focused more attention on these foolishly opinionated comments of Edward than he obviously ever intended, while ignoring the rather amazing accomplishments of the founding first president of Washington and Lee. In one case, he criticizes his older brother for being too concerned with wealth acquisition and he also questions his brother's reading habits in his later life, suggesting that his brother read too little, and too easily dismissed the writings of others. Even Edward's criticisms of his brother, however, were so significantly qualified as to render them virtually meaningless.

In regards to Edward's single significant error, it is of paramount importance to emphasize that even though he made this mistake concerning the sequence of establishment between Liberty Hall and Hampden Sydney, he still correctly identifies the date of the origins by connecting the founding of the academy to the decision of the Hanover Presbytery at its October 1774 autumn meeting to establish a public school in Augusta. It is also significant that Edward made no reference whatsoever to either Robert Alexander, Rev. John Brown, or their private preparatory schools. The reader will discover in the subsection below that Rev. Archibald Alexander likewise made no significant mention of either of these men or their schools, and of course Robert Alexander is his paternal grandfather's brother.[301] Surely had there been any connection or link between these schools

---

300 It is most probable that young Edward (11 yrs. in 1776) traveled from Pennsylvania to Virginia with his father and several of the children shortly after his father, Michael Graham Sr. (immigrant), sold his farm at Paxton Twp. In 1776. The father's destination was North Carolina, but he stopped and presumably lingered in Lexington for a time to visit with his son, William. When the father moved on to North Carolina to join his eldest daughter Mary's family (Edward Sharp family) in the Guilford/Randolph Counties vicinity (Haw River), Edward was left in the care of his older brother, William. Another of Edward's older brothers, Michael Graham (Jr.), had recently returned from his service in the Revolutionary War and he also left his father's caravan, and stayed behind in Lexington with his older brother, William.

301 Archibald [Sr.] and Robert Alexander were brothers and both provided educational instruction to young men in the neighborhood of Timber Ridge and New Providence congregations during

and Alexander's alma mater, Liberty Hall Academy, Rev. Alexander would surely have mentioned it.

****

2. REV. ARCHIBALD ALEXANDER (b. April 17, 1772, d. 1851)

(Archibald Alexander, DD, Mss "Memoir of the Rev. Wm Graham" [written in longhand]. The Rev. Graham portions of this manuscript constitute the largest part of a writing entitled *"Great Valley of Virginia."* The auditor's photocopy came from the Princeton Seminary Library in 1989. It is also available in spiral-bound form at the Leyburn Library, Washington and Lee University; and "Address delivered before the Alumni Association of Washington College," Virginia, delivered June 29, 1843, Lexington, Va.; R. H. Glass, 1843, pp. 31. Also published in *Washington and Lee University Historical Papers,* No. 2, Lexington, Va., 1890; and, James W. Alexander DD, *The Life of Archibald Alexander, DD*, New York, Charles Scribner, 1854.

Note: Error no. 3 is included here because this book includes text by both Archibald, and his son, James Alexander. Importantly, some text that is represented by James to be Archibald's words are not; they are the words of James himself. James, acting as editor, took the liberty of modifying his father's actual wording, and yet represented the words as being those of his father.[302] The unique nature of this report caused the auditor to include this shocking material under the general rubric of the father's error, even though it is actually the error of his son, James W., editor and author of the book. It is also worthy of note that the reason that the auditor repeats Archibald Alexander's full name in the commentary below is that his son, James, who figures so large in the commentary, was also a Presbyterian minister, and it was deemed proper to take extra care lest there be confusion about which of these two Alexanders is being referred to at any one place in this section of the report.

A Confounding Circumstance Created by Rev. Alexander's Son, James W. Alexander

In 1854, three years after the death of Rev. Archibald Alexander, his son, James W. Alexander, published a biography of his father that included numerous important and valuable letters written by his father. Unfortunately, James committed a serious breach of ethics when he decided to correct what he

---

the mid-eighteenth century. Rev. Archibald Alexander, the grandson of Archibald Sr., was a noted historian who published a history of the early educational endeavors of the Presbyterians in America (Archibald Alexander, DD, Biographical Sketches of the Founder and Principal Alumni of the Log College, Philadelphia, 1845 and reprint, 1851), but importantly, nowhere in his many writings does he claim a link between his family's private educational endeavors and the founding of Liberty Hall Academy from whence he matriculated.

302 *James points out in his book that his father's manuscript memoir of William Graham was to be destroyed at his father's death. James, however, used the manuscript in preparing his book and undoubtedly assumed that after the biography was published, he would destroy the manuscript. Unfortunately for him but fortunately for history, James disregarded his father's instructions and then later for unknown reasons either changed his mind or forgot about the manuscript. In any event, the manuscript survived and passed down from generation to generation until in the 1980s it was donated to the Princeton Theological Seminary in Princeton New Jersey. James, never believing that his editorial alterations would be subjected to comparison with his alterations, made changes that he deemed appropriate. Of course, what he did was not appropriate or, accurate.*

obviously believed were historical mistakes made by his father when writing his manuscript memoir of William Graham, and misguidedly, James altered quotes found in his father's manuscript, "Memoir of Rev. William Graham." In so doing, James Alexander misled many important later historians who held his father in high esteem as a historian of Presbyterians in Virginia in the eighteenth century. Additionally, the biography had a great impact on later nineteenth-century historians due to its wide circulation and consequent ease of access. James's published biography of his father unfortunately served to repudiate his father's earlier accounts of the origins of Washington and Lee University, which were only accessible to very limited audiences. Readers, therefore, were misled to believe that Archibald Alexander had connected Liberty Hall Academy to earlier preparatory private schools before Mr. William Graham arrived in Virginia, but of course, Archibald Alexander had written no such thing. He did note in his manuscript memoir of William Graham that there had existed earlier schools in the Valley, but he admitted that the lack of evidence prohibited drawing hardly any conclusions about the schools or the men who conducted them, but at no time did he assert that there was a connection or link between the presbytery's seminary, Augusta Academy, and any other school, public or private. One thing that is certain is that when Mr. Graham arrived in Virginia in response to the call and appointment from the Hanover Presbytery to take charge of its prospective new seminary, there was no school then operating at the place called locally "Mount Pleasant."

The earlier Latin school of Rev. John Brown that had once been located at Mount Pleasant had been moved to Brown's newer residence next door to the New Providence Presbyterian meeting house in the later 1760s. This move to New Providence was occasioned by Brown's deteriorating relationship with his congregation at Timber Ridge and his eventual request to be dismissed from that pastorate. The presbytery granted Brown's request in 1767 and by then Brown's move to New Providence several miles away was a fait accompli. At this point in time, there was no longer any school operating at Mount Pleasant near Fairfield, Virginia. Sometime in early 1775, the presbytery's new seminary in Augusta County initiated its earliest operations in temporary headquarters at "Mount Pleasant," and in so doing caused many later authors to confuse Brown's private Latin school with the Hanover Presbytery's newly established public academy, which was initially and informally referred to by the presbytery as Augusta Academy.[303] The only two things these two schools had in common were that their administrative leaders were both Presbyterian ministers and they both were located for a time at the place called locally "Mount Pleasant," albeit in two different decades. Brown's Latin school in the 1760s and Graham's academy

---

303 As noted elsewhere, the name Augusta Academy was not used in eighteenth-century Virginia to refer to any school other than the presbytery's seminary under the direction of William Graham at Mount Pleasant. Nevertheless, many post-1850 historians have insisted that Robert Alexander's school or Brown's Latin school, or both, were called Augusta Academy. Those who did were wrong and none of them have ever offered any credible evidence to support their claims in this regard.

in 1775 and 1776. Importantly, both of these schools were operating at different locations during 1775.[304]

The auditor, unfortunately, could find no sensible explanation for how James could have honestly misquoted his father concerning the founding of Liberty Hall Academy. The truth is, it is rather obvious that James came to believe that William Henry Foote had published an accurate accounting of the college's founding, and rather than paint his father as having been in serious error, he modified his father's account to correspond to that of Mr. Foote.[305]

James Alexander should have given his father more credit, because it was his father who had discovered the truth and published it in 1843 in his, "Address to the Alumni of Washington College." Unfortunately, at that time, it was only published in a limited- edition pamphlet. By the time that Alexander's address containing his accurate account was re-printed fifty years later in the _Washington and Lee Historical Papers_ of 1890, untold hundreds of historians had relied upon the mistaken unauthenticated representation of William Henry Foote. The accurate version only published in a limited edition pamphlet was generally unknown or fell prey to selective perception. That is no excuse for James Alexander, however, because he was aware of his father's "Address to the Alumni of Washington College," printed in a limited- edition pamphlet in 1843.[306] He therefore must have deemed that his father had been in error and decided to correct what he believed was his father's mistake. By falsely representing what his father had written, the history of Washington and Lee University was magically extended by twenty-five years, at least in the minds of most mid-nineteenth-century historians. James's forged representation, coupled with Foote's similarly fabricated account, caused the public to be understandably led astray. Henceforth, Washington and Lee's life was inappropriately extended by twenty-five years, an extension neither deserved nor accurate. The actual birthday of October 13, 1774, was thereafter ignored by a credulous series of historians and Washington and Lee professors, administrators, and tTrustees who repeatedly and embarrassingly represented the origins as being dated from 1748, or thereabouts. That representation, however, is devoid of any supporting documentary evidence from the eighteenth century and it is in direct

---

304 A fact clearly described by the eyewitness, Rev. Philip V. Fithian, in his journal, which was written in 1775 and 1776. See the report's bibliography.

305 The auditor offers as a possible explanation (not a justification) for James's misquote of his father's manuscript, the following: James was working at the Princeton Theological Seminary where Rev. William Hill was, for a time, a professor, and Rev. Hill had written a history of Washington College in Virginia (see bibliography) wherein he mistakenly included a reference to a "visit" that the Hanover Presbytery had made to Rev. John Brown's school and he left the false impression that the school they visited was the presbytery's new seminary, when it was not. Rev. Hill then later became the pastor of the Presbyterian Church in Winchester, Virginia. He was succeeded by Rev. William Henry Foote, who later published his first volume of _Sketches of Virginia_, in which he essentially makes the same mistake that his predecessor, Rev. Hill, had made in his earlier article. Mr. Foote, however, expands upon Rev. Hill's mistake. If this occurred, Mr. Foote, as is usual for him, does not bother to credit his source, but the close association between these men make this scenario entirely plausible.

306 James Alexander in fact refers to the pamphlet in his biography of his father.

contravention of every representation that had been made by the cCollege from the day the institution was created on October 13, 1774, up to and including the day that President George Junkin was inaugurated in 1749. President Junkin's published iInaugural address was ordered printed by the college's bBoard of tTrustees and that publication includes an aAppendix entitled "A Brief Sketch of the Early History of Washington College." [307] This was the college's first authorized and published history, and it clearly explains that the college was established by the Hanover Presbytery in the autumn of 1774.

Archibald Alexander's true account:

> When the Presbytery of Hanover determined to establish a school in this Valley, for the rearing of young men for the ministry, they applied to the Reverend Samuel Stanhope Smith, then itinerating in the State, to recommend a suitable person to take charge of their school, upon which he at once recommended Mr. Graham; and at their request wrote to him to come on to the Valley of Virginia. *Before this time*, a classical school had been taught at the place called Mount Pleasant, near the little town of Fairfield. ***Here*** Mr. Graham commenced his labours (sic) as a teacher; *and **here*** we find the germ whence sprung this college.[308] (Alexander, Address to the Alumni, p. 128) (Italics and underling added for emphasis)

This correct statement probably misled some historians because it would be relatively easy to conclude that Alexander meant that the earlier classical school was the germ from whence sprung the college, when what he actually says is that it was "here," in this place (i.e., Mount Pleasant), that the germ of the college is found, which is true, but the germ he refers to is is the grammar school organized by Rev. Graham as the institution's footings upon which the foundation was to be laid, and upon which the superstructure of the college was to be built. Archibald Alexander's explanation of the founding is punctuated by this meaningful comment:

---

307 .Rev. George Junkin, DD, *Christianity the Patron of Literature and Science: An Address Delivered February 22, 1849, On the Occasion of the Author's Inauguration as President of Washington College, Virginia*, Philadelphia, The Board of Trustees, 1849 [pamphlet p. 39]. The Junkin Inaugural Address includes an important appendix: "A Brief Sketch of the Early History of Washington College" (ordered printed by the board of trustees). This constitutes the college's first authorized, published history.

308 Alexander, Archibald DD, An Address before Alumni of Washington College, Delivered June 29, 1843, *Washington and Lee Historical Papers,* No. 2, Lexington, Va., 1890 [Note: The auditor's copy is in wraps and includes two articles: Alexander's Address, delivered June 29, 1843, and "The Founders of Washington College" by Hon. Hugh Blair Grigsby, delivered June 22, 1870.] (See bibliography)

"I cannot conclude this address without pronouncing a brief eulogy on the man who deserves to be called the Father of the College, and whose memory should be venerated by all its Alumni. I mean the Rev. William Graham." (Alexander, Address to the Alumni.., pg. 128, Washington and Lee University Historical Papers Vol. 2, 1890. It was also published in a limited edition pamphlet in Lexington in the same year it was delivered, 1843.)

If those misguided mid-nineteenth-century historians who asserted a founding date of 1748 had been correct, Archibald Alexander would likely have insisted that his great-uncle, Robert Alexander, was the man who deserved to be called the father of the college. He insisted, however, that the honor belonged to his preceptor, Rev. William Graham, an insistence consistent with all the known documentary records of the eighteenth century upon which the various accurate histories had been formulated during the college's first seventy-five years, all of which date the establishment as having occurred on October 13, 1774.[309]

James W. Alexander's Maddening Falsification: His own words passed off as the words of his father.

The reverend William Graham, a graduate of the College of New Jersey, had set up an academy at Timber Ridge Meeting-House, and had obtained an ample charter from the Legislature. . . . Several small neat buildings were erected for the use of the students, and a good house for the rector . . . . ***The school indeed existed before Mr. Graham came into the state,***[310] ***but had its seat at Mount Pleasant, near to the site of the village of Fairfield, six or seven miles to the east of Timber Ridge and Hall's Meeting-House. Here Mr. Graham taught for a year or more,*** but ***being a man of much enterprise, he wished to rear a seminary after the model of Princeton College.*** Having received a call from Timber Ridge and Hall's Meeting House, ***he removed the school to the former place, where he conducted it for several years.*** (James W. Alexander, *The Life of Archibald Alexander, DD*, New York, Charles Scribner, 1854, pp. 15–16) (Emphasis in bold italics here indicates errors)

---

309   The one notable exception is in the appendix to President Junkin's inaugural address, "A Brief Sketch of the Early History of Washington College," p. 35, it was only mistaken by one day (October 12, 1774 instead of October 13, 1774.)

310   *.This is interesting because these words are NOT Archibald Alexander's words, but rather those of his son, James, who as editor of this biography of Archibald Alexander, liberally altered and added to the original manuscript left by his father. The original manuscript does not claim any connection between the earlier school at Mount Pleasant, nor to the educational endeavor of Robert Alexander or Rev. John Brown.*

The rendition above, shockingly placed in quotation marks by the son, is pure rubbish and could not possibly have been written by Archibald Alexander who knew full well that Mr. Graham did not move any school to any "former place.,..." Archibald Alexander also did not represent what his son suggests that he did, in any other known publication, letter, or memorandum. James clearly created this fiction, believing that he was covering up his father's mistake.[311] The mistake, however, was James' error in judgment, not his father's failure of memory.

Note: Rev. Graham did move from his temporary quarters at Mount Pleasant, but that move came when the first permanent campus's buildings were fairly completed. This move began in late autumn of 1776 and culminated in the winter months of 1777. This was the only move of the college[312] from Mount Pleasant. Once again, a misguided author confused Brown's private Latin school at New Providence with the presbytery's public seminary at Mount Pleasant. Even then, Brown's private Latin school is only known to have been moved once and that was from Mount Pleasant (circa 1767) to New Providence where it remained as long as it existed.

Here is what Archibald Alexander wrote in his unpublished "Memoir of Rev. William Graham":

> The writer [referring to himself] **has an impression**, however, that Mount Pleasant Academy had a teacher of languages, **before Mr. Graham came, but information on the subject is wanting***; and **if there was such a teacher**, he was probably a man of no distinction, and has left no memorial of himself behind. (Archibald Alexander, D. D., Mss, "Memoir of the Rev. William Graham," [written in longhand] the Rev. Graham portions of this manuscript constitute the largest part of a writing entitled *Great Valley of Virginia*. Pg. 51. The auditor's photocopy came from the Princeton Seminary Library in 1989. It is also available in spiral-bound form at the Leyburn Library, Washington and Lee University. It was hand-paginated by the auditor for easier use.)

Here below is what appears to be Archibald Alexander's marginalia in longhand highlighted with an asterisk, but the handwriting in the notation is strikingly different than that found in the main text, calling into question whether

---

311 What James thought was his father's mistake was written in his father's unpublished manuscript, "Memoir of Rev. William Graham," which was part of a larger work, none of which Archibald intended to be published. In fact, he left instructions that it be destroyed upon his death. James seemingly had no reason to fear that his correction of his father's words would ever be discovered, but as it happened, the manuscript was used by James while writing his father's biography and he reprinted what he deemed useful and informative. Obviously intending to destroy the manuscript after the biography was published. His assumption, however, was incorrect. The manuscript survived and in the 1980s it was gifted to the Princeton Theological Seminary by one of Alexander's descendants. A photocopy of the item was obtained by the auditor shortly thereafter.

312 *Technically a college, this incipient form of its first emendations was in the form of a grammar school, which was an appendix to the college continued throughout Rev. Graham's tenure. Colleges, of course, are not built in a day. They are constructed and formed in phases as freshmen become sophomores and so on and so forth. The grammar school was merely phase one of the envisioned college created on October 13, 1774.*

this notation was actually A. Alexander's or possibly someone else's.[313] If someone else, it's difficult to imagine that it was anyone other than his son, James, who was the author of his father's biography. James quotes from his father's manuscript liberally in his biography of his father, and this note is in many ways consistent with the ridiculous re-write James made of portions of his father's manuscript as concerns the origins of Washington and Lee. It should pointed out, however, that this parenthetical does not contain an assertion that Ebenezer Smith taught at the pPresbytery's patronized, "Augusta Academy." Instead, the note merely says that this Mr. Smith "taught _a_ school" at Mount Pleasant, which is true, although it was not, as James suggests, the Hanover Presbytery's school.

> * "Ebenezer Smith taught a school at Mt. Pleasant before Mr. Graham came into the state."

Smith obviously conducted Brown's Latin school, but it is unclear when or at which location.

The reader's attention is directed to the poignant use of the words "a school" instead of the words "the school.". If Archibald Alexandere meant to assert that Ebenezer Smith taught at the same school that was under Graham's direction, he would have referred to it as "the school." In truth, when Alexander first wrote this section of his memoir of Graham, he clearly wasn't certain about the subject, hence, his reluctance to pronounce the historical sequence with any degree of certainty. Later, when he published his address to the alumni, he had obviously discovered the true series of events and he suggests no links of any kind between Liberty Hall and any other school.

In Archibald Alexander's commentary on this subject, he also says this, referring to the Hanover Presbytery's meeting minutes:

> "...at a meeting of the presbytery held at Cub Creek October 1774, they adopted the following resolution, "'To establish & patronize a public school which shall be confined to the county of Augusta, in this colony... . . . At present it shall be managed by Wm. Graham, a gentleman properly recommended to this Presbytery.'" (Archibald Alexander DD., unpublished "Memoir of Rev. William Graham., pp. 51--52)

Note: Archibald Alexander noticeably left out of this quote from the pPresbytery's minutes the final phrase that says, "and under the inspection of Rev. John Brown.," and he did so for a good reason, which is that it tends to mislead because. Brown never accepted this appointment, whatever it may have meant. Importantly, Edward Graham had earlier (1821) done the same thing and deliberately

---

313 Of course, the apparent difference in the handwriting between the main text and the referenced footnote could have resulted from Archibald Alexander's age and health. It does appear that the footnote was added to the manuscript sometime after the manuscript was originally written. Researchers interested in the early history of Washington and Lee University will, no doubt, discover that William Henry Ruffner added numerous footnotes to his father's manuscript entitled "Early History of Washington College," although in that case, the son initialed his additions, as follows "WHR."

did not refer to the pPresbytery's qualifying phrase, "..under the inspection of Rev. John Brown" presumably for the same reason. (Emphasis added)

It is abundantly clear that what Archibald Alexander wrote in his manuscript memoir of his preceptor, William Graham, is vividly dissimilar from what his son claims that he said. Moreover, it is also apparent from his careful language that Archibald Alexander was, at the time of his writing, very unsure of the precise history of this important phase of the college's institutional history. Later, when Archibald wrote and then delivered his address to the alumni of Washington College, on the subject of the founding, he said this:

> When the Presbytery of Hanover determined to establish a school in this Valley, for the rearing of young men for the ministry, they applied to the Rev. Samuel Stanhope Smith, then itinerating in the State, to recommend a suitable person to take charge of their school, upon which he at once recommended Mr. Graham; and at their request wrote to him to come on to the Valley of Virginia. Before this time, a classical school had been taught a place called Mount Pleasant, near to the little town of Fairfield. Here Mr. Graham commenced his labours [sic] as a teacher; and here we find the germ whence sprung this college.
> (Archibald Alexander, DD, An Address before Alumni of Washington College, Virginia. Delivered June 29, 1843, Washington and Lee Historical Papers No. 2, Lexington, Va., 1890, p. 129)

While Alexander's words are somewhat misleading, when referencing the classical school, his emphasis is appropriately on the place, Mount Pleasant, and he does not claim that the presbytery's seminary and the "classical" school were one and the same. Indeed they could not have been the same because the classical school to which Alexander refers is Rev. Brown's Latin school, and that school was not located at Mount Pleasant when Graham came to Virginia to set up the presbytery's new seminary of learning. Brown had some time earlier moved to Brown's farm at New Providence. Alexander's very specific use of the qualifier "before this time" means that at the time in question, the classical school was not at Mount Pleasant. Alexander demonstrates that he knew this by his careful descriptions, but his son James did not. We know that James altered his father's words because we now have his father's manuscript and can compare James's account with what his father said. The words James represents as being his father's contained mistakes that his father did not make.

In fact, the Hanover Presbytery had not yet formally "established" their prospective seminary when they applied to Samuel S. Smith for a recommendation for someone to take charge of the intended school. We know this because the decision to formally establish the school was only made official on the day that the presbytery also announced their appointment of Graham. Obviously, Smith had to have had time to write to William Graham communicating the presbytery's offer that he take charge of implementing their planned seminary. Graham, in turn, had to have communicated his acceptance of the offer in order for the presbytery to prudently make his appointment official. Both decisions were made official at the autumn meeting, which took place at Cub Creek Meeting House in Charlotte County, on October 13, 1774. Of paramount historical importance is the well-established fact that at the time that these decisions were made by the presbytery, Brown's Latin school was operating at New Providence.

The several erroneous comments published by James were mistakes of his own making, and he was dishonest to have claimed that they were the words of his father. Researchers of tomorrow will need to take great care when reading James's biography of his father and they must obtain a copy of Archibald's handwritten manuscript, "Memoir of Rev. William Graham" and his *Address to the Alumni of Washington College* in order to understand what James's father actually said about the founding of Washington College.

****

Having provided the complicated explanation above concerning the most widely published and available resource containing information about Archibald Alexander, and why it is often unreliable when it is addressing Archibald Alexander's claims about the founding of Washington and Lee University, the report below will now address the actual errors made by Archibald Alexander.

This subsection of the audit report offers a more in-depth treatment than most of the subsequent subsections because the author under review, Rev. Archibald Alexander DD, is a critically important source of information pertaining to the early history of Washington and Lee University. An early student of the institution under Graham, Rev. Archibald Alexander stands as one of its preeminent alumni, who is probably also the single most-published man of all of the school's early alumni, and is clearly its most distinguished graduate dating to the eighteenth century.

At a very early age, Alexander was elected the third president of Hampden Sidney College. From this position, Alexander was elevated to the eminent position of founder and first president of the Princeton Theological Seminary. He served in this capacity from 1812 to 1840. Mr. Alexander's unpublished manuscript, "Memoir of Rev. William Graham," is a source rich in personal recollections and firsthand experiences in and around the region near Washington and Lee.

Rev. Alexander's numerous publications include his history of the early Presbyterian colleges in America, short-titled, *The Log College*.[314] It is clear, therefore, that few men of his age were more familiar with the nuances of creating Presbyterian educational institutions in eighteenth-century North America than was Alexander. Hence, his importance as an eyewitness to so many of the early experiences associated with the establishing and early operations of Liberty Hall Academy, where he was a student for several years, first as a preparatory student, then as a matriculating undergraduate, and finally as a postgraduate student

---

314 *Alexander, Archibald DD., Biographical Sketches of the Founder and Principal Alumni of the Log College*, Philadelphia, 1851.

of theology. At this period in his life he was boarded in the home of President Graham along with his schoolmate, Mr. Edward Graham, the rector's younger brother, who later became Archibald's brother-in-law by marrying Alexander's older sister, Margaret.

This significant historical document written by Alexander is one that he never published, to wit: Archibald Alexander, DD, Mss "Memoir of The Rev. Wm Graham" [written in longhand]. The Rev. Graham/Liberty Hall Academy portions of this manuscript constitute the largest part of a writing entitled *Great Valley of Virginia*. It is worthy of emphasis that the only significant factual errors that were discovered during this investigation that are actually attributable to Rev. Archibald Alexander were found in his memoir of William Graham, which was never intended for publication. Several of the mistakes found in the Alexander manuscript were merely extractions taken from his brother-in-law, Edward Graham's earlier published memoir of Rev. William Graham.

No material mistakes were identified in any of Archibald Alexander's published works during the course of the audit that pertain to the founding of Washington and Lee University. In addition, in none of Alexander's works or the manuscript "Memoir" does he date the origin of the college earlier than the actions of the Hanover Presbytery in October of 1774. Neither does he claim in any of his writings that Mr. Robert Alexander, or Rev. John Brown, played any role in the founding of Liberty Hall Academy or its predecessor the "Augusta Academy," as it was informally known while it was located at the academy's temporary headquarters on the farm of Mr. James Wilson known locally as "Mount Pleasant."

In the unpublished manuscript "Memoir," however, Mr. Archibald Alexander describes an event that transpired during his youth wherein he went beyond description and ventured into analysis, and in this case, he offers his judgment on the cause of certain aspects of this event. In so doing he assigns some measure of blame on his preceptor, Rev. William Graham. In our view, his assessment is inconsistent with the very facts of the case, which Alexander himself described. The result of the assessment of his analysis justifies, in our view, a repudiation of Alexander's conclusions. The event and his analysis, together with the audit report's assessment, are detailed below concerning the New Providence congregation and a communion service conducted by the visiting Rev. William Graham.

ERROR no. (1): The biography of Rev. Archibald Alexander contains an assertion, ostensibly made by the subject of the biography, that Rev. Archibald Alexander wrote in his unpublished manuscript memoir of Rev. William Graham, that the Hanover Presbytery's patronized seminary, Augusta Academy, located at "Mount Pleasant" near Fairfield, Virginia, existed before 1774, which is patently untrue.

Note: We include this error by the son, James, in this part of the subsection because, unfortunately, the quote that embodies the error is so often attributed to the father by later historians. As already explained above, the essence of the assertion is false for reasons already explained, and the assertion is quite clearly that of the son, not one made by the father.

Any serious researcher who reads an account of the origins of Washington College (Va.), written by Archibald Alexander, are herein forewarned that they should read all three known versions attributed to him. The only one to rely on concerning the origins of Washington and Lee University, however, is his last published account, which appears in his *Address to the Alumni Association of Washington College*, delivered in June of 1843.[315] The other two earlier versions should not be relied upon in this regard: The earliest one is based, in large part, on Edward Graham's published memoir of Reverend William Graham," which, as has been pointed out above, is particularly in error concerning the sequence of establishment between Liberty Hall Academy and Hampden -Sydney Academy.

Because of the importance of the error made by James Alexander, we have provided Archibald's earlier, and also incorrect, "draft" statement below in order to demonstrate the difference in text between Archibald's draft language and that which eventually found its way into print. The manuscript draft actually contains the following errorneous comment by Archibald Alexander:

> *[They] [Hanover Presbytery] now determined that another literary institution by whatever name it might be called, should be located in Augusta County.* The resolution of Presbytery was, as I mentioned, prior to Mr. Graham's coming to Virginia. For the Presbytery having declared that they were entirely at a loss for a suitable person to take charge of the institution judged to be expedient, on the west of Blue Ridge, Mr. Smith informed them that he knew a young man, in Pennsylvania, whom he thought eminently qualified for the station, and who he supposed, would accept the offer. At their request, therefore, he wrote immediately to Mr. Graham and informed him of the state of things in Virginia, and of the opening which there was for a literary institution in the Valley, on the west of the Blue Ridge; and urged him to come on, without delay. He accordingly came and commenced a classical school at a place called Mount Pleasant, an eminence in the vicinity of the place where the village of Fairfield now stands. This spot was then in the county of Augusta, but since the county of Rockbridge was erected, it falls within the bounds of this county. It was also within the limits of New Providence congregation[316] of which,

315 Alexander, Archibald, DD, Biographical "Sketch of Rev. William Graham" in Wm. Sprague's Annals of the American Pulpit, Vol. III, New York, Robert Carter & Brothers, 1858 [but dated in the text as 1849], pp.365–370. Note: A sketch drawn from the 1843 "address" of Dr. Alexander and is consistent with this address. This brief sketch was submitted for publication just two years before Archibald Alexander's death in 1851. In regards to the founding of Washington and Lee University, the father was as correct as he was consistent.

316 Rev. Brown had earlier been pastor jointly of both Timber Ridge and New Providence Congregations, and in that time, circa 1760–67, New Providence would certainly have been within the bounds of the joint pastoral appointment. After Brown's falling out with the Timber

as was before said, the Rev. John Brown, a graduate of Nassau Hall, was the pastor. (Archibald Alexander, Mss. "Memoir of William Graham," pp. 43--- 44.) (Eemphasis here indicates errors.)

At the time that Archibald Alexander wrote this first-draft paragraph, he was obviously operating under more than one misconception, including his error concerning the sequence of establishment. He also seems to have thought it somehow relevant that Graham's new classical school was located in an area "within the limits of New Providence congregation" when that fact, if indeed it was a fact, was completely irrelevant, and possibly even untrue.[317] What is true, however, is that the Mount Pleasant location was intended only as temporary headquarters for the new seminary, which the presbytery had every intention of erecting upon lands adjacent to the Timber Ridge congregation. The presbytery's rather obvious plan was to facilitate the licensing of Rev. Graham and subsequently to ordain Mr. Graham as the pastor of the vacant pastorate of the Timber Ridge Church. By including the irrelevant allusion to New Providence congregation in this paragraph, Archibald Alexander may have added to his son's later confusion concerning the early years of Augusta Academy (i.e., Liberty Hall Academy). Any confusion on the part of James Alexander, however, does not mitigate his guilt for having falsely represented his own words for those of his father.

(Note: At the time in 1775 and early 1776 that the "Augusta Academy" was operating temporarily at Mount Pleasant, and it was from its inception "under the care and tuition" of William Graham, and so it remained for the next twenty-two years, until Rev. William Graham submitted his letter of resignation to the Liberty Hall Academy Board of Trustees, in 1796. This fact is revealed in the original meeting minutes of both the Hanover Presbytery and the Liberty Hall Board of Trustees, for the entire twenty-two years of Graham's tenure at the college.)

CONCLUSION OF THE ASSESSMENT OF ERROR no. 1
(IMPORTANT POINTS)

(A) William Graham did initially [1775] conduct a grammar school, of sorts at Mount Pleasant, but not, as James Alexander says, "at Timber Ridge." At Mount Pleasant, he initially prepared students for studying the college classes that he would be conducting once the prospective buildings were erected at Timber Ridge.[318]

Ridge congregation and his voluntary dismissal from his charge at Timber Ridge, it is not clear to us whether the Mount Pleasant site fell within the bounds of Timber Ridge or New Providence, but it really does not bear upon any of the issues with which this audit is concerned.

317   Jurisdictional boundaries in the Valley were rarely precise in that era as they relate to Presbyterian churches located nearby one another.

318   The Hanover Presbytery referred to these initial classes as a grammar school in the meeting minutes of 1775 and early 1776, as did Rev. Graham when he drafted the letter to President George Washington on behalf of the trustees in 1796. This grammar school aspect of the college became a permanent fixture of Liberty Hall during the tenure of Rev. William Graham as the administrative head of the college. In this, Rev. Graham was following the same method adopted by his preceptor, Rev. John Witherspoon of Princeton College, who understood the

(B) "The school" alluded to by Archibald's son, James, in fact, did not exist before Mr. Graham came into the state, as is made clear by Archibald Alexander's manuscript, and his later aAddress to the Alumni Association, and more importantly, by the official meeting minutes of the Hanover Presbytery and the meeting minutes record book of the trustees of Liberty Hall Academy. Indeed, as Rev. A. Alexander so carefully stated it, *"a school," not "the school"* was conducted at Mount Pleasant before Graham's arrival in the state. The earlier school, however, was a private school organized by Brown, and conducted there by hired tutors. This transpired when Brown was pastor of Timber Ridge Church, and when he and his family resided on a farm nearby the school. This school was consistently referred to by its creator as a "Latin sSchool."[319] This school, which has no connection to the pPresbytery's seminary, was moved to Brown's home on Moffett's Creek adjacent to his home and the cChurch. Once established at New Providence, it remained there until Brown closed it sometime in late December of 1775 or early January of 1776. Brown wrote to his brother-in-law, William Preston, in 1782 announcing that he was intent on reopening the school now that the Revolutionary War was coming to a close. The auditor found no evidence to suggest that the school was actually reopened as was planned.

When Rev. Brown's relationship with Timber Ridge Church deteriorated in the 1760s, he voluntarily severed his connection to the Timber Ridge congregation. Sometime during this drawn-out termination process Brown moved his home, his family, and his school to a new location near New Providence Church on Moffett's Creek, several miles distant. This change took place several years before the presbytery established their new seminary in Augusta County and well before Mr. William Graham arrived in Virginia to commence the educational activities associated with the new seminary. In fact, one of Brown's sons was born at Brown's new farm on Moffett's Creek several years before Mr. Graham organized the presbytery's temporary headquarters at Mount Pleasant in early- to mid-1775.

In the interim between Brown's departure from Mount Pleasant and the presbytery's decision to create a college in Augusta County somewhere west of the Blue Ridge Mountains, there was no school being conducted at the place near Fairfield, Virginia, which was in those days known locally as "Mount Pleasant." This remains a critically important fact unknown or appreciated by the historians of the latter nineteenth and twentieth centuries. The failure to recognize and appreciate this fact led to most of the mistakes made by historians who incorrectly linked earlier private educational endeavors to the founding of Liberty Hall Academy.

---

value of such an endeavor, both for recruiting and for enhancing a student's likelihood of success once accepted into the college's regular academic program.

319   Rev. Brown's references to his "Latin school" can be found scattered among his many letters preserved in the Draper Collection housed in Madison, Wisconsin. For examples, see Stuart, John White, *The Rev. John Brown of Virginia (1728–1803): His Life and Selected Sermons,* Doctoral Dissertation, University of Massachusetts, 1988.

(C) The process by which the decision was made to locate the new seminary's temporary headquarters on that portion of Mr. James Wilson's farm called locally, "Mount Pleasant," is not known with any degree of certainty because the process was informal and no records appear to have been kept on that subject. It seems clear, however, that the decision was not formally made by the Hanover Presbytery because if it had, such a decision would have been recorded in their meeting minutes, and the minutes book contains no reference to such an action on its part.

In all likelihood, these earlier decisions were made by Mr. Graham in collaboration with various members of the Presbyterian community located in and around the Timber Ridge and New Providence congregations. That deduction is based on a few known facts, including that William Graham, like so many Presbyterians traveling to that geographic area, lodged temporarily at the home of Rev. John Brown.[320]

ERROR no. 2: In his unpublished manuscript memoir of William Graham, Alexander attempts to explain the arrival of Samuel Stanhope Smith in Virginia, but unfortunately, he relied on Edward Graham's published memoir of his older brother, William Graham, which was mistaken in this regard.

Here is Archibald Alexander's unfortunate, albeit unpublished, passage:

> "About this time Mr. Samuel Stanhope Smith who had been for several years a professor in Nassau Hall, and had acquired a high reputation for classical & elegant English literature, formed the plan of visiting Virginia . . ."

Note: The page break here, in the copy of the manuscript, suggests something may be missing, for the next page in my copy of the manuscript begins: [321]

> were speedily directed to Mr. Graham, with whose talents & attainments he was well acquainted: He therefore without delay, made the proposal, which was favorably received; for Mr. Graham, by the loss of his beloved mother, who was to him as a guardian angel, felt that the tenderest tie wh. [ich] bound him to his native spot was severed; and being, moreover, of an enterprising disposition, he entered into the scheme with ardour [sic]. It is proper to remark, however, that prior to this proposal to Mr. Graham from Mr. Smith, the latter had, on a missionary

---

320 This is discussed by Archibald Alexander in his unpublished memoir of William Graham.

321 *The auditor consulted with Princeton Theological Seminary's library on this anomaly, and after they reviewed the original manuscript, they assured the auditor that his copy is identical to the original. The text in this instance, then, will be treated as an anomaly. Of course it is entirely possible that the original, such as it is, may have a few missing pages. The original is not paginated, but the auditor took the liberty of paginating it in pencil at the upper-right-hand corner of each page, in order to be able to reference certain text by a page number.*

tour passed thro' Virginia, and had preached everywhere with uncommon acceptance & admiration.

The Presbyterians now became numerous in the colony, had for some time wished for a literary institution of their own; especially for the preparation of young men for the ministry; for it was inconvenient for many of the candidates to resort to Princeton for their education; and as to college of William & Mary, it was at this time little more than a school of law, & infidelity. The fact is indisputable that for many years, (??.....) any young man however piously educated, left that seminary without being infected with the Doctrines of Hume & Voltaire.

The Presbyterians in the southern part of the state, judging that Mr. Smith would be eminently qualified to be placed at the head of such an institution, entered upon the enterprise with spirit & promptitude; and fixed upon a spot not far from the Court House of Prince Edward County. (A. Alexander, "Memoir of Rev. William Graham," p. 41)

Note: This information above is wrong and was taken from materials supplied to him by Edward Graham, who was also incorrect in this regard concerning Rev. Samuel Stanhope Smith. Obviously, Rev. Alexander at some point discovered the error, and in the text following the above quoted text, he crossed out with lines forming an X through the remainder of this page and three-fourths of the following page.

When Alexander resumes his text immediately after that which was crossed out, he begins thus:

At the time, the presbytery of Hanover, covered not only the whole state, but extended indefinitely to the south & west. This judicatory entered warmly into the new enterprise; *and having already fixed on a site for the college over which Mr. Smith was to preside, they now determined that another literary institution by whatever name it might be called and should be located in Augusta County.* This resolution of presbytery was, as I now [??][322] prior to Mr. Graham's coming to Virginia. For the presbytery having declared that they were entirely at a loss for a suitable person to take charge of this institution judged to be expedient, on the west of the Blue Ridge, Mr. Smith informed them that he knew a young man in Pennsylvania whom he thought eminently qualified for the station, and who, he supposed, would accept the offer. ...He accordingly came and commenced a classical school at a place called Mount Pleasant, on an eminence in the vicinity of the place where the village

---

322 Indecipherable.

of Fairfield now stands. (A. Alexander manuscript, "Memoir of William Graham" pp. 40–44) (Emphasis added in bold italics reflects here a serious mistake, Archibald Alexander in his unpublished memoir of his preceptor is following his brother-in-law, the mis-guided Edward Graham, who on this issue, has the sequence of establishment between Liberty Hall and Hampden Sydney in reverse order. In fact, the Seminary in Augusta County [Liberty Hall] was established first, on Oct. 13, 1774. The seminary in Prince Edward was not established until the following year on February 1, 1775. While numerous nineteenth-century authors repeated this mistaken sequence of establishment but the correct sequence is now, almost universally correctly understood.) [323]

The audit report does not delve deeply into the important ramifications of this sequence of events, but the sequence of events associated with the founding of Liberty Hall Academy and Hampden Sydney are addressed elsewhere in this report. Suffice to say here that initially, there was but one seminary anticipated. The Hanover Presbytery very early in the establishment process determined that its seminary should be fixed west of the Blue Ridge Mountains, and decided upon William Graham of Pennsylvania to take charge of their first patronized seminary in Virginia.[324] Late in the process, the monied interests east (or, as some prefer, south) of the Blue Ridge began agitating for a second school. When that issue was taken under consideration, the presbytery looked to Rev. Samuel Stanhope Smith as a candidate to take charge of a second academy.

Mr. Graham and Mr. Smith were both from Pennsylvania. Mr. Smith grew up in Pequea not too far from Philadelphia, and Mr. Graham grew up in a frontier settlement in Paxton (Paxtang) Township on the Susquehanna River [now, Harrisburg]. Graham's father was a farmer who was one of the volunteer rangers

---

323 In the 1990s, Professor John L. Brinkley seemingly attempts to re-open the matter in his lengthy history of Hampden Sydney entitled *On This Hill: A Narrative History of Hampden-Sydney College, 1774–1994*, by suggesting that Liberty Hall Academy was a college merely on paper at the time that Hampden Sydney was established. Mr. Brinkley fails to acknowledge that this is typically true of all colleges at their inception. It was certainly true in the case of Hampden Sydney. His poor attempt to establishment an invidious distinction does not square with easily demonstrable facts. His argument is as unpersuasive on this subject as it is devoid of any material evidence to support his foolish notion. The auditor is unaware of any eighteenth-century evidence that supports the late Dr. Brinkley in this regard. This rather ridiculous digression by Dr. Brinkley aside, his valuable history is of exceeding importance and appears to be generally reliable and informative.

324 It may be that, technically, Liberty Hall Academy was the first Presbyterian patronized seminary in America, the existence of the College of New Jersey (Princeton) and its antecedents notwithstanding, because the auditor is not competent to render a judgment on that question. Whether the Presbyterian Church in America had ever taken formal action to patronize Princeton is a question that is outside the scope of the auditor's objective, but that Church's close attachment to Princeton may have been merely an informal connection. Certainly, Princeton's trustees and rectors in its earliest emendations were mostly, if not exclusively, Presbyterian.

called into service whenever the settlement was threatened by marauding Indians passing through the area. Mr. Smith's father was a Presbyterian minister who conducted an academy for preparing young men for the ministry. It seems their backgrounds were entirely consistent with their new surroundings in Virginia, where both men oversaw the raising of institutions of higher learning. Smith's constitution was somewhat frail from his youth and better suited to the more settled eastern part of Virginia, while Graham was a robust frontiersman as comfortable with a rifle or a plow as he was with a volume of Thucydides, Pythagorus, or Euclid, and therefore a better fit for the rugged settlements west of the Blue Ridge mountains. Samuel Smith's tenure at Hampden Sydney was rather brief and insignificant, due mostly to the interruption of the school's activities by the Revolutionary War. By the war's end, Smith had left for greener pastures in New Jersey, where he was hired to succeed his recent father-in-law, Dr. John Witherspoon, as president of Princeton. Rev. Graham, on the other hand, remained at Liberty Hall Academy during his entire professional career as an educator, lasting for twenty-two years.

Mr. Graham resigned his position as president (rector) after the close of the 1796 school year. His former student, Dr. Samuel L. Campbell, who was then a trustee, assumed the role of "acting president" while he and his fellow trustees searched for Mr. Graham's successor. Eventually, the trustees settled on another former student of Mr. Graham's, George Addison Baxter, and he was appointed as Mr. Graham's successor late in the year 1799. In effect, Mr. William Graham was the college's only eighteenth-century president. Rev. Graham remained, however, an active Presbyterian minister throughout the remainder of his life.

Error no. 3: Rev. Alexander describes an event that transpired at Rev. John Brown's New Providence Church in 1787, but errs in his analysis of the event at which a hymn written by Mr. Isaac Watts was introduced by Graham and which was inappropriately deemed by Alexander to have constituted an offense on the part of Graham.

(Note: This judgment by Archibald Alexander, while understandable, is nevertheless, a rather ridiculous judgment as our assessment will demonstrate. Alexander's poor judgment in this instance is inconsistent with both the known pertinent facts and with rather basic reasoning.)

Here is Archibald Alexander's written but unpublished account of the Watts Affair:

> On this occasion while Mr. Graham was serving at the Lord's table and much feeling seemed to be manifest in the congregation, he gave out one of Watts' Sacramental hymns which was sung by most, but one of the elders was so offended, that he made an attempt to stop the preacher from proceeding.[325] ***The innovation***

---

325   The auditor was late to discover the identity of two disruptive elders that Rev. Alexander chose not to name. One is Patrick Hall and the other was a member of the McCormick family. See: McCormick, Leander James, *Family Record and Biography*, Chicago, 1896 pp. 337–338 [pdf file Google]

was unauthorized[326] *[indecipherable word] and consequences such as might have been expected.* One whole district of the congregation with the elder before mentioned withdrew from the congregation; and immediately joined with some seceders in the neighborhood in forming a church in connection with that denomination. *All impartial men*[327] *censured*[328] *the conduct of Mr. Graham in this affair.* (Alexander, Archibald, Mss., "Memoir . . .," pp. 217–218) (Emphasis in bold italics here represents a series of questionable conclusions by Mr. Alexander.)

Archibald Alexander opines that William Graham's introduction of Watts's hymn was improper and affords significant importance to a seeming non-event. On this issue, the auditor fully admits that he cannot provide conclusive empirical evidence that Mr. Alexander is wrong, but the facts as Alexander himself presents them render that unnecessary. His judgment on this occasion was made in his youth, and was undoubtedly shaped in large measure by close relatives. His opinion on this matter, as expressed, is pregnant with prejudice.

Graham, on this occasion, was invited to preside at this, the most sacred of all Christian services (i.e., communion), and an elder was so offended by Rev. Graham's selection of one hymn that he took it upon himself to interrupt this service. Not being successful in his attempt to disrupt the service, the elder stormed out, followed by a small group of dissidents. Reason alone asks what kind of person, who is not unduly influenced by others, concludes from this limited set of facts that it is altogether appropriate for a person to interrupt such a service simply because they object to a particular hymn, and in so doing, leads a few associates or family members in a move to punish their existing pastor (Rev. John Brown) by reducing his income, and also reduces the church's revenues by reducing its congregation, simply because of the decision by a visiting minister to introduce a hymn to which they object? To behave in this way is simply irrational. Who can doubt but that there was an existing rift between factions in

---

326 *An invited minister is not expected to obtain specific authorization for every aspect of a service, which are commonly used aspects that are well-known and accepted practices of the general assembly of the Presbyterian Church, and this is especially true when the invitee is the leader of a current revival, which was the very reason that Rev. Graham had been invited to preside at this communion service, a fact provided by Rev. Alexander himself as a prelude to his description of this event.*

327 *By "all impartial men," he obviously means his close relations who had some connection with the disaffected rump caucus.*

328 *It is unfortunate that Alexander used the word "censured" in this context because in Presbyterian institutional affairs, a censure is a very serious disciplinary act taken by an ecclesiastical court, after a defendant has had due process and an opportunity to be heard. No complaint, however, was lodged against Rev. Graham on this occasion, and he was not then, before, or ever afterward censured by his church. A more appropriate word might have been "criticized," but even then the auditor would contend that Graham's actions in conducting this service, as described by Alexander, were entirely proper and consistent with all established policies of the national general assembly as they related to the use of psalmody in a Presbyterian service.*

this congregation which existed long before Graham was invited to conduct this service?

Assessed more broadly, Rev. Alexander's conclusion seems even more silly. Alexander himself admits that Graham was invited to preside at this service because he was the leading Presbyterian minister in the Valley of Virginia and was also the leader of the current revival movement then sweeping the state of Virginia. One of the well-known components of that revival was the use of Watts's hymns. Watts's hymns by the way, had earlier been deemed entirely acceptable by the Presbyterian Church's national general assembly. In addition, Presbyterians were admonished by the general assembly to refrain from disruptions and disputations concerning the hymns of Davis Rouse and Isaac Watts, an admonition ignored by those who disrupted the communion service at New Providence.

The pastor of New Providence at the time was Rev. John Brown, who, as was well known, had no great fondness for Graham, so if, as Mr. Alexander asserts, Graham's call for a hymn by Watts was unauthorized and worthy of censure, then the person who was in the best position to complain to the presbytery was Rev. Brown, who had, ostensibly just lost a portion of his congregation because of Graham's conduct. Of course, Rev. Brown made no such complaint because he knew full well that Rev. Graham's actions were entirely within the accepted policies of the church. The truth is, Rev. Brown would have realized that his congregants who had permanently departed clearly had far greater grievances than their objections to a particular hymn. It is far more likely that the rump caucus were opposed in general to the revival, and were angry because the larger part of the congregation had insisted on inviting Rev. Graham, as the leader of that revival in the Valley, to preside at this communion service, over their objections. These facts came from Archibald Alexander himself in the introductory commentary presented just prior to his description of this event.

Another commentator, James L. McCormick, is a descendant of the disruptive elder referenced obliquely by Rev. Alexander. Mr. McCormick informs as follows:

> "When our grandparents came to this country, they and their friends, connected with the New Providence Church, Rockbridge County, Virginia.
>
> "At this time, the Psalms of David were used almost exclusively in all the churches. After some years, there came to the church, a minister who introduced Watts' hymns. **Grandfather (Patrick Hall)** thought that nothing should be sung in the worship of God but the Psalms of David, and, as soon as the hymn was given out, he picked up his hat and left the church, and a number of others followed him.[329]

---

329 If Mr. McCormick did hold this view regarding psalmody, he did so at odds with the national general assembly of the Presbyterian Church for they had for some time been admonishing their members to refrain from such contumacious behavior among their brethren over the subject of psalmody. Both authors, David Rouse and Isaac Watts, had long been received by the general assembly as acceptable to the church. Rev. Alexander should have directed his censorious

"They immediately determined to build a church in which worship should be to their minds, would be most acceptable to God, and prove to the building up and edification of His church." (Leander James McCormick, _Family Record and Biography, Compiled by Leander James McCormick,_ Chicago, 1896 p. 247) (Emphasis added)

Imagine a small group attempting, but failing, to interrupt a communion service for the sole reason that a visiting minister calls for the singing of one lone hymn that they find objectionable. If anything, this small group obviously had an ongoing dispute with their fellow parishioners, their minister, or both. According to Dr. Alexander, these men also objected to their fellow parishioners' inviting into their church a representative, Rev. Graham, of the then-current revival. The group in question apparently used this opportunity to justify their leaving the congregation and forming their own congregation. In all, Graham's role in this event constitutes a relatively uneventful occurrence. What was noteworthy was the obvious manifestation of an ongoing struggle between two competing caucuses. Alexander very likely based his analysis of this event in large part on secondhand information because he was a very young and impressionable man at the time that it occurred, although he was not a member of this congregation. His immediate family worshiped at Timber Ridge.

It is apparently true that a disturbance took place during the service, but to lay upon Rev. William Graham the blame for a true schism resulting from this disturbance, as has been done by later authors, is contrary to reason and old-fashioned common sense. In order for the disgruntled to have been so disaffected as to cause them to leave Rev. Brown's congregation, they surely had to have already had a bone to pick with either Rev. Brown or, alternatively, with some other individual or group of individuals within that congregation. Otherwise, they would have simply filed a complaint with the Presbyterian Church against the visiting Rev. William Graham. The fact is, neither the disgruntled Presbyterians nor their minister, Rev. Brown, filed any complaint with the higher church authorities. That Alexander's unpublished words included a judgment call on his part that Rev. Graham was wrong to distribute a hymn says more about Mr. Alexander than it does about William Graham. Graham, after all, was a leading figure in the presbytery, the Virginia Synod, and the national general assembly. As such, he was well aware that the established national policy on what was then referred to as psalmody was that the church recognized both Watts's hymns, and the older and more traditional Rouse's versions as eminently acceptable for use in any service. They also admonished their membership to refrain from such acrimony over the use of these two approaches to psalmody as that which had occurred at New Providence.

Alexander's error, in this regard, is one of incorrect analysis undoubtedly caused by cognitive dissonance brought about by his having close family members

---

assessment toward the offending elder, Mr. Hall, not toward the visiting adherent of the current revival who had been invited to conduct the service because of his role in carrying the revival to the various congregations.

who had some connection to the rump caucus members of New Providence Church. Of course, Alexander's censorious assessment did not include a judgment that his preceptor was the proximate cause of the schism that followed this disruption, but his comments were undoubtedly relied upon by those later authors who did go so far. Alexander's comments in this regard makes no sense whatsoever. Oddly enough, numerous historians have repeated this anecdote and concluded that Rev. Graham caused the schism. They did so as though this judgment made sense, when obviously, it makes no sense at all.

Note: Irrespective of one's view on this subject, it is important to keep in mind that this is a rather minor and unimportant point in history in general. The mistake, if indeed it is a mistake, is not one of fact but merely of opinion. It is a matter, however, that relates to the college's founder, Rev. William Graham's reputation. Rev. Graham knew that his selection of a Watts hymn was entirely within keeping with the policies of the Presbyterian general assembly. That would help to explain why neither the New Providence congregation nor their regular pastor, Rev. John Brown, bothered to file a complaint with the presbytery against Rev. Graham subsequent to the disrupted communion service. It is surprising that Alexander failed to recognize that his preceptor had every right to select a hymn by Mr. Watts on this occasion.

ERROR no. 4: Rev. Alexander mistakenly and ponderously suggested in his manuscript that he knew Rev. William Graham's views concerning slavery. What he ponderously surmised, however, was clearly wrong, and apparently he too came to realize that he had been mistaken on this subject because he struck through those remarks with a bold cross-out of this aspect of the manuscript.

There is no good reason to quote from this section that Alexander *crossed out*, and for that reason, it has not been included. Still, it had seemed to Alexander, for a time, that perhaps Graham, who Alexander says arrived in Virginia believing that slavery was an abomination, but over time he seemed to have become resigned to its existence in Virginia. On that score, Alexander was wrong, but fortunately, he obviously became aware of his mistake. Hence his bold cross-out of that provision.

Alexander's initial notion in this regard seems to have been something he deduced from the fact that Graham was a slaveholder. But as Alexander came to realize himself, many who eschewed slavery in the South became slave owners themselves but their slaves were slaves in name only. That is, slaves sometimes approached Presbyterian ministers they knew and requested that they be purchased by them in order to avoid a family, or a couple from being separated, when the slaves knew or suspected that one or all of them were likely to be sold and separated.

In Graham's case, he had taken possession of two household servants named Davy and Esther.

Later, he reported having four Negro tithables, and presumably the additional two were children of Davy and Esther. Memoranda submitted to Washington and Lee University by a daughter of Rev. Graham and her Presbyterian minister husband stating therein that the Graham family had but two household servants.[330]

---

330   This memorandum was entitled "Lest We Forget." The auditor obtained it from W&L's librarian, Ms Betty Ruth Kondayan, in the 1970s.

When Alexander was appointed as the first president of the Princeton Theological Seminary, he moved from Virginia to New Jersey, but accepted a call to the pastorate of a church in Philadelphia. His own family's female slave's name was Daphne, and both she and her husband, in time, accepted the open invitation to be emancipated. Previously, that option was not a reasonable one for them in Virginia because the law, as it existed in Virginia, required any emancipated slave must leave the state. As fortune would have it, Daphne and her husband separated, and soon thereafter Daphne called upon the Alexanders requesting their assistance in arranging for her to return to Virginia where she had extended family. Alexander informed Daphne that in order to do what she wanted, she had to voluntarily return to a state of slavery. According to Rev. Alexander this was a condition set forth in law, and a condition which she willingly accepted. With this experience, Mr. Alexander began to comprehend some of the perplexing difficulties associated with slavery in Virginia.

Graham's successes could not have been achieved in Virginia had he not been a man of great self-discipline, resourcefulness, and sound judgment. Such a man, in that day, would not have typically shared his personal views on controversial social or political issues of great moment with his young students. Alexander, in his youth, witnessed his preceptor's house servants and initially presumed their existence evidenced a predisposition to the peculiar institution. Alexander admits in his memoir of Graham that he was well aware that when Graham emigrated to Virginia, he abhorred slavery. His youthful and later rejected speculation that Graham *"apparently became reconciled to the institution"* is without foundation, and was a grave mistake, as Graham's 1786 letter to his old friend, Col. Arthur Campbell in Kentucky, makes abundantly clear by his reference therein to "the horrors of slavery,"[331] a letter that Alexander was obviously unaware existed.

Graham's reference to the "horrors of slavery" are his only known written words on the subject of slavery, but by inference one may discover much more about his views on the subject, because when he was asked by some of his friends and earlier students then residing in the area known as Frankland to prepare for them a proposed state Constitution, he gladly consented, and his Constitution was adopted provisionally, but when it came to a vote at a convention called to ratify the Constitution, it became the subject of such heated debate, that those who successfully rose in opposition to it later hung in effigy the likenesses of both Graham and the man who advocated for Graham's Constitution. Perhaps, it was caused by the one aspect of Graham's Constitution, which is rarely mentioned by historians, which is the unprecedented absence of a specific provision that protected slaves as property. Whether this absence of such a provision was the reason that great opposition to the proposed Constitution arose in such a violent fashion is not known. What is known is that a mob was formed in the streets and the mob burned Graham in effigy. If the absence of a slave protection provision was the cause, it is doubtful that the participants in that ugly affair were surprised to later hear that Graham had enrolled into Liberty Hall Academy's regular

---

331   William Graham letter to Col. Arthur Campbell, currently housed in the archives of the Filson Club in Kentucky, dated Sept. 24, 1788.

academic program, the first black student ever to grace the halls of academia in North America.

That man, Mr. John Chavis, went on to complete his education at Liberty Hall Academy (i.e., Washington and Lee University) and with Rev. Graham's assistance and guidance was enrolled into Rev. Graham's Lexington Theological Seminary, allowing him to become the only black Presbyterian minister in the United States of America. Imagine, the first black college student and the first black Presbyterian minister educated and prepared for the gospel ministry in the largest slaveholding state in the nation. In the northern states, including New England, the likes of Harvard, Princeton, Columbia, and Yale thought about this unique innovation for approximately one hundred more years before they deigned to follow Graham's lead by allowing a black student in any of these colleges.

Note: The citizens of greater Lexington were so proud of Mr. Chavis's unprecedented accomplishment that they memorialized the fact of Mr. Chavis' shaving gone through their college's regular academic program by creating a court order recognizing his accomplishment, which was then signed by all of the sitting magistrates, including one who was also a trustee of the college. This constitutes what may be the single most impressive college graduation credential ever obtained by an American undergraduate college student. To see the particulars of this Rockbridge County Court record, see the appendix devoted to the Reverend Mr. John Chavis. Lexington and Washington and Lee University can take great pride in the fact that all of these accomplishments took place in Lexington, Virginia, nurtured from beginning to end, by the college's first president, Rev. William Graham.

Conclusion concerning Archibald Alexander's errors

Rev. Archibald Alexander left much for posterity about the early history of Washington College. His few errors were mostly personal assessments of his preceptor, Graham, that he had no intention of ever publishing. His one error of consequence is also found in the unpublished memoir of Graham, and it concerns the sequence of the Hanover Presbytery's establishment of its two eighteenth-centuryacademies in Virginia, Liberty Hall and Hampden Sydney. His error in this regard resulted from his adoption of one aspect of his brother-in-law Edward Graham's published memoir of Graham. As has already been discussed in the previous section about the errors of Edward Graham, Edward mistakenly believed that Hampden Sydney was established before Liberty Hall when the reverse is clearly the case.

Alexander has little culpability for these few unpublished errors. Moreover, in Alexander's published works, he either corrected his earlier mistakes or decided not to publish on the subjects involved. The one seemingly serious error found in a published book and attributed to Archibald Alexander is the one mentioned above, but that error was actually made by Archibald's son, James, and not by Rev. Archibald Alexander.

As for Archibald Alexander's published works, the auditor found no significant historical error concerning the founding of Washington and Lee or about the college's founder and first president, Rev. William Graham. Alexander's 1843 address to the Alumni Association did repeat Alexander's rather silly criticism of his otherwise venerated preceptor by suggesting that Mr. Graham perhaps read too little or cared little for books. Those interested in this petty and terribly inconsistent criticism by Alexander are referred to the appendix devoted to Graham and books, where it will be shown that the best rejoinder to Mr. Alexander's rather odd statement about Graham and books come from his own inconsistent pen. Alexander makes clear that Graham was very familiar with the contents of all the great books studied at Princeton, and he mentions several other books Graham provided to him during his theological studies. Moreover, Alexander also refers to Graham's knowledge in the various sciences and philosophy. Graham's writings on the politics of government demonstrate that he was well versed in the political philosophy of both Hobbes and Locke. It is doubtful if there was any man west of the Blue Ridge Mountains in the 1780s or 1790s that was more widely read than was the president of the college (Graham) during his residence there in the last quarter of the eighteenth century.

Of the greatest importance here is the fact that both Archibald Alexander and his schoolmate and later brother-in-law, Edward Graham, asserted consistently that Washington College (i.e., W&L) was founded on October 13, 1774, by the Hanover Presbytery. Noteworthy as well is the fact that neither of these eyewitness early scholars ever mentioned in print or in letters that Liberty Hall Academy had a link to any earlier schools in the Valley, and neither mentions Rev. John Brown or Robert Alexander in connection with Liberty Hall Academy. The reason for this is that both men knew Brown and they were well aware of the strained relations between Brown and Graham and the related fact that Brown refused to participate in the affairs of Liberty Hall Academy, or its antecedent temporary preparatory school at Mount Pleasant, which the presbytery unofficially referred to as "Augusta Academy."

3. REV. JOHN BLAIR HOGE (b. April 1790 d. March 31, 1826)

John Blair Hoge, *The Life of Moses Hoge*, The Library, Union Theological Seminary, Richmond, Virginia, 1963, with index, composed by Pansie N. Cameron, p. 179. (In wraps with taped binding. The work was written circa 1823.)

ERROR no. 1: John B. Hoge confused the presbytery's new public seminary at Mount Pleasant with Rev. John Brown's private "Latin school" at New Providence.

Here below is J. B. Hoge's comments in this regard:

> And as soon as practicable they [the Presbytery] began to entertain the project of establishing a literary institution among themselves [1771]. This subject received the contemporary notice of *the Presbytery of Hanover, who in 1774 erected under the general inspection of one of their members a grammar school at New Providence in Augusta which was successively transferred to Timberridge [sic] & to Lexington.* Its more

immediate superintendence was committed to Mr. William Graham, a gentleman who having completed at New Jersey College his literary course & intending to be a minister of the gospel came to Virginia with a mind ardently determined to expend its resources in promoting the interests of learning & religion.
(pg. 16) (Emphasis added here indicates error.)

This statement by John B. Hoge, is incorrect in five important ways:

1. The seminary was not "erected" *at New Providence,* but rather was erected at Mount Pleasant; and,

2. It was not "erected *by the Hanover Presbytery*," but was rather, "established" by the Hanover Presbytery in Augusta County, Virginia, but its initial placement was not decided by the presbytery. A temporary headquarters was placed at Mount Pleasant, which was a decision obviously determined by Rev. Graham in cooperation with the local residents and members of the Timber Ridge Church nearby because if the Hanover Presbytery itself had taken any action in this regard, it would have been recorded in its minutes but it was not;

3. The seminary was not *"erected under the general supervision of one of their members,"* but was rather under the direction of Graham from the day of its creation[332] (October 13, 1774);

4. The only school at New Providence in the 1770s was Brown's private Latin school, which was never moved from New Providence once it had been moved there from Mount Pleasant by Brown about 1767. The move from Mount Pleasant to New Providence was occasioned by Brown's requested dismission from his pastorate at Timber Ridge, as the presbytery's meeting minutes clearly evince; and

5. 5) The presbytery's seminary, Liberty Hall Academy, was not *successively transferred to "Timberridge* (sic) *& to Lexington,"* but was rather, successively transferred from Timber Ridge to Rev. Graham's farm at Whistle Creek. It was located first at his home, then into a frame building erected nearby, which was later burned, and subsequently replaced by the stone buildings on Mulberry Hill outside of Lexington. About a decade later, the main stone building on Mulberry Hill was also burned. The school's final location was fixed at Lexington where it has remained ever since. Of paramount significance is the fact that from the days that classes were first held by Graham at his "Mount Pleasant"[333]

---

332 While the presbytery did nominate (i.e., appoint) Rev. John Brown as an "inspector," Mr. Brown demurred in that regard, as he did in regard to all appointments he received in connection with this seminary that he opposed in his own neighborhood.

333 The auditor found no evidence confirming the specific date on which Augusta Academy's classes were first held, but it is reasonable to assume that the classes were first held in the spring

temporary headquarters, Washington and Lee University has had an uninterrupted history. It has remained open from before the American Revolution War up to and including nearly the twenty-first century's first two decades.

4. REV. WILLIAM HILL (b. March 3, 1767, d. Nov. 16, 1852)

("The History of Washington College,"[334] of the Life and Character of The Reverend Dr. Moses Hoge of Vir American Historical Quarterly, Vol. X, [1838], pp. 145–150;
Autobiographical Sketches of Dr. William Hill, together with his account of Revival of Religion in Prince Edward County, and Biographical Sketches ginia, The Library, Union Theological Seminary in Virginia, Historical Transcripts No. 4, 1968 .)

Dr. William Hill's recounting of actions in Virginia, especially in the 1780s and 1790s, are generally quite accurate. His historical accounts of activities related to the Presbyterian Church in that period and before had obviously not been carefully researched and are, in a couple of important instances, in error. He made two significant mistakes that pertain to this audit.

ERROR no. 1: He made an inappropriate reference to Rev. John Brown's "private" Latin school.

Rev. Hill wrote a very early history of Washington College (1838), which is the first published article that was exclusively devoted to the history of Washington College (i.e., Liberty Hall Academy),[335] and in this article, he made the serious mistake of failing to differentiate between the affairs of the Hanover Presbytery that led directly to the establishment of the college and the completely unrelated

---

of 1775. This guess is based on several presumptions: (1) The idea that Mr. Graham would probably not have left Pennsylvania for Virginia until the presbytery had formally established its new seminary and appointed Graham as its manager which occurred on October 13, 1774; (2) the idea that Graham would have had to gather together his worldly possessions and made travel and lodging arrangements; (3) the notion that once he arrived in Virginia, he would have had to meet with representatives of the Hanover Presbytery and discuss his initial plans; (4) the idea that he would have had to decide upon a location for his initial headquarters and a site for holding preliminary classes that would enable him to assess the potential students and to assure that they were properly prepared for college-level instruction. All of these things together would surely have taken a few months to accomplish. Hence the auditor's guess at the spring of 1775.

334 Rev. William Hill, "The History of Washington College," American Historical Quarterly, Vol. X [1838], pp. 145–150, March 3, 1769 d. Nov. 16, 1852 [Author attributed to Rev. William Hill]. Cited in Crenshaw, Ollinger, *General Lee's College* [unpublished footnotes (typescript) Washington and Lee University Archives/Library] "Vol. II, "Appendix "A"] [hand-paginated in pencil as pg. no. 526., based in large measure upon an article by Rev. Dr. William Hill [Hampden Sydney] in **Southern Religious Telegraph** [Richmond] Dec. 19, 1834, Jan. 2, 23, Feb. 6, 1835 [serialized form], and also relying on a letter to the unnamed author from Edward Graham, Esq. of Lexington, Virginia. This auditor has a photo-copy of the article from the American Historical Quarterly but not the 1834 serialized articles. These articles, according to Dr. Ollinger Crenshaw, both date the history of the college from the 1770s and the actions of the Hanover Presbytery. See the appendix to Crenshaw's typescript version of **General Lee's College**.

335 Ibid p. 145 et seq.

"visit" the presbytery made to the private Latin school of Brown following the presbytery's April meeting in 1775.

This mistake by Rev. Hill may have been the reason why some later historians came to mistakenly believe that Brown's Latin school and Liberty Hall Academy were one and the same, but nothing could be further from the truth. Here is how Rev. Hill constructed his misleading and inappropriate paragraph:

> *April 13, 1775, the affairs of our public school were then taken under consideration,* and after the most mature deliberation, the presbytery find that they can do no more at this session than recommend it, in the warmest manner, to the public, to make such liberal contributions as they shall find compatible with their circumstances, for the establishing of said school. And the Presbytery as guardians and Directors, take this opportunity to declare their resolution to do their best endeavors to establish it on the most catholic plan, that circumstances will permit." April 15th, the presbytery, finding that they cannot of themselves forward subscriptions in a particular manner, do, for the encouragement of the academy to be established in Augusta, recommend it to the following gentlemen to take subscriptions in their behalf.* (A footnote at the bottom of p. 146 lists the names taken from the minutes.) *"As the presbytery have now an opportunity of visiting the school under the direction of Mr. Brown, they accordingly repaired to the school-house, and attended a specimen of the proficiency of the students in the Latin and Greek languages, and pronouncing orations, with which they were well pleased"* [336]

---

336 *American Historical Quarterly,* "The History of Washington College," Vol. X, [1838], pp. 145–150 [Authorship attributed to Rev. Wm. Hill] cited in Crenshaw, Ollinger, General Lee's College [unpublished footnotes (typescript) Washington and Lee University Archives/Library] "Vol. II, "Appendix "A"] [hand-paginated in pencil as pg. no. 526 [based in large measure upon an article entitled by Rev. Dr. William Hill [Hampden Sydney] in **Southern Religious Telegraph** [Richmond] Dec. 19, 1834, Jan. 2, 23, Feb. 6, 1835. [serialized form] and also relying on a letter to the unnamed author from Edward Graham, Esq. of Lexington, Virginia. This bibliographer has a photocopy of the article from *The American Historical Quarterly* but not the 1834 serialized articles. These articles, according to Ollinger Crenshaw, date the history of the college from the 1770s and the actions of the Hanover Presbytery.

(William Hill, "The History of Washington College,"[337]

Note: In the presbytery's meeting minutes, each of the dated items in the above paragraph are found separate from one another, but by placing them all in the same paragraph, Mr. Hill leaves the impression that there is a progression linking each of the selected items to all the others, but the truth is that the final item has no connection to those selections that came before it, and the "visit" to Brown's school was a social visit, not an official visit. Never before and never after was the subject of Brown's school mentioned by the presbytery in its meeting minutes. To have even mentioned this social call in the meeting minutes covering the April meeting was an unfortunate error in judgment because it left readers with a false impression that there was a connection between Brown's school and the Hanover Presbytery when there was no connection whatsoever. It is also of paramount significance that Rev. Caleb Wallace's documentary history of the founding of Liberty Hall Academy, that was authorized to be written by the Hanover Presbytery, and which contains all of the pertinent parts of the presbytery's meeting minutes related to the school's founding, does not contain the paragraph in its minutes of April 1775, which alludes to the visit to Brown's school at New Providence. If this was an oversight, it would surely have been noticed by one of the trustees and if that paragraph had been pertinent to the founding, someone would have insisted that the history be corrected. Nothing of the sort transpired.

Rev. Hill should not have made any reference whatsoever to Brown's private school because that school had no official connection to the Hanover Presbytery and the referenced "visit" to Brown's school was not an official visit, but was rather a social call of the members in politeness to their eldest member and the host of most parts of this spring meeting. Obviously, Hill mistakenly believed that Brown's school and the presbytery's new seminary were one and the same, otherwise he would not have included the reference to that school in the same paragraph describing events leading up to the establishment of the seminary (i.e., academy). Hill appears to be the first person to have ever made this mistake in print, and for that reason he very well may bear great responsibility for the vexatious and perennial mistake of dating the college's origins to a time prior to October of 1774 that took place from 1850 forward to the present.

Twelve years later, William Henry Foote went even further than Hill, and he went so far down the road to historical perdition as to boldly assert a direct link. Below are two mistaken notions:

> In the fall of 1774, on the recommendation of Rev. Samuel Stanhope Smith, employed in founding Hampden-Sidney College, in Prince Edward, ***Mr. Graham was invited to engage***

337   .[Author attributed to Rev. William Hill] cited in Crenshaw, Ollinger, General Lee's College [unpublished footnotes (typescript) Washington & Lee University Archives/Library] "Vol. II, "Appendix "A"] [hand-paginated in pencil as Pg. no. 526. [based in large measure upon an article entitled by Rev. Dr. William Hill [Hampden Sydney] in **Southern Religious Telegraph** [Richmond] Dec. 19, 1834, Jan. 2, 23, Feb. 6, 1835. [serialized form] and also relying on a letter to the unnamed author from Edward Graham, Esq. Of Lexington, Virginia. This bibliographer has a photocopy of the article from the Am. Hist. Quarterly but not the 1834 serialized articles. These articles, according to Ollinger Crenshaw, date the history of the college from the 1770s and the actions of the Hanover Presbytery.

in a classical school, in Augusta County,
under the direction of the Rev. John Brown,
pastor of New Providence and formerly of
Timber Ridge. (Emphasis here indicates error)

ERROR no. 2: Rev. Hill wrongly describes the roles of Rev. William Graham and Rev. John B. Smith in the struggle for religious liberty in Virginia.

Hill was a student at Hampden Sydney College at the time of the final phase of the struggle for religious liberty that took place in Virginia. His knowledge about the final phase of the struggle undoubtedly came to him filtered by his preceptor or his preceptor's adherents. However Mr. Hill came to understand his preceptor's role, his understanding was, at best, incomplete, but more likely distorted.

Dr. Hill is wrong when he says, in regard to the presbytery's position in 1784:

> "Patrick Henry that powerful orator was a member of the Legislature and a strenuous advocate of the assessment, so from the general character of that body it was thought the bill [assessment bill] would certainly pass into law. ...
>
> Different meetings or convention of the Presbyterians were summoned upon this agitating subject, & different Memorials or remonstrances were sent to the legislature; for it was pending more than a year before that body. The presbyterians were nearly unanimous against this plan. ***But Mr. Graham as was common in those days took the opposite side to Mr. Smith, but Dr. Smith ultimately carried the point, & drafted a memorial to his mind, & was appointed....***"
> (Wm. Hill, Autobiographical Sketches...) (Bold italics underlined above indicate an error.)

When viewed in the proper context, and with more complete information, Rev. Hill, is technically almost correct, but as presented above, his statement is utterly false. Mr. Hill suggests incorrectly that "Mr. Graham" was on the side of those *who did not* adhere to the Presbyterian's view in opposition to the proposed assessment (tax) advocated by Mr. Patrick Henry. To the contrary, it was Rev. John B. Smith who was initially out of step, as it were, with the general population of Presbyterians. And, while it is also somewhat true that Mr. Smith "carried the point," he only carried "the point" when in 1784 the Hanover Presbytery changed their position on assessment in what was widely deemed an acquiescence on assessment question.[338] In the final debate on assessment, Rev. Hill is incorrect as to which particular point, because Mr. Smith had actually led the 1784 movement to modify the Presbyterian's long-standing and unequivocal opposition to assessment to support the Church.

Smith persuaded his colleagues of the cloth to follow his lead in refining the Presbyterian position in hopes that when the bill passed, as it was believed would happen, that the Presbyterians would get their fair share of the taxes collected. Smith carried the point among his brethren in October of 1784, but he did so over Graham's objections. Both Smith and Graham were appointed by presbytery to a committee to draft a revised position paper (i.e., Memorial), but Graham refused this appointment and immediately instigated a campaign to overturn Smith's new position.

By the following spring, Smith's position, that had been adopted by a majority of the Virginia Presbyterian clergymen, was now to be put before a general convention of Virginia Presbyterians led by Graham, and this body soundly repudiated the position advocated and drafted the previous October by Mr. Hill's preceptor, Rev. John B. Smith. This fact has been thoroughly studied and analyzed by the most credible scholars of the twentieth century who published their understandings of the struggle for religious liberty in post-revolutionary Virginia. (See Eckenrode, Buckley, Sellers and Hood in the bibliography, and other parts of this report which address Virginia's struggle for religious liberty. This group of scholars uniformly rejected Hill's thesis on this subject and in rebuttal, by inference, eviscerate Hill's contention. Hill's erroneous contention is annoyingly reflected in many important histories too many to mention.)

Historians of today and tomorrow should take great care to correct this aspect of the history of Virginia's important role in providing the nation with freedom of religion. This includes one of Patrick Henry's few political blunders in sponsoring the bill that would have taxed all citizens for the support of an established church. Graham's advocacy to defeat Henry's proposal being so successful saved Henry from eternal infamy. It is no surprise that Liberty Hall Academy's president became intimate friends despite Graham's role in defeating Henry's bill. Ironically, it was Patrick Henry who later attempted to persuade Graham to leave the college in Lexington and become the president of Hampden Sydney, where Henry had become a trustee.

Professor Charles Grier Sellers of Princeton, and the University of California at Berkeley, explains the Presbyterian convention's repudiation of Smith's earlier proposal this way:

---

338 Certainly James Madison viewed the changed position as an acquiescence, and he fumed over it. Graham on this occasion broke with Smith and the majority of members of the presbytery that passed Smith's recommended changes. Graham thereafter launched a successful campaign to overturn Smith's changed position by calling for an unprecedented general convention of Virginia Presbyterians. The convention sided with Graham and authorized him to draft the Presbyterians' final message to the Virginia legislature (general assembly), and on advice of Graham, the convention added to the final message the Presbyterians' support for passage of Jefferson's long-stalled Bill for Religious Freedom. As a result, the assessment bill was allowed to die a quiet death and Jefferson's bill was passed.

> **Smith's defeat was a triumph for William Graham, who drafted the convention's vehement denunciation of any legislation on religion. . .** The final blow to assessment was the loss of its strongest legislative champion through Patrick Henry's election as governor. **"It was . . . In July, 1788, that Smith, . . . withdrew from active supervision of the College [Hampden-Sydney] . . . With Smith out of the way, Patrick Henry undertook to get the state's grants to William and Mary divided with Hampden-Sydney, and Henry's crony and fellow opponent of the Constitution, William Graham, was offered the Presidency.** [339] (Bold/italics and underlining added for the sake of emphasis.)
>
>   [Dr. Charles G. Sellers Jr., Princeton]

Dr. Fred Hood added this:

> Graham, on the other hand was at least one Presbyterian minister who had consistently opposed the assessment.[340]

> In October, [1785] [Rev.] John Blair Smith and [Rev.] William Graham presented the new Presbyterian position in the Assembly at a meeting of a committee of the whole.[341]

Fred J. Hood, also in his essay *"Revolution and Religious Liberty,"*[342] included an important footnote:

> Smith at one time favored the assessment [1784]. Graham on the other hand was at

---

339   Charles G. Sellers, Jr., "John Blair Smith," Journal of the Presbyterian Historical Society, Vol. XXXIV, No. 4, Dec. 1956, pp. 201–225)] esp. p. 214, 217–18. Graham's opposition to Mr. Henry's position on assessment caused no rift in their friendship.

340   Hood, Fred J., *"Revolution and Religious Liberty: The Conservation of the Theocratic Concept in Virginia,"* Church History, Vol. 40, No. 2 (Jun. 1971) pp. 170–181 esp. at p. 180 footnote no.39.

341   Sellers, Charles G., Jr., "John Blair Smith" in *Journal of the Presbyterian Historical Society*, Vol. XXXIV, No. 4, Dec. 1956 pp. 212–214. The committee of the whole is importantly distinguishable from the General Assembly meeting in regular session.

342   *Hood, Fred J.[Church History, vol. 40, No. 2 (June 1971) pp.170–181, Cambridge University Press.*

least one Presbyterian minister who had consistently opposed the assessment. Graham was of western Pennsylvania and a radical democrat who wrote the Constitution for the proposed state of Franklin.[343]

One can easily see that Rev. Hill failed to grasp the entire picture. He mistakenly reported the following aspect of the struggle this way:

> When the Bill was taken up by the house [*in Committee of the whole*] Dr. Smith . . . asked permission to be heard... . . . The debate was conducted chiefly between Patrick Henry, on one side, & Dr. Smith on the other... . . . when they ceased, the question was called for, *& Smith carried his point & defeated the Assessment bill, by a majority of only three votes*[344][345] . . . Alexander White a lawyer of great intelligence who was a delegate from Winchester in Frederick County, & who afterwards filled high offices of trust under Washington, declared when he returned, that he thought that debate between Henry & Smith one of the ablest & most interesting he had ever listened to *& that he thought that Smith deserved the victory he had gained.*[346]
>
> [Rev. William Hill, Autobiography . . . p. 118.]

What Mr. Hill, and by extension, Rep. Alexander White, get wrong here is that while it is true that Rev. Smith presented the presbytery's position, he can hardly be given such full credit because the point that he ostensibly "carried" was not his own, but was that of his opponent on the question, Rev. William Graham. Smith deserves credit for being an effective messenger and proxy advocate, of course, but but only highly qualified credit, because his own personal view was not the point being debated, and the arguments he presented were those of his opponent and of the Presbyterian General Convention. If Mr. Smith had truly achieved what he had set as his objective, every taxpayer in Virginia would have been assessed a

---

343 .Op cit, pp. 180–81.

344 *It is more accurate to say that Rev. Smith carried Rev. Graham's hard won point in 1785, that soundly repudiated Mr. Smith's temporarily won point the year before.*

345 It is more accurate to say that Rev. Smith carried Rev. Graham's hardwon point in 1785, that soundly repudiated Mr. Smith's temporarily won point the year before.

346 *Rev. William Hill, Autobiographical sketches of Dr. William Hill: together with his account of the revival of religion in Prince Edward County, and biographical sketches of the life and character of the Reverend Dr. Moses Hoge of Virginia,* Richmond, 1968, pg. 118

tax to support one of the recognized churches then operating in that state.[347] The credit for ensuring that this did not happen goes first and foremost to the man who led the fight to overturn Rev. Smith's ill-advised new position on assessment. That man was Rev. William Graham, president of Liberty Hall Academy (later, Washington and Lee University). In addition, Rev. Hill's description of the event wrongly suggests that a vote on Patrick Henry's bill advocating for an assessment (i.e., tax) in support of the churches was taken in the Virginia General Assembly, but the auditor/author suggests otherwise, and contends that Henry's bill was never passed out of the committee of the whole with a recommendation that it pass, but rather was simply allowed to quietly die in that committee.[348] This final resolution resulted from two important occurrences: (1) The fact that the William Graham-led campaign for a general convention to overturn the Smith plan previously adopted by the Hanover Presbytery, had been emphatically successful in repudiating the Smith plan; and (2) the statewide petition campaign associated with the Presbyterian Convention, and subsequently joined by the Baptists and others, had culminated with the Virginia legislature receiving signatures of more than ten thousand Virginians opposing the assessment bill.

Note: Graham's friend and anti-federalist colleague, Patrick Henry who had ill-advisedly sponsored the assessment bill had, during the long running debate on assessment, been elevated to the position of Governor. As a result, after it became apparent that there was such widespread opposition to Mr. Patrick's bill, the Committee responsible for religious matters allowed the bill to simply die by inaction rather than embarrass the new Governor by defeating the bill.

Conclusion regarding Rev. William Hill

Quite clearly, Rev. William Hill held an uneducated view of the struggle for religious liberty in Virginia at the time he wrote this entry into his journal, which was when he was recently graduated from Hampden Sydney College under his preceptor, John B. Smith. Apparently, Rev. Smith's adherents at the college had presented the president's students with a very creative interpretation of the struggle for religious liberty in Virginia in 1784 and 1785. Mr. Hill appears to have adopted the view of others without questioning its accuracy. In the parlance of twenty-first-century mass media, Rev. Hill's description of this momentous event

---

347 Namely, the Episcopal Church, which had earlier been the Church of England (i.e., then the Anglican Church).

348 This important procedural maneuver allows the members of either House to obtain a read on other members' sentiments without having to embarrass the bill's sponsoring member in case there are an insufficient number of votes to ensure its passage in the main body of the House of Delegates. In this case, the sponsoring member was Patrick Henry, who had only recently become governor. The bill for assessment (taxing of Churches) did not ever get to the floor of the House of Delegates, where the bill originated several years earlier, and therefore never made it to the Senate. The only significant change of circumstances that might account for the bill's sudden support by members of the House is the Presbyterian-led campaign opposing assessment and urging support for the religious liberty bill, a campaign initiated by and led by the president of Liberty Hall Academy, Rev. William Graham.

in American history was a highly creative *spin* probably developed by President Smith's adherents at Hampden Sydney College. Rev. Hill's understanding was, no doubt, obtained while he was a student at Hampden Sydney, and he credulously accepted the version presented by the authorities to whom he answered. If so, he was as wrong in this regard as were those who had expressed this distorted characterization. This struggle and the language of the Virginia Declaration of Rights were incontestably the intellectual underpinnings of the religious freedom provision of the First Amendment in the American Bill of Rights. It is difficult to believe that James Madison could have persuaded his fellow members of the U.S. Congress to agree to adopt a provision ensuring religious liberty, if Madison's own state taxed their citizens for support of churches and church-patronized schools. Mr. Madison was only able to secure the passage of Virginia's Bill for Religious Freedom after William Graham's campaign against taxing Virginia's citizens produced over ten thousand signatures on petitions opposing the taxation for churches, and also urging passage of the absent Mr. Jefferson's Bill for Religious Freedom, a point, apparently missed by Rev. William Hill and most nineteenth-century historians.

Rev. William Hill, it is fair to say, later became a serious and professional historian[349] who relied typically upon documentary sources. In his history of Washington College, he also relied heavily on information supplied to him by Professor Edward Graham of Washington College. Mr. Hill was the first author to publish a strict history of Washington College (Virginia) and the college's origins. In addition, Rev. Hill also knew the founder and rector, Rev. William Graham, under whose guidance he carried out his own missionary responsibilities. Rev. Hill's extensive documentary History of Washington College (Liberty Hall), like all the other early histories, explains that the college was founded on October 13, 1774, by the Hanover Presbytery. He also left to posterity these insightful comments concerning the college's founder and first president, Rev. William Graham:

> Mr. Graham, of Lexington, was present and preached on Saturday; and on Sabbath, Mr. Graham preached in the forenoon, one of the greatest sermons I ever heard. I sat under it with great delight, and its fruit was sweet to my taste. [Rev. William Hill, from his journal and published, in part, here in Foote, second Series, p. 185]

> Mon July 25 1791 *I rode to Lexington, spent the day with Mr. Graham.* [Wm Hill., Autobiographical Sketches . . . p. 79]

---

349 See Rev. William Hill's *A History of the Rise, Progress, Genius, and Character, of American Presbyterianism: Together with a review of the "Constitutional History of the Presbyterian Church in the United States of America; by Chas. Hodge, D. D., Professor in the Theological Seminary, at Princeton Theological Seminary, N.J."*, Washington City, J. Gideon Jr., 1839 .

> Fr. July 29, 1791 *I rode to Lexington, **spent***
> ***the day, enjoying the edifying conversation***
> ***of the great and good man Mr. Graham.***"
> [Wm. Hill Autobiographical Sketches . . . p. 79.]

It is unfortunate that Rev. Hill misunderstood the respective roles played by the two Presbyterian leaders and Virginia college presidents in the Virginia struggle for religious liberty, and it is also unfortunate that Mr. Hill mistakenly implied that Liberty Hall Academy had some connection to Rev. John Brown's private Latin school located at New Providence, because that implication is patently false. Mr. Hill simply misread the Hanover Presbytery's meeting minutes for the April 1775 spring meeting, and in so doing confused Liberty Hall Academy (then Augusta Academy) at Mount Pleasant with Rev. Brown's school located several miles from the academy, but confusingly in the same general neighborhood of New Providence and Timber Ridge Presbyterian churches.

5. DR. SAMUEL L. CAMPBELL (Interim acting president, Washington College) [1838]
(b. 1766, d. Apr. 24, 1840)

("Washington College, Lexington, Virginia," *Southern Literary Messenger*, June 1838, 7 pp.] *(Note: The article's author is listed as "Senex," but Dr. Campbell is the unquestioned author. Thomas W. White was the editor. It is our assumption that the three footnotes that are included as endnotes designated "Note A" etc. were written by the author, Dr. Campbell.[350])*

Introduction:

Dr. Campbell's article represents the first published account of the early operational aspects of Liberty Hall Academy, and provides the first published eyewitness accounting of the students and their preceptor, Rev. William Graham, in the school's first emendations at Mount Pleasant in 1775 and 1776.[351] The article's importance cannot be overstated at least, as a descriptive narrative. The article, however, is not necessarily reliable as to time and place because it is not a documentary history but a memoir of a well-educated early graduate who enjoyed a long association with the college, and a close relationship with the college's

---

350   *The details included in these notes suggest a degree of familiarity with Washington College not likely possessed by the magazine's editor, Mr. White, and therefore, by default, the auditor assumes they were all written as afterthoughts by Dr. Campbell.*

351   What Dr. Campbell witnessed and described in his memoir of the earliest days of "Augusta Academy," as Liberty Hall was called while at "Mount Pleasant," is the first and only published account of these earliest days. Edward Graham's memoir of his elder brother, Rev. Wm. Graham, reflects the operations after the school had been moved into the first permanent quarters at Timber Ridge, which was then formally given the name Liberty Hall Academy by the school's first board of trustees. These first trustees were appointed by the Hanover Presbytery on May 6, 1776, which is the same governing entity that created the new seminary by declaration on October 13, 1774. Temporary classes were not begun until sometime in early 1775 in temporary quarters on the farm of Mr. James Wilson, at a spot called locally "Mount Pleasant." Classes began moving to their new building at Timber Ridge in November of 1776.

founding first president, Rev. William Graham. Dr. Campbell clearly did not consult the official records of the Hanover Presbytery or the college's board of trustees, and accordingly is wrong about several institutional facts. The great value of this article is in what Dr. Campbell was an eyewitness to, and what he came to know. He errs when he ventures into discussing institutional facts that occurred outside of his presence. On that score, he obviously relied on hearsay and traditions, some of which are incorrect.

Archibald Alexander provides a valuable and insightful commentary on Dr. Samuel L. Campbell's value as an eyewitness, who was an early Liberty Hall Academy Alumnus, later a trustee, and also an acting president of the academy, in the interregnum between the resignation of Rev. William Graham and the appointment of George Baxter as rector/president of Liberty Hall Academy.

> "Doctor Samuel L. Campbell, of Rockbridge, who enjoyed opportunities of acquaintance with Mr. Graham equal to those enjoyed by any other man. The father of Doctor Campbell, Charles Campbell, Esq. was one of Mr. Graham's most intimate friends, who agreed with him in all his sentiments, and at whose house he made his home when in the neighborhood. And Dr. Campbell was brought up under the tuition of Mr. Graham from his youth, and was perfectly acquainted with all his excellencies and his foibles. He not only pursued his academical studies under the direction of Mr. G, but also studied theology under his guidance for several years. . ." [Alexander, Mss. "Memoir of William Graham," pp. 48–49].

Dr. Campbell errs in his "Memoir" by incorrectly describing the very significant early actions of the Hanover Presbytery when establishing its first-ever seminary in Augusta County. The auditor's assessment revealed two significant errors.

ERROR no. 1

Dr. Campbell mistakenly asserts that the board of trustees was responsible for the initial design and implementation of the incipient seminary (Augusta Academy) conducted at Mount Pleasant by William Graham. He says:

> About threescore years ago, the Hanover Presbytery, . . . taking into consideration the low state of literature in this commonwealth, conceived a project of establishing a seminary of learning in the upper country . . . would afford to all classes an opportunity of acquiring liberal education, thereby rendering unnecessary the inconvenience and extra expense of resorting to northern colleges.

> The Presbytery, however, considering the necessity of the case, thought that something might be done; and on making experiment,

something was done. *The trustees soon determined to erect a building; and the site chosen was in a grove, on the summit of Timber-ridge about one mile northwest of the present village of Fairfield*[352]. . . .[353] (Campbell, Hist. Washington College, 1838, p. 361)

The error made here by Dr. Campbell is in his improperly assigning responsibility to the trustees, which is known to have taken place prior to 1776, and is a fact problem because the board of trustees was not created by the Hanover Presbytery until May 6, of 1776. The responsibility for selecting the Mount Pleasant site for the college's initial and temporary headquarters was obviously carried out by Mr. William Graham in cooperation with local area residents, especially Mr. James Wilson, who owned the farm upon which the spot called "Mount Pleasant" was located. It is known that these things were done informally, because it occurred between the two annual regular meetings of the Hanover Presbytery, and the meeting minutes for the year in which this event took place (1775) make no mention of the presbytery selecting this site. Of course, the site selection was probably discussed informally, and the rector, Mr. Graham, presumably felt confident that the temporary site would meet with the trustees' approval. Nevertheless, the trustees did not take the matter up at any of their meetings, as the meeting minutes clearly reveal.

William Graham left his home in Pennsylvania and arrived in Augusta County at a now uncertain date but sometime in late 1774 or early 1775. The initial site selection at Mount Pleasant was probably occasioned by the fact that this new seminary endeavor would necessitate the employment of its manager as a minister in order to supplement his income from the meager funds expected from tuition in such a remote location. Timber Ridge and nearby Hall's Meeting House both being in need of a pastor, Mount Pleasant was viewed as a likely location. Here, in earlier days, a private Latin school was operated by these two churches' previous pastor, Rev. John Brown. As the Hanover presbytery minutes indicate, around 1765, relations between the congregation of Timber Ridge and Rev. John Brown became strained and as a result Rev. Brown asked to be dismissed from his position as the pastor of Timber Ridge. The presbytery authorized the separation in 1767. In the meantime, Rev. Brown sold his farm near Fairfield and moved several miles distant to a commodious abode on a farm adjacent to the New Providence Presbyterian Church near Moffett's Creek. From this time, Rev. Brown devoted all of his ministerial energies exclusively to the New Providence congregation. At the same time, Rev. Brown's Latin school was also transferred to the New Providence location close to his home.[354]

352

353 Samuel LeGrand Campbell, (M.D.) [i.e., "Senex"], "Washington College, Lexington, Virginia," *Southern Literary Messenger*, June 1838 [7 pp.] [Auditor's copy is a photocopy of the original] Thomas W. White was the editor at that time. Campbell, as author, is taken from a graduate paper written by Prof. G. Ray Thompson on Rev. William Graham submitted circa 1967.

354 Rev. Brown's Latin school was peripatetic in nature due to the unusual fact that Rev. Brown did not perform the teaching function. He relied upon others to serve as the instructor, and as the

At the Mount Pleasant site, the new seminary's preliminary work began several years after Mr. Brown's departure. The operations of the new school were all conducted under the direction of William Graham. By 1776, the school was actually well underway, but involved, of necessity, only raw recruits with inconsistent preparation for higher-level instruction. In 1776, the Hanover Presbytery was busy coordinating the permanent site selection along with shepherding through William Graham's licensing as a minister in the Virginia Presbytery process. Soon everything was in order, and Mr. Graham was "called" by both the aforementioned churches in the greater Timber Ridge area. Once Rev. Graham was formally installed as the pastor of Timber Ridge and Hall's Meeting House congregations, the presbytery went ahead and selected Timber Ridge as the permanent site for the new campus.

It was only after this phase of the college's incipiency was completed that the presbytery appointed the men who it was hoped would serve as the board of trustees. The presbytery's board of trustees was created to take over general responsibility for governance of the seminary, now for the first time officially given a name. The name selected by the new trustees was Liberty Hall Academy."[355] The name selection was announced by at the opening of their first meeting, which was held May 13, 1776.[356]

An early twentieth-century historian of the Campbell and Wilson families, Margaret Campbell Pilcher, offers this instructive commentary:

> *"**Elder** (Capt. Charles Campbell) **in New Providence Church** [Rev. John Brown's church]**, with James Wilson, and with him was appointed by Hanover Presbytery, in 1775, to collect funds_to establish Augusta Academy on the land of James Wilson, on Mount Pleasant, afterwards inherited by his son, Moses Wilson." This was the germ of Washington and Lee University. Captain Campbell was trustee of the same twenty-nine years, with many of our relatives, the Campbells, and Wilsons. Two months before the Declaration of Independence he voted with the Trustees to change the name of Augusta*

---

school's administrator, he left no known records as to the tutors' tenures. When an instructor left their position, Rev. Brown was in the unenviable position of having to secure a replacement and qualified candidates were few. Some were recent graduates of the College of New Jersey and most stayed but for a brief period.

355 "Academy" was still the term in use for a school that was, in effect, a college, but as a temporary hold-over after the revolution, the term "college" was still reserved for "chartered" institutions. In the case of Liberty Hall Academy, it chose to keep their name unchanged during its first president's tenure, despite its having received the new Virginia's first college charter in 1782. In Virginia, only the College of William and Mary is older than Liberty Hall Academy, having received its charter by agents of the British Crown prior to the American Revolution. Hampden Sydney received its charter the year following that of Liberty Hall (1783).

356 See the first record book of the meeting minutes of the Liberty Hall Academy's Board of Trustees on file at the archives of the university's Leyburn library. The library provided the auditor with a photographic copy in an electronic format.

Academy[357] *to Liberty Hall, while the British flag was still floating over the Capital.*"[358] (Margaret Campbell Pilcher, p. 205) [Bold and italics were added for emphasis and does not indicate an error.)

This, as with most genealogical studies, must be used more as a guide, and for purposes of formulating postulates, and much of the material requires independent verification using, wherever possible, documentary supporting evidence. Ms. Pilcher's account, however, is consistent with several other well-documented historical accounts on many of the issues she discusses. More importantly, we did not note any serious inconsistencies with well-established documented histories related to the origins of Washington and Lee. She may have exceeded her knowledge, however, in one regard, and that is her final point made in the item reproduced above. The meeting minutes of the board of trustees do announce the decision to name the school Liberty Hall Academy, but contrary to Ms. Pilcher's assertion, the minutes do not indicate who voted "yes" and who, if any, voted "no" on the question. If the decision on so important a matter was unanimous, the trustees failed to note that important detail in their minutes. She is probably correct, however, because the first board meeting had but six trustees in attendance and her relation, Capt. Charles Campbell, was one of them (trustees' minute book, p. 11). It is not suggested here that Ms. Pilcher was incorrect on this matter, but only that her representation concerning her relation, Charles Campbell, cannot be confirmed by any documentary evidence known to the auditor.

ERROR no. 2: Campbell inaccurately designated Rev. William Graham's initial role at Liberty Hall Academy as "teacher" instead of "manager."

Dr. Campbell mistakenly claims that William Graham was initially hired as a "teacher" by the board of trustees, when in fact he was appointed by the Hanover Presbytery to "manage" the new seminary, although they certainly assumed that he would also be the principal teacher. Mr. Graham's responsibilities, however, were far more extensive than merely being a teacher. This fact is clearly demonstrated in the

---

357 *.Technically, the school in its incipiency had no official name. It was, however, referred to unofficially, and as a mere convention, as "Augusta Academy" or similar denominations by the Hanover Presbytery after the presbytery created a second seminary in Prince Edward County, which occurred the year following the establishment of the one in Augusta County, west of the Blue Ridge Mountains. This convention was no doubt occasioned by a need to carefully discriminate between the two academies in the presbytery's meeting minutes. The 1770s minutes of the presbytery therefore have numerous references to these new schools as either "Augusta Academy" or "Prince Edward Academy," respectively.*

358 *Historical Sketches of the Campbell, Pilcher and Kindred Families* by Margaret Campbell Pilcher, Nashville, Tenn., 1911, p. 205. [Note: Much of the information in this book was taken from the papers of Governor David Campbell containing many letters and rare manuscripts, and from an interview of Catherine Bowen Campbell, daughter of Gov. William B. Campbell of Tennessee, the author's father, b. February 1, 1807 – d. August 19, 1867. This Tennessee governor studied law in Virginia with his father's cousin, Gov. David Campbell of Virginia. Her book would have been much more useful to historians had the author cited more specific authorities.

Hanover Presbytery meeting minutes for 1775 and 1776, wherein the minutes contain the substance of discussions between Mr. Graham and the presbytery concerning the procurement of a library and the purchase of scientific laboratory equipment associated with higher education in the eighteenth century. The nature of this business certainly exceeds the responsibilities normally associated with a mere "teacher."

ERROR no. 3: Campbell awkwardly implied that Graham may have had a predecessor.

Note: Campbell may have meant that there had been earlier schools that were located in that vicinage. Surely, Campbell knew or should have known that the public college, even in its infancy, had no direct connection to any of the private preparatory schools that operated in that general location, all of which were unconnected to the college or to Rev. Graham.)

The following quotation from Campbell's article set forth in error no. 1 is his following comment:

> "By contributions from the vicinity, of labor, &c., a building was soon reared . . . .

> "A teacher was now employed. *The first whose name I remember was William Graham.*" (Campbell, History of Washington College, *Historical Papers . . . [W&L]*. Vol. 1, pp. 107–108) (Emphasis in bold italics here indicates error.)

Campbell's comment hints at their having been a possible predecessor to Graham when that was not possible because Graham was the first and only person hired by the presbytery until the presbytery sometime later hired John Montgomery as an assistant to Graham. As written, it may be that Campbell's statement is technically correct, but in effect, its implication probably encouraged those who repudiated the earlier history by leaving an impression that there may have been an earlier teacher at the academy. The indisputable truth, however, is that there was no earlier person conducting the presbytery's new seminary. Of course, there were earlier teachers who provided instruction at that general location, but that was when Brown had overseen a Latin school that had long ago been moved from Mount Pleasant to New Providence. Obviously, Campbell had heard his elder family members and other local residents refer to that earlier school, which served to confuse him about the earlier times as they could, in theory, have related to Liberty Hall, but they did not. Both schools had, at altogether different times, been located at the same essential location, and this fact served to confuse many historians, including, in some degree, Mr. Campbell.

Conclusion Concerning Dr. Campbell's Important Memoir of Augusta Academy

Dr. Campbell's memoir importantly provided the only eye-witness mental snapshot of the college's earliest activities at "Mount Pleasant." The two errors described above demonstrate that Dr. Campbell's narrative was based on his experiences, but that while his observations cannot be questioned, his subject was obviously not carefully researched for his article contains a few errors of fact. His errors, therefore, are of a technical nature. They are important and could possibly mislead future historians. Hence, the importance to identify and correct his few errors.

There is no reason, however, to question the authenticity of the colorful descriptive aspect of his historical account of the school in its infancy.

6. REV. HENRY RUFFNER (b. 1790, d. 1861) (president of Washington College) (Henry Ruffner, D. D., "Early History of Washington College," _Washington and Lee University Historical Papers_, Vol. 1, Baltimore, John Murphy & Co., 1890 [written in the 1840s]. Unpublished for fifty years, it was re-edited and revised in 1857 by the author, then further edited and annotated with notes by the author's son, William Henry Ruffner, in preparation for publishing by Washington and Lee University in 1890, which is the date of its first printing.)

Introduction:

President Henry Ruffner was a major contributor to a process of unintentionally dissembling the college's accurate early history. He initially represented the founding accurately, but thereafter he inserted an erroneous qualifier that essentially destroyed his first representation. Here below is his accurate depiction:

**Ruffner's Mostly Accurate and Important Statement
on the Founding of Washington College**

> "Common schools arose among them [the Scotch-Irish] as soon as the state of the population admitted of them. But some considerable time necessarily elapsed before schools of a higher order could be sustained. *About the year 1772,*[359] thirty-four years after the settlement first began, *private* teachers are reported to have commenced in two or three places to instruct pupils in the elements of classical learning.[360] But these were

359   There is nothing significant about the year 1772 concerning private educational endeavors of the Scotch-Irish in Virginia. Such endeavors existed before and after that date. The brothers, Archibald and Robert Alexander, provided private instruction before 1772, but neither were college graduates. Rev. John Brown organized a private Latin school that he oversaw but did not teach, neither before nor after 1772. Neither of these, or any other private educational endeavor, had any link to the Hanover Presbytery's seminary (i.e., academy/college) created on October 13, 1774, which was an entirely new venture operationally launched by William Graham on behalf of the presbytery initially at a place unofficially called Mount Pleasant.

360   Ruffner is alluding to private educational endeavors that began as early as 1748 or thereabouts. By 1772, the Hanover Presbytery was in the early stages of conducting the feasibility study that was to culminate in the establishment of a seminary of liberal education (i.e., an academy of higher learning). This first such seminary established by the presbytery was initially located

transient efforts, and resulted in nothing more than to prepare the way for a permanent academy which was established a few years later, through the agency of the presbytery. (Ruffner, Henry, "Early History of Washington College," *Washington and Lee Historical Papers*, Vol. 1, Baltimore, John Murphy & Co. 1890, p. 11.) (**Bold** is added here for emphasis only. The bold & italics are added here to indicate error.)

Ruffner's Equivocating Emendation

In the extract below can be seen the effects of William Henry Foote's two volumes written in 1850 and then in 1855, but after Ruffner's 1840 draft had been revised in 1857. It is not known for certain, but it seems reasonable to assume that Ruffner's comments below were inserted by Ruffner in an attempt to make his earlier assertion somehow reconcile with Foote's narrative on the same subject. The shame of it all lies in the fact that Ruffner was right in the first instance. Foote, on the other hand, completely misunderstood the sequence of events that led up to the Hanover Presbytery's decision to establish a seminary in October of 1774.

Ruffner's allusion to the April 1775 meeting of the presbytery, discussed below, constitutes very strong evidence that he had been persuaded that there must have been something to Mr. Foote's assertions concerning the presbytery's "visit" to Rev. Brown's school, which the members made shortly after the April 1775 meeting had adjourned. In fact, Foote had been somehow been misled. Most likely Mr. Foote was misled, in part, by Rev. William Hill, who in 1838 had authored a history of Washington College[361] wherein he listed what he deemed were the pertinent extracts embedded in the presbytery's meeting minutes, which related to the establishment of the college. The only problem with Mr. Hill's list is that the "visit" referenced at the conclusion of the meeting minutes for the April 1775 meeting had nothing whatsoever to do with the presbytery's seminary at Mount Pleasant. The problem with Ruffner's account lies in the fact that Rev. Hill was incorrect on this one particular point. The business of the seminary had been addressed earlier at that meeting.

While Ruffner does not cite Mr. Hill or his article as his authority, Mr. Hill's history is the only known publication wherein it was suggested that Rev. John Brown's Latin school was somehow connected to Liberty Hall Academy. Of course, Rev. William Hill had no direct knowledge of the affairs of Liberty

---

at Mount Pleasant and was unofficially referred to by the presbytery as the Augusta Academy in its meeting minutes. The earlier private efforts alluded to by Ruffner had no names and had no connection whatsoever to the presbytery's new seminary, which was subsequently officially named Liberty Hall Academy by its first board of trustees in May of 1776. The name was announced at the May 13, 1776, first meeting of the Liberty Hall Academy Board of Trustees and seems to have been the first order of business (See Trustees 1st record book, pages no. 8 and 13).

361   Rev. William Hill, "History of Washington College, Virginia," *American Historical Quarterly*, Vol. X, [1838], pp. 145–150 [Authorship attributed to Rev. William Hill by Ollinger Crenshaw, *General Lee's College* [unpublished footnotes (typescript) Washington and Lee University Archives/Library]

Hall Academy. Hill had matriculated at Hampden Sydney over the mountain. His research focused primarily on the meeting minutes of the Hanover Presbytery. On this one point, he simply misinterpreted the minutes. Anyone who lived in that part of the Valley

Both Ruffner and Foote overlooked that this meeting opened on the first day at Timber Ridge, which was the closest meeting location to their new seminary at Mount Pleasant, but after the first day's meeting, the members moved several miles to New Providence where the subsequent days' meetings were held in the home of Rev. John Brown.

At the conclusion of their several days of meeting, the presbytery adjourned, and presumably at their host's invitation, the presbytery members walked next door to "visit" Rev. Brown's Latin school, which was then in session. Mr. Foote, probably following Rev. William Hill's 1838 history of Washington College, made the fundamental error of transforming, in his mind, a mere "visit" into a formal institutional decision to adopt and patronize Mr. Brown's school even though the presbytery did no such thing. This fact is clearly demonstrated in the presbytery's meeting minutes.

Note: The meeting minutes for eighteenth-century meetings were not published and were therefore not necessarily easily accessed. Presumably, most authors writing in the nineteenth century relied upon extracts that had been quoted in others' published works. Any errors made in early nineteenth-century publications that were based upon misinterpretations of the minutes or erroneous transcriptions taken from the original meeting minutes were likely to be repeated by later authors, and indeed mistakes of this sort were commonly made by nineteenth-century authors who did not have ready access to the presbytery's meeting minutes.

The presbytery's new seminary was not located at New Providence in 1775, it was located at Mount Pleasant, which was much closer to Timber Ridge. Dr. Ruffner and numerous others mistakenly assumed that the seminary was located first at New Providence and then later moved to "Mount Pleasant," an assumption that is provably wrong.

The presbytery's meeting minutes for October of 1774 demonstrate that the presbytery agreed to establish and patronize the new seminary, and the details are written down with great specificity. The meeting minutes covering the April meeting do not contain any mention of their agreeing to "adopt," "merge with," or "establish" Rev. Brown's school. Indeed, the only mention of Rev. Brown's school in the minutes was when the clerk casually mentions their "visit" to Brown's school at the conclusion of the meeting. In retrospect, Rev. Irwin's decision to reference this "visit" was a serious error in judgment because historians understandably assumed that the reference suggested that there was some business aspect to the visit, when nothing could be further from the truth. The truth, however, is that the presbytery did not have any official connection to Brown's Latin school. If the presbytery had not held their meeting at Brown's home, there would never have been any reference to Brown's school in the minutes.

Note: Mr. Foote, in all likelihood, assumed that because the presbytery even deigned to mention their "visit" to Rev. Brown's school that this reference must have had some official significance, when in fact it had none. Foote, in this case, was misled by Rev. Irwin who, acting as clerk, decided to refer *to this unofficial "visit" in the minutes because he and the other members understood that their host, Rev. Brown, opposed the presbytery's actions in regard to the new seminary and further, he believed that the new seminary was unnecessary. This fact is revealed in the extant letters of Rev. Brown housed in the Draper Collection in Madison, Wisconsin. The reference to the "visit" in the minutes was a mistake because it misled readers who thereafter confused Rev. Brown's school with the new seminary. It is not surprising, however, that this was the last mention ever made to Rev. Brown's private Latin school in the presbytery's minutes. Nine months later, Rev. Philip Vickers Fithian, while staying at Rev. Brown's home adjacent to Brown's Latin school, mentions in his journal (Dec. 12, 1775) that an old schoolmate, Samuel Doak, was conducting the classes at Brown's private Latin school, and a week or two later, he wrote that "Mr. Graham lately initiated a brother is appointed director of a school in the neighborhood of Mr. Browns."* In January, he also mentions his visit to the presbytery's seminary under the direction of. Rev. Graham.*

* (Fithian's Journal 1775–76, p. 150)

ERROR no. 1: Ruffner mistakenly claims that the Augusta Academy was in some undefined way private, at least "in part."

Below is how Ruffner attempts to reconcile his own understanding of how Liberty Hall was established with Mr. Foote's new theory:

> While the school was thus going on, ***partly as a private establishment,*** yet recognized and patronized by the Presbytery, in April 1775, they named several laymen in various parts of the country to assist in forwarding the subscriptions. (Henry Ruffner, "Early History of Washington College," *Washington and Lee University Historical Papers*, Vol. 1, Baltimore, John Murphy & Co. 1890, p. 19.) (The erroneous and confusing part of this sentence is highlighted by bold italics.)

Of great importance here is the unvarnished fact that the presbytery's new seminary was designated by its creators as a "publick" [sic] seminary from its very inception. There is not one scintilla of evidence to suggest otherwise. Here is precisely what the presbytery said on this subject on the day the college was created:

> October 13, 1774: "The presbytery resume the consideration of a school for the liberal education of youth, judged to be of great and immediate importance. **We do therefore agree to establish and patronize _a publick_ [sic] _school_,** which shall be confined to the county of Augusta. At present, it shall be managed by William Graham, a gentleman properly recommended to this presbytery . . .

Worth emphasizing here is that earlier meeting minutes make it clear that the only consideration before the presbytery, in this regard, was the establishment of a "seminary of learning," which in the parlance of that time was tantamount to referring to a college in all but the name.[362] In the eighteenth century, the

---

362 As already pointed out, the term "college" at the time was generally reserved for schools of higher learning conducted under the auspices of the established Church of England.

presbytery, as a rule, took no official cognizance of preparatory schools. These were deemed as private endeavors principally conducted by local Presbyterian pastors. What Ruffner is discussing above is the new seminary, which the presbytery created for the specific purpose of providing a Virginia alternative to the College of New Jersey. To be clear, the presbytery knew all too well that an undertaking of this magnitude could not be completed in one fell swoop. Just as had been the case with the College of New Jersey, the Virginians would necessarily experience more than one emendation. The man selected by the presbytery to oversee the implementation of this work in progress, Mr. William Graham, had discovered and embraced an important maxim concerning an institutionally attached grammar school, insightfully expressed by Dr. Samuel L. Campbell, one of the college's early students:

> "Here," said he [Mr. Graham], "should be laid a substratum on which to build a superstructure of learning." (Dr. Samuel L. Campbell, "Washington College, Virginia," Southern Literary Messenger, June 1838; re-printed in W&L Hist. Papers No. 1, 1890, p. 115)

The college's incipiency included multifarious and simultaneous tasks, including designing a campus and its prospective buildings, organizing a grammar school, integrating the several roles of the manager, Mr. Graham, as chief operations officer, instructor, fund-raiser, and general contractor, as well as his complementary role as that of supplicant going through the process called "trials," which was the period during which an applicant for licensing as a Presbyterian minister completes various assignments designed to prove a candidate's worthiness to be a minister of the gospel. A process that was completed expeditiously and subsequently, the new reverend William Graham was called to the pastorate of both Timber Ridge and Hall's meeting house congregations.

During this embryonic phase of the college's development, the physical operations would have resembled in appearance a local grammar school to observers unfamiliar with the inner machinations of the much more complex institutional development of the new college. Of course, this phase would also have appeared in much the same manner as has been true for most our nation's colleges in the rudimentary form. Every college, like Rome, was not built overnight. For example, a sophomore class cannot be had without their having first been a freshman class, and those are typically fully formed over the course a full academic year, and so on and so forth. So, too, were the routine activities carried on at Mount Pleasant during much of 1775 and 1776. In fact, the presbytery, in its minutes covering 1775 and 1776, actually referred to the school's operations at Mount Pleasant as the grammar school. As such, the grammar school was merely the substratum or foundation upon which Mr. Graham was planning to erect the superstructure or college.

Note, including an important caveat: *Dr. Henry Ruffner's "Early History of Washington College" was originally written in the 1840s at the behest of the college's board of trustees, but it was not published as originally planned. Dr. Ruffner says, in some introductory remarks written for yet another prospective publication of the article, that he revised his original draft of the "Early History . . ." in 1857.*[363] *By this time, Ruffner had obviously read William Henry Foote's two volumes of his* Sketches of Virginia. *Foote's two books, however, were in conflict with Ruffner's earlier draft account of the college's founding. Presumably, some of Ruffner's errors listed in this audit report were editorial modifications designed to fine-tune his original text in light of Foote's assertions. On the subject of the college's founding, however, Ruffner correctly continued to maintain that it occurred in October of 1774 by action of the Hanover Presbytery. Most assuredly, Mr. Foote's two books must have affected Ruffner's editorial revisions in several ways, but unfortunately, the auditor was not able to discern in just what specific ways Ruffner made changes in his original draft as a result of Foote's assertions.*[364]

Henry Ruffner's "Early History of Washington College" is an extensive, important, and valuable article that, nevertheless, includes numerous mistakes of vast importance. His several negative comments about the activities of the college's first president, William Graham, are in every case factually incorrect.[365] His several errors in this regard were mostly based on mistaken hearsay given to him by mostly unknown persons. Ruffner also contributed in numerous ways to the confusion surrounding the college's earliest days[366] by mistakenly claiming that the school was a "partly private" endeavor.[367] The college, however, was

---

363   *This prospective publication also went awry and did not occur as had been originally envisioned. It was finally published in the university's Historical Papers series (Vol. 2) in 1890, at which time the editors decided to include in that volume Ruffner's earlier written introductory remarks prepared after he made his 1857 revisions to his history of the college.*

364   *There is a longhand version of Ruffner's article copied into a ruled book in the archives at Washington and Lee, but it is very likely not Ruffner's original manuscript. Most likely, it constitutes his 1857 revised and edited version copied into the referenced book because it is attributed to the "Late Henry Ruffner." It is also possible that Foote had obtained some parts of Ruffner's early drafts, so Ruffner and Foote might very well have been influencing each other, but such information is wanting. Ruffner and Foote were, after all, both presbyterian ministers of similar ages, and both lived in Virginia. It may be of some interest to note that Ruffner named his son "William Henry Ruffner." Of course, that may be merely coincidental.*

365   Ruffner, in this regard, took some critical comments made by Edward Graham in his "Memoir of the Late Rev. William Graham," and then by embellishing them as he did, contorted the original slights beyond reason. In that way, he renders them unrecognizable.

366   This probably resulted in the revisions Ruffner made in 1857 after having *read Sketches of Virginia . . .* Series One and Two (1850 and 1855, respectively), written and chronicled by William Henry Foote. By making revisions about the founding of the college or about the character of the college's first president, Ruffner mangled what is otherwise a very valuable contribution to history.

367   The auditor suspects that Ruffner may have added this qualifier (i.e., "partly private") as part of the editing process, which he alludes to in his introductory remarks concerning revisions. In any event, it was a mistake because the college was a strictly public institution from inception, as is stated in the Hanover Presbytery's meeting minutes, and so it remained during the entire eighteenth century. Of course, it functioned much like a private school during part of the Revolutionary War, but the school's 1782 petition to the new Virginia Legislature asking for an Act of Incorporation while drafted by Rev. Graham, it was written "on behalf of the Liberty Hall Academy Board of Trustees."

exclusively created by the Hanover Presbytery as a "public" institution from the date of its establishment (Oct. 13, 1774). The errors in this regard, are discussed in detail below. Washington and Lee University, it can be safely said, was never in any sense a "private" educational endeavor. It was created by the organization known as the Hanover Presbytery, and has been under the control of a governing board of trustees since May of 1776.[368] Prior to the creation of the board of trustees, the school was under the direct control of the Hanover Presbytery and their appointed manager, William Graham. From the date of the college's establishment until early 1797, the institution had only one chief administrator, who was William Graham. Graham arrived in Virginia in late 1774 or early 1775, and he immediately began to lay out his plan to open the state's first institution of higher learning west of the Blue Ridge Mountains.

An early president of Washington College, Ruffner is frequently referred to as the college's "first historian."[369] President Ruffner's treatment is the first extensive history of the college to have been published. Written in the 1840s, it was not published until approximately fifty years later in 1890. In the interregnum, it had been revised and edited at least once. The primary focus of this audit is the false history of the college's origins that first appeared in print in 1850 in addition to the numerous false characterizations of the college's first president, William Graham, that began in earnest with Dr. Ruffner. Ruffner, in this regard, was mistaken about every one of the commonly repeated errors about Rev. Graham, save one.[370] Indeed, many, if not most, of the published errors concerning the college's first president can be argued to have begun with Dr. Ruffner. His other errors most assuredly served in some degree as a germ in the progressive falsification of the history of the college.[371] His role in that process, however, pales in comparison to the egregious falsifications perpetrated by William Henry Foote

---

368 For a brief period in the early nineteenth century, there was some uncertainty about the school's legal status arising from an unfortunate action by the Virginia legislature, but the matter was quickly resolved. This legislative mix-up had no impact on the issues under consideration herein.

369 This is not to suggest that Ruffner's history is the first appearance of a publication that included historical accounts of the origins of the college, for there were several others, all of which are referenced in this audit report. None of the early histories suggest that there was a link between either Robert Alexander's or Rev. John Brown's schools. Neither did any of the early accounts date the college's origins to a time prior to October of 1774. The mistaken notion that the school's origins are traceable to the date 1748 or thereabouts emanated in the fertile imagination of William Henry Foote and first appeared in print in 1850, seventy-five years after the institution was created (see bibliography).

370 Ruffner did not assert that the college's founding took place prior to October of 1774, but some of his inconsistent and inexplicable commentary causes confusion surrounding that important topic.

371 While Ruffner correctly attributes the founding to actions of the Hanover Presbytery in the early 1770s, he made some rather ridiculous comments that mistakenly hinted that the college was partly a private concern. In that, he was surely mistaken, and the mistake clearly served to reinforce those seeking to improperly link earlier private schools to the presbytery's seminary in Augusta.

in the world of letters and of trustee Col. Bolivar Christian within the confines of the college. Ruffner's mistakes in general, and in regard to Rev. Graham's character in particular, appear to have been mistakes he believed to be true.[372] Still, the mistakes made by Ruffner are inexcusable lapses in applying well-established professional and academic methodologies that would have served as a corrective had he elected to apply them.

Both Ruffner and Foote, working on their respective treatments in the same decade, were contemporaries, and both had been seriously misled by unknown sources that were possibly the same. Ruffner seems to have failed as a result of faulty research and severe credulity. Foote's failures are treated with in the subsection of this Section devoted exclusively to Foote. Foote was clearly a better chronicler than an historian. Because of serious discrepancies discovered by the auditor in Foote's published extracts, ostensibly taken from what Foote claims was an undated letter supposedly written by Rev. Samuel Houston, his professional integrity in this regard is now open to question. Suffice to say here that in one volume (1850), Foote claims that the Houston letter says one thing, then five years later, he publishes an extract from the same paragraph, but this time the paragraph's concluding statement is markedly different. In fact, the concluding phrase of the same quoted sentence has been completely changed. In the process, Foote removed the text that had appeared in the original volume (1850) within quotation marks and replaced it with an entirely different assertion, but the entire new extract is again published within quotation marks.[373] See the subsection devoted to Mr. William Henry Foote.

Dr. Ruffner's article provides the public with useful and important historical information about the school. His numerous errors, however, are of paramount significance, and therefore, deserve to be identified and corrected. It is noteworthy that Dr. Ruffner deftly sidestepped discussing education in the valley of Virginia prior to the founding of the presbytery's seminary (college) in Augusta County, Virginia, on October 13, 1774.[374]

Ruffner's refusal to accept Foote's nonsense concerning the college's origins is demonstrated by his insistence that the school was created by the Hanover Presbytery in October of 1774. That he never altered this representation can

---

372   This is in contrast to Trustee Col. Christian's activities surrounding the significant rewrite of the college's early history, which involves activities on his part that seem to be shockingly devious and tantamount to maladministration. His actions constitute unjustifiable nullification of a seventy-five-year documentary history that was palpable to all but the purposely blind (see the subsection devoted to Col. Bolivar Christian).

373   The letter could not have been corrected in the interim between the publication of Foote's two volumes (1850 and 1855) by the letter's claimed author because Rev. Houston died prior to the publication of either of Foote's two volumes on Virginia history. It is reasonable to presume that this significant alteration of the claimed letter's contents was made by Mr. Foote himself. As such, he committed a serious breach of ethics and is guilty of knowing misrepresentation and deceit.

374   William Henry Foote, DD, *Sketches of Virginia, Historical and Biographical*, Philadelphia: J. B. Lippincott & Co., 1850, First Series, and *Sketches of Virginia, Historical and Biographical*, Second Series, 1855.

only be attributed to the fact that he was not persuaded by several of Foote's representations on that subject, all of which are contained in his two volumes of *Sketches of Virginia* . . . (1850 and 1855 respectively). It also has to mean that he was similarly unpersuaded by the ostensible letter, supposedly written by Rev. Samuel Houston and ostensibly reproduced in part within Foote's *Sketches of Virginia* . . . [375] Otherwise, Ruffner would have included these representations in his 1857 editorial revisions referenced in the article's introduction in the *Washington and Lee University, Historical Papers*, Vol. 1, 1890. If Ruffner believed that Foote's account was accurate, he certainly would not have submitted for publication a contrary account.

It seems strange that Ruffner did not comment on the letter supposedly written by Rev. Houston, but then perhaps he realized that even if there was such a letter, and if indeed it did contain a suggestion that there was a link between Liberty Hall Academy and Rev. John Brown's Latin school, that by acknowledging it he would then need to explain it and repudiate it. Ruffner quite likely determined that it was a subject best left unaddressed because he had no need to exacerbate an existing resentment toward him in certain parts of the county that was an outgrowth of his public attack on the institution of slavery.[376]

Perhaps Ruffner presumed that his own history, once it was published, would serve as a corrective to Foote's gross mistake in regard to the establishment of the college. If so, he was sorely mistaken. Ruffner died long before his history of the college was published,[377] and in the meantime, a vast number of consequential books repeated Foote's preposterous claim that Washington and Lee University was an outgrowth of the school of Robert Alexander. Ruffner obviously knew this proposition was demonstrably false as it was in direct conflict with the college's own earliest records.

Note: Ruffner's wife, Sarah (Lyle) Ruffner, was the granddaughter of Mr. Samuel Lyle, who was among the original trustees of Liberty Hall Academy, and for many years, Mr. Lyle served as the college's treasurer. She was also the daughter of Capt. William Lyle, another trustee of the college and a magistrate of the Rockbridge County Court. Ruffner had access to several eyewitnesses to early college events that took place in and around Lexington, including Prof. Edward Graham, and additionally to Edward's 1821 "Memoir of the Late Rev. William Graham," as well as Rev.

---

375 As the result of Foote inconsistently quoting from the exact same portion of the dubious letter he attributed to Rev. Samuel Houston on the important subject of the college's founding, his professionalism, if not worse, is called into question. The so-called letter suspiciously has never been reproduced in its entirety or located for reference purposes. Importantly, even if it did exist, the contents concerning the establishment of the presbytery's seminary, at least as represented by Mr. Foote, would be demonstrably incorrect and inconsistent with all the known official documentary evidence that relates to that subject.

376 Henry Ruffner, *An Address To The People of West Virginia: Shewing that Slavery is Injurious To The Public Welfare and That It May Be Gradually Abolished Without Detriment To The Rights and Interests of Slaveholders, By A Slaveholder of West Virginia*, Lexington: R. C. Noel, 1847 [pdf via Archive books & by HaithiTrust]

377 Ruffner died in 1861, but his history of the college was not published until 1890. By the time it was published, Mr. Foote's two volumes had already caused most of the twentieth-century historical damage to the college's true history.

Archibald Alexander and his "Address to the Alumni," delivered and published in 1843. It is worth noting in this regard that neither of these eyewitness accounts included a claim to a link between Liberty Hall Academy and any school other than the Hanover Presbytery's school created by it on October 13, 1774. Ruffner, no doubt, was aware of the published accounts written by Dr. Samuel L. Campbell (history of the college published in 1838) and Rev. William Hill (history of Washington College, Virginia) also published in 1838. He had then four reputable sources upon which to rely, all of whom dated the institution's origins to the 1770s by an act of the Hanover Presbytery. Neither Rev. Archibald Alexander, Prof. Edward Graham, trustee, Dr. Campbell, nor Rev. Hill specifically mentions the private schools of Robert Alexander or Rev. John Brown. This would explain why Dr. Ruffner elected not to adopt Mr. Foote's claims made initially in 1850 and then further embellished in 1855, which stated that the school was an outgrowth of earlier private schools under Robert Alexander and/or Rev. John Brown. Dr. Ruffner obviously understood that his colleague of the cloth, Rev. William Henry Foote, had blundered badly in this respect As president of the college, Ruffner surely had access to the institution's early records including the school's first authorized history written by Rev. Caleb Wallace and the trustees' first authorized published account published as an appendix to his predecessor's inaugural address, neither of which dates the college's founding prior to October of 1774, or claims generally that a link exists between the college and to any previous school. And neither mentions either Robert Alexander or Rev. John Brown as having had any connection to the college. It comes as no surprise then that Dr. Ruffner was unwilling to repeat the unsupported revolutionary narrative published by Mr. Foote.

Ruffner began composing his history in the 1840s at the suggestion of the school's trustees, but prior to its publication, he published a controversial pamphlet on slavery.[378] According to Dr. Crenshaw in his <u>General Lee's College</u>, Ruffner's stated views on the subject resulted in a serious rift between some of the trustees and Dr. Ruffner. As a consequence of this conflict, the board set aside any thoughts of underwriting and sponsoring any additional publications written by the then-controversial Dr. Ruffner, including his important history of the college. Several years later, another prospective publishing of his history caused Dr. Ruffner to review and edit his earlier manuscript. He explained in a preface (contained in the <u>Washington and Lee Historical Papers</u>, Vol. 1, 1890) that he revised it for publication in 1857, but that anticipated publishing venture likewise never came to fruition.

Ruffner was undoubtedly able to review Foote's terribly incorrect accounts of the origins of the college prior to making his 1857 revisions because both of Foote's books were in the public sphere by 1855. Nevertheless, Dr. Ruffner did not elect to revise his assertion that the college's founding took place in October of 1774 when the Hanover Presbytery announced its decision to establish and patronize a new seminary of learning. This important fact has not been acknowledged in any publication that the auditor has been able to discover, including all the major published accounts of Washington and Lee University. That Ruffner did not revise his earlier assertion that the college's founding took place by an act of the Hanover Presbytery in October of 1774 should have

---

378 Ruffner had delivered an address before the Franklin Society in 1847, which led to his publishing a printed version, which was entitled "<u>An Address to the People of West Virginia: Shewing that Slavery is Injurious to the Public Welfare and that it may be Gradually Abolished Without Detriment to the Rights and Interests of Slaveholders</u>." It was published in Lexington, Virginia and printed by R. C. Noel, with an imprint date of 1847. The publication's unattributed authorship's identity, however, was well-known in Lexington.

served as a cautionary red flag to later historians and college representatives. Alas, it did not. Even the college's in-house historians have, with one exception, adopted the unauthenticated nonsensical and preposterous assertions instead of relying on the college's early institutional records, as well as the published accountings written by early graduates the college who had become recognized scholars (i.e., Prof, Edward Graham and Rev. Dr. Archibald Alexander). He also failed to acknowledge the college's first true historian, whose account conflicted with those of Mr. Foote. By refusing to acknowledge Mr. Foote's serious errors concerning the founding, Ruffner seemingly gave tacit approval. Had Ruffner publicly challenged Foote's erroneous accounts, he very well may have deterred the later trustees who in 1865 repudiated all the early accurate accounts, both published and unpublished, from the founding in 1774 to the end of the Civil War. The trustees did this without bothering to publicly acknowledge what they had done or why they did it.[379] Thirty-six years later, a trustee of the college and two-term attorney general of Virginia wrote to the board and therein explained that Gen. William N. Pendleton, a "lifelong personal friend of Gen. Lee . . . wrote to General Lee, advising his acceptance of the position [president of the college] and assuring him, as he had been authorized to do by Prof. White [James J.] that the institution would in the future be absolutely undenominational." This illuminating revelation, as important and interesting as it is, is also somewhat embarrassing in that Attorney General Anderson certainly must have understood that Professor White, the acting president of the college, was in no position to bind the college or future trustees on this, or hardly any other subject outside of lawful contracts.

While it is important to recognize President Ruffner's adherence to the early histories respecting the establishment of the college, it is equally important to point out the numerous ways in which he unjustifiably sullied the reputation of the vastly significant founding first president, Rev. William Graham. His traducements in this regard were both professional and personal. Professionally, his actions in this

---

379 These historians' reasons, however, are palpably obvious. In 1865, the trustees wanted to persuade Gen. Robert E. Lee to accept their offer of the presidency of the college, but General Lee had already spurned a previous offer based on the fact that the earlier offer was from a religious affiliated college. Consequently, the trustees wanted to be able to approach General Lee with their offer of the presidency and be able to assure him that their college was nondenominational. They authorized the printing of a radically new history of their origins that same year (1865), which therein presented a false history that predated their true origin by twenty-five years (1748). It also falsely claimed that the college was an outgrowth of private nondenominational schools in the valley and, apparently, declined to mention that the college's own official records clearly demonstrate that the founding did not occur until October of 1774, that it was created by the Hanover Presbytery, and was exclusively administered by presbyterian ministers during its entire eighteenth-century existence. They also, apparently, conveniently failed to mention that during the college's first fifty years of existence, it was administered by rectors who were Presbyterian ministers, or that all of the regular religious services attended by the students were conducted by presbyterian ministers. In addition they, presumably, did not explain to General Lee that the college's board of trustees was also created by the Hanover Presbytery, and that all of its original trustees were appointed by this same official body, comprised exclusively of Presbyterian ministers and ordained elders of that church.

regard unquestionably violated long-recognized standards of the Presbyterian Church related to how one minister treats another minister. Surely, Rev. Ruffner understood that to viciously attack the character of a deceased brethren without having indisputable evidence to support his claims was behavior beyond the pale. This Ruffner did repeatedly. His actions in this sense are made more odious by the fact that he had never known Rev. Graham. Ruffner's knowledge of Mr. Graham's personal character was often gleaned by nothing more persuasive than gossip. Moreover, in some cases, his claims about Mr. Graham can be demonstrated to be palpably false. For primary sources, readers are directed to the memoirs of Rev. Graham written by Archibald Alexander, Edward Graham, and Dr. Samuel L. Campbell (Washington College) listed in the bibliography. Alexander and Edward Graham were both early students at Liberty Hall and also lived in the home of Rev. Graham's family for extended periods of time.

ERROR no. 2: Ruffner confused the private preparatory school of Rev. John Brown located at New Providence with the Hanover Presbytery's Public Academy located at Mount Pleasant.

Ruffner mistakenly confused something that happened at a meeting held at Timber Ridge pertaining to Liberty Hall Academy with something else that had transpired the year before at New Providence. The error concerns Rev. Brown's unnamed, private Latin school. It should be mentioned here that many authors later made this same mistake, and it very well may be that Dr. Ruffner's mistake was an underlying cause.[380] In the extract below, Ruffner further complicates his already problematic account of events surrounding the college's establishment. Both of these extracted paragraphs below are riddled with significant errors.

> The next May, 1776, they [the presbytery] met **again** at ***Providence church***, five or six miles from the academy, and visited the school for the purpose of examining the classes. They expressed a high degree of satisfaction with both teachers and pupils. [Ruffner, "Early History . . . Hist. Papers," v. 1, p. 20] (Emphasis added)
> (Here, bold italics indicate error.)

This quote vividly demonstrates just how confused Dr. Ruffner had become about the presbytery's seminary under the direction of William Graham. The meeting he refers to above was not held at Rev. Brown's New Providence church; it was held at Rev. Graham's church at Timber Ridge. Here below is the pertinent comment from the meeting minutes of the Hanover Presbytery:

---

380 The first person to make this mistake was probably Rev. William Hill in his 1838 published history of Washington College. Although Mr. Hill doesn't expressly make the mistake, he certainly infers it, and by association leaves it as an impression. See the auditor's treatment of Rev. Hill in this section.

May 1, 1776. Presbytery met at <u>Timber Ridge</u>
according to appointment. (Hanover Presbytery
meeting minutes, pp. 72–80.) (Underline added)

The above extract, being in direct conflict with Dr. Ruffner's account, is
highly suggestive that Ruffner was not consulting the presbytery's actual meeting
minutes because they are quite clear as to where the presbytery met, hence his
confusion in this regard. Relying on secondary and incomplete sources plays a
significant role in the gradual misshaping of the college's early history. That spring
meeting was a five-day meeting. It met on May 1, 2, 3, 4, and 6. May 5 being the
Sabbath, the presbytery understandably did not meet on that day. These minutes
do not suggest that the meeting was ever moved from Timber Ridge. This is a
significant fact because Timber Ridge was the closest church to the presbytery's
seminary then temporarily located at "Mount Pleasant," and it was the church
where Rev. Graham, the seminary's director, was the pastor. On the last day of
that singularly important meeting, Rev. Graham's position as the seminary's chief
administrative officer was made permanent, and he was accordingly given the
title of rector. The presbytery also created the seminary's board of trustees at that
meeting, and numerous men were named as prospective trustees, and the director
was ordered to seek each nominated trustee's acceptance of that position. This
final directive makes clear that such appointments were not considered as official
until an appointee accepted the role.

*Note: It appears that many descendants of the named appointees mistakenly assumed that simply
because their ancestor was appointed to the position of trustee that they were in fact a trustee. Many
appointed were never consummated. A fairly accurate check may be had by reviewing the trustees'
meeting minutes to learn whether their ancestor was ever in attendance. Attendance is virtually
tantamount to acceptance. A conspicuously missing name from the list of attendees at Liberty Hall
Academy's trustees' meetings is that of Rev. John Brown. His permanent absence status endured
for twenty years, at which time he departed Virginia and moved to be near his family in Kentucky.*

The presbytery on this auspicious occasion "fixed," as they said, the school's
intended permanent location at Timber Ridge and also created a trustee executive
committee to oversee the routine but important duties associated with creating the
college's first permanent campus and its buildings. It is not unimportant that there
is one member of the presbytery and a nominated trustee who was not appointed
to this all-important executive committee, and he is Rev. John Brown.

Ruffner was wrong about where this important meeting took place, and it
was also an error, one of omission to fail to bring attention to the fact that Rev.
John Brown was not appointed to the vastly significant executive committee of
the newly created board of trustees, because if he had, that fact might very well
have caused others to question the efficacy of Foote's false contention that Rev.
Brown had played an integral role in the college's earliest days.

The likely reason that the presbytery did not appoint Rev. Brown to the
trustees' executive committee is that the members knew fully well that Rev.
Brown was opposed to the presbytery creating the college, and therefore, he would
not accept such an appointment. The presbytery had nominated him, along with
many others, as a trustee as a sign of respect and honor to its eldest member, but

it is hardly likely that anyone of the members thought that he would accept the appointment. In that, they would have been correct for he did not. That is why his name is never found in the trustees' meeting minutes among those listed as being present. That is a fact seemingly missed by all historians who suggested that Rev. Brown and/or his school were, in some fashion, linked to Liberty Hall Academy.[381]

ERROR no. 3: Dr. Ruffner mischaracterized the role played by Rev. Samuel Stanhope Smith concerning the appointment of William Graham to lead the presbytery's effort to create a college-level institution in Virginia.

Dr. Ruffner, in this regard, mistakenly said:

> Mr. Samuel S. [Stanhope] Smith, whose studies were in advance of Mr. Graham's, *came to Virginia immediately after he had been licensed by the Presbytery of New Castle . . .*

> "An elder brother of his, named Ebenezer, had sometime before come from Princeton at the call of the Rev. Jno. [John] Brown, of New Providence Church, and had taught a classical school in the bounds of Mr. Brown's charge. *Thus, a beginning had been made;* but Ebenezer Smith having left the country, his pupils were without a teacher under whom they could pursue their studies which they had begun. When Samuel S. Smith visited the valley, *the young men and their fathers applied to him to recommend them a teacher. He recommended Mr. Graham, first to them, and afterwards to the presbytery,* when they resolved to establish an academy. [Ruffner, "Early History . . ." Hist. Papers, v. 1, pp. 16–17] (Here again, bold italics indicate error.)

*Note: In the above extracts, the reader will observe in **bold italics** the several submistakes embodied in error number 1 that were made by Dr. Ruffner.*

The submistakes are identified below:

(1) The presbytery did not meet "*again*" in May of 1776 at New Providence;

---

381   This fact was also overlooked by all the Brown family historians who mistakenly link Rev. Brown to Liberty Hall Academy. Especially those who mistakenly assumed that the newly created board of trustees named their new college, Liberty Hall Academy, to honor their one member who opposed its creation. The idea is beyond absurd.

(2) The presbytery did not meet "again" to *"examine"* students, nor did they meet at New Providence in 1776[382];

(3) Mr. Smith did not come to Virginia *"immediately"* after being licensed;

(4) Samuel Smith's brother's teaching experience in Augusta County did not constitute *"a beginning"* of anything, let alone a new educational endeavor; and

(5) There is no known evidence that Samuel Smith ever recommended Rev. Graham to *"students"* or to *"student's parents"* in the valley as a potential replacement for Samuel's brother, Ebenezer, and the possibility of that being true is nigh unto impossible.

Samuel Stanhope Smith was licensed to preach by the New Castle Presbytery in May of 1773,[383] and since the presbytery did not announce that he was to go Virginia until the 26th of May in 1774,[384] then Ruffner was obviously wrong to say that following his licensure, Mr. Smith **"came *immediately* to Virginia . . ."** Mr. Smith received instructions from the church to go to Virginia a full year after he was licensed. This fact is confirmed by the records of the Presbyterian Church and is incontestable. The notion that he came "immediately after being licensed was concocted by Dr. Ruffner in order to explain certain timeline difficulties occasioned by Mr. Foote's erroneous account of the college's founding. False premises inevitably lead to false conclusions, and many of Ruffner's premises were unfortunately based on faulty assumptions rather than well-documented facts. Had Ruffner consulted the trustees' meeting minutes and Rev. Caleb Wallace's complete documentary history of the founding, he would have realized his error and he could have corrected Mr. Foote's the erroneous claims, respecting the founding of the college.

When Mr. Smith arrived in Virginia in the summer of 1774, his first order of business would obviously have been to contact the Hanover Presbytery, and since all but one of its members then resided east of the Blue Ridge Mountains, and since no official meeting was held near that time, it must surely have been at an informal gathering of a select number of the presbytery's members east of the

---

382 It did meet at New Providence in April of 1775, but that meeting began at Timber Ridge. The presbytery moved to New Providence after the first day's meeting.

383 Rev. D. K. Turner, *History of Neshaminy Presbyterian Church*, Philadelphia, 1876, p. 126. [Pdf file GoogleBooks]

384 Records of the Presbyterian Church In The United States of America, Philadelphia: Presbyterian Board of Publication, 1841, p. 460; **May 26, 1774:** *"Mr. Samuel Smith, a probationer, under the care of New Castle Presbytery, is appointed to supply four months between this and the next meeting of Synod, on the frontier parts of Pennsylvania, and in Virginia, if his state of health shall admit of it."* (Emphasis added)

mountains that Smith learned of the presbytery's earlier (1773) stated intention to establish a seminary west of the Blue Ridge Mountains.[385] It also must have been at a location east of the mountains that a select group of some of the presbytery's members, solicited recommendations from Mr. Smith for a person to take charge of such a monumental task as creating a college in Virginia that they hoped would be conducted using the College of New Jersey as a template.

It is rather ludicrous to believe that Rev. Smith would have traveled first to Augusta County on his missionary tour since there was but one of the presbytery's members located in that vast, mostly unsettled area of the state. That area was an immense country stretching from the Blue Ridge Mountains to what is now the eastern boundary of Ohio. Even if Smith had initially itinerated west, however, he still would have quickly learned that the presbytery had already determined to establish a seminary in that country. If he had learned that, why would he recommend his friend and colleague William Graham to a few local residents as a likely candidate to take over a local common school, when he obviously believed that Mr. Graham was the ideal candidate to take charge of the prospective college (i.e., seminary)? The notion is simply nonsensical. Once again, the scenario described by Ruffner was conjured up so as to explain the idea of their having been some connection to Rev. Brown's private Latin school, but of course there was no such connection, and Ruffner's scenario was but a fiction. If Ruffner had any compelling evidence to support his contentions in this regard, he clearly would have authenticated his claims. Of course, he did no such thing. This nonsense constitutes yet another missed red flag for later historians, none of whom apparently thought to authenticate Ruffner's claim by referring to the college's early documentary records.

Mr. Smith would have had interacted with a significant contingent of the presbytery in order for him to have taken seriously a suggestion that he write to Mr. Graham on the presbytery's behalf, and therein urge Mr. Graham to accept an appointment to direct the presbytery's new seminary.

Since the Hanover Presbytery announced their appointment of Mr. William Graham at the autumn meeting of 1774, therefore, it was highly unlikely that Smith had previously met in the Valley with *"the young men and their fathers* [who] *applied to him to recommend them a teacher,"* or that Smith recommended Mr. Graham as a prospective teacher for their little preparatory school. Ruffner's suggested scenario extracted above was his own mistaken notion that had no basis in fact or in evidence. The truth is that the events leading up to the final stages of the presbytery's decision to establish a seminary west of the mountains that could provide a college education for their sons without sending them to New Jersey,

---

385   The Hanover Presbytery in 1774 only met twice, in May and October of that year; therefore, Mr. Smith's recommendation of Mr. William Graham as a person well-suited to take charge of this prospective new seminary could not have transpired at an official meeting of that body. The May meeting had transpired before he arrived, and Mr. Graham was appointed at the October meeting. The only time for Mr. Smith to have written to Mr. Graham conveying the presbytery's offer and for Mr. Graham to respond with his acceptance had to have occurred between June at the earliest, and early October at the latest.

did not occur as Dr. Ruffner described above. Ruffner offered no evidence or authority to support the notion because there was none.

A man of genius, like Mr. Graham,[386] who possessed so many scholarly attainments, theological expertise, and significant teaching experience under the illustrious President John Witherspoon, would hardly have left his home in Pennsylvania to accept a position in the remote mountainous region of Virginia to serve as a mere tutor in a small private Latin school. A position such as this would have constituted a major demotion for Mr. Graham, who by this time had been conducting Princeton's preparatory school under the prestigious Rev. Dr. John Witherspoon for several years. Prior to that, Mr. Graham is believed by his brother Edward to have taught under Dr. Witherspoon's predecessor, Samuel Finley,[387] either at Finley's Nottingham Academy or at the college. Mr. Graham's prospects in the summer of 1774 were indeed bright, and he was as ambitious as he was sagacious.

Rev. Dr. Archibald Alexander informs that Mr. Graham's reputation as a theologian was such that immediately upon his arrival in the valley, students who had preceded him or had been his schoolmates at Princeton put themselves under his guidance and instruction in preparing themselves for the Gospel. Alexander neglected to mention that this happened even before Mr. Graham was ordained or even licensed as a probationer. Such were the widely recognized attainments of the man who was provided his newly adopted state with chartered degree-granting college nestled into the Blue Ridge Mountains.

The source of Dr. Ruffner's confusion

Dr. Ruffner's comments above demonstrate his utter confusion about what took place and where, on the momentous culmination of the presbytery's several years' process designed to erect a college in their own state. The Hanover Presbytery did not meet at New Providence Church in May of 1776, as suggested by Ruffner; rather, it met on that day at Timber Ridge Church, where the college's director, Rev. William Graham was the new pastor, and where the college's first permanent campus was to be constructed. This meeting was of paramount significance for it was when the rector's position was made permanent, a board of trustees was created, and numerous trustees were nominated (appointed) pending their acceptance.[388] The May 1776 meeting concluded with the presbytery members' examination of its school and its students' performance. That Dr. Ruffner could have failed to grasp why it would have been ludicrous to hold such a meeting at any other location clearly demonstrates that he had no real appreciation for what

---

386 A status assigned to Mr. Graham by Dr. Samuel L. Campbell, who according to Dr. Archibald Alexander, knew Mr. Graham as well as anyone. It is doubtful if anyone who knew Mr. Graham personally would have openly challenged this designation.

387 There was an interim president who served but briefly, before stepping aside for Dr. Witherspoon.

388 The presbytery also appointed John Montgomery, Rev. Graham's assistant. Mr. Montgomery had earlier been appointed as a tutor, and he taught some of the classes while studying theology under Rev. Graham.

was transpiring at that meeting. It is inconceivable that the Hanover Presbytery would hold this very special meeting glorifying the final coming to fruition of the only such college in Virginia at the one pastor's church, Rev. John Brown's New Providence Church, who was opposed to the college being created. This fact is clearly set forth in Rev. Brown's extant correspondence written during this period.[389] Ruffner's suggestion, in this regard, boggles the mind. That no historian encountered by the auditor picked up on this inconsistency is as exasperating as it is inexplicable.

Dr. Ruffner appears to have confused this official attendance and examination of the students matriculating under Rev. Graham, with an *unofficial* visit to Rev. Brown's private Latin school that took place the year before in April of 1775. That meeting too began at Timber Ridge, but the 1775 meeting was moved after the first day's session to the home of Rev. Brown adjacent to the New Providence meeting house. This is a fact that was seemingly overlooked by Dr. Ruffner and many who came after him. Presumably, Dr. Ruffner obtained his misperception from Rev. William Hill and his "History of Washington College, Virginia" published in 1838 (see the bibliography).[390]

The 1776 meeting referred to by Dr. Ruffner was not held, as Ruffner claims, "at Providence church . . . five or six miles from the academy." It was at the Timber Ridge Church, "five or six miles from the academy" (seminary). It was here at the academy under the direction of Rev. William Graham[391] that the presbytery "visited the school *for the purpose of examining the classes.*"

---

389 John White Stuart, *The Rev. John Brown of Virginia (1728–1803): His Life and selected sermons*, Doctoral Dissertation, University of Massachusetts, 1988. Dr. Stuart includes numerous extracts from Rev. Brown's correspondence that clearly demonstrate Mr. Brown's animus for both Liberty Hall Academy and for its director, Rev. William Graham. Brown never attended a meeting of the academy's board of trustees and refused to send any of his sons to attend the academy.

390 Rev. Hill's history of Washington College, published in 1838, includes an annoying paragraph in which he lists what he believed were the pertinent events leading up to the creation of the Liberty Hall Academy's first board of trustees, and in that paragraph he includes the presbytery's unofficial visit to Rev. Brown's private Latin school. This uncalled reference of the unofficial visit in the official meeting

minutes obviously led to Mr. Hill's confusion. There is a likely reason why the presbytery's clerk included a reference to the visit, but discussing here it would likely serve as a distraction. It is enough to say that Mr. Hill confused Rev. Brown's private school at New Providence, with the presbytery's new school at Mount Pleasant under the direction of Rev. Graham several miles away. Rev. Hill's mistake in this regard likely misled both William Henry Foote and Dr. Ruffner. They in turn misled the credulous Trustee Col. Bolivar Christian, and collectively, they all misled nearly everyone else that followed.

391 It should be noted here that the seminary's (academy) quarters were not located at Timber Ridge until the new buildings were completed in late 1776. Therefore, at the time of the May 1776 meeting of the presbytery, the school, such as it was, was operating in temporary quarters nearby on that aspect of Mr. James Wilson's farm called "Mount Pleasant." Importantly, however, the presbytery's meeting was conducted at the Timber Ridge meeting house nearby, where the school's new buildings were in the midst of being constructed on land adjacent to the church. The incipient public seminary at Mount Pleasant and its later emendation at Timber Ridge were unrelated to Rev. Brown's "Latin school" at New Providence, which had been left

This 1776 meeting had nothing to do with the private "Latin school" of Rev. John Brown, which was located at New Providence Church, a fact made clear by both the Hanover Presbytery meeting minutes and also by Rev. John Brown in various letters written at this time. Many of Brown's letters have been extracted and published in John White Stuart's *The Rev. John Brown of Virginia (1728–1803): His Life and selected sermons* (see bibliography).

There was no second "visit" by the presbytery to its academy located at Mount Pleasant, as Ruffner suggests in his comments shown above. The presbytery visited its academy only once before creating a board of trustees to take charge of most of the administrative duties, as its meeting minutes clearly evince. It is therefore reasonable to conclude that Dr. Ruffner mistakenly believed that the presbytery's meeting minutes that referred to visiting the school of Rev. John Brown meant that Rev. Brown's school and the Hanover Presbytery's school were one and the same.

There was, after all, no other reference in the meeting minutes to the presbytery having attended or visited any school but on these two occasions. Dr. Ruffner's confusion then helps to explain his curious reference to the presbytery having met at New Providence *again*, but in this case he is demonstrably wrong. The two visits, like the two schools, were different and took place at entirely different locations. When the presbytery "visited" Rev. Brown's private Latin school the year before (1775) at New Providence, it was merely a social call undoubtedly precipitated by an invitation extended by the presbytery's host, Mr. Brown.[392] In light of what transpired, it was clearly a mistake for the person who drafted the meeting minutes to have even mentioned that "visit" in the minutes. The "visit," after all, came at the very conclusion of a several-day meeting, and it was an entirely unscheduled visit to Mr. Brown's private school that had nothing to do with the business of the presbytery. It had not been previously scheduled,

---

without a tutor in late December of 1775. Rev. John Brown, being incapable of conducting the instruction at his private Latin school, appears to have thereafter closed his school for the duration of the Revolutionary War, but he wrote letters in 1782 advising his relatives of his intention to reopen his school and therein solicited their assistance in procuring books and other supplies. See John White Stuart's biography of Rev. John Brown. In early December of 1775, however, both Rev. Brown's private Latin school at New Providence and the presbytery's new seminary (Augusta Academy) at Mount Pleasant were both operating albeit in different locations, under entirely different directors, and with distinctly different missions or objectives. One (Brown's) is a preparatory, and the other one (the presbytery's seminary under Rev. Graham) designed from inception to provide a college level program of instruction.

392 Mr. Brown's home was a large and commodious one where presbyterian clergy frequently lodged when visiting in the region. On this occasion, the presbytery's meeting was moved from Timber Ridge after the first day's events to New Providence, where several members took their lodging, and where the remainder of the meetings were held over the course of several days. Rev. Brown opposed the presbytery's plan to erect a seminary in his neighborhood, and he, no doubt, took this occasion to invite his colleagues to his school. Schools such as his in conjunction with Princeton, he is known to have believed, was preferable to creating a college in his neighborhood. If this was why he invited his brethren to visit his school, the tactic failed, and the process already underway continued as had been planned. It was a rather transparent stratagem destined from inception to fail.

and because it was unofficial, it occasioned no formal action by the presbytery. By mentioning it in the minutes, the misguided Clerk caused a great deal of confusion on the part of later researchers.

To be sure, the presbytery did have jurisdiction to attend and examine their students at the seminary (Augusta Academy), which was under the direction and care of Rev. Graham, because the presbytery created and patronized it, and they appointed Mr. Graham to oversee it. Rev. Brown's school, on the other hand, is an entirely different matter because the presbytery never had an official connection to it.

Serious researchers are referred to pages 58–63 of the Hanover Presbytery meeting minutes for the specific minutes relating to the April 1775 meeting, and also the minutes for the meeting held on May 3, 1776, which appear on page 76, para 2. (See bibliography for information on accessibility of these records.)

ERROR no. 5: Ruffner mistakenly assumed that Hanover Presbytery's appointment of Rev. William Graham as its "manager" was "under the inspection of Rev. John Brown," when that is clearly wrong,[393] **notwithstanding the meeting minutes that seemingly suggest otherwise.**

Here below is Dr. Ruffner's quotation from the presbytery's meeting minutes:

> October 13, 1774: "The presbytery resume the consideration of a school for the liberal education of youth, judged to be of great and immediate importance. We do therefore agree to establish and patronize a publick school, which shall be confined to the county of Augusta. At present, it shall be managed by William Graham, a gentleman properly recommended to this presbytery,—and under the inspection of Reverend John Brown.[394]

---

393 While this appointment was intended to take place, whatever it may have meant, it never came to fruition because Rev. Brown refused the appointment by virtue of the fact that he never accepted it. The matter is never again mentioned in the presbytery's meeting minutes because Rev. Brown was opposed to the school being created in his neighborhood, and he was intransigent on the subject. The reason why Mr. Brown remained aloof was very personal and resulted from a broken engagement between his daughter and the seminary's director, Mr. Graham, which has been explained in detail elsewhere in this report. The auditor's source is Rev. Archibald Alexander's unpublished "Memoir of Rev. William Graham." See the bibliography.

394 It is noteworthy that in their respective memoirs of Rev. William Graham, neither Archibald Alexander nor Edward Graham included the qualifying phrase: "and under the inspection of Rev. John Brown." Oddly, Dr. Ruffner not only includes the phrase, he footnotes it and in the note provides background on Rev. Brown when he either knew or should have known, that Rev. John Brown had no connection to the presbytery's seminary in Augusta County. A disconnect, by the way, that was of Brown's own choosing. Questions about the qualifying parenthetical, *"and under the inspection of Reverend John Brown . . ."* are rendered moot by Rev. Brown, having never accepted the presbytery's assignment, consistent with his attitude concerning all

While this quote is accurate as far as it goes, it does not go far enough because Rev. Brown paid the presbytery's suggestion no heed, as the subsequent meeting minutes of that body makes abundantly clear. What is also clear is that the meeting minutes include nothing further in that regard, but if indeed Rev. Brown had served as the presbytery's inspector, the minutes would have included the essence of a report by the named inspector, but as it's clear from its meeting minutes that the reason the minutes do not contain the essence of Rev. Brown's report is the fact that Rev. Brown never served in the role of the presbytery's inspector. Instead, Rev. Brown remained aloof from all activities related to the presbytery's seminary from its very inception, as is pointed out elsewhere in this report. The personal relationship between Rev. Graham and Rev. Brown was not congenial due to Mr. Graham's request to break off his marriage proposal to Rev. Brown's daughter Betsy. This request by Mr. Graham was precipitated by Rev. Graham having discovered that Rev. Brown's wife, Margaret (Preston) Brown, had been disparaging Rev. Graham in a design to scuttle this impending marriage. This rather scandalous affair gave Mrs. Brown her desired objective, but did so at the expense of the happiness of both the prospective bride and the groom. This rather scandalous affair also severely strained a previously happy, personal, and professional relationship between Rev. Graham and Rev. Brown. The affair is thoroughly described in Archibald Alexander's manuscript, "Memoir of Rev.

---

attempts by the presbytery to draw him into the seminary project, which he had consistently opposed. That is why both Edward Graham and Rev. Archibald Alexander did not bother to include the parenthetical when discussing the presbytery's actions to establish the academy in their respective memoirs of William Graham, both of which were written well after it was apparent that Rev. Brown was intransigent on all matters concerning Liberty Hall and its rector, William Graham. Mr. Graham, according to Archibald Alexander, had asked Brown's daughter to release him from the understanding they had concerning marriage, after he discovered her mother's demeaning comments about him to others. This breach in their personal relationship was never healed. (See Alexander's "Memoir of Rev. William Graham." pp. 65–66.)

William Graham," which was never intended
to reach the public eye. See footnotes in
this subsection as well as the bibliography
attached to this report.

Dr. Ruffner had no good reason to include this confusing and deceptive
qualifier (i.e., "Under the inspection of Rev. John Brown") because in point
of fact, William Graham's position as "manager" of the new seminary in
Augusta County was never "under the inspection of Rev. Brown." This fact is
indisputable. The presbytery's intended appointment never came to fruition,
as is abundantly clear from a review of the presbytery's subsequent meeting
minutes during the school's incipiency, which reveal that Rev. Brown's name
never again is mentioned in any of those meeting minutes in connection with
the presbytery's seminary, nor in the board of trustees' minutes as a member
in attendance, a fact of paramount significance seemingly missed by every
historian or author who addressed the early days of Washington and Lee
University since 1850.

Note: Both Edward Graham and Rev. Archibald Alexander in their respective memoirs of William
Graham quoted from the section of the presbytery's minutes alluded to above, and in so doing
deliberately excluded the phrase "and under the inspection of Rev. John Brown," and presumably
they did this because they both knew that the appointment was never accepted and they would have
realized that by including it, their readers would most likely have been confused unless they went to
great lengths to explain why the phrase was irrelevant.

**ERROR no. 6: Dr. Ruffner repeats Edward Graham's *sequence of
establishment* error by mistakenly asserting that Hampden Sydney College
was established before Liberty Hall.**

This error was first made by Edward Graham (1821), who was apparently Dr.
Ruffner's source for this erroneous claim. Readers will find a detailed explanation
of why it is an error above in the subsection devoted to Edward Graham's errors. In
sum, Dr. Ruffner made a serious mistake in this case, which could only be made
by someone who failed to consult the Hanover Presbytery's official records. No
one today is likely to make that same mistake. Dr. Ruffner's mistake is illustrated
in these lines from his history of Washington College (Virginia):

In the year 1771, the presbytery made the first record on the
subject in the following words **(this statement was written by
Dr. Ruffner):**

The presbytery, being sensible of the great
expediency of a seminary within their
bounds, do recommend to all their members
to take the matter into their consideration
and report their thoughts thereon at the
next meeting, especially respecting the best
methods of accomplishing it . . .

But the Presbyterians of the valley needed
an academy among themselves . . . . they
adopted no measure for carrying into effect
until their meeting in October, 1774.

**The first result of this movement was the
establishment in Prince Edward County
of an academy, which was afterwards
incorporated as Hampden Sydney College.
(This unattributed quote is presumably
taken from Edward Graham's memoir of
his brother, Rev. William Graham, and it
is factually incorrect.)** [395]

(Henry Ruffner, "Early History of Washington College,"
W&L Historical Papers, No. 1, 1890, p. 13) (Bold italics
above represent a colossal mistake.)

In fact, the "first result" was not the establishment of Hampden
Sydney because the first result was the establishment of the
academy in Augusta County, afterward named Liberty Hall
Academy. Liberty Hall was established by the Hanover
Presbytery in 1774, while Hampden Sydney was established
the following year. These dates are clearly delineated in the
meeting minutes of the Hanover Presbytery, which created
both academies. See the appendix devoted to the sequence of
establishment question. Had Dr. Ruffner deigned to review the
actual institutional records, he would probably have avoided
making this serious mistake.

ERROR no. 7: Dr. Henry Ruffner incorrectly analyzes the so-called psalmody affair (i.e., New Providence schism)

*Note: The narrative below is a more in-depth discussion of this psalmody affair than what appears
above in the Archibald Alexander treatment of a similar error by Alexander, but Dr. Ruffner
expanded upon Alexander's errors on this subject, necessitating a more extensive refutation.*

Dr. Ruffner inaccurately described the oft-repeated erroneous account of the
psalmody affair at New Providence Church, as it related to the rector of Liberty
Hall Academy, Rev. William Graham. He also draws incorrect conclusions
about the cause of the schism at New Providence, which was apparently initiated
sometime after a communion service that had conducted by Rev. William Graham
pursuant to a request by a majority of Rev. John Brown's congregation.

---

395 **Dr. Ruffner does not provide here a specific citation of authority for this statement printed
within quotation marks, but he does refer to Edward Graham as a principal source upon
whom he frequently relied.**

In his "Early History of Washington College," Ruffner provides a distorted account of Rev. Graham conducting a service at the New Providence Church of Rev. John Brown. It occurred sometime after 1789 or 1790 when the visiting Rev. Graham called for the singing of a hymn written by the widely accepted Presbyterian hymnal author, Isaac Watts. At the time in question, the use of Watts's hymns and psalms was common in many Presbyterian churches for over twenty-five years. Moreover, the national general assembly on more than one occasion admonished Presbyterians to refrain from disputations on the subject of psalmody. Here below is what Ruffner erroneously wrote about this particular service: (Bold and italics below indicate error.)

> The Rev. Jno. Brown, pastor of New Providence Church, a good, easy man,[396] *invited Mr. Graham to assist* at a sacrament, or meeting for the administration of the Lord's supper. Mr. Graham, warm with a recent revival determined, on this occasion, to *introduce Watts's <u>hymns</u>. He was so very indiscreet as to do this without notice at the beginning of the communion service.* Some of the elder members immediately left the church, and many were offended. *The consequences were* agitation and ill feeling during the communion, *a schism among the members, terminating in a secession of the most discontented, and the formation of a church by the seceders* called old providence. The division has not yet been healed." (Ruffner . . . Early Hist . . . *W&L Historical Papers*, no. 1, p. 59.) (*Bold italics and <u>underline</u>* above indicate error.)

Mistakes included in this paragraph:

> 1. Rev. Graham conducted the service; he did not, as Ruffner suggests, "assist." (See A. Alexander's Mss. "Memoir of Rev. William Graham.")

---

396 Brown may have been "a good, easy man," but he was also the only known opponent of the presbytery's proposed creation of the seminary that was later named Liberty Hall Academy and subsequently Washington and Lee University. Moreover, Liberty Hall Academy was initially located in Brown's own neighborhood, and yet he refused to send any of his sons to the academy, opting instead to send them to other distant seminaries of learning. For over twenty years, Mr. Brown refused to even visit the presbytery's patronized college located in his own backyard, so to speak. Moreover, Dr. John White Stuart demonstrates with extracts from Mr. Brown's extant correspondence that he urged his relatives not to send their sons to Liberty Hall. (See bibliography.)

2. According to Rev. Archibald Alexander, it was not Rev. Brown's decision to invite Graham to conduct this communion service. It was a decision made by a majority of the divided congregation.

3. Graham introduced a hymn, not "hymns."

4. It was not "indiscreet" to fail to give "notice" of the hymns that had been selected together with the authorship of each at the beginning of the service.

5. The schism was not, as Ruffner suggests, the "consequence" of Rev. Graham's selection of a hymn.

Ruffner has taken liberties in the paragraph provided above concerning Graham's communion service at the New Providence Church. For example, there is no known evidence that Graham was "invited *to assist*" in conducting the communion service as indicated by Ruffner in the paragraph above. Instead, Rev. Archibald Alexander informs that, for all intents and purposes, Graham conducted this service in place of Rev. Brown, and an important, if not the only, reason for this substitution was the desire of a majority of the congregation to witness Graham's revivalist orientation[397] to a religious service had become very popular in the valley at that time.[398] One common feature of services conducted as part of the revival was the use of Watts's hymns and psalms. Graham's use of one particular hymn by Isaac Watts therefore could hardly have come as a surprise to those in attendance.

The use of hymns by Isaac Watts had long been recognized as an acceptable practice in Presbyterian services by the national body of the Presbyterian Church as its records clearly demonstrate. Moreover, the national church policy severely admonished its members against disrupting religious services over disputes on this subject. Those members of Brown's congregation who attempted to disrupt Rev. Graham's communion service in response to his selection of a hymn written by Mr. Isaac Watts acted contrary to the church's policy.[399]

---

397   It is not unimportant that William Graham had become, by this time, the unquestioned titular leader of the Presbyterians in the valley and also the leader of the revival west of the Blue Ridge Mountains.

398   Alexander, Archibald DD. "Memoir of The Rev. William Graham" (Mss. written in longhand, circa 1840). The Rev. Graham portions of this manuscript constitute the largest part of it.

399   The leader of the disrupting contingent of the congregation is apparently in dispute. One source says it was an elder by the name of Patrick Hall. Another infers that it was Robert McCormick. See Leander James McCormick, "Family Record and Biography, Compiled by Leander James McCormick," Chicago, 1896 (Google Books pdf). Regarding New Providence Church schism and Cyrus H. McCormick, see esp. pp. 237–238 and also pp. 247–248. In all likelihood, both

In addition, there was no requirement for Graham to provide a detailed explanation of just what all the various aspects of a revival-oriented service was going to include as a prelude to the service, contrary to what Ruffner suggests above. On that subject, Ruffner is in error. Visiting protestant ministers do not make it a practice to prepare a detailed syllabus for the congregation's review prior to conducting a service. A defining characteristic of a revival-influenced service is that it varies from what is normally expected, and Graham was the acknowledged leader of the revival west of the Blue Ridge Mountains. Ruffner was clearly mistaken in that regard.

As we detail below in an extract from Alexander's memoir of his preceptor, William Graham, Ruffner inappropriately uses the plural form of the term "Watts's hymns," which is an error. Presumably then, Ruffner had been led to believe that Graham put all of Rouse's hymns aside and used only those attributable to Watts, but that assumption was a gross mistake according to the only written eyewitness testimony that is known to exist, which is that of Rev. Archibald Alexander. Alexander, as has been already explained, assured his readers that Graham introduced but one single hymn by Watts during the service in question. Of course, the number of Watts's hymns used that day is really not the important point. Even if Mr. Graham had used Watts's hymns exclusively, he still would have been entirely within the accepted standards of the church. If there is fault to be found on this occasion, attention should be given to the attempt by the elders, Patrick Hall, and Robert McCormick, who are known to have been leaders of the members who objected to the hymn offered by Graham, and who, in response, improperly attempted to disrupt the communion service. This caucus of dissident congregants knew or should have known that Presbyterians had been repeatedly admonished by the national Presbyterian general assembly not to engage in disruptions over disagreements concerning psalmody.

The eyewitness account the auditor has reviewed of this event was provided by Alexander, and it is shown below:

> On this occasion, while Mr. Graham was serving at the Lord's table and much feeling seemed to be manifest in the congregation, he gave out one of Watts's sacramental hymns, which was sung by most. But one of the elders was so offended that he made an attempt to stop the [preacher?] from proceeding. **The innovation was unauthorized and rash**, and the consequences were such as might have been expected. One whole district of the congregation with the elder before mentioned withdrew from the congregation, and immediately joined with some seceders in the neighborhood in forming a church in connexion [sic] with that denomination. **All impartial men censured the conduct of Mr. Graham in this affair**. (A.

---

elders, Mr. Hall and Robert McCormick, were part of this group of dissidents and neither was a denominated "leader." Descendants of both men, however, claim that the leader of the group was their own relative.

> Alexander, Mss. "Memoir of William Graham" pp. 217–218 (hand-paginated
> by me) (Emphasis in **bold italics** here indicate, error(s).)

The concluding sentence above tells far more about the timid Mr. Alexander than it does about his preceptor, Rev. William Graham. Alexander's account of what he observed on this occasion is reliable, but his judgment of the implications cannot be sustained by reason. Imagine a couple of elderly men in Rev. Brown's congregation attempting to interrupt the most sacred Christian sacrament of all, Holy Communion, and these two old, agitating elders initiate a disruption simply because an invited minister gives out one single hymn that the men found offensive. It is an illogical proposition that this lone act by a visiting pastor could have precipitated a schism within that congregation.

Why would any sane person seek to punish an entire congregation and his own minister for a minor, inconsequential, and surely anticipated act of a visiting minister? Further, Alexander's conclusion that the use of a hymn by Isaac Watts was "unauthorized" is specious on its face. Mr. Alexander was still a teenager at the time he witnessed the event he described, so how would he have known whether the use of the hymn in question was or was not authorized?[400] Moreover, it begs the question, not authorized by whom? He certainly does not refer to the Presbyterian Church because its known policy on psalmody had for some time authorized the use of Watts's hymns. If he meant that it wasn't authorized by Rev. Brown, that too would hardly make sense because Rev. Brown was the best judge of that question, and if he judged Graham's action in this regard to be worthy of "censure," he was the person who was in the best position to lodge a complaint against Mr. Graham with the governing presbytery. Had Rev. Brown agreed with Alexander's interpretation that it was Graham's use of a Watts's hymn that precipitated the schism in his congregation, there would have been no apparent reason why he would not seek relief from the presbytery. Yet the records of the church indicate no such complaint was ever lodged against Rev. Graham by anyone in the valley concerning this, or indeed any other matter. As Alexander's testimony and the family records of the McCormick family demonstrate that there were actually two aging elders of that congregation who left the service that day in response to the use of Watts's hymn, and either one of these gentlemen were, as elders, capable of lodging a complaint with the presbytery. That neither did suggests that there was far more to this event than Alexander realized.

---

400 Admittedly, Alexander was not a teenager when he wrote this commentary, but he wrote based on his memory of the event, and his memory did not provide him with the status of church's policy on psalmody at the time in question. It is highly unlikely that the question of the existing policy concerning psalmody at the time of this service was foremost in young Alexander's considerations or that he bothered to research the question, since it apparently hadn't occurred to him when this event was being described. Moreover, his judgment as to Graham's culpability in this affair surely wasn't of his own making as a teenager, but was more likely a criticism that he heard expressed by others at the time the event transpired. It is doubtful if it ever occurred to Alexander to research the chronological history of the church's policy and how the pertinent dates may have affected Rev. Graham's decision to use a hymn by Isaac Watts. It seems rather clear that the youthful Alexander suffered from cognitive dissonance when his preceptor's views came into conflict with certain members of Alexander's family.

The man ultimately in charge was the congregation's pastor, Rev. Brown, who made no claim to church authorities that Graham's actions on that day were unauthorized and or inappropriate. The presbytery's records contain no record of Brown or anyone else in the New Providence congregation having filed a complaint against Graham in this matter. Alexander's hubris is all too evident on this occasion. Who was he, a mere teenage student, to render judgment in this regard? It is truly amazing that in all the years that had passed between the actual incident and his recalling of it, that Dr. Alexander had not come to realize that his initial assessment had been utterly baseless. A rather timid man, especially in his youth, Alexander seems to have eschewed all animated disputations, while his preceptor, Mr. Graham, had no scruple in following the path that he had determined was the right path, irrespective of the consequences, at least within reason. Alexander was a far better recorder of facts than a judge of the adults' behavior in regard to church policy and church politics.[401] Moreover, the church's policy on the psalmody question was promulgated when Mr. Alexander was still a teenager, so it is reasonable to accept that he was unaware of the policies of the national body of Presbyterians at the time that he formulated his opinion. Later, it probably didn't occur to him to research the precise history of that policy's development. What he did know, however, was what he observed on that day, and about that he appears to have been entirely accurate.

Here below is the Presbyterian Church's national policy taken from the following publications:

> "Part XII. General Decisions., CHAPTER I (of psalmody)
> *Sect. 1 The use of Watts's psalms allowed by the late Synod of New York and Philadelphia, in 1787."* (*A Digest, Compiled from the Records of the General Assembly of the Presbyterian Church in the United States of America . . .* Philadelphia, 1820 printed for the trustees of the assembly by R. P. M'Culloh, 1820, p. 313.) (Bold italics below are added for emphasis, *not error*.)

> > ***The Synod did allow, and do hereby allow, that Dr. Watts's imitation of David's Psalms, as revised by the Rev. Mr. Barlow, be sung in the churches and families under their care***. *But they are, at the same time, far from disapproving of Rouse's version, commonly called 'The Old Psalms,' in those who are in*

---

401   The auditor does not mean to suggest that the eminent theologian, Archibald Alexander, was unaware of the church's policies at the time that he wrote his memoir, but rather that his judgment was probably made at the time of the incident when he was still a youth, and he probably didn't bother to do a retrospective analysis of the policies on psalmody that had evolved over the course of several decades and then superimpose his views onto the events of many years earlier. If he had, he would doubtlessly have discovered his error in judgment and made the appropriate modifications.

*use of them, and choose to continue; but are of
opinion that either may be used by the churches,
as each congregation may judge to be most for
their peace and edification.* ***And do, therefore,
highly disapprove of severe and unchristian
censures being passed on either of said systems
of psalmody.*** *(Emphasis added here <u>does not</u>
indicate an error)* (Drawn from p. 314.)

*Note: This policy published by order of the assembly in 1803 had already been in effect for some time.
The policy had evolved over the course of many years, and during those years, the church had never
eschewed the use of Isaac Watts's psalms or hymns. Indeed, these hymns were in wide use in Virginia
even during the earlier time of the venerable Rev. Samuel Davies, who personally preferred Watts's
hymns and distributed them broadly in Virginia. According to Rev. Davies, Watts's hymns were, in his
time, particularly favored by the slaves as well as the free black people[402] who attended his services.*

**ERROR no. 8 Dr. Henry Ruffner failed to recognize William Graham's
authorship of the initial constitution for the State of Frankland.**

Ruffner wrongly doubts William Graham's authorship of the proposed
Frankland Constitution, but does so based on faulty assumptions and not on any
established facts.

Here below are Ruffner's mistaken words on this subject:

About this time, a new state, to be called Frankland, was
projected on the upper waters of the Tennessee River, . . . A
Committee was appointed to draft the form of a constitution
for the projected state. There is a report that Mr. Graham was,
by request of the committee, the draftsman, ***but this is not
probable; for after the proposed constitution was published,
he wrote and published a pamphlet in which he speaks of
this constitution as the production of the committee and not
his own pen, and praised it far too highly to comport with
the modesty of an author when speaking of his own work.***
(Ruffner, Henry, "Early History of Washington College," <u>Washington and Lee
University Historical Papers</u>, Vol. 1 Baltimore, John Murphy & Co., 1890. p.
60.) (Emphasis is added here in ***bold italics*** to indicate error.)

Ruffner, in his "Early History of Washington College," speculated that
Graham was probably not the author of the proposed constitution for the State of
Frankland/Franklin.[403] His speculation, however, was wrong. Today, Graham's

---

402   *The auditor has used the terminology that Rev. Davies would have used instead of the term
      African Americans in use today. Davies ministered to many African Americans, both free and
      slave, but the term African American would have been foreign to him.*

403   William Graham's proposed constitution is reprinted in the <u>American Historical Magazine</u>, 1,
      (1896), William R. Garrett, ed., Nashville, Tennessee. Tennessee University Press, pp. 48–63.
      It is entitled, "The Provisional Constitution of Frankland."

authorship of the proposed constitution is widely recognized by virtually all scholars concerned with the subject. From one eminent scholar and contemporary of that period, Archibald Alexander, can be seen the manner in which this constitution became the subject of great debate. Alexander knew both Graham and Houston very well, and he left a brief but insightful comment on the subject, which confirms that Graham was indeed the author of the proposed constitution.

He explains in his unpublished memoir of Rev. William Graham that:

> The people however disregarded their old charter boundaries and felt it their right and privilege, without regard to North Carolina, to form a constitution for themselves. This independent proceeding was very much in accordance with Mr. Graham's sentiments and wishes. And he being acquainted with many of the people and having correspondence with some of the leading men, **he drew up the form of a constitution to be proposed to the convention.** This was entrusted to the care of the Rev. Mr. Houston already mentioned with directions how to proceed; at the same time enjoining upon him the utmost secrecy. **By some means, however, it came to be known that Mr. Graham had taken upon him to prepare a constitution for Frankland.** (Alexander, "Memoir of Rev. William Graham." unpublished Mss. p. 163.) (Emphasis added.)

Alexander obviously knew a great deal about the Frankland proceedings for he discusses the matter with great confidence and in some detail. At the time of the occurrence, Alexander was still in regular contact with Mr. Graham, under whom he was carrying out his postgraduate theology studies at the college. Alexander's sister, Margaret, married Edward Graham, the younger brother of Rev. William Graham. Alexander and his brother-in-law were regular correspondents who collaborated in the study of the college's early history. These brothers-in-law both wrote memoirs of Rev. William Graham, but Edward, for some unknown reason, does not mention any of his brother's various political activities engaged in during the critical years surrounding the Revolutionary War.

Rev. Alexander and Rev. Samuel Houston both grew up in the greater Lexington, Virginia community and both were active members of the Virginia Synod of the Presbyterian Church. Alexander was an intimate member of the Graham family circle of that period. While at Liberty Hall Academy, both Edward Graham and Archibald Alexander lived in President Graham's home. Few individuals knew President Graham better than these two closely related scholars that maintained close connections to the school, which evolved from Liberty Hall Academy to Washington and Lee University. On matters of fact, these historians of the university's first and founding president were more reliable than any later nineteenth-century historians who relied heavily on the unreliable William Henry Foote. (See Foote subsection of the author's errors section of this report.)

ERROR no. 9 Dr. Henry Ruffner mistakenly claims that Rev. William Graham was censured by his church.

Ruffner incorrectly represents that Graham was censured by the Presbyterian Church when, in fact, he was not censured in the case to which he refers or, for that matter, ever.

Note: In the Presbyterian Church, the term "censure" has a very specific denotative meaning. A censure arises through a very prescribed process. For example, the censure process involves a formal complaint, due process, and a formal hearing in a narrowly restricted jurisdictional forum. The term, in this context, does not mean "to be criticized," willy-nilly by one person or another. Unfortunately, Alexander sometimes uses the term in its connotative sense as a synonym for "criticized." Alexander, as president of the Princeton Theological Seminary, should have known better. His error in this regard seems to have misled numerous authors.

The oft-repeated "censure" mistake associated with Rev. William Graham's role in the Frankland movement arises from confusion surrounding the convention held to consider adopting a constitution for the proposed new state of Frankland/ Franklin. The basic facts of this subject are published in numerous places and need not be reintroduced in detail here.[404] Ruffner's erroneous conclusions, in part, however, deserve some measure of consideration.

Ruffner offers the following mistaken account:

> after the proposed constitution was published, he (Rev. Graham) wrote and published a pamphlet . . . .Either this laudatory pamphlet or the constitution so lauded—***probably the former***— was violently assailed by the Rev. Hezekiah Balch, a member of the Abington Presbytery, which was mostly within the projected state. Mr. Graham in turn addressed a printed letter to Balch, in which he satirized him most bitterly. ***The synod, before whom the case was brought, inflicted but a light censure on Graham***, because the ***provocation was considered as more than a man of Graham's irascible temperament could well bear. But the people who opposed the project of a new state did not let him off so easily. His defence*** [sic] ***of the scheme so irritated some of them, that they assembled tumultuously and burnt him in effigy. These and similar acts of Graham made him many enemies, and caused some good people to question the sincerity of his religion.*** Mr. Graham's love of rectitude and zeal for the glory of God and the welfare of man

---

404 See, for example, Williams, Samuel Coles, *History of the Lost State of Franklin*, New York: Press of the Pioneers, 1933. (Contains valuable information pertaining to Rev. William Graham's limited participation in the plan to establish the state of Franklin. Rev. Graham is the author of the draft of the proposed Constitution for the lost state of "Frankland."

were strong enough *generally to overcome his irascibility and restrain his natural love of wealth and power.*[405] (Ruffner, "Early Hist . . . .", *Washington and Lee University. Historical Papers*, No. 1, pp. 60–61] (Above the *bold italics* indicate error.)

It is quite clear on this matter that Ruffner waded into unknown waters, for it can be seen that in this paragraph, he has waded in well over his head and out of his depth of knowledge. Certainly, he gets more wrong than right in his description of what actually transpired in and around the only formal complaint ever brought against Graham, as well as about Graham's character generally. The reader is reminded of this description of Rev. William Graham made by a man who Rev. Archibald Alexander said knew him as well as anyone, Dr. Samuel L. Campbell:

> "Mr. Graham came to this country with the character of a gentleman of genius, scholarship, and piety, which character he supported through life." (Dr. Samuel L. Campbell, (M.D.) [i.e., "Senex"], "Washington College, Lexington, Virginia," *Southern Literary Messenger*, June 1838)

This characterization of President William Graham is of paramount significance, for Dr. Campbell not only knew Graham better than any other man in that valley, but also he was a man of such an admirable character and reputation that he was chosen to oversee the college's affairs during the interregnum between Graham's tenure and President Baxter's appointment nearly three years later. So much did the trustees trust in Dr. Campbell's ability and affection for the college with which he remained closely connected nearly all of his life. Campbell left the only published eyewitness memoir of Liberty Hall's infancy operations during its first two years at Mount Pleasant.

It is inconceivable that Ruffner had not read the venerable Dr. Campbell's published history of Washington College, that he disregarded Dr. Campbell's characterization of Rev. Graham is indeed puzzling, keeping in mind the fact that Dr. Ruffner did not know Rev. Graham. If Ruffner believed he possessed contrary information from a more credible source, he had an obligation to share that source's identity with his readers. He did not, however, identify his sources, upon which he relied in describing Graham's general character. According to Archibald Alexander, there was no more credible source than the venerable Dr. Campbell, who the college's trustees selected as their interim president after Rev. Graham's resignation in 1796, in which position he remained until three years later when President Baxter was elected to succeed President Graham.

In regard to Ruffner's treatment of the Graham vs. Balch affair, it is important to understand that Balch's response to Graham's published letter castigating Balch for his role in the riotous conduct, which culminated in the public burning

---

405 Dr. Ruffner here has taken the core of his attack on Mr. Graham from a comment made by Graham's younger brother Edward and then amplified by Ruffner in a way that completely altered what Edward had said in his memoir of William Graham.

in effigy of Messrs. Rev. Graham and Rev. Samuel Houston, was to file a formal complaint against Graham. Balch's complaint was about the contents of the public letter condemning Balch's involvement in inciting the riot that culminated in the burning in effigy of Graham and Houston, two Balch's fellow Presbyterian clergymen. Ruffner's account was offered without authority and is completely inconsistent with the known timeline of the events that had transpired leading up to and following the convention at which the proposed constitution was debated and finally decided upon. Ruffner provided nothing to support his contradictory depiction. Since Ruffner was not an eyewitness and provides no authority for his claim, there is no good reason to believe his contradictory account. Moreover, the published Presbyterian records contradict Mr. Ruffner's account as will be shown in the auditor's explanation below.

The auditor cannot say anything meaningful about the actual content of Graham's published letter addressed to Balch, however, because he has not seen a copy. Contacts with the Presbyterian Historical Society were unsuccessful in obtaining a copy, and the numerous histories of the valley that were reviewed for this audit were all devoid of even an extract from that letter. Not even Dr. Crenshaw, Dr. Diehl, or Dr. I. Taylor Sanders seems to have ever seen a copy. If any one of them did, they did not reference that fact. Hezekiah Balch's career as a Presbyterian minister can be legitimately characterized as one of persistent disputations with other Presbyterian ministers. During Balch's career as a clergyman, he was censured by the church on several occasions, albeit in regard to other disputes and for numerous offenses committed at different times in his career. Graham, on the other hand, was never censured by the Presbyterian Church.[406]

When Balch filed his complaint against Graham, for example, Balch knew or should have known, as a Presbyterian minister, the appropriate process to follow and the proper jurisdiction to which a complaint should be addressed. Balch, however, chose to use an old lawyer's trick and engaged in what members of the American Bar Association would currently refer to as "court shopping."[407] "Court

---

406 There is a published collection of Presbyterian Church records that is very incomplete and contains an entry that very much appears to constitute a censoring of Graham by a committee initially assigned to deal with the matter, but this record is misleading because the case had been filed in the wrong jurisdiction, and the synods came to recognize that fact before both parties' cases had been heard on the complaint. The printed remarks already alluded to were improperly made. They were premature and not based on a full and fair hearing on the complaints particulars. Once these due process requirements had been met, the church acquited Rev. Graham and decided a censure was not warranted. These facts were eventually recorded, and Dr. Diehl gives a fairly detailed account of the entire affair in his biography of Rev. Samuel Houston. See bibliography for a full citation.

407 Rev. Balch filed his complaint against Graham with the New York and Philadelphia Synod, but such complaints are supposed to be filed with the presbytery to which the defendant is attached. Every presbyterian minister in America in the eighteenth century would have known where to file a complaint against a fellow member of the church. The New York and Philadelphia Synod initially referred this complaint to a committee, which proceeded, albeit improperly, to take testimony from the complainant contrary to well-established rules pertaining to jurisdiction. The committee only heard one side of this case before reporting to the larger body of the

shopping" is an illegitimate filing of a complaint in a jurisdiction one believes is most likely to be favorable to the complainant, hoping to get action from that jurisdiction, notwithstanding that it is not the correct jurisdiction to hear and decide the issue in dispute.[408] Rev. George West Diehl does an admirable job in presenting this case brought by Balch and how it proceeded over time in his published biography of the Rev. Samuel Houston, DVM.[409]

As has already been depicted, the case was improperly filed with the wrong authorities by Balch. The improper synod (New York and Philadelphia) initially stumbled and referred it to a committee, but then realizing that they did not have jurisdiction in the matter, referred it to the proper authorities in Virginia. Here are the final words from the Synod of New York and Philadelphia,[410] provided by Dr. George W. Diehl in his biography of Rev. Samuel Houston:

> . . . the synod do order the Presbytery of Lexington to cite Mr. Graham before them and make due enquiry whether he be the author and into the reasons for his conduct in that matter and *censure or acquit him as the nature of the case may appear.*[411]
> Dr. Diehl cites as his source for the quotation the records of the Presbyterian Church, 1904, p. 525. (See bibliography) (Emphasis added.)

The above quotation settles the question as to whether the Philadelphia and New York Synod censured Rev. Graham. They clearly referred that decision to the Presbytery of Lexington, and that entity declined to censure Graham. In the following chapter of his biography of Houston, Diehl informs his readers of the final outcome of this hanging in effigy affair:

synod. In the meantime, the synod realized its jurisdictional misstep and had concluded not by censuring Graham, but instead referred the complaint to the proper Virginia authorities. Thereafter, the Virginia authorities received evidence from both sides of the dispute, and its decision was to acquit Graham. By clear inference, the Virginia authorities obviously believed that Rev. Balch and his chief witness had perjured themselves before the New York and Philadelphia Synod. Once the matter was before the proper tribunal, Balch and his witness elected not to attend the hearing, but it is presumed that the earlier synod had transmitted the record of their testimony and evidence to the proper Virginia authorities for its review.

408   Those who might challenge this explanation on the basis that surely one always has an opportunity to challenge the issue of jurisdiction would be failing to consider that such challenges are both costly and inordinately time-consuming, and those who engage in such duplicitous tactics are hoping that the defendant will simply give up in despair.

409   George West Diehl, *The Reverend Samuel Houston*, V.D.M., Verona, Virginia: McClure Printing Company Inc., 1970.

410   Confusingly, the committee to which the synod initially assigned the matter issued a preliminary report; the content of which was later published in the synod's records. This report improperly handled the matter, and the synod should have expunged the report insofar as they had come to realize that they did not have proper jurisdiction. The report's content misled many to believe that Graham had been censured when that is not the case. After a proper review, the appropriate presbytery declined to censure Graham.

411   Ibid p. 49. The reader will note that Diehl's book was published a full decade before Dr. David W. Robson's horrific article attacking Graham was published by the *William & Mary Quarterly*. See the subsection devoted to Robson and the bibliography.

In October of that same year (1786), the Lexington Presbytery met and, pursuant to the directive of synod, made the previous May and made the enquiry into the Graham-Balch affair. The Lexington Presbytery's conclusions are set forth in their response letter:

> "William Graham acknowledged the letter addressed to Rev. Hezekiah Balch and signed William Graham to be his production— he produced several depositions to prove the truth of the charges against Balch and especially his approving of the conduct of the mob in Frankland in burning effigies of Messrs. Graham and Houston . . . Although they could wish Graham had been more temperate in his satyr and more gentle in his expostulations, yet the treatment he met with was so grossly injurious that *presbytery cannot suppose him to merit a formal censure on account of said letter.*" "Thus," says Diehl, "the matter was closed."[412] (Diehl, *The Reverend Samuel Houston, V.D.M.,* 1970, p. 54.)

According to the Presbyterian Church records of that time, Graham was not censured by his church in this matter. Indeed, he was never censured by his church. The complaint brought by the ever-vexatious Hezekiah Balch[413] was the only complaint ever filed against Graham during his tenure as a Presbyterian minister. With Graham having had such a stellar and unblemished career, it is truly astounding that Ruffner, a president of the college, would be so reckless and imprudent as to sully the reputation of the college's first and founding president based apparently on nothing other than hearsay, and without bothering to consult the appropriate church records. His behavior in this regard was inconsistent with his typically careful professionalism.

The published records of the proceedings of the New York and Philadelphia Synod include text from a preliminary committee that chastises the author of the published letter (Rev. Graham) for its "unchristian treatment of a brother." The decision by the committee to draw a critical conclusion was both improper and premature because it violated the long-established rules of procedure designed to provide a minister with due process in any complaint proceeding. It is always considered improper for any entity to issue judgmental comments without having first established that they had proper jurisdiction, and secondly, without having held a proper hearing that includes an opportunity for both parties to a dispute to present evidence.

---

412   Ibid, p. 49

413   Not to be confused with his cousin Hezekiah James Balch.

In this case, the committee heard only from Balch and his witness. Once the synod realized its error by even accepting Balch's complaint, the proper thing for the synod to have done was to vacate any report from the assigned committee before referring the case to the proper jurisdiction. To publish comments like it did was highly prejudicial and unfair to the defendant, who had not yet been heard before a proper tribunal. The result of this egregious error was that many authors relying on the preliminary committee's unjustifiable prejudging of a matter about which they had only information from one of the two parties in dispute was to understandably misconstrue what had transpired. Apparently, none of the many misled mid-nineteenth-century and even later authors understood that the ecclesiastical court's final disposition was to acquit, not censure Rev. Graham. After the proper ecclesiastical court heard all the evidence, the results in this case turned out to be just the opposite of what the earlier committee seemed predisposed to, and what is often mistakenly reported to have been the case's final disposition.

Note: It is not known to the auditor whether Graham had been given notice and an opportunity to be heard, but since the jurisdictional problem was probably realized by Graham and his friends, he may have declined to appear before the improper tribunal for fear that his appearance would be interpreted as acceptance of the jurisdiction. If he appeared, he obviously and wisely declined to participate on jurisdictional grounds.

Unfortunately, Graham's acquittal seems to have gone unnoticed by most nineteenth- and twentieth-century historians, except of course, Dr. Diehl. Unlike what Ruffner reported, the church did not impose a "light censure" on Graham, nor could they have, because in the Presbyterian Church, there is no such thing as "a light censure." A "light censure" is analogous to a criminal court finding a defendant "somewhat guilty." Dr. Ruffner then was incorrect and he improperly traduced the college's president, William Graham. Ruffner's serious mistake here is surprising insofar as he was a Presbyterian minister himself, and as such, it should have occurred to him that Balch had filed his complaint in an improper ecclesiastical court. It is well known by the Presbyterian clergy that the church is dedicated to the proposition that their members should have the right to be judged by those who know them best. When the final decision was made by the appropriate church entity, these Presbyterian leaders acquitted Rev. Graham and therefore, not censured, as was mistakenly reported by Ruffner. President Graham was not censured then, or indeed ever.

ERROR no. 10 Dr. Henry Ruffner gives a seriously incorrect account of the Virginia Synod's consideration of a proposed resolution concerning the so-called whiskey rebellion, and in so doing, mistakenly paints Rev. William Graham in a false light.

Note: The issue in dispute at this meeting of the Virginia Synod was not about whiskey drinking but only about the newly imposed federal tax policy implications associated with the new tax on whiskey.

Dr. Ruffner incorrectly described the important aspects of a meeting of the Virginia Presbyterian Synod at which it had addressed the so-called Whiskey Rebellion. In so doing, he inappropriately and inaccurately portrayed Liberty

Hall Academy's president, William Graham, in a poor light by suggesting
that he was out of step with his colleagues when precisely the opposite is true.
Perhaps more important than any other question pertaining to this event is what
explains the presence of a contingent of soldiers at a meeting of the Virginia
Presbyterian Synod consisting in the main of Presbyterian clergymen and church
elders. This question is one that Ruffner apparently failed to recognize was
of paramount importance. In any event, he failed to mention the curious and
seemingly inexplicable appearance of troops at a sitting of an ecclesiastical court.
He also seems to have misunderstood the significance of the political issues that
precipitated the *"Whiskey Insurrection."* This event constituted a major political
protest of no small political significance that involved the new U.S. government's
early taxation policies.

Ruffner's general characterization of Graham's role in the affair was far
less reliable than the only credible account included in W. H. Foote's *Sketches
of Virginia* . . . (1850 and 1855). The more credible source for the best and most
accurate account of this affair is also the most central character involved in the
Whiskey Rebellion dispute, Rev. Moses Hoge. Frankly, it is unclear what sources
of information Ruffner relied upon for his treatment of this subject, but certainly
no one was in a better position to report upon that day's events than Rev. Moses
Hoge, who initiated the dispute by proposing a resolution that after discussion, and
contrary to Ruffner's assertion, was defeated. Rev. Hoge's son's biography of his
father was based on a manuscript left by his father, and Hoge's account differed
considerably from Ruffner's mistaken account, which was offered gratuitously.
It remains a mystery why Ruffner obviously ignored the Moses Hoge account as
described by Hoge's son, given that it was based on memoranda left by the man
who initiated the dispute by submitting to his brethren a proposed resolution
chastising the so-called whiskey boys.[414] Hoge's account is also consistent with the
synod's records pertaining to this event. In light of the known evidence, Ruffner's
mistake in this regard is inexplicable.

In sum, the Rev. Moses Hoge, an early pupil of Graham, had proposed a
resolution to the Virginia Synod that would have served as a chastisement in the
main of another Synod's members by admonishing them to cease their resistance
to the new tax that the federal government had approved on whiskey. Graham,
the titular head of the Virginia Synod, argued that the whiskey tax dispute was
a purely civil matter, and as such, it was an inappropriate issue to be judged
in an ecclesiastical court. Graham's view in this regard is unassailable, and
his colleagues agreed with that assessment. They thereafter defeated Hoge's
motion, contrary to Ruffner's account of the affair. Here below is what Ruffner
erroneously said:

> Another illustration of Mr. Graham's bold and independent
> spirit was a scene which occurred at Harrisonburg at a meeting

---

414   The so-called whiskey boys were made up of a large contingent of mostly western Pennsylvania
       Presbyterians of Scotch-Irish ancestry. They came under the jurisdiction of a synod other than
       the Virginia Synod.

of the Synod of Virginia in the year 1794, when a company of soldiers arrived there on their way to put down the whiskey insurgents of Pennsylvania. The Rev. Moses Hoge, warm with patriotic zeal, moved that the synod should adopt an address to the people, inculcating obedience to the laws. *Mr. Graham opposed all synodical action on the subject and boldly avowed that 'the whiskey boys,' as they were usually called, were not rebels, but a suffering people whose grievances ought to be redressed . . . .****The address was carried by a small majority***. The soldiers were exasperated against Mr. Graham and his party, ***and threatened violence against him, insomuch that he felt it expedient to retire privately from the same tumult***.

(Henry Ruffner, "Early History . . .," W&L *Historical Papers*, Vol. I, p. 60.)

(Here, emphasis in ***bold italics*** represents error.)

Where Ruffner makes his greatest mistake in the paragraph above is in his claim that Hoge's "address" "was carried by a small majority." The truth of the matter is that Hoge's proposed resolution concerning the "Whiskey Insurrection" lost as a result of Graham's opposition to the proposal. In other words, Graham's colleagues agreed with him and not, as Ruffner intimates, with Hoge. This mistake is not inconsequential because the college's president was portrayed by Ruffner as a someone being out of step with his colleagues and something of a radical gadfly, when the truth is he was a respected leader in the synod, and in this case as was true generally, his colleagues followed his lead and defeated Hoge's proposal. The issue also resonated well beyond the bounds of the whiskey tax issue.

The Presbyterian Church was a well-established advocate of religious freedom and opposed governmental interference in the affairs of the church. Graham and the Virginia Presbyterians were perhaps the single most influential opponents of the state's interference in the affairs of the church during the struggle for religious freedom that culminated in 1784 and 1785. The issue, as proposed by Hoge, was clearly one that could have brought the Presbyterian Church into ridicule for hypocritically violating their own strictures regarding separation of church and state. The synod agreed with Graham, and Hoge's resolution was defeated. This fact is well-established in the official records of the Virginia Presbyterian Church that are housed in several different locations. Our conclusions in this regard are incontrovertible.

The auditor cannot say that Ruffner is demonstrably wrong to claim that Graham was threatened by the soldiers with violence on this occasion, but the suggestion strains credulity. Gossip of this sort, after all, is as difficult to prove as it is to disprove. One thing is for certain—every historical treatment written by those who lived in the latter quarter of the eighteenth century in the Valley of Virginia and who left a known account of Graham universally attest to his fearless and courageous nature in the face of danger. If it is true that soldiers threatened Graham on this occasion, it is highly unlikely that Graham would have been in any degree intimidated by such improper threats. For one thing, Graham undoubtedly knew that these soldiers, whatever their rank, clearly served under the command of his old friend, General "Light-Horse Harry" Lee.[415] Graham was not likely to have been intimidated by unruly subordinates of his old friend and classmate, Gen. Henry Lee. Lee, who Graham had tutored[416] on one important occasion at Princeton in 1773, was the father of Gen. Robert E. Lee. It is perhaps instructive that Mr. Foote's published account explains that a high-ranking officer associated with the soldiers in attendance sent a note to the synod during this meeting demanding the yeas and nays cast by its members that defeated Hoge's motion, and according to Hoge's son, relying on his father's record of the event, the synod rejected the officer's demand as being an improper assumption of power. Apparently, none of these ministers in attendance felt particularly intimidated by these impudent soldiers.

W. H. Foote's books on Virginia include two different accounts of this event. One account is based on a submission to Foote by Hoge's son, and on a memorandum left by the eyewitness father, Moses Hoge, who was the other central character involved in the event under consideration. Mr. Hoge, an earlier student of Mr. Graham and longtime admirer of his preceptor, was the member who put forward the motion in question. The younger Hoge's submission to Mr. Foote concerning the disputed resolution on the whiskey rebellion says in part:

> "Mr. Hoge, after conference with some of his brethren, proposed—that the synod prepare an address to the people under their care, inculcating upon them the duty of obedience to the laws of the country. He continues, Mr. Graham opposed the resolution as uncalled for, and as prejudging in an ecclesiastical court the case of a people that felt themselves aggrieved politically by the practical working of a law of Congress, that pressed as tyrannically upon them as the Stamp Act upon the colonies. The proposition [Hoge's motion] *lost by a small majority.*
>
> "An officer of high grade residing in Rockingham sent a demand of the yes and nays on the question, and the reasons for the decision. <u>This was refused by the synod as an assumption of power.</u>" (W. H. Foote, *Sketches of Virginia* . . . first series, 1850 pp. 560–61.) (Emphasis in bold italics indicates an error, while the underline is strictly for emphasis, and does not constitute an error.)

---

415 Edward Graham "A Memoir of The Late Rev. William Graham, A.M." *The Evangelical and Literary Magazine and Missionary Chronicle*, IV, (1821), p. 75 et Seq., passim.

416 Perhaps "tutored" is not the best word to have been used, but Henry Lee, Graham's classmate at Princeton, is said to have requested that Graham serve as his tutor for purposes of preparing for his final exams. According to the author of the first published memoir of William Graham, by way of compensating Graham, Gen. Lee gave Graham his personal copy of a book after striking through his own name on the flyleaf, and in its place Lee wrote Graham's name. The book was said to have become a family heirloom after Graham's death.

In conclusion in regard to the so-called Whiskey Rebellion affair, we note that William Henry Foote in this case provided good service because, by providing his readers with the essence of the Rev. Moses Hoge's account, he allowed the accurate accounting to emerge, which provided a bit of clarity on a small but not insignificant matter of history. It is significant because this error along with several others about Rev. Graham, when taken together, has served to besmirch the character of President William Graham. The grossly inaccurate characterizations of Graham portray a completely false portrait of a vastly important eighteenth-century Virginian and first president of Washington and Lee. President Graham's leadership role on this day in 1794 was wise and prudent, and in addition, it avoided the embarrassment of the Virginia Synod being labeled as an organization of hypocrites because the issue of taxing whiskey was indeed, as Graham had contended, a purely civil issue and not a religious matter. His clerical colleagues on that day agreed with Liberty Hall's rector, and Graham's view, as usual, prevailed. Contrary to Dr. Ruffner's claim, Rev. Hoge's impolitic[417] and inappropriate motion on this occasion was defeated, while Graham's view on this question prevailed. It is truly disappointing that Dr. Ruffner could have misconstrued the events surrounding the synod's brief consideration of the whiskey boys affair.

ERROR no. 11 Ruffner traduces Rev. William Graham by inaccurately claiming that he was sometimes rash and imprudent.

Ruffner has a curious habit of descending into the realm of gossip, especially when he assaults the character of Washington and Lee's first president, Rev. William Graham, which he typically does without giving any indication as to how he arrived at these judgments. At times, however, it seems as though he is describing two separate and entirely different persons, when in reality he is only dealing with one. If Graham was given to acting both rashly and in a manner one might call "imprudent," as Dr. Ruffner and subsequently Mr. Joseph Waddell both assert,[418] then one or the other ought to have given us some good examples of Mr. Graham's actions that led them to this conclusion. Sadly, neither gentleman meets this normally requisite burden.

The auditor's research into the life of Graham and the early history of the college unearthed no pertinent or significant actions on the part of Graham that could justify such a conclusion with one important and possible theoretical exception. We refer to Mr. Graham's decision to enroll a black man, Mr. John Chavis, as a student in the regular academic college program at Liberty Hall Academy. This was a decision that some living in the eighteenth century might

---

417 Hoge's resolution was impolitic because the Virginia Synod had recently (1792) established two prospective theological seminaries, one in Virginia under Rev. William Graham at Liberty Hall Academy, and the other to be in western Pennsylvania under Rev. John Macmillan, and this resolution was clearly an admonishment of the Presbyterians in western Pennsylvania where Rev. Macmillan was the titular leader. The potential for Rev. Macmillan to view such an admonishment as a direct attack on his leadership was apparent to a man such as Rev. Graham. He, however, astutely did not base his opposition on this likely concern.

418 See this report's subsection devoted to Mr. Joseph Waddell.

have indeed said was impudent, especially in Virginia, but certainly few who live in the twenty-first century would agree with that judgment. That Rev. William Graham decided to enroll a black man in the regular academic program of the chartered college, Liberty Hall Academy, in the then-largest slaveholding state in the Union, is as remarkable, as it is generally unheralded. Whether it was imprudent, however, is an entirely different question. In the case of the college's president (rector), Mr. Graham, imprudent does not seem to be a proper description because his action had no known negative repercussions on Mr. Chavis, the community, or the college; at least none that have come down to us. On the other hand, Mr. Chavis completed his academic program, which prepared the way for his theological training, also at the college and under Graham, which in turn allowed Chavis to present himself before the Lexington Presbytery for training and trials in preparation for becoming a licensed Presbyterian minister.

In the eighteenth century in Virginia, those who successfully completed their regular academic course at a chartered college were, by definition, deemed to have received their bachelor of arts degree, whether a commencement exercise was held or not. There are multiple examples of students who had finished their programs during the early periods when few commencement exercises were held, and subsequently found a need to substantiate their status of graduate for disparate reasons. The extant early records do not appear to include any cases wherein the alumnus was denied their request for confirmation of their graduate status. Ruffner's son, and a later trustee of the college, left an unpublished manuscript essay describing Mr. Chavis's matriculation wherein he makes a clear affirmation of Chavis having received his BA degree.[419] There is additional information on this remarkable circumstance that took place at Liberty Hall Academy in an appendix devoted to the case of Rev. John Chavis, the nation's first black college student and only black eighteenth-century college student in North America. He was enrolled by Graham at Liberty Hall and he went through the regular academic program during the 1790s. This decision may have caused Ruffner to conclude that Graham was, at times, "rash and imprudent," but if that decision formed the basis upon which Ruffner concluded his judgment, then he was merely the victim of his time, and his claim against Graham cannot be sustained.

Ruffner also alludes to Graham's investment in land upon which he intended to retire, and he seems to have concluded that Graham's actions in this regard was also an example of his tendency to rashness. This may be his single most tawdry attack on Mr. Graham because the pertinent facts are that within a couple years of Mr. Graham's investment, the sellers of the land initiated a lawsuit seeking to redeem the land. Unfortunately, history can never know how the case might have resulted because Mr. Graham died during the early stages of its pendency and he was therefore unable to prosecute his case.

It seems Ruffner was willing to blame Graham for having the temerity to unexpectedly die. When Graham died, he was in Richmond where he had gone

---

419 William Henry Ruffner's manuscript article,"*An Educated Negro Preacher of a Century Ago*" n.d. cite: William Henry Ruffner Papers, 1848–1907, Accession 24814, personal papers, collection, The Library of Virginia, Richmond, Virginia., p. 5. [no.88]

on business related to his land. He contracted pneumonia and died despite his otherwise seemingly robust state of health. It hardly seems justified to hold someone accountable for being rash or imprudent based on a case that had an uncertain outcome at the time of his death. Early setbacks and unforeseeable roadblocks were common to most successful American leaders in the eighteenth century, and Graham's numerous prior successes in the face of formidable challenges stand as hallmarks of this one man's ability to succeed where most others would likely have failed. Ruffner provided no persuasive justification for judging Graham to be either rash or imprudent. His judgment in this regard flies in the face of Graham's having been consistently selected to the highest leadership positions concerning the national Presbyterian Church and his colleagues in higher education. Moreover, he was undoubtedly the most sought-after minister in Virginia during the last quarter of the eighteenth century. He was offered the pastorship of three congregations east of the Blue Ridge Mountains and the presidency of Hampden Sydney College. He was also unquestionably the single most sought-after Presbyterian theologian by young men in Virginia who were contemplating the ministry. That's one of the reasons why Graham was selected by his clerical colleagues in the Virginia Synod to take the presidency of the Presbyterian Church's first patronized theological seminary in the country. Being consistently selected for such important leadership positions seems entirely inconsistent with Ruffner's unsupported contention that he was a sometimes "rash and imprudent man." Odd too that the men who enlisted in the militia from Rockbridge County selected their minister to lead them during the Revolutionary War.

Ruffner is the only author who published the unsubstantiated claim that Graham was possessed of an irascible temperament. In this, Ruffner stands alone without having bothered to explain upon what evidence he indicted his college's first president. To be sure, Graham's earliest biographers pointed out that Graham did not suffer fools lightly and he would as likely upbraid a community leader as he would any of his fellow farmers who openly strayed from the path of righteousness. His firmness and objectivity did not always sit well with individuals of wealth and position who sometimes expected deference in matters of public morality, especially as it related to public drunkenness. See Edward Graham's and Archibald Alexander's memoirs of President Graham listed in the report's bibliography.

Conclusion Concerning President Henry Ruffner

Ruffner made numerous mistakes in his "Early History of Washington College," but it should be remembered that he also provided the most in-depth version of such a history written by anyone during the nineteenth century. In so doing, he was severely handicapped by the dearth of readily obtainable official institutional records. Moreover, much of his "Early History . . ." took place during the lead up to and the culmination of nearly eight years of the Revolutionary War. Perhaps even more importantly, some of the letters and journals written during that period by individuals familiar with the valley of Virginia in the latter quarter of the eighteenth century would not be published until the late nineteenth or twentieth centuries. In addition, Rev. Archibald Alexander's unpublished "Memoir of Rev. William Graham," which is indispensable to gaining a full and complete understanding of many of the salient nuances embodied in the early affairs of Liberty Hall Academy and its first president, Rev. William Graham, has never been published. Ruffner probably did not have access to the invaluable original and complete unpublished manuscript of Alexander's "Memoir of William Graham." If anything, he had read James W. Alexander's exceedingly valuable but also seriously flawed biography of his father. James W. Alexander, as explained elsewhere, included some important improper editing of his father's memoir of William Graham, especially concerning the origins of Liberty Hall Academy.[420] In any event, Henry Ruffner obviously did not have access to Archibald Alexander's complete manuscript.

Ruffner's "Early History of Washington College" is a rich source of mostly reliable information about the college itself—its locations, campus buildings, instruction, trustee administrative actions, etc. Importantly, he also identified the college's establishment as having been the direct result of the actions of the Hanover Presbytery in the 1770s, and he does not, like Mr. Foote, assert that the school's origins are traceable to earlier peripatetic preparatory schools. He seriously fails, however, in respect to the initial operations of the presbytery's new seminary during its first two years of operation at Mount Pleasant (1775–1776), and seems to have been persuaded in later years that there may have been some link that existed between the college and the private Latin school of Rev. John Brown, albeit mistakenly.[421] Ruffner does not, however, go so far as to assert that Liberty Hall Academy's origin dates back further than the mid-1770s. In addition, Ruffner is often mistaken in regard to the college's first president and chief administrative officer, William Graham.

In regard to Ruffner's understanding of the character of Graham, he failed in many ways to properly assess the nature of the man who, more than any other, nurtured the infant seminary through its incipiency and then molded it into the institution of higher learning that its creators had dreamed of one day realizing. Such mistakes are difficult to understand given that Ruffner's wife's father and grandfather were both early trustees of the college. His comments about Graham lack the specificity and the citations of authority essential for one who did not know the subject of his characterizations. In order to understand the essence of Graham the man, history should only rely upon Graham's writings, eyewitness testimony, official records of his deeds, and written accounts left by those who

---

420　Fortunately, the auditor had obtained a photocopy of the original manuscript of Archibald's "Memoir of Rev. William Graham," which allowed for discovery of James's unfortunate manipulations of his father's words.

421　Ruffner did not actually assert a link between Rev. Brown's school and Liberty Hall, but he also did not challenge Mr. Foote's mistaken assertions in that regard as he ought to have done. Indeed, he thereby subtly lent some credence to the fiction by his reference to the school being "partly private," which, as has been explained elsewhere, it never was.

knew him. In that, history has but a few sources upon which to rely, namely the writings of Edward Graham, Archibald Alexander, Samuel L. Campbell, and Rev. William Hill, plus a few fragments from Graham's students in the college, and the official records of the Presbyterian Church and those of the college. Ruffner relied upon some of these, of course, but on occasion, he also relied upon gossip and hearsay testimony of unreliable persons.[422] It is also clear that Ruffner relied upon secondary source material including extracts from official records that had been extracted and abridged by others. Finally, there does exist some scattered letters that are extant which contain important references to Graham written by trustees of the college and colleagues of Graham's within the Presbyterian Church, most of which were not available to Ruffner, including the informative journal of Rev. Philip Vickers Fithian, a schoolmate of Graham's at Princeton who visited with Graham while on a missionary tour to the valley of Virginia in late 1775 and early 1776. This richly endowed journal of Mr. Fithian was not available for Ruffner's use because it was not published until 1934.

It would appear that Ruffner fell under the influence of some significant person(s) whose family(ies) despised Graham, and he seems to have accepted their animus-based characterizations that bear no resemblance to reality, or at least insofar as established facts would tend to indicate. Another factor that may have impacted Ruffner is a conflict that Crenshaw says existed between Ruffner and Graham's younger brother, Edward. Whatever the cause of this conflict, Ruffner, when he was president of the college, apparently went out of his way to force Edward off of the faculty. It is difficult to imagine how Ruffner's assessment of a man he never knew wouldn't have been somewhat colored by these factors. At the same time, Ruffner was married to the granddaughter of Samuel Lyle, who was one of Graham's longest and consistent supporters.[423] These varying factors quite likely played a hand in fostering in Ruffner a somewhat schizophrenic notion of the man that is clearly reflected in his many seemingly conflicting references to the man Graham.

Ruffner's every published criticism of Graham's character is demonstrably false and is not of a legitimate sort. His several attacks on Graham's character, in every case, have no basis in fact or credible evidence. His criticisms are easily disproved, as it is hoped the auditor has clearly demonstrated. It should be remembered that Ruffner did not know Graham, and most of his criticisms are based on secondhand information from unidentified sources. Ironically, at

---

422 A good example being Ruffner's reference to an anecdote that he had heard about from the aged Mr. William Patton. Ruffner, "Early History of Washington College," _W&L Historical Papers_, No.1, p. 59. Ruffner quotes this elderly gentleman, whose recollection is presented as a verbatim quotation of a comment made by Graham several decades before. In addition, Ruffner fails to mention that many members of the Patton family were bitter enemies of Graham. For Ruffner to repeat such prejudicial testimony as though it were a verbatim quote calls into question his own objectivity.

423 Alexander suggests that despite Samuel Lyle's support for the academy, he also indicates that Samuel Lyle felt that Graham ought to have stuck to his role as chief administrator and left politics to others.

least two of Ruffner' negative comments concerning Graham can be traced to the work of the man he forced off of the faculty, Edward Graham, the rector's younger brother, whom he cites as one of his basic sources of authority. Ruffner, however, took the liberty of embellishing Edward's mild and significantly qualified criticisms of his older brother and recast them as central characteristics of the man he never knew. In so doing, Ruffner severely diminished the usefulness of his early history by raising serious doubt as to his objectivity and reliability; an unfortunate reality because for all his mistakes, he also presents much valuable and accurate information. The difficult task with Ruffner is in the sorting of wheat from chaff.

Because Dr. Ruffner is so often referred to as Washington and Lee University's first true historian, it is essential to reemphasize that despite the fact that Dr. Ruffner provides the only nineteenth-century in-depth, research-based history of the college, and even though he clearly studied Mr. Foote's two volumes of Virginia history, he nevertheless did not adopt Foote's erroneous assertions that the college's origins are linked to either Robert Alexander's private school or Brown's private Latin school. He did, however, provide a cursory description of the events leading up to the Hanover Presbytery's appointment of Graham to manage their new seminary,[424] which unfortunately fails to clearly delineate the process. His description is misleading, and his language can easily be misinterpreted to mean that a school earlier taught by Ebenezer Smith was essentially the same school that Mr. Graham oversaw when he first arrived in Virginia. This reading would be importantly incorrect because the only schools[425] under Graham in Virginia were entirely new endeavors. In addition, the presbytery's new seminary in Augusta County operated contemporaneously with Brown's Latin school in 1775, as is evidenced by Fithian in his 1775–1776 journal. For this reason alone, it is obvious that the presbytery's seminary could not have evolved from Brown's school. More importantly perhaps is the fact that Brown opposed the new presbytery's decision to create the seminary and the personal rift between Brown's family and the seminary's superintendent. Mr. Graham was the proximate reason why Brown refused to participate in the affairs of the Augusta Academy (i.e., Liberty Hall Academy.) This fact explains why Brown refused to send any of his sons to the academy and encouraged his relations to follow his lead in that regard, and also why the school's earliest records demonstrate that Rev. Brown never attended a meeting of the board of trustees. See bibliography.

Note: The possible implication of Ruffner's confusing description of the origin that would link Brown's school to the presbytery's new academy at Mount Pleasant is an unfortunate one, if for no other reason than that the school taught by Mr. Ebenezer Smith was a private preparatory school organized and overseen by Brown. Graham's educational endeavor was a far more extensive project designed to pattern its curriculum after Princeton's. Smith was appointed by Brown in his private

---

424 This confusing description appears on page 17 of the edition of Ruffner's extensive article that appeared in volume one of the Washington and Lee University Historical Paper (see bibliography).

425 There were but two such schools, which were the presbytery's seminary in Augusta County (1774) and the Virginia Synod's-created Virginia Theological Seminary (1792).

capacity, while Graham was appointed by the Hanover Presbytery then representing the entire Presbyterian Church of the vast Commonwealth of Virginia, which stretched beyond the Appalachian Mountains all the way to the Ohio River. In addition, Brown's "Latin school," as he called it, had long before been moved from Mount Pleasant to his New Providence farm on Moffett's Creek several miles away. Brown's school, which was the one in which Smith taught,[426] was still in operation at New Providence in December of 1775, so the academy (college) being organized at Mount Pleasant could hardly have evolved from Brown's private Latin school at New Providence, Confusingly, Brown's school too had at one time operated at Mount Pleasant, albeit at an earlier date, and since Smith's teaching has not been dated, it is difficult today to determine where the school was located when he was teaching there. However, it was most likely at New Providence.

It is entirely possible that Ruffner simply straddled the fence on this thorny issue and wrote his account in a way that made for him the fewest enemies. He should have explained that all documentary evidence makes clear that the presbytery's school (seminary or academy) was created by the presbytery on October 13, 1774, and that there is no credible evidence to support any contrary narrative. That was the truth in the 1840s when Ruffner first wrote his article, and it remains the case today.

No person who was a participant in the creation of the presbytery's academy in Augusta County left any record that suggests a link between the school informally called "Augusta Academy" (later Liberty Hall Academy) and any other school. There has only been one person who attended the school in the eighteenth century who may have claimed otherwise,[427] and he was but a late teenage farm boy (Rev. Samuel Houston) at the time the school was created, so he had no firsthand institutional knowledge on the subject of the founding. He therefore based his one lone possible reference* on hearsay obtained from others, none of whom could have been a participant because the participants knew fully well that no such link existed . . . Moreover, neither Brown nor the college's first rector, Graham, ever suggested in their letters or other writings that such a link existed.

The first history of the founding of Washington and Lee University, however, was written by a participating member, Rev. Caleb Wallace, who was also the clerk of the organization that created the school. Wallace's account was drawn from all the pertinent meeting minutes of the institution that created the college, the Hanover Presbytery, and nowhere in that important history is there the slightest hint of a link between the new college and any other school. The history comprises the first several pages of the board of trustees' record book, which contains the trustees' meeting minutes. This book contains the college's first institutional records[428] after the presbytery created the board of trustees, and in

---

426 *The auditor was not able to discover whether Ebenezer Smith conducted classes at Brown's school when it was at Mount Pleasant or at its final location at New Providence, but that mystery is nonetheless irrelevant since in either location, the school had no connection to the presbytery's school under Graham.*

427 *The source for the claim is Rev. Houston's somewhat dubious letter, which Foote rendered of no real value through his serious mishandling* of the evidence as has been discussed at length elsewhere in this report.

428 *"Rev. Caleb Wallace, Memorandum History of Liberty Hall Academy," a handwritten document copied into the record book of the newly established board of trustees of Liberty Hall Academy,*

conjunction with that creation, also transferred most of the administrative rights and responsibilities to those trustees that accepted their appointment.

* *The legitimacy of this letter as represented by W. H. Foote in both of his books on Virginia is now open to question. See subsection on Foote.*

Having been the president of the college, it is inexplicable why Ruffner did not consult with his own institution's official early records, including its first authorized history written by the Hanover Presbytery's clerk, Caleb Wallace, which comprises the first several pages of the college's oldest primary record.[429] If by chance he did consult this vastly important record and concluded that it was unreliable, then he had a responsibility to point out in his history why he discounted it. Since he does not even mention it, it must be assumed that he was not even aware of its existence. It is puzzling that the president of the college would fail to be aware of its first authorized written history since he elected to compose for publication a comprehensive early history of the college.

Ruffner's errors of judgment in regard to Graham's character are more understandable insofar as he did not know Graham personally. Most of Ruffner's errors are simply due to careless research. For example, the Presbyterian Church's records quite clearly demonstrate that Graham was never censured by his church,[430] as was asserted by Ruffner, and from the records of the Virginia Synod, he could have learned that the synod's involvement in addressing the Whiskey Insurrection affair was not as he described it. As for the schism at New Providence, Graham's use of Watts's hymn during the service, which he conducted at the congregation's invitation, was authorized by the national general assembly's policies on this subject, and the supposed schism which transpired sometime after this communion service could hardly have resulted from his use of this hymn by the author of the renowned hymn, "Joy to the World." If it had, the disaffected would hardly punish their own pastor for the deeds of a visiting minister. As for Graham's supposed imprudence, Ruffner failed to cite any specific instance and also failed to explain why Mr. Graham was an "imprudent man" with an "irascible

---

in which are found the original meeting minutes of the board of trustees, and is housed at the Leyburn Library of Washington and Lee University, pp. 3–7, and signed, "Caleb Wallace, Clerk, May 1776." Here, Wallace was acting as clerk of the Hanover Presbytery. Rev. Caleb Wallace makes for a witness of the highest caliber for he is the only member of the Hanover Presbytery that created Liberty Hall Academy and the second seminary in Prince Edward County [later Hampden Sydney] who was subsequently appointed a trustee of both Liberty Hall Academy and Hampden Sydney Academy. Wallace afterward became a justice of Kentucky's highest court.

429   The important caveat to this being that it accepts the Hanover Presbytery's meeting minutes and the presbytery's authorized subscription documents, many of which are still extant and housed at the university's archives at the Leyburn Library.

430   It is true that a committee of the Philadelphia and New York Synod made the mistake of commenting on one piece of evidence in the complaint brought against Graham by Hezekiah Balch, which was by inference critical of its author (Rev. Graham), but the comment was procedurally inappropriate, and it was made by an inappropriate committee that had not yet heard from the defendant and prior to having received all the relevant evidence. While critical in nature, the comment did not in any sense constitute a censure.

temperament." Hampden Sydney College, in the last decade of Graham's life, repeatedly sent delegations to Lexington for the avowed purpose of persuading Graham to accept their offer of the presidency of that college, and further why the synod of Virginia selected Graham to head their newly established theological seminary, which at the time was the first such official Presbyterian theological seminary in the nation (i.e., patronized by the church.) Ruffner's mistake in ascribing these traits to Graham, thereby unjustifiably sullied his reputation. Ruffner's unsupported accounts on this subject were contrary to the commonly accepted reputation of the college's president.

Below, the auditor has provided numerous statements from highly credible authorities that demonstrate what was commonly said of Graham by people who either knew him personally or whose close family members knew him, mostly the former:

Note: Archibald Alexander's view of Samuel. L. Campbell vis-à-vis William Graham:

. . . Dr. Samuel L. Campbell of Rockbridge, who enjoyed opportunities of acquaintance with Mr. Graham equal to those enjoyed by any other man. The father of Dr. Campbell, Charles Campbell, Esq., was one of Mr. Graham's most intimate friends, who agreed with him in all his sentiments and at whose house he made his home when in the neighborhood. And Dr. Campbell was brought up under the tuition of Mr. Graham from his youth and was perfectly acquainted with all his excellencies and his foibles. He not only pursued his academical studies under the direction of Mr. G., but also studied theology under his guidance for several years . . . (A. Alexander, Mss. Memoir of William Graham, pp. 48, 49.)

With Alexander's explanation of Dr. Samuel Campbell's value as a witness, the report provides numerous assessments of Graham that contradict Ruffner's unsupported attacks on Graham's character.

1. "Mr. Graham came to this country with character of a gentleman of genius, scholarship, and piety, which character he supported through life." (Samuel L. Campbell, (MD) [i.e., "Senex"], "Washington College, Lexington, Virginia," *Southern Literary Messenger,* June 1838, pp. 107–108)

2. "Especially when the most enthusiastic patriot in all the county was William Graham."[431] (Dr. Henry Ruffner himself in "Early History of Washington College.")

3. "Mr. Graham preached in the house crowded to excess—and yet many could not

---

431 Henry Ruffner, "Early History of Washington College," *Washington and Lee University, Historical Papers,* No.1, 1890, p. 24.

get in. His text was, 'Comfort ye, comfort ye my people.' He began calmly but seriously; and as he preached on his discourse, his feeling as was usual with him, rose gradually until an awful solemnity was spread over the large congregation . . . The writer does[n't] remember ever before or since, to have seen a whole congregation more fully under an impression as tender as it was solemn; but reigned a breathless silence through the house, only interrupted occasionally by the sound [of] a suppressed sigh. Perhaps Mr. Graham never exceeded the sermon preached on this occasion. ***Dr. Smith said to the writer that take it altogether; it was the best sermon he ever heard.***"[432] (Archibald Alexander Mss. "Memoir of William Graham," pp. 206–216.) (Emphasis added.)

4. ". . . On October 22, 1788, Hall's congregation . . . once again called on Graham 'to take charge of them so long as he may continue in this place.' At the same meeting of presbytery, Lexington residents, who wanted to establish their own house of worship, also requested Graham's services." (I. Taylor Sanders, *Now Let The Gospel Trumpet Blow*, Lexington, Virginia; New Monmouth Presbyterian Church, 1986. p. 18.]

5. "And having undergone these trials with high approbation of the presbytery, he [W. Graham] was licensed to preach the Gospel at a meeting in Rockfish on the 20th of October, 1775. **It was soon perceived that he was a preacher of no ordinary kind. The clearness and depth of his reasoning, and the warmth of his applications, placed him in the estimation of judicious hearers, in the first class of pulpit orators.**" (Archibald Alexander Mss. Memoir of William Graham, p. 54, and in the article by Dr. Campbell.) (Emphasis added.)

---

432 This is no small praise, for Smith was raised among educated ministers, and at Princeton had the opportunity to hear some the country's finest preachers.

This emphasized statement was drawn from Edward Graham's memoir of his brother, William.

6. "Mr. Graham now resumed the business of the academy, over which he had heretofore watched with parental care and solicitude. He had led it cautiously and tenderly through many difficulties to a certain stage of its existence. ***Besides the labor of teaching, and governing, there devolved upon him the task of planning buildings; making contracts with the workmen; attending to the faithful execution of the contracts; the devising ways and means for fulfilling those engagements; and, in a word, all that was to be done for the academy fell chiefly on him . . .***

"During this long period he had, for the most part, performed all the duties in person, which in other public seminaries are confided to a faculty consisting of several professors. He not only gave instruction in the scientific and classical departments, but paid special attention to the grammar school. 'Here, said he, should be laid a substratum on which to build a superstructure of learning.'" (Dr. Samuel L. Campbell, "Washington College," *Southern Literary Messenger*, Vol. IV, Richmond, Thomas W. White, 1838, p. 364 (col. 1) and also reprinted in *W & L Hist. Papers* No. 1, 1890, p. 115.) (Emphasis added.)

7. ". . . the dignity of the preceptor; the industry, proficiency, and decorous demeanor of the students, soon gave eclat to the institution . . . the dignity of the preceptor, and his well-known fitness for the station, gave him respectability, and he was respected." (Samuel L. Campbell, (MD) [i.e., "Senex"], "Washington College, Lexington, Virginia," *Southern Literary Messenger*, June 1838, pp. 361–362.)

8. ". . . it was judged expedient to apply to the legislature for an act of incorporation, which was accordingly done, and the petition

of the trustees was granted and they were incorporated in October of 1782. Mr. Graham himself, no doubt, was the author of the act of incorporation; which contained one provision or privilege which I have never known to exist in the case of any other mere academy, in that or any other state. That was the power of conferring the usual degrees in the arts. The truth is, this act of incorporation made the institution a college in everything but the name." (A. Alexander, Mss. "Memoir of William Graham," pp. 92–93.)

9. "Mr. Graham is here—*sage, deep-studied Mr. Graham.* He is director of the small academy in this neighborhood. *He retains, with dignity, the inherent gravity which he always supported in every part of his conduct while he was a student at Nassau [Princeton]. The lines of method and discipline have been inscribed and are yet visible and legible upon his countenance!*" (Philip V. Fithian, *Journal* 1775–1776, p. 171.) (Emphasis added.)

10. "Mr. Graham's next step was to improve the singing in public worship. His efforts in this were crowned with success. The teacher he obtained, Mr. Lemus Chapin, for a few months gave great satisfaction and remained in the county a number of years, occupied in his profession. From whom all the knowledge of church music in Rockbridge and some of the neighboring counties for a number of years was derived." (W. H. Foote, *Sketches of Virginia,* . . . p. 464.)

11. "And as at that time every candidate before receiving license to preach was required to [acquire?] a diploma from some college, or submit to a public examination by a committee of the synod, the young men in Virginia who aspired to the ministry had to go to New Jersey College (Princeton), and there finish their education. Accordingly, Mr.

John Montgomery, Mr. Edward Crawford, Mr. Samuel Doak, and Mr. Archibald Scott went to Princeton soon after Mr. Graham was graduated, and in the year 1775, these with several others who entered the ministry took their first degree at Nassau Hall (Princeton); and then returned to the valley, where they pursued the study of theology under the direction of William Graham. **For although they were nearly of his own age, his reputation as a theologian had risen so high that they gladly availed themselves of his assistance in preparing for the same calling."**[433] (Archibald Alexander, Mss. "Memoir of William Graham," p. 95.)

Note: (?) means that the longhand script is seemingly indecipherable.

12. "After leaving the mountain, they fell down upon the James River near where it takes that name, that is, just below the junction of the Jackson and Cow Pasture rivers. Mr. Graham preached to these scattered people with a clearness which made all understand, and with an earnestness and affection which caused deep feeling." (James W. Alexander, _The Life of Archibald A . . ._ p. 87) (Note: James Alexander's comments are drawn from his father's memoir of Rev. Graham.)

13. "When the poor German had proceeded thus far, we had reached the place of meeting

---

433 Graham is listed as a graduate of the College of New Jersey (Princeton) in an 1827 catalog of alumni [mostly in Latin] for the year 1773, with a degree of AM. This designation, "AM" was given to those whose BA emphasized additional study in preparation for the ministry. The title of Edward Graham's memoir of his brother is, "Memoir of the Late Rev. William Graham, AM (_The Evangelical and Literary Magazine and Missionary Chronicle_, IV (1821), p. 75 et Seq.) Both of these early publications assign to Graham the AM degree. Only by this method could Graham have established such a high reputation in theology by the year 1775. We know that he also studied theology under Rev. John Roan in 1774, but by October, Graham had been appointed to manage the new school in Augusta, Virginia. He could not have established his theological reputation in less than one year in rural Dauphin County, Pennsylvania. To obtain such a high reputation would require his having been near Princeton and the numerous other students studying theology at the College of New Jersey under Dr. Witherspoon. It is also apparent that Graham received instruction under Samuel Finley, Witherspoon's predecessor at Princeton.

and found the house full. We were very solicitous that Mr. Graham might be led to choose a subject suited to the case of our German brother, for such we esteemed him. And it was so ordered that the text led him to open the way of salvation, and to describe the exercises of a soul when closing with Christ on the terms of the Gospel. That day, we heard more for the afflicted man than for ourselves. He never took his eyes off the preacher, and during the hour of the sermon they were full of tears." (James W Alexander, *The Life of Archibald A* . . . p. 89.)

14. "Mr. Graham of Lexington was present and preached on Saturday; and on Sabbath, *Mr. Graham preached in the forenoon, one of the greatest sermons I ever heard.* I sat under it with great delight, and its fruit was sweet to my taste." (Rev. William Hill, from his journal (i.e., Autobiographical Sketches) and published, in part, in Foote, Second Series, p. 185.) (Emphasis added.)

15. "For some time, he [Graham] devoted himself entirely to the work of the ministry, and preached not only within the bounds of his own congregation, but in the neighboring congregations; for the religious awakening, though more powerful in and around Lexington, extended to almost every congregation in the valley in a greater or lesser degree. He was in most instances sent for to assist at communion season; for the custom in all that country was to have public service during [???] when the Lord's Supper was administered: Even where the clergyman was not well affected towards him, the solicitude and impartiality of the people commonly prevailed to procure an invitation for him to attend. His preaching at this time [???] occasions, was very evangelical and very powerful. The writer is now of the opinion that he never heard from any man a clearer or stronger exhibition of the Gospel than in the sermons of Mr. Graham at this time . . ." (A. Alexander Mss. "Memoir of William Graham," pp. 215–216.)

16. "During the preparation for one of the public examinations [at Princeton], the late General Henry ['Light-Horse Harry'] Lee,[434] then a student, requested permission to review with Mr. Graham . . . assigning as a reason for this request that he knew Mr. Graham had been more studious than himself; *and he considered him better qualified than any of the class, to explain any difficulties that might occur in the course of the review.* At the examination, Lee distinguished himself. When it was over, he came into Mr. Graham's room and said, 'Well Graham, I have stood a glorious examination, and I know that I am indebted for it in great measure to you . . . '" (Edward Graham, "Memoir of . . ." pp. 150–151.)

17. "A theological class was now formed, whose reading he directed, and who attended at his study on one day in the week, where they read their compositions on prescribed subjects, and discussed subjects previously given out, he presiding and in the conclusion giving his own views of the matter discussed. By this kind of training, a number of young men, who afterwards were well known and esteemed in the church, were prepared. Though Mr. Graham had a scientific turn and delighted much in experimental philosophy, and yet the philosophy of the mind was his favorite study; and this he had long pursued, not by reading books written on the subject, but by paying close attention to the exercises of his own mind, and he had reduced his thoughts into a system, which he was fond of unfolding to his pupils, from which [?} contrasted a fondness for [??] department of philosophy, and [?] opinion that it was of great service to them in their theological studies." (A. Alexander, Mss. "Memoir of William Graham," pp. 220–222.)

---

434   This Henry Lee is the father of General Robert E. Lee.

18. "As a clear and cogent reasoner, he [W. Graham] had no superior among his contemporaries; and his preeminence in the exercise of this faculty was acknowledged by all unprejudiced persons." *(A. Alexander. Mss. "Memoir of Rev. William Graham," p. 134.)*

19. "A convention of Presbyterians was held at Bethel, August 10, 1785, and a final memorial drawn by Mr. Graham was adopted on the 13th. The legislature met October 17, 1785, and on December 17, Mr. Jefferson's bill to establish religious freedom became law."[435] (Joseph A. Waddell, *Annals of Augusta County, from 1726–1871,* C. R. Caldwell, 1901 [Original Edition, J. W. Randolph, 1888.] Caldwell as publisher may be second edition revised and enlarged, 1901. Auditor's copy is dated 1902, p. 304.)

20. "The extent of the influence exerted by this one man over the literature and religion of this region cannot be calculated. As the stream which fertilizes a large district is small in its origin, but goes on continually increasing until it becomes a mighty river; so the influence of Rev. Graham did not cease when he died but has gone on increasing, by means of his disciples who have been scattered far and wide over the west and the south." (A. Alexander, "Address Delivered Before . . . Alumni . . .," in *Hist. Papers of W & L,* p. 135.)

21. "Accordingly, I [A. Alexander] went to Mr. Graham with a request that he would direct my studies. He smiled and said, 'If you mean ever to be a theologian, you must come at it not by reading but by thinking.' He then ridiculed the way of taking our opinions upon

---

435   The president of Liberty Hall Academy, Graham led this movement, which was unexpectedly successful and is largely responsible for the passage of Jefferson's theretofore bogged-down bill. This statute became Madison's template for drafting the religious freedom section of America's Bill of Rights. Absent the interdiction of the Presbyterians led by Graham, it is likely that Henry's proposed tax to support churches would have passed and that, in turn, would have doomed Jefferson's bill for religious freedom because these two proposals were in direct conflict with one another. Moreover, without the passage of Jefferson's bill, it is questionable whether the religious freedom provision in the Bill of Rights would have been included.

the authority of men, and deciding questions by merely citing the judgments of this or that great theologian; repeating what he had just said, that I must learn to think for myself, and form my own opinions from the Bible. This conversation discouraged me more than if he had told me to read half dozens of folios. For as to learning anything by my own thoughts, I had no idea of its practicality. But **it did me more good than any directions or counsels I ever received**." (James W. Alexander, *The Life of Archibald Alexander* . . . pp. 82, 83.) (Emphasis added.)

22. "One important outcome of the patronage of the presbytery was the appointment of William Graham as the manager of the school. Graham led the institution for . . . twenty-two years and singlehandedly sustained it through the tumult of the Revolutionary War and [the concomitant] financial destitution, staving off its near collapse." (Royster Lyle Jr. and Sally Hemenway Simpson, Charlottesville, University Press of Virginia, 1977, p. 145.)

23. ". . . And he [W. Graham] being acquainted with many of the people [Franklinites] . . . **he [Graham] drew up the form of a constitution to be proposed to the convention**. This was entrusted to the care of the Rev. Mr. [Samuel] Houston . . . with directions how to proceed at the same time enjoining upon him the utmost secrecy. **By some means, however, it came to be known that W. Graham had taken upon him to prepare a constitution for Frankland**." (A. Alexander, Mss. "Memoir of William Graham," p. 163.) (hand-paginated in pencil by the auditor for reference purposes.) (Emphasis here does not indicate error.)

24. "Archibald Stuart and Thomas Lewis on the one side, and **William Graham, the Ajax Telamon of the Presbyterians of the valley**, are instances illustrative of the fact stated in the text." (Hugh Blair Grigsby, *The History of the Federal*

Convention of 1788, Two Vols., Richmond, Virginia Historical Society, 1890, pp. 22–23.)[436] (Emphasis added.)

25. "Under these two laws . . . Rockbridge was subject to the draft . . . Mr. Graham attended, and addressed the meeting in favour [sic] of filling up the required quota by volunteers. John Lyle, a captain of one of the militia companies, stepped forth . . . followed by a few . . . Mr. [Rev. W.] Graham stepped forth and joined the band; in a few moments, the required numbers were completed . . . **Mr. Graham was chosen captain.**" (W. H. Foote, Sketches of Virginia . . ., First Series, p. 451.) (Emphasis added.)

26. "Such was William Graham, cradled in the forests of extreme frontier civilization, exposed to the incursions of savages. He resolved to preach the Gospel, and without means, sustained himself and won the applause of Witherspoon and his classmates. **He was one of the great powers of his generation.**

Posterity bends with reverence at his grave and looks with interest at the moldering ruins of his infant seminary and traces careers of thousands, whose genius was kindled by his instruction, who cast the benignant light of letters and love around many a domestic hearth, whose sword flamed on the field of battle, whose eloquence was heard from the pulpit, the bar, and on the floor of assemblies, which decided the questions of the age and whose patriotism, waked into vigor by his voice and example, has been the pride and bulwark of their country. (Henry Boley,

---

436 Grigsby, Hugh Blair, The History of the Federal Convention of 1788, two volumes, Richmond, published by the Society, 1890. [pub. In collections of the Virginia Historical Society, new series, Vol. IX. Note: Vol. II is contained in the collections of the Virginia Historical Society, Vol. X., 1891] [The auditor's copy is a photocopy printed from Google digitized books.] This quote is drawn from Vol. II, p.11, pp. 22–23.

Lexington in Old Virginia, Richmond, Garrett and Massie, 1936, p. 46.) (Emphasis added.)

27. "Monday, July 25, 1791, I rode to Lexington, spent the day with Mr. Graham." (Rev. William Hill *Autobiographical sketches of Dr. William Hill: together with his account of the revival of religion in Prince Edward County, and biographical sketches of the life and character of the Reverend Dr. Moses Hoge of Virginia*, Richmond, 1968. p. 79.)

28. "Friday, July 29, 1791, *I rode to Lexington, spent the day enjoying the edifying conversation of the great and good man, Mr. Graham.*" (William Hill *Autobiographical sketches of Dr. William Hill:* . . . Richmond, 1968. p. 79.) (Emphasis added.)

It is also instructive to see what the twentieth-century scholar at Princeton and the University of California at Berkeley, Prof. Charles Grier Sellers, concluded in his study of the eighteenth-century struggle for religious liberty in Virginia as concerns Graham. Professor Sellers says:

Smith's defeat was a triumph for William Graham, who drafted the convention's[437] vehement denunciation of any legislation on religion . . . The final blow to assessment [taxes] was the loss of its strongest legislative champion through Patrick Henry's election as governor. It was . . . in July 1788 that Smith . . . withdrew from active supervision of the college [Hampden-Sydney] . . . With Smith out of the way, Patrick Henry undertook to get the state's grants to William and Mary divided with Hampden-Sydney, and Henry's crony and fellow opponent of the constitution, William Graham, was offered the Presidency.[438] (Emphasis added.) (Dr. Charles G. Sellers Jr. (Princeton), "John Blair Smith," *Journal of the Presbyterian Historical Society*, Vol. XXXIV, No. 4, December 1956, pp. 201–225.

---

437 He is referencing here the general convention of Virginia Presbyterians, led by Rev. Graham, who met in 1785 to repudiate the actions of the Hanover Presbytery that had recently moderated the church's long-standing opposition to taxing the people to support the church.

438 [Charles G. Sellers Jr., "John Blair Smith," Journal of The Presbyterian Historical Association, Vol. XXXIV, No. 4., Dec. 1956, pp. 201–225.)] esp. pp. 214, 217–18.

Finally, the auditor offers these words from the board of trustees of Liberty Hall Academy written in response to several entreaties by Patrick Henry and his associated trustees at Hampden Sydney College made in an attempt to purloin the services of Graham for their college and three local Presbyterian congregations seeking to have Graham become their pastor. Here are some of the sentiments expressed by Liberty Hall's trustees:

Petition to the Virginia Synod

> "Through the presbytery of Lexington, we are informed of the attempts of the board of trustees of the college of Hampden Sydney to deprive us of our rector, the Rev. W. Graham, in order to convince him to take the presidency of their college. We also are informed that the [issue?] of this event depends upon a decision of your reverend body. In our objecting to the removal of Mr. Graham, we would not in the least reflect on trustees of Hampden Sydney for attempting to obtain our rector from us, for we think him qualified for such a place and that they need such a gentleman. But this so far from leading us to freely give him up as they wish does considerably increase our desire to retain him over our academy . . .

> **"For it was under W. Graham that our academy first received its existence, and it is chiefly owing to his extraordinary exertions that it has persevered through all the convulsions of a calamitous war and the many vicissitudes, which have taken place through the operations of various causes for the space of about sixteen years**, and here we cannot forebear asking the question would it be wisdom or duty in synod to destroy our academy, which has been the most useful to the church of any in the state and which is at this time more promising to the church in point of numbers than ever it has been, and this too on the bare probability that another may or nearly so must be the consequence unless providence preserveth it if our rector be removed at this juncture . . . .

"For these and such reasons your petitioners earnestly pray that this reverend synod would not remove W. Graham from his present charge of the academy, and we hope and trust that you will see reasons to grant the prayer of your petitioners. And that the great head of the church may direct you in all things to seek and promote his glory as the object and prayer of the trustees of Liberty Hall." . . .

Samuel Lyle
Alex. Campbell
Wm. McKee
Wm. Alexander
James Ramsay
Jno. Wilson
Joseph Walker
John Lyle
Samuel Houston
Andrew Moore[439]

"Petition presented to

Andrew Moore*
the synod from the
board of trustees
Sept. 1792"

****

These numerous examples provided above are offered as a repudiation of Ruffner's view of the college's first president, Rev. William Graham. Most of the comments above were written by men who knew Mr. Graham. Ruffner's several negative characterizations of Graham do not square with the comments provided above. His stated beliefs in this regard are mostly asserted gratuitously and are either based on comments of others taken out of context, or they are based on Ruffner's faulty interpretations of official records (e.g., his faulty interpretation of the Whiskey Rebellion affair as described in William Henry Foote's *Sketches of Virginia* . . . Series One and Two). Ruffner claimed that Graham lost this struggle and was out of step with his brethren, when just the opposite was true. The same can be said about Ruffner's claim that Graham was censured by the Presbyterian Church. In truth, Graham was never censured by the Presbyterian Church.

It is eminently clear that someone had inordinately influenced Ruffner in regard to the college's first president, and as a result he did not accurately describe events that he had heard about from others concerning Graham. He even refused to accept that Graham authored the proposed constitution for the state of Frankland

---

439 Andew Moore's name was subsequently added.

based upon his analysis of an essay he assumed incorrectly had been written by Graham.[440] Ruffner's important source, Edward Graham's memoir of his brother, unfortunately did not include information about his brother's role in the Franklin affair, and he failed to consult with Archibald Alexander or Col. Arthur Campbell about the matter, either of whom would have been able to correct him.

Ruffner went so far as to accuse Graham of being sometimes rash and imprudent, but importantly, he provided no competent evidence of his being either. Ruffner's capstone traducement of his subject relates to Graham's purchase of a large tract of land at Point Pleasant on the banks of the Ohio River, where, according to Graham's younger brother, he intended to launch a settlement. Ruffner suggests that the plan was a disastrous failure, but his assessment is based upon the fact that Graham was engaged as a defendant in a lawsuit brought by the sellers of that tract who were attempting to recover that six-hundred-acre parcel. The outcome was still pending at the time of Graham's completely unexpected death while attending to business affairs in Richmond. To criticize Graham as a failure in the early stages of the planned development ignores the fact that most of Graham's grand designs that he carried out while in Lexington were viewed, in the early stages, by many of his contemporaries as likely failures, and yet in most every case, Graham succeeded in the end. At his death, he had created and nurtured a college in the virtually mountainous wilderness; had designed, financed, and overseen the construction of the college's four campus[441]; led the campaign to rebuild two Presbyterian churches; had established on behalf of the Virginia Synod the first Presbyterian Church-patronized theological seminary in the United States; led the unprecedented and successful campaign to overturn the actions of his Presbyterian brethren concerning religious freedom, and at the same time provided the impetus for passing Jefferson's Bill for Religious Freedom;

---

440   See Samuel Coles Williams, *History of the Lost State of Franklin*, New York, The Press of the Pioneers, 1933. [Contains valuable information pertaining to Rev. William Graham's participation in the plan to establish the state of Franklin. Graham is the author of the draft of the proposed constitution for the lost state of Frankland; and, Rev. William Graham, *Essay on Government*, Philadelphia (1786); and Joshua W. Caldwell, *Studies in the Constitutional History of Tennessee*, Cincinnati, Ohio, The Robert Clark Company, 1895.]

   Note: the above is housed at Leyburn Library, Washington and Lee University, Lexington, Virginia. This photocopy bears a note in longhand that asserts "Printed in Philadelphia 1786 . . . Wm. Graham Author." Note the that the printed title is merely "Essay &c." The article's beginning page is numbered 3, and it runs through to page 37, and at the conclusion says, in bolder and larger font, "A Citizen of Frankland." On a following page, there is a written note in longhand: "*This essay was written by the Rev. Wm Graham, who then lived in Franklin, now Tennessee. He would not call that territory Franklin as it was generally called but Frankland, for he never liked Dr. Franklin and there were no bounds to his prejudices.*" The notation is unsigned. It is incorrect in part because Graham never lived in the proposed state of Frankland/Franklin, but it may be true that he owned land there, purchased for him, at his request, by Rev. Samuel Houston, but evidence on that point is lacking.

441   If one were to count the academy's use of an unoccupied house in the earlier days at Graham's farm outside Lexington, then the number would increase by one to five campus'. This campus preceded the frame building built by Graham and local residents during the Revolutionary War, which later burned.

he was chosen by his brethren to chair a committee to oversee the missionary program instituted in conjunction with the creation of a theological seminary in Virginia; and he enrolled and oversaw the matriculation of the nation's first black college graduate in North America.[442] In addition, Graham enrolled into his regular academic program the nation's first female college student.[443] All these achievements were, at their inception, thought to be rash and imprudent. None are viewed as such today.

Perhaps Graham's many and varied attainments were the basis of Gov. Patrick Henry's decision to lead the campaign to persuade Graham and the Virginia Synod to allow Graham to accept Henry's proposal for Graham to accept the presidency of Hampden Sydney College, and the pastorate of three of Virginia's churches near the campus of Hampden-Sydney. An offer was made on successive occasions, but all of which Graham declined. It is also instructive that the board of trustees of Liberty Hall mounted a spirited campaign to keep their rector in Lexington, which campaign included a written appeal to the Virginia Synod designed to keep Graham in Lexington and at Liberty Hall Academy.

Graham's final accomplishment on behalf of the college was his successful advocacy on behalf of his fellow trustees to secure a prospective endowment from the president of the United States, Gen. George Washington. Prior to President Graham's resignation of his presidency of the college, he received word that his letter to President Washington was responded to in the affirmative, and Liberty Hall Academy thereby had become the recipient of the largest such endowment that had ever been received by any chartered college in the United States. The acknowledgment was received just prior to President Graham's retirement.

It is rather clear that Virginia, in the last quarter of the eighteenth century, had the good fortune of having had, in particular, the services of two graduates of Princeton who were schoolmates under the illustrious Dr. John Witherspoon, namely, William Graham and James Madison. These two Princeton men were perhaps most responsible for the passage of Thomas Jefferson's Bill for Religious Freedom, which was the template from which the religious liberty provision of the First Amendment of the nation's Bill of Rights was designed. Their mutual friend, Patrick Henry, would certainly not agree with Dr. Ruffner's careless treatment of his illustrious predecessor, Rev. William Graham. Ironically, President Graham had, on occasion, been an active opponent of both President Washington and Patrick Henry. Gen. Washington, a Federalist, supported ratification of the proposed new United States Constitution, while Graham was a well-known anti-Federalist who opposed the Constitution as originally written, which, at the time, did not include a Bill of Rights. Patrick Henry, on the other hand, was the author of the proposed bill to tax the people of Virginia in support of the church, while Graham led the campaign which brought about its defeat. Nevertheless, and despite their past differences, Graham obtained the favor of President Washington

---

442   Mr. John Chavis, whose matriculation was memorialized by the Rockbridge County Court.

443   Sarah (McBride) Priestley was a student who interacted at the college on numerous occasions with Archibald Alexander.

in securing the college's endowment, and Patrick Henry became Mr. Graham's friend and, as a trustee of Hampden Sydney College, sought to purloin the services of Graham from Liberty Hall for the benefit of his own college and three local Presbyterian congregations.

Ruffner should have known his subject better if he was determined to the sully Rev. William Graham's reputation as he did. It is safe to say that Ruffner's "Early History of Washington College" contains many significant errors of fact concerning the college's first president. Those seeking specific information about Pres. William Graham would be well advised to look someplace other than Ruffner's valuable, but certainly flawed history of Washington College. Those who wrote about Graham and who knew him well include Dr. Samuel L. Campbell, Rev. Dr. Archibald Alexander, and Prof. Edward Graham Esq. Their applicable works are referenced in the attached bibliography.

7. REV. ROBERT DAVIDSON [1847]
(History of the Presbyterian Church in the State of Kentucky, **with a Preliminary Sketch of the Churches in the Valley of Virginia**, New York: Robert Carter, 1847.) (Emphasis added.)

Intro:

Davidson's important history includes what appears to be the first published treatment of the churches in the Valley of Virginia during the eighteenth and early nineteenth centuries. It is also important because of its account of some aspects of the early history of Liberty Hall Academy (Washington College, Virginia) and its first president and founder, Rev. William Graham. Davidson, however, made several important errors in regard to the college's founding and concerning Graham himself.

Davidson's five serious errors are:

> 1. Davidson was confused about distinguishing differences between the Hanover Presbytery's patronized academy (college) in its infancy at Mount Pleasant and the Rev. Brown's private Latin school at Mount Pleasant, several miles from Mount Pleasant. (He failed to comprehend that at the very same time these two schools were independently being conducted at different locations by different men, which renders it impossible that either grew out of the other, or that they had ever merged.[444])

---

444 Confusingly, Brown's private Latin school had in earlier times been located at the same general location where the Hanover Presbytery's academy was housed during the school's initial two years, at which time the academy's prospective buildings were being constructed. It is understandable why some of the residents in the academy's neighborhood might have assumed that these two schools were one and the same, especially if no one in their family was attending either school and/or if they were reflecting back on much earlier days. Also adding to the confusion is the fact that just as the presbytery's academy at Mount Pleasant was settling in and taking form, Samuel Doak informed Rev. Brown that he had agreed to accept a substitute position at the Prince Edward Academy (Hampden-Sydney) under Samuel S. Smith. This was in late December of 1775, and the Revolution was becoming a foregone conclusion. As a

2. Davidson incorrectly publishes an erroneous sequence of establishment as regards Liberty Hall Academy and Hampden-Sydney Academy, incorrectly placing Hampden-Sydney before Liberty Hall.

3. Davidson errs by falsely asserting that Mr. Robert Alexander possessed certain academic credentials when there is no good reason or known evidence to support this gratuitous claim or any claim that he was formally educated. Dr. Crenshaw while researching for his book *General Lee's College*, investigated similar claims on this subject and proclaimed that Robert Alexander did not attend either of the college's referenced by the individuals who published such claims.

4. Davidson errs by adopting and repeating a false notion about President Graham concerning his views on the value of books and reading. Davidson misconstrued the memoirs of Rev. William Graham written by Edward Graham and Archibald Alexander. Their comments in this regard were mostly only applicable to the study of theology. They did not apply to literature, natural philosophy (the hard sciences), mathematics including geometry, or to government, history, surveying or law.

5. Davidson also follows the error made by Rev. William Hill, wherein Hill mistakenly includes a visit to Rev. John Brown's private school at New Providence in April of 1775 in a paragraph listing the presbytery's actions leading up to its establishment and early activities of the academy.[445] This mistake leaves the false impression that Brown's school and the presbytery's seminary were one and the same. If Davidson actually believed this to be true, he was terribly mistaken. They existed at the time in two different locations under two very different men; Brown's private Latin school at New Providence and the presbytery's seminary (Augusta Academy) at Mount Pleasant

---

result, Rev. Brown was apparently unable to secure a replacement for Doak, and he therefore temporarily suspended his Latin school at New Providence. Presumably, any of the students who had been attending classes at Brown's school considered applying to Mr. Graham, whose school at Mount Pleasant was preparing students for entry into the academy once its campus buildings were complete. This could easily appeared to some as Brown's school merging with Graham's operation at Mount Pleasant. If so, they would have been mistaken. A student transferring is not an effective merging. To be sure, Brown attempted to reopen his school at New Providence in 1783 as his extant correspondence proves beyond a shadow of a doubt

Had a merger occurred, as some have speculated, the presbytery's minutes would undoubtedly have referenced such a significant occurrence, but of course they do not.

445   Rev. William Hill, "History of Washington College, Virginia," *American Historical Quarterly,* Vol. X, [1838], pp. 145–150.

under William Graham. (See the subsection in this report
devoted to Hill for an assessment of the confusing paragraph
on this subject.) It is quite likely that Davidson followed Hill in
this regard because prior to Hill's article, no other publication
known to the auditor had ever intimated such a notion.

*Note: The inclusion of a reference to Brown's school in the paragraph mentioned above mimics the
mistake made originally by Hill that misinterprets the presbytery's April 1775 "visit" to Rev. Brown's
private school unfortunately mentioned in their meeting minutes.[446] The presbytery's clerk should
not have included a reference in the presbytery's meeting minutes because it was a mere social
call with no official business implications. This unfortunate reference was the first and thankfully
last reference to Brown's private school ever made in the organization's meeting minutes. Almost
needless to say, this "visit" did not have any policy implications and, therefore, the presbytery took
no action and made no decisions related to the "visit." The exasperating effect of the clerk's mistake
was to create confusion in the minds of later researchers, who understandably assumed that since the
minutes included a reference to Brown's school in the same meeting minutes wherein the presbytery's
seminary's affairs played such a prominent part, that the referenced "visit" must necessarily mean to
refer to the school the members bothered to visit. Of course, it did not refer to the seminary at Mount
Pleasant but rather to the school located but a few yards from where the meeting had just taken
place, which was at New Providence. To visit Augusta Academy, the members would have all had to
travel several miles out of their way. Moreover, the minutes would not have referred to the school
as "the school under the direction of Mr. Brown." Indeed, the following year (1776), the presbytery
did attend and examined its school and its students under Rev. Graham, but then, understandably,
they held their meeting at Timber Ridge, which was so much closer than if they had once again met
at Mr. Brown's home at New Providence.*

For all of Davidson's errors, it is, nevertheless, important to note that nowhere
does he actually claim that Brown was an administrator of Liberty Hall Academy.
On the subject of the presbytery's school's early history, Davidson notes that he
relied heavily upon letters from Edward Graham, Graham's younger brother who
was raised by Graham from early adolescence. He also relied upon correspondence
from Rev. John Lyle who had been a student under Graham at Liberty Hall. Had
either Edward Graham or John Lyle informed Davidson that Liberty Hall's origin
predated the actions of the Hanover Presbytery in 1774, then it is highly unlikely
that Davidson would have failed to mention it because he relied so heavily upon
them concerning the early history of the college.

ERROR no. 1 Davidson clearly errs at page 41 of his own account by saying that
the presbytery "twice attended the examinations," referring therein to what he
called "the school," and thereby indicating his confusion about the two different
schools in the neighborhood of New Providence and Timber Ridge churches.

---

446 *The reference to the members of the presbytery visiting Rev. Brown's school after the April
1775 was a monumental administrative error because the "visit" was not the organization's
business. The "visit" was purely social, but by referencing it, any reader would very likely
conclude that this activity was official when in reality the members merely accepted their host's
invitation to stop in at his school next door for a few minutes. Because the presbytery had no
connection to Mr. Brown's school, the clerk who prepared the minutes should not have included
this reference. The clerk, however, was a longtime acquaintance of Brown's, and he may have
noted the "visit" at Brown's request.*

Davidson's mistaken claim in this regard is as follows:

> In 1776, the presbytery, who had shown much interest in the
> school and had **twice attended the examinations**, made the
> appointment [Graham's] permanent, and as Mr. Graham had
> now taken charge of Timber Ridge congregation in connection
> with Hall's Meeting House, the academy was transferred
> thither, and suitable buildings provided." (Robert Davidson, _History_
> _of The Presbyterian Church in The State of Kentucky; with a preliminary_
> _Sketch of the Churches in the Valley of Virginia_, New York, Robert Carter,
> 1847 . . . p. 41) (Here, bold italics indicate error.)

Davidson here is obviously following William Hill, who clearly had misinterpreted the presbytery's unfortunate and confusing meeting minutes for the April 1775 meeting of the Hanover Presbytery already discussed above.

The Hanover Presbytery's meeting minutes for 1775 and 1776 demonstrate that the presbytery only "visited" their new seminary (Augusta Academy) once during the academy's incipiency, not "twice" as Davidson suggests. Davidson, like Hill before him, mistakenly assumed that the presbytery's unofficial "visit" to Brown's school at New Providence in April of 1775 was also a "visit" to their new seminary, but it was not. One thing that may have confused these gentlemen was the fact that both of the spring meetings (1775 and 1776) were initially convened at Timber Ridge. However, the 1775 meeting was moved after the first day, and the subsequent days of that spring meeting were held several miles away from Timber Ridge, at New Providence. While there, the members met at Brown's home, while his private "Latin school" was conducted next door. This school, being private, had no connection to the Hanover Presbytery, but the presbytery did accept their host's invitation to unofficially "visit" it. As previously stated, the clerk made a serious mistake by mentioning the unofficial "visit" in their minutes.

It is easily discernable how Davidson's mistake concerning the unwise reference to the presbytery's "visit" to Brown's school[447] may have contributed to Foote's identical error in associating the school at New Providence with the presbytery's new seminary "Augusta Academy" initially located at Mount Pleasant. Foote after all had probably consulted both Hill's "History of Washington College, Virginia" and Davidson's history of Kentucky, which also included a special treatment of the churches in the Valley of Virginia that included a consideration of the founding of Liberty Hall Academy (i.e., Washington College).

An important point to remember is that the Hanover Presbytery made no recorded "visit" to their patronized seminary in Augusta County at any time in 1775, and that there were two separate schools in the neighborhood of New Providence and Timber Ridge churches in 1775 and 1776, and importantly, these

---

447 Davidson in turn may very well have read Rev. Hill's 1838 article, "The History of Washington College, Virginia" _American Historical Quarterly_, Vol. X, (1838), pp. 145–150. [Authorship attributed to Rev. William Hill. See bibliography.] Hill does not make a direct assertion linking the schools, but his chronological organization of one paragraph in particular implies it.

schools had no link or connection to one another. This fact is made abundantly clear by reviewing the actual meeting minutes of the Hanover Presbytery covering the years 1775 and 1776, and also by reviewing the personal journal of Rev. Philip Vickers Fithian written in 1775 and 1776 when he was visiting the Valley of Virginia and frequently lodging with Brown, and also interacting with his old Princeton schoolmate, Graham. Both of these sources make it abundantly clear that these were two entirely separate and distinctly different educational endeavors having no link between them. Moreover, Rev. Archibald Alexander's unpublished "Memoir of Rev. William Graham" explains why Brown refused to participate in the affairs of the presbytery's new academy under Graham. The explanation, as it relates to Brown's attitude toward all things related to Liberty Hall Academy, is inferential, but nevertheless, patently obvious.

(Note: Graham had broken off his engagement to Brown's daughter, which brought about a breach in the relationship between Graham and Brown's family. The breach between Brown and Graham does not seem to have seriously affected their ability to conduct their pastoral duties with all professional decorum. Beyond that, it would serve no useful purpose to say anything more about the matter other than that the broken engagement left both the prospective bride and groom brokenhearted. What is significant about this rupture in their earlier happy relationship is that it goes a long way toward explaining why Brown, contrary to modern representations, was never connected to the presbytery's seminary, Liberty Hall Academy, and why he sent his own sons elsewhere for their higher education.)

ERROR no. 2 Davidson erred regarding the sequence of establishment of Liberty Hall and Hampden-Sydney. Davidson, following Edward Graham's earlier error on this point, mistakenly claims that Liberty Hall was established following the establishment of Hampden-Sydney.

Davidson errs by falsely representing that Hampden-Sydney Academy was established prior to the Hanover Presbytery's establishment of Liberty Hall Academy. The correct sequence is just the opposite. This fact is discussed in detail in the subsection devoted to Edward Graham and also in an appendix devoted to this subject.

Davidson's error in this regard can be seen in his discussion on page 40 of his history, where he says:

> "A single seminary being deemed inadequate to the growing wants of so extensive a country, ***another was opened under the patronage of Hanover Presbytery in what is now Rockbridge County*** . . ." [Robert Davidson, *Hist. of the Presb. Church..Ky* . . ., p. 40.] [Bold italics are added here to indicate error.]

The above statement is patently incorrect. The seminary established by the Hanover Presbytery in Rockbridge County was the first seminary ever established and patronized by the Presbyterian Church in Virginia. It was established on October 13, 1774 (see Hanover Presbytery meeting minutes). The presbytery subsequently (1775) established another seminary east of the Blue Ridge

Mountains that is currently conducted under the name Hampden-Sydney College. Its creation took place, in effect, on February 1 of the next year, 1775.[448] This report has already set forth its explication of the nature and source of this error in the earlier entry devoted to Edward Graham, above. Rather than repeat the explication and argumentation here, the auditor refers the reader to the Edward Graham subsection above that addresses the sequence of establishment error in some detail. The correct sequence is: Augusta Academy was established by the Hanover Presbytery on October 13, 1774, and the second seminary was established by the presbytery on February 1, 1775. These two indisputable facts are set forth in the Hanover Presbytery meeting minutes.

Note: The correct sequence of establishment is not a matter in dispute today notwithstanding Prof. John L. Brinkley's erroneous discussion in his book, "On This Hill,"[449] first at page 7 and secondly, on pages 308–309 and his related footnote number 63.

ERROR no. 3 Davidson misrepresents the educational credentials of Robert Alexander.

Davidson wrongly asserts that Alexander, who conducted a school of an unknown type in Augusta County in the neighborhood of Timber Ridge and New Providence Presbyterian churches, was a known graduate of a specific college. Referring to Robert Alexander, he says:

> "[Robert Alexander] *was a graduate of Dublin University* and a good classical scholar. He taught the first *Latin School* west of the Blue Ridge . . ." (Davidson, *History of the Presbyterian Church in Kentucky . . .* p. 20.)

Davidson, like numerous others, mistakenly assumed that Robert Alexander was a formally trained scholar, but Dr. Ollinger Crenshaw debunks this general claim about Alexander having attended a European university, the most often-cited place of his education. He reports his findings in his "Appendix A: The

---

448   The Presbyterian Church investigated the expediency of establishing a patronized college (seminary) in Virginia on a par with the College of New Jersey for three years, and then decided in favor of establishing one such college and establishing it west of the Blue Ridge Mountains. Once it was established, it took under consideration the expediency of establishing a second college east of the mountains. Afterward, a special meeting was called (pro re nata) on February 1, 1775, at which the members appointed Samuel S. Smith to superintend the college they had in mind, forgetting, however, to officially decide to "establish" it. See presbytery minutes.

449   John Luster Brinkley, *On This Hill: A Narrative History of Hampden-Sydney College, 1774–1994,* Hampden-Sydney, 1994. (Note: The section entitled "A Stiff Upper Lip," and especially the erroneous footnote no. 63, the essence of which is incorrect. The school did not, as Brinkley suggests, begin in December of 1775, but rather it began in January of 1776. [This is not a matter of insignificance to the early history of Washington and Lee. Brinkley here mistakes a promise with a fact. Smith was unable to keep this promise. This too is not open for debate. The records are perfectly clear that classes did not begin at Hampden-Sydney until January of 1776. In this case at least, Brinkley relied on secondary sources instead of more reliable "primary sources."

Problem of The Origins."[450] Crenshaw refers to one of several references to various issues of the _Catalogue of the Alumni of Washington and Lee University_, Lexington, Virginia, 1749–1788, and an article included therein, "Historical Sketch" [of Washington and Lee University]. In reference to the sketch, he notes that it "follows closely the pattern of succession as set forth by Bolivar Christian in 1869." Crenshaw cites in this regard the "Catalogue of 1888," and thereafter says, "The Catalogue of 1897 repeats earlier categorical statements . . ." Later, Crenshaw says:

> This little article declares, contradicting an earlier assertion that Robert Alexander had been educated with the MA degree from Trinity College, Dublin, that he had attended the University of Edinburgh. The cautious historian, Joseph A. Waddell, merely has it that Alexander had been educated in Edinburgh, **and the truth is that he attended neither university** . . . Inquiry at the University of Edinburgh (E. Staples to writer, August 6, 1946) and at the University at Dublin (Denis Devlin to writer, June 11, 1946) reveals no evidence that Robert Alexander had attended either institution."
>
> (Crenshaw, _General Lee's College_, typescript version Vol. II, Appendix A, "The Problem of the Origins," pp. 8–9.) [Paginated in pencil by the auditor for entire Vol. II as p. 531.] (Emphasis added.)

Note: The auditor was not able to locate any cited authority referred to by any author who claimed that Robert Alexander was formally educated at a chartered or otherwise recognized college. All such claims were offered gratuitously. With that fact, and Crenshaw's research in mind, there appears to be no good reason to conclude that Robert Alexander was formally educated. Like his brother Archibald ("Ersbel"), they were obviously given ample instruction by a local European clerical scholar, but his identity is unknown.

Embellishments like Davidson's concerning Robert Alexander begin at some point to build on themselves, until truth becomes so tangled up in fancy that larger false narratives predictably overcome more plain and simple facts. What history knows about the educational activities of Robert Alexander and his brother Archibald is very little and more general than specific with but a few exceptions, none of which shed any meaningful light on the subject. To be sure, both brothers aided local residents by providing some measure of elementary education, but there is scant evidence that has surfaced as to the specific nature of their educational contributions. If anything, there is more information in that

---

450 Ollinger Crenshaw, _General Lee's College._ Typescript, unpublished version in two volumes with Appendix A, "The Problem of The Origins." (Page 524 of the entire typescript, but Appendix A is also paginated separately as pages 1–13.)

regard to Archibald ("Ersbel") Alexander's efforts as they relate to Samuel Lyle's youth, as described by Trustee Lyle to the younger Rev. Archibald Alexander, who then included some of these anecdotes in his unpublished "Memoir of Rev. William Graham."

Importantly, there is no known eighteenth-century evidence of a link between any school and Liberty Hall Academy, which was an entirely new endeavor initiated by the Hanover Presbytery.[451] This fact is made quite clear by reading the presbytery's meeting minutes between 1771 and 1775. The creation was the culmination of a lengthy and prudent process designed to ensure that there was both a desire and a willingness of the various congregations to support such a monumental endeavor to be carried out in nearly wilderness territory. That the endeavor was successful is a testament to the prudence of conducting that investigating process.

Note: As previously pointed out, Liberty Hall Academy was initially referred to as Augusta Academy by clerks of the Hanover Presbytery when they were writing out their meeting minutes in order to distinguish between their two seminaries. As a convention, they referred to the new schools as the Augusta Academy and the Prince Edward Academy respectively, but these denominations were unofficial because the presbytery itself had not officially decided on these names or any other names. The presbytery had apparently decided informally not to name the schools, reserving that honor for the future boards of trustees that they intended to create once it was clear that their new schools were likely to succeed. Therefore, some later authors failed to appreciate that Augusta Academy was the same entity as Liberty Hall Academy. There was a difference, but the difference was in its functionality. As Augusta Academy, it was the grammar school component according to Graham served as the academic foundation of the college. It was patterned after the structure of Princeton when Graham, as a student himself, was its principal overseer under the college's president, Witherspoon. At the conclusion of 1776, the college's new buildings were completed at Timber Ridge, and the grammar school and the college began operations at the Timber Ridge campus. The grammar school, however, was simply phase one of Graham's design of the college. The grammar school remained an integral component of the college from its inception through Graham's entire twenty-two-year tenure at the college.

ERROR no. 4: Davidson mistakenly follows Edward Graham's misguided assertion in reference to William Graham, that he was "not a great reader: perhaps he did not read enough."

Note: Although the statement is quite vague in substance, it leaves an entirely unjustified and obviously false impression.

---

451 The temporary instruction at Mount Pleasant is no exception because this school operating in the form of a grammar school was an integral aspect of the presbytery's new seminary, which was referred to informally as Augusta Academy, and which was transferred from Mount Pleasant to Timber Ridge after the campus buildings were completed. The grammar school facet of Liberty Hall was patterned after the similar operations at Princeton when Graham was a student there. Simultaneously, Graham served as the Princeton's grammar school Tutor and as an undergraduate student. So he knew exactly how important a function the grammar school element could be to a college. Hence, his decision to construct the same foundation in Virginia as that upon which Princeton's superstructure was built. This important feature was one understood by Dr. Samuel L. Campbell, who explained it in his 1838 history of the college. See bibliography.

Rev. Davidson followed Archibald Alexander's and Edward Graham's misconstruction of William Graham's views about books and reading. Both Edward Graham and Archibald Alexander provide inconsistent claims in this regard. Both failed to explain that they were only discussing Graham's views on books and reading in the narrow context of Christian theology. Graham emphasized reliance on the scriptures and on each individual contemplating the scriptures rather than relying on the views of religious writers. Davidson says:

> **Mr. Graham was not in the habit of wielding the pen _or of reading many books_**; but he was **a nervous** and independent thinker. (Davidson, _Hist. . . . Ky._ p. 46.) (Bold italics here represent error.)

Davidson's notion about books and reading is preposterous in its implications, but Davidson's source for saying this is clearly Edward Graham, his subject's younger brother, who did hint at this in his published memoir of his older brother. Edward's misguided attempt to appear objective has led many to conclude that Rev. William Graham read little, when in fact the record demonstrates otherwise. What Edward was obviously referring to was his older brother's views about current writers on theology, which he mostly found of little use outside of their table of contents, which served as suggestions for his contemplation. Edward's comment in this regard is exceedingly vague and terribly misleading. His brother William was clearly capable of teaching college-level courses in virtually every subject area one then found in American colleges or universities; a virtual impossibility for someone who was not widely read in classical literature, mathematics, natural philosophy (sciences), and basic jurisprudence and government. That William was an extraordinary theologian was widely accepted. Moreover, the militia unit formed in the Rockbridge area during the Revolution selected William to serve as its captain by popular vote, which suggests that he possessed a sound understanding of topography. How then could such a man not be well-read? It is doubtful if any man living west of the Blue Ridge Mountains in the Valley of Virginia during that last quarter of the eighteenth century was more widely read than the president of Liberty Hall Academy and president of the Lexington Theological Seminary. The Hanover Presbytery appointed him to head their college, while the Virginia Presbyterian Synod appointed him as president of its patronized theological seminary. Of course, Samuel Stanhope Smith, who served in Virginia briefly as president of Hampden-Sydney, and Graham possessed similar academic attainments. Smith's knowledge of medicine, however, undoubtedly exceeded Graham's. Similarly, the two presidents of William and Mary in Graham's time, Rev. John Camm and Bishop James Madison, were both eminent scholars trained in Europe, but then both of them and Samuel Smith were not living west of the Blue Ridge Mountains. The same can be said as pertains to several men of great education then living in Tidewater in Virginia, including Graham's schoolmate, James Madison, and Madison's colleague, Thomas Jefferson. Jefferson, of course, exceeded them all in the field of law. As for reading books, it seems nonsensical to suggest that any one of the men herein listed was more widely read than any of the others. Graham's only critic in this regard was his younger brother, Edward, who was in no position to make such a judgment about his far more accomplished brother, William.

Davidson's likely source was Edward Graham's "Memoir of the Late Rev. William Graham A.M.," as well as his letters to Davidson. Edward said this:

> "*He was not a great reader: perhaps he did not read enough.* Books he said were of little use to him, except they served as indexes to direct his mind to subjects to think upon, and, as to many of them, he thought reading over the table of contents, at the beginning of a book, answered this purpose as well as reading the book regularly through." (Edward Graham, "Memoir of the Late Rev. William Graham A.M.," p. 410) (Emphasis added.)

Note: This comment by Graham's younger brother is rather absurd. Graham taught natural philosophy (i.e., science), mathematics, moral philosophy, and Greek and Latin grammar and literature, and he was the most noted theologian of long-standing in Virginia in the eighteenth century. Such accomplishments would not be easily obtained by someone who was never much of a reader. In addition, Graham had read enough of the great literature on politics that he could publish his own article on government and create a proposed state constitution that was imbued with the ideas of John Locke and Jean-Jacques Rousseau. This comment by Edward Graham is rather inexplicable. It is true that William Graham's numerous professional responsibilities in his later years left him with little leisure time for reading current literature, but by that time he had fairly well mastered virtually all the great classics of Western literature. Edward Graham's views in this regard undoubtedly reflect his honest opinion, but in light of the known facts of Graham's life, the opinion appears to be rather irrational. Perhaps the fact that he lived with his brother after his life at Princeton when his energies were devoted more to his roles as college president, professor, and pastor of various congregations, as well as a farmer providing the necessities of life for his extended family and those poorer students whom he took into his home fed and educated at his own expense, left him little time for casual reading of current popular literature. He was, however, quite familiar with the major academic treatises of his time, a point made abundantly clear by Edward's brother-in-law, Archibald Alexander, who as president of Princeton Theological Seminary was clearly more widely read than Edward Graham.

Here is a comment from Graham's most scholarly student at Liberty Hall Academy, which helps to clarify Rev. William Graham's literary attainments obtained by reading:

> Mr. Graham possessed a mind formed for profound and accurate investigation. He (W. Graham) **had studied the Greek and Latin classics with great care,** and relished the beauties of these exquisite compositions. **With the authors taught in the school** [Princeton], *he was familiar by long practice in teaching, and always insisted on the importance of classical literature as the proper basis of a liberal education* . . . *The science, however, which engaged his thoughts more than all others except theology, was the philosophy of the mind. Though acquainted with the best treatises which had then been published, he carried on his investigations **not so much***

by books, as by patient and repeated analysis of the various processes of thought as those arose in his own mind, and by reducing the phenomena thus observed to a regular system. The speaker is of the opinion that the system of mental philosophy which he thus formed was in clearness and fullness superior to any which had been given to the public in the numerous works recently published on this subject. (Archibald Alexander, in his Address to the Alumni Association of Washington College, 1843, limited edition pamphlet; also quoted in Alexander, James W. [*The Life of Archibald Alexander, DD,* New York, Charles Scribner, 1854, pp. 17–19.] (Note: The quote is Archibald Alexander's.) Also reprinted in *W&L Hist Papers* no. 2, p. 132.) (Emphasis added.)

Taking Alexander at his word, it may be instructive then to consider what books were being studied at Princeton in Graham's time as well as the only real textbook used at Liberty Hall in the eighteenth century, which were the transcribed lectures of Rev. John Witherspoon. In order to master John Witherspoon's lectures on moral philosophy, the student, and especially Witherspoon's tutors, had to familiarize themselves with the works upon which these lectures were based including those listed in Witherspoon's list of authors attached to the lectures. These included: *"Leibniz, his Théodicée, and his letters . . . Hutcheson's An Inquiry into the Original of Our Ideas of Beauty and Virtue . . . Wollaston's The Religion of Nature Delineated, Collins on human God-given rights to life and liberty, Nettleton on virtue and happiness, David Hume's essays, Lord Kaimes's essays, Smith's Theory of Moral Sentiments, Balfour's delineation of morality, Butler's Analogy and Sermons, Balguy's tracts, Beatty on truth, essay on virtue and harmony . . . In politics and government, Grotius, Puffendorf, Cumberland, Selden, Burlamaqui, Hobbes, Machiavel, Harrington, Locke, Sydney . . . Montesquieu's "Spirit of the Laws," Ferguson's history of civil society, Lord Kaimes's political essays, etc."* [See Broderick, Francis L., *Pulpit, Physics* . . . footnote no. 68, pp. 65–66.]

Edward Graham on this point seems a bit inconsistent when he explains that:

> The study of human nature, in a philosophical point of view, was one to which his thoughts had been frequently turned ever since he left college. While there, he was very much delighted with the study of natural philosophy. He saw that the Newtonian plan of philosophizing must be right; and the certainty which in this way had been attained was highly gratifying to his mind." (Edward Graham, Memoir of . . . p. 398.)

This, together with the fact that Graham was selected by President Witherspoon to present an address at his commencement in 1773 on the question,

"Is matter infinitely divisible," is a clear indication that Graham was widely read in Newtonian physics. His mastery of Latin and Greek grammar and literature had to have been recognized by President Witherspoon in order for him to have been hired by Witherspoon to teach the Princeton grammar school while at the same time matriculating with the undergraduate class of 1773. Indeed, Graham was so thoroughly read in all the subjects taught in the senior class at Princeton that Witherspoon excused him from attending classes during his senior year. Nevertheless, his classmate, Henry Lee (later Gen. Light-horse Harry) implored with Graham to allow him to study with him for the seniors' final examination, which Graham reluctantly did. Lee, according to Edward Graham, later attributed his success in passing his examination, in large measure, to Graham's assistance.

Quite obviously, Graham was so well and widely read in his youth that he spent his later years on other matters of greater importance to himself: his congregations, his family, and his country. Of course, Graham's mastery of theology was such that, in the last quarter of the eighteenth century, he was the most sought-after instructor of theology in Virginia by those who had decided to seek the Presbyterian ministry; a fact memorialized by his colleagues (the Virginia Synod) who selected him to serve as the founding first president of the Lexington Theological Seminary, which, at the time, was the only Presbyterian-patronized seminary in the country. One other, in Pennsylvania, had been decided upon, but it had failed to come to fruition for many years. Eventually, the other seminary was conducted by Rev. John McMillan in Pennsylvania.

Having mastered the great books of the Western world of his time, it would hardly seem appropriate to question Graham's devotion to the written word. After all, he rode on horseback from the Blue Ridge Mountains to Philadelphia during the first year of the Revolutionary War in order to purchase three hundred books for his new college's library.

It is also worth noting that Dr. Alexander, who was the most widely published Presbyterian scholar of his age as well as the president of the Princeton Theological Seminary, provided a much clearer and more accurate portrayal of the literary attainments of Rev. William Graham than that presented by Graham's younger brother Edward. As a source on this subject, few were in a better situation to evaluate Graham's grasp of the great books than Archibald Alexander, who was long under Rev. Graham's tutelage. He also boarded in Mr. Graham's home during most of the same time that Edward Graham was living with his older brother. We suggest that Edward heard from Alexander and others about his brother's comments to his theological students in preparation for the ministry when he said that they must come to that subject not by reading books, but by thinking in light of the Scriptures. Edward apparently assumed the comment carried more meaning than it did.

Conclusion of the assessment of Rev. Robert Davidson's historical treatment of the churches of the Valley of Virginia included in his book, "History of the Presbyterian Church in the State of Kentucky: With a Preliminary Sketch of the Churches in the Valley of Virginia":

In sum, if Davidson hadn't made his unfortunate allusion to the irrelevant "visit" to Brown's Latin school at New Providence or referred to Edward Graham's mistaken idea about the sequence of establishment between Washington and Lee and Hampden-Sydney, he would have presented a fairly accurate history of the churches in the Valley of Virginia during the eighteenth century as well as the way in which Washington College came to be established. Fortunately, Rev. Davidson did not make the mistake of claiming that Liberty Hall Academy was in any way connected to either Robert Alexander or Rev. John Brown's schools. He did mistakenly imply, however, that Washington College was somehow linked to an earlier school by virtue of his misguided reference to the presbytery's unconnected and nearly irrelevant "visit" to Brown's school.

Davidson's history was published in 1847, and then two years later (1849), Washington College published its first authorized institutional history. Neither of these two histories represents the founding of Washington College, Virginia, to have been earlier than October 13, 1774, and neither asserts a link between Liberty Hall Academy (then Washington College) and any earlier preparatory school in the valley.

8. WILLIAM HENRY FOOTE (1850 and 1855)

(William Henry Foote, DD, *Sketches of Virginia, Historical and Biographical*, Philadelphia, J. B. Lippincott & Co., 1850 First Series, John Knox Press reprint edition 1966, with index; *Sketches of Virginia, Historical and Biographical*, Philadelphia: J. B. Lippincott & Co., 1856 (originally published in 1855). Second Series,* Second Edition revised.)

No single person bears more responsibility for the destruction of Washington and Lee University's true early history than the chronicler William Henry Foote. Long viewed as a highly significant and important contributor to the eighteenth-century history of Virginia, Foote will undoubtedly be reevaluated in light of the revelations embodied in this audit report. From this time forward, his two Virginia history books cannot legitimately be cited as unquestioned authority without independent verification from other sources, at least not until or unless someone can explain and justify Foote's apparent deception in quoting from a letter on two different occasions and, in so doing, representing that the letter says one thing in 1850 and something very different five years later.

Described below is the shocking revelation that Foote inconceivably misrepresented the contents of a seemingly important letter concerning the founding of Washington and Lee University. Foote's gross malfeasance was inadvertently realized when the auditor was editing what was assumed to be the same extract from a letter reprinted once again in his second volume of Virginia history, "*Sketches of Virginia, Historical and Biographical*," Series Two, 1856. If the original letter or a true photocopy of the alleged letter was readily available, it could be compared with Mr. Foote's two versions of the same letter, but it appears that the original letter has been lost. Nevertheless, there cannot be two accurate yet different versions of the exact same letter. This matter is discussed in detail below, and both variants are presented for easy comparison. Unless someone can find a seemingly comprehensible and justifiable explanation for how an author can quote from a letter at one point in time and then several years later quote the exact same sentence but contend that it says something entirely different, without notice or explanation, then the author's veracity must necessarily be called into question.

To be sure, on the subject of the founding of Washington and Lee University, Foote is seriously mistaken. Of course, mistakes are common to all historians on occasion, but to knowingly alter someone else's work in order to have it fit more nicely with one's own narrative is beyond the pale. Still, the auditor has chosen to continue to cite Mr. Foote where there exist sufficient supplemental authorities and well-established supporting authorities to confirm that his reprints may be assumed to reasonably accurate. Attempts have been made to avoid drawing broad conclusions, however, wherever Foote is the lone source and the implications of his claims are inconsistent with other well-established counternarratives.

The Houston letter incident calls to mind Foote's presumptuous declaration in the introduction to Volume One of his "*Sketches of Virginia, Historical and Biographical*" wherein he asserts, in effect, that he could not be bothered to resort to citing his authorities or to including footnotes in his work. The discovery of the exceedingly problematic Houston letter serves as a cogent reminder of why Foote's fellow historians adopted citations of authority in the first instance.[452] As any adult reader can see, the differences in the two versions of the same so-called Houston letter are not simply typographical errors. In one particular case, Foote actually removes from the previously reprinted letter's text a name of someone who had earlier been listed as a student.[453] Presumably, Foote did this because he had discovered that the named student had actually been an instructor, not a student. By extricating the named student, Foote corrects the letter writer's gross error, which, if reprinted as it originally existed, would have served to undermine the letter writer's credibility. By correcting the error, Foote enhances the writer's reliability, and that in turn served to better justify Foote's abandonment of the

---

452   This is Foote's shocking explanation of what he did in regard to citations of authority and why he did it: "To a great extent, and generally as far as practicable or useful, the important facts are given in the words of the original writer or author of the tradition, that the reader may make his own construction. By this means, numerous footnotes are avoided, the searching out authorities for verification less necessary, and the liability to misconstruction greatly lessened." (William Henry Foote, DD, *Sketches of Virginia, Historical and Biographical*, First Series, Philadelphia, J. B. Lippincott & Co., 1850, p. 4, John Knox Press reprint edition, 1966.) It is true that in Foote's methodology, footnotes were "avoided," but otherwise, he could hardly have been more mistaken. In fact, Foote frequently intersperses his own words with those of his numerous contributors, usually using quotation marks to distinguish between his words and others, but in some important cases, he does so confusingly.

453   The name Ebenezer Smith was part of the list of students ostensibly attending the academy in Augusta. This Mr. Smith, however, was not a student at any school in Virginia. Ebenezer Smith attended his father Robert's academy in Pennsylvania prior to entering Princeton. Ebenezer Smith served for a time as a tutor in Brown's private Latin school. To have mistakenly claimed that he was a student when he was actually the tutor leads any reasonably skeptical historian to conclude that the author was actually providing hearsay information rather than information that he had obtained from firsthand knowledge or from official records of any school or its sponsoring entity. Foote's motive for surreptitiously correcting his lone source in regard to his novel narrative about the school's founding is patently transparent.

traditional historical narrative that the college was founded in 1774. To correct the error without noting what he had done, and why he did it, is both dishonest and unprofessional.

Note: The auditor makes the above assertion somewhat reservedly because of Foote's long-standing reputation among historians, but the conclusion was presented to several others and in no case was there any dispute as to the aptness of the assertion based on the relevant facts.

Foote's potentially valuable collection of rare manuscripts may have served to preserve for posterity materials that otherwise would likely have been lost to history. For most of the last 160 some odd years, Foote's reprints of these documents have been assumed to have been accurate reproductions, but with the issuance of this report, that assumption must be swept aside. As will be explained in this subsection of the report, Foote seriously undermines his credibility by committing an obvious and inexcusable perjury in the form of at least one and possibly three forgeries of an alleged letter supposedly written by Rev. Samuel Houston. A series of seemingly insurmountable difficulties exists for those who might attempt to determine which version, if any, is accurate. One such difficulty is that none of the more than seventy author's works that were reviewed by the auditor contains a reference to the original letter's whereabouts. Without the original, a researcher is not able to determine which version is the one that contains the true sentiments of the supposed author. Interestingly, no early author who wrote about the college's origins, and no early nineteenth-century institutional record of the Hanover Presbytery or of the college, makes any reference to such a letter until after the publication of Foote's two books on Virginia.

The historical damage that accrues to Foote's reputation as a result of this discovery of malfeasance, if not wholesale fraud, is immense, because he is one of, if not the most cited historical sources by those who have written about the history of the Valley of Virginia or about the Presbyterians in Virginia during this period. Any of these authors' works that were based in whole or in part upon the representations of Mr. Foote will hereafter need to be reviewed, and determinations made as to whether the material provided by Foote can be independently verified. If not, the material must be considered to be a possible fraud. Of course, many of the oft cited materials were fragile and later lost, leaving only the word of Mr. Foote as to whether the content of many old documents is accurate. Once a witness in a court proceeding has clearly perjured themselves, courts usually will advise jurors sitting in judgment of the case that they may legitimately assume that all of that witness's testimony is unreliable. Of course, the matter being dealt with here is not a court case, but the underlying principles are precisely the same.

In the past, the seemingly obvious value of Foote's preservation and reprinting of so many rare and fragile documents probably gave to Foote's numerous editorial additions, subtractions, and interpretations, far more credibility than was deserved. The result was that, Foote's numerous errors are of great significance concerning the origins of Washington and Lee University because most of these errors have unfortunately been accepted as gospel by virtually all mid-nineteenth-century historians and thereafter. These misguided historians were, in turn, accepted without reservation by later twentieth-century historians of the Valley of Virginia and, in no small part, because they had relied on the historically "gifted" Mr. Foote.

It is not the purpose of this historical performance audit to posit a hypothesis as to what led Mr. Foote astray on the subject of the early history and founding of Washington and Lee. That subject is ought to be carried out by history scholars. We will, however, note that by all outward appearances, Mr. Foote appears to have eschewed wide reading of many of the then-extant original documentary records as well as the existing published articles that dealt directly with the subject of the early history of the college. If that is true, it would certainly account for how he became misled by information he gleaned from sources that he usually refused to identify. A methodology, he amazingly admitted to using in the introduction to his first book on the history of Virginia published in 1850. Had later historians paid closer attention to Mr. Foote's open admission of his rejection of the standard historical methodology of citation of authority, they might have avoided the predictable embarrassment which, frankly, is justly applied to most of the historians who addressed the eighteenth-century history of Washington and Lee University and who published between 1850 and today, 2015. Most recent historians rely, at least to some degree, on Foote's "*Sketches of Virginia, Historical and Biographical*." Today, however, no one should rely on anything Mr. Foote says about Washington and Lee's origins without having obtained independent verification from pre-Foote sources, if possible. Even then, they could be led astray concerning the sequence of establishment between Washington College (VA) and Hampden-Sydney College.

Note: Washington College was established before Hampden-Sydney College. This is an incontrovertible fact easily demonstrated by examining the pertinent meeting minutes of the Hanover Presbytery between 1771–1777, which is discussed in several other places in this report.

The auditor offers one additional comment about Mr. Foote's two books on the history of Virginia in hopes of explaining why Foote's errors are so very important to understanding how and why the early history of Washington and Lee University has become so embarrassingly wrong. The dust jacket for a twentieth-century reprint edition of Mr. Foote's "*Sketches of Virginia, Historical and Biographical*" includes the following comment from the preeminent Presbyterian historian, Ernest Trice Thompson,[454] then professor emeritus at Union Theological Seminary:

> "This is the most valuable book we have dealing with early Presbyterianism in Virginia, valuable **not only because of Dr. Foote's gifts as a historian**, but because he quotes from so many sources, and with access to others no longer available." (Ernest

---

454   Ernest Trice Thompson, *Presbyterians in the South*, three volumes, Vol. One: 1607–1861, Richmond, The John Knox Press, 1963, p. 629.

Trice Thompson, author, *Presbyterians in the South*)
(Emphasis added.)

Thompson made a serious mistake in regard to Foote as a historian. At the time Thompson rendered this opinion of Foote, it did appear that he was correct. Once this report becomes public, however, it will no longer be acceptable to consider Foote's books to be the "most valuable we have on early Presbyterianism in Virginia," because every representation Foote makes therein will need to be seriously vetted for accuracy.

An important nineteenth-century historian does not refuse to cite his authorities because it takes too much time and effort. Moreover, a historian with bona fides does not edit substance and content of earlier authorities prior to reprinting quotes from that authority, and in so doing reshape the authorities' views so as to better conform to the would-be historian's assertions. Mr. Foote, as has already been shown, did exactly that. Thompson's bona fides, however, are a given, even though he too made mistakes concerning Washington and Lee University. Thompson's errors in this regard were most likely made by his having followed the frequently misguided Mr. Foote.

Note: Thompson is one of the authors who were originally assessed for this report, but the auditor has reserved his comments on Thompson and numerous others for a possible subsequent volume. Thompson's errors are the result of his unfortunate reliance on Foote.

Here, from "Dr. Foote's" introduction to his first volume, is his shocking admission:

> "To a great extent, and as far as practicable or useful, the important facts are given in the words of the original writer or author of the tradition, that the reader may make his own construction. **By this means, numerous footnotes are avoided, the searching out authorities for verification less necessary, and the liability to misconstruction greatly lessened.**" [455] (William Henry Foote, 1850)

Here above, Mr. Foote preposterously provides the personification of the non sequitur. His admission underscores just how important it is to read an author's introduction and preface. Mr. Foote has admirably provided a warning as much as an explanation; the warning being that whatever appears in his text should be taken with a proverbial grain of salt. However, what is of equal importance is what he does not inform his readers, which is that he sometimes edits substance without bothering to note what he has done, and he also, at times, inserts inaccurate prepositional commentary that substantively alters the apparent meaning of the quoted extract that follows. Specifically, he did this in a way that altered the

---

455 Foote, William Henry, DD, *Sketches of Virginia, Historical and Biographical*, Philadelphia, J. B. Lippincott & Co., 1850. First Series, John Knox Press reprint edition 1966, with index on page 4 of the introduction.

accurate history of the founding of Washington and Lee University. In American jurisprudence, what he has done is referred to in some important circles as "a failure to reveal material facts in light of positive representations." This concept refers to unfair and deceptive acts and practices. *For example, a Nebraska seller of goods or services says, "This product is of the highest quality and will last a lifetime," but fails to point out that it is illegal to use the product in Nebraska.* What Foote did was to fail to disclose that he had provided extracts from the works of others within quotation marks, but which he had made gratuitous alterations to that effectively altered the original author's intent. His edits, in this regard, were not mere typographical errors but were substantive alterations that turned facts into fictions posing as facts. Note: The auditor's findings are exceedingly important and equally disappointing. Nevertheless, nothing was found to suggest any intentional misrepresentations. Foote's motivations, whatever they may have been, are beyond the scope of this investigation.

Foote's errs concerning all of the following:

1. The founding of Washington and Lee University.
2. Rev. John Brown's Latin school, its location, and its nonexistent relationship to the Hanover Presbytery.
3. The two different unconnected eighteenth-century schools in the "neighborhood" of Timber Ridge and New Providence Presbyterian Churches.
4. The presbytery's two different types of visits to two different schools in 1775 and 1776. One, unofficial visit to Brown's school at New Providence, and the other, an official visit to the presbytery's own seminary (Augusta Academy) at Mount Pleasant.
5. Incorrectly assigning the presbytery's "patronage" to Rev. J. Brown's private, Latin school, which never occurred.
6. The so-called New Providence Watts's hymns-based schism.
7. The Virginia Synod's involvement in the so-called Whiskey Rebellion (i.e., Graham vs. Hoge dispute.[456])
8. An allegation that William Graham was censured by the Presbyterian Church. *(He was not.)*
9. The vastly important role played by Graham in Virginia's struggle for religious liberty.
10. The relatively insignificant role played by Rev. John Blair Smith in Virginia's struggle for religious liberty.

---

456 This error assigned to Foote is particularly complicated because he provides more than one account. Parts of these two accounts are correct, and parts are not. Foote deviates from his typical methodology concerning one account, which he explains is based on a submission by John B. Hoge, the son of Rev. Moses Hoge. Hoge's submission, in turn, was ostensibly based on manuscripts left by his father in his own possession. This account is reasonably consistent with Hoge's biography of his father written circa 1823. (See bibliography.)

Note: Foote collected materials from a vast array of sources, which he then published by cutting and pasting extracts that he may or may not have identified with specificity. This multitude of varying accounts appear in different sections of his books, often in unidentified quotations, providing thereby a virtual grab bag of conflicting material from which later authors could select and attribute to him. He also extracted material from obscure sources without necessarily even bothering to place the material within quotation marks, leaving the false impression that Foote was responsible for much that he was not. Foote himself obviously had access to large portions of Archibald Alexander's unpublished mss "Memoir of Rev. William Graham," which he often draws from verbatim but without attribution. While we can also say that much of the accurate history about Washington and Lee and its first president, William Graham, is also included in Foote's two books, the difficulty lies in selecting only the accurate accounts and discarding the inaccuracies. A good example is found in the extracts taken from the meeting minutes of the Hanover Presbytery pertaining to the founding of Liberty Hall Academy. These extracts taken by themselves are accurate, but then at times he feebly and inaccurately describes the contents of these extracts. Some of these resulted in his mistaken formulation of links between Rev. John Brown's Latin school at New Providence and the presbytery's seminary (Augusta Academy/Liberty Hall) at Mount Pleasant, which did not and could not exist. Unfortunately for Washington and Lee's accurate history, most, if not all, post-1850 historians relied upon the chaff and discarded the wheat, resulting in one historian after another attempting in vain to explain these supposed links that never were. These vain attempts, in some cases, border on being comical. The auditor will now explain the nature of the more significant inaccuracies provided by Foote concerning the early history of W&L.

Note: *FOOTE'S UNDOING*

The following material, presented as "ERROR no. 1-A," was written based on a revelation that only materialized very late in the auditor's review and analysis, and was nearly overlooked. By its very nature, this seeming anomaly cannot be attributed to a typographical error, a memory lapse, or to an administrative slipup, because this gross forgery required that someone create text that did not otherwise exist, and superimpose that text into what had been represented as the contents of a letter supposedly written by Rev. Samuel Houston; a letter that rather conveniently does not appear to be extant, and which apparently was never actually examined by any of the authors who published treatments of the founding of Washington and Lee or about the college's first president (rector), Rev. William Graham. That is not to question the fact that Rev. Houston wrote a letter to Rev. Morrison of the New Providence Presbyterian Church, but rather that the precise content of that letter is open to serious question because no copy is known to exist.

ERROR no. 1 Foote misrepresented the content of what he referred to as a letter written by Rev. Samuel Houston, and in so doing, he attempted to create a more credible source of authority than was justified. His actions were presumably taken to enhance the credibility of the only source, upon which he appears to have relied in support of his false narrative of the events that supposedly led up to the founding of Washington and Lee University. His action in this regard appears to have been knowingly calculated to justify his complete repudiation of the college's history as it had then (1849) been consistently represented by the college's founders, the Hanover Presbytery, and its guardians, the board of trustees, during the institution's then entire existence of seventy-five years.

Note: It would be exceedingly difficult to construct a credible explanation that would be in any degree plausible and that could be perceived by a rational mature adult as an innocent and inadvertent mistake.

In order to explain his discombobulation, it seems necessary to provide the pertinent extracts taken from both of the editions of Foote's "*Sketches of Virginia, Historical and biographical*" that appeared first in 1850 and then in a second series in 1855. These two books under the same main title are each unique volumes, but both contain representations of what the so-called Houston letter contained. In order for the reader to realize the full import of the forgery presented by Mr. Foote, the following extracts are presented for comparison. The mischaracterizations of what Mr. Houston's alleged letter contained are of such a nature that it could hardly be labeled as a mere mistake, as will be seen below:

William Henry Foote, in his *Sketches of Virginia* . . . Series no. 1, 1850, said this:

> "The Rev. Samuel Houston in his letter to Rev. James Morrison tells us—
>
> ". . . that shortly before the war, some men whose sons were growing up, felt a desire for having them or part of them educated liberally, chiefly with a view to the ministry of the Gospel. Accordingly, a small grammar school was formed in the neighborhood of Old Providence, composed of Samuel Doak, John Montgomery, Archibald Alexander James Houston, William Tate, Samuel Greenlee, William Wilson, Ebenezer Smith, and some others, which greatly increased and drew youths from distant neighborhoods. This grammar school was moved to the place near Fairfield called Mount Pleasant, *about which time the presbytery of Hanover patronized it*."[457] (Foote, *Sketches of Virginia* . . . series 1, pp. 442–443) (Emphasis added.)

---

457   Houston, if he actually wrote what Foote claims, has mixed apples and oranges. All of the men the author named as students of the presbytery's seminary, in truth, attended a school other than Augusta Academy. There was no school at Mount Pleasant at the time that the presbytery created its new seminary (Augusta Academy), and the presbytery did not "fix" the location for its initial operations. (Although it did preliminarily "fix" a site in Staunton, which was later abandoned before the school was even established.) The actual initial placement decision was made by the new seminary's "manager," William Graham, in cooperation with local residents living within the bounds of the Timber Ridge congregation. The new seminary's temporary headquarters was located on the farm of Mr. James Wilson, on a spot that local residents called Mount Pleasant. Here, some years earlier, Brown had organized a "Latin school" while pastor of Timber Ridge Congregation. When Brown moved and relinquished his pastorate of Timber Ridge (circa 1767), he moved his school to his new residence on Moffett's Creek several miles from Mount Pleasant. The school referenced by Houston was conducted from that time forward at New Providence, not at Mount Pleasant. Most importantly, the private school attended by those men Houston names was not patronized by the Hanover Presbytery, nor was it ever moved to Timber Ridge. Those named by Houston, attended, if at all, Rev. Brown's Latin school, not Augusta Academy. One of those named, Ebenezer Smith, was an instructor, not a student; a fact that suggests that Houston's knowledge of that school's history was based more on community

Foote, in his *Sketches of Virginia* . . . Series no. 2, 1855, quotes below from the same letter and same paragraph, but now informs his readers quite differently that Houston's letter said this:

> "That shortly before the war, some men, whose sons were growing up, felt a desire for having them, or part of them, educated liberally, chiefly with a view to the ministry of the Gospel. Accordingly, a small grammar school was formed in the neighborhood of Old Providence, composed of Samuel Doak, John Montgomery, Archibald Alexander, James Houston, William Tate, Samuel Greenlee, William Wilson, and others, which greatly increased and drew youths from distant neighborhoods. This grammar school was moved to the place near Fairfield called Mount Pleasant; *it was, in 1776, established at Timber Ridge meeting house and named Liberty Hall.*

"Sincerely Yours,
"S. Houston."

(Foote, *Sketches of Virginia* . . . series 2, p. 60) (Emphasis added.)

These alleged statements, ostensibly written by Houston, are demonstrably inconsistent quotations, and either one version or the other *(or both)* is therefore necessarily incorrect. In addition, both conclusions to this paragraph are factually incorrect. The school to which the author refers in the first quotation was not then or ever patronized by the Hanover Presbytery, and the school referred to in the second paragraph's conclusion was not established at Timber Ridge in 1776.[458] Foote further fails to inform his readers of the discrepancy, let alone explain it. His rather obvious two misrepresentations both contradicted seventy-five years of well-established documentary and mostly published history of the origins of Washington and Lee University (then Washington College, Virginia). This is an astounding reality, and yet in some ways predictable because Foote, as pointed out earlier, did not feel obliged to provide any authority to support his claims and assertions concerning the establishment of Washington and Lee. Of course, the result of his having adopted this ridiculous notion is that latter historians had no easy way to validate these claims. Historians foolishly took him at his word, but his word was incontrovertibly false. In at least one instance, Foote reprints what

---

hearsay than documentary evidence or firsthand knowledge. Houston was an early student of Liberty Hall, but he was not a student under Graham at Mount Pleasant. He was an earlier preparatory student at the Latin school. After completing his preparatory studies, he returned to the family farm, and shortly thereafter, he served in the militia, which activities he recorded in a journal or diary. His account of this expedition into North Carolina has been preserved. See Diehl's biography of Rev. Samuel Houston. After Houston's stint in the militia, he returned to the family farm and thereafter enrolled in the first class of students gathered together at the new campus buildings located on Timber Ridge. Again, see Diehl's biography of Houston listed in the bibliography.

458   It was established by the Hanover Presbytery on October 13, 1774 at its meeting held at the Cub Creek Meeting House in Charlotte County, as its meeting minutes clearly demonstrate.

he represents to be a letter written by Houston incorrectly, the manner in which he presents these excerpts dictates that at least in one case, he did so falsely and either deceitfully or incompetently. What Foote and possibly Houston failed to appreciate is the clear fact that the school that Mr. Doak, Mr. Montgomery, and any other named students attended, whatever it may have been, was not the same school that the presbytery created in 1774, which was only located at Mount Pleasant in 1775 and 1776.

The school in the valley that Doak and Montgomery had attended was most likely Brown's Latin school. But it must be remembered that Brown's school had, at an earlier time (late 1760s), been moved from Mount Pleasant to New Providence. This move happened long before Graham came to Virginia to launch the presbytery's patronized new seminary. It is a mere coincidence that Rev. Brown's school and the presbytery's seminary had, at one time, both been located for a time at Mount Pleasant, but one school was located there prior to 1770 and the other after 1774. The presbytery's seminary was only located at Mount Pleasant temporarily in part of 1775 and 1776 while the campus was being built.

From this day forward, all aspects of Foote's two books on Virginia will require independent verification in order for readers to have any confidence in them. This fact will become abundantly clear as this report details how his narrative is often at odds with incontrovertible facts concerning serious and important matters.

Below are various assessments of Foote's two books on Virginia as they concern the early history of the college.

ERROR no. 2: Foote falsely assigns to Graham, the institution's first president, a subservient role under the "supervision" or "direction" of Rev. John Brown.

Here is what Mr. Foote said in that regard:

> "The Presbytery having, in 1771, taken up the subject of education, and in 1772, having deferred action, and in 1773, having *located it in Staunton,* and in 1774, having determined to locate the school in another place, *appointed Rev. William Graham the tutor under supervision of Mr. John Brown* of New Providence, *and directed the seminary to be carried on near Fairfield, where Brown had been conducting a classical school.*" (Foote, W. H., *Sketches of Virginia, Historical and Biographical,* Series One, p. 393.) (Here, the bold and italics emphases were added to indicate error.)

Foote made a colossal mistake by misinterpreting the meeting minutes of the Hanover Presbytery as they relate to the years 1775 and 1776. During these two years, the presbytery had occasion to refer to two different schools then located in the same neighborhood of the Timber Ridge and the New Providence Presbyterian Churches. Unfortunately, Foote mistakenly assumed that the two different events, occurring in two different years and at two entirely different locations, involved only one school, which is absolutely incorrect. The 1775 event was an unofficial "visit" to the private Latin school of Rev. John Brown located at New Providence. The second event in 1776 refers to the Hanover Presbytery's public seminary (academy), which operated under the "care and tuition" of its "manager," Rev. William Graham. Foote, failing to comprehend the fairly clear meeting minutes, failed to notice that the two events took place at two different locations, and further, that the first event had no relationship to the second. Indeed, Foote incomprehensibly conflated the two different schools into one, and then attempted to rationalize rather obvious inconsistencies by positing the preposterous idea that Graham was a "tutor" under the "supervision" of Rev. John Brown. This theory only gained ready acceptance by later nineteenth-century historians because by then all the principals involved in the establishment of the college were dead. Had Foote's proposition been offered to the public at the dawn of the nineteenth century, it would have been universally and immediately rejected by the many participants that were still living.

Foote's mistake about the two schools may have been occasioned, at least in part, by an earlier history of Washington College written by Rev. William Hill.[459] Hill incorrectly included a reference to the presbytery's "visit" to Brown's Latin school in a paragraph devoted exclusively to pertinent extracts from the presbytery's meeting minutes covering the years 1774–1776 that related to the establishment of the seminary. Hill's inclusion of the reference to Brown's school strongly implied that the reference meant that Brown's school at New Providence and the presbytery's seminary at Mount Pleasant were one and the same, but of course, they were not, and Hill's reference to this part of the meeting minutes constituted a monumental error in judgment. At the same time, Hill did not specifically assert the mistaken notion that Brown's school was linked to Liberty Hall; he merely implied it. In that, Hill was grievously incorrect. He was probably confused by the unusual fact that the meeting, which began at Timber Ridge, was thereafter moved from there to Rev. Brown's home at New Providence several miles away.

Graham, as the facts will attest, came to Virginia as a widely recognized scholar of high theological attainments. He was also a thoroughly prepared educator who trained under the eminent Dr. John Witherspoon at Princeton, and before him, the earlier president of the College of New Jersey, Rev. Samuel Finley. Witherspoon was so impressed with young Graham that he hired him as a student instructor of the preparatory program at Princeton. Graham shouldered this responsibility while he was himself a matriculant in the college. Moreover, Witherspoon was so thoroughly convinced of Graham's scholarly attainments that he waived his entire senior year of classes, requiring him to only sit for the

---

459 Rev. William Hill, "History of Washington College, Virginia," *American Historical Quarterly*, Vol. X [1838], pp. 145–150 [Authorship attributed to Rev. William Hill] cited in Crenshaw, Ollinger, General Lee's College [unpublished footnotes (typescript) Washington and Lee University Archives/Library], "Vol. II," ["Appendix "A"] [handpaginated in pencil as page no. 526.], based in large measure upon an article entitled by Rev. Dr. William Hill [Hampden-Sydney] in *Southern Religious Telegraph* [Richmond] Dec. 19, 1834, Jan. 2, 23, Feb. 6, 1835 [serialized form], and also relying on a letter to the unnamed author from Edward Graham Esq. of Lexington, Virginia.

senior class examinations. All this is well described in the "Memoir of the Late Rev. William Graham A.M." written by his brother, Edward Graham, as well as by Archibald Alexander in his unpublished "Memoir of Rev. William Graham." (See bibliography.)

Brown, on the other hand, came to Virginia with two years of instruction in theology but no known instruction in college-level mathematics, philosophy, or science. Brown attended the College of New Jersey during its first two rather discombobulated years when instruction was interrupted by the deaths of two early presidents and when records were only sketchily kept. In fact, during his tenure as a minister, Brown merely organized his preparatory Latin school. He had to hire more recent graduates of the College of New Jersey to carry out the actual instruction at his Latin school. Rev. John Brown was a country parson in every sense of that term, and did not possess the requisite training or experience to even provide elementary instruction in Latin and Greek grammar, let alone to supervise a man of Mr. William Graham's abilities as an educator and as a theologian.

Indeed, even before Mr. Graham had been licensed and ordained by the Hanover Presbytery, young college graduates seeking to become Presbyterian ministers sought out Mr. Graham for theological instruction in preparation for their trials in that regard. This is learned from the testimony of Archibald Alexander in his informative "Memoir of Rev. William Graham" preserved at the Princeton Theological Seminary Library. (See bibliography.) Of course, Graham and Brown resided in the same general neighborhood, but Mr. Graham's scholarship in theology was so widely recognized that the young would-be ministers soon called upon Graham's assistance and guidance in preparation for the ministry. Alexander, in his "Memoir of Rev. William Graham," provides a sample of the names of some of the men who sought out Mr. Graham for his assistance, which includes the names Samuel Doak, Edward Crawford, John Montgomery, and others. (See Alexander's "Memoir of Rev. William Graham" in the bibliography.) It is noteworthy that these named young men and their families had long been members of Brown's New Providence Church, but it was not their longtime pastor that they sought out for assistance in preparing for the ministry; it was the newcomer Graham.

Apparently, this disparity in educational and theological training that existed between Graham and Brown had no apparent direct negative impact on the professional relationship between these two eminent Presbyterian ministers. The differences were so readily apparent, however, as to require no taking notice of it, at least initially. At the same time, it is also clear that from the time of Mr. Graham's arrival in the Valley of Virginia, Brown's stature in the community became far less significant than it had been previously, while Graham's prominence became increasingly more apparent. So much so that according to Alexander, Mrs. Brown came to resent Graham's rise and her husband's corresponding decline in social standing. The resentment grew, and Mrs. Brown was unable to hide her feelings, which were manifested in the form of ridicule and sarcastic aspersions voiced to others about Graham. Indeed, Mrs. Brown shared her private feelings among many in her family as well as among her influential friends. To make matters worse, Graham, who had been lodging with the Brown family, had become the Brown's prospective son-in-law.

Mrs. Brown's vituperative attacks against Graham eventually came to his attention, and he immediately thereafter asked his fiancée's permission to be released from his matrimonial proposal, which she obviously granted to the great disappointment of the two young lovers, both of whom were crushed. This tragedy ruptured forever the prior friendly relationship between Mr. Brown and Mr. Graham, although it did not seem to affect their ability to remain somewhat above the fray in their clerical relationship as pastors of nearby congregations.

In short order, Rev. Graham became a leading member of both the surrounding community, and in fact, in the state. In both the affairs of the church and the state, Rev. Graham became a man of ever-increasing importance. At the same time, the aging Rev. Brown was less and less active in both social affairs and the policy questions related to the church, a fact highlighted by Dr. John White Stuart III in his biographical study of Brown.[460]

Brown, recognizing the realities of the professional disparities between himself and Graham, understandably recused himself from all activities related to the presbytery's new infant seminary, and that is why his name is never found among those appointees to the board of trustees who actually attended trustee meetings. This is a rather embarrassing fact for those who claim that Rev. John Brown was an early president of the college. Those who have clumsily asserted that Rev. Brown was closely affiliated with the college in its early days obviously failed to consult the institution's original records, including the trustee's minute book. If they had, they would have discovered that Brown never once attended a board of trustees meeting from the day of its creation. Just how historians since the appearance of Foot's two books on the history of Virginia first appeared could have failed to take notice of this striking reality is indeed astounding. These historians as well as the university after 1850 were obviously blinded by some preconceived notion(s), but wishing Rev. Brown had been involved in the founding of the college does not make this falsehood true.

Note: Brown's grandson, John Mason Brown of Kentucky, mistakenly believed that his grandfather's Latin school was directly linked to the college and said so in a letter to Herbert Adams.[461] *Brown's grandson was wrong in this regard, but it isn't difficult to understand why he might have believed this. His grandfather's Latin school located at New Providence was under a tutor named Samuel Doak in December of 1775 when the new academy in Prince Edward County suddenly and unexpectedly lost their prospective tutor, and desperate to obtain a substitute, sought out Mr. Doak, who was a*

---

460 Stuart, John White, *The Rev. John Brown of Virginia (1728–1803): His Life and Selected Sermons,* Doctoral Dissertation, University of Massachusetts, 1988.

461 *Herbert Baxter Adams, Thomas Jefferson, and the University of Virginia, Washington, 1888 [see especially Chap. XXII (Washington And Lee University by Professors White and Harris) [i.e., W&L professors, Carter J. Harris and James J. White] and Chap. XXIII (Bibliography of Washington and Lee University) pp. 293–308. The whole supplemented by a letter from John Mason Brown [great grandson of Rev. John Brown that is riddled with errors and false assumptions]; part of: U.S. Bureau of Education Circular of Information No. 1, 1888; Contributions To American Educational History, Edited by Herbert B. Adams, No. 2.;* The letter begins on p. 305.

recent graduate of Princeton. Doak agreed to accept what constituted a promotion to the higher-level institution of learning. Brown was now without a tutor for his Latin school, and with the impending Revolutionary War, his prospects for obtaining a young man from Princeton were disappointing, so Brown's preparatory school, like so many such schools, was forced to close for the war's duration. At the same time, Graham was conducting the grammar school component of the new college as a prelude and foundation of the next phase in the construction of the college (Liberty Hall Academy). Insofar as the grammar school aspect of the college was only a few miles from Brown's now defunct Latin school, it is rather predictable that those students who were abandoned at Brown's school would gravitate to Graham's operations at Mount Pleasant. Years later, a person describing these events to others might very well portray the circumstances surrounding these events as a sort of "merging" of the two schools even though no such merger ever actually transpired.[462] *Moreover, as late as 1782, Brown was still in charge of his own private school, and he wrote letters seeking assistance for reopening his Latin school. Quite clearly, no earlier merger had transpired, which is consistent with the absence of any reference to Brown's school in the presbytery's meeting minutes outside of the one meager reference to the members visiting his school following the April 1775 meeting that had been held in Brown's home, next door to Brown's school. The Hanover Presbytery, as you can see, had no connection whatsoever with Brown's private school any more than with all of the myriad in such preparatory schools in Virginia that were commonly conducted by local Presbyterian ministers. Brown, very much alone, however, as previously mentioned, was not able to conduct such classes at his school and was forced to hire young graduates from Princeton to serve as tutors. That is the reason why, when Mr. Doak accepted the offer to serve as a temporary substitute at Hampden-Sydney, Brown couldn't just take over the conducting of classes but instead was forced to suspend the school for several years during the Revolutionary War.*

Just as embarrassing for these mistaken adherents to a false history is the demonstrable fact that Brown elected not to send any of his several sons to the presbytery's academy (Liberty Hall) under Graham, which was located in his own neighborhood. Every meeting of the Liberty Hall Academy board of trustees took place without Rev. John Brown having ever even bothered to attend as an observer. Indeed, it also appears that the same is true with respect to Brown's sons, but clear evidence on that issue is lacking.

Again, in the same volume but in a different section, Foote erroneously said this:

> In the fall of 1774, on the recommendation of Rev. Samuel Stanhope Smith, employed in founding Hampden-Sidney [sic] College in Prince Edward. ***Mr. Graham was invited to engage in a classical school in Augusta County, under the direction of the Rev. John Brown***, pastor of New Providence and formerly of Timber Ridge. (W. H. Foote, *Sketches of Virginia* . . . Series One, p. 441)
>
> (Here, the bold and italics emphases are added to indicate error.)

As the Hanover Presbytery minutes clearly reflect, William Graham was not, as Foote contends, "invited to engage in a classical school," nor was he appointed "under the direction of the Rev. John Brown," at any time. He was,

---

462 *At the conclusion of the Revolutionary War, Rev. Brown (1782) initiated a process for reopening of his Latin school, as his correspondence clearly demonstrates. Certainly, Rev. John Brown was still in charge of his own educational endeavor while at the same time Liberty Hall Academy was petitioning the legislature for a charter with degree granting authority. See John White Stuart's dissertation biography of Rev. John Brown.*

however, appointed as a "manager" of the Hanover Presbytery's'work-in-progress', seminary[463] (i.e., academy), but he was never "under the direction" of any individual. During the early phase of the academy's operations, the school was under the exclusive administrative oversight of William Graham, who kept the Presbytery and later, the trustees advised of the school's activities. Of course, he was subject to the oversight of these twoinstitutional entities but he was the chief operations officer of the college from its inception. Foote failed to comprehend that the Presbytery's reference to Rev. John Brown in its October 1774 meeting minutes was both non-specific and importantly never effectuated.

During Graham's entire twenty-two year tenure from October 13, 1774, until 1796, Rev. John Brown had no connection whatsoever with the affairs of the presbytery's academy in Augusta County other than being one of the many ministers comprising the presbytery. This is a plain and relatively easily determined fact that was inexplicably unknown to Foote. The indisputable false narrative that Rev. John Brown was involved in the affairs of Augusta Academy, Liberty Hall, or Washington College is directly traceable to William Henry Foote. Rev. Brown, in all of his extant correspondence from that period, often discusses his Latin school's affairs, but he never even hints at his having been involved in the affairs of the presbytery's seminary in his neighborhood.[464] Brown's uninvolvement was by his own choice that grew out of a broken engagement between Rev. Brown's daughter and Rev. Graham. A private matter that is carefully explained elsewhere in this report.

ERROR no. 3: Foote creates a related but compounding and equally damaging error regarding Washington and Lee University (i.e., Liberty Hall) and its president, William Graham, when discussing the events of the third day of the presbytery's spring meeting in 1775.

Foote mistakenly depicts the April 1775 meeting of the Hanover Presbytery in such a way that he creates the false impression that the private Latin school of Rev. John Brown is the seminary that the presbytery created the prior October, which is not true.

Here is how the paragraph looks in Foote's book:

> The opportunity of visiting ***the school under their patronage being so favorable***—"The Presbytery repaired to the school house, attended a specimen of the proficiency of the students in the Latin and Greek language, and pronouncing their orations in which they

---

463   The new seminary was to be patterned after the academic program at the College of New Jersey, not a preparatory "classical school." This fact is quite obvious from the presbytery's meeting minutes between 1771 and 1775.

464   After Liberty Hall Academy was moved from Timber Ridge closer to what was later, Lexington, the academy (college) was no longer located in the neighborhod of Timber Ridge and New Providence congregations, but it's still within ten to fifteen miles of Brown's residence.

were well pleased." (Note: This is a quote
within a quote. Foote's words are in standard
quotation marks, while the presbytery's
meeting minutes extract is shown with
a single quotation mark. The erroneous
<u>underlined</u> words above are those of Foote,
but of course, the underlining was added by
the auditor.)

The school being referred to above (Brown's Latin school) was definitely
not "under their patronage," referring, of course, to the Hanover Presbytery,
and there are no eighteenth-century records suggesting otherwise. Those later
historians who made this claim relied on the mistaken Mr. Foote or Foote's
likely source, Rev. Samuel Houston,[465] who, if he suggested that, was similarly
mistaken. Houston often relied on hearsay and or gossip, which he rarely, if ever,
bothered to validate by consulting official records. Long a friend and a trustee of
the college, Houston preferred yarn-spinning over scholarly research of official
records. Importantly, Houston's authorship here is seriously open to question, as
has been already explained elsewhere in this report. In the final analysis, whether
Houston wrote it or not, is not all that significant because the statement is, in any
event, demonstrably incorrect.

Here below are the actual meeting minutes:

The Pby think it expedient, as they now have
an opportunity of visiting the School under
the Direction of Mr. Brown, accordingly
the Pby repaired to the School House, and
attended a Specimen of the proficiency of the
Students, in the Latin and Greek languages,
and pronouncing orations with which they
were well pleased. (Hanover Presbytery meeting
minutes p. 63.)

The above quoted statement comprises all the action that the eighteenth-
century Hanover Presbytery ever took in regard to Brown's private preparatory
Latin school. The reader will no doubt notice that the Hanover Presbytery made no
mention here of *"under their patronage"* because this preposterous introductory
phrase was created in the mind of Mr. Foote. Rev. Brown's private Latin school
was never under the patronage of the Hanover Presbytery, hence its denomination

---

465   Foote may have also read Rev. William Hill's 1838 article on the history of Washington
College, in which Hill mistakenly included a reference to the 1775 meeting of the presbytery.
This reference, by inference, suggested a link between Liberty Hall and Brown's school. Hill
did not specifically assert this, but his mistaken reference certainly implied it. In sum, it was
a disastrous mistake by someone who meant well, but who misread the meeting minutes. Hill,
of course, had no direct connection to Liberty Hall, having attended Hampden-Sydney under
Rev. John B. Smith.

as "private." Mr. Foote, however, failed to recognize that this "visit" was an unofficial social visit that had nothing to do with the business of the presbytery. The school's director, Rev. John Brown, was also the presbytery's host for the final three days of the four-day meeting, which began at Timber Ridge. The presbytery, having concluded their meeting, no doubt acted in response to an invitation extended to them by their host, Rev. Brown. The members then walked next door to observe his students' orations.[466] This constitutes the single lone act that the presbytery ever took in regard to this school. Of course, the presbytery's visit to this private school had no official objective and therefore was never again mentioned in the presbytery's meeting minutes. This is not merely the auditor's opinion, but is rather an undeniable fact of history.

This error caused other later historians to mistakenly believe that the presbytery had established a business relationship with Brown's Latin school when it had done no such thing. The presbytery simply paid Brown's school a courtesy call after their spring 1775 meeting. The school was located in another building at the same place where the meeting had been held, which was referred to as New Providence.[467] The school was then being conducted by Samuel Doak as evidenced by Rev. Philip Vicker Fithian in his journal of 1775–1776 (see bibliography). This school at the New Providence Church was not the presbytery's new seminary (Augusta Academy) located, at that time, at the place called locally as Mount Pleasant.

Mount Pleasant was the seminary's first and temporary location, which was on the farm of James Wilson. Once the new buildings were erected, the school was moved (in late 1776) into its first permanent campus buildings at Timber Ridge. The academy/seminary was conducted there during the second and third years of the Revolutionary War, but vicissitudes occasioned by the war necessitated that the operations be shifted from Timber Ridge toward Lexington, where it continued operations in various buildings until the conclusion of the war.

ERROR no. 4: Foote incorrectly assigns the presbytery's "patronage" to Brown's Latin school.

Here is Foote's error on patronage taken from the 1966 photographic reprint of the original 1850 edition:

> "The opportunity of visiting the school ***under their patronage*** being so favorable"—"The Presbytery repaired to the schoolhouse and attended a specimen of the proficiency of the students in the Latin and Greek language and pronouncing

---

466 As evidenced by his private correspondence, Brown had opposed the presbytery's October 1774 creation of Augusta Academy and had earlier contended that such a seminary was unnecessary, and that his school in conjunction with Princeton was sufficient to meet the church's need to prepare prospective Virginia students for the gospel ministry. Inviting his colleagues to visit his school just six months after they had decided to move forward with a new seminary may very well have been his last ditch effort to abort the seminary plan while it was still in the embryonic state.

467 New Providence was the name of Brown's presbyterian congregation.

orations, with which they were well pleased." (Foote: Sketches of Virginia . . . Series One, p. 444.) (Emphasis added.)

The preceding paragraph begins with Foote's own introductory qualifying phrase, "The opportunity of visiting the school *under their patronage* being so favorable . . ." [sic] (Standard quotation marks here are the auditor's and are used to emphasize that these are the words of Foote. Readers will see above that immediately following Foote's erroneous introductory phrase beginning with "the opportunity . . ." that there is yet another set of quotation marks, but these are shown here by the auditor in single quotation marks to indicate a quote within a quote. These words are quoted by Foote and are from the presbytery's meeting minutes at page 69.

What is so troubling about the entire paragraph is that the introductory phrase by Foote is patently false, but by linking it to the words taken from the presbytery's meeting minutes, it is very likely that readers have associated Foote's introductory phrase, which is a gross mistake, with those of the presbytery that follow. The words within standard quotation marks are the precise words taken from the presbytery's official meeting minutes. Structurally, the linking of Foote's words with those from the presbytery's minutes seemingly gave credence to a notion that is entirely false (i.e., that Rev. Brown's school was "under their patronage." Of course, Brown's school was not then or ever under the presbytery's patronage. Foote had confused the private school of Brown at New Providence with the presbytery's public seminary (Augusta Academy) at Mount Pleasant. Thereafter, literally hundreds of writers, blindly following Foote over the course of a hundred and fifty years, made the same mistake that Foote made in 1850.

This particular patronage passage led to much confusion by later historians, hence its great importance, notwithstanding the technical nature of the way in which it was presented and the difficulty in explaining both the substantive error concerning the false claim of patronage, and the erroneous way it was structured, which the auditor contends to suggest to casual readers that the entire paragraph represents words from the Hanover Presbytery, when the single most important aspect of the paragraph is the error of fact that came from Mr. Foote's faulty understanding of these events. This important mistake by Foote helps explain how so many later historians came to believe that Brown and his Latin school were linked to Augusta Academy (later Liberty Hall) when neither Brown nor his school had any such link. If, however, one were to believe such nonsense, then it is not a great leap to see a connection of Rev. Brown's Latin school to the earlier educational endeavors of Robert Alexander. This is mere speculation, of course, but one can easily see how Mr. Foote's errors evolved into the grossly incorrect early history that came to exist.

It may also explain why Dr. Henry Ruffner's revised "*Early History of Washington College*" contained this seemingly inexplicable comment:

"While the school was thus going on, *partly as a private establishment, yet recognized and patronized by the Presbytery*, in April 1775, they named several laymen in various parts of the country to assist in forwarding the subscriptions."[468]

(The erroneous and confusing part of this sentence is highlighted by bold italics.) (Emphasis is added.)

Presumably, Ruffner added this awkward comment to his original unpublished manuscript after he read Foote's two books on Virginia. If so, he might better have left the subject alone because he simply made things worse. The school to which Ruffner refers to was never "partly private," as he suggests above, and the presbytery did not agree to patronize any school in April of 1775, as its meeting minutes clearly evinced. The Hanover Presbytery only patronized two schools in the eighteenth century: its seminary in Augusta County on October 13, 1774 (Augusta Academy) and later its seminary in Prince Edward County (Prince Edward Academy) on February 1, 1775.[469] To Ruffner's credit, his 1857 editorial amendment did not go so far as to positively link Brown's school to Augusta Academy, but his carefully selected wording, nevertheless, unfortunately suggested that this was a possibility.

As is discussed elsewhere in this report, the presbytery's seminary in Augusta was a public institution from its inception, and it was patronized and established simultaneously on October 13, 1774, not in April of 1775 as gratuitously suggested by Ruffner. Brown's Latin school at New Providence, which the presbytery visited in April of 1775, however, was a private school that was never patronized by the Hanover Presbytery. For some unknown reason, Foote was not able to distinguish between these two entirely different educational entities with altogether different objectives, and under two different Presbyterian ministers at two unique locations. His confusion in this regard obviously affected Ruffner's decision to revise his original manuscript as is suggested by the above quotation. Fortunately, Ruffner refused to go so far as to repudiate his view that the college was founded in October of 1774.

It is important to keep in mind that while Ruffner originally composed his history in the 1840s, he revised the original after 1857, but his final manuscript version was not published until it was released posthumously by the university in its first volume of historical papers in 1890. This means that Ruffner had the opportunity to read Foote's first book after his own original draft had been written, and make any revisions he deemed appropriate. It is obvious that Ruffner was not persuaded by Foote's accounts of the founding of Washington and Lee, and, by and large, let his original version stand. His oddly worded comment above suggests that he was willing to accept the remote possibility of some connection

---

468 Henry Ruffner, "Early History of Washington College," *Washington and Lee University Historical Papers*, Vol. 1. Baltimore: John Murphy & Co., 1890, p. 19.)

469 The presbytery's establishment of Prince Edward County took place at a special meeting pro re nata, and as a result, the meeting minutes were lost for a while and later written in after the fact. Its actions at that meeting were designed to establish and patronize the Prince Edward Academy as is made clear by subsequent meeting minutes, but the minutes for the special meeting are deficient due, no doubt, to the special circumstances, but the presbytery's intentions are nonetheless quite clear.

existing between Brown's school and Liberty Hall. Of course, there was no such link, and Ruffner might better have left his manuscript unrevised.

As the auditor has pointed out elsewhere, no one asserted in print or in a known letter the idea of a connection between either Robert Alexander's school or Brown's private Latin school, and Liberty Hall Academy prior to 1850, with one possible exception. The possible, although unlikely exception, being Rev. Samuel Houston, who may have suggested such a link. If he did, as Mr. Foote says that he did, he was sorely mistaken, and such a claim would be inconsistent with the pertinent records of both the Hanover Presbytery and the earliest records of the board of trustees of the college.

Finally on this point, Brown's extant correspondence contains nothing that hints at such a connection even though he frequently discusses his Latin school and its affairs, nor is such a connection hinted at by the two early biographers of William Graham, Edward Graham and Archibald Alexander, both of whom lived in the rector's home during their time as students of Liberty Hall. Every specific claim that there was a connection or link between the private schools of either Brown or Alexander or both emanate in the minds of nineteenth-century post-Foote writers, none of whom were able to cite any eighteenth-century evidence to support their novel narratives. Not in the nineteenth-century, not in the twentieth-century, and not, as yet, in the current century. That anyone still believes this unsupported preposterous nonsense simply boggles the mind.

ERROR no. 5: In Foote's second volume of "_Sketches of Virginia_," he further embellishes the factually incorrect account of the origins of Washington and Lee University offered in his earlier book. Beyond his earlier declaration that the Hanover Presbytery patronized Brown's private Latin school, he subsequently claimed that in 1774, the presbytery adopted Brown's school, and then in conjunction with this adoption, appointed Graham as a mere teacher under Brown. None of this is true, for reasons made abundantly clear in several other places in this report.

Note: The presbytery at the time had not been searching for a "teacher" and did not appoint Graham for that purpose alone. What it wanted was someone who could take its stated dream of erecting a college in Virginia and shape that idea into an institution of higher learning. This fact is made clear in the presbytery's meeting minutes between 1771 and 1775. Moreover, the presbytery would hardly have solicited a man of Graham's unusual talents and attainments, both academic and theological, to leave Pennsylvania and come to the mountains of Virginia, if he was only coming to serve in a subordinate position to someone who had no experience in teaching or in conducting the responsibilities associated with overseeing a contingent of numerous college-age young men. Brown's educational activities in the valley were limited to organizing a preparatory Latin school, which was then conducted by a tutor hired by Brown. In connection with that activity, Brown also solicited from the community their support in supplying certain elementary Latin and Greek books to be used by the students. In addition, he made periodic visits to the classroom, but it is doubtful if he ever oversaw a class in more than a role as temporary substitute. Frankly, Brown lacked the requisite academic skills. This fact is strongly implied by Brown's eldest son in one of his extant letters as well as by Johm White Stuart in his biography of Rev. John Brown. See the bibliography.

Here is what Mr. Foote wrongly imagined:

> Before the time of Mr. Brown, *there was a classical school at New Providence, and Mr. Robert Alexander taught in the bounds of Timber Ridge, the first classical school in the Valley.* Mr. Brown kept up a flourishing *grammar school* near his residence . . . In 1774, *the Presbytery of Hanover adopted the school, and appointed William Graham teacher, under the care of Mr. Brown.* In 1777, the school was removed to Timber Ridge. From thence it was removed to the neighborhood of Lexington. For a series of years, its history is interwoven with the life of William Graham. It is now Washington College.
>
> (Foote, <u>Sketches of Virginia</u>, Series Two, 1855, pp. 96–97.) (Emphasis in bold italics here indicate error[s].)

This constitutes a complete unadulterated fabrication by Mr. Foote. There is no known credible eighteenth-century evidence that there was ever a "classical school"[470] in the neighborhood of New Providence and Timber Ridge congregations prior to Mr. Graham's arrival in Virginia in 1774. The modifying term *classical* suggests that Foote means to refer to something more than just a common school. Admittedly, there was no clear definition of that term in eighteenth-century Virginia, but it could hardly have meant a common school imparting basic elements of reading, writing, and mathematics. In all probability, Robert Alexander's educational efforts entailed a little more than conducting a common elementary curriculum with perhaps some enhanced mathematical instruction. It is noteworthy that none of his students appears to have left any evidence to the contrary, nor did anyone else. The result is that the only real eighteenth-century evidence that pertains to Alexander's educational activities are fragmentary county records, which are generally unilluminating.

Brown's school, on the other hand, appears to have been definitely a Latin school, for that is how Brown consistently refers to his school in his eighteenth-century correspondence, much of which is housed in the Draper collection in Madison, Wisconsin. Brown's school was not, as Foote suggests, a "grammar school." Grammar schools were schools designed to prepare young men for college. Latin schools were narrowly designed to provide instruction in basic elementary Latin and Greek grammar, and this fundamental knowledge was then a prerequisite for acceptance into a regular academic program at a college.

---

470   The auditor challenges, in general, the appropriateness of Foote invoking the denomination of "classical school" in connection with any school in the valley of Virginia prior to the presbytery's establishment of its seminary in 1774, but in particular as it relates to Brown's private school because his extant extensive correspondence indicates that he consistently identified his school as a "Latin school." As for Alexander's educational endeavors, history has not unearthed anything from the eighteenth century that indicates the nature of his or his brother Archibald's educational background or his educational activities. It is important that the noted education and church historian Rev. Dr. Archibald Alexander did not claim in print that his grandfather or his grandfather's brother Robert ever conducted a "classical school" or had even attended college.

There is scant evidence pertaining to the various private efforts made in Virginia, west of the Blue Ridge, prior to the founding of Augusta Academy. The term "classical school" connotes a broad curriculum taught by a recognized scholar. There is no credible evidence that any such school existed in the Valley of Virginia prior to the establishment of Augusta Academy in 1774 by the Hanover Presbytery. At best, it can be said that various efforts by such men as Archibald[471] and Robert Alexander were made to provide instruction to select young men in the rudiments of basic education. To be sure, Rev. John Brown did not keep up a grammar school, but he did organize a "Latin school" as he was wont to describe it. See John White Stuart's biography of Rev. Brown.

Rev. Brown's school was clearly a preparatory school for those who intended to go on to college because it was devoted particularly to the teaching of the language prerequisites of all colleges in the colonies. But as for other general education requirements, students had to obtain those elsewhere. In fact, Brown explains to his brother-in-law, Col. William Preston, in one of his letters that he was sending one of his sons to an "English school," rather than relying on the tutor at his Latin school for such general education. In many cases, college-bound students polished their basic educations at the grammar school affiliated with the College of New Jersey (Princeton), which coincidentally was for several years taught by William Graham during his time at Princeton under Rev. John Witherspoon.[472]

In the eighteenth century, the Hanover Presbytery's did not involve itself in educational initiatives lightly, but when it did it, was scrupulous about maintaining a clear record of their actions in that regard. The records were written into their meeting minutes, as can easily be seen in the Hanover Presbytery's meeting minutes between 1771 and 1776. A review of those minutes will easily reveal that the presbytery, contrary to the representations of Mr. Foote, did not "adopt" any existing school during those years. Moreover, the only two schools that were patronized by the presbytery in Virginia during that century were its two "public" seminaries in Augusta County (Augusta Academy and Prince Edward Academy). Both of these schools were entirely new ventures created by the Hanover Presbytery, and neither of them had any connection to the private schools of Robert Alexander or Rev. John Brown. This fact is demonstrated in the presbytery's meeting minutes, which apparently were seldom reviewed by nineteenth- or twentieth-century historians concerned with the early history of Washington and Lee. When these authors quoted from the presbytery's minutes,

---

471   This Archibald Alexander was the grandfather of the eminent theologian and early student of Liberty Hall Academy, Rev. Archibald Alexander. According to Dr. Ollinger Crenshaw, Robert Alexander did not attend either of the colleges that several nineteenth-century historians averred that he had either attended or from which he had graduated.

472   It is also known that William Graham served as a tutor while himself a student under Samuel Finley, Witherspoon's predecessor, but facts in this regard have not been sufficiently uncovered to be able to describe this activity with particulars. It appears that Graham also studied under Finley prior to Finley's short-lived presidency of Princeton. He very well may also have served as a tutor at Finley's Nottingham Academy.

they were typically quoting from secondary sources, not from the actual meeting minutes' record book. As a result, they lacked the text in its larger context, which severely handicapped them in terms of understanding the true meaning of the material being quoted.

Finally on this error, Rev. William Graham was appointed by the presbytery as the first chief administrator of the presbytery's first prospective seminary in Virginia. He was not hired as a "teacher," and he certainly wasn't under the "direction" or the "care" of Brown, as has been explained in detail previously in this report. Brown, as has been already explained, eschewed all involvement in the affairs of the seminary (Augusta Academy) created by the Hanover Presbytery within the bounds of the congregations of both Rev. Brown and Rev. Graham.

ERROR no. 6: Mr. Foote mischaracterized Liberty Hall scholars.

Foote offered his own opinion on the scholarship of the students at Liberty Hall Academy instead of reporting the facts and views of those more familiar with the early history of the college. He suggested that Liberty Hall produced subpar scholars. Consider, for example, this comment:

> "If Liberty Hall did not make so full and complete scholars as the more richly endowed college has done, she laid the foundation for scholarship and awakened that thirst for knowledge, which precedes eminence in attainments, and may be named with exultation as the germ—the strong root from which Washington College sprung."[473] (Foote, Sketches of Virginia . . . Series One, 1850.)

While this poor attempt at damning with faint praise is merely Mr. Foote's opinion on a highly subjective matter, he appears to be treading here on rather thin ice. It is, after all, rather difficult to ascertain a precise meaning of such words as "full" and "complete," so the auditor simply points out, by way of example, the views of several scholars and eminent professional men who matriculated at Rev. Graham's Liberty Hall, including the noted and widely published author, president of Hampden-Sydney College, and founding first president of the Princeton Theological Seminary, **Rev. Archibald Alexander DD. Rev. George A. Baxter**, president of Washington College, VA (i.e., successor to Rev. W. Graham at Liberty Hall Academy); Rev. **James Priestley**, noted educator and president of Cumberland College; **Rev. Moses Hoge,** president of Hampden-Sydney College; **Rev. Conrad Speece**, author and educator; **Rev. John Holt Rice**, author, editor, publisher, and president of the Union Theological Seminary in Richmond; **Rev. Samuel Doak,** founder of Washington College, Tennessee; **Archibald Roane**, governor of Tennessee; **Rev. John Lyle,** educator; and **Rev. John Chavis**, first black college graduate,

---

473   Foote, William Henry, DD, _Sketches of Virginia, Historical and Biographical_. Philadelphia: J. B. Lippincott & Co., 1850. First Series, John Knox Press reprint edition, 1966, pp. 449–450.

first black Presbyterian minister in the United States, and an eminent educator and theologian in North Carolina, just to name a few from the numerous eminent scholars who went through either the regular academic program or the theological seminary at Liberty Hall Academy in the eighteenth century. In addition, those Presbyterian ministers that emigrated to the Carolinas, Georgia, Tennessee, and Kentucky, and there oversaw schools and founded colleges in those states who obtained some measure of their educational training at Liberty Hall under Rev. William Graham, including Rev. Samuel Doak, Rev. Edward Crawford, Rev. Samuel Houston, Rev. Adam Rankin, and, Rev. Samuel Carrick. Also worthy of mention is the rector's younger brother, **Edward Graham,** a long-serving professor at Washington College who was instrumental in founding the Ann Smith Academy for women in Lexington, and who served as the first president of New London Academy in Bedford County, Virginia.

These early scholars and divines built churches, academies, and colleges throughout the expanding nation both west and south. There is simply no justification for Mr. Foote's disparagement of these early graduates of Liberty Hall Academy, many of whom were widely regarded for their eminence in the field of higher education and the church.

ERROR no. 7: Foote incorrectly reports the Graham vs. Balch affair, and in so doing lends some measure of credence to the false claim that Graham was censured by his church.

Admittedly, this enumerated error is unique because it is in his overall presentation and description of the Graham vs. Balch controversy. Foote failed by omission to explain facts that are exculpatory, and thereby altered how later historians viewed Graham's character. The materials Foote presents on pages 463 and 464 of his "*Sketches of Virginia*" Series One concerning this matter are essentially correct, but there are some comments included that came out of a committee proceeding that was only part of a meeting of the Philadelphia and New York Synod held in May of 1787. These comments are critical in nature and are clearly referring to Graham. In this instance, Foote's error lies not in what he includes in his book, but what he leaves out.[474] What Foote does not explain but surely understood as a Presbyterian minister was that there were two very important undisclosed facts that bear importantly on this matter, to wit:

> 1. The activity that took place in Philadelphia, to which Foote refers, should not have been allowed because it involved a complaint against William Graham in an improperly albeit deliberate submission to the wrong jurisdiction by Rev.

---

474   Much of the exculpatory material that debunks the notion that Graham was censured by the church is not included in the section in which the most damaging and improper information appears concerning him. To be fair, Foote should have placed the exculpatory extracts from church records in conjunction with the totally improper disparagement of Graham.

Hezekiah Balch. Balch's complaint, as it was filed, was a transparent attempt to obtain a lopsided review of a matter in an improper ecclesiastical court. The Philadelphia and New York Synod did not have proper jurisdiction to even accept receipt of the complaint. This fact has never been disputed in print by anyone as far as can be determined by the sources relied upon by the auditor, which are extensive enough to include most known sources.

Note: A complaint against a Presbyterian minister is supposed to be filed with the principal Presbyterian entity to which the defendant minister is attached. This fact is so fundamental that all active Presbyterian ministers at that time knew fully well to which Presbyterian entity they should direct their complaint. Balch, however, adopted an old lawyer's trick by which one files papers with a court that they believe will be most favorable. Balch went "court shopping" and filed his complaint with his own synod in hopes of obtaining more favorable treatment in one manner or another. In fact, Balch's trick worked to some degree at least, because this improper court assigned the complaint to a committee that mistakenly only received evidence presented by Balch and his acolytes. The committee thereafter made some entirely improper critical comments in writing before the synod acknowledged that they did not have jurisdiction in the matter.

The synod compounded its mistake of commenting on certain aspects of the merits of the case by neglecting to expunge the committee's inappropriate comments before they referred the matter to the appropriate presbytery in Virginia. As a result, the committee's comments were unfortunately printed in the records of the synod, but the church's final disposition acquitting Graham were not included in that volume of the church's records. What Foote should have done is highlight this very important, improperly conducted, half-hearted, and one-sided review. If Foote (also a Presbyterian minister who knew, or should have known, that the proceeding was improper) decided that it was worth including the comments emanating from this improper court, then he should have put these comments in a footnote and labeled them as improper. Moreover, Foote should also have known about Graham's acquittal that was published in a subsequent volume of the Presbyterian Church's records. The only person who was injured by this bureaucratic bungling was William Graham, but as was characteristic of the man, once acquitted, he let the matter die. Historians, however, continue to this day to repeat Foote's false claim that Graham was censured by his church. One notable exception is David Diehl, author of the biography of Rev. Samuel Houston. Diehl may be the only author who bothered to delve into this case deeply enough to ascertain the case's ultimate outcome. He describes the case in detail in his biography of Rev. Samuel Houston. See the attached bibliography.

2. This audit review reveals that Rev. William Graham was acquitted following the proper court's finding. Thus, the disposition in the Graham vs. Balch matter was that the Virginia ecclesiastical court that sat in judgment of Balch's complaint against Graham determined that the published letter addressed to Balch did not warrant Graham's censure. The evidence from both the complainant and the defendant demonstrated and

persuaded the proper ecclesiastical court that Rev. Graham's published accusations against Balch were, in essence, true, and the clear inference to be drawn from this finding is that Balch and his chief witness, Col. Cocke, had perjured themselves before two ecclesiastical courts. Graham was exonerated, not censured. Following the decision, Graham let the matter stand rather than file a countercomplaint against Balch. These are the indisputable facts of this case, and Foote should have revealed them rather than traduce the founder of Washington and Lee as having been censured. The calumny has been repeated by numerous misguided historians, and these false claims have served to diminish the reputation of Washington and Lee's founding first president, Rev. William Graham. In truth, Rev. Graham was one of the few Presbyterian pastors of that period (eighteenth century) who was never censured by the Presbyterian Church. He was so esteemed, in his day, by his colleagues that they selected him to lead virtually every major endeavor taken by his church in Virginia, a fact revealed in the pages of the church's records covering the last quarter of that century.

Note: There appears to be some difference of opinion as to whether Rev. Graham's acquittal of all charges lodged by Rev. Hezekiah Balch took place before the Lexington Presbytery or before the entire Virginia Synod. The auditor relied upon a primary source, the published records of the Presbyterian Church (general assembly), and some secondary sources like Alexander's manuscript, "Memoir of Rev. William Graham," Diehl's biography of Rev. Samuel Houston, and Foote's first volume of Sketches of Virginia . . ., which contain copies of important selected documents related to this incident. Alexander claims that he attended the meeting and asserts that it was comprised of the Virginia Synod and that it was the synod's first meeting. It's entirely possible that it was a joint meeting of the Lexington Presbytery and the organizational meeting of the Virginia Synod.

It hardly matters in the last analysis whether the ecclesiastical court was the Lexington Presbytery or the Virginia Synod because on the substantive findings and the final outcome of the complaint. All the above-referenced eyewitness sources agree that Rev. Graham was acquitted of all charges in this sad affair. It is worthy of note that this was the one and only complaint ever lodged before the Presbyterian Church against Rev. William Graham, and that it was brought by the single most disputative member of the Presbyterian Church in America at that time, Rev. Hezekiah Balch[475] (i.e., during the latter part of the eighteenth and early part of the nineteenth century, as the church's records will attest).[476]

Note: Readers are referred to David W. Robson, "An Important Question Answered: William Graham's Defense of Slavery in Post-Revolutionary Virginia," William and Mary Quarterly, Third Series, 37, No. 4 (October 1980), pp. 644–652. This contains a scurrilous attack on Graham's

---

475   In fairness, this troublesome Hezekiah Balch of the Abington Presbytery should not be confused with his cousin Hezekiah James Balch of Mecklenburg County, NC.

476   *Records of the Presbyterian Church in the United States of America, Embracing the Minutes of the General Presbytery of Philadelphia 1706–1716, Minutes of 1717–1758, Minutes of the Synod of NY 1745–1758, 1758–1788*, Philadelphia: The Presbyterian Board of Publication, 1841.

character, which falsely claims that Graham was censured by his church on multiple occasions. Such a claim cannot be supported by any credible evidence. Indeed, the entire article is comprised of unprofessional and false assumptions, as the auditor explains in detail in the appendix devoted to it. It is truly astounding and an embarrassment that the article passed muster by the editors of that fine journal. Not content to slander Graham on the slavery issue, Robson picked up on Foote's false claim that Graham was censured by his church, although Robson went Foote much better by falsely claiming that Graham was censured on several occasions, proving thereby the ancient adage that a repeated lie will inevitably expand upon itself. Predictably, Robson's principal source is none other than William Henry Foote. Of course, Robson also relied upon his own interpretation of a written lecture, which he mistakenly attributes to Rev. Graham. See appendix devoted to Robson's slander of William Graham.

ERROR no. 8: Foote misrepresents the views and involvement of both Graham and Rev. John B. Smith on religious liberty. Both Smith and Graham were presidents of their respective Virginia colleges, Liberty Hall and Hampden-Sydney.

Foote falsely claims that Liberty Hall's rector, Rev. William Graham, acted in concert with Hampden-Sydney's rector, Rev. John B. Smith, along with the majority of the Presbyterian clergy during Virginia's struggle for religious liberty in the autumn of 1784. At this time, the clergy acquiesced and capitulated from the presbytery's long-standing rigid opposition to taxing the public for support of the church and its schools (i.e., separation of church and state). The presbytery on this occasion modified its stance on the issue and included as a caveat, that if the legislature acted to approve the assessment bill that, in that case, they sought equal treatment in the distribution of the revenues received from the assessment. In fact, Graham opposed this decision by his colleagues and led a revolt that successfully repudiated his brethren's foolhardy acquiescence.

Graham's significant role in Virginia's struggle for religious freedom is mistakenly depicted by Foote. He assigns to Graham views that he did not hold, and he fails to comprehend Graham's preeminent leadership role in defeating Smith's 1784 advocacy for modifying their position on assessment. Foote's retrospective analysis of this event makes little sense and is in direct conflict with the view held by James Madison, which was revealed in his correspondence written at the time that the event transpired. Madison was furious with the capitulation of the Presbyterians in 1784. It is not known whether Madison ever came to understand that it was his old schoolmate from Princeton, William Graham, who undid his fellow clergymen's temporary surrender on the struggle for religious liberty.

Foote mistakenly avers that Graham agreed with and participated in advancing the actions of the Hanover Presbytery to repudiate their long-standing unequivocal position opposing any interference by the state in the affairs of the church. Graham believed that the state should not have any authority in determining church policy, and that by taxing the people to support the church, the government would later predictably use its power of the purse to leverage the church into adopting measures that were purely ecclesiastical.

It is a well-known and widely held view by professional politicians that when any interest group alters a position of opposition to any proposed public policy issue and replaces the existing policy with one that says, "We still oppose X," but if the legislature decides to go in another direction, then in that circumstance, our view would be something else, then that change is viewed by legislators as the functional equivalent of surrender. In other words, such actions are typically deemed to reflect an acquiescence on the part of said advocacy group. It is, in all political circles, related to public policy development tantamount to having accepted defeat, irrespective of how the actions may be spun by public relations professionals. That explains why James Madison was livid when he learned of the presbytery's decision in 1784 to change its position as it did.[477] Madison's schoolmate at Princeton, Graham, however, successfully challenged his brethren's foolhardy change of position by launching a campaign to circumvent them, and he did so by calling successfully for a general convention of Presbyterians in conjunction with a statewide petition campaign. The convention met early the following year, and in short order repudiated the acquiescence of most of their clergymen. The petition campaign was joined by Baptists and others, and collectively over ten thousand signatures were obtained opposing the proposed assessment. As a result, the assessment measure facing predictable defeat was allowed to quietly die in deference to the venerable Patrick Henry, the assessment bill's sponsor.

The 1785 convention of Presbyterians soundly repudiated the prior decision by most of its pastors and appointed William Graham, their titular leader, to draft their final position paper (memorial) on religious liberty. At the same time, Graham, with the convention's approval, added to this memorial a request that the legislature pass Mr. Jefferson's bill for religious liberty. Jefferson's bill, at the time, was being managed by James Madison.[478] With the assessment (taxation) bill's defeat, Mr. Jefferson's bill was then resurrected from committee and thereafter passed by both houses of the legislature. Prior to this campaign, Mr. Jefferson's bill had been logjammed in the religion committee for several years because the Anglican Church lobby still held out hope that it would be deemed the state's established church, and as such, would receive the lion's share of the revenue that would result from the proposed bill on assessment. With the defeat of the assessment proposal, the way was then clear for Jefferson's religious liberty bill to be approved.

Power and influence in the Virginia legislature at the time was predominately with the Anglicans (later denominated Episcopalians), and the Presbyterians were nearly as influential. The Episcopalians were initially disposed to the idea

---

477   This is a fact that has been referenced in many of the articles and books that have been published on Virginia's struggle for religious liberty. See Thomas Buckley, Charles Sellers, Mark Noll, Fred Hood, Charles F. James, and William Wirt Henry in this report's bibliography.

478   James Madison had agreed to take responsibility for managing the bill when Jefferson was appointed ambassador to France. As a practical matter, the bill had insufficient support as long as the Episcopal Church had any prospect of being appointed by the legislature as the state's established church. The vigorous campaign waged by Graham's Presbyterians along with the Baptists ended any Episcopalian hopes in that respect. This in turn allowed James Madison to bring up Jefferson's bill, and it easily passed and became law within weeks. Virginia's bill for religious liberty became Madison's template for the religious freedom provision in the first amendment of the nation's Bill of Rights.

of the state establishing a particular church (themselves, of course), and in that way they hoped to maintain the status quo ante that had been in place prior to the Revolution. The Virginia Presbyterians officially sought religious liberty [479] as early as 1774, and vigorously opposed any plan that included the establishment of any church.

This is Foote's specious claim:

> When the bill for a general assessment was brought forward with such an advocate as Patrick Henry, and with the Episcopal Church to support it, it was generally supposed that it would certainly become law. To those who had been paying to support their own church and another foreign to it, this bill proposed relief; they were to pay only for the support of the church of their choice. As it was a relief from their former burdens; and as the Presbyterian congregations would not be called on to pay more for the support of their own ministers than they would cheerfully give by voluntary subscription, ***Mr. Graham was agreed with his brethren to send up the memorial,*** *which gives their sentiments on the subject of the support of religion, disclaiming all legislative interference; and under the conviction, that the law would in some form pass, proposing the least offensive form in which the assessment could be levied.* (William H. Foote, Sketches of Va . . . . Series I One, p. 455.) (Emphasis in *bold italics and or* <u>underline</u> indicates, in this case, an error.)

Foote's assertion that Graham was "agreed with his brethren" on revising the long-established unequivocal opposition to assessment (taxing for the benefit of churches) by the state is incorrect. At that period, it seems that the presbyteries, when confronted with dissension among its members, often made attempts at reconciliation by appointing proponents and opponents to the same committee created to draft appropriate documents pertaining to disputed policies. In this case, the presbytery appointed Graham to the committee to draft the memorial to reflecting the policy change that he had opposed. Graham ignored the appointment as did his colleague and earlier theology student, John Montgomery.[480] The presbytery's minutes contained language later printed in Mr. Foote's "*Sketches of Virginia*" that misleadingly said this:

---

479   See the Hanover Presbytery meeting minutes for 1774.

480   Montgomery had at an earlier date been Graham's teaching assistant at Liberty Hall.

> The Presbytery approves of the memorial and
> ordered it to be recorded in the Presbytery
> book. Messrs. Graham[481] and Smith were
> appointed a committee to prepare a memorial
> to be presented at the present session of the
> General Assembly of the State, and to produce
> it tomorrow for the inspection of the Presbytery.
> "On the next day, a memorial was presented"—
> "complaining of, and praying a redress of
> certain grievances." "The Presbytery approved
> it and ordered it to be sent to the Assembly
> then in session." [Note: quote within a quote.] (Foote,
> *Sketches of Virginia* . . . Series One, 1850, p. 335.)

This language has been understandably misinterpreted by numerous nineteenth-century historians who assumed that the minutes meant that Graham had agreed with his brethren concerning the newly modified position, when in fact he had not. Graham immediately, after this misguided decision had been made, initiated a major campaign designed to undo what the association of Presbyterian ministers had done.

Fortunately, several twentieth-century authors have perceived Graham's role correctly, including Thomas Buckley, Dr. Charles G. Sellers, and Dr. Fred Hood. In that regard, the following is from Dr. Sellers's biography of Rev. John Blair Smith:

> <u>Smith's defeat was a triumph for William
> Graham,</u> who drafted the convention's vehement
> denunciation of any legislation on religion . . .
> The final blow to assessment was the loss of its
> strongest legislative champion through Patrick
> Henry's election as governor. "It was . . . In
> July 1788 that Smith, . . . withdrew from active
> supervision of the college [Hampden-
> Sydney] . . . With Smith out of the way, Patrick
> Henry undertook to get the state's grants to
> William and Mary divided with Hampden-
> Sydney, <u>and Henry's crony and fellow opponent
> of the constitution, William Graham, was
> offered the presidency.</u>[482] (Emphasis added.)

> [Dr. Charles G. Sellers Jr., Princeton]

---

481 Graham, however, opted instead to lead an internal revolt against his brethren's ill-advised policy change. This fact was eventually recognized by Sellers and referenced in his biography of Rev. John Blair Smith, as well as by Hood in "Revolution and Religious Liberty." (See bibliography.)

482 Charles G. Sellers Jr., "John Blair Smith," *Journal of the Presbyterian Historical Association*, Vol. 34, No. 4. (Dec. 1956), pp. 201–25, especially pp. 214, 217–18.

Note: Graham declined his friend Henry's offer of the presidency, electing instead to remain in Lexington at Liberty Hall.

Here below are several pertinent and rather poignant extracts from Thomas Buckley on this subject:

> The two ministers [W. Graham and John B. Smith] were widely divided in their views on the church-state relationship. John Smith had succeeded to the presidency of Hampden-Sydney College when his brother had gone to the College of New Jersey. Like his brother [Samuel S. Smith[483]], John believed that civil government should support religion, provided it was done on the basis of equality for all religious groups and without interference in their system of worship or government.[484]
>
> **Over in the Valley, where Presbyterians comprised the dominant religious group, William Graham, President of rival Liberty Hall College, was unalterably opposed to an assessment, an incorporation, or any other measure which would intrude the government into the affairs of the church. The disagreement would rupture their relationship for several years.**
>
> That fall of 1784 Smith dominated the Presbytery, and the ministers and elders authorized a memorial reflecting his viewpoint . . . The most significant section of the memorial dealt with the justification for an assessment and, in effect, requested one . . . The Presbytery then appointed four members, Smith, Graham, Todd, and Montgomery, to attend the session and present both the memorial and the assessment plan.[485] **But it is likely that only Smith and**

---

483   Samuel S. Smith was at this time president of Princeton, and John B. Smith was president of Hampden-Sydney.

484   The Smith brothers were naive in this respect. By "support," Foote meant "financial support," and the Smith brothers' qualified support in this respect is oxymoronic because it is axiomatic that whenever a government provides financial support to any entity, interference at some point thereafter inevitably follows.

485   FN no. 63 reads as follows: "Minutes of the Hanover Presbytery, October 28, 1784."

Todd remained at the session as they were the only ones who signed the letter to the assembly. (Thomas Buckley, E. S. J., *Church and State in Revolutionary Virginia*, 1776–1787, Charlottesville, Virginia, University Press of Virginia, 1977, pp. 93–96.) (Emphasis added.) "Father" Buckley, as he is oft referred to, is a widely recognized scholar of matters pertaining to the politics of church and state in post-Revolutionary America.

The point missed by many historians is that both Graham and Montgomery, who were closely aligned as friends, educators, and ministers, both refused to sign this memorial that was written and signed by Smith and Todd on behalf of the presbytery, because they opposed what it stood for. They ignored the presbytery's appointment to assist in drafting it in 1784.[486] To outside observers, however, the minutes seem to suggest that all disputation had come to a close when nothing could be further from the truth. Messrs. Graham and Montgomery left the meeting, and Graham thereafter initiated a rebellious campaign to overturn this misguided action on the part of his brethren. It is surprising that Foote, who was himself a Presbyterian minister, was not aware of how such matters can appear to be one thing when they are quite another.

Hood adds this observation by Dr. Buckley, one of the widely recognized experts on the subject of public policy issues pertaining to the subject of church and state in general and on the assessment (tax) issue in particular as it related to the Presbyterians in Virginia, especially in 1785 and 1785.

"Smith at one time favored the assessment. *Graham, on the other hand, was at least one Presbyterian minister who had consistently opposed the assessment. Graham was of western Pennsylvania and a radical democrat who wrote the Constitution for the proposed state of Franklin."*[487] (Hood

---

486 The presbytery frequently made vain attempts to reconcile opponents following their resolution of formal disputes. The unsuccessful disputants were then appointed to a committee created to implement the matter, hoping the losers become reconciled to their differences. Perhaps it was successful in some cases, but it appears that more often than not, the losing side members ignored their appointments. Unfortunately for historians, unaccepted appointments were rarely, if ever, noted in subsequent meeting minutes. Consequently, later researchers incorrectly assumed that all the named appointees were essentially of one mind.

487 *Fred J. Hood, "Revolution and Religious Liberty: The Conservation of the Theocratic Concept in Virginia," Church History, Vol. 40, No. 2 (June 1971), Cambridge University Press, pp. 180–181. The comment is located in one of Dr. Hood's footnotes crediting Dr. Buckley. Finally, someone had assessed Rev. Graham's roles correctly, although it should be pointed out here that Mr. Graham's draft constitution for the proposed state of Frankland was not adopted. The convention before which it was considered rejected Graham's draft and adopted instead a modified version of North Carolina's existing*

citing Thomas Buckley in footnote no. 39 pp. 180–81,
Fred J. Hood, "Revolution and Religious Liberty: The
Conservation of the Theocratic Concept in Virginia,"
Church History," Vol. 40., No. 2 (June 1971), Cambridge
University Press, pp. 170–181.)

Foote's description of the events leading up to and following the Graham led coup d'état (an unprecedented call for a general convention to review the actions of the presbytery's movement led by Rev. John B. Smith, in which the general convention repudiated the 1784 decision advocated by Rev. John B. Smith.) Graham's movement began in the valley, where he was the undisputed leader of the Presbyterians. Graham, after all, by this time had trained several of the young Presbyterian ministers serving in Virginia west of the Blue Ridge Mountains.

This revolt culminated in a Presbyterian-inspired, statewide petition drive that was joined by the Baptists and even some Episcopalians.[488] In all, the legislature received over ten thousand signatures in opposition to the Patrick Henry's assessment (i.e., tax) bill for the benefit of churches. This opposition was led, in the main, by Graham, president of Liberty Hall Academy, and joined by many of Graham's adherents and prior students at Liberty Hall.

The general convention (1785) of Presbyterians repudiated the Hanover Presbytery's actions taken in October of 1784, and it selected Graham to write the Presbyterian's final position on religious freedom and liberty. To the credit of Smith, he took his defeat with grace and even offered to present the church's final position to the legislature written, in this case, by his opponent on this occasion, William Graham.

The final decision of the church included two parts: (1) The opposition to any interference in church affairs by the state, and (2) Support for the long logjammed Bill for Religious Freedom, sponsored by the absent Mr. Jefferson.[489] Foote, followed by many after him, falsely represented the respective roles of Graham and Smith concerning this important historical event. Foote also falsely suggests

---

constitution. **A faction of the attendees led by John Sevier, William Cocke, and Rev. Hezekiah Balch believed that Graham's draft was not friendly to their financial and political interests, and by their efforts, they successfully defeated those advocating for Graham's more democratic constitutional model. Sevier's faction was also successful in changing the proposed new state's name from Frankland to Franklin.**

488   After the initiation of the American Revolution, Anglicans (the Church of England) became known as Episcopalians.

489   Thomas Jefferson submitted his Bill for Religious Freedom several years earlier, but it had little support and was sent to committee, where it sat undisturbed and unacted upon for several years. James Madison had agreed to serve as the bill's chief advocate in Mr. Jefferson's absence in France as Secretary of State. Madison had little hope for the bill until Rev. Graham mounted his successful campaign to overturn his brethren's misguided acquiescence on the religious tax issue. When Graham drafted the Presbyterians' final position paper, he had obtained the convention's authorization to include a provision calling for Jefferson's Bill to be passed. The ten thousand petitions received by the legislature gave Madison the leverage he needed to obtain enough support for Jefferson's Bill to secure its passage. That bill became the template for the First Amendment in the Bill of Rights' provision for freedom of religion.

that Smith was mostly responsible for the final actions of the Presbyterians on this occasion when just the reverse is the true picture.

What has been overlooked by most historians is that absent the timely decisive leadership of Liberty Hall Academy's rector, William Graham, Virginians and quite possibly most Americans might now will be paying additional taxes for the needs of the various Christian churches in America because absent the defeat of Henry's assessment bill, Mr. Jefferson's bill could not possibly have passed because it was in direct conflict with the assessment bill. If Virginia's law had provided for assessments to support the church, and if Jefferson's bill had not become law in Virginia, then James Madison could hardly have advocated for a religious freedom provision that conflicted with his own state's law, and, moreover, he would not have had the persuasive template for the religious liberty provision that he included in his draft of the new nation's Bill of Rights.

As a result of Rev. Graham's successful campaign on this occasion, not only was the taxation issue defeated, but the Presbyterians also provided, as part of the effort, the absolutely essential support required for passing Thomas Jefferson's long-stalled Bill for Religious Freedom. Of course, it is this very bill of Jefferson's that served as the template for Mr. James Madison when he crafted the First Amendment's religious "establishment" provision in the American Bill of Rights. Until the Presbyterians weighed in on Jefferson's bill, it remained in a permanent state of inertia. The Presbyterians' support for Jefferson's bill was part and parcel of the Rev. Graham-led coup d'état. To date, few have recognized the pivotal role played by Washington and Lee University's founding president, William Graham. Keeping in mind that Graham's schoolmate at Princeton, James Madison, was given the responsibility for overseeing Jefferson's bill for religious freedom when Jefferson was appointed ambassador to the French Court, and for several years, despite Madison's best efforts, the bill languished in committee. One of the major reasons why Madison had failed in this regard was that the powerful Anglican (Church of England) presence in the Virginia legislature was effectively lobbying for the legislature to restore its previously long-held status as Virginia's established church.

As a result of the American Revolution, the church's status was understandably up in the air, so to speak, despite the church having changed its own designation to that of "Episcopalian." This church held vast sums of property purchased with financial support of the Crown's representatives in Virginia; revenues obtained from taxes paid by Anglicans, as well as by Presbyterians, Baptists, and Methodists. Obviously, the new Episcopalians were pressing as best they were able to retain these valuable properties and the exclusive right to perform marriages and other sacraments for which the interested parties were expected to pay a fee; fees from Anglicans and dissenters alike. So too the privilege to charter institutions of higher learning. In short, much was at stake and most expected, at the time, that the Anglicans ("Episcopalians") would have their way.

In short order, Liberty Hall Academy's rector organized a massive petition drive accompanied by a call for a general convention of the state's Presbyterians. The Virginia Legislature was faced with a deluge as they received petitions with over ten thousand signatures opposing any "establishment" and any taxation for the purpose of supporting any religious organization. These petitions were accompanied by a statement from the state's Presbyterians drafted by Liberty Hall Academy's president, Graham, stating in the strongest terms their unequivocal opposition to any state involvement in the internal affairs of any church of any denomination, including the receipt of funds. At President Graham's urging, the convention of Presbyterians added their desire that the legislature finally bring up and pass Mr. Jefferson's Bill for Religious Liberty.

Graham's campaign was a glorious success for within weeks, the assessment (tax) bill was allowed to quietly die, and shortly thereafter the committee on religious matters finally found the requisite support to pass it out of committee, which, as is well known, was then easily passed into law. None of this would likely have happened without the efforts and leadership provided by Liberty Hall Academy's president, Rev. William Graham.

Foote, as has been shown above, got this subject entirely wrong. Thereafter, a bevy of historians followed the misguided notion of Mr. Foote on this subject. Not so later on when Dr. Charles Grier Sellers, then at Princeton, and later, Father Buckley and also Dr. Fred Hood, all of whom had to have been aware of Mr. Foote's treatment, appropriately refused to blindly follow Foote's assertions on such an important topic as religious freedom in America. Here is a short list of key works published by these scrupulous researchers who didn't take the easy way of following William Henry Foote, and instead sought to discover more fundamental sources of information. These authors' key works on this subject are:

- Sellers, Charles Grier, "John Blair Smith," *Journal of the Presbyterian Historical Society*, vol. XXXIV, no. 4, December 1956, pp. 201–225.

- Hood, Fred J., "Revolution and Religious Liberty: The Conservation of the Theocratic Concept in Virginia, *Church History*," vol. 40, no. 2 (June 1971), Cambridge University Press.

- Buckley, Thomas E. S. J., *Church and State in Revolutionary Virginia, 1776–1787*, University Press of Virginia, Charlottesville, Virginia, 1977.

Also worthy of mention on this topic is this important work:

- James, Charles F., *Documentary History of the Struggle for Religious Liberty in Virginia*, Lynchburg, VA, J.P. Bell Company, 1900.

Mr. James is an avid supporter of the Baptists, but despite his admirable overall efforts, he unfortunately follows the mistaken and misguided Mr. Foote about the Presbyterian's momentary equivocation that did not include Rev. William Graham. His work, however, contains an impressive collection of important documents. Mr. James came close to the truth by providing this important quotation from James Madison, who was Jefferson's assigned substitute advocate for the bill while he was in France as Secretary of State:

> The opposition to the general assessment
> (taxation) gains ground . . . The Presbyterian
> clergy have at length espoused the side of the
> opposition,[490] being moved either by fear of
> their laity or a jealousy of the Episcopalians . . .
> (Writings of Madison, I., 175.") (James, Doc. Hist . . .
> p. 139)

There is an irony in Madison's statement, which is that despite the fact that both Rev. William Graham and James Madison were at Princeton in 1773 (albeit in different classes), Madison seems to have been completely unaware of the critical role being played by Graham (his old schoolmate) over in the valley on these two vastly important legislative matters in which Madison played a key role in the legislature. This despite the fact that Madison was a trustee at Hampden-Sydney, and despite the well-known fact that John Smith's older brother, Samuel Stanhope Smith, his predecessor at Hampden-Sydney and later, the president of Princeton, who knew both Graham and Madison, corresponded with Madison on this issue. The Smith brothers, at the time, were advocating for the change in policy by the Presbyterians, while Graham and Madison were against it. It's unimaginable that Samuel Smith never mentions Graham's role as the valley's leader who opposed his and his brother's gambit in acquiescence that so infuriated Madison. Nevertheless, no evidence has emerged that Madison either knew about or appreciated Graham's efforts to return the Presbyterians to the fold of unequivocal opposition to assessments for support of the church. Of course, the basis of their mutual support for religious liberty was not the same. Graham's views were based upon his belief that monies received through the offices of the state came with undesirable strings attached. Madison's concerns were more philosophical.

Apparently, unbeknownst to Madison, his schoolmate from Princeton, Graham was providing him with the necessary political support that he had anxiously hoped would eventually emerge. Madison's suspicion as to motives of the Hanover Presbytery's momentary lapse of judgment in October of 1784 was only partly correct. He seems to have been unaware that the majority of the ministers who maneuvered to modify the church's long-standing opposition to an assessment to support the church were repudiated by a general convention

---

490 It is difficult to comprehend Mr. Madison's statement in this letter because he should have known that the Presbyterians had long opposed any interference by the government into the affairs of the church as expressed in several earlier memorials to the legislature beginning in 1776. Of course, the Presbyterians made the colossal mistake of modifying their theretofore opposition in the autumn of 1784, but Rev. Graham's opposition had soon reversed his brethren's error, as is expressed in the final memorial of October 1785. It is surprising that both Mr. Madison and Mr. Jefferson failed to comprehend the Presbyterian's mostly supportive position; a position consistently held for nearly a decade and only briefly modified in 1784.

instigated by Graham, which restored the Virginia Presbyterian's rigid opposition to any involvement by the government in the affairs of the church. The equivocation led by Hampden-Sydney's president, Rev. John B. Smith, was extremely short-lived, and quickly reversed by the fast-acting president of Liberty Hall, Rev. William Graham. Graham sagaciously moved to call for an unprecedented general convention of all Presbyterians, who responded vehemently to the suggestion that they might be taxed to support churches and church-patronized schools.

The primary motivating factor for the great body of the Presbyterians was their desire for unequivocal religious freedom for every sect of Christian Protestants and broad tolerance for others, the Hanover Presbytery's short-lived acquiescence on assessment notwithstanding. Mr. Foote, like both Jefferson and Madison, misread the Presbyterians during the struggle for religious liberty in Virginia. Mr. Foote erroneously reported the Presbyterians' activities in this regard and utterly misunderstood the respective roles played by the presidents of both Liberty Hall Academy and Hampden-Sydney.

Hampden-Sydney's president, Rev. John B. Smith, was the principal advocate in Virginia for altering the presbytery's long-standing opposition to assessment, while Liberty Hall's president, William Graham, vehemently opposed Smith's advocacy. Smith's brother, Samuel, who had earlier preceded John as president of Hampden-Sydney, also supported in absentia his brother's efforts to change the Hanover Presbytery's position on assessment. Smith initially succeeded in persuading his brethren, but Mr. Graham outmaneuvered Smith and the Hanover Presbytery by successfully calling for a general convention, which overturned the presbytery's ill-advised acquiescence on the issue. Foote, however, refused to accept that Smith's role amounted to a reversal of position. Despite Foote's efforts to portray Smith's position as only providing for a nominal clarification, Mr. Madison's statement above proves that the legislature interpreted the presbytery's actions at the behest of Rev. John Smith in this regard to constitute a surrender on the issue. It is rather interesting the lengths to which Foote went to obfuscate Smith's role in this affair.

Fortunately, Graham's quick and decisive action saved the day for religious liberty, and presumably restored the Presbyterians' standing in the legislature especially with Mr. Madison. This fact went unacknowledged by the credulous Mr. Foote, who gave all the credit for the Presbyterians' success on this issue to the politically foolish instigator, Rev. John B. Smith; credit which rightfully belonged to Liberty Hall's president, William Graham.

It seems apropos, in summing up this monumental blunder by Foote, to reiterate Professor Seller's astute observation on this subject:

> **<u>Smith's defeat was a triumph for William Graham</u>**, who drafted the convention's vehement denunciation of any legislation on religion . . . The final blow to assessment was the loss of its strongest legislative champion through Patrick Henry's election

> as governor. "It was . . . in July 1788 that
> Smith, . . . withdrew from active supervision
> of the College [Hampden-Sydney] . . . With
> Smith out of the way, Patrick Henry undertook
> to get the state's grants to William and
> Mary divided with Hampden-Sydney, and
> Henry's crony and fellow opponent of the
> Constitution, William Graham, was offered
> the Presidency. [491] (Emphasis added.)

[Dr. Charles G. Sellers Jr., Princeton]

Conclusion concerning Mr. Foote's errors:

Several of Foote's errors were of the same type but are repeated in several different parts of his two books with variations of one type or another. They are sometimes treated here as though they are different because they are presented in different contexts. Importantly, because of Foote's awkward historical methodology, his books contain much that he received as submissions from others, and his sources sometimes give differing accounts of the same events but Foote does not typically explain this to his readers. Nor does he normally identify the source of many of his quoted extracts. Worse, he sometimes mixes in one account with others and without explaining which quotation is attributable to whom. Moreover, Foote occasionally inserts his own words in the midst of quotations from others, and he does this in such a way that he sometimes seriously alters the meaning of the quoted author's text. He may have believed that his input was helpful, but in some cases, he bungled history terribly; his treatment of Washington and Lee's early history as well as his passing along false attacks on the character of the college's founding first president, William Graham, being two prime examples.

His major mistake, however, is of such a magnitude that all his other mistakes pale in comparison. His major misstep completely undermines his credibility as a reliable chronicler and historian. What he did is not easy to explain, but it is of great importance that historians are advised of his shocking prestidigitations.

Foote informs his readers in volume one of his two-part history of Virginia[492] that Rev. Samuel Houston said one thing about the origin of Washington and Lee (then Washington College), to wit:

> "This grammar school was moved to the place, near Fairfield,
> called Mount Pleasant; *about which time the Presbytery of
> Hanover patronized it.*"

---

491 Charles G. Sellers Jr., "John Blair Smith," *Journal of the Presbyterian Historical Association,* vol. 34, no. 4. (Dec. 1956), pp. 201–25, especially pp. 214, 217–18.

492 William Henry Foote, *Sketches of Virginia, Historical and Biological,* series one, 1850.

Then in his second volume, he informs his readers that the same part of the earlier quoted letter says something entirely different in its conclusion. To wit:

"This grammar school was moved to the place near Fairfield, called Mount Pleasant; *it was, in 1776, established at Timber Ridge meeting house, and named Liberty Hall.*"

Note: The auditor added the emphasis in bold italics to make certain the readers take notice of Foote's inexcusable altering of text. It is bad enough that he did this; it is made worse by his failing to bring attention to what he had done.

In both cases, he quotes a particular portion of a paragraph from a letter as saying X, and then in volume two, quoting the same portion of that paragraph, he says that Rev. Houston said Y, which is something entirely different about the origin of the college. Both versions are placed by Mr. Foote inside of quotation marks. The question for historians is, *did he lie when he quoted Rev. Houston in volume 1, or did he lie when he quoted him in volume 2?*

It is even possible that he misquoted Rev. Houston in both volumes because the letter to which he refers is not known to exist. All too conveniently, neither the original letter nor a photocopy is now available for comparison. The most important aspect of this fiasco is that Foote says that the quoted paragraph from a letter contains a sentence with two different conclusions, which is, of course, an impossibility. One or both of the two concluding phrases, of necessity, must be a mistake or a fraud. Here, it must be a fraud because one of these conclusions had to have been created. It cannot, therefore, be a mere typographical mistake.[493]

It is frankly difficult to imagine how Mr. Foote could possibly have blundered so badly in this way. What makes things historically worse is that most historians following Mr. Foote's publication of volume one relied on that version, which is the most clearly mistaken, and yet, without question, Mr. Foote has been one of the most commonly relied upon sources on matters related to the activities of the Scotch-Irish in Virginia in the eighteenth century. The mid-nineteenth century rewriting of Washington and Lee's early history can mostly be traced directly back to Mr. Foote's monumental discombobulations and falsifications.

Making things even more confusing and annoying in this regard is the shocking fact that the so-called letter written by Rev. Houston has never been dated, or apparently even been seen by any author who referred to it, with the possible exception of Foote. It may even be a great hoax since no one is known

---

493   In all likelihood, Foote had been advised that the letter's claim that the school referenced by Houston was in fact not patronized by the Hanover Presbytery, as the letter as first quoted said. Foote, realizing that if this quote was false, had no grounds whatsoever to proclaim his new theory that the college was founded twenty-five years earlier than the founders themselves had been representing for the previous seventy-five years. He, therefore, decided to change the quote to say something that seemed true but did not undermine his theory. If so, he failed again, because the second emendation is as false as the first. The school to which the letter-writer referred was Brown's Latin school then at New Providence, not the Augusta Academy at Mount Pleasant. His shame, however, lies in his decision to alter someone else's work at all. To do so without notice is grossly unethical.

to have seen it, except possibly Mr. Foote, and possibly the person to whom Houston ostensibly wrote it, Rev. Morrison of the New Providence Church. The result of this fiasco is that until, and unless, someone can produce the letter for authentication, it must be presumed to be a fraud. If not a fraud, it represents, at best, a gross malfeasance on Foote's part. The auditor cannot fathom how someone unintentionally copies a letter twice and represents the letter to say one thing in 1850, and then five years later, it says something mostly the same but with a conclusion that is entirely different,[494] as discussed above.

Another significant mistake made by Foote was occasioned by his failure to understand the true nature of three entirely different educational endeavors that existed in the valley of Virginia in and around the Lexington area during the last half of the eighteenth century that preceded the establishment of the Augusta Academy by the Hanover Presbytery. These are the one overseen by Archibald (Ersbel) Alexander;[495] and those of Robert Alexander and Rev. John Brown, which were nominal basic educational endeavors offered privately, and which involved no institutional support. There were several other nominal efforts, too numerous to mention, but about these, almost nothing certain is known. For example, Rev. Robert Sanders, a Liberty Hall alumnus residing in Kentucky in 1837, explained in a written memorandum that:

> "1st. With respect to the place and under whom he commenced his education. It was in Rockbridge County at a private grammar school in the neighborhood of my father. A number of neighbors determined to institute a grammar school for the education of their children, and applied to Mr. Graham to furnish them a teacher. He sent them a Mr. Hamilton, of whom you may have had some knowledge. This school was composed of twelve boys, two of whom were Dr. Campbell and myself. I being twelve years old, and he a little older. This school continued one year under Hamilton, and six months under Mr. McPheeters, afterwards a physician . . ." [496]

---

494   The auditor here is not referring to separate sections of the letter, but rather he is referencing the exact same concluding couple of sentences of the same paragraph. This fact is an impossible contradiction suggesting either chicanery or incompetence. In either case, the now dubious letter, such as it is, cannot be afforded any historical value because without the actual letter, no one can know for certain what the author, assuming there is one, actually said. Incidentally, the inconsistent texts is demonstrably incorrect in both variants.

495   The auditor here is referring to Rev. Archibald Alexander's venerable grandfather, Archibald.

496   Robert Stuart Sanders, _The Rev. Robert Stuart, DD 1772–1856: A Pioneer in Kentucky Presbyterianism and His Descendants_, Louisville, The Dunne Press, 1962, p. 83. [Google/ Archives Books]. The author of this piece is father to Emeritous Professor, I. Taylor Sanders, of Washington and Lee. This extract was originally published as part of three articles written by Robert Stuart and published in _The Western Presbyterian Herald_ in April of 1837.

Such were the myriad of peripatetic educational endeavors of these Scotch-Irish settlers in the valley before, during, and after the establishment of Liberty Hall Academy. None of which were institutionally linked to Liberty Hall. The exception being the institutionally created Lexington Theological Seminary, as Edward Graham called it, which was created by the Virginia Synod in the early 1790s, which was under the direction of Liberty Hall Academy's president, William Graham. This theological seminary was an appendage of Liberty Hall Academy as long as it existed. It became defunct upon the unexpected death of Rev. Graham in 1799.

The efforts of the Alexander brothers appear to have taken place in mid-century and extending into the 1760s. Somewhat later, Rev. John Brown organized what he consistently labeled as a "Latin school" that, like the earlier models, were private endeavors supported only by the individuals providing the instruction: the parents and private patrons. Also, like the earlier endeavors, their principals kept few, if any, records, none of which are known to be extant with, but a couple of unimportant exceptions. Mr. Foote, for his own reasons, failed to consistently and accurately distinguish among the early endeavors, and at times he confused one endeavor with another. Mr. Foote's numerous failures in this regard is the proximate cause of the exceedingly discordant and exasperating attempts by later nineteenth- and twentieth-century historians to provide a reasonably accurate accounting of the institutional history of Washington and Lee University. Some like the eminent Herbert B. Adams[497] actually gave up the effort in despair.

For unknown reasons, Mr. Foote failed to comprehend that beginning in 1771 and culminating in 1774, the then only presbytery in Virginia (Hanover) first considered and ultimately decided to revolutionize education in Virginia by creating and patronizing an institution designed from inception to be patterned after the College of New Jersey (Princeton). At the point of culmination in October of 1774, it resolved to establish a public seminary west of the Blue Ridge Mountains in what was then the vast county of Augusta. On the following day, it expressed the desirability of establishing a second seminary on the opposite side of the mountains and thereafter decided to investigate the feasibility of such a school, especially the likelihood of obtaining the requisite financial support for a second seminary. The presbytery then authorized a subscription campaign in their name, which ultimately resulted in the presbytery creating a second seminary in Prince Edward County in 1775. It also agreed at that time to patronize the second established school, a process which is clearly described in the meeting minutes. Foote, however, obviously failed to comprehend the plain meaning of the minutes.[498] The result is that Foote, having ignored all prior published and

---

497   Herbert B. Adams, *Thomas Jefferson and the University of Virginia*, Washington, 1888 [See especially chapter XXII (Washington and Lee University by Professors White and Harris)] [i.e., W&L professors, Carter J. Harris and James J. White], and chapter XXIII (Bibliography of Washington and Lee University) pp. 293–308. Also discussed by Dr. Crenshaw in his appendix, "The Problem with the Origins." See bibliography.

498   The meeting minutes, which describe the presbytery's formal establishment of its first seminary (Augusta Academy), is located on page 55 of the handwritten meeting minutes. The minutes,

written records, superimposed what in the parlance of today would be construed as a deconstruction and a rewrite of history so that it fits the notions and prejudices of unknown and uncited persons in whom he placed great confidence, but who obviously knew very little about the school's true institutional history.

Foote thereafter became the pied piper of misinformation about the origins of and the founding of Washington and Lee University. Additionally, Foote mangled the truth about what might be denominated the "Graham-Balch dispute," and unfortunately by including extracts from an inappropriate and incomplete phase in an institutional review of an internal church matter, he left the false impression that Liberty Hall Academy's rector was censured by his church when in truth, the final disposition was an acquittal, not a conviction. Foote's books suggest that he selectively extracted from the complete record and then rearranged the extractions so that Graham seems to have been censured by the church, when in fact he was not censured. Moreover, Foote leaves the impression that the church's final conclusions were that Balch was blameless,[499] but the final disposition of acquittal, by inference, leaves a contrary impression, which is that Balch of Abington Presbytery, along with his chief witness, William Cocke, had both perjured themselves before two ecclesiastical courts (i.e., the New York and Philadelphia Synod and the Virginia Synod acting in conjunction with the Lexington Presbytery).

Foote also presented a fairly detailed yet utterly false depiction of the roles played by Graham and Rev. John B. Smith, the presidents of the Hanover Presbytery's two seminaries in Virginia, during the famous and politically important struggle for religious liberty in Virginia in 1784 and 1785. Foote entirely fails to appreciate that in the final and most important part of this struggle that these two college presidents and leading Presbyterian ministers in Virginia were opponents concerning the question of taxing the citizens to support the church.

Smith, president of Hampden-Sydney altered his earlier position of firm opposition to assessment in 1784 and adopted a qualified position in which he still opposed assessment but was now also seeking a fair share of the revenue in

---

which describe the presbytery's action to hire Samuel S. Smith to take charge of a new seminary in Prince Edward County, are located, out of proper sequence, on page 135. The February 1775 meeting was a special, previously unscheduled meeting (pro re nata), and for sometime the minutes were deemed to be lost. Later, the minutes were discovered or reconstructed and inserted into the presbytery's record book, but necessarily out of chronological sequence. Technically, the presbytery appointed Samuel Smith to take charge of a nonexistent seminary because the members in attendance at this pro re nata meeting failed to recall that a motion to establish a second school had never actually been made and voted on. At the previous meeting, the members simply stated their *willingness* to establish such a school, provided certain conditions were met. An understandable oversight given the vicissitudes occasioned by the American Revolution, but an embarrassing omission nonetheless.

499   Indeed, the initial committee's communication does say that it appeared to the committee that Balch and Cocke were blameless, but as already pointed out, that committee was improperly empaneled, and moreover, its comments were only based on testimony given by the complainant and his own witness, which is contrary to the idea of due process. The proper entity to hear the matter had evidence from both parties, and its conclusion leaves no doubt that the deciding members did not believe Rev. Balch or W. Cocke.

the event that the legislature were to approve such a tax. In other words, Smith changed his view and agreed to take the revenue benefit of the assessment if his position failed, provided it was done in a manner guaranteed to ensure that those in positions like himself benefited financially on a fair distribution basis. Graham, on the other hand, remained unalterably opposed to assessment period. He therefore opposed Mr. Smith's efforts to alter the Presbyterian's long-standing unequivocal opposition. Smith persuaded a majority of his colleagues, and the presbytery modified their position.

The more politically astute Graham was intransigent and led a revolt among the common Presbyterians to repudiate Smith's efforts in this regard. While Graham was persuading the Presbyterians of the valley to convene a general convention of Presbyterians to challenge the actions of their ministers, Rep. James Madison was writing blistering letters to his colleagues, calling out the Presbyterians for being all too willing to sell their principles in exchange for lucre. Madison manifested the views that Foote so desperately insisted, which were not what Smith's Presbyterian ministers had meant, but once again, Foote was wrong. For Foote to presume that James Madison did not know what Smith's changed message meant in a congressional context was presumption personified. Was not James Madison Americas's paragon of political process? Graham was exactly correct in assessment, and Liberty Hall's president prevailed. At the Presbyterians' request, Graham wrote the church's final message on the issue ("A Memorial"). One person who seemingly completely misunderstood what had transpired during this struggle was William Henry Foote.

Smith accepted his defeat gracefully, and even agreed to argue the church's final position before the Virginia Legislature, which held its meetings nearby Smith's college and his church.[500] Anyone with practical legislative experience knows that presentations or debates that take place just prior to a vote are, more often than not, mere formalities because by the time the debates are allowed, the legislative leaders have mostly ascertained how their members will be voting. Legislators in this case already knew that having received 10,000 signatures on petitions opposing the "assessment" proposal to tax the people to support the church, it would be political suicide to vote for the proposal, and in fact the proposal was allowed to die a quiet death by way of withdrawal of the proposal before it was even voted on by the full body of the legislature.[501]

---

500 Much has been made of Smith's apparently admirable defense of the Presbyterians' position before the legislature, but in fact his presentation is much ado about nothing because, as all political insiders know, debates in a legislative body of any configuration (i.e., committee, subcommittee, etc.) is for the public's benefit alone, because debates of this type only transpire, as a general rule, after all the votes have been privately counted. Legislators' votes are so rarely determined by rhetoric and passion that exceptions are few.

501 Incidentally, the Presbyterians' message opposing the assessment bill, drafted by William Graham, also contained the Presbyterians' plea that the legislature now pass Mr. Jefferson's bill for religious liberty that had been tied up in committee for several years, despite the best efforts of the bill's substitute manager, James Madison, filling in for the absent Mr. Jefferson, who had been appointed ambassador to France. Two weeks after receiving the petitions and the Presbyterian's final memorial, Virginia passed Mr. Jefferson's bill. It would later serve as

The seeming great value of Mr. Foote's two books on Virginia history in the eighteenth century gave him great credibility, which caused many later historians to blindly follow him in regard to the founding of Washington and Lee University and about the college's founding first president, Rev. William Graham. Foote's grave false characterizations, adhered to by hundreds of later historians, underscore the importance for historians to verify sources and double-check anything that contradicts original primary sources and institutional records.

The first several identified central errors of Mr. Foote, taken together, provide a false picture of the founding or "establishment" of Washington and Lee University. These errors were presented by Mr. Foote in contravention of a long-established, well-documented history, as demonstrated in detail above. He cites but one lone authority in support of his rewrite of the institution's founding, which is not in the least credible, while ignoring the contradictory compendium of institutional records of the institution's founding authority. The evidence that Mr. Foote was wrong to assert a connection or link between the Hanover Presbytery's newly established seminary (academy) in Augusta County, Virginia with any prior private school is incontrovertible. His several additional mistakes, while of less significance to the university's early history, have been addressed as the auditor deemed appropriate.

That Foote falsely represented the contents of one of his selected authorities is so eminently clear that his actions in this regard calls into question forever his credibility as either a chronicler or as a historian. As previously noted, his malfeasance in this regard undermines the integrity of any document included in his two volumes' absent independent verification. Indeed, every document he reprinted in his two volumes will hereafter require that another copy be located for comparison.

9. REV. SAMUEL HOUSTON[502] (b. Jan. 1, 1758; d. Jan. 20, 1839 [81 years])

This section was originally created based on what appeared to be a letter in which Rev. Houston, by inference, ostensibly claimed that the Hanover Presbytery patronized an already existing school. The letter and much of its content was provided by William Henry Foote in his _two volumes entitled "Sketches of Virginia, Historical and Biographical"_ series one in 1850, and series two in 1855. Recently, however, it became clear that Mr. Foote's testimony on the contents of the letter was perjured, because what Mr. Foote had represented in series (volume) one was altogether different than what he represented in series (volume) two. It was altogether different in several important ways, as is discussed in detail in the section above devoted to Mr. Foote's errors and also in an appendix on that same subject. At best, a possibly well-meaning Mr. Foote foolishly attempted to correct an error he assumed Mr. Houston had made by claiming that the Hanover Presbytery adopted Rev. Brown's Latin school. If so, Foote's attempted fix was just as erroneous as was Houston's, if in fact either version of the dubious

---

Mr. Madison's template for the religious liberty provision embodied in the Bill of Rights' first amendment.

502 **No date given for this partial letter of Rev. Samuel Houston's, printed by Foote.**

letter was actually written by Rev. Houston. Whatever may be the cause of Foote's colossal failure to accurately depict the content of Houston's letter, as it is said to pertain to the school attended by several named students, the effect serves to undermine anything that Mr. Foote ever published. Whether he acted incompetently or concocted a hoax is of little importance in this context. What is important, however, is that historical researchers can no longer depend upon the published word of William Henry Foote. Any reference to his works must hereafter be taken with the proverbial grain of salt. Mr. Foote, having perjured himself on this subject, is deemed by the auditor to be expedient and appropriate to delete the remainder of this section that was originally devoted to what appeared to be an error made by Rev. Samuel Houston.

In truth, Rev. Houston as an author was not a reliable source on anything historical beyond his own experiences because he was clearly a glorified yarn spinner whose material was typically based entirely on hearsay and local gossip. The serious researcher will search in vain for a footnote or citation of authority in any of the known writings of Rev. Samuel Houston, excepting those letters or memoranda written by him in his official capacity as a trustee of Liberty Hall Academy.[503] His works are amusing, perhaps, but they are unreliable for historical purposes.

Houston did not publish anything that pertained to the founding of Washington College, Liberty Hall Academy, or Augusta Academy. He was, however, an eyewitness to much of what transpired at the college after his return to Virginia from where he had resided for a time in Kentucky. He thereafter became a trustee of the college. The auditor discovered nothing troublesome in the actions of Rev. Houston in his role as a trustee.

As a trustee of the college he was a signatory to two important documents, both of which address the subject of the founding of the college. Perhaps the most important document he signed as a trustee was a petition sent to the Presbyterian Synod of Virginia in 1792. Here below is the most pertinent extract from that petition:

> "But this so far from leading us to freely give him [W. Graham] up as they wish does considerably increase our desire to retain him over our Academy. . . .

> "**For it was under W. Graham that our Academy first received its existence and it is chiefly owing to his extraordinary exertions that it has persevered through all the convulsions of a calamitous War and the many vicissitudes which have taken place through the operations of various causes for the space of about 16 years** . . ."

---

503   The auditor does not include in this assessment the pamphlet that Dr. Diehl attributes to Rev. Houston in his biography, *The Reverend Samuel Houston, VDM*, Verona, Virginia, McClure Printing Company Inc., 1970 because he was unable to locate a copy.

(Board of trustees' petition to the Virginia Presbyterian
Synod, dated September 1792. The original on file is at
the Leyburn Library of W&L.) (Emphasis added.)

The auditor submits that if one seeks to know what Rev. Samuel Houston
believed about the founding of Liberty Hall Academy (later, Washington College,),
then you need look no further than this vastly important document which Houston
signed along with every member of the board of trustees, which was to be submitted
to the highest authority in the Virginia Presbyterian Church, of which he was a
member. It is fruitless to speculate on a mysterious or dubious letter that Houston
may or may not have written, especially given that its contents are substantially and
inconsistently reported. This alleged letter now appears to be missing, and only one
man, William H. Foote, may have ever seen it, and even he could not make up his
mind as to what the letter said. See the subsection above devoted to William Henry
Foote. Finally, on this point, Rev. Houston never referred in writing to his family's
pastor, Rev. John Brown, as having had anything whatsoever to do with Liberty
Hall Academy. The same is true with respect to Robert Alexander and his role as an
educator. That is, as far as history has discovered, Houston made no such assertion.

Finally on this point, Houston signed the letter written by President Graham
addressed to the president of the United States of America, George Washington,
in early 1796 that contained a very cursory sketch of the college's history, and
this sketch never mentions the college being linked to any earlier schools that had
existed in the valley prior to the establishment of Augusta Academy (i.e., Liberty
Hall Academy.) Had Houston actually believed that the man who baptized him
(Brown) was deserving of credit as the founder of Liberty Hall Academy, it is highly
unlikely that he wouldn't have insisted on that monumentally important letter to
at least mention him. Even if that had happened and was an oversight missed by
Houston, he would not have failed to include such a reference in the letter he wrote
to Rev. Brown on behalf of the Lexington Presbytery containing the presbytery's
approval of Brown's request to be dismissed from his duties associated with his
long service as a member of that presbytery and as the pastor of New Providence
congregation. This was effectively Brown's retirement from his pastoral duties, and
it is customary to acknowledge a retiring pastor's extraordinary accomplishments
during their service, but Houston's letter includes no reference to Brown having
been associated with the affairs of Washington College or Liberty Hall Academy.
This is yet another oversight made by virtually every historian who addressed the
early history of Washington and Lee University and therein mistakenly asserted
Brown's important contributions to the establishment of the college.

10. Charles Campbell [1860][504]

(*History of the Colony and Ancient Dominion of Virginia, Philadelphia*, J. B. Lippincott and Co.,
1860 [Google Books pdf], p. 677. This is one of the few books cited as an authority in this report that
the auditor does not have in his own collection.)

---

504 **No reference is made here to Mr. Campbell l's earlier one-volume history of Virginia
because he did not address the subject of education in the valley of Virginia in this version.**

Mr. Campbell makes several mistakes worthy of mention in connection with Washington and Lee University's early history. His greatest error in that regard is located on page 677 in the third paragraph, wherein he improperly assigns to Rev. John Brown a role he never had nor desired.

ERROR no. 1: Campbell mistakenly claims that Rev. John Brown held an administrative position (superintendent), and that Rev. William Graham held the position of "tutor."

Mr. Campbell makes the classic mistake of asserting that Rev. Brown was connected to the presbytery's new seminary (academy) in Augusta County when he had no such connection, and he mistakenly believed that Rev. John Brown was connected as a supervisor at the new academy, but that is entirely false. Rev. Brown never accepted any role in connection with the presbytery's "public academy," and Rev. William Graham was the chief administrative officer from the school's inception until his resignation twenty-two years later.

Here are Mr. Campbell's mistaken words:

> A year or two before the rupture with the mother country, the Presbytery of Hanover established a seminary in Augusta, beyond the Blue Ridge. The Rev. Samuel Stanhope Smith . . . was at this time a missionary in Virginia, **and the school was founded upon his recommendation.**[505] (Campbell, _History of Virginia_, p. 677.) (**Bold** emphasis here indicates error.)

Mr. Campbell was in error concerning Rev. Samuel Stanhope Smith's role in the establishment of Washington and Lee University as well as in respect to Rev. Mr. Brown's involvement in that school, which did not exist. The academy (seminary) in Augusta County, Virginia established by the Hanover Presbytery was not founded upon Rev. Smith's recommendation. The school was founded as the culmination of a feasibility and desirability study initiated sua sponte in 1771 by the presbytery, as can be seen in the institution's meeting minutes for 1771, and Mr. Smith was at that time teaching in New Jersey at Princeton. Mr. Smith did not come to Virginia until 1773, at a time well after the presbytery had decided to establish an academy. It was, however, before it had made a final decision as to the school's location, and also prior to its having identified a suitable person to manage the work in progress.[506]

What Mr. Smith did recommend, of note, was a prospective manager or director, who was William Graham of Pennsylvania. Smith believed that Graham was uniquely capable of designing and implementing a plan to create a college patterned after Princeton. Smith was well aware of Mr. Graham's scholarly attainments, and he knew that Graham's instructional experiences were of such a quality that he could teach virtually any subjects likely to be offered. Smith's

---

505 Campbell, Charles, _History of the Colony And Ancient Dominion of Virginia_, Philadelphia, J. B. Lippincott and Co., 1860 [Google, pdf], p. 677.

506 These facts are easily seen in the Hanover Presbytery's meeting minutes passim.

opinion was sought because the presbytery had not yet been able to locate a candidate it believed suitable for the great challenge. See especially Edward Graham's "Memoir of the Late Rev. William Graham" and the Hanover Presbytery meeting minutes covering the two 1774 meetings.

ERROR no. 2 Mr. Campbell mistakenly links Rev. John Brown to the presbytery's new seminary in Augusta County, Virginia.

> "A year or two before the rupture with the mother country, the Presbytery of Hanover established a seminary in Augusta, beyond the Blue Ridge. The Rev. Samuel Stanhope Smith . . . was at this time a missionary in Virginia, *and the school was founded upon his recommendation. <u>The superintendent was John Brown, and the tutor William Graham.</u>*"[507] (Campbell, History of Virginia, 1860 ed., p. 677.) (Bold italics and underline emphases added here indicate errors.)

The school, as Mr. Campbell mistakenly claims, was not founded upon Mr. Smith's recommendation, and Rev. John Brown was not the superintendent of the Hanover Presbytery's seminary in Augusta County. Campbell was obviously relying on the mistaken Mr. Foote, but may have even misinterpreted the mistaken Mr. Foote.

Creating a college-level seminary was initially contemplated by the Hanover Presbytery as early as 1771, as reflected in the meeting minutes of that date. Additionally, the presbytery was so far persuaded to establish such a school by 1773, that they had already indicated a predisposition to fix its location at Staunton.[508] In 1774, Mr. Smith, then residing in New Jersey, decided that he was healthy enough to itinerate[509] in Virginia in pursuance of his probationary status as a Presbyterian minister. It was, therefore, not possible that the presbytery's new seminary was established upon the recommendation of Mr. Samuel Stanhope Smith because he was in New Jersey at the time that the presbytery was deciding upon the establishment of a college in Virginia. By the time Smith had arrived in Virginia, the decision was already clear in the members' minds. The only remaining sticking points when Smith came on the scene were location and finding the right qualified person who could be expected to oversee such an enormous task.

---

507   Campbell, Charles, *History of the Colony and Ancient Dominion of Virginia*, Philadelphia, J. B. Lippincott and Co., 1860 [Google pdf], p. 677.

508   The following year, the presbytery abandoned any hope of fixing the intended school's location at Staunton.

509   A term used to describe the movements of a minister functioning as a missionary in a distant location and where he/she is moving about.

Mr. Smith, however, is known to have recommended to the presbytery in 1774 the name of Mr. William Graham as the person to take charge of its new endeavor. Mr. Graham had been a colleague of Mr. Smith at Princeton, where both men occupied teaching responsibilities under their mutual preceptor president, Dr. John Witherspoon. Mr. Graham was of a robust constitution and had been reared in his youth on the Pennsylvania frontier, where life was not unlike that of most people then reared in the valley of Virginia, west of the Blue Ridge Mountains.

Campbell was also incorrect in naming Rev. John Brown as a superintendent of the presbytery's seminary. Brown, by his own choice, had nothing whatsoever to do with the seminary's operations.

ERROR no. 3 Mr. Campbell mistakenly assigns formal education attainments to Robert Alexander when the facts reveal that his formal education, if any, remains nearly a complete mystery.

Of far less importance than the previous two mistakes by Mr. Charles Campbell is that pertaining to the educational attainments of Mr. Robert Alexander of Augusta County, Virginia. On this subject, Mr. Charles Campbell says this:

> "Robert and Archibald Alexander also settled in the Rockbridge region. ***Robert, a graduate of Trinity College***, Dublin, taught the first classical school west of the Blue Ridge."[510] (Campbell, _History of . . . Virginia_, 1860, p. 677.). (Emphasis added.) (Emphasis here denotes an error.)

The subject of Robert Alexander's alleged connections with various European universities was investigated in depth by Dr. Ollinger Crenshaw in conjunction with his research conducted for his important book, _General Lee's College_, cited elsewhere. (See bibliography, especially in regard to the two-volume typescript version of the book as well as the appendix A located in vol. II, wherein Dr. Crenshaw asserts that he had contacted the two variously cited European colleges, where it was alleged that Robert Alexander had matriculated, and both colleges informed Dr. Crenshaw that this Robert Alexander had not been of one their students.)

Since Robert Alexander apparently left no autobiographical information, and no other documentary evidence on the subject of his formal education, if any, is known to have been unearthed, we must presume for the present that history knows little if anything about the educational attainments of Robert Alexander. We do know, however, that Robert Alexander and his brother, Archibald Alexander (the elder[511]), both provided some kind of preparatory instruction for youth in the valley of Virginia in the eighteenth century. That information comes from the great-nephew and grandson, respectively, of these two brothers, and indirectly from Mr. Samuel Lyle, who informed the younger Archibald that in his (Lyle's) youth, old

---

510   Charles Campbell . . . ibid, p. 429.

511   Not to be confused with his grandson, Rev. Archibald Alexander, the venerable alumnus of Liberty Hall Academy.

Archibald Alexander gave him some basic instruction and inspired in him a bit of an obsession for books.[512] Mr. Samuel Lyle is one of the original trustees of Liberty Hall Academy and an original member of the executive committee of the board of trustees. In addition, Mr. Lyle was the college's first treasurer, an office he held for virtually the remainder of his life. At his death, the trustees immediately filled Samuel Lyle's position with Samuel's son, Capt. William Lyle.[513], [514]

It is difficult to believe that Robert Alexander was formally educated and held a degree from any college because, if he had, that fact would have been widely known, and certainly his great-nephew, Rev. Archibald Alexander, would have mentioned such a singularly important fact about his grandfather's brother. Rev. Archibald Alexander was, after all, one of a few published authors who wrote about the early American Scotch-Irish and Presbyterian educational institutions in such accounts as *"The Log College."*[515] In conclusion concerning Charles Campbell, his three identified errors are all repeats of the same or similar errors made by Edward Graham in his memoir of his brother, Rev. William Graham, and or by Mr. William Henry Foote. His work on the history of Virginia, as it pertains to Washington and Lee, involves no new revelations indicating any significant original research. Campbell's errors therefore require no in-depth explanations because such discussions were included in several of the above assessments and in the prolegomenon.

****

11. Anon., *The Charter and Laws and Trustees and Faculty of Washington College*, Richmond, 1865.
(Article entitled "Historical Statistics," p. 3.)

It is tempting to speculate on the authorship of this article. Absent some objective criteria, however, we will only point out that this erroneous piece is the first in-house Washington College document that the auditor has located that repudiates the earlier known historical accounts of the college's founding, both in-house and even most all of those that had been published, with the lone exception being W. H. Foote's colossal blunder that asserted a date for the founding of the college earlier than October 1774.

---

512 Alexander, Archibald DD, Mss "Memoir of The Rev. Wm. Graham" [written in longhand]. The Rev. Graham portions of this manuscript constitute the largest part of a writing entitled "Great Valley of Virginia." The original manuscript is housed at the Princeton Theological Seminary Library. A photocopy is also available in spiral-bound form at the Leyburn Library, Washington and Lee University. This copy, supplied by the auditor, is handpaginated by him, in pencil, for reference purposes.

513 Young Archibald Alexander provides this insight in his unpublished memoir of Rev. Graham.

514 This Samuel Lyle is the auditor's fifth great-grandfather.

515 *Archibald Alexander DD, Biographical Sketches of the Founder and Principal Alumni of the Log College*, Philadelphia, 1851.

The date presented in this institutionally published article contained in "*The Charter and Laws* . . ." is foolishly premised on the false belief that the college's founding is linked to the school conducted by Robert Alexander in the valley of Virginia. So too does the next published article that emanated from the college four years later, said by Dr. Crenshaw to have been authored by Col. Bolivar Christian, a trustee of the college. It is noteworthy that Colonel Christian was a trustee at the time that the anonymous article appeared in 1865, but admittedly, the first article dates the origin as being 1752, while the later article dates the founding as 1749. Both of these dates are directly associated with Robert Alexander and his school, and both incorrectly assume that Alexander's school was linked to Liberty Hall Academy.

The likelihood that Colonel Christian is responsible for both the 1869 article and also the 1865 article is quite high, but we cannot actually assign the 1865 authorship to Colonel Christian without having more definite proof. Without a doubt, both of these publications are in error and are presented without any credible evidence to support their dubious claims. Mr. Christian's interest in the topic during the time frame in which these articles were written is palpable as he was then the only person known to possess such an interest in the topic, and at the same time, Colonel Christian was one of the central players in the cabal established to bring General Lee to Lexington to take charge of the college as its president.

This objective was deemed by the cabal to be intimately connected to important issues related to the school's history and its connections, if any, to the Presbyterian Church. The new history advanced by Colonel Christian de-emphasized the role of the church in the affairs of the school, but it was clearly a disingenuous affair involving misdirection and deception. The intrigue was hardly necessary because any institutional connection of the college to the Presbyterian Church had, by that time, been completely severed.

Note: The cabal's members were very likely not aware of Colonel Christian's deceptive machinations exercised in altering the college's early history. For certain, General Lee played no part in this unseemly aspect of the process that brought him to Lexington. In fact, it is unlikely that President Lee was ever made aware of the trustees' actions to repudiate the school's long-standing history.

Note: The article "Historical Statistics" in Charter and Laws . . . contains a false historical account of the origin of Liberty Hall Academy, dating the founding to Robert Alexander's school in 1852. This is a unique date that is later designated to be 1749, but both of these dates are incorrect, as is the alleged connection between Mr. Alexander's school and Liberty Hall Academy. This article contains numerous errors concerning the college and is in direct contravention of all of its earlier records. It cannot be considered as anything better than a hoax.

This one-page 1865 article constitutes the college's first repudiation of its long-standing and consistent representation of its founding and origins maintained in the original official records. However, the repudiation is only by inference because its authors disappointingly neglect to point out that numerous others, including representatives of the college, had consistently identified the college's origin as having taken place in October of 1774. Issued anonymously, the "Historical Statistics" article fails to even notice that this representation is at odds with all prior statements of the institution's founding, let alone provide some semblance of a justification for engaging in a complete rewrite of th college's founding.

Error no. 1: The college's unnamed author misdated the college's founding by twenty-five years

The anonymous author asserts incorrectly that the "germ" of the college was Robert Alexander's "classical school,"[516] and incorrectly dates its founding as having occurred in 1752. There is no applicable "germ" in the case of Washington and Lee University because it was created out of whole cloth by the Hanover Presbytery in 1774. As such, it was an outgrowth of no other prior educational entity, although from its inception it was intended to provide the same kind of educational opportunity then being offered at the College of New Jersey, a fact reflected in various meeting minutes of the presbytery between 1771 and 1776.

It should be remembered that as a general rule, institutions of higher learning do not emerge fully developed like Athena in an instant. They typically evolve like the construction of a building. From the planning stage to the laying of a foundation, the process requires constant supervision and periodic revision. In some cases, a college will result from an unpredictable expansion of a preexisting common or preparatory grammar school, but more often, colleges and universities are preordained as an institution of higher learning by a sponsoring entity, like a church or a governmental body that resolves to establish and patronize the prospective school.

In the case of Washington and Lee University, the sponsoring entity was an association of Presbyterian leaders in Virginia called the Hanover Presbytery comprised, in the main, of all the active Presbyterian ministers in Virginia and some selected and ordained elders. This body usually met twice a year, in the spring and in the autumn. In 1771, the Hanover Presbytery initiated what today might very well be called a feasibility and desirability study designed to discover whether it would be expedient for the presbytery to establish and patronize a school for providing the kind of education then being offered by the College of New Jersey (Princeton). Further, to learn whether there was sufficient support among their congregations to support such an endeavor financially.

By 1773, the presbytery's meeting minutes revealed that the congregations favored such an establishment, and that the people would pledge their financial support. They also seemed to be disposed to fix the school's location west of the Blue Ridge Mountains, but it soon became clear that the greatest obstacle facing these Presbyterians was in finding a suitable person to take charge of planning, implementing, and overseeing such an endeavor. By the time the members of the presbytery met in October of 1774, they believed that they had found their man. On

---

516 There is no known credible evidence that Robert Alexander's school was considered as a "classical school." The exact nature of this endeavor is more unknown than known. It would only seem legitimate to refer to it as a "classical school" if that term possessed little meaning and was applicable to any educational activity of any kind. Presumably, at the time in question, however, it did have meaning for some, but its denotative meaning is now rather elusive given the wide varations of its use.

the recommendation of Rev. Samuel Stanhope Smith, an itinerating probationer who was then under the New Castle Presbytery, the presbytery made a provisional decision to appoint Mr. William Graham to lead this effort and memorialized their decision as follows (From the Hanover Presbytery meeting minutes):

> October 13, 1774:[517] "The presbytery resume the consideration of a school for the liberal education of youth, judged to be of great and immediate importance. **We do therefore agree to establish and patronize a publick school**, which shall be confined to the county of Augusta. **At present, it shall be managed by William Graham, a gentleman properly recommended to this presbytery**—and under the inspection of Rev. John Brown,[518] and the presbytery reserve to themselves the liberty at a future session, more particularly to appoint a person by whom it shall be conducted, and the place where it shall be fixed, which they are induced to do notwithstanding a former presbyterial appointment—because there is no person take the management of it in the place first agreed on—and it is very uncertain whether there ever will be." (Hanover Presbytery's meeting minutes record book, p. 55.) (Emphasis is added, but here it does not indicate an error.)

Error no. 2: The article wrongly asserts that Robert Alexander's school was adopted by the Hanover Presbytery on October 12, 1774.

The article "Historical Statistics" contains errors no. 1 and no. 2:

> "The *germ of Washington College was a classical school established about 1752 (?) By Robert Alexander*, at first near Greenville, Augusta County; and '*was the first classical school in the Valley of Virginia.*' It was removed '*shortly before revolution*' to *Mt. Pleasant, near Fairfield*, Rockbridge

---

517 The meeting was held at Cub Creek Meeting House located in Charlotte County, Virginia, and it began on October 12, 1774.

518 Questions about the qualifying parenthetical "*and under the inspection of Reverend John Brown . . .*" are rendered moot by Rev. Brown, having never accepted the presbytery's assignment, consistent with his attitude concerning all attempts by the presbytery to draw him into the seminary project, which he had consistently opposed. That is why both Edward Graham and Rev. Archibald Alexander did not bother to include the parenthetical when discussing the presbytery's actions to establish the academy in their respective memoirs of William Graham, both of which were written well after it was apparent that Rev. Brown was intransigent on all matters concerning Liberty Hall and its rector, William Graham. Mr. Graham, according to Archibald Alexander, had asked Brown's daughter to release him from the understanding they had concerning marriage after he discovered her mother's demeaning comments about him to others. This breach in their personal relationship was never healed. (See Alexander's "Memoir of William Graham." pp. 65–66.)

> County, where, ***October 12th, 1774, it was
> formally adopted by Hanover Presbytery***,
> with its original name of Augusta Academy,
> and arrangements were made to support it,
> while it remained under the patronage of the
> presbytery, by 'liberal contributions.'" _{(Anon.,}
> _{"Historical Statistics," _Charter & Laws_, p. 3.] (Emphasis in bold}
> _{italics is added here to indicate error.)}

Note: The quotes within the quote are designated by single quotation marks.

This representation, published under the imprimatur of the college, is incorrect and erroneous in the extreme. First, there is no "germ of Washington College," which was an entirely new institution created by the Hanover Presbytery on October 13, 1774, not on the 12th as the author of the article asserts. In two hundred years, not one author has located any credible evidence of a link between Robert Alexander's school and Augusta Academy, and the same is true as regards a link between Brown's Latin school and the presbytery's seminary. Second, the Hanover Presbytery's meeting minutes contain no reference to an action by the Hanover Presbytery to "adopt" any school, not by that specific referenced term, nor by any other term remotely similar to it. Rather, they announced on October 13, 1774, their decision to create an entirely new public school and to patronize the school they established on that day. In addition, no school was ever moved to "Mt. Pleasant"[519] (sic). Brown did establish his private Latin school there during that time when was pastor of Timber Ridge Congregation but after his separation from Timber Ridge Congregation he moved his school.

Afterwards (circa 1767), Rev. Brown moved his Latin school from Mount Pleasant to his new home on Moffett's Creek, near his church and congregation of New Providence. That school thereafter continued to operate at New Providence late into December of 1775. This fact is evidenced by several entries in the famous journal of Rev. Philip Vickers Fithian, who visited the valley in late 1775 and early 1776, and who frequently lodged in Rev. Brown's home. Brown's "Latin school" discontinued operations during the Revolutionary War, but resumed once again, albeit briefly, at New Providence at or near the conclusion of the War, as is evidenced by his correspondence with Col. William Preston. [See John White Stuart, *The Rev. John Brown of Virginia (1728–1803): His Life and Selected Sermons*, Doctoral Dissertation, University of Massachusetts, 1988.]

ERROR no. 3 This publication (Charter and Laws) incorrectly identifies five persons as representing either "rectors, presidents, . . ." etc. on page 4, and suggesting therein that there were four earlier presidents of the college before the appointment of (Rev.) William Graham, which is patently untrue and contrary to all credible eighteenth-century extant evidence.

---

519 "Mount Pleasant" is the proper designation.

The following appears on page 4 under the general heading of:

"Rectors, Presidents, Professors, &c."
  "Augusta Academy (1752–1774)"

"Robert Alexander (1752–1765);
_____ Edmondson, MD (1765);
Rev. John Brown DD,[520];
Ebenezer Smith;
_____ Archibald (??–1774)"

(Charter and Laws . . . p. 4.)[521]

Contrary to this listing in the Charter and Laws book, the "Augusta Academy" did not exist prior to October 13, 1774.[522] The subtitle "Augusta Academy (1752–1774)" is bogus. The editor of this publication added five names on this page and associated these gentlemen with an Augusta Academy that, at the time, had not yet been established. None of the above-named gentlemen had any connection to Liberty Hall Academy or its precursor, that was unofficially and as a mere convention, denominated "Augusta Academy." The name was first used by the presbytery's clerk in order to distinguish the two recently established seminaries one from the other, in its 1775–76 meeting minutes, hence the two unofficial names, "Augusta Academy" and "Prince Edward Academy."

That this was included in the _"Charter and Laws"_ page listing past college officials is no doubt the tomfoolery of Col. Bolivar Christian, who had taken upon himself the task of rewriting the college's seventy-five-year-old documentary history. In this, he probably relied on Foote's falsification published in 1850. He then repeated most of his errors and expanded and embellished this fiction in a second volume published in 1855. Neither Mr. Foote nor Christian had any credible evidence to justify supplanting seventy-five years of consistent history, as represented by the very institution that created the college on October 13, 1774[523] and by the college's administration from its inception in 1774, until the travesty herein under consideration was published in 1865.

---

520 A specious designation. Rev. Brown did not hold a degree of Doctor of Divinity, either real or honorary, unless granted posthumously, but even of this type none are known to exist. In the eighteenth century, it was not common to grant such degrees to someone who was not a scholar of unusual talent and theological attainment. Rev. John Brown was an ordinary Presbyterian parson who did not aspire to obtain such lofty heights of scholarship.

521 _Charter and Laws and Trustees and Alumni of Washington College at Lexington, Virginia, AD 1865,_ Richmond, 1865.

522 The misuse of the name "Augusta Academy," no doubt, is a common feature found in many of the false histories of the origins of Washington and Lee. That term will not be found in Virginia literature or in letters prior to October of 1774 because none of the schools in Virginia prior to that time was ever referred to as "Augusta Academy." Few of the earlier precollege schools had ever been given a name because that was the custom of the time.

523 A few years after the "Charter and Laws" was published, an unnamed author (probably Mr. Christian) published an article in the college paper (Southern Collegian Feb. 7, 1874 et seq.),

Interested readers are referred to the subsection of this general section under the entry devoted to William Henry Foote as well as the appropriate appendix item for a more detailed explanation with all the requisite evidentiary authorities necessary to settle the question beyond any reasonable doubt.

ERROR no. 4 The anonymous (B. Christian) author omits any reference to the long-standing history of the college that had been well established and consistently represented in several published formats and in several institutional records that state the college's date of establishment as having occurred in October of 1774. Some of which were written by officials of the organization that created the college and who participated in the establishment; officials and clergymen whose reputations were then and remain impeccable.

The unknown author[524] of this erroneous historical sketch in the Charter and Laws document also committed an error of omission, which is that the author failed or refused to acknowledge that the college had a contrary institutional history dating back to the school's first authorized written history created by Rev. Caleb Wallace in 1776. Wallace's history functions as an introduction to the first meeting minutes of the board of trustees of Liberty Hall Academy. The history is the first text in the board of trustees' first-ever record book, which contains their earliest meeting minutes. The author compounds this error of omission by failing to explain upon what basis the established official history had been rejected, and what historical evidence the author relied upon to support the major change in the institution's history. Surely, this anonymous author had read the college's first published historical sketch, which had been published in connection with the inaugural address of President George Junkin in 1847, [525] or, if not that article, he surely reviewed the history contained in the board of trustees' first meeting minutes record book written by the noted jurist, Caleb Wallace, on behalf of the organization that created the school. If not, then he was derelict in his duty and unfit to carry out such a responsibility as to write for publication a history of the college's founding.

Given the enormity of the errors contained in this brief sketch, it comes as no real surprise that the author elected to remain anonymous. Still, in that a rewrite of their own history was an event of such import, and because it was

---

and therein perpetrated a hoax designed, no doubt, to create evidence where none existed. See subsection devoted to Bolivar Christian. The article is an amusing display of pettifogging and distorted logic.

524   The auditor strongly suspects that the author is Col. Bolivar Christian, who wrote similar pieces containing the same themes in and around the time this was written. He was also a trustee of the college at this time, and an amateur historian who was a better writer than he was a historian.

525   Junkin, Rev. George, DD, _Christianity The Patron of Literature and Science: An Address Delivered February 22, 1849, On the Occasion of the Author's Inauguration As President of Washington College, Virginia,_ Philadelphia, The Board of Trustees, 1849. The Junkin inaugural address includes an important appendix: "A Brief Sketch of the Early History of the College." (Ordered printed by the board of trustees.) [Pamphlet appendix pp. 35–39.] This appendix constitutes the college's first published history.

published under the college's imprimatur, the college should not have allowed its appearance without attribution. Its mistake in this regard has multiplied in significance over the last 150 years because it has contributed to the ongoing misrepresentation of the school's history ever since. Perhaps one of the reasons the error has been perpetuated for so long is that historians could hardly believe that a history so long repeated without challenge by so many of the college's officials, including the many professors of history that have passed through its halls, could possibly have been untrue. If so, it was a sorrowful false assumption. The article is incontrovertibly erroneous concerning the college's origins. The basic thrust of the article is to repudiate seventy-five years of solid documentary-based history, but its repudiation was made without notice and without explanation. Its appearance smacks of intrigue and chicanery, and its premise lacks even a pretense of having any evidentiary foundation.

12. COL. BOLIVAR CHRISTIAN [1869]
(b. April 26, 1825; d. July 17, 1900)
"Historical Sketch," _Catalogue of Alumni of Washington College of Virginia for the year 1869_, Baltimore, John Murphy & Co, 1869. Especially at pp. 3–13.], Bolivar Christian Esq. is the presumed author of three unsigned articles on the origins of Washington and Lee in the "Southern Collegian" [Washington And Lee University college newspaper, volume VI, no. 9, Feb. 7, 1874; volume VI, no. 10, Feb. 1874; and volume VI, no. 12, March 1874]. The auditor has accepted Dr. Ollinger Crenshaw's presumption concerning Mr. Christian's authorship of these articles.

Note: As pointed out above, it is very possible that Colonel Christian also wrote the 1865 article referenced in the section immediately above (Historical Statistics," Charter and Laws . . .), but evidence on the matter is lacking. The article was published without attribution, and while it differs concerning certain details related to the founding, the general theme based on erroneous assumptions is much the same as what is found in the 1869 version.

INTRODUCTION CONCERNING COL. BOLIVAR CHRISTIAN

Trustee "Col." Bolivar Christian's contribution to the historically incorrect rewrite of the university's early history was to engineer the college's institutional repudiation of its long-standing history. He then shepherded that rewrite's adoption into the college's institutional records. Cloaking himself in anonymity, he manipulated the rewrite into the first section of the college's new and primary publication, ___Charter and Laws and Trustees and Alumni of Washington College at Lexington, Virginia, AD 1865___, (later, _Catalogue of the Officers and Alumni. . .)._

There are three historic occurrences in which Christian played a central role, although one of them, the auditor concedes, is somewhat speculative:[526]

The three occurrences are:

---

526 Of the two or three other possible "persons of interest" potentially responsible, he is the only suspect that had both motive and opportunity to accomplish or carry out this infamous act.

1. The rewrite of the college's early history that appeared in the college publication, _Charter and Laws_ . . . (1865), later revised in the _Catalog of Alumni_[527] in 1869. The revision was thereafter embodied in annual publications that through annual repetition from 1869 forward, reinforced for alumni, faculty, and administrations a completely false and untenable representation of the institution's founding. The "Historical Sketch" in the Catalogue of Alumni (Washington College) originally written by Christian in 1869 was repeated, with variations on numerous occasions in subsequent editions of the catalogue, which has long been republished annually.[528]

2. The perpetration of the "Edward Graham Manuscript" hoax[529] in the February 21, 1874 edition of the "Southern Collegian," in which Mr. Christian, the presumptive author, wrote a preposterously false article anonymously, but his authorship is suggested by Dr. Ollinger Crenshaw in the appendix A of his typescript version of _General Lee's College_.

3. The unauthorized defacing of the university's earliest official record book by inserting ex post facto, a dubious document of no known provenance or authorship into that place of honor and distinction reserved for a book's first page. The book's use was inaugurated in May of 1776, and Trustee Christian pasted in the dubious document sometime after the Civil War, nearly a

---

527 _The Catalog of Alumni_ publication seems to have been issued subsequently as a replacement for _Charter and Laws_.

528 Virtually everything Trustee Christian has written about the early history (origins) of Washington and Lee University is patently and demonstrably wrong. This article may constitute the single most egregiously erroneous account ever published. We have then, in some cases, lumped several errors into one general category. It surely warrants remedial action as soon as is practicable.

529 This handwritten document is unsigned and undated, and whatever it is, it is not a representative of Edward Graham's views concerning the founding of Washington and Lee. This is explained in detail elsewhere in this report.

century after the book's first pages were
used to convey the college's first authorized
history of its establishment. Today, the first
page[530] of this venerable book containing any
text is the document Christian pawned off as
the true history of the college, but which is an
utterly false claim that is entirely inconsistent
with all known eighteenth-century evidence
on the subject. The auditor's primary source
of authority for establishing Christian's role
in this affair is Dr. Crenshaw's appendix A,
from his two-volume typescript version of
General Lee's College,[531] but this report's
conclusions in this regard are based on a
careful analysis of the applicable facts.

Christian, a trustee of the college from 1858, was a law partner of J. Randolph
Tucker. Four years later, he wrote a historical sketch of Washington College
published in the *Catalogue of Alumni,* 1869, again anonymously, but Crenshaw
identifies him as the author. It is a ten-page sketch, but the serious errors with
which this audit is concerned are found at the article's outset and deal with the
founding of the college. Christian stands as the central personality responsible for
the institution's serious mistake in repudiating their previous institutional history
of the founding. The history that was repudiated is a documentary-based one that
was of seventy-five years' duration. The narrative embodied in the institutional
history first formulated in Caleb Wallace's historical memorandum,[532] written
in 1776, is consistent in all the pertinent particulars asserted in all the published
histories known to exist prior to the publication of Foote's two volumes on Virginia
history (1850 and 1855.) Christian ignored all of these earlier sources and focused
completely on the unauthenticated and preposterous claim made by William
Henry Foote. Somewhat later, Christian sought to bolster his claim's legitimacy
by foisting upon an unsuspecting public the Edward Graham manuscript hoax.

Christian compounded his guilt in this regard by advancing the revolutionary
rewrite without bothering to provide any public notice of the full import of what
he was doing, and furthermore, he was bold enough to refuse to provide any
justification for his impertinence. Nowhere in his writings on this subject does he

---

530   It appears to be located on the front endpaper which, of course, is on the verso of the front cover.

531   It is noteworthy that Dr. Crenshaw too was confused and in error concerning the founding of
the college. Surprisingly, Dr. Crenshaw nowhere mentions the college's first authorized history
included in the meeting minutes record book, which was written by Rev. Caleb Wallace on
behalf of the Hanover Presbytery in May of 1776.

532   Rev. Caleb Wallace, "Memorandum History of Liberty Hall Academy," a handwritten document
copied into the record book of the newly established board of trustees of Liberty Hall Academy,
in which are found all the pertinent extracts taken from original handwritten meeting minutes
of the board of trustees that relate to the college's founding, is housed at the Leyburn Library
of Washington and Lee University, pp. 3–7, signed, "Caleb Wallace, Clerk, May 1776."

even hint that he has discarded the consistently presented history of the founding during the college's first seventy-five years.

In so doing, he placed himself above the venerable members of the Hanover Presbytery that created the college; and the venerated alumni **Rev. Archibald Alexander DD**,[533] president of Princeton Theological Seminary; and Washington College's alumni as well as officer and longtime trustee, **Prof. Edward Graham**, who was the younger brother of the college's first president, William Graham. Christian also repudiated the institution's first authorized documentary history written by Rev. and, later, Justice, **Caleb Wallace**[534] in May of 1776. Christian went so far as to refuse to even acknowledge the existence of the college's first *authorized and published* institutional history that appeared in print in 1849.[535]

Christian's transparent attempt to create a false impression that Washington College was not the creation of the Hanover Presbytery of Virginia, was adopted by various credulous College officials including, his fellow Trustees, all of whom wanted the Anglican (Episcopalian) Gen. Robert Edward Lee to accept the Trustees' offer of the Presidency of the College. This group apparently feared that the institution's long-standing connections to the Presbyterian Church might negatively affect Lee's attitude towards accepting the college's offer of the Presidency.

Christian, in concocting his false scenario of the college's founding, failed to realize that the presbytery's plan did not involve patronizing any private preparatory or common schools. The notion that the presbytery adopted or merged with earlier schools is a nonsensical one concocted in the fertile imaginations of mid-nineteenth-century mischief-makers. It is important to remember that every novel post-eighteenth-century hypothesis concerning the founding of Washington and Lee was offered by its proponent without a shred of documentary evidence to support the new notion. In any event, the presbytery's meeting minutes make it abundantly clear that the presbytery never agreed to patronize any existing Virginia schools in the eighteenth century, an undeniable fact which its meeting minutes clearly evince.[536]

---

533 Alexander, Archibald DD, "Address Delivered before the Alumni Association of Washington College, Virginia," delivered June 29, 1843, Lexington, VA, R. H. Glass, 1843, p. 31. Also in: *Washington and Lee Historical Papers* no. 2, Lexington, VA, 1890.

534 **Caleb Wallace op cit. Wallace was the only member of the Hanover Presbytery who served as a trustee of both Liberty Hall and Hampden-Sydney Academies (colleges).**

535 Rev. George Junkin, DD, *Christianity the Patron of Literature and Science: An Address Delivered February 22, 1849. On the Occasion of the Author's Inauguration as President of Washington College, Virginia*, Philadelphia, The Board of Trustees, 1849 [pamphlet p. 39]. The Junkin inaugural address includes an important appendix: "A Brief Sketch of the Early History of Washington College." (Ordered printed by the board of Trustees.) This constitutes the college's first authorized published History.

536 Despite this fact, Rev. William Hill obviously misread the presbytery's April 1775 minutes, and consequently, he created great confusion when his article, "The History of Washington College, Virginia" was published in 1838. See bibliography. He included in a list of events leading up to the establishment of Augusta Academy, a "visit" to Brown's Latin school, which had no connection whatsoever to the establishment of Augusta Academy. Hill's mistake was

Both of the seminaries created in Virginia at this time were stated by their creators (Virginia's Presbyterian clergymen) to be "public" academies[537] under the patronage of the Hanover Presbytery. Just as the seminary in Prince Edward County had no connection with any of the local private Latin or grammar schools, so too was the case with the presbytery's first established seminary in Augusta County, which the presbytery unofficially referred to as the "Augusta Academy."[538] Had the presbytery deemed it desirable to associate their first established seminary with a private preparatory school, they undoubtedly would have followed suit when they established their second seminary in Prince Edward County. The fact is, it only patronized the two schools that the presbytery established. Trustee Christian failed to discern the embarrassing fact that in December of 1775, a reliable eyewitness, Rev. Philip Vickers Fithian, had recorded his observations into his journal, wherein he references the then concurrent operations of Brown's Latin school and the presbytery's academy under the direction of Graham.

As presented in previous entries, here is some of Fithian's revealing testimony:

> Dec. 12, 1775 "Tuesday, 12th (December), I rode on further twenty miles to Mr. Brown's—extreme cold—Young Mr. Trumble was along. We came to Mr. Brown's just when the sun was going down. Mr. Hunter was there before me. On Sunday, he preached below Stanton[539] (sic). We were glad to meet. Here, we met Mr. Doak, who is now over the Latin school in this neighborhood."[540] [Footnote no. 18] (Fithian Journal, pp. 1775–1776, 140.)

Approximately two weeks later, on Christmas Eve, Fithian had returned to the previous vicinity, and while residing briefly at Rev. Brown's home, he wrote:

---

due to his confusing Brown's private school at New Providence with the presbytery's seminary, under Graham, at "Mount Pleasant."

537 A "pubic academy" did not mean then what it does today. It simply meant that it was open to all qualified prospective students and that its instructors were subject to the oversight of a governing body representing a community or region. Private school were typically governed by the person who created the school who, more often than not, was also the instructor.

538 Since the denomination "Augusta Academy" was merely a convenient convention and not an official name, some referred to the school as "the seminary in Augusta" or "our school in Augusta," variations on a theme, but all referring to the same school under William Graham's direction. Use of this convention lasted for less than two years (1775–1776), after which, the academy was given the official name, "Liberty Hall Academy." The naming of the school was the first recorded action taken by the academy's newly created board of trustees, a Board created by the Hanover Presbytery in May of 1776.

539 Mr. Fithian spelled the name of Staunton the way it is to this day pronounced in the Valley (i.e., *Stanton.*)

540 The editors for this volume issued by The Princeton University Press were incorrect in challenging Fithian's use of the term "neighborhood" in connection with Mr. Doak. Fithian was correct; the editors were wrong. The neighborhood Fithian refers to is the vicinity of the two adjoining congregations of Timber Ridge and New Providence. The editors were misled, probably by Mr. W. H. Foote. Doak was where Fithian puts him at the time in question.

Dec. 24, 1775 "Mr. Graham, lately initiated a brother, is appointed director of a school <u>in the neighborhood of Mr. Brown's</u>[541]—He thinks to enlarge his method of education so much as to finish youth in their classical, philosophical studies—" (Fithian's Journal 1775–1776, p. 150.)

The assessment, which follows of Christian's various works related to the early history of the college, are arranged differently from all the other authors we have audited for accuracy because there remains some question about the authorship of the articles that appeared anonymously in the Southern Collegian, which address the college's origins and connections to the Presbyterian Church in Virginia. We believe that Dr. Ollinger Crenshaw is probably correct to suspect that Christian is the author, but there remains at least some doubt on that question. Therefore, that component of this assessment is separated from the rest.

In some cases, a numbered error actually represents several mistakes made in the same sentence or the same paragraph.

ERROR no. 1: Christian avers incorrectly that the school conducted by Robert Alexander in the valley of Virginia (circa 1760s) was an institution of some permanence, and that it evolved into Washington College.

Here below is Christian's erroneous assertion:

> **The germ of Washington College was a Mathematical and Classical School, called the Augusta Academy, established in 1749, by Robert Alexander,** and first located two miles southwest of the site of Greenville, in Augusta, and near the interlacings of the head springs of the Shenandoah on the eastward, and of the James River on the westward. **"It was the first classical School in the Valley of Virginia," and was continued by an uninterrupted succession of principals and assistant instructors, on successive sites, increasing in usefulness and influence, until it gradually developed into Washington College.** (Col. Bolivar Christian, *Catalogue of the ... Historical Sketch*, 1869, pp. 3–4.)[542] (Bold italics emphasis here indicates error.)

This preposterous assertion by Christian is uttered in direct contravention of every known historical treatment written from the college's founding in October of 1774 through 1849. All published and all internal documentary records of the

---

541 Fithian here is referring here to "Brown's" school, and his reference to "finish youth in their classical philosophical studies" means to complete their college education. The same phraseology can be seen in the literature of that period in reference to the College of New Jersey and other colleges in British North America.

542 Published anonymously, the authorship is attributed to Christian by Dr. Ollinger Crenshaw in both his footnotes to *General Lee's College* (typescript version) on file at Washington and Lee Archives/Leyburn Library, and also in his appendix A to vol. II of the version, neither of which is included in the Random House version.

college up to the time of Christian's rewrite of the college's early history are essentially concordant and contradict every representation made by Christian about the college's establishment that appears above. Contrary to Christian's claim (above), Robert Alexander's school was never known as "Augusta Academy,"[543] and it was not the "germ of Washington College."

Concerning Christian's claim that Alexander's school was "a mathematical and classical school," it is important to point out that he offers not one shred of evidence in support of this claim. His failure in this regard is understandable, however, because no such evidence is known to exist, except in the Colonel's own mind. He refers to no book, article, or letter in support of his remarkably novel claim, and he conveniently fails to acknowledge that history knows very little, if anything about Alexander's school. Moreover, history contains not one bit of evidence that would distinguish Robert Alexander's school from any one of the vast array of country peripatetic primary schools that existed in Virginia during the eighteenth century. It is not even known with any credible degree of certainty where the school was located, let alone what constituted its curriculum. In fact, history contains no reliable information on when his school was established or when it was either closed or transferred to another. The few court records that refer even indirectly to his school convey little information that is of interest historically. If Christian had unearthed some reliable information on the subject of Alexander's school, he should have shared it with his readers. Instead, he offers us nothing but wild speculation devoid of facts and or reason, and inconsistent with all the known documentary evidence that exists. Since it was Christian who was proffering a radically new history, there was a burden to provide some compelling argument as to why the world should accept his presumptuous ideas. Alas, he offers nothing in support of his claim. We have no choice then but to reject his notion as the ravings of a would-be historian. His credulous fellow trustees chose to accept his repudiation of the then long-standing existing history and supplanted their previously adhered to documentary history with their own rather ridiculous counterversion.

Note: Christian studied the early history of the Scotch-Irish settlement in the valley of Virginia and deemed himself somewhat of a historian of the subject. In fact, he published at least two articles on the subject, one for the Scotch-Irish society and one for the Washington and Lee University Historical Papers.[544] In so doing, any argument that might be made that his misrepresentations were simply an honest mistake is clearly lost.

ERROR no. 2: Christian mistakenly represents that there was a "germ" from whence the academy evolved.

---

543 And why would it be, since it was a local neighborhood operation and in no way was it ever known, in the eighteenth-century, to be an academy.

544 *Of course, he is also the most likely author of the serialized unsigned article on the origins of Washington and Lee in the "Southern Collegian." [Washington and Lee University college newspaper, vol. VI, no. 9, Feb. 7, 1874, and vol. VI, no. 10, Feb. 21.]*

Christian avers incorrectly in the opening lines of his quotation shown above that:

> "***The germ of Washington College*** was a Mathematical and Classical School, called the Augusta Academy, established in 1749, by Robert Alexander . . ." (Col. Bolivar Christian, *Catalogue of the* . . . "Historical Sketch," 1869, pp. 3–4.)
>
> (Bold italics emphasis here indicates error.)

In truth, the school had no germ, as such, for it was designed and implemented from the beginning to be a college that could prepare young men for the Presbyterian ministry. This fact lies in plain sight, embedded in the official meeting minutes of the Hanover Presbytery. Therein is described the process by which the presbytery evaluated the initial proposal to establish such a college-level school in Virginia.

The school or seminary operated initially with an unofficial name, "Augusta Academy," in its rudimentary form as a "grammar school"[545] conducted in temporary quarters awaiting completion of the college's first permanent buildings, which were then being constructed on lands adjacent to the Timber Ridge Meeting House. The college's first board of trustees were nominated en blanc in May of 1776, and thatboard, once constituted, acted to name the school "Liberty Hall Academy." This action was first announced on May 6, 1776, a name choice clearly in concert with the times.[546] Two months later, the prospective new nation was formally at war with the mother country, but the school continued on, and by dint of the undaunted efforts of William Graham, instruction continued throughout the long and troublesome conflict. In that time, implementation of the college continued albeit more slowly than had been everyone's desire at the outset.

Unstated in Christian's fabulous sketch is his clear but mistaken belief that the Alexander school he refers to was directly linked to a private Latin school that was at one time organized by Brown, but which was conducted by an unrecorded line

---

545   This is the denomination adhered to by the presbytery's clerk and used in writing these minutes. In the course of the1771–1774 series of presbytery meetings, the various clerks referred to the prospective patronization of an educational program referred to their object as a "seminary of learning," a "public school," "a seminary," "our intended seminary," "the public seminary," and "a public School." Every one of these references allude to what the presbytery intended to be a college, patterned after the College of New Jersey. When the Hanover Presbytery decided to "establish" this school and agreed to patronize it, they also authorized a fund-raising campaign in its name for the purpose of purchasing laboratory equipment and a library the likes of which were then only used in a college setting.

546   Descendants of Brown living in Kentucky would later mistakenly contend that the college's trustees named the academy after a homestead of one of Rev. Brown's ancestors in Ireland. This notion is beyond absurd because Brown is the only known member of the Hanover Presbytery that consistently opposed the creation of the seminary later named Liberty Hall Academy, but he was also the only member of the Hanover Presbytery that rejected his appointment as a trustee of the college. The trustees would hardly have named its academy to honor an avowed enemy of the school and its first president (rector), William Graham.

of various instructors, initially at a place near Rev. Brown's home called by local residents as "Mount Pleasant," but later (circa 1767) moved to New Providence on Moffett's Creek.[547] No historian concerned with this vicinity in Virginia has produced any credible eighteenth-century evidence that any such link ever existed. Brown's peripatetic private school was focused on providing the very basic Latin and Greek grammar that was then a prerequisite for being accepted into Princeton, where those young men interested in becoming a Presbyterian minister most generally matriculated.

In the 1770s, in the vicinity or "neighborhood" of Timber Ridge and New Providence churches, there was but one known school being conducted prior to October of 1774, and that school was first organized by Brown and was located on the farm of James Wilson, at or near a spot referred to by local residents as "Mount Pleasant." This is one fact on which most all local histories agree. Also well-established is the fact that instruction at this peripatetic educational endeavor was not conducted by Brown, but by various individuals, about which little is known with any degree of certainty. The published local histories offer varying accounts with only scant particulars, but none of these accounts are based on identifiable credible evidence. What history does know in this regard is that the school was a private "Latin school," and we learned this from the school's creator, Rev. John Brown, who consistently identified it as a Latin school in his extant private correspondence from that period.

It is also known from the Hanover Presbytery's records that in the 1760s, Brown was pastor of both Timber Ridge and New Providence churches, and from Brown's correspondence, he lived on a farm near by the Latin school initially located at Mount Pleasant. From the records of the Hanover Presbytery (meeting minutes), however, it can be learned that there came a time in 1763 when Brown's relationship with certain members of the Timber Ridge Church became so untenable that Brown petitioned the presbytery, seeking their permission to separate himself from the Timber Ridge pastorate. Again, from the correspondence of Brown and the presbytery's records, it is clear that he had purchased a farm near the New Providence Church on Moffett's Creek and had obtained an agreement with the members of the New Providence congregation to be their exclusive pastor, if the presbytery would grant him permission.[548]

In the interim, Brown moved his farm, family, and his Latin school from Mount Pleasant to the new location on Moffett's Creek, several miles distant from its earlier location. In the meantime, the presbytery having failed to obtain a mediated resolution of the dispute between Brown and the Timber Ridge congregation, granted Brown's request, and the bonds between him and the

---

547 According to J. R. Hildebrand's 1973 "Historical Map of Rockbridge County," published by the Roanoke Valley Historical Society, the New Providence Church, which was adjacent to Brown's school, was located between Raphine and Moffett's Creek, but it was probably somewhat closer to Moffett's Creek. Hildebrand's map probably locates "Old Providence," and New Providence was most likely closer to Moffett's Creek, as described by many of the eighteenth-century authors, including Philip V. Fithian in his 1775–1776 journal. See bibliography.

548 John White Stuart, dissertation, op cit.

Timber Ridge congregation were permanently severed, effective 1767. Thereafter, the neighborhood's school was no longer conducted at "Mount Pleasant," but was instead now conveniently located at New Providence on Moffett's Creek and adjacent to the Brown's second family home. Contrary to various similar assertions made by later nineteenth-century historians, Brown's Latin school was never again moved or relocated after it was moved to New Providence, a fact made clear by his extant correspondence housed in the Draper collection in Madison, Wisconsin.[549] Those who later represented otherwise did so based on mere speculation spurred, in the main, by their vain attempts to explain how Brown's school could have returned to its earlier location at "Mount Pleasant." Simply put, they were demonstrably wrong. Brown's Latin school was never moved from New Providence, and there is ample evidence to prove this fact. The evidence can easily be gleaned by reviewing Brown's extant correspondence from the period in question. See John Whites Stuart's biography of Rev. Brown listed in the attached bibliography.

The misguided historians who insist on finding a link between Alexander's private common school, as it clearly was, and Brown's private Latin school, have not and cannot produce one shred of competent evidence that any such link ever existed between Alexander's and Brown's two entirely different kinds of schools. Without establishing link between these two peripatetic common schools, no theory of connection between Washington and Lee and Robert Alexander's school could possibly be sustained, in part because no such link exists.

The problem with the theories that would link either school to Liberty Hall is that there is no known evidence that supports a link between Washington and Lee and either of these early common schools independent of one another, or as taken together, as if they were linked, but of course, that too is unverifiable nonsense.[550]

In pursuit of these fanciful theories, every historian who tried has failed, and in so doing, they generally deftly avoid mentioning this glaring insufficiency. Finding themselves without any requisite evidence, they fall back on either a straightforward gratuitous assertion, or they attribute their premise to "traditions." In fact, there are no "traditions" to support these notions either, if one accepts that "traditions" are supposed to be traceable to the time period in question. Here, the so-called traditions did not surface during the time period in question, but rather nearly a century later. Such phenomena as this are not traditions; they are fanciful fictions formulated in the credulous minds of wishful thinkers.

In this case, the only claim possibly traceable to the eighteenth century that is known to exist that is apparently based on tradition is a legendary letter ostensibly written by Rev. Samuel Houston, but even that paltry piece of evidence, such as it is, is said by its proponent Foote to say one thing in 1850, and then later

---

549 Ibid.

550 Even if one assumes for the sake of argument that Alexander's school and Rev. John Brown's school were linked, and that Brown's school evolved from Alexander's, it would still be demonstrably false to suggest a link between Washington and Lee's earliest form as Augusta Academy/Liberty Hall, and any earkier school, for such a thing never happened and there is no known evidence to the contrary.

(1855) said by the same source, Foote, to say something entirely different. Such inconsistent representations typically render the so-called evidence inadmissible and unreliable, absent production of the original so as to allow for comparison and authentication. Apparently, no one but the inconsistent Mr. Foote has seen this mystery letter. Over and above this consideration is the fact that Houston, the supposed source of the letter, which may or may not assert a link between Rev. Brown's Latin school and the Hanover Presbytery's Academy established in Augusta County, is not a particularly credible source. What Houston is claimed to have said could only be based on hearsay insofar as Houston was a mere lad in his teens at the time the Hanover Presbytery established the school, and their actions in that regard took place at the Cub Creek Meeting House approximately eighty miles from young master Houston's father's farm. Moreover, young Mr. Houston was not a student at Liberty Hall until that time in 1777 when he began his instruction at the new academy, and even then he shortly thereafter left the school and volunteered to serve in the early stage of the Revolutionary War. What he believed he knew was in fact hearsay, and obviously failed to consult the Hanover Presbytery's records because their own official records are in significant conflict with the varying accounts(s) Mr. Foote attributes to Houston.[551] As has been pointed out elsewhere, Houston was not given to historical research, relying instead on folklore and community gossip upon which he formulated his amusing but unreliable "yarn spinning."

The myth that Liberty Hall Academy grew from a germ, and that the germ was either Alexander's school (circa 1760s) and/or Brown's Latin school, is belied by two important and incontestable facts: (1) Robert Alexander's school was long defunct at the time that the Hanover Presbytery established their seminary in Augusta County on October 13, 1774, and (2) that "'Augusta Academy," as it was then called, was in operation at Mount Pleasant in 1775, and Brown's Latin school was simultaneously in operation at New Providence. The one school could hardly have evolved into the other if they were both operating at the exact same time at two different locations. And it is an incontestable fact that these two schools were operating at entirely different locations at the very same time. (See Philip Vicker Fithian's 1775–1776 journal.) (See bibliography.)

For the sake of those "doubting Thomas" that might still exist, we offer this insight from a highly credible eyewitness, Rev. Philip Vickers Fithian, testifying in 1775 and early 1776:

---

551 Foote strangely quotes the same part of the same paragraph with two entirely different concluding phrases. These differing phrases significantly alter the paragraph's meaning, and even more strangely, he fails to notice or explain the amendment. This serious discrepancy appears first in his 1850 volume of *Sketches of Virginia, Historical and Biographical,* series one. Then five years later, in what amounts to volume two (1855), he quotes from the same mysterious letter, but quotes the same material altogether differently. This is rather thin evidentiary reed of evidence upon which to formulate an entirely different history than what everyone else had previously written over the course of seventy-five years.

Dec. 12, 1775:

"We came to Mr. Brown's. Hunter was there before me . . . Here we met with Mr. Doak, who is now over the Latin school[552] in this neighborhood." (Fithian's Journal 1775–1776, p. 140.)

Dec. 24, 1775:

Mr. Graham, lately initiated a brother, is appointed **Director of a school <u>in the neighborhood of Mr. Brown's</u>—He thinks to enlarge his Method of Education so much as to finish Youth in their classical, Philosophical Studies—** (Fithian's Journal 1775–1776, p. 150.)

Jan. 12–20, 1776:

Mr. Graham is here— – Sage, deep-studied Mr. Graham. **He is Director** of a small **Academy** in this neighborhood. He retains, with Dignity, the inherent Gravity which he always supported in every Part of his Conduct while he was a Student at Nassau [Princeton]. The Lines of Method & Discipline have been inscribed & are yet visible & legible upon his countenance!

Thursday, <u>at his school,</u> he gave us a sermon. He spoke with Propriety; he preached, I believe, orthodox Divinity; & he seemed zealous. I was entertained, I hope a little improved. (Fithian's Journal 1775–1776, p. 171.) (Emphasis added.)

The above raises the question of why Fithian would refer to the school as being Graham's school if, in fact, it was Brown's school especially when Fithian makes it clear that Rev. Brown was in attendance for this prayer-group session?

---

552 There was only one Latin school in the neighborhood of Timber Ridge and New Providence congregations, and it was Brown's Latin school. The designation Latin school was what Brown consistently used when referring to his school in his extant correspondence. See John White Stuart's biography of Rev. John Brown.

The answer is, that Fithian, obviously knew that the school to which he was alluding was Graham's school and that it was not Brown's school.

Earlier that same year, the Hanover Presbytery was meeting at Brown's home, and after the meeting, members went from there to visit Brown's school next door. The school was most likely conducted at the New Providence Meeting House (i.e., church). So there were two schools at two separate locations. One, Brown's private Latin school at New Providence, and the other, the presbytery's new "public" academy under Mr. Graham at Mount Pleasant. Both operated under different auspices, and each of a distinctively different character. This comes from the eyewitness testimony of Philip Vickers Fithian, who wrote the entry at or about the time the events occurred (i.e., December and January of 1775 and 1776).

> Note: This entry by Fithian is of paramount significance. Fithian and William Graham were schoolmates at Princeton. Fithian makes clear in this journal that he felt kindly toward Rev. Brown and his family, and he lodged with them whenever he passed through that community. He therefore would not have cavalierly referred to Graham as the "director" of the seminary school or have referred to the school as "his school" if Rev. Brown was the director of the school. Moreover, Fithian would not have referred to the seminary as "his school" if Rev. Brown was Graham's supervisor. *This journal entry was not written from memory, but was written and entered into the journal on the day, or day after the event took place.* The dispute does not arise until seventy=five years later when W. H. Foote published his "*Sketches of Virginia,*" which contained the bogus account of the school's origins. *All subsequent assertions that are at odds with the early correct accounts are based, in the main, on Foote's bogus account either directly, or indirectly.* (All italics and bold fonts are added here by the auditor for emphasis only.)

Remembering that Fithian knew both Graham and Brown and that he recorded his monumentally important statement in his journal, his comment bears repeating:

> Mr. Graham, lately initiated a brother, *is appointed Director* of a school *in the neighborhood of Mr. Brown's*. (Bold underlined italics are strictly for emphasis.)

Fithian is clearly saying here that there were two schools in the neighborhood of Timber Ridge and New Providence churches, one being Brown's school and the other under Graham. Both schools were also obviously operating simultaneously and somewhat near one another.

> Query: How does Fithian's eyewitness testimony square with Mr. Christian's allusion to the interesting but irrelevant "germ" theory as it relates to Washington and Lee?

Answer: It is in direct contravention. Christian is palpably wrong, as is the source upon who he relied, who is most likely Foote. Foote was the identified source relied upon by a long list of authors, who followed him in several matters of great importance concerning the founding of Washington and Lee University, many of which are incorrect.

ERROR no. 3: Several errors in the same paragraph.

Here below is the way in which Christian, again following Mr. Foote, crafts his own false assertion:

> "As Principal of Augusta Academy, *Mr. Alexander was succeeded by Rev. John Brown, DD*, his pastor, who was called to Providence and Timber Ridge Churches in 1753. During the administration of Mr. Brown, *the Academy was successively removed a few miles westward, first to Old Providence, then to New Providence Church, and 'shortly before the Revolution,' to Mt. Pleasant,* near Fairfield, in Rockbridge County, where in 1774, <u>*Mr. William Graham became his assistant*</u>, and in 1776, succeeded him as Principal." (Col. Bolivar Christian, *Catalogue of the* . . ." Historical Sketch, 1869, pp. 3–4)
>
> (Bold italics and underline here indicate error(s).)

Erroneous claims made by Colonel Christian in this one sentence, in the following order:

1. Alexander's school did not have any name, let alone the specific name "Augusta Academy." The name Augusta Academy was only in use during 1775–1776 in reference to the presbytery's new seminary, initially located at Mount Pleasant. The name is not found in any eighteenth-century sources as referring to any other school. The name reappears in the nineteenth century in works written by misguided historians and chroniclers, who used the name willy-nilly and in reference to schools that were not known by that name in the eighteenth century.

2. There is no known eighteenth-century evidence indicating that Brown succeeded Alexander or that their two schools had any institutional connection. (See McDaniel et al., *Liberty Hall Academy, The Early History of the Institutions which Evolved into Washington and Lee University*, Lexington, Virginia, Liberty Hall Press, 1979.)

3) There is no known eighteenth-century evidence suggesting there was a link between Alexander's mysterious school and Brown's Latin school in Augusta County.

4) William Graham was never Brown's assistant, and there is no known evidence from the eighteenth century suggesting otherwise.

In the quoted extract above, Christian made four demonstrably incorrect statements, and he offered no credible evidence to support any one of these four mistakes. The auditor, however, offers the following arguments challenging Christian's assertions:

Comments regarding Christian's errors listed above beginning with his error number 1:

1. It is instructive to learn that no known eighteenth-century source contains the name "Augusta Academy" in conjunction with Alexander's school, including books, articles, letters, and institutional records. No published author who later (i.e., post-1850) used this name in conjunction with Alexander's school has ever given a citation to support his or her use of that name. Moreover, no one ever published an account of the schools or a history of the valley of Virginia that contained this false claim, until at least seventy-five years after Liberty Hall Academy was established in 1774. Unsupported claims such as this only surfaced after all the original principals involved and the eyewitnesses to the founding were long dead. The name Augusta Academy was not applied to any school in Virginia other than the academy established by the Hanover Presbytery in 1774. In the eighteenth century, the name is only found when it is in reference to the presbytery's academy at Mount Pleasant during 1774 and 1775, and even then only in the meeting minutes of the presbytery covering those same two years.[553]

---

553 As has been pointed out elsewhere in this report, the names Augusta Academy and Prince Edward Academy were unofficially adopted as a convention by the presbytery's clerks who were responsible for keeping the organization's meeting minutes and who sought to distinguish between the two new academy's when referencing them in the presbytery's minutes. Before this use, the names are not known to have existed in Virginia. Schools like Alexander's and Brown's were then common in Virginia and were intended to service local residents. Precollege preparatory or common schools were not intended to service entire counties, so adopting a name referencing the county by name would have been grossly inappropriate. Similarly, such schools were not, at that time, typically deemed "academies." These private preparatory schools were more properly referred to as grammar schools, English schools, classical schools, or Latin schools. There were no clear lines of distinction between such private schools during this period. Schools of higher learning were rarely allowed to use the label college unless the school in question was affiliated with the established Anglican Church. Therefore, prior to the Revolution, schools of the higher sort were labeled seminaries of learning or academies.

Indeed, no one is known to have made this serious mistake until after the mid-nineteenth century when it was manufactured by authors credulous enough to accept Foote's mistakes about the founding of the college. These later authors simply conjecture that the earlier schools were called "Augusta Academy," when in fact they were not. Moreover, in eighteenth-century Virginia, no one is known to have referred to either Alexander's endeavors or Brown's Latin school as an "academy." Once again, these mistakes originated in the fertile imaginations of mid-nineteenth-century figures like Foote and Christian, and then embellished by many others.

> 2. From the well-funded, extensive archaeological study conducted at Washington and Lee University under the supervision of Professor McDaniel emerged an important publication, *Liberty Hall Academy, The Early History of the Institutions Which Evolved Into Washington and Lee University*, by John M. McDaniel, Charles N. Watson, and David T. Moore, Lexington, Virginia, Liberty Hall Press, 1979, which includes the following finding:

> > **The fact remains, then, that evidence of direct ties between the sites [Alexander's school and Brown's school(s)] has not been found in eighteenth-century sources.**[554]
> > (McDaniel et al., Liberty Hall Academy . . . p. 4).

> This important archaeological study team combed the institution's archives alongside a vast array of known sources and could find nothing to support this oft-repeated erroneous assertion. Their 1979 finding comports with our forty years of intermittent research. The team's bibliography demonstrates wide-ranging research. On this point, at least, we agree with Professor McDaniel's group. The auditor, however, regrets that what was said in regard to the nonexistent link between Robert Alexander's school and that of Rev. John Brown had been extended to include the similarly nonexistent link between Brown's school and Liberty Hall.

> 3. The evidence relied upon to disprove this false assertion includes that which was proffered in the prior citation. In sum, the auditor's finding expands upon the finding of the McDaniel group as concerns the possibility of there being a link between Alexander's and Rev. Brown's schools. The auditor asserts with

---

554 **McDaniel, John M., Watson, Charles N., Moore, David T.,** *Liberty Hall Academy, The Early History of the Institutions Which Evolved into Washington and Lee University*, Lexington, Virginia, Liberty Hall Press, 1979.

great confidence that there is also no known eighteenth-century credible evidence that there was a link between Brown's Latin school and the Hanover Presbytery's Augusta Academy. (See no. 2 immediately above.)

4. The evidence to disprove the notion that Graham was Brown's assistant is located throughout this report. No person has ever alluded to any source that would verify this impossible assertion, and for good reason: no such evidence exists. Brown had but one unimportant connection to Liberty Hall Academy, which is that he was one of the numerous members of the Hanover Presbytery that established the academy in 1774, but the presbytery did so over his publicly silent opposition. Moreover, he refused his appointment as a trustee, as can be seen by the fact that he never attended a meeting of the board of trustees, and he refused to send any of his sons to Liberty Hall Academy.[555]

The notion is preposterous because Brown's scholarly attainments were known to be of the most limited kind, while Graham's scholarship was remarkable in a vast array of subjects including theology, natural philosophy, Newtonian physics,[556] Latin and Greek literature, political philosophy, mathematics, and astronomy.[557] In addition, Graham had several years of experience as an instructor under the direct supervision of two Princeton's presidents, Samuel Finley and John Witherspoon. Brown, on the other hand, had no classroom experience. It is therefore difficult to imagine the subject about which Brown would have been in a position to supervise Graham.

Brown's extant correspondence demonstrates that his animus toward Liberty Hall Academy and its rector, William Graham,

---

555 Several authors have claimed that one or another of Brown's sons had attended Liberty Hall, but in every case these misguided writers were incorrectly assuming that the name Augusta Academy referred to the these boys' father's Latin school when it did not. No eighteenth-century evidence to the contrary has ever surfaced in official records, letters, or known writings from the time in question. All such references are mid-nineteenth-century ex post facto ones, and they are all false assertions. Certainly, neither Rev. Brown nor any of his sons ever made that claim in writing. Any claim of that type that was made by a Brown family member were later descendants, and none of them cites any credible evidence to support the specious assertion. These are mere gratuitous assertions having no basis in fact (e.g., John Mason Brown).

556 Graham was selected to speak at his Princeton commencement on the question: "Is matter infinitely divisible."

557 In 1776, Graham purchased for the school an orrery for studying the solar system, various laboratory equipment used in the study of mathematics and Newtonian physics, and also a telescope with a double reflector. (See Crenshaw, General Lee's College, p. 11.)

was so deep and long-lasting that he went so far as to advise close relations to follow his lead in this regard. History has Dr. John White Stuart III to thank for extracting the pertinent parts of Rev. Brown's letters from the period in question. See John White Stuart III, *The Rev. John Brown of Virginia (1728–1803): His Life and Selected Sermons*, Doctoral Dissertation, University of Massachusetts, 1988, passim. History has also been well-served by the descendants of Rev. Archibald Alexander, who joyously ignored his admonition to destroy his unpublished manuscript, "Memoir of Rev. William Graham," in which Alexander explains how the estrangement between the immediate family of Brown and Graham, as well as how Liberty Hall came about. Finally, in this regard, history will forever be indebted to those who preserved the original handwritten eighteenth-century meeting minutes of both the Hanover Presbytery and Liberty Hall's board of trustees.

Note: During Brown's life, he is not known to have directly supervised any instructor who was teaching a college-level course and, without doubt, he never taught a college-level class by himself. When Rev. Graham organized a temporary program of instruction in the form of a grammar school at Mount Pleasant while buildings for the academy were being constructed at Timber Ridge, Brown had no connection to the presbytery's educational endeavor.[558] From its inception, the school was under the direction of William Graham, as the presbytery's meeting minutes will attest, provided the reader examines these minutes closely.

As a pastor, Brown was expected by his congregants to conduct a school for the congregation's young people. His scholarly attainments, however, were so limited that he was forced to organize a school that relied entirely on the expertise of others for the instruction of the students. When, in late December of 1775, Brown lost his instructor, Samuel Doak, Brown had little choice but to close his school insofar as young instructors were mostly unavailable. As events unfurled, the closing was, like for most schools, for the duration of the Revolutionary War.[559] Liberty Hall was one of the few exceptions, and technically, it was never closed during Graham's twenty-two-year tenure, representations to the contrary notwithstanding.

Had Brown possessed the requisite teaching skills, he would, no doubt, have taken the instruction responsibility temporarily upon himself. As things stood, however, Mr. Brown's students had no choice but to seek other educational alternatives. Presumably, some of the younger students gravitated toward the recently established grammar school directed by Rev. Graham only a few miles

---

558 *Brown did attend a prayer service at the new school in January of 1776, as is evidenced by Fithian in his journal. His attendance was probably a professional obligation that he believed he had to attend.*

559 *When the Revolutionary War was coming to a close, Brown wrote to his brother-in-law, Col. William Preston, announcing that he was reopening his Latin school at New Providence, and sought his assistance in securing essential supplies. See John White Stuart's Dissertation Biography of Rev. John Brown.*

away, but still, in Brown's neighborhood. If so, some local residents might very well have misinterpreted these facts and concluded that the two schools had merged, or that the presbytery had adopted Brown's school, but fortunately, Brown's letter to his brother-in-law, William Preston, rather vividly illustrates Brown's understanding that his Latin school's closure in December of 1775 was merely a temporary suspension due to exigent circumstances precipitated by the war. He communicated his intention to reopen his school in 1782, and this fact eviscerates the accuracy of any contention that Brown's school was in some way linked to the presbytery's academy at Mount Pleasant.

These facts are aptly discussed and explained by Dr. John White Stuart in his biography of Rev. John Brown. See the bibliography. Stuart provides numerous pertinent facts that shed important light on Brown's activities, but he mistakenly ignores the implications of these facts and surprisingly misrepresents Brown as having been associated with the presbytery's seminary.

Simply stated, Brown could not abide the presence of the presbytery's academy in his own neighborhood. Had any of the post-1850 historians interested in Washington College's origins bothered to actually consult the official records of the college's board of trustees, they could hardly have missed the glaring absence of Rev. Brown's presence at these meetings for twenty consecutive years. Trustees who accepted their appointments as a trustee did not typically refuse to attend any of the board meetings, especially so in the case of Brown, given that these meetings were held in his own neighborhood.[560] It is noteworthy that Brown sent none of his sons, all of whom were college educated, to his presbytery's established and patronized seminary that was located in his own community.

ERROR no. 4 Christian compounds his previous errors by claiming a clear link between Robert Alexander's private school and the private Latin school of Brown. Moreover, he bestows on Brown a degree of Doctor of Divinity, which he is not known to possess. Trustee Christian also errs here by falsely asserting that Graham became Brown's assistant.

Here below is Christian's false and unsupported assertion:

> *.As principal of Augusta Academy, Mr. Alexander was succeeded by Rev. John Brown, __DD__,* his pastor, who was called to Providence and Timber Ridge churches in 1753. During the administration of Mr. Brown, *the academy was successively removed a few miles westward, first to Old Providence, then to New Providence*

---

560 *The term neighborhood, at the time, referred, in this case, to the locale of Timber Ridge and New Providence Presbyterian churches, which were adjacent to one another and only a few miles apart. At the same time, Brown, as a member of the Hanover Presbytery, often traveled eighty miles or so to attend meetings of that body of clergymen and selected elders. Brown's absence at all meetings of the trustees of Liberty Hall Academy, as the saying goes, speaks volumes about his views as they relate to Liberty Hall Academy.*

Church, and shortly before the Revolution,
to Mt. Pleasant, near Fairfield, in (now)
Rockbridge County, where in 1774, Mr.
William Graham became his assistant, and
in 1776, succeeded him as Principal. (Bolivar
Christian, Catalogue of the Alumni . . . "Historical
Sketch," 1869, pp. 3–4.)

In regard to trustee Mr. Christian, the pertinent facts are these:

(1) There is no known eighteenth-century evidence that
the name "Augusta Academy" was ever used in the valley
of Virginia before it appears in the meeting minutes of the
Hanover Presbytery following the establishment of a seminary
in Augusta County, Virginia. The use of the term unofficially,
"Augusta Academy," only occurred after the Hanover
Presbytery agreed to establish a second seminary in Prince
Edward County, Virginia, thereby necessitating that they adopt
some means by which to distinguish them when constructing
its meeting minutes. The presbytery had apparently already
decided to give the honor of naming these schools to a board of
trustees, yet to be appointed. The presbytery minutes referred to
the schools, thereafter, informally as "Augusta Academy" and
"Prince Edward Academy" respectively, although sometimes
the names are somewhat varied.

(2) No known evidence exists as to when, or where the school
operated by Alexander, was conducted, or what kind of
instruction was offered at the school.

(3) Neither Alexander nor Brown was ever the principal of
Augusta Academy, and there is not one shred of evidence from
the eighteenth century to indicate otherwise.

(4) Graham was never anyone's assistant at Augusta Academy
or Liberty Hall Academy because he was, from its inception,
the chief operations officer, and any assistant at that school
worked under rector, Graham, and finally, in regard to this
error-ridden paragraph.

(5) Brown's eighteenth-century school at New Providence
was never moved from that location, and especially not, as
suggested, back to Mount Pleasant. This fact is evidenced by
Brown's correspondence from that period housed in the Draper
manuscript collection in Madison Wisconsin. See John White
Stuart, *The Rev. John Brown of Virginia (1728–1803): His Life*

and Selected Sermons, Doctoral Dissertation, University of Massachusetts, 1988, which contains numerous letters and letter extracts of Rev. John Brown.

Until and unless any party who adheres to the proposition that there was a link between Alexander's school and or Brown's Latin school, or between either school and the presbytery's seminary (academy) at Mount Pleasant produces some credible evidence that either one of these two private preparatory schools was actually linked to the seminary in Augusta, this rather absurd notion should be dropped from all publications sponsored by Washington and Lee University. There is simply no good reason to perpetuate this ahistorical myth that is demonstrably untrue. The fact that Houston may have suggested that a grammar school attended by Samuel Doak et al. was "patronized" by the Hanover Presbytery does not constitute compelling evidence that Houston's obviously mistaken assertion was in fact true. Houston, as we have clearly demonstrated in other parts of this report, was clearly mistaken on that point, if, that is, he actually ever made this claim, which is open to question. No known author has ever seen the letter alluded to by Foote. Foote suggests that he had it, or a copy, but in either event, he significantly altered his representations of its contents from one volume to another, and as a result, his value as a witness to its very existence is severely limited. See the subsection devoted to Foote. This inconsistent representation by Mr. Foote calls into question the reliability of Mr. Foote's representations in this regard, and presumably, in regard to everything he has ever written or chronicled.

In regard to number four above, it is pointed out that William Graham was never anyone's assistant from the day of his arrival in Virginia to take the management of the Hanover Presbytery's recently established seminary (academy).[561] No pre-Civil War record of the presbytery indicates or even remotely suggests a possibly different scenario, excepting the meeting minutes of the presbytery that do say that Mr. Graham's appointment as "manager" is to be "under the inspection" of Brown. This provision in the minutes, however, is of no consequence insofar as Brown did not accept any of the presbytery's appointments that were related to the presbytery's new seminary.[562] A full reading of the minutes will make that abundantly clear because all interactions between the presbytery and its academy in Augusta County are described in its meeting minutes as interactions solely between the presbytery and Graham. When Brown's name appears in the minutes in connection with the school (Augusta Academy), it only

---

561 Of course, Graham answered to Hanover Presbytery in the very beginning and later to the board of trustees, but he was never in a subordinate position at the academy, as the institutional records all clearly demonstrate.

562 Brown, along with several others, was appointed to participate in the early fund-raising efforts of the presbytery, and the facts and evidence reviewed by the auditor are deemed to constitute an insufficient basis upon which to conclude whether Brown participated in these activities. If he did, the auditor is unaware of it. His correspondence with his brother-in-law, Col. William Preston, strongly suggests that he chose to disparage the fund-raising effort rather than encourage contributions.

pertains to certain appointments of Brown, none of which he accepted.[563] The only reference in the minutes to his (Brown's) Latin school is a fleeting reference to some members of the presbytery's mere social "visit" to Brown's private Latin school after its April 1775 meeting at New Providence had concluded. Numerous authors have confused Brown's school at New Providence with the presbytery's public school at Mount Pleasant.

Since Brown was never a teacher or instructor, it is impossible that the experienced instructor, Graham, could have assisted him in that regard. Moreover, as a theologian is well-known in the last quarter of the eighteenth-century, the two most eminent Presbyterian theologians in Virginia were William Graham and Samuel Stanhope Smith. It is therefore difficult to comprehend how Graham could possibly have been Brown's assistant in any capacity. Certainly not in any matter academic because Graham's attainments in that regard stood preeminent even at Princeton, let alone in the rural Blue Ridge Mountains, while Brown's scholarly attainments were unusually rudimentary. See John White Stuart's biography of Brown. Brown had no classroom experience at any level, let alone in an environment of higher education. Christian's suggestion in this regard invites unnecessary invidious distinctions that are rather embarrassing and serve little purpose.

Note: As pointed out by Rev. Fithian in his journal, Rev. Brown was in attendance at a prayer meeting held at Mr. Graham's school in its earliest days. It was a meeting of the local ministers and church elders in that neighborhood, and Brown probably only attended because he assumed that his absence would surely have been deemed both discourteous and unchristian under the circumstances. It appears that this was the only time Brown ever visited the presbytery's patronized academy (Augusta Academy), which was later named Liberty Hall Academy.

ERROR no. 5: Christian avers incorrectly that:

> "[On] the 6th of May, 1776, the trustees direct the record . . . to be entitled 'Liberty Hall'—as this academy is hereafter to be called instead of Augusta Academy." (Bolivar Christian, Catalogue of Alumni of Washington College, Virginia, for the year 1869, Baltimore, John Murphy & Co. 1869, p. 4.)

Christian is incorrect in saying that the board of trustees met and made decisions on May 6, 1776, because on May 6 of that year, the board of trustees did not yet exist. The meeting he refers to took place a week later, on May 13, 1776. The Hanover Presbytery, however, did meet on May 6, 1776, and on that day created the board of trustees. The board of trustees met for the first time, a

---

563 The one possible exception is an early (1774) appointment of Brown to take charge of the fund-raising campaign in a specific geographical area, which he may or may not have carried out. The records are very incomplete, but the auditor have reviewed those subscription sheets bearing signatures that he could locate, and they did not contain the name of Brown. Whether the extant lists represent all that ever existed, the auditor was unable to ascertain.

week later, on May 13, 1776. This fact would have been very obvious to anyone who had a true copy of the presbytery's meeting minutes in front of them when they wrote the above quoted sentence. Therefore, the auditor seems justified in concluding that Mr. Christian was either relying on his memory, imprecise notes, or he was relying on a secondary source, which might explain why he was so very mistaken about the origin of the college.

The only meeting held on May 6, 1776, pertaining to Augusta Academy was a meeting of the Hanover Presbytery, not, as represented by Mr. Christian, *the board of trustees*. As the presbytery's meeting minutes for that date reveal, the presbytery decided to "fix" the academy's location at Timber Ridge, and they also named a board of trustees for the academy. Additionally, they also appointed an executive committee comprised of a select few members, and directed the executive committee to meet one week later on May 13th, 1776. It is eminently clear here that Mr. Christian was no expert on the subject of the origins of the college because he could not even distinguish between the Hanover Presbytery and the college's board of trustees.

Christian, and most of those authors who followed him in this regard, should have wondered why the Hanover Presbytery did not appoint Brown to the all-important executive committee of the board of trustees. Christian might also have asked himself why Brown's name does not appear as having been present on the day the new board of trustees held its first official meeting. If Christian had, he might well have looked more closely into Brown's overall participation in the academy's affairs and discovered that, indeed, Brown did not participate in any of the academy's business affairs, not once, not ever.

The board's executive committee met on May 13, 1776, not May 6 as suggested by Christian, and on that day, they chose Graham to be their chairman and Mr. McKee their clerk. It does not appear that it had dawned on Christian that if he was correct in claiming that Graham was Brown's assistant, then why wasn't Brown selected to be the board's chairman of the executive committee? Indeed, he should have inquired as to why Brown wasn't even selected to be a member of this all-important committee.

The new board also assigned the name Liberty Hall Academy to the school, thereby replacing the informal use of the term "Augusta Academy." Importantly, the action by the executive committee to adopt the formal name, Liberty Hall Academy, was carried out by the six patriots comprising the executive committee. This was two months before the signing of the Declaration of Independence, and while the British flag still flew over the capitol of Virginia. It was a bold and courageous act of defiance.

Some have suggested that the trustees named the school Liberty Hall Academy to honor Rev. Brown because it is supposed that Brown had an ancestor in Ireland whose homestead was called Liberty Hall. The board, however, certainly did not select the name Liberty Hall Academy to honor an ancestral home of one of Brown's ancestors because Brown is the only known member of the Hanover Presbytery that opposed the creation of the school. The mere idea of such a ridiculous notion strains credulity. Anyone who suggested such an idea obviously had no idea that Brown was opposed to the creation of the school, had refused his appointment as a trustee, and had refused to send any of his sons to the presbytery's school located in his own neighborhood.

This mistake by Christian demonstrates that he did not have a clear view of what was happening in Virginia among the Presbyterians concerning the creation of two educational institutions in the eighteenth century. It is difficult to comprehend how the board of trustees allowed such an ill-informed fellow trustee to so mislead them that they chose to repudiate their long, honorable, and previously well-established history.

Christian then falsely claimed a link between Alexander's school and Brown's school that did not exist, preposterously asserted the germ theory wherein Alexander's school is viewed as being the germ from whence Washington and Lee grew, mistakenly claimed that Brown was the principal of Augusta Academy, and bizarrely claimed that Rev. Graham was Brown's assistant. All claims are purely gratuitous, and none of which are remotely possible for reasons already elucidated. He was so confused and so terribly ignorant about the institutional affairs of Liberty Hall Academy in its earliest days, that he claimed the board of trustees named Augusta Academy as Liberty Hall Academy before the board of trustees existed. He has no credibility whatsoever as a historian of the early days of Washington and Lee University. What he did do was to serve as an advocate or attorney representing clients bound and determined to establish that the Presbyterian Church played no important role in the creation of Washington College, and he used a lawyer's bag of tricks designed to create silk purses out of sow's ears. He refused to acknowledge the school's own complete early documentary records as well as those of the Hanover Presbytery for the years 1771–1776, and instead relied upon hearsay, gossip, and yarn-spinning folklore. All of his main points are easily disputed by compelling eyewitness testimony of highly respected individuals who were actually involved in the establishment of the college.

***** SEPARATE ASSESSMENT OF THREE ARTICLES FROM *THE SOUTHERN COLLEGIAN* *****
(Putative author, Col. Bolivar Christian[564]):

In 1874, there were three articles published in *The Southern Collegian* that attempted to justify the then recently adopted false view about the founding of Washington College. Bolivar Christian Esq. is the presumed author of the three related articles on the origins of Washington and Lee, published in Washington and Lee University's college newspaper, vol. VI, no. 9, Feb. 7, 1874; vol. VI, no.

---

564 Dr. Ollinger Crenshaw speculated that these articles were written by Bolivar Christian. His speculation is bolstered by the fact that the initial article describes in detail a sheet of paper, later dubiously dubbed "The Edward Graham Memorandum" or words similar, which Dr. Crenshaw asserts was pasted into an official record book of the board of trustees, ex post facto by trustee, Mr. Christian. This action by Mr. Christian was grossly inappropriate for numerous and rather obvious reasons.

10, Feb. 1874; and vol. VI, no. 12, Mar. 1874. The first article contains the text of an unsigned manuscript said to be in the handwriting of Edward Graham, brother of William Graham. The author provides a very brief sketch of a series of schools evolving into Liberty Hall Academy. It contains a list of early students, to wit: "Samuel Doak . . . etc. and Archibald Alexander, son of Robert's . . ." etc. This comment is not referring to Rev. Archibald Alexander, DD . . . but rather to his second cousin of the same name. More importantly, the unsigned author's hypothesis and reasoning is absurd in the extreme.

The article's (presumably B. Christian) hypotheses in the last analysis are based merely upon a one-page, unsigned, and undated memo about which almost nothing is known or knowable. No known provenance of this curiosity exists. Its legitimacy, therefore, is beyond dubious, and it is of no historical value whatsoever. It could be almost anything the mind can conjure up, but what it is not is a sound basis upon which to revise seventy-five years of both published and documentary history left by historians and custodians of institutional records of reputable bodies. Nevertheless, this meaningless, unsigned, undated memorandum mortared together with W. H. Foote's unevidenced and unauthenticated revised version of Liberty Hall's founding formed the very foundation of the postmodern-like version of a history of the college's founding that has been represented by the university since 1869.

Colonel Christian, if he be the author, as is suggested by Dr. Crenshaw, presents in this article nothing particularly persuasive or worthy of challenge. It is pure pettifogging enshrined in petty rubbish. It ostentatiously pronounces a dubious unsigned and undated document to represent the true story of the founding of Washington and Lee despite the unvarnished fact that the sum and substance of the document's argument is offered in contravention of every previously written document known to exist prior to Foote's similarly preposterous and unauthenticated history of the founding of Washington College. Surprisingly, he claims that the author of the documents is Edward Graham; this, despite the indisputable fact that every known document written by Edward Graham during the last twenty years of his life that pertained in some part to the subject of the founding of Washington college, contained Edward's assertion that the college's origins are traceable to the actions of the Hanover Presbytery in October of 1774 in direct contravention of what Christian's mystery document claims. Christian makes no attempt to explain how this contradiction is possible. The auditor, therefore, declined to waste the readers' time, attempting to dissect and analyze these three absurd articles that cannot possibly be accurate or representative of Edward Graham's views on the origins of Washington and Lee.

Christian's embraced document also contradicts every piece of documentary evidence ever created by the Hanover Presbytery or the college's board of trustees from the date of the college's founding through the year 1849 when the trustees released its first authorized published history of its own origins. The 1849 historical sketch located in the pamphlet containing Dr. Junkin's inaugural address states in no uncertain terms that the college was established in October of 1774. Christian would have his readers accept his own novel narrative without one shred of accompanying credible evidence.

Conclusion regarding Col. Bolivar Christian:

Trustee Bolivar Christian was at the very center of the mid-nineteenth-century movement to purge the seventy-five-year consistently represented documentary history of Washington and Lee University. In order to accomplish this within the college's administration, he and those who joined his effort had to ignore all the pertinent early records of the college and the records of the Hanover Presbytery from 1771 through 1776. He also had to completely ignore the only published histories that addressed the origins of the college published prior to 1850, including Edward Graham's "Memoir of the Late Rev. William" published by the eminent editor, Rev. John Holt Rice. The cabal also ignored the private manuscript "Memoir of Rev William Graham" written by the founder and first president of the Princeton Theological Seminary and early alumnus of the college, Rev. Archibald Alexander, DD.[565] In addition, they paid no heed to the college's first authorized and documentary history written by the Rev. Caleb Wallace, who later became a justice of Kentucky's highest appellate court.

At the same time, Mr. Christian relied principally on suppositions and wishful thinking to support his claims. On the few occasions when he refers to documentary records,[566] he obviously relied on extracts written down from records by others instead of reviewing the actual official records. The records, when viewed in the proper context, provide eminently clear evidence of Christian's serious errors. The official records, for example, do not even remotely suggest that John Brown's private Latin school was ever patronized by the Hanover Presbytery, and there was never a merger of Augusta Academy or Liberty Hall Academy with any other entity prior to the school obtaining a charter and incorporation from the new legislature of Virginia in 1782. By inference, the entire 1865 board of trustees accepted Trustee Christian's repudiation of the college's earlier history, or they were guilty of benign neglect.

In the aftermath of the 1865 revision of the college's early history, one author after another repeated and often embellished the new and yet utterly false history. The actions of these gentlemen trustees resulted in an institutional embarrassment that yet remains to be corrected. Provided that Dr. Crenshaw was correct when he identified Bolivar Christian as the person who pasted the so-called Edward Graham memorandum into the first record book of the board of trustees, then that act suggests gross malfeasance by an official of the university. It warrants a special commission to examine the pertinent evidence and thereafter make

---

565 To be fair, Archibald Alexander's unpublished memoir formed the basis of his son's biography of his father, and the son's treatment misrepresented his father's memoir in regard to the founding of Washington College, and the son's distortions were widely distributed and more readily available than his father's unpublished memoir. So while this fact mitigates Christian's culpability in this regard, the facts are the most important. The facts demonstrate that the college technically began in 1774, although its operations at "Mount Pleasant" under W. Graham began the following year, 1775.

566 The documentary evidence being referred to are the official eighteenth-century records of the Hanover Presbytery and those of Liberty Hall Academy, which are comprised, in the main, of their respective meeting minutes.

recommendations to the trustees as to what actions in that regard, if any, may be warranted. At a minimum, the appropriate archivists should be directed by the administration to remove the so-called Edward Graham memorandum from the trustees' first record book, which should never have been allowed to have been pasted into that book in the first place. It should be preserved, of course, but it should be handled carefully and stored separate from the official record book. To be certain, the university should sponsor an investigation into this unsigned and undated memorandum and the role it played in undermining the institution's inappropriate repudiation of its early history.

13. HUGH BLAIR GRIGSBY LLD [1870] (b. Nov. 22, 1806; d. April 28, 1881) Hugh Blair Grigsby, "The Founders of Washington College," an address delivered June 22, 1870, *Washington and Lee University Historical Papers* no. 2, Lexington, VA, 1890.

Note: Riddled with serious errors, generally unreliable concerning historical facts pertaining to the origins of Washington and Lee University, but contained much interesting and useful information on other aspects of the college's history.

Hugh Blair Grigsby was a historian of no little fame and vast experience and, at one time, was a president of the Virginia Historical Society. It is readily apparent that Grigsby relied heavily on the two works of William Henry Foote in preparation for his address because he refers to both books therein. Had he used his own powers as a historian, he might well have avoided the several important mistakes included in his address to the Lexington community and the faculty and students of Washington College on June 22, 1870. It is to be regretted that he did not carry out the research himself. As a result, his reputation suffered in some degree but in no wise does the damage to himself compare to the damage that was done to the true history of Washington and Lee University. Library shelves are now filled with books, magazines, and pamphlets that have relied on this eminent historian's numerous false depictions, most of which resulted from his failure to rely upon primary sources that were readily available.

Grigsby, early in his address, makes the following mistake:

ERROR no. 1: Grigsby errs by describing an origin of Washington and Lee that does not exist, dating its founding as 1749.

By drips and drabs, Grigsby presents his mistaken account of the origins of Washington and Lee:

> In 1749 was opened the first classical school
> west of the Blue Ridge . . . (p. 9)

> The site of this classical school was two miles
> southwest of Greenville in Augusta [county]
> as Augusta then was, and which included
> Rockbridge, and its first teacher was Robert
> Alexander. ***That school was the origin of the***

> **noble institution whose massive buildings
> cast their shadows from this glorious
> eminence** . . . (p. 10)
>
> And who was he who taught the infant mind
> to know those immortal productions of Greek
> and Roman genius . . . (p. 10)
>
> His name was Robert Alexander. **He was a
> man of thorough training in the schools** . . .
>
> **Robert was educated at Edinburgh . . .**"
> (Grigsby, "The Founders of Washington College . . .,"
> _Washington and Lee University Historical Papers_, no.
> 2, pp. 10–11.) (Emphasis added here indicates error.)

All that is emphasized by bold italics above is patently incorrect. Robert Alexander's school was not the origin of Washington and Lee, which is the institution Mr. Grigsby is alluding to in the extracts above. Any known retrospective, mid-nineteenth-century and later representations by historians treating with the early history of Washington and Lee are, in most every case, based on the false assertions of William Henry Foote or are mere speculation and of no evidentiary value whatsoever, excepting Dr. Crenshaw, who despite having thoroughly researched his subject, declined to publish the rather clear implications of his study. Fortunately, his surviving family contributed his unpublished writings on the subject to the university.

Dr. Crenshaw has ably demonstrated that history knows virtually nothing about Robert Alexander's educational attainments. Crenshaw, author of "_General Lee's College_," researched Robert Alexander's educational background and discovered that he attended neither of the universities that several historians have gratuitously suggested was where he obtained his education. In truth, nothing of consequence is known today about that subject, except what is not true. Robert's grandnephew, Rev. Dr. Archibald Alexander, the noted theologian and historian, briefly referenced the educational endeavors of his namesake and grandfather, Archibald ("Ersbel") Alexander, as well as those of his grandfather's brother, Robert, but in neither case did he remotely suggest that either relative had any connection whatsoever to his own alma mater, Liberty Hall Academy. If there had been a connection, it is hardly imaginable that Rev. Alexander would have failed to mention it. If nowhere else, at least in his important "Address to the Alumni of Washington College," wherein he eulogizes his own preceptor at Liberty Hall Academy and declares him to be the founder and first president of the college. Here below is what Rev. Alexander said on this momentous occasion in 1843:

> I cannot conclude this address without
> pronouncing a brief eulogy on the man
> who deserves to be called the Father of

the College, and whose memory should be venerated by all its Alumni. I mean the Rev. William Graham. (Archibald Alexander, "Address to the Alumni, p. 128, W&L Hist. Papers, vol. 2, 1890.)

On the same subject, Dr. Alexander somewhat earlier said this:

Mount Pleasant should be considered as a kind of consecrated spot; and altho' it is now, like Shilo of old,[567] a desolation; yet it would be well, **especially for the surviving pupils of Mr. Graham, to erect a monument on that spot, as a memorial of the first classical school instituted in the Valley,** But stone, marble, & brass are perishable substances: we want a memorial more enduring than those; and this can only be erected by a faithful history of this institution & its founder (William Graham) which we are now attempting to furnish. (Emphasis added does not in this case indicate an error.)

(Rev. Archibald Alexander DD, Mss. "Memoir of Rev. William Graham" p. 45.)[568]

Dr. Alexander would hardly credit William Graham with being the founder of Washington College if there was any reason to believe that the honor belonged to either his grandfather or his grandfather's brother, Robert. It is difficult to imagine how this reality has escaped the attention of so many historians who have repeated the nonsensical notion that the college was founded by anyone other than William Graham and the Hanover Presbytery.

Continuing on with Grigsby's error-ridden account:

The successor of Robert Alexander was the Rev. John brown . . .

"It is stated that the academy in the time of Mr. Brown was successively moved a few miles westward, first to near Old Providence, and then shortly before the Revolution to Mount Pleasant, near Fairfield, in the present county of Rockbridge. He conducted the school until 1774, when he was assisted by William Graham, who two years later,

---

567   "Shiloh of old" is ancient biblical references found in the Old Testament books of Joshua and Judges, and refers to ancient ruins of the capital of Israel before Jerusalem.

568   Mss, "Memoir of Rev. William Graham," handwritten by A. A. & paginated by this writer, p. 45.

> *became the principal."* (pp. 11–12) (Emphasis
> here indicates error. Indeed, the entire extract can be
> viewed as erroneous. His unknown source was seriously
> misinformed on the subject.)

Virtually the entire extract above is provably false. The early history of the university sections of this sketch is based on the mistakes of many nineteenth-century authors, most of whom unfortunately relied upon the misguided William Henry Foote. Nevertheless, a great deal of Grigsby's article is useful and accurate. The challenge for the reader is to sort wheat from chaff. Below is another example of a Grigsby error:

> *His five sons were educated here and at Princeton.* (Grigsby, "The Founders of Washington College . . .," *Washington and Lee University Historical Papers*, no. 2, pp. 11–12.) (As was true above, the emphasis in bold italics represents statements that are erroneous.)

The above representation about Brown's sons is a preposterous misstatement. In fact, none of Brown's sons attended Washington and Lee University or any of its antecedents. This mistake assumes incorrectly that Augusta Academy, Liberty Hall Academy, and Washington College were in some manner linked to Robert Alexander's school, Rev. John Brown's Latin school, or both. There was never any such link, and that is why no credible evidence in two hundred years has ever surfaced indicating that there was such a link. Unsubstantiated speculations or assertions, even from noted authors with admirable reputations, are not credible evidence unless it is based on their eyewitness observations relating facts as opposed to their analysis of facts.[569]

As it happens, there is no eighteenth-century evidence that Brown succeeded Alexander, or that there is any link between their two schools. This fact was recognized by Professor McDaniel and his research group at Washington and Lee that carried out an extensive research on the subject. (See John M. McDaniel, Charles N. Watson, David T. Moore, *Liberty Hall Academy, The Early History of the Institutions Which Evolved into Washington and Lee University*, Lexington, Virginia, Liberty Hall Press, 1979; and John M McDaniel, Kurt C. Russ, and Parker B. Potter, *An Archaeological and Historical Assessment of the Liberty Hall*

---

569 A good example of the analysis of facts differentiation is A. Alexander's relaying observations of Rev. Graham's communion service at Rev. Brown's New Providence Church, where he provides an accurate depiction of the service, but his analysis, which concludes that Rev. Graham's use of a hymn written by Isaac Watts was improper, is erroneous. Graham's use of Watts was consistent with the policies of the Presbyterian Church and was predictable, given that Watts's hymns were a key component of the the Presbyterian Revival, and it was because of Graham's position as the leader of the Revival in the valley that he had been invited by a majority of Brown's congregation to conduct this service. This fact was revealed by Alexander in the same document.

Academy Complex 1782–1803, Lexington, Virginia, The Liberty Hall Press, 1994. [The James G. Leyburn Papers in Anthropology, vol. II, 1994.])

Grigsby is also incorrect in his description of the movement of Brown's school. For example, Brown's school was never "moved to Mount Pleasant." Instead, about 1767, Brown moved his school from Mount Pleasant to his home and church on Moffitt's (Moffett's) Creek. Moreover, Brown did not "conduct" his school at any location. He merely organized the school and left the "conducting" to his hired instructors as has been discussed in several previous subsections of this section. In addition, Rev. Brown was never assisted by William Graham with the possible exception being on the occasion when Graham was invited by Brown's congregation to conduct a communion service at Brown's new Providence Church. Still, this was merely as a visiting fellow clergyman, not as Brown's assistant. Graham at that time was president of the academy and pastor of two congregations. His playing second fiddle to a country parson is a ludicrous, nonsensical notion lacking any demonstrable foundation.

Grigsby, by following the mistaken Mr. Foote, wrongly assumed that Brown's Latin school and Graham's academy were one and the same school when, in fact, they were not. Moreover, neither Brown's school nor Alexander's school was ever named "Augusta Academy." Augusta Academy was the unofficial name used by the Hanover Presbytery to distinguish between the new seminary in Augusta County from that academy located in Prince Edward County. This convention adopted by presbytery clerks of using unofficial names associated with the counties in which the schools were located was only used in 1775 and 1776. By mid-1776, the schools were officially named Liberty Hall Academy in Augusta County, and Hampden-Sydney Academy in Prince Edward County.

There is no eighteenth-century evidence of that the denomination "Augusta Academy" having ever been used in connection with any Virginia school other than Liberty Hall Academy under William Graham. That is, not until seventy-five years after the school was founded and all the original members of the Hanover Presbytery had died. The name "Augusta Academy" will not be found in any eighteenth-century Virginia sources, except in the minutes of the Hanover Presbytery between 1771 and 1776 or in works referring to the academy created by the Hanover Presbytery in October of 1774.

Inaccurate and inappropriate uses of the name Augusta Academy in connection with the private schools of Alexander or Brown only began to appear in the mid-nineteenth century, and mostly, if not exclusively, after the appearance of Foote's two "*Sketches of Virginia, Historical and Biographical*" issued in two series beginning in 1850 and concluding in 1855.

Brown, as discussed by Rev. Philip Vickers Fithian and John White Stuart, no longer lived adjacent to Fairfield and Timber Ridge in 1770. His permanent move to Moffitt's Creek (New Providence) took place sometime around 1767.[570]

---

570   The move was permanent with regard to Brown's Latin school. Brown and most of his family moved to Kentucky. The semiretired Rev. Brown followed in 1796, but his Latin school had, long before that time, become defunct. Indeed, there is scant if any reason to believe Brown's school was ever again viable after the American Revolution.

Knowledge of these several critical facts is paramount to understanding why so many historians confused these two schools, one with the other.

Another critical fact that Grigsby might have discovered if he had done his own research on this early period of the university's history is the nature of Brown's alienated feelings about the Hanover Presbytery's new project to establish a seminary in Augusta County. Feelings that emerged during the mid-1770s remained with him through the remainder of his residence in Virginia. Brown's feelings in this regard are easily discernable in his private correspondence from that period, as is discussed in some detail by John White Stuart III in his biographical dissertation on Rev. John Brown. Unfortunately, Dr. Stuart misinterpreted some of these letters. His misinterpretations were likely due to his having accepted many of Foote's errors in regard to Rev. Brown and Rev. Graham. Stuart missed the glaring fact that Brown never accepted his appointment as a trustee of Liberty Hall and was never present at a meeting of that August body. His error was predictable because it was also missed by all other historians who followed the erroneous Mr. Foote from 1850 up to today.

Had Grigsby deigned to review the minutes of the institution that founded Augusta Academy covering the period from 1771 through 1776, he would likely have noted the peculiar absence of Mr. Rev. Brown in regard to any of the presbytery's several appointments of Brown to various positions related to the new seminary, appointments which Brown uniformly ignored.

ERROR no. 2: Grigsby formulated a faulty time frame, ostensibly encapsulating the early history of the college.

Grigsby says in the "Founders of Washington College":

> "The theme presents *three well-defined historic* periods: *From 1749, the foundation of Augusta Academy* –for Rockbridge had not then been set apart from Augusta – *to 1782*, when the charter was granted to Liberty Hall Academy; from 1782 to 1860, the beginning of the late war; and from 1860 to the present date." (Grigsby, Address,[571] delivered in 1870 but published in 1890, p. 2.)

As has already been explained, the period from 1749 to "the foundation of Augusta Academy" is a historical disconnect because the date 1749 has no significance in the history of Augusta Academy. The date 1749 predates the founding of Augusta Academy by twenty-five years. Grigsby's error in this regard is an embarrassment for the otherwise well-thought-of historian, especially insofar

---

571 Grigsby, Hugh Blair, "The Founders of Washington College," an address delivered June 22, 1870, Washington and Lee University Historical Papers no. 2, Lexington, VA, 1890. [Riddled with serious errors, generally unreliable concerning historical facts pertaining to the origins of Washington and Lee University, but containing much interesting and useful information on other aspects of the college's history.]

as his own father was Rev. Graham's favorite student at Liberty Hall Academy, or so Archibald Alexander believed and reported in his memoir of his preceptor.

ERROR no. 3: In the opening line of the concluding paragraph of Grigsby's discussion about the founding of Liberty Hall Academy, he repeats his earlier error concerning the origin.

Grigsby mistakenly says this:

> Such is a brief outline of the Academy *from its foundation in 1749* to 1796, a period of forty-seven years . . . (Grigsby, Address . . .
> p. 14.) (Here, the *bold italics* represents an error.)

It is interesting to see Grigsby in the first paragraph of his next section on Graham, referring to him as "our founder," which is an entirely accurate designation, but in designating Graham as the "founder," he is being entirely inconsistent with his several representations in the first section. This inconsistency may indicate that Grigsby was initially mostly correct, but that he added the early history treated with above after the fact of an earlier draft. In other words, someone influenced him after the fact, and he may have added the pre-1774 information after the initial draft had been prepared.

ERROR no. 4: In the subsection of Grigsby's address subtitled, "William Graham," Grigsby relies on the now-infamous Mr. Foote concerning much of the early life of Graham. From the incidents Grigsby relates, it is readily apparent that, at least in this regard, Mr. Foote's material is mostly a repeat of that given by William Graham's younger brother Edward Graham Esq. in his 1821 published "Memoir of the Late Rev. William Graham A. M.," published by yet another student of Graham's, Rev. John Holt Rice.[572] The initial portion of this subsection is mostly correct. Then on the second page of this subsection, Grigsby returns to an earlier erroneous foundation and repeats the Brown as supervisor mistake when he says:

> "On leaving college, Graham returned to
> his father's house, and entered on the study
> of theology under his pastor, Mr. Roan, and
> in 1774 he was invited to engage *a classical
> school* in Augusta *under the direction of the
> Rev. John Brown* . . ." (Grigsby, Address . . . p. 17.)
> (*Bold italics* here represents error.)

As has been related elsewhere, any fair reading of the Hanover Presbytery's minutes covering the time period 1771–1776 will reveal a very clear picture of the relationship of the Hanover Presbytery and their appointed "manager," William Graham, and it is not that of an underling working at the direction of another. Brown was not the "director" of Augusta Academy, and he certainly was not

---

572 Edward Graham, "Memoir of Rev. the Late Rev. William Graham, AM." *The Evangelical and Literary Magazine and Missionary Chronicle*, IV, (1821), p.75 et seq. [serialized format]

William Graham's supervisor. In fact, he held no position whatever in connection with the presbytery's new seminary, (i.e., Liberty Hall), and it was by Brown's own choice that this was the case.

ERROR no. 5: Mr. Grigsby mistakenly claims that Brown's Latin school at New Providence was moved from that location when it was not.

Here are Grigsby's words on this subject:

> "It is stated that the academy in the time of Mr. Brown was successively removed a few miles westward, first to near Old Providence, and then shortly before the Revolution to Mt. Pleasant, near Fairfield, in the present county of Rockbridge."

(Grigsby, "Founders . . .," pp. 11–12.)

Mr. Grigsby once again gets his basic facts wrong. In that, he follows closely the mistaken Mr. Foote.

ERROR no. 7: Grigsby presents an inaccurate portrayal of William Graham's role in the struggle for religious liberty that transpired in Virginia in the 1770s and 1780s.

Here below are Grigsby's words:

> "But the question which particularly interested clerical men was our legislation in respect of religion. When the scheme of an assessment for support of religion was brought forward, and was sustained by Patrick Henry, Richard Henry Lee, and other prominent men, ***Graham, who viewed even religious questions with the eye of a statesman, was not indisposed to approve it, and he was governed by the same reasons that led Henry to favor the policy.*** (Grigsby, Founders . . . p. 27) (Emphasis added in bold italics in this instance indicates error.)

In all likelihood, Grigsby came to this erroneous conclusion by relying on Foote, who also completely misunderstood the role played by Graham in Virginia's struggle for religious freedom. In this regard, Grigsby makes the same error made by numerous others not familiar with the meeting minutes of the Hanover Presbytery during this important period. There are numerous examples found in the presbytery's minutes, which suggest that named members listed in one regard or another were all of one mind and were acting in concert with one another, when in many cases there was great division among the members.

The confusion in this regard results from a peculiar methodology of the Hanover Presbytery in managing their members during disputes. When fashioning a final decision on a matter in dispute, the presbytery was predisposed to appoint members representing conflicting viewpoints to a committee charged with preparing a memorial or some such other document designed to memorialize the final decision. The obvious intent was to smooth over ruffled feathers. That is probably what led Grigsby astray on the issue of religious "assessment" in Virginia. When he reviewed Foote's treatment of this subject, he no doubt noticed Foote's emphasis on the presbytery's minutes, and because Graham was appointed to the committee directed to draft the presbytery's message to the Virginia Legislature explaining their recent modification of its position on assessments, he must therefore have been in the majority. Graham, however, vehemently opposed the majority on this occasion. He did not accept the appointment to that committee. Instead, he mounted a vigorous campaign to repudiate his colleagues' equivocation, which was entirely successful. By following Foote at his word, Grigsby repeated Foote's error.

Grigsby and Foote both drew an incorrect conclusion in this regard, because as later scholars discovered, William Graham opposed the modification of the long-standing opposition to any interposition of the state into the affairs of the church.

ERROR no. 8: Mr. Grigsby again mistakenly places Graham "under the supervision of Brown," which never happened.

> In 1774 he [W. Graham] was invited to engage in a classical school in Augusta **under the direction** of the Rev. John Brown . . . and on the 6th of May, 1776, the headship of the academy devolved upon him, with the title of Rector, and John Montgomery as his assistant. (Emphasis added.) (Grigsby, Address, "The Founders of Washington College." Delivered June 22, 1870, Washington and Lee University Historical Papers, no. 2, 1890, p. 17.)

Graham was not invited to engage a classical school, but rather was invited to take charge of implementing a plan to create a college in Virginia on a plan similar to that at Princeton. Brown, having refused all appointments with respect to the presbytery's new seminary (i.e., academy), played no role in the affairs of the presbytery's new academy, focusing instead on his own private Latin school at New Providence.

ERROR no. 9: Grigsby repeats his error concerning his mistaken understanding of the relationship between Graham and Brown as it related to education, which, in fact, did not exist. Their only relationship that existed after the breakup of the prospective connubial connection between Graham and Brown's daughter, Betsy, was with respect to their roles as Presbyterian ministers with adjoining pastorates.

Much later in the piece in a subsection dedicated to Mr. Andrew Moore, Grigsby says:

> "He [Moore] probably received his early training at the *Academy before it assumed the name of Liberty Hall, under the Rev. Dr. Brown . . .*" (Grigsby, "Founders . . .," p. 57)
> (Emphasis here represents error.)

Grigsby speculates on where Mr. Moore went to school, and then before mistakenly assigning Brown as his teacher, he mistakenly bestows a doctorate degree on Brown that has otherwise alluded historians for two hundred years. Brown was not "Rev. Dr. Brown" then or ever, and Brown had no connection to "the academy."

ERROR no. 10: Grigsby assigns Washington and Lee University alumnus status to several notable persons who resided in the vicinity of Liberty Hall, but many of these persons' status is at best dubious and probably incorrect because the alumni status is merely inferred by Grigsby from these individuals' association with Brown's Latin school, which Grigsby incorrectly connects to Liberty Hall.

Grigsby's brief sketches of various trustee "founders" include several representations that the referenced "founder" was an alumnus of the college, whose only imagined connection was based on their connection to a private school that was never connected to the college. It appears that in every such case, the named "founder" had been a student at either Robert Alexander's school or Brown's Latin school. If that is the case, these founders' connection is strictly as a trustee, not as an alumnus.

In the case of one trustee, Mr. Samuel Lyle, he is reported to have been educated by Robert Alexander's brother, Archibald, but as best as the auditor was able to discover, no one claims that his educational efforts constituted the functional equivalent of a "germ" of Washington and Lee University.[573]

Note: The audit's scope of review was not established with the view to investigate the possible connections of Virginians with Augusta Academy or its successor, Liberty Hall Academy. It is very likely that none of the original trustees of Liberty Hall Academy were alumni of the college under Rev. William Graham, the many representations to the contrary notwithstanding.

Conclusion Regarding Hugh Blair Grigsby

We learn from the eminent divine Rev. Archibald Alexander, DD, the founder and first president of the Princeton Theological Seminary, that the father of Hugh Blair Grigsby, Rev. Benjamin Grigsby, was the favorite student of Liberty Hall Academy's rector, Rev. William Graham. It is therefore with some degree of unease that the auditor found so many fundamental errors in the published

---

573   Rev. Dr. Archibald Alexander includes such an anecdote in his unpublished "Memoir of Rev. William Graham." See bibliography.

commencement address of his well-known son, Hugh. His mistakes concerning the founding of Washington and Lee, it seems, result from his having followed the ignominious Foote, whom Grigsby unfortunately relied upon for information pertaining to the founding. In this, Grigsby is in good company including the Virginia Historical Society and the Virginia Synod of the Presbyterian Church, as well as most nineteenth-century authors who touched upon this subject after 1850. Unfortunately, the failures in this regard spilled over into all of the twentieth century. Grigsby might well have stemmed this tide had he bothered to do his own research and consulted the meeting minutes of the Hanover Presbytery and the minutes of the Washington College's board of trustees during its embryonic period instead of simply assuming that Foote's representations were accurate. As president of the Virginia Historical Society, Grigsby set a very poor example of the historian's responsibility to exercise due diligence by challenging those who rely upon secondary sources or no sources at all, as was the case with respect to William Henry Foote.

Note: Grigsby's article on the Founders of Washington and Lee contains much useful and interesting information on many of the school's early alumni, but his treatment of the actual founding is replete with error.

14. REV. E. D. JUNKIN [1871] (Not to be confused with his father, George Junkin of Washington College fame)
Junkin, Rev. E. D., *The History of the Church and Congregation of New Providence, Lexington Presbytery, Virginia*, published by request of the congregation, 1871. (The auditor only has the section dealing with Rev. John Brown and the origins of Washington and Lee University.)
(Pamphlet) In this section of the pamphlet, Junkin makes two errors in regard to the establishment of Washington and Lee University (then Washington College).

Junkin's history of the New Providence Church misrepresented the founding of Washington and Lee University and mistakenly links the college to the schools of both Robert Alexander and Rev. John Brown, and he invokes the "germ" theory when that innovative nineteenth-century notion had no applicability to the founding of Washington and Lee.[574]

ERROR no. 1: Mr. Junkin improperly titles Rev. William Graham as "principal."
Rev. Junkin inappropriately referred to the Hanover Presbytery's appointment of Graham as a "principal," which is technically inaccurate because Graham was

---

574 If one stretched the boundaries of the germ theory in regards to Washington and Lee, it could be argued that the college's incipient format as an unnamed grammar school that was unofficially referred to as "Augusta Academy" during 1775 and 1776 was the institution's germ, but technically, the institution was an entirely new venture created on October 13, 1774. The grammar school was simply the college's temporary form taken during the period when its permanent buildings were being constructed. From inception, the institution's institutional guardians were the members of the Hanover Presbytery and their first chief operations manager, William Graham. Universities, after all, don't spring forth in one fell swoop like a goddess fully formed from the head of Zeus. That's why their published histories typically avoid discussing such institution's first two or three years of existence. A college with nothing but freshmen does not lend itself to much interesting discussion.

appointed as a "manager." This would normally be written off as a perfunctory mistake of no consequence, but given one hundred and fifty years of authors falsely representing the origins of Washington and Lee University, it seemed to be a good idea to correct errors wherever we find them, and especially if they are made in ways that might fit into the series of false scenarios. It is also important because so many have falsely represented that Graham served under Rev. John Brown in a series of different roles, such as "director," "supervisor," etc. The auditor determined therefore to get the matter precisely correct. Of course, the demonstrable truth on this subject is that Rev. Brown eschewed participation in the presbytery's seminary, which he opposed from the very beginning. His position in opposition to the seminary is one that he adhered to as long as he lived in Virginia. This easily proven fact belies all the false representations that have been made that would have the public believe that Brown played a crucial role in its early operations. The truth is that he played no role whatsoever in the affairs of Liberty Hall Academy.

Rev. Junkin says, on page 16, the following:

> On October 27th, 1775, Mr. Graham who had been licensed to preach the day before, was appointed the Principal of the school.

The fact is, on October 27, 1775, the presbytery did something else in regard to Graham. The presbytery did not use the term "principal." Rather, they said this:

> The Pby met according to adjournment, . . . The Augusta school is taken under consideration. *We agree that Mr. William Graham continue*[575] *to have the care and tuition of said school.*
> (Hanover Pby. minutes, p. 67)

The above demonstrates that Junkin did not rely on original sources, which explains why his representations are generally suspect. Of course, he was merely following in the path of virtually all post-1865 historians that addressed the early history of Washington and Lee up to the present day.

William Graham from October of 1774 had been appointed as the college's "manager." Following Graham's 1775 licensing and ordination, this temporary title was altered on May 6, 1776, to that of "rector," thereby, indicating in clear terms that Graham already was the principal administrator or, more accurately, the "manager." Mr. Junkin's description suggests that William Graham's role, on that day, was made something new and different. In fact, Mr. Graham was always the presbytery's appointed head of their new seminary. At no time was any other person appointed to an administrative position at the presbytery's

---

575 *An interesting question here is, "continue" from when? What is meant here is that his care and tuition continue from the school's very inception. Its actual operations, after all, did not begin until about the time of the presbytery's last meeting in April of the same year. Therefore, this language fairly well disposes of the notion that Brown had been in charge. If this were not enough to answer that question, the complete content of the presbytery's meeting minutes clearly do because there is no mention whatsoever of Brown in regards to the school's operations. Of course, the minutes do mention certain appointments, but these references are of no consequence insofar as Brown did not accept any of those appointments.*

new seminary superior to the administrative position of William Graham.[576]
To this, the presbytery's minutes attest from the institution's inception (i.e.,
"establishment) on October 13, 1774. No other name appears in these minutes as
an administrative head during these early years, and this is consistent with all
the minutes during these early years. Every aspect of business with which the
school and the presbytery was concerned is discussed in terms of the presbytery
and their manager, William Graham, with the one exception of its references
to Presbyterians selected to oversee the initial fund-raising efforts. These
appointments, however, were not permanent appointments.

A common misunderstanding concerning the school's early days relates to
the presbytery's language appointing William Graham, the "manager" of the
new seminary, alongside the qualifying phrase "and under the inspection of the
Rev. John Brown." In order to fully comprehend the meaning of this qualifying
and unfortunate qualifier, it is helpful to engage in an investigation and possible
debate over the meaning and intent of this qualifying phrase because Rev. Brown
did not accept this appointment, and there is no evidence that he ever accepted
that responsibility either. It must be remembered that all appointments made by
the Hanover Presbytery in connection with either of these two seminaries were, in
effect, more akin to a nomination, and these nominations only technically became
official upon the nominees' acceptance.

The careful researcher will note immediately upon reviewing the meeting
minutes of the board of trustees from the school's very inception, the absence of
Brown at every meeting of the trustees. Perhaps, more to the point, the presbytery
did not even bother to appoint Brown to the all-important executive committee
of the board of trustees. An odd occurrence if Brown, the only "nominated"
trustee then living in the vast Augusta County, is purposely left off the working
committee that was responsible for launching this new endeavor.

Finally, in this regard, the meeting minutes of the Hanover Presbytery from
October of 1774 through 1776 demonstrate that in regards to the affairs of the
Prince Edward Academy (Hampden-Sydney) under Samuel Stanhope Smith,
the presbytery's minutes only describe activities between Smith, the seminary's
rector, and the presbytery. The same is true with respect to Augusta Academy and
its rector, William Graham. All activities of the Augusta Academy were reported
to the presbytery by Graham, and for a very good reason, which is that in all of
its operational concerns, there was no distinction between the roles of William
Graham and Samuel Stanhope Smith as they relate to their respective positions
as the administrative heads of their seminaries.

s' titles was more of a formality, which was based on the fact that at the
time, Samuel Smith was a licensed probationer awaiting ordination while Mr.
Graham was on trials (application) before the presbytery to be licensed and made

---

576 Technically, of course, the collective Hanover Presbytery was in charge of the school from
its inception on October 13, 1774, as was the collective board of trustees, from May 6, 1776,
forward. Although it is instructive to know that one of the earliest actions by the newly created
board of trustees was to establish an executive committee and they elected William Graham
as chairman. An incredibly inexplicable thing to do if Reverend Brown was in charge.

a probationer. Smith initially could conduct religious services as a probationer minister while Graham's religious activities were more restrictive for a few months. Mr. Smith, it should be remembered, arrived in Virginia at least a year in advance of Mr. Graham. Graham's trials, meanwhile, were completed in short order, and his licensing followed quickly thereafter in 1775. Any differences between Smith and Graham as regards their educational responsibilities were mostly technical and only lasted a few months.

Note: Even though Smith obtained his license to preach in advance of Graham, and even though Smith arrived in Virginia prior to Graham, nevertheless, the presbytery established their first seminary in Virginia on October 13, 1774, and fixed its location west of the Blue Ridge Mountains. Their second seminary was somewhat of an afterthought. It was established the year after the creation of the Augusta Academy, and it was fixed by the presbytery in Prince Edward County, east (or south) of the Blue Ridge. Smith was appointed February 1, 1775.

ERROR no. 2: Rev. E. D. Junkin inappropriately invoked the germ theory of institutional development.[577]

Junkin says this:

> "After Mr. Brown became pastor of New Providence and Timber Ridge and established his home near Fairfield, the school was removed to that neighborhood, where its site can still be pointed out. This was the germ from which grew Washington and Lee University. (Rev. E. D. Junkin, *A History* . . ., p. 16) [Emphasis here in bold italics represent error.]

Brown's Latin school was not the germ of Washington and Lee University because the school to which he refers, he admits, is Brown's Latin school, and Brown's school had been moved from the location to which he refers (Mount Pleasant, near Fairfield) to a subsequent location ten to twelve miles away to New Providence, which was the name of Brown's congregation at the time. The new location was at Brown's new farm on Moffett's Creek. This move was made sometime before 1770. There, Brown's school remained until after the Revolutionary War, as is evidenced by Brown's surviving letters from that period.[578] The most important fact about the location of Brown's school is that it was nowhere near Mount Pleasant when the presbytery in 1771 began its discussions about whether to establish and patronize a seminary in Virginia patterned after the College of New Jersey. From this location, the Latin school was never again moved, the efforts of numerous later authors to suggest otherwise notwithstanding. This is an incontrovertible fact that is evidenced by Rev. Brown's

---

577 In the paragraph that precedes the the one from whence this extract was taken, Junkin refers to the infamous so-called Rev. Samuel Houston letter ostensibly reprinted, in part, in Foote's two histories on Virginia. Junkin took Foote's representations at face value and places certain parts in quotation marks, but it does not appear that Junkin possessed the letter or a copy of it. He simply relied on Foote's hearsay claims in that regard.

578 See bibliography for a reference to John White Stuart's dissertation, which constitutes a biography of Rev. John Brown.

extant correspondence from the period in question. See John White Stuart's biography of Brown.

Washington and Lee's first emendation was erected at Mount Pleasant well after Brown's school had been relocated at New Providence. Moreover, there was no other school located at Mount Pleasant after Brown's departure and prior to Graham's arrival. This is a fact that has never been refuted based upon any competent evidence. During 1775, both of these schools were operating separately under their directors, Rev. John Brown and Rev. William Graham. This situation is aptly described by Fithian in his journal covering the years 1775 and 1776. Fithian's descriptions are provided in-depth in several earlier subsections of this section. See bibliography.

ERROR no. 3: Mr. E. D. Junkin, again on page 16, says this:

> A committee, such as had been appointed in previous years, was again appointed to collect more money for its more complete equipment. *Of this Committee Rev. John Brown was Chairman.*

On this day, October 27, 1775 (or, for that matter, any other day), Rev. John Brown was definitely not appointed as "chairman" of anything. The presbytery did direct that "the gentlemen appointed by the Pby last Spring, still continue to take subscriptions." They then appointed several individuals including John Brown, William Graham, and several others to collect subscriptions taken out in the prior campaign. Rev. Brown's appointment in this regard was probably never activated by virtue of his refusal to accept such appointments, but in this specific case, evidence is lacking on the subject. What is abundantly clear, however, is that Brown was not appointed as the chairman of this committee, and nothing in the minutes suggests that he was. Indeed, this committee was more of a group of named individuals than a working committee that might have benefited from having a chairman. In any event, the minutes do not refer to anyone as chairman.

15. SAMUEL DAVIES ALEXANDER [1872]
(Samuel Davies Alexander, _Princeton in the Eighteenth Century_, New York, Anson D. F. Randolph & Co., 1872.)

Introduction:

Samuel Davies Alexander is a younger son of Rev. Dr. Archibald Alexander. His history of Princeton, which is mostly in the form of brief biographical sketches of Princeton alumni, is often quoted by historians, but his biographical sketch of his father's preceptor, William Graham, is erroneous in several important ways.

Alexander makes three mistakes that were selected for inclusion in this section. He twice mistakenly asserts an origin of Washington College (Virginia) as being earlier than October 13, 1774, and he mistakenly asserts a connection between Rev. John Brown and Washington College that does not exist. Rev.

Brown's only connection, if one could call it that, was as a member of the Hanover Presbytery that created the college. Importantly, Brown was estranged from both the college, or academy, and its rector, William Graham from a very early period in the school's existence. Alexander incorrectly links his father, Rev. Archibald Alexander, DD, president of Princeton Theological Seminary, to the Latin School of Brown, but no such connection exists. Samuel relies hereupon on his older brother James, who made numerous similar mistakes when comprising their father's biography.

At Princeton, the college has an important manuscript including many biographical sketches including one of Rev. William Graham, class of 1773, which was apparently written by Samuel's brother, James. James's account of Graham is erroneous and varies significantly from what his father wrote about his preceptor, William Graham. Unfortunately, Princeton's institutional histories do not provide an accurate portrayal of one of their most distinguished eighteenth-century graduates, William Graham, and either one or both of these two sons of Archibald Alexander are to blame. Most of the subsequent mistakes made about William Graham are traceable to these two erroneous accounts written by Rev. Archibald Alexander's sons, both of whom were obviously misled by William Henry Foote's two Virginia histories.

Three of Mr. S. D. Alexander's errors appear in his preface as follows:

> In 1776 John Brown. A graduate of the class of 1749 [College of New Jersey, now Princeton] started a grammar school at Timber Ridge, Virginia, *at which Dr. Archibald Alexander attended among the first scholars. This school grew into Liberty Hall*, and that into Washington College, over which we find the first President William Graham, a graduate of the class of 1773. (Samuel Davies Alexander, *Princeton in the Eighteenth Century*, preface, p. xiii) [Emphasis here indicates error.]

In brief, (1) Brown did not start a grammar school at Timber Ridge, but he did create a private "Latin school" there but which was later moved several miles to New Providence; (2) young Archibald Alexander, the author's father, had not even been born when Brown moved his "Latin school" from Timber Ridge to New Providence, and his father was only three years old when Brown closed his Latin School at New Providence for the duration of the Revolutionary War[579]; and (3) no school with which Rev. John Brown was attached grew into Liberty Hall Academy.

---

579 Brown's school at New Providence closed in December of 1775. It remained closed during the Revolutionary War, and while he indicated an intent to reopen it after the war, nothing much, if anything, became of his plan to reopen. By then, most potential students were choosing to attend Liberty Hall Academy or its associated grammar school, both of which were conducted in the same buildings on various campuses in the greater Lexington vicinage.

16. REV. J. G. CRAIGHEAD, DD (1878)

(Craighead, Rev. J. G., DD, *Scotch And Irish Seeds in American Soil: The Early History of the Scotch and Irish Churches,* Philadelphia, Presbyterian Board of Publication, 1878.)

Error no. 1: Mr. Craighead mislabeled the Latin school organized by Rev. John Brown and, in so doing, mischaracterizes the nature of the school.

> In most of their congregations pastors established ***classical and scientific schools***. West of the Blue Ridge *such a school was carried on at New Providence, by Rev. John Brown,* while east of the Ridge a similar institution was conducted by the Rev. John Todd, under the patronage of Dr. Samuel Davies. (Craighead, *Scotch and Irish Seeds,* 1878, p. 307)

Unlike John Todd's school, Brown's school at New Providence was not a "classical" nor a "scientific" school. In his extant correspondence (see Stuart's Dissertation on the Life of Rev. John Brown in bibliography), Brown consistently referred to his school as a Latin school, a classical school connoted at the time, a school with a general curriculum including basic English, elementary mathematics, Latin and or Greek grammar, and geography. A Latin school was typically focused on basic Latin and Greek grammar for students seeking to meet prerequisites for applying to a college. Of course, there were no rigid classifications for common schools, so this mistake is a relatively minor one.

Error no. 2: Mr. Craighead inaccurately locates Rev. John Brown's Latin school and mistakenly describes the order in which the school was moved, which has the effect of creating an entirely incorrect impression about the school's location at the time the Hanover Presbytery established and patronized their new seminary under the care and tuition of William Graham.

> "The first of these, (i.e., Brown's Latin School) ***after removals to Mount Pleasant, where it was known as Augusta Academy,*** and then to Timber Ridge, as Liberty Hall, finally became Washington College. (Craighead, *Scotch and Irish Seeds,* pp. 307–308, 1878)

Mr. Craighead here is simply wrong about Rev. Brown's Latin School having been moved from New Providence to Mount Pleasant. The fact is, Brown's school was moved from Mount Pleasant to New Providence (circa 1767), not the other way around. More importantly, Craighead is mistaken to claim that Brown's school was known as Augusta Academy because it was not. In fact, the only school that was ever known as Augusta Academy was the Hanover Presbytery's seminary during its incipiency (1775–1776) at Mount Pleasant. This subject has been discussed in detail in several of the above subsections above and need not be repeated here.

ERROR no. 3: Rev. Craighead errs in asserting that the Hanover Presbytery took steps as early as 1771 to establish an academy in Prince Edward County.

Here is what Craighead said:

> The widespread desire for literary institutions of a high order led the *presbytery of Hanover, as early as 1771, to take measures to establish an academy in Prince Edward County, which subsequently was chartered as Hampden Sidney [sic] College.*
> (Craighead, *Scotch and Irish Seeds*, p. 308)

In 1771, the Hanover Presbytery initiated a study within the Presbyterian churches of Virginia to ascertain the desirability and feasibility of establishing a single seminary like that at Princeton in New Jersey, Virginia. As the study progressed, they began to indicate a predisposition toward such an establishment; but contrary to the representation of Rev. Craighead, the presbytery took measures to establish an academy in the county of Augusta, west of the Blue Ridge Mountains, not in Prince Edward County. The seminary east of the Blue Ridge was an afterthought of the Hanover Presbytery. The subject of a second seminary is not referred to in any of the presbytery's meeting minutes until October 14, 1774, the day after Augusta Academy had been formally established on October 13, 1774.

As the meeting minutes of the presbytery clearly explain, the establishment of the Prince Edward Academy took place at a special pro re nata meeting of the presbytery, called in February of 1775. Contrary to Craighead's assertion, this establishment was an afterthought as can be seen by reviewing the presbytery's meeting minutes between 1771 and 1776. Moreover, the presbytery appointed William Graham to oversee the actualization the presbytery's dream of establishing a seminary akin to the College of New Jersey in Virginia.

Craighead, like so many others, somehow believed, albeit mistakenly, that Smith's appointment preceded that of William Graham. That mistake was not made by the presbytery's clerk Caleb Wallace, however, who wrote Liberty Hall's first authorized and documentary-based history,[580] about which he was a uniquely qualified eyewitness insofar as the establishment of Liberty Hall Academy, which took place at the same meeting at which he was ordained as the new pastor of the very church where the meeting was held (i.e., the Cub Creek Meeting House in Charlotte, County, Virginia). It is amazing to realize that in the two hundred years since Washington and Lee was created, not one author has cited Wallace's authorized history. This is despite the fact that this history comprises the first five pages of Liberty Hall Academy's first record book containing the meeting minutes

---

580   Rev. Caleb Wallace [later, Justice], "Memorandum History of Liberty Hall Academy," a handwritten document copied into the record book of the newly established board of trustees of Liberty Hall Academy, in which are found the original handwritten meeting minutes of the board of trustees at the Leyburn Library of Washington and Lee University, pp. 3–7, signed, "Caleb Wallace, Clerk, May 1776." This constitutes the first written and first authorized history of Liberty Hall Academy.

of the Board of Trustees of Liberty Hall Academy. It is difficult to comprehend how anyone reviewing these minutes could have missed this venerable document.

ERROR no. 4: Craighead errs concerning the movements of Brown's Latin school.

Mr. Craighead is also wrong in saying that Brown's school was moved sequentially first from *New Providence* to *Mount Pleasant* and then from Mount Pleasant to Timber Ridge. See no. 2 above.

In conclusion on Rev. J. G. Craighead, he, like so many others, represents a false history of the origins of Liberty Hall Academy (Washington and Lee University). Mr. Craighead chose to present a history of the origins of Washington and Lee University that is entirely inconsistent with the early records of the presbytery that established the academy, and those of the early board of trustees that was created by the presbytery in May of 1776. He generally cites no authorities because, says he,

> it is impossible to state with any accuracy all the sources of information from which I have derived the materials for this volume. (James G. Craighead, _Scotch and Irish Seeds in American Soil_, Philadelphia: Presbyterian Board of Publication, 1878)

Given Mr. Craighead's attitude concerning citation of authority, it is no mystery why his representations concerning the origins of Washington and Lee University are completely unreliable and mostly demonstrably false. As concerns the early history of Washington and Lee, his book should be considered more as a novelty than as a legitimate history. The book's utility with respect to other subjects is beyond the scope of this study.

17. [Mrs.] **S. P. McD., MILLER** (1883)
(Mrs. S. P. McD Miller, "A Virginian University Town," _Overland Monthly_, Jan–June, (May) 1883, vol. 1, Second Series pp. 488–502)

Mrs. Miller provides much information of interest, but she knew very little about the founding of Washington and Lee and mistakenly links the eighteenth-century Rev. John Brown and his immediate family with the college. Ironically, according to Rev. Archibald Alexander, president of the Princeton Theological Seminary, the Brown family came very close to having been intimately involved on the founding of Washington and Lee because the founding first president, while residing with the Brown family when he first arrived in Virginia, became engaged to Rev. Brown's highly sought-after daughter. Betsy. This couple's eventual breakup was brought about by the interference of the would-be bride's mother who had come to resent Mr. Graham's sudden influence within the rural community.

One hates to denigrate this otherwise valuable article, but the auditor is obligated to identify the several important mistakes made by Mrs. Miller concerning the origins of Washington and Lee University. Her article, in the main, does not contain any citations of authority; therefore its historical value must remain severely limited. Most of her errors can be traced to the infamous William Henry Foote, but whether directly or by way of one of his several acolytes, is uncertain.

In one case, the author commits an error that was, at the time, unprecedented, to wit: She claims on page 490 that Senator James Brown of Louisiana, who was an ambassador to France, was an alumnus of Washington and Lee. To be very clear on this matter, he was not an alumnus of Washington and Lee or of any of its earlier forms, including Augusta Academy, Liberty Hall Academy, Washington Academy, or Washington College. Those, including Mrs. Miller, who have made similar claims about Rev. Brown's sons rely upon the fallacious contention that the college was an outgrowth of either Robert Alexander's or Rev. Brown's local preparatory schools. As has already been demonstrated, there is no credible eighteenth-century evidence that either contention is true, and all documentary evidence from that century on the subject clearly evinces that Liberty Hall Academy was not an outgrowth of any other school. Not one of Rev. John Brown's several sons had any attachment to the school established by the Hanover Presbytery in Augusta County, Virginia. James's father, Rev. John Brown, was estranged from both the college and its President William Graham from the college's very inception, as has been explained above in great detail, and Rev. Brown did not send any of his sons to Liberty Hall Academy. This fact is all too clear from Brown's eighteenth-century correspondence. See John White Stuart's biography of Rev. John Brown listed in the bibliography.

Here below is Mrs. Miller's 1883 contention:

> In 1749 *a classical school of high grade* was founded in Augusta County, *by Mr. Robert Alexander, A.M., of Trinity College, Dublin University* . . . in 1753 he resigned *and his pastor, Rev. Dr. John Brown . . . became its principal. It was known then as the Augusta Academy . . . until in 1774, when he relinquished it to Rev. William Graham, whom he employed as an assistant.* (Mrs. S. P. McD. Miller, "A Virginian University Town," p. 489; emphasis in bold italics represents error.)

Virtually nothing is known about the character of Robert Alexander's educational endeavor, and there is no known evidence to support her contention that Robert Alexander ever attended any college. But for certain, he did not attend Trinity College in Dublin, as has been explained by Dr. Crenshaw in his unpublished version of General Lee's College in an appendix entitled "The Problem with the Origins." See bibliography. In addition, Rev. John Brown was not a "Dr." of any type, and Rev. William was never his assistant, nor was he ever employed by Brown, a point that has been addressed several times in earlier subsections. It is equally untrue that any school in the Valley of Virginia was ever known as Augusta Academy other than the Hanover Presbytery's seminary at Mount Pleasant during 1775 and 1776.

Her final mistaken claim that has been identified in this audit is that the name Liberty Hall Academy was given to the school by its president, William Graham. Technically, that responsibility fell to the board of trustees, which is a fact that was announced in the trustees meeting minutes for its very first meeting on May 13, 1776. William Graham, however, was the chairman of the executive committee, but his role as trustee was strictly ex officio so he could not have had a direct role in the naming of the school. While this may seem to be a terribly minor error and hardly worthy of note, it still underscores that Mrs. Miller was obviously seriously uninformed about the early institutional history of Washington and Lee.

18. ALFRED NEVIN, DD, LLD (1884)

(Alfred Nevin, DD (Editor) _Encyclopedia of the Presbyterian Church in the United States_, Philadelphia, Presbyterian Encyclopedia Publishing Co., 1884, pp. 1248)

Principal Error(s):

The entries for Rev. William Graham and Rev. John Brown, while not absolutely correct, avoid the common errors concerning the origins of Washington and Lee University. A closer look at this behemoth of a book, however, finds that Mr. Nevin falls into the common traps under the entries labeled "Academies" and also under "Washington College." Here, the reader will find the common mistakes that follow the worst parts of William Henry Foote wherein he links the founding to Rev. Brown and his private Latin school.

Mr. Nevin as editor undoubtedly depended upon submissions for his multitude of biographical sketches. In this case, his source is not identified. Had Mr. Nevin bothered to consult William Sprague's well-known comprehensive _Annals of the American Pulpit_ (vol. 3, New York, Robert Carter & Brothers, 1858) he would have discovered that his nameless source was seriously misinformed. Sprague's source, on the contrary, was named, and it was none other than the president of Princeton's Theological Seminary, Rev. Archibald Alexander. Alexander, an early student under Graham, was the Presbyterian church's preeminent church historian accepting for his student and assistant, Rev. Charles Hodge, author of _The Constitutional History of The Presbyterian Church in the United States of America_ (Philadelphia, William S. Martien, 2 vols., 1839–1840).

ERROR no. 1: Nevin incorrectly states that a grammar school was moved to Mount Pleasant, which is an erroneous statement.

> Accordingly a small **grammar school** was formed in the neighborhood of Old Providence . . . This school was moved to a place called Mount Pleasant, near to the little town of Fairfield. **Here** the Rev. William Graham ...at the request of the Hanover Presbytery commenced his labors **as a teacher**, and here we

find the germ of whence sprung Washington College. (Nevin,_
Encyclopedia, p. 11)

Mr. Nevin's assertion that the school conducted near Old Providence was
moved to Mount Pleasant is pure conjecture. There is no known evidence to support
this contention. Moreover, the easily demonstrated fact is that the presbytery's
seminary was not fixed at Mount Pleasant by the Hanover Presbytery and that
there are no eighteenth-century documentary records suggesting otherwise. The
place where Augusta Academy was originally located (Mount Pleasant) was not
discussed by the Hanover Presbytery, as is made clear by the presbytery's meeting
minutes. That decision was obviously made between its two annual meetings in
1775. It was therefore the sole responsibility of the manager Mr. Graham, although
it was undoubtedly a decision made in consultation with other local residents,
especially the land's owner, Mr. James Wilson. The subject is never mentioned
in the presbytery's minutes.

, it is from such erroneous statements that gross errors will predictably follow.
It hints at an evolution, and in that lies its danger. In fact, there is no link between
the oldest-known educational endeavor of Robert Alexander and the Latin school
later organized by Rev. John Brown, first at "Mount Pleasant" near Fairfield.
Later (circa 1767), Rev. John Brown moved his home, family, and school to be
adjacent to his then-permanent pastorate at New Providence, which was located
on Moffett's Creek. From that location, the school was never again moved.[581]

The school being referenced here and said by the author to have been conducted
in the neighborhood of Old Providence was a school of unknown type that was,
however, some sort of primary educational endeavor, and it is generally believed
to have been conducted by Robert Alexander. The school, if indeed it truly was a
school, is not known to have been moved to "Mount Pleasant" near Fairfield. No
eighteenth-century evidence exists to support that contention. In fact, there is no
known eighteenth-century evidence to establish much of anything about Robert
Alexander's school, but for certain, his educational efforts had no connection
whatsoever to the Hanover Presbytery's seminary established in October of 1774
because by that time, Alexander was no longer engaged in educational activities
due to his well-known health concerns. Moreover, no known link has ever been
established between Robert Alexander's educational activities and those of Rev.
John Brown, a fact well established by Professor McDaniel at Washington and
Lee. See especially McDaniel group in bibliography.

ERROR no. 2: Mr. Nevin gratuitously downgrades William Graham's new
position as "manager" to that of a mere teacher.

*Note: It is true that Graham provided instruction and he did, in fact, function
as an instructor, but that, however, was only one of numerous functions he
carried out in his position as manager. The only operational difference between
Graham's role as manager and then shortly thereafter as rector would be the*

---

581 John White Stuart, *The Rev. John Brown of Virginia (1728-1803): His Life and Selected Sermons*, doctoral dissertation,
University of Massachusetts, 1988. Reverend Brown's various letters confirm this account.

nature of the religious activities he oversaw prior to his ministerial licensing in October of 1775. The limitations he placed on himself in that regard during his initial months at the school are not known. Had Graham been licensed when he arrived in Virginia, he would no doubt have been given the title of rector, just as that title was bestowed on Samuel S. Smith by the presbytery when they appointed him to oversee the affairs of the new seminary in Prince Edward County. The only meaningful difference between these two new chief operations officers was that Smith was licensed shortly before he arrived in Virginia while Graham was licensed shortly afterward.

William Graham was not "requested" by the Hanover Presbytery **to be their teacher**, but rather to be their **manager** of an intended new seminary. He taught classes among his many other duties associated with his overall "*care and tuition*" of the seminary, granted to him by the presbytery, which was confirmed by them in their meeting minutes for both 1775 and 1776, until, having been ordained as pastor of Timber Ridge and Hall's Meeting House congregations, he was named rector in early 1776.[582]

ERROR no. 3: Nevin errs concerning the date of "establishment."

Nevin says this:

> In 1776 the school was established at Timber Ridge Meeting-House. (p. 11)

The referenced school here above was "established by the Hanover Presbytery Oct. 13, 1774," therefore, it was not "established" in 1776" and it was definitely not established at Timber Ridge. Timber Ridge is where the already "established" seminary was moved to from its place of nativity called locally "Mount Pleasant." Classes at Timber Ridge were held in the school's new main building, not at the church.[583]

ERROR no. 4: This is perhaps more misleading than erroneous, but the original board of trustees was created on May 6, 1776. In 1782, with the Act of Incorporation approved by the Virginia legislature, the board of trustees was afforded corporate status with all that this would entail.

> In the year 1782, application was made to the Legislature for an Act of Incorporation, and accordingly a number of Trustees were formed into a body corporate, to have charge of the

---

582 The label "rector" is generally reserved for those who are licensed Presbyterian ministers because the label implies, or connotes, one who, in addition to being chief administrative officer, also conducts all religious services for those in his charge. Hence, the label "manager" adopted by the presbytery during the interregnum between Mr. Graham's initial appointment and his subsequent ordination as pastor of the two aforementioned congregations.

583 When the school's various components were transferred from Mount Pleasant, it is possible that a few classes were held in the Timber Ridge Meeting House, but if so, there is no evidence that appeared in print during or near the time in question that supports that notion. If anything like that transpired, it is more likely that the preparatory classes were held in the meeting house.

Academy, which received the name of *Liberty Hall*, which name it retained until it was endowed by General Washington. (p. 11)

ERROR no. 5: Nevin leaves a false impression that the college's name, Liberty Hall Academy, was bestowed upon the school when it was incorporated in 1782, but that name was given to the school by the original board of trustees on May 13, 1776.

The name "Liberty Hall" was not received in conjunction with the incorporation by the Virginia legislature (i.e., general assembly) that took place in October of 1782. Rather, the name "Liberty Hall Academy" was adopted in May of 1776 by the executive committee of the newly appointed board of trustees. Prior to the trustees' naming the academy "Liberty Hall Academy," it been informally called "Augusta Academy" by the Hanover Presbytery. Presumably, this convention was adopted by the presbytery in order for them to distinguish between the seminary in Augusta County and the seminary in Prince Edward County when constructing their meeting minutes.

When Rev. William Graham, the rector, and Samuel Lyle, the treasurer of the board of trustees, submitted the application for a Charter for Liberty Hall Academy to the Virginia General Assembly, they did so in the name of the board of trustees of what had been named "Liberty Hall Academy" since May of 1776.[584]

ERROR no. 6: Nevin repeats in a different context the erroneous linking of Rev. John Brown's Latin school with Liberty Hall.

Here is how Nevin accomplishes this:

> *On the nucleus of a school taught by Rev. John Brown*, pastor of New Providence Church, *the presbytery organized the Augusta Academy*, <u>*retaining Mr. Brown in its general inspection*</u>, and <u>employing Mr. William Graham, . . . as teacher.</u>
> (Nevin, *Encyclopedia*, p. 984)

Rev. John Brown did not teach at his private "Latin school," as he himself always referred to it. Rather, Mr. Brown organized his school and then arranged for others to teach the students. The Hanover Presbytery did not "organize" any school associated with Rev. John Brown. Instead, that presbytery "agreed to establish and patronize a publick Seminary" that was intended, from its inception,

---

584   That record reads as follows: "May 13, 1776, Pursuant to an Order of the Pby of Hanover, relative to the Academy of Liberty Hall as it is hereafter to be called instead of Augusta Academy appointing a Committee for purposes herein mentioned" (page 11 of the old record book used for maintaining the trustees' meeting minutes). This record book is maintained today by the Leyburn Library, Archives Section. This is the record of the first meeting of the board of trustees. In attendance were Rev. Wm. Graham, Alexander Stuart, Samuel Lyle, Charles Campbell, John Houston, and Wm. McKee. Noticeably absent is the appointed trustee, Rev. John Brown, a condition that became a perpetual indicator of his failure to accept the appointment.

to become an institution of higher learning for the preparation of Presbyterian ministers among other things. Toward that end, the presbytery initiated a fund-raising campaign at the same time they "established" the seminary, the purpose of which was to finance the purchase of the beginnings of a library, as well as to purchase various laboratory equipment ("apparatus" as they then called it) associated with instruction in the sciences, mathematics, surveying, and philosophy. Mr. Brown's Latin school was intended only as a preparatory school for such seminaries as Augusta Academy and the College of New Jersey (i.e., Princeton).

In addition, Mr. Brown was not retained by the presbytery in any capacity concerning Augusta Academy because the term "retained" implies an agreement between two parties for specific services to be rendered, and Rev. Brown had made no such agreement. Not then, not ever. The presbytery did announce that Graham's appointment as manager was to be "under inspection by Rev. John Brown," but there is no record that this appointment was ever accepted by Rev. Brown, and certainly he never performed the duties of "being the Presbytery's 'eyes & ears'" during Mr. Graham's initial period of managing the presbytery's new seminary.

That the presbytery would desire such an "inspector" is obvious since none of the presbytery's members had yet met the highly recommended Mr. Graham,[585] and Brown, being then their only member living in the county of Augusta, was the likely candidate. Unfortunately, Rev. Brown demonstrated no interest in performing such a role, and as good fortune would have it, it soon became obvious that his services would have been superfluous at best, for Graham was almost immediately well received in the community and his genius and ability was quickly recognized after his arrival in Virginia.

19. CHARLES A. [Alfred] **GRAVES** (Dean W&L Law School) [1885]
(Charles A. (Alfred) Graves, "Washington and Lee: Views of this University," _The Richmond Dispatch_, Richmond, August 14, 1885, p. 2) [Chronicling America - pdf)

In the opening paragraphs of Dean Graves's article, he mistakenly adopted the 1749 date of the college's founding and by inference mistakenly suggests that the college's founding first president, Rev. William Graham, had a predecessor when he did not. Dean Graves also incorrectly identifies the college's founders as the Scotch Irish settlers of the valley, when that honor rightfully belongs to the Hanover Presbytery, which established the institution on October 13, 1774, as their official meeting minutes clearly evince. Of course, the Hanover Presbytery was comprised of mostly Scotch Irish, but some of the members may have emigrated directly from Scotland. Graves's mistaken idea on this point is minor in comparison to his other serious mistake of predating the founding to 1749.

Technically, Dean Graves also erred by claiming the school was called Augusta Academy until the Revolutionary War when in fact, the school was unofficially

---

585 It is entirely possible that Rev. Caleb Wallace, the presbytery's then most recently inducted member, had met Graham at Princeton, but information on that subject is wanting.

called Augusta Academy only until May 13, 1776, when the newly created board of trustees bestowed upon the institution its first official name, Liberty Hall Academy. The first eighteenth-century appearance of the name Augusta Academy in Virginia emerged in 1775, and it ceased being used on May 13, 1776. The academy then predates the United States' Declaration of Independence by a year and a half. The naming of the school predates the Declaration of Independence by a month and a half. A seemingly minor difference, but one pregnant with distinction because by openly naming the school Liberty Hall Academy when it did, all the trustees who adopted this name, by unanimous consent, presumably, would have been deemed guilty of treason by Great Britain, whose flag still flew over Virginia's capitol. Their open defiance deserves to be recognized by posterity for the courageousness that it was. Had the revolution failed, the entire board of trustees might well have been hung by the British authorities.

20. WILLIAM McLAUGHLIN [1888]
(Catalogue of the Officers and Alumni of Washington and Lee University, Lexington, Virginia, 1749–1888, Baltimore: John Murphy & Co., 1888)

This catalog appears to be a major rewrite prepared by a committee chaired by Trustee William McLaughlin, according to the preface on page 3. The catalog, however, is embarrassingly wrong. It manifests this in the "Historical Sketch" that follows the table of contents. Also demonstrably incorrect is the list of "Rectors and Assistants" and the list of "Trustees," which begins on page 34 of the catalog.

Note: Mr. McLaughlin chaired the committee overseeing this publication, and for that reason, he is the focus of this assessment. For the purpose of the audit, he is deemed to be the person responsible for editorial footnotes that appear without attribution. The auditor apologizes if Mr. McLaughlin was not personally responsible, but since he was ostensibly in charge, the responsibility would naturally and normally be considered to be his. Still, the preface reminds the readers that John L. Campbell, the college's treasurer, and Mr. Jacob Fuller, the librarian, were integrally involved in the development of the catalog.

ERROR no. 1: McLaughlin asserts mistakenly that the historical sketch is a full, accurate, and valuable record of the early students and overseers of the academy when in fact the sketch is not accurate but rather grossly inaccurate, and it is also not a valuable record but rather a hodge-podge of absurdities based on delusion and misapprehension. Which is not to say that nothing in the book is accurate, but the errors made concerning the early history of the college and the men who were instrumental in its founding are so terribly flawed that everything that follows cannot be considered to be reliable and therefore must be independently verified.

The preface concludes with this statement:

> Much of this work has been done by John L. Campbell, Esq. Treasurer,[586] and Jacob Fuller, Esq. Librarian of the University.

---

586 In deference to John L. Campbell, he apparently died in 1886. If this is accurate, and without knowing what changes or modifications had been made to the early work on the book, he cannot reasonably be held personally responsible for the myriad of mistakes highlighted in this audit report. The lion's share of the responsibility then falls to Messrs. McLaughlin and Fuller.

Other friends have assisted materially in the work. *But the whole has been under supervision and direction of the Hon. William McLaughlin of the Board of Trustees, and it is but just to say that the unsparing and enthusiastic labors and untiring energy of this gentleman is due this very full, accurate and valuable record of the sons of our Alma Mater.*

The initial parts of the catalog are riddled with inexcusable errors on subjects that are of paramount significance to any accurate history of the founding of Washington and Lee University. The highlighted and underlined statement above is substantively wrong. The essence of the "Historical Sketch" of the institution's founding is patently incorrect and demonstrably false.

Those responsible for this publication added twenty-five years to the institution's history without any sound basis for their action. The formulations of this false history were constructed without any acceptable evidentiary foundation and are at variance with all the official documentary records of those well-recognized institutions responsible for the college's creation and governance during its formative years, namely, the Hanover Presbytery and the Liberty Hall Academy's Board of Trustees.[587]

To be sure, the institution's records suffered in great measure during the Civil War, and it seems very unclear what the status of the college's official records were when this publication was being developed. Presumably, they were mostly extant and had been restored to their rightful place in the archives by the 1880s when this project began. After all, many of the most important records were quoted in this publication's text, which means they were obviously available to the architects of this largely erroneous volume.

Given the effects of the civil war, it's difficult to know when the early records of the college were reassembled and available for use by the institution's librarians and record keepers. Still, those who prepared publications like the one under consideration could have consulted early published histories like those written by Edward Graham, Archibald Alexander, Samuel L. Campbell, Rev. William Hill, and Rev. Robert Davidson; and any one of these sources' works should have served as cautionary red flags for anyone considering notions or suggestions to extend backward the history of Washington and Lee's founding.

If someone thought there were grounds for believing that their existing history was wrong, then the first step should have been to establish beyond all reasonable doubt that this was true. In fact, no such process is known to have taken place. It comes as no surprise then that those who moved to revise the college's history completely bungled the project. The result of the revision was to mangle the true history beyond recognition. And so it remains a statement of history completely baseless and embarrassingly incorrect.

---

587 The Virginia Synod altered the history of the college in *Contributions to the History of the Synod of Virginia* (Waddell, Rev. James A., ed. Waddell, James A., Washington: John F. Sheiry, Printer, 1890). This is an embarrassing rewrite devoid of evidence to support it.

ERROR no. 2: The "Historical Sketch" begins with an erroneous sentence that contains multiple mistakes about the origin of Washington and Lee University.

Here is the error-ridden first sentence:

> *The germ of Washington and Lee University was a Mathematical and Classical school,* called *Augusta Academy,* established in 1749, by Robert Alexander, and first located two miles southwest of the site of Greenville, in Augusta, and near the interlacings of the headsprings of the Shenandoah on the eastward, and of the James River on the westward."
> (McLaughlin, Ed., *Catalogue of the Alumni,* 1888, p. 7)

First and foremost, Washington and Lee University did not have a "germ" from whence it sprang.[588] Beyond this, there is no need to address this issue again since the point has been already been put to rest in numerous earlier subsections of this section.

ERROR no. 3: McLaughlin's committee erroneously asserts that Robert Alexander's school was called "Augusta Academy." This error also appears in the opening paragraph's first sentence. (See the sentence quoted above.)

Again, this false claim has already been debunked.

ERROR no. 4: McLaughlin wrongly asserts, again in the first sentence, that Augusta Academy was founded by Robert Alexander when that claim is provably untrue.

Already debunked.

ERROR no. 5: McLaughlin inadvisably identifies Alexander's school as a "mathematical and classical school."

The term "classical school" is a very broad term and has only a connotative meaning, but as it is generally used in that period, it connoted a building or rooms dedicated to formal instruction in a wide range of subject matters, from English grammar to basic mathematics and geography. Certainly, some degree of English composition and literature and at least a smattering of history.

In the case of Robert Alexander, history has no idea whether he even typically instructed more than one student at a time. Moreover, we only know the name of one of his students. That is, Alexander may have taken students in for specific instructions in basic mathematics or surveying without holding classes for several

---

588 The first emendation of the college emerged shortly after Graham's arrival in Virginia. Appointed in mid-October of 1774, the Pennsylvanian emigrated in the autumn of that year, but the specific date of his arrival is unknown. By the spring of 1775, Graham was forming a grammar school component of the college to serve as its foundation. Located at Mount Pleasant, it was unofficially referred to by the presbytery as Augusta Academy. If anything could arguably be considered a germ of the college, this grammar school would be it. But technically, the grammar school was merely a component of the prospective seminary (i.e., college or academy) and was patronized by the Hanover Presbytery on October 13, 1774, with Graham as its chief operations officer (manager).

students, much as his brother Archibald did when he served as a kind of tutor to Samuel Lyle when Lyle was a young man. The Reverend Dr. Archibald Alexander is the source of information about his namesake grandfather. Importantly, there are no known contemporary or even backdated memoirs that describe either of these brothers conducting a school as schools are typically thought of. At least none that were written by individuals with firsthand knowledge.

If Robert Alexander's school was of any real significance, it most certainly would have been described to us by his illustrious grandnephew, Rev. Archibald Alexander, who made a study of the important early schools in America conducted by Presbyterians. In the various and sundry books, articles, and addresses of Archibald Alexander, he never even mentions Robert Alexander by name and never suggests that his great-uncle conducted any regular school. He did, however, refer to his namesake grandfather who was Robert Alexander's brother who, he explains, gave private instructions to one of Liberty Hall Academy's original trustees, Samuel Lyle. Presumably then, Rev. Archibald Alexander would have mentioned Robert's educational endeavors, whatever they may have been, if he deemed them worthy of notice. In addition, the college's first true historian, Henry Ruffner, made his view perfectly clear in the following words:

> "About the year 1772, . . . private teachers are reported to have commenced in two or three places to instruct pupils in the elements of classical learning. **But these were transient efforts, and resulted in nothing more than to prepare the way for a permanent academy which was established a few years later, through the agency of the Presbytery.** (Henry Ruffner, "Early History of Washington College," written in the 1840s but not published until 1890. See bibliography.) (Emphasis added.)

ERROR no. 6: McLaughlin incorrectly claims that there was a direct link of the schools of Robert Alexander, Rev. John Brown, and Rev. William Graham.

McLaughlin's "Historical Sketch"[589] makes this assertion in regards to the school of Robert Alexander:

It was the first "Classical school in the Valley of Virginia,"[590]

> "and was continued by an uninterrupted succession of principals and assistant instructors on successive sites, increasing in usefulness and influence, until it gradually developed into Washington and Lee University." (William McLaughlin, *Catalogue of the Officers and Alumni of Washington and Lee University, Lexington, Virginia 1749–1888,* Baltimore, John

---

589 It is entirely possible this sketch was actually written by John B. Campbell, Esq., the treasurer of Washington and Lee University, because he was one of the three that made up the committee referenced in the preface; but since the article indicates no attribution, the auditor assigns responsibility to the committee's chairman, Mr. McLaughlin.

590

> Murphy & Co., 1888, p. 7) (There is no authorship attribution in the book, but in the preface, it is stated, *"Much of the work has been done by John L. Campbell, Esq. Treasurer, and Jacob Fuller Esq., Librarian of the University* . . . But the whole has been under the supervision and direction of the Hon. William McLaughlin of the Board of Trustees" <u>Catalogue</u>, preface, p. 3) Note: The auditor ascribes the errors listed in this section to Mr. McLaughlin, but while the book was under his supervision and direction, it may be that the erroneous text was created by someone else.

McLaughlin asserts this, but he provides no credible evidence to support his contention because no such credible evidence exists. If this claim were to be believed, we should be able to recite the pertinent dates of succession, the names of the instructors and principals involved, and the locations of the applicable schools. Nothing along these lines exists that is not the product of gratuitous grandiose and gratuitous expostulations lacking any specificity whatsoever. What we know is that many have made myriads of gratuitous assertions, but no one has provided anything remotely resembling facts or evidence on this subject. The most in-depth study made prior to 1850 was conducted by President Henry Ruffner during the 1840s, which much later was published in the Washington and Lee University Historical Papers. (See bibliography.) Here is what the college's first true historian, Henry Ruffner, said in this regard:

RUFFNER'S PERTINENT COMMENTS ON THIS SUBJECT

I.   "About the year 1772, thirty-four years after the settlements first began, private teachers are reported to have commenced in two or three places to instruct pupils in the elements of classical learning. But these were transient efforts, and resulted in nothing more than to prepare the way for a permanent academy which was established a few years later, through the agency of the Presbytery." (Henry Ruffner, "Early History of Washington College," W&L Hist. Papers No. 1, p. 11.)

> The Presbyterians of the Valley needed an academy among themselves. The Presbytery therefore resolved to *"fix a seminary for the education of youth in Staunton"* But they adopted no measure for carrying this resolution into effect until their meeting in October of 1774.

II.   **In the form of a handwritten footnote:**

> I had this from the late Andrew Alexander, Esquire. Before this time Ebenezer Smith, elder brother of S. S. (Samuel Stanhope)

> Smith had taught a classical school for a
> short time in the Providence Congregation."
> *Note: Since the editor of this publication was*
> *Henry Ruffner's son, Wm. Henry Ruffner,*
> *the footnote may have been added by him,*
> *but usually the son gave his initials to any*
> *footnote that he added, which are not present*
> *in this instance.*

III.   Note: *The comment below seems to be one of the revisions*
Ruffner made in 1857 after having read Foote's two books, but this is purely
subjective on the part of the auditor. Irrespective, the qualifying phrase below,
"partly as a private establishment" is pure rubbish. This may very well be an
edit inserted by Ruffner's often misguided son and later a trustee of the college,
William Henry Ruffner, who edited his father's manuscript for publication
in the University's Historical Papers, No. 1. His son, William, like Archibald
Alexander's son, James, were both responsible for editing their fathers' works on
the early history of the college and both son's had been taken in by Foote's hoax
on this subject. The auditor believes that neither Archibald Alexander or Henry
Ruffner believed that there was any link between Augusta Academy and either
Robert Alexander or Rev. John Brown. With that having been said, the published
version is presented below:

> While the school was thus going on, ***partly as a private***
> ***establishment, yet recognized and patronized by the Presbytery,***
> in April 1775, they named several laymen in various parts of
> the country to assist in forwarding the subscriptions. (Henry
> Ruffner, Washington & Lee University Historical Papers, vol.
> 1, "Early History of Washington College" Baltimore, John
> Murphy & Co., 1890, p. 19) (the erroneous, and confusing part
> of this sentence is highlighted by bold italics[591]) (The emphasis
> is not original but was added by the auditor.)

The truth of the matter is that the statement above attributed to Henry Ruffner
is wrong and McLaughlin too is wrong about his assertion about their having been
uninterrupted successions. There was no succession from Alexander to Brown
and finally to Graham. History actually knows more about Robert Alexander's
brother Archibald (Old Ersbel) as he was apparently called, who we learn from his
grandson and namesake, Rev. Archibald Alexander, was Samuel Lyle's teacher.
Dr. Crenshaw also relates some interesting details taken from county records that
show that Old Ersbel noted to the court some outstanding or unpaid debts he was
owed for teaching local resident's children. About Robert Alexander we know

---

591   The school was not "partly as a private" establishment. It established by the Hanover
      Presbytery as a "public" seminary. The initial funds were raised by subscription under the aegis
      of the presbytery, and the school's management was appointed by the presbytery. Finally, the
      presbytery "fixed" its location and at the same time created the school's board of trustees. As
      such, it is difficult to see just how it could be viewed by anyone as a "partly private" endeavor.

nearly nothing with any degree of certainty, but there does exist some sketchy traditions that seem to support that he knew enough about mathematics to have taught some young men about that subject.

ERROR no. 7: McLaughlin incorrectly asserts in the opening of his second paragraph of the historical sketch that

> "Robert Alexander was a Master of Arts of Trinity College, Dublin University. (McLaughlin, *Catalogue*, 1888, p. 7)

Mr. McLaughlin's assertion here is incorrect because Robert Alexander is not known to have even attended an institution of higher learning, let alone a university. McLaughlin's assertion, in this regard, was offered gratuitously. He provided no citation of authority because no such authority exists.

Dr. Ollinger Crenshaw alludes to one of several references to various issues associated with the "Catalogue of the Alumni of Washington and Lee University, Lexington, Virginia, 1749–1788" and an article included therein, "Historical Sketch" (of Washington and Lee University); and in reference to the sketch, he says that it "follows closely the pattern of succession as set forth by Bolivar Christian in 1869 (cites Baltimore, 1888) and thereafter Crenshaw says this:

> "The Catalogue of 1897 repeats earlier categorical statements ... then Crenshaw says this: This little article declares, contradicting an earlier assertion that Robert Alexander had been educated with the M. A. Degree from Trinity College, Dublin, that he had attended the University of Edinburgh. The cautious historian, Joseph A. Waddell, merely has it that Alexander had been educated in Edinburgh, **and the truth is that he attended neither University** ... Inquiry at the University of Edinburgh (E. Staples to writer, Aug. 6, 1946) and at the University at Dublin (Denis Devlin to writer, June 11, 1946) reveals no evidence that Robert Alexander had attended either institution.[592] (Emphasis added)

In other words, McLaughlin attributes academic credentials to Robert Alexander without having any evidence to support his assertion. It is to be regretted that the full version of Crenshaw's history was not that which was published by Random House in 1969 because Crenshaw's footnotes as well as his important appendix A, "The Problem with the Origins," was never made available to the general public.

Note: Crenshaw's comments on the founding of Washington and Lee included in the Random House edition are discombobulated and nearly nonsensical. Presumably, what he said in his original unpublished typescript version that is included in the appendix "The Problem with the Origins" he deemed too controversial and potentially problematic, and he therefore attempted to obfuscate

---

592   Ollinger Crenshaw, *General Lee's College*, typescript version, vol. 2, appendix A, "The Problem of the Origins, pp. 8–9 (paginated by hand for entire vol. 2, as p. 531 in pencil).

the whole question rather than instigate an uproar in the Lexington community where they had been so long misled as to the actual founding of the university. Irrespective of his motivations, history is indebted to him for his comprehensive and insightful research on the subject of the founding of the college. He provided the keys that unlocked the mystery even if he was happy to leave it to others to explain the solving of the mystery. In chapter 1 of his typescript version, he had claimed a founding that is also without merit but different in some respects to the Random House version. It seems that late in his writing process, he discovered or came to realize that the university's post-1865 version made no sense and was not sustainable when subjected to established methods for authentication. He left an appendix that is admirable and illuminating, but of course, the appendix, "The Problem of the Origins," never made it into the Random Housed edition. It is, however, extant and on file in the Leyburn library at Washington and Lee.

Note: It is shocking that not even Dr. Crenshaw seems to have discovered Caleb Wallace's first authorized history of Liberty Hall Academy. At least, he never mentions that primary source of authority in either version of his book, General Lee's College. See this report's assessment of Crenshaw and his work, General Lee's College, attached to this subsection, albeit out of chronological order.

no. 8:

McLaughlin fails to note a curious fact about Robert Alexander's school, which is that according to McLaughlin's own account, Alexander's school began its operation in 1749. History has determined that was still active in the community until 1760, and yet Bolivar Christian, McLaughlin's fellow trustee, could only offer up the names of half a dozen students that supposedly attended Alexander's school during the eleven years of its apparent operation. This error then is one of omission rather than the typical incorrect assertion, but this omission can hardly be excused if in fact Robert Alexander's school was of any historical importance. A school with only six or seven students over the course of eleven years hardly constitutes a "mathematical and classical school." It suggests rather that Alexander possessed enough understanding in mathematics that he was able to serve as a private teacher to a handful of students looking to obtain enough understanding to be able to serve as a surveyor's apprentice. Given McLaughlin's apparent definition of classical school, a vast number of Valley mothers were professors of theology and home economics. Moreover, Archibald Alexander only mentions one of his family as an educator of sorts, and that was Robert Alexander's brother, Archibald ("Old Ersbel") who gave private instruction to Mr. Samuel Lyle. This information was provided to him by Samuel Lyle himself. Lyle, in this context, accredited the elder Archibald with his fondness for reading and his contracting bibliomania.

Note: This Archibald Alexander was Rev. Archibald Alexander's grandfather, and his student, Samuel Lyle, was one of the few original trustees of the college and its first treasurer. He passed on his bibliomania to his fifth great-grandson,

*who is the author of this report and the auditor who conducted the research
necessary for its completion.*

ERROR no. 9: McLaughlin repeats the false assertion of an institutional succession,
which mistakenly assumed that Robert Alexander was formally succeeded by
Rev. Brown and then also claims erroneous sequential movements attributed to
Brown's school. In the process he falsely claims for Brown an honorary Doctor's
degree he did not possess. He embellishes further by erroneously asserting that
Rev. William Graham somehow became Rev. Brown's "assistant."
McLaughlin says,

> **As Principal of Augusta Academy,** *Mr. Alexander was
> succeeded by Rev. John Brown, D. D.* His pastor, who was called
> to Providence and Timber-Ridge Churches, in 1753. During the
> Administration of Mr. Brown, the Academy was successively
> moved a few miles westward, first to Old Providence, then to
> New Providence Church, and "shortly before the Revolution"
> to Mt. Pleasant, near Fairfield, in (now) Rockbridge County,
> where in 1774 Mr. *Wm. Graham became his assistant*, and
> in 1776 succeeded him as Principal. (McLaughlin *Catalogue*,
> 1788, p. 8)

Neither Robert Alexander nor Rev. Brown was ever the "principal" of a
school named Augusta Academy. There is no known or published evidence that
Robert Alexander's school, whatever makeup it might have been, was anything
more than a local individual with no known credentials teaching a few young
people basic mathematics.

Archibald Alexander, first President of Princeton Theological Seminary puts
it this way:

> While engaged in teaching he (referring to John Montgomery)
> was pursuing his own studies with a view to the Holy ministry.
> And as at that time every candidate before receiving license to
> preach was required to obtain a diploma from some college, or
> submit to examination by a committee of Synod, the young men
> in Virginia who aspired to the ministry had to go to the New
> Jersey College and there "*finish their education.*" *Accordingly
> Mr. Montgomery, Edward Crawford and Mr. Saml Doak,
> and Mr. Archibald Scott went to Princeton*[593] *soon after Mr.*

---

593   *It is more likely that these four Valley students went to Princeton sometime earlier than what
McLaughlin suggests and studied there in the grammar school under William Graham that
was associated with the college of New Jersey (Princeton), although any of them may have
studied their basic Latin and Greek grammar at Rev. Brown's Latin school. If so, who the
instructor might have been at Brown's school is unknown, but possibly Ebenezer Smith,
whose two brothers, Samuel and John, would follow in Mr. Graham's footsteps as director
or rector of a Presbyterian college in Virginia. Augusta Academy preceded its younger sister
Academy in Prince Edward County by less than a year. Samuel was the first rector (president)*

> *Graham was graduated, and in the year 1775, these, with several others entered the ministry, took their first degree at Nassau Hall* [Princeton]*; and then returned to the Valley, where they pursued the study of theology under the direction of Mr. Graham, For altho they were nearly of his own age, his reputation as a theologian had risen so high, that they gladly availed themselves of his assistance in preparing for their sacred calling.* (A. Alexander, *Mss Memoir*, pp. 94, 95) (Emphasis added)

At least two of the men mentioned by Rev. Alexander in the above quotation had been students at Mr. Brown's Latin school, but they nevertheless repaired to Mr. Graham for theological instruction instead of their old parson, Rev. Brown, and for good reason, that being that Rev. Brown was not much of a scholar although his extant correspondence makes it clear that he did assist a few young men in preparing for the ministry, at least prior to Rev. Graham's arrival in Virginia. After Graham's arrival, most every young man living in Virginia beyond the Blue Ridge Mountains interested in preparing for the Presbyterian ministry went to Mr. Graham for their theological studies.

ERROR no. 10: McLaughlin quotes from meeting minutes of both the Hanover Presbytery and the earliest meetings of the Liberty Hall Board of Trustees and thereby assures his readers that he is familiar with both and, importantly, by doing so reveals that his false history representations may not have been innocent, but rather may well have been a knowing misrepresentation. The auditor does not charge him in that regard, however, and leaves it to the readers to decide for themselves. Here are what we deem the pertinent facts:

* McLaughlin's history (Historical Sketch[594]) quotes the trustees' meeting minutes as follows:

> On the first meeting after the battle of Lexington, the Trustees direct the record for the 6th of May, 1776,[595] to be entitled "Liberty Hall—as this Academy is hereafter to be called instead of the Augusta Academy." ("Historical Sketch," *Catalogue of the Alumni*, p. 8)

Note: The above quote is from the trustees' first meeting minutes, which would seem to establish that the author had seen and read these meeting minutes

---

of Prince Edward Academy (now Hampden Sydney College) who only served in that capacity briefly, who was followed by his younger brother John Blair Smith.

594 The auditor credits the historical sketch to the chair of the committee responsible for the publication of the catalog because the article lacks any attribution.

595 The author (McLaughlin) has the date wrong—the quote is from the trustees' meeting minutes for May 13, not May 6. The author then discusses subjects that he says were treated with at the trustees' meeting when in fact the matters were dealt with by the Hanover Presbytery, not the trustees and at an earlier meeting. See Hanover Presbytery meeting minutes for 1775 and 1776.

of the trustees. The reason that this fact is important is that it demonstrates that the writer elected to ignore the vastly important first authorized history of the seminary that begins on page 3 of the book and concludes on page 7. It is followed by pages 8–10 containing important extracts copied from the Hanover Presbytery's minutes that also pertain to the seminary. In other words, for McLaughlin, or whoever wrote this for McLaughlin, to read the page from which he quotes, but ignore the last page of the college's first authorized history, which is located on the opposite side of the opened record book, is rather preposterous. Such a stretch is hardly plausible. The fact is that McLaughlin constructed his false published early history of the college with the true history written on the pages immediately preceding the page from which he quotes. The first authorized history as written by Rev. Caleb Wallace completely contradicts what McLaughlin published under the imprimatur of the college. McLaughlin, therefore, is presumptively guilty of perpetrating a fraud on the public and on all of then-current students of Washington and Lee University, unless, that is, he relied upon a secondary source for copying the extract taken from his own college's board of trustees' meeting minutes record book. As chairman of the board of trustees, one would think he had easy enough access to his own board's record books of their meeting minutes. So even if one suggests that he relied upon a secondary source when the primary source was at his fingertips would strain credulity beyond reasonable limits. His guilt in perpetrating this historical hoax is nearly as certain as it could be.

Note: The history written by Caleb Wallace constitutes the first four pages of the record book containing the trustees' minutes. Wallace's history is followed by selected extracts from meetings of the presbytery, occupying pages 8–10.

Surely McLaughlin did not carelessly turn to page 11 of the earliest record book of the trustees and ignore the institution's first written history along with pertinent extracts from the presbytery's minutes pertaining to the seminary appearing on the book's first ten pages. While it is theoretically possible that the author did not read anything in the book's first ten pages, the likelihood of that being true seems to be terribly remote.

William McLaughlin, as the committee chairman, was responsible for the Catalogue of the Officers and Alumni of Washington and Lee University, Lexington, Virginia, 1988. Located in the preface is this explanation: *"But the whole has been under the direction of the Hon. William McLaughlin of the Board of Trustees"* (p. 3). As the director and supervisor, he is presumed to know the contents of the publication, which effectively rewrote the history of the university's founding and origins; and even though prior editions of the catalog had contained similar erroneous assertions dating back to the false sketch prepared by McLaughlin's fellow trustee, Col. Bolivar Christians, as early as 1869, McLaughlin's sketch includes direct quotations from the first meeting minutes of the board of trustees for May of 1796. Therefore, it is fair to assume that McLaughlin also read the few pages from the trustees' meeting minutes that appear just before the entry from which he quotes, for after all, they are the first few pages of the book. What McLaughlin undoubtedly found there is the very first account of the founding of the university, written into this book by the clerk of the presbytery that created both the institution and the institution's first board of trustees, and that account differs entirely from that account given by Mr. McLaughlin and the committee under his direction. There is one caveat to this near indictment, which is that someone could have handed McLaughlin a copy of the meeting minutes that only included the minutes from which he quotes. If so, McLaughlin may only be guilty of malfeasance for failing to consult a primary source where the primary source is readily available for review. If Mr. McLaughlin had simply read pages 3 through 10 in addition to page 11, he would have found on the very first leaf of this book the following:

> **"The present Academy of Liberty Hall _began under the_**
> **_Direction and Patronage of the Presbytery of Hanover_ as the**
> **following Minutes fully evince.** (Emphasis added)

This clear statement is followed by Clerk Wallace's extracts of all those pertinent parts relating to the establishment, which were taken from the minutes of the Hanover Presbytery and which we have compared to the actual handwritten minutes and found to be in all important points a verbatim transcription. The first extract is as follows:

> At a Session of the Pby. Of Hanover at Cub Creek October 13, 1774 (quoting initially Caleb Wallace) now, the extract:
>
> **The Pby resumed the consideration of a school for the liberal education of youth which we unanimously Judge to be of great importance. We do therefore agree to establish and patronize a public school which shall be confined to the County of Augusta in this Colony. At Present it shall be managed by Wm. Graham a gentleman properly recommended to this Pby.** (The original memorandum was signed and dated, Caleb Wallace, Clerk, May 1776,[596] p. 3 [the books first leaf, i.e., page].)

Note: The above is followed by the unfortunate qualifying statement "and under the inspection of Rev. John Brown."[597] We elected to follow the decisions of Edward Graham and Rev. Archibald Alexander who both did not include this qualifying phrase, and while they did not explain this to their readers, it is easy to

---

596 Wallace's signature is not actually present because his memorandum was copied into the minutes book by whoever was acting as clerk for that particular meeting.

597 _Both Edward Graham and Archibald Alexander wrote memoirs of William Graham, and both excluded the qualifying statement_ "and under the inspection of Rev. John Brown" because both realized that it had no applicability, nor importance because Rev. Brown did not accept this appointment, nor did he act on it in any way whatsoever—a fact made clear by all subsequent minutes wherein all communications, noted in the minutes, between the school and the presbytery, and later, the trustees, were between those two bodies and Mr. Graham. Moreover, Rev. Brown eschewed activities related to the seminary, save one unimportant prayer meeting.

understand why they left it out of their quotation from these minutes. The simple and obvious reason is that they both understood that Rev. Brown had declined to perform any "inspection" responsibility, irrespective of what was intended by the presbytery's decision in this regard. Most likely, they intended for Rev. Brown to observe the events taking place in Augusta County concerning Mr. Graham's activities to initiate their new seminary because Rev. Brown was the presbytery's only member then living in Augusta County and was the only person available to function as the presbytery's eyes and ears during this initial phase in the implementation of their new educational endeavor, but it matters little for Rev. Brown remained intransigent in his opposition to the presbytery's initiative to create a seminary and elected to not participate in any way. For either of these two biographers to include this now-superfluous language would only serve to confuse their readers. The printed word, after all, was then an expensive proposition; and the fewer the words used, the better.

It is quite clear what the Hanover Presbytery thought about the subject of the origins of Liberty Hall Academy, as is demonstrated by these words of their clerk, Caleb Wallace. Words that Mr. McLaughlin elected to ignore despite their prominent placement in the single most import historical record in the university's possession. McLaughlin may not have intended to intentionally mislead his readers, the other trustees, and the alumni of the college, but based on the compelling evidence shown herein, it is exceedingly difficult to conclude otherwise. Here are Clerk Wallace's words:

> **"The Present Academy of Liberty Hall began under the Direction and Patronage of the Presbytery of Hanover as the following minutes fully evince.**
>
> "At a session of the Pby. Of Hanover at Cub Creek Oct. 13, 1774, the Pby resumed consideration of a school for the liberal education of youth which we unanimously judge to be of great importance. We do therefore agree to establish and patronize a publick school which shall be confined to the county of Augusta in this colony. At present it shall be managed by Mr. William Graham, a Gentleman properly recommended. (Rev. Caleb Wallace's record book containing the minutes of the Board of Trustees of Liberty Hall Academy, p. 3. This opening is written down and organized by Rev. Caleb Wallace, clerk of the Hanover Presbytery. The second paragraph is a quote from the Hanover Presbytery's meeting minutes.) (Emphasis added)

ERROR no. 11: McLaughlin's historical sketch inaccurately describes the movements of a mythical school from one location to another that supposedly represents the movements of Washington and Lee, but which are neither true nor accurate. It should also be noted that in support of this asserted chronology of movement, McLaughlin offers no supporting authority.

During the administration of Mr. Brown, the Academy was
successively removed a few miles westward, first to Old
Providence, then to New Providence Church, and "shortly
before the Revolution"[598] to Mt. Pleasant, near Fairfield, in (now)
Rockbridge County, where in 1774 Mr. Graham became his
assistant, and in 1776 succeeded him as Principal. (McLaughlin,
"Historical Sketch," pp. 7–8)

The description of movements described above are completely unreliable
and, in some cases, absurdly false. It is premised on the falsehood that Brown
succeeded Robert Alexander as principal of Alexander's school. The terms
succeeded and principal are terribly problematic because Alexander's endeavor
was certainly a one-man show, meaning he organized and administered whatever
his operation was, and he was not the instructor. Brown, on the other hand, was
no instructor, and there is no known evidence that he was either inclined or able
to conduct classes. Therefore, he could hardly have taken over from Alexander
his role as principal. Moreover, McLaughlin identifies Alexander's school as a

Additionally, according to McLaughlin (see error no. 2 above), Alexander
conducted a mathematical and classical school; Brown consistently described
his school as a Latin school. Moreover, Brown's school was operating at New
Providence in December of 1775, as is evidenced by Philip Vickers Fithian in his
1775–1776 journal, written during his visit to the Valley.[599] While lodging in Rev.
Brown's home, he describes meeting with Samuel Doak, who was then conducting
the classes at Brown's Latin school at New Providence. Meanwhile, Graham was
conducting the presbytery's seminary at Mount Pleasant. It would have been
ridiculous for Brown to move his school back to Mount Pleasant because Mount
Pleasant is where it had been moved to New Providence from several years earlier.
Therefore, Brown's school was not moved to "Mt. Pleasant [sic]" shortly before
the Revolution, as McLaughlin claims. The author here is terribly confused, and
his explanation is filled with absurdities and false assumptions. That explains why
he offers no citations of authority to support his numerous false claims.

ERROR no. 12: McLaughlin inaccurately describes the chronology of campus
locations, beginning with the academy's move from Timber Ridge during the
Revolutionary War, and fails to mention one of the several campus locations
during the eighteenth century. His error lies not in what he says, but is an error of
omission that fails to mention two of the schools' locations as described by one
of its students of that period, Archibald Alexander. Below is how McLaughlin
describes the college's moves during this period:

---

598   The author places these words between quotation marks, but provides nothing to indicate where
      the quote comes from.

599   Philip Vickers Fithian, *The Journal & Letters of Philip Vickers Fithian, "Written on the Virginia-Pennsylvania Frontier and in the Army Around
      New York, [1775-1776]*] (Princeton, Princeton University Press, 1934).

"It was removed to this location in 1777, but was again removed, in 1785, to near Lexington, —to where yet stand the picturesque stone ruins of Old Liberty Hall, burned in 1802, "—and was removed finally, in 1803, to its present site within the limits of Lexington."

The true picture is rather more detailed. When Liberty Hall departed their intended permanent campus at Timber Ridge due to the vicissitudes occasioned by the Revolution, the critically important laboratory and mathematical equipment was transported to the rector's home on his new farm at Whistle Creek. The remaining students were housed at Rev. Graham's home and in the homes of various local residents. Classes initially were held at the rector's home but in time were moved into an abandoned home that was somewhat refurbished for the academy's use. Thereafter, funds were raised to construct a framed building dedicated to the school's operations. This building served for a time, but then it was destroyed by fire. The McLaughlin sketch omitted the refurbished abandoned home and the newly constructed framed structure.

After the fire, Rev. Graham initiated discussions with the Synod of Virginia that led to the Synod of Virginia deciding to establish a theological seminary under the synod's patronage and in conjunction with Liberty Hall Academy. This arrangement was complicated, but it provided the school with fund-raising opportunities that allowed Graham to build a replacement for the school that previously burned. The new school buildings were built of stone and included a central hall with an attached dormitory and a refectory where students took their meals and the steward boarded. This campus was located on Mulberry hill, and it too was destroyed by fire in 1802 or 1803. The remains of two walls are still standing.

ERROR no. 13: McLaughlin mistakenly authorized the false entries included in the first section of the catalog entitled "Rectors and Assistants" and the second section entitled "Trustees, Previous to Charter of 1782" on pages 34 and 35.

Here below is a rough facsimile of the page in question:

AUGUSTA ACADEMY AND
LIBERTY HALL

Rectors and Assistants
Previous to Charter of 1782.

ENTERED OFFICE.

1749......   Robert Alexander, A.M.   1762
1752......   John Buchanan, Assistant   1760

1760......	J. Edmundson, MD	1770
1762......	John Brown, DD	1776
1770......	Ebenezer Smith	1774
1774......	Rev. Robert Archibald	1775
1774......	William Graham, A. M.	1799
1776......	John Montgomery, AB	17??

****

The only names listed in the illustrated chart above that are not incorrect are William Graham and John Montgomery.[600] All the others are incorrect, and none of the other named individuals had any connection whatsoever to the Hanover Presbytery's seminary in Augusta County. In the last two hundred years, no one has located any document or other credible evidence to show otherwise. Moreover, there is ample evidence to demonstrate that there could not possibly be any connection of these individuals and the seminary called at the time Augusta Academy.

None of the people listed was either a rector (president) or an assistant at the Hanover Presbytery's patronized seminary in Augusta. That means that Robert Alexander, John Buchanan, J. Edmundson, John Brown, Ebenezer Smith, and Rev. Robert Archibald should never have been listed in this chart. All of these gentlemen are said to have been associated with Rev. John Brown's Latin school, which may or may not be true, but nonetheless, they had no connection whatsoever to the Hanover Presbytery's seminary in Augusta Academy. That is why there is no reference to any of them as having had a connection with the school in the academy's board of trustees' meeting minutes[601] or the Hanover Presbytery's meeting minutes, with the lone exception of Rev. John Brown, but in Brown's case, he refused acceptance of any appointment related to the presbytery's academy.

Note: William Graham was the rector of Liberty Hall, and for a time, John Montgomery was Graham's assistant. (See Hanover Presbytery meeting minutes for May 6, 1776, p. 78.)

McLaughlin expands on these mistakes by including a list of trustees identified as having been trustees prior to the college's 1782 charter. The list is not correct, however, because the list is comprised of all the gentlemen appointed, or nominated, for the position of trustee; and numerous of the men appointed never accepted their appointments and therefore should not be considered to have

---

600   Technically, John Montgomery was assisted by Graham as a tutor in 1775, and his role does not
      seem to differ from 1775 to 1776.

601   It is true that Rev. Brown's name does appear in these minutes as one who was appointed to
      a fund-raising effort and as an "inspector," but as the minutes clearly evince, Brown did not
      accept any of these appointments. If any of these gentlemen are mentioned in the presbytery's
      meeting minutes, it is only in their capacity as a minister, not as having been associated with
      the presbytery's academy in Augusta County.

been a trustee. It seems that McLaughlin apparently failed to read all the minutes covering that meeting because on the page following the one upon which the appointees' names appear is found this critically important parenthetical:

> Ordered that Mr. Graham inform the gentlemen we have chosen Trustees, of the contents of these Minutes, *& solicit their acceptance in behalf of the Presbytery*. *(See Hanover Presbytery meeting minutes for May 6, 1776, p. 79.)* (Emphasis added)

As subsequent trustees' meeting minutes reveal, many of the named trustees never bothered to register their acceptance by bothering to attend a meeting of the trustees. That includes Rev. John Brown, who lived in the neighborhood where the trustees held their meetings but never attended a meeting and never accepted his appointment as a trustee. This is another fact that was obviously and inexplicably missed by most, if not all post-1850 authors who addressed the early history of Washington and Lee.

Note: Those trustees listed that have the notation "reappointed 1782" are trustees that accepted and participated as trustees between May of 1776 and October of 1782. Those who were not reappointed can safely be assumed to have refused their earlier appointment or had died in the interim.

The important points here are that all those listed above as rectors or assistants save Graham and Montgomery were neither rectors nor assistants, and many that are identified in the subsequent list as trustees were never in fact trustees, including Rev. John Brown. As for Graham having been an assistant to Rev. Brown, it need only be pointed out that there is no evidence that Rev. John Brown ever taught a class on any subject in any type of school during his entire life. This fact is underscored by his extant correspondence located in the Draper collection of rare manuscripts housed in Wisconsin–Madison, a reality reflected quite clearly in John White Stuart's biography of Rev. Brown. See bibliography. Brown was not much of a scholar, and he had no inclination to teach.[602] Graham's impressive scholarship and teaching experience under such venerated educators as Dr. Samuel Finley and Dr. John Witherspoon, both presidents of Princeton, renders the idea of Graham being Brown's assistant perversely nonsensical.

****

---

602 That very well may explain why he organized a Latin school, but he did not conduct the classes. Overseeing a school was an assumed responsibility of a pastor in that period, so it very well may be that Brown's reluctance to conduct a school in connection with his early pastorate over Timber Ridge and New Providence congregations was the source of the tension that arose between Brown and some members of the Timber Ridge congregation that resulted in Brown's departure from the Timber Ridge congregation.

An Attachment to this subsection of Select
Important Twentieth-Century Historians
(Extracted from the Reports' Comprehensive Chronologically Arranged List)[603]

Introduction

The original plan for this publication envisioned an assessment of seventy-four authors who the auditor has assessed and whose works were found to include substantive errors concerning the origin of the university or about the character and life of the university's founder and first president, Rev. William Graham.

21. HERBERT B. ADAMS [James J. White & Carter Harris[604]] & John Mason Brown (1888)

(Thomas Jefferson and the University of Virginia, U.S. Bureau of Education Circular of Information No. 1 (sub-numbered No. 2), Washington, Government Printing Office, 1888, [see especially chap. 22 (Washington And Lee University by professors White and Harris, i.e., W&L professors, Carter J. Harris & James J. White) & chap. 23 (bibliography of Washington and Lee University), pp. 293–308. The whole is supplemented by a grossly inaccurate letter from John Mason Brown (great-grandson of Rev. John Brown).

Note: This monograph by Dr. Adams was one aspect of a much larger envisioned project of the U.S. Bureau of Education, and the entire project is discussed in **"The Executive Documents of the House of Representatives for the first session of the Fiftieth Congress 1887–88 in thirty-two volumes."** *This history prepared under the direction of Dr. Herbert B. Adams is of paramount importance in the history of American higher education. The profound errors contained therein with respect to the founding of Washington and Lee University contributed to perpetuating the grossly false history of one of Virginia's premier universities.*

---

603 The original list of more than seventy authors was severely reduced, mostly due to unacceptable redundancies.

604 Notice in the "Alumni Bulletin of the University of Virginia [May 1894, vol. 1, no. 1]" mentions the recent passing of two professors at Washington and Lee University, both of whom were alumni of [U.Va.]: "Carter Johns Harris, born in the same year, (1828) ..and entered the University [U. Va.] in 1847–49, where, equally with his friend and associate, White, he studied under Courtenay, McGuffey, and Harrison, and was afterwards thrown with him, as professor of Latin, in the same faculty and institution, for five and thirty years. He died August 2d, 1894. . . . The two men were the most striking personalities in the faculty of Washington and Lee University, yet so absolutely different that the contrast between them was even picturesque. An intimacy of nearly eighteen years between the writer and them enabled him to study and record the contrast. . . . Seldom indeed has an institution been more bitterly bereaved than Washington and Lee in the death of these twin professors, whose benign influence long antedates the war" James A. Harrison, Wash. And Lee Univ" (p. 84).

Introduction

It were better had this book's chapters 22 and 23 not been written. Taken together, they are a complete failure. They stand as exemplars of poor historical treatment. Adams, in this project at least, shunned primary sources[605] in favor of secondary unauthenticated sources and second-guessed in significant ways the selected authors who were asked to provide a brief history of the founding of Washington and Lee. Adams adds a so-called bibliography, which is a narrowly select and highly annotated one that is error-ridden and unreliable in its annotations. Rounding out these examples of poor editorial judgments, he completes these two chapters by inexplicably reprinting an error-laced letter from John Mason Brown, whose self-admitted ignorance permeates his entire communication. While this may seem to be an overly strong critique for an objective audit review, it may be illuminating to share the letter writer's opening admission:

> "*...my information as to the organization and history of Augusta Academy*, in Virginia, *is quite limited....*," (John Mason Brown; emphasis added)

Given the writer's admitted ignorance, it strains credulity that Dr. Adams chose to further confuse what Adams refers to as obscurity, referring to the founding of Washington and Lee, by including extracts from ill-informed authors whose only real contribution to the college's early history is repeating erroneous assertions of William Henry Foote and various mid-nineteenth-century documents published by the university, none of which are supported by the institution's earliest records.

Adams's unjustifiable second-guessing of his own handpicked authors was simply wrongheaded because any confusion or obscurity about the founding of Washington Lee is the fault of all the nineteenth-century historians who relied upon William Henry Foote's _Sketches of Virginia_ instead of relying on the primary documentary and pre-1850 histories, all of which were essentially correct and in concert with one another, at least, about the time frame in which the college was created. To be sure, there were a few perfunctory mistakes made by the earliest authors, but not about the fact that the college was created by the Hanover Presbytery in the autumn of 1774. The official documentary records also date the founding as having occurred in October of 1774. Unfortunately, a few later historians relied upon the actual records but were satisfied with relying on others' published extracts, many of which were misleading. The reprinted letter from John Mason Brown demonstrates that Brown had never seen any of the official records of the Hanover Presbytery or the college trustees' meeting minutes from the period of the college's founding.

Adams's judgment in deciding to reprint this letter is even more inexplicable in light of the fact that the chapters in question are about the subject that the writer admits he knows little about. Astoundingly, Adams nevertheless reprints the letter and then compounds his mistake by praising Brown's letter and labeling

---

605 Adams's bibliography, which he took responsibility for.

it as a "valuable memoranda." The letter, however, is anything but a valuable contribution to the literature about the institution.

In regards to the early history of Liberty Hall Academy, or, as it was first called, Augusta Academy, Mr. Brown's letter is replete with error and is hardly correct about any aspect of the school. Mr. Brown's character is not in question here for his bona fides in regard to history are widely accepted; rather it is his knowledge about the founding that is seriously lacking.

Mr. Brown mistakenly assumed that his great-grandfather, Rev. John Brown, was intimately connected to an academy he actually opposed from its very inception and one he so despised that he refused to send any of his sons there even though it was conveniently located in his own neighborhood. Appointed a trustee and an inspector, Rev. Brown refused to accept either appointment.

John Mason Brown would no doubt have been surprised to learn that the name, Liberty Hall Academy, was given to the school by the new board of trustees at the trustees' first meeting on May 13, 1776. At this historic meeting held in John Brown's own neighborhood, the following members of the board proudly attended: William Graham, Alexander Stuart, Samuel Lyle, Charles Campbell, John Houston, and William McKee. It was these six men who gave the school the name *Liberty Hall Academy*, and they certainly did not name the school in honor of the most noticeably absent appointed trustee, Rev. John Brown, as the letter writer speculates.

That Rev. Brown never accepted his appointment is an easily demonstrated fact, embarrassingly missed by both John Mason Brown and Dr. Adams. Indeed, missed by virtually all historians treating the subject since 1850. The reason it was missed is that no one bothered to look at the primary documentary sources, relying instead on what others wrote in those records. Even a cursory review of the trustees' earliest meeting minutes confirms Rev. Brown's perpetual absence from every meeting of the Trustees.

The letter-writer unsurprisingly, asserted a demonstrably false history of the college's early history and his paucity of knowledge, it seems, was far greater than he even realized. One can only imagine these two equally misguided historians' (Adams and John Mason Brown) shock and dismay were they to have seen Rev. Brown's letters to his bother-in-law, Col. William Preston advising him to not send his sons to Liberty Hall and his prediction that the school would not likely succeed.

Fortunately, scholars now have access to Rev. Archibald Alexander's unpublished, handwritten manuscript "Memoir of Rev. William Graham" wherein he explains why Rev. Brown and most of his immediate family were estranged from Rev. William Graham, the founding first president of Augusta Academy (Liberty Hall Academy). A photostatic copy, paginated in pencil by this auditor, now resides in the Leyburn Library at Washington and Lee University.[606]

---

606 The auditor's copy was obtained in the nineteen eighties and was provided by the library at Princeton Theological Seminary, which had obtained the original from a descendant of Archibald Alexander.

Adams compounded his egregious error of printing John Mason's specious letter by appending a note of his own, a note that contains one erroneous representation after another. One cannot help but question why Adams bothered to employ Messrs. White and Harris to author the chapter on Washington and Lee if he intended to add extensive extracts and commentary that mostly serve to nullify the comments of White and Harris, to wit:

> "One of the earliest, if not the very earliest school established, was known first as Augusta Academy, ***then as Mount Pleasant***, and during the Revolutionary War as Liberty Hall. (Adams, _The History of the University of Virginia_, chapter 22 [written by professors James J. White and Carter Harris, p. 295]; emphasis in bold italics here represents error, albeit a minor and seemingly harmless one.)

The author's mostly accurate words above are footnoted by the editor after "Augusta Academy," and in a lengthy footnote, he reprints a selection from Joseph Waddell's _Annals of Augusta County_, which is one of the most unreliable sources he could have selected on this subject. For example, the extract Adams selected for his footnote lists three dates associated with the founding of Washington and Lee, two of which are of relative unimportance and the third inaccurate. Indeed, Mr. Waddell failed to comprehend the importance of Washington and Lee University or its founding first president, William Graham, who he misrepresents and mistakenly traduces in several different ways. For details, see the subsection of this section devoted to Waddell's work.

It is a mystery why Adams inserts himself into the chapter at all. The content of his lengthy footnotes conflict with the assertions of the chapter's authors on the greatest central question of the chapter, which is the question of the college's founding and early history. Adams, however, does not explain in any of the footnotes that the conflict even exists, let alone why he believed that further elucidation was necessary. The White and Harris chapter is essentially correct. Adams's commentary on the same subject is demonstrably inaccurate.

Perhaps Adams was troubled by the White and Harris assertion that the college's virtual founder is William Graham because he presents an alternate narrative in the subsequent chapter (his bibliography) that supports the specious notion that the college was not founded by the Hanover Presbytery but by Rev. John Brown. Adams obviously did not know that Brown opposed the creation of the Augusta Academy (Liberty Hall) and that he refused all attempts to persuade him to join his brethren of the Hanover Presbytery in supporting the new college. Adams, like so many other misguided historians of the later nineteenth century, failed to realize that Brown never attended a single meeting of the college's board of trustees and he refused to send any of his sons to the college. See John White Stuart's biography of Rev. John Brown and his heavily extracted letters housed in the famous Draper Collection in Wisconsin–Madison.

Had Dr. Adams or any of the authors he selected to extract in his annotated bibliography been aware of the well-known fact in the Valley that Rev. John

Brown's family were mostly all seriously estranged from Rev. William Graham,[607] they would have reconsidered their speculations about Brown having been in some way connected to the college in his neighborhood.

Conclusion Concerning Dr. Adam's Book and the Chapters Related to Washington and Lee University

There are approximately a dozen significant errors about the early history of Washington and Lee contained in Dr. Adams's book. Most of them are attributable to Dr. Adams rather than the authors (professors White and Harris) of the chapter designated:

"CHAPTER XXII.

WASHINGTON AND LEE UNIVERSITY.

By PROFESSORS WHITE AND HARRIS[608]

The authors curiously say this:

> *One of the earliest, if not the very earliest school established, was known first as Augusta Academy, then as Mount Pleasant,* and during the Revolutionary War as Liberty Hall. This school, after occupying other neighboring localities, *was finally established in the vicinity of Lexington, Va., May 6, 1776*, under the name of Liberty Hall Academy with William Graham, its virtual founder, as its rector. (Adams, *The History of the University of Virginia*, chapter 22, "Washington and Lee University" by Professors James J. White and Carter Harris, pp. 294–295)

> The two author's statement concerning the school's founding contains several mistakes. There were other private local schools that existed prior to the Presbytery's creation of Augusta Academy in October of 1774. Augusta Academy, was never known as "Mount Pleasant" The school was not named Liberty Hall Academy after the Revolutionary War but was

---

607 The estrangement was occasioned by Mr. Graham requesting to be relieved of his proposal of marriage to Reverend Brown's highly sought-after eldest daughter, Betsy, a romance destroyed by the actions of Mrs. Brown who resented her would-be son-in-law, Mr. Graham. See Archibald Alexander's Mss. "Memoir of Rev. William Graham." Alexander was an early student who resided in the president's home and whose family were neighbors of the Brown family in that area that encompassed the congregations of Timber Ridge and New Providence Presbyterian congregations.

608 Professors James J. White and Carter Harris of Washington and Lee University.

rather given that name by the College's first Board of Trustees in May of 1776, before the Continental Congress' adoption of the Declaration of Independence. It was the Board of Trustees' first official action recorded in its meeting minutes record book which was dated May 13, 1776.

By inserting numerous footnotes, an annotated bibliography, and a reprinted erroneous letter by John Mason Brown, the editor, Dr. Herbert B. Adams, embarrassingly and unprofessionally altered the essence of the history that the authors he had selected carefully created. This mistake by Adams left a false impression that the error-ridden chapter 22 was the responsibility of professors White and Harris. Adams selected erroneous extracts, written by later historians, and printed them in his bibliography. These extracts are in direct conflict with the history of the origins of Washington and Lee as told by the professors labeled as the authors. In addition, he elected not to include extracts written by eyewitnesses that in the main supports the account given by White and Harris pertaining to the institution's founding. Oddly, Adams failed to include in his bibliography these two authorities:

* The first authorized history of the founding of Liberty Hall Academy, written by the clerk of the Hanover Presbytery, Caleb Wallace.[609]
* The first authorized published history of Washington and Lee (then Washington College), published in the pamphlet containing the inaugural address of Rev. George Junkin[610] as an appendix entitled, "A Brief Sketch of Washington College."[611]

Both of these seminal sources constitute official records of the institution that created the college, and both contradict the contents of most of the extracts inserted by Adams, as well as the erroneous letter of John Mason Brown. Moreover, Adams fails to even mention in his bibliography the record books containing the official meeting minutes of the Hanover Presbytery and the Liberty Hall Academy Board of Trustees. He also conveniently left out of the bibliography the 1796 letter written by President William Graham to President George Washington on behalf of the board of trustees, which also contradicts the later accounts of the various sources who followed the erroneous William H. Foote's accounts.

These two chapters of Adams's magnum opus, _History of the University of Virginia_, are the personification of the twentieth-century communications theory labeled as "selective perception." Adams simply saw only that which he wanted

---

609 Later, Wallace became a justice of Kentucky's highest appellate court.

610 Adams does list the inaugural address itself, but he neglects to mention the all-important appendix that contradicts Adams's narrative account.

611 Rev. George, Junkin, DD, _Christianity the Patron of Literature and Science: An Address Delivered February 22, 1849. On the Occasion of the Author's Inauguration as President of Washington College, Virginia,_ Philadelphia, The Board of Trustees, 1849 [pamphlet pp. 39]. The Junkin Inaugural Address includes an important Appendix: "A Brief Sketch of the Early History of Washington College" ("ordered printed by the Board of Trustees").

to see. Hence, this writer's introductory proclamation that it were better had these chapters never been included in Adams's history.

Note: Detailing Adams's numerous mistakes regarding Washington and Lee was deemed unworthy and deleted from this audit. Moreover, it was also decided to delete the details of the several errors made in the chapters devoted to Hampden-Sydney College that relate to that institution's founding, especially where it discusses its founding. The reader should simply remember that the first college created by the Hanover Presbytery is Washington and Lee, and Hampden-Sydney was an afterthought that was created the year after the founding of Washington and Lee. W&L was founded in 1774, and Hampden-Sydney in 1775. They are often considered to be sister colleges given that they were founded by the same group of Presbyterian ministers (Hanover Presbytery), their establishments separated by only a few months. These two colleges' founding presidents, Rev. William Graham and Rev. Samuel Stanhope Smith, were teaching colleagues at Princeton under its president, Rev. John Witherspoon.

22. JOSEPH A. WADDELL (1888–1902)

(Joseph, A. Waddell, *Annals of Augusta County, from 1726-1871*, C. R. Caldwell, 1901 [original edition, J. W. Randolph, 1888. Caldwell as publisher may be the second edition revised and enlarged in 1902; Article, "Scotch-Irish of the Valley of Virginia" in the Scotch-Irish in America Proceedings and Addresses, Nashville, Tenn.: 1895, pp. 79–99.)

Mr. Waddell made errors in both his *Annals of Augusta County* and his article, "Scotch-Irish of the Valley of Virginia." The errors in his book are treated first.

ERROR no. 1: [Annals...] Mr. Waddell provides an incorrect chronology of the schools in the Valley of Virginia in the eighteenth century. He also incorrectly links the Robert Alexander School to the Rev. John Brown Latin school and also incorrectly links Rev. Brown's Latin School to the Hanover Presbytery, when the only connection of the Latin school of Rev. John Brown was a single visit of the presbytery to observe Rev. Brown's school in April of 1775. This visit has been misunderstood by many historians. It took place after the several days' business spring meeting of the presbytery. It was occasioned by the presbytery's having met at Mr. Brown's home on their second day onward and undoubtedly at the invitation of their host, Rev. John Brown. There is no subsequent reference to Rev. Brown's private Latin school in any of the presbytery's meeting minutes. No action was either called for or taken in regard to Rev. Brown's school, which was being taught by Samuel Doak, as noted by Rev. Philip Vickers Fithian, during his visit to the Valley at that time [Dec. 1775].[612]

Mr. Waddell set forth the following on page 69 of his *Annals of Augusta County* (1902 ed.):

> *The first classical school* west of the Blue Ridge was opened in 1749, by Robert Alexander, two miles southwest of the present village of Greenville. The teacher was educated in Edinburgh, it is believed. He immigrated to Pennsylvania in 1736, and to

---

612   Philip Vickers Fithian, The Journal & Letters of Philip Vickers Fithian, "Written on the Virginia-Pennsylvania Frontier and in the Army Around New York, [1775-1776], Princeton, Princeton University Press, 1934.

the Valley in 1743. How long Mr. Alexander conducted the school we do not know. *He was succeeded by Rev. John Brown, and the school was removed first to Old Providence, then to New Providence, and shortly before the Revolutionary war to Mount Pleasant,* near Fairfield. *It was latterly under the care of Hanover Presbytery.* (Joseph A. Waddell, *Annals of,* p. 69; emphasis in bold italics here represents error and is added.)

Mr. Waddell, and all those who preceded him on this point, were presumptuous and ahistorical in pronouncing Robert Alexander's school a "classical" school because in truth, history has no idea what kind of school Mr. Alexander conducted. Neither Mr. Waddell, nor any of his predecessors on this point, bothered to cite any authority for this contention. The reason he failed to provide any authority in support of his assertion is that no credible authority exists. All representations of this absurdity were published many decades after the principals had been laid to rest; and the principals left no known letters, manuscripts, documents, or publications containing anything that might reasonably allow one to conclude that his school was a "classical school." Indeed, from what we do know, Mr. Alexander had no known formal education, and his instruction was quite elementary, excepting perhaps in mathematics and surveying. Alexander's brother, Archibald, the grandfather of Rev. Archibald Alexander, also provided local boys with some elementary instruction. The elder Archibald's grandson, Archibald, is a well-known and well-published historian of early Presbyterian schools.[613] Robert Alexander's great-nephew, Rev. Archibald Alexander, had ample opportunity to give credit to his grandfather and or his great-uncle as early instructors, but noticeably abstained in that regard. Instead, Rev. Archibald Alexander focused his historical study on those institutions that provided "classical studies." Archibald Alexander makes it abundantly clear that he commenced his "classical studies" at Liberty Hall under Rev. William Graham during the Revolutionary War, and he did so along with several others.[614]

("it is believed"), the specious idea that Mr. Alexander was "educated in Edinburgh." Dr. Ollinger Crenshaw explains, embarrassingly for several authors, that he investigated such claims and determined that they were all bogus. Again, on the subject of Robert Alexander's education, history is, was, and likely always will be completely ignorant.

On the subject of the movement of schools, Dr. McDaniel and his team investigating this subject concluded, "The fact remains, then, that evidence of direct ties between the sites [Alexander's school & Brown's school(s)] has not been

---

613 Archibald Alexander, DD, Biographical Sketches of the Founder and Principal Alumni of the Log College, Philadelphia, 1845.

614 Archibald Alexander, Mss "Memoir of William Graham," passim [written in longhand]. The Reverend Graham portions of this manuscript are part of a larger writing entitled, *Great Valley of Virginia.* My photocopy came from the Princeton Seminary Library in 1989. It is also available in spiral-bound form at the Leyburn Library, Washington and Lee University.

found in eighteenth-century sources"[615] (McDaniel et al., *Liberty Hall Academy*, p. 4).

On the movements of the schools, Waddell said, "*And the school was removed first to Old Providence, **then to New Providence**"* (Waddell, *Annals of*, p. 69). On this, he is incorrect. No author has presented any evidence that there was ever a move to "Old Providence," but that point is unimportant to the history of Liberty Hall Academy's founding. Mr. Waddell then goes on to say that it was "then moved to New Providence," obviously referring to the school of Rev. John Brown, and in that he is absolutely incorrect because Rev. Brown's Latin school was being conducted first at the place called locally "Mount Pleasant" near Fairfield, Virginia, and then subsequently it was moved from Mount Pleasant to New Providence, where it continued for several years. This we know from Rev. Brown's correspondence so well laid out and described by Mr. John White Stuart in his *The Rev. John Brown of Virginia (1728-1803): His Life and Selected Sermons*. See bibliography.

Importantly, Messrs. Waddell and Stuart mistakenly assumed the Hanover Presbytery adopted and patronized Mr. Brown's Latin school at New Providence. It did not, and there is nothing in the official records to suggest otherwise.

ERROR no. 2: [Annals..] Joseph Waddell mistakenly asserts that Rev. William Graham was a "somewhat imprudent man."

> In the latter part of the century the Presbyterian churches of the Valley were disturbed by dissensions in regard to psalmody. The version of the Psalms by Rouse* had been universally used, and when the smoother version by Dr. Isaac Watts was introduced, there was strenuous opposition to it on the part of many people. It is related that, in 1789 or 1790, the Rev. William Graham, <u>a somewhat imprudent man</u>, precipitated a controversy on the subject in New Providence Congregation. Rouse's version had been used there as elsewhere, but Mr. Graham, while assisting the pastor at a communion service, without conferring with any one, **introduced Watt's psalms and hymns**. Some of the older members left the church immediately, and a schism occurred.

> (Waddell, referring to Ruffner's *History of Washington College*; see Waddell's *Annals*, p. 343) (Emphasis added)

Waddell is wrong on several points about the history of the psalmody issue, but is seriously mistaken to conclude from this incident that Graham was imprudent. On its face, Waddell's conclusion is clearly ridiculous. Why would church members punish Rev. Brown for the decision of a visiting minister to circulate one hymn by Isaac Watts? This conclusion by Waddell makes no sense whatsoever.

---

615 John M. McDaniel, Charles N. Watson, David T. Moore, <u>Liberty Hall Academy, The Early History of the Institutions which Evolved into Washington and Lee University</u> (Lexington, Virginia: Liberty Hall Press, 1979).

The anecdote he references he based on Dr. Ruffner's *History of Washington College*, but the anecdote first appeared in Archibald Alexander's unpublished "Memoir of William Graham." Ruffner's knowledge is based on hearsay testimony of others while Archibald Alexander's account was a youthful remembrance of a scene in which he had been an eyewitness. Waddell incorrectly assumed Graham had introduced Watts's psalms and hymns, when in truth he introduced just one hymn by Mr. Watts. More importantly, Rev. Graham's conducting of this service at Rev. Brown's church (New Providence) was at the invitation of a majority of the congregation who desired to see firsthand the leader of the then-popular "revival,"[616] and the introduction of Watts's hymns was one of the defining features of that revival—a fact that most were fully apprised of even before this communion service began.

Alexander, while an accurate reporter, was a mere youth when this event transpired and as such was obviously unaware that the national assembly of the Presbyterian Church had authorized the use of either Rouse or Watts's hymns and had admonished Presbyterians against disruptions and disputation on the controversy. If there was imprudence on this occasion, it was that of the minority members of Brown's congregation who left the congregation and formed a new one. Quite obviously, these disaffected members were spoiling for a fight when they arrived at the service.

If there had been a legitimate beef against Graham's use of this one hymn, either Rev. Brown or any one of the members of Brown's congregation could have lodged a complaint against Graham with the appropriate presbytery, but tellingly, none did.

> On this occasion while Mr. Graham was serving at the Lord's table and much feeling seemed to be manifest in the congregation, *he gave out **one** of Watt's Sacramental hymns* which was sung by most, but one of the elders was so offended, that he made an attempt to stop the preacher from proceeding. ***The innovation was unauthorized*** [indecipherable word] and consequences such as might have been expected. One whole district of the congregation with the elder before mentioned withdrew from the congregation; and immediately joined with some seceders in the neighborhood in forming a church in connection with that denomination. All impartial men censured the conduct of Mr. Graham in this affair. (Archibald Alexander, Mss., "Memoir of William Graham, pp. 217–218; emphasis added, the underlined emphasis an error)

Alexander's judgment in this affair notwithstanding, the idea that a group of Rev. Brown's congregants would disrupt a communion service and resign from the Church because a visiting minister invoked the use of one hymn by Isaac Watts, whose hymns were formally recognized by the General Assembly of the

---

616 Graham was the leader of the revival in the Valley of Virginia while Rev. John Blair Smith was its leader east of the Blue Ridge Mountains.

national Presbyterian Church, is patently absurd. One can only conclude that Archibald Alexander's assessment resulted from his close familial connection to someone who joined in the disruption and schismatic turbulence that ostensibly was a reaction to the signing of one hymn. It would seem here that Alexander, who was a young adolescent at the time the event took place and faced with cognitive dissonance, he decided to side with his family over his preceptor. Nevertheless, Alexander gives a full and detailed account of the event and the facts speak for themselves.

ERROR no. 3: ["Scotch-Irish in the Valley..."]

Introduction: Mr. Waddell in this address makes several mistakes concerning the origins of Washington and Lee University, many embodied in this extract:

> "In the meanwhile, as early as 1749, sixteen years after the first settlement, *a classical school* had been opened by Robert Alexander, a native of Ulster, *educated in Edinburg*, [*sic*] some twelve miles from Augusta C. H. *This school was subsequently moved, under different teachers, from place to place, and finally located in the vicinity of Lexington. Here it assumed the name of Liberty Hall Academy, and presided over by Rev. William Graham.*[617] (Waddell, *Scotch-Irish of*, p. 86)

The first error in this extract is his denomination of Robert Alexander's educational endeavor as a "classical school." The fact is that virtually nothing of substance is known about Robert Alexander's educational activities in the Valley, and the few miscellaneous court records that do mention it indirectly do not touch upon the nature of the school, nor its location, or when it began, or when it ended, let alone the nature of is curriculum, if any. This then constitutes error no. 3, but there are others that emanate from the same extract which are as follows:

ERROR no. 4: ["Scotch-Irish in the Valley..."]
Mr. Waddell says above that Robert Alexander was "educated in Edinburg [*sic*]," but the truth is there is no known evidence concerning Robert Alexander other than what was gleaned by Dr. Ollinger Crenshaw and that evidence only confirms that Robert Alexander was not a student at the University in Edinburgh. (See Crenshaw's appendix A to his unpublished two-volume typescript of General Lee's college included in the audit's bibliography.)

ERROR no. 5: ["Scotch-Irish in the Valley..."]
Mr. Waddell's claim above that "this school was subsequently moved, under different teachers, from place to place, and finally located in the vicinity of Lexington" is both factually incorrect and also misleading beyond just the subject

---

617   Joseph A. Waddell (Addison), "Scotch-Irish of the Valley of Virginia," pp. 79–105, in *The Scotch-Irish In America: Proceedings and Address of the Seventh Congress*, Lexington, Va., June 20–23, 1895, Nashville, Barbee & Smith Agents, 1895, pp. 79–99.

of his errors of fact. First, it is not clear from known facts that there was ever a connection between the educational efforts of Robert Alexander and those initiated by Rev. John Brown. Secondly, Rev. Brown's school was located in two different locations but is only known to have moved once, from "Mount Pleasant" (near Fairfield) to New Providence on Moffett's Creek. Finally in this regard, the school(s) to which Mr. Waddell obviously refers were never located near Lexington. Mr. Waddell, like so many others who preceded and succeeded him, became discombobulated by their efforts to reconcile known facts with faulty assumptions about there being a link between earlier preparatory schools and Liberty Hall. Their error in this regard was predictable because there were no such links. It is absolutely certain that there was no link between Brown's Latin school and Liberty Hall, and it must also be assumed that there was no link between Robert Alexander's school and Rev. Brown's school because there is no known credible evidence to support that assertion. In two hundred years of endless searching, no one has located any eighteenth-century evidence that Alexander's educational efforts in the Valley had any connection to the Latin school organized by Rev. John Brown.

Moreover, in all of Rev. Brown's eighteenth-century correspondence in which he discusses his school, he never once mentions Robert Alexander or his school. Moreover, Rev. Archibald Alexander's extensive historical writings are devoid of any hint of there being a connection between the educational efforts of his great-uncle Robert Alexander and Brown's Latin school despite Alexander's serious interest in the history of early schools with connections to what he termed log colleges.[618]

Most likely, the Alexander endeavor was located near Greenville while Rev. Brown's "Latin school" was certainly initially located close to his first residence near Fairfield at "Mount Pleasant," but then about 1767, it was moved to its permanent location adjacent to the New Providence Presbyterian Church close by his home. Rev. Brown had moved to that location after severing his connection to the Timber Ridge congregation in the 1760s.[619]

Waddell added to the growing number of nineteenth-century historians who had mangled the early history of Washington and Lee University.

23. HENRY ALEXANDER WHITE (1861–1926)
Publications (1890, 1895, 1911):

10. "The Scotch-Irish University of the South: Washington And Lee," published in *The Scotch-Irish In America:*

---

618   Archibald Alexander, DD, *Biographical Sketches of the Founder and Principal Alumni of the Log College*, Philadelphia, 1845 and reprint, 1851.

619   The breach between Reverend Brown and his Timber Ridge congregation first surfaced in 1763, and the agitation culminated in his official separation in 1767. Brown's move from his home near Fairfield (Timber Ridge) to his home on Moffatt's Creek (New Providence) was completed during 1763 and 1767. Initially, Brown served as pastor of both congregations; but by 1767, he was assigned exclusively to the New Providence congregation. Both congregations were deemed to have been within the same general neighborhood although they were several miles apart.

Proceedings and Addresses of the Second Congress, May 29 to June 1, 1890, published by order of the Scotch-Irish Society of America (Cincinnati, Ohio: Robert Clark & Co, 1890), 223–246.

11.   ."The Presidents of the Washington College in Virginia" in *The Scotch-Irish in America, Proceedings and Addresses of Seventh Congress*, 1895, pp. 100–122, and

12.   *and 3), Southern Presbyterian Leaders* (New York: Neale Publishing Company, 1911).

Introduction

Rev. Henry Alexander White graduated from Washington and Lee and served as faculty at his alma mater from 1889–1902. He later became a faculty member of Columbia Theological Seminary.

Errors in Henry Alexander White's article: "The Scotch-Irish University of the South: Washington And Lee," *The Scotch-Irish in America: Proceedings and Addresses of the Second Congress*, **May 29 to June 1, 1890.**

ERROR no. 1: Mr. Henry A. White erroneously and with no justification whatever assigns a meaning to the minutes of the Hanover Presbytery that cannot be justified by the content of the minutes. Mr. White, acting as a sitting judge in a juvenile court, presumes to take child of one Presbyterian minister and transfers custody to another without establishing a record upon which to base his decision. Acting sua sponte, Mr. White, with no petition having been placed before him setting forth the purpose of the meeting and without taking any evidence, simply decides that an adoption has just taken place and puts his imprimatur on the entire affair.

> "Thus the academy of Robert Alexander, presided over by Rev. John Brown, **became the child of Hanover Presbytery.**[620] (Henry Alexander White, "The Scotch University of the South," 228)

It is truly astounding how Mr. White could get so much right and still err by misguidedly claiming that there is a link between Robert Alexander's and Rev. John Brown's altogether different private schools and then somehow mysteriously wrapping these two schools in the same blanket with the presbytery's new

---

620 *Rev. Henry Alexander White,"The Scotch-Irish University of the South: Washington And Lee," The Scotch-Irish In America: Proceedings and Addresses of the Second Congress*, **May 29 to June 1, 1890, published by order of the Scotch-Irish Society of America, Cincinnati, Ohio, Robert Clark & Co, 1890, p. 228.**

seminary that evolved into Washington and Lee University. Of course, he cites no credible evidence to support this ridiculous notion because in truth, no such evidence exists. Every known documentary record from the eighteenth century makes it abundantly clear that no such link ever existed between the university in its first forms (i.e., "Augusta Academy" and Liberty Hall Academy) and any other school west of the Blue Ridge Mountains. All representations to the contrary, with one unimportant exception,[621] originate with authors writing seventy-five years after the school was created and none citing any credible evidence to support such a notion.

A few paragraphs later, Mr. White says,

> "One week later, May 13, 1776, the Trustees, at their first meeting, left this record: "Pursuant to an order of the presbytery of Hanover, relative to the Academy of Liberty Hall Academy as it hereafter to be called, instead of Augusta Academy, . . . *the following members of the Trustees met.*"

> "So does this old record speak *regarding the act of adoption*, whereby the presbytery, younger by six years than the school, assumed control of the latter."

Perhaps Mr. White may have been a bit more careful as to the details of this adoption had the adoptee in question been his own.

If Mr. White had included the members' names that he just referred to, his readers would learn that here at this very first meeting of the board of trustees, one name is noticeably absent, which is Rev. John Brown. Just as that name continues to be absent ad infinitum thereafter. He might have asked why. The answer, if he had bothered to ask, would have been, in effect, "because Mr. Brown, was no friend of the Presbytery's new seminary and reacted with disdain and disinterest in response to all attempts by the Presbytery to involve him in the affairs of the seminary." Rev. Brown accepted no appointments in connection with the academy; he attended no trustee meetings; he refused to send any of his children to the academy; he made no reports to the presbytery concerning the affairs of the academy; and he never accepted the responsibility to serve as an "inspector" in connection with the academy.

In sum, there was no adoption of Mr. Brown's school by the Hanover Presbytery. Had Mr. White had the opportunity to read Rev. Philip Vickers Fithian's journal entries for 1775 and 1776, made while he was lodging at Rev. Brown's home in the Valley, which he did not, he would have found rather illuminating a few of Rev. Fithian's eyewitness comments:

---

621 See appendix on the erroneous letter of Rev. Samuel Houston. A dubious document, but still riddled with errors. It is not credible evidence of anything pertaining to Washington and Lee University.

Dec. 12 1775

Tuesday, 12ᵗʰ (December)I rode on further twenty miles to Mr. Brown's—Extreme cold—Young Mr. Trumble was along. We came to Mr. Browns just when the sun was going down. Mr. Hunter was there before me; On Sunday he preached below Stanton. We were glad to meet. **Here we met Mr. Doak who is now over the Latin School in this neighborhood.**[Footnote no. 18] (Fithian's Journal, p. 1775–1776, 140)

Jan. 1776

Mr. Graham, lately initiated a brother, is appointed Director of a school in the neighborhood of Mr. Brown's—*He thinks to enlarge his Method of Education so much as to finish Youth in their classical, Philosophical Studies.* (Fithian's Journal, 1775–1776, p. 150)

Approximately two weeks later, and close to Christmas, Fithian returns to the previous vicinity. While residing briefly at Rev. Brown's home, he says,

Jan. 18, 1776

Mr. Graham is here—*Sage, deep-studied, Mr. Graham.* **He is Director of the small Academy in this neighborhood.** *He retains, with Dignity, the inherent Gravity which he always supported in every Part of his Conduct while he was a Student at Nassau [Princeton]. The Lines of Method & Discipline have been inscribed & are yet visible & legible upon his countenance!* (Jan. 18, 1776, Fithian's Journal 1775–1776, p. 171)

Jan. 18, 1776

Thursday, **at his school,**[622] *he gave us a sermon. He spoke with Propriety; he preached, I believe, orthodox Divinity; & he seemed zealous.—I was entertained, I hope a little improved.* (Fithian's Journal)

---

622 *Here, Mr. Fithian's phrasing seems eminently important as regards the controversy of the alleged connection of Brown's school to the presbytery's "Augusta Academy." If as asserted in* Foote's Sketches of Virginia, *Series One,* Graham was "under the direction of John Brown" [get quote exactly] why would Fithian refer to the school as being Graham's school, especially when Fithian makes it clear that Reverend Brown was in attendance for this prayer group session? Fithian obviously knew that the school was Graham's school and not Brown's school. Earlier that same year, the Hanover Presbytery were at Brown's home and went from there to visit "Brown's school." So there were two schools at two locations, under two different auspices, each distinctively different in character. This comes from the best witness testimony which was written down at the time the event occurred.

Here is Rev. Fithian, who had been lodging with the Rev. Brown family, referring to Rev Graham as the "director" of the academy. So Rev. Fithian interacted with Rev. John Brown, his host on several occasions, and Rev. William Graham with whom he spent Christmas Eve in Dec. of 1775, referring to Rev. Graham as the "director" of the academy. Now, to punctuate Fithian's meaning, reconsider this statement given above by Fithian, but with yet a different emphasis:

> Mr. Graham, lately initiated a brother, is appointed Director of a school *in the neighborhood of Mr. Brown's*. (Fithian's Journal)

Not only has Rev. Fithian informed us that Mr. Graham is the obvious leader of the presbytery's seminary (academy), but he also makes clear that the academy is distinguishable from the school of Rev. Brown and further that both schools are located in what Fithian considered as the same neighborhood. Two schools with separate locations under two different leaders, but within a few miles of one another.

Unfortunately, for the true history of Washington and Lee University's early history, Philip Vickers Fithian's Journal wasn't published until 1934, so Mr. White did not have the benefit of this highly persuasive eyewitness testimony written down at the time that the events occurred.

ERROR no. 2: ["The Scotch-Irish University of the South: Washington and Lee"[623]] White opens his interesting article with a serious mistake. In his opening paragraph, he mistakenly claims the following:

> *In 1749 . . . —in that year was laid the foundation-stone of Washington and Lee University.* Beneath the shadows of the Blue Ridge, in the Valley of Virginia, Scotch-Irish brawn upreared a rude cabin of oaken logs, and with fervent prayer did set apart this temple of the wilderness as the school for the training of Scotch-Irish prophets. *Over the little "mathematical and classical school" was called the name Augusta Academy. Her founder and ruling spirit was from the North of Ireland, and bore that typical Scotch name, Alexander [Robt. Alexander].* (White, "The Scotch-Irish University of the South: Washington and Lee, pp. 236–237; emphasis in bold italics and underlining here represents error.)

This moving opening of Mr. White's article is nevertheless error-ridden. The "foundation-stone," as it were, was not laid in 1749 but rather in 1774, for White confuses Robert Alexander's school with the Hanover Presbytery's seminary of learning created out of whole cloth in October of 1774. Alexander's private educational endeavors had no connection to any other school, and no person

---

623 Rev. Henry Alexander White,"The Scotch-Irish University of the South: Washington And Lee" published in: *The Scotch-Irish In America: Proceedings and Addresses of the Second Congress*, May 29 to June 1, 1890, Published by order of The Scotch-Irish Society of America, Cincinnati, Ohio, Robert Clark & Co, 1890, pp. 223–246.

claiming otherwise bothered to reference any evidence upon which they had made such a termination. All and each of these claims were offered gratuitously and by authors who had no firsthand knowledge of the events they describe.

Moreover, Alexander's school, which may or may not have been a "mathematical and classical school," was not named at all, let alone named "Augusta Academy." Indeed, the name Augusta Academy does not appear in the literature or records of Virginia until in 1775, the presbytery adopted as an unofficial convention that label for use in its meeting minutes, which was thereafter used in that way during the academy's incipiency at the place called locally Mount Pleasant. When the Augusta Academy was installed in its "permanent" campus buildings at Timber Ridge (January 1777), the limited use of that denomination was terminated, and thereafter it embraced its first official name, Liberty Hall Academy.[624]

ERROR no. 3: White errs by linking Rev. John Brown to the Hanover Presbytery's new seminary of learning, which they unofficially referred to as Augusta Academy.

White explains,

> "The energy of Rev. John Craig had appeared that solid sanctuary after a pastoral work of eight years. In 1740, he had entered the Valley, "the first pastor of the American Synod in the Colony of Virginia." Then came Rev. John Brown, in 1753, to shepherd the flock at New Providence *and to exercise supervision over Augusta Academy.* (White, "The Scotch-Irish University of the South: Washington and Lee," p. 236–237; emphasis in bold italics here represents error.)

The major mistake here is that Rev. John Brown never exercised "supervision" over the Augusta Academy. In fact, he had nothing whatsoever to do with the Augusta Academy or for that matter any academy.

ERROR no. 4: "The Presidents of the Washington College in Virginia."[625] White asserts an incorrect date of origin for the institution.

Mr. White says this:

> "Before receiving the title of college, *this school of the prophets had lived for many years as an academy during the period of four and sixty years, from 1749, to 1813.* (Henry A. White, "The Presidents of," p. 100; the bold italics here represent error.)

The school, however, did not exist prior to October 13, 1774.

---

624   These facts are all embedded in clear language in the meeting minutes of the Hanover Presbytery between 1771 and 1777.

625   Henry Alexander White, "The Presidents of The Washington College in Virginia" in, _The Scotch-Irish In America, Proceedings And Addresses, Seventh Congress,_ 1895, pps 100-122.

ERROR no. 3: Mr. White errs in linking the founding of the Hanover Presbytery's first patronized seminary in Virginia to a private school conducted by Robert Alexander.

> ***Augusta Academy was the title applied to the log school of the colonial era by the founder, Robert Alexander, in 1749.***
> (Henry A. White, "The Presidents of," p. 100; bold italics here represent error.)

There is no eighteenth-century evidence to suggest, or prove, that the private primary school of Robert Alexander ever had a name of any sort, let alone the lofty title of "academy." In the literature of the time of Mr. Robert Alexander, there is not one reference anywhere to Robert Alexander's school by any name whatsoever.

ERROR no. 4: White repeats his error immediately above in these words:

> ***Around this rude frontier academy in 1755, was made fast one end of the ecclesiastical chain, known as the Hanover Presbytery***, which was afterwards on the eastern side of the Blue Ridge made fast to the Prince Edward Academy. (Henry A. White, "The Presidents of," p. 101; bold italics here represent error)

First, as is already established, Alexander's school was neither an "academy," nor was it in any fashion linked to the Hanover Presbytery or the academy created by the presbytery in Augusta County, Virginia, on October 13, 1774. Mr. White's "ecclesiastical chain," if one can be said to exist, linked the presbytery's two newly established academies in Augusta County and Prince Edward County, respectively, that were only created a few months apart: Augusta in October of 1774 and Prince Edward, in February of 1775. A link illustrated in the 1770s meeting minutes of the Hanover Presbytery.

ERROR no. 5: Mr. White honors the wrong entity by asserting that the name of Liberty Hall Academy was bestowed upon the college by Hanover Presbytery.

Here is what Mr. White says on page 101:

> ***It was the Hanover Presbytery that named the Liberty Hall Academy*** and furnished it with teachers, students, and financial and moral support. (Henry A. White, The Presidents of," pp. 101–102; the ***bold italics*** emphasis is added here to indicate an error.)

Mr. White is mistaken in this regard. The Hanover Presbytery did not name either one of their two academies in Virginia, at least not officially. Instead, they held that honor in abeyance until such time as they deemed it appropriate to appoint for each academy a board of trustees upon which they intended to convey the authority to oversee each academy's routine affairs as carried out and directed by their respective rectors or presidents. The board of trustees for the academy in Augusta County, west of the Blue Ridge Mountains, was created by the Hanover Presbytery on May 6, 1776. The new board of trustees of that school referred to unofficially by the presbytery as "Augusta Academy" the school its first official name, "Liberty Hall Academy." This was the first official act of the newly established board of trustees at their very first meeting on May 13, 1776. This first act was duly recorded in the official record book of the board of trustees on page 13, which follows the brief historical sketch of the founding of the academy written by the Hanover Presbytery's clerk, Rev. Caleb Wallace, which is dated "May 1776."

This brief historical sketch by Rev. Wallace constitutes Washington and Lee University's first authorized and official historical accounting of its origins. The credibility of the author of this sketch is beyond question for he is a widely recognized cleric of the very highest reputation for both scholarship and veracity. A graduate of Princeton under the venerable Dr. John Witherspoon, Rev. Wallace rose to become the chief judge of the supreme appellate court of Kentucky. The events which he describes in his account took place at the same meeting where he was first ordained as a Presbyterian minister, and as a result, he is highly unlikely to have been mistaken about the date on which the Augusta Academy was created. Moreover, that specific and historic meeting took place at the Cub Creek Church, which had that very day received Rev. Wallace as their new pastor. This then is the author of the first authorized history of Washington and Lee University. Mr. Wallace, it is fair to point out, is the only man in the eighteenth century to serve as a trustee on the boards of trustees of both Liberty Hall Academy and her younger sister academy, Hampden-Sydney Academy in Prince Edward County, east of the Blue Ridge Mountains.

It is fair to add that the perpetrator of the hoax extending Washington and Lee's birth date by twenty-five years, William Henry Foote (*Sketches of Virginia, Historical and Biographical*, Series One and Two, 1850 & 1855) reprinted extensive extracts from the minutes of the Hanover Presbytery, but failed to provide extracts from the Liberty Hall Academy's board of trustees' meetings that began in May of 1776. By excluding these important meeting minutes, he cleverly also avoided having to mention the existence of Rev. Wallace's premier historical account that appears immediately before the meeting minutes for the board of trustees' first meeting held on May 13, 1776.

Note: Foote also failed to note that the Hanover Presbytery's meeting minutes extracts that he reprinted contradict his own account. For a more detailed account of Foote's misdeeds in regard to the early history of Washington College, see the subsection above that deals exclusively with his errors.

ERROR no. 6: Mr. White is in error by linking the schools of Robert Alexander and Rev. John Brown.

> Mr. White inappropriately refers to "pupils" of Robert Alexander and "*his successor, Rev. John Brown*." (Henry

A. White, "The Presidents of..."; bold italics here represent a gratuitous assertion lacking any supporting evidence and which is therefore presumptively wrong.)

This error appears on page 101 of Mr. White's article and is found in the paragraph referring to the presbytery's actions to create or "establish" their two presbytery-patronized seminaries in Virginia because the presbytery's actions in this regard had nothing whatever to do with the private schools of Robert Alexander in the 1760s or the "Latin school" organized by Rev. John Brown first at Mount Pleasant, near Fairfield, Virginia, in the mid to late 1760s and then later in the 1770s at New Providence. Facts made abundantly clear by both the official records of the presbytery and the presbytery's academy, and also by the eyewitness-recorded testimony of Rev. Philip Vickers Fithian, whose recorded testimony was unfortunately not published until 1934.[626] Rev. Fithian, in 1775 and 1776, discriminates between the "Latin school" of Rev. John Brown at New Providence from the academy (seminary) under the direction of Rev. William Graham at Mount Pleasant in fairly clear language for those who elect to read his journal with some care.

ERROR no. 7: Mr. White inappropriately and misleadingly designates Dr. George A. Baxter as the first president of Washington College.

Note: Perhaps Mr. White on this occasion elected to differentiate between president and rector, in which case, he would be technically accurate, but his distinction would also be one of no meaningful difference. Both titles are operationally the same for they merely identify the chief administrative officer of the college. Mr. Baxter's role was identical to the role exercised by his predecessor and preceptor, Rev. William Graham. During Graham's tenure, the institution operated under the names Augusta Academy and then shortly thereafter as Liberty Hall Academy. After Graham's letter to President Washington requesting the president's endowment, written on behalf of the trustees, successfully persuaded the president to grant this endowment to Liberty Hall, the trustees, in gratitude for the president's largess, determined to change the school's name in honor of the president.

Here is White's misleading statement:

> In the curve of the well-closed lips terminate the lines of strength that furnish a frame for the countenance which beams upon us from the old portrait of Dr. George A. Baxter, ***first President of Washington College***. (Henry A. White, "The Presidents of . . ."; bold italics here represent a gratuitous assertion lacking any supporting evidence and which is therefore presumptively wrong.)

When Mr. Baxter received his appointment to be the chief administrative officer of the college, the institution had not experienced any important structural changes other than the name change from Liberty Hall Academy to Washington

---

626 Fithian, Philip Vickers, The Journal & Letters of Philip Vickers Fithian, "Written on the Virginia-Pennsylvania Frontier and in the Army Around New York, [1775-1776]", Princeton, Princeton University Press, 1934.

Academy since the departure of the institution's _president_, William Graham. The college's organizational framework had not changed in any way that would justify assigning to the institution's second rector the honor of being hailed as "the first president." The first administrative leader was Rev. William Graham, and it was under his leadership that the college received its charter from the new Virginia legislature in 1782, which charter bestowed upon the institution all the powers of a college including degree-granting authority.

Errors of Professor Henry Alexander White Contained in His Book, _Southern Presbyterian Leaders_[627]

ERROR no. 8: Mistakenly attributes the presbytery's "visit" to Rev. Brown's Latin school in April of 1775, with the presbytery's seminary under Rev. Graham. White says,

> *At the close of Graham's first year as a teacher in the academy,* that is, *in the spring of 1775,* as we have just seen, *the presbytery held one of its daily sessions in the school house and there listened to recitations, by Graham's students in the Latin and Greek languages.* (White, _Southern Presbyterian Leaders,_ p. 127)

Mr. White, like many of those who erred before him, is seriously confused and misconstrues these meeting minutes. This "visit" occurred at New Providence, and the school referenced is Rev. Brown's "Latin school," which was located at New Providence. Graham's academy was then in its incipiency at "Mount Pleasant," several miles from New Providence. Moreover, the presbytery's session for the day was not held in the schoolhouse, but rather at Rev. Brown's home. The "visit" took place after the presbytery had concluded all their business. The presbytery, of course, took no subsequent action in regard to Rev. Brown's private school. This was clearly nothing more than a courtesy call by the presbytery who had been lodging at and meeting at Rev. Brown's home.[628] The presbytery's spring meeting was held at Timber Ridge Meeting House on the first day, however, and those who failed to read the minutes carefully failed to note that the meeting place had changed after the first day's meeting had concluded.

The presbytery's new seminary was located nearby the Timber Ridge Meeting House. Some apparently assumed, however incorrectly, that the school referenced was the presbytery's school under William Graham, but of course, they were actually referring to Brown's private Latin school, which was next door. A careful reading of the minutes makes this quite clear. Still, many became confused and

---

627   Rev. Henry Alexander White, **Southern Presbyterian Leaders**, New York, Neale Publishing Company, 1911.

628   Confusingly, the Presbytery had held its first day's meeting at Timber Ridge Meeting House. After that session ended, the members traveled to New Providence where, in Rev. Brown's capacious home, at least some of the members lodged and where the subsequent day's meetings were held. Brown's Latin School was conducted in quarters adjacent to his home.

assumed that the minutes referred to the presbytery's public seminary and thereafter mistakenly treated these two schools as though they were one and the same.

Brown obviously wanted to showcase his private Latin school for his colleagues. Many authors have made this same mistake, and it is likely due to the fact that the presbytery met at Timber Ridge, near Mount Pleasant, on the first day of this several days' session, but which then moved several miles' distant to Rev. Brown's home at New Providence. One important reason why it was important for Rev. Brown to showcase his school's students is that Rev. Brown opposed the presbytery's actions to create the new seminary, as is made quite clear by this extract from one of Rev. Brown's letters, written during this time to his brother-in-law, Col. William Preston, shown below.

Dr. John White Stuart provides the following extract wherein he quotes from one of Brown's letters: "Brown wrote respectfully of his Alma Mater in 1775 (Stuart Diss..., pp. 45–46)."

> ### *A private school and The College of New Jersey will pollish a young man & fit him for usefulness better than any semenary we can expect in Virginia.* (John Brown letter to Wm. Preston, Aug. 24. 1775, Draper Collection no. 4QQ31, n60; emphasis added)

The author of the above statement, Rev. John Brown, operated at the New Providence Church, the type of "private school" to which his letter refers and which he consistently labeled a "Latin school." This letter also refers to the "semenery" conducted by William Graham at, "Mount Pleasant," a few miles distant from his Latin school.

It is also important to correct Mr. White concerning his opening comment. Mr. Graham's appointment to lead the presbytery's educational endeavor to establish a seminary in Virginia that would obviate the need for Virginia's youth to have to travel to New Jersey in order to obtain a college education was made at a meeting of the Hanover Presbytery at Cub Creek on October 13, 1774. Therefore, Mr. White cannot be correct that the following spring would constitute the "close of Graham's first year as a teacher in the Academy." Mr. Graham was living with his family in Pennsylvania (Harrisburg) at the time of his appointment. Unless, of course, Mr. Graham had an iron-clad agreement with the presbytery that is otherwise unknown to history; he was unlikely to uproot himself and travel to the mountains of Virginia based on the supposition that the presbytery might hire him. If Mr. Graham came to Virginia after the presbytery made their decision in October of 1774, then he probably did not arrive in Virginia until after the first of the year 1775. The precise date of his arrival has not been ascertained.

Some form of communication between Mr. Graham and the Hanover Presbytery had to have transpired informing Graham of the presbytery's decision because it is hardly reasonable to think that Mr. Graham would have traveled from Pennsylvania to Virginia without having reached an understanding that he was being hired to launch this important new enterprise that encapsulated his rather clear life objective to teach and to preach.

These preliminaries would undoubtedly have been followed by Mr. Graham preparing a permanent move from the home of his birth and leaving behind his entire family, as well as making plans for locating a place to reside once he arrived in the Valley. There is nothing in the extant literature to suggest Mr. Graham arrived in Virginia before the onset of 1775. He could not then have possibly concluded his first year as director of the academy (i.e., seminary) in the spring of 1775 as Professor White suggests. The presbytery's spring meeting of 1775 included a last-minute effort by Rev. Brown and his few allies to dissuade the presbytery from completing the launch of its new seminary at Mount Pleasant near Fairfield, Virginia.[629]

After the first day of the presbytery's spring meeting (1775), the presbytery moved the location of the meeting from Timber Ridge to Brown's capacious home at New Providence on Moffett's Creek. Here, Rev. Brown could provide lodging for the traveling members. The host would later invite his guests to sit in on a class at his private Latin school, which was conducted at the same general location. The polite members agreed to "visit" Rev. Brown's school following their last day's meeting. By giving the members a firsthand view, he obviously hoped they would see that there was no real need to continue their new educational program. Rev. Brown's school was, at this time, conducted by Mr. Samuel Doak, a recent graduate of Princeton.[630] The gambit, if that is what it was, failed, and the presbytery paid their courtesy visit to Rev. Brown's Latin school in deference to their host and eldest member. But by that time, the die was cast, and the presbytery had gone so far as to create two new seminaries (i.e., academies): the first at Mount Pleasant under William Graham, west of the Blue Ridge Mountains (1774), and the second under Samuel Stanhope Smith east of the mountains (1775).

Rev. Brown, as already mentioned, opposed the creation of even one such endeavor. This courtesy visit by the presbytery to Rev. Brown's Latin school at New Providence is the only mention of Rev. Brown's Latin school in the minutes of the Hanover Presbytery in the eighteenth century. Rev. Brown's last-ditch gambit failed to dissuade his colleagues, and the initiative to provide College educational opportunities in Virginia under the patronage of the Presbyterian Church continued. Given the confusion that has emerged over the course of time from this one inappropriate visit to a private school, it seems in retrospect that it would have been far better if the presbytery had declined Rev. Brown's invitation to visit his school after they concluded their spring meeting of 1775. If they had,

---

629 The launching of the seminary (Academy) necessitated careful planning because, the Presbytery's new Director, (Mr. Graham) would have to licensed and ordained as a pastor of a congregation in order to provide him with an income. The Presbyterian Timber Ridge pastorate was then vacant but Mr. Graham would first have had to be found acceptable to the congregation. It all went off without a hitch and in short order. Mr. Graham was licensed and ordained as pastor of Timber Ridge and Hall's Meeting House Congregations by the time of the Presbytery's October meeting in 1775.

630 Doak's teaching at the Latin school is referenced by Rev. Philp Vicker Fithian in his 1775 Journal.

perhaps the myth of Rev. Brown's school being linked to the new academy, which evolved into Washington and Lee University, might never have emerged.

ERROR no. 9: Professor White unfortunately repeats from Henry Ruffner's "Early History of Washington College" Ruffner's quotation from Archibald Alexander's unpublished memoir of William Graham,[631] Archibald Alexander's unfortunate comment concerning Rev. William Graham's preaching.

Here are Professor White's words concerning the preaching of Rev. William Graham:

> ".. *Rather feeble and embarrassed* (Henry A. White, <u>Southern Presbyterian Leaders</u>, p. 135. White here is following one comment by Archibald Alexander.)

This assessment was time-specific and, like with most preachers in their earliest days, are not a fair reflection of their preaching over the length of their careers. We have added several other comments from a cross-section of those who had occasion to hear Mr. Graham's preaching, most of whom were Presbyterian preachers.

We begin by quoting the same man who had said about Mr. Graham's early preaching that it was "rather feeble and embarrassed."

> "The writer [Archibald Alexander] *is now of opinion*, that *he never heard from any man a clearer and stronger exhibition of the gospel than in the sermons of Mr. Graham during this period* [i.e., the 1780s]. (James W. Alexander, *The Life of A. Alexander*, p. 90)

Apparently, Rev. Graham had improved with experience. At about that same time, the same Rev. Alexander, now president of Princeton Theological Seminary, shares these thoughts:

> *Mr. Graham preached in the house crowded to excess*—*and yet many could not get in.* His text was "Comfort ye Comfort ye my people. He began calmly but seriously; and as he preached on his discourse, *his feeling as was usual with him, rose gradually until an awful solemnity was spread over the large congregation. . . . The writer does[n't] remember ever before or since, to have seen a whole congregation more fully under an impression as tender as it was solemn; but reigned a breathless silence through the house, only interrupted occasionally by the sound [of] a suppressed sigh.* Perhaps Mr. Graham never exceeded the sermon preached on this occasion. *Dr. Smith said to the writer that take it altogether; it was the*

---

631 Alexander, Archibald D. D., Mss "Memoir of William Graham," [written in longhand]. My photocopy came from the Princeton Seminary Library in 1989.

best sermon he ever heard.[632] (A. Alexander Mss. "Memoir of William Graham." pp. 206–216)

Here are the words of Rev. Graham's first biographer, Edward Graham, Esq. Professor at Washington College:

It was soon perceived that he [Wm. Graham] ***was a preacher of no ordinary kind. The closeness and depth of his reasoning and the warmth of his applications, placed him in the estimation of those who heard him, in the first class of pulpit orators.***[633] (Edward Graham, "Memoir....," p. 254, 1821)[634]

Once again from Edward Graham's brother-in-law, Archibald Alexander:

As the travelers approached their destination, there was an interesting meeting between the two great preachers of Virginia.[635] (Referring to Rev. Wm. Graham and Rev. John B. Smith, this is a quote from Archibald, as presented by his son in his biography of his father.)

During the year I paid one visit to my friends in Lexington, ***and heard Mr. Graham preach a sermon on the text, "For our righteousness are as filthy rags."*** The utter insignificancy [*sic*] of our own works, and the need of a better righteousness than our own, were of course the subjects. ***It was the first intelligent discourse to which I had listened since my new understanding of the doctrines in question, and it gave me great satisfaction.*** (James W. Alexander, *The Life Archibald Alexander*, p. 52, referring, of course, to Archibald Alexander's words)

His preaching was always interesting and instructive, often impressive in the highest degree.[636] (Edward Graham, Memoir of,[637] p. 411, col. II, para 2)

Rev. William Hill, a well-known Presbyterian divine, scholar, and historian, who graduated from Hampden-Sydney Academy, informs as follows:

---

632 Smith was the president of Hamden Sydney college who had broad experience with Presbyterian preachers of that day.

633 Edward Graham, "A Memoir of The Late Rev. William Graham, A.M." *The Evangelical and Literary Magazine and Missionary Chronicle*, IV, (1821), p.75 et Seq.

634 Edward Graham,"A Memoir of The Late Rev. William Graham, A.M." *The Evangelical and Literary Magazine and Missionary Chronicle*, IV, (1821), p.75 et Seq..

635 Alexander, James W., *The life of Archibald Alexander, DD*, New York, Charles Scribner, 1854.

636 *Edward Graham, Op Cit*

637 Edward Graham, Op Cit

Mr. Graham, of Lexington, was present and preached on Saturday; and on Sabbath, *"Mr. Graham preached in the forenoon, one of the greatest sermons I ever heard. I sat under it with great delight, and its fruit was sweet to my taste."*[638] (Rev. William Hill, from his journal and published, in part, in W. H. Foote's *Sketches of Virginia*, Second Series, p. 1855)

And in connection with the above, this:

William Hill was the only one of four of the Hampden-Sydney students with whom the revival began who left a record of his activities. **He spent two or more years as a missionary under the direction of the synod's commission** (i.e., the Synod's Commission on Missions, chaired by Rev Graham), the details of which he recorded in a Journal.[639]

We have here above the testimony of several credible sources, including Edward Graham, Rev. Graham's first biographer; Rev. Archibald Alexander's, given on several different occasions; Rev. John Blair Smith, Graham's colleague, classmate at Princeton and president of Hampden-Sydney Academy in Prince Edward County; and Rev. William Hill. Given the testimony of these accomplished gentlemen, it is, we believe, fair to say that it was indeed unfortunate that Dr. Henry Ruffner selected the only negative reference we have seen concerning the preaching of Rev. William Graham, which was clearly made in reference to Mr. Graham's earliest sermons as a young and recently licensed minister. It is unfortunate because several authors have reprinted or referenced this one lone critical comment, and as best as we can determine, that is the only comment on Graham's preaching to have been published over the last one hundred and fifty years, this despite the numerous glowing comments that are known to exist. Quite clearly, Rev. William Graham developed into one of the finest pulpit orators of his lifetime. Perhaps this was one of the reasons he was selected by the Presbyterian Church to be the founding president and chief operating officer of the Presbyterian Church's first patronized theological seminary in America, which was created by the Virginia Synod and located just outside the town of Lexington, Virginia. It was conducted by Graham in conjunction with Liberty Hall Academy.[640]

Note: The close relationship of the new Presbyterian Theological Seminary in Lexington with Liberty Hall Academy was not well received by some influential citizens in and around Lexington who were adherents of the Episcopal

---

638   Rev. William, Hill, <u>Autobiographical sketches of Dr. William Hill: together with his account of the revival of religion in Prince Edward County, and biographical sketches of the life and character of the Reverend Dr. Moses Hoge of Virginia</u>, Richmond, 1968

639   Howard McKnight Wilson, *The Lexington Presbytery Heritage*, McClure Press, 1971.

640   As noted elsewhere the Synod attempted to create two seminaries at this time, but the one envisioned to be conducted by Rerv. John McMillan in western Pennsylvania did not come to fruition for several years.

*Church, and this fact was probably why the connection was later severed after the resignation of Rev. William Graham. This ongoing tension between the Presbyterians and the Episcopalians may very well account, in part, with the otherwise seemingly inexplicable actions of the college to change the college's official history following the Civil War when the chairman of the board of trustees, Judge John Brockenbaugh (an Episcopalian), was sent to offer the presidency of the college to Gen. Robert E. Lee (also an Episcopalian). The first known author of the college's revised history was another trustee, Col. Bolivar Christian (an Episcopalian). Colonel Christian's revised historical account did not include a notice that this account completely repudiated the college's official authorized history that had been in place from the school's founding until 1865. Moreover, Colonel Christian's new and revised history provided no citation of authority for having altered the institution's long-standing and documentary history. The first historian to note this discrepancy in the college's history was the preeminent historian of the college, Dr. Ollinger Crenshaw, whose full-length typescript history, <u>General Lee's College</u>,[641] contained extensive footnotes and a vastly important appendix entitled, "**<u>The Problem of the Origins</u>**." Unfortunately, the published version put out by Random House contained neither Dr. Crenshaw's footnotes, nor the important appendix A. The auditor found no evidence during the audit that suggest there was any attempt to deliberately falsify the institution's history. The motivations that led to this historical travesty may very well have been wishful thinking by parties desperately seeking to obtain General Lee's acceptance of the college's presidency. It is doubtful that General Lee and the board of trustees had any idea that they were representing a false history because the college's official records were in such terrible disarray after the war, and restoring them was an ongoing process that took years to accomplish.*

ERROR no. 9: Mr. White incorrectly states that Theological Seminary in Lexington, Virginia, was discontinued when Rev. Graham resigned his position as rector of Liberty Hall Academy. (See p. 137 of Henry Alexander White's *Southern Presbyterian Leaders*.)

This is inaccurate, according to Rev. Conrad Speece's biographer, Rev. William Brown, who says Speece continued his theological studies under Mr. Graham in Lexington as late as 1797. This is consistent with Rev. Graham's attendance at several meetings of the Lexington Presbytery, up to and including a meeting shortly before Graham died in June of 1799. (See especially Foote series 2, 1855, chapter 29, p. 349, et seq.)

Mr. Foote, who was wrong about the founding of Washington and Lee University, nevertheless provides very valuable information on the subject of the Lexington Theological Seminary's continuing existence after William Graham's resignation as rector of Liberty Hall Academy. His section on Rev. Conrad Speece, which is based upon numerous memoranda left by Rev. Speece,

---

641   *Ollinger Crenshaw, General Lee's College, typescript, unpublished version in two volumes with Appendix A, "The Problem of The Origins," (pg. 524 of entire typescript but Appendix A is also paginated separately as pages, 1-13.)*

provides important clarity on several important historical topics including William Graham's connection to the seminary after his resignation as president of Liberty Hall Academy. Mr. Foote provides in this chapter numerous extracts from Rev. Speece's memoranda, including the following:

> I went to Liberty Hall in May, 1795. New studies in which I engaged eagerly.... I heard the preaching of William Graham, our rector, with intellectual pleasure. . . . Towards the end of summer, I gradually became again anxious about my eternal interests; I felt myself a sinner, and set out more earnestly than ever to seek salvation. I was soon driven to the brink of infidelity, by some of the more mysterious doctrines of Scripture. Jenyn's Internal Evidences and Beattie's Evidences, providentially put into my hands by our rector (Rev. Graham) fully convinced me of the truth of Christianity.

> In April, 1796, I was received into communion in the Presbyterian Church of New Monmouth. (Rev. Graham's Church)

> October 20, together with George Baxter, he received the degree of AB at the Hall; on the same day the Rector, William Graham's resignation was received by the Trustees.... In the same month, I was received by the Lexington Presbytery as a candidate for the ministry. . . . **The ensuing Winter (1797) I studied Theology under the instruction of our Rector.**[642] (Wm. H. Foote, *Sketches of Virginia: Historical and Biographical*, Series 2, pp. 351–352; emphasis added)

> (Note: "Our Rector," of course, refers to Rev. William Graham for Mr. Speece had no other rector.)

These quotes taken from memoranda left by Rev. Conrad Speece are of great importance for he states categorically that he studied under his rector (William Graham) in the winter of 1777, which was well after Rev. Graham had resigned his presidency of Liberty Hall Academy. So while Mr. Graham resigned his post as president of the college and his pastorate of New Monmouth and the Lexington Presbyterian Church, he remained active with the Lexington Presbytery as demonstrated by their meeting minutes from the time of his resignation in the fall of 1796 until just a few weeks before he died in 1799. He also remained in

---

642 Rev. Graham was the rector of both Liberty Hall Academy and the Lexington Theological Seminary in 1796 but Rev. Graham tendered his resignation as rector of Liberty Hall Academy in the fall of 1796. Mr. Speece's memorandum here is referring to the Presbytery's patronized Seminary and not Liberty Hall Academy. After Rev. Graham's resignation as rector of Liberty Hall, he continued to oversee his responsibilities as the administrative head of the theological training as related by Mr. Speece in this memorandum. Rev. Graham, of course, remained an active member of the Lexington Presbytery as can be seen in the minutes of the Lexington Presbytery even in the weeks immediately before his death in 1799.

charge of his Lexington Theological Seminary, which was created and patronized by the Virginia Synod of which Rev. Graham remained a member.

> In April, 1796, he [Conrad Speece, DD] was admitted to the communion of the Presbyterian Church at New Monmouth, and in September following, was received a candidate under the care of the Presbytery of Lexington. His teacher in Theology was Mr. Graham.

Note: If the author, Rev. William Brown, is correct, this shows that Graham was still operating his theological seminary AFTER he had submitted his resignation to the board of trustees at Liberty Hall/Washington College. It follows then that Chavis's training was also continued under Graham insofar as his application for being examined for licensure followed closely the unexpected early death of Graham in 1799, Graham's interests in developing his property in Western Virginia at that time notwithstanding.

(Sprague's *Annals of the American Pulpit*, vol. IV [Presbyterians], p. 285, submitted by Rev. William Brown, Augusta County, VA, 1856)

Professor White's book is of great importance. It is regrettable, however, that he erred as he did in regards to the origins of Washington and Lee University and as regards Rev. William Graham's preaching.

To sum up on Professor White, he has painted two pictures of Rev. William Graham: one a well-documented and accurate depiction and one that inaccurately portrays Rev. Graham's talents as a preacher and unfortunately repeats out of context Rev. Graham's view of the value of books and reading, which was only applicable to the study of theology. In addition, he foolishly adopted Mr. Wm. H. Foote's erroneous views on the date of origin of the college.

24. OLLINGER CRENSHAW (1968)

(Ollinger Crenshaw, *General Lee's College*, New York, Random House, 1969; Crenshaw, *General Lee's College*, typescript unpublished early version in two volumes at Washington and Lee University Library, with footnotes. Appendix A, "The Problem of The Origins," (p. 524 of entire typescript, but appendix A is also paginated separately as pages 1–13)

Introduction

Dr. Crenshaw's work is truly remarkable and currently still stands as the most thoroughly researched comprehensive and definitive history of the university. Anyone interested in the subject of Washington and Lee University will be forever in his debt for the exhaustive research he has preserved in the published and unpublished versions of this history. His history, however, must be read with one vastly important caveat, which is that his account of the origins of the university is demonstrably and patently incorrect in every important way.*

Especially valuable to students of the early history of the university during its formative years is his appendix A to volume 2 of the typescript version of

General Lee's College. What is not useful, valuable, or accurate is Dr. Crenshaw's treatment of the origins of Washington and Lee in chapter 1 of either the Random House edition or in his typescript original version of *General Lee's College*.

One particularly striking aspect of Crenshaw's footnoted manuscript version of chapter one is that all the published sources that he relied upon were published after Foote's two volumes of *Sketches of Virginia: Historical and Biographical*, 1850 & 1855 respectively. By selectively eliminating from his own account all the early published histories (1821–1849) and all the documentary records of the Hanover Presbytery and the Liberty Hall Academy Board of Trustees' records compiled during the 1770s, he was destined to repeat the errors of Foote and his multitude of misguided adherents. Since the decision to do this is contrary to reason and established enlightenment logic, the mostly reasonable explanation for his inexplicable decision is political provincialism. He obviously chose to leave resolution of the conflicting historical accounts to posterity.[643]

* Caveat: The entire first chapter of the Random House published version of General Lee's College *is preposterously without merit. The chapter is entitled "The Origins," but the contents of the chapter often have no basis in fact or in evidence. Crenshaw's cursory treatment of the origins of the college is palpable poppycock and is riddled with demonstrably false assumptions. Similarly, Crenshaw's typescript version of chapter one is a major disappointment and woefully wrong. Crenshaw undoubtedly wrote his typescript version of chapter 1 while he was still researching his general history because what he wrote in his appendix A, "The Problem of the Origins," reveals that in time, Crenshaw came to comprehend that the version of the institution's founding that he had adopted in his text was not based on accepted standards of historical research, but he was obviously unwilling to begin again at the end of his lengthy historical research project. His important appendix hints at his dilemma thus:*

> **"It is evident even from cursory investigation that the institution [W&L]** *had adhered to one version of its history [prior to 1865], and to another in the post-bellum era.* (Note: This footnote makes clear that the Crenshaw footnotes [typescript version, vol. 1, p. 37, n60] did not limit his investigation on this question to a cursory review but rather that he "investigated such educational directories, journals devoted to education, almanacs, etc., of the first half of the nineteenth century as could be located in the Library of Congress.") (See Crenshaw's unpublished footnotes maintained as a typescript in two volumes at the Washington & Lee University Archives,

---

643 To be blunt, Crenshaw obviously had no desire to be the bearer of bitter news to his employers, colleagues, and the community that their adopted history of the college's founding is a fairytale. It is frankly, inconceivable that he did not at least suspect the truth given his unpublished Appendix A, "The Problem of the Origins."

n60, p. 37 of chapter 1; see also appendix A, "The Problem of the Origins.) (Emphasis added here does not indicate error.)

He knew full well that what he was describing was an indefensible conflict that necessitates, at some point, a resolution. Crenshaw further illuminates as follows:

> "*It was not until 1869 that the school which became Washington and Lee University officially asserted that it had its origins in the rude, bucolic school of Robert Alexander*; and it was not until then that the year 1749 was officially and categorically accepted as the year in which the "Alexander school", "the germ" of Washington and Lee, had its inception. (Crenshaw, unpublished typescript version, *General Lee's College*, chapter 1, p. 9 [actually pp. 16–17]; emphasis added.) (Emphasis in bold italics and underlined here represents error.[644])

The opening phrase is patently incorrect, as the college's first catalogue of officers and alumni published in 1865 states in clear terms:

> "<u>*The germ of Washington College was a classical school established about 1752 (?) by Robert Alexander*</u> at first near Greenville, Augusta county; and "<u>*was the first classical school in the Valley of Virginia." It was removed "shortly before the revolution" to Mount Pleasant*</u>; near Fairfield, Rockbridge county, where, <u>*October 12, 1774*</u>, it was formally adopted by Hanover Presbytery, <u>*with its original name of the Augusta Academy*</u>, and arrangements were made to support it, while it remained under the patronage of the Presbytery, by liberal contributions.[645] (That which is in <u>***bold italics and underlined***</u> is erroneous.)

---

644   The erroneous date that Crenshaw alludes to here (1869) obviously refers to Bolivar Christian's historical sketch included in the 1869 Catalogue of the Alumni, but Crenshaw ought to have referred to the similar sketch included in the 1865, <u>Charter and Laws</u> pamphlet published by the post-war administration, that also references Robert Alexander's school but dates its founding as 1752. So, five years later, the College decided to add a few more years to its history. A shocking and embarrassing exercise in literary and historical selective perception. for which the University owes an admission and an apology because there is no credible evidence to support the fairytale.

645   <u>Charter and Laws and Trustees and Alumni of Washington College at Lexington, Virginia, A. D. 1865</u>, Richmond, 1865, includes a sketch of the early history of the college under the strange title, *"Historical Statistics."* It is the first article in the book. While the pamphlet lists no author or editor, the copy reviewed by the auditor is housed in the Leyburn Library of Washington and Lee University, and it is bound in a volume which bears the following legend upon its spine,"Washington and Lee University, Catalogs, 1865- - 1879." The volume includes an 1855 catalogue and also catalogues for 1865-1879 in order, along with a few miscellaneous items. The auditor has accepted the authenticity of these various catalogues as having been produced at the behest of the University's administration.

There was no germ of Washington and Lee University as was claimed by the college in 1865. To be sure, the university had altered its name from time to time, but it began at its nativity on October 13, 1774, and has remained the same school since 1774. Its charter and incorporation in October of 1782 changed its legal status, but the school remained as it began as one operation. Contrary to so many varying accounts, the school's operation has been continuous and uninterrupted from 1774 until the present day. It has no connection to either Robert Alexander, Rev. John Brown, or any other school of any type. The school's incipient form as a grammar school was merely the creation of its foundation upon which the superstructure was erected at the college's campus at Timber Ridge. This methodology was based upon a plan formulated by William Graham shortly after his arrival to take charge of the prospective institution envisioned by the Hanover Presbytery that established the new seminary and appointed William Graham from Pennsylvania to manage all of its affairs. It was described by Dr. Samuel L. Campbell in his 1838 history of Washington College, Virginia.[646]

The academy's administrative leader from the school's inception in 1774 was William Graham, and so that circumstance remained until the trustees accepted Graham's resignation in late 1796. There are no records from the eighteenth century indicating that Robert Alexander's educational endeavors were assumed by Rev. John Brown or that the school was ever moved. This fact was also revealed by Professor McDaniel and his research team, which is discussed in detail in that subsection of the Author's Errors section of this report.[647]

Later, official school historians also have explicitly denominated this Alexander school "the Augusta Academy," but there is no justification for such claims. Alexander's meager educational efforts in the Valley of Virginia, whatever form they may have taken, were clearly not designed to serve the vast extensions of Augusta County that then stretched all the way west to the Ohio River and some contend to the Mississippi. Moreover, whatever Alexander's educational activities were, they cannot be considered to have constituted an academy as that term was used in the eighteenth century. Academies were schools of the highest sort, lacking only recognition from the British authorities for them to be denominated a college.[648]

---

646 Samuel L. Campbell, M.D.[i.e., "Senex"], "Washington College, Lexington, Virginia," Southern Literary Messenger, June 1838, beginning at pg. 364. [the auditor's original copy is a photocopy of the original] Thomas W. White was the editor of the publication at that time. Campbell's article was taken from a graduate paper written by Prof. G. Ray Thompson on Rev. William Graham submitted circa 1967.

647 John M. McDaniel, Charles N. Watson, David T Moore, Liberty Hall Academy, The Early History Of The Institutions Which Evolved Into Washington and Lee University, Lexington, Virginia, Liberty Hall Press, 1979. (Of course the sub-title is inappropriate insofar as there was no evolution of the institution except as to form, size, name, and location, and it had no connection whatsoever with any other school.

648 We don't mean to imply that all academies were functional equivalents of chartered college, but they provided some instruction at the college level. Students from Academies like Robert Smith's Academy in Pennsylvania, and Samuel Finley's Nottingham Academy in Maryland had prepared their students so well that when they transferred to the College of New Jersey were

It is astounding that Crenshaw's original manuscript version with corresponding footnotes reveals that with all of his citations of authority related to chapter one's treatment of the institution's origins, he fails to cite any official record of either the Hanover Presbytery or those of the Board of Trustees of Liberty Hall Academy. His "chapter 1" included in the Random House published version presents an essentially identical narrative as the grossly mistaken "chapter 1" of his typescript original version. Both are wrong for precisely the same reasons. Perhaps Crenshaw would not have been so seriously in error if he had relied on the published histories of Washington College written by scholars who actually attended the college in its early years, like Archibald Alexander and Edward Graham. Perhaps even more important is the institution's own histories written by Caleb Wallace, President William Graham, and the unnamed historian who penned for the board of trustees its first authorized published history of the college (1849).[649] Crenshaw does mention the history published by Samuel L. Campbell but conveniently omits the telling fact that the eyewitness Dr. Campbell makes no mention the schools of Robert Alexander or Rev. John Brown in his early history of Washington College. Campbell, an eighteenth-century trustee who was an eyewitness to the school's first incipient phase at Mount Pleasant, was so respected by his peers and fellow trustees that he was appointed as an interim president of the college after Graham's sudden and unexpected resignation.

Ollinger Crenshaw admits in his unpublished appendix A, "The Problem of the Origins," that he was aware of all these sources because he refers to them. What he does not explain is why he ignored them when writing his chapter 1 on the origins and asserts therein a history inconsistent with all the most knowledgeable authors who had written histories that are completely at odds with his own. It would seem that he owed his readers some kind of explanation. At the same time, history owes him a great debt for at least having written his appendix A wherein he admits that institution had adhered to two entirely different accounts of their origins. The university's early historical accounts all agree with its earliest records. The version adhered to after 1865 and adopted without explanation in General Lee's College is not a true account and is not supported by any competent historical evidence.

---

able to begin their matriculation at the Junior year level. No one prior to 1850 is known to have suggested that Robert Alexander's students had from him that degree of academic preparation. His school was not an Academy. The same is true concerning Brown's Latin school, and that is why Brown in his correspondence from the 1770s onward, always referred to his school as a "Latin school.," not an Academy. Those who made errors in this regard are all post-Foote historians who had no direct connection to either school.

649 Whoever actually wrote this first authorized and published history of the college, they certainly availed themselves of the manuscript history of Rev. Henry Ruffner, the immediate past President who was still an active instructor. His history had been written but the school refused to publish it as had originally been planned. It was later edited and slightly revised in 1857 but was not published until 1890. In the University's first volume of its Historical Papers. Unfortunately, Ruffner's history, by then had been foolishly revised. His original did not mistakenly even hint at a link between the college and Rev. Brown's school. Later, he was somewhat misled on this point by his son and other adherents of the mistaken Mr. Foote.

Crenshaw was careful, however, to admit the following:

> **"The continuity from Latin school to university cannot therefore be demonstrated by official record**. But it is evidenced in letters and other writings of the early nineteenth century by men who learned the story from older residents and who were familiar with local traditions.[650] Such traditions are often well preserved through oral transmission. (O. Crenshaw, *General Lee's College*, Random House, 1969, p. 4; emphasis added)

Note: Of course, there was no continuity from Latin school to university because the college (academy) had no link to any Latin school, and no credible eighteenth-century evidence is known to exist that suggests otherwise.

Crenshaw was correct to say that the Latin school of Rev. Brown's supposed link to Augusta Academy (Liberty Hall) cannot be demonstrated by official record. He was not correct, however, in saying that the link is evidenced in letters and other writings of the early nineteenth-century men who had heard that there was a link. His concluding statement in the extract shown above constitutes little more than obfuscation personified. Said in more concrete terms, what he actually meant was this: There is no documentary evidence to support the notion that there was any link, let alone a direct link between Rev. Brown's Latin school and the presbytery's new seminary, not from the eighteenth-century records of the Hanover Presbytery or the Liberty Hall Board of Trustees. There is, however, supposedly, a letter attributed generally to Rev. Samuel Houston, which suggests that he had heard from others older than himself that the school attended by certain named students was patronized by the Hanover Presbytery. If the alleged letter did in fact exist, and if Rev. Houston wrote that this patronization took place, then his hearsay testimony would simply be incorrect because he was a man of sterling reputation who would not perjure himself although as a writer, he frequently related hearsay testimony of others as though they were facts and he rarely bothered to fact-check traditions related by close friends and relations. In this case, he would simply have been in error because all the official records of the Hanover Presbytery and those of the board of trustees are congruent on the founding of the university. The official records of either entity would be compelling evidence, but the official records of both entities, taken together, are in agreement on every particular about the founding. These records were recorded by numerous eyewitnesses to the events in question. These men were all of the highest character and paragons of virtue, which renders their representations virtually incontrovertible, men like Rev. Philip Vickers Fithian, Justice Caleb

---

650 Curiously, Crenshaw neglects to provide posterity with any specific references to the "older residents" and or to the so-called "letters" to which he refers. If there were such letters, they have miraculously disappeared. As such, they must be relegated to the ash-heap of dubious hearsay.

Wallace, Samuel Lyle,[651] and Rev. William Graham. Not one of these men or the many others associated with the college in its infancy, including the entire board of trustees in 1792, ever suggested or hinted at a link between Augusta Academy and any earlier school.

Crenshaw failed his readers on this point in another significant way, which is that he failed to reveal in this context material facts in light of his positive representations about Liberty Hall's origins dating further back than October of 1774. One glaring omission is that he did not mention his unpublished but entirely accurate appendix A, "The Problem of the Origins," which accompanied his typescript version of *General Lee's College*. This appendix vividly demonstrates the two histories of Washington and Lee. He also knew, but did not mention, the fact that not one of the published histories of the college that appeared between 1774 and 1850 suggested that the college's origins were traceable to a date before October of 1774, and not one of these early histories mentioned the schools of Robert Alexander of Rev. John Brown.[652] Most importantly, he neglected to mention that there was not one shred of credible evidence upon which to base an entire repudiation of nearly a century of consistent representations of the school having been created on October 13, 1774. These representations were also made in the public press until 1850 and the appearance of William Henry Foote's fallacies on this subject.

The true facts are that Washington and Lee University was never a Latin school, and that is why such a fictional account cannot be demonstrated by official records. The only Latin school conducted in the Valley of Virginia in the last quarter of the eighteenth century was the one organized by Rev. John Brown, which in 1775 was located at New Providence. This situation was clearly described by Rev. Philip Vickers Fithian in his 1775–1776 journal that he wrote while lodging in Rev. Brown's home. Published for the first time in 1934, this highly important and well-known publication is one Dr. Crenshaw conveniently ignored despite the fact that it is the only such written testimony by an eyewitness to the events under our consideration that was written in the eighteenth century other than the ones written by Justice Caleb Wallace and the one written by the college's

---

651 Samuel Lyle was one of the original Trustees appointed in 1776, a member of its first Executive Committee, a benefactor and the institution's first Treasurer, who, along with President Graham petitioned the new Virginia Legislature seeking incorporation and a Charter for the Academy, in 1782. His is the first signature appearing on the Board of Trustees' petition to the Virginia Synod of the Presbyterian Church sent by the Trustees in 1792.

652 Rev. Hill's History of Washington College (1838), as discussed earlier, did allude to a "visit" to Rev. Brown's school but this was a demonstrable error by Hill which was caused by his failure to note that the Presbytery's meeting had been moved after its first day meeting, from Timber Ridge to New Providence causing him to mistakenly conclude that a visit to their host's school at New Providence was a visit to the Presbytery's seminary at Mount Pleasant, which was much closer to Timber Ridge, and the location where they met on day one. Hill, however, did not suggest that the seminary's origin pre-dated October of 1774. Some, mistook this "visit" for a decision by Presbytery to patronize Brown's school. They seem to have failed to note that his school was never again mentioned in the Presbytery's meeting minutes. Rev. Fithian, however, noted that Brown's Latin school was still in operation in Dec. Of 1775, under the tutelage of Samuel Doak. A strange circumstance if Brown's school had "merged" with Augusta Academy, as some have suggested based on the April 1775 "visit."

president William Graham in his letter to President George Washington on behalf of the board of trustees of the college. It was no accident that all these writings produced by eyewitnesses in the eighteenth century were in complete agreement that the university's nativity can be traced directly to the actions of the Hanover Presbytery, taken on October 13, 1774, to "establish" and "patronize" Virginia's second college and the first Virginia college to be incorporated and chartered by the State (Commonwealth) of Virginia, following the American Revolution, this momentous occasion occurring in the late fall of 1782.

In Re the Random Housed Edition of *General Lee's College*

ERROR no. 1: Inexplicably, Crenshaw confused Robert Alexander's school with "Augusta Academy." On page 4, Crenshaw mistakenly said this:

> "Augusta Academy was established by Robert Alexander, a native of Ulster, who migrated to America in 1737.

This statement is pure fiction.

Dr. Crenshaw concludes this sorrowful chapter 1 with this caveat and embarrassing attempted self-exculpatory declaration:

> "Thus far we have viewed the formative years of Augusta Academy dimly, through a mist of tradition and sketchy information. Now we turn to the advent of William Graham and the emergence of the academy into the clear light of history.

ERROR no. 2: Crenshaw mistakenly asserted that the Hanover Presbytery "assumed responsibility" for Rev. Brown's private "Latin school" (O. Crenshaw, *General Lee's College*, Random House edition, p. 9).

Here are Crenshaw's words in this regard:

> Although the presbytery resolved "to establish" a school, it is evident that, ***in fact, the body assumed responsibility for continuing an educational enterprise already in being under supervision of the Reverend John Brown.*** <u>The minutes of the presbytery do not make this clear.</u> (Emphasis in bold italics here indicates error; the underline does not indicate error, but was merely added for emphasis.)

Crenshaw here is clearly mistaken because, ***in fact***, the body did not assume responsibility for continuing an educational enterprise already in being under supervision of the Reverend John Brown. For one thing, Brown's Latin school was located at New Providence, not at Mount Pleasant. The presbytery's newly established seminary under William Graham was located at Mount Pleasant. In addition, Brown's Latin school was being conducted that December of 1775 by Samuel Doak, at New Providence, as is explained by Rev. Philip Vickers Fithian in his journal, written at the time in question but only published in 1934.

Crenshaw here had the facts before him, but he drew the wrong conclusions. It is astounding that Crenshaw said, "The minutes of the presbytery do not make this clear." Of course, "the minutes of the presbytery do not make this clear" because it did not happen. Crenshaw obviously misinterpreted the minutes. Apparently, he overlooked the fact that the meeting, which convened at Timber Ridge, had moved to New Providence after the conclusion of the first day of a multiday autumn session. Missing that point in the meeting minutes casts the overall context of the next few days into an entirely different light.

What is important is that nowhere in these minutes does the recorder of the minutes suggest that the presbytery acted on any policy that related to Brown's Latin school. Believing that the presbytery acted in regard to Brown's school is a colossal mistake. It is gross speculation that assumes facts that are nonexistent. This is a mistake Crenshaw probably would not have made if he had read Caleb Wallace's 1776 history written into the trustees' record book on its first several pages of text. It is inexplicable that he neither cites Wallace's treatment nor explains why he did not.

Here below, once again, are the opening lines of the university's first authorized history of its founding:

> **"The present Academy of Liberty Hall <u>began under the Direction and Patronage of the Presbytery of Hanover</u> as the following Minutes fully evince.**
>
> (Rev. Caleb Wallace, Clerk Hanover Presbytery, Liberty Hall Academy, Board of Trustees' record book no. 1, May, 1776; emphasis added)

ERROR no. 3: Crenshaw assigned an inappropriate significance to the presbytery's use of a future infinitive ("to be established") and, in so doing, incorrectly assigned a connection between schools that did not exist.[653]

The meeting minutes of the Hanover Presbytery for April 15, 1775, say this:

> The Pby met according to Adjournment . . . The Pby finding that they cannot of themselves forward Subscriptions in a particular manner, do for the encouragement of the *Academy to be established* in Agusta, recommend to the following Gentlemen to take in Subscriptions in their behalf. (Minutes, p. 62; emphasis added here is not indicative of error.)

Now, below, see the comment made by Dr. Crenshaw:

> The minutes of February 1, 1775, contain a brief reference to "the school in Agusta, and those of April 15 mention the "academy to be established in Agusta. The future infinitive appears especially significant because the presbytery was

---

653 This appears on page 9 of the Random Hgouse edition of General Lee's College.,

meeting at the time in the vicinity of the existing school "under the Direction of Mr. Brown." (O. Crenshaw, *General Lee's College*, p. 9)

Contrary to Crenshaw's notion that there is something significant in the clerk's use of the future infinitive because the presbytery was meeting in the vicinity of Rev. Brown's school, the auditor finds the "future infinitive" mostly irrelevant, keeping in mind that this meeting is the first mention of the new school's manager William Graham and that Mr. Graham's public academy was then being launched at Mount Pleasant, several miles' distant from Brown's private Latin school at New Providence. These two educational entities had very little, if anything other than geography, in common. Brown's endeavor was strictly a preparatory Greek and Latin basic grammar school. The academy then being established was just taking shape and was in its infancy. Nevertheless, Graham's academy was intended from inception to be a college program patterned after the College of New Jersey.

Brown's private Latin school was a peripatetic operation dependent for instruction on tutors who rarely stayed long at Brown's school. Graham's academy (Augusta Academy) was established and patronized by the Hanover Presbytery while Brown's school had no official connection to the Hanover Presbytery. Indeed, Brown's school is only once even mentioned in the presbytery's minutes and then only because the presbytery had been holding its spring meeting at Rev. Brown's home next door to his school.

Finally on his point, the Hanover Presbytery established and patronized two seminaries during this brief period of several months. In each case, the minutes include specific information pertaining to the establishment and patronizing of these two schools, including the men they chose as the school's administrative leaders, Rev. William Graham and Rev. Samuel Smith. Both of these men were charged with securing books for their academies as well as laboratory apparatus for instructing in the fields of mathematics and science. In both cases, the presbytery authorized subscription (fund-raising) campaigns to underwrite the construction of buildings to house their chief administrators and families, a steward, the students, and classrooms, all of which is detailed in the presbytery's meeting minutes.

With respect to Rev. Brown and his private school, the presbytery devoted but one sentence in its minutes to his school, and even then, it was as an afterthought concerning a "visit" next door to honor a request of their host.[654]

---

654 At this time, Brown opposed the Presbytery's plan to create a "seminary of learning"/college in Virginia, believing it were better to send young men to Latin schools like his own, and thereafter on to Princeton. This sentiments he expressed in letters to his friends and family members. By inviting his guests to visit his school next door to his home where the Presbytery had been meeting he obviously hoped to impress his colleagues and further his goal of defeating the proposal before it became a fait accompli. This stratagem, however, failed to persuade his colleagues who pressed forward with their plan. In this earliest phase, the plan included completing their new Manager's installation as the new Pastor of the then vacant pastorate of the nearby Timber Ridge Congregation. All related plans were then tentative as the organizers

The problem here lies in the board of trustees and Wm. Graham's attempt to be perfectly accurate, hence the troublesome parenthetical. The school truly was operating only as a grammar school initially, but not unlike most every new college without seniors, juniors, and sophomores. Moreover, by referencing the initial two years as "previously operated as a grammar school," they were able to accurately and honestly show an uninterrupted history that predated the Revolution—a not unimportant fact in their view and they believed, probably accurately, that it would be important to President George Washington. Crenshaw is unjustifiably wrong to assert that the board must have meant a time period greater than the two years prior to their move to Timber Ridge. He merely asserts this as a fact but provides no argumentation or evidence to support his assertion. This awkward comment is likely Crenshaw's undeft avoidance of a reality that might have lit a firestorm reaction in parts of the greater Lexington community. Some of that community's oldest and most prestigious families' claims of attachment to the university from its earliest days are based on the fiction that anyone who attended either Robert Alexander's school or Rev. John Brown's school were automatically considered alumni of Washington and Lee. To have any credence, this notion depended upon unquestioned links of both schools to Liberty Hall Academy. Crenshaw undoubtedly saw that this was an untenable premise but chose not to challenge this fictitious orthodoxy. Hence, his rather feeble and obfuscational commentary about what the trustee's letter must have meant. In this, Crenshaw offers an almost nonsensical dodge. Here it is again:

> "It is hardly reasonable to believe that the Trustees would not have bothered to include that parenthetical allusion unless it referred to a longer span than the two years between the appointment of William Graham as manager of a classical school in 1774 and the titular designation of academy in 1776. (Crenshaw, *General Lee's College*, Random House edition, para 3, p. 10)

It apparently escaped Crenshaw's attention that the letter writer's author, Rev. Graham, astutely avoided referring to the Presbyterian Church's early involvement because the college no longer operated under the aegis of that church; and yet at the same time, he wanted to accurately describe the school's history, which indeed was operating initially "in the form of a "grammar school." The letter, after all, was addressed to the noted Anglican and president of the United States and the fact that its name, Liberty Hall Academy, predated the Declaration of Independence would likely impress the nation's paragon of patriotism. Still, the school's official meeting minutes covering the pre-revolutionary brief period did, at the time, refer to the school as a "grammar school." Of course, Graham understood that the college buildings were under construction during this period, and the grammar

---

attempted to bring the numerous variables into a state of synergy. Brown's tactic failed and within a year the tentive nature of the strategy was made permanet as Graham was ordained as Timber ridge's new Pastorate, and the campus buildings were nearing completion on lands adjacent to the Timber Ridge Meeting House.

school was viewed by its creators as "the foundation" upon which Graham would construct "the superstructure."[655] The trustees understood full well that they were competing for an endowment and knew that their competitors would likely attack if Liberty Hall were to play fast and loose with the facts.

ERROR no. 4: Crenshaw inappropriately linked the term "Augusta Academy" to Rev. Brown's private Latin school. (p. 6, 10 et seq.)

Crenshaw mistakenly uses the name loosely in chapters 1 and 2 as though it was used in that time in connection with the schools of either Robert Alexander or Rev. John Brown or both. There is no known evidence to support the notion because it is not true. Neither school is known to have had a name of any sort and certainly not Augusta Academy. The few known students who attended either of these two local schools were virtually all local residents at the time of their schooling.

ERROR no. 5: Crenshaw inappropriately assumed that Rev. John Brown's intention to reopen yet another phase in his peripatetic Latin school offerings, which he alluded to in a letter in 1782, to fruition when that plan may not have ever been realized. Facts on the subject are wanting, but his attempt would likely have failed in this regard because during the eight years of the Revolutionary War, the academy continued uninterrupted despite the war and the site being moved a few miles toward what is now the town of Lexington. During this interregnum, the school had solidified its form, which included both the college and the college's associated preparatory grammar school. The college and its grammar school were able to secure from the new Virginia legislature the new state's first charter as a degree-granting college. This momentous occasion took place the same year that Brown announced to his brother-in-law Col. William Preston his intent to reopen a Latin school. The new well-received college, however, appears to have met all of the Valley's educational needs for everything other than elementary education for young children. The public records do not give any insight as to how long it took for Mr. Brown to abandon his design for yet another Latin school. From the little contemporary information extant, it appears that Brown's school closed during all of the Revolutionary War and was never revived after the war. History has not provided us with the name of any student who might have been educated at Brown's school after 1775.

ERROR no. 6: Crenshaw confuses the presbytery's established seminary at Mount Pleasant with Rev. Brown's Latin school operating near his home on Moffett's Creek close by the New Providence Church. (O. C., *General Lee's College*, p. 11). Crenshaw also erred by accepting that Brown's school at New Providence moved from New Providence to Mount Pleasant though it never did.

This mistake is rather self-evident given all that has gone before.

---

655   Dr. S. L. Campbell, "Washington College, Lexington, Virginia," *Southern Literary Messenger*, June 1838.)

ERROR no. 7: Crenshaw inexplicably assigns as "evident" an otherwise undocumented action to "assume responsibility for continuing an educational enterprise already in existence under the supervision of the Reverend John Brown." In fact, Brown's school was still in operation at New Providence as late as December of 1775 under the tutoring of Samuel Doak (*General Lee's College*, Random House, 1969, p. 8).

As has been thoroughly explained elsewhere, Brown organized his school but played no direct role in its instruction. His "supervision," such as it was, had nothing whatsoever to do with Augusta Academy operating at "Mount Pleasant" in the mid-1770s.

ERROR no. 8: Crenshaw mistakenly attributes a student's lecture notes as being taken from William Graham's lectures, but in fact, they are the lectures of Dr. John Witherspoon transcribed from a master copy made by Graham while student at Princeton and then later used by students at Liberty Hall (O. C., *General Lee's College*, Random House, 1969, p. 2).

As related earlier, both of Graham's early biographers, Edward Graham and Archibald Alexander, specifically asserted that William Graham's lectures were never written down or transcribed. These men were eyewitnesses, and both lived in Graham's home during this period.

ERROR no. 9: Crenshaw briefly discusses Graham's political opinions and certain activities in one paragraph and leaves his readers with a vastly incomplete, inaccurate, and uncalled-for unpleasant characterization of Graham's politics and unnecessarily cast some degree of doubt as to his piety. He curiously omits his most significant political activity concerning Virginia's Act for Religious Liberty (O. C., *General Lee's College*, Random House, 1969, p. 15).

Most of these referenced political activities have been adequately dealt with in earlier comments in this section and in earlier sections as well. Suffice to say that Graham generally kept a low profile in regards to political matters. He wrote a proposed constitution for the proposed state of Franklin (see bibliography) but did so anonymously. He wrote an essay on government during the period in which we were forming the current US Constitution (see bibliography), and he led the Virginia Christians' struggle for religious liberty and was perhaps the most significant person responsible for the adoption of the state's Bill for Religious Freedom that served as the template for the establishment section of the First Amendment of this nation's Bill of Rights, an ardent anti-federalist in Virginia, joining with his friend Patrick Henry, George Mason, and numerous others who opposed the adoption of the Constitution for several reasons not least of which was the failure to have adopted a Bill of Rights as part of the Constitution. Nevertheless, there has been no serious attempt to amend the later added Bill of Rights since its adoption shortly after the ratification of the Constitution. His brief foray into political affairs was limited to the period during which our nation was being formed.

ERROR no. 10: Crenshaw failed to correct Charles Campbell's history of Virginia concerning Samuel Stanhope's role in the founding of Washington and Lee.

Campbell credits Smith with instigating the college's founding, and Crenshaw reprints this nonsense without bothering to correct it. The founding of the school had already been agreed upon by the Hanover Presbytery before Smith even arrived in Virginia in 1773. Smith, however, deserves the credit for recommending his friend and colleague at Princeton, William Graham, as the right person to take charge of this dream and bring it to fruition; and without doubt Smith's prescience in this regard, it is doubtful if the institution would exist. He is worthy of honor and praise for this by every friend of Washington and Lee University. Later, their friendship may have suffered as a result of their differences concerning separation of church and state.

Note: Because of its importance to perpetuating another error in regards to the origins and because Crenshaw addresses the point without noting its erroneous nature, we add here the basic information and then cross-reference the matter in the section devoted to lesser authorities. The author referenced by Crenshaw is Charles Campbell, and the work cited is History of the Colony and Ancient Dominion of Virginia *(Philadelphia, 1860). Crenshaw's quote taken from Campbell is as follows:*

> *"The Rev. Samuel Stanhope Smith . . . was at this time a missionary in Virginia, and the school [Augusta Academy]* **was founded upon his recommendation** *. . . From this seminary Washington College, at Lexington, arose. (p. 677; emphasis added)*

Dr. Crenshaw's error here is in not correcting Campbell's mistake in inappropriately assigning to Rev. Samuel Stanhope Smith the honor of being the instigator of this great plan to establish what we now know as Washington and Lee University. Crenshaw undoubtedly knew full well that the idea to establish this seminary was a group effort of the Hanover Presbytery, and while Rev. Smith may have concurred in the presbytery's evolving plan, Smith's important role, as reflected in the presbytery's own records (meeting minutes), was to recommend someone to manage their effort and, in so doing, bring the plan to fruition. That he did by recommending Mr. William Graham of Paxton Township, Pennsylvania, a man who was Smith's schoolmate at Princeton and who he knew from his role as instructor at Princeton's preparatory academy, a distinguished scholar, and as a personal friend. This not to belittle Smith's role or his wisdom in this regard, for as a prognosticator in this regard, the university stands as ample evidence of his value to the institution and its legacy.

Conclusion Regarding Dr. Crenshaw

The auditor reminds the reader that Dr. Crenshaw's extensive research into the history of Washington and Lee University is without parallel. Its historical value cannot be underestimated. Having said that, we cannot help but conclude that Crenshaw's great failure is that he either failed, or refused, to confront the ugly provincialism that allowed a false history to emerge and go uncorrected from 1850 and the publication of William Henry Foote's *Sketches of Virginia*, first and second series, 1850 and 1855. Mr. Foote, who is said by one family historian to have known both the Rev. John Brown and his wife, Margaret Preston, took receipt of historical information from an unknown or unidentified source that inappropriately inserted Rev. Brown and his private Latin school into the history of what was then deemed "Washington College" without naming his source or the factual basis upon which he had challenged all prior historical accounts of the institution. This stands as a disappointment because there is no justification, in this case, for such a lapse in judgment.

The auditor reluctantly found fault with Dr. Crenshaw given his stature as a historian, but it is clear from the two versions of his book, *General Lee's College*, including his unpublished footnotes, that Crenshaw knew, or should have known, that Rev. Brown consistently opposed the Hanover Presbytery's actions in establishing the new seminary in Augusta County and that he was no friend of that school during his lifetime. In the auditor's view, Crenshaw had a duty to disclose the content and implications embedded within his unpublished appendix A, but instead, he turned his back on the inescapable truth that there is no credible evidence of a direct link between Robert Alexander's school and Reverend's altogether different Latin school and the other related fact that Rev. John Brown's alienation from Liberty Hall Academy explains why he refused to have any connection to the academy or its director, William Graham.

Note: Crenshaw may not have discovered the truth about Rev. Brown not having a connection to Liberty Hall Academy during the last stages of writing his history and was simply unwilling to rewrite the early chapters. Whatever his reasons, Dr. Crenshaw had to have known that when the final draft of the manuscript of *General Lee's College* went to the publishers, his representations about the college's origins were not true. That the book contained no errata slip pointing out this mistake is not forgivable.

25. JOHN M. McDANIEL[656] (1979) (1994)

(John M. McDaniel, Charles N. Watson, and David T. Moore, *Liberty Hall Academy, The Early History of the Institutions which Evolved into Washington and Lee University* [Lexington, Virginia: Liberty Hall Press, 1979]; John M. McDaniel, Kurt C. Russ, and Parker B. Potter, *An Archaelogical and Historical Assessment of the Liberty Hall Academy Complex 1782-1803* [Lexington, Virginia; Liberty Hall Press, 1994]; The James G. Leyburn Papers in Anthropology, vol. 2, 1994)

We identify three particularly significant errors in the McDaniel project's first publication, *Liberty Hall Academy, The Early History of the Institutions which*

---

656 These publications are attributable to several participants in each of the two projects that culminated in a publication. The other participants are listed in the bibliography and elsewhere but Professor Mcdaniel was the project direction in both cases, hence our listing of McDaniel. Obviously, much of the material was prepared by other participants and some of the errors are more attributable these participants.

Evolved into Washington and Lee University,[657] two of which pertain to the origins of the school and the other pertaining to Rev. William Graham and lectures mistakenly attributed to him, but which were actually the intellectual property of Rev. John Witherspoon, president of Princeton. Graham's copy of Witherspoon's lectures was used repeatedly at Liberty Hall as a template from which students copied the lectures for use as a textbook. In all likelihood, Mr. Graham's personal copy had Mr. Graham's name on it for the purpose of identification, and someone obviously mistakenly concluded that he had written the attached lectures.[658] As has been explained elsewhere in this report, the cover page of this packet of lectures was created by a copyist in 1890. We know the cover page was not created by the student (Joseph Glass) who originally transcribed these lectures because he could not have been unaware that the school's rector did not give regular lectures in 1796, as the cover page asserts. The rector spent much of 1796 in extreme western Virginia arranging his retirement on lands that he had purchased on the Virginia-Ohio border.

There are numerous errors contained in this monograph and some are somewhat duplicative, but while the basis of the error may be the same, the statements might vary by the language used and by the context in which they appear. Hence their separate identification.

ERROR no. 1. This error has two parts: part 1, the McDaniel group mistakenly concluded that the Hanover Presbytery in 1774 patronized an existing school and part 2, the McDaniel group mistakenly concluded that Graham was appointed to a position "under the direction of Rev. John Brown." In both cases, the McDaniel group was mistaken.

The two most significant errors in the *Liberty Hall* book, pertaining to the origins, appears on page 6 where the author(s) say,

> Paragraph 2, *"In 1774, however, the presbytery **decided instead to patronize the existing school at Mount Pleasant**. William Graham was designated to operate it, **under the direction of Reverend John Brown.**"* (n. 25, p. 6; errors here are indicated by bold italics)

The above assumes incorrectly and without authority that the school established by the Hanover Presbytery in 1774 existed at the time the Hanover Presbytery established their new seminary, which it did not. Indeed, there had been a private Latin school at Mount Pleasant at one time, but it was closed, or rather, transferred by Rev. Brown when he left the Timber Ridge congregation. Brown moved it to a location nearby the New Providence Church at Moffatt's

---

657   John M. McDaniel, Charles N. Watson, David T. Moore, Liberty Hall Academy, The Early History Of The Institutions Which Evolved Into Washington and Lee University, Lexington, Virginia, Liberty Hall Press, 1979

658   Edward Graham and Archibald Alexander both explained that President Graham's lectures were regretfully never written down for posterity, and both pointedly asserted that Witherspoon's lectures were copied by all students at Liberty Hall for use as a textbook.

(Moffett's]) Creek circa 1765–7. See John White Stuart's dissertation on the life of John Brown.

The group further errs by conferring on Brown an authority and position superior to William Graham, which did not happen. Importantly, the presbytery's appointment of Brown as "inspector" was never accepted by Mr. Brown. The more careful reader will note that in these meeting minutes, all business that transpired between the presbytery and the administrator of the seminary was between the presbytery and Mr. Graham, not between the Presbytery and Rev. Brown. There are representations by authors to the contrary but only by a few authors, and in each case, these representations arise from the author confusing the school at New Providence with the academy at Mount Pleasant. No such representation has ever been accompanied by any competent supporting authority.

ERROR no. 2. The auditor identifies another error, one in two parts: part 1, the McDaniel group mistakenly concluded that Liberty Hall Academy descended from another and prior private school, and part 2, the McDaniel group mistakenly concluded that Rev. John Brown was directly involved in the affairs of Liberty Hall Academy, which is inaccurate.

The second most significant error in McDaniel et al.'s book, _Liberty Hall_, is located on page 4, paragraph 1, where the authors inappropriately link two partially correct statements in a way that creates a false impression. Here are the two comments:

> 1. owever, it is not until we reach the Mount Pleasant location that we come across a line of descent that leads clearly and without interruption to Liberty Hall."

> 2. **_"Both schools were conducted by Presbyterian ministers;_** _at Mount Pleasant, by John Brown, who became pastor of the nearby New Providence Church in 1753."_ (McDaniel, _Liberty Hall_, p. 4.)

This paragraph on page 4 refers to schools conducted by Robert Alexander and John Brown. Robert Alexander, however, was not a Presbyterian minister, and his name does not appear in any of the Presbyterian church records in America covering the years in which he lived. Rev. John Brown was a Presbyterian minister, but his "Latin school," as he was wont to call it in all of his correspondence referring to the school, was not located at Mount Pleasant when the Hanover Presbytery established its seminary in Augusta County. At that time, Brown's school was located at New Providence where his home and church were located on Moffett's Creek.

The error lies in mistaking the school at Mount Pleasant operated by John Brown prior to 1764 with the school at Mount Pleasant under William Graham from early in 1775 to the latter part of 1776. The line of descent referenced by McDaniel et al. in item "1" above is from Graham's school at Mount Pleasant, not Brown's school, which had been abandoned at Mount Pleasant by Rev. Brown prior to 1770 and thereafter located at New Providence from whence it was never again moved.

Brown's school ceased to exist at Mount Pleasant after Brown had a falling-out with his Timber Ridge congregation in 1763, a fact easily discerned from a review of the Hanover Presbytery minutes. When Brown's school was conducted at Mount Pleasant, he lived nearby. Brown, by his own choice, had no real connection to the school at Mount Pleasant under Graham. Brown was a member of the Hanover Presbytery that created the school under Graham, but his private correspondence makes it abundantly clear that Brown was no friend of the Mount Pleasant school (Augusta Academy) under William Graham. He advised his close relations, as early as 1775, to send their sons elsewhere for schooling, advice that Brown himself adhered to from the time of the presbytery's establishment of this new school in 1774. Brown's correspondence makes it crystal clear that he did not support the presbytery's decision to create what in time became known as Washington and Lee University.

In December of 1775, Rev. Philip Vickers Fithian wrote into his now-famous journal references to Brown's Latin school then located at New Providence. He also refers to the presbytery's public seminary (Augusta Academy), which was under his old schoolmate William Graham. This eyewitness testimony was written into the journal at the time when Fithian was lodging in the home of Rev. John Brown. It is not unimportant that Philip V. Fithian was also a schoolmate at Princeton of Mr. Samuel Doak who was at the time of Fithian's December entries, conducting the classes at Rev. Brown's Latin school. His eyewitness testimony of events occurring before his very eyes, and recorded at the same time, is of the highest credibility. Of course, this testimony was not considered by the nineteenth-century historians who mistakenly believed that Rev. Brown was connected to Augusta Academy or that his school either evolved into or was merged with Augusta Academy because Fithian's Journal while written in 1775 and 1776 was, unfortunately, not published until 1934.

Fithian's Journal is not, by itself, definitive proof that the presbytery's seminary was not in any way related to Augusta Academy, but it aids posterity in understanding how things were at the time the academy was created. More definitive in that regard are the meeting minutes of the Hanover Presbytery and those of the board of trustees of Liberty Hall Academy in conjunction with the extant correspondence of Rev. John Brown written around the time the academy was created. Also helpful is the manuscript memoir of Rev. William Graham written by Archibald Alexander. So too the memoir of Rev. Graham written by his brother Edward, longtime professor at Washington College. Indeed, every source known that was written or published prior to 1850 makes no mention of Rev. Brown or his school having had any connection to Liberty Hall Academy. None of them more pertinent and revealing than the university's first authorized history of its founding authored by Rev. (later, Justice) Caleb Wallace and copied into the institution's first record book in May of 1776. Taken together, these early records form an incontrovertible case for proving that Washington and Lee University's founding took place on October 13, 1774, a fact no one doubted during the college's first seventy-five years.

Note: The twentieth-century editor(s) who doubted the accuracy of Rev. Fithian's record of Samuel Doak's teaching at Rev. Brown's Latin school was wrong to have challenged Fithian's account without having solid credible evidence to support his challenge. In fact, the editor in question, was himself in error. His challenge was based upon two fallacious assumptions: (1) That Hampden-Sydney was opened in 1775 when it was not and (2) that Samuel Doak was in Prince Edward County teaching classes at Hampden-Sydney in December of 1775 when he was not. Hampden-Sydney did not open until sometime in January of 1776, by which time Mr. Doak had indeed arrived to serve as a temporary substitute. The editor's basis for challenging the author's journal entry was fallacious. It was based on a published advertisement that announced that the opening of classes would begin in December, which proved to be incorrect. In fact, the academy would not open for classes until January of 1776.

ERROR no. 3: This error concerns a mistake that pertains to Rev. William Graham and a set of handwritten lectures mistakenly thought by some to have been lectures prepared by Graham. What was revealed by several of his early students, including Graham's younger brother Edward, was that William Graham made use of the lectures of Dr. John Witherspoon at Liberty Hall Academy. These were lectures that Graham had copied down while a student under Witherspoon at the College of New Jersey. None of Graham's own lectures were ever written down.

This fact was attested to in writing by both Archibald Alexander and Edward Graham in their respective memoirs of Rev. William Graham. The only evidence to the contrary is a cover page created in 1890 by a copyist, and the text of that cover page has no known provenance earlier than 1890. The copyist created a cover page for the lectures, and the copyist asserts mistakenly that the lectures were delivered by Rev. William Graham in 1796. In 1796, however, President Graham was in his last year at Liberty Hall; and during that year, he was frequently absent tending to property he had purchased on the Ohio River. In that year, he rarely lectured to students in the regular academic program. The copyist obviously just assumed the lectures were written and delivered by William Graham. The eyewitnesses, however, assert in no uncertain terms that Graham's lectures were never written down by anyone. These eyewitnesses were not only students at Liberty Hall, but they both lived in the president's home and saw him daily. If any of Graham's lectures had been written down by Rev. Graham or anyone else, both of these two eyewitness' would have known about it.

Here then is what the McDaniel group said, in part, in this regard:

> Another example of the nature of education at Liberty Hall is provided by ***records of a series of lectures Graham offered in the 1790s on the subject of human nature.*** George Johnston was a member of a class in 1795, when he recorded in his notebook, for Lecture Four: "What is perception . . . what is to be considered in every perception? (N14, p. 25 of the monograph;[659] this footnote refers to a copy of Johnston's notebook held in the archives of the Washington and Lee University Library, which bears little on the question of the source of the lectures.)

---

659   McDaniel et al, Liberty Hall Academy... pg. 25

While it's true that Graham, as rector, can be said to have "offered" a series of lectures, it is an error, however, to contend as McDaniel does that

> Graham distinguished between original beauty, possessed by the object itself, and derived beauty, or "fitness as a means to an end. (McDaniel, et al., *Liberty Hall Academy*, p. 26)

That statement clearly means to attribute to William Graham the essence of the concepts embodied in the quotation, but those notions were penned by another, namely, Dr. John Witherspoon. Witherspoon's lectures were copied down from a template and used for purposes of study by the students at the College of New Jersey (Princeton). William Graham, like other students of Witherspoon who went on to become instructors, later used those lectures of Witherspoon with their own students. At some point in time over the course of two hundred years, someone fashioned a sort of title page, which they used as a cover page for the packet of lectures. And because the original was the property of William Graham, it was somehow conceived that he actually wrote them, and consequently, the title page was mistakenly fashioned in a way that presented Graham as the author when, in fact, he was not. If his name (Wm. Graham) was ever located on or in the original packet, it would have been there to merely indicate that he was the owner of the original template set.

ERROR no. 4. The McDaniel Group mistakenly concluded that a reference made by Rev. John Brown in one of his extant letters to a student and that student's standing was concerning the school at Mount Pleasant when, in fact, the reference was to Brown's Latin school at New Providence, and the student he referred to was his own son, John.

Note: It appears that the McDaniel group, despite all of its important efforts and work concerning Liberty Hall Academy, completely failed to grasp an all-important reality concerning Rev. John Brown and Liberty Hall Academy. What they missed is that Rev. John Brown and virtually his entire immediate family were personally alienated from both Rev. William Graham and Mr. Graham's academy, Liberty Hall. While Rev. Brown does not appear to have allowed this personal breach to affect his professional relationship with Rev. Graham as a fellow Presbyterian minister, it is an easily ascertainable fact that Rev. John Brown never accepted any appointment of the presbytery in connection with their patronized seminary, Liberty Hall Academy. That is why Rev. Brown is never recorded as being present at any meeting of the board of trustees from the time of the board's first meeting on May 13, 1776, until Rev. Brown left Virginia in 1796. Moreover, Brown sent every one of his sons to schools other than Liberty Hall Academy. He went so far as to recommend to the most powerful and influential man in the Valley of Virginia, his brother-in-law, Col. William Preston, that he send his sons somewhere other than to Liberty Hall Academy.

The McDaniel Group mistook Brown's private "Latin school" at New Providence as being the same school that was created by the Hanover Presbytery in October of 1774 and which was the other educational establishment in the neighborhood of New Providence and Timber Ridge Presbyterian churches.

Note: There are two entirely different kinds of schools, one a private and preparatory primary school, the other under the direction of William Graham, a public seminary (academy) designed to provide college education to Virginia youth and which opened in temporary quarters at a place located on the farm of Mr. James Wilson in 1775, which was then called Mount Pleasant. Mount Pleasant, coincidentally, was where Rev. John Brown had directed his private "Latin school" sometime earlier when he was pastor of Timber Ridge Church, but when his association with Timber Ridge was discontinued, it was moved to the Rev. Brown's new home on Moffett's Creek at New Providence.

Here below is the McDaniel group's mistaken comment:

> The school that was located at Fairfield was first referred to in 1773 when . . . *The Reverend Mr. John Brown, talked of the program of one of the students at the **Mount Pleasant school** by saying he was "so far through his education that he [was] fit to enter college"* (McDaniel, Watson, Moore, (Liberty Hall Academy: The Early History...) 1979: p. 5], "This comment demonstrates that in 1773, the education offered by Brown was preparatory in nature." (John M. McDaniel, Kurt C. Russ, and, Parker B Potter, <u>*An Archaeological and Historical Assessment Of The Liberty Hall Academy Complex 1782–1803*</u>, Liberty Hall Press, Washington and Lee University Press, Lexington, Virginia, 1994 pp. 166.)

Authority for this exceedingly important quote is found in the listed authorities to the first McDaniel publication cited above and which is footnote no. 18: "John Brown to William Preston, New Providence, January 13, 1773, in William Preston Papers, Series QQ, Draper Collection, State Historical Society of Wisconsin, p. 141 (microfilm copy in the Washington and Lee University Library), p. 48 of *Liberty Hall Academy: The Early History*, seen above. It is also cited by Dr. Crenshaw in his *General Lee's College* and by John White Stuart in his biographical dissertation on Rev. John Brown. See the bibliography.

*Note: The highlighted "**Mount Pleasant school**" is the error because Brown's reference is to a student (his son) at his Latin school at New Providence and **not at his earlier location at Mount Pleasant**. Brown left that location shortly after 1767 when his connection to the Timber Ridge congregation was severed. When Brown left his farm near Fairfield and Mount Pleasant, he took his family and his Latin school to his home on Moffett's Creek and close by the New Providence Church.*[660]

---

660 *See John White Stuart's unpublished doctoral Dissertation, <u>The Rev. John Brown of Virginia (1728-1803): His Life and selected sermons</u>, Doctoral Dissertation, University of Massachusetts, 1988. Stuart's research includes the most detailed study of Rev. Brown's correspondence which clarifies much of our assertions, and when viewed in conjunction with Philip Vickers Fithian's Journal for 1775-1776, it is difficult to imagine how one could not see clearly that there was no connection between Brown's Latin School and Liberty Hall Academy. Still, Mr. Stuart managed to misconstrue the clear meaning of these materials concerning the founding of Liberty Hall. When these materials are viewed in light of the meeting minutes of the Hanover Presbytery from 1771-1776, and the Board of Trustees meeting minutes covering 1776, its hardly possible to believe Rev. Brown, or his school, had any connection whatever to Liberty Hall. That is what explains Brown sent all his sons elsewhere for their educations.*

The authors scrupulously, and quite correctly, avoid referring to Brown's school as Augusta Academy, leaving that designation to William Graham's school. McDaniel et al. say this:

> In 1776 Graham's school officially called Augusta Academy, was moved . . . to Timber Ridge. (See McDaniel, Russ, and Potter above; emphasis added)

Note: The quote is correctly given here, but the quote is in error because the designation "Augusta Academy" was never official but rather was an unofficial convention used in their meeting minutes by the presbytery to distinguish between their two eighteenth-century patronized seminaries. Providing official names for these seminaries was left to the school's respective boards of trustees when the presbytery created these governing boards.

Sometime after 1850, nineteenth-century historians began to repeat the mistake of unknown origin that used the name Augusta Academy in reference to earlier eighteenth-century common primary schools that had been located in the Valley of Virginia, but that mistake is unknown to have occurred in the eighteenth century. In the eighteenth century in Virginia, the word *academy* was used to designate schools of the higher order that were not Anglican and were therefore rarely afforded an official charter.[661] The term *college* was then used by schools that were chartered by the crown, and charters were generally reserved for only Anglican-patronized schools. The first school in Virginia that was granted a charter after the Revolution was Liberty Hall Academy. In the eighteenth century in Virginia, there were only two true academies: Liberty Hall Academy (earlier called unofficially "Augusta Academy") and Hampden Sydney Academy (earlier unofficially called "Prince Edward Academy").

Only someone ignorant of the eighteenth-century Virginia uses of the term "academy" would have applied the term academy in conjunction with the schools under Rev. John Brown and Mr. Robert Alexander. Certainly, neither of these gentlemen would have made this mistake, and neither did so far as is known.

ERROR no. 5. On page 7, McDaniel et al., in paragraph 2, present a somewhat oblique picture that leaves the reader with the false impression that Rev. Samuel Stanhope Smith accepted an appointment of director of Prince Edward Academy prior to the appointment of William Graham as director of the new academy in Augusta County. The true sequence was that the academy (seminary) in Augusta constitutes the first post-Revolution establishment of an institution of higher learning in Virginia. Prince Edward Academy was established the following year (1775).

McDaniel et al. continue to mistakenly refer to a preexisting school upon which Graham constructed his new academy. It should suffice to know that had one visited the site of Graham's new school (i.e., Mount Pleasant) prior

---

661   The auditor is aware of only one exception, that being the College of New Jersey which for political reasons was an exception to the rule.

to Graham's arrival circa January 1775, they would have found, at that time (1774/1775), no operating educational endeavor. Graham therefore did not expand a curriculum of someone else's making or merge with another existing school; rather, he created one from his own fertile mind cultivated by his experience under Dr. Witherspoon at Princeton.

ERROR no. 6. In the "Timber Ridge Location" section of McDaniel's et al. monograph *Liberty Hall Academy*, the ever-emergent Rev. John Brown connection once again surfaces in yet another form. This time from these several authors, the reader is invited to join in with their speculation regarding the origin of the name, "Liberty Hall Academy." It begins as follows:

> The popular thesis has been that the name change came in response to the patriotic fervor then seeping the Colonies; it is probable that this analysis is accurate, However, Liberty Hall was also the name of the Reverend Mr. Brown's ancestral home in Ireland [citing FN # 58]. **The adoption of the name, therefore, might have been intended as a final tribute in recognition of his early contributions to the development of the school. But the conflict between Graham and Brown over the future of the Academy, together with the now-dominate Graham's own interest in and commitment to the cause of freedom,** make it seem unlikely that the name change would have been adopted solely as a tribute to Brown. (McDaniel et al., *Liberty Hall Academy*, p. 10, para 3)

Until and unless someone can demonstrate an actual connection of the new academy under William Graham at Mount Pleasant (near Fairfield and Timber Ridge) to Mr. Brown's Latin school operating at New Providence some six or seven miles distant, then it is erroneous to assert a connection where none appears to exist. The fact that Brown once operated a private school at Mount Pleasant and lived nearby while he was a minister at Timber Ridge does not mean that after Brown moved his family and his school to another location, his descendants may properly lay claim to an involvement in, and a contribution to, a completely different educational endeavor established by the Hanover Presbytery.

Rev. Brown himself never made such a claim to this distinction. That dubious task was taken up by others who only emerged after Graham and Brown were dead. In fact, it means just the opposite, to wit: Any credit for having made a contribution to the newly established seminary in Augusta County must be earned and demonstrated by typical historical methodology. In all the published accounts prior to 1850 there was never demonstrated a recognized contribution of Brown to the establishment and success of Liberty Hall Academy.

Of course, Brown was never the president, rector, inspector, or any other officer in connection with Liberty Hall Academy. The reason has been explained in several locations of this report. There was an estrangement that came to exist between Rev. Brown's family and the academy's rector, Rev. Graham, occasioned by Mr. Graham's request to be relieved of any obligation concerning marriage to Brown's highly sought-after daughter, Betsy. This sad affair is explained elsewhere in this report, and the authority is Rev. Dr. Archibald Alexander, founding president of Princeton Theological Seminary, who was an early student of Liberty Hall Academy and a favorite of the academy's rector. As a source for historical facts, Alexander's bona fides are of the highest caliber.

ERROR no. 7. In re "the Timber Ridge Location," this section of the monograph, _Liberty Hall Academy_, begins with a definition of terms, and here we find one significant error. Only significant perhaps because of the ubiquitous and repetitive false assertions by so many different later nineteenth-century authors that mistakenly associate the term "Augusta Academy" with the Latin school operated by Rev. John Brown.

Note: Other later nineteenth-century authors refer to Robert Alexander's school as "Augusta Academy." In fact, neither school was ever referred to as Augusta Academy in the literature of eighteenth-century Virginia, including all the generally known letters from Augusta County residents during the last quarter of that century. That is because neither one of these schools was an academy, as that term was used in that period.

The McDaniel Group sets forth the following definition:

> "Augusta Academy—_**the official name**_ of the school at the time of its location at Timber Ridge in 1776. (McDaniel's group, _Liberty Hall Academy_, p. 10; bold italics here indicate error.)

In truth, the presbytery's new seminary, which began its operations in temporary quarters at a place called Mount Pleasant on the farm of Mr. Wilson, near Fairfield, Virginia, never had an official name before it was given the name Liberty Hall Academy by the executive committee of the board of trustees, acting on behalf of the entire board, at its first meeting held on May 13, 1776. The name "Augusta Academy" does not appear in any known eighteenth-century document, publication, or known letter of that period until it was used **_unofficially_** by the Hanover Presbytery and where it appears in various forms in the meeting minutes of the period beginning with October 1774 and ending upon May 6, 1776.

During this period, the presbytery determined to establish a second seminary in Prince Edward County east of the Blue Ridge Mountains. Thereafter, the presbytery adopted a convention, and unofficially, the presbytery began referring to these seminaries as "Augusta Academy" and "Prince Edward Academy" respectively, and obviously did so for the sole purpose of distinguishing one academy from the other in their meeting minutes. They undoubtedly withheld officially naming either school because they had apparently also decided to reserve the honor of naming these schools for their prospective boards of trustees after they had been both nominated and had accepted their nominations. It is quite clear from a review of the meeting minutes of the Hanover Presbytery between October 1774 and May of 1776 that the presbytery took no formal action to name either of their new seminaries, so the name "Augusta Academy" was not an "official name," as suggested in the quotation above.

One body that was not confused on this point was the Hanover Presbytery, whose minutes demonstrate that on the very first day they decided to "establish and patronize" their new school, they also initiated a fund-raising campaign to purchase the beginnings of a library and various laboratory equipment, all of which were essential tools associated with college-level instruction. Rev. Philip Vickers Fithian provides some additional insight on all this in his valuable journal:

> **Mr. Graham, lately initiated a brother, is appointed Director of a school in the neighborhood of Mr. Brown's—He thinks to enlarge his Method of Education so much as to finish Youth in their classical, Philosophical Studies.** (Fithian's Journal, 1775–1776, p. 150[662])

If primary or preparatory schools were labeled as an academy, the academy's trustees would hardly have decided to label its seminary, designed from inception to provide college-level instruction, as an academy. The cavalier use of the term "academy" did not begin to appear commonly until long after the end of the American Revolution. Certainly, Rev. Brown never used the term *academy* in connection with his school in any of his extant eighteenth-century correspondence. He consistently referred to his school as a "Latin school."

ERROR no. 7. McDaniel et al. incorrectly attribute an assertion concerning the location of the Alexander school to Samuel Doak. Here is the assertion:

> The Reverend *Samuel Doak,* a presbyterian minister who had studied under Alexander, *indicated* that the school was first located at Alexander's house but was moved later two or three miles to the south. (This quote is followed by footnote 11; see McDaniel et al., *Liberty Hall Academy*, p. 2 para 3.)

McDaniel et al.'s assertion is incorrect because Samuel Doak is not known to have "indicated" anything whatsoever on this subject. The cited authority for McDaniel's assertion in footnote no. 11, references the Judge James T. Patton, "Letter on the Location of Robert Alexander's School, John Brown's Residence, and Mount Pleasant," printed in the Washington and Lee University Historical Papers, Vol. 1, Baltimore: John Murphy & Co., 1890. P. 125, but Judge Patton was also incorrect in the same way. When we reviewed this published letter of Judge Patton, we found the following at the cited page 125:

> In a sketch of the Rev. Samuel Doak, in Foote's History of North Carolina, it is stated that when he was sixteen years of age,

---

662 Fithian, Philip Vickers, The Journal & Letters of Philip Vickers Fithian, "Written on the Virginia-Pennsylvania Frontier and in the Army Around New York, [1775-1776], Princeton, Princeton University Press, 1934 [considered by publisher to be vol. II] While this volume stands alone and has its own index, it is volume two, the first volume being published in 1900.

(1764) he commenced a course of classical studies with Robert Alexander, who resided about two miles from his father's house. This grammar school, _he says_, was soon after removed two or three miles farther south, to about where the Seceder meeting House, called, Old Providence, now stands. About this time the school came more immediately under the charge of the Rev. John Brown, by Mr. Brown the school was removed to Pleasant Hill, within about a mile of his dwelling, and about the same distance north of Fairfield. (Continuing on the next page [126], Judge Patton includes this assertion: "The Old Providence Meeting house, _alluded to by Mr. Doak_, is about a mile in a southwesterly direction from the Alexander house."[663]) (Patton Letter, W&L Historical Papers, v. 1; emphasis added)

Here, Judge Patton contributes to the ever-expanding misconstruction. The reader will note the words we've highlighted in line 4, "_he says_," which clearly must refer to Mr. Foote, the author of the book, incorrectly cited by Judge Patton as the authority (i.e., Patton cites _Foote's History of North Carolina_, but which should read W. H. Foote, _Sketches of North Carolina, Historical and Biographical_, New York, 1846).

Judge Patton, then referring back to his own "_he says_," shifts the meaning of "_he_" to Samuel Doak, which cannot be accurate because the book from which this is drawn contains no content from Samuel Doak. All the information in this section of Foote's book on North Carolina is written by Foote himself, and he offers no authority whatsoever for this material. Foote, however, is not a credible source of material about the founding of Washington and Lee University, notwithstanding his reprinting of many important documents created by others. Foote on several occasions fails to accurately analyze or correctly interpret the content of material written by others. For details, the reader is referred to the subsection of the Author's Errors section of this report that is devoted to Foote's serious mistakes.

A review of Foote's book herein cited finds that on pages 309–311 is where the sketch of Rev. Samuel Doak appears, and nothing in that section, or in the introduction that addresses many authorities used by the author Foote, refers to any material supplied to Foote by Samuel Doak. In short, none of the comments attributed to Samuel Doak can be said to have come from him. The actual source, as far as Foote informs us, is Foote himself. Upon what or whom he relied is, at this time, pure conjecture, Judge Patton's incorrect assertion to the contrary notwithstanding. All this was missed by McDaniel's working group who, unfortunately, passed on this series of missteps and in so doing leaves their readers with an incorrect understanding that Samuel Doak, in fact, is not a source of information on the location of the eighteenth-century primary schools in Augusta County. Doak left no known writing on that subject.

---

663 Washington and Lee University Historical Papers, Vol. 1, Baltimore: John Murphy & Co., 1890. pps. 125-126.

Judge Patton himself is also not a credible source on the subject of the founding of the school because the events in question took place in the time of his grandfather. Patton's letter relies on the unreliable Mr. Foote who typically failed or refused to cite authorities for his own assertions, and Foote's errors concerning Washington and Lee (Liberty Hall) and its rector, Mr. Graham, are legion. Oddly, he chronicles numerous important rare documents that he apparently either did not bother to read or he read them carelessly. Many of his errors can be discovered by simply examining his own reprints of important early records, especially extensive extracts from meeting minutes of the Hanover Presbytery. These errors are discussed in detail in the subsection concerning Foote's mistakes.

Note: This is not say that all of Patton's information is incorrect because some of it may indeed be accurate. Sorting wheat from chaff is the problem.

ERROR no. 7. McDaniel et al. include two footnotes that are incorrect, in part, that are seemingly perfunctory, but in the context of our audit have serious potential for misleading others, hence our pointing out footnote numbers 55 and 56 in John M. McDaniel et al.'s <u>Liberty Hall Academy, The Early History Of The Institutions Which Evolved Into Washington and Lee University</u> (Lexington, Virginia: Liberty Hall Press, 1979).

McDaniel et al. footnote numbers 55 and 56 read as follows:

> Trustee' Minutes 1774–1873, ***meeting of May 6, 1776.*** The men chosen to serve were . . . [his is followed by a list of numerous men. Then]

> "(Grigsby, Washington, and Lee, Historical Papers, II, pp. 12–13.) (See page 49 of the *Liberty Hall Academy*, monograph, 1979)

The nature of this error is mislabeling because the source cited as *"**Trustees' Minutes, occurring on May 6, 1776**"* cannot be accurate because the trustees did not, at that time, yet exist. The day the board of trustees was created by the Hanover Presbytery was May 6, 1776. The trustees named on that day had probably not yet even been advised of their appointment. Moreover, the board of trustees' first meeting was held on May 13, 1776, exactly one week after the board was appointed. It appears that McDaniel et al. erred, in part, by relying on a secondary source, if that is what the concluding parenthetical means at the end of footnote 55. Footnote 56 simply repeats that part of the error in footnote 55, labeling it as a meeting of the board of trustees when the meeting to which they refer was a meeting of the Hanover Presbytery, which indeed was held on May 6, 1776.

What's most important about this error is that it highlights just how important it is for historians to use original sources whenever possible. Had the McDaniel working group done that, in all likelihood, they would have noticed that preceding the minutes for the Board of Trustees very first meeting was a memorandum written by the Hanover Presbytery's Clerk, Caleb Wallace wherein he presents the first written history of the founding of Liberty Hall Academy, and by reviewing that memorandum they would have learned that Liberty Hall Academy began by act of the Hanover Presbytery on October 13, 1774. The result then, would have been that they could have written the first accurate history published of the origins of Liberty Hall Academy in well over a century and probably in 150 years. Unfortunately they did not.

ERROR no. 8: The McDaniel Group is mistaken in several ways when it presumes that the Presbytery's 1775 visit to the school under Rev. Brown was the same school that they examined at Mount Pleasant, under William Graham, the following year. Here is how the McDaniel Group explains these two circumstances:

> In contrast to Brown's reaction, The Presbytery was pleased with Graham's work, and with education being offered *at the school*. In Feb. 1775, it met *at Mount Pleasant* and heard representative orations, "with which they well pleased.[Fn #43]

> In May 1776, the Presbytery met _**again** to attend examinations_, and applauded the diligence and abilities of the teachers. [FN # 44]

The first error in this paragraph is in asserting that these two separate events involved one school, when in fact it involved two entirely different schools, one a private Latin school under Rev. Brown,[664] the other a public seminary (academy) under Rev. William Graham. The second error is in dating the initial event that McDaniel et al. gave as February 1775, when in truth it took place on April 15, 1775. The third mistake relates to the location of the first event mentioned, and here, McDaniel et al. place it at Mount Pleasant when in truth, it was at New Providence. This is evidenced by the presbytery's meeting minutes on pages 62 and 63. They may have missed this because this multiday meeting began on April 12, 1775, and the first day's meeting was held at Timber Ridge near the Mount Pleasant school under Graham, but it moved to Rev. Brown's home and New Providence after their initial day's meeting. Thereafter the members met at Rev. Brown's home on April 13, 14, and 15. After the last day's business was completed, the presbytery accepted Rev. Brown's invitation to visit his school near his home. The final error in the above quoted paragraph is found in the words "to attend examinations," which is far different from what actually occurred. Here are the presbytery's actual words from their minutes of the meeting that took place at New Providence concerning the third day's meeting (April 15, 1775):

> The Pby. Think it expedient, as they now have an opportunity of visiting the school under the <u>Direction of Mr. Brown</u>, accordingly the Pby repaired to the school house, and attended a specimen

---

664 While this private Latin school was Brown's, Brown did not conduct classes at the school. He used hired tutors.

of the proficiency of the students, *in the Latin and Greek language*, and pronouncing orations with which they were well pleased. (Hanover Pby. Meeting minutes, p. 63; emphasis added)

The reader will note that here, at New Providence, the presbytery merely observed the students' work in grammar, which is the focus of a Latin school, like Mr. Brown's, but they did not "examine" Brown's students; they merely observed. This is in contrast to the presbytery's "examination of the students" in their own academy under William Graham a year later, this time assessing their student's work in "classical studies" indicating a far broader curriculum of studies. Here below is that contrast:

> "The Presbytery *proceeded to examine* the School under the Care of Mr. Graham, and having attended a specimen of their Improvement *in their Classical Studies*, and pronouncing Orations, the Pby highly approve of the Proficiency of the Students and the Diligence and Abilities of the Teachers. (Hanover Pby. meeting minutes, p. 76)

Here, the presbytery examined the school's students and their teachers under the "care of Mr. Graham." In the case of the prior event, the presbytery merely took the opportunity to "visit" the school "under the direction of Mr. Brown." The minutes also make clear that they merely "attended" the school in session. The careful reader of the entire associated meeting minutes will note that these schools were both different in type and situated at two different locations several miles apart from one another.

The most important point in all this is that the McDaniel group, like so many authors before them, failed to grasp that these two events did not concern one school, but two entirely different schools and, further, they failed to note that these events took place at two different locations and also incorrectly described them as both occurring at Mount Pleasant when, in fact, only the presbytery's seminary was located at Mount Pleasant in the years 1775 and 1776.

ERROR no. 9.   McDaniel et al. mistakenly found a contradistinction between the accounts of Rev. Archibald Alexander and Edward Graham concerning instruction that took place after the school was moved from the location at Timber Ridge in consequence of the Revolutionary War. Below is the paragraph in which the error is found and then an explanation of what actually took place. Here then is the McDaniel group's commentary on this point:

> "During the Revolutionary war, a few students remained in the area and studied under Graham at his North River farm. Some are reported to have received boarding from him as well as instruction." (FN # 74, citing Edward Graham's memoir of William Graham[665])

---

665 Edward Graham, "Memoir of the Late Rev. William Graham, A.M." *The Evangelical and Literary Magazine and Missionary Chronicle*, IV, (1821), p.75 et Seq..

They continue, "...Support for the notion that classes were taught in Graham's home, however, is found in an Address delivered to the Alumni of the school in 1843 by Archibald Alexander. (FN #75[666])

Continuing, "*But his account is contradicted by an article in the Evangelical and Literary Chronicle, published in Richmond in 1821*, which states: "The students were taught for some time in an old house that once had been used as a dwelling." (FN#76; bold italics here represents error)

The error here is that the McDaniel group finds in these two cited sources a contradiction when there is none. Both of these sources were eyewitnesses to the events being described, and both lived in Rev. Graham's home at the same time. Moreover, these two men were later brothers-in-law. Edward Graham was Rev. Graham's much younger brother who lived with his older brother from approximately late 1776 or early 1777 until he completed his college studies. Archibald Alexander boarded in Rev. Graham's home during the Revolutionary War, along with Edward Graham. Edward Graham later married Archibald Alexander's sister Margaret. Both Alexander and young Edward were lifelong friends and correspondents. The reason these two sources did not contradict each other about where classes were held is that classes were often held in an assortment of places during those times, sometimes even out of doors as described by Dr. Samuel L. Campbell in his article "Washington College, Lexington, Virginia."[667] Presumably, however, classes were initially held in Rev. Graham's home but were later moved into an abandoned home nearby.

When the Graham family made their move from Timber Ridge to their new farm on North River, classes were held in Mr. Graham's home as suggested by both Edward Graham and Archibald Alexander and as suggested by the McDaniel group. The McDaniel group, however, finds that their source for footnote 76 contradicts their source for footnote 74. The problem with this is that these sources are the same author writing on the same subject in different parts of the same article. In other words, the McDaniel group says that Edward Graham is contradicting Edward Graham on the same subject in the same article. The truth of the matter is that Liberty Hall classes were held in both places but at different times. There is then no contradiction.

In addition, Archibald Alexander admits in his unpublished memoir of Rev. Graham that he relied heavily on Edward for much of the material found in his own memoir. On this subject at least, the readers have two eyewitnesses testifying on the same subject and essentially agreeing with one another. McDaniel's group were overthinking this issue. In fact, it appears there were two different frame

---

666 Alexander, Archibald DD, An Address before Alumni of Washington College, Delivered June 29, 1843, Washington and Lee Historical Papers No. 2, Lexington, Va., 1890

667 Samuel L. Campbell, (M.D.)[i.e., "Senex"], "Washington College, Lexington, Virginia," Southern Literary Messenger, June 1838, beginning at pg. 364.

buildings used for instruction during the lengthy Revolutionary War, the first being an abandoned home near Graham's farm at Whistle Creek and another that was built to replace the abandoned home.

Both of these frame buildings are said to have been destroyed by fire. As an issue, these questions, while interesting to ponder, have very insignificant bearing on the school's early history.

ERROR no. 10. The McDaniel group asserts that Rev. William Graham's real estate venture at Point Pleasant was "unsuccessful."

Here is how they put it:

> "After leaving Liberty Hall, he [Mr. Graham] did move his family to the Ohio River, near Point Pleasant in what is now West Virginia, where he sought—*unsuccessfully*—to bring his plan into being. (McDaniel group, *Liberty Hall Academy*, p. 42)

There appears to be no shortage of those in the Valley of Virginia who were predisposed in the nineteenth century to assign negative attributes to Rev. Graham. In this case the assignation seems inappropriate given the fact that the matter was still in litigation at the time of Mr. Graham's untimely and totally unexpected death. What the outcome of that litigation may have been cannot now be known and therefore the ultimate outcome of Graham's plans are similarly unknowable. Many ventures that begin with difficulty were eventually a success. A pattern similar to the incipiency of what is now known as Washington and Lee University.

Those who have experience with real estate litigation, especially in eighteenth-century America, know full well that in civil law, "it ain't over till the ample woman sings," and in this case, the matter was in what can only be called an embryonic state. After all, Graham only began negotiations to purchase six hundred acres of land on the Ohio River in the spring of 1776, and he died in the early summer of 1799. Therefore, his development plan was only in play for roughly two-and-a-half years; and in that time, he was dealing with a lawsuit brought by the sellers who wanted to rescind the sale.

Given Mr. Graham's numerous successes in matters that were often labeled "doomed from the start" and especially insofar as he had a proven ability to turn desperate circumstances into successes, like those pertaining to Liberty Hall Academy. One might think that he had earned the right to a bit of forbearance in regard to making final judgments on major projects. We call to mind the anecdote shared by Dr. Samuel L. Campbell in a footnote to his history of Washington College, attached as "note A." "*A gentleman of Kentucky, Col. W. McKee, who formerly resided in this county, and who long acted as a trustee of the academy, expressed himself thus in a letter to a friend.*" Note: The above is a prelude to the following:

> "I rejoice to hear that Gen. Washington has placed Liberty Hall on a permanent foundation. ***This recalls to my mind the saying***

of Mr. Graham many years ago. I had often myself almost despaired of the academy, and on one occasion expressed my apprehensions to him. He in usual concise manner replied, 'there are people working for this academy, who don't know it. (*Southern Literary Messenger*, p. 366, col. 1, from Campbell's article, "Washington College, Lexington, Virginia," June 1838)

Consider the case of Thomas Edison. The patent litigation and other expenses associated with his lightbulb cost Edison over $200,000, but by 1882, he merely sold approximately three thousand lightbulbs to about two hundred customers. Ten years later, he had only increased his sales to about seven hundred. The sales results were occasioned by the costs associated with preliminary requirements related to the use of lightbulbs. Had Edison died in the early stages of litigation over his patents, would we then have identified his efforts *"unsuccessful"*? Continuing our illustration, the reader will note that despite the fact that Edison obtained a patent for his phonograph in 1878, he failed to develop it into a working machine until Alexander Graham Bell and his associates had created a similar machine several years later wherein a cardboard cylinder that was coated with wax was employed. Had Mr. Edison died unexpectedly in 1800, would we now label his efforts *"unsuccessful"*? The point is that to judge an investment a failure in the eighteenth century simply because a land purchase is tied up in litigation is a rash judgment. And even though the McDaniel group were technically correct by using the term "unsuccessful" as opposed to a "failure," in the context of the paragraph, the comment clearly connotes a failure.

The McDaniel group seems to have had sufficient grounds for concluding as they did on this subject because many other authors before them had said much of the same thing. We contend, however, that there is insufficient evidence upon which to pronounce Graham's activities after his resignation from Liberty Hall Academy "unsuccessful." At worst, the plan was slow to launch and embroiled in a vexatious lawsuit.

How Mr. Graham might have handled his affairs had he lived is beyond anyone's ability to predict. From the few memoirs of William Graham's life and from the various histories of the greater Lexington community in the late eighteenth century, it seems rather clear that if Mr. Graham had succumbed to the anxieties and dire predictions of many of his contemporaries in the Valley in those years, there would probably be no such thing as Washington and Lee University and probably no such thing as Hampden-Sydney College or Union Theological Seminary in Virginia. Moreover, many, if not most, of the colleges in Kentucky and Tennessee that trace their roots to the late eighteenth century would not have come to fruition. Many of the early Presbyterian churches of that region too would not have emerged but for the efforts of the numerous Presbyterian ministers that had been Mr. Graham's students. For certain, some of the early Presbyterian Church structures in the area might never have been built had Rev. Graham not persisted over the concerns of so many who thought such projects could not then be accomplished.

The advancement of music in the Valley is also traceable to the efforts of Mr. Graham who virtually hog-tied a young music teacher just passing through Lexington and convinced him to alter his designed course and instead remain in greater Lexington for several years where he brought about so many well-known music-related innovations to the Valley.

Conclusion Concerning the McDaniel group's errors

The major mistake made by the McDaniel group was in accepting that Rev. Brown and his Latin school had a connection to Liberty Hall Academy when there is no eighteenth-century evidence to support that notion, and nothing since that time has surfaced that serves as credible evidence to support the idea that there was any connection between Liberty Hall Academy and any other local school.

26. RICHARD HARRISON (Editor, *Princetonians*) (1980)

(Richard A. **Harrison**, Ed. *Princetonians, 1769–1775*, Princeton University Press, Princeton, New Jersey, 1980. This is volume 2 in a five-volume series. **W. Frank Craven**, author of the article on Rev. William Graham. See also Professor John M. Murrin's introduction to *Princetonian 1784-1790*, p. liii of the introduction)

Note: The errors of Mr. Harrison are particularly troubling because the series, the *Princetonians*, is a most important reference tool used by many important historians seeking background information on important historical graduates of Princeton from the period of our nation's founding. Harrison relied upon an in-house manuscript with information collected together by one or two of the sons of Princeton Theological Seminary's founding first president Archibald Alexander. The material they wrote about their father's preceptor, William Graham, is seriously in error. Unfortunately, this manuscript appears to have been Harrison's principal resource for compiling the brief biographical sketch of Rev. William Graham of the class of 1793. Interestingly, Dr. Craven wrote the biographical sketches of both William Graham and John B. Smith, both of whom were of the class of 1773. Craven mistakenly describes Smith's position at Hampden-Sydney Academy much differently than he does Graham's position at Liberty Hall Academy even though the schools were very much the same.

ERROR no. 1. Harrison is responsible for Dr. Craven's mistakenly describing President Graham as simply a schoolmaster and Presbyterian minister.

In stark contrast to John B. Smith's tenure at Hampden-Sydney, Graham's tenure and professional attainments in Virginia far and away exceeded those of his classmate, John Smith. Although both were celebrated scholars and fervid patriots who volunteered and served on occasion in the militia as captains of their local units during the Revolutionary War, Graham was held in high esteem by his board of trustees, as demonstrated by the board's petition nearly twenty years after he was first appointed to head this college:

Through the Presbytery of Lexington we are informed of the attempts of the Board of Trustees of the college of Hampden Sydney to deprive us of our Rector the Rev. Wm. Graham in order to convince him to accept the presidency of their college. . . . In our objecting to the removal of Mr. Graham, we would not in the least reflect on Trustees of Hampden Sydney for attempting to obtain our Rector from us for we think him qualified for such a place and that they need such a gentleman. But this so far from leading us to freely give him up as they wish does considerably increase our desire to retain him over our Academy. . . . Hampden Sydney can plead the necessity. On this [??] surely we are not behind them. ***For it was under Wm. Graham that our Academy first received its existence and it is chiefly owing to his extraordinary exertions that it has persevered through all the convulsions of a calamitous War and the many vicissitudes which have taken place*** through the operations of various causes for the space of about 16 years, and here we cannot forebear asking the question would it be wisdom or duty in Synod to destroy our Academy which has been the most useful to the church of any in the state and which is at this time more promising to the church in point of numbers than ever it has been, and this too on the bare probability that another may or nearly so must be the consequence unless providence preserveth it if our Rector be removed at this juncture. . . .

For these and such reasons ***your petitioners earnestly pray that this Rev'd Synod would not remove Wm Graham from his present charge of the Academy and we hope and trust that you will see reasons to grant the prayer of your petitioners***. And that the great head of the church may direct you in all things to seek and promote his glory as the object and prayer of the Trustees of Liberty Hall.

This petition was signed by all the trustees of Liberty Hall Academy as a testament to their sentiments about their long-serving president (rector).

That same year (1792), the Virginia Synod[668] appointed Rev. Graham as the president of its new theological seminary and authorized Graham to select the presidency of either Hampden-Sydney College or remain at his current location in Lexington and conduct the new theological seminary in conjunction with his role of the college of his choice. Smith, on the other hand, while president of Hampden-Sydney, had become embroiled in controversies with his trustees and had become in such deep debt that he was forced to resign his presidency.

This is not intended to engage in invidious distinctions for its own sake, but in fairness to Liberty Hall and its founding first president, William Graham, the

---

668 Virginia Synod of the Presbyterian Church representing all Presbyterians in the state.

factual contrasts of the careers of these two educators and Presbyterian clergymen make it abundantly clear that Graham's presidency began and ended in glory while Smith's much briefer tenure concluded in rancor and shame. To compare the two as Dr. Craven has done is foolish, and to hold Smith in higher esteem in their alma mater's historical sketches of its early alumni than that of William Graham is totally unwarranted by facts and historical evidence.

When Dr. Craven describes William Graham as a "schoolmaster and Presbyterian minister" (p. 287) is historically unfair. In contrast, Craven's description of John B. Smith is as follows: "Schoolmaster, Presbyterian clergyman, and college President." In fact, both of these academies were colleges lacking only an official charter.[669]

ERROR no. 2. Harrison is responsible for Dr. Craven's mistakenly describing William Graham's beginnings in Virginia.

Dr. Craven said this:

> "Graham was engaged in October 1774 to manage, for the time being and under the general supervision of Reverend John Brown (A. B. 1749) a "publick school" in Augusta County that had the sponsorship of the Hanover Presbytery.

In this, Craven was mistaken in several ways: (1) At the Hanover Presbytery's new "publick school," William Graham was never under the supervision of anyone, let alone Rev. John Brown; (2) Rev. John Brown's Latin school," as Brown consistently labeled it, was a private school, not a "publick school"; and (3) Rev. Brown's private school was located at New Providence near his home and the congregation's New Providence "meeting house" located several miles away from the Hanover Presbytery's patronized new academy under the exclusive management of William Graham, as the Hanover Presbytery's meeting minutes clearly delineate.

(Note: The presbytery's vague appointment of Rev. Brown as "inspector" went unaccepted and unacted upon by Brown, who opposed the creation of Graham's academy from its inception. The presbytery's minutes also demonstrate that all of the new academy's business was conducted by Mr. Graham, and those activities were reported upon at the presbytery's meetings exclusively by Mr. Graham.)

ERROR no. 3 Harrison is responsible for Dr. Craven's mistakenly vilifying Graham's preaching based on an ill-advised inconsistent comment made

---

669 In Virginia, at that time (pre-Revolution) only Academies affiliated with the *established* Anglican Church were in a position to obtain a charter from the British authorities. William and Mary, therefore was the only chartered school that could assume the mantle of *college*. In 1782, Graham's Liberty Hall obtained the new state's first charter as a school with college degree granting authority, other than William and Mary. The following year, John B. Smith's academy was also chartered.

by a student of Graham's, which student (Archibald Alexander) in numerous publications rendered his lone criticism a nullity. Here below is but one example:

> *"And having undergone these trials with high approbation of the Presbytery he [W. Graham] was licensed to preach the gospel at a meeting in Rockfish on the 20th of October, 1775.* **It was soon perceived that he was a preacher of no ordinary kind. The clearness and depth of his reasoning, and the warmth of his applications, placed him in the estimation of judicious hearers, in the first class of pulpit orators.** (Archibald Alexander Mss. Memoir of William Graham, p. 54, and in the article by Dr. Campbell)

In other sections of this report are listed a large number of testimonials to the greatness of Graham's preaching in the view of a myriad of eminent educators and clergymen of that time, all of whom were eyewitnesses. Here is another observation by Rev. Archibald Alexander, the very source unfortunately relied upon by Dr. Craven:

> *Mr. Graham preached in the house crowded to excess—and yet many could not get in. His text was "Comfort ye Comfort ye my people. He began calmly but seriously; and as he preached on his discourse, his feeling as was usual with him, rose gradually until an awful solemnity was spread over the large congregation. . . .* **The writer does[n't] remember ever before or since, to have seen a whole congregation more fully under an impression as tender as it was solemn; but reigned a breathless silence through the house, only interrupted occasionally by the sound [of] a suppressed sigh.** *Perhaps Mr. Graham never exceeded the sermon preached on this occasion.* **Dr. Smith said to writer that take it altogether; it was the best sermon he ever heard.** (Alexander Mss. "Memoir of William Graham," pp. 206–216; emphasis added)

Dr. Craven could not have selected a worse example to feature in his sketch regarding Rev. William Graham. It is not only inconsistent with every account this author has encountered from eyewitnesses who remarked on Graham's preaching, but it is even inconsistent with all the many other statements made by the source upon whom Craven relied. It is also unwarranted selective attribution.

In conclusion on the biographical sketch, the auditor/author concludes that the academic selected to write this sketch apparently developed an animus for his subject that colored the entire tone of his sketch, resulting in an unfair, biased treatment that cannot bear scrutiny for accuracy in regards to the character of a man much venerated by most of the Valley of Virginia's leading men of that day. He can be excused in some measure by the multitude of historical errors committed by so many nineteenth-century misguided historians, many of whom have been exposed herein.

27. I. TAYLOR SANDERS [1986]

(I. Taylor Sanders, _Now Let The Gospel Trumpet Blow_, Lexington, Virginia, New Monmouth Presbyterian Church, 1986)

Introduction

It seems inevitable that in assessing Dr. Sander's book, _Now Let the Gospel Trumpet Blow,_ as it treats with the early history of Washington and Lee University, that we would discover a plethora of errors concerning the college's first rector, Rev. William Graham given Sanders's decision to focus so much attention on Rev. Graham and his critical role in the founding of the university. There have been many mistakes made and then repeated, ad nauseam, about Rev. Graham's role in that regard. These mistakes have been made by nearly every author writing on that subject since 1850. Sanders naturally relied on a certain select few of these authors because the most respected authors' errors had not yet then been discovered.

Dr. Sanders devotes two entire chapters to Rev. Graham and the early history of the college and, in so doing, presents more material about Mr. Graham than any twentieth-century author. In so doing, he had unknowingly waded into a virtual swamp of error-infested historical mistakes and misimpressions that formed an ahistorical minefield. Recognizing the debt owed to Dr. Sanders for his impressive wide-ranging research, we will now highlight some of the oft-repeated errors also passed on by Dr. Sanders.

ERROR no. 1. Dr. Sanders seems to imply that William Graham was recommended by Samuel Stanhope Smith for a teaching post at an existing academy in Augusta County, which is not an accurate depiction of what transpired.

Below is how Dr. Sanders mistakenly expresses it:

> At Princeton Graham tutored classes for younger students at a school connected with the College. His reputation as an effective teacher prompted, Reverend Samuel Stanhope Smith, his friend at Princeton and a founder of Hampden Sydney College, to recommend Graham **for a teaching post at an Academy in Augusta County located near the present town of Fairfield**.
>
> (I. Taylor Sanders, _Now Let the Gospel Trumpets Blow_, p. 16)

The place being referred to by Sanders, in that time, was called "Mount Pleasant" by many local residents that formed the neighborhood located within the bounds of Timber Ridge and New Providence Presbyterian congregations. In fact, there was no existing "academy" located at Mount Pleasant when William Graham was appointed by the Hanover Presbytery to oversee the erection of a "seminary of learning" in Augusta County, Virginia. Graham was not appointed to merely "teach," but was also expected to mold the presbytery's dream of a college patterned after the College of New Jersey (Princeton) into a reality. At that time (1774), the only school that was then in existence in this neighborhood was Rev. John Brown's private Latin school that was located at New Providence several miles away from Mount Pleasant. Ironically, and confusingly, Brown's school had at an earlier time also been located at Mount Pleasant, but the school had been moved to New Providence in the latter part of the 1760s.[670]

Insofar as Brown's Latin school was a private preparatory school, its governance fell outside the jurisdiction of the Presbyterian Church. It was organized by Brown, but conducted as an adjunct operation in connection with his pastorate of the New Providence congregation. It was not, however, patronized formally by the New Providence Church. Rather, the patronage came from individual members of the congregation or by the students' parents unless the student was an adult. The school's policies were those set by Rev. Brown and the tutors he appointed to teach the classes. Most of the students that attended instruction at Brown's school were older boys or young men who were intending to go on to college-level programs and many with an eye toward a career in the Presbyterian ministry. Before the creation of Liberty Hall Academy, such students who were able went on to matriculate at the College of New Jersey. Once Liberty Hall Academy was in full operation, such students as had earlier attended Brown's Latin school were then able to obtain their college education in Virginia. Some attended Liberty Hall Academy while others were able to attend Hampden-Sydney in Prince Edward County on the eastern side of the Blue Ridge Mountains.

The envisioned school to which Graham was called by the Hanover Presbytery was envisioned by its establishing authority to serve as an alternative to the College of New Jersey for young men from Virginia and even beyond toward the south and west. This fact is made quite clear in a series of the Hanover Presbytery's meeting minutes written between 1771, when the idea was first broached, and 1774, when the presbytery finally decided to formally "establish" their seminary of learning.[671] Moreover, contrary to Sanders' representation, Graham was appointed to manage the physical and academic creation of this new educational venture. Hence, the nominal initial title of "manager." Graham's initial duties are revealed in the presbytery's meeting minutes describing the reports made by Graham to the presbytery. It is patently obvious from these minutes that from the outset, the seminary had but one administrator in charge because all reporting on the subject of the seminary was from Mr. Graham directly to the presbytery. Just as

---

670 Brown moved the school from Mount Pleasant to New Providence when he gave up his pastorate of the Timber Ridge Church and devoted himself exclusively to the New Providence congregation.

671 As has already been mentioned in other parts of this report, "a seminary of learning" was a euphemistic phrase meaning college level instruction in an Academy that, for whatever reason, was not able to receive a formal charter from the governing authorities. In this case, and prior to the American Revolution, Presbyterian Academies were rarely ever recognized for chartering by the British authorities because they were not operated by Anglican clergymen. Hence, the term Academy instead of College. In Graham's case, his new school was to be endowed with such laboratory and mathematical apparatus as was in use elsewhere by colleges. In addition the prospective funds were intended to provide the new Academy with an appropriate library for college level instruction. A list of the Titles purchased by Graham for and on behalf of the Hanover Presbytery will demonstrate beyond any question just what the Presbytery's objectives were in regards to their new seminary.

importantly, all revenues received from the presbytery's sponsored fund-raising campaign were placed in the care of Mr. Graham who then disbursed the funds. That changed in later years when the academy's trustees appointed one of their own, Samuel Lyle, as its treasurer.

To be sure, Graham often taught the classes at Liberty Hall Academy, but teaching was not the only focus of his responsibilities. He was the chief operations officer responsible for every facet of the academy's activities, from handling property transfers to letting contracts for the building of the school's several successive campuses. Graham designed the buildings as well as the curriculum.[672] Soon after his arrival in Virginia, the presbytery appointed an assistant for Mr. Graham, John Montgomery. Montgomery was a recent graduate from Princeton. This allowed for Graham to travel north and east on a fund-raising campaign during which he appealed to many Presbyterian congregations for their assistance in endowing this new college in Virginia.

The records are exceedingly clear that William Graham was to Augusta Academy what Samuel Stanhope Smith was to Hampden-Sydney Academy in Prince Edward County. Once the presbytery licensed Graham,[673] they changed his title to that of "rector." As rector, he also conducted religious services for the students. At the same time, Graham had assumed the pastoral duties over the congregations of Timber Ridge and Hall's meeting house. This all took place during his first year in Virginia, and there is every indication that this was precisely as it was planned between Mr. Graham and the Hanover Presbytery.

Mr. Graham, therefore, did not assume "a teaching post" at an existing academy as is suggested by Dr. Sanders. The only academy that existed at Mount Pleasant after Graham arrived in Virginia was the one he created, at the behest of the Hanover Presbytery that established and agreed to patronize it on October 13, 1774, at Cub Creek meeting house in Charlotte County.

ERROR no. 2. Dr. Sanders incorrectly represents that the Hanover Presbytery patronized the private "Latin school" under the direction of Rev. John Brown, but that was not the case.

Dr. Sanders informs as follows:

> "For a number of years Hanover Presbytery *had sponsored the school*, which *was under the guidance of Reverend John Brown*, pastor of New Providence Church. (Sanders, *Now Let*, p. 16, para 4)

---

672 This all-encompassing responsibility is aptly described by Samuel L. Campbell, in his 1838 published history of the college, Graham, Campbell say, was responsible for virtually every aspect of Liberty Hall Academy's major responsibilities.

673 Graham was licensed as a probationer in the same year that he arrived in Virginia, 1775, and in that same year classes were first instituted. Created in October of 1774, the college, like all colleges, took several years to reach its full complement of Freshmen through senior classes. Graham's Academy was visited in early 1776 by the Rev. Philip Vickers Fithian who recorded his visit in his Journal for 1775-1776. See bibliography.

On this point, Dr. Sanders was clearly mistaken, relying no doubt upon his then-deceased colleague Dr. Crenshaw, who in turn was misled by the ever-present and infamous William Henry Foote.

In the eighteenth century, the Hanover Presbytery did not sponsor any of the many private preparatory schools like Brown's Latin school. These kinds of schools were typically associated with the various congregations that made up the presbytery. Rev. John Brown's Latin school was one of numerous preparatory schools organized by pastors in connection with their pastorates. The only two schools in Virginia in the eighteenth century that the Hanover Presbytery ever decided to patronize were those two public academies they established in 1774 and 1775, the one under William Graham in Augusta County (1774) and the other under Samuel S. Smith in Prince Edward County (1785). The presbytery's records specifically reflect their decisions to patronize these two schools in their official meeting minutes written in its record book created for maintaining these records. The Virginia Synod would patronize but one school in that century, which was the Lexington Theological Seminary,[674] which was conducted by William Graham as an adjunct to Liberty Hall Academy in its new stone quarters built on Mulberry Hill.

Contrary to Dr. Sanders, the presbytery did not "sponsor" the private Latin school under John Brown, and the presbytery's eighteenth-century records are devoid of any suggestion to the contrary.[675] In all likelihood, Dr. Sanders again relied on Dr. Crenshaw and the mistaken Mr. Foote for his authority. A mistake made by most every writer on the subject after 1850.

ERROR no. 3. Dr. Sanders confuses Rev. John Brown's private "Latin school" then located at New Providence with the Hanover Seminary's new "public school" (seminary), which was initially operating out of temporary quarters at "Mount Pleasant."

---

674 The name Lexington Theological Seminary was assigned to this duly recorded theological venture by the author of the first biographical treatment of Rev. William Graham, published by the rector's younger brother Edward Graham in his posthumous biographical memoir of the college's first president/rector, entitled "Memoir of the Late Rev. William Graham, A. M." published in 1821.

675 The Virginia Synod, in the late nineteenth century mistakenly relied upon the histories written by William H. Foote in a retrospective publication whrein it mistakenly asserted the false history of Washington and Lee University. Their error in this regard stems from the failure of the Presbyteries to have forwarded copies of their past meeting minutes for the Synod's use in constructing this history. The relied instead on a secondary source which was sorely mistaken. The missing minutes demonstrate the Synod's error in this regard. See Rev. James A. Waddell, ed. "Contributions to the History of The Synod of Virginia" Washington: John F. Sheiry, Printer, 1890. Waddell was one of three Committee Members who, it appears functioned as writers, editors, and collators. This is not the famous eighteenth-century "blind preacher," James Waddell, rather, it is his grandson. Who lived at Lexington Va. and was pastor of the Lexuington Presbyterian Church and President of the Ann Smith Academy. His errors as editor of the previously mentioned Synod publication are simply inexplicable, and inexcusable. He was the son of Littleton Waddell of Albemarle County, Virginia. He was first cousin of Joseph A. Waddell, author of Annals of Augusta County. These cousins both published false accounts of the origins of W&L.

Dr. Sanders mistakenly describes it, in part, this way:

> "In October, 1774, the Presbytery appointed Graham to manage *the school* and urged its patrons to begin raising money for a library and other new buildings. (Emphasis added)

The above is a mistake because the Presbytery appointed Graham to oversee the creation of their newly established seminary of learning (college) which they initially denominated "Augusta Academy." Sanders, like so many others, incorrectly interpreted the Presbytery's Oct. 13, 1774, meeting minutes qualifier "under the inspection of Rev. John Brown" and in so doing failed to appreciate that Brown never accepted this appointment, whatever it meant, and the fact that Graham never served under any one person at the Presbytery's seminary created west of the Blue Ridge Mountains. He reported directly to the Presbytery in the beginning and then later under the Board of Trustees. During his tenure there, he was the only chief operations officer.

Above we have purposely included only one of two related mistaken assertions of Dr. Sanders in order to emphasize these two important mistakes. Hopefully, in this way, the importance of the mistakes become more understandable. When the two statements are reunited in one paragraph, as originally presented by Dr. Sanders, the reader will see this:

> "For a number of years Hanover Presbytery had sponsored the school, **which was under the guidance of Reverend John Brown, pastor of New Providence Church**. In October, 1774, the Presbytery appointed Graham to manage *the school* and urged its patrons to begin raising money for a library and other new buildings. (Sanders, *Now Let*, p. 16, para 4; emphasis added indicates error)

Above, appearing reunited, Dr. Sanders's meaning becomes quite clear and it is, according to Sanders, that the school to be managed by Mr. Graham was the *private Latin School* "under the guidance of Reverend John Brown." This, however, is not the case, as Rev. Philip Vickers Fithian makes all too clear in his journal entries written in and around the Valley of Virginia at the time these important events were occurring. Here is how Rev. Fithian explains these two different schools located at separate locations but not far from one another. *Note: Below we emphasize key words and phrases using a mix of bold, italics, and underscores, but the emphasis is our own.*

Dec. 12, 1775

Tuesday, 12th (December) I rode on further twenty miles to Mr. Brown's—Extreme cold—Young Mr. Trumble was along. **We came to Mr. Browns just when the sun was going down. Mr. Hunter was there before me;** On Sunday he preached below Stanton. We were glad to meet. **Here we met Mr. Doak who is**

now over the Latin School in this neighborhood.[676] Footnote
18 (Fithian, *Journal, 1775–1776*, p. 140)

Approximately two weeks later, on Christmas Eve, Fithian returned to the previous vicinity. While residing briefly at Rev. Brown's home, he says,

Dec. 24, 1775

> **Mr. Graham,** lately initiated a brother, **is appointed Director of a school in the neighborhood of Mr. Brown's**—He thinks to enlarge his Method of Education so much as to finish Youth in their classical, Philosophical Studies. (Fithian, *Journal 1775–1776*, p. 150)

Notice that Fithian is saying here that Graham's school was located in the same neighborhood as Brown's school. This underscores that there are two different schools, Brown's and Graham's. One, Brown's, was a private preparatory school at New Providence and the other a public seminary (academy) patronized by the presbytery under Graham at Mount Pleasant.

Jan. 18, 1776

> Mr. Graham is here—Sage, deep-studied, Mr. Graham. **He is Director of the small Academy in this neighborhood.** He retains, with Dignity, the inherent Gravity which he always supported in every Part of his Conduct while he was a Student at Nassau [Princeton]. The Lines of Method & Discipline have been inscribed & are yet visible & legible upon his countenance!

It was obviously clear to Rev. Fithian that Graham was in charge of the presbytery's academy in Augusta County.

Jan 18, 1776

> Thursday, **at his school,**[677] he gave us a sermon. He spoke with Propriety; he preached, I believe, orthodox Divinity; & he

---

676 The only Latin school being conducted in the Valley at this time was John Brown's school at New Providence.

677 Here Mr. Fithian's phrasing seems eminently important as regards the controversy as to Brown's school's alleged connection to the Presbytery's "Augusta Academy." If, as asserted in Foote's, Sketches of Virginia, Series One, Graham was 'under the direction of John Brown' [get quote exactly] why would Fithian refer to the school as being Graham's school, especially when Fithian makes it clear that Rev. Brown was in attendance for this prayer-group session? Fithian obviously knew that the school was Graham's school and not, brown's school. Earlier that same year, the Hanover Presbytery were at Brown's home and went from there to visits "Brown's school." So, two schools, at two locations, under two different auspices, each distinctively different in character. This comes from the best witness' testimony and written down at the time the event occurred.

seemed zealous. –I was entertained, I hope a little improved."
(Jan. 18, 1776, Fithian, *Journal 1775-1776*, p. 171)

It is unfortunate that Rev. Fithian's Journal was not published until in 1934, Princeton University Press released it to the public. Many of the errors made from 1850 forward until 1934 might well have been avoided had the historians been aware of this important eyewitness testimony written at the scene and at the time of the events described. The full measure of the significance of these extracts are as palpable as they are persuasive concerning these two schools in the Valley of Virginia in December of 1775. One final notation on this issue: Readers who consult Rev. Fithian's Journal, as published, should ignore the unfortunate footnote inserted on page 140 concerning Mr. Samuel Doak. The editors were demonstrably wrong in this footnote, as we have demonstrated in several other places in our report. Their incorrect note is based on false information concerning the opening of classes at Hampden-Sydney Academy. The false information resulted from individuals relying on a published advertisement submitted for publication by the then-president Samuel Stanhope Smith who intended to open the school earlier than he was able. The advertisement contained a promised date of opening that Smith was unable to meet. This is a currently widely recognized fact not open to debate.

ERROR no. 4. Dr. Sanders mistakenly claims that the "lectures" used by students at Liberty Hall during Graham's years as rector were written by William Graham and that they represent Graham's personal views. But they were not written by Mr. Graham, and his own personal views cannot be ascertained from the content of these lectures written by someone other than William Graham. Certainly, most, if not all of them, were written by Dr. John Witherspoon, president of Princeton. Graham's sentiments on slavery were never published, but he does to refer to slavery in a letter written in the late 1780s to Col. Arthur Campbell in which Graham refers to "the horrors of slavery." See bibliography for a listing of Graham's writings.

Dr. Sanders discusses the lectures in question on page 20, wherein he says this:

> "Graham, who had seen the positive side of revivalism, refused to condemn its excesses ranging from weeping to loss of consciousness. *In his series of college lectures on human nature, he discussed the connection between the body and the mind. . . . He believed the connection accounted for the "commotions" at religious meetings, when sinners terrified by the "awful majesty of God" fell down, cried, and feinted twitched, and jerked and lost consciousness. . . .* (Sanders, Now Let the Gospel, p. 20)

> *Graham urged his students to keep open minds.* (n43, p. 22)

Dr. Sanders's statement that "he (Rev. Graham) believed" is footnoted as being derived from the cited lectures (lectures on human nature), but these lectures are not William Graham's lectures; rather, they were copied by Graham's students from Graham's own copy of Witherspoon's lectures.[678]

ERROR no. 5. [Preaching] Dr. Sanders joins with Dr. Ruffner and others who judge William Graham's preaching based on only one of numerous comments on that subject made by Rev. Archibald Alexander but, a careful reading of Alexander's manuscript "Memoir of Rev. William Graham" reveals that the lone negative comment made by Alexander referred to his early preaching. Like most preachers, their talents for preaching evolve over time and are typically much improved with maturity and experience. In Graham's case, this tendency was obviously one that ripened during his second decade as a minister. Here is Dr. Sanders only comment on Graham's preaching:

> Graham had always delivered tightly knit, intellectual sermons, but prior to 1789 his preaching had met with little success. A friend said prior to the revival that a person converted by Graham's preaching was "a thing unknown." (Sanders, *Now Let the Gospel*, p. 15)

A fair question in response to this curious statement is this: What Christian minister in all the world believes that a man may become truly converted as the result of a particular pastor's particular sermon? The answer should be no sane experienced minister would, or could, believe otherwise. Certainly, anyone familiar with the clerical history of Rev. William Graham of Virginia would know that William Graham would have rejected that notion. Graham was known to question the validity of any such apparent overnight conversion.

Dr. Sanders does allow that Mr. Graham's preaching could be impressive, but he seems to limit this positive aspect of Rev. Graham's career to only a brief period during the revival. Perhaps we are being too severe by questioning Dr. Sanders in this regard. Nevertheless, it would appear from this section of his book that Sanders's concluded that Rev. Graham's preaching was of little significance.

---

678   To be as clear as possible, this particular set of Witherspoon's lectures was very likely originally written, in the main, by President John Witherspoon, then copied by William Graham while he was a student at Princeton. Rev. Graham took his copy to Virginia and used his copy as a template for his students et al, to be used as a text-book. Some early students later became instructors at Liberty Hall, and they in turn made their own copies available to their students and once again, used as text-books. It is predictable that some instructors might have added lectures to their packets. As mere pedagogical tools, these packets were not copyrighted or officially attributed to any particular person, although the earliest students always referred to them as Witherspoon's lectures. The set discussed by Sanders appears to have been copied by a student named Joseph Glass, who is known to have had a close connection to his professor, Edward Graham. Edward was the younger brother of Rev. William Graham. Edward wrote an essay as a student to be judged for a potential prize to be awarded by Gov. Randolph. Edward won the contest and he may have included a slightly modified version of huis essay on slavery to his packet copied by Mr. Glass. None of Rev. Graham's lectures were ever written down or preserved for posterity, according to both Professor Edward Graham in 1821 and Rev. Dr. Archibald Alexander in the 1840s. See the bibliography.

We believe the following additional quotes from Dr. Alexander, and others leave a far different impression.

Importantly, the man upon whom Ruffner and others relied,[679] including Sanders, altered his views about Graham as a preacher in later life. Here are a few examples, mostly from that same source (Rev. Archibald Alexander). A few comments from others were added to reinforce the point that William Graham's preaching was, more often than not, deemed to be of the highest caliber. It hardly seems just for anyone to cherry-pick one critical comment, especially since the person quoted had praised the same man far more often than he criticized him. It is not unfair to say that as a general rule, Archibald Alexander almost always needed to balance praise with at least one critical comment. It is an obvious idiosyncrasy of his. Oddly, Alexander's brother-in-law Edward Graham seemed driven by a similar compulsion, and they were collaborators in writing memoirs of their preceptor Rev. William Graham.

Note: In each extract provided below, the auditor has added the emphasis in bold, italics, and underlining.

> 1. "And having undergone these trials with high approbation of the Presbytery he [W. Graham] was licensed to preach the gospel at a meeting in Rockfish on the 20th of October, 1775. _**It was soon perceived that he was a preacher of no ordinary kind. The clearness and depth of his reasoning, and the warmth of his applications, placed him in the estimation of judicious hearers, in the first class of pulpit orators.**_" (Archibald Alexander Mss. "Memoir of Rev. William Graham," p. 54, quoting, in part, the published "History of Washington College, Virginia" by Dr. Samuel L. Campbell. Both Campbell and Alexander on this subject seem to have principally relied on Edward Graham's published "Memoir of the Late Rev. William Graham" published in 1821. See bibliography.)
>
> 2. "Mr. Graham preached in the house crowded to excess— and yet many could not get in. His text was "Comfort ye Comfort ye my people. He began calmly but seriously; and as he preached on his discourse, his feeling as was usual with him, rose gradually until an awful solemnity was spread over the large congregation.... _**The writer does[n't] remember ever before or since, to have seen a whole congregation more fully under an impression as tender as it was solemn; but reigned a breathless silence through the house, only interrupted**_

---

679   Sanders refers here to Archibald Alexander who mostly heard his preceptor's preaching when a very young lad. Alexander was a precocious but immature youngster who may not have yet obtained the ability to render a mature judgment. Certaily, Alexander's view in this regard changed as he matured.

occasionally by the sound [of] a suppressed sigh. Perhaps Mr. Graham never exceeded the sermon preached on this occasion. *Dr. Smith said to writer that take it altogether; it was the best sermon he ever heard.*" (Alexander, Mss. "Memoir of William Graham," pp. 206–216)

Note: Rev. Smith was raised near Philadelphia and had occasion to hear most of the great preachers of his time. For John Blair Smith to say that "take it altogether; it was the best sermon he ever heard" is no slight praise. But he is yet another example of James Alexander having edited his father's memoir without bothering to notify his readers about what he had done, thereby creating the false impression that his father's quotation of John Blair Smith's comment was more qualified than what it was.

3. "Where Mr. Graham was preaching . . . Dr. Smith [Rev. John B. Smith, Pres. Hampden Sydney College] afterwards said to me of this sermon, that it was the best he had ever heard, **except one . . .*** from this time, Mr. Graham was considered one of the ablest preachers in the land." (James W. Alexander, *The Life of Rev. Archibald Alexander DD*, New York, Charles Scribner, 1854)

*This unfortunate qualifier, "except one," was inserted by Rev. Alexander's son, James, who was his father's editor and biographer. The qualifier does not appear in his father's manuscript version of the "Memoir of Rev. William Graham." It appears to have been editorially added inappropriately by the subject's son.

4. "After leaving the mountain they fell down upon the James River near where it takes that name, that is, just below the junction of the Jackson and Cow Pasture Rivers. Mr. Graham preached to these scattered people with a clearness which made all understand, and with an earnestness and affection which caused deep feeling. (James W. Alexander, *The Life of Archibald Alexander*, p. 8)

5. "When the poor German had proceeded thus far, we had reached the place of meeting, and found the house full. **We were very solicitous that Mr. Graham might be led to choose a subject suited to the case of our German brother, for such we esteemed him.** And it was so ordered that the text led him to open the way of salvation, and to describe the exercises of a soul when closing with Christ on the terms of the Gospel. That day we heard more for the afflicted man than for ourselves. *He never took his eyes off the preacher, and during the hour of the sermon they were full of tears.*" (James W. Alexander, *The Life of Archibald A*, p. 89)

6. "For some time he [Graham] devoted himself entirely to the work of the ministry, and preached not only within the bounds of his own congregation, but in but in the neighboring congregations; for the religious awakening, tho more powerful in and around Lexington extended to almost every congregation in the Valley, in a greater or lesser degree. He [Rev. Graham] was in most instances sent for to assist at communion season; for the custom in all that country was to have public service during [???] when the Lord's Supper was administered: *Even where the clergyman was not well affected towards him, the solicitude & impartiality of the people commonly prevailed to procure an invitation for him to attend. His preaching at this time [???] occasions, was very evangelical & very powerful. The writer is now of opinion that he never heard from any man a clearer or stronger exhibition of the gospel than in the sermons of Mr. Graham at this time.*" (Alexander, Mss. "Memoir of William Graham," pp. 215–216)

7. "The company went onward by the way of York, and at length reached the little town of Pequea . . . Here the venerable Doctor Robert Smith, the father of the President (Samuel Stanhope Smith), was still pastor. Here likewise the sacrament was to be celebrated on the approaching Sabbath. The congregation was large, . . . *On Monday in conformity to the old Scottish practice, Mr. Graham discoursed; his sermon was powerful and pungent, and a certain young man was struck to the heart, and came to the house inquiring what he should do to be saved.*" (James W. Alexander, *The Life of Archibald A*, p. 94)

"Mr. Graham was preaching. Little did I think, that I should ever preach in that pulpit, [Briery Congregation] and become pastor of that people . . . His text was Isaiah xl. 1, 'Comfort ye, comfort ye my people,' etc. . . . The good people of Briery were entranced . . . Dr. Smith [Rev. John B. Smith, Pres. Hampden Sidney College] afterwards said to me of this sermon, that it was the best he had ever heard, *except one;** and the one excepted was preached during the revival by the Rev. James Mitchell . . . Every mouth was filled with expression of admiration, and *from this time [circa 1789], Mr. Graham was considered one of the ablest preachers in the Land.*" (James W. Alexander, *The Life*, p. 58)

8. "His preaching was always interesting and instructive, often impressive in the highest degree."[680] (Edward Graham,

---

680 Edward, Graham, "Memoir of Rev. William Graham, A.M." The Evangelical and Literary Magazine and Missionary Chronicle, IV, (1821), p.75 et Seq.[published in a series.]

"Memoir of the Late Rev. William Graham A. M.,"[681] p. 411)
(Edward was William Graham's younger brother.)

9. *"Mr. Graham is here—Sage, deep-studied, Mr. Graham. He is Director of a small Academy in this neighborhood.* He retains, with Dignity, the inherent Gravity which he always supported in every Part of his Conduct while he was a Student at Nassau [Princeton]. The Lines of Method & Discipline have been inscribed & are yet visible & legible upon his countenance!

He spoke with Propriety; he preached, I believe, orthodox Divinity; & he seemed zealous. –I was entertained, I hope a little improved."

(Philip Vickers Fithian, *Journal . . . 1775-1776*, p. 170)

10. "Fri. April 1st 1791 . . . Sab 3. [April 3] . . . *Mr. Graham preached in the forenoon, one of the greatest sermons I ever heard. I sat under it with great delight, & its fruit was sweet to my taste. I had a sweet time at the communion."* (Rev. William Hill, <u>Autobiographical Sketches</u>, p. 64)

that we have provided above came from the same source Dr. Sanders relied upon in concluding that Graham's sermons

"lacked spark and his delivery was flawed."

Fortunately, Sanders provided this important clarification:

"During the revival, however, he became a new man and in 1794 he was "all alive." (Sanders, <u>Now Let the Gospel</u>, p. 15 col. 2, para 1)

It appears then that during Graham's earliest years as a pastor and educator, he, like most clerics, was less captivating than he later became. Most clerics, however, never receive the kind of preaching accolades that Graham would one day receive from some of the more gifted preachers in the land.

In the auditor's view, it is a mistake to evaluate a minister's preaching based on critical comments referring to a minister's earliest days in the pulpit.

ERROR no. 6. (Psalmody) Dr. Sanders relates an event that took place at New Providence congregation concerning psalmody in a way that adopts a version adverse to the reputation of Rev. Graham that which frankly, strains credulity. More importantly, his unnamed source got his facts twisted so as to be unrecognizable.

"Graham tried to pass out Watts' edition at the start of the service, *but an elder intervened, a confrontation ensued* and many worshipers walked out. Even Graham's friends

---

681 Ibid

believed that his innovation was unauthorized and rash" and
all "impartial men censured his conduct."[682]

*Caveat: Dr. Sanders relies on a normally reliable source, so
he can hardly be too strongly criticized on this point. See the
important extract below taken from Archibald Alexander's
memoir of his preceptor, William Graham.*

Alexander's statement includes the following:

For a number of years previous to this, there had been
much conversation and disputation about psalmody; and the
consequences were in most congregations, a transition from the
use of Rouse's version of the Psalms and Hymns to Dr. Watts.
But Mr. Brown had never thought it expedient to propose a
change, **tho the majority of his congregation were in favor
of the new psalmody.**[683] On this occasion, while Mr. Graham
was serving at the Lord's table and much feeling seemed to
be manifest in the congregation **he gave out one of Watt's
Sacramental hymns**, which was sung by most; **but one of
the elders was so offended, that he made an attempt to
stop the [preacher?] from proceeding. The innovation was
unauthorized & rash**, and the consequences were such as might
have been expected. One whole district of the congregation with
elder before mentioned, withdrew from the congregation; and
immediately joined with some Seceders in the neighborhood
in forming a church in connexion with that denomination. _"**All
impartial men censured the conduct of Mr. Graham in this
affair.**"_ (A. Alexander, Mss. "Memoir of William Graham," p.
217–218, hand paginated by the auditor; emphasis added with
underlined emphasis indicating error)

Sanders left out the fact that the majority of the congregation favored the
new psalmody by Isaac Watts and also left out the rather important fact that

---

682 I. Taylor Sanders, Now Let The Gospel Trumpet Blow,

683 Mr. Alexander was an eye-witness to the affair and he accounting of the facts we have no
reason to dispute, but it is also true that Mr. Alexander suffered on this occasion what some
refer to as, '**cognitive dissonance**', wherein Party A feels positive about parties B & C who are
in conflict. Alexander's preceptor, William Graham is involved in an incident involving some
of Alexander's close family members. Alexander's reliability on the facts of the matter are not
necessarily replicated on his assessment of, or judgment about fault in the matter. Alexander
was a teenager at the time of the incident and undoubtedly was unaware at that time as to the
policies of the Presbyterian General Assembly who had repeatedly studied the psalmody issue
and had admonished Presbyterians against the very actions taken by the caucus that attempted
to disrupt this holy communion service over Rev. Graham's use of one specific hymn. A fact
given here by Alexander. The idea of breaking up a congregation permanently and punishing
Rev. Brown and the congregation for this totally acceptable use of a hymn by Isaac Watt's, by
a visiting minister, is absurd on its face.

Graham merely handed out "one" hymn, not hymnals, as suggested by Sanders. In addition, Sanders neglected to inform his readers that the national Presbyterian Church had admonished all Presbyterians not to disrupt services over disputes centered around psalmody, a subject that was earlier addressed in great detail.

It is striking, however, to read words so critical coming from Archibald Alexander, whose youthful memory of the event obviously left an indelible impression upon his mind. Presumably, Alexander, at the time he experienced this event, was not aware of the National Church's policy authorizing the use of both versions of the Psalms in question, and it apparently had not occurred to his youthful mind that it is of great significance that the congregation in question's pastor, Rev. John Brown, obviously didn't share Alexander's concerns because neither he nor any of his congregants took the trouble to file a complaint with the presbytery. Sanders may not have been aware that Brown's congregation was already on the verge of a schism when the majority caucus invited Rev. Graham to preside at this communion service, a division that was no doubt inflamed by the recent revival going on throughout Virginia and Graham was then the leader of the revival in the Valley since the use of Watts's hymns was an integral aspect of that revival. Surely, everyone in the congregation knew that Watts's hymns would play some part in the service even before the service began. What is really amazing is that Graham was so moderate in his handling of this issue that he merely called for the singing of one hymn by Mr. Watts. This fact was admitted by Alexander in the above extract.

On this one occasion, Rev. Alexander's youthful conception of the political underpinnings of this event clouded his judgment as a reporter of the event. Unfortunately, Dr. Sanders failed to appreciate how Alexander's youth might affect his retroactive remembrance. It should also be pointed out that visiting pastors do not typically submit their sermons or hymns to congregations prior to conducting a service for the congregation's approval. Moreover, it was not "rash" to use a hymn written by an approved hymnist. Sanders's source on this occasion rendered a faulty judgment.

ERROR no. 7. Whiskey Rebellion Affair. Dr. Sanders presents an account of this well-known affair in the history of the Valley of Virginia in the eighteenth century that is based on one of Foote's two differing accounts. Unfortunately, he selected to wrong one.

Sanders selected the less reliable version presented by Foote and the one that unfairly paints the college's president William Graham in a far less attractive light than the facts warrant. Sanders's selected version was presented without any citation of primary authority, which is understandable because his source, Mr. Foote, also offered this account without reference to any authority. The other version Foote reprinted was written by the son of Rev. Moses Hoge, who relied on facts written by his father who had been an eyewitness to the event. Moses Hoge, the original source, played a critical role in the meeting of the Virginia Synod at which the "Whiskey Boys" controversy within the Synod took place. On this one occasion, the writer, Rev. Moses Hoge, had disagreed with his old preceptor, but

Moses's account of the dispute contradicts the version relied upon by Dr. Sanders. It is difficult to understand why Dr. Sanders relied on an unauthenticated account of this event. Perhaps he overlooked the second version located in a different section of Foote's book(s) and was therefore unaware of the contradictory account.

Dr. Sanders concluded as follows:

> "He [Rev. Graham] may have won few friends among his more affluent parishioners in 1794, **when he publicly supported the Pennsylvania "Whiskey Boys"** who had taken up arms to oppose the excise **tax on the drink**. (Sanders, *Now Let the Gospel*, p. 2; emphasis added)

In the above, Sanders is somewhat off the mark. First, there is no reliable evidence that Rev. Graham "publicly" took partisan sides in the controversy over the whiskey excise tax, which had been recently adopted by the federal government. Second, Sanders may have gone a bit too far by invoking the word *drink* because this dispute had little, if anything, to do with the proverbial "devil's brew." Instead, it was about the federal government taxing whiskey that was often made in order to be able to transport a valued commodity from the frontier settlements to the markets nearer the coast far more quickly, inexpensively, than grain, with the added advantage of no spoilage.

The farmers who grew the grain from which the whiskey was made were singled out by the new Congress and were the first of Americans to be taxed on a product by the federal government. The dispute was mostly about the federal government's authority to directly tax the American citizenry instead of their being taxed by their states. In sum, the issue had great public policy implications that extended well beyond whiskey.

As Moses Hoge pointed out in his private papers, Graham's primary argument on the subject centered around two separate issues. One was that the issue that the matter was a purely civil one and therefore beyond the jurisdiction of an ecclesiastical court like the Virginia Synod of the Presbyterian Church. The other issue centered around the concern about the federal government's authority to tax citizens directly.

Whiskey was in those days often used as currency in the marketplace. The tax was intended to raise necessary revenue for paying down the debts incurred by the various states during the course of the Revolutionary War. Whiskey, at the time, was made by farmers who did not have the ability to store their crops, and travel to better markets was exceedingly burdensome with grains. The tax therefore was asking a particular part of the public to pay a tax when it might have more fairly been applied to the general citizenry. That argument aside, Graham's opposition to Hoge's motion was actually focused on the more persuasive argument that the taxation of any product was a political and civic issue that was not properly a subject within the jurisdiction of an ecclesiastical court such as the Virginia Synod. These clerics and ordained elders quite rightly saw that Graham's view was the more persuasive position and therefore defeated Hoge's proposal.

Here is the way that Mr. Hoge, the son, presents the story of that day's activities as they related to his father's motion. The son's description is based on material left by the father in his journal:

> Mr. Hoge, after conference with some of his brethren, proposed—"That the Synod prepare an address to the people under their care, inculcating upon them the duty of obedience to the laws of the country. . . . *Mr. Graham opposed the resolution as uncalled for, and as prejudging in an ecclesiastical court the case of a people that felt themselves aggrieved politically by the practical working of a law of Congress, that pressed as tyrannically upon them as the Stamp Act upon the colonies.* The proposition [Hoge's motion] lost by a small majority. . . . An officer of high grade residing in Rockingham sent a demand of the yes and nays on the question, and the reasons for the decision. This was refused by the Synod as an assumption of power.
>
> (Foote, first series (1850) later reprint pp. 560–61; emphasis added)

Graham, according to this source above, had simply stated the case being made by the rebellious and so-called "Whiskey Boys" of western Pennsylvania. It is not inferred herein above what Graham's own view on the matter was. Hoge's meaning here is clear that Graham believed that the subject was a political matter outside the jurisdiction of the synod. In that, Graham was assuredly correct.

The locus of Graham's contention was clearly on the jurisdictional aspect of the matter not on the tangential question of how the "people" may or may not have felt about the issue. Sanders's description seems to focus more on the hyperbolic use of the descriptive "tyrannically" in drawing his conclusion that Graham may have won few friends among his more affluent parishioners, but of course, those are Sanders's words, not necessarily Graham's. Moreover, as Archibald Alexander made clear, his old preceptor was a man whose considered opinion did not alter let alone falter on the basis of what others might think, and Alexander believed that this tendency in Graham cost him potential allies. Graham was admittedly not a man who feared making enemies when a serious issue was at stake. By way of example, Graham actively opposed Gov. Patrick Henry on Henry's bill for taxing the people to support the church(s), and yet Henry became a major supporter and friend of President Graham. On the same vastly important issue of religious freedom, Graham openly challenged his clergymen colleagues and went over their heads to the people achieving in the process a great victory for the religious freedom that formed the basis of the "establishment clause" embodied in our nation's Bill of Rights. In the process he made several temporary enemies, but over time, his colleagues repeatedly selected Graham to lead their most important new programs including overseeing the committee to administer the church's internal missionary program and overseeing as president their only patronized theological seminary in the new nation.

Conclusion Regarding Sanders

Professor I. Taylor Sanders's *Now Let the Gospel Trumpet Blow*, despite its many virtues, failed to portray an accurate view of Washington and Lee's founding first president, Rev. William Graham and, unfortunately, perpetuates several myths that serve to wrongfully impugn the founder's reputation, myths that cannot be sustained and cannot bear close scrutiny. These myths in most cases are attributable to a campaign that was originally initiated by a few powerful and influential enemies and thereafter perpetuated by gossip and inexcusable selective perceptions fueled by agenda driven but otherwise well-meaning scholars unwilling to conduct scholastic investigation normally expected of professional historians.

By the time Dr. Sanders initiated his treatment of the early days of Washington and Lee, his predecessors had spun the same tall tales so many times that it is understandable that he could not comprehend how so many could possibly have been so wrong for nearly two centuries and therefore neglected to conduct the normally requisite investigations based on primary sources.

It goes somewhat without saying that if you begin with a faulty foundation, your superstructure is destined to collapse one day. Such is the case with Dr. Sanders's portrayal of Rev. William Graham. Sanders has painted a false picture of the man's scholarship, his ability as a clerical divine, as a pioneer in higher education, and his vast importance as one of the nation's founding fathers. Moreover, he overlooked the significance of Graham's few but astoundingly prescient published political works.[684]

Still, Sanders presented much important detail that had been neglected by most others, which will undoubtedly assist others yet to come who will hopefully one day construct a full and complete image of a truly remarkable person that trained many of the brightest stars who went forth on a quest west and south to accomplish our nation's manifest destiny.

Many of those who came under Graham's influence in the critical training periods of their lives built colleges and congregations throughout the emerging south and west. Colleges in Tennessee and Kentucky were built by men that he had trained. Two of the nation's earliest theological seminaries were built by men who trained under Graham and took with them the template he designed for the first theological seminary south of the Potomac. The originators of both Princeton Theological Seminary and Union Theological in Richmond were both students under Graham who patterned their seminaries after Graham's in Lexington. Editors, physicians, lawyers, judges, and professors had obtained their professional educations under Graham at Liberty Hall in Lexington.

---

684 Although published anonymously, his authorship has never been seriously contested by anyone other than Pres. Dr. Henry Ruffner, whose doubts were thinly based and demonstrably wrong on this point. See the sub-section devoted to Dr. Henry Ruffner.

Dr. Sanders seems to have also failed to acknowledge the courage that President Graham displayed in the field during the Revolutionary War when he served as the local militia's captain on two separate occasions and also in providing a college education to the first black college student and graduate in the nation, an act that was unparalleled and unequaled in the eighteenth century. That he accomplished this in the then-largest slaveholding state of the Union seems worthy of note and acclimation, but in Sanders's treatment, it receives but a faint tip of the hat. That Graham enrolled the nation's first female college student, for some reason, didn't even warrant Sanders's attention. Finally, like so many of those who went before him, Sanders failed to mention the college's first authorized history written by Rev. Caleb Wallace. This brief but documentary history is located at the very beginning of the record book containing the university's earliest meeting minutes, a source not easily missed when researching the college's earliest days. Of course, he only missed what every other historian before him either missed or dismissed.

Sanders's book is a good one and a thoroughly researched one, but the college's founder got short shrift by the author. Sanders could have and should have done better by him.

Note: Sanders and those before him did not have the ready use of computers that the auditor has had in the last couple of decades of his research. At the same time, original records dispel many of the myths that collectively explain the 1865 evisceration of the university's true and documentary-based history. Those records were extant and readily available to both Dr. Sanders and to his colleague, Dr. Ollinger Crenshaw. It seems that well-educated citizens of the great Valley of Virginia have developed over time an unusual fondness for their sleeping dogs.

28. JOHN WHITE STUART III

(John White Stuart, *The Rev. John Brown of Virginia (1728-1803): His Life and Selected Sermons*, doctoral dissertation, University of Massachusetts, 1988)

ERROR no. 1. Dr. Stuart mistakenly credits Rev. John Brown as a founder of the school that evolved into Washington and Lee University.

While nearly accurate, Stuart's quoted extract below is misleading because while it is true that Brown was a member of the alluded-to institutions, he was the only known member of the Hanover Presbytery that opposed the presbytery's creation of the seminary referred to as Augusta Academy. The presbytery meeting minutes rarely, if ever, recorded its members' votes, so his opposition is not reflected in the minutes, but Rev. Brown's opposition to the school is well-known to those familiar with his letters from that period. He would personally therefore never have publicly represented that he was a "founder" of a school whose founding he opposed.

> He [Rev. John Brown] was a founding member of the Hanover Presbytery, Lexington Presbytery, and the Synod of Virginia; and in a ministry notable for its **support and direction of classical education** in the Valley of Virginia, *he served as a founder of the school that evolved into Washington and Lee*

University. (Stuart dissertation, p. 1) (The underlined portion of this quote, technically the only correct assertion by Stuart on the subject of Rev. Brown's role vis-a-vis, Augusta Academy. The bold italics above, however, represents fundamental error.)

Dr. Stuart's assertion above is erroneous in large measure because he was, at the core, not a founder of the school that evolved into Washington and lee University, unless his role as an opponent of the founding of the school can be properly viewed as a founder. He was a clear and unquestioned opponent of the founding of Augusta Academy by the Hanover Presbytery, as his correspondence from that period proves. Nevertheless, he was a member of the Hanover Presbytery that did found the school and he may not have cast a dissenting vote when the final vote was taken, but then no record was made that reflects dissenting opinions so there is no way of proving the point. What is known, however, is that Brown voiced his opposition in written correspondence prior to the establishment of the college, and for twenty years after the Board of Trustees met for the first time on May 13, 1776 Rev. John Brown never attended a meeting of the Board of Trustees that met on every occasion in his own neighborhood.

ERROR no. 2. Dr. Stuart apparently assumed that Rev. Brown's letter to William Preston in 1783 announcing that he was reopening his Latin school was reflective of what actually transpired. It was not.

Technically, the Latin school may have opened, but if so, it was a lackluster event that only lasted for a very brief time. The fact is that there was no longer a need for such precollege instruction in basic Latin and Greek grammar because William Graham's preparatory grammar school located at the Liberty Hall Academy was providing that service and more nearby at the Timber Ridge location of the college. When Graham was having the academy's campus constructed, he offered a grammar school operation at "Mount Pleasant"; and when the college moved into its campus buildings at Timber Ridge, he moved the preparatory grammar school into the same quarters with the regular academic program. As Dr. Campbell explains in his *History of Washington College* (1838),

> "Mr. Graham now resumed the business of the academy, over which he had heretofore watched with parental care and solicitude. He had led it cautiously and tenderly through many difficulties to a certain stage of its existence. Besides the labor of teaching, and governing, there devolved upon him the task of planning, buildings; making contracts with the workmen; attending to the faithful execution of the contracts; the devising ways and means for fulfilling those engagements; and, in a

word, all that was to be done for the academy fell chiefly on him . . .

"During this long period he had, for the most part, performed all the duties in person, which in other public seminaries are confided to a faculty consisting of several professors. He not only gave instruction in the scientific and classical departments, **but paid special attention to the grammar school**. **"Here," said he, "should be laid a substratum on which to build a superstructure of learning**." (Dr. Samuel L. Campbell, "Washington College, VA," reprinted in W&L Historical Papers No. 1, 1890, p. 115.; emphasis here is not an error.)

Graham had learned from his own preceptor at Princeton, Dr. John Witherspoon, the multifarious value of conducting a grammar school as an auxiliary to a college. First, the college learns firsthand each student's preparedness when enrolling them into the college's regular academic program; plus, it serves as a valuable marketing device for the college since it operates as an obvious feeder channel into the college. Moreover, students with discipline or severe emotional issues can be removed before they become a distraction to the college's students and instructors.

ERROR no. 3. Dr. Stuart's speculations, shown in the extract that appears below, are at least misleading, if not technically incorrect.

> **"In 1783 Brown instituted a new "Latin school at N. Providence meeting house."** He may have conducted an English school without interruption, but he apparently had not sponsor college preparatory education **since Augusta Academy's move to Timber Ridge in 1776**. (John White Stuart, *Dissertation, John Brown*, p. 104; bold italics and underline here represents error.)

The fact is that by 1783, Liberty Hall Academy was functioning as both a chartered college and operating with an attached preparatory school. These two separate but closely linked entities were both under the direction of the rector (president) Rev. William Graham; therefore, there was by this time no real need for Brown to reopen his Latin school at New Providence. Brown's school had always suffered from its peripatetic nature occasioned by the predictable coming and going of its instructors.[685] Graham, who had conducted the grammar school at Princeton while himself a student at the college, was an experienced academic and scholar of the highest order. For that reason, only parents who may have had a grudge against Graham would have sent their sons to Brown for their preparatory

---

685 As Stuard has explained, Rev. Brown was himself not qualifies as an instructor and relied instead on the assistantance of recent graduates from Princeton, none of whom stayed very long at his school.

education once Graham was well ensconced at Liberty Hall in the same general neighborhood as Rev. Brown.

There is no indication in the valley of Virginia's records showing that Brown's Latin school ever reopened after the Revolutionary War. It appears the reopening was merely a dream that never materialized. This disappointing reality may explain why Rev. Brown's descendants chose to depict the then-defunct Latin school at New Providence as having merged with Liberty Hall Academy. In truth, if anything, some of Brown's pre–Revolutionary War students may have transferred to Graham's Academy after he closed his school in December of 1775. There is, however, no known record indicating any instruction taking place at New Providence after December of 1775, and by then Graham's Augusta Academy was already operating in temporary quarters at "Mount Pleasant." See the 1775–1776 journal of Rev. Philip Vicker Fithian, on page 170 listed in the bibliography. Fithian visited Graham's academy on January 18 of 1776. Fithian had already referenced Graham as the director of this academy on Christmas Eve day in 1775 (see page 150 of Fithian's Journal).

ERROR no. 4 - Stuart repeats Joseph Waddell's mischaracterization of the so-called New Providence congregation schism.

Both Stuart and Waddell before him mistakenly relied upon William Henry Foote's incorrect depiction of this event. For a more detailed explanation, the reader is directed to the subsections herein devoted to Rev. Archibald Alexander on this subject. **(*See also Stuart p. 124 and Joseph Waddell, Annals of Augusta Academy, 2nd ed., 1902, p. 342.*)**

ERROR no. 5: Stuart wandered outside the field of his expertise when referencing the character of William Graham and the early history of Washington and Lee University and in so doing misrepresented important aspects of both of these subjects.

Stuart's research was focused on the activities of Rev. John Brown, not on William Graham. He was obviously not aware of the animus toward Graham held by the matriarch of the Brown family, Mrs. John Brown (Margaret Preston Brown), who was mother to several influential sons, who naturally adopted her views about a man she despised and with whom they had little, if any, exposure. Most of the traducing of Rev. Graham are attributable to her, much of it indirectly through her sons and other descendants, who were fed with her gossip from childhood.

Had Stuart been exposed to more of the primary source material about the affairs of greater Lexington in the last quarter of the eighteenth century, he would likely have realized his errors regarding the university's founding first president. Had he been apprised of the fact that Graham withdrew his offer of marriage to Mrs. Brown's highly sought-after daughter "Ms. Betsy Brown" for the sole reason that her mother's vexatious meddling had doomed the young couple's likely successful marriage, Stuart would probably have reserved judgment about Graham.

Stuart's research about Rev. Brown, however, unearthed important historical information pertaining to that period, and his dissertation helps us to better understand the early history of the Presbyterian Church in Virginia during the period surrounding the founding of both our nation and Washington and Lee University.

As for Stuart's assertion of their existing a conflict between Mr. Brown and Mr. Graham, I find in all the published accounts of the affairs of the Presbyterian Church and of Liberty Hall nothing to suggest a conflict between these two men. Conflict, after all, implies the active involvement of two or more persons. Mr. Brown's actions and his correspondence suggests an animus, but I have yet to see any evidence of like feelings or behavior on the part of Mr. Graham. Admittedly, there may have been some bad feelings held by Mr. Graham, but there is no known evidence of that fact. I have not found support for this notion in the records or literature of that time. As for contemporary sources, I found the same result, the lone exception being an unsupported assertion by Dr. Sanders in his book, *Now Let the Gospel Trumpet Blow*. (See bibliography. See I. Taylor Sanders's, *Now Let the Gospel Trumpet Blow*, p. 22, n42.)

Note: Something important that was missed by Stuart and many others are the several implications of the so-called New Providence schism affair. Long after the breakup of Mr. Graham and Ms. Brown, Graham was invited by Rev. Brown's congregation to preside at the all-important communion service held at Brown's New Providence meeting house (church), which suggests that Rev. Brown and Rev. Graham were able to carry out their respective clerical responsibilities without incident. Based upon the facts surrounding this event, upon which there seems to be no disagreement, it is noteworthy that no complaint was ever filed with the governing presbytery by either Rev. Brown or any of the elders in his congregation.

Like the implications in Conan Doyle's The Hound of Baskervilles *and again in "Silver Blaze," Sherlock Holmes found great meaning in the fact that a dog did not bark. If there truly was a serious rift between Rev. Brown and Rev. Graham, as has been suggested by Dr. Stuart, it is difficult to imagine Rev. Brown's congregation inviting their minister's enemy to conduct their communion service; and given the apparent disruption that occurred during that service, the fact that neither Rev. Brown nor any of his elders bothered to file a complaint with the governing presbytery says a great deal on the subject.*

In this auditor's view, the animus that existed was held mostly by Mrs. Brown rather than by her husband. Whatever animus may have existed on the part of Rev. Brown, he does not appear to have allowed it to interfere with these two Presbyterian ministers' professional affairs. As concerns Rev. Graham, there is no evidence to suggest that he held any serious personal resentments toward Rev. Brown. All in all, the relations between the Brown and Graham families of that period appear to amount to nothing of consequence.

The College in Rockbridge County (Liberty Hall) succeeded far beyond the expectations of most, and its endurance has always been deemed to be attributable to the extraordinary efforts of its founder, Rev. William Graham. Certainly that was the view of the college's board of trustees in 1792 when they expressed their views in the quoted extract below, which is **Board of Trustees of Liberty Hall Academy** petition re Wm. Graham 1792 (on file at Washington and Lee's Leyburn Library [archives, file 41]). The emphasis that was added in the extract below are no case indications of error. Below then is a most insightful expression of sentiment given unanimously by the entire board of trustees, all of whom placed their signatures on this document. As such, it is perhaps the best evidence known to exist on the subject of how Rev. Graham was viewed by this broad cross-section of the small community's leaders.

> *Through the Presbytery of Lexington we are informed of the attempts of the Board of Trustees of the college of Hampden Sydney to deprive us of our Rector the Rev. Wm. Graham in order to convince him to accept the presidency of their college. . . . In our objecting to the removal of Mr. Graham, we would not in the least reflect on Trustees of Hampden Sydney for attempting to obtain our Rector from us for we think him qualified for such a place and that they need such a gentleman. But this so far from leading us to freely give him up as they wish does considerably increase our desire to retain him over our Academy. . . . Hampden Sydney can plead the necessity. On this [??] surely we are not behind them. **For it was under Wm. Graham that our Academy first received its existence and it is chiefly owing to his extraordinary exertions that it has persevered through all the convulsions of a calamitous War and the many vicissitudes which have taken place** through the operations of various causes for the space of about 16 years, and here we cannot forebear asking the question would it be wisdom or duty in Synod to destroy our Academy which has been the most useful to the church of any in the state and which is at this time more promising to the church in point of numbers than ever it has been, and this too on the bare probability that another may or nearly so must be the consequence unless providence preserveth it if our Rector be removed at this juncture. . . .*
>
> *For these and such reasons **your petitioners earnestly pray that this Rev'd Synod would not remove Wm Graham from his present charge of the Academy and we hope and trust that you will see reasons to grant the prayer of your petitioners.** And that the great head of the church may direct you in all things to seek and promote his glory as the object and prayer of the Trustees of Liberty Hall.*

We appoint Mr. John Wilson a member of our Board [??]* on our behalf to present our petition and to give such information as may be required.

> Samuel Lyle
> Alex. Campbell
> Wm. McKee
> Wm Alexander
> James Ramsay
> Jno. Wilson
> Joseph Walker
> John Lyle
> Samuel Houston

Petition presented to
the Synod from the
Board of Trustees
          Sept. 1792

These trustees' sentiments were underscored many years later by the man who presided over the academy after Rev. Graham's resignation and retirement.

*The words here are indecipherable by the auditor.

Dr. Samuel L. Campbell, an alumnus, trustee, and acting president of the college, wrote this in 1838:[686]

> "Mr. Graham now resumed the business of the academy, over which he had heretofore watched with parental care and solicitude. He had led it cautiously and tenderly through many difficulties to a certain stage of its existence. Besides the labor of teaching, and governing, there devolved upon him the task of planning, buildings,; making contracts with the workmen; attending to the faithful execution of te contracts; the devising ways and means for fulfilling those engagements; and, in a word, all that was to be done for the academy fell chiefly on him . . .

> "During this long period he had, for the most part, performed all the duties in person, which in other public seminaries are confided to a faculty consisting of several professors. He not only gave instruction in the scientific and classical departments, but paid special attention to the grammar school. "Here," said he, "should be laid a substratum on which to build a superstructure of learning." (Dr. Samuel L. Campbell, "Washington College, Va.," reprinted in W&L Historical Papers No. 1, 1890, p. 115)

---

686 Samuel L. Campbell, (M.D.)[i.e., "Senex"], "Washington College, Lexington, Virginia," Southern Literary Messenger, June 1838, at pg. 364.

29. MAME WARREN (1998)

(Mame Warren, _Come Cheer for Washington and Lee: The University at 250 Years_, Meridian Printing, East Greenwich, Rhode Island, 1998)

ERROR no. 1. Incorrect assumption of the university's date of origin.

The most significant error in Mame Warren's book, _Come Cheer for Washington and Lee: The University at 250 Years_ is found in the subtitle of the book because the subtitle assumes, incorrectly, that the school's origin is traceable to Robert Alexander's school founded circa 1749. Ms. Warren can hardly be held responsible for this mistake, however, since the university based the project on that inaccurate assumption, which was not made by the book's editor, Ms. Warren, but by the university and its guardians.

The institution originally, however, held that its date of origin was October 13, 1774, a position it held for approximately seventy-five years beginning with the Hanover Presbytery's meeting minutes for October 13, 1774. Tellingly, there is nothing that emanates from any person or institution prior to October of 1774 suggesting that the college existed prior to that time. Neither Robert Alexander nor Rev. John Brown left any representation in a letter or document of any type that indicates or asserts that their schools had any connection to the academy established by the Hanover Presbytery in October of 1774.

The college's first authorized written history appeared in May of 1776, and the college's first authorized and also published historical sketch appeared in 1849 in an appendix attached to the inaugural address of Rev. George Junkin. Both of these historical sketches were written by order of the institution's then governing authority. Initially, that was the Hanover Presbytery, but after the presbytery created a board of trustees in 1776 and once the new Virginia legislature granted an act of incorporation and a charter with degree-granting authority in 1782, the governing authority passed strictly to the board of trustees.

In each case, these two earliest authorized histories proclaimed that the school was created in October of 1774. So these matters remained until William Henry Foote challenged this orthodoxy by introducing a new view extending, as it were, the institution's life by twenty-five years, an innovation he failed to explain or justify. He simply asserted it as a fact, which the governing board of trustees in 1865 credulously adopted without comment. Five years later, one of the trustees who authorized the new history in 1865, Col. Bolivar Christian, added to the fiction with further nonsensical embellishments. In the process, he foisted a documentary hoax on the institution and on Virginia historians by concocting a fairy tale in which an early trustee and professor, Edward Graham, it was mistakenly asserted, played an important part. Of course, the evidence that dispels this fiction is well-known to most historians, but virtually, none appear to have appreciated the fact that the evidence refutes trustee Colonel Christian's mischievous pretensions. Christian pawns off a mysterious unsigned and undated sheet of foolscap with notations that contain speculations about the earliest days of the college, as being a manuscript history of the college's founding, listing several early instructors and students.

The document he believed to be a true and accurate history, however, is not anything of the sort. It does not reflect the considered views of Edward Graham on this subject. It is a ponderous set of preliminary notes that is fanciful and error-ridden.

Moreover, it constitutes a contradictory claim from those views published by the man Colonel Christian insists was its author. Edward Graham published a contrary account in 1821 in his memoir of his late brother Rev. William Graham (see bibliography). Moreover, other published authors corresponded with Edward Graham on the subject of the college's origins after Graham's memoir was published and relied upon him in that regard, a fact they all mention in their later published works. In every case, these authors give the college's origins as having occurred in the autumn of 1774, the last of these appearing shortly after Edward's death in 1840. Christian's unsigned and undated sheet of notes then had to have been created well before Edward Graham ever publicly opined on the subject. These facts disprove Colonel Christian's novel hypothesis.

In 1869, trustee Bolivar Christian wrote a historical sketch of Washington College that was in direct contravention of all previously published histories of Washington College, save the one written in the *Charter and Laws* pamphlet published by the college in 1865 without attribution, but which was most likely also written by trustee Bolivar Christian. Information on this, however, as pointed out by Dr. Crenshaw in his appendix to the unpublished two-volume version of *General Lee's College* is lacking.

Colonel Christian made no mention in his 1869 sketch that in effect, he was repudiating all the consistently represented documentary histories dating from the college's inception to the end of the Civil War. Christian also failed to mention that he was doing so without bothering to explain his radical departure from all published histories and all the official records of the board of trustees from 1776 to 1864, as well as the official records of the institution that created the school and created its first board of trustees. The same is true with regard to the 1865 article in *Charter and Laws* that was oddly entitled, "Historical Statistics." This the original institutional repudiation of the college's long-standing documentary history was, as previously noted, issued without attribution.

Aside from this, we find but one factual error, which has at its core the same issue with regard to the origin of Washington and Lee. The first entry in the "Chronology" section of the book on page 318 is incorrectly about Robert Alexander's school in Augusta County in 1749. To Ms. Warren's credit, she points out that dating the origin to Alexander's school is done based on "meager" evidence. She would have been correct if she had said "no credible evidence," because there is no eighteenth-century evidence that supports this notion. All evidence amounts to nineteenth-century ex post facto dreams that bear no resemblance to the truth and will not stand up to scrutiny.

In conclusion concerning Mame Warren's book *Come Cheer for Washington and Lee*, we note two additional errors, but both are errors only of omission. One is that Ms. Warren fails to note the vastly important role of the college's founder, Rev. William Graham. Mr. Graham appears on her pages as a minor player in a drama with a gargantuan cast. Certainly not a picture that would be recognized by the greater Lexington community of 1776.

Secondly, Ms. Warren's text is fairly devoid of any mention of the institution that created the college in October of 1774, namely, the Hanover Presbytery. This is the same entity that created the first board of trustees on May 6, 1776. Before the actions of the Hanover Presbytery, Mount Pleasant was a part of Mr. James Wilson's farm near Fairfield, where some years before, Rev. John Brown had overseen the organizing of a "Latin school" as he called it, but after separating himself from the Timber Ridge Church, Rev. Brown moved his private little preparatory school to his new farm surroundings on Moffett's Creek near his New Providence Church—a scene well drawn by Rev. Philip Vickers Fithian in his journal written down in late 1775 and early 1776.

> school" during the Revolutionary War after losing his tutor, Samuel Doak, to Hampden-Sydney.

The inferred connection between Robert Alexander's school and Liberty Hall depends entirely upon there having been a similar link between Alexander's school and Rev. Brown's Latin school, and here too there is no evidentiary chain linking any of the three entities. Ms. Warren's reference to Robert Alexander's school as constituting the first link in a chain misses the point that no such chain exists, a fact thoroughly examined in earlier sections of this report. In fairness to Mame Warren, her assertions in regards to the date of founding is entirely consistent with the current history adhered to by the university. She can hardly be blamed for its mistake.

Error no. 2. Ms. Warren includes in her chronology of the university at its beginning the educational endeavors of Robert Alexander. Her statement, as written, is not technically incorrect, but its mere inclusion as the chronology's first entry implies that there is a direct link when no such connection exists.

The entire purpose of Warren's book is to celebrate the university's 250th birthday when in point of fact, that celebration won't be appropriate until the year 2025. This celebratory book-publishing event took place approximately a quarter of a century too soon. The correct date for such a celebration is October 13, 2025. That is because the college's first birthday was celebrated on October 13, 1775, exactly one year after its nativity on October 13, 1774.

30. THEODORE DELANEY (2001)
(Theodore DeLaney, PhD, "Founders Day Lecture" [in regard to Rev. John Chavis] Washington and Lee University, 2001)

Still online in April 2017.

Caveat: While it's clear that Professor DeLaney was misled about the university's founder William Graham by the misguided Dr. David W. Robson (indirectly) and by Dr. William Cooper (directly), he deserves credit for illuminating a brighter light on the matriculation of John Chavis at W&L.

Dr. DeLaney's Founder's Day lecture delivered on January 19, 2001, is an important address that features the university's first black student, John Chavis, and yet it is flawed with respect to the university's first president, William Graham, who made the remarkable decision to enroll this black applicant in what was then the largest slaveholding state of the Union. DeLaney's mistake in this regard is somewhat understandable because he followed William Cooper's *Liberty and Slavery: Southern Politics to 1860* and Cooper, in turn, followed the then seriously misguided David W. Robson.[687]

Dr. DeLaney mistakenly says this about the college's first president:

> ***"Chavis' first year at Liberty Hall was the last year that William Graham served as rector***. (DeLaney, W&L Web site article based on DeLaney's lecture, p. 2, para three; emphasis here in bold italics and underline represents error.)

The university's records are incomplete, but the 1795 class list is extant showing Chavis as a member of the regular academic program so he was clearly there at least a year earlier than DeLaney represents. More importantly, Chavis was most likely there in 1794 as well. Most of DeLaney's sources who commented on Chavis's college preparedness mistakenly believed that Chavis was at Princeton for at least some of his college experience, but about that, they are all mistaken as has been shown in the attached appendix devoted to Mr. Chavis. In sum, on this point, the plan to prepare Chavis, advanced by Messrs. Samuel Smith and his brother John, went awry due to the serious illnesses of Dr. Witherspoon, whose maladies included complete late-life blindness and numerous serious bouts of vertigo that caused him to fall. As Princeton professor, John Murrin discovered there is no evidence at Princeton that Chavis ever attended instruction there of any kind. Indeed, there is only one term where that is even remotely possible. This auditor has not been able to locate any evidence that John Chavis was ever in the state of New Jersey. Here below are Murrin's comments on Chavis at Princeton:

> On September 27, 1792, the trustees voted to use the Lesley Fund ("for the education of poor and pious youth with a view to the ministry of the Gospel in the Presbyterian Church") on behalf of John Chavis, a light-skinned free black and Revolutionary War Veteran from Virginia. One of the most remarkable African-Americans of the antebellum era, Chavis

---

687 David W. Robson, "An Important Question Answered": William Graham's Defense of Slavery in Post-Revolutionary Virginia," *William And Mary Quarterly*, 3rd Series, 37, No. 4, (October 1980), pp. 644-652. (Note: An erroneous piece throughout based on the an incorrect assumption that the Joseph Glass "lecture notes" were transcriptions of Graham's lectures. There is no credible evidence that this notion is correct. Moreover, the evidence that does exist, suggests that they were not written by Graham but rather, were transcribed by Graham from the Witherspoon master copy during Graham's time at Princeton. Graham's lectures were never written down and were lost to history according to Graham's most important and earliest biographers, Professor Edward Graham, William's younger brother and Rev. Archibald Alexander, founding first President of Princeton Theological Seminary.

became a noted Latinist and a tutor to prominent white boys, particularly in the Magnum family of North Carolina. His name appears on no class list, but strong family tradition insists that he attended.[688] If so, he was the College's only black student before the mid-twentieth century, but he did not stay long. The one semester he would most likely have been at Princeton was the summer term of 1793, for which no class list survives. In other words, the family tradition may well be accurate and has been accepted by several generations of archivists at Princeton University. But unless Chavis entered with junior class standing, which seems highly improbable, he would necessarily have been assigned to the class of 1795 or 1796. For this reason, his biography does not appear in these volumes. (Dr. John M. Murrin, *Princetonians, 1784–1790* [Princeton, NJ: Princeton University Press, Introduction, p. lii)

The Rockbridge County court record referred to by both DeLaney and Chavis's biographer, Helen Chavis Othow, concerning John Chavis, was created by John Chavis's "own motion" wherein he himself asserts that he went through the regular academic program at Liberty Hall Academy (later, Washington College); and Chavis's representation in this regard was affirmed by the signatures of every sitting magistrate of the Rockbridge County court, including that of the college's trustee, William Lyle. Presumably, both Chavis and trustee Lyle knew very well where Mr. Chavis earned his college degree. Interestingly, another trustee, William Henry Ruffner, and superintendent of public education in Virginia would later affirm this in an article he wrote to posterity about John Chavis.[689]

What is of paramount importance here is that Chavis was not simply someone who attended a class or two at Liberty Hall Academy, but rather that he obtained his entire college education at Washington and Lee. Helen Chavis Othow, John Chavis's biographer, made the same mistake, believing incorrectly that Chavis received his education at Princeton, a belief that is not supported by one whiff of credible evidence. Ms. Othow, a descendant of John Chavis, relied upon supposition rooted in the Princeton early records that demonstrate that there was indeed a plan there to educate Chavis privately under the tutorship of the retiring president John Witherspoon. This flawed plan was advanced by acting president, Samuel Stanhope Smith. Smith, Dr. Witherspoon's son-in-law,

---

688   The known family traditions referred to only surfaced in the twentieth century are all are mere speculations. Chavis suffered from vision problems, which may explain the lack of extant correspondence from that period. In addition, several sources indicate that the Smith brother's plan was to have Chavis educated by Witherspoon privately. There was no known plan to have him matriculate in the regular academic program. At Liberty Hall, however, Chavis "went through the regular academic program" as evidenced by the Rockbridge County Court. See Chavis appendix.

689   William Henry Ruffner, *Manuscript Article "An Educated Negro Preacher of a Century Ago,"* n.d., cite: William Henry Ruffner Papers, 1848-1907, Accession 24814, personal papers, collection, The Library of Virginia, Richmond, Virginia. 5pg. [no.88?]

proposed to fund Chavis's studies from expected proceeds of the prospective Lesley fund.

The Chavis plan was destined to fail completely for three well-established facts that are indisputable. First, Dr. Witherspoon's health was precarious. He suffered from serious and dangerous dizzy spells complicated by blindness. Secondly, the Lesley fund was to be underwritten by proceeds of the late Mr. Lesley's estate, which became embroiled in legal disputes and was therefore not available at the time when it was most needed. Lastly, during this last period of Dr. Witherspoon's life, his affairs were complicated by serious financial questions that precipitated a detailed financial audit of the college's financial status that hinted at Witherspoon having acted improperly with respect to the college's funds. This scandal induced Dr. Witherspoon to spend much of his waking hours preparing for the detailed audit, and shortly after being cleared of any financial wrongdoing, President Witherspoon died. This calamitous close to Dr. Witherspoon's illustrious career at Princeton hardly fit him for carrying out his son-in-law's fanciful plan regarding John Chavis. That is why Princeton's records make no reference to John Chavis as a student there. Nor is there any reference to him by anyone associated as an official with Princeton in the eighteenth century.

Another serious mistake by DeLaney is his treatment of the college's first president, William Graham. DeLaney claims in a paragraph concerning Graham that he was a "proslavery apologist," but here he is simply following William Cooper's *Liberty and Slavery*. Cooper and his source, David W. Robson, were sorely mistaken about Rev. William Graham. The mistake of all three of these authors is rooted in the false belief that Graham delivered a lecture to his students on slavery and that a packet containing this lecture, which is housed in the archives at the Leyburn Library, are, in fact, the lectures of William Graham when they are obviously not. The lectures in question are actually copies made by a student, Joseph Glass, who copied them from someone else's copy of the original packet of Witherspoon's lectures that had belonged to Rev. William Graham. These were lectures written by Dr. John Witherspoon, president of Princeton, who was President Graham's own preceptor. Graham copied the lectures while a student at Princeton, and like at Princeton, the lectures were used as a kind of eighteenth-century textbook. Confusingly, in 1896, a professor at Washington and Lee University, Harry Waddell Pratt, copied this packet of lectures and created what served as a title page that was attached to the packet, but the horribly inaccurate text of that page was clearly written by Mr. Pratt.

Unfortunately, the version from which Pratt copied this currently held packet does not seem to exist. On the other hand, history has the testimony of the named student copyist's professor, Edward Graham, who makes it abundantly clear that Graham's lectures were never written out or transcribed and were lost to history. Moreover, Edward Graham also makes it unmistakably clear that Liberty Hall students copied Witherspoon's lectures and that they were used as a sort of textbook. Edward Graham's account of these lectures squares perfectly with those of his brother-in-law, Rev. Archibald Alexander, who relates much the same story as regards the use of Witherspoon's lectures at Liberty Hall.[690] Since both of these gentlemen lived in the rector's home during their matriculation at the college, they were in a particularly advantageous position to know about such matters. Fortunately, both of these early alums of W&L left published accounts that attest to the real facts that relate to the handwritten lectures from the eighteenth century that are extant.

Continuing to follow the aforementioned Mr. Cooper, DeLaney suggests that Graham "referred to black slaves as savages . . . and unfit for liberty." This is a loose translation, however, gleaned by Mr. Cooper translating David Robson. In truth, Graham wrote nothing known to history on the subject of African slavery in America that could be construed to be a defense of that peculiar institution. He did, however, write referring to "the horrors of slavery"[691] and also these words in his published "Essay on Government" in 1786:

REVEREND WILLIAM GRAHAM

"A Republic is a government, by equal and just laws, made by common consent, for the common benefit, *__and not the dominion of one community over another community__*, . . . which is founded in the perfect, political equality of all the citizens.

"Every violation of the perfect equality of the citizens, is a step towards tyranny.

"That government is excellent, which inviolably preserves the equality of the citizens, both in civil and a religious respect.

"Let us try to know our rights and assert our privileges, free from the heat of passion, or the prejudice of party. *__Let us remember that we are acting for ages; and let us endeavour to secure the applause and gratitude of posterity, by securing to them a precious birth right of perfect freedom and political__*

---

690 As if the subject wee not complicated enough, it is a fact that Edward Graham also had his own copy of Witherspoon's lectures and as a Professor at Washington College, he likely used the lectures of Witherspoon just as he had when he was a student at Liberty Hall. Since the packet's actual lectures do not identify the source of the lectures, each professor who elected to use them as a text-book, were also free to edit them and add a lecture of their own, if they so chose. Moreover, since the lectures were viewed simply as an educational tool, presumably some did do this. In Edward's case, he had once written an essay on slavery while a student and it was written as a submission in a contest sponsored by Governor Randolph, which he won. He may very well have added a slightly edited version of his essay to the packet he used with his students. It is more important, however, that whatever the lecture on slavery represents it does not represent a lecture by Rev. William Graham,

691 Mss signed letter from Graham to Col. Arthur Campbell, see bibliography.

equality. (Rev. William Graham, "An Essay on Government,"
Phil. 1786; emphasis added)

These are words that Graham not only wrote, but were also published in conjunction with a proposed state constitution. This constitution, unlike most every state constitution, did not provide a provision that protected a property right in slaves. Rev. Graham's views on slavery are best gleaned by his actions because he left no writing devoted exclusively on the subject.

DeLaney also unfortunately posited this thought in his web-published "Founder's Day Lecture" first presented in 2001:

"Apparently, Graham found free born blacks like Chavis much more acceptable.

Since Mr. Graham left no specific commentary on the subject of blacks or black slaves, neither history nor Dr. DeLaney really has any standard by which to make such a comparison. It were better had DeLaney not commented on this aspect of Graham's character because there is no known credible evidence upon which one might justifiably proffer such an odious thought, especially since such speculation flies in the face of the material provided above. To engage in such rank speculation about the only eighteenth-century college president in the United States who had the courage to enroll a black man into the regular academic program of a chartered institution with degree-granting authority is unwarranted treatment of the college's founding first president.

Graham's one written comment on the subject makes it abundantly clear that he viewed slavery as a "horror" and given his courageous act to enroll a black man into both his regular academic program and into his theological seminary at Liberty Hall, it would seem far more appropriate to honor the man's unmatched selfless acts in these regard and extend credit where it is undeniably due. To act as he did, as a leader in higher education in the United States while living and presiding over Liberty Hall in the largest slaveholding state in the nation, is remarkable in and of itself; but having done so in conjunction with his decision to enroll a married woman nearly hundred years before any of his fellow college presidents in the nation makes Graham a man worthy of the highest kind of praise. It took far less courage, after all, to admonish others from a great distance when to do so placed the critic in no real personal or professional danger. To act as Graham did under the circumstances was the personification of undaunted courage. If that were not true, why was no one else willing to follow his lead? Why also did it take his professional colleagues nearly a century to finally accept his prescient professionalism?

It should also be pointed out that it is indeed curious that about the time that Chavis would have completed his regular academic studies, Graham shocked the college and the Lexington community by resigning from the presidency of the college. Also interesting is the fact that while Graham resigned from the presidency, he did not resign from his presidency of the Lexington Theological Seminary.[692]

---

692 A worthy subject for a historian might well be, whether Graham presented Chavis' name to the Board of Trustees and some of the Trustees refused to sign his Diploma which could possibly

Chavis, having completed his theological training under Rev. Graham, applied to the Lexington Presbytery to be taken on trials for licensing as a Presbyterian minister at the first regular meeting of the presbytery following the unanticipated death of his preceptor, Rev. William Graham. He was quickly accepted by this presbytery and, in due course, became the nation's first black licensed Presbyterian minister in the nation. While on trials, Chavis traveled and preached to various congregations throughout Virginia. In this capacity, Chavis stood as proof positive of the ability of a black man to become a scholar, an educator, and a minister of the gospel, a feat not witnessed in that day in any New England state for nearly a century afterward.

DeLaney mistakenly informs his readers that the Graham and Chavis relationship "lasted only one year," but on this, he is also obviously mistaken. As shown earlier, DeLaney's timeline for drawing this conclusion is based on the false notion that Chavis had already been at Princeton before his enrollment at Liberty Hall. What is far more likely is that Chavis was under Graham's "care and tuition" in the regular academic program for at least 1795 and 1796 and probably in 1794 as well. Thereafter, he was under Graham's care and tuition in the theological seminary for two to three years. It was there that Chavis continued on under Graham for his theological instruction in preparation for the Presbyterian ministry. This conclusion is based on the reality that Graham is known to have continued on in training his theological students as explained by a fellow student, Conrad Speece,[693] who was a contemporary of Rev. Chavis.

Graham resigned from his duties as president of the college in 1796, but as explained by Rev. Conrad Speece, Graham continued to carry on his theological seminary in Lexington well beyond 1796. Rev. Graham was the preeminent theologian in Lexington where Chavis received his training. It was no accident that Chavis applied to the Lexington Presbytery for licensure as a probationary minister at the presbytery's first regular meeting following Mr. Graham's untimely and unanticipated death from pneumonia in 1799. Chavis was obviously studying directly under Graham at least during the years 1795–1799, some of that time at Liberty Hall in the regular academic program and some of the time devoted to theological study.

It is worth remembering that Graham as preceptor at Princeton impressed upon his students that were destined for the Presbyterian ministry that if their ministries took them into the Southern slave states that their primary concerns were with the souls of those under their care and that were of little value in that regard if they were driven from their communities over political controversies like the slavery controversy. At the same time, the slavery question was ever present

---

explain Graham's sudden unanticipated resignation. Chavis was accepted into the Theological Seminary over which Graham continued to lead, as evidenced by Conrad Speece's biographical sketch included in Sprague's Annals of the American Pulpit; or Commemorative Notices of Distinguished American Clergymen..Volume III, New York, Robert Carter & Brothers, 1858, pg. 366, [note appears on pg. 365, [This sketch submitted by Rev. Archibald Alexander D. D., Nov. 23, 1849.] The sketch is also re-printed in Foote's, Sketches of Virginia: Historical and Biographical, Series 2, 1855 pp. 351-352.]

693   See the entry for Rev. Conrad Speece in Sprague's Annals list in the bibliography.

in the councils of the national church during Graham's active role in the church. The church's policies were thoroughly discussed and debated in those years and one thing they consistently agreed upon was that slavery was both a political and a moral issue. On the moral question, it was agreed that as it was practiced in the colonies of Great Britain and later in the States, it was a blight on humanity but that as a political question, it was exceedingly difficult to find a real solution given the reality of a large segment of the population in several states that were in lawful bondage. That together with the fact that in large slaveholding states there were vast numbers of slaves that if simply emancipated en masse, vast numbers of them would thereby perish in short order for a host of practical reasons, including rampant illiteracy, lack of agricultural lands and tools, and language barriers between slaves and the rest of the communities.

In Virginia in the last quarter of the eighteenth century, there was a large slaveholding contingent, and radical emancipation would predictably bring emancipated slaves and the remainder of the community into direct conflict between the races that would likely result in the slaughter of slaves who rarely owned a firearm.

The Presbyterian Church urged their members to attempt to bring meaningful education to the slave community as a prelude to emancipation. Little in this regard was actually implemented, and what efforts existed were dedicated mostly to very elementary education. In Rockbridge County (Lexington), William Graham initiated a program designed to educate a free black man as both a teacher and a minister who could then carry both religious and regular education among both the black citizenry as well as the white. He began the program by experimentation, which proved eminently successful.

When Rev. John Chavis completed his regular academic program, Graham took him into his care for theological training. Once licensed, Chavis entered the Presbyterian missionary program that had him preaching to congregations, both black, white, and mixed, throughout Virginia. Chavis's very presence among these practicing Presbyterians demonstrated in the most vivid terms the reality that a black man had every bit as much chance of becoming educated as a white man. Thus far, Graham's plan was working as designed. Unfortunately, no one followed in his footsteps. Then quite unexpectedly, the noted educator and theologian William Graham caught pneumonia and died. His death came so suddenly that he never had an opportunity to hear his famous student preach the gospel that he had taught him. Chavis returned to North Carolina where his career suffered in the aftermath of slave rebellions and consequent legislative restrictions on blacks that severely limited his effectiveness. Nevertheless, Chavis remained connected to the Presbyterian Church throughout the remainder of his life, and he educated many young men both black and white in North Carolina.

Conclusion Regarding the Founder's Day Lecture of Dr. Delaney

There is great irony in Dr. DeLaney's sadly mistaken Founder's Day lecture because instead of honoring the founder of his university for his prescient and courageous leadership manifested by his decision to enroll a black man into a regular academic program at a chartered institution of higher learning with legislatively established degree-granting authority, he elected to traduce the only educator in America in the eighteenth century who had the standing within his community and among his clerical colleagues to fend off whatever criticism must surely have been heaped upon him and the college. His standing was so great that he was able to ensure that the student, John Chavis, was able to matriculate successfully and complete his academic program without any known disruptive incident impeding Chavis's completion.

At this time, the early to mid-1780s, Liberty Hall Academy had been reunited with the Virginia Presbyterian Church (Virginia Synod) who cosponsored the funding of the new stone buildings on the campus at Mulberry Hill. As cosponsors, the Virginia Synod of that church established the Lexington Theological Seminary, which shared facilities with the academy. This is the place where Mr. Chavis received his academic training and subsequently his theological training, with William Graham sitting as president of both entities in the same building.

There is no school record showing that the Liberty Hall Academy Board of Trustees extended a formal diploma to Mr. Chavis, but in that time, there were few formal commencements held at the college. Nevertheless, Mr. Chavis petitioned the Rockbridge County Court in 1802 as was then required by all free blacks, and therein he represented that he went through the regular academic program at Liberty Hall; all the sitting magistrates validated his petition by signing this court record. Among those magistrates was Captain William Lyle, a Revolutionary War veteran and a trustee of Liberty Hall Academy. William Lyle was the son of Samuel Lyle, an original trustee of Liberty Hall Academy, and William was appointed trustee to replace his father. Chavis's approved petition constitutes what is probably the best-evidenced successful matriculation at Liberty Hall Academy of any alumnus of the eighteenth century, with the possible exception of Professor Edward Graham, the president's younger brother, who, as an alumnus, served as a steward, an officer, trustee, and professor of the college.[694] Of course, President George A. Baxter, Dr. Samuel L. Campbell, and Rev. Samuel Houston's successful matriculation is also well established, but none of their descendants can point to a signed court record affirming their successful matriculations. John Chavis alone has such a distinction. Perhaps in due course the modern-day trustees will take steps to formally assert their well-deserved status as the only eighteenth-century college in the United States whose alumni includes a black graduate.

It seems entirely appropriate here to reiterate these published words written by the College's founder, Reverend William Graham taken from his published Essay on Government in 1786:

---

694   The auditor speculates that Edward Graham, the first Steward at the College on Mulberry Hill, probably shared quarters with Mr. Chavis in the Refectory building where the students took their meals. Mr. Chavis and Edward Graham were both mature men, and it is doubtful if the president would have invited the kind of unnecessary criticism that undoubtedly would have arisen had he moved Chavis in with the much younger students housed in the dormitory. Edward, being legally trained might very well have assisted Mr. Chavis in preparing his petition to the Court in 1802. Evidence to confirm this speculation, however, is lacking.

> **"A Republic is a government, by equal and just laws, made by common consent, for the common benefit, and _not the dominion of one community over another community_, ...which is founded in the perfect, political equality of all the citizens."** (Rev. William Graham, <u>An Essay on Government</u>, Phil. 1786.)

This sentiment expressed by the college's founder was written in defense of the proposed state Constitution that he had earlier drafted for publication which just happened to be the only such Constitution written in that time for a southern state that failed to include a provision for protecting a person's right to property in slaves. An omission that was the most likely reason he was burned in effigy by a riotus mob for having had the audacity to author such a Constitution. It is unfortunate that Dr. DeLaney decided not to reference these significant sentiments expressed in writing by his University's founder and first President in his Founder's Day Lecture.

Conclusion to the Author's Errors Section

The auditor decided to issue the first part of this report with only twenty-eight listed authors despite having assessed at least seventy. All the significant errors that have been published about the founding of the college and about its founding first president, William Graham, are found within the assessments of the included twenty-eight. Moreover, most of the errors are repeated in numerous variant forms, but very similar in their essence.

The most egregious early error made by authors before 1850 centers on the sequence of establishment of Augusta Academy (Liberty Hall Academy) and Prince Edward Academy (Hampden-Sydney Academy). Edward mistakenly assumed Hampden-Sydney was established before Augusta Academy. This error began with the president's younger brother Edward who first advanced this mistake. It was due to the fact that Edward had not yet arrived in Virginia at the time these actions took place. By the time Edward's father, Michael Graham, dropped Edward off at the home of Edward's older brother in late December or early January in 1776, both schools had already been established. Having learned that Hampden-Sydney's president Samuel Stanhope Smith had recommended William Graham to be the director of the new academy in Augusta, Edward must have assumed that Smith's academy was then already established. If so, he was wrong. Of course, when Edward took up his pen to draft his published memoir of his late brother in 1821, most of the eyewitnesses were no longer living, and Edward apparently did not have access to the original records of the Hanover Presbytery, which was the institution that created both of these academies.

The official records that did exist were apparently not easily accessed in this period; and when Mr. William Henry Foote initiated his extensive chronicle entitled, *Sketches of Virginia: Historical and Biographical*, which he issued in two series in 1850 and 1855, it completely mangled both the history of the college's founding and his professional reputation and credibility, as demonstrated in the above portions of this report. His motivations have not, as yet, surfaced, but he clearly was misled by individuals in whom he placed great trust. But whoever they may be, they seriously misled Mr. Foote, who, in turn, misled hundreds of subsequent historians.

The university, however, is blameless from the institution's inception up to and including 1849 when the college released its first authorized published history identifying the college's founding as being in the autumn of 1774 by the Hanover Presbytery.[695] This account accompanied the inaugural address of President George Junkin listed in the bibliography under President Junkin's name.

This account varies only slightly from the first authorized history located in the board of trustees' record book on it first few pages of text. It was written by the clerk of the Hanover Presbytery, Rev. Caleb Wallace, in May of 1776. This and the 1849 account are identical in all-important particulars. The very next year, William Henry Foote completely eviscerated the college's early history, and historians ever since have mostly danced to his miserable tune, most seemingly having never bothered to check any of the primary sources. At least not until Dr. Ollinger Crenshaw, late in his studies, smelled a rat, the stench being so odious that he couldn't bring himself to share the stench with the public.

His widow had the good sense to leave his papers to the university and therein this auditor discovered Dr. Crenshaw's shocking stock of startling earlier documentary evidence showing just how a credulous 1865 board of trustees instituted an Orwellian *"Newspeak"* revision that replaced fact with fiction. This outlandish mid-nineteenth-century scheme was foisted on an all-too-ready and credulous board of trustees by one of their own in the person of one Col. Bolivar Christian, whose colonelcy was apparently as dubious as was his postmodern baseless fairy tale about the founding of Washington and Lee University.

Having debased the original history of the origins of the college, the post-Foote historians haphazardly began their deconstruction of the college's founder, William Graham. Not willing to conduct their own original research, they appear to have engaged in a historical version of the old telephone trick wherein a written message is conveyed to someone verbally who then retells the story to another and so on and so forth until the original message becomes unrecognizable. Of course, in the case of Rev. William Graham, there are original documentary records with which to compare the later nineteenth-century traducement of the man most responsible for erecting an institution that became the Valley of Virginia's crown jewel, Washington and Lee University. The reader has been presented above with the documentary-based evidence that disproves many currently accepted falsehoods. What emerges are the following now well-established facts:

> * Washington and Lee University's nativity occurred on October 13, 1774, by the act of the Hanover Presbytery to

---

695 As evidenced earlier, this account was mistaken but only in terms of weeks.

establish and patronize a college in Virginia, west of the Blue Ridge Mountains.

* The two known educators that operated preparatory instruction mechanisms in the Valley of Virginia during the latter half of the eighteenth century, Robert Alexander and Rev. John Brown, had no connection to or involvement with Augusta Academy, Liberty Hall Academy, Washington College, Virginia, or Washington and Lee University.

* The first administrative leader of Augusta Academy, Rev. William Graham, had no predecessor and during the institution's first twenty-two years of existence was its only administrative leader.

* The founder and first president of Washington and Lee University, William Graham, was responsible for the erection of five successive campuses in the Rockbridge County vicinage between 1775 and 1796.

* As the uncontested leader of the Virginia Presbyterian Church during most of the last quarter of the eighteenth century, the college's president, William Graham, eventually emerged to lead the fight in Virginia to establish religious freedom and liberty as reflected by the defeat of the initiative to reestablish the Church of England in Virginia (now called the Episcopal Church). His successful campaign was a key to the adoption into the law the principle of religious freedom and liberty that shortly thereafter became the template for the establishment clause (i.e., separation of church and state) in our nation's Bill of Rights.

* Washington and Lee University's first president, William Graham, contrary to repeated claims to the contrary, was never censured by the Presbyterian Church.

* Washington and Lee's first president, William Graham, personally enrolled the first and only black college student into a regular academic undergraduate program in the United States in the eighteenth century.

* Washington and Lee University's first president, William Graham, enrolled the first and only female college student into a regular academic undergraduate program in the United States.

* Rev. William Graham was not the proximate cause of the schism that took place at the New Providence congregation of Rev. John Brown.

* The first president of Liberty Hall Academy established the first theological seminary in the United States of America south of the Potomac River at Liberty Hall Academy, having been appointed its president by the Virginia Synod of the Presbyterian Church. This seminary located at Liberty Hall Academy also enrolled into its regular class the graduate of Liberty Hall Academy, John Chavis. Thereafter, Mr. Chavis with his theological credentials from the Lexington Theological Seminary[696] intact was accepted and licensed as the nation's only black Presbyterian minister in America.

* Rev. William Graham embraced the Presbyterian Church's national policy on African slavery and facilitated the education of the nation's first black college graduate and prepared that student, after graduation, for the Presbyterian ministry, this feat accomplished in the largest slaveholding state in the nation.

* President William Graham left no written lectures for posterity and indeed never wrote one out. Moreover, there exists no evidence that he ever spoke publicly on the subject of African slavery in North America.

* As a direct result of President Graham's unmatched courage to enroll a black man into his regular academic program, Graham and the student, John Chavis, proved to the world that the black man was just as educable as are those of the Caucasian race. That student, having also been trained theologically by Graham, went on to become the nation's first black Presbyterian minister, and he preached the gospel to Presbyterian congregations throughout many regions in Virginia. The symbolism of this graduate of Washington and Lee University (the Liberty Hall) standing before congregations of persons of all races in America belied the racist denigrations of the Negro as uneducable and dispelled this myth forever. To his colleagues' and successor's shame, none would rise to follow in the first president's footsteps for over a century.

---

696 This name was adopted informally by Edward Graham in his published "Memoir of the the Late Rev. William Graham." See bibliography.

president, William Graham, traveled on a perilous journey to Philadelphia soon after his arrival in Virginia (1775–1776)[697] with funds to purchase a library and various laboratory apparatus requisite for providing advanced college-level instruction. The list of the books purchased reflects those with which he was thoroughly familiar from his days as a student and instructor at Princeton under the renowned Dr. John Witherspoon, his own preceptor. The list is extant at the university's Leyburn Library.

The above are conclusions reached during the course of this audit. The various errors identified in this section have been authenticated as well as can be accomplished with the sources now known to us. The fact that so many errors by so many authors have been made over the course of more than two centuries should not detract from the well-earned praise and respect the listed authors deserve for their many efforts, with but a very few exceptions where we discovered what seems to be unmistakable deceptions.

The university and its staff, faculty, and administrators have gladly made their records available for this project; and without doubt, the discoveries made herein were only made because of their commitment to openness and administrative cooperation.

---

697 Skirmishes between colonists and British forces were already taking place in the days leading up to the Declaration of War (Declaration of Independence.)

Conclusions and Recommendations

This audit had revealed that the history of Washington and Lee University as presented by the institution since 1869 is unquestionably incorrect. All known documentary evidence demonstrates beyond any reasonable doubt that the university's origins are precisely determined to be October 13, 1774. The erroneous representations to the contrary have been repeated by the university since it was first introduced into *The Charter and Laws and Trustees and Faculty of Washington College* in 1865.

The error in this regard is no harmless administrative or perfunctory mistake, but rather a monumental failing on the part of an institution that prides itself on scholarship and professionalism. The gross errors, while most likely unintentional, are nevertheless of such great importance to the history of Virginia that it clearly calls for forceful action to acknowledge the error and to make appropriate amends for allowing a false history to be presented to the public for over a hundred and fifty years.

What makes these mistakes doubly embarrassing is that there were at least ten written historical accounts of the institution's early history published during its first seventy-five years of existence that were all basically correct and widely known at the time. In addition, there were accurate institutional accounts of the school's origins dating to as early as May of 1776 and as late as 1849. In the ensuing years, there have been a myriad of opportunities to identify and correct the mistakes, but by failing to apply basic elementary tests of proofs, an unsupportable deviation in the historical account of the institution's founding was allowed to persist, unchecked by generations of historians, both within and without the walls of the institution.

Since the institutional error emerged in 1865, hundreds of publications from books to newspapers have been distributed to hundreds of thousands of researchers and readers, including the university's alumni, containing an utterly inaccurate history and date of origin. A tainted history, of course, will eventually be revealed, and when it does, the revelations cannot help but taint an institution's reputation. Any professional public relations expert will readily admit that when faced with such a reality, redemption will only be realized following institutional recognition of the error. In the aftermath, an active program to remedy the problem is the only way to convince a suspicious public that true recognition has indeed occurred. Our report includes a set of recommendations designed to remedy the numerous problems that exist as a direct result of the inaccurate history foisted on an unsuspecting public.

Discovering the reasons why such important historical errors were made and then allowed to persist over time is beyond the scope of our audit's original objectives. It is nevertheless important to appreciate the climate of the times in which the historical mistakes were allowed to become accepted orthodoxy in light of earlier accurate published and unpublished but well-known accounts.

The first significant errors that surfaced were presented to the public in two widely acclaimed and often-cited books published by Rev. William Henry Foote under the titles _Sketches of Virginia, Historical and Biographical_ and issued as series 1 and series 2 in 1850 and 1855 respectively. A reader can find in these two books accounts that are reasonably accurate and others that are egregiously wrong. Unfortunately, Mr. Foote received numerous proposed contributions and simply included them based presumably on his whim. So much of what he included was printed without attribution or citation of authority that it is difficult for anyone to sort the wheat from chaff. The public, however, is indebted to Mr. Foote for collecting and publishing a vast array of critically important documents that otherwise would likely have been lost. This indebtedness, however, does not excuse his abandoning well-established norms that call for citing authority when the authority is known, nor does it excuse misleading methodology wherein the chronicler inserts his own notions in the midst of original material that has the effect of altering in significant ways the original material's clear meaning. This report includes sufficient examples to make the point.

The mistakes made by Mr. Foote do not, however, exculpate the guardians of the institution's well-being, the board of trustees, to ensure that sloppiness or mischief making do not contaminate an otherwise pristine long-established history gifted to the institution by its fathers.

There were two inescapable realities that surfaced during our extensive research that frankly shocked the auditor. One was the discovery of the first written account of the establishment of the institution, which appears on the first few pages of the record book that houses the original meeting minutes of the board of trustees, and second, our discovery of the first institutionally authorized published sketch of the history of the institution, both of which were inexplicably contradicted by the revised institutional accounts since 1869. The historical account set forth in the very beginning of board of trustees' record book containing the board's minutes was constructed directly from the pertinent meeting minutes of the Hanover Presbytery, which few have ever disputed, was responsible for establishing the institution. This account details the events leading up to the establishment. It was written by Rev. Caleb Wallace, acting as secretary of the Hanover Presbytery, and dated May 1776. As such, its historical value is beyond measure. The second historical sketch is included as an appendix to the inaugural address of President George Junkin, all printed by order of the board of trustees.[698]

---

[698] No authorship attribution attaches to this sketch, but it can accurately be represented as the product of the Board of Trustees irrespective of who actually drafted the sketch. It was almost certainly based on the original manuscript history of Washington College written by President Henry Ruffner who was still an integral part of the college when Dr. Junkin was inaugurated as Ruffner's successor. Ruffner's history remained, at the time, unpublished. Slightly revised in 1857, Ruffner's lengthy article was not published until 1890. Ruffner has been acknowledged by many nineteenth and twentieth century historians as the college's first true historian. See _Washington and Lee University Historical Papers_, Vol. 1, 1890.

Importantly, these two primary sources are virtually never cited by historians. On the subject of the origins or "establishment" of the Washington and Lee University, they are in absolute agreement as to the year and the month of the establishment. They vary only on the specific day and then only by a single day, a difference attributable to the fact the meeting of the Hanover Presbytery took place over the course of several days. These two institutionally recorded accounts only differ from what is today being represented by the university by a quarter of a century. The university was founded on October 13, 1774. The university over the years has represented that the school was founded in 1749, or alternatively 1748, and one even claims 1752 as the date of the founding. All representations made by the university since 1865 have been false.

This gross error has served, among other things, to obscure the true significance of the university's founder and first president, Rev. William Graham. The assertion that William Graham is the founder and first president is not an original idea of this audit report; it was an idea propounded by, among others, one of Washington and Lee University's most illustrious alumni, Dr. Archibald Alexander, founder and first president of the Princeton theological seminary while appearing before the alumni of Washington College on June 29, 1843, when he said,

> I cannot conclude this address without pronouncing a brief eulogy on the man who deserves to be called the *Father of the College,* and whose memory should be venerated by all its Alumni. I mean the Rev. William Graham. (Address to the alumni, W&L Historical Papers, vol. 2, 1890, p. 128; also published in a limited edition in Lexington, 1843, p. 128) (Emphasis added)

In his unpublished "Memoir of William Graham," Dr. Alexander added the following comment, which was also included in his son's biography of his father. Alexander says this:

> "Mount Pleasant should be considered as a kind of consecrated spot; and altho' it is now, like Shilo of old,[699]a desolation; yet it would be well, **especially for the surviving pupils of Mr. Graham, to erect a monument on that spot, as a memorial of the first classical school instituted in the Valley,** But stone, marble, & brass are perishable substances: we want a memorial more enduring than those; and this can only be erected by a faithful history of this institution & its founder, (William Graham) which we are now attempting to furnish. (Emphasis added here does not indicate error.)

(Rev. Archibald Alexander D. D.)[700]

---

699 "Shilo of old" is ancient biblical references found in the Old Testament books of Joshua and Judges and refers to ancient ruins of the capital of Israel before Jerusalem.

700 Mss, "Memoir of William Graham," hand-written by A. A. & paginated by this writer. Pg. 45.

Recommendations

1. Adopt and publish the essence of the "Brief Sketch of the Early History of Washington and Lee University" that is located in this report or publish an entirely new history based on the official records of the Hanover Presbytery between 1771 through 1776 and the official records of the first board of trustees as found in the first record book of Liberty Hall Academy.

2. Circulate a memorandum of error from the current board of trustees and include the publication referenced in number 1 to at least all of the following:

> * All departments and programs at Washington and Lee
> * The Virginia Historical Society
> * *The Virginia Magazine of History and Biography*
> * The Virginia Department of Education
> * The Library of Congress
> * *The Chronicle of Higher Education*
> * *The William and Mary Quarterly*
> * The Virginia congressional delegation

* The Governor of Virginia

> * The leaders of each house of the Virginia General Assembly

* The standard press outlets
* All universities in Virginia
* Union Theological Seminary in Richmond, Virginia

3. Create a fund-raising committee to underwrite the erection of a monument honoring the university's founder and first president, Rev. William Graham, whose contribution to the university's very existence is unmatched.

4. Formally reinstate the school's initial date of origin as October 13, 1774, by resolution and issue a press release to the state and national media announcing this action with appropriate apologies for having failed as guardians of the institution's history to protect a clear and well-documented original history of the university's founding.

5. Fund the creation of a professional restoration of the university's original and true history.

6. Establish a dedicated endowment fund to build a replica of the old Liberty Hall Building on Mulberry Hill to house a university museum and to maintain that museum in perpetuity.

7. Name the new museum as the William Graham Historical Center (Old Liberty Hall).

8. Fund a bronze sculpture of the likeness of William Graham to be mounted on a large granite monument to stand in front of the colonnade. The monument

should have a mounted bronze tablet that identifies the lifelike sculpture as "Washington and Lee University's Founder and First President, Rev. William Graham (1746–1799)"

9. Initiate negotiations to purchase the parcel of land once known as Mount Pleasant, which is where the university's birth took place in 1774 and where the institution located its temporary headquarters during 1775–1776 for launching Liberty Hall Academy, which included conducting preparatory classes in the form of a grammar school for students wishing to matriculate once the construction of the new buildings were completed at Timber Ridge, which took place between November of 1776 and early 1777. (Note: The location is described in John M. McDaniel, Kurt C. Russ, and Parker B. Parker's *An Archaelogical and Historical Assessment of the Liberty Hall Academy Complex 1782-1803* [Lexington, Virginia; Liberty Hall Press, 1994], James G. Leyburn Papers in Anthropology, vol. 2, 1994.)

10. Formally recognize that Mr. John Chavis earned his BA degree in 1796 and conduct a special ceremony to honor him as the first black college student and graduate in America.[701]

the auditor's discovery of the early Rockbridge County Court Order memorializing the fact that Mr. John Chavis, who was well known to the court, was believed by the court to have gone "through a regular course of academical studies," signed by all sitting magistrates including trustee Capt. William Lyle. This order was from the court's April term of 1802. See Rockbridge County, Virginia Order Book, 1802–1802, p. 10 (reel 36) (Archives Research Services, the Library of Virginia).[702]

---

701 As explained elsewhere in this report, Rev. John Chavis filed with the Rockbridge County Court a affidavit attesting to the fact that he went through the regular academic course at Washington College [Liberty Hall Academy] when it was a chartered with full degree granting authority by the Virginia Legislature. This affidavit was agreed to by all the sitting Magistrates, one of whom, Capt. William Lyle was a Trustee of the College. I has also been attested to by President Henry Ruffner in a mss. Entitled, Article "An Educated Negro of a Hundred Years Ago," n.d., cite: William Henry Ruffner Papers, 1848–1907, Accession 24814, personal papers, collection, The Library of Virginia, Richmond, Virginia.

702 *This record is copied in the biography of John Chavis, by Helen Chavis Othow, but the copy does not reveal the name of Magistrate William Lyle, as does the auditor's copy which was obtained directly from the Library of Virginia.*

Audit Bibliography

(* Items found in the writer's personal collection)

* **Abernathy, Thomas Perkins**. *From Frontier to Plantation in Tennessee, A Study in Frontier Democracy*. Chapel Hill: University of North Carolina Press, 1932.

*————. *Historical Sketch of the University of Virginia*. Richmond, VA: Dietz Press, 1948. Wraps, 61.

* **Adams, Herbert Baxter**. Thomas Jefferson and the University of Virginia, Washington, 1888 (see especially chap. 22 [Washington and Lee University by Professors White and Harris, i.e., W&L professors Carter J. Harris and James J. White] and chap. 23 [bibliography of Washington and Lee University] pp. 293–308. The whole supplemented by a letter from John Mason Brown [great-grandson of Rev. John Brown that is riddled with errors and false assumptions] part of US *Bureau of Education Circular of Information No. 1, 1888; Contributions to American Educational History, edited by Herbert B. Adams, No. 2*. The letter begins on page 305.

*Alexander, Archibald, DD. "Address delivered before the Alumni Association of Washington College, Virginia," delivered June 29, 1843, Lexington, VA. R. H. Glass, 1843, 31 pp. Also in Washington and Lee Historical Papers No. 2, Lexington, VA, 1890. (Note: My copy is in wraps and includes two articles: Alexander's address, delivered June 29, 1843, and "The Founders of Washington College" by Hon. Hugh Blair Grigsby, delivered June 22, 1870.)

*————. "An address before Alumni of Washington College, Virginia. Delivered June 29, 1843, limited edition, and also in Washington and Lee University Historical Papers, No. 2, Lexington, VA, 1890. (Note: Auditor's copy is in wraps and includes two articles: Alexander's "An address . . .," delivered June 29, 1843, and "The Founders of Washington College" by Hon. Hugh Blair Grigsby, delivered June 22, 1870.)

*————. Biographical Sketch of Rev. William Graham in Wm. Sprague's Annals of the American Pulpit, Vol. 3. New York: Robert Carter & Brothers, 1858 (but dated in the text as 1849), pp. 365–370.

*————. _Biographical Sketches of the Founder and Principal Alumni of the Log College_, subtitled and referred to by many as "The Log College," Philadelphia, 1845, and reprinted in a second edition in 1851.

*————. Mss "Memoir of The Rev. Wm Graham," [written in longhand] the Rev. Graham portions of this manuscript constitute the largest part of a writing entitled, _Great Valley of Virginia_. My photocopy came from the Princeton Seminary Library in 1989. It is also available in spiral-bound form at the Leyburn Library, Washington and Lee University.

*————. Letter to his sister Margaret (Alexander) Graham (wife of Edward Graham). July 19, 1803. (See Alexander's biography by his son James, p. 274.)

"Dear Sister:-" "By John Chavis I received yours, and pass over all the rest to answer that part in which you express some uneasiness at my entertaining doubts respecting the genuineness of the Kentucky revival. (Alexander, James, W., _The Life of Archibald Alexander, DD_ [New York: Charles, Scribner, 1854], p. 274)

*Alexander, James W., DD. _The Life of Archibald Alexander, DD_. New York: Charles Scribner, 1854.

*————. _Forty Years' Familiar Letters of James W. Alexander_ (2 Vols., New York, 1860), edited by Dr. John Hall. [pdf]

*Alexander, Samuel Davies. _Princeton College during the Eighteenth Century_. New York: Anson D. F. Randolph & Company, 1872. _(On p. 163, he includes a brief sketch of Rev. Wm. Graham, which is mostly correct, but mistakenly implies that his school already existed when he arrived in Virginia, but it was entirely new and designed from its inception by Mr. Graham. He also erred by suggesting that Graham was not much given to reading books, which was only true as regards the study of theology, and here he stressed thinking in light of the scriptures.)_

Alexander, James A., J. Carnahan, and A. Alexander. MS "Notices of Distinguished graduates," referring, of course, to graduates of Princeton. (This item is suspect in those parts represented to be written by Archibald Alexander because they may have been altered by his son, James W. Alexander, something James did in his biography of his father and, in so doing, made egregious mistakes in his father's name.)

John De Witt, John. "Archibald Alexander's Preparation for His Professorship." _Princeton Theological Review_ 3 (1905).

Alexander, Samuel Davies. _Princeton College During the Eighteenth Century_. New York: Anson D. F. Randolph & Company, 1872. _(On p. 163, he includes a brief sketch of Rev. Wm. Graham, which is mostly correct, but mistakenly implies_ *that his school already existed when he arrived in Virginia, but it was an entirely new endeavor and designed implemented and overseen from its inception by Mr. Graham. He also erred by suggesting that Graham was not much given to reading books, which was only true in the limited context of the study of theology, and here he stressed thinking in light of the scriptures.)*

*American Historical Quarterly. "The History of Washington College, Virginia." Vol. 10, 1838, pp. 145–150 (Authorship attributed to Rev. William Hill), cited in Ollinger Crenshaw's *General Lee's College* (unpublished footnotes [typescript] Washington & Lee University Archives/Library). "Vol. II, "Appendix "A"] hand-paginated in pencil as p. 526 (based in large measure upon an article entitled by Rev. Dr. William Hill [Hampden-Sydney] in **Southern Religious Telegraph** [Richmond] Dec. 19, 1834, Jan. 2, 23, Feb. 6, 1835 [serialized form] and also relying on a letter to the unnamed author from Edward Graham, Esq., of Lexington, Virginia). This bibliographer has a photocopy of the article from the *Am. Hist. Quarterly*, but not the 1834 serialized articles. These articles, according to Ollinger Crenshaw, date the history of the college from the 1770s and the actions of the Hanover Presbytery.

*Garrett, William R. Ed. "The Provisional Constitution of Frankland." *American Historical Magazine* 1 (1896). Nashville, Tennessee. Printed by the University Press. 48–63. (from the Filson Club)

An Article, "Rev. William Graham, Founder, and Rector of Washington and Lee" in the *Lexington Gazette*, Vol. 107, No. 19, May, 10, 1911; An article "William Graham, Founder of Washington and Lee, Teacher, Preacher, and Patriot," *Rockbridge County News*, May 5, 1911, Trustee [W&L], (see I. Taylor Sanders's *Now Let The Gospel Trumpets Blow*, p. 74). The *Rockbridge County News* article is an abridged version of an address delivered by Mr. Anderson in conjunction with the reinterment of the remains of Rev. William Graham, which took place on May 5, 1911. The complete address is located in the *Lexington Gazette*. The difference in the two versions is of vast historical importance even though the complete version is error ridden and the abridged version, as far as it goes, is essentially accurate. The *Rockbridge County News* abridgment of the complete address is not identified in the newspaper as being abridged.

Anderson, William A. A letter from trustee Anderson to the Board of Trustees, typed and dated June 17, 1901, and addressed to the Rev'd G. B. Strickler, DD, rector of Washington and Lee University.[703] (This letter is very important and mostly accurate historically although the author's principal argumentation is fundamentally flawed insofar as he claims the trustees were bound, in honor, if nothing more, to maintain the institution nondenominational in perpetuity,

---

703 Probably "rector" is here an inappropriate designation because, that term was discontinued for the chief operations officer, and replaced with the title "president" many years earlier, and thereafter the term "rector" was used to designate the leader of the Board of Trustees.

which, as he well knew, as a lawyer, one group of governors may not bind future governors to any such pledge excepting perhaps by the exercise of a legal contract, but a contract of that sort may not bind future governors on any matters of policy.)

*Archives of the State of New Jersey, First Series, Vol. XXIX, [Tenth Volume of Extracts From American Newspapers Relating to New Jersey, Paterson, N.J., The Call Printing and Publishing Co., 1917, p. 52.]

*"Augusta Academy." *West Virginia Historical Magazine*, vol. 5, no. 1 (January 1905): 9–15. (Pdf Google Books)

Banning, Lance. "James Madison, the Statute for Religious Freedom, and the Crises of Republican Convictions, pp. 122–123, *The Virginia State for Religious Freedom, Its Evolution and Consequences in American History*. Merrill D. Peterson and Robert C. Vaughan, editors (Cambridge NY: Cambridge University Press, 1988).

***Baxter, Hon. Sidney S.** "Notes on the History of Washington Academy and College from 1799 to 1829." W&L Hist. Papers, Vol. 3, pp. 45–63.

***Beadie, Nancy and Kim Tolley.** *Chartered Schools: Two Hundred Years of Independent Academies In the United States, 1727–1925*. New York and London: Routledge Farmer, 2002, 364.

***Beam, Dr. Jacob Newton.** "Dr. Robert Smith's Academy at Pequea, Pennsylvania." *Journal of the Presbyterian Historical Society*, vol. VIII, no. 4 (Dec. 1915): 145.

***Bean, William Gleason.** "Liberty Hall Volunteers: Stonewall's College Boys." University Press of Virginia, 1964, 227. Also "Civil War History," vol. 11, no. 4 (December 1965).

***Boley, Henry.** *Lexington in Old Virginia*. Richmond, Garrett and Massie, 1936.

***Bowden, Henry Warner.** "Science and the Idea of Church History: An American Debate.: *Church History*, vol. 36, no. 3 (Sept. 1967). (Imp re Herbert B. Adams the historian (T. J. and the Univ. of VA). (Photocopy)

***Bracken, R. J.** "Lest We Forget," article memorandum subtitled "A condensed compilation of persons and events made by R. J. Bracken, of Pittsburgh, Pa., in the year 1967." On file in the William Graham folder of the Leyburn Library at Washington and Lee University. Mr. Bracken is a descendant of Rev. William Graham through his grandmother Mary (Graham) Bracken (dau' of Rev. Wm. Graham founder of W&L University) who married Rev. Reid Bracken on May 1, 1806.

*Bradshaw, Herbert C. *History of Hampden-Sydney*. Privately printed 1976, one of the oldest private colleges in the US, Michael Graham's (the younger) son, Rev. Samuel Lyle Graham, was an early professor there and is buried in the college's cemetery. In 2006, it is still an all-male college.

*Brinkley, John Luster. *On This Hill*: *A Narrative History of Hampden-Sydney College, 1774-1994*. Hampden-Sydney, 1994, 880 pp.

*Broderick, Francis L. "Pulpit, Physics and Politics: The Curriculum of the College of New Jersey, 1746–1794." *The William and Mary Quarterly*. 3rd Series, vol. 6, no. 1 (Jan. 1949): 42–68. (jstor copy)

Brown, John (Rev). Letters to William and John Preston. 8 June 1764–26 Feb 1784. MS. Preston Papers of the Draper Manuscripts, State Historical Society of Wisconsin, Madison, 2QQ49-5QQ119. (See extracts in John White Stuart III's Dissertation biography of Rev. John Brown in this bibliography.)

*Brown, John Mason. This entry taken from **Herbert Baxter Adams**'s Thomas Jefferson and the University of Virginia, Washington, 1888. (See especially chap. XXII [Washington and Lee University by Professors White & Harris, i.e., W&L professors, Carter J. Harris and James J. White] and chap. XXIII (bibliography of Washington and Lee University) pp. 293–308, *the whole supplemented by a letter from John Mason Brown [great-grandson of Rev. John Brown] [riddled with errors and false assumptions].*) (**Note: KW's copy is a photocopy.**)

*Brown, John Mason. *Memoranda of the Preston Family*, printed at Frankfort, KY, 1870 by S. I. M. Major, pp. 64. (Photocopy only)
(KW has not seen this item referenced in "John Mason Brown, 1837-1890," Filson Club, vol. 13, no. 3, 1939, by Preston Brown.)

*Brown, Preston. "John Mason Brown, 1837-1890." *Filson Club History Quarterly*, vol. 13, no. 3, Louisville, Kentucky (July 1939) 125–133. (Photocopy)

*Brown, Robert E. and Katherine B. Brown. *Virginia 1705-1786: Democracy or Aristocracy?* East Lansing, Michigan: Michigan State University Press, 1964.

*Buckley, Thomas E. S. J. *Church and State in Revolutionary Virginia, 1776-1787*. Charlottesville, Virginia: University Press of Virginia, 1977.

*Burgess, John W. *The Civil War and the Constitution*. New York: Charles Scribner's Sons, 1901.

*Burgess, John W. *Reconstruction and the Constitution*. New York: Charles Scribner's Sons, 1902/1911.

Calendar of the Virginia and Preston Papers of the Draper Collection of Manuscripts. Madison: Wisconsin Historical Society, 1915: (see also Brown, John, Letters to William and John Preston. 8 June 1764–26 Feb 1784. Ms. Preston Papers of the Draper Manuscripts, State Historical Society of Wisconsin, Madison, 2QQ49-5QQ119, this bibliography)

*Butterfield, L. H., *John Witherspoon Comes to America*. Princeton, NJ: Princeton University Press, 1953, pp. 99.

*Caldwell, Joshua W. *Studies in the Constitutional History of Tennessee*. Cincinnati, Ohio: Robert Clark Company, 1895.

Campbell, Charles. Introduction to the History of the Colony and Ancient Dominion of Virginia Richmond: B. B. Minor, 1847.

*Campbell, Charles. History of the Colony and Ancient Dominion of Virginia, Philadelphia, J. B. Lippincott and Co., 1860. (Mistakenly claims Rev. John Brown was "superintendent" of "Seminary in Augusta" and understandably lacks any citation of authority), 677. (Note: Campbell also mistakenly asserts that the Augusta Seminary was founded upon Rev. Samuel S. Smith's recommendation. The decision, however, had been made prior to Smith's coming to Virginia. Smith did recommend William Graham as the person to take charge of the project. Campbell obviously relied on William Henry Foote's erroneous two *Sketches of Virginia*).

*Campbell, Rev. Robert F. (Fisburne). Some Aspects of the Race Problem in the South, A Paper, Asheville, NC, 1899. (Basically a sermon preached at the First Presbyterian Church, in Asheville, on Christmas 1898). Campbell was from Lexington, Virginia.

*Campbell, Samuel L. (MD) (i.e., "Senex"). "Washington College, Lexington, Virginia," Southern Literary Messenger, June 1838, beginning at p. 364. [Kw's copy is a photocopy of the original] Thomas W. White was the editor at that time. Campbell as author is taken from a graduate paper written by Prof. G. Ray Thompson on Rev. William Graham submitted circa 1967.]

*Campbell, Samuel L., MD., "Memoir of the Battle of Point Pleasant" taken from *The Southern and Western Literary Messenger and Review: Devoted to Every Department of Literature and the Fine Arts*, vol. XIII, Richmond, Virginia, 1847. (Photocopy) But this reprint in *So. Lit. Messenger* is extracted from Charles Campbell's *History of the Colony and Ancient Dominion of Virginia*, 1860. This appendix item was also included in Campbell's earlier *Introduction to the History of the Colony and Ancient Dominion of Virginia*, published in Richmond by B. B. Minor in 1847.

*The Centennial Memorial of the Presbytery of Carlisle, 2 Vols., (The presumed editor or committee chairman was apparently George Norcross who signed both the preface and the introduction [Harrisburg: Meyers Printing Company, 1889].) PRINCETONIE: TYPIS D. A. BORRENSTEIN 1827 (Catalogue of Alumnus of Princeton) (Note: On page 21 the entry of William Graham reads, "Gulielmus (William) Graham, A. M.") So as late as 1827, Princeton lists William Graham's degree as AM, which merely refers to BAs with a ministerial/theological emphasis.

*Catalogue of the Alumni of Washington and Lee University, Lexington, Virginia 1749-1888. Baltimore: John Murphy & Co., 1869. (Includes a historical sketch of the college that is absurdly incorrect and which falsely dates the origins of the institution to 1749.)

*Catalogue of the Officers and Alumni of Washington and Lee University, Lexington, Virginia 1749-1888. Baltimore: John Murphy & Co., 1888. (There is no authorship attribution.)

*"Ceremonies Connected with The Inauguration of the Mausoleum and the Unveiling Of the Recumbent Figure of General Robert Edward Lee at Washington and Lee University, Lexington, Va., June 28, 1883"; Oration of John W. Daniel, LL.D., Historical Sketch of the Lee Memorial Association, Richmond, VA.: West Johnson & Co., 1883. (Contains a brief sketch of Liberty Hall Academy)

*Charter and Laws and Trustees and Alumni of Washington College at Lexington, Virginia, A. D. 1865. Richmond, 1865, includes a sketch of the early history of the college under the strange title, "Historical Statistics." It is the first article in the book. While the pamphlet lists no author or editor, the copy reviewed by the auditor is housed in the Leyburn Library of Washington and Lee University, and it is bound in a volume which bears the following legend upon its spine, "Washington and Lee University, Catalogs, 1865–1879." The volume includes an 1855 catalogue and also catalogues for 1865–1879 in order, along with a few miscellaneous items. The auditor has accepted the authenticity of these various catalogues as having been produced at the behest of the university's administration.

*Christian, Col. Bolivar. "The Scotch-Irish Settlers in the Valley of Virginia," Alumni Address at Washington College, Alumni Association, 1860. (Also published in the book below.)

*Christian, Bolivar. Washington and Lee University. Historical Papers, no. 3, 1892. "The Scotch-Irish Settlers in the Valley of Virginia" originally published by the Alumni Association, 1860, 33 pp., pages 3–43. (Note: Contains nothing that directly bears upon the founding and early history of Augusta Academy [Liberty Hall Academy].)

*Christian, Col. Bolivar. "Historical Sketch." *Catalogue of Alumni of Washington College of Virginia for the year 1869*. Baltimore: John Murphy & Co., 1869. Esp. at pp. 3–13.

*Christian, Col. Bolivar. Note: Christian Bolivar, Esq., is the presumed author of an unsigned article on the origins of Washington and Lee in the *Southern Collegian* (i.e., *Washington and Lee Univ. College* newspaper, vol. VI, no. 9, Feb. 7, 1874, and vol. VI, no. 10, Feb. 21). The article contains a quote (within the article) from an unsigned manuscript said to be in the handwriting of Edward Graham, brother of William Graham, setting forth a very brief sketch of a series of schools evolving into Liberty Hall Academy and referring to a list of early students, to wit: "Samuel Doak etc. and Archibald Alexander, son of Robert's . . ." so not referring to Rev. Archibald Alexander, DD. More importantly, the unsigned author's hypothesis and reasoning is absurd in the extreme. The contentions in the last analysis is merely about a one-page unsigned and undated memo about which almost nothing is known or knowable. Its legitimacy is beyond dubious and is of no historical value whatever. (See Catalogue of the Alumni of Washington College, sketch of the origins by Bolivar Christian.)

Christie, John W., and Dwight L. Dumond. *George Bourne and the Book and Slavery Irreconcilable*, Historical Society of Delaware and the Presbyterian Historical Society, Wilmington and Philadelphia, 1969.

*Collins, Varnum Lansing. *President Witherspoon, A Biography*, 2 vols., 1st London edition (Oxford University Press). Princeton: Princeton University Press, 1925, 217.

Come, Donald Robert. "The Influence of Princeton Higher Education in the South before 1825," William and Mary Quarterly, Third Series, 2 (October, 1945) pp. 367-368.
* Contributions to the History of The Synod of Virginia, Waddell, Rev. James A., ed. Waddell, James A., Washington: John F. Sheiry, Printer, 1890. Waddell was one of three Committee Members who, it appears functioned as writers, editors, and collators. Of this Article. Other Committee members were, Rev. Wm. Wirt Henry and Rev. P. B. Price, both Trustees of Hampden-Sydney College. Henry, grandson of Patrick, was Pres. American Historical Association. This unfortunate piece is riddled with errors and omissions concerning the origins of Washington and Lee University; Another included article is a reprinted Address by John Randolph Tucker given originally at the Centennial Meeting of the Virginia Synod in October of 1888 at New Providence Presbyterian Church in Rockbridge County, Virginia.

*Cooper, Richard. *John Chavis, To Teach a Generation*. Raleigh, NC: Creative Productions, 1985. (This is categorized as juvenile literature, which it is, but it is also seriously inaccurate.)

*Cooper, William J. *Liberty and Slavery*: *Southern Politics to 1860*. New York: Alfred A. Knopf, 1983, 309 pp. (Cites David Robson in footnotes to Chapter 5, "The 1790s also witnessed one of the first publicly expressed defenses of slavery. The advocacy of slavery came from the Reverend William Graham, rector and principal instructor of liberty Hall Academy. (Now Washington and Lee University) in Lexington, Virginia." P. 98. A false assertion directly attributable to David W. Robson who relied upon by Dean Cooper Professor of History at Louisiana State University.)

*Craighead, Rev. J. G., DD. Scotch And Irish Seeds In American Soil: The Early History of the Scotch and Irish Churches..., Philadelphia, Presbyterian Board of Publication, 1878. [Contains incorrect info re the establishment of Washington and Lee University, then Liberty Hall Academy.]
The Craighead Family:
A Genealogical Memoir of the Descendants of Rev. Thomas and Margaret Craighead, 1658-1876
Rev. James Geddes Craighead. Philadelphia, 1876. Simon & Company, Printers. 173 pages, with index of primary and secondary persons.
The Rev. J. G. Craighead was quite the Presbyterian, and the history and politics surrounding the presbytery of Ireland occupies a good portion on the introduction of this work. The body includes individual listings for each Craighead descending from Rev Thomas & Margaret Craighead, who came over on the ship Thomas & Jane to Boston in 1715. Some of the passages are quite interesting in themselves, genealogy aside. However, it should be noted that, when this book was written, **the number of Craigheads in the Tennessee and Virginia branches heavily outnumbered those recorded in this work, and the Rev J. G. must have been aware of their existence, yet chose not to include them.** One can make one's own speculation as to why.... but it makes the work sadly incomplete.

Availability: LDS microfiche at 6060572

*Craven, Wesley Frank. Published in Richard A., Ed. _Princetonians, 1769-1775_, Princeton University Press, Princeton, New Jersey, 1980. W. Frank Craven, author of the article on Rev. William Graham.

*Craven, Wesley Frank. _"On the Writing of a Biographical Dictionary."_ Proceedings of the American Philosophical Society, Vol. 122, No. 2 (April 24, 1978), pp. 69-74.

*Crawford, Earle, W. _Samuel Doak; Pioneer Missionary in Tennessee_. Johnson City, TN: Overmountain Press, 1980 (reprint 1999) 58 pp.

*Crawford, Earle, W. _An Endless Line of Splendor: Profiles of Six Pioneer Presbyterian Preacher-Educators_. Wichita Falls, Texas, 1983, pp. 238. (A chapter on Rev. William Graham)

*Crenshaw, Ollinger. _General Lee's College, The Rise and Growth of Washington and Lee University_. New York: Random House, 1969.

*Crenshaw, Ollinger. _General Lee's College, The Rise and Growth of Washington and Lee University_ (typescript unpublished early version in two vols., with footnotes and appendix, at Washington and Lee University Library).

*Crenshaw, Ollinger. _General Lee's College_. Typescript, unpublished version in two volumes with Appendix A. "The Problem of the Origins" (page 524 of entire typescript but appendix A is also paginated separately as pages 1–13).

*Couper, William. _One Hundred Years at V. M. I._ 4 vols. Richmond, 1938 (auditor only possesses the first two volumes).

*Davidson, Rev. Robert. _History of the Presbyterian Church in the State of Kentucky; with a preliminary Sketch of the Churches in the Valley of Virginia_. New York, Robert Carter, 1847. A PDF file and a reprint edition.

*Dayton, Ruth Woods. _Pioneers and Their Homes on the Upper Kanawha_. Charleston, West Virginia: West Virginia Publishing Company, 1947. (Contains a few references to Edward Graham, brother of Rev. Wm. Graham, and political positions he held.)

*DeLaney, Theodore, PhD. "Founder's Day Lecture" (in regard to Rev. John Chavis). Washington and Lee University, 2001.

*De Witt, John. "Archibald Alexander's Preparation for His Professorship." _Princeton Theological Review_ 3 (1905).

*Diehl, George West. *The Reverend Samuel Houston, V.D.M.* Verona, Virginia: McClure Printing Company Inc., 1970.

*————. *The Brick Church on Timber Ridge.* Verona, Virginia, 1975.

*A Digest Compiled from the Records of the General Assembly of the Presbyterian Church in the United States of America**, Philadelphia for the Trustees** by R. P. M'Culloh, 1820.
See also Records of the Presbyterian Church below under "Records . . ."

Doak, Samuel. *Lectures on Human Nature; To which Is Added an Essay on Life by John W. Doak.* Jonesboro, Tennessee: F. Gifford & Co., 1845.

*Drakeman, Donald L.** The Church Historians Who Made the First Amendment What It Is Today, Religion and American Culture: A Journal of Interpretation, vol. 17, no. ! (Winter 2007): 27–56.

*Eckenrode, H. (Hamilton) J. (James). *Separation of Church and State in Virginia: A Study in the Development of the Revolution*, Richmond, 1910. (Photocopy)

*Egle, William Henry, Ed. *Pennsylvania: Genealogies; Chiefly Scotch-Irish and German.* Harrisburg: Harrisburg Publishing Company, 1896. (2nd edition, revised; 1st edition 1886).

*Egle, William Henry, Ed. *Centenary Memorial of the Erection of the County of Dauphin, at the Founding of the City of Harrisburg, Harrisburg.* Telegraph Printing House, 1886, 397.

*Farnham, Christie Anne. *The Education of the Southern Belle: Higher Education and Student Socialization in the Antebellum South.* New York and London: New York University Press, 1994, 257.

*Farrar, Emmie Ferguson, and Emilee Hines. *Old Virginia Houses: Shanandoah.* Charlotte, NC: Delmar Publishing Co., 1976. (Note: contains an entry for "Whistle Creek," the home of Rev. William Graham. Owned in the seventies by Robert P. Cooke and Major and Mrs. Chester Goolrick.)

*Fea, John. *The Way of Improvement Leads Home, Philip Vickers Fithian and the Rural Enlightenment in Early America.* Philadelphia: University of Pennsylvania Press, 2008.

First Presbyterian Church, Staunton, Va., Staunton. The Ross Printing Co., 1903. (Wraps, 114 pp.)

*Fithian, Philip Vickers. *The Journal & Letters of Philip Vickers Fithian, 1773–1774: A Plantation Tutor of the Old Dominion.* Williamsburg: Colonial Williamsburg, Inc., 1943 (2nd edition revised). (Note: The first edition was published in 1900.)

*Fithian, Philip Vickers. *The Journal & Letters of Philip Vickers Fithian, "Written on the Virginia-Pennsylvania Frontier and in the Army Around New York, [1775–1776].* Princeton: Princeton University Press, 1934. (Considered by publisher to be vol. II.) While this volume stands alone and has its own index, it is volume 2, the first volume being published in 1900. *(The editors, in a footnote, erroneously challenged Mr. Fithian concerning Samuel Doak being in Augusta in December of 1775. The editors' challenge is not supported by the demonstrable facts surrounding the starting date of classes at Hampden Sydney Academy. Simply put, the Princeton editors were wrong to challenge Mr. Fithian in this regard. Philip Vickers Fithian was a scholar and eyewitness to the events he describes in his journal written at the time in question. The Princeton editors, writing more than a century after the fact, rather foolishly challenged a highly credible source with firsthand knowledge.)*

*Foote, William Henry, DD. *Sketches of Virginia, Historical and Biographical.* First Series. Philadelphia, William S. Martien, 1850. See also John Knox Press reprint edition 1966 with index.

*Foote, William Henry, DD. *Sketches of Virginia, Historical and Biographical.* Second Series. Second edition revised. Philadelphia: J. B. Lippincott & Co., 1856. This second series was first published in 1855.

*Ford, Henry Jones. *The Scotch-Irish in America.* Princeton, NJ: Princeton University Press, 1915.

*Foster, Sydnor Franklin JR. *A History of Hat Creek Presbyterian Church, 1742-1953* (1954) master's thesis. Paper 79. University of Richmond, Richmond, Virginia. *Note: The first footnote is comprised of a citation of authority naming William Henry Foote's Sketches of Virginia, and yet unlike most every other historian of the twentieth century, Mr. Foster ignored Foote's false history of Washington and Lee University, opting instead, as one should, to rely upon primary sources and in two locations refers to the meeting minutes of the Hanover Presbytery and quotes therefrom and, in so doing, correctly identifies the date of the founding of the institution as being October 13, 1774.*

*Futhey, J. Smith. *Historical Discourse Delivered on the Occasion of the One Hundred and Fiftieth Anniversary of the Upper Octorara Presbyterian Church.* Philadelphia, 1870.

*Gaines, Elizabeth Venable. *Cub Creek Church and Congregation 1738-1838,* published for the author, Presbyterian Committee of Publication. Richmond, VA, Texarkana, Ark. Tex.

*Gillespie, Robert Goggin, Jr. *Rev. William Graham, Presbyterian Minister and Rector of Liberty Hall Academy.* Master's thesis. University of Richmond, 1970. (Photocopy). Tazewell High School (VA); BA degree Hampden-Sydney College, 1962; MA Univ. of Richmond, VA, 1970; died November 1976; lived in Richmond; worked for VA Employment Commission.

(Note: Mr. Gillespie, in preparing to write his master's thesis, read fairly extensively, but more importantly, his research focused on most of the most important original source materials pertaining to Rev. William Graham's long association with Liberty Hall. Unfortunately, he failed to appropriately sort the wheat from the chaff, as it were. He gave far more credence to William Henry Foote than he should have and too little to the official records of the Hanover Presbytery and the Liberty Hall Board of Trustees' meeting minutes book. At the same time, he deserves credit for his careful scrutiny among the Graham Family Papers at the Perkins Library at Duke University for his citations, and important quotations from letters from Rev. Matthew Lyle to Edward Graham provide some material not included in any other publications that we are aware of. Nevertheless, we did not include Mr. Gillespie in our list of author's audit for possible errors. He made several, but those of significance he made in deference to the misguided Mr. Wm. H. Foote. Like President Ruffner, he misjudged Mr. Graham's view of both reading and his first position at Augusta Academy, not realizing that Rev. Graham was the chief executive officer from the very beginning of the school. Finally, he failed to grasp that the dispute between Rev. Graham and Rev. Hezekiah Balch resulted in Graham's acquittal, and Balch, by clear inference, was clearly guilty of perjury in an ecclesiastical court. He should have read more broadly on this subject if he was intent on quoting from an incomplete record taken, improperly, in an improper ecclesiastical court that had no jurisdiction and one that had no business speaking (writing) on an incomplete record of evidence, while at the same time transferring the case to the ecclesiastical court with the proper jurisdiction. For such a body to comment on a case, under any circumstance, is highly improper and entirely irregular. The improper ecclesiastical courts uncalled for commentary has been reprinted on several occasions to the completely innocent defendant's harm and to the utter shame of the court that had no jurisdiction to even consider the matter. Mr. Gillespie made the mistake of repeating words that should have been written. Mr. Gillespie does not refer to the preeminent historian Dr. Ollinger Crenshaw, author of General Lee's College, which apparently came out just as Mr. Gillespie was finishing his final editing of his master's thesis on Rev. William Graham. Moreover, it is highly likely that Dr. Crenshaw's typescript two-volume version of that book, which includes a vast number of detailed, important explanatory notations footnotes and the all-important appendix A, "The Problem of the Origins," which may well have caused Mr. Gillespie to rethink several of his mistakes before the thesis was submitted. Ironically, approximately fifteen years prior to Gillespie's thesis, master's student Sydnor Franklin Foster Jr., wrote a thesis on the Hat Creek Presbyterian Church wherein he explains the history of the founding of Washington and Lee University correctly by relying on primary

sources instead of William H. Foote. Gillespies should have consulted his fellow alumnus, Mr. Foster. See above entry for Mr. Foster.
His youth and inexperience may also explain why he erred, but it doesn't mitigate the harm to Rev. Graham's reputation and legacy.)

*Glise, Morton Graham. *A History of Paxton Church 1732–1976.* Paxton Presbyterian Church, Harrisburg, PA, 1976 (199 pp.).

*Graham, David. *History of the Graham Family.* Clayton, West VA, 1889.

*Graham, Edward. "A Memoir of the Late Rev. William Graham, A.M." *The Evangelical and Literary Magazine and Missionary Chronicle* IV (1821): 75 et seq. No authorship attribution appears in the magazine. (Note: Attributed to Edward Graham [Rev. Wm.'s brother] by Archibald Alexander upon whom one can rely. Moreover, the authorship has been generally accepted by the historians of this locale and this period.)

Graham Family Papers. ALS from David W. Brown, assistant, William R. Perkins Library, Manuscript Department, August 10, 1973, in which Mr. Brown describes the Graham Family Papers contents. He also mentions that 1,113 items and 12 volumes kept in six boxes are "entered in the National Union Catalog of Manuscripts as Graham Family Papers."

*Graham, Michael. (Immigrant) His Bible includes a family history page in Michael's handwriting, which was compared with his handwriting in his last will and testament.
A handwritten note attached to this photocopy says it is from Michael Graham's Bible at Washington & Lee University. The page I have before me only lists Michael's children, and the spelling of his eldest daughter's name appears to be "Cristan" while the printed version supplied by Mrs. Alice (Aunspaugh) Kyle of Lynchburg, VA, shows the name as "Christian." Mrs. Kyle has apparently corrected Michael's spelling as evidenced by his spelling of Christian in exactly the same way in his handwritten last will and testament when he adopts the common phrase "Cristan [Christian] burial."

*Graham, Michael (Jr.).[704] (1758–1834). Deposition (Rev. War pension application). Bedford, Virginia, 24 December (Christmas Eve day) 1832. Note: Several-page deposition outlining some of his family's history in Pennsylvania, VA, and North Carolina before, during, and after the Revolutionary War. Michael, son of Michael the immigrant and brother of Rev. William Graham, enlisted in the Pennsylvania "Flying Camp" prior to the signing of the Declaration of Independence (i.e., last of May or first of June 1776). He served a total of nine

---

[704] This is the son of Michael Graham, immigrant, from Paxton Twp. Pa., and who was born in 1758 and fought in the American Revolution on two separate occasions, including at the beginning from Pennsylvania, and near the War's conclusion from Rockbridge County, Virginia.

months, six in Pennsylvania at the beginning of the war and three in a Virginia company when he was deployed near Yorktown where Lord Cornwallis surrendered to General Washington, effectively ending the war although technically it was not formally ended for yet another year. Revolutionary War Pension Claim S.8621. Recorded in Bedford County, VA. Clerk's Book "D," vol. 7, p. 99.

*Graham, Rev. William. *Petition for Charter (1782).*

*Graham, Rev. William. *The proposed Charter of Liberty Hall Academy (1782).*

*Graham, Rev. William. *Memorial In Re to Opposing P. Henry's Proposed Bill on Assessment, & in Support of Jefferson's Bill for Religious Liberty* (1785).

*Graham, Rev. William. *Proposed Constitution, State of Frankland.*

*Graham, Rev. William. *"Essay on Government."* Philadelphia, 1786.
Note: The above is housed at Leyburn Library, Washington and Lee University, Lexington, Virginia. This photocopy bears a note in long hand that asserts "printed in Philadelphia 1786 . . . Wm Graham Author." Note the printed title is merely "Essay &c." The article's beginning page is numbered 3, and it runs through to page 37 and at the conclusion says, in bolder and larger font, "A Citizen of Frankland." On a following page, there is written this note in long hand: "*This Essay was written by the Rev. Wm Graham, who then lived in Franklin, now Tennessee. He would not call that Territory Franklin as it was generally called but Frankland, for he never liked Dr. Franklin & there were no bounds to his prejudices.*" The notation is unsigned. It is incorrect because Wm. Graham did not ever live in the proposed state of Frankland/Franklin, but it may be true that he owned land there, purchased for him, at his request, by Rev. Samuel Houston, but evidence on that point is lacking.

*Graham, Rev. William. *Address to the Presbyterian General Assembly* (see Foote's *Sketches of Virginia*, Series One, 1850).

*Graham, Rev. William. *Letter to Zachariah Johnston.* Leyburn Library, Washington and Lee University.

*Graham, Rev. William. *Letter to Col. Arthur Campbell.* The letter is housed in the archives of the Filson Club in Kentucky; the letter is dated Sept. 24, 1788.

*Graham, Rev. William. *Letter to President George Washington with historical sketch of the college* (for the board of trustees) (1796). (The letter's content is reprinted in full in William Henry Foote's *Sketches of Virginia, Historical and Biographical*, Philadelphia, William S. Martien, 1850, pp. 479–482.)

*Graham, Rev. William. *"The Scriptural Doctrine of Water Baptism: Shewing 1. The Scriptural Substance of that Ordinance; II. The Scriptural Mode of Its*

Administration; III. And, Lastly, Answering Some Questions for the Satisfaction of Serious Enquirers, Richmond, Virginia, Printed by William Alex. Rind, 1799, 41 pp. (A copy from an original is housed at Leyburn Library, Washington and Lee University, Lexington, Virginia.)

Graham, Rev. William. *"Essay on Government."* Philadelphia, 1786.

*Graves, Charles A. (Alfred). "Washington and Lee: Views of this University." *The Richmond Dispatch*, Aug. 14, 1885, Richmond, August 14, 1885, p. 2. (Chronicling America PDF)

*Grigsby, Hugh Blair. *"The Founders of Washington College."* An address delivered June 22, 1870, Washington and Lee University Historical Papers No. 2, Lexington, VA, 1890 (riddled with serious errors, generally unreliable concerning historical facts pertaining to the origins of Washington and Lee University, but containing much interesting and useful information on other aspects of the college's history).

*Grigsby, Hugh Blair. The History of the Federal Convention of 1788, vol. I (of two), Richmond, published by the Society, 1890. (Published in Collections of the Virginia Historical Society, New Series, vol. IX.) (Note: Vol. II is contained in the Collections of the Virginia Historical Society, Vol. X.) My copy is a photocopy printed from Google digitized books.

*_Hand-Book of the Presbyterian Church_. Staunton, VA. (1804–1903)

Hageman, John Frelinghuysen. *History of Princeton (the Town, not the College, but some info re College)*. 2 vols. Philadelphia: J. B. Lippincott & Co., 1879.

*Hagy, James William. "Democracy Defeated." *Tennessee Historical Quarterly*, vol. 40, no. 3 (Fall 1981): 239–256. (PDF Jstor)

*Hanna, Charles A. *The Scotch-Irish or The Scot in North Ireland, And North America*. 2 vols. New York: G. P. Putnam's Sons, 1902.

*Hanna, Charles A. *The Wilderness Trail*. 2 vols. New York and London: G. P. Putnam's Sons, 1911.
*Hanover Presbytery meeting minutes, 1771–17776. (These are scanned copies by William Smith Morton Library, Union Presbyterian Seminary, Richmond, Virginia, scanned in 2013.) (See also??)
Contact: Dr. Paula Skreslet, Reference/Archives, William Smith Morton Library, Union Presbyterian Seminary.

*Hardin, Bayless. "The Brown Family of Liberty Hall." *The Filson Club History Quarterly*, vol. 16, no. 2 (April 1942) (reprint pamphlet not dated but appears to be contemporary with the original publication of the Filson Club).

*Harrison, Richard A., ed. _Princetonians, 1769-1775_. Princeton, NJ: Princeton University Press, 1980. W. Frank Craven, author of the article on Rev. William Graham. See also Professor John M. Murrin's introduction to _Princetonian 1784-1790_, page liii of the introduction.

*Hart, Freeman. _The Valley of Virginia_. Chapel Hill: University of North Carolina Press, 1942. (See esp. pp. 30–32.)

Hawks, Francis Lister. _Contributions to the Ecclesiastical History in America_. 2 volumes. New York: Harper & Brothers, 1836–1839. (Author, rector of St. Thomas Church Episcopal, New York)

*Heinricks, Johann of the Hessian Jager Corps 1778–80 (see entry "Extracts from," above) in re "Scotch-Irish Rebellion."

*Hening, William Waller. _The Statutes at Large, . . . Laws of Virginia_, vol. XI, Richmond. Printed for the editor, 1823.

*Hill, William, DD. _A History of the Rise, Progress, Genius, and Character, of American Presbyterianism: Together with a review of the "Constitutional History of the Presbyterian Church in the United States of America; by Chas. Hodge, D. D., Professor in the Theological Seminary, at Princeton Theological Seminary, N.J._ Washington City, J. Gideon, JR., 1839, pp. 224. (BiblioLife reprint)

Hill, William. _Autobiographical sketches of Dr. William Hill: together with his account of the revival of religion in Prince Edward County, and biographical sketches of the life and character of the Reverend Dr. Moses Hoge of Virginia_. Richmond, 1968.

*Hill, Rev. William. "History of Washington College, Virginia." _American Historical Quarterly_, vol. X (1838): 145–150 (Authorship attributed to Rev. William Hill) cited in Ollinger Crenshaw's _General Lee's College_ (unpublished footnotes [typescript] Washington & Lee University Archives/Library), "Vol. II, "Appendix "A," hand-paginated in pencil as page 526 (based in large measure upon an article entitled by Rev. Dr. William Hill [Hampden Sydney] in **Southern Religious Telegraph** [Richmond] Dec. 19, 1834; Jan. 2, 23; Feb. 6, 1835 [serialized form], and also relying on a letter to the unnamed author from Edward Graham, Esq., of Lexington, Virginia. This bibliographer has a photocopy of the article from the _Am. Hist. Quarterly_ but not the 1834 serialized articles. These articles, according to Ollinger Crenshaw, date the history of the college from the 1770s and the actions of the Hanover Presbytery.

J. R. Hildebrand Map see below.

*Historical map of the Roanoke Valley Historical Society, showing Rockbridge County, Virginia, 1778-1865. Author, J. R. Hildebrand, Donald Orth Collection.

(A wonderful map that identifies many of the owners and their property location in the eighteenth century. BUT it unfortunately repeats the erroneous notion that Washington and Lee University began in 1749 (it was Oct 13, 1774) and further that an earlier common school conducted by Robert Alexander was named "Augusta Academy," which is an error.

*"**History of Washington College**" (ordered printed by the board of trustees) 1849. This constitutes the college's first published account of the early history of the college. As such, it is of paramount significance. It is likely, but undocumented as far as this writer knows, that this article is based primarily on notes in the possession of the college or some of the trustees by the immediate past president Henry Ruffner. Ruffner is known to have been researching the topic in question. President Ruffner's estate contained a lengthy manuscript entitled, "Early History of Washington College."

***Hodge, Charles.** *The Constitutional History of the Presbyterian Church in the United States of America.* 2 volumes. Philadelphia: William S. Martien, 1839–1840.
***Hoge, Arista, ed.** *The First Presbyterian Church, Staunton, Virginia.* Staunton, VA, 1908.

***Hoge, John Blair.** The Life of Moses Hoge, The Library, Union Theological Seminary, Richmond, Virginia, 1963, with index, composed by Pansie N. Cameron, pp. 179. (In wraps with taped binding. The work was written circa 1823.)

***Hoge, Peyton Harrison.** *Moses Drury Hoge.* Richmond: Presbyterian Committee of Publications, 1899.

***Hood, Fred J.** "Revolution and Religious Liberty: The Conservation of the theocratic Concept in Virginia." *Church History,* vol. 40, no. 2 (June 1971), 170–181. Cambridge Univ. Press. (My copy is a photostatic copy.) (**Note**: Very Important re Rev. William Graham's role in the adoption of Jefferson's bill [Virginia] for the establishment of religious freedom. This bill forms the infrastructure for the religious freedom portion of the First Amendment of our nation's Bill of Rights. Hood is useful and gets much right, but he fails to recognize that Wm. Graham overturned the 1784 Memorial and was the driving force for calling the general convention that overturned the presbytery's position. He fails to comprehend that Wm. Graham played no role in the 1784 Memorial despite being appointed to the committee; he turned his back on that approach and successfully reversed it by grassroots means. Basically an important and insightful article.

***Houston, Rev. Samuel.** Letter to Rev. Morrison, New Providence Church. Printed in part in Foote's *Sketches of Virginia,* Series One and Series Two; also, MSS letter to Sidney S. Baxter, an elder of the New Monmouth Presbyterian Church, written in 1837 and referenced in Dr. I. Taylor Sanders's book, *Now Let the Gospel Trumpet Blow,* 1986, p. 9, at footnote no. 28. This item was obtained by the auditor from the Virginia Historical Society (ref. no. VIH MSS. 2H 8184a.1). Dr. Sanders says in his footnote: "The paper appears to have been the last thing Houston wrote."

Howe, Henry. *Historical Collections of Virginia; A Collection of the most interesting facts, Traditions, Biographical Sketches, Anecdotes, & c. Relating to Its History and Antiquities, together with Geographical and Statistical Descriptions. To which is appended, An Historical and descriptive Sketch of the District of Columbia.* Charleston, SC: Babcock & Co., 1845, esp. at pp. 448, et seq.

*Hume, Edgar Erskine. "The Virginia Society of The Cincinnati's Gift to Washington College." *The Virginia Magazine of History and Biography,* vol. 42, no. 2 (April 1934): 103–115. *(Note includes an erroneous sketch of early history of Washington & Lee.)*

*Hunter, Robert F. *Lexington Presbyterian Church 1789 – 1989.* Lexington: Lexington Presbyterian Church, 1991.

*James, Charles F. Documentary History of the Struggle for Religious Liberty in Virginia, Lynchburg, Virginia, 1900.

*Johnson, Patricia Givems. *William Preston and the Allegheny Patriots.*

*Johnson, Thomas Cary. Virginia Presbyterianism and Religious Liberty in Colonial and Revolutionary Times. Richmond, Presbyterian Committee of Publication, 1907. (PDF Google)

*Junkin, D. X., DD. *The Reverend George Junkin, DD, LLD, A Historical Biography.* Philadelphia: J. B. Lippincott & Co., 1871.

Junkin, Rev. E. D. *A History of The Church and Congregation of New Providence, Lexington Presbytery, Virginia,* published by request of the congregation, 1871. (KW has only the section dealing with Rev. John Brown and the origins of Washington and Lee University in photocopy.) *(E. D. Junkin b. 02/08/1829; d. July 31, 1891.)*

*Junkin, Rev. George, DD. *Christianity the Patron of Literature and Science: An Address Delivered February 22, 1849. On the Occasion of the Author's Inauguration as President of Washington College, Virginia.* Philadelphia, Board of Trustees, 1849 (pamphlet, pp. 39). The Junkin inaugural address includes an important appendix: "A Brief Sketch of the Early History of Washington College" (ordered printed by the board of trustees). This constitutes the college's first authorized published history.

*Kaleidoscope (Annual), vol. 1, Hampden-Sydney College, vol. 1, 1893.

Kemper, Charles E. "The Early Westward Movement of Virginia, 1722-1734 As Shown by the Proceedings of the Colonial Council," vol. 13, no. 4 (April 1906): 351–374; "Settlement of the Valley," *Virginia Magazine of History and Biography*, vol. 30, April 1, 1922; "Early Settlers in the Valley of Virginia," *The William and Mary Quarterly*, vol. 6, no. 1 (January 1926): 57–62; Historical notes from the records of Augusta County, Virginia, Part II (concluded) by Charles E. Kemper.

Kercheval, Samuel. *A History of the Valley of Virginia.* Winchester, Samuel E. Davis, 1833, pp. 455 plus three appendices. (PDF file Google Books) (Nothing related directly to Washington and Lee.)

Knight, Edgar W. "Notes on John Chavis." *North Carolina Historical Review* 7 (January–October 1930): 326–45.

*Kondayan, Betty R. (Ruth). MS letter to the auditor dated June 1, 1973. This one-page letter is in response to an inquiry originally directed to the widow of Dr. Ollinger Crenshaw. It lists various resources used by Dr. Crenshaw and lists some writing on file that were written by Rev. William Graham. The letter also included an enclosed copy of a typed memorandum sent to the university by Rev. Reid Bracken entitled "Lest We Forget" with a series of anecdotes concerning his wife's (Mary [Graham] Bracken) family. His wife was the youngest daughter of Rev. William Graham. The entire enclose runs thirteen pages.

*Kondayan, Betty R. *A Historical Sketch of the Library of Washington and Lee University: From the Beginnings in 1776 through 1937.* Lexington, Virginia, 1980, (University Publication No. 7), pp. 50.

Lee, Gen. Robert Edward (Pres. W&L). SEE "Ceremonies Connected with the Inauguration of the Mausoleum and the Unveiling of the Recumbent Figure of General Robert Edward Lee" in alphabetical order, this bibliography.

Lexington Presbytery. "Records of the Presbytery of Lexington" copied and attested to by Rev. D. L. Beard, 193. Typescript/probably a carbon copy, from Leyburn Library and Archives, Washington and Lee University, a PDF-scanned file (pp. 20–149 covering minutes between April 26, 1771–April 14, 1803).

*Leyburn, James G. *Scotch-Irish: A Social History*, 1962??
"Liberty Hall Volunteers: Stonewall's College Boys," **Bean, William Gleason**, University Press of Virginia, 1964, pp. 227; also Civil War History, vol. 11, no. 4, December, 1965.

*Lyle, Royster Jr. and Pamela H. Simpson. *The Architecture of Historic Lexington*, Charlottesville, pp. 314 with index and selected bibliography, 1977.

*Lyle, Oscar K. *Lyle Family.* New York, 1912.

Note: Lyle genealogy including information on the four immigrant Lyles from Northern Ireland to Augusta (Rockbridge) County, Virginia.

*McAlarney, Mathias Wilson. _The History of the Sesquicentennial of Paxtang Church._ Harrisburg: Harrisburg Publishing Company, 1890.

McCluskey, Vincent S. _The Life and Times of Philip Vickers Fithian: Revolutionary War Hero._ PhD dissertation, New York University, 1991 (read and analyzed entire text July 2014).

*McCook., Rev. H. C., DD. _Historic Decorations at the Pan-Presbyterian Council._ Philadelphia: The Presbyterian Publishing Company, 1880.

McCormick, Leander James. _Family Record and Biography._ Compiled by Leander James McCormick, Chicago, 1896 (PDF Google Books). In re New Providence Church schism and Cyrus H. McCormick, see esp. pp. 247–248. Note:

*McCullough, David. _1776._ New York, NY: Simon & Schuster, 2005. (Contains an extract from Michael Graham's Revolutionary War pension application. He requested no pension but only applied for historical record-keeping purposes. This Michael Graham was a younger brother of President Graham who lived with the president for a decade in the Lexington area.)

*McDaniel, John M., Charles N. Watson, and David T. Moore. _Liberty Hall Academy, The Early History of the Institutions Which Evolved into Washington and Lee University._ Lexington, VA: Liberty Hall Press, 1979.

*McDaniel, John M., Kurt C. Russ, and Parker B. Potter. _An Archaeological and Historical Assessment Of The Liberty Hall Academy Complex 1782-1803,_ _Lexington._ Virginia: The Liberty Hall Press, 1994 (The James G. Leyburn Papers in Anthropology, Vol. II, 1994).

*McLaughlin, William. _Catalogue of the Officers and Alumni of Washington and Lee University, Lexington, Virginia 1749-1888._ Baltimore, John Murphy & Co., 1888. (Author(s) unknown, but the pattern of succession of the administrative heads of the institution closely follows that which was written by Bolivar Christian in 1869, as made clear by Dr. Ollinger Crenshaw in his appendix A to the typescript version of _General Lee's College,_ later published without footnotes and without appendix A by Random House in 1969. (Also listed under "Catalogue...")
Note: Contains a false historical account of the origin of Liberty Hall Academy, dating the founding to Robert Alexander's school in 1752. A unique date that is typically 1749, both of which are as incorrect as the alleged connection that does not exist. Contains numerous errors concerning the college. (One-page three-paragraph historical sketch in narrative format strangely titled, "Historical Statistics." This sketch is followed by a two-page collection of names and dates

categorized as rectors, presidents, and professors &c. (There is no authorship attribution in the catalog.)

*Maclean, John. *History of the College of New Jersey, from its origin in 1746 to the Commencement of 1854.* 2 vols. Philadelphia: J. B. Lippincott & Co., 1877. PDF.

*Maier, Pauline. *American Scripture: Making the Declaration of Independence.* New York: Alfred A. Knopf, 1997. Maier explains that "the more alterations Congress made on his draft, the more miserable Jefferson became," p. 149.

Martin, Francois Xavier. *The History of North Carolina, from the Earliest Period.* 2 vols.

Maxwell, William, Esq. *A Memoir of Rev. John H.[olt] Rice, DD, First Professor of Christian Theology in Union Theological Seminary.* Virginia, Philadelphia: J. Whetham, 1835. (Note: Includes some important letters by Rice that address his views on slavery and the politics of slavery in the South as it pertains to the Presbyterian Church in general and Presbyterian clergy more specifically.)

*Maxwell, William. *An Oration Commemorative of the Late Rev. John Holt Rice, DD, Spoken before the Literary and Philosophical Society of Hampden-Sydney College, At their Anniversary Meeting, on Thursday the 27ᵗʰ of September, A.D. 1832.* Richmond, Robert I. Smith, 1832. (Google Books PDF)

Melton, Julius Wemyss. *Pioneering Presbyter: Collection and Analysis of the letters of John Holt Rice.* Imprint 1959, pp. 393, typescript, dissertation/thesis (Th.M.) Union Theological Seminary, Richmond, Virginia. *(An important work that includes many important letters. He merely summarizes many so it is helpful to refer also to the earlier memoir of Rice by William Maxwell, which includes some important letters by Rice that address his views on slavery and the politics of slavery in the South as it pertains to the Presbyterian Church in general and Presbyterian clergy more specifically.)*

*Miller, Mrs. S. P. McD. Miller. "A Virginia University Town." *Overland Monthly.* (Jan–June 1883), vol. I, Second Series, pp. 488–502. *(This article is error-ridden with respect to the origins of Washington and Lee. She provides much information of interest but knew very little about the founding of the college and mistakenly links the eighteenth-century Rev. John Brown family with the college.)*

*Mills, Scott A. History of West Nottingham Academy 1744 – 1981. Maryland Historical Press, Lanham, Maryland, 1985.

*Minutes of the General Assembly of the Presbyterian Church in the United States of America from Its Organization A. D. 1789 To A.D. 1820 Inclusive.

Philadelphia: Presbyterian Board of Publication, n.d., editor, William M. Engles. Advertisement dates the publication as 1847. (Archive/Google Books PDF file)

*Records of the Presbyterian Church in the United States of America, Embracing the Minutes of the General Presbytery of Philadelphia 1706–1716, Minutes of 1717–1758. Minutes of the Synod of NY 1745–1758, 1758–1788. Presbyterian Board of Publication, Philadelphia, 1841.

*Minutes, Hanover Presbytery of Virginia, 1771–1776, scanned images from William Smith Morton Library, Union Presbyterian Seminary, Richmond, VA.

*Monk, Samuel H. "Samuel Stanhope Smith, Friend of Rational Liberty" (appearing in the book, *The Lives of Eighteen From Princeton*).

*Morgan, George H., ed. (or compiler). *Annals, Comprising Memoirs, Incidents, and Statistics of Harrisburg from the Period of Its First Settlement.* Harrisburg: Geo. A. Brooks, 1858, pp. 399.

*Morrison, Alfred. J. The College of Hampden-Sidney, Calendar of Board Minutes 1776-1876. Richmond, VA: The Hermitage Press, 1921

Morrison, Alfred. J. *The Beginnings of Public Education in Virginia, 1776 - 1860,* Richmond: Superintendent of Public Instruction, 1917.

*Morton, Oren F. *A History of Highland County, Virginia.* Reprint. Baltimore: Regional Publishing Company, 1979. Originally published, Monterey, Virginia, 1911.

*Morton, Oren. *A History of Rockbridge County, Virginia.* Reprint. Baltimore: Regional Publishing Company, 1973. Originally published, Staunton, Virginia, 1920.

*Murrin, John M. *Princetonians 1784-1790.* Princeton, NJ: Princeton University Press, 1991, p. liii of the introduction. Important information pertaining to John Chavis.

*Neely, Mark E., Harold Holzer, and Gabor S. Boritt. *The Confederate Image: Prints of the Lost Cause.* University of North Carolina Press, Chapel Hill, 1987. *(Note: Contains a copy of the Lee engraving on page 58 found in the Kent S. Wilcox collection.)*

*Nelson, Professor A. L. "Personal Recollections of Washington College" in the *RING-TUM PHI,* vol. II, Feb. 11, 1899, p. 1, et seq.

*Nevin, Rev. Alfred. *Churches of the Valley.* Philadelphia, Joseph M. Wilson, 1852.

***Nevin, Alfred, DD.** _Encyclopedia of the Presbyterian Church in the United States_. Philadelphia: Presbyterian Encyclopedia Publishing Co., 1884.

"Notices of Distinguished Graduates." (Alexander, J. A., J. Carnahan, and A. Alexander) referring, of course, to graduates of Princeton. (This item is suspect in those parts represented to be written by Archibald Alexander because they may have been altered by his son, James W. Alexander, something James did in his biography of his father.)

***Nybakken, Elizabeth.** "In the Irish Tradition: Pre-Revolutionary Academies in America." History of Education Quarterly, vol. 37, no. 2, Special Issue on Education in Early America (Summer 1997): 163–183.

***Othow, Helen Chavis.** John Chavis, African American Patriot, Preacher, Teacher, and Mentor, _1763-1838_. Jefferson, North Carolina, and London: McFarland & Company, 2001.

Patteson, Roy K., Jr., "New Providence Presbyterian Church: 1746-1856, in Larry I. Bland, ed., Proceedings of the Rockbridge Historical Society, [Lexington, Virginia: Rockbridge Historical society, 1979], VIII, pp. 13-21.

***Patton, Jacob Harris.** A Popular History of the Presbyterian Church in the United States of America. New York: R. S. Mighill and Company, 1900.

Patton, Jacob Harris. The Triumph of the Presbytery of Hanover; or, Separation of Church and state in Virginia (NY, 1887).

***Patton, Judge James T.** "Letter on the Location of Robert Alexander's School, John Brown's Residence, and Mount Pleasant" in Washington and Lee University Historical Papers, No. 1 (Baltimore: John Murphy & Co., 1890. (Photocopy)

***Pennsylvania Archives, 2ⁿᵈ Series, Vols. 1, 2, and 3.** (John Linn and Wm. H. Egle, editors), Harrisburg, 1874, 1875, 1876 respectively.

***Peterson, Merrill D. and Robert C. Vaughan, editors.** The Virginia Statue for Religious Freedom, Its Evolution and Consequences in American History. New York: Cambridge University Press, 1988, 373.

*"Petition for Charter for Liberty Hall Academy." William and Mary Quarterly Historical Magazine, vol. 13, no. 4 (Apr. 1905): 265–266 for contents of the petition.

Peyton, J. Lewis. History of Augusta County, Virginia. Staunton, Virginia: Samuel Yost & Son, 1882.

*Pilcher, Margaret Campbell. Historical Sketches of the Campbell, Pilcher, and Kindred Families. Nashville, TN: Press of Marshall & Bruce Co., 1911. 444 pp. *(Important because she locates the property on which Rev. Wm. Graham's "Augusta Academy" was first located at Mount Pleasant, near Fairfield, VA re Rev. John Brown, Rockbridge County.) (Auditor's copy is part photocopy and part electronic file copy.)*

Preston, Margaret Junkin. "A Ballad in Reply to Tupper's Ballad to Columbia." Oxford, Nov. 5, 1848. (See Mary P. Coulling's Margaret Junkin Preston Notes, p. 222. [Martin Farquhar Tupper's "New Ballad to Columbia"])
Princetonians see Harrison, Richard A., editor.

*Pruett, Rebecca K. The Browns of Liberty Hall. Masonic Home Printing Office, Masonic Home, Kentucky, 35 pp., 2nd ed., October 1,1967 (1st ed. Aug. 24, 1966). *Her treatment addresses, in the main, those descendants of Rev. John Brown of Augusta County, VA, and the term Liberty Hall is usually in reference to the home of one of Rev. Brown's sons in Kentucky. It does erroneously assert a connection of Rev. John Brown to Washington and Lee University, but it doesn't develop the assertion.*

*Ramsey, J. G. M., A.M., M.D. The Annals of Tennessee to the end of the Eighteenth Century: Comprising the Settlement, as the Watauga Association, from 1796 to 1777; A Part of North Carolina, from 1788 to 1784; The Territory of the U. States, South of the Ohio, from 1790 to 1796; The State of Tennessee, from 1796 to 1800. Charleston: John Russell,1853.

*Records of the Presbyterian Church in the United States of America, Embracing the minutes of the General Presbytery of Philadelphia 1706-1716, Minutes of 1717-1758. Minutes of the Synod of NY 1745-1758. 1758-1788. Presbyterian Board of Publication, Philadelphia, 1841.

*Read, Daisy I. *New London, Today and Yesterday.* Lynchburg, Virginia: J. P. Bell Company, 1950. (Concerns New London Academy where Edward Graham of Lexington, VA, was an instructor.)

*The Ring-tum Phi (Washington and Lee University student newspaper), vol. XIV, no. 25, May 9, 1911. "William Graham's Body Re-Interred: Remains of First President of the Institution Laid to Rest on the Campus."

*The *Ring-Tum Phi* (Washington and Lee student newspaper), vol. XIV, no. 23, May 9, 1911. "William Graham's Body Re-Interred." (Article describes the service and the associated reinterrment.)

*Rives, William C. History of the Life and Times of James Madison. Second edition. 3 Vols. Boston: Little Brown and Company, 1881. (Pdf Google)

*Roan, Rev. Notes from his papers re William Graham, published in Wm. Henry Egle's, *Notes and Queries*, Series 3, vol. 3, pp. 88–90.

*Robson, David, W. "An Important Question Answered: William Graham's Defense of Slavery in Post-Revolutionary Virginia." William and Mary Quarterly 37, no. 4 (October 1980): 644–652. (Note: An erroneous piece throughout based on the incorrect assumption that the Joseph Glass's "lecture notes" were transcriptions of Graham's lectures. There is no credible evidence that this notion is correct. Moreover, the evidence that does exist suggests that they are not written by Graham but rather were transcribed by Graham from the Witherspoon master copy during Graham's time at Princeton. Graham's lectures were never written down and were lost to history.)

*Ruffner, Henry, ed. "Early History of Washington College." Washington & Lee University Historical Papers, vol. 1. Baltimore: John Murphy & Co., 1890.

*Ruffner, Henry. An Address to the People of West Virginia: Shewing that Slavery Is Injurious to the Public Welfare and That It May Be Gradually Abolished Without Detriment to the Rights and Interests of Slaveholders By A Slaveholder of West *Virginia*. Lexington. Printed by R. C. Noel, 1847. (PDF via Archive)

*Ruffner, William Henry. *Manuscript Article "An Educated Negro Preacher of a Century Ago."* n.d. Cite: William Henry Ruffner Papers, 1848–1907, Accession 24814, personal papers collection, Library of Virginia, Richmond, Virginia. 5 pp. [no. 88?].

Ruffner, William Henry. Unpublished anecdotes of George Washington by Henry Ruffner, n.d. **Folder: 10** 4 pp. (Stories told to Ruffner by Edward Graham of Washington College. The Library of Virginia, Richmond, Virginia. [no. 94?]

Ruffner, William Henry. Washington & Lee University Historical Papers, vol. 4, "Continuation of the History of Washington College." Baltimore: John Murphy & Co., 1893.

Ruffner, William Henry. Third Annual Report of the Superintendent of Public Instruction, for the year Ending Augusta 31, 1873. Richmond, 1873. (Includes an appendix article by Ruffner entitled "Washington and Lee University, pp. 138-141." *(It is a brief sketch that reviews important events related to the college from the 1796 endowment bestowed upon the college by President Washington up through the then-current year, 1873.)*

*Rupp, I. Daniel. The History and Topography of Dauphin, Cumberland, Franklin, Bedford, Adams, and Perry Counties. Lancaster City, PA, Gilbert Hills, 1846.

*Sanders, I. Taylor II. Now Let the Gospel Trumpet Blow. Lexington, Virginia: New Monmouth Presbyterian Church, 1986. (Contains a chapter on Rev. Wm. Graham of Washington College, now Washington & Lee fame.)

*Sanders, Robert Stuart. The Rev. Robert Stuart, DD, 1772–1856: A Pioneer in Kentucky Presbyterianism and His Descendants. Louisville: Dunne Press, 1962. (Pdf file) *(Important piece but repeats the ".Janet Brown sister of Rev. John Brown" error, debunked by John White Stuart in his dissertation on Rev. John Brown; see this bibliography.) (Note: This book has copy of Stuart's Liberty Hall Academy diploma and copy of licensure by Lexington Pby. with Wm. Graham & Samuel Houston signature.)*

*Scruggs, Philip Lightfoot. The History of Lynchburg, Virginia 1786–1946. Lynchburg, J. P. Bell Co., Circa 1971

*Sellers, Charles Grier. "John Blair Smith." *Journal of the Presbyterian Historical Society*, vol. 34, no. 4 (December 1956): 201–225. (Auditor's copy is a photostatic copy.)

*Shaw DD, James. The Scotch-Irish in History. New York and London (for the author), 1899.

*Sipes, C. Hale. The Indian Wars of Pennsylvania. First Edition. Harrisburg, PA: The Telegraph Press, 1929.
Dr. Robert Smith's Academy at Pequea, Pennsylvania: See Beam, Dr. Jacob Newton entry.

*Smylie, James H. "Jefferson's Statute for Religious Liberty: The Hanover Memorials." American Presbyterians, vol. 63, no. 4 (Winter 1985): 355–373. *(Inaccurately attributes the October 1784 acquiescent Hanover Memorial to John Smith and William Graham; this was Smith's memorial. W. Graham, however, opposed this memorial.)*

*Spangler, Jewel L. "Pro-Slavery Presbyterians: Virginia's Conservative Dissenters in the Age of Revolution." The Journal of Presbyterian History (1997–), vol. 78, no. 2 (Summer 2000): 111–123. (JSTOR) (Yet another attack on Virginians who opposed slavery but who failed to devote their lives to immediate abolition at any cost. In other words, if you're not an active advocate for immediate abolition, you are, by definition, a defender of slavery.) (In addition, his facts are seriously wrong concerning Rev. William Graham who he libels by asserting that lectures written by Dr. John Witherspoon, president of Princeton, were Graham's lectures when they were not and concerning Rev. Henry Patillo who collaborated with Wm. Graham in the scheme to enroll the nation's first black college student, Rev. John Chavis, and to enlist Mr. Chavis as the nation's first black Presbyterian minister.)

*Speece, Rev. Conrad. Sprague's Annals of the American Pulpit, extract reprinted by Wm. H. Foote's Sketches of Virginia: Historical and Biographical, Series 2, pp. 351–352.

*Sprague, William B. Annals of the American Pulpit; or Commemorative Notices of Distinguished American Clergymen . . . Volume III, New York, Robert Carter & Brothers, 1858, p. 366 (note appears on p. 365, sketch by Rev. Archibald Alexander DD, Nov. 23, 1849).

*Stokes, Anson Phelps and Leo Pfeffer. Church and State in the United States. New York, Evanston, and London: Harper & Row, 1950 & 1964. Revised edition in one volume. (Stokes is an Episcopal bishop, who provides a rather cursory treatment of the struggle for religious liberty in Virginia in the 1780s & demonstrates a rather limited understanding of the events in Virginia at that time.)

*Stokes, Durward T. "The Reverend John Brown and His Family." Filson Club Quarterly, vol. 44, January 1970. (Photocopy)

*Stokes, Durward T. "Henry Patillo of North Carolina." (Article *North Carolina Historical Review*, vol. 44 (1976), 373–391 [from internet (2010) "The Colonial Records Project, Jan-Michael Poff, Editor, Historical Publications Section, Raleigh, NC 27699-4622. Note: Useful for Rev. Wm Graham & John Chavis; and, Haw River Graham historians. [photo-copy]

*Stokes, Durward T. A History of the Graham Presbyterian Church, *1850–1983*. Durward Stokes, Burlington, North Carolina, 1984, 102.

*Stuart, John White. The Rev. John Brown of Virginia (1728–1803): His Life and selected sermons. Doctoral dissertation. University of Massachusetts, 1988.

*Swaim, William C. Facts Are Strangers in the Histories of the Early Years of Paxton and Derry Presbyterian Churches. Harrisburg, Pennsylvania, 1989.

*Smyth, S. Gordon. The Journal of The Presbyterian Historical Society, vol. 11, no. 6, 2 vols. (March 1922 and June 1922), "The Pioneer Presbyterians of New Providence, Virginia." Vol. 1, 178–186, Vol. 2, pp. 193–204.

*Symmes, Rev. Frank R. History of the Old Tennant Church. Freehold, New Jersey: James Yard & Son [Printers], 1897.

*Thompkins, M. D., Edmund P. (Fishwick, Marshall W., Ed.) Rockbridge County, Virginia: An Informal History, Richmond, VA, 1952. *(Mr. Thompkins was the librarian of the Rockbridge Historical Society.)*

*Thompson, Ernest Trice. Presbyterians in the South, vol. 1: 1607–1861. Richmond: The John Knox Press, 1963, 629.

*Thompson, G. Ray. "William Graham: Virginia Educator and Theologian, 1746 -1799, (Paper with bibliography written while a graduate student at the University of Kansas.) Photocopy of typescript.

*Thorp, Willard, ed. *The Lives of Eighteen from Princeton.* Princeton, New Jersey: Princeton University Press, 1946. (Very important article about of Rev. Samuel Stanhope Smith by **Samuel Holt Monk**, but also very misleading regarding the "establishment sequence between the two colleges, Washington and Lee University and Hampden-Sydney College.)

*Tucker, John Randolph. "Address by John Randolph Tucker, Delivered before the Centennial Meeting of the Synod of Virginia, at New Providence Church, Rockbridge Co., Virginia, October 24, 1888. (Note: This address is published with **Waddell, Rev. James A.,** ed. Waddell, James A., "Contributions to the History of the Synod of Virginia" Washington: John F. Sheiry, Printer, 1890. Tucker's address begins at page 63 and concludes at page 105.)

*Tucker, St. George. "A Dissertation on Slavery: With a Proposal for the Gradual Abolition of It in the State Of Virginia." New York, reprint of 1861 (originally published in Phil. by Mathew Carey, 1796.

*Turner, Charles W. Old Zeus: Life and Letters (1860-1862) of James J. White. Verona, VA, 1983.

*Turner, Henry S., DD. Church in the Old Fields. Chapel Hill, University of North Carolina Press, 1962.

**The Virginia Teacher*. (Harrington Waddell,) "William Henry Ruffner, vol. V, no. 10–11 (October–November 1924): 268–274. (PDF/Google Books) See also under Waddell, Harrington.

*Waddell, Rev. James A., ed. "Contributions to the History of the Synod of Virginia." Washington: John F. Sheiry, Printer, 1890. *(Waddell was one of three committee members who, it appears, functioned as writers, editors, and collators of this article. Other committee members were Rev. Wm. Wirt Henry and Rev. P. B. Price, both trustees of Hampden-Sydney College. Henry, grandson of Patrick, was president of American Historical Association; this unfortunate piece is riddled with errors and omissions concerning the origins of Washington and Lee University.)*

*Waddell, Harrington. "William Henry Ruffner, *The Virginia Teacher*, vol. V, no. 10–11, October–November 1924, pp. 268–274. [pdf/Google Books] See also under Virginia Teacher above.

*Waddell, Joseph, A. Annals of Augusta County, from 1726-1871. C. R. Caldwell, 1901 (Original edition, J. W. Randolph, 1888. Caldwell as publisher may be second edition revised and enlarged in 1901. My copy is dated 1902.)

*Waddell, Joseph A. [Addison]. "Scotch-Irish of the Valley of Virginia," pp. 79–105 in _The Scotch-Irish In America: Proceedings and Address of the Seventh Congress_, Lexington, VA, June 20–23, 1895, Nashville Barbee & Smith Agents, 1895, pp. 79–99.

*Wallace, Rev. Caleb. Memorandum history of Liberty Hall Academy, a handwritten document, written into the record book of the newly established Board of Trustees of Liberty Hall Academy in which are found the original handwritten meeting minutes of the board of trustees at the Leyburn Library of Washington and Lee University, pp. 3–7, signed, "Caleb Wallace, Clerk, May 1776." _(Here Rev. Wallace was acting as clerk of the Hanover Presbytery. Rev. Caleb Wallace makes for a witness of the highest caliber for he is the only member of the Hanover Presbytery that created Liberty Hall Academy and the second seminary in Prince Edward County [later, Hampden Sydney] who was subsequently appointed a trustee of both Liberty Hall Academy and Hampden-Sydney Academy. Rev. Wallace afterward became a justice of the Kentucky Supreme Court.)_

*Warren, Mame. Come Cheer for Washington and Lee: The University at 250 Years. East Greenwich, Rhode Island: Meridian Printing, 1998.

Washington & Lee University Historical Papers, No. 1. Baltimore, John Murphy Co., 1890. Note: My copy is an online partial copy including two of the three included items, namely, "Early History of Washington College" by Rev. Henry Ruffner, late president of the college and Washington College, Lexington, Virginia by Samuel Lyle Campbell, MD, taken from the _Southern Literary Messenger_, 1838. _Not included is "Letter on the Location of Robert Alexander's School, John Brown's residence, and Mount Pleasant" by Judge James T. Patton._

*Washington and Lee University Historical Papers, No. 2. Baltimore, John Murphy Co., 1890. (My copy in wraps, contains "The Founders of Washington College" by Hon. Hugh Blair Grigsby, delivered June 22, 1870, and "Address before the Alumni Association of Washington College" by Rev. Archibald Alexander, delivered June 29, 1843.

*Washington & Lee University Historical Papers, No. 3. Baltimore, John Murphy Co., 1892. Note my partial copy is a contemporary online printed piece, compliments of Google. My partial online digitized copy by Google _(Contains sketches of selected trustees). Others published but not included in my copy include "Memorial Tribute to the Rev. Geo.[rge] A.[ddison] Baxter"; "The Scotch-Irish Settlers in the Valley of Virginia" by Col. Bolivar Christian; "Notes on Washington College: Prepared in 1873, ..." by Sidney S. Baxter._

*Washington & Lee University Historical Papers, No. 4. Baltimore, John Murphy Co.,1895, A Continuation of W. H. Ruffner's "History of Washington College" and "Sketches of Trustees Continued."

*Washington & Lee University Historical Papers, No. 5. Baltimore, John Murphy Co.,1895. Note: my copy of 1/4 red leather contains a continuation of W. H. Ruffner's "History of Washington College" and "Sketches of Trustees Continued."

*Webster, Rev. Richard. A History of the Presbyterian Church in America: From Its Origin until the Year 1760; with Biographical Sketches of Its Early Ministers, Philadelphia, Joseph M. Wilson, 1857. (*Makes no mention of Rev. Brown having any connection to Liberty Hall in his bio sketch.*) (PDF file)

Weeks, Stephen B. "John Chavis: Antebellum Negro Preacher and Teacher." Southern Workman (February 1914): 101–6.

*The West Virginia Historical Magazine. "Augusta Academy," vol. 5, no. 1, January 1905, pp. 9–15. [Pdf Google Books]. *(This article is based, in part, on Henry Ruffner's, "Early History of Washington College" but errs by linking Robert Alexander's and Rev. John Brown's schools to Liberty Hall. It is also based upon the errors of Wm. H. Foote, Sketches of Virginia, 1850 and 1855 Series One and Series Two).*

*White, Rev. Henry Alexander. "The Scotch-Irish University of the South: Washington and Lee" published in The Scotch-Irish in America: Proceedings and Addresses of the Second Congress, May 29 to June 1, 1890, published by order of the Scotch-Irish Society of America, Cincinnati, Ohio, Robert Clark & Co, 1890, pp. 223–246.

*White, Rev. Henry Alexander, PhD, DD. "The Presidents of The Washington College in Virginia" in The Scotch-Irish in America, Proceedings and Addresses, Seventh Congress, 1895, pp. 100–122.

*White, Rev. Henry Alexander. Southern Presbyterian Leaders. New York: Neale Publishing Company, 1911.

*White, James J. (Herbert Baxter Adams, Thomas Jefferson and the University of Virginia, Washington, 1888 *(See especially chap. XXII [Washington And Lee University by Professors White & Harris, i.e., W&L professors, Carter J. Harris & James J. White] and chap. XXIII (bibliography of Washington and Lee University) pp. 293–308. The whole supplemented by a letter from John Mason Brown [great-grandson of Rev. John Brown] [riddled with errors and false assumptions.)* Note: Auditor's copy is a photocopy] *(This is a duplicate of the entry listed under Herbert Baxter Adams)*

White, James J. "Regimental History of the Liberty Hall Volunteers." Box 870266; Tuscaloosa, Alabama, 35487-0266; 205.348.0500; archives@ua.edu.

*Whitsitt, William, H. The Life and Times of Judge Caleb Wallace, Filson Club Publications, Number Four, Louisville: John P. Morton & Company, 1888, 149. Note: Errs reestablishment of Liberty Hall and Hampden-Sydney Academies by misinterpreting W. H. Foote's _Sketches of Virginia_ Series 1, in re dates of Hanover Presbytery meetings; see esp. Whitsett, p. 63, paragraphs 2 and 3.

*William A. Anderson. Trustee "William Graham, Founder of Washington and Lee, Teacher, Preacher, and Patriot." See reference in I. Taylor Sanders's _Now Let the Gospel Trumpets Blow_, p. 74.

*Williams, Samuel Coles. History of the Lost State of Franklin. New York: Press of the Pioneers, 1933. (Contains valuable information pertaining to Rev. William Graham's [of Washington & Lee fame] participation in the plan to establish the state of Franklin. Graham is the author of the draft of the proposed constitution for the lost state of Frankland.)

*Wilson, Howard McKnight. The Lexington Presbytery Heritage, McClure Press, 1971. (errors re founding of W&L)

*Wing, Rev. Conway, A. History of the First Presbyterian Church of Carlisle, PA. Carlisle, "Valley Sentinal" Office, 1877.

*Withers, Robert Enoch. Autobiography of an Octogenarian. Roanoke, Virginia: Stone Printing & Mfg. Co. Press, 1907

*Witherspoon, Rev. John, DD. Lectures on Moral Philosophy. Princeton, NJ: Princeton University Press, 1912.

*Woods, David Walker, Jr., MA. John Witherspoon. New York: Fleming H. Revell Company, 1906.

Appendix 1

W&L Origins Timeline

(A Documentary History Drawn from the Minutes of the Hanover Presbytery and Liberty Hall Academy's Board of Trustees)

*(Note: References to Rev. John Brown, pastor of the Presbyterian New Providence congregation in Rockbridge County, Virginia, are only included in this timeline to aid in facilitating **this report's debunking of the widely held, but utterly false belief that Mr. Brown was a principal party to the establishment of "Liberty Hall Academy" when in fact, he opposed its creation and refused all efforts by his colleagues to obtain his participation in the activities associated with it operations**. Rev. Brown was appointed to several tasks related to the school, including one as trustee, but he did not accept any of these appointments— a view he obstinately held throughout the remainder of his life, a view reflected in the absence of any reference to him in any of the meetings of the Liberty Hall Academy's board of trustees. Nevertheless, histories that address Washington and Lee University's origins persist in representing that Rev. Brown's Latin school at New Providence was a forerunner of the university. Many also suggest that a corresponding link exists backward to the educational endeavors of one Robert Alexander. This claim, like the Rev. Brown school claim, are both devoid of any documentary or other credible evidence in support of the claims. The truth in this regard is that no such link of either type exists. Perhaps that is why no one ever suggested that such a link during the school's first seventy-five years of existence only surfaced after all the actual participants were dead and therefore could not challenge the nonsensical notions. These facts are demonstrated in tiresome, but essential detail repeatedly throughout this report.)*

1767 Rev. John Brown on Oct. 11, 1767 (Hanover Pby. minutes), requested that his pastoral relations with Timber Ridge congregation be dissolved. His request was approved. Rev. Brown had already begun to move his home, his family, and his Latin school from near Fairfield, Virginia (Mount Pleasant) to Moffett's Creek near New Providence, from where it never again moved.

1767   William Graham was studying under Rev. John Roan (see Wm. Henry
                Egle's _Notes and Queries_, Series 3, vol. 3, p. 248, 1896, quoting from
                old papers of Rev. John Roan.)
                "Wm. Graham enter'd 10 br 23, 1767."

1767

June 13   Wm. Graham, student, returned to Rev. Roan after several weeks' absence.

1768   Rev. John Witherspoon comes to America from Scotland to accept
                the presidency of the College of New Jersey (Princeton).

1769   Samuel Brown, b. Jan. 30, 1769, at Rev. John Brown's Moffett's
                Creek home.

                *These dates are included only because they help to debunk the
                alleged connection of Rev. Brown's private Latin school to "Augusta
                Academy" (Liberty Hall Academy).

1769   William Graham left Pennsylvania, went to Princeton, thereafter
                selected to conduct the college's grammar school, under the direction
                of the college's president, John Witherspoon, while at the same time
                matriculating at the college (class of 1773).

May **1770**   Orange Presbytery created in North Carolina.

1771   William Graham continues matriculating at Princeton and teaching
                at the attached grammar school.

                First mention in the Hanover Presbytery meeting minutes of
                consideration of establishing a **seminary** in Virginia to be patterned
                after the College of New Jersey (Princeton). (Hanover Presbytery
                meeting minutes, p. 36)

April 8,   "The consideration of the [meeting] minute concerning the New
1772   Ark Academy [College of New Jersey], and a **Seminary** amongst
                ourselves is defered [_sic_] until our next Sederunt [scheduled meeting]."
                (Hanover Pby. Minutes, p. 40)

                Note: Once again, the presbytery makes it clear that it intended its
                school to be a "Seminary of Learning" (i.e., college) and not a mere
                preparatory school, a stated intent made from the beginning.

, 1773   The Hanover Pby.:

                "The presbytery think it prudent to defer the fixing of a particular
                place of our intended **seminary** until our next stated presbytery,
                which is to be held at Rockfish."

. 4, 1773   (At Rockfish as previously announced?)

                "The presbytery agree to fix the public seminary for the liberal
                education of youth in Staunton, Augusta county."

Oct. 13, 1774

> Hanover Presbytery agreed to "establish" and "patronize" a new academy, in Augusta County, Virginia, which they informally denominated, in their minutes, "Augusta Academy."

> Hanover Presbytery ordained that the academy newly established "shall, at present, be managed by Mr. William Graham." (Hanover Pby. meeting minutes, p. 55)

Oct. 14, 1774

> The College of Hampden Sydney was created as Prince Edward Academy only a few months after the creation of Graham's academy. Hampden-Sydney's historian, Herbert Bradshaw, explains these early days this way:

>> On the day following the action to establish a school in Augusta (October 14, 1774), Hanover Presbytery **gave its blessing** to the founding of a second school within its bounds, east of the Mountains.

>> Further, "The pby taking into consideration the great extent of this colony [*sic*] judge that a publick school for the liberal education of youth would be of great importance on the south side of the blue ledge,[ridge] ***notwithstanding the appointment of one already in the County of Agusta [sic]***."[705]

> *(Importantly, this statement by the presbytery did not create or establish Hampden-Sydney. Rather, the statement is merely an expression of a willingness and desire to establish a second seminary, provided money can be determined to be readily available and provided a suitable person could be found to take the management of it. The presbytery called a special unscheduled meeting to actually establish the second seminary the following year [1775], in February.)*

> Washington and Lee appears to hold the unenviable distinction of being an institution that backdated their origins for some, seemingly, inexplicable reason. It is all the more striking that

---

705 Bradshaw, Herbert C., History of Hampden-Sydney College, N.P., [privately Printed]1976, pg.12.

the institution waited approximately seventy-five years before completely reconstructing their early history.

It does not seems to have occurred to Bradshaw to attempt to antedate their institution's birth date by magically connecting the local grammar school initiated by Patrick Henry et al. and then announce that their first president was Patrick Henry. Others who do not claim a date of origin earlier than that which is supported by documentary evidence are Harvard University, Yale University, and King's College (Columbia).

Feb. 1, 1775

Cub Creek congregation, but session held at Captain Venable's home.

"The presbytery proceed to consider how it would be most expedient to lay out these monies, and when to establish an Academy." (Foote, *Sketches of Va.*, First Series, p. 394)

"Hanover Synod establishes a 2nd school in Prince Edward County." (Meeting at home of Nathaniel Venable)[706]

Feb. 3, 1775

Cub Creek congregation, but session held at Captain Venable's home:

> On Feb. 3rd Presbytery chose Mr. Samuel Stanhope Smith, Rector of the Prince Edward Academy. (Foote, *Sketches of Va.*, First Series, p. 395)

April 12, 1775

The Hanover Presbytery met at Timber Ridge Meeting House.

> April 12, 1775, the Presbytery commenced its Spring Sessions at Timber Ridge; on the 13th, it met at the house of Rev. Mr. Brown; present Messrs. Todd, Brown, Rice, Leake, Irwin, Waddell, and Wallace, with John Logan elder. (Foote, *Sketches of Virginia*, p. 443)

---

706 Gaines, Elizabeth Venable, [**Cub Creek Church and Congregation**, ... pg.23]

April 13, 1775

The presbytery announced that Mr. William Graham offered himself on trial for the gospel ministry and that he had "produced sufficient testimonials of his good standing in the churches where he lived to the northward, and having been interrogated on his views for the gospel ministry, and also on his acquaintance with practical Piety, and on these points having satisfied the Psby, he is continued on tryals [*sic*]." (Hanover Pby. meeting minutes, p. 61). Mr. Graham attended his first meeting of the Hanover Presbytery on this day.

> The affairs of our public school were taken under consideration, ..the presbytery find that they can do no more at this session than recommend it, in the warmest manner, to the public, to make such liberal contributions, as they shall find compatible with their circumstances, for the establishing of said school. And the presbytery, as guardians and directors, take this opportunity to declare their resolution to do their best endeavors to establish it on the most catholic plan, that circumstances will permit. (*American Quarterly Register*, p. 146)

Apr. 15, 1775

> he presbytery, finding they cannot of themselves forward subscriptions in a particular manner, do, for the encouragement of the academy to be established in Augusta, recommend it to the following gentlemen to take subscriptions in their behalf.* [List follows in a footnote.]

Note 1. This entry and the entry preceding it is interesting in that they are but two days apart. The meeting of the thirteen[th] was held at Timber Ridge Church nearby.

Minutes of April 15, 1775:

> As the presbytery have now an opportunity of **visiting** the school under the direction of Mr. Brown, they accordingly repaired to the schoolhouse, and attended a specimen of

the proficiency of the students in the **Latin
and Greek languages**, and pronouncing
orations, with which they were well-pleased.
(The *American Quarterly Register*, vol. 10
[Boston: Perkins & Marvin, 1838], p. 146)

Note 2: The presbytery held its session and conducted their
business at Timber Ridge Church and then proceeded to travel
six or seven miles to the home of Rev. John Brown who often
entertained traveling Presbyterian clergymen who were passing
through. Here, Brown obviously sought to have these brethren
observe his private Latin school. It is important because it
demonstrates that Brown's school was located near his home.
Those who have asserted a connection between Rev. Brown's
school and Washington and Lee mistaken believed that Brown's
school was still operating at Mount Pleasant. The only school
operating at Mount Pleasant in the 1770s was the presbytery's
new seminary under William Graham. It is also noteworthy
that the presbytery's minutes make clear that their only role at
Rev. Brown's school was that of a *visitor*. The following May,
the Presbytery's role when visiting their sponsored school under
William Graham was one of **"examination."**

Aug. 24, 1775

Rev. Brown's biographer, John White Stuart III (PhD
dissertation)[707] describes another of Brown's letters to Col.
Wm. Preston (his brother-in-law) as asserting pessimistic views
regarding "Augusta academy."

> In the summer of 1775, Brown expressed
> pessimism "that the times are not favorable
> to the design of the semenary" [*sic*] and "the
> Expectation is too high for the plan that is
> laid. (Stuart, . . ., p. 102, n42, chap. 5; quote
> within quote)

Brown also said this:

*Note: The quote above provides an explanation as to why Rev. Brown had invited the presbytery to
visit his Latin school at New Providence during the immediately prior meeting of the presbytery.
Rev. Brown clearly believed that Liberty Hall Academy, as it would soon be named, was a near-
certain failure. His school, he apparently hoped, would serve as a viable alternative. Of course, in
this, he was wrong, as events would soon evince. By the same date, the following year (1776), Brown
would have closed his Latin school at New Providence, and it remained closed for the duration of
the Revolutionary War while Liberty Hall Academy was flourishing in their new quarters at Timber*

---

707   John White Stuart III, The Rev. John Brown of Virginia (1728–1803): His Life and selected
      sermons, Doctoral Dissertation, University of Massachusetts, 1988.

Ridge, and the preparatory program conducted temporarily as a "grammar school" at Mount Pleasant while the new buildings at Timber Ridge were being constructed was to continue throughout the tenure of the academy's rector, Rev. William Graham.

When Rev. Brown's tutor, Samuel Doak, abandoned his role at Rev. Brown's school to take a temporary position at the other academy, Hampden-Sydney, at the end of December of 1775, Rev. Brown had little hope of obtaining a replacement instructor in light of the rapidly approaching hostilities with the mother country. Not being capable of performing that task himself, he had no choice but to close the school. Any students remaining when Mr. Doak left, who were so young that they could not serve as a soldier and who desired to pursue his studies, likely transferred to Rev. Graham's grammar school a few miles distant at Mount Pleasant. Of course, Rev. Brown's sons were sent elsewhere, demonstrating Rev. Brown's obvious disdain for all things associated with Liberty Hall Academy.

Oct. 26, 1775

> *William Graham licensed as a minister by the Hanover Presbytery. (Hanover Pby. meeting minutes, p. 65)

Oct. 27, 1775

> *The Augusta school was taken under consideration. The presbytery agree that Mr. William Graham **_continue to have the care and tuition_** of said school. (Hanover Pby. meeting minutes, p. 67)

Note: The academy was "established at the autumn meeting of 1774 followed by the Spring meeting of 1775," and the minutes for that meeting are devoid of any reference to the "care and tuition" of the academy having changed. Therefore, the only reasonable interpretation of the presbytery's use of the phrase "to continue to have the care and tuition" must necessarily mean that the presbytery's view was that it had been with Mr. Graham from the school's date of establishment. If not, when could Mr. Graham have received from the presbytery the "care and tuition of the academy"?

Nov. 23, 1775

> Rev. Samuel S. Smith corrects his earlier advertised promise to open Hampden-Sydney Academy in November of 1775.
>
> ***Rev. Samuel Stanhope Smith's written announcement that Hampden Sydney's first-ever classes would begin in January*** and that before the first of January, the steward, with assistance of a few neighbors, who live well within less than two miles of Hampden Sydney," would be "able to accommodate all the young gentlemen who may be put under my care. I presume we shall not need the assistance of the neighborhood longer than till next summer, when the buildings will be chiefly erected."[708]

---

708   Alfred J. Morrison, *The College of Hampden-Sidney: Calendar of Board Minutes 1776–1876*, Richmond, VA., The Hermitage Press, 1912, pg. 18

(Emphasis added for those who may have been misled by Dr. John Luster Brinkley, in his dubious tome, *On This Hill: A Narrative History of Hampden-Sydney College, 1774–1994*, Hampden-Sydney, 1994, 880 pp. The dubious and error ridden section is located on pages 307–310.)

In a subchapter or subsection of his third chapter entitled "Toilers of the Sea," which Brinkley identifies as "A Stiff Upper Lip," he challenges the college's decision to change their date of establishment. In this, Brinkley is correct, but for the wrong reason. Brinkley mistakenly asserts that the date of founding or "establishment" is October 4, 1774, but the accurate date of establishment cannot be before February 1 of 1775. The reason the board of trustees cannot legitimately change the date of establishment is because that function must emanate with the entity that created the college, which was the Hanover Presbytery, and we think that it is entirely appropriate to point out that the Hanover Presbytery is the same entity that created the first board of trustees of Hampden-Sydney.

It is the auditor's view that the date of establishment is a question of historical fact, not policy. The question as to when the college was established is clearly one that is within the sole province of the entity that "established" it. Of course, the trustees may decide to represent to the public a false date of establishment, just as they may represent to the public that the sun rises in the west, but the fact that they choose to represent a falsehood doesn't alter the actual facts of the matter. To exercise that which they may falsely do, however, is an act of institutional absurdity.

In the final analysis, it is an empirically based historical fact that the trustees of Hampden-Sydney did not establish the college. The Hanover Presbytery established the college, and the date of the establishment is provided in the meeting minutes for Feb. 1, 1775. The first time the school is mentioned as an actual entity in the presbytery's minutes is in the meeting minutes of a pro re nata meeting held on Feb. 1, 1775. Prior to that date, the presbytery was merely considering the feasibility of raising sufficient funds and obtaining a sufficiently qualified person to manage such an anticipated possible school. Indeed, the first mention of the possibility of establishing a second academy east of the Blue Ridge Mountains was on October 14, 1774. The presbytery, however, did not "agree to establish and patronize" a second academy at that meeting. They merely authorized a feasibility study to determine if they could raise sufficient funds and to determine the availability of Samuel S. Smith to manage such an operation, if one were established.

The board of trustees may not legitimately alter the date of establishment of the institution ex post facto. After all, the board of trustees of Hampden-Sydney did not exist prior to February of 1775. As a body, the board of trustees was initially a mere theoretical construct, which was created by fiat, by the Hanover Presbytery; and every member of the first board of trustees were only trustees by virtue of an appointment given to them by the Hanover Presbytery. The trustees then may not legitimately alter the date that the Hanover Presbytery created the college.

Note: The same may be said with respect to Washington and Lee University. The Hanover Presbytery created Washington and Lee, and that body set forth the date when the college was established in its first authorized institutional history, which may be located in the Liberty Hall Academy's first record book containing the meeting minutes of the first board of trustees. This history written by the presbytery's clerk, Rev. Caleb Wallace, in May of 1776, and a copy of it begins on the record book's first page of text, and it is identified as page 3. It covers pages 3 through 7 and is comprised, in the main, of extracts from those sections of the Presbytery's meeting minutes that are pertinent to the establishment of the college. A similar memorandum of history should be located in the first record book used by the Hampden Sydney College's board of trustees because the presbytery directed Mr. Wallace to provide it to them, according to their minutes.

May 1776

*Hanover Presbytery met and noted "A Call[709] from the United Congregations of Timber Ridge and Hall's Meeting House, for William Graham." [Mr. Graham accepted the call on May 4.] (Hanover pby. minutes pp. 72, 76)

**"The Presbytery proceeds to examine the School under the Care of Mr. Graham. . . . The Pby highly approve of the proficiency of the Students and the Diligence and abilities of the Teachers." (Hanover Pby. Minutes, p. 76)

The Presbytery "fixed" the permanent location of the "Augusta Academy" at Timber Ridge" and "we choose Mr. William Graham, Rector"[710] and they also created the Board of Trustees

---

709 A "Call" in this context refers to a formal invitation proffered by a Presbyterian Congregation(s) to a licensed minister, to become their pastor. To be "ordained" typically means that the minister accepted the "Call" with the Presbytery's blessing. Such an ordination is memorialized by a formal ceremony.

710 There followed a parenthetical qualifier, "and under the inspection of Rev. John Brown," that qualifier, however, was rendered meaningless insofar as Brown did not accept this, or for that matter, any appointment that related to the new seminary (i.e., Academy.)

and appointed the members. (Hanover Pby. meeting minutes, p. 78)

May 4, 1776

Mr. Graham accepts the call from Timber Ridge and Hall's meeting house. (Hanover Pby. Meeting Minutes p. 77)

May 13, 1776

*The Board of Trustees of the Augusta Academy, announced at their first meeting that they had selected the school's first official name, "Liberty Hall Academy." (Hanover Pby meeting minutes, p. 11)

Note: During the American Revolution, Liberty Hall changed its location from Timber Ridge to the rector's farm on Whistle Creek several miles from Timber Ridge toward what is now the city of Lexington. Here, its classes took place first in the rector's home then in an abandoned home. Thereafter, a frame building was constructed for the academy's college classes, but it was burned. Finally, in the early 1790s, several more permanent stone structures were constructed on Mulberry Hill, including one which housed the students, classrooms, and the library. One building served as a refectory, and it also had rooms for a steward. Technically, the students matriculated at six different campus locations under the Graham administration: Mount Pleasant, Timber Ridge, the rector's home, an abandoned house, a new frame building, and the stone campus on Mulberry Hill.

May of 1776

The clerk of the Hanover Presbytery, Rev. Caleb Wallace, writes the first authorized history of Liberty Hall Academy. This history was created from the official records of the Hanover Presbytery by Rev. Caleb Wallace, pastor of Cub Creek congregation in Charlotte County, Virginia, at the direction of the Hanover Presbytery.[711]

Liberty Hall Academy campus moved to Mulberry Hill.

---

711   Technically, the Presbytery directed Clerk, Wallace to prepare such a history for the Trustees of Hampden Sydney Academy, but it was obvious to Wallace that such a history should also be prepared for the Trustees of Liberty Hall Academy, which he did. These historical memoranda were then copied into the new record books of each of the Presbytery's new patronized Academies for historical recording of the events which led up to each school's creation. Oddly, no published history of Washington and Lee University, or the same school by any of its various denominations from Augusta Academy to Washington and Lee University has ever cited this the most significant historical artifact that exists outside of the official meeting minutes of the Hanover Presbytery during this period.

1782   President Graham and two others donate land at Mulberry Hill for purpose of constructing a frame building for housing the academy.

The new Commonwealth of Virginia's first legislature enacts a bill granting Liberty Hall Academy the first charter[712] and granting the college formal (legal) degree-granting status.

1782

(Autumn) On application made by Rev. William Graham, in the name of the Board of Trustees of Liberty Hall Academy, the school becomes the first "chartered college authorized by the legislature of 'New' Virginia," with the authority to grant the degree of Bachelor of Arts.

In December, the charter was formally approved by VA legislature [note Washington College in Maryland chartered Oct. 15, 1782 according to their web site]. Liberty Hall Academy appears to have been the first College chartered by the Virginia after the Revolution and apparently the second college chartered in the United States of America by an American authority. Harvard, Yale, William and Mary, and Princeton etc. having been chartered by the British authorities prior to the American Revolution.

October 1782—Rev. William Graham, Rector [i.e., President] of Liberty Hall Academy, drafted a Petition seeking to have the Legislature grant to Liberty Hall Academy, an Act of Incorporation with degree granting authority and submitted the petition to the Legislature in the name of the Board of Trustees, under his signature.[713]

Rev. William Graham also drafted the proposed Act of Incorporation and submitted this along with the petition alluded to above. The Legislature granted the petition by enacting an Act of Incorporation on [October—, 1782] This action by the Virginia Legislature gave to Liberty Hall Academy the important distinction of being the first chartered institution of higher learning in "free[714]" Virginia.

---

712 Earlier, the British government granted William and Mary College the only formal Charter as a college. Typically, under British dominion, only colleges affiliated with the Church of England (Anglican) were granted an official Charter. William and Mary was the first and only institution in Virginia the British government recognized as a college. Other institutions providing college level instruction, like Liberty Hall in the Valley were referred to as an "Academy."

713 A copy of this petition can be seen at, William and Mary College Quarterly Historical Magazine, Vol. 13, No.4, (Apr., 1905), pp. .265-266 .

714 "Free" meaning after the formation of The United States of America following the Revolutionary War.

(Note: Several have dated the charter as October 21, of 1782.[715] This is accurate.)

New board of trustees appointed as part of the legislative charter.

Trustees of Liberty Hall, Mulberry Hill, near Lexington:

Joseph Walker (1782–1815); William Alexander; Alexander Campbell; Col. Arthur Campbell; Rev. Edward Crawford; Samuel Doak; Benjamin Erwin; Maj. John Hays; John Lyle; James McConnell; James McCorkle; Rev. John Montgomery; Gen. Andrew Moore; Rev. Archibald Scott; Archibald Stuart; John Trimble; James Trotter; Caleb Wallace; John Wilson; Rev. William Wilson; Rev. Samuel Carrick (1784–1791), who was replaced by Rev. Samuel Houston (1791–1826).

Note: Not reappointed were those men who never accepted the original appointments made by the Hanover Presbytery and those who had departed the Valley in the ensuing years or had died. Rev. John Brown was not reappointed for the obvious reason that he had never accepted his original appointment and had no desire to be appointed. Rev. Brown had no affiliation with the presbytery's created and patronized college whether known as Augusta Academy or as officially named Liberty Hall Academy.

1783

The new Commonwealth of Virginia's first legislature enacts a Bill granting Hampden-Sydney Academy the second charter (after the Revolution) and granting the college formal (legal) degree-granting status. Thereafter, the college's name is Hampden-Sydney College.

Liberty Hall's main building destroyed by fire. Arson is suspected. Burned building is rebuilt.

1785   In September, the college held its first formal commencement for twelve graduates.

---

715   See *Charter and Laws and Trustees and Alumni of Washington College at Lexington, Virginia, A. D. 1865*, Richmond, 1865. While the pamphlet lists no author or editor, the copy reviewed by the auditor is housed in the Leyburn Library of Washington and Lee University, and it is bound in a volume which bears the following legend upon its spine, "Washington and Lee University, Catalogs, 1865- - 1879," pg. 5, it says, as parenthetical in brackets under the Article's title, "[Passed October 21ˢᵗ, 1782.]"

Sept. 24, 1788

> Rev. Graham writes important letter to Col. Arthur Campbell of Kentucky, referring therein to the "horrors of slavery." Colonel Campbell was a close confidant and friend of Graham's from the days when Campbell lived in the Valley.

1790

> A second framed college building was destroyed by fire. Apparently, this fire was accidental.

1792

> The Virginia Synod enters into a new agreement to create the first Presbyterian patronized theological seminary in the United States. An important aspect of that agreement was the synod's sponsored fund-raising effort that allowed for the college to erect a new limestone campus on Mulberry Hill. This realignment between the Presbyterian Church and the college was controversial as both the college and the theological seminary were conducted in the same buildings comprising Liberty Hall Academy. Rev. Graham was president of both entities (i.e., Liberty Hall and "the Lexington Theological Seminary," as Prof. Edward Graham referred to it in his "Memoir of the Late Rev. William Graham"). (*The Evangelical and Literary Magazine_and Missionary Chronicle*, IV [1821], p. 75, et seq.)

1793   Limestone buildings completed.
1793
(or 1794)

> John Chavis enrolled at Liberty Hall Academy. He was probably enrolled in late 1793 for the 1794 academic year.[716]

1798   Liberty Hall Academy's name changed to "Washington Academy."

1813   Washington Academy's name changed to "Washington College."

1849

> Washington College trustees published the college's first authorized history of its founding as an appendix to *Christianity the Patron of Literature and Science: An Address Delivered February 22, 1849. On the Occasion of the Author's [Pres.]*

---

716 Many of the college's records for this period were lost or destroyed by fire during this period. Fortunately, the meeting minutes of the Lexington Presbytery are extant and importantly illuminating with regard to the educational affairs of Rev. John Chavis.

George Junkin] Inauguration as President of Washington College, Virginia, Philadelphia, the Board of Trustees, 1849 (pamphlet, pp. 39). The Junkin inaugural address includes an important appendix: "A Brief Sketch of the Early History of Washington College" (ordered printed by the board of trustees).

1865

First appearance of an institutional false history of the origins of Washington College (Virginia).

Washington College Board of Trustees publish *The Charter and Laws and Trustees and Faculty of Washington College at Lexington, Va. A. D. 1865*, Richmond: Chas. H. Wynne, Printer, 1865. This publication's first section is curiously labeled:

"HISTORICAL STATISTICS"

Its content constitutes a repudiation of the history of the founding of the college previously and consistently adhered to from its inception on October 13, 1774. This 1865 rewrite was offered without notice that it constituted a repudiation of the college's long-standing traditional history, and the repudiation was published without explanation or justification. The revised history begins with this bald-faced fiction:

> The **germ of Washington College was a classical school established about 1752 (?) By Robert Alexander**, at first near Greenville, Augusta County; and **"was the first classical school in the valley of Virginia"** It was removed **"shortly before the revolution" to Mt. Pleasant**, near Fairfield, Rockbridge County, where October **12, 1774, it was formally adopted by Hanover Presbytery**, with its original name of the Augusta Academy, and arrangements were made to support it, while it remained under the patronage of the Presbytery, by "liberal contributions." In its records of May 13, 1776, it is styled "Liberty Hall Academy as it is hereafter to be called, instead of The Augusta Academy," and lands were accepted for its "new site," near the Timber Ridge Church. In 1785, it was removed to near Lexington, where yet stand the ruins of Liberty Hall, burned in 1803. It was promptly rebuilt,

but on its present site, within the limits of Lexington.

The university has not published an accurate history of its founding since 1865.

Oct. 9, 1771

(First mention in the minutes of consideration of establishing a seminary in Virginia)

Hanover Presbytery's first acknowledged consideration of establishing a seminary patterned after Princeton, in Virginia. Pby. solicited feedback from their various congregations concerning the desirability, and feasability of such an endeavor.

> The presbytery being very clear of the great expediency of erecting a seminary of learning somewhere within their bounds do recommend to all their members to take this matter under consideration, report their thoughts at our next meeting; especially respecting the best method of accomplishing it.[717]

> The matter [establishment of a seminary in Virginia] was introduced at the session at the Dee Ess Church on October 9, 1771. The desirability of establishing a school in Virginia was recognized, but more thorough deliberation was deemed advisable.[718]

Presbytery being very sensible of the great Expediency of erecting a Seminary of Learning within the bounds of this presbytery, do recommend it to all the Members to take this matter under Consideration, and report their tho'ts at our next, especially respecting the best method of accomplishing it.[719]

---

717 "History of Washington College," *The American Quarterly Register*, B. B. Edwards and W. Cogswell, eds., Vol. 10, Boston, 1838, pg.145.

718 *"The matter* [establishment of a seminary in Virginia] *was introduced at the session at the Dee Ess Church on October 9, 1771. The desirability of establishing a school in Virginia was recognized, but more thorough deliberation was deemed advisable:"* [Bradshaw, Herbert C., *History of Hampden-Sydney College*, N.P., [privately Printed]1976, pg.11.] [Hanover Presbytery Minutes, II, 37, Oct. 9, 1771]

719 Hanover Presbytery Minutes, II, 37, Oct. 9, 1771

April 8, 1772

> Hanover Presbytery deferred consideration concerning the possibility of establishing an academy for preparing young men for the professions, especially the ministry.

April 17, 1771

> Rev. Dr. Archibald Alexander is born (1st president, Princeton Theological Seminary)

1772

> William Graham's mother died; he completes his junior year at Princeton and then is deemed by President Witherspoon to have completed all his essential instruction, thereby skipping the senior class instruction, but requiring that he sit for examinations at the conclusion of the 1773 academic year. (Note: he graduates high in his class.)

April 8, 1772   The Hanover Presbytery

> The consideration of the minute concerning . . . and a seminary among ourselves, is deferred until our next *sederunt*.[720] (i.e., a formal meeting of an ecclesiastical body) (Hanover Pby. minutes)

January 1773

> Letter from Rev. John Brown to his brother-in-law, Col. Wm. Preston, in which he discusses his "overseeing the school & sometimes hearing classes, and that there are 14 or 15 of *our school* reading Greek" (13 Jan. 1773[721]). He is referring in this letter to his "Latin school" at New Providence.

*Note: This "Latin School" had operated briefly in the 1760s at Mount Pleasant near Fairfield when Rev. Brown was also the pastor of Timber Ridge Presbyterian Church. **He was voluntarily dismissed from that pastorate in 1767. He had moved from near Fairfield to a farm on Moffett's Creek near his congregation of New Providence. He had also moved his family and his "Latin school" from the earlier location, a fact frequently overlooked by nineteenth-century historians.***

June 2, 1773   Hanover Presbytery deferred locating the seminary.

1773

> Wm. Graham returns to Princeton and agrees to tutor Henry (later Gen. "Light-Horse Harry") Lee in preparation for both

---

720   "History of Washington College"...op cit

721   Ibid. Pg. 100.

of them taking their final exams. (Note: Mr. Lee happily passes his exams); Wm. Graham selected to give presentation at the commencement exercises on the proposition, "Matter is not in any sense infinitely divisible." (See William Graham entry in *Princetonians, 1769-1775* volume edited by Richard A. Harrison, article on Graham by W. Frank Craven, p. 290) (See esp. Professor Murrin's introduction to the *Princetonians* cited in the bibliography.)

1773

Sept.   William Graham graduates from College of New Jersey (Princeton) under Dr. John Witherspoon.

1773

Oct. 4   Hanover Presbytery announced intent to establish seminary (i.e., academy) at Staunton, VA (note: a decision later revised by striking the reference to Staunton).

1773   Wm. Graham continues his theological instruction under Rev. John Roan.

1773

Nov. 15   Rev. John Roan loan to William Graham of ten shillings noted in Roan's account ledger, a fact published by Wm. H. Egle in his famous *Notes and Queries* series (see bibliography).

D e c .   Liberty Hall trustees met concerning the completion of the construction
1773   of the new campus on Mulbery Hill, the steward (Edw. Graham) to accept students the first of January

1774
Feb. 18

John White Stuart III, dissertation published on Rev. John Brown (1988), diss. references 1774 letter: From John Brown to Wm. Preston:

> *In 1774 Brown reported to Preston, "Our school floorshes [sic] there is now 23 hopful boys at it pulling away ambitiously.* (Stuart, dissertation . . . pp. 100–101, n38, chap. 5, references a letter: Rev. John Brown to Wm. Preston, Brown's brother-in-law)

August 22, 1774

J. W. Stuart, dissertation on John Brown, says (on p. 101),

> This school was clearly a Latin grammar, classical, or secondary school and ***was almost***

> *certainly conducted at the New Providence meetinghouse or nearby.* <u>Brown also ran an English school at new Providence</u> in which writing and figures were taught, apparently a primary school but one where John Brown Jr., also could review some basics before entering college. ***Brown Sr., had conducted similar schools** at Mount Pleasant **when he lived there*** and may have operated either a primary or secondary school throughout his ministry; but the evidence for such is not complete. (Stuart, dissertation . . ., p. 101; emphasis added, underline here representing an error)

Note: Underlining in the extract above indicates an error. Rev. Brown did not organize an "English school" at New Providence, but he did organize a Latin school at New Providence. It is well established that Presbyterian ministers were typically expected to operate primary schools as part of their ministerial obligations. Most conducted the classes in these schools, and they were conducted at or adjacent to their meeting houses or churches. Rev. Brown briefly ran, or rather organized, but did not teach, a "Latin school" at Mount Pleasant, but there is no evidence that he organized any other schools at that time. Mr. Stuart's supposition concerning this is not supported by any evidence, and he is clearly in error on this point. Rev. Brown's Latin school was never moved back to Mount Pleasant after leaving there in the late 1760s. Mr. Brown's Latin school at New Providence was still operating there as late as December 1775 and was taught, at that time, by Samuel Doak, as evidenced by the eyewitness testimony of Rev. Philip Vickers Fithian (see his journal 1775–1776 [ref. in bibliography]). Which "English" (i.e., teaching basic English and elementary mathematics, and history etc., essential for preparing students for college) school Rev. Brown was referring to is unknown to history, but for certain, Rev. Brown neither organized nor taught at any such school. Mr. Brown was not inclined, nor qualified for such an endeavor.

1774
Aug. 22

Letter of Rev. John Brown to Col. Wm. Preston (Brown's brother-in-law):

> ***Johny is so far thro his Education that he is fit to enter College*** & I have had him this month past at ***the English School learning to write and figure with a design to prepare him.*** But I have received a Letter from Mr. Waddell that he intends to open a school &

desires me find him an assistant as my son is so young & unexperience, I design to send him as I know he can make improvement under observation of such a man as Mr. Waddell & he will be young enough next year & if I am able to send Billy with him they will be company for one another, for I expect he will be ready.[722]

****

Below: The Date of Origin of Washington and Lee University

****

1774

Oct. 12, 13, and 14

(At Cub Creek Presbyterian meeting house [church], in Charlotte County, VA)

The presbytery resume the consideration of a public school for the liberal education of youth, judging it to be of great and immediate importance. *We do, therefore, agree to establish and patronize a public school* which shall be confined to the county of Augusta. At present it shall be managed by Mr. William Graham, a gentleman properly recommended to this presbytery, *—and to be under the inspection of the Rev. John Brown.*[723]

(*This appointment of Rev. Brown to be the presbytery's eyes and ears in Augusta County was refused by Rev. Brown just as he shunned all such attempts to reconcile him to the establishment of their seminary. The meeting minutes of both the Hanover Presbytery and the later Liberty Hall Academy Board of Trustees, demonstrate quite clearly that Rev. Brown had no connection to the activities of Augusta Academy (later, Liberty Hall Academy). Mr. Brown was also appointed a trustee of Liberty Hall Academy, but during the school's first twenty years of*

---

722 Rebecca K. Pruett, The Browns of Liberty Hall., Masonic Home Printing Office, Masonic Home, Kentucky, 1966 (2nd Printing, 1967 [, pg.5, referencing in FN # 11, Draper Mss. No. 3QQ81, State Historical Society of Wisconsin. Madison.

723 *From a copy of the hand-written Minutes of the Hanover Presbytery, October 14, 1774, housed at Union Theological Seminary, Richmond, Virginia, pg. 55. Provided by: Dr. Paula Skreslet, Reference / Archives, William Smith Morton Library, Union Presbyterian Seminary*

existence, he never attended a meeting of the trustees, a fact embarrassingly
overlooked by all historians of the college who mistakenly asserted a link between
Rev. Brown and Liberty Hall Academy.)

Oct. 14, 1774 (Third day of a meeting which began on Oct. 12, 1774)

> The Hanover Presbytery discussed the possibility of establishing
> yet another academy east of the Blue Ridge Mountains and
> authorized an investigation into the question including whether
> sufficient funds could be raised for such an endeavor.

1775   Sometime in the first quarter of 1775, William Graham arrived in the
Valley of Virginia.

> Note: At least for some appreciable time, Mr. Graham was
> invited to join the Rev. Brown's household, a benefit Rev. Brown
> extended to virtually all itinerating Presbyterian ministers and
> probationary minister who came to the Valley. We learn this
> from the illuminating "Memoir of Rev. William Graham"
> written by Archibald Alexander (unpublished). Alexander
> explains that during this period, Mr. Graham formed an
> alliance of mutual affection with the eldest daughter of Rev.
> Brown, and in time, an understanding was reached between
> this young couple concerning marriage. Without descending
> into the realm of gossip, we nevertheless learn from Rev.
> Alexander that Mr. Graham came to know of his prospective
> mother-in-law's disapproval in this regard and further of her
> sharing her feelings about Mr. Graham with many in her family
> and with others. In response, Mr. Graham requested that his
> prospective bride release him from any obligations concerning
> marriage, and despite the great disappointment for both the
> prospective bride and the would-be groom, the daughter, Betsy,
> reluctantly granted Mr. Graham's request. Such events usually
> result, albeit unfairly, in social embarrassment, most of which
> fell upon the bride and her family, a result which apparently
> the Brown family inexplicably blamed on Mr. Graham, and it
> caused a rupture in their relations that never healed. With this
> information, it becomes far easier to comprehend the animus
> felt by the Brown family toward Liberty Hall Academy and
> its rector, Rev. William Graham. There is no known evidence
> that the rupture in this young couple's marriage was due to
> either the prospective bride, Betsy, or her intended groom, Rev.
> William Graham. The affair seems not to have affected the
> professional relationship between the Rev. Mr. Brown or his
> colleague in the Presbyterian ministry, the Rev. Mr. Graham.
> Mr. Alexander, president of Princeton Theological Seminary,

suggests that the cause of Mrs. Brown's animus toward Rev. Graham stemmed from her husband's loss of social standing that resulted from Mr. Graham's rather obvious higher professional standing in both scholarly and educational attainments. The two clerics' differences were admittedly palpable, but whether her assessment concerning community social standing was accurate is not knowable.

1775

Feb.   On the first day (Feb. 1) of a special "pro re nata," and theretofore unscheduled, meeting of the Hanover Presbytery, it was decided to establish a second seminary (academy) to be located east of the Blue Ridge Mountains. Without actually "deciding to establish and patronize the seminary (the presbytery's intent to do so can be inferred from their decision on this day to hire Samuel Stanhope Smith to manage this endeavor), this second academy would, in time, become Hampden-Sydney College.

April 13, 1775

William Graham's application for licensing and trials for becoming a minister was announced by the Hanover Presbytery in their regular spring meeting minutes.

> "Mr. William Graham having offered himself on tryal for the gospel ministry produced sufficient testimonials of his good standing in the churches where he lived to the northward, and having been interrogated on his views for the gospel ministry, and also on his acquaintance with practical Piety, and on these points having satisfied the Psby, he is continued on tryals. (Hanover pby. meeting minutes, p. 61)

April 14, 1775

Presbytery re William Graham and Augusta Academy:

> The Pby do also appoint to Mr. Graham a Discourse on 1 Tim. ?? 10 also a Homily on this subject "How far knowledge is necessary to salvation, to be delivered at a Pby to be held at the Dee Ess (Church) on the last Wednesday of June, Anno 1775 . . .

> ___The Affairs of our publick school___ is taken under Consideration, and after the most

mature Deliberation the Psby find that they can do more at this session to recommend it again in the warmest manner to the Publick to make such liberal contributions as they shall find compatible with their circumstances, for the establishing said School and the Psby as Guardians and Directors, take this opportunity to declare their Resolution to do their best Endeavors to establish it, on the most Catholic plan that circumstances will permit of. (Hanover pby. meeting minutes, pp. 61–62; emphasis added)

April 15, 1775

The presbytery appointed a subscription committee members to carry out the fund-raising campaign. The presbytery then lists many significant persons in various communities attached to the Presbyterian Church and directs

> **Mr. Brown**, Mr. Irwin, and Mr. Wallace *are to give the above named gentlemen Notice of this Appointment and to Solicit their favor* (i.e., acceptance)**. (Hanover pby. meeting minutes)

Note: Here the presbytery is very specific and directs the named members to "solicit their favor." Appointments made by the presbytery are usually not ordinations or directives, but nominations must always be "accepted" before they become official in the technical sense, an important point often missed by historians, researchers, and other various writers. Often, members of the presbytery are appointed to a committee, but that notice in the minutes of the presbytery's meetings does not indicate that the members necessarily "accepted" the appointment. For example, several of the men named as trustees of Liberty Hall Academy on May 6, 1776, did not accept their appointments and never participated as a trustee. One striking case in that regard is with the appointment of Rev. John Brown who never accepted his appointment as trustee and never attended a trustee meeting. It is possible, however, that Rev. Brown attended a meeting of the Lexington Presbytery that was held in the new stone main building of Liberty Hall Academy in the early 1790s, so at least on this one occasion he probably saw with his own eyes the college whose creation he opposed and refused to support that was conducted in his own neighborhood. He went so far as to send his sons to Pennsylvania, New Jersey, and Williamsburg, far from home, to obtain schooling they could have received while living at home.

April 15, 1775

Presbytery foolishly references in their meeting minutes a postmeeting "visit" to Rev. John Brown's private "Latin School" then operating next door to their host's home at New Providence meeting house.

Note: The auditor uses the term *foolishly* above for two reasons: (1) The "visit" was not official since Rev. Brown's school was an entirely private affair and, as such, the presbytery had no jurisdiction over its affairs and (2) by referencing in their official minutes an entirely private operation, the meeting's cursory minutes had potentially misled any nonmember into thinking the school had an official connection to the presbytery when it did not. Indeed, that is precisely what happened, for when Rev. William Hill wrote for publication a brief history of Washington College, he confused this private preparatory school of Rev. Brown's at New Providence with the new academy just being organized by William Graham at "Mount Pleasant." In his confusion, he then referred to this unofficial postmeeting "visit" in an extensive paragraph listing a series of actions taken by the presbytery in connection with their new academy and in so doing left the appearance that the two different were in fact the same endeavor when they were not. To further confound later nineteenth-century readers, the new academy, which operated temporarily at "Mount Pleasant," is the same location where Rev. Brown's private "Latin school" had earlier been conducted before he moved to his New Providence location. From this, it is entirely understandable how later readers of these official records misread them.

An important aspect of the meeting minutes overlooked by Rev. Hill and subsequent authors is that the spring meeting session met on the first day at Timber Ridge Meeting House several miles from Rev. Brown's home. After they adjourned the first day's session, they all traveled several miles to Rev. Brown's capacious home where traveling members took their lodging and where the subsequent meetings were held. Those who misread the meeting minutes in this regard often only read extracts. In that way, the important aspects of the minutes that separated the activities and discussions pertaining to the presbytery's new academy from the foolish last-minute reference to Mr. Brown's private unaffiliated school weren't sufficiently differentiated and therefore appeared to be the same school when they were not. Here is what they said, which, of course, they should not have said:

> The Pby think it expedient, as they now have an opportunity of *visiting* the School under the Direction of Mr. Brown, accordingly the Pby repaired to the school House, and attended a Specimen of the Proficiency of the Students, in the Latin and Greek languages, and pronouncing orations with which they were well pleased. (Hanover pby. minutes, pp. 63)

Note no. 1: Those readers who may ask themselves, "Why would the presbytery bother to visit Rev. Brown's school?" The auditor reminds them that they were guests at their longest-serving and oldest member, Rev. John Brown, whose private "Latin school" was obviously threatened in some degree by the presbytery's new academy that would be operating in the same neighborhood as was his "Latin school," and presumably he understood that just like Princeton, the academy would no doubt create an affiliated "grammar school" that like his "Latin school" is designed to polish the studies of students anticipating enrollment at the presbytery's new academy, where they would finish their education. This reality, no doubt, affected Rev. Brown's attitude concerning the establishing of the new higher education endeavor. This was an opportunity for him to show off his own school in hopes that the presbytery would reevaluate their earlier decision to patronize the new academy, which was just then beginning to organize at "Mount Pleasant."

Note no. 2: So the presbytery at a three-day meeting starting at Timber Ridge moved to John Brown's home for the second two days (where they presumably lodged since most traveling Presbyterian ministers visiting the area in those days stayed at Brown's commodious home) here. Rev. Brown obviously took the occasion to invite the members to visit his "Latin School" as he always referred to his private school. They politely accepted their host's invitation and visited, but these records make no further mention of Brown's school thereafter.

Note no. 3: From a letter of Rev. Brown, it can be seen just how Rev. Brown carried out his direction from the presbytery to notice the presbytery's prospective appointees to both raise funds for their school and to "solicit their favor," concerning their appointment as trustees. In other words, trustee appointments only came to fruition upon the appointees' acceptance of the position, usually confirmed by their attendance as a trustee at a meeting of that board. *Importantly, the meeting minutes confirm that neither Rev. Brown nor his brother-in-law, Col. William Preston, accepted the presbytery's appointment of them as trustee. Neither ever attended a board meeting of the trustees to accept their appointment, an embarrassing fact for those who have represented that Rev. Brown was an early president, or rector, of Washington and Lee University, including the university itself from 1865 to the present, a fact that someone at the university's history department should have discovered and brought to the university's attention, but apparently they all either failed, or refused, to carry out this important responsibility.*

August 24, 1775

> -Rev. John Brown revealed some of his views concerning the Hanover Presbytery's new academy created in October of the previous year (1774).

>> A private school & the college of New Jersey will pollish [*sic*] a yong man & fit him for usefulness better than any semenery [*sic*] that we can expect in Virginia. (p. 46) (Letter to William Preston, 24 August 1775, Preston Papers of the Draper Manuscripts, State Historical Society of Wisconsin, Madison,

4QQ31 [see footnote 60 for chap. 3]; Stuart,
dissertation, p. 220)

Brown also said this:

> A private school & the college of New Jersey
> will pollish [*sic*] a yong man & fit him for
> usefulness better than any semenery [*sic*] that
> we can expect in Virginia. (p. 46) (Letter to
> William Preston, 24 August 1775, Preston
> Papers of the Draper Manuscripts, State
> Historical Society of Wisconsin, Madison,
> 4QQ31 [see footnote 60 for chap. 3]; Stuart,
> dissertation, p. 220)

Stuart's footnote says,

> John Brown, Letter to William Preston, 24
> August 1775, Preston Papers of the Draper
> Manuscripts, State Historical Society of
> Wisconsin, Madison, 4QQ31. (Stuart,
> dissertation, p. 220)

Oct 2, 1775

- Death of Rev. John Roan.

Roan was William Graham's early teacher and subsequent
instructor in theology in preparation for the Presbyterian
ministry. Rev. Roan was also an occasional correspondent of
Rev. John Brown, pastor of New Providence congregation. Rev.
Roan, the family pastor of Rev. William Graham's family in
Paxton Twp., Pennsylvania, and William Graham's theological
preceptor, undoubtedly provided one of the testimonials
recommending William Graham to head up the new seminary
(Liberty Hall), referred to in the minutes of the Hanover
Presbytery of October 13, 1774.

Oct. 26, 1775 William Graham licensed by the Hanover Presbytery.

Oct. 27, 1775 Hanover Presbytery explains who has been in charge of Augusta
Academy from date of "establishment."

> The Augusta school was taken under
> consideration. The presbytery agree that Mr.
> William Graham *continue to have the care*

and tuition of said school. (Hanover pby.
meeting minutes; emphasis added)

Note: The academy was "established at the autumn meeting of 1774 followed
by the Spring meeting of 1775," and the minutes for that meeting are devoid of any
reference to the "care and tuition" of the academy having changed; therefore the
only reasonable interpretation of the presbytery's use of the phrase "to continue
to have the care and tuition" must necessarily mean that the presbytery's view
was that it had been with Mr. Graham from the school's date of establishment. If
not, when could Mr. Graham have received from presbytery the "care and tuition"
of the academy?

Nov. 23, 1775

Rev. Samuel S. Smith corrects his earlier advertised promise to
open Hampden-Sydney Academy in Nov. of 1775

> *Rev. Samuel Stanhope Smith's written
> announcement that Hampden Sidney's first
> ever classes would begin in January*, and
> that before the first of January the Steward,
> with assistance of a few neighbors, who live
> well within less than two miles of Hampden
> Sidney," would be "able to accommodate
> all the young gentlemen who may be put
> under my care. I presume we shall not need
> the assistance of the neighborhood longer
> than till next summer, when the buildings
> will be chiefly erected."[724] *(Emphasis added
> for those who may have been misled by Dr.
> John Luster Brinkley in his dubious, but
> gargantuan tome, <u>On This Hill: A Narrative
> History of Hampden-Sydney College, 1774-
> 1994</u>, Hampden-Sydney, 1994, 880 pp.; the
> dubious and error-ridden section is located
> on pages 307–310.)*

In a subchapter, or subsection, of his third chapter entitled
"Toilers of the Sea," which subchapter Mr. Brinkley identifies
as "a Stiff Upper Lip," he challenges the college's decision to
change their date of establishment. In this, Brinkley is correct,
but for the wrong reason. Brinkley mistakenly asserts that the
date of founding, or "establishment," is October 4, 1774; but
the accurate date of establishment cannot be before February

---

724 Alfred J. Morrison, <u>The College of Hampden-Sidney: Calendar of Board Minutes 1776–1876</u>,
     Richmond, VA., The Hermitage Press, 1912, pg. 18

1, of 1775. The reason the board of trustees cannot legitimately change the date of establishment is because that function must be with the entity that created the college, which was the Hanover Presbytery, and we think it is entirely appropriate to point out that the Hanover Presbytery is the same entity that created the board of trustees.

It is the auditor's view that the date of establishment is a question of historical fact, not policy. The question as to when the college was established is clearly one that is within the sole province of the entity that "established" it. Of course, the trustees may decide to represent to the public a false date of establishment, just as they may represent to the public that the sun rises in the west; but the fact that they choose to represent a falsehood doesn't alter the actual facts of the matter. To exercise that which they may do falsely, however, is truly an act of institutional absurdity.

In the final analysis, it is an empirically based historical fact that the trustees of Hampden Sydney did not establish the college. The Hanover Presbytery established the college, and the date of the establishment is provided in the meeting minutes as Feb. 1, 1775. The first time the school is mentioned as an actual entity in the presbytery's minutes is in the meeting minutes of a pro re nata meeting held on Feb. 1, 1775. Prior to that date, the presbytery was merely considering the feasibility of raising sufficient funds and obtaining a sufficiently qualified person to manage such a school. Indeed, the first mention of the possibility of establishing a second academy east of the Blue Ridge Mountains was on Oct. 14, 1774. The presbytery, however, did not "agree to establish and patronize" a second academy at that meeting. They merely authorized a feasibility study to determine if they could raise sufficient funds and to determine the availability of Samuel S. Smith to manage such an operation, if one were established.

The board of trustees may not legitimately alter the date of establishment of the institution ex post facto. After all, the Board of Trustees of Hampden-Sydney did not exist prior to February of 1775. As a body, the board of trustees is merely a theoretical construct that was created by fiat by the Hanover Presbytery, and every member of the first board of trustees were only trustees by virtue of an appointment given to them by the grace of God and the Hanover Presbytery.

Dec. 1775

Rev. Brown's Latin School at New Providence witnessed by a Princeton graduate, Presbyterian minister, schoolmate of William Graham, who importantly recorded his observations for posterity which, by itself, disproves the notion that Rev. John Brown's Latin school and the presbytery's new seminary in Augusta County were the same schools.

This is one of the most significant times in the history of Liberty Hall Academy because this is when Rev. Philip Vickers Fithian writes in his vastly important journal his eyewitness testimony that clearly demonstrates to the careful reader that at this time, there were two entirely different schools being conducted in the neighborhood of Timber Ridge and New Providence congregations in Augusta County, Virginia. One, a public seminary, or academy, named unofficially "Augusta Academy," which was established by the Hanover Presbytery and that was under the "direction" of Rev. William Graham, the other, a private "Latin School" of Rev. John Brown, then conducted at New Providence by Mr. Samuel Doak. So many of the errors that found their way into print as a result of William Henry Foote's colossal mistake suggesting that Rev. Brown's "Latin School" and "Augusta Academy" were one and the same, when that was not possible. Doak was Brown's last teacher, he resigned in late December, of 1775 to accept an offer to serve as a temporary substitute for another, a Mr. John Springer who had become embarrassingly indisposed. After he returned to the Timber Ridge neighborhood, Doak completed his theological studies privately under Rev. Graham. Doak's new brother-in-law, John Montgomery was then Rev. Graham's assistant at the Academy. All three of these men had known one another at Princeton.

"Rev. Fithian uses the term "Latin School" in referencing Rev. Brown's school because that is the label consistently used by Rev. Brown as evidenced by his extant letters still housed at the Wisconsin Historical Society in the famous Draper Collection, and Fithian would obviously have known that because he was lodging in Rev. Brown's home at the time that he wrote these important entries into his Journal. Moreover, Rev. Fithian was a school-mate of both Rev. Graham and Samuel Doak at Princeton although he was of an earlier class.

Note: The footnote in Fithian's Journal questioning Fithian's account as it concerns Mr. Doak should be ignored because the notation interjected by the journal's 1934 editors was a serious error on the part of the editor(s) who relied on faulty information about when Hampden-Sydney Academy began their classes. This mistake is described in detail in other parts of this audit report. Documentary records of Hampden-Sydney and the Hanover Presbytery demonstrate the editor's obvious mistake in this regard. The editors also must not have known that Mr. Samuel Doak's family were all members of Rev. Brown's Church and that on October 31, 1775, Mr. Doak was married to a Ms. Montgomery who was the sister of Rev. Graham's assistant, John Montgomery (also a schoolmate at Princeton). At "Augusta Academy" located at "Mount Pleasant" in 1775–1776 and informally referred to as "Augusta Academy," after moving into its new campus buildings on Timber Ridge, the school's new trustees named the academy (college)"Liberty Hall Academy" on May 6 of 1776. This was the college's first board of trustees. Rev. Fithian correctly refers to the academy under the direction of his friend, Rev. William Graham, as being located in the same neighborhood as Rev. Brown's school and, in this way, distinguishes between the two schools both of which were being conducted within a few miles of one another, but very distinguishable from one another. One, Rev. Brown's was appropriately and consistently denominated by Brown as a "Latin school." It was a private endeavor that was peripatetic in nature because Brown was not qualified to provide the preparatory instruction himself, relying instead on young graduates from Princeton to instruct the students. The other, Graham's new academy was designed and created to serve as a public college-level academy. William Graham, on the other hand, was a noted scholar who was so far advanced in his studies at Princeton that President Witherspoon offered him a position as an instructor of the school's preparatory grammar school while he was matriculating as an undergraduate. At the beginning of his senior year, Witherspoon recognized that Graham was so far advanced that he was not required to attend classes, but he only had to sit for the final exams at the end of the academic year.[725]

May 1, 1776

- Opening day of the spring session of the Hanover Presbytery meeting at Timber Ridge meeting house.

> Present Rev. Mssrs. Brown, Waddell, Rice, Irvin, Wallace, and Smith; with Elder Charles Campbell. (Hanover Pby. minutes)

May 1

Rev. William Graham called to Timber Ridge and Hall's meeting house.

> "Presby met at Timber Ridge, Rev. Brown chosen moderator; "A call from the united congregations of Timber Ridge and Hall's Meeting House, for the services of Mr. Graham was given in to the Pby." (Hanover Pby. meeting minutes, p. 72)

---

725 *The facts concerning William Graham's experience at Princeton were published in the first biographical "Memoir of the the Late Rev. William Graham" written by Professor Edward Graham and published in the "A Memoir of The Late Rev. William Graham, A.M." The Evangelical and Literary Magazine_and Missionary Chronicle*, IV, (1821), p.75 et Seq. No authorship attribution appears in the magazine.[Note: attributed to Edward Graham (Rev. Wm.'s brother) by Archibald Alexander upon whom one can rely. Moreover, the authorship has been generally accepted by the historians of this locale and this period.]

May 3

> Hanover Presbytery announces their first assessment of Rev.
> William Graham and Mr. Graham's assistant as well as the
> performance of the students under his "care and tuition."

> Session met at Graham's school. "<u>The Presbytery Proceeded to
> examine the school under the care of Mr. Graham </u>and having
> attended a specimen of their improvement in their classical
> studies, and pronouncing orations, the Pby highly approve of
> the proficiency of the students and the Diligence and abilities of
> the teachers." (Pby. minutes, p. 76; emphasis added)

Note 1: The part of the quote above NOT ITALICIZED are the words of Dr. Foote,
not the presbytery. Importantly, while Foote is technically correct, he could easily
be misinterpreted because Graham's school was in its infancy; and during the
period during which the college's buildings were being constructed, the first phase
of the institutional development was to form the college's institutional foundation
in the form of a grammar school. As the college's intended and stated foundation, it
was an integral part of the college; and for that reason, it is included in the college's
history. Foote later confused this phase during which the presbytery referred
to its embryonic form as a grammar school when creating its meeting minutes.
Once the buildings were finished, the students were moved into the college's
buildings where regular college classes were conducted by Rev. Graham and his
new assistant, John Montgomery. Unfortunately, many authors misinterpreted
these early minutes and Mr. Foote's careless use of the term "grammar school"
and confused Graham's school at Mount Pleasant with Rev Brown's Latin school
at New Providence.

Note 2: To invoke the term "examine" in the quotation immediately above is of paramount
significance. Use of that term clearly implies a superintending connection to the school.

May 4, 1776

> - Rev. William Graham accounts to the Hanover Presbytery of
> his management activities at Augusta Academy.

> Graham accepted the call of Timber Ridge and Hall's meeting
> house at the meeting of the Hanover Presbytery. Note: Rev.
> Samuel Stanhope Smith was in attendance at this meeting of
> the Hanover Presbytery. The presbytery meeting minutes also
> includes the following:

>> "Mr. Graham informs, that agreeable to the
>> commission of Pby. He has purchased Books,
>> and apparatus for the use of the academy to the
>> amount of £ 160- 10 - 9½ which he has paid
>> and £2.1 which he has lost in change which

monies, with the purchase of the Books, the Apparatus, and all other valuable expenses the Trustees hereafter to be appointed, are directed to account with Mr. Graham for, and pay him the Balance. (Hanover Pby. minutes, p. 77)

May 4, 1776

- Below is Foote referring to the minutes of the Hanover Presbytery.

"..And afterwards were informed by Mr. Graham "That agreeable to the commission of presbytery, he had purchased books and apparatus for the use of the Academy to the amount of £ 160 10 s.9 ½ d., which he has paid, and £ 2 4s. Which he has lost in change. Which monies, with the potage of the books, the apparatus, and all other reasonable expenses, the Trustees hereafter be appointed, are directed to account with Mr. Graham for, and pay him the balance. Mr. Graham informs, that the gentlemen appointed last fall have collected and paid into his hands about £ 128, which he will be ready to account for more accurately with the Trustees of the Augusta Academy when they are appointed." *At the opening of this meeting of Presbytery, a call from the United congregations of Timber Ridge, and Halls Meetinghouse, for the services of Mr. Graham, was handed in*; and being put into his hands, he asked time for consideration. *On the fourth day of the session* (May 4, 1776) *he accepted the call,*—and,—on" our next stated Presbytery is appointed at Concord, on the fourth Tuesday of October next, the time and place of Mr. Grahams ordination, at which Mr. Wallace is to preside, and Mr. Rice to give the charge.[726]

May 5, 1776

*Rev. John Brown Writes to Col. Wm. Preston asserting his negative views regarding Augusta Academy.

---

726 Foote, Sketches of Va., First ser., pps. 447-448.

Dr. John White Stuart describes it thus:

> Brown confided to Preston, his "fear the scheme is too contracted & not upon as catholic [universal] a plan as to answer the best purposes"; and he further noted the unencouraging results of fund raising for the seminary, the disagreement regarding its location, and the presbytery's appointment of leading citizens like Preston "to assist in raising money."[727]

Note: What is important here is that this communication from Brown to Preston was in response to the presbytery appointing Brown and others to solicit the active participation of various potential fund-raisers. Instead, in the seminary's initial few months after "establishment," Rev. Brown is acting in contradistinction to his instructions and appointment. Instead of encouraging Preston's involvement, he takes the opportunity to undercut the presbytery's educational initiative.

May 6, 1776

- [Minutes of the Hanover Presbytery:

> "On Monday, May 6th, 1776, the presbytery determined to remove the academy from Mount Pleasant, for want of accommodations, and made the following arrangements for its location, and for its management by Trustees. ***The Presbytery, finding, that as the Augusta Academy is circumstanced, it is highly necessary now to fix on the place for its situation, and the person by whom it shall be conducted;*** and as this congregation of Timber Ridge appears to us to be a convenient place, and they have obtained a minister, whom we judge qualified; and Capt. Alexander Stewart, and Mr. Samuel Houston, each offering to give forty acres of land, for the purpose, convenient to the place of public worship; and the neighbors offering to build a hewed log-house, twenty eight by twenty four feet, one story and a half high, besides their subscriptions, and assuring us of the probability of fire-wood and timber for

---

727 Stuart, John White, Dissertation...Rev. John Brown.... pg. 101] He footnotes this paragraph with reference to a letter from Brown to Preston dated May 5, 1775]

buildings will be furnished gratis, for at least twenty years,—**we agree that the Augusta Academy shall be placed on Timber Ridge, upon those land; and we choose Mr. William Graham rector, and Mr. John Montgomery, his assistant.**[728] (In addition, they appointed the first board of trustees.)

May 6, 1776

- Creation of the Board of Trustees of Liberty Hall Academy by Hanover Presbytery

*Note: The institutional entity that created "Augusta Academy" (i.e., Liberty Hall Academy), the Hanover Presbytery, met and created the first board of trustees; appointed twenty-four trustees (of which Rev. Brown was one); **and also appointed an executive committee; and despite Rev. Brown being the only member of the presbytery from Augusta County other than Rev. Graham, he [Brown] was, noticeably, not appointed to the Executive Committee of the Board of Trustees.*** (Emphasis added)

Note: Rev. John Brown did not accept this or any other of the Hanover Presbytery's appointments that directly involved the affairs of the Presbytery's seminary in Augusta County, Virginia, a fact made readily apparent by his consistent absence from any and all official activities of the presbytery's academy. (Emphasis added)

Note: The executive committee of the board of trustees was comprised of the members who were charged with the important business of launching the school and all the important business associated with that task, including perfecting the legal paperwork associated with the land transfers, hiring contractors, designing the school buildings, hiring and overseeing the steward who would care for the student's housekeeping needs, and obtaining food, preparing food, and all these tasks associated with feeding and housing the students. That Rev. Brown had no hand in any of these activities is a fact inconsistent with the representations of so many nineteenth-century historians who insist on claiming that Brown either "directed," "supervised," or otherwise assumed a position at the academy superior to that of the rector, William Graham. In fact, Rev. Brown assumed no role whatever in conjunction with the school.

May 6, 1776

After creating the Liberty Hall Academy's board of trustees and then appointing (i.e., nominating) the prospective trustees, the presbytery directs these hoped-for trustees as follows:

The Trustees are to meet together stately, Twice in the year, *and have the students examined before them, at these times.* They are also to choose their own Chairman,

---

728 Ibid, pg. 447-48;. Also, set forth in "History of Washington College," *The American Quarterly Register*, B. B. Edwards and W. Cogswell, eds., Vol. 10, Boston, 1838, pg, pg. 147.

Treasurer, and Clerk, and appoint a
Committee, who shall have power to call
a Meeting of the Trustees, as often as any
emergency shall make it Necessary. (Hanover
Pby. minutes, p. 80)

*Note: There exists a vastly important distinction between two separate actions
by the Hanover Presbytery taken in 1775 and 1776 respectively. The historical
importance is directly related to the many entirely incorrect assertions made after
1849 that Liberty Hall Academy and the Latin school of Rev. John Brown were
one and the same, which false abomination continues even to this day. Claims not
made by historians who knew the principals nor who were eyewitnesses to the
founding events surrounding the establishment of Liberty Hall.*[729]

*The first occurred in April of 1775, when the presbytery accepted a last-
minute invitation, extended by their host, Rev. John Brown to pay a social "visit"
to Rev. John Brown's private "Latin school" at New Providence. The other action
was that described above, taken in 1776, which involved the presbytery's "public
seminary" (academy) at the place called "Mount Pleasant" near Fairfield,
Virginia. In the second action, the presbytery's action was clearly an official
one noted in advance as an upcoming event that was clearly a scheduled and
official one.*

*The minutes include vastly different content in regards to both of these
events. In the "visit" to Rev. Brown's private school, the members are accurately
described as observing visitors. In the matter of the second separate action, the
trustees, as the governing authority, attended the academy for the express purpose
of "examining" the administration, the students, and the assistant instructor,
which was an important prelude to their subsequent action to "fix" the location
for the permanent campus (i.e., Timber Ridge) and to decide whether to make their
earlier appointment of their chief administrator (manager) permanent or to select
another and a similar decision concerning the appointment of Rev. Graham's
assistant and tutor, Mr. John Montgomery.*

*The "visit" and the "official examination" were two entirely different kinds
of events, but several important historians beginning in 1850 confused these two
events and mistakenly presumed that the two events were not only of the same
type, but that they involved the same school. Of course, they were not in any
sense similar—not in nature, nor in purpose—and they were operating at entirely
different locations, several miles distant, one from the other.*

---

729 *The partial undated letter said to have been written by Rev. Samuel Houston will undoubtedly
be raised an objection in this regard, but even if one accepted the existence of such a letter, it
is, if an exception, one of utterly little, if any, consequence because the venerable Rev. Houston,
pious clergyman that he was, was not an historian and he made little, if any, use of documentary
research methods to verify the accuracy of his 'yarn-spinning,' as it were. Moreover, his
cursory comment, conflicts with incontrovertible documentary records of both, the Hanover
Presbytery, and the Liberty Hall Academy Trustee records. Moreover, his testimony is clearly
the unverifiable hearsay, made by one who was a teen age boy at the time of the institutional
events he describes.*

The word "examine" in the context of this discussion is of paramount importance, and it can readily be seen that the presbytery only invoked that term in regards to their own public academy and for good reason, which is that they were keenly aware of the fact that over Mr. Brown's school, like all such private preparatory schools, they had no jurisdiction whatsoever, let alone the authority to "examine" either the students, the administrators, or the tutors. That is why the minutes are virtually riddled with comments, appointments, and directions of the members in regards to Rev. Graham's academy while the only mention ever made in the minutes to Rev. Brown's private school was the cursory explanatory announcement of their "visit" to Brown's school in April of 1775, despite Mr. Brown's membership in the presbytery from its inception until his departure more than forty years later.

May 13, 1776

Trustees announce that they have named the academy "Liberty Hall Academy."

*The executive committee, pursuant to the order of presbytery, met May 13, 1776, and at this meeting the name Liberty Hall first appears. In the proceedings of the Presbytery which was in session only the week before, the school is then called **Augusta Academy**.*

(Pres. Henry Ruffner, "Early History," p. 23)

Note: Rev. Brown, not being a member, appears to have had no part in selecting the name of Liberty Hall.

Nov. 22, 1776

Nov. 22 Rev. Samuel Houston began his education at Liberty Hall Academy.

On the margin of Houston's wee-worn Greek and Latin testament is written the statement.

Samuel Houston entered on his classical education at Liberty Hall Academy, Nov. 22, 177, and graduated 1780, being then twenty-two years of age.

(George W. Diehl, *The Reverend Samuel Houston V.D.M.* [Verona, VA: McClure Press, 1970], p. 71)

1777   Augusta Academy's temporary quarters at Mount Pleasant are moved to
the school's first "permanent campus" at Timber Ridge.

The initial seminary quarters at Mount Pleasant were moved in early 1777
into the newly constructed buildings at Timber Ridge, which, however,
were not actually completed until late 1777.[730]

1778   Additional actions concerning the opening of the academy at Timber
Ridge.

Liberty Hall Academy Board of Trustees continue to raise
money but not very successfully. Two or three lodging rooms
were added as attachments to the "Academy House." [731]

1780

-BELOW IS A REFERENCE TO AN ACTION THAT IS ASSERTED TO HAVE
TRANSPIRED IN 1780, BUT IT WAS WRITTEN (ASSERTED) MUCH EARLIER
OR PERHAPS LATER, EITHER IN THE 1840S, OR CIRCA 1890.

The error was committed by either President Henry Ruffner or his son,
William Henry Ruffner, who edited his father's manuscript when he prepared
for publication many decades after it was originally written. This matter is
further confused by the fact that in 1857 long after it was originally written,
Henry Ruffner made a number of edits to the original. This fact was revealed
by Henry Ruffner in a notice printed along with the publication of his "History
of Washington College" that is located in volume 1 of the Washington and Lee
University Historical Papers.

An erroneous representation by one of the Ruffners, (father &
son); it isn't clear which was is responsible for this error ". . .
__in the course of the year 1780, the operations of the academy__
__were wholly suspended, and were never resumed at Timber__
__Ridge.__ Thus in the fourth year of its new existence, the this
young seminary of learning fainted under the hard pressure
of the times; . . . But some of the students being anxious to
complete their studies, the library and apparatus were removed
to Mr. Graham's residence, where he continued to give private
instruction. . . . Among the pupils who followed their teacher,
were Moses Hoge and Archibald Alexander . . . This private
school prevented extinction of the academy . . . While the
academy lay in this state of suspended animation, the people of
Virginia were more than ever agitated by the alarms of war.[732]

---

730   Henry Ruffner, Early History of Washington ..., [W&L Historical Papers no.1, pg. 26]

731   Ibid, pg. 28

732   Ibid, [Note: It is unclear to this auditor, why Pres. Ruffner invokes the term, "private" here
because it appears the only real change is that of place. This appellation, "private" in this
context is what the U.S. Supreme Court has called "a distinction without a difference." Aren't
the Mssrs. Hoge and Alexander who both matriculated for a time at Graham's home, considered

This entry is included for reference purposes only. It seems to be entirely misleading because the school never closed; it was merely relocated, a distinction of the greatest significance to the school's true history.

May 29, 1781

> - Rev. John Brown reveals his animus concerning Rev. William Graham and Liberty Hall Academy.

> Letter of John Brown to William Preston, discussed in Stuart's dissertation. Dr. Stuart presents an extract from a Rev. Brown letter:

>> Graham may have received mostly praise from the Rev. Archibald Alexander and others who had studied under him; but in 1781 Brown cautioned Preston that:

>> *it will by no means suit to send them* (Preston's sons) *to Mr. G* (i.e., Wm. Graham, for their education). (N46, John White Stuart III, dissertation, p. 103; so this is a quote within a quote)

April 22, 1783

> Rev. John Brown censured by the Hanover Presbytery.

> A complaint was entered that,

>> *The Revd. Jno. Brown had baptised the child of a certain William Brown who resided in their bounds, and who at the same time was held in Suspension, by them as a session. The Presbytery pronounce it wrong and the Revd Mr. Brown acknowledges that it is so too.* (N5 & 6, Stuart, John White, dissertation, p. 118)

---

by all, to be graduates of Liberty Hall Academy? The point is, that due to the American Revolution, Liberty Hall Academy avoided going into suspended animation by continuing classes under William Graham at his home a few miles south of the original campus. When Graham petitioned the new Virginia Legislature (General Assembly) for a charter afer the Treaty of Paris, concluded hostilities, he did so in the name of Liberty Hall Academy and its Trustees. Moreover, classes by then were being held in separate quarters from Graham's home.

Jan. 28, 1783

Rev. John Brown confirms the fact that his "Latin school" at
New Providence was never "adopted" or "patronized" by the
Hanover Presbytery and that he had not moved it back to Mount
Pleasant after abandoning that site in 1767. Instead, his school
remained at New Providence and was reopened following the
Revolution.

Letter: John Brown to William Preston, discussed in Stuart's
dissertation.

> "He (Rev. Brown) mentions **the new Latin
> school** at New Providence and invites Preston
> to have his son Billy lodge at the Brown home
> while studying there. He asks Preston to
> send "all the Rudiman's gramers you can &
> Cordy's & Esop's & Erasmus's . . ." (Preston
> Papers, 5QQ113) (John White Stuart III,
> dissertation, p. 113, chap. 5; so this is a quote
> within a quote, and the words "the new Latin
> School" are not Rev. Brown's words, but are
> Mr. Stuart's words.)

April 23, 1783

Rev. Wm. Graham proposed a motion that they (Rev. Cumins
and Rankin) not

> *be allowed to preach at Sinking Spring
> until Pby shall have met to compromise the
> differences subsisting.* (N7)

> Whatever those "differences" were, Brown
> voiced dissent, but Graham's proposal
> passed overwhelmingly. (John White Stuart,
> dissertation, Rev. John Brown of Virginia,
> p. 118)

The quote above is of singular importance. Rev. Brown's New
Providence Latin school, taught by Samuel Doak, in December
1775, closed when Doak left to become a substitute teacher at
Samuel S. Smith's presbytery-sponsored academy in Prince
Edward County in January of 1776. Doak's departure was
not foreseen so there was no time to locate a replacement.
The country was on the verge of war with Great Britain, and

uncertainty was the order of the day. The Revolutionary War was only a few months away. It isn't until after the surrender of Cornwallis at Yorktown and the opening of peace negotiations to end the war in 1782 that Brown attempts to revive his Latin school. He did so despite the fact that Liberty Hall had received its degree-granting charter by the Virginia legislature the year before.

Dec. 1785

VA legislature passed the Bill for Religious Freedom (vote 67 to 20).

Graham, a candidate for ratification convention, lost to William McKee.

Sept. 26, 1786

William Graham wrote a letter to Col. Arthur Campbell wherein he refers to the "horrors of slavery"

Oct. 22, 1788[733]

Virginia Synod formed with four presbyteries, Hanover, Lexington, Redstone, and Transylvania.[734]

1789

Wm. Graham pastor of New Monmouth and Lexington Presbyterian Churches. (SPL, p. 135, i.e., Henry Alexander White's _Southern Presbyterian Leaders_)

Synod of Virginia establishes a seminary for religious instruction at Lexington under Rev. William Graham, president (rector) of Liberty Hall Academy.

1789 (possibly 1790)[735]

The Watts controversy takes place in 1789 or 1790 at Rev. John Brown's New Providence Presbyterian Church (i.e., meeting house).

Note: This controversial communion service administered by the visiting Rev. Graham is discussed in several sections of this report and especially in the "Key Errors" chapter.

---

733 William Graham letter to Col. Arthur Campbell, currently housed in the archives of the Filson Club in Kentucky, dated Sept. 24, 1788.

734 See Geo. W. Diehl, _The Reverend Samuel Houston, V.D.M._ (Verona, VA: McClure Printing Company Inc., 1970), p. 50.

735 John White Stuart III, Dissertation, Rev. John Brown . . . p. 124.

Oct. 1, 1791

> -Archibald Alexander commissioned by the Presbyterian
> Church to preach the gospel.

September 1792

> September - Princeton Board of Trustees authorizes the
> enrollment of John Chavis on the Leslie fund.

Note: The plan was to have Chavis educated privately by the retiring president
John Witherspoon, but the plan never came to fruition due to Witherspoon's
rapidly failing health. The Princeton trustees were obviously not willing to accept
Chavis into the regular academic program.

1794

> It was sometime in this year that Mr. John Chavis from North
> Carolina was enrolled as a member of the regular academic
> class at Liberty Hall.

*Note: Few W&L records exist from this period, but his name is found in the school's class records
that pertain to 1795, but the plan to have Mr. Chavis educated was one advanced by Messrs. Rev.
Wm. Graham; Rev. Samuel Stanhope Smith and his brother Rev. John B. Smith; and Mr. Chavis's
preparatory preceptor, Rev. Henry Pattillo, all of whom had at one time been members of the
Hanover Presbytery and all of whom were colleagues of the cloth. The initial plan, hatched by the
Smith brothers at Princeton, provided for Mr. Chavis to be educated privately there by the retiring
Dr. Witherspoon. Witherspoon, however, proved unable due to his rapidly declining health and a
financial scandal that consumed his energies in his last year of life on earth. The Smith brothers
and Rev. Pattillo brought Mr. Graham into their confidence, and Mr. Graham went so far as to
invite Mr. Chavis to join the regular academic class at Liberty Hall. Here, Mr. Chavis had the
decided advantage to be located much closer to his home in northern North Carolina and many of
his extended family in Virginia in counties only a few miles from the college. Mr. Chavis's complete
matriculation at Liberty Hall Academy is officially recognized and entered into the record by the
Rockbridge County Court in a matter initiated by Mr. Chavis, which is recorded and approved by
several sitting magistrates including one that was also a trustee of the college, Capt. William Lyle.
The record demonstrates that Mr. Chavis claimed his matriculation at Liberty Hall; was well-known
to the court as a citizen in the community; and was a graduate of the chartered college (Liberty Hall
Academy); and while the college had few commencements in this era, the court recognized that Mr.
Chavis's assertion that he "had gone through the regular academic program" at Liberty Hall was a
certifiable fact, a fact attested to by a sitting magistrate who was also a trustee of the college, a fact,
therefore, that is incontrovertible and which makes Mr. Chavis unquestionably the first black man
ever enrolled into a chartered institution of higher learning in America and the only black man to
have "gone through the regular Academic program at a chartered college in the eighteenth century
in North America."[736]*

---

736 *Rockbridge County Court Order Book 6, pg. 10, April Term 1802, The Library of Virginia., Reel
36. A photocopy of this official Court record can be seen on pg. 45 of Helen Chavis Othow's
book, John Chavis, African American, Patriot, Preacher, Teacher and Mentor (1763-1838),* but
this copy has unfortunately cropped off part of the name, "William Lyle," rendering it nearly
indecipherable. The Library of Virginia's copy does not have this defect. In addition, Mr.
John Chavis was also a student at the Lexington Theological Seminary, an adjunct to Liberty
Hall and was licensed by the Lexington Presbytery based on his educational and theological

Sept. 1794

Whiskey Rebellion Affair" at Winchester meeting of the Virginia Synod.[737]

Meeting at Harrisonburg, VA (Winchester) meeting of the Synod of Virginia.

Whiskey Boys affair see: Foote: Account no. 1pg 476 [Graham bio] & Account no. 2 p. 560 from Moses Hoge bio sketch written by his son based upon a mss left by Moses Hoge." This is the most credible account because it is written by Moses Hoge who is the member who introduced the controversial motion which was opposed by his old preceptor, Rev. Graham, and was defeated based primarily on jurisdictional grounds, which upon reflection was an indisputable point.

(Note: The issue had virtually nothing to do with the intoxicating liquor aspect of liquor, but rather was a subject of taxation by the new federal government on a substance easily transported and widely used in trade. As such, it was viewed by many as an improper method of taxation by the new federal government and was seen by some as analogous to the attempt by the prior British government to tax tea. Rev. Graham properly pointed out that the issue was a purely civil matter, not a proper subject for review in an ecclesiastical court.)

Jan. 1796

William Graham in Lexington calls together board of trustees in regards to Pres. George Washington's prospective endowment opportunity.

Jan. 1796

Rev. William Graham signs letter to Pres. George Washington (i.e., application for endowment) along with Rev. Samuel Houston, clerk, the letter written on behalf of the Board of Trustees of Liberty Hall Academy.

June 1796

Southwest Territory becomes the state of Tennessee, John Sevier governor, William Blount senator.

---

preparations under the direction of Rector, William Graham. Rev. Chavis was the first black Presbyterian minister in America. Like so many early W&L Alumni, Mr. Chavis has not as yet received, posthumously, an acknowledgment of his formal degree.

737   The authority for the date is Dr. Henry Ruffner, "Early History...", W&L <u>Historical Papers.</u> <u>Papers,</u> p. 60.

1796

> George Washington awards **Liberty Hall** an endowment gift of
> one hundred shares of canal stock, valued at between $25,000
> and $50,000—*at that time the largest gift ever made to a
> private educational institution in America*, the principal to
> remain in the present endowment.

Oct. 20, 1796

> Conrad Speece and George Addison Baxter receive diplomas
> at end of course of study under Graham. (Henry A. White,
> *Southern Presbyterian Leaders,* p. 233)

Note: This is probably the same time that John Chavis received his diploma.
Chavis, thereafter, was taken into the theological studies at the Lexington
Theological Seminary[738] by Rev. Graham along with Messrs. Speece and Baxter.
It is strange that Henry Alexander White failed to note that Mr. Chavis, a black
man, subsequently became the first black Presbyterian minister in America. Rev.
Chavis received both his undergraduate degree and his theological studies at
Liberty Hall Academy. He was taken on trials for the Presbyterian minister at the
Lexington Presbytery's first regular meeting following Rev. Graham's unexpected
death from pneumonia in 1799.

1797

> Conrad Speece still studying theology under rector, Rev.
> William Graham.

> > "In the same month (September)(1796) I was
> > received by the Lexington Presbytery as a
> > candidate for the ministry. They appointed
> > me, as trials, a homily on original sin, and
> > a Latin exegesis on the question, in quo
> > consistat coeli felicitas. The ensuing winter
> > I studied Theology under the instruction of
> > our Rector. In April 1797, our Presbytery
> > accepted my first trials, and further appointed
> > me a lecture on Isiah 11th: 1–9; and a popular
> > discourse on John 3:7. Reluctant to engage
> > too early in preaching, I obtained leave of the

---

738 This name was adopted informally by Edward Graham in his memoir of his late brother, Rev.
William Graham. The Theological Seminary was an adjunct to Liberty Hall Academy from its
inception and during Reverend Graham's tenure as president. This connection was official and
grew out of the Presbyterian Church's agreement to repatronize the academy. The fund-raising
campaign that provided, in part, the underwriting of the Academy's new Stone buildings on
Mulberry Hill, and it is for that reason that the Lexington Presbytery held some of its meetings
in the 1790s at the academy.

Presbytery in September to defer delivering
these exercises until the ensuing spring.[739]

Sept. 1799

Rev. William Graham died in Richmond.

1821–

First published account of the origins of Liberty Hall Academy
(i.e., W&L).[740]

Edward Graham's "Memoir of the Late Rev. William Graham,
A.M." published by John Holt Rice in Richmond (see
bibliography).

December 12, 1838

Rev. Robert Davidson writes letter to Edward Graham
concerning Edward's valuable letters about the early history of
Liberty Hall Academy.

> *Your last, relating to the College, (i.e.,
> Liberty Hall Academy) is particularly rich
> in valuable details (Davidson to Graham),
> Lexington, Ky., December 12, 1838, MS,
> Graham Family Papers, Duke University.*
> (The Graham family papers are housed at
> Duke University's Perkins Library.)

The importance of Davidson's letter cannot be underestimated in importance
for it puts lie to the rather ridiculous assumption that an undated, unsigned sheet
of foolscap with notations purporting to account for a sequence of events leading
up to the establishment of Liberty Hall is, in fact, a representation by Edward
Graham that contradicts all of Edward's known assertions that are in direct
conflict with the mysterious unsigned document, a document someone foolishly
and inappropriately pasted in the beginning of the board of trustees meeting
minutes' record book. What is of singular interest in this regard is the fact that the
letter from Rev. Davidson to Edward Graham is dated December 12, 1838. And
yet Davidson obviously reported his historical account of the origins of Liberty
Hall in direct conflict with the mystery document some assume was written by
Edward Graham. Given Davidson's representation to Edward of the great value
of his letters, he would hardly have written an account, which, in effect, would

---

739 William H. Foote, *Sketches of Virginia...* new series (1855), pp. 351–352. The words here are
     extracts taken from a memorandum in the private papers of Conrad Speece, then in possession
     of Mr. Foote, but the whereabouts of these papers are unknown to the auditor.

740 Edward Graham, "A Memoir of The Late Rev. William Graham, A.M." *The Evangelical and
     Literary Magazine and Missionary Chronicle*, IV, (1821), p.75 et seq.

repudiate Edward's published contentions unless, of course, Edward had good reason to repudiate his 1821 account. If he had such evidence, then Davidson would not have adopted Edward's earlier account. Edward Graham died a year after receiving Davidson's letter, hardly leaving enough time for Edward to have had an epiphany that resulted in his complete reversal of his views about the founding of Liberty Hall, which he had held throughout his adult life.

Finally, if Edward had changed his mind on the founding of Washington College at the close of his life, he would undoubtedly have informed his friends and relations in the Lexington vicinage, and the college would not have subsequently published its first authorized history of its founding and asserted therein that its founding took place in the autumn of 1774.[741]

*****************************Finis*************************

---

741 Rev. George Junkin, DD, _Christianity the Patron of Literature and Science: An Address Delivered February 22, 1849. On the Occasion of the Author's Inauguration as President of Washington College, Virginia_, Philadelphia, The Board of Trustees, 1849 [pamphlet pp. 39]. The Junkin Inaugural Address includes an important Appendix: "A Brief Sketch of the Early History of Washington College" (ordered printed by the Board of Trustees). This constitutes the college's first authorized, published history.

Appendix no. 2

Checklist of President William Graham's Writings

* Graham, Rev. William. Petition for Charter (1782)
* Graham, Rev. William. The proposed Charter of Liberty Hall Academy (1782)
* Graham, Rev. William. Memorial in re to opposing P. Henry's proposed Bill on Assessment, & in Support of Jefferson's Bill for Religious Liberty (1785)
* Graham, Rev. William. Proposed Constitution, State of Frankland
* Graham, Rev. William. Essay on Government, Philadelphia, (1786)
* Graham, Rev. William. Address to the Presbyterian General assembly (see Foote's *Sketches of Virginia*, Series One, 1850)
* Graham, Rev. William. Letter to Zachariah Johnston, Leyburn Library, Washington and Lee University.
* Graham, Rev. William. Letter to Col. Arthur Campbell; the letter is housed in the archives of the Filson Club in Kentucky; the letter is dated Sept. 24, 1788.
* Graham, Rev. William. Letter to President George Washington with historical sketch of the college (for the board of trustees) (1796) (The letter's content is reprinted in full in William Henry Foote's *Sketches of Virginia, Historical and Biographical*, Philadelphia, William S. Martien, 1850, pp. 479–482.)
* Graham, Rev. William. "The Scriptural Doctrine of Water Baptism: Shewing 1. The Scriptural Substance of that Ordinance; II. The Scriptural Mode of Its Administration; III. And, Lastly, Answering Some Questions For The Satisfaction of Serious Enquirers, (Richmond, Virginia, Printed by William Alex. Rind, 1799, 41 pp.)

Petition for Charter

PETITION FOR CHARTER FOR LIBERTY HALL ACADEMY* (From the State Archives. Presented to the Legislature in Oct. 1782)

> To the Speaker and Gentlemen of the House of Delegates, the petition of the Trustees of Liberty Hall Academy most humbly showeth:
>
> That your petitioners, very sensible of the great utility arising from the regular education of youth, have for some time been associated for that purpose, and finding our efforts attended with good success, are induced, from the experiment made, to believe that a Seminary may here be conducted to very general advantage. And we are reather inclined to be more fully of this

opinion when we consider the extensive fertile country around the place, the fine air and pure water with which it is blessed, contributing so powerfully to health of body.

Having also procured one hundred and twenty acres of land in the neighborhood of Lexington for the use of the Academy, a valuable library of well-chosen books, and a considerable mathematical & philosophical apparatus. Under these advantages, and many more that might be named, we doubt not, should we be so happy as to obtain the approbation & patronage of the Honorable house, of being instruments under smiles of heaven, of conveying down to posterity, the most valuable blessing, and the surest pledge of true patriotism we are capable of.

We therefore pray the honorable Assembly to take the matter under consideration, and grant us an Act of Incorporation, with such powers and privileges as will enable us and our successors more effectually to carry on the laudable design and give all possible encouragement to a polite and solid education.

We hope also that a patriot Assembly will see the reasonableness of, and grant an exemption from militia draughts to the professors and Masters of the said Seminary, and to all students thereto belonging, under the age of twenty-one years. And your petitioners, as in duty bound, shall pray.

Signed in behalf of the Trustees.

> Wm. Graham C.M.
> James Lyle, Jr., Clerk[742]

****

* Graham, Rev. William. "The Proposed Charter of Liberty Hall Academy." *William and Mary Quarterly*, Vol. 13, No. 4 [April 1905], pp. 265–266)
* Graham, Rev. William. Memorial in re to opposing P. Henry's proposed Bill on Assessment, & in Support of Jefferson's Bill for Religious Liberty [1785]. (reprinted in Foote's Sketches of Virginia, Series One, 1850.)
* Graham, Rev. William. Constitution, State of Franklin The American Historical Magazine, Vol. 1. Note: The proposed Constitution written by Wm Graham was also printed in, The American Historical Magazine, 2nd edition. (1st ed. Printed in Jan. 1896), Nashville, Tenn: The University Press, Nashville, 1896, pp. 48-63.

---

742 "Petition for Charter for Liberty Hall Academy," *William and Mary Quarterly*, vol. 13, no. 4 (April 1905): 265–266.

* Another format: This is not likely to be Graham's version, *but* it is curious that it was published in Philadelphia like Graham's "Essay on Government," and it is even more curious that the title page and the Declaration of Rights uses the name Frankland, which was thought to have been idiosyncratically linked to William Graham, whose personal animus for Benjamin Franklin was palpable. Graham's animus grew out of Franklin's attacks on the Paxton Boys concerning the Conestoga Indian affair.

Graham, Rev. William. Declaration of Rights, A Prelude to his proposed Constitution, or Form of Government Agreed to, and resolved upon by the Representative Freemen of State of Frankland: Elected and chosen for that particular purpose, in Convention assembled at Greenville, 14th of November 1785; Philadelphia, Printed by Francis Bailey, at Yorick's Head, MDCCLXXXVI. [1786]

[*State of Franklin Constitution, published in its entirety by the American Historical Magazine, vol. 9, 1904. (Note: This is not the provisional constitution of Frankland written by Wm. Graham; it is the later one adopted, which is based on the N. Carolina Constitution. This entry is only here because some have mistakenly believed it is the constitution written by William Graham)

* Graham, Rev. William. "Essay on Government." Philadelphia, (1786)
Note: The above is housed at Leyburn Library, Washington and Lee University, Lexington, Virginia. This photocopy bears a note in long hand that asserts "printed in Philadelphia 1786 . . . Wm Graham Author." Note the printed title is merely "Essay &c." The article's beginning page is numbered 3, and it runs through to page 37, and at the conclusion says, in bolder and larger font, "A Citizen of Frankland." On a following page, there is written this note in long hand: "This Essay was written by the Rev. Wm Graham, who then lived in Franklin, now Tennessee. He would not call that Territory Franklin as it was generally called but Frankland, for he never liked Dr. Franklin & there were no bounds to his prejudices." The notation is unsigned. It is incorrect because Wm. Graham did not ever live in the proposed state of Frankland/Franklin, but it may be true that he owned land there, purchased for him at his request by Rev. Samuel Houston, but evidence on that point is lacking.

* Graham, Rev. William. Address to the Presbyterian General assembly (see Foote, *Sketches of Virginia*, Series One, 1850.)

* Graham, Rev. William. Letter to Zachariah Johnston. (Auditor's copy came from Leyburn Library at Wa&L)

* Graham, Rev. William. Letter to Col. Arthur Campbell; the letter is housed in the archives of the Filson Club in Kentucky; the letter is dated Sept. 24, 1788.

* Graham, Rev. William. Letter to President George Washington with historical Sketch of the College (for the Board of Trustees, 1796)

* Graham, Rev. William. "Letter of Resignation to the Trustees of Liberty Hall," September 25, 1796.

* Graham, Rev. William. "The Scriptural Doctrine of Water Baptism: Shewing 1. The Scriptural Substance of that Ordinance; II. The Scriptural Mode of Its Administration; III. And, Lastly, Answering Some Questions for the Satisfaction

of Serious Enquirers, Richmond, Virginia, printed by William Alex. Rind, 1799, 41 pp. (a copy from an original housed at Leyburn Library, Washington and Lee University, Lexington, Virginia)

There are, no doubt, other letters written by Rev. William Graham that have yet to be discovered. The envisioned "piece" referenced in Rev. Graham's letter to Zachariah Johnston probably became the basis of his "Essay on Government," or alternatively, it was to form the basis of the envisioned piece that was to propound a rationale for the anti-federalist's opposition to the ratification of the proposed US Constitution. In any event, it is not believed to have ever been written as originally envisioned.

William Graham's Letter to George Washington

"The Trustees of Liberty Hall Academy, in Rockbridge county, and State of Virginia, his Excellency George Washington, President of the United States of America.

> "Sir: — We have lately heard of your generous and disinterested conduct, in refusing as private emolument, the shares in the Potomack and James River Companies, presented to you by the Legislature of Virginia, as a testimony of their approbation and gratitude.

"We have also heard of the wise and beneficent purposes to which you wished to have the profits arising from these shares applied, —the endowment of a Seminary on the waters of each of these rivers for the education of youth, and that you referred the appropriation of the hundred shares in the James River Company to the wisdom of the Legislature of Virginia; who after deliberating on the important subject, agreed that the whole should be applied to one Seminary up the country,—but some differences of opinion arising respecting the particular place to which it should be applied, referred the ultimate decision to your excellency.

> "Supposing our information just, we are constrained by the duty we owe the public, as well as the Seminary we have long had the honour to patronize, to address you on this very interesting subject.

> "And here we cannot allow ourselves to think it proper to pray you to grant the donation for the support of education in this Seminary, as a matter of honour or emolument to ourselves, or emolument to the neighborhood where it stands. This would be selfish and invidious and inconsistent with the feelings of that mind, which always overlooks private interest to embrace and secure the public good. We beg leave only to state a few facts for your Excellency's information, that you may be enabled to decide the important question with greater precision.

> From a conviction of the necessity and utility of a public Seminary to complete the education of youth in this upper part of the State; as early as the year 1776, a Seminary before conducted in these parts under the form of a grammar school, received the nominal title of an Academy, and money was collected to purchase the beginnings of a library, and some of the most essential parts of a philosophical and mathematical apparatus.

> "The question then was, where should the Seminary be fixed? Staunton was proposed by some, to be the proper place, as

the most ancient and populous town, and nearest the centre [*sic*] of the population in the upper part of the State as it then stood. But considering that a public Seminary, which was to be of permanent duration and general utility, ought not to be affected by local circumstances arising from temporary causes;—and viewing the extensive lands upon the drains of [the] Holstein to the south-west, and of the Kanawha to the west, we were of opinion that the time was not very far distant when the population upon these lands must equal, if not exceed the population upon the drains of the Potomac to the northeast, upon one of which drains Staunton stands. We therefore considered the waters of James River as forming a kind of natural and common centre. We also felt a conviction, that the extensive and fertile lands upon James River, would at a period not far remote, point out the necessity and practicability of rendering its streams navigable above the mountains, and we have been happy in seeing our expectations realizing every day.

"We therefore concluded that some spot in the tract of country now known as Rockbridge county, would be the proper place. We therefore organized the Seminary, and set it in motion, hoping that the public would one day aid our exertions and enable us to perfect what had been honestly begun.

"Through the calamities of a long and dangerous war, and the deceptions of a paper currency, together with other misfortunes, great obstructions were experienced, but being happy in able and diligent teachers, we were enabled to preserve the Academy in a state of considerable reputation and usefulness until the year 1782, when we were aided by an act of incorporation from the Legislature of Virginia, which was the first granted after the Revolution.

"In 1793 we found it necessary to fix the spot where the buildings should finally stand, and which was determined to be in that fine tract of country formerly known by the name of the Wood's Creek lands, in the Forks of James River, one mile from the navigation of the North Branch, and on an eminence about three-quarters of a mile from Lexington, —so that whilst it enjoys an extensive prospect of the circumjacent country, and a view of the town, it has agreeably to its great design, an undisturbed retirement for study.

"The situation of the neighborhood for health and fertility as well as pleasantness, yields to no lands in the upper part of the State.

"If our information of the state of the dispute respecting the place, as it existed before the Legislature, be accurate, it went a great way to determine the propriety of our original opinion. It is said that Fincastle on the one side, and Staunton on the other, were the extremes which made any vigorous claims. Fincastle is situated thirty-seven miles south west from Liberty Hall. Add Staunton thirty-five miles north east. Therefore, Liberty Hall is as near the centre [*sic*] as local situation would admit.

"There is one more fact which we would beg leave to state. In 1793, by voluntary contributions, and some sacrifices of private property, we were enabled to erect and finish plain neat buildings, sufficiently capacious to accommodate between forty and fifty students, and the business of education is now in full train, and the Seminary in as high reputation as could be expected without funds. Many young gentlemen have finished their education here, who are now serving their country with reputation and usefulness, in different professional departments, and a number are now collected from different parts of the country for the same end.

"The buildings and other furniture of the Academy could not be estimated at much less than two thousand pounds. If the seat of the academy is changed, the young gentlemen must be interrupted for some time in their studies, and the buildings totally lost, as they can applied to no other purpose. The destruction of so much property, procured with considerable difficulty, unless a much greater preponderating good can be secured to the public, will doubtless be seriously weighed. And as the public good is the only object which can influence your determination it is unnecessary to add any thing further, but fully confiding in your wisdom, we shall entirely acquiesce in your decision.

"That all possible happiness, present and future, may attend your person, and every public blessing your administration, is the desire and prayer of all your Excellency's humble servants, the Trustees of Liberty Hall. By order and in behalf of the Board,

William Graham. C.M.
Samuel Houston, C. B. T.

January, 1796.

****

Graham, Rev. William, Memorial in re to opposing P. Henry's proposed Bill on Assessment, and in Support of Jefferson's Bill for Religious Liberty (1785)

Memorial no. 5 from the Hanover Presbytery to the legislature of (in this case the new [i.e., post–Revolutionary War]) Virginia General Assembly. (The final memorial on these two important subjects: (1) assessments (taxation) to support religion and (2) Jefferson's the bill for religious freedom.

*****

"To The Horourable The General Assembly of the Commonwealth of Virginia,

"The ministers and Lay Representatives of the Presbyterian Church in Virginia, assembled in Convention, beg leave to address you.

"As citizens of the State, not so by accident but choice, and having willingly conformed to a system of civil policy adopted by our government, and defended it with the foremost at the risk of everything dear to us, we feel ourselves deeply interested in all the measures of the Legislature.

"When the late happy Revolution secured to us an exemption from British control, we hoped that the gloom of injustice and usurpation would have been forever dispelled by the cheering rays of liberty and independence. This inspired our hearts with resolution in the most distressful scenes of adversity and nerved our arm in the day of battle. But our hopes have since been overcast with apprehension when we found how slowly and unwillingly, ancient distinctions among the citizens on account of religious opinions were removed by the legislature. For although the glaring partiality of obliging all denominations to support the one which had been the favourite of government, was pretty early withdrawn, yet an evident predilection in favour of that church, still subsisted in the Acts of the Assembly. Peculiar distinctions and the honour of an important name, were still continued,; and these are considered as equally partial and injurious with the ancient emoluments. Our apprehensions on account of the continuance of these, which could have no other effect than to produce jealous animosities, and unnecessary contentions among different parties, were increased when we found that they were tenaciously adhered to by government notwithstanding the remonstrances of several Christian societies. To increase the evil a manifest disposition has been shown by the State, to consider itself as possessed of supremacy in spirituals, as well as temporals,; and our fears have been realized in certain proceedings of the General Assembly at their last sessions. The engrossed bill for establishing a provision for the teachers of the Christian religion and the act for incorporating the Protestant Episcopal Church, so far as it secures to that Church, the churches, glebes, &c. procured at the expense of the whole community, are not only evidence of this, but of an impolitic partiality which we are sorry to have observed so long.

"We therefore in the name of the Presbyterian Church in Virginia, beg leave to exercise our privilege as freemen in remonstrating against the former absolutely, and against the latter, under the restrictions above expressed.

"We oppose the Bill,

"Because it is a departure from the proper line of legislation;

"Because it is unnecessary, and inadequate to its professed end—impolitic, in many respects—and a direct violation of the Declaration of Rights.

"The end of government is security to the temporal liberty and property of mankind, and to protect them in the free exercise of religion. Legislators are invested with powers from their constituents, for this purpose only; and their duty extends no farther. Religion is altogether personal, and the right of exercising it unalienable; and it is not, cannot, and ought not to be resigned to the will of the society at large; and much less to the Legislature, which derives its authority wholly from the consent of the people, and is limited by the original intention of civil associations.

"We never resigned to the control of government, our right of determining for ourselves, in this important article; and acting agreeably to the convictions of reason and conscience, in discharging our duty to our Creator. And therefore, it would be an unwarrantable stretch of perogative, in the Legislature, to make laws concerning it, except for protection. And it would be a fatal symptom of abject slavery in us, were we to submit to the usurpation.

"The Bill is also an unnecessary, and inadequate expedient for the end proposed. We are fully persuaded of the happy influence of Christianity upon the morals of men; but we have never known it, in the history of its progress, so effectual for this purpose as when left to its native excellence and evidence to recommend it, under the all directing providence of God, and free from the intrusive hand of the civil magistrate. Its Divine Author did not think it necessary to render it dependent on earthly governments. And experience has shown, that this dependence, where it has been effected, has been an injury rather than aid. It has introduced corruption among its teachers and professors of it, wherever it has been tried, for hundreds of years, and has been destructive of genuine morality, in proportion to the zeal of the powers of this world, in arming it with the sanction of legal terrors, or inviting to its profession by honours and rewards.

"It is urged, indeed, by the abettors of this bill, that it would be the means of cherishing religion and morality among the citizens. But it appears from fact, that these can be promoted only by internal conviction of the mind, and its voluntary choice, which such establishments cannot effect.

"We farther remonstrate against the bill as an impolitic measure:

"It disgusts so large a proportion of citizens, that it would weaken the influence of government in other respects, to diffuse a spirit of opposition to the rightful exercise of constitutional authority, if enacted into a law:

"It partially supposes the Quakers and Menomists to be more faithful in conducting the religious interests of their societies, than the other sects–which we apprehend to be contrary to fact:

"It unjustly subjects men who may be good citizens, but who have not embraced our common faith, to the hardship of supporting a system, they have not as yet believed the truth of; and deprives them of their property, for what they do not supposed to be of importance to them:

"It establishes a precedent for farther encroachments, by making the Legislature judges of religious truth. If the Assembly have a right to determine the preference between Christianity, and the other systems of religion that prevail in the world, they may also, at a convenient time, give a preference to some favoured sect among Christians:

"It discourages the population of our country by alarming those who may been oppressed by religious establishments in other countries, with fears of the same in this: And by exciting our own citizens to emigrate to other lands of greater freedom:

"It revives the principle which our ancestors contested to blood, of attempting reduce all religions to one standard by the force of civil authority:

"And it naturally opens a door for contention among citizens of different creeds, and different opinions respecting the extent of the powers of government.

"The bill is also a direct violation of the Declaration of Rights, which ought to be the standard of all laws. The sixteenth article is clearly infringed upon by it, and any explication which may have been given of it by the friends of this measure in the Legislature, so as to justify a departure from its literal construction, might also be used to deprive us of other fundamental principles of our government.

"For these reasons, and others that might be produced, we conceive it our duty to remonstrate and protest against the bill; and earnestly urge that it may not be enacted into law.

"We also wish to engage your attention a little farther, while we request a revision of the act for incorporating the protestant Episcopal Church: and state our reasons for this request. We do not desire to oppose the incorporation of that church for the better management of its temporalities; neither do we wish to lessen the attachment of any of the members of the Legislature, in a private capacity, to the interests of that church. We rather wish to cultivate a spirit of forbearance and charity towards the members of it, as the servants of one common Master who differ in some particulars from each other. But we cannot consent that they shall receive particular notice or favour from government as a Christian Society; nor peculiar distinctions or emoluments.

"We find by the act, that convenience of the Episcopal Church hath been consulted by it, in the management of their interests as a religious society, at the expense of other denominations. Under the former establishment there were perhaps few men who did not, at length, perceive the hardships and injustice of a compulsory law, obliging the citizens of this State by birthright free, to contribute to the support of a religion, from which their reason and conscience obliged them to dissent. Who then would not have supposed that the same sense of justice, which induced the Legislature to dissolve the grievous establishment, would also have induced them to leave to common use, the property in churches, glebes, &c., which had been acquired by common purchase.

"To do otherwise, as we conceive, to suppose that long prescription could sanction injustice; and that to persist in error, is to alter the essential difference between right and wrong. As Christians also, the subjects of Jesus Christ, who are wholly opposed to the exercise of spiritual powers by civil rulers, we conceive ourselves obliged to remonstrate against that part of the incorporating act, which authorises and directs the regulation of spiritual concerns. This is such an invasion of Divine perogative, that it is highly exceptional on that account, as well as on account of the danger to which it exposes our religious liberties. Jesus Christ hath given sufficient authority to his church, for every lawful purpose: and it is forsaking his authority and direction, for that of fallible men, to expect or to grant the sanction of the civil law to authorise the regulation of any Christian society. It is also dangerous to our liberties, because it creates an invidious distinction on account of religious opinions, and exalts to a superior pitch of grandeur, as the church of the State, a society which ought to be contented with receiving the same protection from government which the other societies enjoy, without aspiring to superior notice or regard. The Legislature assumes to itself by that law, the authoritative direction of this church in spirituals; and can be considered in no other light than its head, peculiarly interested in its welfare; a matter which cannot be indifferent to us—though this authority has only as yet been extended to those who have requested it or acquiesced in it. This church is now considered as the only regular church in the view of the law: and it is thereby raised to a state of unjust preeminence over others. And how far it may increase in dignity and influence in the State, by these means, at a future day, and especially when aided by the emoluments which it possesses, and the advantages of funding a very large sum of money without account, time alone can discover. But we esteem it our duty to oppose the act thus early, before the matter be entangled in precedents more intricate and dangerous. Upon the whole, therefore we hope that the exceptionable parts of the act will be repealed by your honourable [sic] House,; and that all preferences, distinctions, and advantages, contrary to the fourth article of the Declaration of Rights will be forever abolished.

"We regret that full equality in all things, and ample protection and security to religious liberty were not incontestably fixed in the constitution of the government. But we earnestly request that the defect may be remedied, as far as it is possible for the Legislature to do it, by adopting the bill in the revised laws for establishing religious freedom. [chap. 82 of the report]

"That Heaven may illuminate your minds with all that wisdom which is necessary for the important purposes of your deliberation, is our earnest wish. And we beg leave to assure you, that however warmly we may engage in preserving our religion free from the shackles of human authority, and opposing claims of spiritual domination in civil powers, we are zealously disposed to support the government of our country, and to maintain a due submission to the lawful exercise of its authority. Signed by order of the convention.

> John Todd, Chairman
> Attest, Daniel McCalla, Clerk.
> Bethel, Augusta County,
> 13th August, 1785

Graham, Rev. William, *Address to the Presbyterian General
Assembly by **Rev. William** Graham* (see Foote)

Presbyterian General Assembly
(Reprinted from Foote's *Sketches of Virginia*, First Series, 1850)

From a report prepared for the general Assembly and spread upon the records
of the Presbytery, April 29, 1793, we may learn his ideas of ministerial public
labours."[743] (Foote, p. 487–488, Foote's intro)

> *1ˢᵗ. That all our members banish the spirit of the world from
> their dress, manners, and conversation, and adopt the plainness,
> simplicity, self-denial, and holiness of life, so remarkably exemplified
> in the first and most successful of preachers of the gospel.*
>
> *2ⁿᵈ, That dry, formal and unaffecting harangues, be banished
> from our pulpits, and that the simple truths of the gospel be
> addressed to every man's conscience in the sight of God,
> with that fervour [sic] and solemnity which the dignity and
> interesting importance require.*
>
> *3ʳᵈ. That our private preparations for the pulpit consist chiefly in
> prayer, self-examination, and a practical study of the Scriptures.*
>
> *4ᵗʰ. That we endeavour always to enter on our public
> ministrations with a deep sense of the presence of God, and
> the awful importance of eternal judgment, in which we and our
> hearers must shortly share; and that we have no other object in
> view, but to recommend the gospel as the only means of escape
> for condemned perishing sinners. That an active persevering
> zeal, in preaching and exhorting in season and out of season, be
> a leading trait in the character of a Presbyterian clergyman. In
> fine let us endeavour to know nothing, in our official character,
> but Christ and him crucified.*
>
> *These appear to us some of the visible means which God has
> blessed for reviving religion in every period of the Church; or
> at least they are inseparable concomitants of a revival; and
> could they be generally adopted would be either forerunner
> of a revival, or a certain indication that a revival was begun.*

****

---

743   William Henry Foote, DD, *Sketches of Virginia, Historical and Biographical* (Philadelphia: J.
B. Lippincott & Co., 1850), First Series (John Knox Press reprint edition 1966, with index).

Report presented to the Presbyterian General Assembly by Rev. William Graham, April 29, 1793, and here reported and published by W. H. Foote in _Sketches of Virginia_, Series One, reprint ed. 1966, pp. 487–488.

Note: We have been unable to authenticate this representation by Foote using the many resources at our disposal, but it is our experience that Mr. Foote is scrupulously accurate in transcribing official documents and records. Unfortunately, Mr. Foote rarely cites his authorities. One should always seek independent verification when relying on Foote.

Appendix no. 3

America's First Black College Student and College Graduate
([Rev.] John Chavis)

Introduction

One of the more remarkable events in the history of American higher education has gone relatively unnoticed by most American historians. The subject matter involved is the education of the nation's first black college student. For some time, there have been numerous references in American historical publications to John Chavis, but typically, these references are surrounded by vagaries and qualified careful comments, which merely suggest that Mr. Chavis was an early student at Princeton and that he may have had some degree of theological instruction at Washington and Lee University in its early years. More recently, Washington and Lee has begun to recognize that Chavis was, indeed, once a regular student at the college. This, however, belies the actual truth of the matter for his appearance in Lexington was far more significant than a mere student who may have had some connection to the university. So why then the mystery, and why the reluctance to directly address his obviously curious presence?

What Led to John Chavis's Coming to Liberty Hall Academy

This report sets forth the proposition that the first black college student and graduate in the United States received his college education in the then-largest slaveholding state in America at Washington and Lee University, then Liberty Hall Academy, a chartered and degree-granting college in Lexington, Virginia. Chavis's enrollment was authorized by the institution's president (rector) William Graham because he was the only person authorized to enroll a prospective student. Moreover, Chavis's matriculation was most likely the proximate cause of the university's founding first president's surprising and rather inexplicable sudden resignation after twenty-two years. Several historians have hinted at Graham having had an additional or different reason for resigning than his resignation letter asserts. Frankly, the timing of his resignation and Chavis's astounding matriculation being so in concert with one another suggests a definite link between the two events. Since the resignation did not come about until after the completion of Chavis's regular academic studies, it raises a question about the trustees' willingness to publicly acknowledge Chavis as an alumnus.[744] Of course,

---

744 While the president (rector) approved each student's enrollment, the granting of the diploma at most colleges of that era was typically within the province of the trustees.

there is no known evidence that this was the case, but race relations being what they were at the time, one cannot avoid considering if perhaps the trustees, or some number of them, were unwilling to make a public representation of Chavis's successful completion of his studies at their academy. To be sure, there was no public acknowledgment of his presence at Liberty Hall during Graham's tenure or for a hundred years thereafter.[745]

We now know for certain, however, that Chavis was a student during 1795 and 1796. He probably began a year earlier than 1795 because the plan to educate Chavis privately at Princeton was likely aborted before the 1794 classes began. This was due to the rapidly deteriorating health condition of President Witherspoon. In 1793, Chavis resided in North Carolina near Virginia's southern border. Chavis could easily have traveled the approximately one hundred miles to arrive in Lexington for the 1794 session. In addition, many of the college's alumni were so well prepared at their enrollment that they completed their regular program within two years. Chavis is said to have been so thoroughly prepared for college by Rev. Pattillo that the Smith brothers at Princeton were willing to champion his admission there although only for private study under the retiring Dr. Witherspoon.

It is not known precisely when Chavis's matriculation began at Liberty Hall, but then we don't know precisely when most of the Liberty Hall Academy students began their studies. The important things to know in this regard is that the student in question attended in the regular academic program and the approximate date when his studies were completed. Those students who intended to pursue theological studies in preparation for the ministry typically went directly from the regular program to theological instruction. Further, we know that they completed their college studies when the presbytery to which they attached themselves accepted them for trials as a prospective probationer minister because obtaining a college education was deemed a prerequisite for ministers. This was because most congregations expected any new minister to be able to offer to oversee a grammar school for a congregation's younger members.

The Sociopolitical Implications of Chavis's Enrollment

Once enrolled at Liberty Hall, Chavis became the only black college student in the nation. Indeed, he was the only such distinguished American student during the eighteenth century. He was accepted into "the regular academic program" by the college's president, William Graham. Once Chavis had "gone through the regular academic program," the president enrolled him as a student in the

---

745 William Henry Ruffner, Manuscript Article *"An Educated Negro Preacher of a Century Ago,"* n.d., cite: William Henry Ruffner Papers, 1848-1907, Accession 24814, personal papers collection, Library of Virginia, Richmond, Virginia, 5 pp.

Lexington Theological Seminary,[746] which, at the time, was an integral, albeit adjunct, part of the college.[747]

While many of the college's early records have been lost, there are enough extant records to establish beyond any reasonable doubt that John Chavis received his college education exclusively at Liberty Hall Academy. In fact, only a very few descendants of early alumni of the university could be said to possess better academic credentials proving their ancestor's status as a graduate than those of John Chavis because most of the institution's early records were lost or destroyed. Among the college's alumni, Chavis is unique in having his status reflected in an official Rockbridge County court record, a record signed by all the several sitting magistrates including Capt. William Lyle,[748] a then-current trustee of Liberty Hall Academy. Lyle's signature on this court record punctuates the record's singular importance in settling any question as to whether Chavis "went" through the regular academic program at Liberty Hall Academy under Rev. William Graham.

There are no known records of the events that transpired leading up to Rev. William Graham's momentous decision to accept Rev. Pattillo's uniquely well-prepared charge, John Chavis, into the regular academic program at Liberty Hall, but there are a number of facts that may well have played some significant role in this intriguing process. First, it is well-known that Pattillo was, at one time, the pastor of Haw Fields Presbyterian Church in North Carolina. He accepted a call from that church in 1764. One of his new congregants at Haw Fields was Col. Edward Sharp, whose wife, Mary (Graham) Sharp is Rev. William Graham's older sister Mary (Graham) Sharp. Two of Rev. Graham's brothers, James and John, were also living in the area although the date of their arrival in North Carolina is unknown to this writer. In all probability, they resided for a time with Colonel Sharp and their older sister Mary (Graham) Sharp after their arrival. In

---

746   The name of this theological seminary was assigned to it by the rector's brother, Edward Graham. His reference to the seminary by that name can be seen in his 1821 published memoir of his late brother, William Graham. (See bibliography.)

747   In the early 1790s, the Presbyterian Virginia Synod entered into an agreement with Liberty Hall to sponsor a fund-raising campaign that would help pay for constructing a new campus to replace the frame structure recently destroyed by a fire. In exchange for the Synod's sponsorship, the college agreed to attaching a newly established Theological Seminary as an auxiliary of the college. The president, it was agreed, would serve as the president of the seminary. This action was not taken without controversy in the greater Lexington community.

748   William Lyle was appointed to replace his father, Samuel Lyle, who was one of the original trustees appointed in 1776. Almost needless to say, John Chavis's presence as a student at Liberty Hall would be a fact with which any of the colleges trustees would have been intimately familiar. In this case, it was absolutely certain insofar as William Lyle's sister, Elizabeth, was married to the Rectors brother, Michael Graham (Jr.). Moreover, Edward Graham, another of the rector's brothers, was the college's steward. Magistrate William Lyle then was brother-in-law to all three of these Graham brothers. Even more important, the mother of William Henry Ruffner, who wrote "An Educated Negro of a Hundred Years Ago" (see bibliography), was Captain William Lyle's daughter. These family members of trustee William Lyle were obviously aware of John Chavis's extraordinary status at the college. Lexington (Rockbridge County was very rural in that day, and this was an extraordinary occurrence.)

fact, even William Graham's widowed father was for a time living in the same general vicinity.

Rev. Pattillo would assuredly have known that this aspect of the Graham family was closely related to the rector of Liberty Hall Academy. The connections between William Graham's close family relations and Rev. Pattillo would very likely have played some role in bringing Graham into the coterie of Presbyterian ministers committed to providing this black man the opportunity to obtain a college education. Of course, the most significant common denominator with respect to all the Presbyterian ministers involved is that they were all members of the Hanover Presbytery, the same institution that created both Liberty Hall Academy (now W&L) and Prince Edward Academy (now Hampden Sydney), where the Smith brothers were successive presidents of Hampden Sydney during the period when Rev. Graham was president of Washington and Lee (then Liberty Hall).

Given the highly sensitive nature of the plan to educate a black man in that day, it is not surprising that those clergymen involved apparently agreed to avoid bringing any unnecessary attention to the unfolding events. Maintaining a low profile on all racial issues was in keeping with Princeton's president Witherspoon's oft-repeated admonition to his students at Princeton who were intending to enter the Presbyterian ministry, especially those destined to reside in slave states. To Witherspoon, the church's primary concern is with man's spiritual affairs, and clergymen would only be able to attend to these concerns in the slave states if they were welcomed into society's social fabric. They were advised by Princeton's president to avoid becoming politically active in their local neighborhoods and particularly with respect to the divisive slavery issue. Their congregation, of course, would be kept apprised of the church's national policies on that subject so the local minister did not need to invite the question into public debate. Universal emancipation was the church's long-term objective, and the ministers were advised to encourage their congregants to provide opportunities for their slaves' education in order to prepare them for emancipation and acculturation.

Rev. Graham was well aware of government and public policy issues as well as the church's strictures on all political topics. It is indeed strange that he alone among his brethren saw how providing a potential black minister would thoroughly debunk the then widely held but nonetheless ignorant view that blacks were not educable, and he saw how educating Mr. Chavis would serve as an important foundational step toward educating American slaves pursuant to the church's policy on emancipation.

At Liberty Hall, President Graham went much further than the Smith brothers had been prepared to go, and he enrolled Chavis into the regular academic program. At Princeton, Chavis would not likely have been placed in a dormitory setting with the typical college-age freshmen because Chavis was a fully mature adult. In addition, his race would predictably have had incendiary social implications. The same problem was obviously facing President Graham when Chavis arrived in Lexington.

The rector's brother, Edward Graham, had served as the first steward at the newly constructed campus on Mulberry Hill. The buildings, including the main one that housed the classroom(s) and the dormitory, were of stone construction.[749] Also of stone was the refectory building that contained quarters for the steward and space where the students took their meals. In all likelihood, Mr. Chavis lodged there along with the steward. Chavis may also have served as a part-time instructor in the grammar or preparatory school component to the college, much like Graham had done at Princeton, as a means by which to offset his tuition expenses. If Chavis was as well prepared for college as the Smith brothers at Princeton apparently believed he was, then Graham probably afforded him a similar opportunity as that which Dr. Witherspoon gave Graham when he was matriculating at Princeton. It is believed that Chavis paid no out-of-pocket tuition expenses at Liberty Hall, but still, Chavis would probably have been expected to make some form of contribution toward his otherwise free education.[750]

Mr. Chavis's Theological Instruction at Liberty Hall

As has been explained elsewhere in this report, Conrad Speece left autobiographical memoranda used later by Rev. Archibald Alexander when preparing a biographical sketch of Speece for inclusion in the compilation of sketches of Presbyterian ministers published in Sprague's *Annals of the American Pulpit* extract and also reprinted by Wm. H. Foote in his *Sketches of Virginia: Historical and Biographical* (Series 2, pp. 351–352). This biographical sketch was written by Rev. Archibald Alexander, DD, on Nov. 23, 1849, Alexander, who knew Speece would also have relied upon personal knowledge. This sketch makes clear that Rev. Graham continued his postgraduate theological instruction in Lexington even after his resignation as president of the college in the fall of 1796. It is inconceivable that Chavis would not have continued his theological studies under Graham given that his collegiate preceptor Graham conducted the only church patronized Presbyterian Theological Seminary in the nation,[751] and Chavis was already functioning without any known serious racial repercussions at Liberty Hall.

---

749   While it is entirely speculative on the auditor's part, it makes perfect sense that Graham would have insulated Chavis from potential conflict over Chavis lodging with the younger students by simply placing him with his brother, Edward in the refectory building. Moreover, Edward was both a scholar and graduate of Liberty Hall. Professionally, Edward was trained for the law and was a member of the Bar. As such, Edward may very well have prepared Chavis's 1802 court documents that became so important to proving Chavis's status as a graduate of the academy. About that same time, Edward became a member of the faculty of the college founded by his late brother, William.

750   There is no record suggesting that the proceeds of the Lesley fund that was to be used to pay Chavis's expenses at Princeton were used to remunerate Mr. Graham at Liberty Hall, and there was no likelihood that the Smith brothers would have been inclined to use those funds in that way because Mr. Lesley's Will was specifically designed for defraying tuition costs of poor Princeton students.

751   The possible exception being Princeton, but Princeton did not as yet have a formally established and patronized theological seminary. In fact, the Princeton Theological Seminary's founding first president was one of Graham's students, Rev. Dr. Archibald Alexander.

Of course, Chavis, like all other theological students must have regularly engaged in instructive conversations with his peers and other relatively local clergymen, but for his formal instruction, he would have relied upon the services of his educational benefactor, William Graham, just as Mr. Speece and all the other church-bound Liberty Hall students. In addition, it is well-established that Chavis applied to the Lexington Presbytery to be taken on trials for licensing as a probationary Presbyterian minister at the first regular meeting of the Lexington Presbytery following the unexpected sudden death of his preceptor, Graham, who died suddenly in June of 1799. Chavis applied to the Lexington Presbytery at its autumn meeting of that year, which was the first opportunity after the death of Mr. Graham. The presbytery titular leader was Rev. Graham, and his role in that regard had been consistent since Graham led the effort to create that presbytery. There was no reasonable opportunity for Mr. Chavis to continue with his theological training after Mr. Graham's death, so it was understandable that Chavis immediately applied to the presbytery in hopes of securing his license as a probationer. Moreover, Chavis knew many, if not most, of the Lexington Presbytery's members, and he would have had confidence in their ready acceptance of him. In that, he was perfectly correct. Presumably the members, who had all also been trained by Liberty Hall's president, had been kept apprised of Chavis's educational progress by their old preceptor and were ready to receive Mr. Chavis's application. This helps to explain Chavis's smooth transition from student to clergyman in Virginia.

Following his trials,[752] Chavis was licensed by the presbytery and began a missionary tour in Virginia. In that capacity, Chavis preached to numerous congregations of varying racial mixes as well as exclusively white congregations. From the reports made by Chavis to the church, it appears these events were held without any serious incidents. This subject is admirably dealt with in Ms. Othow's biography of her ancestor. Her treatment together with the Presbyterian Church historical records demonstrate conclusively that the presbytery that oversaw Chavis's regular collegiate educational preparation and his theological instruction as well as his licensing did not carry out that mission with a design to limit his ministrations to "people of his own color." That mischaracterization was obviously and unfortunately made by Presbyterians who had no direct involvement with Mr. Chavis and the administrative operations of the Lexington Presbytery. The Lexington Presbytery's records reflect the true nature of Chavis's role as a Presbyterian minister during his years in Virginia.

Conclusion Regarding Chavis

Much that has been written about Chavis is flawed. The most extensive of the published biographical treatments **is** _John Chavis, African American Patriot, Preacher, Teacher, and Mentor, 1763–1838_ (Jefferson, North Carolina, and London: McFarland & Company, 2001) by Helen Chavis Othow; but

---

752 These "trials" were the intensive investigation into a prospective minister's theological views and knowledge. In addition, the members inquired into the applicant's character and faith.

unfortunately, Ms. Othow mistakenly concluded that Chavis was principally educated at Princeton, which did not happen. She deserves credit, however, for unearthing valuable primary research material. For whatever reason, selective perception dominated her analysis and led her astray. As a result, following the publication of her ancestor's biography, his highly significant connections to Washington and Lee University remained hidden in obscurity.

Most academics are unfamiliar with the use of legal documents and often fail to fully grasp the significance of certain aspects of court procedures. For example, the Rockbridge County court record she unearthed is of far greater importance than she realized. Indeed, the photocopy of the document reprinted in her book cut off so much of the signatures of certain sitting magistrates that the name William Lyle cannot be ascertained by the reader simply by referring to her book's reprint of that document. William Lyle, however, is the most significant signature contained on this document because he was not only a magistrate, but he was also then a current trustee of the college. His approval of the document that was prepared by Chavis or someone representing him confirms Chavis's representation that "he went through the regular academic program" at Liberty Hall Academy.[753]

The document in question was filed by Chavis as required by a then-recent state law affecting all adult free persons of color. To misrepresent the basic facts in such a filing is tantamount to perjury so, in essence, this document is Chavis's declaration, under oath, which was accepted and approved by the Rockbridge County court. The final wording may have been slightly reworked by the court's clerk, but the facts are drawn from what Chavis filed.

Clearly, Chavis knew where he received his collegiate education, and his own testimony, approved by one of the trustees of the college, pretty well settles the question as to where Chavis matriculated. Additionally, Chavis's theological preparation could hardly have been obtained anywhere else at the time. What this means in sum is that the education of the first black college student and college graduate was all carried out in Lexington, Virginia, at Liberty Hall Academy. In addition, that student's theological preparation for the Presbyterian ministry took place at the location because the Hanover Presbytery's Theological Seminary in Virginia was created under its patronage in a joint arrangement with the college. This arrangement included a church-sponsored fund-raising campaign designed to underwrite the construction of a stone campus to be constructed on Mulberry

---

753   Court records of this sort are, in essence, depositions containing the filer's statement of facts as he or she knows them. In some cases, the Court or a Court Clerk will edit the filed document but not change the substance of the filed document presented under the filing party's signature. The record then, represents a statement of the filing party submitted to the Court under Oath. Viz, the representation that Chavis "went through the regular Academic Program" at Liberty Hall," reflects John Chavis' knowledge of where he attended college. If he had been a graduate or even a student at Princeton he certainly would have said so in such a vastly important permanent court record. Since, in over two hundred years, no evidence has ever surfaced suggesting otherwise, it is high time that the suggestion that Chavis attended college at Princeton should be discarded to the ash-heap of bad history.

Hill, and the institution of a new theological seminary under the direction of Rev. William Graham was to also be housed on this campus.

Rev. William Graham was the only college president in the eighteenth century who had the courage to enroll the only black college student in the United States, and he oversaw both his undergraduate program and his postgraduate theological studies that allowed Chavis to join the exclusive club of Presbyterian ministers. Exclusive because to be a Presbyterian minister, one had to prove that they were possessed of a college education. Chavis ably presented himself before a Presbyterian committee of scholars (Lexington Presbytery), most of whom were educated by Mr. Graham at Liberty Hall, and this conclave of scholars accepted Mr. Chavis for trials. This action too was tantamount to a finding that Chavis was fully prepared in his collegiate course work.

What William Graham and John Chavis accomplished together was to establish with certainty that a black man was every bit as educable as a Caucasian student, which was a powerful message to make in the then-largest slaveholding state in the nation. Congregations throughout many regions of Virginia witnessed firsthand the evidence that debunked the notion of the racial inferiority of blacks. William Graham and Liberty Hall Academy in Lexington, Virginia, allowed John Chavis the opportunity to prove that the Presbyterian Church's national policy encouraging slaveholders and ministers to provide educational opportunities to the slaves within their jurisdiction was a valid policy. Education, according to the church's policy was essential as a means by which to emancipate slaves responsibly because this policy increased significantly the newly emancipated slave's successful transition from slavery to freedom. Acculturation, after all, would depend upon slaves having a common language with the dominant cultural establishment and at least a modicum appreciation for the social mores and customs of the society with which it would be acclimating, if they were to survive in this somewhat foreign land.

William Graham's unanticipated death from pneumonia denied him the opportunity to witness Chavis's licensing and preaching, but he had overseen enough of his training to realize that the experiment was a complete success. Thankfully, he died before the slave interests intervened politically and successfully subverted the plan. The proverbial cat, however, was now "out of the bag."

Chavis stood as symbol from that day forward, and even though his talents and attainments were restricted by the political interventions designed to thwart his ability to preach and teach, he still managed to advance the idea that racial integration was entirely possible if sufficient educational opportunities are extended to the nation's African immigrants and universal emancipation in America was indeed an achievable goal. In that sense, it is difficult to argue that any other American in the eighteenth century accomplished more than William Graham at Liberty Hall Academy in Lexington, Virginia, did to advance the objective of universal emancipation of American African slavery.

It is amazingly ironic then that nearly two hundred years after William Graham welcomed the first black college student into a chartered institution of higher learning, a young academic, Dr. David Robson, would publish these patently false words:

> **William Graham was the first late eighteenth-century**
> **Virginia clergyman to defend slavery and, so far as I can**
> **determine, the only college professor in the country during**
> **the era who supported the institution.** *His was a powerful,*
> *if little known, advocacy. It should be considered when*
> *examining the resurgence of proslavery sentiment in the post-*
> *Revolutionary South.*(
>
> David, W. Robson, "An Important Question Answered: William
> Graham's Defense of Slavery in Post-Revolutionary Virginia,"
> *William and Mary Quarterly*, 3rd Series, 37, no. 4, [October
> 1980], pp. 644–652; emphasis added)

(Note: The above quotation is from an erroneous piece throughout. It is based on an incorrect assumption that the Joseph Glass "lecture notes" were transcriptions of William Graham's lectures. While the recopied version of these lectures contains a new "cover page" identifying the contents as being lectures of William Graham delivered at Liberty Hall in 1796, this description is from the fertile imagination of the 1896 copyist, Mr. Harry Waddell Pratt.[754] Why Pratt mistakenly believed the lectures were Graham's is unknown, but it is simply untrue, a fact made certain by the testimony of both Edward Graham and Rev. Dr. Archibald Alexander, two of Graham's early students. They were both students who wrote memoirs of William Graham after his death. Edward Graham was the younger brother of William Graham, and both of these scholars lived in William Graham's home while students at Liberty Hall Academy. There is no credible evidence to suggest that Robson's notion is correct. Moreover, the evidence that does exist suggests that they are not written by Graham but rather were transcribed by Graham from the Witherspoon master copy during Graham's time at Princeton. Graham's lectures were never written down and are lost to history. No contemporary of William Graham ever claimed that William Graham was a defender of slavery.)

Here, however, are some things that William Graham did write and publish:

> *A Republic is a government, by equal and just laws, made*
> *by common consent, for the common benefit, and not the*
> *dominion of one community over another community, . . .*
> *which is founded in the perfect, political equality of all the*
> *citizens.*
>
> *Let civil government be the common guardian and protector*
> *of all; but the patron of none.*

---

754 The recopied packet of lectures has a handwritten note from Mr. Waddell identifying himself
      as the copyist.

Every violation of the perfect equality of the citizens, is a step towards tyranny.

That government is excellent, which inviolably preserves the equality of the citizens, both in civil and a religious respect.

Let us try to know our rights and assert our privileges, free from the heat of passion, or the prejudice of party. Let us remember that we are acting for ages; and let us endeavour to secure the applause and gratitude of posterity, by securing to them a precious birth right of perfect freedom and political equality. (Rev. William Graham, "An Essay on Government," Phil. 1786)

The above extracts are hardly the sentiments of a defender of slavery. The first extract in particular is obviously directed at the institution of slavery. The United States should have adopted this provision into the Constitution and thereby avoided the bloodiest war in our nation's history.

It is also worth mentioning here that William Graham, while president of Liberty Hall Academy, wrote a proposed state constitution for his friends and earlier students then living in what is now mostly eastern Tennessee, which was rejected. It is very unique in many respects, but one way in particular because this proposed constitution does not contain any provision protecting a property right to hold anyone in slavery. A rather odd omission for someone who is said to have defended slavery. Perhaps that explains why Graham's proposed constitution was rejected in favor of another, and also why, after the convention had rejected Graham's proposed constitution, a mob formed and burned Graham's image in effigy.[755]

Together, Liberty Hall's president William Graham and the amazingly unique black student, John Chavis, took a monumental step forward in race relations in the United States. Chavis's successful completion of his regular academic program debunked forever the ridiculous notion that blacks were uneducable and as inferiors could be held in perpetual bondage. Washington and Lee University (then Liberty Hall), as a chartered degree-granting institution of higher learning, stands tall and alone as a landmark of social progress and the only such educational institution in the United States in the eighteenth century. Its status, in this regard, was soon shrouded in darkness, but in the full sunlight of the present, it is once again revealed as a beacon illuminating a glorious past in which her sons and daughters may take well-deserved pride in what took place at Liberty Hall on Mulberry Hill. May her current guardians never forsake the legacy of the founder

---

755   Samuel Coles Williams, *History of the Lost State of Franklin* (New York: The Press of the Pioneers, 1933). (Contains valuable information pertaining to Rev. William Graham's [of Washington & Lee fame] participation in the plan to establish the state of Franklin. Graham is the author of the draft of the proposed constitution for the lost state of Frankland).

and father of this great university, Rev. William Graham, nor that of her first black alum, Rev. John Chavis, two men of great character, courage, and faith.

****

Additional and Miscellaneous Notes on Chavis

Notes taken from the minutes of the general assembly of the Presbyterian Church of America:

Item no. 1.

> "That in order to attain one important object of the contributions, (the instruction of blacks,) Mr. John Chavis, a black man of prudence and piety, **who has been educated and licensed to preach by the presbytery of Lexington, in Virginia**,[756] be employed as a missionary among people of his own colour, until the meeting of next General Assembly. And that for his better direction in the discharge duties which are attended with many circumstances of delicacy and difficulty, some prudential instructions be issued to him by the Assembly, governing himself by which, the knowledge of religion among that people may be made more and more to strengthen the order of society. And the Rev. Messrs. Hoge, Alexander, Logan and Stephenson, were appointed a committee, to draught instructions to said Chavis, and prescribe his route. (Minutes of the general assembly of the Presbyterian Church of the United States of America, from its Organization AD 1789 to AD 1820 inclusive, Philadelphia: Presbyterian Board of Publication, p. 229; emphasis added)

The above is of great significance because it confirms that the Presbyterian National Assembly recognized that Chavis was educated and licensed to preach by the presbytery of Lexington.

In Re the Pby. of Lexington and Rev. John Chavis

> They have lately dismissed Mr. John Chavis, a licentiate, to put himself under the care of Hanover Presbyter. (Minutes, General Assembly, 1802, p. 240)

---

756   The assembly may have believed that Chavis was to be employed as mssionary to people of his own people, but the Lexington Presbytery and the Virginia Synod where the most influential members had been William Graham had no intention of limiting Chavis's responsibilities to only people of his own color.

That the Journal of Mr. John Chavis, a black man, licensed by the Presbytery of Lexington, in Virginia, was read in the Assembly. He appears to have executed his mission with great diligence, fidelity, and prudence. He served nine months, and received fifty-eight dollars and sixty-four cents. (Minutes, General Assembly, p. 254)

Item no. 2: Chavis is well known to the Lexington community including Archibald Alexander family

Archibald Alexander wrote to his sister Margaret [Alexander] Graham [wife of Edward Graham, Rev. Graham's brother] July 19, 1803 (see Alexander's biography by his son James, p. 274):

> *Dear Sister:—By John Chavis I received yours, and pass over all the rest to answer that part in which you express some uneasiness at my entertaining doubts respecting the genuineness of the Kentucky revival.*
>
> (Alexander, James, W., The Life of Archibald Alexander, DD [New York: Charles, Scribner, 1854], p. 274. This is an extract from a letter written by the subject of James W. Alexander, who is his father, Rev. Archibald Alexander.)

Item no. 3: Chavis not at Princeton

On September 27, 1792 the trustees voted to use the Lesley Fund ("for the education of poor and pious youth with a view to the ministry of the Gospel in the Presbyterian Church") on behalf of John Chavis, a light-skinned free black and Revolutionary War Veteran from Virginia. One pf the most remarkable African-Americans of the antebellum era, Chavis became a noted Latinist and a tutor to prominent white boys, particularly in the Magnum family of North Carolina. His name appears on no class list, but strong family tradition insists that he attended. If so, he was the College's only black student before the mid-twentieth century, but he did not stay long. The one semester he would most likely have been at Princeton was the summer term of 1793, for which no class list survives. In other words, the family tradition may well be accurate and has been accepted by several generations of archivists at Princeton University. But unless Chavis entered with junior class standing, which seems highly improbable, he would necessarily have been assigned to the class of 1795 or 1796. For this reason, his biography does not appear in these volumes. (Dr. John M. Murrin, *Princetonians, 1784–1790*, [Princeton, NJ: Princeton University Press], introduction, p. lii)

Item no. 4: Edgar Knight's poignant observation about the Chavis-at-Princeton notion?

The comment below was reprinted in John Hope Franklin's, *The Free Negro in North Carolina*, page 170.

> "***There is no clear proof . . . that Chavis was ever a student at Princeton****. Beyond the known fact that he was not graduated the institution has no genuine record of the man. (Edgar, W. Knight, "Notes On John Chavis," *North Carolina Historical Review*, vol. 7, no. 3 [January–October 1930]: 326–45; emphasis added)

Note: Mr. Knight acknowledges that there is a Chavis family tradition that claims John Chavis went to Princeton. Tradition or not, the fact remains that there is no evidence that John Chavis ever attended Princeton or that he was educated by Princeton's retiring president John Witherspoon. Mr. Knight also says that the institution lists Mr. Chavis as a "non-graduate," but it is readily apparent that this is merely a public relations stunt by the university because once again, there is no proof that John Chavis ever attended Princeton.

Item no. 5: Here below is particularly compelling evidence of Mr. Chavis's complete matriculation at Liberty Hall Academy:

> 1. The Rockbridge County Court's recognition in 1802 that John Chavis had completed his undergraduate education at Liberty Hall and was a member in good standing of the Lexington Community.[757] (Rockbridge Co Ct Order, Book 6, p. 10)

Below is the complete text of that court record:

---

757 This court document was published in full including a photostatic facsimile in 2001 in *John Chavis, African American Patriot, Preacher, Teacher, and Mentor (1763-1838)* by Helen Chavis Othow, although this particular copy unfortunately cuts off enough of the names of two magistrates that they are indecipherable. The auditor, however, secured a photostatic copy from the Library of Virginia in November of 2012, which includes the names of all the sitting magistrates that comprised this court, which were James Gilmore, John Gay, Joseph Grigsby, and William Lyle. This record taken from the Rockbridge County Coutt Order Book, 6, p. 10. This record can be found also in the Personal Papers of W. H. Ruffner at the same library.

"April Term 1802

"Rockbridge Co. Ct. Order Book 6, p. 10.

"***On the motion of Rev. John Chavis***, a black man, It is ordered that the Clerk of this Court certify that the said Chavis has been known to the Court for several years last past, and that he has always since known to the Court, been considered as a free man, and they believe him such, and that he has always while in this County, conducted himself in a decent orderly and respectable manner, ***and also that he has been a student at Washington Academy where they believe he went through a regular course of academical studies.*** The Justices comprising this Ct. Were James Gilmore, John Gay, Joseph Grigsby & ***William Lyle***. [[758]] (here the emphasis is simply that and does not represent an error)

Note: The above text is from a copy obtained from the Library of Virginia pursuant to the auditor's request on November 24, 2012.

There are two points worth noting about this record: (1) The record and its content exists pursuant to a motion brought to the court by Mr. John Chavis, and therefore, its content reflects the views of Mr. Chavis and are simply agreed to by the magistrates of the court and (2) the order was signed and therefore agreed to by Mr. William Lyle, who was a trustee of Washington College during the latter part of Mr. Chavis's matriculation, and he was appointed a trustee to replace his father Samuel Lyle. As father and son, these two trustees would not have failed to note and discuss the unprecedented matriculation of a black student at the college. Trustee Lyle's status as a signatory of this court record is tantamount to the eyewitness affidavit of a trustee of the Washington College affirming under oath the fact that Rev. John Chavis had completed successfully his academic program at the college.

Item no. 6: Article written by William Henry Ruffner

(William Henry Ruffner, *Manuscript Article "An Educated Negro Preacher of a Century Ago,"* n.d., cite: William Henry Ruffner Papers, 1848-1907, Accession 24814, personal papers, collection, Library of Virginia, Richmond, Virginia. 5pps.)

In this handwritten piece by Washington College trustee, Wm. Henry Ruffner, he says,

---

758 William Lyle, one of the sitting magistrates, was also a trustee of Washington Academy. He was appointed to succeed his father Samuel Lyle, who was one of the original trustees of Liberty Hall Academy, appointed on May 6, 1776. Their combined service formed an unbroken chain for many decades. Without a doubt, magistrate and trustee, Mr. Lyle, would not have perjured himself by signing on to this court order if he had any doubt as to Mr. Chavis's status as a student who had gone "through a regular course of academical studies" at his college.

"Owing to defective records it does not appear when he was graduated, but his scholarship as subsequently shown *authorizes the belief that he rec'd the degree of Bachelor of Arts.* (Wm. H. Ruffner, "An Educated Negro...; emphasis added)

(Note: Ruffner then includes a parenthetical or marginalia reference to the county court record, which obviously is a reference to the record discussed in no. 1 above. Following that, Mr. Ruffner sets forth the various exercises John Chavis went through before the Lexington Presbytery as part of those trials required by all candidates for the Presbyterian ministry, which include several means by which the candidate demonstrates his scholarly and theological attainments.

Mr. Wm. H. Ruffner's father, Henry, was president of Washington College. President Ruffner wrote the first lengthy history of Washington College in the 1840s, but it was not published until 1890 in the historical papers of Washington and Lee University. The article "The Early History of Washington College" is the first article in the first volume of the university's historical papers series (see "Audit Bibliography"). His son William Henry Ruffner was an amateur historian, and he added several footnotes to his father's *"Early History of Washington College."* President Henry Ruffner's first wife Sarah was the daughter of that Samuel Lyle who was an original trustee of Washington College (earlier Liberty Hall Academy) and was also William Lyle's sister. It seems readily apparent that this Ruffner family, including both father and son, both of whom were so closely connected to Washington College, were thoroughly convinced as to the education of Rev. John Chavis at Washington College and equally as assured that he successfully completed his regular academic program at the academy (i.e., Liberty Hall Academy) in Lexington. Hardly any family in Virginia connected to the college in the nineteenth century, excepting the William Graham and Samuel Lyle families, would have been in a more advantageous position to understand what had transpired in regard to John Chavis's education than the Ruffner family.

The institution's name change no doubt took place after Mr. Chavis's initial enrollment and during his matriculation at the then-associated theological seminary, which in that time was under the patronage of the Virginia Synod of the Presbyterian Church and yet was conducted at Liberty Hall Academy's main campus building. The remains of that structure are visible today on Mulberry Hill.

Remembering that William Henry Ruffner's mother was the daughter of an original trustee of Liberty Hall Academy, Samuel Lyle, and a sister of trustee William Lyle who had signed the court record affirming John Chavis's affidavit that asserted that Mr. Chavis had gone through the regular academic program at the college, it is hardly likely that the early historian of Washington College, Henry Ruffner, failed to accurately represent the matriculation of the nation's first black college graduate to his immediate family, including his son William Henry who penned the brief sketch of that happy event referenced above. Especially since President Ruffner's father-in-law Samuel Lyle was a trustee at the time that the college's rector, William Graham, enrolled this rather unique new student.

Of course, trustee William Lyle was William Henry Ruffner's uncle, and trustee Samuel Lyle was his grandfather.[759]

Note: It is probably appropriate here for the auditor to remind his readers that Samuel Lyle is also the auditor's fifth great-grandfather, a fact noted earlier in the auditor's "Statement of Purpose."

Item no. 7: Rev. John Chavis's ministerial activities in Virginia

The year following the licensing of Mr. John Chavis by the Lexington Presbytery, he was employed by the national Presbyterian Church as a missionary as the following extracts from the minutes of the general assembly for the year 1801 clearly evince:

> "Mr. John Chavis, a black man, of prudence and piety, who has been educated and licensed to preach by the Presbytery of Lexington, in Virginia, be employed as a missionary among people of his own color, until the meeting of next General Assembly. (Minutes of the general assembly,[760] p. 229)

> "The committee appointed for that purpose, reported a set of special instruction for Mr. John Chavis, the Assembly's missionary in Virginia, which was approved; whereupon

> "Ordered that a copy of the same, certified by the stated Clerk, be transmitted, with his commission, to Mr. Chavis. (Minutes of the gen . . ., p. 233)

> "The Presbytery of Lexington, . . . has lately dismissed Mr. John Chavis, a licentiate, to put himself under the care of Hanover Presbytery. (Minutes of the general assembly, p. 240, 1802)

The extracts above are a part of the actions of a special committee of the general assembly established in connection with the church's desire to carry the word of God among disparate peoples who otherwise would not hear the word of God, including the various North American Indian tribes and the African slaves. The appointment of Mr. Chavis in this regard was a key component of the

---

759 Oscar K. Lyle, *Lyle Family*, New York, 1912. This is a professionally researched and written genealogical study of four immigrant members of the Lyle family that settled in the vicinity of Rockbridge County, Virginia, in the eighteenth century and their descendants. One of these Lyle immigrants, Samuel Lyle, was one of the original trustees of Liberty Hall Academy, who served in that capacity from 1776 to 1796. Samuel Lyle was also the institution's first treasurer and an original member of the executive committee of the board of trustees. His eldest daughter, Elizabeth, married Michael Graham who was a younger brother of Rev. William Graham, the college's founding first president (i.e., Rrector). Michael Graham (Jr.) was a revolutionary soldier and sheriff of Bedford County, Virginia.

760 Minutes of the General Assembly of the Presbyterian Church, Philadelphia: Presbyterian Board of Publication, 1847.

church's national policy regarding slavery, which was dedicated to carrying out a plan for preparing those held in bondage for the hoped-for total abolition of that institution by a peaceful process of acculturation and assimilation, which they believed could only come about through education. A prudent and expedient plan soon interrupted by the likes of the notorious slave Gideon and, later, by Mr. Nat Turner, whose penchant for bloody violence condemned the Presbyterian plan to failure and near extinction.[761] Rev. Chavis requested and received authorization to return to the neighborhood of his closest family and friends in North Carolina and was there received into the care of the Hanover Presbytery where he joined his earliest preceptor, Rev. Henry Pattillo.

Note: The North Carolinians eventually formed the Orange Presbytery.

Item no. 8: John Chavis, Bristol Yamma, and John Quamine

An error from Varnum L. Collins, biographer of Rev. Dr. John Witherspoon:

> In 1774 two free negroes Bristol Yamma and John Quamine, sent by the Missionary Society of Newport, Rhode Island, were enrolled at Princeton for a couple of years of preparation for work in Africa. . . .

> The most remarkable of his pupils in this group was John Chavis, a negro sent to Princeton as an experiment, who became famous as a schoolmaster in North Carolina. (Varnum L. Collins, *President Witherspoon, A Biography*, vol. 2, firˢᵗ London edition, Oxford University Press, [Princeton: Princeton University Press, 1925], p. 217)

Very little is known about the education of Bristol Yamma and John Quamine. In his biography of Witherspoon, it contains but a brief reference to these two would-be missionaries. Like most of the "special students," they were either instructed in the college's grammar school or were under Witherspoon's private instruction or possibly some combination of the two, but there is no official records suggesting any of these special students were enrolled in the regular academic program at Princeton.

---

761   John Hope Franklin points out in his book, *The Free Negro in North Carolina...* that much of what comprised the North Carolina "free black codes" were promulgated prior to Nat Turner's rebellion.

Appendix 4

America's First Female College Student
(Mrs. Sarah Priestley)

The significance of Sarah (McBride) Priestley's matriculation at Liberty Hall Academy in Lexington, Virginia, lies not in her person, nor in her academic profile, but rather it has to do with the singular fact that Rev. William Graham willingly enrolled her into the regular academic program at a chartered college with degree-granting authority and that this took place in America in the eighteenth century. It appears from this fact that Mrs. Priestley is America's first bona fide female college student.

The source of the information that reveals this previously unheralded social innovation is Rev. Archibald Alexander, the founding first president of the Princeton Theological Seminary, a widely published authority on eighteenth-century Presbyterian colleges and seminaries in America and an early alumnus of Washington and Lee University.[762] In the case of Sarah (McBride) Priestley, Rev. Alexander was an eyewitness to her matriculation who was a postgraduate theological student under the college's rector, William Graham. In addition, Mrs. Priestley's husband James was one of his tutors at Liberty Hall and someone whom Rev. Alexander admired greatly.

> He [Priestly] formed a purpose in which she [Mrs. P] concurred, of sending her to W. Graham's to go thro a regular course of classical learning. Being then a student of theology with Mr. Graham, I saw Mrs. Priestly often. She was the mother of two children; the youngest an infant at the breast. There she commenced her Latin grammar; but what thro' dullness of intellect and interruption from the children she never got through the pronouns . . . Great must have been his disappointment when his wife returned to him, without having in any degree realized his wishes and expectations but he never ceased to urge upon her the importance of mental cultivation & altho she never returned to the study of Latin & Greek, she made some progress in geography, arithmetic, and English Grammar; so that some years afterwards, with his assistance she superintended the education of a large class of young ladies,

---

762 Another important fact is that no other institution of higher learning appears to have asserted or claimed to have enrolled a female student into their regular academic program during the eighteenth century.

in Baltimore. (Alexander Mss. "Memoir of William Graham,"
pp. 112–113)

Rev. Alexander was a widely recognized scholar and theologian who held
students to the very highest of academic standards, so his comments about Mrs.
Priestley's difficulties with Latin and Greek grammar should be taken with a
grain of salt. Compared to the college students of today, she would probably
seem like a student with a master's degree who was working on her doctorate.
After all, her husband was one of the finest scholars in North America and a
college president. Comparing Dr. Priestley's wife to the likes of two presidents
of institutions of higher learning is a comparison few would wish to have
made concerning themselves. Without a doubt, Mrs. Priestley was one of the
most educated women in America during her lifetime. Washington and Lee
University can take pride in their progressive attitude and accomplishments
relative to diversity of its student body in the eighteenth century. No other state
and no other chartered college in America permitted blacks and or women as
students in their regular academic programs in the eighteenth century. In this
regard, Washington and Lee University stands as the only example of this
kind of forward thinking, thanks to the wisdom and courage of the college's
president, William Graham.

****

Miscellaneous Tidbits about Dr. James Priestley

History knows far more about Mrs. Priestley's husband James Priestley, and
this added information has been included for reference purposes.

From the internet:

Peg Green's Notes for James Priestley Sr.:

* "JAMES PRIESTLEY, SR.: b. 1760, in Augusta Co., VA, the
son of WILLIAM SR. and MARY (—) PRIESTLEY; d. Feb. 6,
1821, Nashville, TN; Bur. in old cemetery in Hendersonville,
TN, on north side of Gallatin Pike; m. 19 Apr 1788, in Mercer
Co., KY, to **SARAH MCBRIDE** (b. Bef. 1772, in KY) - 6
children

James was born in 1760 in Augusta Co., which later became
Rockbridge County, Virginia. James went to live with Rev.
William Graham, ca. 1774–1776, when he was still a young
man, and would not have been listed in a Priestley household
(or as his own household), in 1778.

James Priestley, Sr., son of William Sr. and Mary, became a member of the first graduating class of Liberty Hall Academy (later became Washington and Lee). As a boy of about 14, his intelligence was noticed in a class by Rev. William Graham, who took James into his household sometime after that (1774), so that he could receive a good education.

William Priestley, Sr., James' father was apparently "indigent" ca. 1774–1776, when James was taken in by Rev. Graham. It was the pre-Revolutionary times. William was a farmer in Rockbridge County and did not have deeds for land until more than 20 years later, on April 12, 1799, when he purchased the 115 acres at Todd Springs Run, on Buffalo Creek and Lot no. 5, in the town of Lexington, Virginia.* James Priestley, the scholar, left Rockbridge County in 1784, for Kentucky.

James Priestley, AB, LL. D., Rockbridge Co., Tutor Liberty Hall Academy, Prof. of Languages and Mathematics, 1782–84. Principal Classical Schools in Bardstown, KY, Georgetown, DD, Annapolis and Baltimore, MD. Pres. of Cumberland College at Nashville. Distinguished for his learning.

Cokesbury College was a college in Abingdon, Maryland and later Baltimore, Maryland that existed from 1787 until 1796. Cokesbury College was founded as the first Methodist college in the United States.

*   In "ROCKBRIDGE HISTORICAL SOCIETY PROCEEDINGS," Vol. IX, pp. 49–50, article on "The First Graduating Class of Liberty Hall Academy," by Charles N. Watson, Jr.: "The last of the graduates of 1785 to be discussed was also a Rockbridge County man, James Priestley. He came from an indigent family, but his intelligence so impressed Reverend William Graham that he took the young man into his own home to insure the boy a proper education. Priestley became a distinguished scholar, devoting his life to the promotion of classical literature. Greek literature was his favorite subject, and he knew the orations of Demosthenes by heart. He was briefly employed as a tutor at Liberty Hall. (Washington and Lee Historical Papers, 2:136)* In 1784, Priestley went to Kentucky where he became principal of Salem Academy at Bardstown. Under his guidance the school enjoyed a high reputation. In 1792, he moved to Baltimore and taught briefly at Cokesbury College. Returning to Kentucky, he taught at an academy in Danville. Finally, in 1809, he accepted the presidency of

Cumberland College in Nashville. This Cumberland College later became Peabody College and even later became a separate college within Vanderbilt University. This Peabody College at Vanderbilt specializes in education.

In 1816, when Cumberland College closed temporarily, Priestley opened a school for young ladies. When the college reopened in December, 1820, he resumed his duties as its president. Two months later he died suddenly at the age of sixty-one. (Cyclopedia of American Biography, 8:130)

(Submitted by M. L. Green [mlgreen@wvinter.net])

****

Conclusion Regarding Sarah (McBride) Priestley

This report reveals openly for the first time a matters of utmost importance, one of which is that

Washington and Lee University has the distinct privilege of being the first chartered college in North America to have enrolled a woman into a chartered college's (Liberty Hall Academy) regular academic course.

It is an error of omission to fail or refuse to appropriately recognize the cultural significance of Rev. William Graham's decision to enroll the first woman, Mrs. Sarah (McBride) Priestley, into a chartered college's (Liberty Hall) regular academic course in the United States of America.[763] The accuracy of this assertion is gleaned from an impeccable source, the founding president of Princeton Theological Seminary, Rev. Dr. Archibald Alexander, one of Liberty Hall Academy's earliest students and a serious historian of the Presbyterian Church's early role in advancing American higher education.

The only evidence we have discovered on this issue is the eyewitness testimony of Rev. Archibald Alexander, who was a divinity student at Lexington under Rev. William Graham, which we provide below:

> *He (James Priestley) formed a purpose in which she [Mrs. P] concurred, of sending her to W. Graham's to go thro a regular course of classical learning. Being then a student*

---

763 The only evidence we have discovered on this issue is the eyewitness testimony of Rev. Archibald Alexander, who was, at the time, a divinity student at Lexington under Rev. William Graham:

Citation: **Alexander, Archibald, DD,** MSS "Memoir of The Rev. Wm Graham" (written in longhand), the Rev. Graham portion of this manuscript constitutes the largest part of a writing entitled *Great Valley of Virginia.* The auditor received a copy from the Princeton Seminary Library in 1989. It is also available in spiral-bound form at the Leyburn Library, Washington and Lee University.

of theology with Mr. Graham, I saw Mrs. Priestly often. <u>She was the mother of two children; the youngest an infant at the breast</u> . . . altho she never returned to the study of Latin & Greek, she made some progress in geography, arithmetic, and English Grammar; so that some years afterwards, with his (Mr. Priestley) assistance she superintended the education of a large class of young ladies, in Baltimore. (Rev. Dr. Archibald Alexander, Mss., "Memoir of William Graham," pp. 112–113; see bibliography)

We know of no other chartered college in America that had, at this time in our nation's progress (circa 1785–1790) agreed to afford a woman the opportunity to obtain a college degree by enrolling her in a regular academic program. It is clear from additional eyewitness testimony by Dr. Alexander that other women, aside from Mrs. Priestley, also benefited from this unprecedented experiment, but their opportunities were more in the form of occasional auditing of lectures and scientific experiments. We regret that we have no further information on Mrs. Priestley or her school for "young ladies" in Baltimore. After William Graham's resignation of the college presidency in 1796, efforts to extend educational opportunities to women were made by Rev. Graham's younger brother Edward, who was instrumental in the erection of the Ann Smith Academy for women in Lexington. It also appears that this academy's principal instructor was Edward Graham, who was also the first administrative head of the New London Academy in Virginia.[764] In addition, one of Graham's graduates from Liberty Hall, Rev. John Lyle, created and oversaw a school for young women in Kentucky.

Note re Rev. James Priestley: b. 1760 in Augusta County, VA, son of William and Mary; d. Feb. 6, 1821, buried in Hendersonville, Tennessee, on north side of Gallatin Pike; married **Sarah McBride** *April 19, 1788, Mercer Co., KY. He became president of Cumberland College. Mr. Priestley was an early graduate of Liberty Hall Academy and was subsequently a tutor at Liberty Hall Academy under Rev. William Graham. Mrs. Priestley and her husband, James, conducted a school for young women in Baltimore and later in other venues as well.*

---

764 Daisy I. Read, <u>New London, Today and Yesterday</u> (Lynchburg, VA: J. P. Bell Company, 1950). (Concerns New London Academy, where Edward Graham of Lexington, VA, was the school's first president.)

Appendix 5

Rev. William Graham's Nonexistent "Defense of Slavery"

Introduction

In 1980, a then-young academic Dr. David Robson presented a vilifying and specious article to the *William and Mary Quarterly*, which included the following mistaken academic indictment:

> **William Graham was the first late eighteenth-century Virginia clergyman to defend slavery** and, so far as I can determine, **the only college professor in the country during the era who supported the institution.**[765]

The above constitutes Mr. Robson's central indictment of Rev. William Graham, but an indictment is merely a charge; it does not constitute a conviction. The main body of this appendix constitutes an examination and analysis of the nature and the quality of the evidence relied upon by Mr. Graham's prosecutor, Dr. Robson. Once identified and assessed, it will become clear that Dr. Robson's evidence in support of his claim is not in any degree credible nor persuasive.

His main theses will hereafter be discredited. Robson ignored his professional responsibility to exercise due diligence in researching his subject; he proceeded instead to unjustifiably attack Graham's character, assuming much in the process but knowing very little.

Robson's article title shown below is an explosive charge. As such, its author bears a heavy burden to present a strong evidentiary case. A defendant so viscously charged should not be relegated to the dust bin of history as a character worthy of infamy without having been given the benefit of being assumed innocent until proven guilty. In this case, not only is Dr. Robson guilty of publicly vilifying an innocent man, but he is clearly guilty of the serious charge of knowingly withholding clear exculpatory evidence. (*See the discussion below concerning the Graham vs. Balch affair.*)

---

765 David, W. Robson, "An Important Question Answered: William Graham's Defense of Slavery in Post-Revolutionary Virginia," *William and Mary Quarterly*, 3rd Series, 37, No. 4 (October 1980): 644–652. (Note: An erroneous piece throughout based on the an incorrect assumption that the Joseph Glass "lecture notes" were transcriptions of Graham's lectures. There is no credible evidence that this notion is correct. Moreover, the evidence that does exist suggests that they are not written by Graham but rather were transcribed by Graham from the Witherspoon master copy during Graham's time at Princeton. Graham's lectures were never written down and were lost to history.)

Dr. Robson's title fairly well explains his main thesis, but beyond that, Dr. Robson makes several demonstrably false assertions that all serve to sully the reputation of Washington and Lee University and its founding first president. In each case, Dr. Robson's claims are grossly inaccurate and are clearly mistakes, mistakes due in part to insufficient research, faulty judgment, or defective analysis. Whether his research was too narrow or too focused, he clearly was out of his depth when he wrote this article, for he seems to have been unaware of much of the then-known literature on the subjects at hand. One thing is for certain: he did not know, nor understand, the central character he elected to write about, Rev. William Graham.

The result of Robson's unprofessional attack has been that other authors have picked up Robson's mantle and have become institutionalized. Those authors who have relied on Robson's thesis have collectively served to sully the reputation of the lone eighteenth-century educator in the United States who had the courage to enroll and provide a college education to the sole black college student in the nation. One of those who joined in by advancing Robson's false account, Dr. Theodore DeLaney, is a faculty member of the very institution where the nation's first black college student, John Chavis, attended as a member of the regular undergraduate program.[766] Chavis's unique presence as a regular student on a college campus was the direct result of the man who Robson has focused on as the **"first late eighteenth-century Virginia clergyman to defend slavery** and, so far as I can determine, **_the only college professor in the country during the era who supported the institution._**" The apparent disconnect seems to have eluded the credulous Dr. Robson.

DeLaney cited as his authority for accepting Robson's thesis William J. Cooper's _Liberty and Slavery: Southern Politics to 1860_ (New York: Alfred A. Knopf, 1983). Cooper, in turn, cited David Robson in one of his footnotes to chapter 5. All three of these published academics were, however, grossly mistaken and indicted the wrong man. This demonstrates quite clearly the existing havoc created by Robson's miscalculations. The damage to the reputations of President Graham and the university that he founded, Washington and Lee, are incalculable.

Dr. Robson misunderstood seven additional subjects concerning Washington and Lee and its first president, William Graham. First, Mr. Robson mistakenly believed that Rev. Graham's Presbyterian colleagues obviated his effort to defeat a motion concerning the infamous and misnamed "Whiskey Insurrection." In fact, his brethren endorsed Rev. Graham's view, and they endorsed, not defeated, the very resolution that Graham opposed. Robson completely misunderstood what transpired at this meeting. He failed to grasp that his source, Mr. Foote, published two entirely different accounts of this affair; but unfortunately, Robson relied on the misleading and unattributed rendition. Had he researched the subject more broadly, this error would not likely have occurred.

Additionally, Mr. Robson mistakenly believed that Rev. Graham was a central character in the movement to establish the proposed state of Frankland when he

---

766 Theodore DeLaney, PhD, "Founder's Day Lecture" (in regard to Rev. John Chavis) Washington and Lee University, 2001.

merely assisted some of his prior students and parishioners who had moved to the area of what is now east Tennessee by drafting a proposed constitution.

Graham's published constitution is very general in its scope and is mostly applicable to virtually any prospective state. This was a time of constitution making in the newly emerging nation. Thomas P. Abernathy, a noted historian, was unaware that Rev. Graham was the sole author of this constitution. Abernathy assumed, incorrectly, from his source, Mr. Samuel Cole Williams, author of *The Lost State of Franklin*,[767] that it was a committee product. It was no more a committee product than Jefferson's Declaration of Independence. The constitution in question is today recognized to be Rev. William Graham. Abernathy, however, importantly, says this about the (Graham's) constitution:

> This was the first original Constitution west of the mountains [Blue Ridge], and, without being fanatical, it was in many respects one of the most democratic ever produced in the United States. Though it retained the property qualifications for members of the single-chambered legislature, manhood suffrage was provided, registration of voters and elections by ballot were required, and all legislation of a general nature was to be referred to the people before being finally enacted . . . this was a sincere attempt to put the reins of power, for the first time, into the hands of the people.[768] (Thomas Perkins Abernathy, *From Frontier to Plantation in Tennessee, A Study in Frontier Democracy*, Chapel Hill, the University of North Carolina Press, 1932, pp. 77, 78)

The proposed constitution for Frankland and the "Essay on Government," both written by Liberty Hall Academy's president, William Graham, stand in stark contrast to the caricature qualities attributed to him by Dr. Robson. This contrast should have alerted Robson to an apparent discrepancy that suggested a need for greater clarification. Apparently, it did not.

Dr. Robson also mistakenly believed that Washington and Lee's rector was censured by his church "for meddling in politics."[769] Dr. Robson several times foolishly moved beyond his main thesis and in so doing undermined his own credibility by being demonstrably wrong on each count. Subjects Robson

---

767 Samuel Coles Williams, *History of the Lost State of Franklin* (New York: The Press of the Pioneers, 1933). Contains valuable information pertaining to Rev. William Graham's (of Washington & Lee fame) participation in the plan to establish the state of Franklin. Graham was the author of the draft of the proposed constitution for the lost state of Frankland.

768 It is noteworthy that this constitution called for the establishment and support of a university that would receive financial support from the state. This does not, however, violate Graham's strong objections to taxing the people to support religiously patronized schools and their teachers.

769 David W. Robson, "An Important Question Answered..." "Early in the contest [Revolution] he [Graham] wrote a piece for the press on Revolutionary themes and was censured by the presbytery for meddling in politics," p. 646.

completely misunderstood at the time are enumerated immediately below. These subjects are also dealt with in other parts of this book. Below is a list of Robson's mistakes made in addition to the false claim regarding Graham being a defender of slavery.

Additional Errors Made by Dr. Robson:

1. The mistaken attribution to Graham of a "piece written for the press on Revolutionary themes, for which he was censured."
2. The often misreported Graham v. Balch dispute.
3. The Whiskey Rebellion/Virginia Presbyterian Synod affair.
4. The nonexistent link between Liberty Hall and Rev. Brown's private Latin school.
5. The inaccurate depiction of Rev. Graham as being fearful of free Negroes.
6. The inaccurate depiction of the political activities of Rev. William Graham.
7. The omission by Robson of any mention of Graham's momentous, unprecedented decision to enroll the first black college student in America into a degree-granting college.

Analysis of Robson's Serious Errors

This appendix is mainly devoted to Robson's erroneous central thesis that Rev. William Graham was a "defender of slavery." The additional errors are identified and explained herein but superficially here because they have been dealt with elsewhere herein in greater depth.

In assessing Dr. Robson's thesis, his citations of authority, such as they are, are analyzed and evaluated and thereafter rejected for good cause. Also assessed herein is Robson's error in simply accepting without question that the lecture packet upon which he relied was truly written and/or delivered by Rev. Graham. A careful investigation of the relevant facts demonstrate conclusively that Dr. Robson's primary source in formulating his thesis concerning slavery is not what he represents it to be. Indeed, William Graham wrote none of the lectures he delivered at Liberty Hall during his tenure. Those to which Robson refers are the intellectual property of Princeton's eminent and venerated president, Dr. John Witherspoon.[770] Robson does refer in a footnote to an essay contest concerning

---

770 The principal lecture Robson relies upon, however, may not have been written by Dr. Witherspoon; but whether it was or was not, for certain there is no credible evidence whatsoever that this particular lecture was written by Rev. William Graham. Moreover, there is no eighteenth-century evidence of any type that suggests that the lecture in question was written by William Graham. It is at least possible, however, that it was originally an essay written by Graham's younger brother, Edward Graham. Prof. Edward Graham may have inserted it into his own packet of Witherspoon's lectures. Edward's essay on slavery was written while he was a student at Liberty Hall and as a submission to a contest which promised a prize, a contest that Edward won. Whether the essay reflected Edward's personal views, however, is entirely unknown and irrelevant to questions pertaining to who wrote most of the lectures comprising

slavery and even suggests that it was the impetus for the lecture. The essay contest Robson refers to is described in some detail by Rev. Archibald Alexander in his "Memoir of Rev. William Graham," and Alexander's commentary based on his own eyewitness experience generated but three essays, all of which were written by students of the college, among which was Edward Graham, the president's much younger brother. If President William Graham had written an essay at any time on slavery, Archibald Alexander and Edward Graham would have known about it and would have referred to it in their biographical sketches of their preceptor. Neither of these published memoirs even hint at such a possibility.

There is no known evidence that the lecture on slavery alluded to and relied upon by Robson reflected any views whatsoever held by the college's president, William Graham.[771] Moreover, being a defender of slavery is inconsistent with numerous published and unpublished statements made by Graham. His published writings do reflect many of President Graham's political views, and those views are entirely at odds with any defense of slavery.

Graham's insignificant connection to Robson's referenced lecture packet was well known to his early students because they all made copies of the packet and used their own copies as textbooks at the college. The template from which the copies were made by students were distributed by both William Graham and other instructors at Liberty Hall. The templates from which students copied the lectures in the earliest days of the college were made up from Graham's own personal copy that he had copied years earlier when he was a student of Dr. John Witherspoon, then president of Princeton.[772]

Without doubt, some later instructors at Liberty Hall may have edited some of Witherspoon's lectures and even added lectures to the packet.[773] The packets

---

the packet relied upon by Dr. Robson. What is relevant, however, is that absent any eighteenth-century evidence supporting this contention, and there is none, Dr. Robson's main thesis must be rejected as pure rubbish.

771   President Graham may have shared some of the sentiments contained in the lecture, such as the legality of slavery under the laws of Great Britain, but in point of fact, even this would amount to pure speculation since he left nothing in writing that specifically addressed this point.

772   The auditor examined copies of several sets of lectures copied by and retained by the student's who originally copied them at Princeton in order to determine whether they were consistent. They all vary from one another because they were copied during different periods and Witherspoon, made frquent changes, additions, and deletions. Therefore, there is no one official set of Witherspoon's lectures. The only published lectures of Witherspoon's lectures were issued without his consent and appeared in print after his death. In addition, instructors who relied upon Witherspoon's lectures may very well have edited them and then inserted items written by themselves or others. It is therefore improper to rely upon any given set as evidence of the sentiments of anyone in particular. *Note: The heavily edited lectures of Witherspoon printed in 1934 by the Princeton University Press should not be relied upon as evidence since they were not authorized by Witherspoon, and while interesting, they vary in many ways from various renditions left by early students at Princeton.* Moreover, Witherspoon himself modified them many times over the years.

773   In fact, Witherspoon himself was constantly editing his lectures. As a result, various copies made and kept by Princeton students that made their way back to the university for keeping vary one from the other in significant ways.

were neither copyrighted nor published during Witherspoon's life, so as a mere pedagogical tool, instructors may have modified the packets as they deemed proper. Presumably, the rector, Mr. Graham, would have expected his tutors to inform him if they were altering the packets in any substantial way, but evidence is lacking on that subject. In any event, none of the packets passed down from that period (eighteenth century) are very useful as evidence because their provenance is, in every case, highly questionable.

At the conclusion of this appendix is presented the only known direct statement ever made by Rev. William Graham on the subject of slavery along with an appropriate citation of authority. In addition, several of Graham's published remarks that indirectly refer to the politics of slavery in America are extracted. Finally, this appendix will review the various known actions of Washington and Lee's rector as they pertain to persons of color, which are in clear contrast with Dr. Robson's thesis.

Robson's Indictment of Rev. William Graham

Dr. Robson's principal thesis:

> William Graham was the *first late eighteenth-century Virginia clergyman to defend slavery* and, so far as I can determine, *the only college professor in the country during the era who supported the institution.* (David W. Robson, "An Important Question Answered: William Graham's Defense of Slavery in Post-Revolutionary Virginia," *William and Mary Quarterly*, 3rd Series, 37, no. 4, pp. 644–652, October 1980).

Dr. Robson's Unpersuasive Evidence in Support of His Principal Claim Concerning Slavery

Robson's evidentiary foundation is a collection of handwritten lecture "notes" housed at the Leyburn Library at Washington and Lee University that have long been mistakenly attributed to Rev. William Graham. Dr. Robson unfortunately assumed that this packet is what the packet's late-nineteenth-century cover page indicates that it is, but what the cover page asserts is demonstrably incorrect. What Dr. Robson and the institution's librarians have long mistakenly assumed is that the packet contains transcribed lectures that were delivered by Rev. Graham at Liberty Hall Academy in 1796. That mistake's most likely culprit is the late-nineteenth-century transcriber, Henry W. Pratt, who appears to have created a cover page out of whole cloth containing false assertions that the packet contains lectures written and delivered by the Rev. William Graham.

The packet's true nature is this: The numbered handwritten lectures' content represents what was collected together in 1796 by the then-current student, Mr. Joseph Glass, not including the gratuitous "cover page" created by the copyist who was one of the university's instructors, Mr. Harry W. Pratt. In 1896, Pratt recopied the originals copied by Mr. Glass one hundred years earlier.[774] Mr. Glass's packet, in turn, were copied from a similar packet originally copied by William Graham while a student at Princeton. The template used by the student William Graham was originally created by Graham's preceptor, who was Princeton's president, John Witherspoon. Similar packets were made by the other students at Princeton and used as a kind of textbook before there were such things. This explains why Graham used them at Liberty Hall.

Whether the original packet belonging to the student Joseph Glass also had a cover sheet is unknown. If so, we do not know the contents of the text, which might have been included in such a theoretical cover sheet. We do know that if it was the product of Joseph Glass, he would not have claimed, as Pratt's cover page does, that the packet constituted his notes for the transparent reason that they are not notes, but rather they are the complete contents of thirty-one lectures. It is obvious from even a cursory review of any one of the individual lectures that these are not a student's "notes." Notes would not include complete sentence after complete sentence like what is found in the packet attributed to Glass. If Glass had made this cover page, he would have described the contents accurately.

In addition, Mr. Glass would have known that these lectures were not, as the Pratt cover claims, "delivered by Rev. William Graham in 1796" for the very fact, well-known to all the students of 1796, that Rev. Graham was rarely in Lexington during that school year. Graham was absent due to his traveling pursuits in western Virginia. He was fully engaged that year in a complex real estate venture to secure property on the banks of the Ohio River of six thousand acres.[775] In 1796, classes were conducted mostly by tutors. This was Graham's final year as president of Liberty Hall Academy. Rev. Graham returned frequently enough, however, to occasionally meet with his theological students who were preparing for the ministry.

The abovementioned errors, taken together persuasively, argue against any notion that the current cover sheet was originally created by Mr. Joseph Glass. It is Mr. Pratt himself who informs that he is the 1896 copyist, and his announcement to that effect appears as a postscript on the current packet's final page. The announcement reads as follows:

---

774 The auditor's analysis too relies on an assumption, that being Mr. Pratt was an hororable man with good intentions who had some sound reason to attach student Glass's name to the packet. We know, for example, from extant records that indeed Mr. Glass was a student in 1796. Whether the original lecture transcriptions were available to Mr. Pratt, we do not know. What can be deduced from what is known is that Mr. Graham did not deliver lectures to the regular academic classes at Liberty Hall in 1796. Therefore, the cover page is factually incorrect because it asserts that the lectures contained in the packet were delivered by Graham in 1796. They were not. At the time, Mr. Graham was, more often than not, elsewhere than Lexington. The student Mr. Glass knew that so he would not have made the assertion found on the 1896 copy with the mistaken cover page. It was probably created by the copyist Mr. Pratt. In any event, the assertion was not made by student Glass, and the assertion is false.

775 The president's activities in 1796 are detailed in Edward Graham's published memoir of his older brother. See bibliography.

"Copied by Harry Waddell Pratt; M. A. In A.D. 1896. W & L
University

It should also be pointed out that for over 150 years, no author has ever suggested that Rev. Graham was the author of this packet of lectures prior to the published assertion made by Dr. Robson. The then-young Dr. Robson, obviously, albeit mistakenly, believed he had stumbled upon a gold mine of historical significance; but in truth, his discovery was merely iron pyrite and of no historical value. Other nineteenth- and twentieth-century researchers may have seen these records at Washington and Lee, but if so, they probably realized that these lectures were not what they appeared to be from the cover page because of the two well-known biographical sketches of Rev. Graham by highly credible eyewitnesses who had known Graham. Both of these eminent scholars explained emphatically that Graham's lectures were never written down or saved for posterity. In addition, the student, Joseph Glass, had a long and close professor-student relationship with one of the referenced biographers, Edward Graham.[776] Glass would not have been mistaken about who actually wrote the packet of lectures because the copy he used as a template when copying them would have been that of his instructor Edward Graham. Surely, Edward Graham would have thoroughly explained to the students under his care what the lectures were and who wrote them. Edward made it abundantly clear in publishing his "Memoir of the Late Rev. William Graham" that the lectures of the eminent John Witherspoon were copied at Liberty Hall and used as textbooks. Even on the remote outside chance that Joseph Glass was mistaken on this score, at some point, Edward would have discovered the error and corrected it because Edward's association with the college began as early as 1777 and only ended at his death in 1840.

It is obvious then that the 1896 copyist Mr. Pratt made up the packet's cover page based on his own misunderstanding as to the original source. Robson, for no sound reason, assigned to Pratt's cover page a degree of credibility that was undeserved. He thereafter also mistakenly assumed that the lecture packet was comprised of lectures written by and delivered by Rev. William Graham.[777]

---

776 Joseph Glass had been a student under Edward Graham when Edward was the president and principal instructor at the New London Academy in Bedford County, Virginia. When Edward was appointed to the faculty of Liberty Hall in Rockbridge County (greater Lexington), young Mr. Glass followed his instructor to Liberty Hall. The use of the Witherspoon lectures were so central a feature of the academic program that no student would not have realized that the principal textbooks they relied upon were the lectures of John Witherspoon copied by their president William Graham while he was a student at Princeton.

777 Robson is not the only person to make this mistake. Betty R. Kondayan, Washington and Lee Uiversity's librarian, also believed the packet contained William Graham's lectures. She obviously perused the packet's cover page and concluded that these were indeed the lectures of Pres. William Graham, and she conveyed that belief to this auditor in a letter written in 1972. In fact, the auditor accepted her interpretation for several years. Later, it became obvious to the auditor that the lectures were not written by or delivered by Mr. Graham.

Some Additional Source Evidence in Regard to the So-Called "Lectures" of William Graham

Below are extracts from the writings of two eighteen[th]-century eyewitnesses concerning these lectures and one published comment from the eminent twentieth-century historian Dr. George W. Diehl:

[A. Archibald Alexander on the "lectures"

"It is a remarkable fact, that this institution, although not honored with the name of a college, by its charter possessed all the powers of a college, being expressly authorized to grant literary degrees; and although there were then no periodical commencements, yet in several instances the degree of bachelor of arts was granted, and in one instance, at least, publicly. The course of study in the Academy was precisely the same as that at Princeton while Mr. Graham was a student in that college; **even the manuscript lectures of Dr. Witherspoon were copied, and studied by the students**. (Alexander, address to alumni, delivered June 1843, published at that time in a small edition, later in the Historical Papers; see bibliography) (Emphasis added)

B. Edward Graham, Esq., on Rev. Graham's writing, generally and in reference to Witherspoon's lectures.

It is to be regretted that he [Wm. Graham] left no written specimens of the peculiar manner of sermonizing; but none have been found amongst his papers. **Indeed, he wrote but little on any subject. His early habits of life were unfavorable to the pen; but in addition to this, he had a tremor in his hand and fingers, which made it very inconvenient and difficult to write. His various occupations also left him but little leisure for writing; and it was moreover no easy matter for him to bring his thoughts to wait for his pen.**

"But when it came to Moral Philosophy he found the case considerably different. Dr. Witherspoon's lectures on the subject, though in many respects excellent, left some things involved in great obscurity, Mr. Graham, endeavored, but ineffectually, to penetrate the mist until the state of his mind became painful and distressing. Dr. Witherspoon, in an Address to his class at the close of his lectures, observed that in moral philosophy there were difficulties which the present state of human knowledge did not enable us to solve; but he had no doubt that the time would arrive and perhaps at no distant day, when these difficulties would be removed, and we enjoy as much certainty and perspicuity in moral as in natural philosophy.[778] (Edward Graham, Esq., "A Memoir of the Late Rev. William Graham, A.M.," *The Evangelical and Literary Magazine and Missionary Chronicle*, IV, (1821), p.75 et seq., esp. at page 398–399; emphasis added)

[C. Dr. George W. Diehl, a historian and frequent writer on historical subjects in the Valley of Virginia, especially in the vicinage in and near Lexington, authored the definitive biography of Rev. Samuel Houston, an early student at Liberty Hall Academy.[779] In his biography of Rev. Houston, Dr. Diehl describes the result, in one regard, of his many years of researching as it regards the early years of Washington and Lee University in this way:

These young men, in their theological study, followed the pattern used at Princeton where William Graham studied and from which he graduated in 1773. **Text-Books were difficult to secure and Graham had his students make their own texts by copying the works [lectures] of John Witherspoon. The copy, made by Houston, is in the library of Washington & Lee University and evidences his excellent craftsmanship.**[780] (George W. Diehl, *The Rev. Samuel Houston, V. D. M.* [Verona, VA: McClure Press, 1970]; emphasis added)

---

778 The lecture packet containing the lecture focused on by Robson, and mistakenly attributed to William Graham, were Withersponn's lectures on moral philosophy. Great care must be taken when comparing published lectures of Witherspoon because none were ever authorized to be published by Witherspoon, due in large measure to the fact he made frequent changes to them during his tenure at Princeton. They were purely pedegogical instruments not meant for publication. This fact is clearly reflected in the important biographies of Witherspoon by Messrs. MacLean and Collins. (John Maclean, *History of the College of New Jersey, from Its Origin in 1746 to the Commencement of 1854*, 2 vols. [Philadelphia: J. B. Lippincott & Co., 1877] and Varnum L. Collins, *President Witherspoon: A Biography*, 2 vols. (1925, repr. 1969).

779 Dr. George W. Diehl was included here despite the fact that he is a twentieth-century author because the subject of his biograohy, Rev. Samuel Houston, was an early student at Liberty Hall under Rev. William Graham.

780 **George W. Diehl, _The Rev. Samuel Houston, V. D. M._ (Verona, VA: McClure Press, 1970), 31. The auditor was not able to locate at the library of Washington & Lee the packet of lectures copied by the student Samuel Houston referenced by Dr. Diehl. The late Dr. George W. Diehl is a well-known local Lexington historian with a stellar reputation and not a man to have said that which he knew to be untrue. *(Note: It is said by Dr. Diehl that an additional copy of the handwritten "lectures" copied by the student, Samuel Houston, is available in the archives of the Leyburn Library at W&L, but the auditor was not able to locate that copy.)***

This important biography by Dr. Diehl was published a decade before Dr. Robson's now-infamous article, so it is curious that Dr. Robson either ignored it or was unaware of its existence. Dr. Diehl is undoubtedly wrong, however, in one respect, which is that the lectures were not used by theology students but those in the regular academic program. Most of the "lectures" have little, if anything, to do with theology. For example, consider these few lecture titles: "On Perception and its Concomitants"; "On Man's Civil Relations"; "Of Common Sense, Reason, Memory, and Recollection"; On Beauty"; "On Instinct, Conception, and Imagination"; On the formation of Government"; and finally in this regard, "Illustration of the Law by which Bodies Moving in Elliptical Orbits Are Governed." These are all subjects one typically would not associate with theology. They are also similar or identical to the topics included in the published "Lectures on Moral Philosophy" of John Witherspoon. That is because that is precisely what the Glass packet of lectures is—a copy he made of Witherspoon's lectures as they existed at Liberty Hall in 1796.

Conclusion of the Assessment of the Lectures Mistakenly Attributed to William Graham

The foundation of Robson's contention that William Graham was a defender of slavery has been shown to be lacking any credible and persuasive evidence that the lectures in question were actually written and delivered by William Graham. Moreover, Robson's insistence that the one lecture on slavery constitutes a defense of slavery is a contention about which reasonable minds could easily disagree. Any attempt to digress into a discussion on that question, however, would serve little purpose here and merely serve as a frustrating diversion. Robson's thesis is neither proven nor credible. It is contrary to what history knows about Rev. William Graham and about the use of lectures at Liberty Hall Academy in the eighteenth century, Mr. Pratt's idle speculations notwithstanding. Robson's personal attack on the character of the first president of Washington and Lee is unwarranted and unsupported and, in this author's view, irresponsible.

Robson's Additional Errors Concerning Rev. William Graham

No. 1: The mistaken attribution to Graham of a "piece written for the press on Revolutionary themes" and "that he was censured by the presbytery for meddling in politics."[781]

As for Graham having been censured by his church, the church's records prove otherwise. Graham was never censured by his congregation, the National General Assembly, the Virginia Synod, the Hanover Presbytery, nor the Lexington Presbytery.[782] Some authors took a careless comment by Rev. Archibald Alexander

---

781   David W. Robson, "An Important Question Answered," p. 646, para 1.

782   Quite the contrary, Graham was repeatedly selected by his peers for almost all of the important posts in Virginia during his tenure that related to higher education or theological and ministerial

about Graham having been "censured" by his enemies and embellished the comment all out of proportion. Of course, Graham was censured by his enemies, but that hardly constitutes being "censured" by one's church.[783] As used by Rev. Alexander, censure is synonymous with *criticized*, but as used by Robson, it is clearly meant to convey an official act of condemnation by his church superiors. Nothing even remotely resembling that ever transpired, but Robson mistakenly insisted that it occurred on multiple occasions. If a record existed showing that Graham had received an official censure, Robson would have cited it. Instead, he relies on secondhand representations, none of which included a citation of a record indicating a censure of Graham by the Presbyterian authorities.

In addition, Graham did not write a piece for the press on revolutionary themes as Robson asserts, and Graham was not censured by the "presbytery" or any other entity within the Presbyterian Church, not on this or any other occasion. Both of these claims are demonstrably false. See Dr. George W. Diehl's biography of Rev. Samuel Houston.[784] In regards to Robson's claim that he wrote a piece on revolutionary themes, he provided no citation of authority and for good reason because there is no known record of his having written such a piece. Needless to say, his claim that he was censured for writing it or for meddling in politics on account of a piece that does not exist is equally devoid of an evidentiary foundation.

No. 2. The often misreported Graham v. Balch Dispute (i.e., false representation that Graham was *censured* by his church)

> Much as had his earlier venture into politics, this effort [Frankland movement] resulted only in disappointment for Graham. The Franklin convention did not adopt the document.

---

instruction. Both of the church-patronized colleges in Virginia desired him for their presidency. Moreover, most of the Presbyterian ministers in Virginia and many in the South during the latter part of the eighteenth century were trained under Graham. If Graham had been a defender of slavery, that fact would have surfaced long before Robson penned his now infamous piece.

783 George West Diehl, *The Reverend Samuel Houston*, V.D.M.(Verona, VA: McClure Printing Company Inc., 1970). "In October of that same year[1786] The Lexington Presbytery met and pursuant to the directive of Synod, made the previous May, and made the enquiry into the Graham-Balch affair. The Lexington Presbytery's conclusions are set forth in their response letter: "William Graham acknowledged the letter addressed to Rev. Hezekiah Balch and signed William Graham to be his production – he produced several depositions to prove the truth of the charges against Balch and especially his approving of the Conduct of the mob in Frankland in burning effigies of Msrs. Graham and Houston. . . . Although they could wish Graham had been more temperate in his Satyr and more gentle in his Expostulations, yet the treatment he met with was so grossly injurious that Prebytery can not suppose him to merit a formal Censure on account of said letter." "Thus," says Diehl, "the matter was closed."

784 Ibid. (and it is likely that Robson was made aware, either directly or indirectly, of Graham's letter to Zachariah Johnston wherein he mentioned that he had been asked to prepare a piece on the proposed ratification of the US Constitution, but he never published one. That letter was concerning the ratification of the proposed US Constitution, not on the earlier revolution.

Once again, the presbytery censured him. (Robson, p. 646,
para 3; emphasis of error is added)

In truth, the Synod of New York and Philadelphia **did not censure** Graham,
nor did the Lexington Presbytery. Robson failed to grasp what had transpired
within the Presbyterian Church growing out of the Graham v. Balch affair. He
cites as his primary source William H. Foote.

> Foote: page 463 "But difficulties of a religious nature were
> connected with it, that were referred to the Synod of New
> York and Philadelphia. On the 26th of May, 1787, the following
> resolution was passed—In respect to the letter addressed to
> Mr. Balch, through the medium of the press, and supposed to
> be written by the Rev. William Graham of Rockbridge County,
> Virginia, the Synod look upon the same as very unchristian and
> unwarrantable treatment of a brother;[785] and the Synod do order
> the Presbytery of Lexington to cite Mr. Graham before them,
> and make due inquiry whether he be the author, and into the
> reasons for the conduct in that matter, **and censure or acquit
> him as the nature of the case may appear**. (Foote, _Sketches of
> Virginia_, Series 1, p. 463; emphasis of error is added)

Here below is the actual record:

> The committee appointed yesterday to converse with the
> brethren of Abington Presbytery [Rev. Balch's Presbytery],
> who were present, and to endeavor to accommodate the matters
> of uneasiness among them, met agreeably to order, and report
> as follows: . . . [_First three unrelated and therefore irrelevant
> items are not included here._]
>
> 4th. In respect to the letter addressed to Mr. Balch, through the
> medium of the press, and supposed to be written by the Rev.
> William Graham of Rockbridge County, Virginia, **the Synod
> look upon the same as very unchristian and unwarrantable
> treatment of a brother**; and the Synod do order the Presbytery
> of Lexington to cite Mr. Graham before them, and make due
> inquiry whether he be the author, and into the reasons for the
> conduct in that matter, and censure or acquit him as the nature
> of the case may appear; and report their proceedings herein to
> the next Synod. This was found in Foote's Sketches of Virginia
> Series 1 and also in **Records of the Presbyterian Church in
> the United States of America, Embracing the minutes of the
> General Presbytery of Philadelphia 1706–1716, Minutes of
> 1717–1758.** (Minutes of the Synod of NY 1745–1758. 1758–1788,

---

785   This is a correct rendition of what the committee report contained, but it should not have said
      it for two reasons: (1) A small committee does not speak.

Presbyterian Board of Publication, Philadelphia, 1841, p. 537; emphasis added)

The above underlined/bold statement does not constitute a "censure" of Rev. Graham. It is a general statement, and while it was included in the committee's report, it was an improper comment insofar as it is a conclusion (albeit general in nature), and it is clearly referencing a letter that was at the center of a dispute about which this synod and especially this committee had no jurisdiction to hear or decide on the merits of the case. This committee, as it freely admits in the report's introduction, only met with representatives of one of the parties in an apparent dispute over which it had no jurisdiction. To comment on the substance of such a matter prior to the matter having been reviewed by the appropriate body (i.e., the Lexington Presbytery[786]) is institutionally inappropriate, and as subsequently revealed evidence demonstrated, the committee's comments were based on false representations, prevarications that might well have been divulged to that committee if they had held a proper two-sided hearing. It goes almost without saying that this committee comment was prejudicial in the extreme and is likely the proximate cause of Robson's colossal error in this regard. As it turned out after the case had been properly adjudicated, the charges against Rev. Balch made by Rev. Graham were actually proven by official depositions from several highly credible eyewitnesses to Balch's central involvement in the mob violence in Frankland, which culminated in the burning of an effigy of the two Presbyterian ministers, William Graham and Samuel Houston (not General Houston).

If any parties were subjected to **"very unchristian and unwarrantable treatment of a brother"** in this affair, it was Messrs. Graham and Houston at the instigation of Rev. Hezekiah Balch.[787] This case shows why it is improper for officials to comment substantively on disputed matters prior to the dispute having been fully and properly adjudicated.

Of critical importance about these two different versions is the conclusion of this complaint after it had been adjudicated in the proper ecclesiastical court. Here below is what the proper entity concluded after having had the opportunity to conduct a full hearing of Rev. Balch's complaint against Graham. Evidence was presented by both sides of the dispute, including the testimony of Rev. Balch and his lone witness. Rev. Graham and several additional eye-witnesses to the events leading up to Graham's writing a public letter addressed to Rev. Balch also testified. On this point, at least, Robson's cited authority, Mr. Foote, actually reported the case accurately. The culmination of the Graham v. Balch dispute appears on the page immediately following the page from which Robson

---

786 According to Rev. Archibald Alexander, the case was actually heard in Lexington, Virginia, before the Virginia Synod. See his unpublished manuscript memoir of William Graham, held in the archives of the Princeton Theological Seminary and a copy of which is in the Leyburn Library at W&L.

787 Given this Reverend Balch's exposed behavior in this matter, it is important that readers not confuse the deeds of this Rev. Hezekiah Balch with the instigator's cousin, the Rev. Hezekiah James Balch of Mecklenburg County, North Carolina.

took his selected extract. Robson must therefore have reviewed the conclusion his own authority provided acquitting Rev. Graham. By failing to report the case's culmination, Robson failed to reveal the exculpatory evidence that clears Graham of his indictment by Balch. Failing to reveal a material exculpatory fact, like what he did in this case, would generally be considered a serious breach of professional ethics. Here then is the case's final exculpatory decision intentionally not disclosed by Robson.

> He [Graham] acknowledged himself the author of the "letter directed to Rev. Hezekiah Balch" which was in question— **"and produced <u>several depositions to prove the truth of the facts with which he charged Mr. Balch, and especially of his approving of the conduct of the mob in Frankland in burning the effigies of messrs. Graham and Houston</u>.**

> The Presbytery therefore, on mature deliberation agree, that although they could wish that Mr. Graham had been more temperate in his satire, and more gentle in his expostulations, **<u>yet that the treatment he met with was so grossly injurious, that they cannot suppose him to merit a formal censure of this Presbytery, on account of said letter.</u>** (Foote quoting presbytery, series 1, p. 464; emphasis added)

This referenced complaint by the disputatious and perpetual disputant, Rev. Hezekiah Balch of Abington Presbytery, is the only known complaint ever lodged against Rev. William Graham during his entire career as a Presbyterian minister. **Importantly, he was not censured.** Not then, not ever. Dr. David Robson was absolutely incorrect when he claimed Graham had been censured by his church, and he was wrong again when he claimed that Graham was censured on other occasions. Indeed, Robson made several separate false claims of censure against Rev. Graham. Embarrassingly, he cited Mr. Foote on the occasion of the Balch complaint, and his own source (Foote) acquits Graham. First, Foote correctly reported that the New York and Philadelphia Synod actually referred Balch's complaint to the proper Virginia ecclesiastical court (i.e., the Lexington Presbytery), and then on the following page, Foote explains that the Lexington Presbytery declined to censure Rev. Graham after having reviewed all the evidence proffered by both parties involved in this dispute. It is rather inexplicable how Dr. Robson could have gotten this so incredibly wrong and why he withheld the true outcome of Rev. Hezekiah Balch's cynically brought complaint.

Robson's error no.No. 3: The Whiskey Rebellion/Virginia Presbyterian Synod Affair

Here below is Robson's unjustified characterization of William Graham's participation in a meeting of the Virginia Synod of the Presbyterian Church

Much as had his earlier venture into politics, this effort resulted only in disappointment for Graham.[788] The Franklin convention did not adopt the document. Once again, the presbytery censured him. A few years later he actively opposed the ratification of the United States Constitution on the Antifederalist ground that Virginia should have sole control over internal taxes and trade regulation. Once more he met defeat. Finally, in 1794, he [Graham] **used the Synod of Virginia, meeting at Harrisonburg, as a forum to criticize the use of troops to put down the Whiskey Rebellion**. A detachment of Virginia militiamen, passing through on their way north, took umbrage at this and threatened to attack Graham, but a moderate minister brought calm to a tense situations. (This quote appears as footnote 10, and he cites Foote, _Sketches of Virginia_, 476; Grigsby, "Founders of Washington College," _Washington and Lee Univ. Papers_, II, 29; Abernethy, _Frontier to Plantation_, 79; Sprague, _Annals of the Pulpit_, 368; William Graham to Capt. Johnston, Nov. 3, 1787, MS, Special Colls., McCormick Lib.") (Robson, "A Question Answered," p. 647)

Robson's quote is supposedly based on several sources, but his only real source is actually Foote because the other named sources provide no new information on this subject, and they too were simply relying on Foote. Robson's mistake here is due to selective perception. As has already been pointed out elsewhere in this report, Foote often accepted submissions from multiple sources that contained conflicting content without bothering to notify his readers. In Robson's case, the author he cites, Mr. Foote, included a somewhat misleading account, and Robson selectively relied on an unnamed source while ignoring the far more credible source's submission.[789] In the Author's Errors section and elsewhere, it has been pointed out that this particular attack on Graham centered around a motion offered and supported by Rev. Moses Hoge at a Virginia Synod meeting, which was intended to admonish other Presbyterians concerning what is often referred

---

788   William Graham's political involvement was short-lived and took place during events related to creating a constitution for the new United States. If he suffered disappointments, he was in good company because almost no one who engages in politics is free of disappointments. Graham's successes far outweighed his disappointments. Robson saw disappointment where it did not exist because he misunderstood what actually took place.

789   The more credible source is the son of Rev. Moses Hoge. Moses was the person who brought the issue of the Whiskey Insurrection to the attention of the other members of the Virginia Synod of the Presbyterian Church and who proffered a motion therein that chastised certain Presbyterians who participated in or gave support to the so-callled whiskey rebels protesting the theretofore unprecedented tax. His son's submission to Foote was compiled for Foote from the father's journal in which Moses had kept a record of the meeting of that meeting of the synod. Since it was Moses Hoge's motion that Graham opposed, this journal's account, being relayed by Hoge's son, is unlikely to have been in error on the central facts of the matter. This information is provided by Foote in the book cited by Robson. Why Robson failed to cite this most reliable source is, once again, inexplicable.

to as "the Whiskey Insurrection." Rev. Graham opposed the motion. Contrary to Robson's clear inference that this event was a defeat for Mr. Graham, Graham's view on this matter was supported by his colleagues, and Hoge's motion was defeated. His suggestion that Graham was intimidated by soldiers who were present is simply ridiculous and unsupported by any known evidence. The synod members dismissed the only known interjection by military attendees by rejecting their inappropriate demand to have a person-by-person vote.

It should be pointed out as well that Robson's commentary on the Whiskey Insurrection matter improperly characterized Graham's motivations on this day by claiming that he "used the Synod of Virginia" meeting on that day as a "forum to criticize the use of troops to put down the Whiskey Rebellion."[790] This criticism is highly suggestive of ulterior motives on the part of Graham with a premeditated plan to criticize the use of troops. There is, however, nothing in the sources he cites in his accompanying footnote that supports this notion. Moreover, there is nothing in Hoge's son's submission to Foote to suggest such a thing. John Blair Hoge's representation was based on his father's journal, wherein it is explained that Graham's primary concern in opposing his father's motion was that the subject (Whiskey Insurrection) was a purely civil matter that fell outside the jurisdiction of an ecclesiastical court. Moreover, there is nothing in either account reprinted by Foote or from Foote that suggests that Graham either "used the Synod's forum" or that his motivation or intent was a desire to criticize the troops under the general command of his friend and classmate, General Henry ("Light-Horse Harry") Lee, the father of General Robert E. Lee.

Graham was an outspoken supporter of religious freedom, and during Virginia's struggle for religious freedom he had led a statewide campaign to defeat attempts to allow the new state of Virginia to designate one particular Christian denomination as the state religion and also to tax all citizens to support that "established church." He had argued on behalf of the Presbyterians that the state should not interfere with the internal affairs of Christian churches irrespective of their denomination. The aforementioned "Whiskey Insurrection" was about the government's tax and revenue policies, and in order for the Presbyterian Synod who supported religious freedom to remain consistent, he argued that the Synod of Virginia should likewise not interject itself into a purely civil matter. As such, Graham's view was deemed both wise and prudent, and Hoge's motion was therefore rejected.

No. 4: The nonexistent link between Liberty Hall Academy and Rev. John Brown's private Latin school

Following Foote's *Sketches of Virginia*, Robson provides his interpretation as follows:

> After a brief stint at home studying theology with the local minister, ***Graham was summoned by the Hanover Presbytery***

---

790   David W. Robson, "An Important Question Answered," p. 646, para 3.

> *to assist with a classical school in Augusta County, Virginia*,
> just beyond the Blue Ridge. By late 1775, the presbytery had
> licensed him to preach and had placed him in charge of the
> school. (Robson, p. 645, para 3; emphasis here indicates error.)

As has been thoroughly explained in many sections of this report, Graham was not appointed to "assist" in the operations of any school in Virginia. He was appointed to manage the newly created academy by the Hanover Presbytery in October of 1774. From its inception, the newly created school was intended by the Hanover Presbytery to be a "public" school under the patronage of the Hanover Presbytery, and its purpose was to provide an opportunity for Virginia youth to be educated on a plan emulating that which was then being provided by Princeton College in New Jersey. These facts are set forth plainly in the meeting minutes of the Hanover Presbytery that cover all of their official meetings between 1771 and 1774. This was the period during which the subject of creating an academy of higher education where young men who desired to obtain a college education could do so without having to travel to New Jersey.

Many authors of the nineteenth century became confused about this subject due to Foote's own confusion. The basis of this confusion was based upon a false notion that the so-called "classical school" must have been the "private" Latin school organized in the Valley of Virginia by Rev. John Brown, but this was not the case. Adding to the confusion is the fact that Rev. Brown's Latin school had at one time been located on a farm called by the local inhabitants "Mount Pleasant," and when Graham first arrived in Virginia, he organized his headquarters on the same lands where Brown's school had been earlier located. Brown's school, however, had been moved several miles away by the time Graham arrived in Virginia.

Robson's mistake in this regard is understandable because most of the mid-to-late-nineteenth-century historians had all followed the misguided Mr. Foote on this point. Indeed, after 1865, the university had come to adopt this nonsensical notion. In this report, the author has completely debunked that idea. There is no institutional connection between Washington and Lee University and any other educational institution of any type other than the direct connection between the college and the Lexington Theological Seminary that only existed in the 1790s under Rev. William Graham. The presbytery that created Washington and Lee in its earliest manifestations moved to create a second such academy (Prince Edward Academy, now Hampden-Sydney College) the year following that in which Washington and Lee was created. That second endeavor has long been considered by many as a sister college of Washington and Lee, but that is the only institution that might be loosely considered as having an institutional connection, but only because they were created within a year of one another by the same institution (Hanover Presbytery). Both seminaries (academies), however, had disparate chief administrative officers and boards of trustees. The only person who served on both of these academy's boards of trustees in the eighteenth century was Rev. Caleb Wallace, but his service in that regard was not simultaneous.

The extant letters of Rev. John Brown together with the records of the Presbyterian Church prove that Brown had no connection to Liberty Hall Academy whatsoever. Moreover, the meeting minutes of the Board of Trustees of Liberty Hall Academy prove that Brown never attended a meeting of the trustees and he never accepted his appointment to that Board.

Robson's error no.No. 5: The inaccurate depiction of Graham as being fearful of free Negroes

Robson said this:

> He [Graham] was acutely sensitive to the "danger in freeing the negroes and thereby putting it in their power of uniting in one body against us . . ." In the context of other pronouncements on slavery in late eighteenth-century Virginia, Graham's anxiety seems to have been genuine, for both antislavery and proslavery attitudes were founded principally on fear, especially of the free Negro.

This conclusion by Robson cannot be justified. He relied here on the lecture on slavery that he misattributes to William Graham. Robson's second footnote refers to an essay contest sponsored by Virginia's governor. He suggests that he learned about the contest from M. E. Rachal, and Robson concluded that it was apparently this contest that prompted the lecture on slavery. If the lecture relied upon by Robson was indeed prompted by the referenced contest, then both Robson and his source are wrong. It was the student, young Edward Graham, who wrote the winning essay resulting from that contest. Whether the essay's content was a reflection of Edward's personal views or was written for the sole purpose of winning a prize is now unknown and likely unknowable.

We remind the reader here of this quote written by Graham in his published "Essay on Government."[791] In this case, the article obviously did reflect its author's views.

Rev. Graham published these sentiments:

> A Republic is a government, by equal and just laws, made by common consent, for the common benefit, **and not the dominion of one community over another community**, . . . which is founded in the perfect, political equality of all the citizens.
>
> **Let civil government be the common guardian and protector of all; but the patron of none.**
>
> **Every violation of the perfect equality of the citizens, is a step towards tyranny.**

---

791   William Graham, "Essay on Government," Philadelphia, 1786, a copy on file at Washington and Lee University's Leyburn Library.

> **That government is excellent, which inviolably preserves the equality of the citizens, both in civil and a religious respect.**
> (Rev. William Graham, "An Essay on Government," Phil. 1786)

Dr. Robson, however, again relying on his false assumption that the slavery lecture he relied upon was written by William Graham, said this:

> If we are to accept his [Graham] own statements, the over-riding consideration was fear. He was acutely sensitive to the "danger in freeing the negroes and thereby putting it in their power of uniting in one body against us . . . (Robson, p. 647)

Based on the author's refutation of the assumption that the lecture in question was written by Graham, the extract from Robson's article is incorrect. Today, there is no good reason to believe that the lecture being referred to by Robson was written or delivered by Rev. William Graham.

If Rev. William Graham was so fearful of "free Negroes" as Robson mistakenly asserts above by inference, then how would Robson explain Graham's unprecedented decision to enroll the free Negro, John Chavis, into his chartered degree-granting college's regular academic program? Additionally, Robson had a responsibility to point out that his claim in this regard is in direct conflict with Graham voluntarily accepting the Negro John Chavis into his Lexington Theological Seminary and essentially sponsoring Chavis's training to become the first black Presbyterian minister in North America.

These are not the actions of a man who was, as Robson asserts, was a "defender of slavery."

It is patently absurd to believe that either Edward Graham or his brother-in-law, Rev. Archibald Alexander, as two respected scholars would not have informed their prospective readers if they knew that William Graham was a defender of African slavery in America. Both of their memoirs were written prior to William Henry Foote's _Sketches of Virginia_, Series 1 and 2, and Foote quoted liberally from both of these authors. Foote, of course, never represented that William Graham defended slavery, nor that he left a written lecture on slavery.

Robson's error no.No. 6: The inaccurate depiction of Graham's political activities

Robson's claims in this regard are scattered throughout the article. These mistakes are therefore not found in any one statement. In brief, his criticism seems to be that Graham was a serial loser. The truth is that Graham's political activities, such as they were, only took place in and around the founding of this country's new government and its associated constitution. While he was an ardent anti-federalist and lost his election to be a delegate to Virginia's ratifying convention, he was nevertheless in good company with many other anti-federalist Virginians, including Patrick Henry, George Mason, Gov. Edmund Randolph, and Richard Henry Lee. These men, together with many like-minded Virginia antifederalists, are considered to have brought about the adoption of our nation's Bill of Rights by their efforts in opposing ratification of a constitution that was presented for ratification without a bill of rights.

In addition, William Graham played one of the most pivotal roles in defeating taxation in Virginia to support the church, ensuring in the process the long-stalled Virginia bill for religious freedom that would serve as the Congress's template for the establishment clause of the First Amendment in the Bill of Rights. See bibliography for Dr. Charles Grier Sellers and Dr. Fred Hood and the footnote below.[792] In regard to Graham's success in regards to both the proposed taxing of the citizenry to support a church or all Christian churches, Graham's success here dwarfs his defeat in the election for delegate to the Virginia ratification convention.

As regards William Graham's published state constitution, which was not adopted by the Frankland delegates, its most glaring aspect is that unlike most proposed constitutions of that era, Graham's deliberately did not contain a provision recognizing a property interest in slaves, an omission that was the most likely reason that some of the Frankland delegates and their friends formed a mob to burn the absent Rev. Graham in effigy. After all, riotous mobs forming with a design to burn an absent minister in effigy had to have been highly agitated by some highly provocative issue. The subject of slavery being the most provocative issue that comes to mind suggests that this was most likely the only subject dealt with in the two proposed state constitutions that might have engendered some people's wrath.

Robson unfairly and inaccurately critiqued Graham's important, albeit brief, role in the nation's political affairs during its most critical period.

Robson's error no.No. 7: The omission by Robson of any mention of Graham's momentous, unprecedented, and courageous decision to enroll the first black college student in America, John Chavis, into a degree-granting college

Insofar as Dr. Robson's unprecedented premise labeling Rev. William Graham as not only a "defender of slavery" but also as the first and likely only college professor in that day who defended slavery was based on nothing more than an assumption that a handmade cover page constructed by a copyist one hundred years after the original packet had been copied from yet another copy was factually correct, it would seem incumbent on Robson to have shared with his readers that the man who he charged with such an infamous act was also the

---

792   Certainly James Madison viewed the changed position as an acquiescence, and he fumed over it. Graham, on this occasion, broke with Smith and the majority of members of the presbytery that passed Smith's recommended changes. Graham thereafter launched a successful campaign to overturn Smith's changed position by calling for an unprecedented general convention of Virginia Presbyterians. The convention sided with Graham and authorized him to draft the Presbyterians' final message to the Virginia legislature (general assembly), and on advice of Graham, the convention added to the final message the Presbyterians' support for passage of Jefferson's long-stalled bill for religious freedom. As a result, the assessment bill was allowed to die a quiet death, and Jefferson's bill was passed.

only college president (rector) in America who had ever been willing to enroll a black man into a regular academic program at a chartered degree-granting college. Robson may not have been aware that the two college presidents he cited as "active abolitionists," Ezra Stiles of Yale and Jonathan Edwards, when contrasting Rev. Graham to his contemporaries, oversaw their "lily white" institutions in such a way that no black college student ever passed through their ivy-covered doors during their tenures despite their abolitionist bona fides.

It should have occurred to Dr. Robson that the mere presence of a black student at the college over which Mr. Graham presided might serve as some degree of exculpatory evidence that would serve in some degree to mitigate, if not suggest innocence, of the charge which he was making about the deceased Rev. Graham. Unless, of course, Robson thought Graham only enrolled Mr. John Chavis in order to demonstrate that a black man was not up to the rigors of academia, which is a machination too cynical to even ponder. After all, Graham was the titular leader of the Lexington Presbytery that licensed John Chavis as the nation's first black Presbyterian minister, an action the presbytery initiated at its first regular meeting after Graham's unexpected death from pneumonia in 1799.

We can safely assume that Dr. Robson would have been familiar with Dr. Ollinger Crenshaw's *General Lee's College*, insofar as it was then the definitive history of Washington and Lee University. Consequently, the auditor therefore concludes that his failure to mention the presence of John Chavis as an undergraduate student at Mr. Graham's chartered institution of higher learning in Lexington, Virginia, was an intentional omission. What remains as a seriously unanswered question is why he omitted such a powerful exculpatory piece of evidence from his article charging Mr. Graham as the nation's premier racist professor and open defender of slavery. Did he fail to see the apparent inconsistency between being a public defender of slavery and at the same time an advocate and enabler of the first black college student in America?

Today, history knows that a Rockbridge County Court record initiated by the black man, John Chavis, claims that "he went through the regular academic program" at Graham's college and that this record was signed by all the sitting magistrates whose collective signatures represent a highly persuasive argument of Chavis's complete undergraduate matriculation. One of the sitting magistrates, Capt. William Lyle, was then a trustee at Graham's college.[793] Could a Trustee of Chavis' college have been unaware of the presence on his own campus of the nation's only black college student? Of course, that could not possibly happen. Had Robson provided this and the other heretofore mentioned exculpatory information about the censure that did not occur, the editors at William and Mary might very well have rejected his article as professionally unpersuasive. In the last analysis,

---

793 This court record is reprinted in Helen Chavis Othow's biography of John Chavis, but it unfortunately cut off the signature of William Lyle. The auditor suspecting this to be the case secured a full copy from the Library of Virginia, which shows the clear signature of William Lyle. William Lyle was the son of one of the original trustees of Liberty Hall Academy, Samuel Lyle, who served as a trustee until shortly before his death. The auditor is the fif[th] great-grandson of Samuel Lyle.

Robson's motives are entirely irrelevant to the legitimacy of his findings about the founding first President of Washington and Lee. Hard facts gathered together comprise the weapon which does in his thesis.

Graham was never a defender of slavery, nor was he ever censured by his church. A repeatedly selected leader of the Presbyterians in Virginia, he was never censured for meddling in politics except perhaps by his opponents. A writer and philosopher, he published one of the most democratic essays on government at the critical period of our nation's founding, and he crafted one of the few state constitutions coming from a southern state that did not include a provision for protecting a property interest in slaves. If Graham had been a defender of slavery, that omission would have constituted one of the few failures of his professional life. The people who actually knew Graham and who left a written account of him provide a picture of a man quite inconsistent with the character of the William Graham that Dr. Robson imagined.

Postscript note: Robson did correctly report a few things about Graham, but none of these instances provided new or important information. On his judgments and accusations about William Graham, he was consistently mistaken. Had any significant number of college presidents in this nation followed the lead of Washington and Lee's founding president, Graham, by embracing black students into their colleges, our nation might have been spared the mass killing of 700,000 of our citizens and the vast economic destruction of half of our country's infrastructure. That's because the millions of black American slaves would have soon received the educational opportunities that had historically been denied, and an educated man is rarely, if ever, a person who can be maintained in slavery.

Appendix 6

Biographical Sketches of President William Graham

BELOW ARE TWO ACCURATE SKETCHES OF WASHINGTON AND LEE'S FIRST PRESIDENT REV. WILLIAM GRAHAM

The first was written by Rev. Archibald Alexander, the second comprised of extracts from W&L trustee, Honorable William A. Anderson, attorney general of Virginia. They were written a century apart. Both are historically accurate and consistent with early documents created by the university's creators.

1. WILLIAM GRAHAM.

1775–1799.

FROM THE REV. ARCHIBALD ALEXANDER, D. D.[794]

Princeton, November 23, 1849.

"Rev. and dear Sir: In complying with your request for some notices of the life and character of my former instructor and friend the Rev. William Graham, I shall avail myself chiefly of an Address which I delivered, some years ago, before the Alumni of Washington College, and which, upon examination, I find to be entirely in accordance with my present impressions.

"William Graham was born on the 19th of December, 1745, in the township of Paxton, near Harrisburg, in Lancaster County, (now Dauphine, [*sic*][795] in Pennsylvania. His father was a plain

---

794 The below biographical sketch of Rev. William Graham written by Archibald Alexander, DD, was published in William Sprague's *Annals of the American Pulpit, Vol. III* (New York: Robert Carter & Brothers, 1858 [but dated in the text by Alexander as 1849], pp. 365–370). It was undoubtedly submitted posthumously bt Alexander's son, James W. Alexander, sometime after his late father's death. If so, James may have taken editorial liberties because we know that James had earlier clearly changed some of his father's manuscripts where he believed his father had been mistaken. He did so when publishing his father's biography. See the *Author's Errors* section of this report in the Archibald Alexander entry for examples. The auditor discovered that in every known case of this, James's material edits are erroneous, due in the main to his adherence to Foote's serious errors. His father, a better historian, was usually correct. The few exceptions are noted in the Author's Errors Section devoted to Archibald Alexander.

795 Correct spelling is "Dauphin."

farmer, in moderate circumstances, and emigrated from the North of Ireland, as did also his mother, whose name before marriage was Susannah Miller. Mr. Roan was the Pastor of the Presbyterian Church in Paxton, which was much larger a hundred years ago than at present, owing to the fact that the Germans have bought out most of the original settlers, who were Scotch and Irish.

"Until the age of manhood, Mr. Graham was brought up in the business of agriculture, which he understood well, and of which he was always fond. But, at this period of his life, having undergone a great change in his religious views and feelings, he resolved to prepare for the work of the holy ministry. The obstacles in his way were indeed great: but being encouraged by the counsels, and aided by the efforts and prayers, of a most excellent mother, to whom he attributed, in a great measure, his success in this important enterprise, he ventured, under all discouragements, to go forward in endeavouring to obtain a liberal education, depending on the guidance and aid of Divine Providence. Having prepared himself for admission to the College of New Jersey, he entered that institution, in company with a number of young men, who became eminent in the Church or State. Among whom, as a scholar, he stood preeminent; for, during the college course, he gained a whole year; that is, he anticipated the studies of the Senior year before the class entered on them, and was permitted to retire from College till the time of the examination of his class, when he attended with them, and was graduated in the year 1773. As his father was unable conveniently to bear the expenses of his son, while at College, he contributed to his own support, by teaching in the grammar school, then under the special direction of Dr. Witherspoon, the President of the College.

"Having completed his college course, he pursued his theological studies under the tuition of the Rev. Mr. Roan, a divine of considerable distinction. But, during the whole period of his education, he was constantly engaged in the study of Theology. Among all his teachers, however, he gave the preference to his excellent mother; and has been heard to say that he learned more of practical religion from her, than from all persons and books beside [the Bible[796]].

---

796 Alexander here had borrowed from Edward Graham's memoir of his late brother, Rev. William Graham.

"He was licensed to preach by the Presbytery of Hanover, on the 26th of October, 1775. When the Hanover Presbytery determined to establish a school for the rearing of young men for the ministry, they applied to the Rev. Samuel Stanhope Smith, then itinerating in the State of Virginia, to recommend a suitable person to take charge of their school,—upon which, he at once recommended Mr. Graham, and at their request wrote to him to come on to the Valley of Virginia. Before this time, a classical school had been taught at a place called Mount Pleasant, near to the little town of Fairfield. Here Mr. Graham commenced his labours [sic] as a teacher; and here we find the germ whence sprung Washington College.[797]

"It was not long, however, before it was judged expedient to remove the infant school to Timber Ridge Meeting-House, where a convenient house for the Rector was built, and also an Academy, and other small buildings for the accommodation of the students. A considerable sum was now raised by subscription for the purchase of books and a philosophical apparatus, and Mr. Graham was entrusted with the business of selecting and purchasing such articles as he should judge most useful and necessary; and, accordingly, he took a journey to Philadelphia, and executed judiciously the trust reposed in him. He also travelled into New England, to solicit benefactions for the rising Academy, and not without some success, though not very considerable.

"At this time, the prospects of the infant institution were very encouraging, and if no untoward events had occurred, there is reason to believe that it would speedily have risen to great eminence and usefulness. But the Revolutionary war having burst on the country, threatening ruin and desolation, the attention of all true men was turned to the defence [sic] of the country; and from no part of the United States, it is believed, did more young men enter the public service, than from the region to which I am now referring. And it may truly be said that the patriotic fire burned in no bosom with a warmer flame, than in that of Mr. Graham himself.

---

797 Importantly, James W. Alexander left his father's allusion to the "germ of Washington College" just as his father intended, and his father makes it very clear that the school taught by William Graham at Mount Pleasant was the true germ of Washington College. At the time this was written by Archibald Alexander, he was in the last years of his life and was esteemed the preeminent historian of the early Presbyterian institutions of higher learning in the United States. It was written six years after his published address too the alumni of Washington College (1843) and four years after his history of the "Log College." See bibliography. It constitutes Archibald Alexander's last word on the founding of Washington College.

"On a certain occasion, when, by invitation of the Executive authority of the State, it was resolved to raise a volunteer company of riflemen, to go into active service, there appeared much backwardness in the men to come forward,—he stepped out, and had his own name enrolled, which produced such an effect that the company was immediately filled, of which he was unanimously chosen Captain; and all necessary preparations were made for marching to the seat of war, when General Washington signified to the Governors of the States, that he did not wish any more volunteer companies to join the army.

"The abandonment of the houses erected at Timber Ridge, appears to have taken place,—though without authority,—as a matter of necessity. The income from the Academy was small, and his salary for preaching to the two Congregations of Timber Ridge and Hall's Meeting-House, (now Monmouth,) being paid in depreciated currency, it was impossible for him to support his family. He, therefore, resolved to return to farming, and, accordingly, he purchased a small farm on the North River, within a mile or two of the present site of Washington College.

"The school at Timber Ridge was, however, continued for some time after Mr. Graham retired to his farm, and he endeavoured [*sic*] to perform the duties of a Rector, by visiting it, and giving instruction, several times in each week. But this being found very inconvenient to himself, and disadvantageous to the school, after due deliberation, he resolved to relinquish the establishment at Timber Ridge, and to open a school in his own house. It was here that, at an early age, I commenced my course of classical learning.

"Even at this time, there was a respectable number of students in the school, most of them having reached the age and stature of men. After some time, a frame edifice was erected on ground given for the purpose, and the school was continued until, in the year 1782, application was made to the Legislature for an Act of Incorporation, and, accordingly, a number of Trustees were formed into a body corporate, to have full charge of the Academy, which received the name of Liberty Hall,—which name it retained until it was endowed by General Washington, when his name was substituted for that which it had before borne. Before this donation was received, Mr. Graham had resigned his office as Rector or President, though it is understood that he used all his influence to secure this important endowment;

and that he was the author of the letter addressed to General Washington, by the Trustees, in favour of this institution.

Though Mr. Graham had some formidable opposers, who had taken up strong prejudices against him, and although, after the close of the war, the character of the students who attended at the Academy was greatly deteriorated, and the difficulties which environed him were many and perplexing; yet it must be conceded that, in resigning his important post at this time, he was not guided by his usual wisdom.

"It is not expedient, perhaps, to bring distinctly into view, in this connection, the disappointment which attended his favourite scheme of planting in the West a little colony of select families of like mind, who might live in peace, far from the contentions, bustle, and turmoil of the world. All such schemes must fail in the present state of human nature.

"Mr. Graham possessed a mind formed for accurate and profound investigation. He had studied the Latin and Greek classics with great care, and relished the beauties of these exquisite compositions. With those authors taught in the schools, he was familiar by a long practice in teaching, and always insisted on the importance of classical literature, as the proper foundation of a liberal education.

"He had a strong inclination to the study of Natural Philosophy, and took pleasure in making experiments, with such apparatus as he possessed; and he had procured for his Academy as good a one as was then possessed by most of the Colleges. In these experiments much time was employed, on which inquisitive persons, not connected with the Academy, were freely permitted to attend.

"As he was an ardent patriot and a thorough republican, the times in which he lived led him to bestow much attention on the science of government; and one of the few pieces which he wrote for the press was on this subject. By some he was censured for meddling with politics; but it should be remembered that, at that time, this country, having cast off its allegiance to Great Britain, and declared itself independent, had to lay the foundation of governments both for the States and for the Nation; and that the welfare of posterity, as well as of the existing inhabitants of the country, was involved in the wisdom with which this work was done. The talents of every man, capable of thinking and judging on such subjects, seemed to be fairly put into requisition. It is a sound maxim that men living at one time must not be judged by the maxims of an age in which all circumstances are greatly changed. At the adoption of the Federal Constitution, which, according to its original draft, he did not approve, he relinquished all attention to politics during the remainder of his life.

"The science, however, which engaged his attention more than all others, except Theology, was the Philosophy of the Mind. In this he took great delight, and to it he devoted much time and attention. Though acquainted with the best treatises which had then been published, his investigations were not carried on so much by books, as by a patient and repeated analysis of the various processes of thought, as they arose in his own mind, and by reducing the phenomena thus observed to a regular system. I am of opinion that the system of mental philosophy which he thus formed, was, in clearness and fulness, superior to any thing which has been given to the public, in the numerous works which have recently been published on this subject. And it is greatly to be regretted that his Lectures were never fully committed to writing, and published for the benefit of .the world. It was, however, a fault in this man of profound thought, that he made little use of his pen. And it was also a defect that, in the latter years of his life, he addicted himself little to reading the productions of other men, and perhaps entertained too low an opinion.

"But you will wish to know something more particularly of Mr. Graham as a theologian and a preacher. From the time of his ordination by the Presbytery of Hanover in 1775, he became a teacher of Theology. Most of those who entered the holy ministry in the Valley of Virginia, pursued their preparatory studies under his direction. And, after the great revival which commenced in the year 1789, he had a theological class of seven or eight members, under his tuition, which was kept up for several years. It was his custom to devote one day in the week to hearing the written discourses of these candidates, and to a free discussion of theological points. In these exercises he appeared to take great delight; and the students were always gratified, and commonly convinced, by his lucid statements and cogent reasonings. As most of those who enjoyed the benefit of his instructions in this incipient Theological Seminary are not now in the world, it may not be improper to say that some of them rose to eminence in the Church, And as Professors or Presidents of literary institutions.

"The influence which he gained over the minds of his pupils, while under his care, was unbounded. Yet he encouraged the utmost freedom of discussion, and seemed to aim, not so much to bring his pupils to think as he did, as to teach them to think on all subjects for themselves. A slavish subjection to any human authority he repudiated; and, therefore, never attempted to add weight to his opinions, by referring to a long list of authors, of great name; but uniformly insisted that all opinions should be subjected to the test of Scripture and reason. Some of his students have been heard to say that the chief benefit which they derived from his instructions, was that, by this means, they were led to the free and independent exercise of their own faculties in the investigation of truth.

"Mr. Graham, in his theological creed, was strictly orthodox, according to the standards of his own Church, which he greatly venerated; but, in his method of explaining some of the knotty points in Theology, he departed considerably from the common track; and was of opinion that many things which have been involved in perplexity and obscurity, by the manner in which they have been treated, are capable of being easily and satisfactorily explained by the application of sound principles of philosophy.

"As a preacher, he was always instructive and evangelical; though in common his delivery was rather feeble and embarrassed than forcible; but when his feelings were excited, his voice became penetrating, and his whole manner awakening and impressive. And his profound study of the human heart enabled him to describe the various exercises of the Christian with a clearness and truth which often greatly surprised his pious hearers; for it seemed to them as if he could read the very inmost sentiments of their minds; which he described more perfectly than they could do themselves.

"When it was his object to elucidate some more difficult point, it was his custom to open his trenches, so to speak, at a great distance; removing out of the way every obstacle, until he was prepared to make his assault on the main fortress: thus, insensibly, he led his hearers along, step by step, gaining their assent, first to one proposition, and then to another, until, at last, they could not easily avoid acquiescence in the conclusion to which he wished to bring them. As a clear and cogent reasoner, he had no superior among his contemporaries; and his preeminence in the exercise of this faculty was acknowledged by all unprejudiced persons. It has been hinted that Mr. Graham had enemies, who often had influence to impede or thwart his favourite schemes; and candour requires that it should be acknowledged that he sometimes imprudently made enemies of those who might have been efficient friends, by too free an indulgence of satirical and sarcastical remarks; which weapon he could wield with great power. And it must also be conceded that towards his opponents he never manifested much of a conciliatory temper, but seemed rather disposed to stand aloof from them, and to set them at defiance.

"In the government of youth, Mr. Graham was, from the first, a rigid and unyielding disciplinarian. He laid it down as a principle that, at every risk, authority must be maintained; and when this was by any one resisted, however formidable the student might be in physical strength, or however many might combine to frustrate the regular exercise of discipline, he fearlessly went forward in the discharge of his duty, and generally triumphed over all opposition; and often inflicted severe castigation on the thought less persons, who dared to rebel against lawful authority. Whether his rigour might not, in some instances, have been extreme, is a question on which judicious men would differ in opinion.

"As has been already hinted, the great error of his life was the relinquishment of the important station in which Providence had placed him, and for which he was so eminently qualified; and that at a time of life when he possessed the ability of being more useful than at any former period. Having removed to the banks of Ohio River, he fell into great embarrassments, in the midst of which ho died, in consequence of a violent fever contracted by exposure to frequent drenching rains, while on a journey to Richmond. "In that city he breathed his last, on the 8th of June, 1799, in the house of his friend, the late Colonel Robert Gamble; and his remains were deposited near the Episcopal Church on the hill, over which a plain marble slab, with a short inscription, is placed.

"Mr. Graham was married to a young woman in Carlisle, by the name of Mary Kerr. They had two sons and three daughters who lived to mature age. His eldest son entered the ministry, and, after licensure, was stationed in Prince George County, below Petersburg, where he contracted a bilious fever that proved fatal. His only other son who grew to man hood, was his youngest child, and was taken by James Priestley, LL. D., and educated out of gratitude for Mr. Graham's kindness in giving him a liberal education. He studied medicine, lived in Georgia, and was hopefully converted among the Methodists, of which society he became a member, and died a few years since.

"The extent of the influence exerted by this one man over the literature and religion of Virginia, cannot be calculated. As the stream which fertilizes a large district is small in its origin, but goes on continually increasing until it becomes a mighty river, so the influence of the Rev. William Graham did not cease when he died, but has gone on increasing by means of his disciples, who have been scattered far and wide over the West and South.

Yours truly,

A. ALEXANDER.

(*Sprague's Annals of the American Pulpit*, vol. 3, pp. 365–370)

****

2. William A. Anderson[798] (Trustee W&L) Article: "William Graham, Founder of Washington and Lee, Teacher, Preacher, and Patriot" from *Rockbridge County News*, May 11, 1911

Below are extracts from Anderson's presentation and his article:

For twenty-three years, from 1774, to 1796. He discharged the duties and performed a work which would have been an ample task for several ordinary instructors.

He [William Graham] was President, and at the same time he was the professor of mental science, of moral philosophy, of the Greek and Latin Languages, of natural philosophy, of belle letters, and of mathematics. For much of the time, he also conducted and taught classes in theology . . .

However, after the election [Ratification of the U.S. Constitution Convention delegates] and the assembling of the convention, the great debate still went on, and under the tremendous logic of George Mason, and Patrick Henry and those who shared their views (i.e., William Graham et al), and under the personal

---

798 Anderson was the Virginia attorney general and an active trustee of Washington and Lee University.

leadership of Patrick Henry, . . . there was a change in popular sentiment in Virginia.

So signal was the change in Rockbridge County under the championship of Graham, that he succeeded in getting the voters of that county to reverse their former judgment and to adopt pre-emptory instructions to Moore and McKee, their delegates in the convention,[799] directing them to oppose and vote against ratification of the constitution–instructions which those courageous gentlemen disregarded by casting their votes for adoption.

And here it is worthy of remark, that but for the support of the trustees of this institution, who were members of that convention, the adoption of the new constitution and establishment of the new government would have failed.

(Remarks made by William A. Anderson on March 5, 1911, in the university chapel during the ceremony associated with the reinterment of the remains of Rev. William Graham.)

When President Graham's remains were reinterred to the campus from Richmond where he had died, trustee, William Anderson, presided over a ceremony held on the campus at the Lee Chapel. Just outside of the Lee Chapel, Graham's remains were buried and a large flat stone was placed over his remains. This stone monument contains an engraved epitaph, the text of which appears below. In later years, a short wrought-iron fence was installed around the monument.

The author of this epitaph is unknown, but it may well be trustee, William. A. Anderson.

Sacred
to the Memory
of the
Rev. William Graham
Founder and twenty years Rector of
Washington Academy
in
Rockbridge County
Virginia
He was born in the State of Pennsylvania
December 19th 1746
And died in the City of Richmond

---

799   This was the convention held for the purpose of considering whether the proposed new United States Constitution should be ratified. This was prior to the nation's adoption of the Bill of Rights.

June 17th 1799
He was distinguished for the strength and
originality of his genius
And the successful tenor of his exertions
in behalf of solid literature and
evangelical piety.

(Emphasis added)

(Remarks made by William A. Anderson on March 5, 1911, in the university chapel during the ceremony associated with the reinterment of the remains of Rev. William Graham.)

****

The above sketches are fairly reliable ones as far as they go. Alexander's contains a few minor mistakes. Where he fails, it is mostly with errors of omission and results from Alexander's disinterest in Graham's efforts to help shape the political foundations of the new American nation. For example, Alexander was but an immature youth when Virginia was forming the new American state; and Alexander, then wrestling with his early theological studies, had little time for participating in Virginia's struggle for religious liberty, and he failed to comprehend the critical role played by his preceptor in fending off the political influence of the Church of England (then only recently restyled as the Episcopal Church).[800]

As the new nation was forming, the Anglicans/Episcopalians sought to ensure that they retained their theretofore privileged position as the country's established church. As the decision-making period approached, most observers assumed the Anglicans would be victorious in this regard; and faced with these prospects, many Presbyterian clergymen in Virginia attempted to obtain some small measure of financial benefit for the Presbyterian Church and especially its clergymen by withdrawing their long-standing unequivocal opposition to taxing the people to support the church. These clergymen therefore agreed to communicate to the new Virginia legislature[801] that if the legislature grants the Episcopal Church with exclusive "establishment" status, then the Presbyterians should receive financial support from the public treasury as well.

This new approach was adopted by the Presbyterian clergymen over William Graham's strenuous objections. Graham, however, rejected this approach and

800 The Church of England (i.e., Anglican Church) had long been the *established* church in British North America, and as such, it was endowed by the British government with many legal privileges rarely afforded to adherents of other denominations. Colleges were almost never "chartered" by the ruling British authorities, and Presbyterian, Congregationalists, etc., were taxed to support the Anglican Churches and marriages were generally required to be administered by Anglican priests.

801 That is, the first Virginia legislature created after the American Revolution.

launched a campaign of opposition by calling for a general convention of Presbyterians. The campaign naturally began in the Valley of Virginia where Graham was the recognized leader of the Presbyterians. The campaign spread well beyond the Valley, and the Valley's petition campaign spread even beyond the Blue Ridge when the Baptists joined the campaign.

In sum, Graham's masterful strategy was wildly successful, garnering, in the end, some ten thousand signatures of Virginians opposed to any establishment of any denomination. Furthermore, these disgruntled petitioners opposed any taxation to support churches. When the Presbyterians' meeting in general convention authorized their leader, William Graham, to draft its final memorial message to the Virginia legislature clarifying the churches' views on establishment, they also authorized Graham to announce their support of Mr. Jefferson's long-stalled "Bill for Religious Freedom.[802]"

Alexander was obviously too disinterested in these worldly events to appreciate the significance of his preceptor's pivotal role in Virginia's struggle for religious liberty. Late-twentieth-century scholars, however, began to realize this fact; but to date, Graham's role has failed to be recognized in the Valley of Virginia. See Dr. Charles Grier Sellers and Dr. Fred Hood's entries in our attached bibliography for important treatments of this vastly important aspect of American history.

Graham's two important writings on constitutions published at such a critical time in the early history of the United States has also been long overlooked. Had Alexander recognized the significance of these publications, they might not have been buried and neglected in the archives of the university's precious documents.

Finally, Alexander failed or withheld mention of Graham's amazingly important decisions to enroll the nation's first black and first female regular college students in North America. Of course, in Alexander's day, few would have recognized the significance of Graham's prescience in regards to blacks' and females' right to participate in the educational and political milieu.

As it stands, the nation's first black college graduate, Rev. John Chavis, obtained his entire college education at Washington and Lee University as a direct result of the courageous decision of Rev. William Graham to enroll Mr. Chavis into a regular class at a chartered higher education institution with authorized degree-granting authority. No other college in America would follow Graham's lead in this regard for nearly a century.

This momentous occasion took place in what was then the largest slaveholding state in the nation. How Rev. Graham was able to oversee the education of a black man in that time (1790s) and in that state without any known disturbances is a subject ripe for investigation by American historians. It is a testament to Graham's courage and sagacity together with the progressive attitudes of the settlers of the

---

802 Jefferson's log-jammed bill, which Mr. Madison had been unable to get passed out of committee, had a new birth as a result of obtaining the Presbyterians' and Baptists' support as seen from the petition campaign. After several years of inaction, Jefferson's bill was now moved quickly out of committee and gained full passage. This bill became the template for the establishment clause included in the First Amendment to the new nation's Bill of Rights.

Valley of Virginia that a black man as well as a married woman with children could be accepted as college students at Liberty Hall Academy in Lexington, Virginia, long before such a right was recognized by any other college in America. It is sorrowful indeed that Graham's initiatives, in this regard, were not carried forth by his immediate successors. His legacy, however, deserves to have a bright and constant light directed toward these monumental accomplishments during the early days of our nation's founding.

*The author of this historical performance audit is grateful to have been allowed to play a small part in revealing these long-lost facts concerning the education of John Chavis and Sarah Priestley as early (eighteenth century) students at the chartered and degree-granting college, Liberty Hall Academy.

Special Acknowledgment

This report could not have been created without the consistent assistance and cooperation of professionals that administer the affairs of the library on the campus of Washington and Lee University and the librarian, Betty R. Kondayan, as early as 1972, as well as Seth Goodheart and especially Lisa McCown, whose cooperation and efforts over the last several years were indispensable to this effort.

************************Finis************************

Index

About The Book

Forty years in the making, this book constitutes an unveiling of hitherto unrecognized archival records pertaining to the founding of Washington and Lee University. These startling records created by men of the highest reputations and character disclose long-held secrets both shocking and at the same time assuaging. In the process, the true character of the university's founding first president is illuminated as is his astounding significance to the history of the Great Valley of Virginia and to all of the nation's lovers of liberty.

Within, a vast array of pearls of wisdom are disclosed, serving to quash long-held but mistaken notions and several myths exposed as utterly false narratives concerning when the institution was founded and by whom. The institution's current mistake on this subject is only wrong by twenty-five years. Some of those who are today heralded as founders, it turns out, had nothing whatever to do with establishing Washington and Lee. Within these pages lies the unmistakable evidence of who was responsible and when the historical miscalculations were committed.

Empty assertions too numerous to mention here are discredited as are many of their perpetrators. Some of those named were merely credulous and or too disinterested to scrutinize unauthenticated assertions of the past. Others, more agenda driven, failed to rise above their predispositions and selective perceptions, but all in all failing to exercise due diligence in preserving the heritage and legacies of their forebears.

The vast majority of the conclusions presented here for the first time since 1850 are virtually incontrovertible, at least by critics employing empirical standards nearly universally accepted since the dawn of the enlightenment.

Footnotes are liberally employed to emphasize facts and uncover truths as well as giving citations of authority. A bibliography is also attached, as are several important appendices. In a few select cases, those with the intent to deceive or cover up are specifically exposed. In the case of one particular false narrative, its exponent is held up to just ridicule for knowingly publishing a malicious and unjust traducement of a noble paragon of virtue, Rev. William Graham.

All in all, Washington and Lee University and its founding first president, William Graham, are shown an entirely new light. The university is compellingly demonstrated to deserve to be considered the most progressive American institution of higher learning of the eighteenth century.

As the new nation gave to the world an unprecedented democratic vision of freedom, so this book reveals, Washington and Lee University in its infancy (Liberty Hall Academy) introduced a vision of higher education for men and women of all races. This chartered degree-granting institution was then the only such institution with its doors open to all. Then, the only campus in America where one might observe a black or female regular undergraduate student was at Lexington, Virginia, a sight never yet seen at Harvard, Yale, or even Princeton in the eighteenth century.

This noble idea, unfortunately, died when the university's founder, William Graham, died. His vision in this regard is but a part of his heretofore mostly unknown legacy. Although unheralded, he was, nevertheless, unquestionably the only educator in America who dared to prove that a black man, if given the opportunity, can succeed in securing a college education—a powerful lesson that once learned remained a powerful and enduring truth.

About The Author

The author grew up in Lansing, Michigan, and resides in East Lansing with his wife, Donna. He is a rare book dealer and amateur historian.

He began his professional career as the director of a state government agency. At the same time, he served on numerous boards and commissions as an active member. As director, he was an adviser to governors and legislative leaders on matters pertaining to public policy. He also served for several years on an advisory committee to the chief administrator of the Michigan Supreme Court and was appointed the chair of a public utility research-funding committee by the chairman of the Public Service Commission.

During this period, he also taught as an adjunct instructor on consumer law and politics at Eastern Michigan University and at a local community college.

After his governmental career, he founded Claverhouse Associates, a national performance auditing firm that conducts federal and state arbitration audits. He has been the president and senior auditor for twenty-five years.

CPSIA information can be obtained
at www.ICGtesting.com
Printed in the USA
LVHW090611071118
596285LV00001B/292/P

9 781984 530493